MW01000823

# Child Development Worldwide

## A Cultural Approach

**FIRST EDITION**

**By Lene Arnett Jensen & Jeffrey Jensen Arnett**

**Senior Portfolio Manager:** Amber Chow/Kelli Strieby
**Content Producer:** Cecilia Turner
**Content Developer:** Nic Albert
**Managing Editor:** Debbie Coniglio
**Portfolio Manager Assistant:** Louis Fierro
**Executive Product Marketing Manager:** Christopher Brown
**Senior Field Marketer:** Debi Doyle
**Content Producer Manager:** Amber Mackey
**Content Development Manager:** Sharon Geary
**Content Developer, Learning Tools:** Christopher Fegan
**Art/Designer:** Blair Brown
**Digital Studio Course Producer:** Elissa Senra-Sargent
**Project Manager:** Gina Linko
**Compositor:** Integra Publishing Services, Inc.
**Printer/Binder:** LSC Communications
**Cover Printer:** Lehigh Phoenix Color/Hagerstown
**Cover Design:** Lumina Datamatics
**Cover Credit:** Noma Bar, Pentagram

Credits and acknowledgments borrowed from other sources and reproduced, with permission, in this textbook appear on pages C-1–C-3.



**Library of Congress Cataloging-in-Publication Data**
Names: Jensen, Lene Arnett, author. | Arnett, Jeffrey Jensen, author.
Title: Child development worldwide / by Lene Arnett Jensen & Jeffrey Jensen Arnett.
Description: 1 Edition. | New York : Pearson, [2017] | Includes bibliographical references and index.
Identifiers: LCCN 2017016776 (print) | LCCN 2017029584 (ebook) | ISBN 9780134635804 (epub) | ISBN 9780134635859 (Revel) | ISBN 9780134014005 (alk. paper) | ISBN 9780134635835 (ala carte : alk. paper) | ISBN 9780134635767 (exam copy : alk. paper)
Subjects: LCSH: Child development–Cross-cultural studies.
Classification: LCC HQ767.9 (ebook) | LCC HQ767.9 .J46 2017 (print) | DDC 305.231–dc23
LC record available at https://lccn.loc.gov/2017016776

1 17

**Student Edition:**
ISBN 10: 0-134-01400-6
ISBN 13: 978-0-134-01400-5

**A la Carte:**
ISBN 10: 0-134-63583-3
ISBN 13: 978-0-134-63583-5

www.pearsonhighered.com

*We dedicate this text to the many thousands of students whom we have taught and who have continuously inspired us to revisit and renew our knowledge of children. With this text, we hope to inspire the next generation of students to appreciate the amazing diversity of children's development, within and across cultures.*

# Contents

# Preface

## Four New Ways to Approach Child Development

*Child Development Worldwide: A Cultural Approach* grows out of our personal, teaching, and professional experiences. Lene grew up in Denmark and Belgium, and Jeff in the United States. Together, we have lived in Denmark, India, France, and the United States. We have shared the wonderful experience of being involved in the development of our twins, now 18 years old, who have traveled with us to all those places and consider themselves fully American and fully Danish. Both of us have taught a wide range of developmental psychology courses, including child development. What is striking to us about the world and the field of child development are the remarkable changes that both have undergone in the last decades. We wrote this text to reflect those changes.

Globalization and technology have been making the world smaller—with distances shrinking and interconnections multiplying. Cultural diversity and globalization are often part of the everyday experiences of today's students—through travel, migration, and study abroad programs, as well as everyday real-life and virtual interactions. We see this vividly in our twins' lives as they learn about different cultures from their teachers, have friends from many different countries, and play Internet games with children from across the globe. These worldwide changes are here to stay and will continue to profoundly impact children's lives.

Today, the field of child development is as fascinating and important as it has ever been—and, like the world, looks much different than it did 15 or 25 years ago. *Child Development Worldwide* speaks to that change. After all, child development does not occur in a vacuum. It happens in numerous communal contexts and cultural settings that are perpetually changing. By encouraging students to see children through a cultural lens, this text balances the universals and Western-centric research that have in the past characterized much of the field with the growing body of research on the development of children from diverse cultures within and across countries. Our experiences of growing up and working in a number of different countries have translated into an approach that emphasizes how universal features of development are shaped by cultural diversity. *Child Development Worldwide* offers this new approach, in four fundamental ways:

1. An emphasis on teaching students to *think culturally* about development;
2. A broadened *scope of child development* and an updated perspective on when children may be considered "grown up";
3. An unprecedented inclusion of *diverse contexts* of child development; and
4. A deep *integration of digital technology* into the text.

## Thinking Culturally

The world's population is about 7½ billion, and the population of the United States is about 330 million—less than 5% of the total. By 2050, the world's population is expected to exceed 9 billion, with almost all growth taking place in economically developing countries. Worldwide, child development is remarkably diverse. In Africa, for example, most children are multilingual because they learn both local and European languages in primary school. In Asia, after centuries of being excluded from educational opportunities, girls are reaching parity with boys in educational achievement. In fact, 15-year-old-girls in many Asian countries outperformed boys on recent international science tests. In Europe, it is now typical for young people in many countries to take a "gap year"—a year devoted to travel and exploration before they commit to higher education or a "real" job—as they enter emerging adulthood. For students, it is more important than ever to have knowledge of the wider world because of the increasingly globalized economy, and because so many issues—issues like climate change, disease, and terrorism—cross borders.

Although this text covers scientific findings from across the world, it aims to do something even more important. The ultimate learning goal is for students to *think culturally* about development. As this text emphasizes, diverse cultures exist both within and across nations, often intersecting in important ways with ethnicity, race, and religion. We hope that through this text students will learn to apply child development to the work they do as well as to their own lives, and to understand that there is—always and everywhere—a cultural basis to development. To be clear, this does not mean that biology is not important. Transcending the old "nature versus nurture" division, students will learn that humans have evolved to be an incomparably cultural and global species, and that current research shows startling ways that genes and the environment influence one another.

## Broadening the Scope of Child Development

The second way that this text takes a new approach corresponds to the historical expansion of the field of child development, from an early, narrow focus on young children to a broader one—one that now encompasses adolescents and emerging adults. This expansion is reflected in the growth of professional organizations supported by instructors, researchers, and practitioners. The oldest, the Society for Research in Child Development (SRCD), was started in 1933. The Society for Research on Adolescence (SRA) and the European Association for Research on Adolescence (EARA) were established about a half-century later, in 1984 and 1988 respectively, as scholars increasingly recognized the importance of the adolescent years. The Society for the Study of Emerging Adulthood (SSEA) is even more recent, begun in 2013, because scholars recognized that it was taking longer than in the past to "grow up" in many countries and that ages 18–25 had become crucial years of change and preparation for adult life. Also, major international organizations dedicated to the well-being of children, such as UNICEF (United Nations Children's Fund) and the WHO (World Health Organization), have recently broadened their focus on younger children to include adolescents and emerging adults.

Here, we provide in-depth coverage from prenatal development through middle childhood, and also cover adolescence and emerging adulthood. The learning goal is for students to know what contemporary child development looks like—to understand how the meanings of childhood, adolescence, and emerging adulthood are dependent on cultural and historical circumstances. For example, emerging adulthood exists in some cultures but not others, and consequently, adult work may be taken on anywhere from middle childhood to the 20s.

## Encompassing Diverse Contexts

Not only has child development broadened in terms of the age groups covered, but today the field also addresses many more contexts of development than previously. From an early focus in the field on family (e.g., Freud) and peers (e.g., Piaget), researchers now address many other contexts such as work, media, and civic organizations. Thus, the third way that this text takes a different approach is by including an unprecedented number of chapters on different contexts: "Family Relationships: Foundations and Variations," "Peers, Friends, and Romantic Partners," "School and Work: Developing Cultural Skills," "Media: Uses, Risks, and Benefits," and "Meaning Systems: Moral, Religious, and Civic Development."

It is not only that we devote five full chapters to different context, but we also cover topics that reflect cultural diversity and change within those contexts. For example, the chapter on "Family Relationships: Foundations and Variations" includes sections on grandparents and sexual minority families. The chapter on "School and Work: Developing Cultural Skills," as indicated by the title, recognizes that many children all over the world work—not just to support their leisure activities but to support their families. The chapter on "Media: Uses, Risks, and Benefits" covers not only long-known risks to children's development, but also benefits to cognitive, emotional, and social development. It also addresses how children, parents, schools, and governments use media for developmental purposes. In the chapter on "Meaning Systems: Moral, Religious, and Civic Development," there is attention to children's lives in the context of political conflict and war. In sum, *Child Development Worldwide* covers a rich array of contexts—what they look like in today's world and how they intersect.

Every chapter also includes "Apply Your Knowledge as a Professional" videos to help students see how what they have learned is applicable across a wide range of contexts and professions. For example, the videos include interviews with an instructor of maternity nursing, a media literacy teacher, a child development researcher, a reproductive endocrinologist, an education coordinator in a language immersion school, and a court-appointed child advocate. In short, the learning goal is for students to know that current theory and research on child development pertain to many contexts and societal roles.

## Embracing Digital Learning

Our fourth approach to offering an up-to-date and innovative text pertains to pedagogy. Today's students are the most tech-savvy generation of college students yet, and we wanted to present materials in a way that was inspired by the opportunities of digital technology. When we wrote the text, we wrote it with digital features in the forefront of our minds rather than as an afterthought.

In addition to a print version, this text is available in Revel format, which provides an immersive digital and interactive learning experience. After all, a digital approach fits well with our cultural approach. Digital content easily travels across boundaries. For example, interactive maps of the United States and the world allow students to explore content across cultures in a more meaningful way. When students engage with content in a lively way, they learn more deeply and effectively.

Revel also allows us to update materials more frequently to provide students access to important cutting-edge knowledge. The text inaugurates a "Breaking Developments" feature that will be available digitally. This feature will provide succinct summaries of landmark new research and significant cultural trends that have direct relevance to theory and research in the text, yet have occurred since the publication of the print text. "Breaking Developments" will be updated at the beginning of each January and July.

# Understanding Children's Lives Today

As parents, we have learned a lot from raising twins, Paris and Miles, who are now entering emerging adulthood. We occasionally share stories from their childhood to illustrate concepts in the text. Just as we draw on our personal experiences, we encourage students to draw on theirs as a source of insights into child development. For example, each chapter ends with a personal journaling prompt.

Furthermore, in every chapter, we include first-person quotes from children, adolescents, and emerging adults from around the world. In videos included with the text, children talk about their lives, including growing up as a Latina girl in the United States, being a child soldier in Congo, and living with a learning disability. We wish for students to hear other individuals' perspectives, and think this adds authenticity to the presentation of theories and research findings. It is also a vivid reminder that, although personal experience is important, it may not be reflective of how most children develop.

The Chinese have an expression for the limited way all of us learn to see the world: *jing di zhi wa*, meaning "frog in the bottom of a well." The expression comes from a fable about a frog that has lived its entire life in a well. The frog assumes that its tiny world is all there is. Only when a passing turtle tells the frog of the great ocean to the east does the frog realize that there is much more to the world. All of us are like that frog—which you can also see depicted on the cover of this text. We grow up as members of a culture and learn to see the world from the perspective that becomes most familiar to us. But look at the cover again. Do you also see how the black dot is the eye in the profile of a child? With *Child Development Worldwide*, we hope that students will come to understand the lives and development of children in ways previously unseen.

Growing up is universal. Every culture differentiates between children and adults, and children across all cultures share common developmental characteristics. Yet, culture also profoundly impacts psychological development. How and when a child reaches adulthood varies widely across the world. By encouraging students to see children from both a developmental and cultural perspective, we hope to inspire an understanding that will be useful and fruitful, not only while students are taking this course but throughout their lives.

# Child Development Worldwide Features

**"Cultural Focus" Features** highlight how culture impacts various aspects of development, such as breast-feeding practices, friendship and play in middle childhood, or what it means to be a teenager in Kathmandu. Students read an overview of the topic, watch a cultural video expanding that topic's discussion, and then answer a review question.

### Cultural Focus: Object Permanence Across Cultures

The knowledge of object permanence is something that all young children need to learn in order to function in the world. In this video, we see demonstrations of children at various ages being tested with Piaget's tasks to see if they grasp the concept of object permanence or not. The results with children from many different cultures indicate that this is a universal concept.

**Review Question**

According to this video, object permanence is universal across cultures. Why would this be such an important concept for children to acquire?

**Watch** OBJECT PERMANENCE ACROSS CULTURES

**"Education Focus" Features** highlight the application of child development research to educational settings, both in and outside of school. Students read an overview of the topic and then respond to a review question.

### Education Focus: Early Multilingual Education Across Contexts

On the basis of a comprehensive review of the research on multilingualism, a group of social scientists has issued policy guidelines for professional caregivers and teachers to ensure that multilingual children in the United States develop strong language skills. The report was endorsed by the American Academy of Pediatrics (McCabe et al., 2013). The report highlights six strategies:

(1) Avoid attributing children's language delays to multilingualism.

(2) Ensure that multilingual children have exposure to rich versions of both the first language and English across a variety of contexts.

(3) Provide support for development of the first language in the childcare environment.

(4) Support the first language by also visiting other contexts and places where it is spoken.

(5) Have the caregiver speak to the child in the language that comes most naturally to ensure a rich language environment.

(6) Develop programs that expose children to high-quality English at an early age. Such exposure may involve home visitation, center-based early childhood education programs, healthcare providers, and mass media.

**Review Question**

The policy report focuses on ways to support multilingual development in immigrant children. Do you think there is need for new policies for professional caregivers and teachers to support multilingual development among American children from families in which only English is spoken? Explain.

**"Research Focus" Features** offer a detailed description of a research study, including its premises, methods, results, and limitations. Each feature is available in both traditional narrative format and as a sketch-art style video. Multiple choice questions appear at the end of the feature to ensure that students have a solid understanding of the research study and methodology.

Research Focus: Observing Everyday Storytelling

Around age 5, children become capable of telling stories. Well before that age, they have also been listening to stories told by the people around them (Miller et al., 2014; Nelson, 1993). Stories are told across cultures and contribute to a language-rich environment. Interestingly, stories also hold both implicit and explicit cultural lessons for children about what to say and how to say it.

Peggy Miller (1996) has studied the stories that parents tell in the presence of their toddlers for many decades. Her observational research involves video-recording the natural, everyday behaviors of families in their home (see Chapter 1). Each family is assigned one researcher who comes for regular visits over the course of an extended period. For example, one study of six families in Taiwan and six families in the United States involved 2 years of observations (Miller et al., 1997, 2008).

In order to address the issue that families react to the presence of researchers by changing their behavior, each researcher first spends considerable time with the families, habituating them to their presence. Only video-recordings taken after the family seems comfortable and back to regular routines are used. Also, in an effort to capture true-to-life interactions, Miller's research team matched up researchers to share key demographic characteristics with the families being studied. For example, they assigned Taiwanese researchers to the six Taiwanese families, and American researchers to the American families. Once the families were comfortable with the researchers, the Taiwanese families referred to the researcher as kin, calling her "aunty," whereas the American families tended to treat the researchers as a first-name family friend.

Although the research in the two countries included only a small number of families, hundreds of stories were recorded and analyzed. Every story was coded independently by two researchers, and inter-rater reliability was calculated (see Chapter 1). The analyses showed that the content of stories—what was said—differed between Taiwanese and American families. Taiwanese families were more likely to tell stories about their children's transgressions, whereas American stories tended to highlight how the children were cute, smart, or unusual. Miller interprets the Taiwanese content as fitting the Chinese maxim that "the deeper the love, the greater the correction" (*Ai zhi shen, ze zhi qie*). In contrast, what was taken to be story-worthy among American families centered more on self-affirmation and entertainment. This does not mean that American families do *not* care about children's transgressions, but that these were not regarded as fitting story topics.

The structure of the stories—how things were said—also differed between the two cultures. Taiwanese adults often ended their stories by explicitly stating the moral of the story. For instance, one Taiwanese mother concluded a story by emphasizing that: "Saying dirty words is not good." American stories seldom ended this way. The structure of the Taiwanese stories, then, *matched* the content. Both elements conveyed the view that a parent has more knowledge than a child, and that the parent has a responsibility to impart this knowledge.

Watch OBSERVING EVERYDAY STORYTELLING

Video

RESEARCH FOCUS

Review Question

1. Taiwanese families called the researcher "aunty." This is an example of:
   a. Infinite generativity
   b. Pragmatics
   c. Social gating
   d. Overextension

# Teaching and Learning Aids

## Learning Objectives

Learning objectives for each chapter are listed at the start of the chapter as well as alongside every section heading. Based on Bloom's taxonomy, these numbered objectives help students better organize and understand the material. The end-of-section summary is organized around these same objectives, as are all of the supplements and assessment material.

### Early Theories

LO 6.3.1 **Describe how behaviorist, innatist, and cognitive theories explain language development, including the extent to which they emphasize nature or nurture.**

Three early theories bring very different perspectives to language development, and continues to influence present-day research.

**BEHAVIORISM.** For language acquisition, as for the development of any other skill, **behaviorism** regards infants as starting out from scratch and learning behaviors based on the responses or "conditioning" of those around them (Skinner, 1957). According to this theory, children learn language based on:

- ***Positive reinforcement:*** when a caregiver encourages a child's behavior by responding positively to it, for example, with praise or a reward.
- ***Negative reinforcement:*** when a caregiver encourages a child's behavior by stopping or removing something negative, such as nagging or being grounded.

SUMMARY: Languages in Today's World

LO 6.1.1 **Provide an overview of languages spoken in today's world.**

The world has about 7,000 living languages. In many countries, more than one language is spoken and children grow up with knowledge of two or more languages. Linguists expect that hundreds of languages will die out during this century. To counteract extinction, preservation efforts geared to children and adolescents have sprung up.

LO 6.1.2 **Describe the impact of globalization on the languages that children grow up to speak.**

Globalization is influencing the language development of children. The use of English is growing worldwide, and the projection is that half of the world's population will be proficient English speakers by the year 2050. In part because of the spread of English, multilingualism is growing. Almost 70% of the world's population understands and speaks two or more languages.

## Section Summaries

Organized by learning objective, a summary now appears at the end of each section.

## Critical Thinking Questions

These questions encourage students to think more deeply and critically about a developmental topic, and to synthesize information across chapters.

**Critical Thinking Question:** Relate the above findings pertaining to brain damage and language development to the "plasticity" of the brain described in Chapter 2.

# Revel for *Child Development Worldwide*

When students are engaged deeply, they learn more effectively and perform better in their courses. This simple fact inspired the creation of Revel: an interactive learning environment designed for the way today's students read, think, and learn. Built in collaboration with educators and students nationwide, Revel is the newest, fully digital way to deliver respected Pearson content. Revel enlivens course content with media interactives and assessments—integrated directly within the authors' narrative—that provide opportunities for students to read about and practice course material in tandem. This immersive educational technology boosts student engagement, which leads to better understanding of concepts and improved performance throughout the course.

## Learn More about Revel

Rather than simply offering opportunities to read about and study child development, Revel facilitates deep, engaging interactions with the concepts that matter most. By providing opportunities to improve skills in analyzing and interpreting research and theory, Revel engages students directly and immediately, which leads to a better understanding of course material. A wealth of student and instructor resources and interactive materials can be found within Revel. Some of our favorites are mentioned in the information that follows.

For more information about all the tools and resources in Revel and access to your own Revel account for Child Development Worldwide, go to www.pearsonhighered.com/revel.

**Interactive Maps, Tables, and Figures** feature Social Explorer technology that allow for real-time data updates and rollover information to support the data and show movement over time. Dozens of other interactivities feature enhanced visuals and exercises that bring important concepts to life such as clickable maps that highlight differences between developing and developed nations, interactive figures, and table- and figure-based exercises that encourage students to check their understanding of materials.

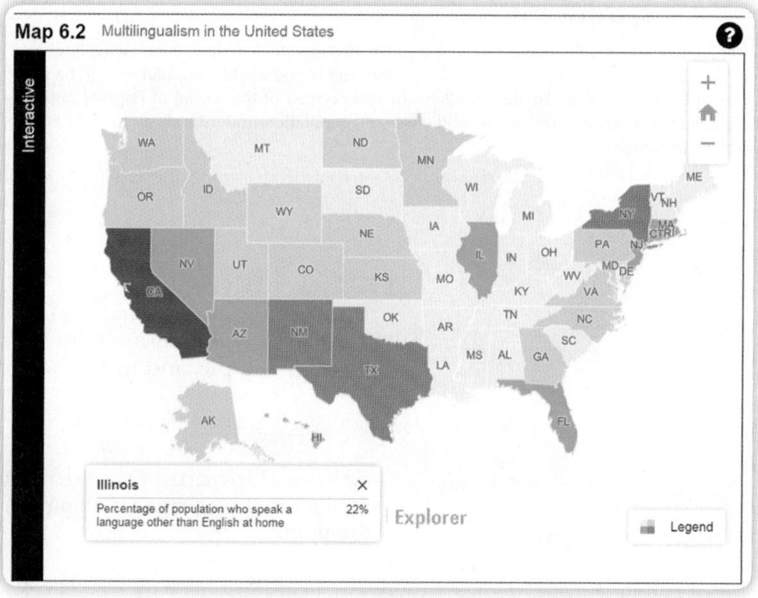

**"Chapter Introduction" Videos** begin each chapter and provide an overview of the developmental topic being covered. The videos feature children and parents from diverse cultural backgrounds discussing their lives and experiences in relation to the topic of a chapter.

ACROSS THE WORLD, PEOPLE SPEAK ABOUT 7,000 DIFFERENT LANGUAGES. Some languages are spoken by large numbers of people, others by small and diminishing communities. Babies come into the world primed to learn to speak any of the languages. In fact, they have an ability to detect differences among the sounds of all languages. By their first birthday, this ability will dramatically diminish as they become attuned to the specific language or languages spoken in their social world. Roughly around 1 year of age is also when children speak their first word, and in the course of the next few years, their skill at stringing together grammatically correct sentences and communicating in accordance with the cultural norms of their community develops with astonishing speed, especially between ages 2 and 3. In today's globalizing world, it is also increasingly common for children to grow up to be multilingual. In this chapter, we cover the unique human ability to go from zero words to fluency in one or more languages in the course of relatively few years. We also look at how children, adolescents, and emerging adults not only learn the languages of the adults in their community, but also take a lead role in creating new forms, including sign language and slang.

**Watch** CHAPTER INTRODUCTION: LEARNING LANGUAGES

Video

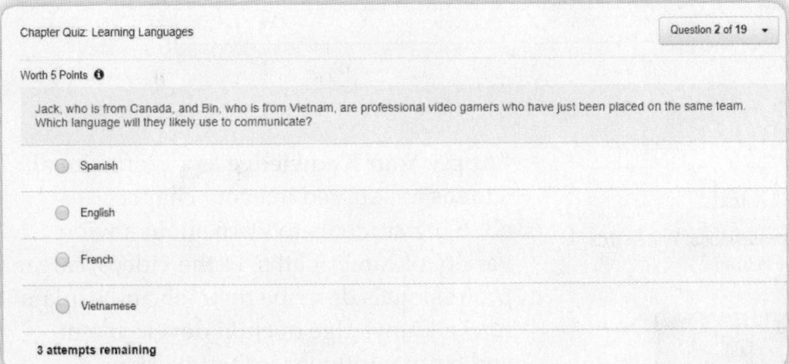

Chapter Quiz: Learning Languages

Question 2 of 19

Worth 5 Points

Jack, who is from Canada, and Bin, who is from Vietnam, are professional video gamers who have just been placed on the same team. Which language will they likely use to communicate?

- Spanish
- English
- French
- Vietnamese

**3 attempts remaining**

## End-of-Section and End-of-Chapter Review Quizzes

Available in our Revel product, multiple-choice practice quizzes appear after each section to help students assess their comprehension of the material. A cumulative multiple-choice test appears at the end of every chapter.

## Shared Writing

Assignable Shared Writing Activities in our Revel product direct students to share written responses with classmates, fostering peer discussion.

Shared Writing: Globalization and Media

Worth 20 Points

How does the global reach of media influence children's cultural values and identity development?

A minimum number of characters is required to post and earn points. After posting, your response can be viewed by your class and instructor, and you can participate in the class discussion.

Post

0 characters | 140 minimum

**"Breaking Developments"** feature author-written summaries of new landmark research and cultural trends. New Breaking Developments will be added to the Revel version of this title at the beginning of each January and July.

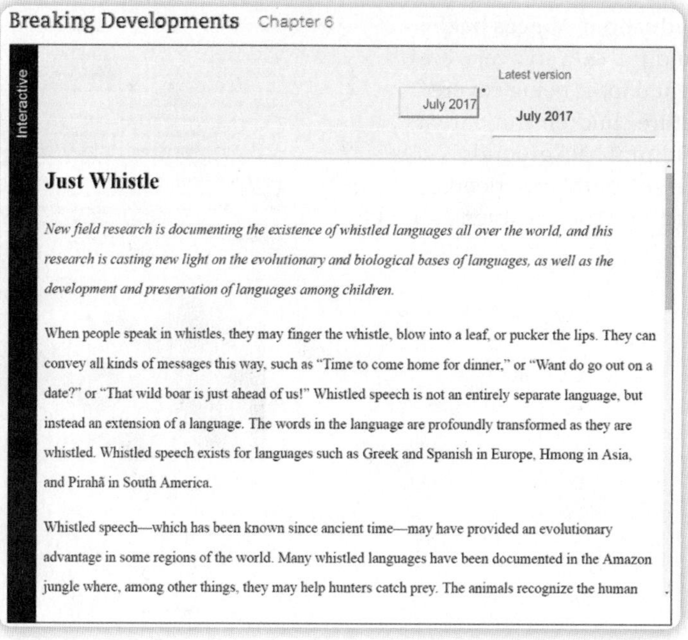

**"Apply Your Knowledge as a Professional" Videos** are offered in every chapter, allowing students to learn about a wide variety of career paths. In the videos, career professionals describe their job and explain how a knowledge of child development and culture influences their work on a daily basis.

**"Journaling Question"** prompts toward the end of each chapter give students an opportunity to apply key concepts and new knowledge to their own experiences.

Journaling Question: Reflect on your own psychological identity. How do you think of yourself? This chapter has introduced a variety of dimensions such as culture, developmental stage, ethnicity, gender, SES, and globalization. Which of these dimensions, and potentially others too, are most important to how you see yourself?

## Teaching and Learning Package

A textbook is but one component of a comprehensive learning package. The author team that prepared the teaching and learning package had as its goal to deliver the most comprehensive and integrated package on the market. All supplements were developed around the textbook's carefully constructed learning objectives. The authors are grateful to reviewers and focus group members who provided invaluable feedback and suggestions for creating a complete and outstanding package.

**TEST BANK** (ISBN: 0134635825) Written by Professor Regina M. Hughes (Collin College), the test bank contains hundreds of multiple-choice and essay questions, each referenced to the relevant page in the book and correlated to the chapter learning objectives. Each chapter of the test bank includes a Total Assessment Guide, an easy-to-reference grid that organizes all test items by learning objective and question type.

The test bank comes with Pearson MyTest (ISBN: 0134625366), a powerful test generation program that helps instructors easily create and print quizzes and exams. Questions and tests can be authored online, allowing instructors ultimate flexibility and the ability to efficiently manage assessments wherever and whenever they want. Instructors can easily access existing questions and then edit, create, and store using simple drag-and-drop and Word-like controls. Data on each question provides information relevant to difficulty level and page number. In addition, each question maps to the text's major section and learning objective. For more information go to www.PearsonMyTest.com.

**ENHANCED LECTURE POWERPOINT SLIDES WITH EMBEDDED VIDEOS** (ISBN: 0134891856) the Enhanced Lecture PowerPoints offer detailed outlines of key points for each chapter supported by selected visuals from the textbook, and include the videos from the video series featured in the text. ADA-compliant Standard Lecture PowerPoints (ISBN: 0134635744) without embedded videos are also available. A separate *Art and Figure* version (ISBN: 0134891864) of these presentations contains all art from the textbook for which Pearson has been granted electronic permissions

**INSTRUCTOR'S MANUAL** (ISBN: 0134635752) Written and compiled by Linda Lockwood, Ph.D. (Metropolitan State University), the Instructor's Manual includes suggestions for preparing for the course, sample syllabi, and current trends and strategies for successful teaching. Each chapter offers integrated teaching outlines and a list of the key terms for quick reference, and includes an extensive bank of lecture launchers, handouts, and activities. Answers to the in-text features are provided. The electronic format features click-and-view hotlinks that allow instructors to quickly review or print any resource from a particular chapter. This tool saves prep work and helps you maximize your classroom time.

**ACCESSING ALL RESOURCES** For access to all instructor supplements for *Child Development Worldwide*, go to www.pearsonhighered.com/irc and follow the directions to register (or log in if you already have a Pearson user name and password). Once you have registered and your status as an instructor is verified, you will be e-mailed a log-in name and password. Use your log-in name and password to access the catalog.

You can request hard copies of the supplements through your Pearson sales representative. If you do not know your sales representative, go to www.pearsonhighered.com/replocator and follow the directions. For technical support for any of your Pearson products, you and your students can contact http://247.pearsoned.com.

# Acknowledgments

Writing a new child development text involves many years of unwavering dedication, and we are profoundly grateful to all of the talented people who contributed to the effort.

We would especially like to thank Amber Chow, the Senior Portfolio Manager, who supported our vision for the text with her characteristic blend of thoughtfulness and enthusiasm. She mobilized all the resources necessary to bring it to fruition. Nic Albert and Julie Swasey performed superbly as the Senior Development Editors, going over every word of our writing and making it better. Thanks also go to the wise and indefatigable Debbie Coniglio at Ohlinger Publishing Services and to Gina Linko at Integra for coordinating all aspects of production. The fabulous videos were filmed by the folks at Cabin 3 Media and New Look Films, and the sketch art videos created by Video Jeeves. Cecilia Turner, the Content Producer, oversaw all aspects of the program and its supplements package, and Chris Fegan, Technical Manager of Learning Tools, and Elissa Senra-Sargent, the Digital Content Producer, coordinated all aspects of digital media production. Chris Brown, Product Marketing Manager, handled the marketing of the text and organized focus groups that provided valuable feedback on the Revel product. Liz Kincaid with SPi Global found the photos that do a fantastic job of reflecting our attention to diversity within and across cultures. Lumina created the cover design. We would also like to thank Noma Bar for the cover illustration, and Stephany Harrington for coordinating reviews.

Finally, we would like to thank all of the reviewers who read chapters, sections, and other materials in the course of the development of the book. We benefited greatly from their careful feedback, and now instructors and students reading the book will benefit, too.

## The Development of *Child Development Worldwide*

This text is the product of the most extensive development effort this market has ever witnessed. *Child Development Worldwide* reflects the countless hours and extraordinary efforts of a team of authors, reviewers, and publishing experts who shared a vision for not only a unique and up-to-date topical child development textbook, but also the most comprehensive and integrated supplements program on the market. Before writing, we reviewed almost 100 syllabi from instructors across the United States in order to understand important learning goals for students. Once writing commenced, dozens of manuscript reviewers provided invaluable feedback for making each chapter as accessible and relevant to students as possible. Every chapter was also reviewed by a panel of subject-matter experts to ensure accuracy and currency. Dozens of focus-group participants helped guide every aspect of the program, from content coverage to the art style and design to the configuration of the supplements. In fact, some of those focus-group participants were so inspired by the project that they became members of the supplements author team themselves. We'd like to thank those individuals by name here:

Katherine Abba, *Houston Community College*
Linda Aiken, *Southwestern Community College*
Laurel Anderson, *Palomar College*
Florencia Anggoro, *Holy Cross College*
Margaret Annunziata, *Davidson County Community College*
Dina L. Anselmi, *Trinity College*
Heather Bachman, *University of Pittsburgh*
Alfred Baptista, *Massasoit Community College*
Ashley Biddle, *University of Hawaii–Manoa*
Heidemarie Blumenthal, *University of North Texas*
Chris Boyatzis, *Bucknell University*
Steve Bradshaw, *Bryan College*
Leilani Brown, *University of Hawaii–Honolulu*
Amanda Cannarella, *Boston College*
Ralph Carlini, *UMASS–Dartmouth*
Johnny Castro, *Brookhaven College*
Shakiera Causey, *Guilford Technical Community College*
Kelly Champion, *Northern Illinois University*
Lover Chancler, *University of Centeral Missouri*
Stacie Christian, *University of Wisconsin–Green Bay*
Carol Connor, *University of California–Irvine*
Maricela Correa-Chavez, *California State University–Long Beach*
Christie Cunningham, *Pellissippi State Technical College*
William Damon, *Stanford University*
Maribel Del Rio-Roberts, *Nova Southeastern University*
Melissa Delgado, *Texas State University*
Allison DiBianca Fasoli, *Middlebury College*
Stacey Doan, *Claremont McKenna College*
Hope Doerner, *Minneapolis Community Technical College*
Dana Donohue, *Northern Arizona University*
Larry Eisenberg, *William Peace University*
Ann Englert, *Cal Poly Pomona*
Caitlin Faas, *Mount St. Mary's University*
Colleen Fawcett, *Palm Beach State*
Constance Flanagan, *University of Wisconsin*
Deb Flynn, *Mitchell Technical Institute*
Natasha Fratello, *American River College–Sacramento*
Amber Gentile, *Cabrini College*
Kim Glackin, *Metropolitan Community College, Blue River*
Christina Gotowka, *Tunxis Community College*
James Guinee, *University of Central Arkansas*
Jamie Harmount, *Ohio University*

Deborah Harris O'Brien, *Trinity Washington University*
Daniel Hart, *Rutgers University, Camden*
Myra Harville, *Holmes Community College*
Vivian Hsu, *Rutgers University*
Nancy Hughes, *SUNY Plattsburgh*
Suzanne Hughes, *Southwestern Community College*
Alisha Janowsky, *University of Central Florida*
Ben Jee, *Worcester State University*
Lee Ann Jolley, *Tennessee Tech University*
Jennifer Kampmann, *South Dakota State University*
Deena "Amy" Kausler, *Jefferson College*
Lisa Kincaid Bailey, *Florida State Community College at Jacksonville*
Pamela King, *Fuller Theological Seminary*
Kathy Kufskie, *Southwestern Illinois College*
Joseph Lao, *Hunter College and Teachers College*
Alyson Lavigne, *Roosevelt University*
Jennie Lee-Kim, *University of Maryland–College Park*
Miriam Linver, *Montclair State University*
Francesca Longo, *Boston College*
Mark Lyerly, *Burlington County College*
Adriana Manago, *University of California–Santa Cruz*
Rebecca Martin, *South Dakota State University*
Kyle Matsuba, *Kwantlen Polytechnic University*
Elizabeth McCarroll, *Texas Woman's University*
Melissa McInnis Brown, *Texas Woman's University*
Jessica McKenzie, *California State University–Fresno*
Tai McMiller, *Patrick Henry Community College*
Krisztina Micsinai, *Palomar College*
Wanda Moore, *Eastfield College*
Kristie Morris, *Rockland Community College*
Vicki Murrell, *University of Memphis*
Simone Nguyen, *University of North Carolina–Wilmington*
Wendy Orcajo, *Mt. San Jacinto Community College*
Laura Padilla-Walker, *Brigham Young University*
Kalani Palmer, *Indiana University of Pennsylvania*
Melissa Paoloni, *Folsom Lake College*
Carrie Pfeiffer-Fiala, *Cleveland State University*
Laura Pirazzi, *San Jose State University*
Nicole Porter, *Modesto Junior College*
Kerry Prior, *Grand Rapids Community College*
Lakshmi Raman, *Oakland University*
Andrea Rashtian, *California State University–Northridge*
Sadhna Ray, *Delgado Community College–West Bank*
Dianne Russom, *College of the Desert*
Brigette Ryalls, *University of Nebraska Omaha*
Beth Sanders-Rabinowitz, *Atlantic Cape Community College*
Carlos Santos, *Arizona State University*
Seth Schwartz, *University of Miami*
Jamie Shepherd, *Saddleback College*
Gaye Shook-Hughes, *St. Edwards University*
Wallace Smith, *Union County College*
Nelly St. Maria, *Suffolk County Community College–Selden*
Carola Suarez-Orozco, *University of California–Los Angeles*
Colleen Sullivan, *Worcester State College*
Moin Syed, *University of Minnesota*
Amber Tankersley, *Pittsburg State University*
Tanya Tavasollie, *George Mason University*
John van Bladel, *Fulton Montgomery Community College*
Marcia Weinstein, *Salem State University*
Delaine Welch, *Frederick Community College*
Marlene Welch, *Carroll Community College*
Patricia Westerman, *Bowie State University*
Karl Wheatley, *Cleveland State University*
Angela Williamson, *Tarrant County College*
Denise Winsor, *University of Memphis*

Lastly, dozens of students compared the manuscript to their current texts and provided suggestions for improving the prose and design. We thank everyone who participated in ways great and small, and hope that you are as pleased with the finished product as we are!

# About the Authors

Lene Arnett Jensen is Associate Professor in the Department of Psychology at Clark University in Worcester, Massachusetts. She received her Ph.D. in developmental psychology in 1994 from the University of Chicago, and did a 1-year postdoctoral fellowship at the University of California—Berkeley. Before coming to Clark University, she taught at the University of Missouri and Catholic University of America.

She aims through scholarship and professional collaboration to move the discipline of psychology toward understanding development both in terms of what is universal and what is cultural. She terms this a "cultural-developmental approach." Her research addresses moral development and cultural identity formation. Together with her students, she has conducted research in countries such as Denmark, India, Thailand, Turkey, and the United States. Her publications include *New Horizons in Developmental Theory and Research* (2005, with Reed Larson, Jossey-Bass/Wiley), *Immigrant Civic Engagement: New Translations* (2008, with Constance Flanagan), *Bridging Cultural and Developmental Psychology: New Syntheses for Theory, Research and Policy* (2011), the *Oxford Handbook of Human Development and Culture* (2015), *Moral Development in a Global World: Research from a Cultural-Developmental Perspective* (2015), and the *Oxford Handbook of Moral Development* (forthcoming).

From 2004 to 2015, she was editor-in-chief for the journal *New Directions for Child and Adolescent Development* (with Reed Larson). She served as program chair for the 2012 biennial conference of the Society for Research on Adolescence (with Xinyin Chen), and currently serves on awards committees for the Society for Research on Child Development (SRCD) and the Society for Research on Adolescence (SRA). For additional information, please see **www.lenearnettjensen.com**.

The authors with their toddler twins, Miles and Paris.

The authors with their twins, now on the cusp of emerging adulthood.

Jeffrey Jensen Arnett is a Research Professor in the Department of Psychology at Clark University in Worcester, Massachusetts. He received his Ph.D. in developmental psychology in 1986 from the University of Virginia, and did 3 years of postdoctoral work at the University of Chicago. From 1992 to 1998 he was Associate Professor in the Department of Human Development and Family Studies at the University of Missouri, where he taught a 300-student lifespan human development course every semester. In the fall of 2005, he was a Fulbright Scholar at the University of Copenhagen in Denmark.

His primary scholarly interest for the past 20 years has been in emerging adulthood. He coined the term, and he has conducted research on emerging adults concerning a wide variety of topics, involving several different ethnic groups in U.S. society. He is the Founding President and Executive Director of the Society for the Study of Emerging Adulthood (SSEA; www.ssea.org). From 2005 to 2014 he was the editor of the *Journal of Adolescent Research (JAR)*, and currently he is on the Editorial Board of JAR and five other journals. He has published many theoretical and research papers on emerging adulthood in peer-reviewed journals, as well as the books *Adolescence and Emerging Adulthood: A Cultural Approach* (2018, 6th edition), and *Emerging Adulthood: The Winding Road from the Late Teens Through the Twenties* (2015, 2nd edition). For more information on Dr. Arnett and his research, see **www.jeffreyarnett.com**.

Lene and Jeff live in Worcester, Massachusetts with their twins, Miles and Paris.

Chapter 1

# Child Development Worldwide: Who, How, and Why

## Learning Objectives

### 1.1 A Worldwide Profile of Humanity Today

1.1.1 Describe the nature of the "global demographic divide" between developing and developed countries, and explain why the United States is following a different demographic path from other developed countries.

1.1.2 Distinguish between developing and developed countries in terms of income, education, and cultural values.

1.1.3 Explain why socioeconomic status (SES), gender, and ethnicity are important aspects of child development within countries.

### 1.2 Humans: The Cultural and Global Species

1.2.1 Identify the evolution of characteristics that make modern humans distinct from their nearest great ape species.

1.2.2 Summarize the major changes in human cultures since the Upper Paleolithic period.

1.2.3 Apply information about human evolution to how child development takes place today.

### 1.3 The Field of Child Development: Emergence and Expansion

1.3.1 Provide some reasons why the field of child development primarily focused on younger children until about the mid-20th century.

1.3.2 Describe when the field of child development began to address adolescence in a notable way, and explain why the age range that Hall had designated for adolescence has been moved downward by contemporary researchers.

1.3.3 Explain how the field of child development has recently expanded anew to encompass emerging adulthood.

1.3.4 Describe the cultural-developmental approach, and why developmental stages and pathways within this approach are somewhat flexible.

### 1.4 How We Study Child Development

1.4.1 Recall the five steps of the scientific method.

1.4.2 Summarize the main measurements used in research on child development.

1.4.3 Distinguish between major types of research designs.

1.4.4 Describe the two major types of research designs distinctive to developmental psychology.

1.4.5 Identify some key ethical standards for child development research.

### 1.5 Why We Study Child Development Worldwide

1.5.1 Explain the three general levels at which child development contributes knowledge.

1.5.2 Give examples of how scientific knowledge can be applied across contexts to improve children's lives.

THE CHINESE HAVE AN EXPRESSION FOR THE LIMITED WAY ALL OF US LEARN TO SEE THE WORLD: *jing di zhi wa*, meaning "frog in the bottom of a well." The expression comes from a fable about a frog that has lived its entire life in a small well. The frog assumes that its tiny world is all there is, and it has no idea of the true size of the world. It is only when a passing turtle tells the frog of the great ocean to the east that the frog realizes there is much more to the world than it had known.

All of us are like that frog. We grow up as members of a culture and learn, through direct and indirect teaching, to see the world from the perspective that becomes most familiar to us. Because the people around us usually share that perspective, we seldom have cause to question it. Like the frog, we rarely perceive how big and diverse our human species really is.

**child development**
the ways individuals grow and change until adulthood

**culture**
the total pattern of a group's customs, beliefs, art, and technology

The goal of this text is for us to lift out of the well, by taking a cultural approach to understanding **child development**, the ways individuals grow and change until adulthood. This means that a central focus of the text is on how children develop as members of a culture. **Culture** is the total pattern of a group's customs, beliefs, art, and technology. In other words, a culture is a group's common way of life, passed on from one generation to the next. From the day we are born, all of us experience our lives as members of a culture, or sometimes more than one. This profoundly influences how we develop, how we behave, how we experience life, and how we see the world. Biology is important, too, of course, and this text provides in-depth discussion of up-to-date research on the interactions between biological and social influences. Nonetheless, human beings everywhere have essentially the same biological constitution, yet their paths from birth to adulthood are remarkably varied depending on the culture in which their development takes place.

As authors of this text, we will be your fellow frogs, your companions and guides as we rise together out of the well to gaze at the broad, diverse, remarkable cultural panorama of child development. The text will familiarize you with many variations in child development and cultural practices, which may lead you to think about your own development and your own cultural practices in a new light.

This chapter sets the stage for the rest of the text by addressing: the who, the how, and the why.

- ***Who?*** In this text, we address child development worldwide. Thus, we begin this chapter with a tour of the global human population. We look at demographic changes over time, today's diversity and interconnections across cultures, and population projections for the future. Additionally, we delve into the history of humanity in order to understand that humans have evolved to be a uniquely cultural and global species. In this text, we also take an encompassing perspective on child development. All cultures differentiate children from adults (Lancy, 2008), but who is considered an adult within a culture and by what age varies. The contemporary field of child development spans from the prenatal period through emerging adulthood, a new life stage in some cultures that comes after adolescence and ends by the mid-20s.

- *How?* The use of the scientific method is the hallmark of how researchers study child development. We will review the steps and tools of this method, including distinctive opportunities and challenges of conducting research with children and across cultures.
- *Why?* As you will realize in the course of reading this chapter, the scientific study of child development has grown tremendously since its birth more than 100 years ago. It is a dynamic field with findings that speak to people's personal and professional lives. We end by addressing the importance of contemporary child development research to understand and improve the lives of children worldwide.

**Watch** CHAPTER INTRODUCTION: CHILD DEVELOPMENT WORLDWIDE: WHO, HOW, AND WHY

# 1.1 A Worldwide Profile of Humanity Today

Because the goal of this text is to provide you with an understanding of how child development takes place in cultures all around the world, let's begin with a demographic profile of the world's human population in the early 21st century.

## Population Growth and Change

**LO 1.1.1 Describe the nature of the "global demographic divide" between developing and developed countries, and explain why the United States is following a different demographic path from other developed countries.**

Perhaps the most striking demographic feature of the human population today is the sheer size of it. For most of history the total human population was less than 10 million (McFalls, 2007). Women typically had from four to eight children. Due to inadequate medical care and nutrition, however, most of the children died in infancy or childhood and never reached reproductive age.

The human population began to increase notably around 10,000 years ago, with the development of agriculture and domestication of animals, but the growth remained slow and steady (Diamond, 1992). It was not until the past century that population growth began to accelerate at an astonishing rate. Around the year 1800, the human population stood at 1 billion. Then came the medical advances of the 20th century, and the elimination or sharp reduction of deadly diseases like smallpox, typhus, diphtheria, and cholera. The human population subsequently reached 2 billion by 1930, then tripled to 6 billion by 1999. The 7-billion threshold was surpassed just 12 years later, in early 2011. In short, population growth between 1800 and today has been exponential. As of 2017, the total human population is about 7.4 billion. If you want to see the exact number at the time that you are reading this, the U.S. Census Bureau keeps a running tally at https://www.census.gov/popclock/.

How high will the human population go? This is difficult to say. Estimates vary, but most projections indicate the total human population will rise to 10 billion by about 2090. Thereafter it will stabilize—perhaps even decline slightly. This forecast is based on the worldwide decline in birthrates that has taken place in recent years. The **total fertility rate (TFR)** (number of births per woman) worldwide is currently 2.5, which is substantially higher than the rate of 2.1 that is the *replacement rate* of a stable population. However, the TFR has been declining sharply for more than a decade and will decline to 2.1 by 2050 if current trends continue (Population Reference Bureau, 2014).

**total fertility rate (TFR)**
in a population, the number of births per woman

The projected population increase from now to 2090 will not take place equally around the world. On the contrary, there is a "global demographic divide" between the wealthy, economically developed countries that make up less than 20% of the world's population, and the economically developing countries that contain the majority of the world's population (Kent & Haub, 2005). Nearly all the population growth in the decades to come will take place in the economically developing countries. In contrast, nearly all wealthy countries are expected to decline in population during this period and beyond, because they have fertility rates that are well below replacement rate.

For the purposes of this text, we will use the term **developed countries** to refer to the most affluent countries in the world. Classifications of developed countries vary, but usually this designation includes Canada, the United States, Japan, South Korea, Australia, New Zealand, Chile, and nearly all the countries of Europe (Organization for Economic Cooperation and Development [OECD], 2017). (The term "Western" countries is also sometimes used to refer to most developed countries because they are in the Western hemisphere, geographically, except Japan and South Korea, which are considered "Eastern" countries). For our discussion, developed countries will be contrasted with **developing countries**, which have less wealth than the developed ones.

**developed countries**
world's most economically developed and affluent countries, with the highest median levels of income and education

**developing countries**
countries that have lower levels of income and education than developed countries but are experiencing rapid economic growth

## Cultural Focus: Niger and the Netherlands: An Up-Close Look at the Demographic Divide

The stark global demographic divide is illustrated by comparing Niger (pronounced NYE-jur) and the Netherlands, two countries with similar population sizes of 17 million in 2013. By 2050, Niger is projected to nearly quadruple its population to 66 million whereas the population of the Netherlands will likely only grow very slowly to 18 million. At the root of this divide are differences in the average number of births per woman and the share of the population in their childbearing years. As Table 1.1 shows, Nigerian women's total fertility rate is more than four times the rate of Dutch women. Also, half of Niger's population is younger than age 15, compared to 17% of the Netherland's population. For more information on the global demographic divide and its implications for children, watch the video *The Demographic Divide*.

**Watch** THE DEMOGRAPHIC DIVIDE

### Review Question

What are some ways that a high ratio of children-to-adults in a country might influence psychological development?

**Table 1.1** The Demographic Divide: Niger and the Netherlands

| | Niger | Netherlands |
|---|---|---|
| Population in 2013 | 17 million | 17 million |
| Population Projected for 2050 | 66 million | 18 million |
| Total Fertility Rate | 7.6 | 1.7 |
| Total Annual Births | 845,000 | 176,000 |
| Total Annual Deaths | 195,000 | 141,000 |
| Population Below Age 15 | 50% | 17% |
| Life Expectancy at Birth | 57 years | 81 years |
| Infant Mortality Rate per 1,000 Births | 51 | 3.7 |

SOURCE: Population Reference Bureau (2013).

Mothers from the Netherlands and Niger with their children.

As the comparison of Niger and the Netherlands exemplifies, an important implication of the global demographic divide is that the age composition of developing and developed countries differ markedly. Take a look at the two population pyramids in Figure 1.1. The proportion of the population that is younger than 25 years of age in developing countries is about 50%. In contrast, the comparable number is less than 30% for developed countries (United Nations, 2013). As we will see in the course of this text, a person's psychological development from birth into the 20s is bound to be affected by the demographic, social, and cultural differences between developing and developed regions of the world.

Although developing countries with particularly rapid population growth are severely constrained in their efforts to address poverty (Population Reference Bureau, 2013), many developing countries are nonetheless improving today. They are experiencing economic growth as they join the globalized economy. For example, India is a developing country, and most of its people live on an income of less than $2 a day (United Nations Development Program [UNDP], 2014). About half of Indian children are underweight and malnourished (World Bank, 2011). Less than half of Indian adolescents complete secondary school. Only about half of adult women are literate, and about three-fourths of adult men. About two-thirds of India's population lives in small rural villages, although there is a massive migration occurring from rural to urban areas, led mostly by older adolescents and emerging adults. However, India's economy has been booming for the past two decades, lifting hundreds of millions of Indians out of poverty (UNDP, 2014). India is now a world leader in manufacturing, telecommunications, and services. If the economy continues to grow at its present pace India will lead the world in economic production by 2050 (Price Waterhouse Coopers, 2011). Life is changing rapidly for Indians, and children born today are likely to experience much different economic and cultural contexts than their parents or grandparents have known.

The current population of developing countries is about 6.1 billion, about 82% of the world's population. In comparison, the current population of developed countries is 1.3 billion, about 18% of the total world population (Population Reference Bureau, 2014). Among developed countries, the United States is one of the few likely to gain rather than lose population in the next few decades. Currently there are about

**Figure 1.1** Population Pyramids in Developing and Developed Countries

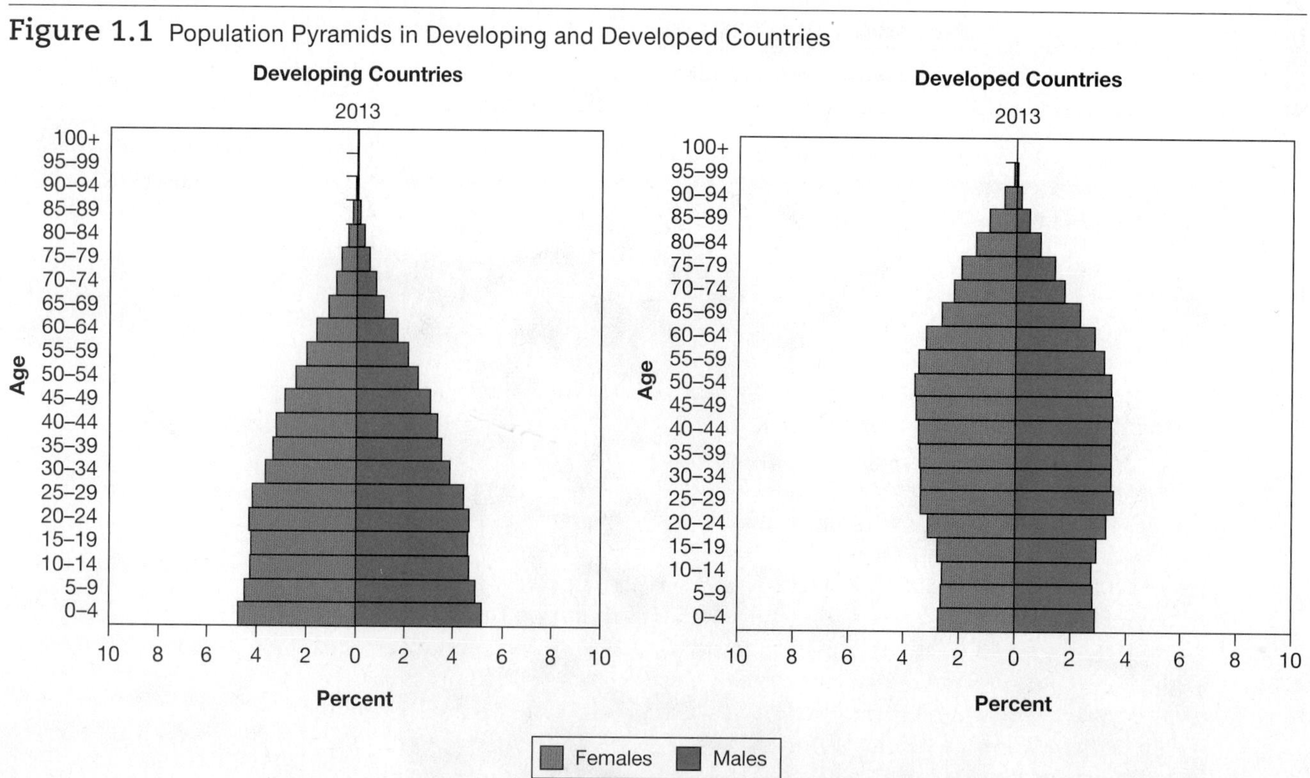

316 million persons in the United States, but the projection is for 400 million by 2050. Nearly all other developed countries—as exemplified above by the Netherlands—are expected to remain fairly steady in population between now and 2050. Some countries, such as Germany, Taiwan, and many eastern European countries are projected to decline. The decline will be steepest in Japan, which is projected to drop from a current population of 120 million to just 97 million by 2050, due to a low fertility rate and virtually no immigration (Population Reference Bureau, 2014).

There are two reasons why the United States is following a different demographic path than most other developed countries. First, the United States has a TFR of 1.9, which is slightly below the replacement rate of 2.1 but still higher than the TFR in most other developed countries (Population Reference Bureau, 2014). Second, and more importantly, the United States allows more legal immigration than most other developed countries do, and there are millions of undocumented immigrants as well (Suárez-Orozco, 2015). The increase in population in the United States between now and 2050 will result entirely from immigration (Martin & Midgley, 2010). Both legal and undocumented immigrants to the United States come mainly from Mexico and Latin America, although many also come from Asia and other parts of the world. Consequently, as Figure 1.2 shows, by 2050 the proportion of the U.S. population that is Latino is projected to rise from 16% to 30%. Canada also has relatively open immigration policies, so Canada, too, may experience an increase in population (DeParle, 2010; Population Reference Bureau, 2013).

**Figure 1.2** Projected Ethnic Changes in the U.S. Population to 2050

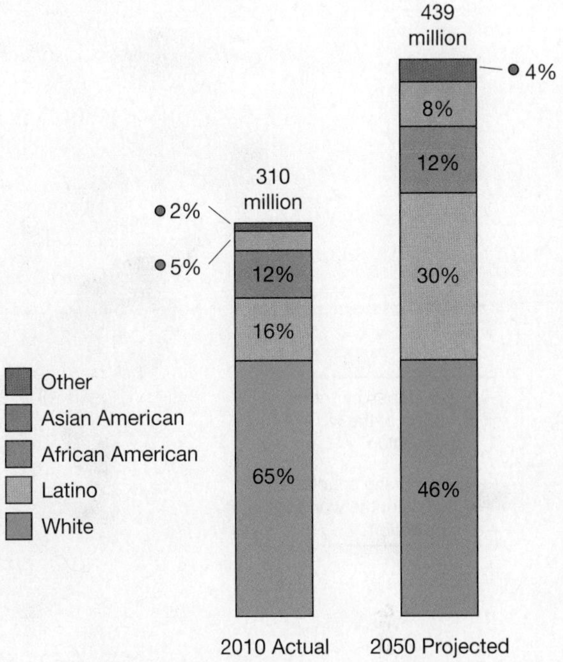

**Critical Thinking Question:** Can you think of three ways that growing up in a country, such as the United States, with a relatively high proportion of immigrants is different from growing up in one, such as Japan, where there are few immigrants?

## Variation Across Countries

**LO 1.1.2 Distinguish between developing and developed countries in terms of income, education, and cultural values.**

The demographic contrast between developed countries and the rest of the world is stark. As you can see from Map 1.1 (next page), this is not only with respect to population but also in other key areas, such as income and education. With respect to income, about 40% of the world's population lives on less than $2 per day, and 80% of the world's population lives on a family income of less than $6,000 per year (Population Reference Bureau, 2014). At one extreme are the developed countries, where 9 of 10 persons are in the top 20% of the global income distribution, and at the other extreme is southern Africa, where half of the population is in the bottom 20% of global income. Africa's economic growth has been strong for the past decade, but it remains the poorest region in the world (McKinsey Global Institute, 2010; UNDP, 2015).

A similar contrast between rich and poor countries exists regarding education. Your experience as a college student is a rare and privileged status in most of the world. In developed countries, virtually all children obtain primary and secondary education, and about 50% go on to tertiary education (college or other post-secondary training). However, in developing countries about 20% of children do not complete primary school and only somewhat more than half are enrolled in secondary school (UNDP, 2014). College and other tertiary education are only for the wealthy elite.

**Map 1.1** Worldwide Variations in Population and Income Levels

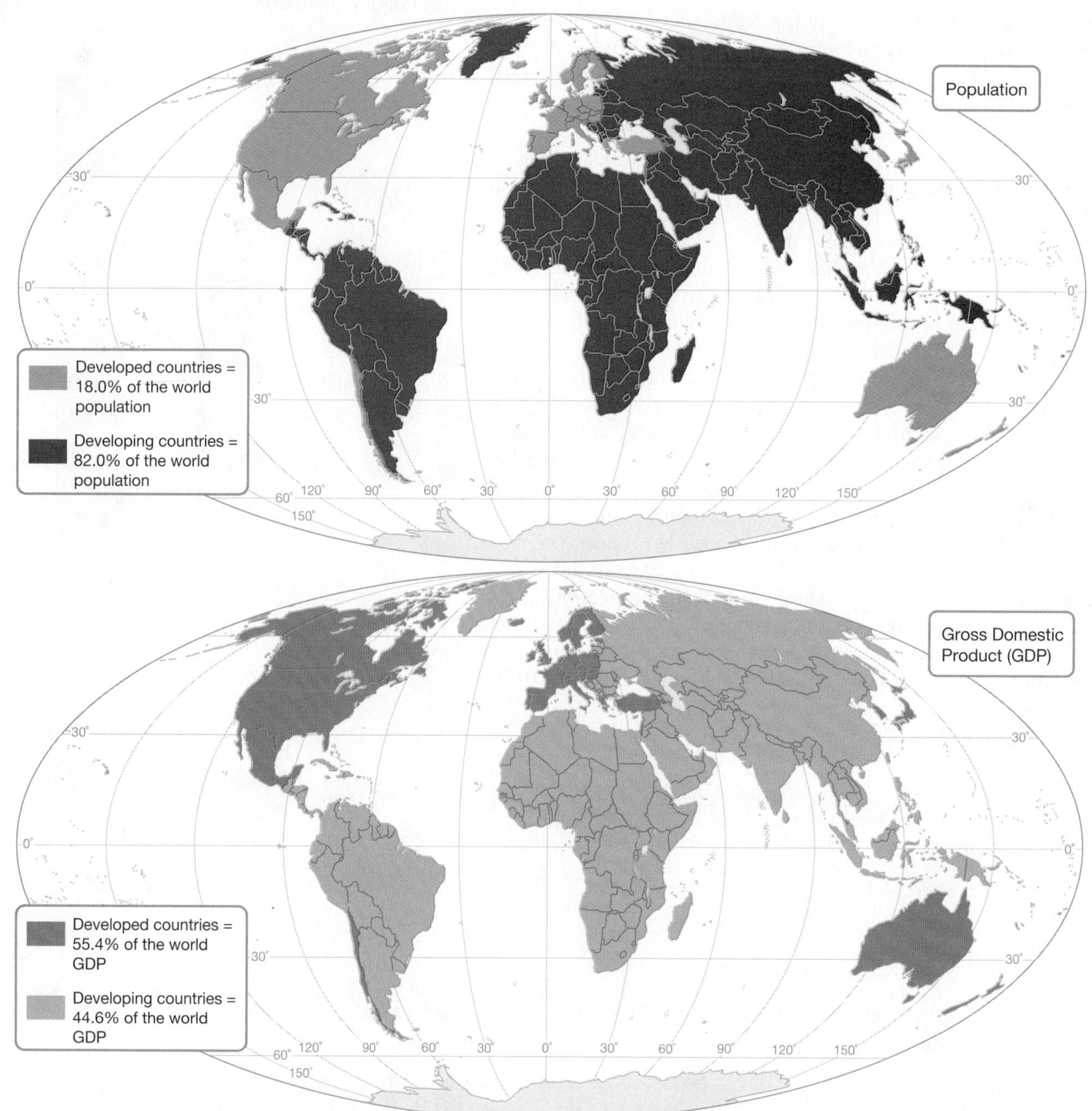


**individualistic**
cultural values such as independence and self-expression

**collectivistic**
cultural values such as obedience and group harmony

There are also some broad cultural differences between developed and developing countries, even though each category is very diverse. One important difference is that the cultures of developed countries tend to be based on **individualistic** values such as independence and self-expression (Greenfield, 2005; Hermans, 2015). In contrast, developing countries tend to prize **collectivistic** values such as obedience and group harmony (Sullivan & Cottone, 2010). These are not mutually exclusive categories and each country has some balance between individualistic and collectivistic values (Kağitçibaşi & Yalin, 2015). Furthermore, most countries contain a variety of cultures, some of which may be relatively individualistic whereas others are relatively collectivistic. Nevertheless, the overall distinction between individualism and collectivism is useful for describing broad differences between cultural groups.

Within developing countries there is often a sharp divide between rural and urban areas, with people in urban areas having higher incomes and receiving more education and better medical care. Often, the lives of middle-class persons in urban areas of developing countries resemble the lives of people in developed countries in many ways, yet they are much different than people in rural areas of their own countries (UNDP, 2014). In this text, the term **traditional cultures** refers to people in the rural areas of developing countries, who tend to adhere more closely to the historical traditions of their culture than people in urban areas do. Traditional cultures tend to be more collectivistic than other cultures are, in part because in rural areas close ties with others are often an economic necessity (Sullivan & Cottone, 2010).

By age 10, many children in developing countries are no longer in school. Here, a child in Cameroon helps his mother make flour.

This worldwide profile of humanity today demonstrates that if you wish to understand psychological development, it is crucial to understand the lives of children and their families in developing countries, who comprise the majority of the world's population. The tendency in most social science research, especially in psychology, has been to ignore or strip away culture in pursuit of universal principles of development (Jensen, 2011; Rozin, 2006). As we will learn in the course of this text, there are universals of child development. To fully comprehend children's development, however, we also need to understand its worldwide variations.

Most research in developmental psychology is on the 18% of the world's population that lives in developed countries—especially the 5% of the world's population that lives in the United States (Arnett, 2008; Henrich et al., 2010). This is changing, and in recent years there has been increasing attention paid in psychology and other social science fields to the cultural side of development (Bornstein, 2010; Jensen, 2015; Goodnow & Lawrence, 2015). By now, researchers have presented descriptions of child development in places all over the world. Furthermore, researchers studying American society have increased their attention to cultures within the United States that are outside of the White middle class.

**traditional cultures**
people in the rural areas of developing countries, who tend to adhere more closely to the historical traditions of their culture than people in urban areas do

## Variations Within Countries

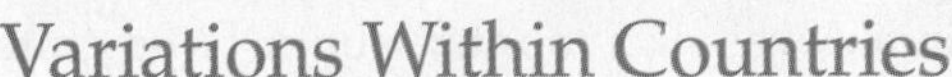

**LO 1.1.3 Explain why socioeconomic status (SES), gender, and ethnicity are important aspects of child development within countries.**

The contrast between developed countries and developing countries will be used often as a general way of drawing a contrast between child development in relatively rich and relatively poor countries. However, it should be noted that there is substantial variation within each of these categories. All developed countries are relatively wealthy, but child development in Japan is quite different from child development in France or Canada. All developing countries are less wealthy than developed countries, but child development in China is quite different than child development in Bolivia or Niger. We will explore variations in child development within the broad categories of developed countries and developing countries.

Not only is there important variation in psychological development within each category of developed and developing countries, but there is additional variation within each country. Most countries today have a **majority culture** that sets most of the norms and standards and holds most of the positions of political, economic, intellectual, and media power (García Coll et al., 1996; Marks et al., 2015). In addition, there may be many minority cultures defined by ethnicity, religion, language, or other characteristics.

**majority culture**
within a country, the cultural group that sets most of the norms and standards and holds most of the positions of political, economic, intellectual, and media power

Variations in child development also occur because of differences within countries in the settings and circumstances of individual lives. The settings and circumstances that contribute to variations in pathways of development are called **contexts**. Contexts include environmental settings such as family, peer groups, school and work, media, as well as civic and religious institutions. In this text, we devote a complete chapter to each of these contexts. Three other important aspects of variation that will be highlighted throughout are socioeconomic status, gender, and ethnicity.

**contexts**
settings and circumstances that contribute to variations in pathways of human development, including SES, gender, and ethnicity, as well as family, school, community, and media

Minority cultures are often defined by ethnicity, religion, and language as well as distinct cultural traditions. Here a Latina girl and her parents in the United States are ready for her quinceañera (coming-of-age) celebration.

The term **socioeconomic status (SES)** is often used to refer to a person's *social class*, which includes educational level, income level, and occupational status. For children and adolescents, because they may not yet have reached the social-class level they will have as adults, SES is usually used in reference to their parents' levels of education, income, and occupation. In most countries, SES is highly important in shaping development. It influences everything from the risk of infant mortality (as we saw for Niger and the Netherlands) to height and weight in infancy and childhood to children's language development and communication styles within families to age of first sexual intercourse and use of contraception in adolescence (as we will see in upcoming chapters).

**socioeconomic status (SES)**

person's social class, including educational level, income level, and occupational status

Differences in SES are especially sharp in developing countries (UNDP, 2014). In a country such as India, or Peru, or Saudi Arabia growing up as a member of the upper-class SES elite is very different from growing up as a member of the relatively poor majority, in terms of access to resources such as health care and education. However, even in developed countries there are important SES differences in access to resources. For example, in the United States infant mortality is higher among low-SES families than among high-SES families, in part because low-SES mothers are less likely to receive prenatal care (Daniels et al., 2006).

Gender is a key factor in development throughout the life course, in every culture (Carroll & Wolpe, 2005; UNDP, 2014). The expectations cultures have for females and males are different from the time they are born (Hatfield & Rapson, 2005). However, the degree of the differences varies greatly among cultures. In most developed countries today, the differences are relatively blurred: Men and women hold many of the same jobs, wear many of the same clothes (e.g., jeans, T-shirts), and enjoy many of the same entertainments. If you have grown up in a developed country, you may be quite surprised to learn in the chapters to come just how deep gender differences go in many other cultures. Nevertheless, gender-specific expectations exist in developed countries, too, as we will see.

**ethnicity**

group identity that may include components such as cultural origin, cultural traditions, race, religion, and language

Finally, **ethnicity** is a crucial part of child development. Ethnicity may include a variety of components, such as cultural origin, cultural traditions, race, religion, and language. Minority ethnic groups may arise as a consequence of immigration. There are also countries in which ethnic groups have a long-standing presence and may even have arrived before the majority culture. For example, Aboriginal peoples lived in Australia for many millennia before the first European settlers arrived. Many African countries were constructed by European colonial powers in the 19th century and consist of people of a variety of ethnicities, each of whom has lived in their region for many generations. Often, ethnic minorities within countries have distinct cultural patterns that are different from those of the ethnic majority. For example, in the Canadian majority culture, premarital sex is common, but in the large Asian Canadian minority group, female virginity until marriage remains highly valued (Sears, 2012). In many developed countries, most of the ethnic minority groups have values that are less individualistic and more collectivistic than in the majority culture (Suárez-Orozco, 2015).

**Critical Thinking Question:** The American Academy of Pediatrics (2016) recommends that parents not share a bed with their baby. Based on what you have read so far, would you expect differences by cultural values, SES, and ethnicity in how likely parents in the United States are to follow this advice?

## SUMMARY: A Worldwide Profile of Humanity Today

**LO 1.1.1 Describe the nature of the "global demographic divide" between developing and developed countries, and explain why the United States is following a different demographic path from other developed countries.**

The total human population was less than 10 million for most of history, but it has been rising exponentially since 1800. The human population rose from 1 billion in 1800 to 7 billion in 2011, and it is expected to increase to 10 billion by 2090. There is a global demographic divide in that nearly all the population growth in the decades to come will take place in economically developing countries. The projection is that the United States, unlike most developed countries, will experience an increase in population during the 21st century, primarily as a result of immigration.

**LO 1.1.2 Distinguish between developing and developed countries in terms of income, education, and cultural values.**

Most people in developing countries are poor and live in rural areas, but these countries are experiencing rapid economic development and a massive migration to urban areas. Only about 50% of children in developing countries are enrolled in secondary school, whereas almost all children in developed countries complete secondary education. In general, cultural values are more collectivistic in developing countries and individualistic in developed countries. These are not mutually exclusive categories and each country has some balance between the two kinds of values.

**LO 1.1.3 Explain why socioeconomic status (SES), gender, and ethnicity are important aspects of child development within countries.**

SES includes educational level, income level, and occupational status. Within both developing and developed countries, SES influences access to resources such as education and health care. Gender shapes expectations and opportunities in most cultures throughout life. Ethnicity often includes a distinct cultural identity, and ethnic minorities within countries often have cultural patterns that are different from those of the ethnic majority.

# 1.2 Humans: The Cultural and Global Species

In the course of this text, you will see that the lives of children, adolescents, and emerging adults are fabulously diverse across and within cultures. But how did this diversity arise? Humans are one species, so how did so many different ways of life develop from one biological origin? Before we turn our attention to the development of individuals—called *ontogenetic* development—it is important to understand our *phylogenetic* development, that is, the development of the human species. As we will now see, humans have evolved to be a singularly cultural species capable of inhabiting almost any part of the globe (Tomasello, 2010). For students who hold religious beliefs that may lead them to object to evolutionary theory, we understand that you may find this section of the text challenging, but it is nevertheless important to be familiar with the theory of evolution and the evidence supporting it.

**natural selection**
evolutionary process in which the offspring best adapted to their environment survive to produce offspring of their own

## From Africa to Distant Destinations

**LO 1.2.1 Identify the evolution of characteristics that make modern humans distinct from their nearest great ape species.**

To understand human origins it is important to know a few basic principles of the theory of evolution, first proposed by Charles Darwin in 1859 in his book *On the Origin of Species*. At the heart of the theory of evolution is the proposition that all species change through the process of **natural selection**. In natural selection, the young of a species are born with variations on a wide range of characteristics. Some young may be relatively large and others

**Watch** NATURAL SELECTION

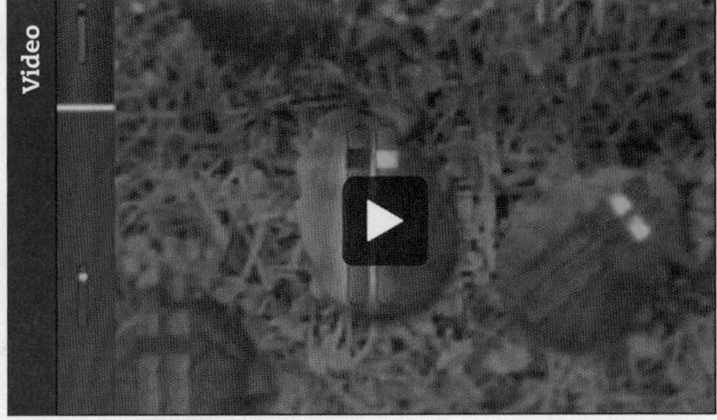

**Figure 1.3** Changes in Brain Size in Early Humans

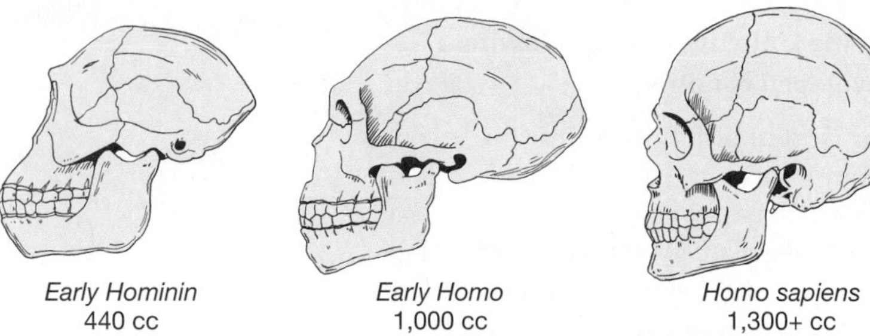


relatively small, some relatively fast and others relatively slow, and so on. Among the young, those who will be most likely to survive until they can reproduce will be the ones whose variations are best adapted to their environment. The video *Natural Selection* has more detail on this process.

According to evolutionary biologists, humans, chimpanzees, and gorillas had a common primate ancestor until 6 to 8 million years ago (Shreeve, 2010). At about that time, this common ancestor split into three paths, leading to the development of humans as well as to chimpanzees and gorillas. The evolutionary line that eventually led to humans is known as the *hominin* line. Early hominins lived in Africa, as chimpanzees and gorillas do today.

***Homo sapiens***
species of modern humans

By 200,000 years ago the early hominin species had evolved into our species, ***Homo sapiens*** (Shreeve, 2010; Wilson, 2012). During the millions of years of evolution that led to *Homo sapiens*, crucial characteristics developed that made us distinct from chimpanzees, gorillas, and earlier hominins. Two of these pertain to the human brain. The size of *Homo sapiens'* brain became about three times as large as the brains of chimpanzees and early hominins. Figure 1.3 shows changes in brain size in cubic centimeters (cc) in early humans.

To allow for the birth of bigger-brained babies, the female *Homo sapiens'* pelvis became relatively wide. However, bipedalism simultaneously required pelvises narrow enough for stable walking and running. This is almost certainly why human children are born at an earlier stage of brain development relative to other African great ape species. The brain of a chimpanzee is at 45% of its average adult size at birth and at 85% by 1 year of age. In contrast, the human infant's brain is merely at 25% of the adult size at birth and not until 6 years of age does it reach approximately 85% to 90% (Hublin, 2005; Stiles & Jernigan, 2010). In short, compared to chimpanzees, gorillas, and early hominins, *Homo sapiens* evolved to have a remarkable brain capacity. Furthermore, the less mature brain of the human child at birth makes for a longer period of dependency, and for extensive brain maturation and learning within local physical and cultural environments (Bjorklund, 2007; Haun 2015).

At some point between 125,000 and 60,000 years ago, *Homo sapiens* migrated out of Africa, and over time these humans replaced other hominin species (such as Neanderthals) who had left Africa earlier (Meredith, 2011). In contrast to their nearest

Humans evolved to establish cultural communities across the globe, from the arctic to tropical rainforests, from deserts to mountains.

great ape relatives, who all still live close to the equator in Africa, humans adapted to life in highly different environments. For example, evidence indicates that at least 45,000 years ago humans lived in the Arctic (Gibbons, 2016). Successfully surviving in vastly different environments, from equatorial Africa to the Arctic, requires the highly flexible set of cognitive skills afforded by the human brain. As we will see next, successful human survival across the globe also requires the ability to form cultural communities and complex social institutions (Tomasello, 2010).

## Early Cultures and Civilizations

**LO 1.2.2 Summarize the major changes in human cultures since the Upper Paleolithic period.**

Physically, *Homo sapiens* has changed little from 200,000 years ago to the present. However, as shown in Figure 1.4 (next page), a dramatic change in the development of the human species took place during the *Upper Paleolithic period* from about 50,000 to 10,000 years ago (Ember et al., 2011; Wilson, 2012).

For the first time, cultural differences developed between human groups, as reflected in their art and tools. Humans began to bury their dead, sometimes including art objects in the graves. There was also a rapid acceleration in the development of tools. For example, the first boats were invented, allowing humans to reach and populate Australia and New Guinea. Also, trade took place between human groups.

Whereas the origin of the revolutionary changes of the Upper Paleolithic remains a mystery (Wrangham, 2009), climate change was a key contributor to dramatic changes during the *Neolithic period*, from 10,000 years ago to about 5,000 years ago (Johnson, 2005). The Upper Paleolithic was the time of the last Ice Age, when glaciers covered Europe as far south as present-day Berlin, and in North America, as far south as what is now Chicago. By the Neolithic period the climate had become much warmer, resembling our climate today.

As the climate became warmer and wetter, new plants evolved that were good human food sources, and humans began to produce more of the ones they liked best. The huge animals that had been hunted during the Upper Paleolithic became extinct, perhaps from overhunting, perhaps because the animals failed to adapt to the climate changes (Diamond, 1992). Domestication of animals may have developed as a food source to replace the extinct animals. Along with agriculture and animal care came new tools: mortars and pestles for processing plants into food, and the spindle and loom for weaving cotton and wool into clothing. Larger, sturdier dwellings were built (and furniture such as beds and tables) because people stayed in settled communities longer to tend their plants and animals.

The final major historical change that provides the basis for how we live today began around 5,000 years ago with the development of **civilization** (Ridley, 2010). The characteristics that mark civilization include cities, writing, specialization into a variety of kinds of work, differences among people in wealth and status, and a centralized political system known as a *state*. The first civilizations developed around the same time in Egypt and Sumer (part of what is now Iraq). Because people in these civilizations kept written records and produced many goods, we have a lot of information about how they lived. We know they had laws and sewer systems, and that their social classes included priests, soldiers, craftsmen, government workers, and slaves. We know they built monuments to their leaders, such as the pyramids that still stand today in Egypt. They produced a vast range of goods including jewelry, sculpture, sailboats, wheeled wagons, and swords. Later civilizations developed in India (around 4,500 years ago), China (around 3,700 years ago), southern Africa (around 3,000 years ago), the Mediterranean area (Greece and Rome, around 2,700 years ago), and South America (around 2,200 years ago).

**civilization**
form of human social life, beginning about 5,000 years ago, that includes cities, writing, occupational specialization, and states

Why did civilizations and states arise? As agricultural production became more efficient, especially after the invention of irrigation, not everyone in a cultural group had to work on food production. This allowed some members of the group to be concentrated in cities, away from food-production areas, where they could specialize as merchants, artists, bureaucrats, and religious and political leaders. Furthermore, as the use of irrigation expanded there was a need for a state to build and oversee the system, and as trade expanded there was a need for a state to build infrastructure such as roadways. Trade also connected people in larger cultural groups that could be united into a common state (Ridley, 2010).

Figure 1.4 Key Changes in Human Species Development Past 50,000 Years

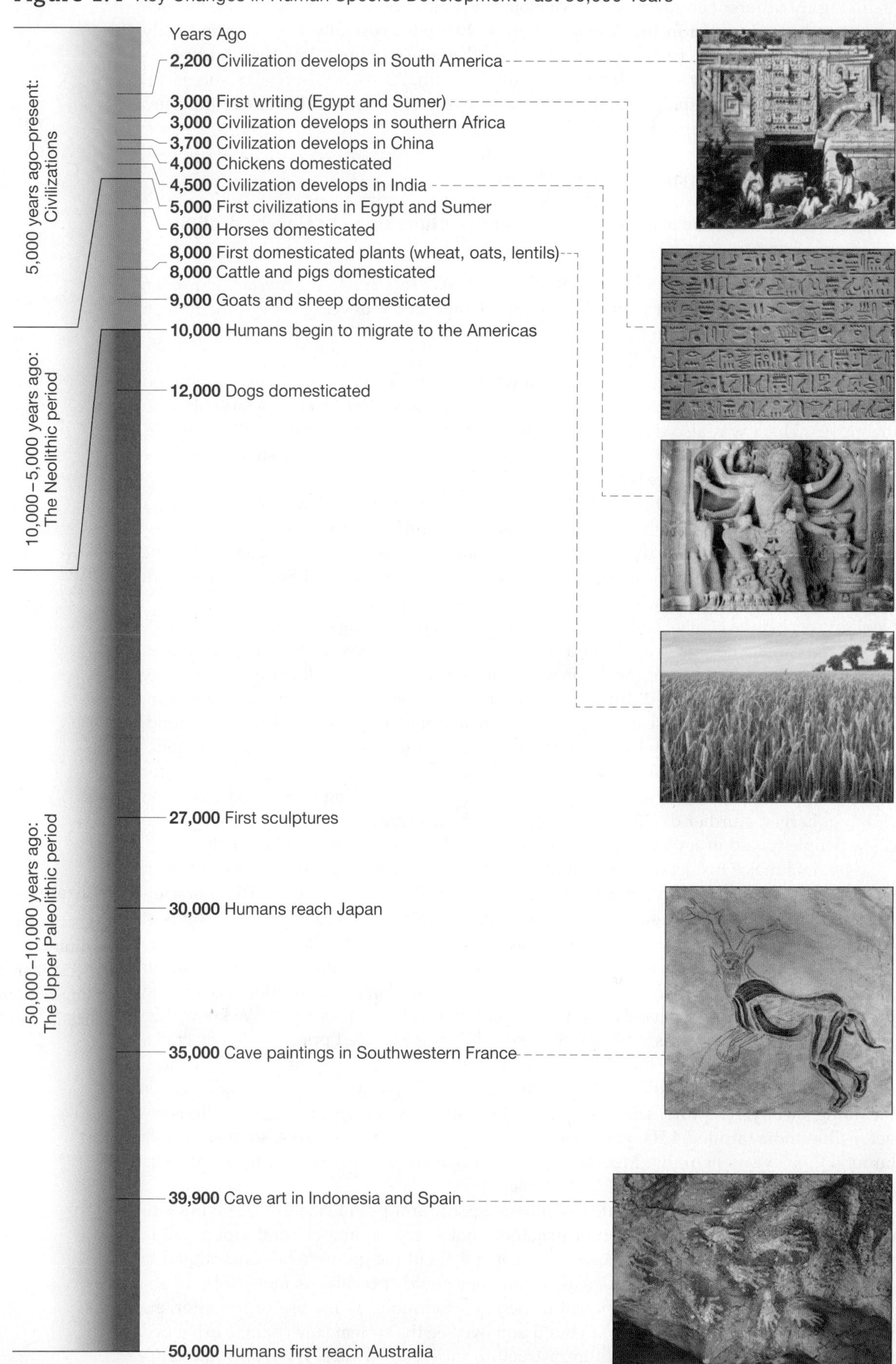


SOURCE: Pearson Education, Inc.

## Evolution, Culture, and Child Development Today

**LO 1.2.3 Apply information about human evolution to how child development takes place today.**

How does the evolution of the human species pertain to child development today? First, it is important to recognize that how we develop and who we are as human beings is based partly on our evolutionary history. Researchers working in the field of **evolutionary psychology** argue that many characteristics of humans are influenced by our evolutionary history, including aggressiveness, empathy, and mate selection (Crawford & Krebs, 2008; De Waal, 2009). We will examine their research in the course of this text.

**evolutionary psychology** branch of psychology that examines how patterns of human functioning and behavior have resulted from adaptations to evolutionary conditions

A second important fact to note about our evolutionary history is that biologically we have changed little since the origin of *Homo sapiens* about 200,000 years ago, yet how we live has changed in astonishing ways (Ridley, 2010; Wilson, 2012). Although we are a species that originated in the grasslands and forests of Africa, now we live in every environment on earth. Although we are a species that evolved to live in small groups of a few dozen persons, now most of us live in cities with millions of other people. Although human females are capable of giving birth to at least eight children in the course of their reproductive lives, and probably did so through most of history, now most women have one, two, or three children—or perhaps none at all. Although children transitioned into adult-like work at an early age for much of history, now that transition often occurs only during emerging adulthood in developed countries and among the urban middle- and upper-classes in developing countries.

As far as we can tell from the fossil record, all early hominins lived in the same way (Shreeve, 2010). Even different groups of early *Homo sapiens* seem to have lived more or less alike before the Upper Paleolithic period, as hunters and gatherers in small groups. Today there are hundreds of different cultures around the world, all part of the human community but each with its distinctive way of life. There are wide cultural variations in how we live, such as how we care for infants, what we expect from children, how we respond to the changes of puberty, and whether we extend the entry into a full sense of adulthood into the 20s. As members of the species *Homo sapiens* we all share a similar biology, but cultures shape the raw material of biology into widely different developmental paths.

It is culture that makes us unique as a species. Other species have evolved in ways that are adaptive for a particular set of environmental conditions. They can learn in the course of their lifetimes, certainly, but the scope of their learning is limited (Haun, 2015). When their environment changes, if their species is to survive it will do so not by learning new skills required by a new environment but through a process of natural selection that will enable those best-suited *genetically* to the new environmental conditions to survive long enough to reproduce, while the others do not.

In contrast, once humans developed the large brain we have now, it enabled us to survive in any environment by inventing and learning new skills and methods of survival, and then passing them along to others as part of a cultural way of life. We also became capable of altering our environments, so that it was no longer natural selection alone that would determine how we would live, but the cultures we created. We can survive and thrive even in conditions that are vastly different from our environment of evolutionary adaptation, because our capacity for cultural learning is so large and, compared to other animals, there is relatively little about us that is fixed by instinct.

### SUMMARY: Humans: The Cultural and Global Species

**LO 1.2.1 Identify the evolution of characteristics that make modern humans distinct from their nearest great ape species.**

*Homo sapiens* evolved to have a remarkable brain capacity. Furthermore, the less mature brain of the human child at birth makes for a longer period of dependency and for extensive brain maturation and learning within local physical and cultural environments. Compared to their nearest great ape species, humans evolved to be a singularly cultural species capable of inhabiting almost any part of the globe.

**LO 1.2.2 Summarize the major changes in human cultures since the Upper Paleolithic period.**

The Upper Paleolithic period (50,000–10,000 years ago) was the first time human cultures became distinct from one another in their art and tools. During the Neolithic period (10,000–5,000 years ago), humans first domesticated plants and animals. The first civilizations around 5,000 years ago marked the origin of writing, specialized work, and a centralized state.

**LO 1.2.3 Apply information about human evolution to how child development takes place today.**

How we develop and who we are as human beings is based partly on our evolutionary history. As a species, however, our large brains have enabled us to adapt to almost any environment by inventing new methods of survival and passing them along to children as part of a cultural way of life. We have also become capable of altering our environments, so that it is no longer natural selection alone that determines how we live, but the cultures we create.

# 1.3 The Field of Child Development: Emergence and Expansion

The field of child development emerged as a science around the turn of the 20th century. Between 1890 and 1910, there was a burst in publications focusing on psychological development (Collins & Hartup, 2013). In this section, we look at how the field of child development over the course of somewhat more than a century has moved from a predominant focus on children to encompass adolescents and emerging adults.

## The Emergence of a Science of Child Development

**LO 1.3.1 Provide some reasons why the field of child development primarily focused on younger children until about the mid-20th century.**

We first zoom in on three scholars who made long-lasting and memorable contributions to the emergence of the field of child development, Sigmund Freud (1856–1939), Alfred Binet (1857–1911), and G. Stanley Hall (1844–1924). They were not the only important contributors, but their work and its historical context elucidate why developmental researchers primarily studied younger children for many decades after the founding of the field, and how attention to adolescents was sporadic.

Freud's focus on early child development had a major impact on the field.

**FREUD'S FOCUS ON EARLY CHILDHOOD.** The earliest scientific theory of psychological development was devised by Sigmund Freud, who was a physician in Vienna, Austria, in the late 19th century (Breger, 2000). Freud's theory became the dominant view of psychological development throughout the first half of the 20th century (Robins et al., 1999), and its supremacy is one reason why the field for many decades focused overwhelmingly on children.

Working with persons suffering from various mental health problems, Freud concluded that a consistent theme across patients was that they seemed to have experienced some kind of traumatic event in childhood. The trauma then became buried in their unconscious minds, or *repressed*, and continued thereafter to shape their personality and their mental functioning even though they could no longer remember it. In an effort to address their problems, Freud developed the first method of psychotherapy, which he called *psychoanalysis*. The purpose of psychoanalysis was to bring patients' repressed memories from the unconscious into consciousness, through having them discuss their dreams and childhood experiences while guided by the psychoanalyst (Freud, 1901/1953). According to Freud, just making the repressed memories conscious would be enough to heal the patient.

Freud's (1905/1953) experiences as a psychoanalyst were the basis of his **psychosexual theory**. He believed that sexual desire was the driving force behind human behaviors throughout life, but that the locus of the sexual drive shifts around the body during the course of early development. He proposed five stages of child development.

**psychosexual theory**
Freud's theory proposing that sexual desire is the driving force behind psychological development

1. The *oral stage* of infancy is when sexual sensations are concentrated in the mouth. Infants derive pleasure from sucking, chewing, and biting.
2. The *anal stage*, beginning at about a year and a half, is when sexual sensations are concentrated in the anus. Toddlers derive their greatest pleasure from the act of elimination and are fascinated by feces.
3. The *phallic stage*, from about age 3 to 6, is when sexual sensations become located in the genitals, but the child's sexual desires are focused particularly on the other-sex parent.
4. The *latency stage*, lasting from about age 6 until puberty, is a period when the child experiences incestuous desires for the opposite-sex parent. Fearing punishment from these desires, the child represses them and instead identifies with the same-sex parent, and focuses on learning social and intellectual skills.
5. The *genital stage*, from puberty onward, is when the sexual drive reemerges, but this time directed toward persons outside the family.

For Freud, everything important in development happens in childhood. In fact, Freud viewed the personality as complete by age 6. In his view, the motives—whether repressed or not—underlying a person's behaviors could be traced back to events during the first three stages of development, especially the child's interactions with parents. Freud is the most popularly recognized psychologist of all time, but most features of his psychosexual theory have not stood the test of time (Breger, 2000). Sexuality is certainly an important part of human psychology, but child development is complex and cannot be reduced to a single motive. Also, family is formative but it is not the sole context of importance in child development. Nonetheless, throughout the first half of the 20th century, the popularity of Freud's theory contributed to the prevailing attention to children in the field of developmental psychology (Robins et al., 1999).

**BINET AND MANDATORY PRIMARY SCHOOL.** Also in Europe at the turn of the 19th century, Alfred Binet, a French lawyer and psychologist, was commissioned by his government to design an instrument to identify children who would have difficulty learning in school and would need special instruction. French society and its educational system was changing significantly at this time, and the commission came on the heels of a law making school attendance mandatory for children between 6 and 14 years of age. Responding to these new societal circumstances, Binet and his colleague Theodore Simon introduced the first intelligence test in 1905 (Binet, 1911; Binet & Simon, 1905). The *Binet-Simon Scale* had features still in use in today's intelligence tests. For example, it focused on children's general knowledge, reasoning, memory, and problem-solving skills. It also assessed children based on how they compared to others their age. The scale was translated and revised in 1916 at Stanford University, and the English version became known as the *Stanford-Binet Intelligence Scale* (Goddard, 1911; Terman, 1916). This intelligence test (updated over the years) remains in common use today.

By 1900, primary school attendance had become mandatory in many American states.

The changes occurring in French society at Binet's time were also taking place in many other of the nations that are considered developed today. In the 1860s, only 30% of Japanese children had some schooling outside the home, a figure comparable to many major European nations. By 1900, however, primary school enrollment in Japan exceeded 90% (Marshall, 1972). Also, as in France, school attendance became mandatory for children younger than age 15 in a number of nations during the decades leading up to the 20th century, including New Zealand in 1877, Norway in 1889, and 30 of the American states by 1900.

We see, then, that Binet's work was a harbinger of the importance that societies increasingly have come to place on children's education and assessments of their academic knowledge. More generally, we see that Binet's work and the emergence of the field of child development occurred in an historical context where children's place and roles in society were changing dramatically. Children were increasingly spending much more time with peers in school rather than working alongside adults, and there was a new understanding that the brunt of their economic contributions to family and society would come later in their lives after primary school education.

**HALL'S PRELIMINARY ATTENTION TO ADOLESCENCE.** While the early field of child development focused on children, there was also preliminary attention to adolescents. Here a key figure was G. Stanley Hall (Modell & Goodman, 1990). Hall was a remarkable person whose achievements included obtaining the first Ph.D. in psychology in the United States, becoming the founder of the American Psychological Association, and serving as the first president of Clark University. Hall wrote the first textbook on adolescence, published in 1904 as a two-volume set ambitiously titled *Adolescence: Its Psychology and Its Relations to Physiology, Anthropology, Sociology, Sex, Crime, Religion, and Education*.

The impact of Hall's writing on adolescence has been mixed. Much of what he wrote is dated and obsolete (Youniss, 2006). To a large extent, he based his ideas on the now-discredited theory of *recapitulation*, which held that the development of each individual reenacts the phylogenetic development of the human species as a whole. Hall believed that the stage of adolescence was full of *storm and stress* because it recapitulated a stage in the human evolutionary past when there was a great deal of upheaval and disorder. No reputable scholar today adheres to the theory of recapitulation. Nonetheless, a number of Hall's observations have also been supported by recent research, such as his description of biological development during puberty, and his claim that adolescence is a time of heightened responsiveness to peers (Arnett, 2006).

Hall did not originate the term *adolescence*, but he contributed to its popularization as it came into use at the end of the 19th century and the beginning of the 20th (Kett, 1977). Before this time, young people in their teens and early 20s were more often referred to as "youth" or simply as young men and young women (Modell & Goodman, 1990). When Hall initiated the study of adolescence, he defined the age range of adolescence as beginning at 14 and ending at 24 (Hall, 1904, vol. 1, p. xix)—an age range that the contemporary field has shifted downward, as we will see in just a moment. Hall's work heralded adolescence as a developmental period preceding adulthood and meriting scientific scholarship. Still, the first many decades of the field of child development were characterized by theory and research centered on younger children.

## Expansion of the Field of Child Development: Adolescence

**LO 1.3.2 Describe when the field of child development began to address adolescence in a notable way, and explain why the age range that Hall had designated for adolescence has been moved downward by contemporary researchers.**

Theories and research specifically addressing the development of adolescents were sparse until about the mid-20th century. Gradually, however, this started to change. For example, Anna Freud (1895–1982), Sigmund Freud's daughter, wrote extensively on adolescence between the 1940s and 1960s. She was a particularly strong advocate of Hall's idea that adolescents go through storm and stress (1946, 1958, 1968, 1969). In her view, the absence of turmoil signified serious psychological problems: "To be normal during the adolescent period is by itself abnormal" (1958, p. 267). Also, from the 1950s to the

1970s, Erik Erikson (1902–1994) proposed a lifespan theory of development and singled out adolescence as the key period for establishing one's identity (1950, 1958, 1959, 1968). As a prerequisite to a healthy entry into adulthood, he proposed that adolescents must develop an awareness of who they are, what their capabilities are, and what their place is within society. Erikson was trained as a psychoanalyst in Freud's circle in Vienna, but ended up departing from Freudian theory in important ways. As we will see later in this text, his theory and especially his ideas about adolescence have continued to inspire researchers (Clark, 2010).

By now, research on adolescence is thriving. Today's scholars generally consider adolescence to begin at about age 10 and end by about age 18. Studies published in the major journals on adolescence rarely include samples with ages younger than 10 or older than 18 (Arnett, 2000). What happened between Hall's time and our own to move scholars' conceptions of adolescence forward chronologically in the life course?

Two changes stand out as explanations. One is the decline that took place during the 20th century in the typical age of the initiation of puberty. At the beginning of the 20th century, the median age of **menarche** (a girl's first menstruation) in Western countries was about 15 (Eveleth & Tanner, 1990). Because menarche takes place relatively late in the typical sequence of pubertal changes, this means that the initial changes of puberty would have begun around ages 13 to 15 for most girls and boys (usually earlier for girls than for boys), which is just where Hall designated the beginning of adolescence. However, the median age of menarche (and, by implication, other pubertal changes) declined steadily between 1900 and 1970 before leveling out, so that by now the typical age of menarche in Western countries is 12.5 (McDowell et al., 2007; Vigil, Geary, & Byrd-Craven, 2005). The initial changes of puberty begin about 2 years earlier, thus the designation of adolescence as beginning at about age 10. In developing countries, the average age of menarche remains somewhat higher. However, in countries that have undergone rapid economic development in recent decades, such as China and India, a corresponding decline in the average age of menarche has been reported (Graham et al., 1999; Rokade & Mane, 2008). Recent research in rural areas of some developing countries, such as Bangladesh, has found a mean age of menarche at just below 13 years of age (Rah et al., 2009).

**menarche**
a girl's first menstrual period

As for when adolescence ends, the change in this age may have been inspired by a social change: the growth of secondary school attendance to a normative experience for adolescents in the United States and other developed countries. For example, in 1890 only 5% of Americans age 14 to 17 were enrolled in high school. As you can see in Figure 1.5, however, this proportion rose steeply and steadily throughout the 20th century. Secondary education had become normative when Anna Freud and Erikson began to theorize about the distinctive psychological features of adolescence in the 1940s and 50s.

By 1985, enrollment in high school leveled out at 95% (National Center for Education Statistics [NCES], 2012). Because secondary education is now nearly universal among adolescents in developed countries and because it usually ends by about age 18, it makes sense for developmental researchers to place the end of adolescence at this time. Hall did not choose 18 as the end of adolescence because for most adolescents of his time no significant transition took place at that age. Education ended earlier, work began earlier, and leaving home took place later. Marriage and parenthood did not take place for most people until their early to mid-20s (Arnett & Taber, 1994), which may have been why Hall designated age 24 as the end of adolescence.

In developing countries, even now a substantial proportion of adolescents do not attend secondary school. In those countries, education beyond childhood is mainly for the urban middle class (just as it was in the West a century ago). The labor of rural adolescents is needed by their families, and they can best learn the skills needed for adult work by working alongside adults rather than by attending school. However, these patterns are changing

**Figure 1.5** Enrollment in High School in the United States, 1890–2010

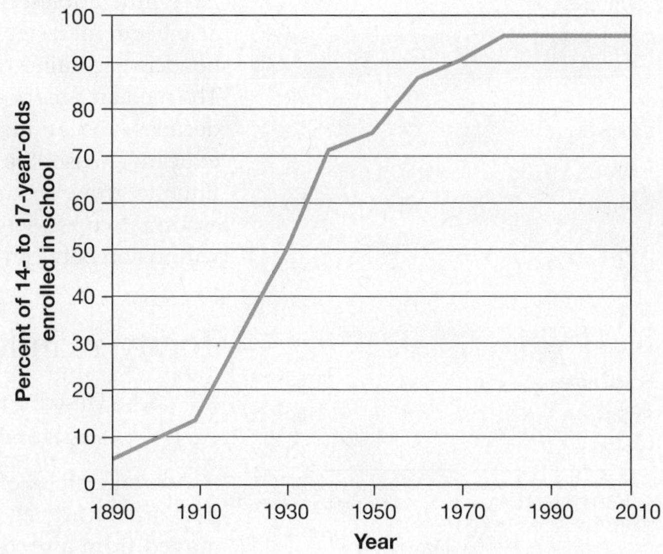

**Table 1.2** Enrollment in Secondary School, Selected Developing Countries, 1980 and 2015

| | 1980 | | 2015 or Latest Year | |
|---|---|---|---|---|
| Country | Females (%) | Males (%) | Females (%) | Males (%) |
| Argentina | 62 | 53 | 87 | 86 |
| China | 37 | 54 | 69 | 69 |
| Egypt | 41 | 66 | 90 | 90 |
| India | 20 | 39 | 77 | 72 |
| Mexico | 46 | 51 | 80 | 76 |
| Nigeria | 13 | 25 | 41 | 47 |

in many countries due to growing economic development. Table 1.2 shows secondary school enrollment in various countries in 1980 and 2015. In the space of less than 40 years, secondary education has risen rapidly in countries such as China, India, and Mexico. Economic development introduces agricultural technologies that make children's and adolescents' labor less necessary to the family, while staying in school brings increasing economic benefits because more jobs become available that require educational skills. Secondary education, then, is becoming normative across developing countries. In turn, adolescence is increasingly recognized as a developmental stage not only in developed countries, but also in developing countries.

## Another Expansion: Emerging Adulthood

**LO 1.3.3 Explain how the field of child development has recently expanded anew to encompass emerging adulthood.**

**emerging adulthood**
new life stage in developed countries, lasting from the late teens through the mid-twenties, in which people are gradually making their way toward taking on adult responsibilities in love and work

Within recent decades, the transition into adulthood has been pushed back again. Especially in developed countries, the end of adolescence no longer marks the entry into adulthood—as Erikson's theory, for example, purported about a half-century ago. Consequently, the field of child development has expanded anew. **Emerging adulthood** is a new stage of life between adolescence and young adulthood, lasting from about age 19 through the mid-20s (Arnett, 2000, 2011, 2015). This new life stage reflects the fact that most people in developed countries now continue their education into their 20s (Padilla-Walker & Nelson, in press). Take a look at Table 1.3. Gross enrollment rates in tertiary education are now above 50% in every developed country. Also, most people now enter marriage and parenthood in their late 20s, rather than in their late teens or early 20s as was true half a century ago. These demographic changes demonstrate that the period from 19 to 25 years of age, which used to be a time of settling into adult responsibilities in work and family roles, is now something else entirely. Emerging adulthood is a life stage in developed countries in which most people are not as dependent on their parents as they were in childhood and adolescence but have not yet made commitments to the stable roles in love and work that structure adult life for most people (Schwartz et al., 2013; Syed & Mitchell, 2013).

Unlike developed countries, it is only a minority of young people in developing countries who currently experience anything resembling emerging adulthood (Arnett, 2015). The majority of the population still marries around age 20 and has long finished education by the late teens or sooner. For young people in developing countries, emerging adulthood exists only for the wealthier segment of society, mainly the urban middle class, whereas the rural poor have no emerging adulthood and may even have little adolescence because they enter adultlike work at an early age and also begin marriage and parenthood relatively early. However, emerging adulthood is becoming more common in developing countries (Jensen et al., 2012). The median ages of entering marriage and parenthood have been rising in recent decades, and an increasing proportion of young people have obtained tertiary education. Also, the urban middle class in developing countries is likely to continue to grow. It may be that a century from now, emerging adulthood will be a normative life stage worldwide, although it will continue to show variations within and between cultures, as childhood and adolescence do today.

**Table 1.3** Gross Enrollment Ratio in Tertiary Education, Selected Developed Countries

| Country | Females | Males |
|---|---|---|
| Australia | 102 | 72 |
| Czech Republic | 77 | 55 |
| France | 71 | 58 |
| Germany | 63 | 68 |
| Greece | 110 | 110 |
| Italy | 74 | 53 |
| Japan | 60 | 65 |
| Lithuania | 82 | 56 |
| South Korea | 81 | 108 |
| Spain | 96 | 82 |
| United States | 101 | 73 |

Note: Gross enrollment ratio is the number of students enrolled in tertiary education divided by the number of persons ages 18–22 in the population.

SOURCE: Based on Arnett et al. (2014).

## Today's Child Development

**LO 1.3.4 Describe the cultural-developmental approach, and why developmental stages and pathways within this approach are somewhat flexible.**

As we take stock of the field of child development since its emergence more than a century ago, we see that it has steadily broadened. The field has moved from a predominant focus on children to encompass adolescents and

## Education Focus: Falling Behind? College Graduation in the United States

While tertiary enrollment has grown markedly in developed countries in recent decades, the United States has slipped behind many other developed countries in college completion. In a recent report, the college graduation rates for 25- to 34-year-olds in both 1995 and 2012 were provided for 15 developed countries. (Researchers look at college graduation rates after the conventional age of college students in order to include the many individuals who take longer to complete their degree). In 1995, the United States, together with New Zealand, led all countries with a 33% graduation rate. By 2012, however, only 4 countries were lower than the 39% graduation rate for the United States. The 4 countries were Germany and Switzerland at 31%, Spain at 29%, and Turkey at 27%. Among those with higher college graduation rates were Iceland at a remarkable 60%, New Zealand at 57%, Denmark at 49%, Japan and the Netherlands at 45%, and the Slovak Republic at 44%. Whereas the United States was in the vanguard in 1995, American college graduation rates have grown at nearly the slowest rate among developed countries and many countries now surpass the United States.

Across developed countries, individuals invest about US$50,000 to earn a tertiary degree. In Japan, the Netherlands, and the United States, average investment exceeds US$100,000 when direct and indirect costs are taken into account. The cost of an American college education is the highest in the world at an average of US$26,000 a year. Although a college education can be expensive, especially in a country like the United States, the recent report by the Organisation for Economic Co-Operation and Development (OECD) estimates that gross earnings benefits from tertiary education, compared with the income of a person with a secondary education, are US$350,000 for men and US$250,000 for women (OECD, 2014) across all OECD countries.

Today, more than half of emerging adults in developed countries pursue tertiary education.

### Review Question

Beyond the financial benefits to an individual of a college degree, what psychological benefits do you think there might be?

emerging adults. This expansion is reflected in the growth of professional organizations supported by instructors, researchers, and practitioners. For example, the Society for Research in Child Development (SRCD) was started in 1933. The Society for Research on Adolescence (SRA) and the European Association for Research on Adolescence (EARA) were established in 1984 and 1988, respectively. The Society for the Study of Emerging Adulthood (SSEA) began in 2013. Also, as we will see in later chapters, major international organizations dedicated to the well-being of children, such as United Nations Children's Fund (UNICEF), have recently expanded their focus on children to include adolescents and emerging adults (Diers, 2013).

This text covers the full spectrum of the field of child development, from prenatal development through emerging adulthood. The following is a guide to common developmental terms and their corresponding ages that we will employ:

- Prenatal development, from conception until birth
- Infancy, birth to age 12 months
- Toddlerhood, ages 12–36 months
- Early childhood, ages 3–6 years
- Middle childhood, ages 6–9 years
- Adolescence, ages 10–18 years
- Emerging adulthood, ages 19–25 years

**cultural-developmental approach**

the study of development within and across cultures in order to understand both what is universal and what is culturally distinctive

These terms and age ranges are a useful conceptual framework. However, throughout this text we will examine child development based on a **cultural-developmental approach** (Jensen, 2011, 2015). In essence, that means three things. First, we will continuously keep in mind that psychological development and developmental periods are profoundly impacted by culture. As we have already seen, adolescence begins with the first evidence of puberty, but puberty may begin as early as age 9 or 10 or as late as age 15 or 16, depending on cultural conditions. To give another example, emerging adulthood exists in some cultures and not others, and consequently, adult responsibilities such as marriage and stable work may be taken on in the early teens or after the mid-20s.

Second, according to the cultural-developmental approach, it is important to study child development across diverse cultures. Clearly, that is the only way to understand how development may occur in distinctive ways within cultures. But just as importantly, it is also the only way to know whether research findings from one culture generalize to other cultures. In other words, focusing on children worldwide renders the field of child development simultaneously more broadly valid across cultures *and* more attentive and applicable to local cultural conditions.

Third, the cultural-developmental approach also highlights that in today's globalizing world, cultural change can be quite rapid, and it is not uncommon for individuals to identify with more than one culture. In this text, you will encounter theories and research that address this. For now, we will end this section with a small personal story to illustrate how this has been our experience. In 2005, we moved from the United States to Denmark with our 6-year-old twins for a sabbatical year. Some months into the year, we visited Copenhagen where we were delighted to find an Indian restaurant. After ordering a selection of our favorite dishes, we were talking away in a mix of Danish and English when the waiter ambled back to our table. With a friendly smile he asked in English: "Where are you from?" Our son, Miles, explained that his mother is Danish and his father American. To which the waiter replied: "Oh, so you are half-Danish and half-American." Almost instantly Miles rejoined: "Oh no, I am 100% Danish and 100% American." This was not a math error. It was an enthusiastic affirmation that he does not consider himself half of anything, but rather a full member of both cultures.

## SUMMARY: The Field of Child Development: Emergence and Expansion

**LO 1.3.1 Provide some reasons why the field of child development primarily focused on younger children until about the mid-20th century.**

The field of child development emerged in a historical context in which children's roles in society were changing dramatically. By 1900, children in developed countries were often required to attend primary school rather than working full-time alongside adults. Thus Alfred Binet, an early French developmental psychologist, was commissioned by his government to design an instrument for identifying children who would have difficulty learning in school. Also, Sigmund Freud, whose psychosexual theory of development dominated the field until the mid-20th century, proposed that everything important in development happens in childhood.

**LO 1.3.2 Describe when the field of child development began to address adolescence in a notable way, and explain why the age range that Hall had designated for adolescence has been moved downward by contemporary researchers.**

Around 1900, G. Stanley Hall proposed that adolescence lasts from age 14 to 24. By the middle of 20th century, when developmental psychologists such as Anna Freud and Erik Erikson wrote extensively on adolescence, Hall's age range was shifted downward. One reason was the decline in the typical age for the onset of puberty that took place in the 20th century, and the other reason was the increase of secondary school attendance to become normative by mid-century. Today's scholars consider adolescence to begin at about age 10 and end by about age 18.

**LO 1.3.3 Explain how the field of child development has recently expanded anew to encompass emerging adulthood.**

Within recent decades, the transition into adulthood has been pushed back again. Emerging adulthood is a life stage in developed countries in which most people are not as dependent on their parents as they were in childhood and adolescence but have not yet made commitments to the stable roles in love and work that often structure adult life. Even though emerging adulthood is becoming more common in developing countries, it is only a minority of young people in these countries who currently experience this new stage of life.

**LO 1.3.4 Describe the cultural-developmental approach and why developmental stages and pathways within this approach are somewhat flexible.**

The cultural-developmental approach recognizes that psychological development and developmental periods are profoundly impacted by culture. Consequently, developmental psychology needs to study children from diverse cultures to understand both how they are similar and different. Furthermore, in a globalizing world, cultures can change rapidly and children increasingly identify with more than one culture.

# 1.4 How We Study Child Development

The field of child development is based on the scientific method, and to understand the research presented in this text, it is important to know the essential elements of this method. In this section, we begin by looking at the five basic steps of the scientific method. Although all investigators of child development follow the scientific method in some form, there are many different ways of investigating research questions and collecting data. In this section, we also examine the major types of research measurements and research designs used in the field of child development, as well as ethical guidelines for research.

## The Five Steps of the Scientific Method

**LO 1.4.1 Recall the five steps of the scientific method.**

In its classic form, the **scientific method** involves five basic steps: (1) identifying a question to be investigated, (2) forming a hypothesis, (3) choosing a research measurement and a research design, (4) collecting data to test the hypothesis, and (5) drawing conclusions that lead to new questions and new hypotheses. Figure 1.6 summarizes these steps.

**scientific method**
process of scientific investigations, involving a series of steps from identifying a research question through forming a hypothesis, selecting measurements and designs, collecting and analyzing data, and drawing conclusions

**STEP 1: IDENTIFY A QUESTION OF SCIENTIFIC INTEREST.** Every scientific study begins with an idea (Machado & Silva, 2007). A researcher wants to find an answer to a question that can be addressed using scientific methods. For example, in research on child development the question might be "Where and by whom do infants most commonly

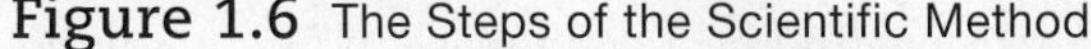

**Figure 1.6** The Steps of the Scientific Method

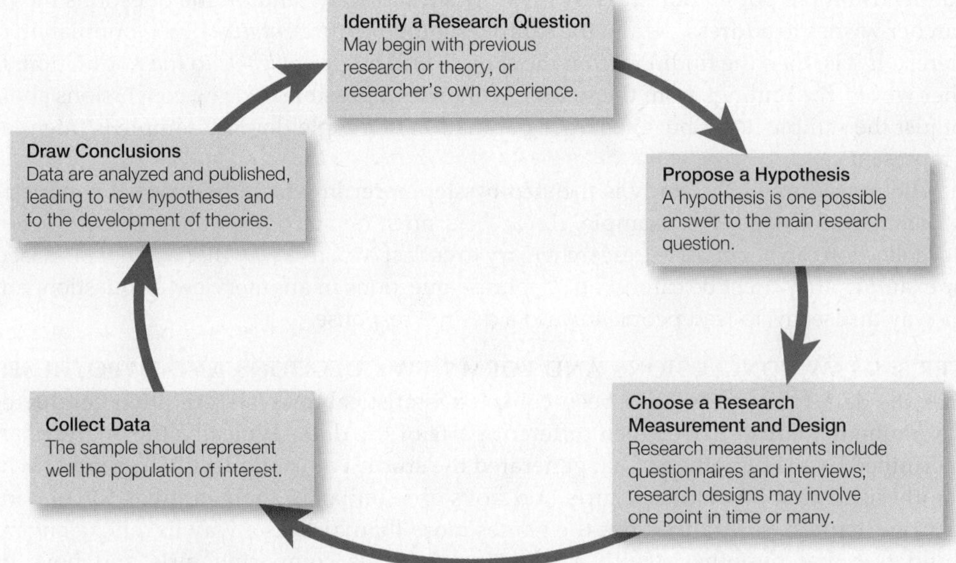

sleep?" or "Does daily physical activity in middle childhood affect cognitive development?" or "Do adolescent girls and boys have similar motives for playing electronic games?" The question of interest may be generated by a theory or previous research, or it may be something the researcher has noticed from personal observation or experience. (In the course of this text, you will find out the answers to these questions.)

**hypothesis**
a researcher's idea about one possible answer to the question proposed for investigation

**STEP 2: FORM A HYPOTHESIS.** In seeking to answer the question generated in Step 1, the researcher proposes one or more hypotheses. A **hypothesis** is the researcher's idea about one possible answer to the question of interest. For example, in answer to the above question about adolescents' use of electronic games, a researcher might hypothesize that "Adolescent girls and boys are similar in their motives for playing electronic games, except boys use the games more than girls as a way to relieve anger." The researcher would then design a study to test that hypothesis. The research questions and hypotheses of a study are crucial, because they influence the researcher's choices about research measurements, research design, sampling, data analysis, and interpretation that follow.

**research measurement**
the approach to collecting data. Examples of common measurements in the field of child development are observations and interviews

**research design**
the master plan for when, where, and with whom to collect the data for a study

**STEP 3: CHOOSE RESEARCH MEASUREMENT AND RESEARCH DESIGN.** Once the hypothesis is proposed, the investigator must choose a research measurement and design (Salkind, 2011). The **research measurement** is the approach to collecting data. Examples of common measurements in the field of child development are observations and interviews. The **research design** is the master plan for when, where, and with whom to collect the data for the study, for example, the decision of whether to collect data at one time point or at more than one point. More detail on research measurements and designs will follow shortly.

**sample**
the people included in a given study, who are intended to represent the population of interest

**population**
the entire group of people of interest in a study, and that the sample aims to represent

**STEP 4: COLLECT DATA TO TEST THE HYPOTHESIS.** After forming a hypothesis and choosing a research measurement and design, researchers who study human development seek to obtain a **sample**, which is a group of people who participate in a research study. The sample should represent the **population**, which is the entire category of people the sample represents. In the example above of the researcher who wants to study adolescents' motives for playing electronic games, adolescents are the population and the specific adolescents who participate in the study comprise the sample.

The goal is to seek out a sample that will be *representative* of the population of interest (Goodwin, 2009). To continue our example, a gaming conference would probably not be a good place to look for a sample, because the adolescents attending such a conference would be quite likely to be more avid electronic gamers than adolescents in general. If the population of interest is adolescents in general, it would be better to sample them through schools or through a telephone survey that selects households randomly from the community. On the other hand, if a researcher were particularly interested in motives for playing electronic games among the population of adolescents who are deeply committed to electronic gaming, then a gaming conference would be a good place to find a sample. It depends on the population the researcher wishes to study and on the questions the researcher wishes to address. Again, the sample should be *representative* of the population of interest. If it is, then the findings from the sample will be *generalizable* to the population. In other words, the findings from the sample will make it possible to draw conclusions about not just the sample itself, but the larger population of people that the sample is intended to represent.

**procedure**
the step-by-step order in which a study is conducted and data are collected. For example, researchers must obtain participants' consent before data collection can begin

The **procedure** of the study is the step-by-step order in which the study is conducted and data are collected. For example, researchers must obtain participants' consent before data collection can begin. Also, researchers try to collect data in a way that will not be biased. For example, they must be careful not to phrase questions in an interview or questionnaire in a way that seems to lead people toward a desired response.

**STEP 5: DRAW CONCLUSIONS AND FORM NEW QUESTIONS AND HYPOTHESES.** Once the data for a study have been collected, statistical analyses are often conducted to examine relationships between different parts of the data. Typically, the analyses are determined by the hypotheses that generated the study. For example, the researcher who hypothesized that "Adolescent girls and boys are similar in their motives for playing electronic games, except boys use the games more than girls as a way to relieve anger," would test that hypothesis with a statistical analysis comparing girls and boys on motives that did and did not pertain to the relief of anger. Once the data are analyzed they must be interpreted. When scientists write up the results of their research for publication in a scientific journal, they interpret the results of the study in light of relevant theories and previous findings.

Depending on the research question, a gaming conference may or may not be a good place to recruit a sample.

After researchers write an article describing the methods used, the results of the statistical analyses, and the interpretation of the results, they typically submit the manuscript for the article to a professional journal. The editor of the journal then sends the manuscript out for review by other researchers. In other words, the manuscript is **peer-reviewed** for its scientific accuracy and credibility and for the importance of its contribution to the field. The editor typically relies on the reviews by the researchers' peers in deciding whether or not to accept the manuscript for publication. If the editor determines that the manuscript has passed the peer-review process successfully, the article is published in the journal. In addition to research articles, most journals publish occasional theoretical articles and review articles that integrate the findings from numerous other studies. Researchers studying child development also publish the results of their investigations in books, and often these books go through the peer-review process.

**peer-review**
in scientific research, the system of having other scientists review a manuscript to judge its merits and worthiness for publication

The results of research often lead to the development or modification of theories. A good **theory** is a framework that presents a set of interconnected ideas in an original way and inspires further research. Theories and research are intrinsically connected: A theory generates hypotheses that can be tested in research, and research leads to modifications of the theory, which generate further hypotheses and further research.

**theory**
framework that presents a set of interconnected ideas in an original way and inspires further research

There is no separate chapter on theories in this text, because theories and research are intrinsically connected and benefit from being presented together. Furthermore, the field of child development has come a long way from its early days where it was dominated by a few key theories and research issues. By now, researchers investigate a large number of theories and research issues. The field is broad and dynamic. Theories will be presented in every chapter in relation to the research they have generated and the questions they have raised for future research.

## Research Measurements

**LO 1.4.2 Summarize the main measurements used in research on child development.**

Researchers study child development in a variety of academic disciplines, including anthropology, education, family studies, medicine, psychology, social work, and sociology. The different research measurements they use have both strengths and limitations. We'll examine major types of research measurements next, and consider an issue that is important across measurements, the question of reliability and validity.

**QUESTIONNAIRES.** The most commonly used measurement in social science research is the **questionnaire** where participants complete printed or written questions (Salkind, 2011). Usually, questionnaires have a *closed-question* format, which means that participants are provided with specific responses to choose from (Shaughnessy et al., 2011). Sometimes the questions have an *open-ended question* format, which means that participants state their response in their own words following the question. One advantage of closed questions is that they make it possible to collect and analyze responses from a large number of people in a relatively short time. Everyone responds to the same questions with the same response options. For this reason, closed questions have often been used in large-scale surveys.

**questionnaire**
written questions where participants typically select among answers chosen by the researcher

Although questionnaires are commonly used, the questionnaire has certain limitations. When a closed-question format is used, the range of possible responses is

Interviews often provide rich data. In what ways do you think a child's responses might be influenced by the characteristics of the person conducting an interview?

already specified, and the participant must choose from the responses provided. The researcher tries to cover the responses that seem most plausible and most likely, but it is impossible in a few brief response options to do justice to the depth and diversity of human experience. For example, if a questionnaire contains an item such as "How close are you to your father? 1. very close; 2. somewhat close; 3. not very close; 4. not at all close," it is probably true that people who choose "very close" really are closer to their fathers than people who choose "not at all close." But this alone does not begin to capture the complexity of the child-parent relationship.

**interviews**

spoken questions where participants typically are free to provide their own answers

**quantitative**

data that is collected in numerical form, usually on questionnaires

**qualitative**

data that is collected in non-numerical form, usually in interviews or observations

**INTERVIEWS.** **Interviews**, where participants answer questions asked directly by the researcher, are intended to provide the kind of individuality and complexity that questionnaires usually lack. An interview allows a researcher to hear people describe their lives in their own words, with all the uniqueness and richness that such descriptions make possible. Interviews also enable a researcher to know the whole person and see how the various parts of the person's life are intertwined. For example, an interview on an adolescent's family relationships might reveal how the adolescent's relationship with her mother is affected by her relationship with her father, and how the whole family has been affected by certain events—perhaps a family member's loss of a job, psychological problems, medical problems, or substance abuse.

Interviews provide **qualitative** data, as contrasted with the **quantitative** (numerical) data of questionnaires, and qualitative data can be interesting and informative. (Qualitative data are nonnumerical and include not only interview data but also data from other measurements such as descriptive observations, video recordings, or photographs.)

However, like questionnaires, interviews have limitations (Shaughnessy et al., 2011). Because interviews do not typically provide a range of specific responses the way questionnaires do, interview responses have to be coded according to some plan of classification. For example, if you asked emerging adults the interview question "What do you think makes a person an adult?" you might get a fascinating range of responses, such as "turning 18," or "having one's first child," or "making decisions independently." However, to make sense of the data and present them in a scientific format, at some point you would have to code the responses into categories—legal markers, social markers, character qualities, biological characteristics, and so on. Only in this way would you be able to say something about the pattern of responses in your sample. Coding interview data takes time, effort, and money. This is one of the reasons far more studies are conducted using questionnaires than interviews.

**observations**

observations and recording of people's behaviors either on video or through written records

**OBSERVATIONS.** Another way researchers learn about child development is through **observations.** Studies using this kind of measurement involve observing people and recording their behavior either on video or through written records. In *naturalistic observations*, the observations take place in the natural environment. For example, a study of aggressive behavior in children might involve observations on a school playground. In *structured observations*, the observations take place in a laboratory setting.

Observational methods have an advantage over questionnaires and interviews in that they involve actual behavior rather than self-reports of behavior. People who self-report their behaviors may not always remember correctly or understand their own motivations. Also, researchers can observe behavior even prenatally, whereas interviews and questionnaires can only be used with children capable of communicating their ideas orally or in writing. However, the disadvantage of observations is that the people being observed may be aware of the observer and this awareness may make their behavior different than it would be under normal conditions. For example, parents being observed in a laboratory setting with their children may be nicer to them than they would be at home. This issue of people behaving in socially desirable ways also applies to questionnaires and interviews. People tend to overreport socially desirable behaviors and underreport undesirable behaviors.

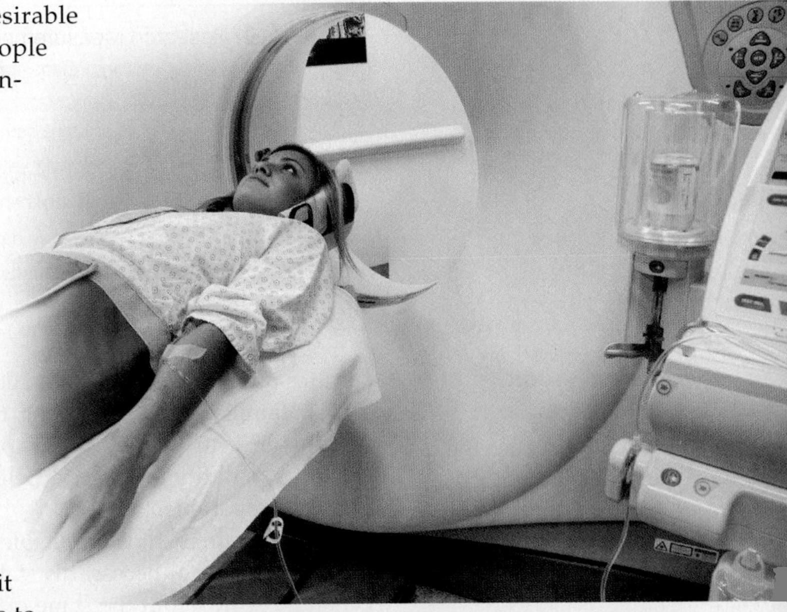

Research on brain functioning, including the use of fMRI, is thriving in the field of child development.

**BIOLOGICAL MEASUREMENTS.** Biological changes are a central part of psychological development, so research includes **biological measurements**. This includes research on the genetic basis of development, hormonal functioning, and brain functioning. Research on genetics increasingly involves directly examining the chemical structure of genes. Research on brain functioning often involves measuring brain activity during different kinds of behavior, like listening to music or solving a math problem. One widely used method, the **electroencephalogram (EEG)**, measures the electrical activity of the cerebral cortex (the most distinctively human part of the brain, as we will describe in the next chapter). Every time a synapse fires in the brain it emits a tiny burst of electricity, which allows researchers to measure the overall activity of the cerebral cortex as well as activation of specific parts of it. Another common method, **functional magnetic resonance imaging (fMRI)**, requires a person to lie still inside a machine that uses a magnetic field to record changes in blood flow and oxygen use in the brain in response to different kinds of stimulation, such as music. Unlike the EEG, an fMRI can detect activity in any part of the brain, not just the cerebral cortex.

Biological measurements can provide precise information about many aspects of human biological functioning. They allow researchers to gain knowledge into how biological aspects of development are related to cognitive, social, and emotional functioning. However, some biological measurements rely on expensive equipment. Also, although biological measurements can be precise, their relation to other aspects of functioning is often far from exact. For example, if levels of a certain hormone are positively associated with aggressive behavior, it may be that the hormone causes the aggressive behavior, or it could be that aggressive behavior causes levels of the hormone to rise. Measurements in brain research yield data from monitoring the brain's electrical activity or recording images of the brain while it is engaged in various activities, but those data can be difficult to interpret (Gergen, 2011).

**RELIABILITY AND VALIDITY.** In scientific research it is important that research measurements have *reliability* and *validity*. There are a variety of types of reliability, but **reliability** generally refers to the extent to which measurements generate consistent results (Salkind, 2011). For example, if a questionnaire asked girls in their senior year of high school to recall when their first menstrual period occurred, the questionnaire would be considered reliable if most of the girls answered the same on one occasion as they did when asked the question again 6 months later (this is also known as *test-retest reliability*). Or, if observations of behaviors were coded into categories by two different researchers, such as whether the behaviors involved aggression, the coding would be reliable if the researchers consistently categorized behaviors the same way (this is also known as *interrater reliability*).

**Validity** refers to the truthfulness of a measurement (Shaughnessy et al., 2011). A measurement is valid if it *measures what it claims to measure.* For example, IQ tests are purported to measure general intellectual abilities, but as we shall see in Chapter 11, this claim is controversial. Critics claim that IQ tests are not valid (i.e., that they do not measure what they claim to measure).

Just as for reliability, there are a variety of types of validity. One type that is particularly important in child development research across cultures is **ecological validity**. An approach to measurement is ecologically valid if there is a fit between the measurement approach and the everyday life of the people being studied. For example, one-on-one interviews where an unfamiliar person asks questions of children are very common in some

**biological measurements**
includes measures of genetic, hormonal, and brain activity

**electroencephalogram (EEG)**
device that measures the electrical activity of the cerebral cortex, allowing researchers to measure overall activity of the cerebral cortex as well as activation of specific parts of it

**functional magnetic resonance imaging (fMRI)**
method of monitoring brain activity in which a person lies inside a machine that uses a magnetic field to record changes in blood flow and oxygen use in the brain in response to different kinds of stimulation

**reliability**
the extent to which a measurement generates consistent results

**validity**
the extent to which a measurement assesses what it claims to measure

**Table 1.4** Research Measurements: Advantages and Limitations

| Measurements | Advantages | Limitations |
|---|---|---|
| Questionnaire | Large sample, quick data collection | Preset responses, no depth |
| Interview | Individuality and complexity | Time and effort of coding |
| Observations | Actual behavior, not self-report | Observation may affect behavior |
| Biological measurements | Precise data | Expensive; relation to behavior may not be clear |

**ecological validity**
the extent to which there is a fit between the measurement approach and the everyday life of the people being studied

cultures but not others (Briggs, 2003). If a measurement approach does not have reasonably similar familiarity and meaning to participants from two different cultures, it is unlikely that it is measuring the same variable for those participants. The measurement may have ecological validity in one culture but not the other. But if that is the case, then the findings are not comparable.

If a measurement is unreliable, it cannot be valid. But notice that even if a measurement is reliable, it is not necessarily valid. It is widely agreed that IQ tests are reliable—people generally score about the same on one occasion as they do on another—but the validity of the tests is disputed. In general, validity is more difficult to establish than reliability. We will examine questions of reliability and validity throughout the text.

Take a moment to review Table 1.4, which lists the advantages and limitations of each of the research measurements we have discussed.

## Research Designs

**LO 1.4.3 Distinguish between major types of research designs.**

Research designs lay out when, where, and with whom to employ the measurements of the study. The researcher makes decisions such as whether data are collected: once or at more than one point in time, in a laboratory or natural setting, and with one individual or one group or more than one group. Research design also involves the question of whether or not the researcher administers some kind of treatment or intervention to participants.

**experimental design**
entails comparing an *experimental group* that receives a treatment of some kind to a *control group* that receives no treatment

**independent variable**
in an experiment, the variable that is different for the experimental group than for the control group

**dependent variable**
in an experiment, the outcome that is measured to calculate the results of the experiment by comparing the experimental group to the control group

**interventions**
program intended to change the attitudes and/or behavior of the participants

**EXPERIMENTAL DESIGN.** An approach used in many kinds of scientific research is the **experimental design**. In its simplest form, participants in the study are randomly assigned to either the *experimental group*, which receives a treatment of some kind, or the *control group*, which receives no treatment (Goodwin, 2009). In an experiment there are independent variables and dependent variables. The **independent variable** is the variable that is different for the experimental group than for the control group. The **dependent variable** is the outcome that is measured to calculate the results of the experiment. For example, in one classic experiment by Albert Bandura and his colleagues (1961), children in the experimental group were shown a film that involved aggressive behavior by an adult, and children in the control group were shown a film that did not portray aggressive behavior. The independent variable was the content of the film each group was shown. In a play session that followed, children in the experimental or treatment group were more aggressive toward an inflated doll ("Bobo") than children in the control group. The dependent variable was the children's aggressiveness. Because the children were randomly assigned to either the experimental group or the control group, it can be reasonably assumed that the two groups did not differ prior to the experiment and that the difference on the dependent variable (aggression) was caused by the independent variable (the film content).

Another area of child development research for which the experimental research method is commonly used is for **interventions**. Interventions are programs intended to change the attitudes or behavior of the participants. For example, a variety of programs have been developed to prevent adolescents from starting to smoke cigarettes, by promoting critical thinking about cigarette advertising or by attempting to change attitudes associating smoking with peer acceptance (e.g., Horn et al., 2005). The adolescents participating in such a study are randomly assigned to either the experimental group receiving the intervention or the control group that does not receive the intervention. After the intervention, the two groups are assessed for their attitudes and behavior regarding smoking. If the intervention worked, the attitudes and behavior of the experimental group should be less favorable toward smoking than those of the control group.

A classic series of experiments involved children in the experimental group watching a film where an adult inflicted violence on an inflatable doll, "Bobo." Here, a girl who seems to have been influenced by what she saw.

The advantage of the experimental design is that it allows the researcher a high degree of control over participants' behavior. Rather than monitoring behavior that occurs naturally, the researcher attempts to change the normal patterns of behavior by assigning some persons to an experimental group and some to a control group. This allows for a clearer and more definite measure of the effect of the experimental manipulation than is possible in normal life. However, the disadvantage of the experimental design is the flip side of the advantage: Because participants' behavior has been altered through experimental manipulation, it is difficult to say if the results would apply in normal life. In normal life, for example, children watch not just one isolated film clip with aggressive content but a wide variety of media with an array of content. Would the presence of aggressive content within this media panoply have the same effect as in the laboratory experiment with a sole film clip that primarily portrayed aggression?

**NATURAL EXPERIMENT.** A **natural experiment** is a situation that exists naturally—in other words, the researcher does not control it—but that provides interesting scientific information to the perceptive observer (Goodwin, 2009). Typically, the situations involve "treatments" that a researcher could not ethically administer, such as premature birth or having major surgery. One natural experiment used frequently in child development research is adoption. Unlike in most families, children in adoptive families are raised by adults with whom they have no genetic relationship. Because one set of parents provide the child's genes and a different set of parents provide the environment, it is possible to examine the relative contributions of genes and environment to the child's development. Similarities between adoptive parents and adopted children are likely to be due to the environment provided by the parents, because the parents and children are biologically unrelated. Similarities between adopted children and their biological parents are likely to be due to genetics, because the environment the children grew up in was not provided by the biological parents.

**natural experiment**
a situation that occurs naturally but that provides interesting scientific information to the perceptive observer

Natural experiments provide the advantage of allowing for exceptional insights into naturally occurring events. For example, research on adoption has been fruitful as to the relation between genes and the environment. However, natural experiments have limitations as well. For example, families who adopt children are not selected randomly but volunteer and go through an extensive screening process, which makes adoption studies difficult to generalize to biological families. Also, natural experiments tend to be rare and to occur unpredictably, and consequently such studies can only provide answers to a limited range of questions.

**CORRELATIONAL DESIGN.** In the **correlational design**, the researcher assesses relations between naturally occurring variables with the goal of finding out whether one variable predicts the other. For example, researchers may ask a sample of adolescents to fill out a questionnaire reporting their physical health and how much they exercise, based on the hypothesis that exercising promotes better physical health. They then analyze the data to see if the amount of exercise is related to physical health. Figure 1.7 (next page) shows a hypothetical illustration of this relationship.

**correlational design**
data collected on naturally occurring variables on a single occasion

The main strength of correlational studies is that they can be completed quickly and inexpensively. Data collection is done on one occasion, and the study is finished. These features explain why the design is widely used among researchers.

**Figure 1.7** Physical Health and Exercise Are Correlated—But Which Causes Which?

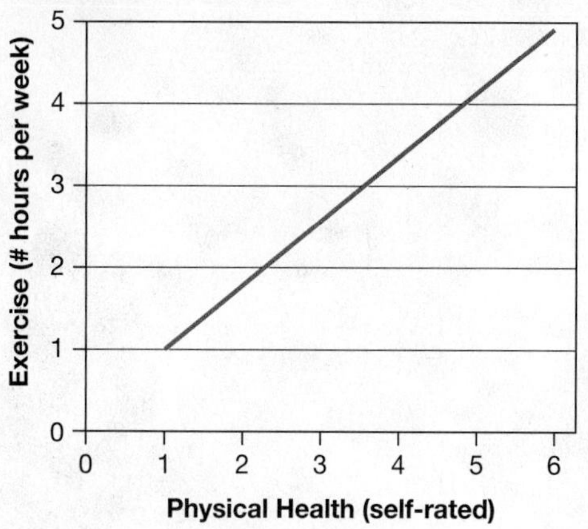


However, there are limitations as well. For this kind of design, researchers often calculate the correlation between variables, and correlations can be difficult to interpret. A **correlation** is a statistical relationship between two variables, such that knowing one of the variables makes it possible to predict the other. A *positive correlation* means that when one variable increases or decreases, the other variable changes in the same direction; a *negative correlation* means that when one variable increases the other decreases. In the example just provided, the researcher may find a positive correlation between exercising and physical health. Figure 1.7 illustrates this positive correlation: as exercise increases, physical health also increases. But does this mean that exercising causes better physical health, or that people with better physical health are more inclined to exercise? Based on correlational research alone, there is no way to tell.

It is a basic statistical principle of scientific research that *correlation does not imply causation*, meaning that when two variables are correlated it is not possible to tell whether one variable caused the other. Nevertheless, this principle is frequently overlooked in research on child development. For example, there are hundreds of studies showing a correlation between parenting behaviors and children's functioning. Frequently this correlation has been interpreted as causation—parenting behaviors *cause* children to function in certain ways—but in fact the correlation alone does not show this (Pinker, 2004). It could be that children's characteristics cause parents to behave in certain ways, or it could be that the behavior of both parents and children is due to a third variable, such as SES or cultural context. We will explore this issue and other *correlation versus causation* questions in later chapters.

**correlation**
statistical relationship between two variables such that knowing one of the variables makes it possible to predict the other. A statistical value of 0 indicates no correlation. Values of 1 and −1 indicate the strongest possible positive and negative correlations.

**ETHNOGRAPHIC RESEARCH.** Researchers also learn about child development through **ethnographic research** (Jessor et al., 1996). In this method researchers spend a considerable amount of time with the people they wish to study, often by living among them. Information gained in ethnographic research typically comes from researchers' observations, informal conversations, and interviews with the people they are studying. Ethnographic research is commonly used by anthropologists, usually in studying non-Western cultures. Anthropologists usually report the results of their research in an *ethnography*, which is a book that presents an anthropologist's descriptions and interpretations of what life is like in a particular culture. Ethnographic research is also used by some social scientists to study particular aspects of their own societies, such as high school peer culture.

**ethnographic research**
research design that involves spending extensive time among the people being studied

The main advantage of ethnographic research is that it allows the researcher to learn how people behave in their daily lives. Other methods capture only a slice or summary of people's lives, but the ethnographic approach provides insights into the whole span of daily experience. The main disadvantage is that ethnographic research requires a great deal of time, commitment, and sacrifice by the researcher. It means that researchers must give up their own lives for a period of time, from a few weeks to years, in order to live among the people whose lives they wish to understand. Also, an ethnographic researcher is likely to form relationships with the people being studied, which may bias the interpretation of the results.

> **Critical Thinking Question:** Anthropologists who travel abroad to do ethnographic work have to learn the language, dress codes, gender norms, customs, and morals of the foreign culture. Can you think of examples of how this too would be the case for an ethnographer who decided to do a case study among domestic high school students?

**case study**
the detailed examination of a particular person, group, or situation over time

**CASE STUDY.** The **case study** entails the detailed examination of a particular person, group, or situation over time. For more on this design, and an illustration from a famous study, see the video *Darwin's Diary: A Case Study* in the Research Focus feature.

# Research Focus: Darwin's Diary: A Case Study

The case study often entails the detailed examination of the life of one person or a small number of persons. The advantage of a case study is in the detail and richness that is possible when only one or a few persons are being described. The disadvantage of the case study is that it is especially difficult to generalize the results to larger groups of people on the basis of only one or a few people's experiences.

Some of the most influential studies in the history of child development research were case studies. For example, Jean Piaget (an influential Swiss psychologist whom we'll meet in future chapters) initially based his ideas about infants' cognitive development on his detailed observations of his own three children. Also, Charles Darwin recorded an extensive case study of the early years of his son William, nicknamed Doddy.

Darwin is best known for his 1859 book *On the Origin of Species*, which laid out his theory of evolution and dramatically changed how humans view themselves in relation to nature. However, 20 years before he published it, Darwin embarked on a different project. He decided to keep a diary record of the development of his first child, Doddy. Already Darwin was intensely interested in how and why animal species differ from one another. By keeping a careful record of Doddy's development, Darwin hoped to find evidence toward answering questions such as: "What is innate and what is learned?" "What skills emerge in the first years of a child's life, and at what ages?" and "How are human children different from other young primates?"

In his diary, Darwin recorded observations and insights concerning Doddy's cognitive, language, social, and moral development. In observing Doddy's cognitive development, Darwin noted that it was at about 4 months of age that Doddy first became able to coordinate simple actions:

> Took my finger to his mouth & as usual could not get it back in, on account of his own hand being in the way; then he slipped his own back & so got my finger in.—This was not chance & therefore a kind of reasoning (p. 12).

About 2 weeks later, at 4½ months of age, Doddy showed further evidence of being able to coordinate his actions: tracking an object with his eyes and reaching for it.

> May 9th a watch held close to face: he extended his hand to it—Had made feeble trials for two or three days before (p. 16).

Beginning to coordinate actions in this way was later recognized by psychological researchers as an important marker of early cognitive development.

With regard to social development, Darwin observed, as later researchers would, that Doddy's first smiles were

**Watch DARWIN'S DIARY: A CASE STUDY**

the expression of internal states rather than being intended as communication. "When little under five weeks old, smiled but certainly not from pleasure" (p. 3). Over the course of the next months, Darwin recorded how smiling changed from an expression of internal feelings to a social act directed toward others.

Darwin also noted Doddy's aggressive behavior. On one occasion when Doddy was 13 months old, he became angry when his nurse tried to take a piece of cake away from him: "He tried to slap her face, went scarlet, screamed & shook his head" (p. 29). Because Doddy had never been physically punished, Darwin concluded that this act of aggression must have been instinctive rather than learned.

Today the case study is sometimes used in mental health research to describe a case that is unusual or that portrays the characteristics of a mental health issue in an especially vivid way. It is also used in combination with other methods, as a way of providing a sense of the whole of a person's life.

## Review Questions

1. Which of these was one of Darwin's goals in keeping a diary of his son Doddy's development?
   - **a.** To see whether he preferred breast-feeding or bottle-feeding
   - **b.** To see how he responded to the family pets
   - **c.** To identify what was innate and what was learned
   - **d.** To give parents guidelines on how to soothe their crying children
2. Which of these emotions did Doddy display vividly at age 13 months, according to Darwin's diary?
   - **a.** Anger
   - **b.** Sadness
   - **c.** Curiosity
   - **d.** Fear

**Table 1.5** Research Designs: Advantages and Limitations

| Designs | Advantages | Limitations |
|---|---|---|
| Experiment | Control, identification of cause and effect | May not reflect real life |
| Natural experiment | Illuminates relations among naturally occurring events. | Unusual circumstances; rare |
| Correlational study | Quick and inexpensive | Correlations difficult to interpret |
| Ethnographic research | Entire span of daily life | Researcher must live among participants; possible bias |
| Case studies | Rich, detailed data | Difficult to generalize results |

Take a moment to review Table 1.5, which lists the advantages and limitations of each of the research designs we have discussed.

## Research Designs in Developmental Psychology

**LO 1.4.4 Describe the two major types of research designs distinctive to developmental psychology.**

Because a key goal of child development research is to examine how variables change as a function of age, there are research designs specific to this purpose. Two major types of research designs in developmental psychology are cross-sectional and longitudinal designs. The hallmark of both designs is that age is the independent variable. An independent variable may be a treatment or an intervention administered by the researcher, as in the case of an experiment. Here, however, the independent variable is simply selected by the researcher since we obviously cannot assign people to be a certain age.

**cross-sectional design**
data with people of different ages are collected at a single point in time

**CROSS-SECTIONAL DESIGN.** The most common of the developmental research designs is a **cross-sectional design**. In cross-sectional research, data with people of different ages are collected at a single point in time (Cozby & Bates, 2015). Then, the researcher examines the relation between age and the dependent variable. For example, researchers may want to compare children in middle childhood and adolescents on depressed mood.

Cross-sectional research has both strengths and weaknesses. The main strength is that these studies can be completed in a relatively affordable and timely manner. Data collection is done on one occasion, and the study is finished. A key disadvantage is that the design can only show a correlation between age and the dependent variable, but it cannot establish causation.

**Critical Thinking Question:** Can you think of an explanation other than age or development as to why 15-year-olds may report more depressed moods than 8-year-olds?

**longitudinal design**
the same persons are followed over time and data are collected on two or more occasions

**LONGITUDINAL DESIGN.** The limitations of cross-sectional research have led some researchers to use a **longitudinal design**, in which the same persons are followed over time and data are collected on two or more occasions. The length of longitudinal research varies widely, from a few weeks or months to years or even decades. Most longitudinal studies take place over a relatively short period, a year or less, but some studies have followed their samples over an entire lifetime, from infancy to old age (e.g., Friedman & Martin, 2011).

The great advantage of the longitudinal research design is that it allows researchers to examine the question that is at the heart of developmental research: "How do people change over time?" In addition, the longitudinal design allows researchers to gain more insight into the question of correlation versus causation. For example, suppose a cross-sectional study comparing adolescents, emerging adults, young adults, and middle adults shows that religiosity goes up with age. Does this mean that growing older causes people to become more religious? From a cross-sectional study, there is no way to tell; it could be that the culture has changed over the years, and that the middle adults grew up in a more religious era than

Longitudinal studies follow the same persons over time. Here, an American girl is pictured in toddlerhood, early childhood, middle childhood, and adolescence.

those in the younger age groups. This kind of explanation for age differences is called a **cohort effect**; people of different ages vary because they grew up in different *cohorts* or historical periods (Cozby & Bates, 2015). However, if you could follow adolescents into middle adulthood using a longitudinal research design, you could see if they became more religious as they grew older. You could then draw more definite conclusions about whether or not aging leads to higher religiosity.

**cohort effect**
in scientific research, an explanation of group differences among people of different ages based on the fact that they grew up in different *cohorts* or historical periods

Longitudinal research designs have disadvantages as well. Most importantly, they take a great deal more time, money, and patience than a cross-sectional research design does. Researchers do not learn the outcome to the investigation of their hypothesis until weeks, months, or years later. Over time, it is inevitable that some people will drop out of a longitudinal study, for one reason or another—a process called *attrition*. Consequently, the sample the researcher has at Time 1 is likely to be different than the sample that remains at Time 2, 3, or 4, which limits the conclusions that can be drawn. In most studies, dropout is highest among people from low-SES groups, which means that the longer a longitudinal study goes on, the less likely it is to represent the SES range of the entire population. Table 1.6 provides you with an overview of the key features of cross-sectional and longitudinal designs.

Throughout this text, studies using a variety of scientific approaches to research will be presented. For now, the measurements and designs just described provide you with an introduction to the approaches used most often. As we will see, researchers have come up with ingenious variations and innovations.

## Ethics in Child Development Research

**LO 1.4.5 Identify some key ethical standards for child development research.**

Imagine that you were a researcher interested in parent-child relations, and you designed a laboratory situation where a parent leaves their toddler alone with a stranger for a brief period of time. You think that toddler's reaction to the return of their parents is indicative of the quality of the relationship. Is this research method ethical?

Imagine that you were a researcher who was interested in moral development among middle and high school students. You set up a research situation where students take a computerized test individually and have what appears to be an undetectable opportunity to gain access to test answers. In fact, you will be able to tell if a student accessed the answers. Is this research design ethical?

**Table 1.6** Developmental Research Designs: Advantages and Limitations

| Method | Definition | Advantages | Limitations |
|---|---|---|---|
| Cross-sectional | Data collected at one time point | Quick and inexpensive | Correlations difficult to interpret |
| Longitudinal | Data collected at two or more time points | Monitors change over time | Time, expense, attrition |

Imagine that you were a researcher interested in the question of what makes romantic partnerships last or not. So, you proposed a study in which you invited couples in their 20s to come into a laboratory situation, where they were provided with a list of possible secrets that partners might keep from each other and asked to pick one of them to discuss, while being filmed by the researchers. Is this research design ethical?

These are the kinds of ethical issues that arise in the course of research on child development. To prevent ethical violations, most institutions that sponsor research, such as universities and research institutes, require proposals for research to be approved by an *institutional review board (IRB)*. IRBs are usually comprised of people who have research experience themselves and therefore can judge whether the research being proposed follows reasonable ethical guidelines. In addition to IRBs, professional organizations such as the Society for Research on Child Development (SRCD) often have a set of ethical guidelines for researchers.

The requirements of IRBs and the ethical guidelines of professional organizations usually include the following components (Fisher, 2003; Rosnow & Rosenthal, 2005):

1. ***Protection from physical and psychological harm.*** The most important consideration in psychological research is that the persons participating in the research will not be harmed by it.
2. ***Informed consent prior to participation.*** One standard ethical requirement of research involving humans is **informed consent**. Participants in any scientific study are supposed to be presented with a *consent form* before they participate (Salkind, 2011). For persons under age 18, the consent of one of their parents or guardians is also usually required. Consent forms typically include information about who is conducting the study, what the purposes of the study are, what participation in the study involves, what risks (if any) are involved in participating, and what the person can expect to receive in return for participation. Consent forms also usually include a statement indicating that participation in the study is voluntary, and that persons may withdraw from participation in the study at any time. In this regard, it has been demonstrated that children tend to be reluctant to stop participation unless the researcher reiterates this freedom to withdraw, such as by explicitly stating that no one would be upset if the child stopped participating (Abramovitch et al., 1995).

**informed consent**

standard procedure in social scientific studies that entails informing potential participants of what their participation would involve, including any possible risks

3. ***Confidentiality.*** Researchers are ethically required to take steps to ensure that all information provided by participants in developmental psychology research is confidential, meaning that it will not be shared with anyone outside the immediate research group and any results from the research will not identify any of the participants by name.
4. ***Deception and debriefing.*** Sometimes research involves deception. For example, a study might involve having children play a game but fix the game to ensure that they will lose, because the objective of the study is to examine how children respond to losing. IRBs require researchers to show that the deception in the proposed study will cause no harm. Also, ethical guidelines require that participants in a study that involves deception must be *debriefed*, which means that following their participation they must be told the true purpose of the study and the reason for the deception.

**Critical Thinking Question:** If you were a member of an IRB, what kinds of concerns—if any—would you have about the three studies described above?

As the field of child development increasingly involves worldwide research, researchers are paying attention to ethical issues that arise in the study of groups with different cultural beliefs, values, and behaviors. With respect to consent, for example, a tendency not to withdraw from a study once it has begun is more characteristic of cultural communities in which individuals are particularly inclined to defer to the authority of the researcher (Miller et al., 2015). With respect to harm, the laboratory study described above where a toddler is left alone in a room with a stranger is intended to evoke mild distress for the child. Typically, however, the distress is judged to be acceptable as a means to gain insight into the parent-child relationship, and the research method—also known as the "Strange Situation"—is routinely approved by IRBs in the United States. However, Japanese researchers have pointed out that mothers in Japan seldom leave their children with another caregiver, even a family member. In research where the Strange Situation was administered to a sample of Japanese 12-month-olds, the anxiety involved was intense (Takahashi, 1986). As you read this text, we would encourage you think about the ethics of research, from both a developmental and cultural point of view.

## SUMMARY: How We Study Child Development

**LO 1.4.1 Recall the five steps of the scientific method.**

The scientific method involves five main steps: (1) identifying a research question, (2) forming a hypothesis, (3) choosing a research measurement and a research design, (4) collecting data, and (5) drawing conclusions that lead to new questions and new hypotheses.

**LO 1.4.2 Summarize the main measurements used in research on child development.**

Researchers studying child development use a variety of measurements. Major types of measurements are: questionnaires, interviews, observations, and biological measures. Each type of measurement has both strengths and weaknesses. It is important that a measurement has both reliability (consistency) and validity (reflects real life).

**LO 1.4.3 Distinguish between major types of research designs.**

Research designs lay out when, where, and with whom to employ the measurements of the study. Major types of research designs are: experimental designs, natural experiments, correlational designs, ethnographic research, and case studies. Each type has advantages and limitations.

**LO 1.4.4 Describe the two major types of research designs distinctive to developmental psychology.**

Two major types of research designs distinctive to developmental psychology are cross-sectional and longitudinal designs. The hallmark of both designs is that age is the independent variable. In cross-sectional research, data with people of different ages are collected at a single point in time. In longitudinal research, the same persons are followed over time and data are collected on two or more occasions.

**LO 1.4.5 Identify some key ethical standards for child development research.**

Developmental researchers must follow ethical guidelines that are laid out by professional organizations and enforced by institutional review boards. The main guidelines include protecting participants from physical and psychological harm, informed consent prior to participation, confidentiality, and debriefing after participation if deception was used.

# 1.5 Why We Study Child Development Worldwide

The field of child development has two central purposes:

(1) to contribute knowledge of children's development, and

(2) to improve children's lives.

These two purposes have been evident since the emergence of the field. Both Alfred Binet and G. Stanley Hall conducted their scientific research as part of the **child study movement** that was beginning to flourish in Europe and the United States around the turn of the 20th century (Collins & Hartup, 2013). Hall, in fact, was one of the initiators of the American child study movement. On both continents, these movements advocated scientific research on child and adolescent development and the improvement of conditions for children and adolescents in the family, school, and workplace.

**child study movement**
European and American movements around the turn of the 20th century that advocated scientific research on child and adolescent development, and the improvement of conditions for children and adolescents in the family, school, and workplace

## Contributing Knowledge

**LO 1.5.1 Explain the three general levels at which child development contributes knowledge.**

With respect to the first purpose, child development research contributes scientific knowledge at three general levels. From the outset, child development researchers have aimed to generate **nomothetic** knowledge. In other words, they have sought to provide universal descriptions, predictions, and explanations of child development. Freud's psychosexual theory of development is a good example. According to Freud, all children—across time and place—pass through his five stages. As you now know, Freud's theory has not stood the test of time. However, as you will see in the course of this text, the field of child development has generated innumerable insights about child development in general. For example, all babies are what we might call universal listeners. They have a remarkable ability to perceive speech sounds in all of the world's languages. By their first birthday, however, infants have become native listeners, only hearing the segments of sound that are meaningful in the language spoken by those around them. To give another example, worldwide research over the course of the last decades indicates that when children and adolescents first gain access to media, such as the Internet or TV, they become more likely to subscribe to individualistic values, emphasizing individual decision-making, achievement, and leadership.

**nomothetic**
research aimed at providing universal knowledge

Since the early days of the field of child development, researchers have also thought it important to gain knowledge at the **idiographic** level. Such research addresses ways in which individuals are unique. This often involves the use of the case study, such as Darwin's study of his son. Contemporary research also addresses how every child's unique genetic makeup influences her responses to the world and the people around her. In turn, a child's surrounding environment will impact the extent to which her genes are "turned on" or "turned off." We will learn a lot more about this in upcoming chapters.

**idiographic**
research aimed at providing knowledge of how individuals are unique

Apart from nomothetic and idiographic knowledge, child development researchers also increasingly aim to provide descriptions, predictions, and explanations at the **sociocultural** level. The focus on what is distinctive about the psychology of particular cultural and social groups. For example, as you will learn, Chinese and American children differ in a variety of ways on their cognitive development, including what they remember and how they process and interpret information. In recent years, researchers have also highlighted that ethnic minority children experience discrimination in ways that children who belong to the majority do not and have called for research on the psychological implications of such discrimination (García Coll et al., 1996; Marks, 2015).

**sociocultural**
research aimed at providing knowledge of particular cultural and social groups

## Improving Children's Lives

**LO 1.5.2 Give examples of how scientific knowledge can be applied across contexts to improve children's lives.**

In addition to contributing knowledge, the field of child development aims for its findings to be translated into practices and policies that will improve the lives of children. The application of knowledge about child development takes place across a large array of contexts: families, schools, health care, media, businesses, nonprofit organizations, and society as a whole. In the course of this text, you will learn about a variety of such practices and policies. Let us take a moment here, however, to preview some of the contributions of child development to practices and policies in regard to children:

- ***Families.*** When parents have clear expectations for their children's behavior and respond to their children with warmth and love, they contribute to their children becoming creative, socially skilled, and academically accomplished.
- ***Childcare Institutions.*** Infants and toddlers who spend some time in early childcare institutions are just as securely attached to their parents as infants and toddlers who are taken care of at home by a parent. It is, however, important that early child care is high quality, including an appropriate ratio of well-trained childcare providers per child.
- ***Schools.*** Successful schools foster a positive "climate" where teachers have high expectations for students while also being attentive to their needs and interests. Compared

to other schools, those with a positive climate have students with better attendance records and achievement test scores.

- *Media.* In the United States, anti–tobacco advertising based on principles from developmental psychology has proven to be effective in decreasing the likelihood that adolescents will begin smoking. However, tobacco companies are now targeting developing countries, where smoking is increasing as wealth increases.
- *Government.* Based on research from developmental psychology and other social sciences showing that today's emerging adults are more likely to remain financially dependent on their parents than in the past, the United States government mandated that as of 2010 most young people may remain on their parents' health insurance plan up to the age of 26.
- *International Nonprofit Organizations.* In recent years, UNICEF and the World Health Organization (WHO) have launched major initiatives to prevent mortality in adolescents and emerging adults. These initiatives arose from developmental research showing that whereas mortality rates had been declining in children in developing countries, this was not the case for adolescents and emerging adults. Also, based on psychological research, adolescents and emerging adults have been consulted in the formulation of preventive policies.

Fresh empire, run by the U.S. Food and Drug Administration, is a public education campaign designed to prevent and reduce tobacco use among at-risk multicultural youth who identify with the Hip Hop peer crowd.

At the heart of this text is also an understanding that we are all becoming global citizens. Increasingly the world is approaching the *global village* that the social philosopher Marshall McLuhan (1960) forecast over half a century ago. In recent decades there has been an acceleration in the process of **globalization**, which refers to the increasing connections between different parts of the world in trade, travel, migration, and communication (Arnett, 2002; Jensen et al., 2012; Hermans, 2015). Consequently, wherever you live in the world, in the course of your personal and professional life you are likely to have many contacts with people of other cultures. For example, those of you pursuing careers in education will likely teach students whose families emigrated from countries in Africa or Europe. Those of you going into the medical profession may one day have patients who have a cultural background in various parts of Asia or South America. Your coworkers, your neighbors, and your friends and family members may include people from a variety of different cultural backgrounds. Through the Internet you may have contact with people all over the world via e-mail, Facebook and other social media, YouTube, and new technologies to come. Thus, understanding child development worldwide may not only be inherently interesting, but it is also likely to be useful in many aspects of life. It will help you to communicate with and understand the perspectives of others in a diverse, globalized world.

**globalization**
increasing worldwide technological and economic integration, which is making different parts of the world increasingly connected

## SUMMARY: Why We Study Child Development Worldwide

### LO 1.5.1 Explain the three general levels at which child development contributes knowledge.

Child development research contributes scientific knowledge of children's development at three general levels. Nomothetic knowledge pertains to all children, idiographic knowledge focuses on individual children, and sociocultural knowledge captures the distinctive characteristics of children from particular cultural and social groups.

### LO 1.5.2 Give examples of how scientific knowledge can be applied across contexts to improve children's lives.

Knowledge of child development contributes to improving children's lives through initiatives such as anti-tobacco advertisement campaigns, guidelines for evaluating the quality of early child care, and programs for fostering a positive school climate.

## Apply Your Knowledge as a Professional

The topics covered in this chapter apply to a wide variety of career professions. Watch this video to learn how they apply to an early learning specialist at an international aid organization.

**Journaling Question:** Reflect on your own psychological identity. How do you think of yourself? This chapter has introduced a variety of dimensions such as culture, developmental stage, ethnicity, gender, SES, and globalization. Which of these dimensions, and potentially others too, are most important to how you see yourself?

# Chapter 2
# Genetics and Prenatal Development

## Learning Objectives

**2.1 Genetic Basics**

2.1.1 Distinguish between genotype and phenotype, and identify the different forms of genetic inheritance.

2.1.2 Describe the sex chromosomes and identify what makes them different from other chromosomes.

**2.2 Genes and the Environment**

2.2.1 Explain how behavior geneticists use heritability estimates and concordance rates in their research.

2.2.2 Explain how the concepts of epigenetics and reaction ranges address gene–environment interactions.

2.2.3 Explain how the theory of genotype → environment effects casts new light on the old nature–nurture debate.

**2.3 Genes and Individual Development**

2.3.1 Outline the process of meiosis in the formation of sperm and eggs, and specify how the process differs for females and males.

2.3.2 Describe the process of fertilization and conception.

**2.4 Prenatal Development**

2.4.1 Describe the structures that form during the germinal period, and identify when implantation takes place.

2.4.2 Outline the major milestones of the embryonic period and identify when they take place.

2.4.3 Describe the major milestones of the fetal period, including when viability occurs.

**2.5 Prenatal Brain Development**

2.5.1 Identify the different regions of the brain.

2.5.2 Describe how brain development during the fetal period involves neuronal migration and communication, as well as the loss of neural elements.

2.5.3 Explain how normal brain development involves both gene expression and environmental input.

**2.6 Prenatal Care**

2.6.1 Compare prenatal care in traditional cultures and developed countries.

2.6.2 Identify the major teratogens in developing countries and developed countries.

**2.7 Pregnancy Problems**

2.7.1 Explain how chromosomal disorders occur.

2.7.2 Describe the four main techniques of prenatal testing and diagnosis, and explain why some prospective parents seek genetic counseling.

2.7.3 Describe psychological and social implications of infertility, and review major causes of and treatments for infertility.

FOR MOTHERS-TO-BE WORLDWIDE, PREGNANCY IS OFTEN EXPERIENCED WITH A COMBINATION OF JOY, HOPE, AND FEAR. Yet here as in other aspects of development, the experience differs substantially depending on the culture and economic context. For most women in rural areas of developing countries, there is little in the way of technology or medical care to promote the healthy development of the fetus. Instead, pregnant women often rely on folk beliefs, a midwife's years of experience, and social support from the extended family. For most women in developed countries, medical care and technological aids are available throughout pregnancy. Yet many prospective mothers and fathers often face challenges in altering their lives to make room for the demands of raising a small child while continuing to pursue their careers.

Pregnancy is experienced in many different ways around the world, but everywhere it is a momentous event. In this chapter we examine the process of prenatal development, from its genetic beginnings until the final months of pregnancy. The chapter starts with a review of the basics of genetics and the role of genes in psychological development. Then, we focus on the beginnings of a new human life. You may be surprised to learn that the forming of a unique human being starts long before an egg and a sperm are joined. We look at this genetic basis of prenatal development, and then turn to the milestones of prenatal development itself. We pay special attention to the way the development of the brain depends both on genes and the prenatal environment. We also discuss prenatal care for both mother and baby to enhance the likelihood that all will go well. Sometimes problems arise in the course of pregnancy or in becoming pregnant in the first place, so the chapter concludes with a description of prenatal complications and infertility, including options for treatment of infertility.

**Watch** CHAPTER INTRODUCTION: GENETICS AND PRENATAL DEVELOPMENT

# 2.1 Genetic Basics

In all organisms, humans included, individual development has a genetic beginning. To understand the role of genetics in human development, it is important to have a basic foundation of knowledge about genes and how they function.

## Genotype and Phenotype

**LO 2.1.1 Distinguish between genotype and phenotype, and identify the different forms of genetic inheritance.**

Nearly all cells in the human body contain 46 **chromosomes** in 23 pairs, with one chromosome in each pair inherited from the mother and the other inherited from the father (see Figure 2.1). The chromosomes are composed of complex molecules known as **DNA (deoxyribonucleic acid)** (see Figure 2.2). The DNA in the chromosomes is organized into segments called **genes**, which are the basic units of hereditary information. Genes contain paired sequences of chemicals called *nucleotides*, and these sequences comprise instructions for the functioning and replication of the cells. There are about 19,000 genes in our 46 chromosomes, the total **human genome**, with all together about 3 billion nucleotide pairs (Ezkurdia et al., 2014). Research on the human genome is advancing at a rapid clip, generating new and surprising knowledge. For example, recent work is focusing on DNA sequences in the human genome that are not genes in the traditional sense, but that nonetheless serve important functions including regulation of gene expression (National Human Genome Research Institute, 2017).

Not all 19,000 genes are expressed in the course of development. The totality of an individual's genes is the **genotype**, and the person's actual characteristics are called the **phenotype**. In part, the difference between genotype and phenotype is a consequence of the person's environment. For example, if you were born with a genotype that included a potential for exceptional musical ability, this talent might never be developed if your environment provided no access to musical instruments or musical instruction. Consequently, the musical potential present in your genotype would not be apparent in your phenotype. On the other hand if, like for Mozart, your parents provided musical instruments and training already by age 4 (Davenport, 1979), then the musical potential might well find phenotypic expression.

Another aspect of genetic functioning that influences the relation between genotype and phenotype is **dominant–recessive inheritance** (Jones & Lopez, 2014). On every pair of chromosomes there are two forms of each gene, one on the chromosome inherited from the mother and one on the chromosome inherited from the father. Each form of the gene is called an **allele**. On many of these pairs of alleles, dominant–recessive inheritance occurs. This means that only one of the two genes—the *dominant gene*—influences the phenotype, whereas the *recessive gene* does not, even though it is part of the genotype. For example, if you inherited a gene for curly hair from one parent and a gene for straight hair from the

**chromosome**
structure in the nucleus of cells, containing genes, which are paired, except in reproductive cells

**DNA (deoxyribonucleic acid)**
long strand of cell material that stores and transfers genetic information in all life forms

**genes**
basic units of hereditary information

**human genome**
the sum total of hereditary information

**genotype**
organism's unique genetic inheritance

**phenotype**
organism's actual characteristics, derived from its genotype

**dominant–recessive inheritance**
pattern of inheritance in which a pair of chromosomes contains one dominant and one recessive gene, but only the dominant gene is expressed in the phenotype

**allele**
on a pair of chromosomes, each of two forms of a gene

**Figure 2.1** The Human Genome

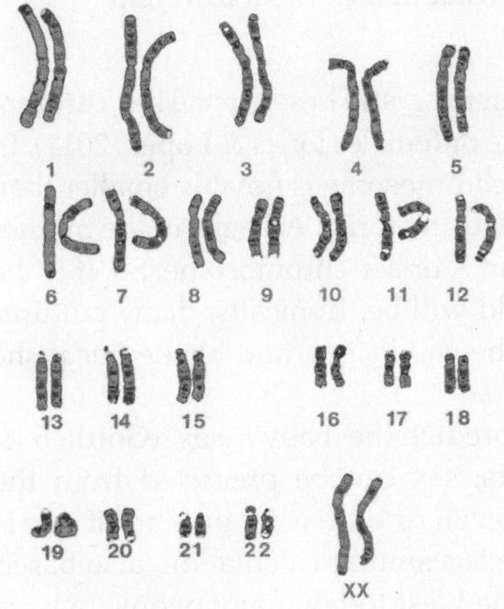


**Figure 2.2** The Chemical Structure of DNA

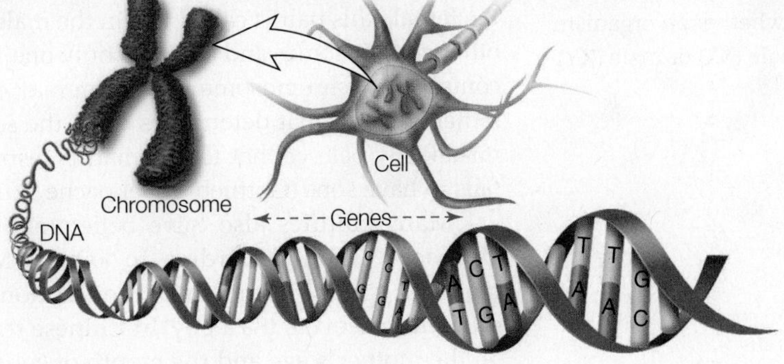

**Table 2.1** Traits With Single-Gene Dominant-Recessive Inheritance

| Dominant | Recessive |
|---|---|
| Curly hair | Straight hair |
| Dark hair | Blonde hair |
| Facial dimples | No dimples |
| Normal hearing | Deafness (some forms) |
| Normal vision | Nearsighted vision |
| Freckles | No freckles |
| Unattached ear lobe | Attached ear lobe |
| Can roll tongue in U-shape | Cannot roll tongue in U-shape |

other, you would have curly hair, because curly hair is dominant and straight hair is recessive. Recessive genes are expressed in the phenotype only when they are paired with another recessive gene. A clear pattern of dominant–recessive inheritance is evident only for traits determined by a single gene, which is not true of most traits, as we will see shortly. Some other examples of dominant and recessive characteristics are shown in Table 2.1.

The table shows clear-cut examples of dominant and recessive genes, but sometimes there is **incomplete dominance**, in which the phenotype is influenced primarily, but not exclusively, by the dominant gene. One example of incomplete dominance involves the sickle-cell trait that is common among black Africans and their descendants such as African Americans. Most blood cells are shaped like a disk, but when a person inherits two recessive genes for the sickle-cell trait, the blood cells become hook-shaped, like the blade of a sickle. This results in a condition called *sickle-cell anemia*, in which the sickle-shaped blood cells clog up the blood vessels and cause pain, susceptibility to disease, and early death. About 1 in 500 Africans and African Americans have this disorder, and it also occurs (less commonly) in people whose ancestors came from India, Saudi Arabia, the Mediterranean region, or Central and South America (World Health Organization [WHO], 2017).

**incomplete dominance**
form of dominant–recessive inheritance in which the phenotype is influenced primarily by the dominant gene but also to some extent by the recessive gene

However, as Figure 2.3 shows, if a person inherits a single recessive gene for the sickle-cell trait, along with a normal dominant gene, the dominance is incomplete, and a portion—but not all—of the person's blood cells will be sickle shaped. This portion is not large enough to cause sickle-cell anemia, but it is large enough to make the person resistant to malaria, a blood disease that is spread by mosquitoes. Malaria is often fatal and, even when it is not, it can cause brain damage and other enduring health problems. It occurs worldwide in developing countries but is especially common in Africa, killing over a million people a year. In many central African countries, over 50% of children are affected (World Health Organization [WHO], 2013). This explains why the sickle-cell trait evolved especially among Africans. Because the effects of contracting malaria are so severe, in evolutionary terms it is a genetic advantage to have the sickle-cell trait to protect against malaria, even if it also raises the risk of sickle-cell anemia.

Most characteristics in human development are not determined solely by a single pair of genes. Despite what you may have heard about the supposed existence of a "gay gene" or "religion gene" or "crime gene," no such genes have been found, nor are they likely to be (Pinker, 2004; "A special report on the human genome," 2010). Although single gene pairs sometimes play a crucial role in development, as in the case of sickle-cell anemia, more commonly the influence of genes is a consequence of **polygenic inheritance**, the interaction of multiple genes rather than just one (Lewis, 2015). This is true for physical characteristics such as height, weight, and skin color, as well as for characteristics such as intelligence, personality, and susceptibility to various diseases (Hoh & Ott, 2003; Karlsson, 2006; Rucker & McGuffin, 2010).

**polygenic inheritance**
expression of phenotypic characteristics due to the interaction of multiple genes

## The Sex Chromosomes

**LO 2.1.2 Describe the sex chromosomes and identify what makes them different from other chromosomes.**

Of the 23 pairs of chromosomes, one pair is different from the rest. These are the **sex chromosomes**, which determine whether the person will be male or female (Jones & Lopez, 2014). In the female this pair is called XX; in the male, XY. The Y chromosome is notably smaller than other chromosomes and contains only one-third the genetic material. All eggs in the mother contain an X chromosome but sperm may carry either an X or a Y chromosome. So, it is the father's sperm that determines what the sex of the child will be. Ironically, many cultures mistakenly believe that the woman is responsible for the child's sex, and blame her if she fails to have sons (Gottlieb & DeLoache, 2017).

**sex chromosomes**
chromosomes that determine whether an organism is female (XX) or male (XY)

Many cultures also have beliefs about how to predict the baby's sex (Gottlieb & DeLoache, 2017). According to ancient Mayan beliefs, sex can be predicted from the mother's age and the month of conception; if both are even or odd, it's a girl, but if one is odd and one even, it's a boy. In Chinese tradition there is a similar calculation, also based on the mother's age and the month of conception. In the West today many people believe

**Figure 2.3** Incomplete Dominance in Sickle-Cell Inheritance

**NOTE:** S = Normal dominant gene, s = Recessive gene for sickle-cell trait.

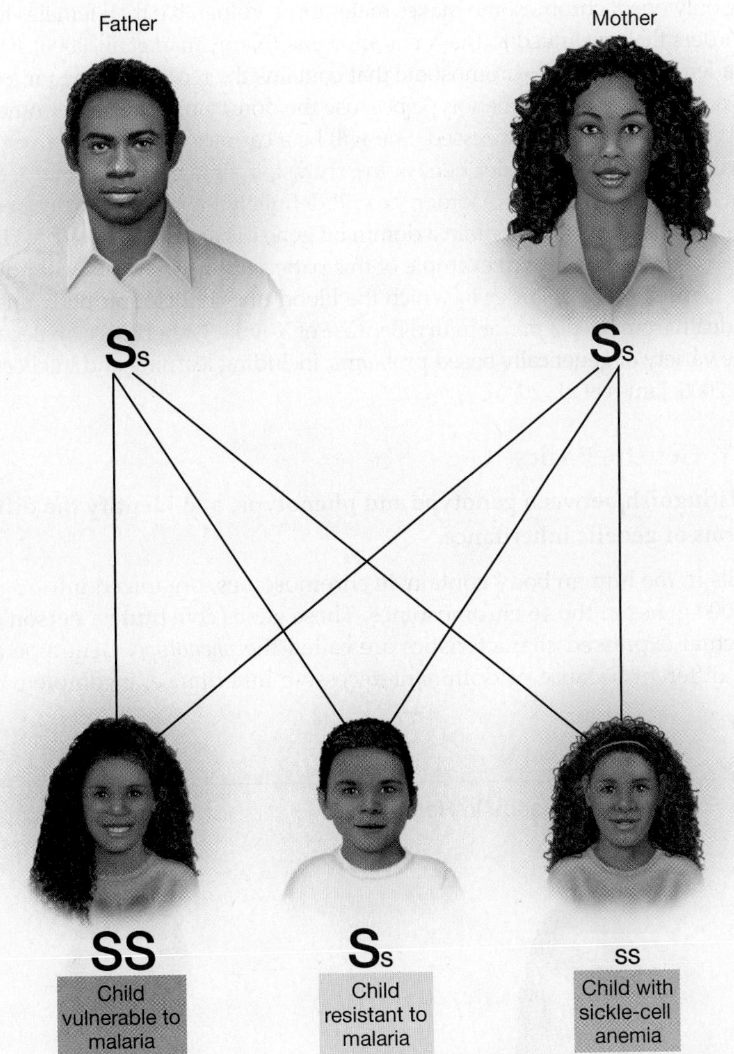


that if the mother is "carrying high"—the fetus feels high in the uterus—a girl is on the way, but if the mother is "carrying low" it's a boy. Another belief is that if the mother craves sweet foods, the baby will be a girl, but if she craves sour or salty foods she will soon have a boy. And in some countries it is believed that if the right breast of the mother-to-be is larger than the left, she will have a boy, but if the left breast is largest she will have a girl. None of these beliefs has the slightest scientific basis, but they demonstrate how important gender is to a child's future in most cultures, even before birth.

Many cultures have a bias in favor of boys, and the use of sex-selective abortion to achieve this is resulting in gender ratios skewed toward boys, especially in Asian cultures where this bias is especially pronounced (Abrejo et al., 2009). For more information on this, watch the video *A Preference for Sons*.

**Watch** A PREFERENCE FOR SONS

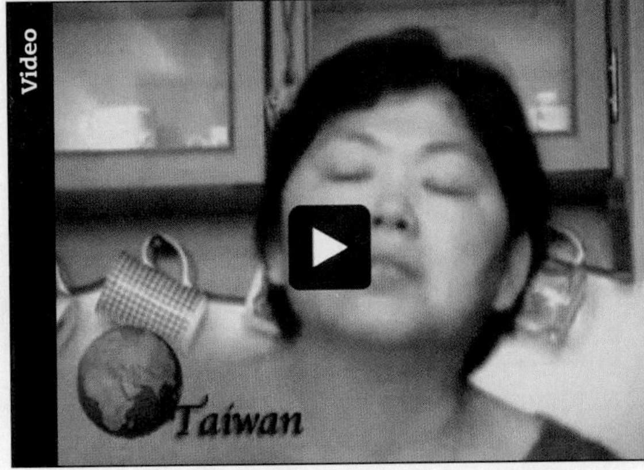


While sex ratios in many countries remain skewed toward more baby boys than girls, census data indicate that the bias against girls is diminishing (Economist, 2017). In China, the sex ratio at birth has declined from a peak of 121 boys per 100 girls in 2004 to 114 in 2015. In South Korea, the ratio has fallen from 116 boys per 100 girls in 1990 to 105 in 2015. In fact, South Korea's current ratio is perfectly normal because even without sex-selective abortion, the sex ratio at birth is skewed. Humans naturally give birth to about 105 boys per 100 girls. Evidently, this is nature's way of compensating for the greater genetic vulnerability of males (World Health Organization, 2017).

The sex of the developing organism also has biological consequences for prenatal development. Having only one X chromosome makes males more vulnerable than females to a variety of recessive disorders that are linked to the X chromosome (Narayanan et al., 2006). The reason for this is that if a female has one X chromosome that contains the recessive gene for a disorder, the disorder will not show up in her phenotype because the dominant gene on her other X chromosome will prevent it from being expressed. She will be a carrier of the disorder to the next generation but will not have the disorder herself. In contrast, if a male receives one X chromosome containing the recessive gene for a disorder, he will definitely have the disorder because he has no other X chromosome that may contain a dominant gene to block its expression. His Y chromosome cannot serve this function. An example of this pattern of **X-linked inheritance** is shown in Figure 2.4 for hemophilia, a disorder in which the blood does not clot properly and the person may bleed to death from even a minor injury. Because of X-linked inheritance, males are at greater risk for a wide variety of genetically based problems, including learning and intellectual disabilities (Halpern, 2000; James et al., 2006).

**X-linked inheritance**
pattern of inheritance in which a recessive characteristic is expressed because it is carried on the male's X chromosome

## SUMMARY: Genetic Basics

**LO 2.1.1 Distinguish between genotype and phenotype, and identify the different forms of genetic inheritance.**

Nearly all cells in the human body contain 46 chromosomes, organized into 23 pairs. There are about 19,000 genes in the 46 chromosomes. These genes constitute a person's genotype. A person's actual expressed characteristics are called the *phenotype*. Genotype and phenotype may be different because of dominant–recessive inheritance, incomplete dominance,

**Figure 2.4** X-Linked Inheritance in Hemophilia

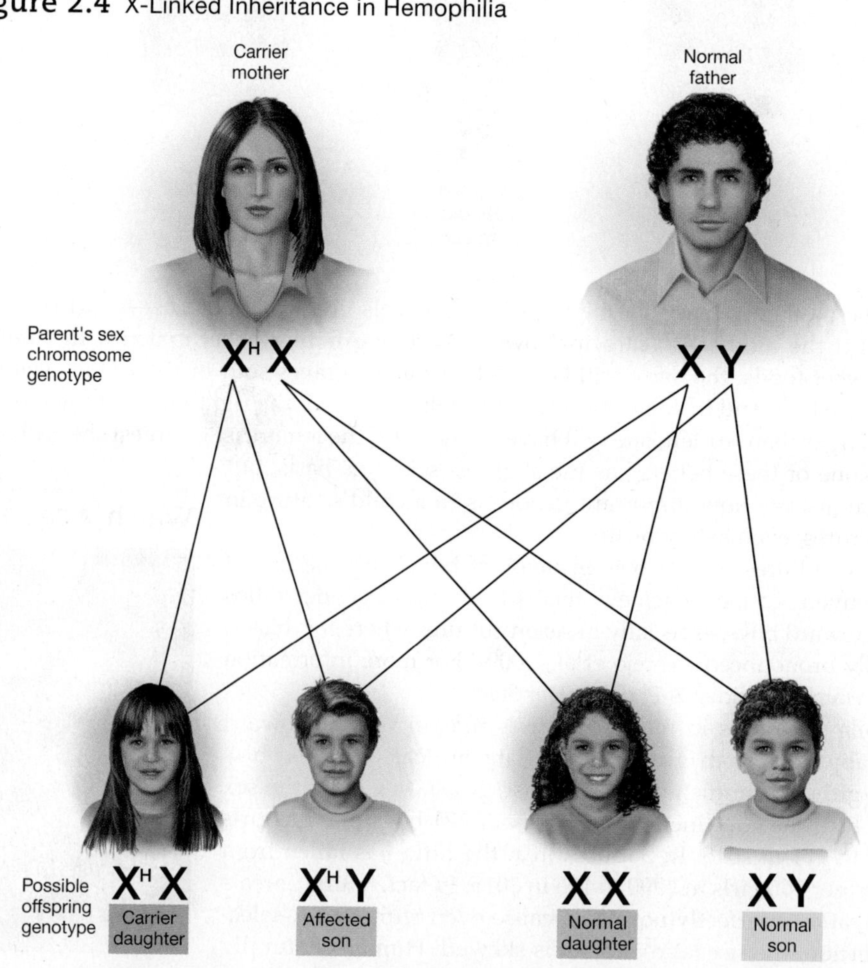

and environmental influences. Most human characteristics are polygenic, meaning that they are influenced by multiple genes rather than just one.

**LO 2.1.2 Describe the sex chromosomes and identify what makes them different from other chromosomes.**

The sex chromosomes determine whether the person will be female or male. In the female this pair is called XX; in the male, XY. Having only one X chromosome makes males more vulnerable than females to a variety of recessive disorders that are linked to the X chromosome.

# 2.2 Genes and the Environment

There is no doubt that genes have some influence on psychological development, but how much? Scholars have long debated the relative importance of genes and the environment in human development. In this **nature–nurture debate**, some scholars have claimed that development can be explained by genes (nature) and that environment matters little, whereas others have claimed that development depends mainly on environmental factors (nurture) (compare Baumrind, 1993; Scarr, 1993). By now, most scholars have reached a consensus that both genes and environment play key roles in human development, although the relative strength of nature and nurture continues to be debated (Dodge, 2007; Lickliter & Honeycutt, 2015; Pinker, 2004).

## Principles of Behavior Genetics

**LO 2.2.1 Explain how behavior geneticists use heritability estimates and concordance rates in their research.**

The question of how much genes influence human development is at the heart of the field of **behavior genetics** (Gottesman, 2004; Plomin, 2009). Researchers who work in behavior genetics estimate the influence of genes on development by comparing people who share different amounts of their genes, mainly through twin studies and adoption studies. Identical or **monozygotic (MZ) twins** have 100% of their genes in common (except in extraordinarily rare cases). Fraternal or **dizygotic (DZ) twins** and siblings have 40%–60% of their genes in common. Consequently, when MZ twins are more similar than DZ twins or siblings on psychological measures, this indicates that genetics play a strong role. Adoptive children have no genetic resemblance to their adoptive families. Consequently, adoption studies allow a researcher to study whether certain behaviors or traits of adoptive children are more similar to those of their biological parents (indicating a stronger genetic influence) or their adoptive families (indicating a stronger environmental influence).

By comparing these different groups, behavior geneticists are able to calculate a statistic called **heritability**. Heritability is an estimate of the extent to which genes are responsible for the differences among persons within a specific population. The value of the heritability estimate ranges from 0 to 1.00. The higher the heritability, the more the characteristic is believed to be influenced by genetics. If a heritability estimate is 0.70, for example, this means that genetic and environmental factors are estimated to contribute 70% and 30% to a trait, respectively.

Behavior genetics has flourished in the past two decades, and heritability estimates have been calculated for a wide range of characteristics. For intelligence, heritability estimates for children and adolescents have been found to be about 0.50, meaning that about half the variation in their IQ scores has been attributed to genetic influences (Turkheimer et al., 2009). With regard to personality characteristics, heritability estimates range from 0.40 to 0.50 for a wide array of characteristics such as sociability, activity level, and even religiosity (Bouchard & McGue, 2003).

**nature–nurture debate**
debate among scholars as to whether human development is influenced mainly by genes (nature) or environment (nurture)

**behavior genetics**
field in the study of human development that aims to identify the extent to which genes influence behavior, primarily by comparing persons who share different amounts of their genes

**monozygotic (MZ) twins**
twins who result from one fertilized egg splitting in two and who, except in extraordinarily rare case, have exactly the same genotype; also called identical twins

**dizygotic (DZ) twins**
twins who result from two eggs that each are fertilized by a sperm; also called fraternal twins

Monozygotic (MZ) twins are genetically identical. Studies that compare MZ twins to other sibling pairs have provided valuable insights regarding child development.

**heritability**
statistical estimate of the extent to which genes are responsible for the differences among persons within a specific population, with values ranging from 0 to 1.00

However, heritability estimates have been criticized for giving a misleading impression of the influence of genetics on development (Collins et al., 2000; Rutter, 2002). According to the critics, to state that a trait is heritable implies that we know with precision how much genes contribute to its development, but this is not so. Heritability estimates are simply estimates based on comparisons of persons with different amounts of genetic material in common, not direct measures of the activity of genes. Heritability estimates are a measure not just of genetic influence but of *how much the environment allows the genes to be expressed*. In other words, heritability estimates measure phenotype rather than genotype.

This can be seen in studies indicating that heritability of intelligence increases from childhood to adulthood (McGue & Christensen, 2002). Obviously genes do not change during this time, but the environment changes to allow greater expression of genetic potentials, as children grow into adolescence and become increasingly able to choose their own environments (such as after-school activities and peer groups). Importantly, research also shows that heritability of intelligence is higher in middle-class families than in poor families in the United States (McCartney & Berry, 2009; Turkheimer et al., 2009). This is not because middle-class families have different kinds of genes than poor families do, but because the greater economic resources of middle-class families make it more likely that children's genotypic potential for intelligence will be expressed in their phenotype. For example, middle-class families are more likely to be able to afford books, board games, electronic devices, and extracurricular activities that support the development of children's intellectual potential. They are also more likely to be able to send their children to well-functioning child care institutions and schools that offer many academic opportunities.

**Critical Thinking Question:** In Chapter 1, we reviewed how the field of child development contributes scientific knowledge at three levels: nomothetic, idiographic, and sociocultural. To which of these levels does a heritability estimate apply?

In short, we need to keep two things in mind. First, a heritability estimate does not describe the contribution of genetic and environmental factors for any one individual. It pertains to a population. Second, a heritability estimate for one population is not valid for another population. It is an estimate that pertains to the particular population of people that is being studied.

**Critical Thinking Question:** As we also saw in Chapter 1, socioeconomic variation occurring within a developed country such as the United States is much narrower than what is found worldwide. What consequences would you expect this to have for heritability estimates from a worldwide perspective?

Heritability estimates pertain to specific populations. For example, heritability estimates for American middle-class families cannot be applied to poor families in the United States.

Another statistic of genetic influence used in behavior genetics is **concordance rate**. This is a percentage that indicates the degree of similarity in phenotype among pairs of family members. Concordance rates range from 0% to 100%. The higher the concordance rate, the more similar the two persons are.

In many studies, comparisons of concordance rates are made between MZ and DZ twins. When concordance rates are higher among MZ than DZ twins, this indicates that the basis for the trait is partly genetic. For example, concordance rates for schizophrenia, a severe mental disorder involving hallucinations and disordered patterns of thinking and behavior, are 50% for MZ twins and 18% for DZ twins (Insel, 2010). This means that when one MZ twin has schizophrenia, 50% of the time the other twin has schizophrenia as well. For DZ twins, when one twin has schizophrenia, the other twin has the disorder only 18% of the time. Adoption studies also sometimes use this statistic, comparing concordance rates between parents and adopted children, parents and biological children, and adoptive or biological siblings.

**concordance rate**
degree of similarity in phenotype among pairs of family members, expressed as a percentage

**epigenetics**
the study of how genetic activity responds to environmental influences

**reaction range**
range of possible developmental paths established by genes; environment determines where development takes place within that range

## Gene–Environment Interactions: Epigenetics and Reaction Ranges

**LO 2.2.2 Explain how the concepts of epigenetics and reaction ranges address gene–environment interactions.**

Studies of heritability show not only that genes influence development but also that the environment influences how genes are expressed. A related idea is **epigenetics**, which means that development results from the bidirectional interactions between genotype and environment (Gottlieb, 2004; 2007). According to epigenetic theory, genetic activity responds constantly to environmental influences.

Here is an example of epigenetics. Girls normally begin menstruating between ages 11 and 16, toward the lower end of this range under healthy conditions and toward the higher end when nutrition is insufficient or the girl is suffering from medical problems (Neberich et al., 2010). Clearly it is part of the human-female genotype for menstruation to be initiated somewhere in this age range, with the timing influenced by environmental conditions. Furthermore, when girls' environmental conditions change, their menstrual patterns may also change. Girls who experience severe weight loss often stop menstruating (Roberto et al., 2008). If their nutritional intake improves, they begin menstruating again. This demonstrates a continuous interaction between genotype and environment, with menstruation being "turned on" genetically as part of puberty but "turned off" if environmental conditions are dire, then turned on again once the nutritional environment improves.

As this example illustrates, often when genes influence human development it is by establishing boundaries for environmental influences rather than specifying a precise characteristic. In other words, genes establish a **reaction range** of potential expression, and environment determines where a person's phenotype will fall within that range (McCartney & Berry, 2009). To take another example, height is known to be influenced by genes. You may well be able to tell this just by looking at your own height in relation to other members of your family. However, the genes for height simply establish the reaction range's upper and lower boundaries, and where a person's actual height ends up—the phenotype—is determined by environmental influences such as nutrition and disease.

Evidence for this is clear from the pattern of changes in height in societies around the world over the past century. In most Western countries, average height rose steadily in the first half of the 20th century as nutrition and health care improved (Freedman et al., 2006). The genes of their populations could not have changed in just a generation or two; instead, the improving environment allowed them to reach a higher point in their genetic reaction range for height. In other countries, such as China and South Korea, improvements in nutrition and health care came later, in the second half of the 20th century, so increases in height in those countries have taken place only recently (Wang et al.,

Genes establish a reaction range for height, and environment determines where a person's height falls within that range. Here, sisters of the Hamer tribe in Ethiopia, a tribe known for being exceptionally tall.

2010). However, people are unlikely ever to grow to be 10 or 20 feet tall. In recent decades in Western countries there has been little change in average height, indicating that the populations of these countries have reached the upper boundary of their reaction range for height.

## The Theory of Genotype → Environment Effects

**LO 2.2.3 Explain how the theory of genotype → environment effects casts new light on the old nature–nurture debate.**

**theory of genotype → environment effects**
theory proposing that genes influence the kind of environment we experience

One influential theory of behavior genetics is the **theory of genotype → environment effects** proposed by Sandra Scarr and Kathleen McCartney (Plomin, 2009; Scarr, 1993; Scarr & McCartney, 1983). According to this theory, both genotype and environment make essential contributions to human development. However, the relative strengths of genetics and the environment are difficult to unravel because our genes actually influence the kind of environment we experience. That is the reason for the arrow in the term *genotype → environment effects*. Based on our genotypes, we *create our own environments,* to a considerable extent.

These genotype → environment effects take three forms: passive, evocative, and active.

**passive genotype → environment effects**
in the theory of genotype → environment effects, the type that results from the fact that in a biological family, parents provide both genes and environment to their children

- ***Passive genotype → environment effects*** occur in biological families because *parents provide both genes and environment for their children.* This may seem obvious, but it has profound implications for how we think about development. Take this father–daughter example. Dad has been good at drawing things ever since he was a boy, and now he makes a living as a graphic artist. One of the first birthday presents he gives to his daughter is a set of crayons and colored pencils for drawing. As she grows up, he also teaches her a number of drawing skills as she seems ready to learn them. She goes to college and majors in architecture, then goes on to become an architect. It is easy to see how she became so good at drawing, given an environment that stimulated her drawing abilities so much—right?

Not so fast. It is true that Dad provided her with a stimulating environment, but he also provided her with half her genes. If there are any genes that contribute to drawing ability—such as genetic propensities for spatial reasoning and fine motor coordination—she may well have received those from Dad, too. The point is that in a biological family, it is very difficult to separate genetic influences from environmental influences because *parents provide both,* and they are likely to provide an environment that reinforces the tendencies they have provided to their children through their genes.

**Critical Thinking Question:** Can you think of parent-child examples from real life that may exemplify a passive genotype → environment effect?

When parents and children are similar, is the similarity due to genetics or environment?

So, you should be skeptical when you read studies that claim that parents' behavior is the cause of the characteristics of their biological children. Remember from Chapter 1: Correlation does not imply causation! Just because there is a *correlation* between the behavior of parents and the characteristics of their children does not mean the parents' behavior *caused* the children to have those characteristics. Maybe causation was involved, but in biological families it is difficult to tell. One good way to unravel this tangle is through adoption studies. These studies avoid the problem of passive genotype → environment effects because one set of parents provided the children's genes but a different set of parents provided the environment. Watch the video *Adopted Twin Studies: The Story of Oskar and Jack* for an extraordinary example of the influence of both genes and the environment.

## Research Focus: Adopted Twin Studies: The Story of Oskar and Jack

The interplay between genes and the environment is one of the most important, complex, and fascinating issues in the study of child development. One approach that has been helpful in unraveling these interactions is twin studies, especially research on twins separated early in life and raised in different environments. Studies of twins reared apart provide a good example of a natural experiment, which is something that occurs without the intervention of a researcher but can provide valuable scientific information.

The Minnesota Study of Twins Reared Apart, led by Thomas J. Bouchard, Jr., of the University of Minnesota, has been studying separated twins since 1979, and the results have been groundbreaking and sometimes astounding. Among the most remarkable cases in the Minnesota study is the story of identical twins Oskar and Jack.

**Watch** ADOPTED TWIN STUDIES: THE STORY OF OSKAR AND JACK

They were born in Trinidad in 1933, but within 6 months their parents split up. Oskar left for Germany with his Catholic mother, while Jack remained in Trinidad in the care of his Jewish father. Thus, unlike most separated twins, who at least remain within the same culture and country, Oskar and Jack grew up with the same genotype but with different cultures, different countries, and different religions. Furthermore, Oskar migrated with his mother to Germany in 1933, the year the Nazis rose to power. And Jack was raised as a Jew, at a time when Jews were targeted for extermination by the Nazis.

In some ways, the twins' childhood family environments were similar—as in similarly miserable. Oskar's mother soon moved to Italy and left him in Germany in the care of his grandmother, who was stern and harsh. Jack's father alternated between ignoring him and beating him. Despite these similarities, their cultures were about as different as could be. Oskar was an enthusiastic member of the Hitler Youth, and he learned to despise Jews and to keep his own half-Jewish background hidden. Jack was raised as a Jew and at 16 was sent by his father to Israel to join the navy, where he met and married an American Jew. At age 21 he and his wife moved to the United States.

What were the results of this extraordinary natural experiment in the two men's adult development? The extensive data collected by the Minnesota team, which included a week of tests and interviews with the men as well as interviews with their family members and others close to them, indicated that they had highly similar adult personalities. Both were described by themselves and others as short tempered, demanding, and absent minded. In addition, they shared a remarkable range of unusual, quirky personal habits. Both read books from back to front, sneezed loudly in elevators, liked to wear rubber bands on their wrists, and wrapped tape around pens and pencils to get a better grip.

However, their cultural identities and worldviews were as far apart as one might imagine, given the vastly different cultures they grew up in. Oskar repented his membership in the Hitler Youth as an adult, and lamented the Holocaust that had taken millions of Jewish lives under the Nazis—but he considered himself very German, and he and Jack disagreed vehemently over the responsibility and justification for bombings and other acts of war conducted during World War II.

Thus, despite all their similarities in personality, because of their different cultural environments they ultimately had very different identities—starkly separate understandings of who they are and how they fit into the world around them. As Oskar told Jack when they met again in adulthood, "If we had been switched, I would have been the Jew and you would have been the Nazi."

### Review Questions

1. Studies of twins raised apart provide a good example of:
   a. Reliability but not validity
   b. Validity but not reliability
   c. Experimental research
   d. A natural experiment
2. Which of the following is NOT one of the ways that Oskar and Jack were similar?
   a. Both were absent-minded
   b. Both were short tempered
   c. Both had a strong Jewish faith
   d. Both read books from back to front

- ***Evocative genotype → environment effects*** occur when a person's inherited characteristics evoke responses from others in their environment. If you had a son who started reading at age 3 and seemed to love it, you might buy him more books. If you had a daughter who could sink 20-foot jump shots at age 12, you might arrange to send her to basketball camp. Have you ever worked or volunteered in a setting where there were many children? If so, you probably found that children differ in how sociable, cooperative, and

**evocative genotype → environment effects**

in the theory of genotype → environment effects, the type that results when a person's inherited characteristics evoke responses from others in the environment

**active genotype → environment effects**

in the theory of genotype → environment effects, the type that results when people seek out environments that correspond to their genotypic characteristics

obedient they are. In turn, you may have found that you responded differently to them, depending on their characteristics. This is what is meant by evocative genotype → environment effects—with the crucial additional assumption that characteristics such as reading ability, athletic ability, and sociability are at least partly based in genetics.

- ***Active genotype → environment effects*** occur when people seek out environments that correspond to their genotypic characteristics, a process called *niche-picking*. The child who is faster than her peers may be motivated to try out for a sports team; the adolescent with an ear for music may ask for piano lessons; the emerging adult for whom reading has always been slow and difficult may prefer to begin working full-time after high school rather than going to a college or university. The idea here is that people are drawn to environments that match their inherited tendencies.

The three types of genotype → environment effects operate throughout the life course, but their relative balance changes over time (Plomin, 2009; Scarr, 1993). In childhood, passive genotype → environment effects are especially pronounced (at least within biological families), and active genotype → environment effects are relatively weak. This is because the younger a child is, the more parents control the daily environment the child experiences and the less autonomy the child has to seek out environmental influences outside the family.

However, the balance changes as children move through adolescence, emerging adulthood, and into adulthood. Parental control diminishes, so passive genotype → environment effects also diminish. Autonomy increases, so active genotype → environment effects also increase. In adulthood, passive genotype → environment effects fade almost entirely (except in cultures where persons continue to live with their parents even in adulthood), and active genotype → environment effects move to the forefront. Evocative genotype → environment effects remain relatively stable from childhood through adulthood.

### SUMMARY: Genes and the Environment

**LO 2.2.1 Explain how behavior geneticists use heritability estimates and concordance rates in their research.**

Heritability estimates indicate the degree to which a characteristic is believed to be influenced by genes within a specific population. Concordance rates indicate the degree of similarity between people with different amounts of their genes in common, such as monozygotic and dizygotic twins.

**LO 2.2.2 Explain how the concepts of epigenetics and reaction ranges address gene–environment interactions.**

Epigenetics is the concept that development results from bidirectional interactions between genotype and environment. The concept of reaction range also involves gene–environment interactions because it means that genes set a range for development and environment determines where development falls within that range.

**LO 2.2.3 Explain how the theory of genotype → environment effects casts new light on the old nature–nurture debate.**

Rather than viewing nature and nurture as separate forces, this theory proposes that genes influence environments through three types of genotype → environment effects: passive (parents provide both genes and environment to their children); evocative (children's inherited characteristics evoke responses from those who care for them); and active (children seek out an environment that corresponds to their genotype). The three types of effects operate throughout the life course but their relative balance changes with time.

# 2.3 Genes and Individual Development

When does the development of an individual begin? The answer may surprise you. The process of forming a new human being actually begins long before sperm and egg or *ovum* (plural, *ova*) are joined. Sperm and eggs themselves go through a process of development. We now turn to this genetic basis of prenatal development, beginning with sperm and egg formation.

## Sperm and Egg Formation

**LO 2.3.1 Outline the process of meiosis in the formation of sperm and eggs, and specify how the process differs for females and males.**

With the exception of eggs and sperm, all other cells in the human body contain 46 chromosomes (arranged into 23 pairs). These cells replicate through the process of **mitosis**, in which the chromosomes first duplicate themselves and then the cell divides to become two new cells (Pankow, 2008).

Egg and sperm, also known as **gametes** (from the ancient Greek "to marry"), consist of 23 single chromosomes. Gametes form in the ovaries of the female and the testes of the male through **meiosis**, a variation of the process of mitosis. In meiosis, cells that begin with 23 pairs of chromosomes first split into 46 single chromosomes, then duplicate and split into two cells, each with 23 pairs of chromosomes like the original cell. So far the process is just like mitosis. But then the pairs separate into single chromosomes and split again, this time into gametes that have 23 unpaired chromosomes instead of the original 46. So, at the end of the process of meiosis, from the original cell in the testes or ovaries, four new cells have been created, each with 23 single chromosomes. Figure 2.5 illustrates the process of meiosis.

There are some important sex differences in the process of meiosis (Jones & Lopez, 2014). In males, meiosis is completed before sperm are released, but in females the final stage of meiosis only takes place when and if the ovum is fertilized by a sperm (more on this shortly). Also, in males the outcome of meiosis is four viable sperm, whereas in females meiosis produces only one viable ovum along with three *polar bodies* that are not functional. The ovum appropriates for itself a large quantity of *cytoplasm*, the fluid that will be the main source of nutrients in the early days after conception, whereas the polar bodies are left with little.

Perhaps you have wondered why you are different from your brothers or sisters, even though both of you have 23 chromosomes each from mom and dad? Here's the explanation for sibling diversity. Something fascinating and remarkable happens at the outset of the process of meiosis. After the chromosomes first split and replicate but before the cell divides, pieces of genetic material are exchanged between the alleles in each pair, a process called **crossing over** (refer again to Figure 2.5). Crossing over mixes the combinations of genes in the chromosomes, so that genetic material that originated from the mother and father is rearranged in a virtually infinite number of ways (Pankow, 2008). Your parents could have had dozens, hundreds, even millions of children together, and none of them would be exactly like you genetically (unless you have an identical twin).

Here is another interesting fact about the production of gametes. Upon reaching puberty, males begin producing millions of sperm each day. There are 100 to 300 million sperm in the typical male ejaculation (Johnson, 2016). In contrast, females have already produced all the ova they will ever have *while they are still in their own mothers' womb.* Because crossing over begins when ova are created, this means that the development of a unique genotype for each individual begins before the individual's mother is even born!

Females are born with about 2 million ova, but this number diminishes to about 300,000 by adolescence, and about 400 of these will mature during a woman's childbearing years (Johnson, 2016; Moore et al., 2015; Norman, 2014). Most women run out of ova sometime in their 40s, but men produce sperm throughout their adult lives (although as we will see later in this chapter, the quantity and quality of sperm declines with age) (Finn, 2001).

**mitosis**

process of cell replication in which the chromosomes duplicate themselves and the cell divides into two cells, each with the same number of chromosomes as the original cell

**gametes**

cells, distinctive to each sex, that are involved in reproduction (egg cells in the ovaries of the female and sperm in the testes of the male)

**meiosis**

process by which gametes are generated, through separation and duplication of chromosome pairs, ending in four new gametes from the original cell, each with half the number of chromosomes of the original cell

**crossing over**

at the outset of meiosis, the exchange of genetic material between paired chromosomes

**Figure 2.5** The Creation of Gametes Through Meiosis

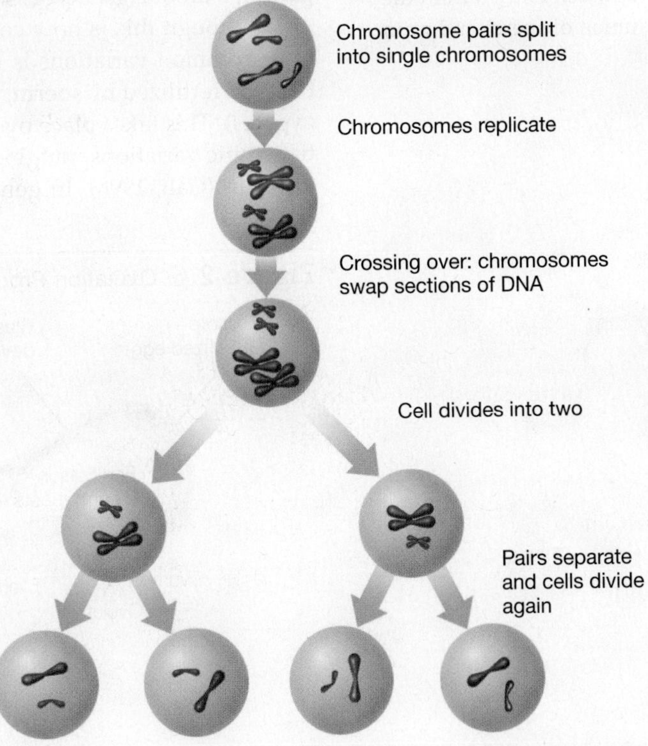

# Conception

**LO 2.3.2 Describe the process of fertilization and conception.**

When sexual intercourse takes place between a man and a woman, many millions of sperm from the man begin making their way through the woman's reproductive organs—first into the vagina, then through the cervix, through the uterus, and up the fallopian tubes toward the ovaries. Hundreds of millions of sperm may seem like more than enough, but keep in mind that sperm are composed of a single cell, not much more than 23 chromosomes and a tail, so they are not exactly skilled at navigation. The distance from the vagina to the ovaries is vast for such a small object as a sperm. Furthermore, the woman's body responds to sperm as a foreign substance and begins killing them off immediately. Usually only a few hundred sperm make it up the fallopian tubes to where fertilization can take place (Jones & Lopez, 2014).

**follicle**
during the female reproductive cycle, the ovum plus other cells that surround the ovum and provide nutrients

Within the woman, there are two ovaries that release an ovum in alternating months. During the early part of the woman's cycle the ovum is maturing into a **follicle**. The follicle consists of the ovum plus other cells that surround it and provide nutrients. About 14 days into a woman's cycle, the mature follicle bursts and *ovulation* takes place as the ovum is released into the fallopian tube (see Figure 2.6). The ovum is 2,000 times larger than a sperm because it contains so much cytoplasm (Johnson, 2016). The cytoplasm will provide nutrients for the first 2 weeks of growth if the ovum is fertilized, until it reaches the uterus and begins drawing nutrients from the mother.

It is only during the first 24 hours after the ovum enters the fallopian tube that fertilization can occur. It takes sperm from a few hours to a whole day to travel up the fallopian tubes, so fertilization is most likely to take place if intercourse occurs on the day of ovulation or the 2 previous days. Sperm can live up to 5 days after entering the woman's body, but most do not last more than 2 days (Johnson, 2016).

When sperm reach the ovum they begin to penetrate its surface, aided by a chemical on the tip of the sperm that dissolves the ovum's membrane. Once a sperm penetrates the membrane, the head of the sperm detaches from the tail and continues toward the nucleus of the cell while the tail remains outside. The moment the first sperm breaks through, a chemical change takes place in the membrane of the ovum that prevents any other sperm from getting in.

**zygote**
following fertilization, the new cell formed from the union of sperm and ovum

When the sperm head reaches the nucleus of the ovum, the final phase of meiosis is triggered in the ovum (Johnson, 2016). Fertilization takes place as the 23 chromosomes from the ovum pair up with the 23 chromosomes from the sperm and a new cell, the **zygote**, is formed from the two gametes. The zygote's 46 paired chromosomes constitute the new organism's unique genotype, set once and for all at the moment of conception.

Although this is how conception usually takes place, there are variations. One of the most common variations is that two ova are released by the woman instead of one, and both are fertilized by sperm, resulting in DZ twins (recall that DZ stands for *dizygotic*—two zygotes). This takes place overall about once in every 60 births, although there are substantial ethnic variations, ranging from 1 in every 25 births in Nigeria to 1 in every 700 births in Japan (Gall, 1996). In general, Asians have the lowest rates of DZ twins and Africans

**Figure 2.6** Ovulation Process

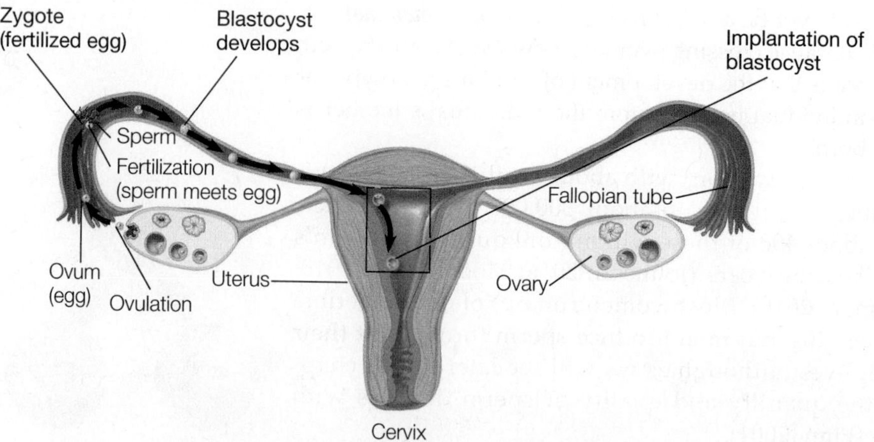

the highest (Mange & Mange, 1998; Smits & Monden, 2011). In addition to ethnic background, some of the factors that increase the likelihood of DZ twins are a family history of twins, age (older women are more likely to release two eggs at once), and nutrition (women with healthy diets are more likely to have DZ twins) (Bortolus et al., 1999). Today, another common cause of DZ twins is infertility treatments, which we will focus on later in this chapter.

Twins can also result when a zygote that has just begun the process of cell division splits into two separate clusters of cells, creating MZ twins (recall that MZ stands for *monozygotic*—one zygote). MZ twins are less common than DZ twins, occurring about 1 in every 285 births (Zach et al., 2001). In contrast to DZ twins, MZ twins are not more common in some ethnic groups than others. They take place at the same frequency all around the world (Quinn, 2013). Also unlike DZ twins, MZ twins are not predicted by age or nutrition, and do not run in families (except in exceedingly rare cases; Machin, 2009).

Across the world, Africa has high rates of dizygotic (DZ) twins. This pair is from South Africa.

## SUMMARY: Genes and Individual Development

**LO 2.3.1 Outline the process of meiosis in the formation of sperm and eggs, and specify how the process differs for females and males.**

In meiosis, cells that begin with 23 pairs of chromosomes split and replicate repeatedly until they form four gametes, each with 23 individual chromosomes. In males, the outcome of meiosis is four viable sperm, but in females, meiosis produces only one viable ovum (along with three polar bodies that are not functional). Also, males produce millions of sperm daily beginning in puberty, whereas females produce all the eggs they will ever have while still in their mother's womb.

**LO 2.3.2 Describe the process of fertilization and conception.**

About 14 days into a woman's cycle, an ovum is released into the fallopian tube. For the next 24 hours, fertilization can occur in which the 23 chromosomes from the ovum pair up with the 23 chromosomes from the sperm and a new cell, the zygote, is formed from the two gametes. The zygote's 46 paired chromosomes constitute the new organism's unique genotype, set once and for all at the moment of conception.

# 2.4 Prenatal Development

When sperm and ovum unite to become a zygote, a remarkable process is set in motion. If all goes well, about 9 months later a fully formed human being will be born. Now we look closely at this prenatal process, from conception to birth. Figure 2.7 (next page) provides an overview of the process.

## The Germinal Period (First 2 Weeks)

**LO 2.4.1 Describe the structures that form during the germinal period, and identify when implantation takes place.**

The first 2 weeks after fertilization are called the **germinal period** (Jones & Lopez, 2014). This is the period when the zygote travels down the fallopian tubes to the uterus and implants in the uterine wall. As it travels, it begins cell division and differentiation. The first cell division does not occur until 30 hours after conception, but after that, cell division takes place at a faster rate. By 1 week following conception there is a ball of about 100 cells known as a **blastocyst**. The blastocyst is divided into two layers. The outer layer of cells,

**germinal period**
first 2 weeks after conception

**blastocyst**
ball of about 100 cells formed by about 1 week following conception

**Figure 2.7** Milestones of Prenatal Development

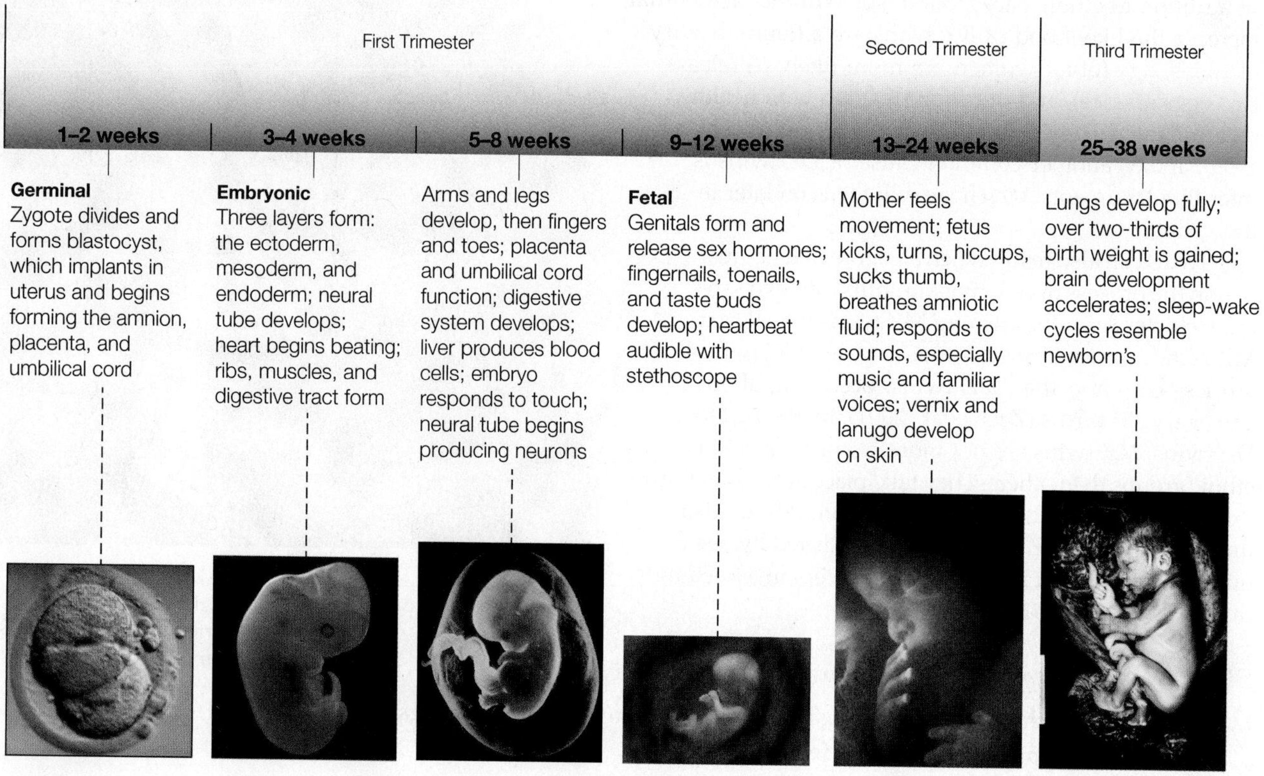

called the *trophoblast*, will form the structures that provide protection and nourishment. The inner layer of cells, the *embryonic disk*, will become the embryo of the new organism.

During the second week after conception, **implantation** occurs as the blastocyst becomes firmly embedded into the lining of the uterus. Since the ovum was released from the ovary, the follicle from which it was released has been generating hormones that have caused the uterus to build up a bloody lining in preparation for receiving the blastocyst. Now the blastocyst is nourished by this blood.

**implantation**
occurs at the end of the germinal period when the blastocyst becomes firmly embedded into the lining of the uterus

**amnion**
fluid-filled membrane that surrounds and protects the developing organism in the womb

**placenta**
structure connecting mother and the developing organism that among other things channels nutrients to the organism, and blocks mother's bacteria and wastes from reaching the organism

**umbilical cord**
structure connecting the placenta to the mother's uterus

The trophoblast begins to differentiate into several structures during this second week. Part of it forms a membrane, the **amnion**, which surrounds the developing organism and fills with fluid, helping to keep a steady temperature for the organism and protect it against impact from the mother's movements (Johnson, 2016). In between the uterine wall and the embryonic disk a round structure, the **placenta**, begins to develop. The placenta will allow nutrients to pass from the mother to the developing organism and permit wastes to be removed. It also acts as a gatekeeper, protecting the developing organism from bacteria and wastes in the mother's blood. The placenta also produces hormones that maintain the blood in the uterine lining and cause the mother's breasts to produce milk. An **umbilical cord** also begins to develop, connecting the placenta to the mother's uterus.

Implantation is the outcome of the germinal period if all goes well. However, it is estimated that over half of blastocysts never implant successfully, usually due to chromosomal problems that have caused cell division to slow down or stop (Johnson, 2016). If implantation fails, the blastocyst will be eliminated from the woman's body along with the bloody uterine lining during her next menstrual period.

## The Embryonic Period (Weeks 3–8)

**LO 2.4.2 Outline the major milestones of the embryonic period and identify when they take place.**

During the germinal period, the trophoblast differentiated faster than the embryonic disk, developing the structures to protect and nurture the organism during pregnancy. Now, differentiation occurs rapidly in the embryonic disk. Over the 6 weeks of the **embryonic period**, or 3–8 weeks' **gestation** (the time elapsed since conception), nearly all the major organ systems are formed (Fleming, 2006).

During the first week of the embryonic period—the third week after conception—the embryonic disk forms three layers. The outer layer, the **ectoderm**, will become the skin, hair, nails, sensory organs, and nervous system. The middle layer, the **mesoderm**, will become the muscles, bones, reproductive system, and circulatory system. The inner layer, the **endoderm**, will become the digestive system and the respiratory system.

The nervous system develops first and fastest (Johnson, 2016). By the end of Week 3 (since conception), part of the ectoderm forms the **neural tube**, which will eventually become the spinal cord and brain. The neural tube begins producing **neurons** (cells of the nervous system) by Week 7 (Stiles & Jernigan, 2010). This **neurogenesis** occurs in immense quantities. Estimates as to how many neurons the average adult brain contains have changed over time, but a study using an improved measuring technique has placed it at about 86 billion (Herculano-Houzel, 2009). Furthermore, research indicates that babies are born with more neurons than adults (Abitz et al., 2007). Most of these billions of neurons will have been produced by the middle of prenatal development (Stiles & Jernigan, 2010).

In the fourth week the shape of the head becomes apparent, and the eyes, nose, mouth, and ears begin to form. The heart begins to beat during this week, and the ribs, muscles, and digestive tract appear. By the end of the fourth week, the embryo is only one-quarter-inch long but already remarkably differentiated. Nevertheless, even an expert embryologist would have trouble at this point judging whether the embryo was to become a fish, a bird, or a mammal.

During Weeks 5–8, growth continues at a rapid pace. Buds that will become the arms and legs appear in Week 5, developing webbed fingers and toes that lose their webbing by Week 8. The placenta and the umbilical cord become fully functional (Jones & Lopez, 2014). The digestive system develops, and the liver begins producing blood cells. The heart develops separate chambers. The top of the neural tube continues to develop into the brain, but the bottom of it looks like a tail in Week 5, gradually shrinking to look more like a spinal cord by Week 8.

By the end of the eighth week, the embryo is just 1 inch (2½ centimeters) long and 1/30 of an ounce (1 g) in weight. Yet all the main body parts have formed, as have all of the main organs except the sex organs. Furthermore, the tiny embryo responds to touch, especially around its mouth, and it can move (Moore et al., 2015). Now the embryo looks distinctly human (Johnson, 2016).

**embryonic period**
weeks 3–8 of prenatal development

**gestation**
in prenatal development, elapsed time since conception

**ectoderm**
in the embryonic period, the outer of the three cell layers, which will become the skin, hair, nails, sensory organs, and nervous system

**mesoderm**
in the embryonic period, the middle of the three cell layers, which will become the muscles, bones, reproductive system, and circulatory system

**endoderm**
in the embryonic period, the inner layer of cells, which will become the digestive system and the respiratory system

**neural tube**
in the embryonic period, the part of the ectoderm that will become the spinal cord and brain

**neuron**
cell of the nervous system

**neurogenesis**
the production of neurons

## The Fetal Period (Week 9–Birth)

**LO 2.4.3 Describe the major milestones of the fetal period, including when viability occurs.**

During the **fetal period**, lasting from 9 weeks after conception until birth, the organs continue to develop, and there is tremendous growth in sheer size, from 1/30 of an ounce in weight and 1 inch long at the beginning of the fetal period to an average (in developed countries) of 7½ pounds (3.4 kg) and 20 inches (51 cm) by birth.

**fetal period**
in prenatal development, the period from Week 9 until birth

By the end of the third month, the genitals have formed. After forming, the genitals release hormones that influence the rest of prenatal development, including brain organization, body size, and activity level, with boys becoming on average somewhat larger and more active (Cameron, 2001). Also during the third month, fingernails, toenails, and taste buds begin to develop. The heart has developed enough so that the heartbeat can now be heard through a stethoscope.

After 3 months, the typical fetus weighs about 3 ounces and is 3 inches long. A good way to remember this is as "three times three"—3 months, 3 ounces, 3 inches. Or, you can think of it as 100 days, 100 grams, 100 millimeters. Prenatal development is divided into three 3-month periods called **trimesters**, and the end of the third month marks the end of the first trimester.

**trimester**
prenatal development is divided into three 3-month periods

During the second trimester, the fetus becomes active and begins to respond to its environment (Henrichs et al., 2010). By the end of the fourth month, the fetus's movements can be felt by the mother. Gradually over the course of the second trimester the activity of the fetus becomes more diverse. By the end of the second trimester it breathes amniotic fluid in

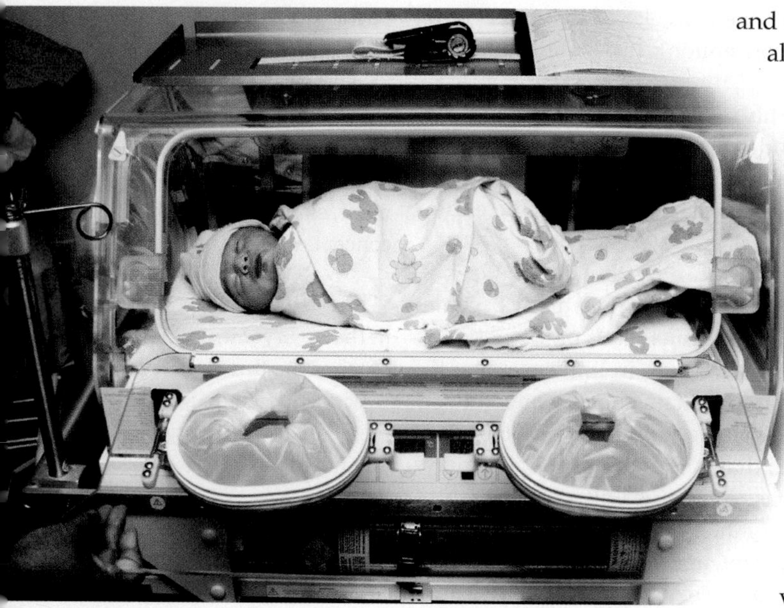

Survival rates for premature babies are much higher for babies born in developed countries than developing countries.

**vernix**

at birth, babies are covered with this oily, cheesy substance, which protects their skin from chapping in the womb

**lanugo**

downy hair that helps the vernix stick to the skin of the developing fetus

and out; it kicks, turns, and hiccups; it even sucks its thumb. It also responds to sounds, including voices and music, showing a preference (indicated by increased heart rate) for familiar voices, especially the voice of the mother. A slimy white substance called **vernix** covers the skin, to protect it from chapping due to the amniotic fluid, and downy hair called **lanugo** helps the vernix stick to the skin. By birth the fetus usually sheds its lanugo, although sometimes babies are born with lanugo still on, then shed it in the early weeks of life.

By the end of the second trimester, 6 months after conception, the typical fetus is about 14 inches long (36 cm) and weighs about 2 pounds (0.9 kg). Although it seems well-developed in many aspects of its behavior, it is still questionable in its *viability*, meaning its ability to survive outside of the womb. Babies born before 22 weeks rarely survive, even with the most advanced technological assistance. The survival rate by 24 weeks is 50%, and by 26 weeks it is 80%. However, the survivors who are born between 22 and 26 weeks often have disabilities, including problems with hearing and sight, intellectual disabilities, and cerebral palsy (which entails extensive physical and neurological disabilities) (Carlo, 2016; Hille et al., 2007; Tyson et al., 2008). And these survival rates are only for babies that happen to be born in developed countries or in a wealthy family in a developing country. In most of the world, babies born before the end of the second trimester have no access to advanced medical care and do not survive (Organisation for Economic and Co-Operative Development [OECD], 2009).

The main obstacle to viability at the beginning of the third trimester is the immaturity of the lungs. The lungs are the last major organ to become viable, and even a baby born in the seventh or early eighth month may need a respirator to breathe properly. Weight gain is also important. During the last trimester the typical fetus gains over 5 pounds, and this additional weight helps it sustain life. Babies born weighing less than 5.8 pounds are at risk for a wide range of problems, as we will see in detail in Chapter 3.

By the third trimester, at 28 weeks, the sleep-wake cycles of the fetus are similar to those of a newborn infant. Fetuses also respond to their internal environment. When the mother is highly stressed, the fetus' heart beats faster and its body movements increase (DiPietro et al., 2002).

The fetus is also increasingly aware of the external environment (James, 2010). In one study, mothers were asked to read Dr. Seuss's *The Cat in the Hat* to their fetuses every day during the last 6 weeks of pregnancy (DeCasper & Spence, 1986). After birth, the babies showed a preference for a recording of their mother reading *The Cat in the Hat*, by sucking on a plastic nipple in order to turn it on. They sucked harder to hear *The Cat in the Hat* than they did for recordings of their mothers reading similar rhyming stories they had not heard before. Research has also shown that newborns prefer tastes, smells, voices, and even languages that they experienced while in the womb (Mennella et al., 2001; Moon et al., 1993; Varendi et al., 2002). Even prenatally, then, fetuses are learning and remembering, and they are developing initial preferences that are culturally shaped, such as for spicy or mild flavors, and for French or Russian.

## SUMMARY: Prenatal Development

### LO 2.4.1 Describe the structures that form during the germinal period, and identify when implantation takes place.

The first 2 weeks after fertilization are called the *germinal period*. During this period the zygote develops into a ball of cells called the *blastocyst* that implants in the lining of the uterus. The blastocyst has two layers, the embryonic disk, which will become the embryo of the new organism, and the trophoblast, which will form the supporting structures of the amnion, placenta, and umbilical cord.

**LO 2.4.2 Outline the major milestones of the embryonic period and identify when they take place.**

During the embryonic period (3–8 weeks after conception) all the major organ systems are initially formed, except the sex organs. This is also the period when neural production, neurogenesis, begins.

**LO 2.4.3 Describe the major milestones of the fetal period, including when viability occurs.**

During the fetal period (Week 9–birth) organ systems continue to develop and there is immense growth in size. Babies born before 22 weeks rarely survive, whereas by 26 weeks the survival rate in developed countries is 80%. The survivors who are born between 22 and 26 weeks often have disabilities. By 28 weeks, the fetus has sleep–wake cycles similar to a newborn baby's and can remember and respond to sound, taste, and the mother's movements.

# 2.5 Prenatal Brain Development

The ability of the fetus to respond to both the internal and external environment provides remarkable evidence of the extent to which the brain develops prenatally. During the fetal period, the basic structures and processes of brain development are formed, even though the brain is malleable and will continue to develop throughout the life course (Stiles & Jernigan, 2010). The production of neurons that began in the embryonic period continues in the fetal period. As they are produced, the neurons migrate to various parts of the brain and *differentiate* into distinct areas.

## Brain Regions

**LO 2.5.1 Identify the different regions of the brain.**

Overall, the brain is divided into three major regions, the *hindbrain*, the *midbrain*, and the *forebrain*. The hindbrain and midbrain mature earliest and perform basic biological functions necessary to life. They will keep your lungs breathing, your heart beating, and your bodily movements balanced. The forebrain is divided into two main parts, the *limbic system* and the *cerebral cortex*. The structures of the limbic system include the *hypothalamus*, the *thalamus*, and the *hippocampus*. The hypothalamus is small, about the size of a peanut in an adult, but plays a key role in monitoring and regulating our basic animal functions, including hunger, thirst, body temperature, sexual desire, and hormonal levels. The thalamus acts as a receiving and transfer center for sensory information from the body to the rest of the brain. The hippocampus is crucial in memory.

The most distinctively human part of the brain is the outermost part of the forebrain, the **cerebral cortex**. This part of the human brain is far larger than in other animals. For example, adult humans weigh about as much as adult chimpanzees, but have a cerebral cortex three to four times larger (Wrangham, 2009). It accounts for 85% of the brain's total weight, and it is here that most of the brain's growth will take place after birth. The cerebral cortex is the basis of our distinctively human abilities, including the ability to speak and understand language, to solve complex problems, and to think in terms of concepts, ideas, and symbols.

**cerebral cortex**
outer portion of the brain, containing four regions with distinct functions

The cerebral cortex is divided into two hemispheres, left and right, which are connected by a band of neural fibers called the *corpus callosum* that allows them to communicate. The fissure between hemispheres begins at about the time of the start of the fetal period and is completed by the end of the second trimester (Stiles & Jernigan, 2010). **Lateralization** is the term for the specialization of the two hemispheres. In general, the left hemisphere is specialized for language and for processing information in a sequential, step-by-step way (Harnad, 2012). The right hemisphere is specialized for spatial reasoning and for processing information in a holistic, integrative way. However, the specialization of the hemispheres should not be exaggerated, because they work together in most aspects of language, emotion, and behavior. No one is mainly a "left-brain" or "right-brain" thinker.

**lateralization**
specialization of functions in the two hemispheres of the brain

Figure 2.8 Lobes of the Brain

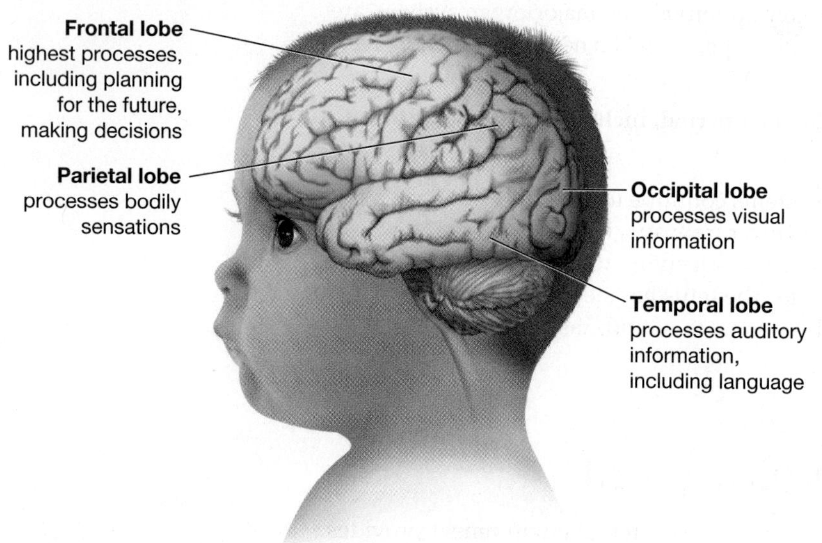


The cerebral cortex is also specialized in that each hemisphere has four regions or lobes with quite distinct functions (see Figure 2.8). The *occipital lobes* at the rear of each hemisphere process visual information. The *temporal lobes* at the lower side of each hemisphere are involved in processing auditory information, including spoken language. The *parietal lobes* above the temporal lobes process information from bodily sensations. The *frontal lobes* behind the forehead are the center of the most advanced human brain processes, including spoken language, planning for the future, and making decisions. This again is a region where a lot of development takes place after birth and for years to come. With the lobes as with the hemispheres, it is important not to exaggerate the degree of specialization, as more than one part of the brain is involved in most brain functions (Harnad, 2012; Knect et al., 2003).

**axon**
part of a neuron that transmits electric impulses and releases neurotransmitters

**dendrites**
arrays of short neural fibers that receive neurotransmitters

**myelination**
process of the growth of the myelin sheath around the axon of a neuron

**synaptic pruning**
process whereby dendritic connections that are unused whither away

## Neural Migration and Communication

**LO 2.5.2 Describe how brain development during the fetal period involves neuronal migration and communication, as well as the loss of neural elements.**

As neurons are produced, they start to migrate to their destinations in different areas of the brain. This *neuronal migration* involves the new cells traveling away from where they originated to new locations where they become part of developing brain structures and regions.

Following migration, the young neurons need to become part of circuits. Neurons differ from other cells in the body in that they are not directly connected to each other. Instead, they are separated by tiny gaps called *synapses*. Neurons communicate across the synapses through the release and reception of chemicals called *neurotransmitters*. Neurotransmitters are released by the **axon** of the neuron and received by the **dendrites** (see Figure 2.9). Dendrites are arrays of short fibers that look like the branches of a tree. Axons are long connecting fibers. Starting early in the fetal period, around the 14th week, axons become wrapped in a white, fatty substance called myelin. **Myelination** increases the speed of communication between neurons (Gale et al., 2004). While myelination starts prenatally, it is especially active in the first year of life but continues at a slower rate into adulthood (Markant & Thomas, 2013).

Figure 2.9 The Synapse

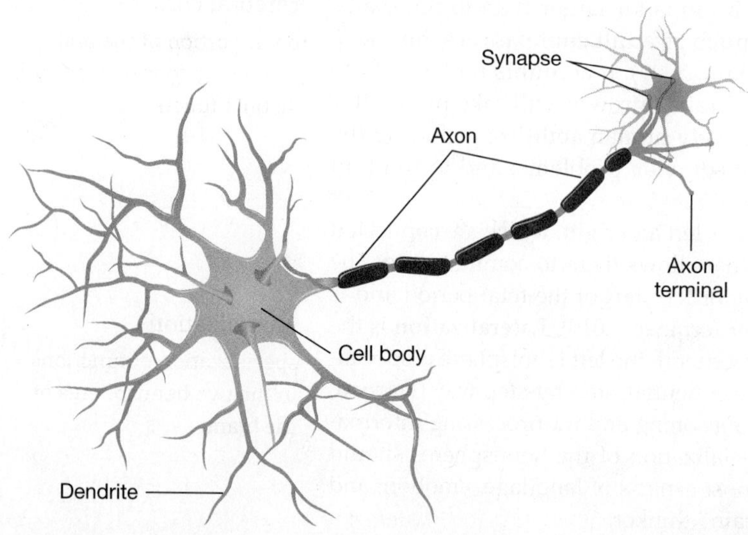


Interestingly, brain development is not simply a matter of adding more neurons and more connections between neurons. There are two normal processes that involve loss of neural elements. One is *neural death*. This is a naturally occurring process where 50% or more of individual neurons within a brain region disappear. One hypothesis is that this loss occurs for neurons that are ineffective in the establishment of circuits (Buss et al., 2006). Neural death mostly occurs during the fetal period.

The other normal process whereby neural elements are lost is through **synaptic pruning**, which

**Figure 2.10** Timing of Neurobiological Processes of the Brain

**NOTE:** Dashed lines indicate periods of active development and bold (purple) lines indicate periods of peak developmental change.

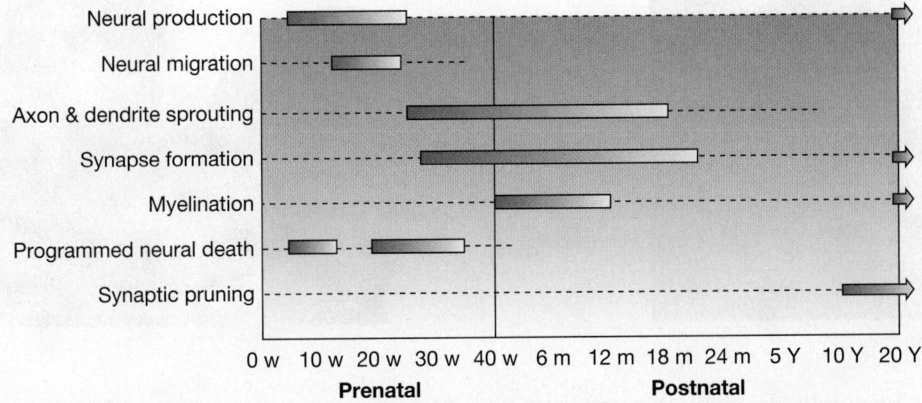


takes place after **synaptic exuberance**. Synaptic exuberance, also called *synaptogenesis*, refers to a period when there is a tremendous spurt in new synaptic connections. This is then followed by pruning, where up to 50% of those connections vanish (Stiles & Jernigan, 2010). "Use it or lose it" is the principle that applies because connections that are used become stronger and faster and those that are unused wither away (Kostovic & Vasung, 2009). If you were growing carrots in a backyard garden and you had planted thousands of seeds, how would you ensure that they would thrive? The best way would be to prune or pluck out the weaker shoots to allow the stronger ones more room and resources to grow on. This is what the brain does with synaptic pruning. Earlier studies had shown that synaptic exuberance and pruning occur during the fetal period and through the first 3 years of life, but now it turns out that it occurs in early adolescence as well (Markant & Thomas, 2013). We will address this neurological change in adolescence in Chapter 5 on cognitive development.

**synaptic exuberance**
also called *synaptogenesis*, refers to a period when there is a tremendous spurt in new synaptic connections

Figure 2.10 summarizes the timing of neurobiological processes in the development of the human brain. As you can see, all of the processes start prenatally, and all but neural migration continue after birth. Also, some of the processes such as myelination will peak in their development after birth.

## The Roles of Genes and Environment in Brain Development

**LO 2.5.3 Explain how normal brain development involves both gene expression and environmental input.**

Normal brain development, both prenatally and after birth, is a result of both gene expression and environmental input (Markant & Thomas, 2013). A disruption of either can fundamentally alter the development of the brain. For example, as we will see, a genetic disorder such as Down syndrome results among other things in intellectual disability and speech problems (Pennington et al., 2003).

The environment is also important. The brain is high in **plasticity**, meaning that it is highly responsive to environmental circumstances. The high plasticity of the human brain makes it adaptable but also vulnerable (Gale et al., 2004). Plasticity of the human brain is high at birth but diminishes steeply over the first few years of life. On the plus side, if a part of the brain suffers some damage in infancy due to an accident or disease, other parts of the brain can often take over the functions of the damaged portion, whereas this becomes less possible later in development when greater specialization has taken place. On the minus side, environmental deprivation that occurs prenatally or in infancy can also result in permanent impairment, whereas later in development such deprivation would not be as profound because the brain would have already matured. For example, as we will describe in more detail below, pregnant mothers whose diet is deficient in folic acid are at risk for giving birth to children with parts of the brain malformed or missing.

**plasticity**
the responsiveness of brain development to environmental circumstances

With respect to both the prenatal and postnatal environment, the development of the brain is shaped by *experience-expectant* processes (Greenough & Black, 1992). This refers to

During prenatal development, the fetus develops initial preferences for the types of foods eaten by the mother. It's likely that Bangladeshi and Japanese newborns favor somewhat different flavors.

how the rapidly developing young brain "expects" or requires certain common and universal experiences in order for development to proceed normally. This includes adequate nutrition and exposure to language. The brain is also shaped by *experience-dependent* processes, that is, experiences that vary across cultures and individuals. For example, the fetus develops initial preferences for specific types of foods and music that are culturally shaped. Once born, of course, children's environments and their experiences become vastly more diverse.

While the brain is already shaped by the prenatal environment, one of the hallmarks of humans is that we are born at an earlier stage of brain development relative to other African great ape species. Recall from Chapter 1 that the brain of a chimpanzee is at 45% of its average adult size at birth and at 85% by 1 year of age. In contrast, the human infant's brain is merely at 25% of the adult size at birth and not until 6 years of age does it reach approximately 85% to 90% (Hublin, 2005; Stiles & Jernigan, 2010). Furthermore, neurological development such as myelination continues past early childhood. For the human child, then, extensive brain maturation takes place within postnatal physical and cultural environments (Bjorklund, 2007; Haun, 2015).

## Education Focus: Biology, Sexism, and Educational Exclusion

In most cultures throughout history, opportunities for enhancing cognitive development through education have been much more limited for females than for males. In the United States and other Western countries, many people in the 18th and 19th centuries were vehemently opposed to the idea that young women should be allowed to attend colleges and universities. Often, the opposition was grounded in a view that women by nature are intellectually inferior to men.

A lot of scientific activity took place in the 19th century, and a lot of pseudoscience, too. Some of the worst pseudoscience attempted to establish biologically based group differences in intelligence (Gould, 1981). Paul Broca, perhaps the most important figure in neurology in the 19th century, claimed that the smaller brains of women demonstrated their intellectual inferiority. He knew very well that brain size is related to body size and that women's smaller brain size simply reflected their smaller body size rather than inferior intelligence, but his prejudice against the cognitive capacities of women allowed him to talk himself out of it:

> We might ask if the small size of the female brain depends exclusively on the small size of her body.... But we must not forget that women are, on average, a little less intelligent than men.... We are therefore permitted to suppose that the relatively small size of the female brain depends in part upon her physical inferiority and in part upon her intellectual inferiority (1861, quoted in Gould, 1981, p. 104).

The pseudoscientific claims got even worse. Gustave Le Bon, one of the founders of social psychology, commented:

> All psychologists who have studied the intelligence of women ... recognize today that they represent the most inferior forms of human evolution and that they are closer to children and savages than to an adult, civilized man. They excel in fickleness, inconstancy, absence of thought and logic, and incapacity to reason. Without doubt there exist some distinguished women, very superior to the average man, but they are as exceptional as the birth of any monstrosity, as, for example, of a gorilla with two heads; consequently we may neglect them entirely (1879, quoted in Gould, 1981).

Keep in mind that Broca and Le Bon were not regarded as cranks or fools, but were two of the most important scholars of their time. Nor were they alone in their views. For example,

Charles Darwin and G. Stanley Hall, who we met in Chapter 1, also wrote of women's nature as placing them beneath men on cognitive capacities (Degler, 1991).

The first American women entered higher education in 1833, at Oberlin College, which was founded as a women's college. By 1875, dozens of institutions accepted female students, and the debate over whether women should be allowed to pursue higher education turned in favor of the proponents (Kerber, 1997). In all Western countries, today, females exceed males' performance on nearly every measure of educational achievement (United Nations Development Programme [UNDP], 2016).

### Review Question

Do you think that the claim that cognitive differences between women and men are based in biology—including references to the brain, evolution, or genetics—is a phenomenon of the past? What lessons do you think the historical account offers for child development today?

## SUMMARY: Prenatal Brain Development

**LO 2.5.1 Identify the different regions of the brain.**

The brain is divided into three major regions, the hindbrain, the midbrain, and the forebrain. The outermost part of the forebrain, the cerebral cortex, is far larger in humans than in other animals. The cerebral cortex is divided into two hemispheres, left and right, which are connected by the corpus callosum. Each of the two hemispheres has four lobes with quite distinct functions.

**LO 2.5.2 Describe how brain development during the fetal period involves neuronal migration and communication, as well as the loss of neural elements.**

Neuronal migration involves new brain cells, neurons, travelling away from where they originated to new locations where they become part of developing brain structures and regions. Following migration, the neurons become part of circuits, where they communicate through the release and reception of chemicals called neurotransmitters. There are two normal brain development processes that involve loss of neural elements. One is neural death, and the other is synaptic pruning.

**LO 2.5.3 Explain how normal brain development involves both gene expression and environmental input.**

Normal brain development, prenatally and after birth, is a result of gene expression. The brain is also highly responsive to environmental circumstances. This plasticity makes it both adaptable and vulnerable to the environment. Although the brain is already shaped by the prenatal environment, extensive brain maturation in humans takes place within postnatal physical and cultural environments.

# 2.6 Prenatal Care

Because prenatal development carries risks for both mother and fetus, all cultures have developed customs and practices to try to promote a healthy outcome. First we look at some of the practices of prenatal care in traditional cultures, then we look at the scientific approach to prenatal care that has developed recently.

## Variations in Prenatal Care

**LO 2.6.1 Compare prenatal care in traditional cultures and developed countries.**

All cultures have customs and beliefs about what a woman should and should not do during pregnancy (Gottlieb & DeLoache, 2017). What kind of guidelines or advice have you heard? You might also ask your mother, your grandmother, and other mothers you know what advice they followed and where they obtained it. Sometimes pregnancy advice seems practical and sensible. The practical advice reflects the collected wisdom that women pass down to each other over generations, based on their own experiences. Other times the advice may seem odd, especially to someone outside the given culture. Customs that seem peculiar to an outsider may arise because pregnancy is often perilous to both mother and fetus. Cultures sometimes develop their prenatal customs out of the intense desire to ensure that pregnancy will proceed successfully, but without the scientific knowledge that would make such control possible.

Here are a few examples. Among the Beng people of the West African nation of Ivory Coast, pregnant women are advised to avoid drinking palm wine during the early months of pregnancy (Gottlieb, 2000). This is wise practical advice drawn from the experience of women who drank alcohol during pregnancy, with unfortunate results. On the other hand, the mother-to-be is also advised to avoid eating meat from the bushbuck antelope while pregnant, and warned that if she does eat it, her baby may emerge from the womb striped like the antelope.

Thousands of miles away, on the Indonesian island of Bali, "hot" foods are to be avoided during pregnancy, including eggplant, mango, and octopus (Diener, 2000). Also, a pregnant mother should not accept food from someone who is viewed as spiritually impure, such as a menstruating woman or someone who has recently had a death in the family. Witches are believed to be especially attracted to the blood of a pregnant woman and her unborn child, so pregnant women are advised to obtain a magic charm and wear it on their belt or hang it on the gate of their yard, for protection.

Some of the examples of prenatal customs just provided may strike you as strange, but they are understandable as humans attempt to control events that are highly important but also mysterious. Even in developed countries, which have a long scientific tradition, not much was known about prenatal care from a scientific perspective until recent decades. As recently as the middle of the 20th century, women in developed countries were being advised by their doctors to limit their weight gain during pregnancy to no more than 15 pounds (Eisenberg et al., 2011). By now, scientific studies have shown that average-weight women should typically gain 25–35 pounds during pregnancy. Women who gain less than 20 pounds are at risk for having babies who are preterm and low birth weight. For women who gain too much weight, their children are at risk for becoming overweight or obese during childhood and developing diabetes, high blood pressure, or heart disease later in life (CDC, 2017). A recent large-scale survey of pregnant American women found that about 20% gained too little weight, and almost 50% gained too much (Deputy et al., 2015).

An extensive body of scientific knowledge has accumulated on prenatal care in recent decades. One key conclusion of this research is that pregnant women should receive regular

## Cultural Focus: Pregnancy and Prenatal Care Across Cultures

Although many cultures have folk beliefs about pregnancy that have no scientific or practical basis, most also have practices that provide genuine physical and emotional benefits to pregnant women. These practices include prenatal visits with a doctor, moderate exercise, and healthful eating. Also, a helpful method of prenatal care common in many traditional cultures is massage (Field, 2014; Jordan, 1994). The prenatal massage is usually performed by a midwife (a person who assists women in pregnancy and childbirth) in the course of her visits to the pregnant woman.

While the massage is taking place, the midwife asks the woman various questions about how the pregnancy is going. As part of the massage, the midwife probes to determine the fetus's position in the uterus. If the fetus is turned in an unfavorable position, so that it would be likely to come out feet first rather than head first, the midwife will attempt an inversion to turn the fetus's head toward the vaginal opening. This is sometimes painful, but as we will see in Chapter 3, a head-first birth is much safer than a feet-first birth, for both baby and mother.

Prenatal massage has a long history in many cultures (Jordan, 1994). In recent years, it has also begun to be used by midwives, nurses, and physicians in developed countries. By now, a substantial amount of research has accumulated to support the benefits of massage for mother and fetus. Benefits to the mother include lower likelihood of back pain, less swelling of the joints, and better sleep (Field, 2010, 2014). Babies whose mothers received prenatal massage score higher on scales of their physical and social functioning in the early weeks of life (Field et al., 2006).

In the video *Pregnancy and Prenatal Care Across Cultures*, expectant mothers from various countries describe their pregnancy experiences. A Mayan midwife also discusses her role in prenatal care and gives an expectant mother a prenatal massage.

**Watch** PREGNANCY AND PRENATAL CARE ACROSS CULTURES

### Review Question

What advantages of having a doctor or midwife for prenatal care are described in the video? Can you think of others that were not mentioned?

**Map 2.1** Ethnic Variations in Prenatal Care Within the United States

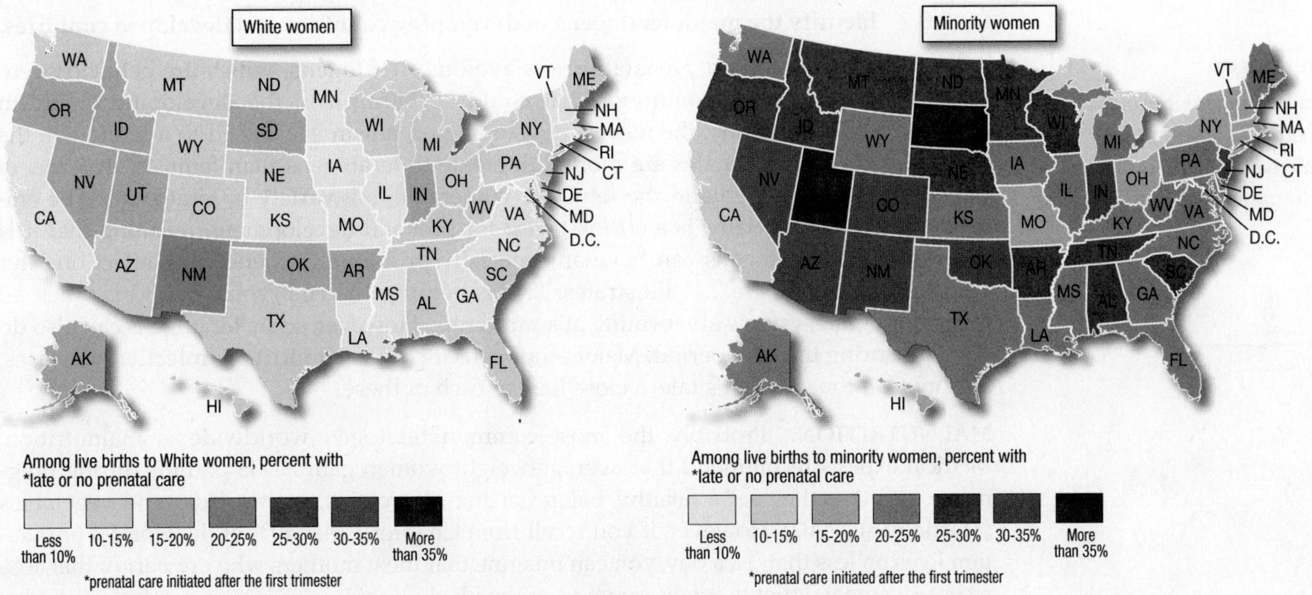

evaluations from a skilled healthcare worker, beginning as soon as possible after conception, to monitor the health of mother and fetus and ensure that the pregnancy is proceeding well. Most women in developed countries have access to physicians, nurses, or certified midwives who can provide good prenatal care. However, some poor women may not have access to such care, especially in the United States. The percentage of women in the United States who begin prenatal care in their first trimester varies greatly based on ethnicity and socioeconomic status (SES), as shown in Map 2.1.

Pregnant women in developing countries are much less likely than those in developed countries to receive prenatal care from a skilled healthcare worker. The World Health Organization's *Making Pregnancy Safer* program has focused on working with governments to set up programs that provide pregnant women with such care (World Health Organization [WHO], 2009). Currently 99% of maternal and infant deaths occur in developing countries—only 1% occur in developed countries—and the WHO program is focused on the 70 countries with the highest death rates, mostly in Africa and South Asia.

As you can see in Table 2.2, guidelines for prenatal care focus mostly on three key areas: diet, exercise, and avoidance of potentially harmful influences called teratogens (CDC, 2017; WHO, 2009).

**Table 2.2** Essentials of Prenatal Care

| Before Pregnancy |
|---|
| • *Medical Care.* Have a medical examination to ensure there are no diseases that may affect prenatal development, and to discuss preconception health care. If not fully vaccinated, obtain vaccinations for diseases, such as rubella, that can damage prenatal development. (Vaccinations may be unsafe during pregnancy.) Take folic acid vitamins every day to help prevent major birth defects of the brain and spine. |
| • *Drugs.* Avoid tobacco, alcohol, and other drugs, which may make it more difficult to become pregnant and are damaging to prenatal development. |
| **During Pregnancy** |
| • *Diet.* Maintain a balanced diet, including protein, grains, fruits, and vegetables. Avoid excessive fats and sugars and obtain sufficient iron and iodine. Gain 25–35 pounds in total; avoid dieting as well as excessive weight gain. Women should also drink more fluids during pregnancy than they normally do, as the fetus needs fluids for healthy development and a pregnant woman's body also requires more. |
| • *Exercise.* Engage in mild to moderate exercise regularly, including aerobic exercise, to stimulate circulatory system and muscles, as well as Kegel exercises to strengthen vaginal muscles. Aerobic exercise, such as walking, jogging, or swimming, stimulates the circulatory and muscular systems of a woman's body (Schmidt et al., 2005). However, it is important to avoid strenuous exercise and high-risk sports, such as long-distance running, contact sports, downhill skiing, waterskiing, and horseback riding. |
| • *Teratogens.* Avoid tobacco, alcohol, and other drugs. Avoid exposure to X-rays, hazardous chemicals, and infectious diseases. |

## Teratogens

**LO 2.6.2 Identify the major teratogens in developing countries and developed countries.**

**teratogen**
behavior, environment, or bodily condition that can have damaging influence on prenatal development

An essential part of good prenatal care is avoiding **teratogens**, which are behaviors, environments, and bodily conditions that could be harmful to the developing organism (Haffner, 2007). Generally, the more a developing organism is exposed to a teratogen, the worse the effect. Also, males are more vulnerable to teratogens than females. In terms of timing, both the embryo and the fetus are vulnerable to a variety of teratogens. The embryonic period, especially, is a *critical period* for prenatal development, meaning that it is a period when teratogens can have an especially profound and enduring effect on later development, as Figure 2.11 illustrates. This is because the embryonic period is when all the major organ systems are forming at a rapid rate. However, some teratogens can also do damage during the fetal period. Major teratogens include malnutrition, infectious diseases, alcohol, and tobacco. Let's take a close look at each of these.

**MALNUTRITION.** Probably the most common teratogen worldwide is malnutrition. Medical experts recommend that average-weight women gain 25–35 pounds during pregnancy and that they eat a healthy, balanced diet of proteins, grains, fruit, and vegetables (Martin et al., 2002). However, if you recall from Chapter 1 that 40% of the world's population lives on less than $2 a day, you can imagine that most mothers who are part of that 40% receive a prenatal diet that falls far short of the ideal.

Furthermore, about half the world's population is rural, and the diet of people in rural areas often varies substantially depending on the time of year. They may eat fairly well during summer and fall when their crops provide food, but less well during winter and spring when fresh food is unavailable. Consequently, prenatal health may depend greatly on when the child was conceived.

Dramatic evidence of this effect has been shown in recent decades in China (Berry et al., 1999). In the 1980s China had the highest incidence in the world of two serious prenatal disorders, *anencephaly*, in which parts of the brain are missing or malformed, and *spina bifida*, which is an extreme distortion in the shape of the spinal column. It was discovered that in both of these disorders the main cause is a deficiency of folic acid, a nutrient found especially in fruits and vegetables. Furthermore, researchers observed that the traditional marriage period in China is January and February, and most couples try to conceive a child as soon after marriage as possible. Consequently, the early months of pregnancy typically take place in winter and early spring, when rural women are least likely to have fruits and vegetables as part of their diet. After this pattern was discovered, the Chinese government established a nationwide program to provide mothers with supplements of folic acid, and since that time, the incidence of anencephaly and spina bifida has been sharply reduced (Centers for Disease Control and Prevention [CDC], 2011).

**Figure 2.11** Timing of Teratogens

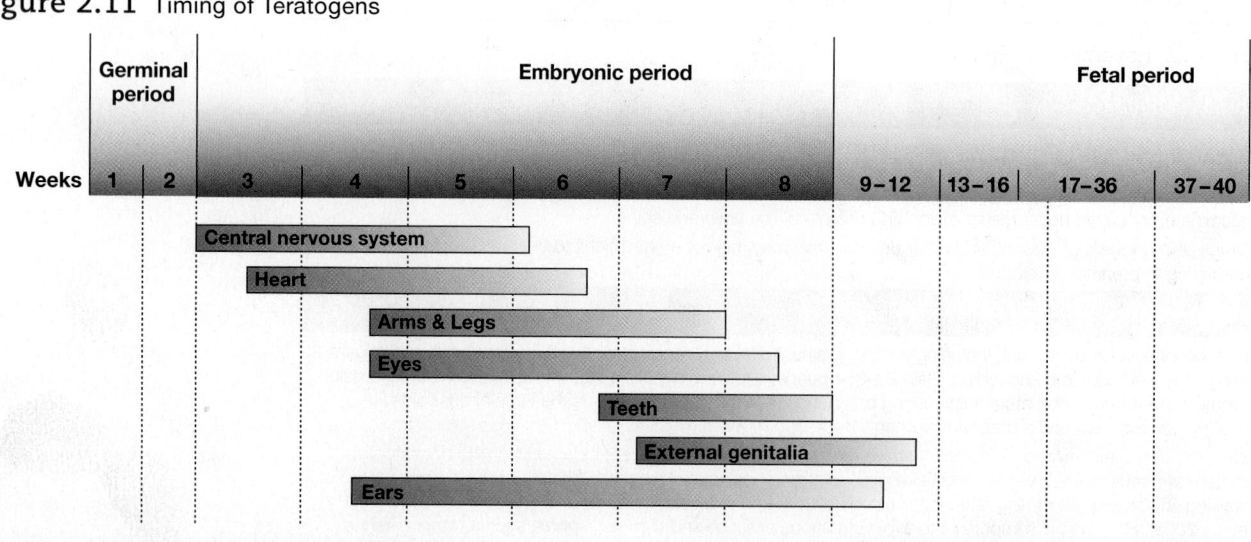


SOURCE: Based on Moore (1974).

Many other countries have also taken steps to reduce folic-acid deficiencies in pregnant mothers. After research established that folic acid was the key to preventing anencephaly and spina bifida, governments in many countries passed laws requiring folic acid to be added to grain products such as cereals, bread, pasta, flour, and rice. Almost immediately, the incidence of both disorders fell sharply (Honein et al., 2001). Medical authorities now recommend that women begin taking folic acid supplements and eating plenty of fruits and vegetables even when they are trying to become pregnant, because the damage from lack of folic acid can take place in the early weeks of pregnancy, before the woman knows for sure that she is pregnant (CDC, 2017; de Villarreal et al., 2006).

Two other common nutritional deficiencies during pregnancy are iron and iodine. Iron-rich foods such as beef, duck, potatoes (including skin), spinach, and dried fruits are important for building the blood supply of mother and fetus. The WHO estimates that nearly one-half of women worldwide are deficient in iron, placing them at risk for having preterm and low-birth-weight babies (WHO, 2009). Even with a healthy diet including iron-rich foods, health authorities recommend an iron supplement from the 12th week of pregnancy onward.

Iodine is also crucial, because low-iodine intake during pregnancy increases the risks of miscarriage, stillbirth, and abnormalities in fetal brain development. In developed countries salt has been iodized since the 1920s, so women receive adequate iodine as part of a normal diet. However, in developing countries most women do not use iodized salt and consequently they often experience iodine deficiencies. The WHO and other major health organizations have made a strong push recently to make iodine supplements available in developing countries, as will be explained in more detail in Chapter 3.

**AIDS (acquired immune deficiency syndrome)**

sexually transmitted infection caused by HIV, resulting in damage to the immune system

**INFECTIOUS DISEASES.** Infectious diseases are far more prevalent in developing countries than in developed ones (WHO, 2009). Many of these diseases influence prenatal development. One of the most prevalent and serious is *rubella* (also known as *German measles*). The embryonic period is a critical period for exposure to rubella. Over half of infants whose mothers contract the illness during this period have severe problems including blindness, deafness, intellectual disability, and abnormalities of the heart, genitals, or intestinal system (Eberhart-Phillips et al., 1993). During the fetal period effects of rubella are less severe, but can include low birth weight, hearing problems, and skeletal defects (Brown & Susser, 2002). Since the late 1960s a vaccine given to children has made rubella rare in developed countries—girls retain the immunity into adulthood, when they become pregnant—but it remains widespread in developing countries where children are less likely to receive the vaccine (Plotkin et al., 1999; WHO, 2009).

Another common infectious disease of prenatal development is **AIDS (acquired immune deficiency syndrome)**, a sexually transmitted infection (STI) caused by the human immunodeficiency virus (HIV), which damages the immune system. HIV/AIDS can be transmitted from mother to child during prenatal development through the blood, during birth, or through breast milk. HIV/AIDS damages brain development prenatally, and infants with HIV are unlikely to survive to adulthood unless they receive an expensive combination of medications rarely available in the developing countries where AIDS is most common. In developing countries mother–child transmission of HIV/AIDS has been dramatically reduced in recent years through three strategies: (1) effective medicines given to mothers prior to birth; (2) cesarean sections for mothers infected with AIDS; and (3) the use of infant formula in place of breast-feeding (Blair et al., 2004; Sullivan, 2003). However, 95% of all HIV infections take place in Africa, and few African mothers or infants have access to the three strategies that are effective against HIV/AIDS (WHO, 2010).

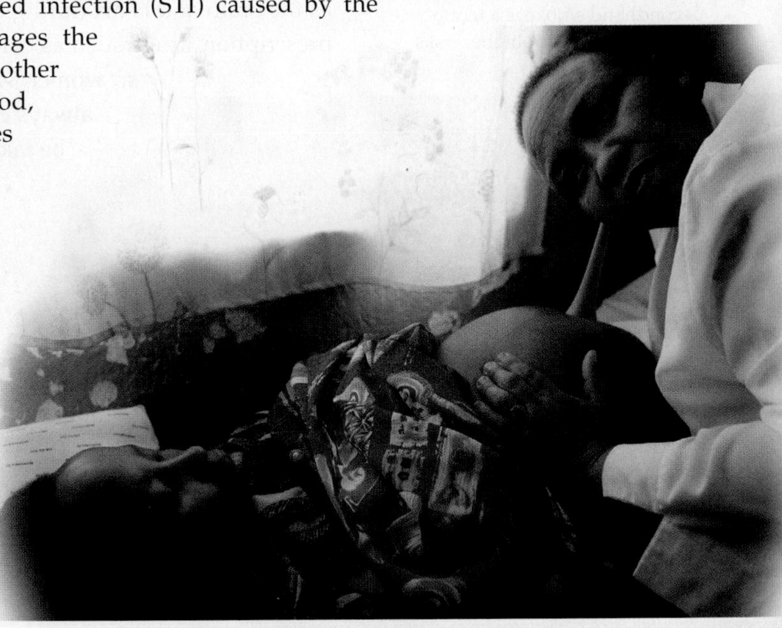

Pregnant women in developing countries who have AIDS rarely receive adequate medical treatment. Here, a woman is being treated at a clinic for HIV/AIDS patients in Lesotho.

**ALCOHOL.** In developed countries, the teratogen that causes the most widespread damage to prenatal development is alcohol (Sokol et al., 2003). Although it used to be believed that moderate alcohol use would cause no harm during pregnancy, recent research has shown that the only safe amount of alcohol for a pregnant woman is *none at all.* Even one or two drinks a few days a week puts the developing child at risk for lower height, weight, and head size at birth, and for lower intelligence and higher aggressiveness during childhood (Willford et al., 2004).

**fetal alcohol spectrum disorder (FASD)**
set of problems that occur as a consequence of high maternal alcohol use during pregnancy, including facial deformities, heart problems, misshapen limbs, and a variety of cognitive problems

When mothers drink heavily during pregnancy, their infants are at risk for **fetal alcohol spectrum disorder (FASD)**, which includes facial deformities, heart problems, misshapen limbs, and a variety of cognitive problems such as intellectual disability and attention and memory deficits (CDC, 2017; Mattson et al., 2010). Infants born with FASD face a lifetime of trouble, and the more alcohol their mothers drank during pregnancy, the worse their problems are likely to be. A review of 25 studies found that adolescents exposed to alcohol in the womb experienced cognitive, behavioral, social, and emotional problems (Irner, 2012). These problems are severe, for example, making it difficult for the adolescents to succeed academically or socially in school (Mattson et al., 2010). Rates of FASD are especially alarming, as high as 10%, in some Native American and Canadian First Nations communities where alcoholism is prevalent (Caetano et al., 2006; Tough et al., 2007).

**NICOTINE.** Maternal cigarette smoking has a wide range of damaging effects on prenatal development. Women who smoke during pregnancy are at higher risk for miscarriage and premature birth, and smoking is the leading cause of low birth weight in developed countries (Espy et al., 2011). Maternal smoking raises the risks of health problems in infants, such as impaired heart functioning, difficulty breathing, and even death (Jaakkola & Gissler, 2004). Prenatal exposure to smoking predicts problems in childhood and adolescence, including poorer language skills, problems with attention and memory, and behavior problems (Cornelius et al., 2011; Sawnani et al., 2004). Maternal smoking is also linked with decreased sperm count in emerging adult men (Jensen et al., 2004).

*Secondhand smoke* from fathers or others leads to higher risks of low birth weight and childhood cancer (Ruckinger et al., 2010). Rates of smoking are generally higher in developed countries than in developing countries, but they are rising rapidly in developing countries around the world as their economies grow (WHO, 2011).

**OTHER TERATOGENS.** Malnutrition and infectious diseases are the most common teratogens in developing countries, with alcohol and nicotine most common in developed countries. However, there are many other teratogens. Some of these include:

- ***Drugs (other than alcohol and nicotine).*** Maternal use of drugs such as cocaine, heroin, and marijuana causes physical, cognitive, and behavioral problems in infants (Messinger & Lester, 2008). Certain prescription drugs can also cause harm. For example, Accutane, a drug used to treat severe acne, can cause devastating damage to major organs such as the brain and heart during embryonic development (Honein et al., 2001). Even nonprescription drugs such as cold medicines can be damaging to prenatal development, so women who are pregnant or seeking to become pregnant should always check with their doctors about any medications they may be taking (Morgan et al., 2010).
- ***Certain kinds of work.*** Work that involves exposure to teratogens such as X-rays, hazardous chemicals, or infectious diseases is best avoided during pregnancy.
- ***Severe maternal stress.*** Pregnant women who experience severe stress, such as the death of a spouse or close family member, are at risk of giving birth preterm and having babies with low birth weight (Class et al., 2011).
- ***Environmental pollution.*** An inventive study, for example, found that when automated toll collection systems were installed on highways in New Jersey and Pennsylvania, it eased traffic and improved air quality. Among pregnant women living within about 1 mile of the toll plaza, premature births fell by 8.6% and low birth weight by 9.3% (Currie & Walker, 2011).

Secondhand smoke is a teratogen contributing to higher risks of low birth weight.

## SUMMARY: Prenatal Care

**LO 2.6.1 Compare prenatal care in traditional cultures and developed countries.**

Cultures develop prenatal customs out of the intense desire to ensure that pregnancy will proceed successfully. In traditional cultures, prenatal care often includes massage as well as folk knowledge that may or may not have practical consequences. For instance, many cultures advise pregnant women to avoid certain types of food. Essential elements of prenatal care in developed countries include regular evaluations by a healthcare professional and guidelines concerning diet, exercise, and avoiding teratogens.

**LO 2.6.2 Identify the major teratogens in developing countries and developed countries.**

The major teratogens are malnutrition and infectious diseases in developing countries, and alcohol and tobacco in developed countries. Generally, the more a developing organism is exposed to a teratogen, the worse the effect. Also, males are more vulnerable to teratogens than females. In terms of timing, the embryonic period is a critical period for exposure to teratogens because all the major organ systems are forming at a rapid rate.

Environmental pollution is a teratogen contributing to premature birth and low birth weight. Here is a pregnant mother on a day when Singapore's smog index reached a critical level.

# 2.7 Pregnancy Problems

Apart from teratogens, there are a variety of other risks to prenatal development. Next, we will look at some common chromosomal disorders and then examine methods of prenatal monitoring and genetic counseling that help identify the risk of disorders. Apart from problems during pregnancy, sometimes problems arise in becoming pregnant in the first place. We conclude this chapter with a description of infertility, including options for treatment of infertility.

## Chromosomal Disorders

**LO 2.7.1 Explain how chromosomal disorders occur.**

In the course of the formation of the gametes during meiosis, sometimes errors take place and the chromosomes fail to divide properly. Consequently, when conception takes place, instead of ending up with 46 chromosomes in each cell, the person has 45 or 47 (or even, in rare cases, 48 or 49), and problems occur. It is estimated that as many as half of all conceptions involve too many or too few chromosomes, but most of the zygotes that result either never begin to develop or are spontaneously aborted early in the pregnancy (Borgaonkar, 1997; Johnson, 2016). In 1 out of 200 live births, the child has a chromosomal disorder. There are two main types of chromosomal disorders: (1) those that involve the sex chromosomes and (2) those that take place on the 21st pair of chromosomes, resulting in a condition known as Down syndrome.

**SEX CHROMOSOME DISORDERS.** The sex chromosomes are especially likely to be involved in chromosomal disorders. A person may have an extra X chromosome (resulting in XXX or XXY), or an extra Y chromosome (XYY), or may have only an X and no second sex chromosome. About 1 in every 500 infants has some type of sex chromosome disorder.

There are two common consequences of sex chromosome disorders (Batzer & Rovitsky, 2009). One is that the person has some type of cognitive deficit, such as intellectual disability (ranging from mild to severe), a learning disorder, or speech impairments. The other kind of problem is that the person has some abnormality in the development of the reproductive system at puberty, such as underdeveloped testes and penis in boys or no ovulation in girls. One of the functions of the sex chromosomes is to direct the production of the sex hormones,

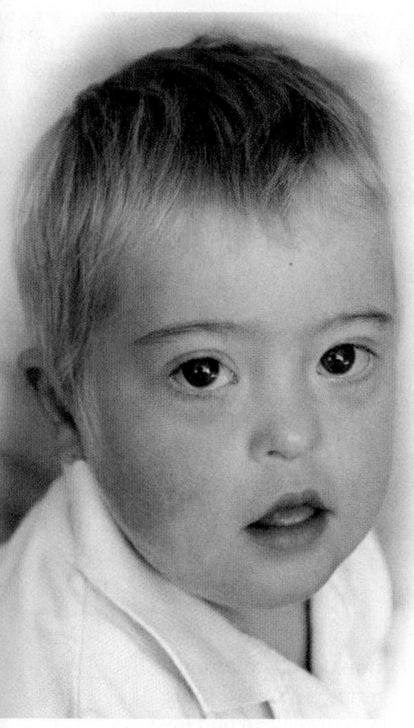

Persons with Down syndrome typically face a wide range of physical and cognitive problems.

**Down syndrome**

genetic disorder due to carrying an extra chromosome on the 21st pair

**multifactorial**

involve a combination of genetic and environmental factors

**genetic mutation**

a permanent alteration of a DNA sequence that makes up a gene

**Figure 2.12** Down Syndrome and Maternal Age

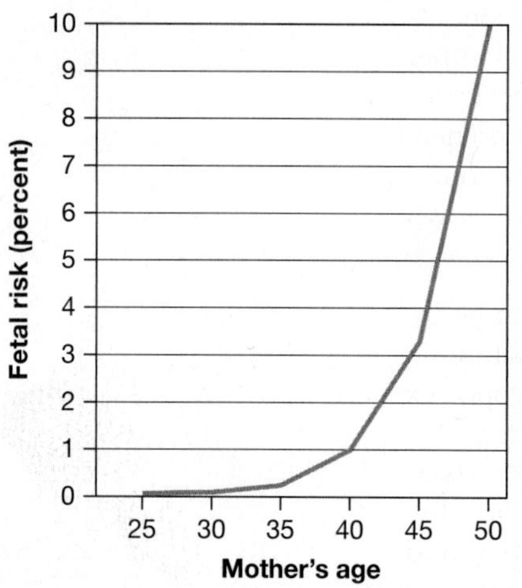


SOURCE: Based on Umrigar et al. (2014).

and having too few or too many sex chromosomes disrupts this process. However, treatment with hormone supplements is often effective in correcting the problem.

**DOWN SYNDROME.** When there is an extra chromosome on the 21st pair, the condition is known as **Down syndrome**, or *trisomy-21*. Persons with Down syndrome have distinct physical features, including a short, stocky build, an unusually flat face, a large tongue, and an extra fold of skin on the eyelids. They also have cognitive deficits, including intellectual disability and speech problems (Pennington et al., 2003). Many also have problems in their physical development, such as hearing impairments and heart defects.

Their social development varies widely. Some children with Down syndrome smile less readily than other persons and have difficulty making eye contact, but others are exceptionally happy and loving. Supportive and encouraging parents help children with Down syndrome develop more favorably (Hodapp et al., 2012; Sigman, 1999). Intervention programs in infancy and preschool have been shown to enhance their social, emotional, and motor skills (Carr, 2002; Hodapp et al., 2012). In adulthood, with adequate support many are able to hold a job that is highly structured and involves simple tasks.

People with Down syndrome age faster than other people (Berney, 2009). Their total brain volume begins to decrease as early as their 20s. Various physical ailments that may develop for other people in late adulthood begin to afflict people with Down syndrome in their 30s and 40s, including leukemia, cancer, Alzheimer's disease, and heart disease (Hassold & Patterson, 1999). As a result, their life expectancy is considerably lower than in the general population. With medical treatment most are able to live into their 50s or 60s (Hodapp et al., 2012).

**PARENTAL AGE AND CHROMOSOMAL DISORDERS.** Children with chromosomal problems are almost always born to parents who have no disorder (Batzer & Ravitsky, 2009). Chromosomal problems occur not because the parents have an inherited problem that they pass on to their children, but usually because of the age of the parents. For example, the risk of Down syndrome rises with maternal age, from 1 in 1,900 births at age 20 to 1 in 30 births at age 45. The risk of chromosomal disorders is very low for mothers in their 20s and rises only slightly in the 30s, but rises steeply after age 40 (see Figure 2.12; Umrigar et al., 2014).

Recall that a woman's gamete production takes place while she is still in the womb of her own mother. The older she gets, the longer the eggs have been in her ovaries. When conception takes place and the last part of meiosis is completed in the ovum, the older the woman, the greater the likelihood that the chromosomes will not separate properly because they have been suspended in that final stage of meiosis for so long. The father's sperm is the cause of the chromosomal disorder in 5%–10% of cases, but it is unclear if the risk increases with the father's age (Crow, 2003; Fisch et al., 2003; Muller et al., 2000).

Recent research, however, has suggested that paternal age is linked to **multifactorial** disorders, such as autism spectrum disorder. Multifactorial disorders involve a combination of genetic and environmental factors. A study of all Swedish individuals born between 1973 and 2001 found that children born to fathers who were 45 years and older were at heightened risk on various cognitive and mental health measures, as compared to children born to fathers in their 20s. The large scale of the Swedish study allowed for many analyses, including comparison of siblings of the same father who were conceived at different paternal ages, thereby increasing its validity. Paternal age was linked, for example, to bipolar disorder, attention-deficit/hyperactivity disorder, autism spectrum disorder, and substance use problems (D'Onofrio et al., 2013). While the causal mechanism remains to be further examined, the hypothesis is that genetic mutations in the sperm are involved (Carey, 2014). A **genetic mutation** is a permanent alteration of a DNA sequence that makes up a gene. Every 16 days, cells in a man's testicles divide and the DNA in each cell is copied into a new one, which is used to make new sperm. The body is highly accurate at making an exact copy, but inevitably it sometimes makes mistakes. Some sperm will be made containing an error in the replication of the DNA. As a man gets older, his sperm contains more mutations. These mutations contribute to problems in the course of development.

## Prenatal Testing and Counseling

**LO 2.7.2 Describe the four main techniques of prenatal testing and diagnosis, and explain why some prospective parents seek genetic counseling.**

Various technologies are used to monitor the health of the fetus in the course of prenatal development. Before pregnancy, some prospective parents who are at risk for genetic disorders seek prenatal genetic counseling.

**TECHNIQUES OF PRENATAL MONITORING.** In developed countries, a variety of **techniques of prenatal monitoring** are widely available to monitor the growth and health of the fetus and detect prenatal problems. Common methods include ultrasound, maternal blood screening, amniocentesis, and chorionic villus sampling (CVS).

In **ultrasound**, high-frequency sound waves are directed toward the uterus, and as they bounce off the fetus, they are converted by computer into an image that can be viewed on a screen. Ultrasound technology has improved in recent years and the 3D/4D (three- and four-dimensional) images are distinct enough to make it possible to measure the fetus's size and shape and to monitor its activities (Merz & Abramowicz, 2012). Studies have also found that viewing ultrasound images helps promote a feeling of parental involvement and attachment even before birth (Righetti et al., 2005).

Ultrasound is sometimes used to screen for Down syndrome, which can be detected 13 weeks into prenatal development (Reddy & Mennui, 2006). It is also used for pregnancies that involve multiple fetuses, because these are high-risk pregnancies in which it is common for some of the fetuses to be developing less favorably than others. However, increasingly, ultrasound is used for normal pregnancies in developed countries, not just for those that are high risk (Merz & Abramowicz, 2012). It is cheap, easy, and safe, and it allows doctors to monitor fetal growth and gives parents the enjoyment of seeing the fetus as it is developing in the womb. It also allows parents to learn the sex of the child before birth, if they wish.

**Maternal blood screening** tests are relatively noninvasive and have become highly accurate. They are administered in the first or second trimesters and sometimes in combination with an ultrasound. Different substances in the blood sample from the mother are examined, such as proteins, hormones, and genetic fragments of DNA from the fetus (Better Health Channel, 2017; Brody, 2013). These tests screen for a variety of risk factors, including spina bifida and Down syndrome. They are considered a screening tool, but not diagnostic. For example, a positive test for Down syndrome will need to be confirmed by amniocentesis or CVS (Brody, 2013).

In **amniocentesis**, a long hollow needle is inserted into the pregnant woman's abdomen and, using the ultrasound image for guidance, a sample of the amniotic fluid is withdrawn from the placenta surrounding the fetus. This fluid contains fetal cells sloughed off in the course of prenatal development, and the cells can be examined for information on the fetus's genotype. Amniocentesis is conducted 15–20 weeks into pregnancy. It is used only for women who are at risk for prenatal problems due to family history or age (35 or older) because it carries a small risk of triggering miscarriage. It can detect 40 different defects in fetal development with 100% accuracy (Brambati & Tului, 2005).

Like amniocentesis, **chorionic villus sampling (CVS)** entails sampling and analyzing cells early in development to detect possible genetic problems. CVS takes place at 5–10 weeks into the pregnancy; the sample is obtained from the cells that are beginning to form the umbilical cord. Guided by ultrasound, a tube is inserted through the vagina and into the uterus to obtain the cell sample. CVS entails a slight but genuine risk of miscarriage or damage to the fetus, so again it is used only when there is a family history of genetic abnormalities, the woman is age 35 or older, or as a follow-up to a blood screening test (Brambati & Tului, 2005). It is 99% accurate in diagnosing genetic problems.

**GENETIC COUNSELING.** If a fetus is found to have a birth defect or a genetic condition during pregnancy, parents may be referred for prenatal genetic counseling to help them gain medical information and know their options (National Center for Biotechnology Information [NCBI], 2017). Even before pregnancy, prospective parents

**techniques of prenatal monitoring**
include ultrasound, maternal blood screening, amniocentesis, and chorionic villus sampling (CVS), which provide the ability to monitor the growth and health of the fetus and detect prenatal problems

**ultrasound**
machine that uses sound waves to produce images of the fetus during pregnancy

**maternal blood screening**
examines different substances in a blood sample from the mother, such as proteins, hormones, and genetic fragments of DNA from the fetus

**amniocentesis**
prenatal procedure in which a needle is used to withdraw amniotic fluid containing fetal cells from the placenta, allowing possible prenatal problems to be detected

**chorionic villus sampling (CVS)**
prenatal technique for diagnosing genetic problems, involving taking a sample of cells at 5–10 weeks gestation by inserting a tube into the uterus

Ultrasound allows medical professionals and parents to monitor prenatal development.

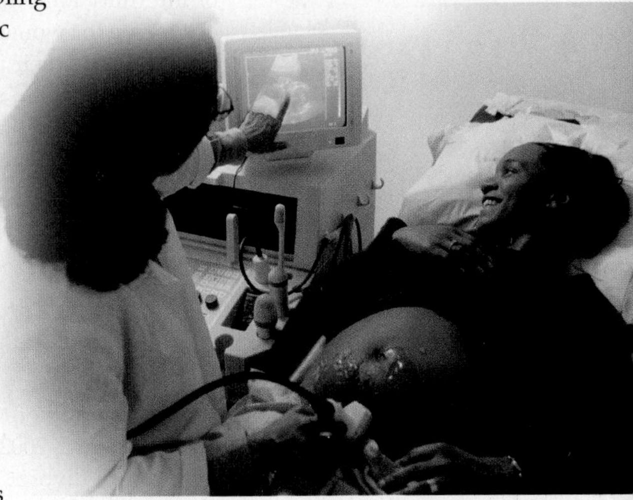

whose family history places them at risk for having children with genetic disorders may seek genetic counseling, which involves analyzing the family history and genotypes of prospective parents to identify possible risks (Coughlin, 2009). Those with risks that merit genetic counseling include persons who have an inherited genetic condition or a close relative who has one; couples with a history of miscarriages or infertility; and older individuals (women over 35 and men over 40) (NCBI, 2017). The decision to obtain genetic counseling may be difficult, because the results may require the couple to make the choice between trying to become pregnant and risking that the child will have a genetic disorder, or deciding not to pursue pregnancy. However, the knowledge obtained from genetic counseling enables people to make an informed decision.

In the first step of genetic counseling, the counselor takes a comprehensive family history from each prospective parent, seeking to identify patterns that may indicate problematic recessive or X-linked genes. Then each partner provides a blood, skin, or urine sample that can be used to analyze their chromosomes to identify possible problems. With the information obtained from genetic counseling, the couple can then decide whether or not they wish to attempt pregnancy (Coughlin, 2009).

## Infertility

**LO 2.7.3 Describe psychological and social implications of infertility, and review major causes of and treatments for infertility.**

**infertility**
inability to attain pregnancy after at least a year of regular sexual intercourse

Most women of reproductive age (roughly age 15–40) who have sexual intercourse on a regular basis will become pregnant within a year or two. However, for some couples becoming pregnant is more problematic. **Infertility** is defined as the inability to attain pregnancy after at least a year of regular sexual intercourse without contraception. Rates of infertility in the United States have been remarkably consistent over the past century at about 10%–15% of couples (Johnson, 2016; Marsh & Ronner, 1996). A worldwide assessment of infertility between 1990 and 2010 also found that rates had stayed consistent at about 9%–13% (Mascarenhas et al., 2012).

**PSYCHOLOGICAL AND SOCIAL IMPLICATIONS.** Across cultures, most people wish to have children, and infertility is experienced as a source of frustration and distress (Balen & Inhorn, 2002). However, there are definite cultural differences in how seriously infertility is viewed and how it is framed socially. In the individualistic West, infertile couples often experience a sense of sadness and loss. In one Swedish study, couples seeking infertility treatments often felt frustration over missing out on a major focus of life, and they experienced a negative effect on their sexual relationship (Hjelmstedt et al., 1999). They felt that they were unable to live up to social and personal expectations for having a child. Other studies have found that infertility often creates strains in the marital relationship; but in the long run, about half of couples report that the experience of infertility made their relationship closer and stronger (Schmidt et al., 2005).

Outside the West, cultures tend to be more collectivistic, and the social consequences of infertility are often more profound. Infertility is often deeply stigmatized. This is especially true for women, who are usually blamed for the problem and for whom motherhood is essential to their identity and their place within the social world (Inhorn & Balen, 2002; Sembuya, 2010). In many cultures, the meaning of infertility involves not only the couple. It may mean that there will be no one to continue the family tradition of remembering and worshipping the ancestors, a responsibility that often falls on the oldest son, especially in Asian and African cultures. It may also mean that the status of the wife is lowered in relation to her husband, her in-laws, and the community, because infertility is viewed more as her failure than his. Even if she has a daughter, she may still be seen as inadequate if she fails to produce a son.

In order to overcome infertility, women may try herbal remedies provided by a midwife. Others may seek supernatural remedies. For example, in Ghana women often consult a shaman (religious leader believed to have special powers), who focuses on trying to appease the wrath of the gods believed to be inflicting infertility on the woman as a punishment (Leonard, 2002). If infertility persists, it is viewed in many cultures as grounds for the husband to divorce his wife or take another wife. For example, in Vietnam it is generally accepted that if a man's wife is infertile he will attempt to have a child with another "wife," even though having more than one wife is actually illegal (Pashigian, 2002). In Cameroon, if a couple cannot conceive a child, the husband's family may encourage him to obtain a divorce and seek the return of the "bridewealth" his family paid to the wife's family when they married (Feldman-Salverlsberg, 2002).

**CAUSES.** Infertility has been regarded almost exclusively as a female problem for most of human history (Marsh & Ronner, 1996). In the West, for over 2,000 years, from about the 4th century BCE to the 1800s, the reigning explanation for infertility was based on a theory that both women and men must produce a seed in order for conception to occur, and that the seed was released through orgasm. Because men generally reach orgasm a whole lot easier than women do, the main advice given to infertile couples was for the husband to give more attention to bringing sexual pleasure to his wife. As one advice writer stated in 1708, "The womb must be in a state of delight" or sex would be fruitless (Marsh & Ronner, 1996, p. 15). This theory was wrong, but at least it did no harm. Other treatments for infertility were not just ineffective but damaging to women's health, including surgery on the woman's reproductive anatomy and bloodletting (which is pretty much what it sounds like: making a cut in a blood vessel in the arm and letting blood run out until the alleged imbalance was restored).

We now know that men and women contribute equally to infertility. This knowledge is very recent, coming only in about the past 50 years. About half the time the source of infertility is in the male reproductive system and about half the time in the female reproductive system (Jones & Lopez, 2014). Among men, there are three main sources of infertility (Jequier, 2011): (1) too few sperm may be produced; (2) the quality of the sperm may be poor, due to disease or defects in the sperm manufacturing process in the testicles; or, (3) the sperm may be low in *motility* (movement) and therefore unable to make it all the way up the fallopian tubes. These problems may be genetic or they may be caused by behavior such as drug abuse, alcohol abuse, or cigarette smoking. Or, they may be due simply to age; it takes three times longer for men over 40 to impregnate a partner than it does for men under 25, because the quantity and quality of sperm production decreases with age (Patel & Niedersberger, 2011).

Among women, infertility is most often caused by problems in ovulation (National Women's Health Information Center, 2011). Inability to ovulate can be caused by disease, or it can be due to drug abuse, alcohol abuse, or cigarette smoking, or to being extremely underweight or overweight. However, age is the most common cause of inability to ovulate (Maheshwari et al., 2008). As you learned early in the chapter, females are born with all the eggs they will ever have in their ovaries, and the quality of those eggs deteriorates gradually after puberty. Fertility decreases for women throughout their 20s and 30s but especially drops after age 40, when they become more likely to have menstrual cycles with no ovulation at all (see Figure 2.13).

**assisted reproductive technologies (ART)**
methods for overcoming infertility that include artificial insemination, fertility drugs, and IVF

**artificial insemination**
procedure of injecting sperm directly into the uterus

**TREATMENTS: ASSISTED REPRODUCTIVE TECHNOLOGIES.** During the course of the 20th century, treatments for infertility have become more scientifically based and technologically advanced. Today there are a variety of approaches to treating infertility. These methods are used by infertile couples as well as by gay and lesbian couples and by single women. A variety of related methods for overcoming infertility are grouped under the term **assisted reproductive technologies (ART)**, including artificial insemination, fertility drugs, and in vitro fertilization (IVF). ART methods are used in response to a wide variety of infertility problems in either the male or female reproductive system, or both.

Before discussing various ART methods, it is important to note that few people in developing countries have access to reproductive technologies like fertility drugs and IVF. There are also disparities within developed countries. Use of ART can be expensive, and hence access depends on income and health insurance coverage (Resolve: The National Infertility Association, 2016).

The oldest effective treatment for infertility is **artificial insemination**, which involves injecting the man's sperm directly into the woman's uterus, timed to coincide with her ovulation (Schoolcraft, 2010). It was first developed in the 19th century when physicians believed the primary cause of infertility was a too-tight cervix (the opening between the vagina and the

**Figure 2.13** Fertility and Maternal Age

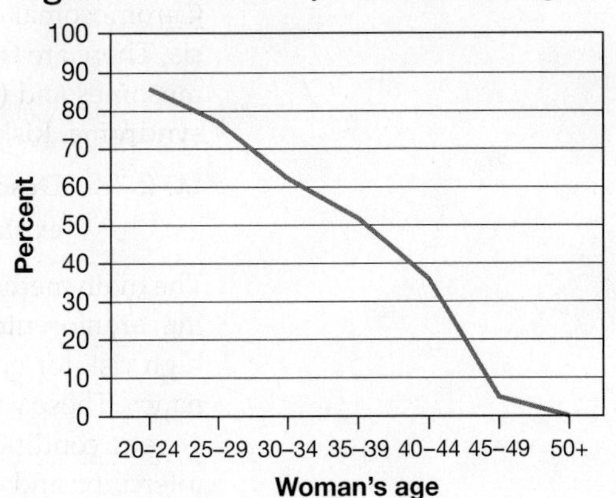

Multiple births often receive extensive media attention, but the consequences of such births are often tragic, with higher risks of miscarriages, premature birth, and serious developmental difficulties.

uterus). Today, artificial insemination most often occurs as *donor insemination*, in which a man other than the woman's husband or partner provides the sperm. Most often this approach is due to problems in the husband or partner's sperm production, but increasingly this procedure is chosen by lesbian couples or single women who wish to have a child. Artificial insemination is the simplest and most effective reproductive technology, with a success rate of over 70% per trial (Wright et al., 2004).

If the primary problem is that the woman does not ovulate properly, the most common approach is to stimulate ovulation through fertility drugs. The drugs mimic the activity of the hormones that normally provoke ovulation. Usually fertility drugs stimulate both the quality and the quantity of follicles in each cycle. Over half of the women who take the drugs become pregnant within six cycles (Schoolcraft, 2010). Fertility drugs work for many women, but they also carry serious risks, including blood clots, kidney damage, and damage to the ovaries (Lauersen & Bouchez, 2000). The purpose of the drugs is to stimulate the development of follicles in the ovaries, but often more than one follicle develops, resulting in the release of two, three, or more ova. Consequently, use of fertility drugs produces high rates of multiple births, about 10%–25% depending on the drug (Schoolcraft, 2010). Usually this means twins, but there is also the possibility of triplets or more. You may have seen magazine stories or television shows about multiple births of six, seven, or eight infants and how adorable they are, but the consequences of multiple births are often tragic. The more babies conceived at once, the higher the risk for miscarriages, premature birth, and serious developmental difficulties.

**in vitro fertilization (IVF)**
form of infertility treatment that involves using drugs to stimulate the growth of multiple follicles in the ovaries, removing the follicles and combining them with sperm, then transferring the most promising zygotes to the uterus

If fertility drugs are unsuccessful in achieving pregnancy, the next step in the ART method is **in vitro fertilization (IVF)**. In IVF, after fertility drugs are used to stimulate the growth of numerous follicles in the woman's ovaries, the ripe ova are then removed from the woman's body and combined with the man's sperm so that fertilization will take place. After a few days it is possible to tell which of the zygotes have developed and which have not, so the most promising one, two, or three are placed into the woman's uterus in the hope that one will continue to develop.

When the first IVF baby was born in 1978 there were concerns that babies conceived in this way might be abnormal in some way. However, by now many of these babies have grown to adulthood without any problems. IVF success rates have steadily improved in recent years. The likelihood of one cycle of IVF resulting in a live birth is currently close to 50% for women under age 35 (Society for Assisted Reproductive Technology [SART], 2017). However, the success rate declines with age to 24% for women ages 38 to 40 and just 4% for women ages 42 and older. Today IVF is the basis of thousands of pregnancies per year, almost entirely in developed countries because of the technology and expense it requires.

## SUMMARY: Pregnancy Problems

**LO 2.7.1 Explain how chromosomal disorders occur.**

Chromosomal disorders occur when the chromosomes fail to divide properly during meiosis. There are two main types of chromosomal disorders: (1) those that involve the sex chromosomes and (2) those that take place on the 21st pair of chromosomes, resulting in Down syndrome. Risks of chromosomal disorders rise with parental age.

**LO 2.7.2 Describe the four main techniques of prenatal testing and diagnosis, and explain why some prospective parents seek genetic counseling.**

The main methods for prenatal testing and diagnosis are ultrasound, maternal blood screening, amniocentesis, and chorionic villus sampling (CVS). Prospective parents who may be at high risk for genetic disorders sometimes seek genetic counseling before attempting pregnancy. Those with risks that merit genetic counseling include persons who have an inherited genetic condition or a close relative who has one; couples with a history of miscarriages or infertility; and older individuals (women older than 35 and men older than 40).

**LO 2.7.3 Describe psychological and social implications of infertility, and review major causes of and treatments for infertility.**

The implications of infertility vary by culture. They include a sense of sadness and loss in some individualistic countries, and stigmatization and ostracism of the woman in some traditional cultures. Female and male factors contribute equally to infertility. Female infertility is most often caused by problems in ovulation, and male infertility may be caused by too few sperm, poor quality of sperm, or low motility of sperm. Treatments for infertility are termed *assisted reproductive technologies* (ART) and include artificial insemination, fertility drugs, and in vitro fertilization (IVF).

## Apply Your Knowledge as a Professional

The topics covered in this chapter apply to a wide variety of career professionals. Watch this video to learn how they apply to a reproductive endocrinologist.

**Journaling Question:** As described in Chapter 1, one aim of the field of child development is to translate its empirical findings into practices and policies that will improve the lives of children and their families. Reflect on one way in your future professional life that you might use information covered in this chapter.

## Chapter 3

# Birth and the Newborn Child

## Learning Objectives

### 3.1 The Stages of Birth

**3.1.1** Describe the three stages of the birth process.

**3.1.2** Name two common types of birth complications and explain how they can be overcome.

### 3.2 Birth Across Times and Places

**3.2.1** Review the costs and benefits to child and mother with the invention of obstetrics.

**3.2.2** Describe cultural variations in who may assist with birth.

**3.2.3** Describe cultural variations in approaches to diminish danger and pain during birth.

**3.2.4** Describe the differences in maternal and neonatal mortality both within and between developed countries and developing countries.

### 3.3 The Neonate's Health

**3.3.1** Identify the features of the two major scales most often used to assess neonatal health.

**3.3.2** Identify the neonatal classifications for low birth weight, and describe the consequences and major treatments.

### 3.4 The Neonate's Physical and Perceptual Functioning

**3.4.1** Describe neonates' patterns of waking and sleeping, including how and why these patterns differ across cultures.

**3.4.2** Describe the neonatal reflexes, including those that have an apparent functional purpose and those that do not.

**3.4.3** Describe the neonate's sensory abilities with respect to touch, taste and smell, hearing, and sight.

### 3.5 Caring for the Neonate: Is Breast Best?

**3.5.1** Describe the cultural customs surrounding breast-feeding across cultures and history.

**3.5.2** Identify the advantages of breast-feeding and where those advantages are largest.

### 3.6 Social and Emotional Aspects of Care for the Neonate and Mother

**3.6.1** Describe neonates' types of crying and how crying patterns and soothing methods vary across cultures.

**3.6.2** Describe the extent to which human mothers "bond" with their neonates and the extent to which this claim has been exaggerated.

**3.6.3** Describe the reasons for postpartum depression and its consequences for children.

ACROSS CULTURES, THE BIRTH OF A NEW HUMAN BEING IS OFTEN REGARDED AS A JOYFUL EVENT, WORTHY OF CELEBRATION (NEWTON & NEWTON, 2003). At the same time, it is a physically challenging and potentially perilous process for both child and mother, especially when modern medical assistance is not available. In this chapter, we first look at the physical stages of the birth process. Because birth is so much more than a physical process, however, we then consider cultural variations in birth beliefs and practices, including a history of birth in the West. As you will see, birth is infused with an abundance of different beliefs. Some of these may seem sensible, others strange or even preposterous, but we will encourage you to think about the underlying psychological reasons for the beliefs and practices. We will also address what birth practices have proven effective in enhancing safe births for child and mother. The chapter then moves on to address the newborn child's physical and perceptual functioning, before ending with recommendations for care of the newborn and mother.

**Watch** **CHAPTER INTRODUCTION: BIRTH AND THE NEWBORN CHILD**

# 3.1 The Stages of Birth

**oxytocin**

hormone released by pituitary gland that causes labor to begin

Toward the end of pregnancy, hormonal changes trigger the beginning of the birth process. Most importantly, the woman's pituitary gland releases the hormone **oxytocin**. When the amount of oxytocin in the expectant mother's blood reaches a certain threshold level, her uterus begins to contract on a frequent and regular basis, and the birth process begins. This process is generally divided into three stages.

## Stages of the Birth Process

**LO 3.1.1 Describe the three stages of the birth process.**

As shown in Figure 3.1, the stages of the birth process are: labor, delivery of the baby, and delivery of the placenta and umbilical cord (Mayo Clinic Staff, 2017; Simkin, 2013). There is immense variability among women in the length and difficulty of this process, depending mostly on the size of the woman and the size of the baby, but in general it is longer and more difficult for women giving birth to their first child.

**labor**

first and longest stage of the birth process

**THE FIRST STAGE OF LABOR.** The first stage of the birth process, **labor**, is the longest and most taxing stage, averaging about 12 hours for first births and 6 hours for subsequent births (Lyon, 2007; Simkin, 2013). During labor, contractions of the muscles in the uterus cause the woman's cervix to dilate (open) in preparation for the baby's exit. By the end of labor, the cervix has opened to about 10 centimeters (4½ inches). The muscles of the uterus contract with increasing intensity, frequency, and duration during labor in order to dilate the cervix and move the fetus down the neck of the uterus and through the vagina. In the early part of labor, as the cervix opens, there may be a thick, stringy, bloody discharge from the vagina known as *bloody show*. Women often experience severe pain from the contractions as well as back pain as labor continues. Nausea and trembling of the legs are also common.

**delivery**

second stage of the birth process, during which the fetus is pushed out of the cervix and through the birth canal

**THE SECOND STAGE OF DELIVERY.** The second stage of the birth process, **delivery**, usually takes a half hour to an hour, but again there is wide variation (Mayo Clinic, 2017; Murkoff & Mazel, 2016). At this stage, the mother's efforts to push will help move the fetus through the cervix and out of the uterus. Contractions continue to help, too, but for most women the contractions are now less frequent, although they remain 60 to 90 seconds long. Usually the woman feels a tremendous urge to push during her contractions.

**episiotomy**

incision to make the vaginal opening larger during birth process

At last *crowning occurs*, meaning that the baby's head appears at the outer opening of the vagina. The woman often experiences a tingling or burning sensation at her vaginal opening as the baby crowns. At this point, if she is giving birth in a hospital she may be given an **episiotomy**, which is an incision to make the vaginal opening larger. The purpose is to make the mother's vagina less likely to tear as the fetus's head comes out and to shorten this part of the birth process by 15 to 30 minutes. However, critics of episiotomies say they are often

**Figure 3.1** Three Stages of the Birth Process

**Stage 1: Labor**

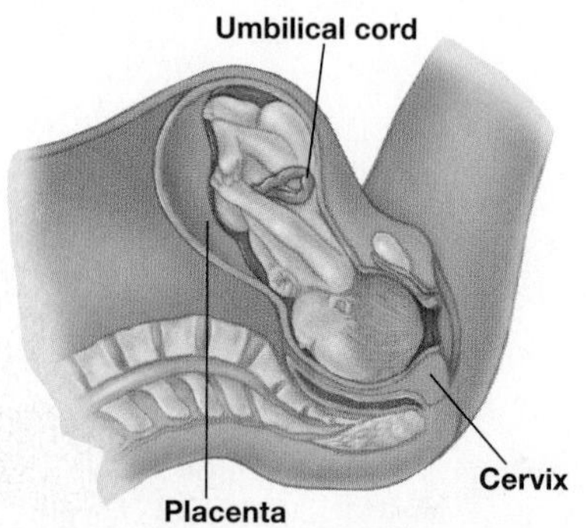


**Contractions increase in duration, frequency, and intensity, causing the cervix to dilate.**

**Stage 2: Delivery**

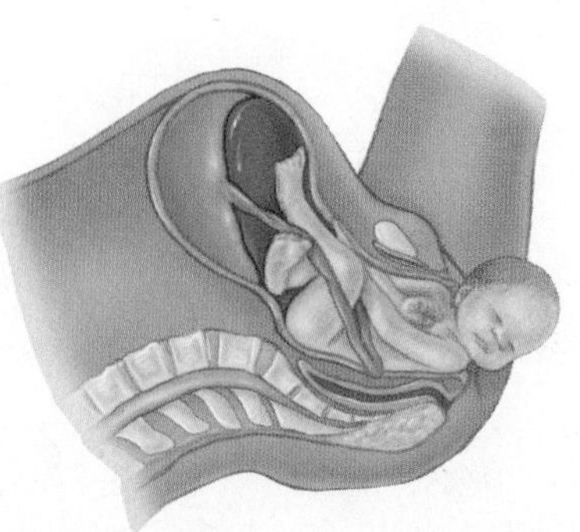

**The mother pushes, and the baby crowns and then exits the birth canal and enters the world.**

**Stage 3: Expelling of Placenta & Umbilical Cord**

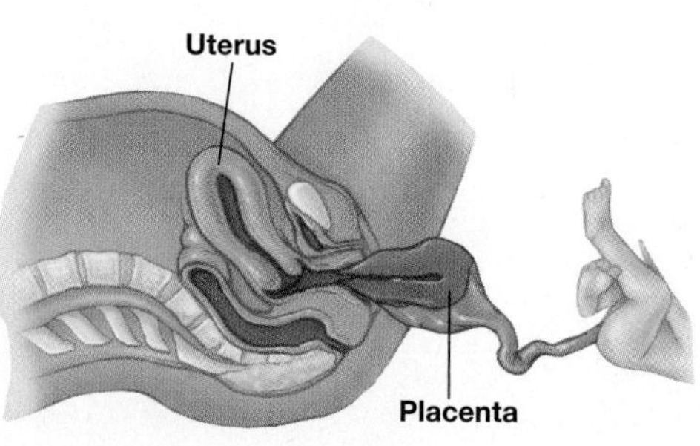


**Contractions continue as the placenta and umbilical cord are expelled.**

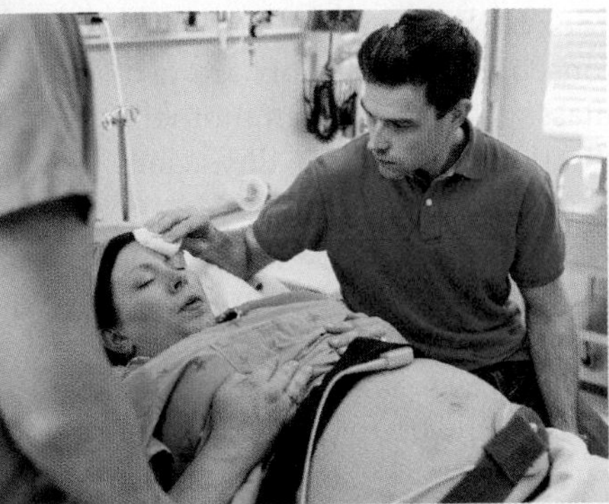

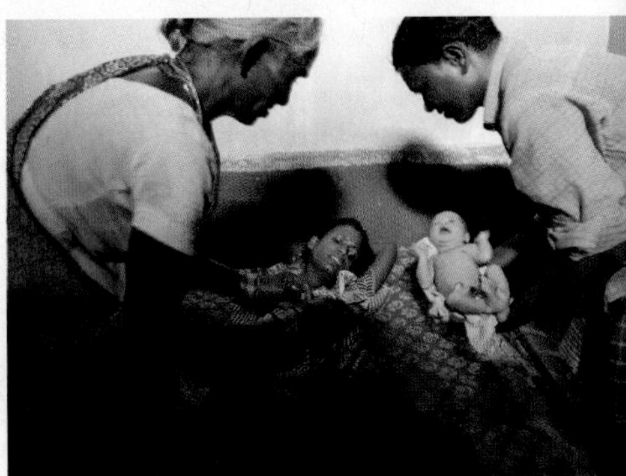

The physical stages of birth are the same everywhere, but the social circumstances vary widely across cultures. These three women are from the United States, Haiti, and India.

unnecessary and, in response to such criticism, the rate of episiotomies in the United States declined from about 90% in 1970 to just 15% in 2012 (Cassidy, 2006; Frankman et al., 2009; Friedman et al., 2015). Rates of episiotomies are associated with ethnicity. In 2012, 8% of black women had episiotomies whereas the rate was 15–16% for other groups (Friedman et al., 2015).

The delivery stage ends as the baby emerges from the vagina, but the birth process is not yet over.

**THE THIRD STAGE OF EXPULSION OF PLACENTA AND UMBILICAL CORD.** In the third and final stage, contractions continue as the placenta and umbilical cord are expelled from the uterus (Lyon, 2007; Simkin, 2013). This process usually happens within a few minutes, at most a half hour. The contractions are mild and last about a minute each. Care must be taken that the entire placenta comes out. If it does not, the uterus will be unable to contract properly and the mother will continue to bleed, perhaps even to the point of threatening her life. Beginning to breast-feed the newborn triggers contractions that help expel the placenta, and when advanced medical care is available the mother may be given an injection of synthetic oxytocin for the same purpose.

If the mother has had an episiotomy or her vagina has torn during delivery, she will have stitches at this time. At this point, too, the umbilical cord must be cut and tied. There are many interesting cultural beliefs surrounding the cutting of the umbilical cord and the disposal of the placenta, as we will see later in the chapter.

The video *Labor and Delivery* shows excerpts from the delivery stage and the expelling of the placenta and umbilical cord, from a live birth. (We would like to mention that some viewers may be somewhat surprised at the reality of what birth looks like.)

## Birth Complications and Cesarean Delivery

**LO 3.1.2 Name two common types of birth complications and explain how they can be overcome.**

**breech presentation**
positioning of the fetus so that feet or buttocks, rather than the head, would come first out of the birth canal

We have just examined the birth process as it occurs if all goes well, but of course there are times when all does not go well. Two of the most common birth complications are *failure to progress* and the *breech presentation* of the fetus.

"Failure to progress" means that the woman has begun the birth process but it is taking longer than normal. The woman may stimulate progress by walking around, taking a nap, or having a warm bath. She may also be given synthetic oxytocin to stimulate her contractions. If delivery is taking place in a hospital setting and the baby is already in the birth canal, then forceps (a pair of tongs) or a "vacuum" (a suction device) may be attached to baby's head to help pull the baby out through the vagina.

**Watch** LABOR AND DELIVERY

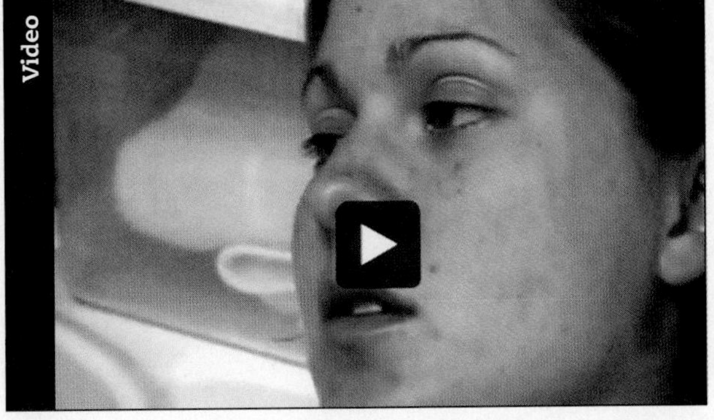


**Breech presentation** is when the fetus is turned around so that the feet or buttocks are positioned to come first out of the birth canal, rather than the head. About 4% of fetuses present in the breech position (Martin et al., 2005). Breech births are dangerous to the baby because coming out feet or buttocks first can cause the umbilical cord to be constricted during delivery, potentially leading to insufficient oxygen and brain damage within minutes. Consequently, attempts are usually made to avoid a breech presentation. Midwives may massage the expectant mother's abdomen and attempt to turn the fetus from breech presentation to headfirst. Physicians also seek to turn breech fetuses at about the 37th week of pregnancy, often using massage along with drugs that relax the muscles of the uterus (Hofmeyr, 2002).

**cesarean delivery**, or **c-section**
type of birth in which mother's abdomen is cut open and fetus is retrieved directly from the uterus

If failure to progress takes place before the baby is in the birth canal, or if a fetus in breech position cannot be turned successfully, or if other problems arise in the birth process, the woman may be given a **cesarean delivery**, or **c-section**. The c-section involves cutting open the mother's abdomen and retrieving the baby directly from the uterus. The c-section has been around for a long time—according to legend it is named for the Roman emperor Julius Caesar, who supposedly was born by this method about 2,000 years ago—but until recent decades mothers nearly always died from it, even if the baby was saved. Today, it is very safe, although it takes women longer to heal from a cesarean than from a vaginal birth (MedlinePlus, 2016). C-sections are generally safe for infants as well, and if the mother has a sexually transmitted infection, such as HIV or genital herpes, it is safer than a vaginal birth because it protects the infant from the risk of contracting the disease during the birth process.

As Map 3.1 shows, rates of c-sections vary widely among countries and do not seem to be related to world region or level of economic development (World Health Organization [WHO], 2014). What is the ideal rate of c-sections in order to lower maternal and neonatal mortality? The World Health Organization recommends that no country's c-section rate exceed 10–15% (WHO, 2009, 2015). A recent analysis of worldwide data suggests that up to about 19% may be ideal (Molina et al., 2015). Many countries exceed these rates, including the United States.

**Critical Thinking Question:** What are some factors that you think influence whether a country has high or low c-section rates?

Some of the countries that have the lowest rates of c-sections also have very low rates of birth complications, which indicates that many c-sections performed in countries with high rates are unnecessary (WHO, 2015). Specifically, the countries that have the lowest rates of birth problems

**Map 3.1** C-Section Rates, Selected Countries

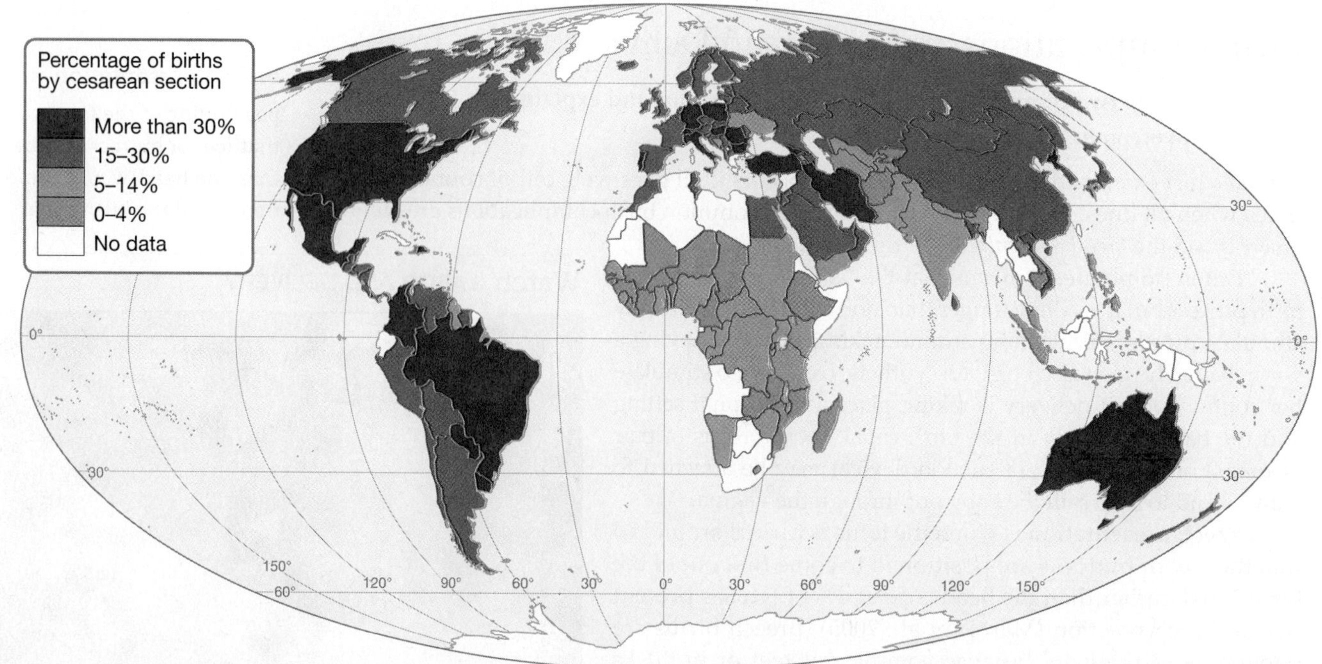

as well as the lowest rates of c-sections are the countries of northern Europe, where doctors and parents-to-be alike share a cultural belief that birth should be natural and that technological intervention should take place only when absolutely necessary (Ravn, 2005). However, rates of c-sections are also very low in countries like India and in most of Africa, where many people lack access to hospital facilities that could provide c-sections when necessary (WHO, 2014).

For women who have had a c-section, there is a possibility of having a vaginal birth with the next baby, a procedure known as a VBAC (*vaginal birth after cesarean section*; Shorten, 2010). In 2010, a National Institutes of Health (NIH) panel reviewed the evidence on VBAC and declared that the procedure is safe for nearly all women.

## SUMMARY: The Stages of Birth

**LO 3.1.1 Describe the three stages of the birth process.**

The three stages of the birth process are labor, delivery, and expelling of the placenta and umbilical cord. During labor, the contractions of the muscles in the uterus cause the mother's cervix to dilate in preparation for the baby's exit. By the end of labor, the cervix has opened to about 10 centimeters (4½ inches). During delivery, the woman pushes the fetus through the cervix and out of the uterus. In the final stage of the birth process, contractions continue as the placenta and umbilical cord are expelled.

**LO 3.1.2 Name two common types of birth complications and explain how they can be overcome.**

Two common birth complications are failure to progress, which occurs when the birth process is taking longer than normal, and the breech presentation of the fetus, which means the fetus is turned around so that the feet or buttocks are positioned to come first out of the birth canal. One way to overcome both complications is through the use of a C-section.

# 3.2 Birth Across Times and Places

Birth inspires especially intense beliefs in every culture because it is often difficult and sometimes fatal, to child or mother or both. The difficulties and dangers of birth are unique to the human species (Cassidy, 2006). Polar bear mothers, who weigh an average of 500 pounds, give birth to cubs whose heads are smaller than the heads of newborn humans. Even gorillas, one of our closest primate relatives, have babies who average only 2% of their mother's weight at birth, compared to 6% for humans. Recall from Chapter 1 that over the course of human evolutionary history, the size of the brain more than tripled. Yet the rest of the female body did not grow three times larger, nor did the female pelvis triple in size. Consequently, birth became more problematic among humans than among any other animal, as it became increasingly difficult for the large-brained, big-headed fetus to make it through the birth canal out into the world.

Humans responded to this danger by developing a wide variety of cultural beliefs and practices intended to explain why labor is difficult and to alleviate the pain and enhance the safety of mother and child. Some of these beliefs and practices were surely helpful; others were indisputably harmful. Some of the most harmful beliefs and practices were developed in the West, through the interventions of the medical profession from the 18th to the mid-20th century. It is only in the past 50 years that scientifically-based medical knowledge has led to methods that are genuinely helpful to mothers and babies in the birthing process.

## The Peculiar History of Birth in the West

**LO 3.2.1 Review the costs and benefits to child and mother with the invention of obstetrics.**

In the West as in other cultures, most births throughout most of history were administered by midwives (Ehrenreich, 2010). In the early 18th century, medical schools were established throughout Europe, and childbirth and the care of expectant mothers became a distinct field within medicine called **obstetrics**. By the 19th century it became increasingly common for doctors in the West to be called on to assist in births.

**obstetrics**
field of medicine that focuses on prenatal care and birth

Unfortunately, medical training and knowledge at the time was often inadequate. For example, all the doctors-to-be were men, and in many medical schools it was considered improper for a man to see a woman's genitals under any circumstances. Medical students learned about assisting a birth only from reading books and attending lectures (Cassidy, 2006). Consequently, obstetrical care could be perilous. By the end of the 19th century, half of all American births involved the use of forceps (Ehrenreich, 2010). In the hands of experienced doctors, forceps are generally safe, but at this time their use frequently resulted in damage to the baby or the mother.

Even worse than the lack of practical training was the lack of knowledge pertaining to infection. Prior to the 20th century, no one understood that it was necessary for doctors to wash their hands before examining a patient to avoid spreading infection. Consequently, hospitals became disease factories. Vast numbers of women died following childbirth from what was called *childbed fever* or *puerperal sepsis*. Records show that in many European and American hospitals in the 19th century, about 1 in 20 mothers died from childbed fever, and during occasional epidemics the rates were much higher (Nuland, 2003).

It was not until the 1940s that childbed fever was finally vanquished in the United States and Europe as it became standard for obstetricians to wash their hands and also wear rubber gloves in examining women. The development of antibiotics at this time cured the cases of childbed fever that did occur (Carter & Carter, 2005).

In the course of the 19th century, doctors increasingly used drugs to relieve pain during birth, but many of these drugs (such as ether and chloroform) had dangerous side effects that could cause maternal hemorrhage and breathing difficulties in babies. In the early 20th century a new drug method was developed that resulted in a condition that became known as *Twilight Sleep* (Cassidy, 2008). After being injected with narcotics (mainly morphine), a woman giving birth in Twilight Sleep became less inhibited, which helped her relax during her contractions and promoted dilation of her cervix, making the use of forceps less likely. Women still felt pain—in fact, screaming and thrashing were so common that women were often strapped in helmets and handcuffed to the birth bed—but afterward they remembered none of it. From the 1930s through the 1960s, use of Twilight Sleep and other drug methods was standard practice in hospitals in Western countries (Cassidy, 2006).

**natural childbirth**
approach to childbirth that avoids medical technologies and interventions

During the late 1960s a backlash began to develop against the medicalization of birth (Lyon, 2007). Critics claimed that medical procedures such as drugs, forceps, and episiotomies were unnecessary and had been created by the medical profession mainly to make childbirth more profitable. These critics advocated **natural childbirth** as an alternative. Natural childbirth methods vary in their details, but all reject medical technologies and interventions as unhelpful to the birth process or even harmful. Natural childbirth encompasses classes in which the parents-to-be learn about the birth process, including how to manage pain by means of relaxation, breathing techniques, and reliance on the physical and emotional support of a spouse or partner or others. No differences have been found in maternal and neonatal health outcomes between natural childbirth and medical methods, as long as the birth takes place in a health facility where medical intervention is available if necessary (Bergstrom et al., 2009).

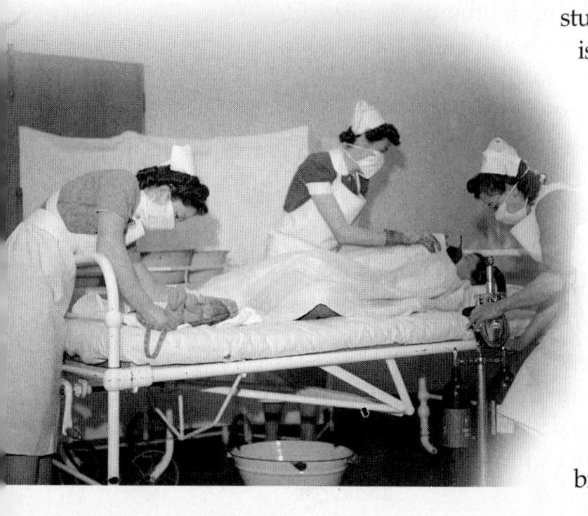

In the mid-20th century, birth in developed countries often took place in a condition of "Twilight Sleep," in which the mother was heavily medicated. This photo from 1946 shows a new mother under sedation after giving birth in a London hospital.

Although natural childbirth can enhance the birth experience for mothers, some studies have shown poorer outcomes of "home birth." The debate over home births is often polarized. A recent study, however, won the praises of both the National Association of Certified Midwives and the American College of Obstetricians and Gynecologists (Belluck, 2015). This study found that the probability of the baby dying during the birth process or in the first month after—though slight—was 2.4 times greater than for women who had hospital deliveries (Snowden et al., 2015). Home births also carried greater risk of seizures in the newborn baby, and greater likelihood that the newborn would need a ventilator and that the mother would need a blood transfusion. On the other hand, home births involved fewer medical interventions, including far fewer c-sections. Home births are not recommended for women with high-risk pregnancies or pre-existing medical conditions, and women are advised to have a plan for transfer to a medical facility, should complications arise. Home births remain rare in developed countries. For example, they account for just over 1% of all births in the United States (Belluck, 2015).

While natural childbirth methods remain popular today, especially in northern Europe (Ravn, 2005), medical interventions are also common. For example, women in labor often receive an **epidural**, which involves the injection of an anesthetic drug into the spinal fluid to help them manage the pain while remaining alert (Vallejo et al., 2007). If administered in the correct dosage, an epidural allows enough feeling to remain so that the woman can push when the time comes, but sometimes synthetic oxytocin has to be administered because the epidural causes contractions to become sluggish. Rates of receiving epidurals for women having a vaginal birth vary widely in developed countries, for example 76% in the United States, 52% in Sweden, 45% in Canada, and 24% in New Zealand (Lane, 2009). The reasons for these variations are not clear.

**Critical Thinking Question:** Based on what you have read so far, can you generate hypotheses as to factors that may account for the different rates of epidurals across developed countries?

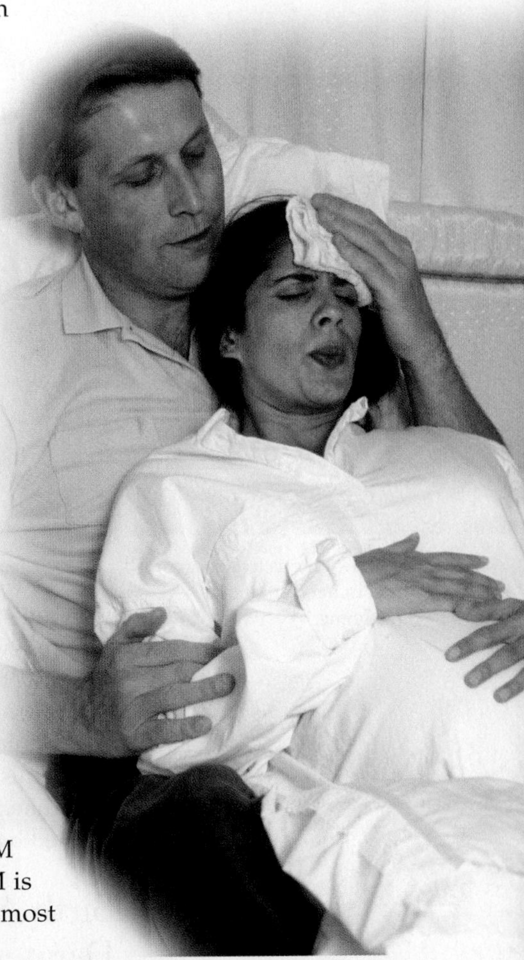

In natural childbirth, husbands or partners often assist with breathing techniques designed to manage pain.

**Electronic fetal monitoring (EFM)** is another common contemporary medical technology. EFM tracks the fetus's heartbeat, either externally through the mother's abdomen or directly by running a wire through the cervix and placing a sensor on the fetus's scalp. In the United States, about 85% of births include EFM (Martin et al., 2005). EFM contributes to making the birth process safer for both child and mother. Changes in the fetal heart rate may indicate distress and call for intervention. However, heart rate changes are not easy to interpret and do not necessarily indicate distress, so use of EFM may increase the rate of unnecessary c-sections (Thacker & Stroup, 2003). EFM is especially useful in preterm or other high-risk deliveries, when fetal distress is most likely to occur.

In developed countries today, the birth process is better than it has ever been before, for both mothers and babies. The natural childbirth movement has had many positive effects on how birth is assisted in mainstream medicine. Although most births in developed countries still take place in a hospital, birth has become less like an operation performed by a physician and more of a collaboration between doctors, nurses (often including nurse-midwives), and mothers. Furthermore, fathers, partners, and other family members and friends are now often involved, too. When fathers are present, mothers experience slightly shorter labor and express greater satisfaction with the birth experience (Hodnett et al., 2007). For fathers, being present at the birth evokes intense feelings of wonder and love, although some fathers simultaneously experience intense fears for the well-being of the mother and baby (Erlandsson & Lindgren, 2009; Eriksson et al., 2007).

**epidural**
during birth process, injection of an anesthetic drug into the spinal fluid to help the mother manage the pain while also remaining alert

**electronic fetal monitoring (EFM)**
method that tracks the fetus's heartbeat, either externally through the mother's abdomen or directly by running a wire through the cervix and placing a sensor on the fetus's scalp

## Birth Across Places: Who Helps?

**LO 3.2.2 Describe cultural variations in who may assist with birth.**

There is relatively little variation among traditional cultures in who assists with the birth. Almost always, the main assistants are older women (Bel & Bel, 2007). In one early study of birth practices in 60 traditional cultures, elderly women assisted in 58 of them (Ford, 1945). Rarely, men have been found to be the main birth attendants, such as in some parts of Mexico and the Philippines. More typically, all men are forbidden from even being present during birth, much less serving as the central helper (Newton & Newton, 2003). However, sometimes fathers assist by holding up the mother as she leans, stands, or squats to deliver the baby.

Although a variety of women are typically present with the mother at birth, especially her relatives, the women who are charged with managing the birth process usually have a special status as midwives. Midwives tend to be older women who have had children themselves but are now beyond childbearing age. They have direct experience with childbirth but no longer have young children to care for, so that they are available and able when called to duty.

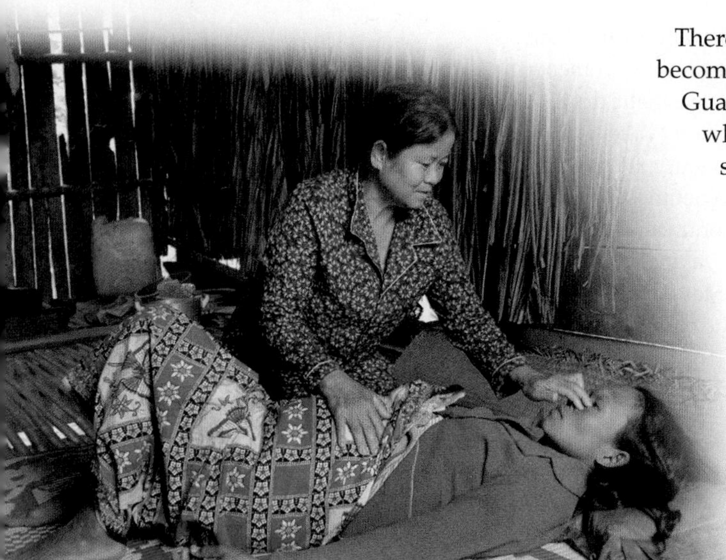
A midwife attends to a pregnant woman in her Cambodian village home.

There are a variety of ways a woman in a traditional culture may become a midwife (Cosminsky, 2003). In some cultures, such as in Guatemala and the Ojibwa tribe of Native Americans, she receives what she believes to be a supernatural calling in a dream or vision. In other cultures, the position of midwife is inherited from mother to daughter. Still other cultures allow women to volunteer to be midwives. Regardless of how she comes to the position, typically the woman who is to be a midwife spends several years in apprenticeship to a more experienced midwife before taking the lead in assisting with a birth. Through apprenticeship she learns basic principles of hygiene, methods to ease the birth, and practices for prenatal and postnatal care.

Across developing countries today, midwives remain the most common assistants with birth. Among those with the highest SES, a change is taking place in which birth increasingly takes place in a medical setting and is overseen by medical personnel (Montagu et al., 2011). Among the less wealthy, however, home birth remains common—either with a midwife present or without any attendant.

In developed countries, midwifery has seen a revival in recent decades. Whereas only 1% of births in the United States were assisted by a midwife in 1973, the current rate is about 10% (Cassidy, 2006; Hamilton et al., 2015; MacDorman et. al., 2010). Many now receive formal training and are certified and licensed as nurse-midwives, rather than simply learning their skills from an older midwife as in the past. In Europe, midwives are much more common than in the United States, especially in northern Europe. In Norway, 96% of births are assisted by midwives (Cosminsky, 2003).

## Birth Across Places: Practices Aimed at Diminishing Danger and Pain

**LO 3.2.3 Describe cultural variations in approaches to diminish danger and pain during birth.**

Perhaps because birth is often risky, many traditional cultures have developed beliefs that giving birth puts a woman in a state of being spiritually unclean (Newton & Newton, 2003). In some cultures, birth must take place away from where most people reside, so that others will not be contaminated by it. For example, among the Arapesh of New Guinea, birth is allowed to take place only at the outskirts of the village, in a place reserved for other contaminating activities such as excretion and menstruation. Many cultures also have beliefs that the mother remains unclean long after the birth and must be kept away from others or ritually cleansed, for her own sake as well as theirs (Newton & Newton, 2003). Until recent decades, for example, the Catholic church had a special ritual for new mothers to purify themselves.

As we have seen, the delivery of the placenta is potentially dangerous, and this may be why many cultures have developed beliefs that the placenta itself is potentially dangerous and must be disposed of properly so that no unpleasant consequences will result (Jones & Kay, 2003). Failure to do so is believed to carry consequences as minor as pimples on the baby or as major as the baby's death. In some cultures the methods for disposing of the placenta are clear and simple: burial, burning, or throwing it in a river, or keeping it in a special place reserved for placentas (Selander, 2011). In other cultures, the traditions surrounding the placenta are more elaborate. For example, in several parts of the world, including Indonesia, Ghana, and Malaysia, the placenta is treated as the baby's semihuman sibling (Cassidy, 2006). Following delivery, the midwife washes the placenta and buries it as she would a stillborn infant. In some cultures the burial includes prayers to the placenta imploring it not to harm the newborn child or the mother.

Why would beliefs develop that placentas and new mothers are dangerous? A frequent motivation for the development of cultural beliefs appears to be the desire for control (Jones & Kay, 2003). Birth is often fraught with peril. Humans, faced with this unpleasant prospect, develop beliefs they hope will enable them to avoid, or at least minimize, the peril. It is a comfort to believe that if certain rituals are performed, the mother, the baby, and everyone else will make it through the process unscathed.

Interestingly, in some places the placenta is recognized as having special value as a source of hormones and nutrients. Hospitals in developed countries give their placentas to researchers, or to cosmetic manufacturers who use them to make products such as hair conditioner (Jones & Kay, 2003). Some people in Western countries even advocate consuming part of the placenta, on top of "placenta pizza" or blended into a "placenta cocktail" (Weekley, 2007)! Maybe this explains why the word *placenta* is derived from the Latin word for "cake"? Well, probably not. More likely, this (rare) practice is inspired by the fact that many other mammalian mothers, from mice to monkeys, eat the placenta. The placenta is full of nutrients that can provide a boost to an exhausted new mother about to begin nursing. It also contains the hormone oxytocin, which helps prevent postpartum hemorrhage. Although not unheard of, few human cultures have been found to have a custom of eating the placenta.

Apart from aiming to diminish the risks of birth, cultures have devised many traditional methods of attempting to ease the pain and difficulty of the birth process. The methods vary, but there are certain common themes. For example, the strategies begin long before birth. As noted in Chapter 2, often a midwife comes for prenatal visits in order to provide advice and give an abdominal massage, which eases discomfort.

When the woman begins to go into labor, the midwife is called, and the expectant mother's female relatives gather around her. Sometimes the midwife gives the mother-to-be medicine intended to ease the pain of labor and birth. Many cultures have used herbal medicines, but in the Ukraine, traditionally the first act of the midwife after arriving at the home of a woman in labor was to give her a generous glass of whiskey (Newton & Newton, 2003). Expectant mothers may be fed special foods to strengthen them for the labor to come. As labor progresses, some kind of upright position is used across many cultures. To make use of gravity to speed up birth, mothers commonly kneel, squat, or stand (Newton & Newton, 2003).

The longer the labor, the more exhausted the mother and the greater the potential danger to mother and child. Consequently, cultures have created a wide variety of practices intended to hasten it. The most widespread approach, appearing in cultures in all parts of the world, is to use some kind of imagery or metaphor associated with opening up or expulsion (Bates & Turner, 2003). For example, in the Philippines a key (for "opening" the cervix) and a comb (for "untangling" the umbilical cord) are placed under the laboring woman's pillow. In other cultures, ropes are unknotted, bottles are uncorked, or animals are let out of their pens. In some traditional cultures, the midwife calls on spiritual assistance from a *shaman*, a religious leader believed to have special powers and knowledge of the spirit world. Among the Cuna Indians, for example, the shaman's job includes singing a song that sends a spirit into the womb to release the baby (Levi-Strauss, 1967).

Do any of these traditional practices do any good to the woman suffering a difficult labor? From a medical perspective, mostly not, but let's be careful before we dismiss the effects of the shaman's song too easily. There is abundant evidence of the *placebo effect*, which means that sometimes if people believe something affects them, it does, just by virtue of the power of their belief. In the classic example, if people are given a sugar pill containing no medicine and told it is a pain reliever, many of them will report experiencing reduced pain (Balodis et al., 2011). It was not the sugar pill that reduced their pain but their belief that the pill would reduce their pain. In the case of the shaman assisting the birth, the mother may feel genuine relief, not only because of her belief in the shaman's song but also because of the emotional and social support the shaman's presence represents (Bates & Turner, 2003).

Current recommendations by health professionals in developed countries for how to handle labor pain in non-medical ways resemble some of the practices used across cultures. These nonmedical strategies include (Mayo Clinic Staff, 2017): 1) Change birth position frequently, including standing upright and walking; 2) Listen to music; 3) Breathe in a steady rhythm, fast or slow, depending on what is most comfortable; 4) Take a shower or bath; and 5) Have a massage between contractions.

It is important to point out that some practices aimed at doing good, actually do harm. For example, some of the traditional customs involved in cutting or treating the umbilical cord connecting the placenta and the baby are unwittingly hazardous (Cosminsky, 2003). Tools used to cut the cord include bamboo, shell, broken glass, sickles, and razors, and they may not be clean, resulting in transmission of disease to the baby. Methods for treating the cut cord include, in one part of northern India, ash from burned cow dung mixed with dirt, which is now known to increase sharply the baby's risk of tetanus.

## Cultural Variations in Neonatal and Maternal Mortality

**LO 3.2.4 Describe the differences in maternal and neonatal mortality both within and between developed countries and developing countries.**

As you can see from Map 3.2, rates of neonatal and maternal mortality are vastly higher in developing countries than in developed countries. In much of the world, birth remains fraught with risk. However, there are some hopeful signs. Maternal mortality has decreased

**Map 3.2** Neonatal and Maternal Mortality Worldwide

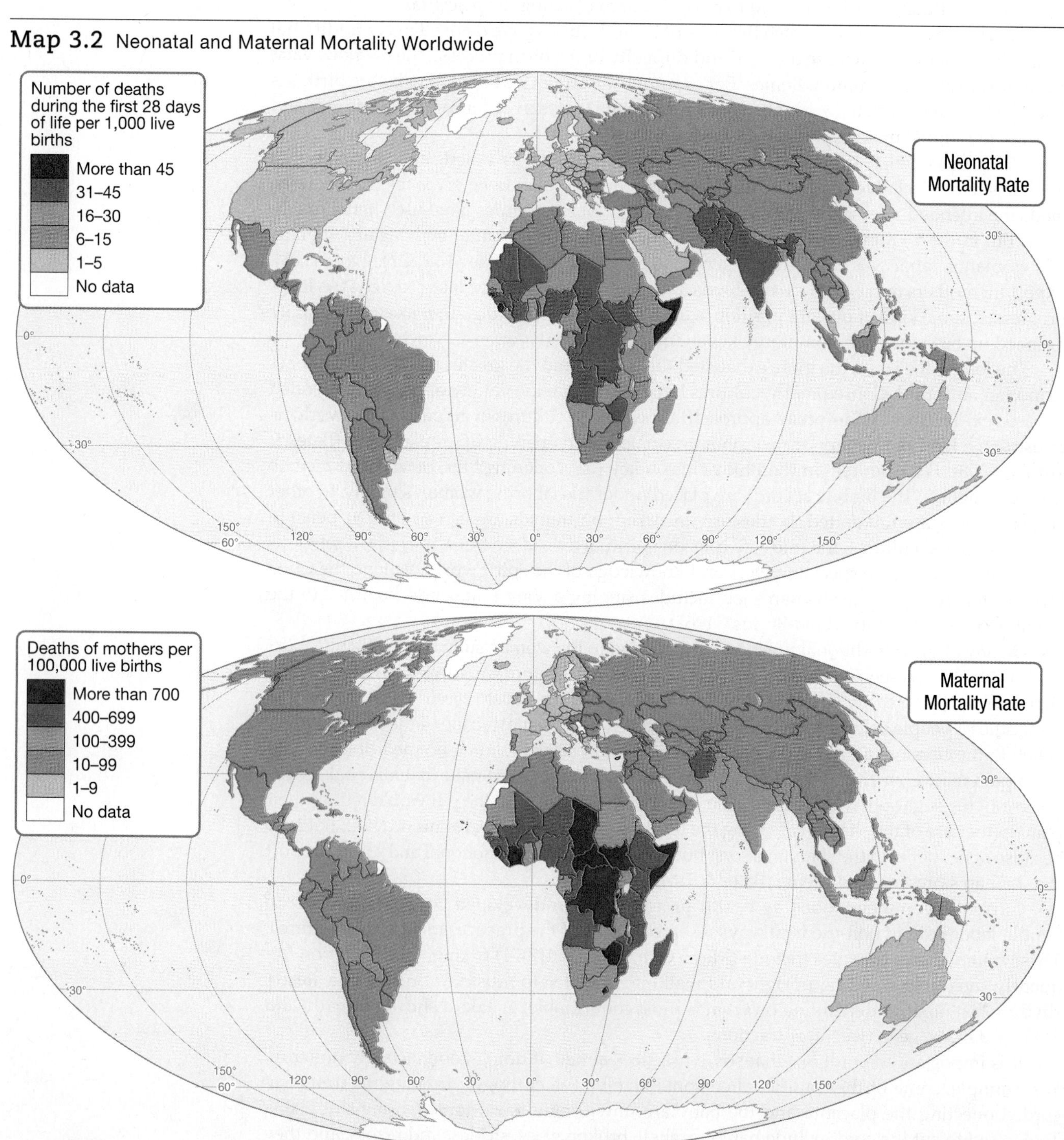

substantially in developing countries over the past 30 years, due to improvements in nutrition and access to health care (Hogan et al., 2010; UNICEF, 2014). The **neonatal period**, the first 28 days of life, is still the most vulnerable time for a child's survival (UNICEF, 2014). To reduce neonatal mortality in developing countries, UNICEF (2015) recommends that for every birth: 1) Hospital care is available in emergencies, 2) Skilled personnel such as trained midwives are in attendance, and 3) There is provision of essential medical items such as drugs for clean umbilical cord care.

**neonatal period**
the first 28 days of a newborn child's life

There is also variation in neonatal and maternal mortality among developed countries. For example, neonatal mortality is about double in the United States, compared to countries such as the Czech Republic, Japan, Finland, and Portugal (MacDorman et al., 2014).

Within the United States, neonatal mortality is over twice as high for African Americans as for Whites, due primarily to greater poverty and lower access to high-quality medical care among African Americans (Centers for Disease Control and Prevention [CDC], 2017). However, neonatal mortality has dropped steeply across ethnic groups in the United States since 1980, by nearly half. Current rates among Asian Americans and Latinos are similar to those for Whites (CDC, 2017). In contrast, maternal mortality has been rising since 1980, for reasons that are not clear (U.S. Bureau of the Census, 2010).

## SUMMARY: Birth Across Times and Places

### LO 3.2.1 Review the costs and benefits to child and mother with the invention of obstetrics.

Obstetrics became a field within medicine in the early 18th century. In the 18th and 19th centuries, however, doctors with unclean hands often spread deadly infections to mothers. In the early 20th century the attempts to make birth safer became overly medical, as birth was taken over by doctors and hospitals, with the maternal experience disregarded. In the past 50 years, most of the West has moved toward a middle ground, seeking to minimize medical intervention but making it available when necessary.

### LO 3.2.2 Describe cultural variations in who may assist with birth.

In developing countries, older women and trained midwives are the most common assistants with birth. For groups with high socioeconomic status (SES), however, a change is taking place where birth increasingly takes place in a medical setting and is overseen by medical personnel. In developed countries, midwifery is seeing a revival. In Europe, midwives are much more common than in the United States, especially in northern Europe.

### LO 3.2.3 Describe cultural variations in approaches to diminish danger and pain during birth.

Because birth is often dangerous, many traditional cultures have developed beliefs that childbirth puts a woman in a state of being unclean and that she must be ritually cleansed or placed away from everyday activities. Also, the placenta is often disposed of carefully in traditional cultures because of beliefs that it is potentially dangerous or even semi-human. In traditional cultures, midwives often aim to ease birth pain through massage techniques, reassurance, and herbal medicines.

### LO 3.2.4 Describe the differences in maternal and neonatal mortality both within and between developed countries and developing countries.

In recent decades, birth has become routinely safe and humane in developed countries, although there is considerable variation based on SES and ethnicity. Childbirth remains highly dangerous in developing countries where little medical intervention is available, although mortality rates are decreasing due to recent improvements in nutrition and access to health care.

# 3.3 The Neonate's Health

Out comes baby at last, after 9 months or so inside the womb. The typical newborn child is about 20 inches (51 cm) long and weighs about 7.5 pounds (3.4 kg). If you were expecting cuddly and cute from the beginning, you may be in for a surprise. The baby's head may be a bit misshapen as a consequence of being squeezed through the birth canal. One

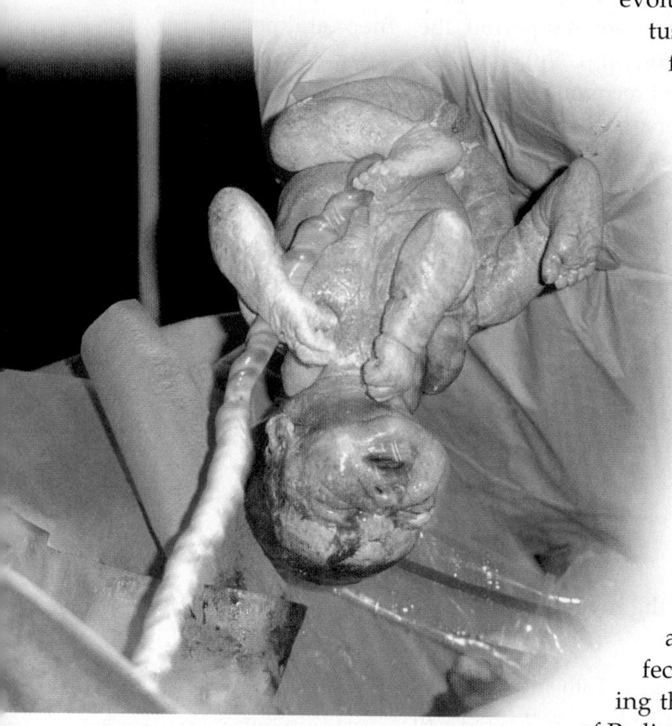

This newborn is covered with vernix, which protects the skin during prenatal development.

evolutionary solution to the problem of getting large-brained human fetuses out of the womb is that the skull of the infant's head is not yet fused into one bone. Instead, it is composed of several loosely joined pieces that can move around as necessary during the birth process. In between the pieces are two soft spots called **fontanels**, one on top and one toward the back of the head. It will take about 18 months before the pieces of the skull are firmly joined and the fontanels have disappeared.

The newborn baby's skin may be covered with fine, fuzzy hair called *lanugo*, a vestige of our hairy primate ancestors. This hair will be shed after a few days, fortunately. The skin may also be coated all over with the oily, cheesy substance called *vernix*, which protected the skin from chapping while in the womb. About half of all neonates have a yellowish look to their skin and eyeballs in the first few days of life. This condition, known as **neonatal jaundice**, is due to the immaturity of the liver (U.S. National Library of Medicine, 2017). In most cases, neonatal jaundice disappears after a few days as the liver begins to function normally, but if it lasts more than a few days it should be treated, or it can result in brain damage (American Academy of Pediatrics [AAP], 2011). The most effective treatment is a simple one, *phototherapy*, which involves exposing the neonate to colored light; blue works best (American Academy of Pediatrics [AAP], 2011).

The neonatal period is a vulnerable time. Consequently, as we will see next, it is important that the health of the neonate is carefully assessed and that treatments are put in place if needed. Low birth weight is one of the most common threats to survival and healthy development.

**fontanels**
soft spots on the skull between loosely joined pieces of the skull that shift during the birth process to assist passage through the birth canal

**neonatal jaundice**
yellowish pallor common in the first few days of life due to immaturity of the liver

**anoxia**
deprivation of oxygen during birth process and soon after that can result in serious neurological damage within minutes

**Apgar scale**
neonatal assessment scale with five subtests: Appearance (color), Pulse (heart rate), Grimace (reflex irritability), Activity (muscle tone), and Respiration (breathing)

## Measuring Neonatal Health

**LO 3.3.1 Identify the features of the two major scales most often used to assess neonatal health.**

In the transition from the fetal environment to the outside world, the first few minutes are crucial. It is especially important for neonates to begin to breathe on their own, after months of obtaining their oxygen through their mothers' umbilical cord. Most neonates begin to breathe as soon as they are exposed to air, even before the umbilical cord is cut. However, if they do not, the consequences can become severe very quickly. Deprivation of oxygen, a condition known as **anoxia**, results in swift and massive death of brain cells. If a neonate suffers anoxia for even a few minutes, the result can be permanent cognitive damage.

Because the transition from the fetal environment is crucial and occasionally problematic, methods have been developed for assessing neonatal health. In Western countries, two of the most widely used methods are the Apgar scale and the Brazelton Neonatal Behavioral Assessment Scale (NBAS).

The **Apgar scale** is named after its creator, the pediatrician Virginia Apgar (1953). In a clever use of her last name, as you can see in Table 3.1, the letters *APGAR* correspond to the five subtests that comprise the scale: Appearance (color), Pulse (heart rate), Grimace (reflex irritability), Activity (muscle tone), and Respiration (breathing). The neonate is rated on each of these five subscales, receiving a score of 0, 1, or 2, with the overall score ranging from 0–10. Neonates are rated twice, first about a minute after birth and then after 5 minutes, because sometimes a neonate's condition can change quickly during this time, for better or worse.

A score of 7 to 10 means the neonate is in good to excellent condition. Scores in this range are received by over 98% of American babies (Martin et al., 2003). If the score is from 4 to 6, anoxia is likely and the neonate is in need of assistance to begin breathing. If the score is 3 or below, the neonate is in life-threatening danger and immediate medical assistance is required. In addition to their usefulness immediately after birth, Apgar scores predict risk of neonatal and infant death (Iliodromiti et al., 2014). This is highly important information as it

**Table 3.1** The Apgar Scale

**Total Score:** 7–10 = Good to excellent condition; 4–6 = Requires assistance to breathe; 3 or below = Life-threatening danger

| Subtest | 0 | 1 | 2 |
|---|---|---|---|
| **A**ppearance (Body color) | Blue and pale | Body pink, but extremities blue | Entire body pink |
| **P**ulse (Heart rate) | Absent | Slow: less than 100 beats per minute | Fast: 100–140 beats per minute |
| **G**rimace (Reflex irritability) | No response | Grimace | Coughing, sneezing, and crying |
| **A**ctivity (Muscle tone) | Limp and flaccid | Weak, inactive, but some flexion of extremities | Strong, active motion |
| **R**espiration (Breathing) | No breathing for more than 1 minute | Irregular and slow | Good breathing with normal crying |

SOURCE: Based on Apgar (1953).

alerts physicians that careful monitoring is necessary. Upon the birth of our twins, one of our very first questions was about their Apgar scores—undoubtedly a testament to our background as developmental psychologists and our anxiety as first-time parents having twins. Even after many years, we still remember those scores and the tremendous relief brought by two simple numbers (8 and 9).

Another widely used scale of neonatal functioning is the **Brazelton Neonatal Behavioral Assessment Scale (NBAS)**. The NBAS contains 27 items assessing *reflexes* (such as blinking); *physical states* (such as irritability and excitability), *responses to social stimulation*, and *central nervous system instability* (indicated by symptoms such as tremors). Based on these 27 items, the neonate receives an overall rating of "worrisome," "normal," or "superior" (Nugent & Brazelton, 2000; Nugent et al., 2009).

**Brazelton Neonatal Behavioral Assessment Scale (NBAS)**
27-item scale of neonatal functioning with overall ratings "worrisome," "normal," and "superior"

In contrast to the Apgar scale, which is administered immediately after birth, the NBAS is usually performed about a day after birth but can be given any time in the first 2 months. The NBAS most effectively predicts future development if it is given a day after birth and then about a week later. Neonates who are rated normal or superior at both points or who show a "recovery curve" from worrisome to normal or superior have good prospects for development over the next several years, whereas neonates who are worrisome at both points or go down from normal or superior to worrisome are at risk for early developmental problems (Ohgi et al., 2003).

For at-risk neonates as well as others, the NBAS can promote the development of the relationship between parents and their infants. In one study of Brazilian mothers, those who took part in an NBAS-guided discussion of their infants a few days after birth were more likely to smile, vocalize, and establish eye contact with their infants a month later, compared to mothers in a control group who received only general health care information (Wendland-Carro et al., 1999). In an American study of full-term and preterm neonates, parents in both groups who participated in an NBAS program interacted more confidently with their babies than parents who did not take part in the program (Eiden & Reifman, 1996).

The NBAS has also been used in research to examine differences among neonates across cultures and how those differences interact with parenting practices (Nugent et al., 2009). For example, studies comparing Asian and White American neonates on the NBAS have found that the Asian neonates tend to be calmer and less irritable (Muret-Wagstaff & Moore, 1989). This difference may be partly biological, but it also appears to be related to parenting differences. Asian mothers tended to respond quickly to neonates' distress and attempt to soothe them, whereas White mothers were more likely to let the neonates fuss for a while before tending to them. In another study, in Zambia, many of the neonates were born with low birth weights and were rated worrisome on the NBAS a day after birth (Brazelton et al., 1976). However, a week later most of the worrisome neonates had become normal or superior on the NBAS. The researchers attributed this change to the Zambian mothers' custom of carrying the baby close to their bodies during most of the day, providing soothing comfort as well as sensory stimulation.

## Low Birth Weight

**LO 3.3.2 Identify the neonatal classifications for low birth weight, and describe the consequences and major treatments.**

**low birth weight**
term for neonates weighing less than 2,500 grams (5.8 lb)

**preterm**
babies born at 37 weeks gestation or less

**small for date**
term applied to neonates who weigh less than 90% of other neonates who were born at the same gestational age

The weight of a baby at birth is one of the most important indicators of its prospects for survival and healthy development. Neonates are considered to have **low birth weight** if they are born weighing less than 2,500 grams (about 5.8 lb). Some neonates with low birth weights are **preterm**, meaning that they were born 3 or more weeks earlier than the optimal 40 weeks after conception. Other low-birth-weight neonates are **small for date**, meaning that they weigh less than 90% of the average for other neonates who were born at the same *gestational age* (number of weeks since conception). Small-for-date neonates are especially at risk, with an infant death rate four times higher than preterm infants (Arcangeli et al., 2012; Regev et al., 2003).

**RATES AND RISKS OF LOW BIRTH WEIGHT.** Rates of low-birth-weight neonates vary widely among world regions (UNICEF, 2014). As Map 3.3 shows, the overall rate worldwide is 15%. Asia and Africa have the highest rates, and Europe the lowest. The current rates in the United States (8%) and Canada (6%) are lower than in developing regions of the world but higher than in Europe. Within the United States, rates of low birth weight are about twice as high among African Americans as among other ethnic groups, for reasons that may include lower likelihood of good prenatal care and higher levels of stress (Casey Foundation, 2010; Giscombe & Lobel, 2005).

**Critical Thinking Question:** Why do you think rates of low-birth-weight neonates are so high in developing countries?

The causes of low birth weight also vary widely among world regions. In developing countries, the main cause is that mothers are frequently malnourished, in poor health, and receive little or no prenatal care. In developed countries, the primary cause of low birth weight is the mother's cigarette smoking (Child Health USA, 2014;

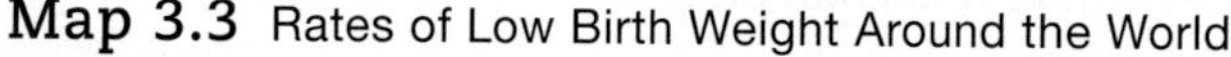

**Map 3.3** Rates of Low Birth Weight Around the World

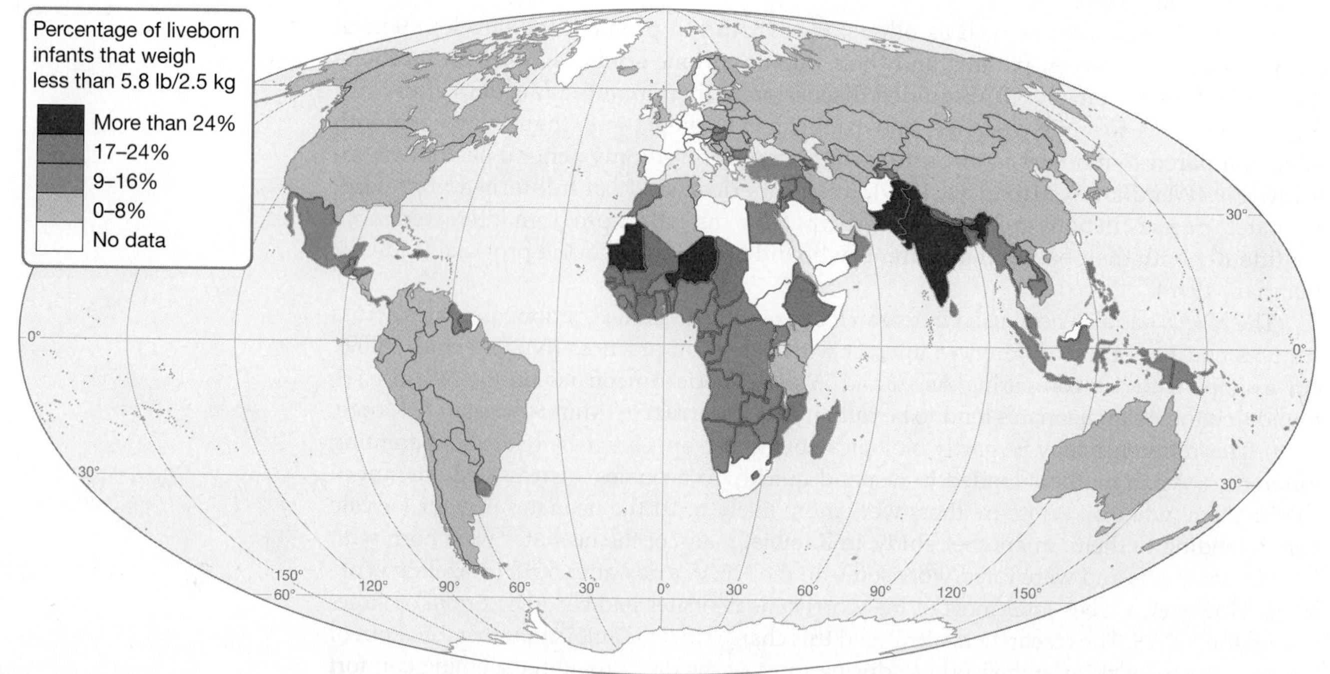

Rückinger et al., 2010). Other contributors to low birth weight are multiple births (the more babies in the womb at once, the lower their birth weights), use of alcohol or other drugs during pregnancy, and low or high maternal age (under 17 or over 40) (Gavin et al., 2011).

Low-birth-weight babies are at high risk of death in their first year of life. Even in developed countries with advanced medical care, low birth weight is the second most common cause of death in infancy, next to genetic birth defects (Martin et al., 2005). *Very low-birth-weight* neonates, who weigh less than 1,500 grams (about 3.5 lb) at birth, and *extremely low-birth-weight* neonates, who weigh less than 1,000 grams (about 2.3 lb) at birth, are at especially high risk for early death (Tamaru et al., 2011). Even in the United States, which has the most advanced medical technology in the world, 24% of neonates who weigh less than 1,500 grams die during their first year, compared to just 1% of those born at 1,500–2,500 grams (Child Trends, 2014). In developing countries, where low birth weight is most common, deaths due to low birth weight contribute to higher overall rates of neonatal mortality.

Babies born with low birth weights are at risk for multiple problems. Unlike this neonate in Uganda, most low-birth-weight neonates in developing countries do not have access to advanced medical care.

Why are low-birth-weight neonates at such high risk for death? If they were small for date at birth, it was likely due to factors that interfered with their prenatal development, such as poor maternal nutrition, maternal illness or disease, or exposure to teratogens such as nicotine or alcohol (see Chapter 2). Consequently, they were already less healthy than other neonates when they were born, compounding their risk.

In most cases, low-birth-weight neonates are born many weeks before full term. For preterm neonates, their physical systems are inadequately developed at birth. Their immune systems are immature, leaving them vulnerable to infection (Stoll et al., 2004). Their central nervous systems are also immature, making it difficult for them to perform basic functions such as sucking to obtain nourishment. Their little bodies do not have enough fat to insulate them, so they are at risk of dying from insufficient body heat. Most importantly, their lungs are immature, so they are in danger of dying from being unable to breathe properly. The lungs of a mature neonate are coated with a substance called **surfactant** that helps them breathe and keeps the air sacs in the lungs from collapsing, but preterm infants often have not yet developed surfactant, a deficiency with potentially fatal consequences (Porath et al., 2011). Where advanced medical care is available, mainly in developed countries, preterm neonates are often given surfactant at birth (via a breathing tube), making their survival much more likely (Mugford, 2006).

**surfactant**
substance in lungs that promotes breathing and keeps the air sacs in the lungs from collapsing

**TREATMENTS AND LONG-TERM OUTCOMES FOR LOW-BIRTH-WEIGHT INFANTS.** What else can be done for low-birth-weight babies? In developing countries, where few of them receive medical treatment, traditional methods of infant care are helpful. In many traditional cultures, young infants are strapped close to their mother's body for most of the time as she goes about her daily life (Small, 1998). In the West, this has been studied as a method called **kangaroo care**, in which mothers or fathers are advised to place their preterm newborns skin-to-skin on their chests for 2–3 hours a day during the early weeks of life (Warnock et al., 2010; Srinath et al., 2016).

**kangaroo care**
recommended care for preterm and low-birth-weight neonates, in which mothers or fathers are advised to place the baby skin-to-skin on their chests for 2–3 hours a day for the early weeks of life

Research has shown that kangaroo care has highly beneficial effects on neonatal functioning. It helps newborns stabilize and regulate bodily functions such as heart rate, breathing, body temperature, and sleep–wake cycles (Ludington-Hoe, 2013; Reid, 2004). Preterm infants who receive kangaroo care are more likely to survive their first year, and they have longer periods of sleep, cry less, and gain weight faster than other preterm infants (Charpak et al., 2005; Kostandy et al., 2008). Mothers benefit as well. Kangaroo care gives them more confidence in caring for their tiny, vulnerable baby, which leads to more success in breast-feeding (Feldman et al., 2003; Ludington-Hoe, 2013). The effects of kangaroo care on low-birth-weight babies are so well established that now it is used in over three-fourths of neonatal intensive

Kangaroo care, here by a father, benefits the neonate in several ways.

care units in the United States, and nearly always with preterm neonates in northern Europe (Ludington-Hoe, 2013). An Italian study found that kangaroo care was practiced in two-thirds of the neonatal intensive care units (de Vonderweid & Leonessa, 2009).

The other traditional method of infant care that is helpful for low-birth-weight babies is *infant massage*. This is a widespread custom in Asia and Africa, not just for vulnerable babies but for all of them (McClure, 2000). In the West, infant massage developed because low-birth-weight babies often are placed in an *isolette*, a covered, sterile chamber that provides oxygen and a controlled temperature. Infant massage, pioneered in the West by Tiffany Field and her colleagues (Field, 1998; Field et al., 2010), was intended to relieve the neonate's isolation. Research has now established the effectiveness of massage in promoting the healthy development of low-birth-weight babies. Preterm neonates who receive three 15-minute massages a day in their first days of life gain weight faster than other preterm babies, and they are more active and alert (Field, 2001; 2014; Field et al., 2010). The massages work by triggering the release of hormones that promote weight gain, muscle development, and neurological development (Dieter et al., 2003; Ferber et al., 2002; Field et al., 2010). In the United States, 38% of hospitals practice massage in their neonatal intensive care units (Field et al., 2010).

Although kangaroo care and massage can be helpful, low-birth-weight babies are at risk for a variety of long-term problems. In childhood, low birth weight predicts physical problems such as asthma and cognitive problems that include language delays and poor school performance (Davis, 2003; Marlow et al., 2005). In adolescence, low birth weight predicts relatively low intelligence test scores, greater likelihood of repeating a grade, and higher risk for dropping out of high school (Black et al., 2007; Martin et al., 2008). In adulthood, low birth weight predicts brain abnormalities, attention deficits, and low educational attainment (Fearon et al., 2004; Hofman et al., 2004; Strang-Karlsson et al., 2008).

The lower the birth weight, the worse the problems. Most neonates who weigh 1,500 to 2,500 grams at birth (3.5 to 5.8 lb) are likely to show no major impairments after a few years as long as they receive adequate nutrition and medical care, but neonates weighing less than 1,500 grams, the very low-birth-weight and extremely low-birth-weight babies, are likely to have enduring problems in multiple respects (Child Trends, 2014; Davis, 2003). With an unusually healthy and enriched environment, some of the negative consequences of low birth weight can be avoided, even for very low-birth-weight babies (Doyle et al., 2004; Martin et al., 2008). However, in both developed and developing countries, low-birth-weight babies are most likely to be born to parents who have the fewest resources to provide such an environment (UNICEF, 2014).

## SUMMARY: The Neonate's Health

### LO 3.3.1 Identify the features of the two major scales most often used to assess neonatal health.

Two of the most widely used methods of assessing neonatal health are the Apgar scale and the Brazelton Neonatal Behavioral Assessment Scale (NBAS). The Apgar scale, which is administered immediately after birth, assesses infants on five subtests with a total rating of 1–10. The NBAS, which is administered any time in the first 2 months, assigns infants an overall rating of "worrisome," "normal," or "superior."

### LO 3.3.2 Identify the neonatal classifications for low birth weight, and describe the consequences and major treatments.

Low-birth-weight neonates weigh less than 2,500 grams (5.8 lb), very low-birth-weight neonates weigh less than 1,500 grams (3.5 lb), and extremely low-birth-weight babies weigh less than 1,000 grams (2.3 lb). Low birth weight is related to a variety of physical, cognitive, and behavioral problems, not just in infancy but throughout life. Close physical contact and infant massage can ameliorate the problems.

# 3.4 The Neonate's Physical and Perceptual Functioning

Physical functioning in the first few weeks of life is different in some important ways when compared to the rest of life. Neonates sleep more and have a wider range of reflexes than the rest of us do. Their senses are mostly well developed at birth, although hearing and especially sight take some weeks to mature.

## Neonatal Sleeping Patterns

**LO 3.4.1 Describe neonates' patterns of waking and sleeping, including how and why these patterns differ across cultures.**

As discussed in Chapter 2, even in the womb there are cycles of waking and sleeping, beginning at about 28 weeks gestation. Once born, neonates' **states of arousal**, or ways of being awake and asleep, are varied and change frequently. When awake, they may be alert, but they may also be fussing and crying, or drowsy. On average, neonates in Western countries spend about 7 to 8 hours alternating between these states of wakefulness.

**states of arousal**
ways of being awake and asleep

Most neonates spend more time asleep than awake. While the average is 16 to 17 hours of sleep a day, there is great variation, from about 10 hours to about 21 (Peirano et al., 2003). Rather than sleeping 16–17 hours straight, they sleep for a few hours, wake up for awhile, sleep a few more hours, and wake up again. Their sleep–wake patterns are governed by when they get hungry, not whether it is light or dark outside (Davis et al., 2004). Of course, neonates' sleep–wake patterns do not fit very well with how most adults prefer to sleep, so parents are often sleep-deprived in the early weeks of their children's lives (Burnham et al., 2002). By about 4 months of age most infants have begun to sleep for longer periods, usually about 6 hours in a row at night, and their total sleep has declined to about 14 hours a day.

Another way that neonates' sleep is distinctive is that they spend an especially high proportion of their sleep in **rapid eye movement (REM) sleep**, so called because during this kind of sleep a person's eyes move back and forth rapidly under the eyelids. A person in REM sleep experiences other physiological changes as well, such as irregular heart rate and breathing and (in males) an erection. Adults spend about 20% of their sleep time in REM sleep, but neonates are in REM sleep about half of the time they are sleeping (Burnham et al., 2002). Furthermore, adults do not enter REM until about an hour after falling asleep, but neonates enter it almost immediately. By about 3 months of age, time spent in REM sleep has fallen to 40%, and infants no longer begin their sleep cycle with it.

**rapid eye movement (REM) sleep**
phase of the sleep cycle in which a person's eyes move back and forth rapidly under the eyelids; persons in REM sleep experience other physiological changes as well

In adults, REM sleep is the time when dreams take place. Are neonates dreaming during their extensive REM sleep periods? It is difficult to say, of course—they're not telling—but researchers in this area have generally concluded that the answer is no. Neonates' brain-wave patterns during REM sleep are different from the patterns of adults. For adults, REM brain waves look similar to waking brain waves, but for infants the REM brain waves are different than during either waking or non-REM sleep (Arditi-Babchuk et al., 2009). Researchers believe that for neonates, REM sleep stimulates brain development (McNamara & Sullivan, 2000). This seems to be supported by research showing that the percentage of REM sleep is even greater in fetuses than in neonates, and greater in preterm than in full-term neonates (Arditi-Babchuk et al., 2009; de Weerd & van den Bossche, 2003).

So far this description of neonates' states of arousal and sleep–wake patterns has been based on research in Western countries, but baby care is an area for which there is wide cultural variation. In many traditional cultures, neonates and young infants are in physical contact with their mothers almost constantly, and this has important effects on the babies' states of arousal and sleep–wake patterns. For example, among the Kipsigis of Kenya, mothers strap their babies to their backs in the early months of life as they go about their daily work and social activities (Anders & Taylor, 1994; Super & Harkness, 2009). Swaddled cozily on Mom's back, the babies spend more time napping and dozing during the day than a baby in a developed country would. At night, Kipsigis babies are not placed in a separate room but sleep right alongside their mothers, so they are able to feed whenever they wish. Consequently, for the first year of life they rarely sleep more than 3 hours straight, day or night. In contrast, by 8 months of age American babies typically sleep about 8 hours at night without waking.

**Watch** NEONATAL REFLEXES

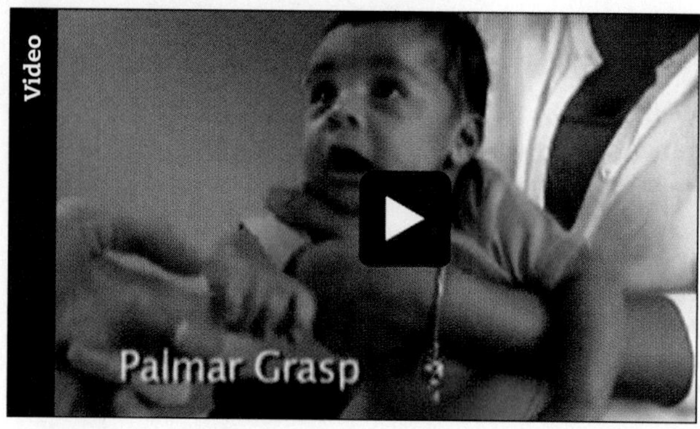


## Neonatal Reflexes

**LO 3.4.2 Describe the neonatal reflexes, including those that have an apparent functional purpose and those that do not.**

Looking at a newborn baby, you might think that it will be many months before it can do much, other than just lie there. Actually, though, neonates have a remarkable range of **reflexes**, which are automatic responses to certain kinds of stimulation. A total of 27 reflexes are present at birth or shortly after (Futagi et al., 2009).

Some reflexes have clear survival value. Sucking and swallowing reflexes allow the neonate to obtain nourishment from the mother's breast. The **rooting reflex** helps neonates find the breast because it causes them to turn their heads and open their mouths when touched on the cheek or the side of the mouth. The grasping reflex helps neonates hang on when something is placed in their palms. The **Moro reflex** serves a similar function, causing neonates to arch their backs, fling out their arms, and then bring their arms quickly together in an embrace, in response to a sensation of falling backward or a loud sound. Reflexes for coughing, gagging, sneezing, blinking, and shivering regulate neonates' sensory systems and help them avoid things in the environment that may be unhealthy.

**reflex**
automatic response to certain kinds of stimulation

**rooting reflex**
reflex that causes the neonate to turn its head and open its mouth when it is touched on the cheek or the side of the mouth; helps the neonate find the breast

**Moro reflex**
reflex in response to a sensation of falling backward or to a loud sound, in which the neonate arches its back, flings out its arms, and then brings its arms quickly together in an embrace

Some reflexes are precursors of voluntary movements that will develop later. The stepping reflex can be observed about a month after birth, by holding an infant under the arms at a height that allows its feet to just touch the floor. Stepping disappears after about 2 months, but will reappear as voluntary movement later in the first year when the infant starts walking. The swimming reflex is one of the most surprising and remarkable. At about 1 month old, an infant placed face down in water will automatically hold its breath and begin making coordinated swimming movements. After 4 months this reflex has disappeared and will become voluntary swimming movements only many years later.

Other reflexes have no apparent purpose. With the *Babkin reflex*, a neonate whose palms are firmly stroked will open its mouth, close its eyes, and tilt its head forward. With the *Babinski reflex*, when the sole of the neonate's foot is stroked, it will respond by twisting its foot inward as it fans out its toes (Singerman & Lee, 2008). Some examples of reflexes are shown in Table 3.2 and in the video *Neonatal Reflexes*.

Most neonatal reflexes fade away after a few months, as they are replaced by voluntary behavior. However, in the early weeks of life, reflexes serve as important indicators of normal development and healthy functioning (Schott & Rossor, 2003). Both the Apgar and the NBAS include items on reflex responses as an indirect measure of the neonate's neurological development.

The Moro reflex is present at birth, but disappears by 3 months of age.

## Neonatal Sensation and Perception

**LO 3.4.3 Describe the neonate's sensory abilities with respect to touch, taste and smell, hearing, and sight.**

The neonate's senses vary widely in how well developed they are at birth. Touch and taste are well developed, even in the womb, but sight does not mature until several months after birth. Next, we focus

**Table 3.2** Neonatal Reflexes

| Reflex | Stimulation | Response | Disappears by |
|---|---|---|---|
| Stepping | Hold baby under arms with feet touching floor | Makes stepping motions | 2 months |
| Moro | Dip downward suddenly, or loud sound | Arches back, extends arms and legs outward, brings arms together swiftly | 3 months |
| Babkin | Press and stroke both palms | Mouth opens, eyes close, head tilts forward | 3 months |
| Sucking | Object or substance in mouth | Sucking | 4 months |
| Rooting | Touch on cheek or mouth | Turns toward touch | 4 months |
| Grasping | Object placed in palm | Holds tightly | 4 months |
| Swimming | Baby is immersed in water | Holds breath, swims with arms and legs | 4 months |
| Babinski | Stroke sole of foot | Foot twists in, toes fan out | 8 months |

on each of the neonate's senses, from the most to the least developed. **Sensation** is the ability to feel stimulation through the physical senses, such as the ears and eyes. We also address the neonate's **perception**, which refers to how sensations are understood or interpreted. For example, a neonate might hear that a person is making sounds. That is a sensation. If the person is speaking, then—as we already know—the neonate will be able to distinguish whether or not those sounds are in a familiar or unfamiliar language. That is perception.

**sensation**
the ability to feel stimulation through the physical senses, such as the ears and eyes

**perception**
refers to how sensations are understood or interpreted

**TOUCH.** Touch is the earliest sense to develop. Even prenatally, as early as 2 months gestation, the rooting reflex is present. By 7 months gestation, 2 months before a full-term birth, all the fetus's body parts respond to touch (Tyano et al., 2010). Most neonatal reflexes involve responses to touch.

Given that touch develops so early and is so advanced at birth, it is surprising that until recent decades, most physicians believed that neonates could not experience pain (Noia et al., 2008). In fact, surgery on neonates was usually performed without anesthetics! Physicians believed that even if neonates felt pain, they felt it only briefly, and they believed that the pain was less important than the danger of giving anesthetic medication to such a young child. This belief may have developed because neonates who experience pain (for example, boys who are circumcised) often either recover quickly and behave normally shortly afterward, or fall into a deep sleep immediately afterward, as a protective mechanism. Also, in response to some types of pain, such as being pricked on the heel, neonates take longer to respond (by several seconds) than they will a few months later (Tyano et al., 2010).

In recent years, research has established clearly that neonates feel pain. Their physiological reactions to pain are much like the reactions of people at other ages: their heart rates and blood pressure increase, their palms sweat, their muscles tense, and their pupils dilate (Warnock & Sandrin, 2004; Williams et al., 2009). They even have a specific kind of high-pitched, intense cry that indicates pain (Simons et al., 2003). Evidence also indicates that neonates who experience intense pain release stress hormones that interfere with sleep and feeding, and heighten their sensitivity to later pain (Mitchell & Boss, 2002). For these reasons, physicians' organizations now recommend pain relief for neonates undergoing painful medical procedures (Noia et al., 2008). To minimize the dangers of anesthetics, local rather than general anesthesia may be used. Also, the combination of having the neonate suck and receiving sugar water has an analgesic effect for about 5 to 8 minutes and can be used for minor procedures such as blood tests and eye examinations (Harrison, 2008; Holsti & Grunau, 2010).

**TASTE AND SMELL.** Like touch, taste is well developed even in the womb. The amniotic fluid that the fetus floats in has the flavor of whatever the mother has recently eaten, and neonates show a preference for the tastes and smells that were distinctive in the mother's diet before birth (Schaal et al., 2000). In one study, when women drank carrot juice during pregnancy, their neonates were more likely to prefer the smell of carrots (Menella, 2000). Neonates exposed to the smell of their mother's amniotic fluid and another woman's amniotic fluid orient their attention to their mother's fluid (Marlier et al., 1998). In fact, neonates

## Watch TASTE

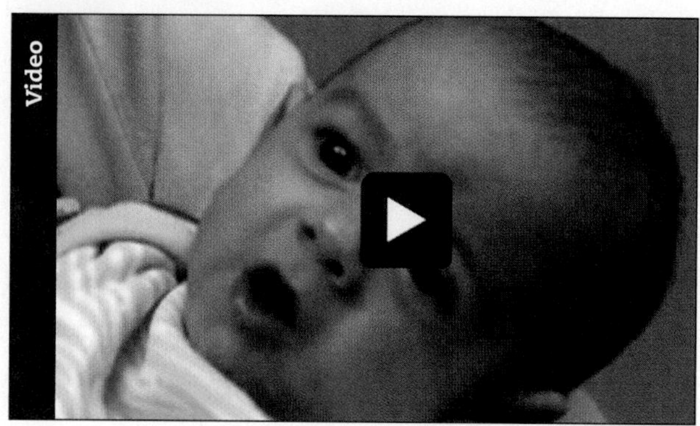


find the smell of their mother's amniotic fluid soothing, and cry less when it is present (Varendi et al., 1998).

In addition to showing an early preference for whatever is familiar from the prenatal environment of the womb, neonates have a variety of innate responses to tastes and smells. Like most children and adults, neonates prefer sweet tastes and smells over bitter or sour ones (Booth et al., 2010). If they smell or taste something bitter or sour, their noses crinkle up, their foreheads wrinkle, and their mouths show a displeased expression (Bartoshuk & Beauchamp, 1994). The video *Taste* shows neonates reacting to various tastes.

Preference for sweet tastes is present before birth. When an artificial sweetener is added to amniotic fluid, fetuses' swallowing becomes more frequent (Booth et al., 2010). After birth, preference for sweet tastes is demonstrated with a facial expression that looks like pleasure and with a desire to consume more. As just noted, sucking on something sweet has a calming effect on neonates who are in pain. In fact, research shows that it triggers the release of endogenous opioid (opiate-like substance produced by the body). Preference for sweet tastes may be adaptive, because breast milk is slightly sweet (Porges et al., 1993). Enjoying the sweet taste of breast milk may make neonates more likely to nurse successfully.

In addition to their innate preferences, neonates quickly begin to discriminate smells after birth. At 2 days after birth, breast-feeding neonates show no difference in response between their mother's breast smell and the breast smell of another lactating mother, but by 4 days they orient more toward their mother's smell (Porter & Reiser, 2005).

**HEARING.** Hearing is another sense that is quite well developed before birth. As we saw in Chapter 2, fetuses become familiar with their mother's voice and other sounds. After birth, they recognize distinctive sounds they heard in the womb.

Neonates have an innate sensitivity to human speech that is apparent from birth (Vouloumanos & Werker, 2004). Studies on this topic typically assess neonates' preferences by how vigorously they suck on a plastic nipple; the more frequently they suck, the stronger their preference for or attention to the sound. Using this method, studies have found that neonates prefer their mother's voice to other women's voices, and their mother's language to foreign languages (Vouloumanos et al., 2010). However, they show no preference for their father's voice over other male voices (Kisilevsky et al., 2003). This may be partly because they heard his voice less while in the womb, and partly because neonates generally prefer high-pitched voices over low-pitched voices.

Neonates can distinguish small changes in speech sounds. In one study, neonates were given a special nipple that would produce a sound of a person saying *ba* every time they

Neonates and infants prefer sweet tastes to sour ones.

sucked on it (Aldridge et al., 2001). They sucked with enthusiasm for a minute or so, then their sucking pace slowed as they got used to the sound and perhaps bored with it. But when the sound changed to *ga*, their sucking pace picked up, showing that they recognized the subtle change in the sound and responded to the novelty of it. Changes in neonates' sucking patterns show they also recognize the difference between two-syllable and three-syllable words, and between changes in emphasis such as when ma-*ma* changes to *ma*-ma (Sansavini et al., 1997).

In addition to their language sensitivity, neonates show a very early sensitivity to music (Levitin, 2007). At only a few days old, they respond when a series of musical notes changes from ascending to descending order (Trehub, 2001). After a few months, infants respond to a change in one note of a six-note melody and to changes in musical keys (Trehub et al., 1985). One study even found that neonates preferred classical music over rock music (Spence & DeCasper, 1987). To babies, evidently, Mozart rocks.

Like language awareness, musical awareness begins prenatally. Neonates prefer songs their mother's sang to them during pregnancy to songs their mothers sang to them for the first time after birth (Kisilevsky et al., 2003). Neonates' musical responses may simply reflect their familiarity with sounds they heard before birth, but it could also indicate an innate human responsiveness to music (Levitin, 2007). Music is frequently a part of human cultural rituals, and innate responsiveness to music may have served to enhance cohesiveness within human cultural groups.

Although neonates hear quite well in many respects, there are also some limitations to their hearing abilities that will improve over the first 2 years of life (Tharpe & Ashmead, 2001). One reason for these limitations is that it takes a while after birth for the amniotic fluid to drain out of their ears. Another reason is that their hearing system is not physiologically mature until they are about 2 years old.

Neonates are unable to hear some very soft sounds that adults can hear (Watkin, 2011). Overall, their hearing is better for high-pitched sounds than for midrange or low-pitched sounds (Aslin et al., 1998; Werner & Marean, 1996). They also have difficulty with **sound localization**, that is, with telling where a sound is coming from (Litovsky & Ashmead, 1997). In fact, their abilities for sound localization actually become worse for the first 2 months of life, but then improve rapidly and reach adult levels by 1 year old (Watkin, 2011).

**sound localization**
ability to tell where a sound is coming from

**SIGHT.** Just as with taste and hearing, neonates also show innate visual preferences (Colombo & Mitchell, 2009). *Preferential looking* is measured by how long they look at one visual stimulus compared to another. The longer they look, the more they are presumed to prefer the stimulus (Berlyne, 1958; Fantz, 1961). Even shortly after birth they prefer patterns to random designs, curved over straight lines, three-dimensional rather than two-dimensional objects, and colored over gray patterns. Above all, they prefer human faces over any other pattern (Pascalis & Kelly, 2009). This indicates that they are born with cells that are specialized to detect and prefer certain kinds of visual patterns (Csibra et al., 2000).

**visual acuity**
clarity of vision

Nonetheless, sight is the least developed of the neonate's senses (Atkinson, 2000). Several key structures of the eye are still immature at birth, specifically, (1) the muscles of the *lens*, which adjust the eyes' focus depending on the distance from the object; (2) the cells of the *retina*, the membrane in the back of the eye that collects visual information and converts it into a form that can be sent to the brain; (3) the *cones*, which identify colors, and (4) the *optic nerve*, which transmits visual information from the retina to the brain.

At birth, neonates' vision is estimated to range from 20/200 to 20/600, which means that the accuracy of their perception of an object 20 feet away is comparable to a person with normal 20/20 vision looking at the same object from 200 to 600 feet away (Cavallini et al., 2002). Their **visual acuity**, or clarity of vision, is best at a distance of 8–14 inches. Vision improves steadily as their eyes mature, and reaches 20/20 sometime in the second half of the first year.

Babies prefer to look at human faces over any other pattern.

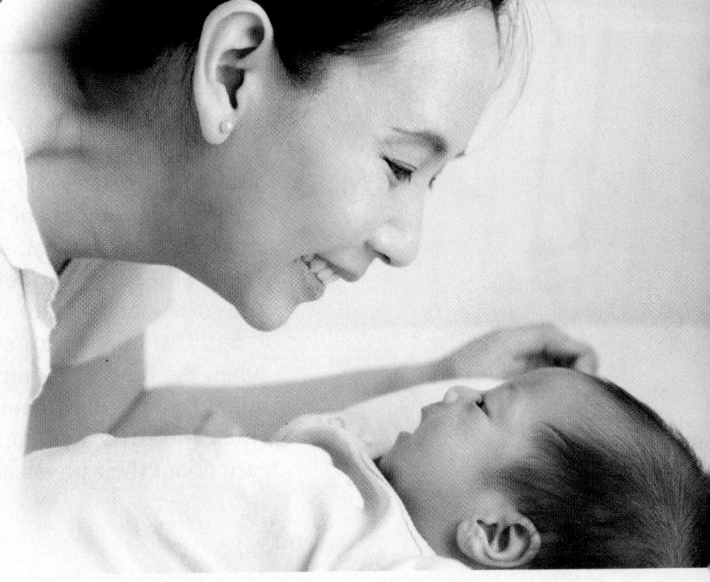

Despite their inability to see clearly objects that are far away, neonates do perceive both size and shape constancy within the first week of life (Atkinson & Braddick, 2013; Cook & Birch, 1984; Slater et al., 2010). **Size constancy** is the perception that two objects are the same size, even if it might look like one is smaller than the other because it is farther away. **Shape constancy** is the perception that the shape of an object is the same, even if it might look differently from different angles.

**size constancy**
the perception that two objects are the same size, even if it might look like one is smaller than the other because it is farther away

**shape constancy**
the perception that the shape of an object is the same, even if it might look differently from different angles

Color vision is limited at birth. Neonates can distinguish between red and white but not between white and other colors, probably because the cones are immature (Kellman & Arterberry, 2006). By 4 months old, however, infants are similar to adults in their perception of colors (Alexander & Hines, 2000).

Neonates' capacity for *binocular vision*, combining information from both eyes for perceiving depth and motion, is evidently also quite limited at birth but matures quickly, by about 3–4 months old (Atkinson, 2000). Binocular vision is important because it allows us to perceive depth. **Depth perception** becomes particularly important once babies become mobile. Once mobile, babies may bump into things or fall off the edge of surfaces unless they can use depth perception to anticipate hazards.

**depth perception**
ability to discern the relative distance of objects in the environment

This was first demonstrated in a classic experiment by Eleanor Gibson and James Walk (1960). They constructed a glass-covered table with a checkered pattern below the glass, but on one half of the table the checkered pattern was just below the surface whereas on the other half it was about 2 feet below, giving the appearance of a "visual cliff" in the middle of the table. The infants in the study (ages 6–14 months) were happy to crawl around on the "shallow" side of the cliff, but most would not cross over to the "deep" side, even when their mothers stood on the other side of it and beckoned them encouragingly. This showed that they had attained depth perception.

However, newly mobile infants were much more likely than experienced crawlers to venture onto the deep side (Bertenthal & Campos, 1984). This suggests a bidirectional relation between perceptual and motor development. In other words, what we perceive influences our movements but we also gain new perceptual knowledge as we engage in physical activities (Adolph & Robinson, 2013; Savelsbergh et al., 2013). Gibson (1988, p. 27) argued that a "cognitive revolution" takes place when we become mobile. An extensive research program by Karen Adolph and colleagues has since supported the idea that infants' and toddlers' experience with crawling and walking influences their understanding of depth and the extent to which they hazard onto dangerous slopes and across risky cliffs (Adolph & Robinson, 2013).

**intermodal perception**
integration and coordination of information from two or more senses

An infant refuses to cross the visual cliff. She clearly perceives depth–and danger.

Even as motor experience is necessary to the development and refinement of perception and cognition, research with the visual cliff that has relied on other measurements indicates that some degree of depth perception exists prior to mobility. For example, 2- to 4-month-olds who are placed on the shallow and deep sides of the visual cliff have different heart rates (Campos et al., 1970).

**INTERMODAL PERCEPTION.** So far we have focused on the senses in isolation from one another. The integration and coordination of sensory information is called **intermodal perception** (Lewkowitz & Lickliter, 2013). Even neonates possess a rudimentary form of this ability. When they hear a sound they look in the direction it came from, indicating coordination of auditory and visual responses. Over the course of the first year, intermodal perception develops further, however. One-month-old infants recognize objects they have put in their mouths but have not seen before, indicating integration of touch and sight (Schweinle & Wilcox, 2004). Four-month-old infants look longer at a video of a puppet jumping up and down in time with music than at the same puppet when the jumping does not match the music, suggesting that the correspondence of visual and auditory stimuli appeals to them (Spelke, 1979). By 8 months, infants can even match an unfamiliar person's face with the correct voice when the faces and voices vary on the basis of age and gender, indicating a developing ability to coordinate visual and auditory information (Patterson & Werker, 2002). Thus, the early development of intermodal perception helps neonates and infants learn about their physical and social world (Lewkowitz & Lickliter, 2013).

## SUMMARY: The Neonate's Physical and Perceptual Functioning

**LO 3.4.1 Describe neonates' patterns of waking and sleeping, including how and why these patterns differ across cultures.**

Neonates sleep an average of 16 to 17 hours a day (in segments of a few hours each), about 50% of it in REM sleep. By 4 months of age, the typical infant sleeps for 14 hours (with about 6 hours straight at night), and the proportion of REM sleep declines to 40%. These patterns may vary across cultures due to differences in parenting practices such as how much time mothers spend holding their babies.

**LO 3.4.2 Describe the neonatal reflexes, including those that have an apparent functional purpose and those that do not.**

There are 27 reflexes present at birth or shortly after, including some related to early survival (such as sucking and rooting) and others that have no apparent function (such as the Babkin and Babinski reflexes). Most neonatal reflexes fade away after a few months, as they are replaced by voluntary behavior.

**LO 3.4.3 Describe the neonate's sensory abilities with respect to touch, taste and smell, hearing, and sight.**

Touch and taste develop prenatally to a large extent, and neonates' abilities are similar to adults'. Neonates quickly begin to discriminate smells after birth, showing a preference for the smell of their mother's breast. Hearing is also quite mature at birth, although neonates hear high-pitched sounds better than other sounds, and their ability to localize sound does not mature until about 1 year old. Sight is the least developed of the senses at birth, due to the physiological immaturity of the visual system, but it reaches maturity by the end of the first year. Neonates possess a rudimentary form of intermodal perception, but this ability develops further over the course of the first year.

# 3.5 Caring for the Neonate: Is Breast Best?

One of the most heavily researched topics regarding neonates is the question of how they should be fed. Specifically, attention has focused on whether breast-feeding should be recommended for all children, and if so, for how long. Here we examine the evolutionary and historical basis of breast-feeding, the extent of evidence for its benefits, and the efforts to promote breast-feeding in developing countries.

## Historical and Cultural Perspectives on Breast-Feeding

**LO 3.5.1 Describe the cultural customs surrounding breast-feeding across cultures and history.**

Both mother and baby are biologically prepared for breast-feeding. In the mother, the preparation begins well before birth. Early in pregnancy the **mammary glands** in her breasts expand greatly in size as milk-producing cells multiply and mature. By 4 months gestation the breasts are ready to produce milk. At birth, the mother's **let-down reflex** in her breasts causes milk to be released to the tip of her nipples whenever she hears the sound of her infant's cry, sees its open mouth, or even thinks about breast-feeding (Walshaw, 2010).

**mammary glands**
in females, the glands that produce milk to nourish babies

**let-down reflex**
in females, a reflex that causes milk to be released to the tip of the nipples in response to the sound of an infant's cry, seeing its open mouth, or even thinking about breast-feeding

In the human past, archaeological and historical evidence indicates that in most cultures infants were fed breast milk as their primary food for 2–3 years, followed by 2–3 more years of occasional nursing. One useful way to understand and remember this is that "baby teeth" in many languages are referred to as "milk teeth," and only by age 6 do children start to lose them (American Dental Association, 2006).

There are also indications that breast-feeding in the human past took place at frequent intervals. Among the !Kung San of Central Africa, a modern hunter–gatherer

Wet nursing has a long history in Europe. Here, a wet nurse is pictured with a baby in France in 1895.

culture, infants feed about every 13 minutes, on average, during their first year of life (Sellen, 2001). In traditional cultures it is typical for infants to be bound to or close to their mothers almost constantly, day and night, allowing for frequent feeding. This has led anthropologists to conclude that this was probably the pattern for 99% of human history (Small, 1998).

Such frequent feeding is, of course, very demanding on the mother, and many cultures have developed ways of easing this responsibility. One common way has been **wet nursing**, which means hiring a lactating woman other than the mother to feed the infant. Wet nursing is a widespread custom as old as recorded human history. European records indicate that by the 1700s in some countries a majority of women employed a wet nurse to breast-feed their babies (Fildes, 1995). Another way is substituting mothers' milk with milk from other species, especially cows or goats, two species that are domesticated in many cultures and so readily available. (According to the American Academy of Pediatrics, cow's and goat's milk should not be fed to infants because of their unsuitable balance of nutrients and risk of indigestion.)

In the late 1800s, manufactured substitutes such as condensed milk and evaporated milk began to be developed and marketed in the West (Bryder, 2009). The corporations claimed that these milk substitutes were not only more convenient than breast milk but also cleaner and safer. By the 1940s only 20%–30% of babies in the United States were breast-fed, and the percentage stayed in this range until the 1970s (Small, 1998). In recent years, rates of breast-feeding have risen to over 70% in the United States and Canada due to government-sponsored campaigns advocating the health benefits. In northern Europe, breast-feeding has become nearly universal (CDC, 2014; Ryan et al., 2006).

In developed countries, the higher the mother's age, educational level, and SES, the more likely she is to breast-feed her infant (Schulze & Carlisle, 2010). Within the United States, rates of breast-feeding are higher among Latinos (80%) and Whites (75%) than among African Americans (58%), but rates have risen across all ethnic groups in recent years (CDC, 2013, 2014b). It should be noted that these rates are for *any duration* of breast-feeding; across ethnic groups, less than half the neonates who initially breast-feed still do so at age 6 months.

## Cultural Focus: Breast-Feeding Practices Across Cultures

For nearly all of human history, until recent decades, breast-feeding has been practiced in all cultures as the method of delivering nourishment in the early months of life. Neonates are ready for breast-feeding as soon as they are born. The sucking and rooting reflexes are at their strongest 30 minutes after birth (Bryder, 2009). As noted earlier in this chapter, within a few days neonates recognize their mother's smell and the sound of her voice, which helps orient them for feeding.

Breast-feeding not only provides nourishment, it also soothes babies when they are distressed. Babies derive comfort from sucking on their mothers' breasts and from the closeness and warmth they experience during breast-feeding, even when they are not hungry. Watch the video *Breast-Feeding Practices Across Cultures* to see how mothers and expectant mothers in three countries view breast-feeding.

**Watch** BREAST-FEEDING PRACTICES ACROSS CULTURES

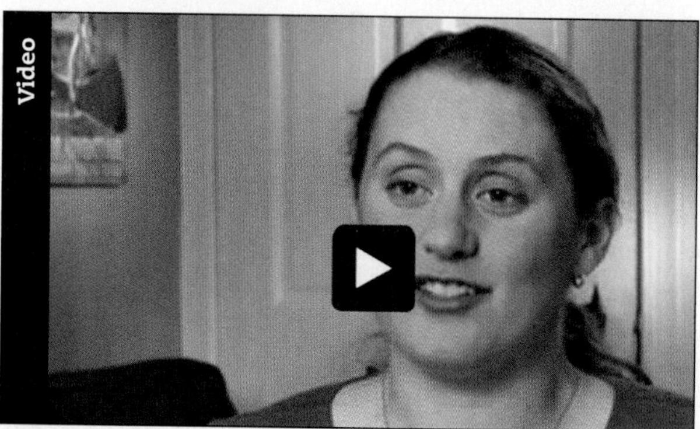


### Review Question

What were the key benefits mentioned in the video for breast-feeding? Can you think of downsides to breast-feeding by mothers in either developing or developed countries?

## Benefits of Breast-Feeding

**LO 3.5.2 Identify the advantages of breast-feeding and where those advantages are largest.**

What benefits of breast-feeding have been demonstrated by scientific research in recent decades? Table 3.3 provides an overview of key benefits for child and mother. As you can see these pertain to physical and cognitive well-being. There is no evidence, however, that breast-feeding influences the emotional development of the infant or the social relationship between infant and mother (Schulze & Carlisle, 2010).

How long should mothers breast-feed their infants? The World Health Organization (WHO) recommends breast-feeding for 2 years, with solid foods introduced to supplement breast milk beginning at 6 months of age. As you can see in Map 3.4, few women today breast-feed for this recommended time. In fact, worldwide only about half of all infants are breast-fed even for a short time (UNICEF, 2011). However, even breast-feeding for only a few days

**wet nursing**
cultural practice, common in human history, of hiring a lactating woman other than the mother to feed the infant

**Table 3.3** Benefits of Breast-Feeding

| ***Benefits for Child*** |
|---|
| • ***Disease protection***. Reduces the risk of illnesses and diseases, such as diphtheria, pneumonia, ear infections, asthma, and diarrhea |
| • ***Cognitive development.*** Improves cognitive functioning, especially for preterm or low-birth-weight infants |
| • ***Obesity.*** Reduces the likelihood of obesity in childhood, if the breast-feeding occurred for at least 6 months |
| • ***Long-term health.*** Promotes long-term health, including bone density, vision, and cardiovascular functioning |
| ***Benefits for Mother*** |
| • ***Uterine health.*** Reduces bleeding in the uterus following birth, and causes the uterus to return to its original size |
| • ***Weight.*** Improves the likelihood of returning to pre-pregnancy weight |
| • ***Long-term health.*** Promotes long-term health, including increased bone density and decreased risk of ovarian and breast cancer. However, breast-feeding has no influence on the emotional development of the infant or the social relationship between infant and mother |

SOURCES: AAP Section on Breast-feeding (2016), Feldman & Edelman (2003), Gibson et al. (2000), Ip et al. (2007), Kramer et al. (2008), Owen et al. (2002), Schulze & Carlisle (2010), Shields et al. (2010).

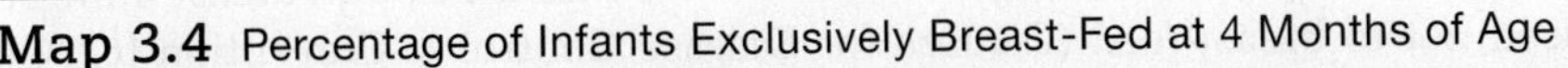

**Map 3.4** Percentage of Infants Exclusively Breast-Fed at 4 Months of Age

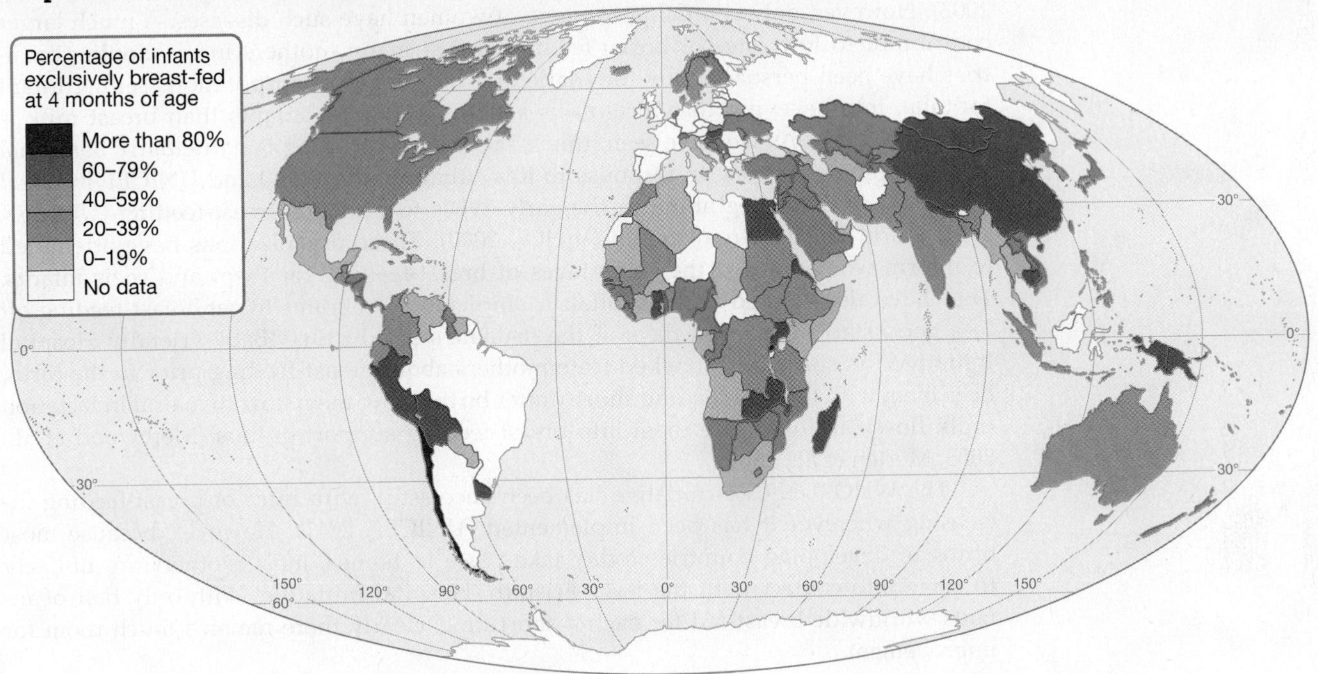

In developing countries, breast-feeding can be literally a matter of life and death. Here, a Namibian mother nurses her baby.

after birth provides important benefits for infants. The first milk the mother produces is **colostrum**, a thick, yellowish liquid that is extremely rich in protein and antibodies that strengthen the neonate's immune system (Napier & Meister, 2000). Colostrum is especially important for neonates to receive, but it lasts only a few days.

**colostrum**
thick, yellowish liquid produced by mammalian mothers during the first days following birth, extremely rich in protein and antibodies that strengthen the baby's immune system

In developed countries, where good health care is widely available, breast-feeding provides advantages for infants and mothers. However, the advantages of breast-feeding are relatively small in developed countries, as we will see in the Research Focus feature and video *Breast-Feeding Benefits: Separating Correlation and Causation*. In contrast, breast-feeding is crucial in developing countries, where risks of many diseases are higher and infants may not receive the vaccinations that are routine in developed countries. In developed countries, breast-feeding helps infants avoid illnesses such as gastrointestinal infections, but in developing countries breast-feeding can be literally a matter of life and death. UNICEF estimates that 1.5 million babies die each year in developing countries because they are bottle-fed rather than breast-fed (UNICEF, 2011). This is not only due to losing the advantages of breast-feeding but to making infant formula with unsafe water, as we will soon see in more detail.

What are the obstacles to breast-feeding? Some women have difficulty with breast-feeding, either because their infant cannot latch on properly (often a problem with low-birth-weight babies) or because they produce insufficient breast milk (Bryder, 2009). However, there are a number of practical obstacles as well. In developed countries, many mothers are employed outside the home, which makes breast-feeding more difficult (but not impossible; some use a breast pump to make milk available in their absence). Breast-feeding also makes it more difficult for fathers to take part in feeding (except via the pumped breast milk) and more challenging for fathers and mothers to share the care of the baby more or less equally, as many couples in developed countries would prefer (Genesoni & Tallandini, 2009; Wolf, 2007). When fathers are able to feed the neonate, it helps mothers recover from the physical strain of giving birth (Simkin, 2013).

In developing countries, sometimes mothers have infectious diseases such as HIV/AIDS, tuberculosis, or West Nile virus that could be transmitted through breast milk, so they are advised not to breast-feed (Centers for Disease Control & Prevention [CDC], 2002). However, only a small percentage of women have such diseases. A much larger contributor to low rates of breast-feeding is that many mothers in developing countries have been persuaded, by the marketing campaigns of corporations selling infant formula, into believing that formula is actually better for infants than breast milk is (Solomon, 1981). As we have seen, this is false. Breast-feeding is particularly beneficial in developing countries. In response to this situation, the WHO and UNICEF initiated a worldwide effort beginning in the early 1990s to promote breast-feeding (UNICEF, 2011; World Health Organization [WHO], 2000). These organizations have attempted to inform women about the advantages of breast-feeding for them and their infants. They have also worked with hospitals to implement programs to get breast-feeding off to a good start in the first days of the neonate's life. In this "Baby-Friendly Hospital Initiative," hospital personnel educate mothers about breast-feeding prior to the birth, help them with the first feeding shortly after birth, show them how to maintain lactation (milk flow), and organize them into breast-feeding support groups (Merewood et al., 2005; Merten et al., 2005).

The WHO/UNICEF initiative has been successful, with rates of breast-feeding increasing wherever it has been implemented (UNICEF, 2011). However, because most births in developing countries today take place in homes, most mothers are unlikely to come into contact with the Baby-Friendly Hospital Initiative. With only half of infants worldwide breast-fed for even a short time, clearly there remains much room for improvement.

# Research Focus: Breast-Feeding Benefits: Separating Correlation and Causation

Numerous studies have found benefits of breast-feeding for children and mothers alike across a wide range of areas. In developing countries, breast-feeding is crucial to infant health because these populations receive little in the way of vaccines and other medical care to protect them from widespread diseases. But what about in developed countries? How much difference does breast-feeding make to the long-term development of children? In the most comprehensive summary analysis (also known as a meta-analysis) of breast-feeding studies yet conducted, Stanley Ip and colleagues (2007) screened over 9,000 studies and selected nearly 500 that met their criteria for valid research methods and design. The conclusions of their analysis of the results of the 500 studies generally support the conclusions stated in this chapter, that breast-feeding is associated with a wide variety of benefits for infants and mothers. However, the authors also warned that readers should not infer causality. Why not? Because most studies of breast-feeding benefits find a correlation between breast-feeding and benefits, but correlation does not imply causation.

One reason to be skeptical of causation claims in studies of breast-feeding is that breast-feeding status is based on self-selection, meaning that women choose to breast-feed (or not), and those who choose to breast-feed tend to be different in many ways than women who do not. Most notably, the authors observed, women who breast-feed generally have more education and higher IQs. Consequently, the differences between the two groups that are attributed to breast-feeding may actually be due to their differences in education and IQ. Education also tends to be connected to a lot of other aspects of mothers' lives, such as attention to prenatal care, access to healthcare resources, likelihood of having a stable partner, likelihood of smoking, and household income, among others. The correlation between breast-feeding and babies' development could be explained by any combination of these differences.

So what can be done to find out accurately how much difference breast-feeding makes in babies' and mothers' outcomes? Ethical standards would prohibit assigning new mothers into breast-feeding and non-breast-feeding groups. However, one study that was conducted by Canadian researcher Michael Kramer and his colleagues in Belarus in Eastern Europe approximated this design. The researchers gained the cooperation of 31 maternity hospitals and clinics and the study involved over 17,000 women who—note carefully—stated their intention to breast-feed.

Kramer and colleagues randomly assigned the women into two groups, with one group receiving an intervention modeled on the "Baby-Friendly Hospital Initiative" and designed to promote and support breast-feeding by providing women with advice, information, and instruction, whereas the women in the control group received no intervention. The women and their babies were then followed up by Kramer and colleagues for the next 7 years (so far). Over the course of the first year, women in the intervention group were more likely to exclusively breast-feed and babies in this group were less likely to have gastrointestinal infections. At age 6, the children in the intervention group had significantly higher IQs, by 6 points. This is especially notable because most studies on the cognitive effects of breast-feeding find that no effects remain after controlling for education and other confounding variables, unless the children were born preterm or low birth weight. The result found by Kramer and colleagues seems to indicate a small but clear positive effect of breast-feeding on children's cognitive development. Crucially, it shows causation rather than merely correlation, because moms and babies were randomly assigned to the two groups, and thus it can be assumed that they were more or less similar in all ways except their group assignment.

**Watch** BREAST-FEEDING BENEFITS: SEPARATING CORRELATION AND CAUSATION

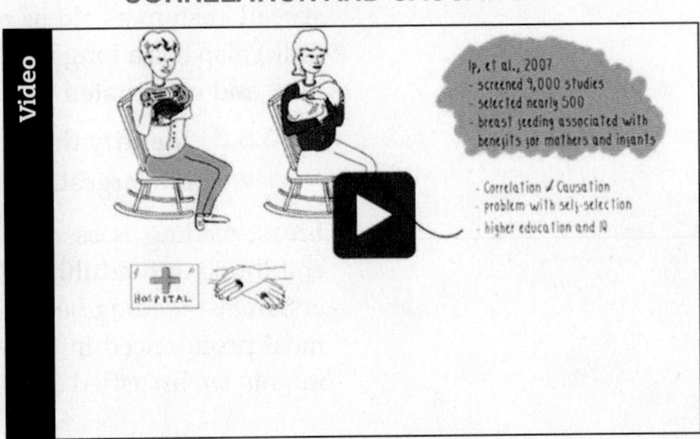


## Review Questions

1. Which of the following is NOT one of the characteristics that has been found to distinguish moms who breastfeed from moms who do not, according to research studies summarized by Stanley Ip?
   **a.** Higher IQs
   **b.** More physically active during pregnancy
   **c.** More likely to have a stable partner
   **d.** More likely to receive prenatal care
2. What was the main finding of the Kramer study that separated moms into an intervention group provided with breast-feeding advice and instruction and a control group who did not receive the intervention, when the children were age 6?
   **a.** Children in the intervention group had more frequent illnesses
   **b.** Children in the intervention group had closer attachments to their moms
   **c.** Children in the intervention group had IQs that averaged 6 points higher
   **d.** Children in the intervention group had IQs that averaged 16 points higher

### SUMMARY: Caring for the Neonate: Is Breast Best?

**LO 3.5.1 Describe the cultural customs surrounding breast-feeding across cultures and history.**

In the human past, evidence indicates that in most cultures children were fed breast milk as their primary food for 2 to 3 years. To ease the burden of frequent feedings, the custom of wet nursing (hiring a lactating woman other than the mother to feed the infant) is a widespread custom as old as recorded human history. Using animal substitutes (cow's or goat's milk) also has a long history. In the late 1800s, manufactured substitutes such as condensed milk and evaporated milk began to be developed and marketed in the West.

**LO 3.5.2 Identify the advantages of breast-feeding and where those advantages are largest.**

Breast-feeding is associated with protection from disease in infancy and better health in childhood and adulthood, healthy cognitive development, and reduced obesity. For mothers, breast-feeding helps their bodies return to normal after pregnancy. The advantages are most pronounced in developing countries. Nevertheless, worldwide only about half of all infants are breastfed even for a short time.

# 3.6 Social and Emotional Aspects of Care for the Neonate and Mother

There are few events that change the life of a person more than having a baby! The two of us had our twins relatively late—when we were 33 and 42—and by then we had been together as a couple for more than 10 years. We were used to late and long dinners, and to leisurely weekends of waking up late, reading for hours, and taking long walks. All that went out the window when the twins were born. In the early weeks it seemed like all we did all day long—and much of the night—was feed them, change them, dress them, walk them, soothe them, and adore them.

Neonates not only need protection and nutrition, they need social and emotional care as well. Here we look at neonates' crying patterns and the soothing methods that cultures have developed, and at the first social contacts between neonates and others, sometimes called "bonding." In closing the chapter we examine the postpartum depression sometimes experienced by new mothers and fathers.

## Crying and Soothing

**LO 3.6.1 Describe neonates' types of crying and how crying patterns and soothing methods vary across cultures.**

Because human newborns are so immature and dependent in the early months of life, they need some way of signaling their needs to those who care for them, and their most frequent and effective signal is crying. Adults tend to find the crying of an infant hard to bear, so they have developed many creative ways of soothing them.

Three distinct kinds of crying signals have been identified (Wood & Gustafson, 2001):

***Fussing:*** This is a kind of warm-up cry, when babies are mildly distressed. If no response comes soon, it develops into full-blown crying. It is fairly soft in volume, an unsteady whimper punctuated by pauses and long intakes of breath.

***Anger cry:*** A cry that expels a large volume of air through the vocal cords.

***Pain cry:*** Sudden onset, with no fussing to herald it. Baby takes a large intake of breath and holds it, then lets loose.

Most parents can tell the difference between an anger cry and a pain cry by the time the infant is about a month old (Zeskind et al., 1992). However, there are lots of other reasons an infant may cry, without a distinctive cry to go with them: hungry, lonely, wet or soiled diaper, tired, uncomfortable, too warm, too cold, or any other kind of frustration. Crying that falls into this general category is usually referred to as a *basic cry* or *frustration cry* (Wood & Gustafson, 2001).

Across a variety of cultures with different infant-care practices, crying frequency follows what is known as the "crying curve" (Barr, 2009): stable for the first 3 weeks of life, rising steadily and reaching a peak by the end of the second month, then declining. Figure 3.2 shows the pattern for American infants. Sometimes crying has a clear source, but there is a lot of crying in the early months for no particular reason. This is important for parents to remember, because distress in neonates often triggers distress in those around them (Out et al., 2010).

**Figure 3.2** Daily Crying Duration in the Early Months

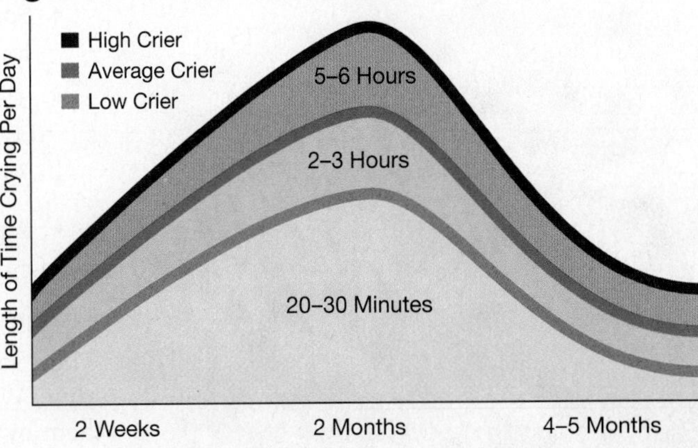


Although daily crying in the early months of life is consistent across cultures, there is wide variation in the *duration* and *intensity* of crying in infancy. Crying episodes are longer and more intense in cultures where infants are left on their own a lot and have relatively little time when they are being carried around. Four out of five American infants have daily crying episodes in the early months of life of at least 15 minutes that do not have any apparent cause (Eisenberg et al., 2011). In contrast, infants in cultures where babies are held or carried around much of the day rarely have prolonged episodes of crying. For example, in a study comparing infants in South Korea and the United States, the American infants cried for much longer periods, and this appeared to be explained by differences in parenting (Small, 1998). Korean infants spent much less of their time alone than American infants did, Korean mothers carried their infants twice as long per day as the American mothers did, and Korean mothers responded immediately to their infants' cries whereas American mothers often let the infant cry it out.

The relation between parenting and infant crying has also been demonstrated experimentally. In one study, researchers divided American mothers and their newborns into two groups (Hunziker & Barr, 1986). The mothers in Group A were asked to carry their babies for at least 3 hours a day, and mothers in Group B were not given any special instructions. The mothers in both groups kept diaries of when and how long their babies cried. When the infants were 8 weeks old, the frequency of crying was the same in both groups, but the duration of crying was only about half as long for Group A, the babies who were held more often, as it was for Group B.

In traditional cultures babies are typically held for most of the day, either by their mothers or by another adult woman or an older sister. When neonates in traditional cultures cry, two common responses are breast-feeding and swaddling (Gottlieb & DeLoache, 2017). Crying often signals hunger, so offering the breast soothes the baby, but even if babies are not hungry they can find consolation in suckling, in the same way that babies in developed countries are soothed by a pacifier.

**Critical Thinking Question:** Can you think of additional reasons why infants might be soothed by being offered the breast, apart from the comfort they derive from sucking?

In **swaddling**, babies are wrapped tightly in cloths so that their arms and legs cannot move. Often the baby is laid on a cradle board and the cloths are wrapped around the board as well as around the baby. Swaddling is an ancient practice, with evidence of it going back 6,000 years (DeMeo, 2006). Swaddling has long been widely used in many cultures, from China to Turkey to South America, in the belief that neonates find it soothing and that it helps them sleep and ensures that their limbs grow properly (van Sleuwen et al., 2007). It fell out of favor in Western cultures in the 17th century, when it became regarded as cruel and unnatural. However, swaddling has recently become more common in the West as studies have indicated that it reduces crying and does not inhibit motor development (Meyer & Erler, 2011; Thach, 2009).

**swaddling**
practice of infant care that involves wrapping an infant tightly in cloths or blankets

What else can parents and other caregivers do to soothe a crying neonate? First, of course, any apparent needs should be addressed, in case the baby is hungry, cold, tired, uncomfortable, injured, or needs a diaper change. For crying that has no apparent source, parents have devised a wide range of methods, such as (Eisenberg et al., 2011):

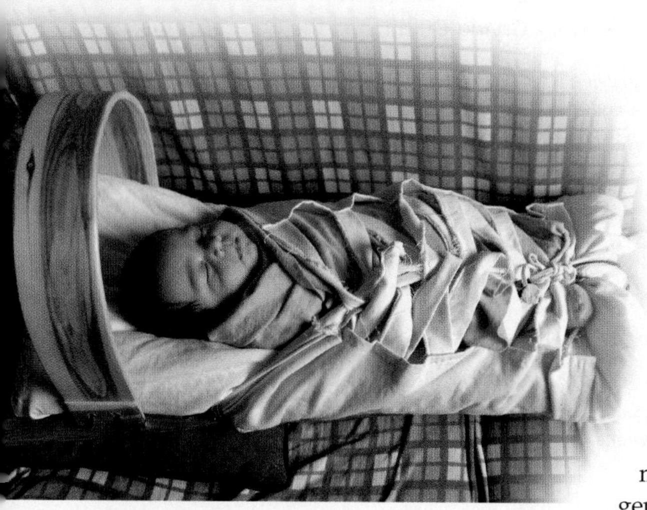

Swaddling babies to reduce crying spells is a long tradition in many cultures. Here, a Navajo baby in Arizona is swaddled to a traditional backboard.

- Lifting baby up and holding to the shoulder
- Soothing repetitive movements such as rocking gently back and forth or riding in a car or carriage
- Soothing sounds such as singing, a fan or vacuum cleaner, or recordings of nature sounds like waves breaking on a beach
- A warm-water bath
- A pacifier or a finger to suck on
- Distraction, with some new sight or sound

The common theme of these methods appears to be offering a new source of sensory stimulation, especially something gently repetitive. When our twins were neonates we usually were able to soothe them by holding them to the shoulder or singing to them, but if those methods did not work, their crying was almost always soothed by the gentle movements of the battery-operated, reclining infant seat we called their "wiggly chair." Parents with a crying neonate will often go to great lengths to make the crying stop, so there are many such items on the market today that promise to help parents achieve this goal. The video *Soothing Methods* shows some of the techniques used by parents and caregivers.

There is also the option of not responding to crying, until the infant stops. For decades, developmental psychologists have debated whether ignoring crying is a good or bad idea. Some argue that ignoring it is a good idea (unless of course the infant has a clear need for food or other care), because parents who respond will reinforce the infant's crying and thus make crying more likely the next time the infant wants attention (Crncec et al., 2010; Gewirtz, 1977; van Ijzendoorn & Hubbard, 2000). Others argue that ignoring crying is a bad idea, because infants whose cries are ignored will cry even more in order to get the attention they need (Bell & Ainsworth, 1972; Lohaus et al., 2004). Different studies have reported different findings (Alvarez, 2004; Hiscock & Jordan, 2004; Lewis & Ramsay, 1999).

**Critical Thinking Question:** As we have seen, infants cry for a variety of reasons and there are also a variety of ways to soothe a crying infant. If you were a researcher, how might you draw on this knowledge to formulate a new research question and hypothesis that elaborates on the issue of whether or not responding to a crying infant is beneficial?

**colic**

infant crying pattern in which the crying goes on for more than 3 hours a day over more than 3 days at a time for more than 3 weeks

About 1 in 10 Western babies have crying patterns of extreme duration, a condition known as **colic**. Babies are considered to be colicky if they fit the "rule of threes" (Barr, 2009): the crying goes on for more than 3 hours a day over more than 3 days at a time for more than 3 weeks. Colic usually begins in the second or third week of life and reaches its peak at 6 weeks, thereafter declining until it disappears at about 3 months of age (Barr & Gunnar, 2000; St. James-Roberts et al., 2003).

The causes of colic are unknown, but it exists primarily in Western cultures, where infants receive relatively little carrying time (Richman et al., 2010). Remedies for colic are also unknown (Hall et al., 2011). Babies with colic are inconsolable. None of the soothing methods described above work with them. Fortunately, there appear to be no long-term effects of colic, in babies' physical, emotional, or social development (Barr, 2009). However, this may be of little comfort to parents who must endure the persistent crying of an inconsolable infant for many weeks. Colic is a risk factor for parents' maltreatment of their babies (Flaherty et al., 2010; Zeskind & Lester, 2001), so it is very important for parents to seek help and support if they feel themselves reaching the breaking point.

## Watch SOOTHING METHODS

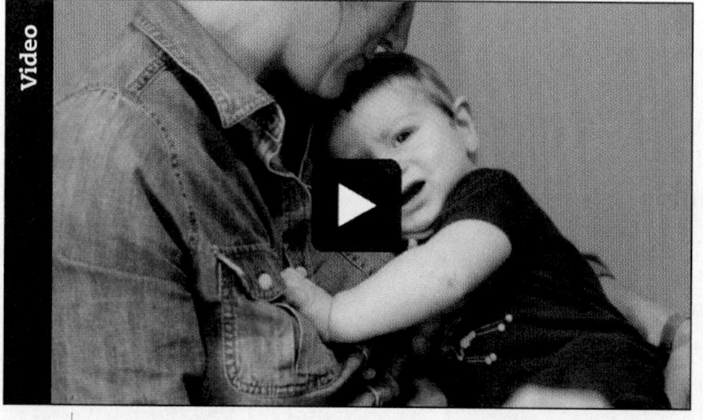

## Bonding: Myth and Truth

**LO 3.6.2 Describe the extent to which human mothers "bond" with their neonates and the extent to which this claim has been exaggerated.**

Goslings will imprint to the first moving object they see, which is usually—but not always—the mother goose. Here, the biologist Konrad Lorenz leads three goslings on a swim.

If you were to peruse parenting Web sites, it would not take long to receive advice such as: "The first few weeks of your baby's life help set the stage for your relationship," or "Try to have skin-to-skin contact with your baby as soon as you can. Your newborn bonds through touch and smell," or "I recommend that parents spend as much time in skin-to-skin and eye-to-eye contact as possible—what I call birth bonding." Is it true that there is such a thing as bonding, and that it requires mother and baby to be in contact as soon after birth as possible?

Well—it is true of some species, such as geese. Especially among birds, the first minutes after birth are a critical period for relations between mother and offspring. Geese form an instant and enduring bond to the first moving object they see, a phenomenon known as **imprinting**. Usually this first object is their mother, of course, and imprinting quickly to her promotes their survival because they will follow her everywhere she goes when they begin waddling around soon after birth. Konrad Lorenz (1957), who first identified the imprinting process, showed that geese would imprint to any moving object they saw soon after birth (including him—see the photo).

**imprinting**
instant and enduring bond to the first moving object seen after birth; common in birds

Some physicians, learning of this research, applied it to humans and asserted that in humans, too, the first few minutes and hours after birth are critical to mother–infant **bonding** (Klaus & Kennell, 1976). Without contact with the mother shortly after birth, these physicians claimed, the baby's future development is jeopardized. However, when systematic research was done to test this hypothesis, it turned out not to be true (Lamb, 1994; Redshaw, 1997; Weinberg, 2004). Humans are not birds, and they are not at risk for later emotional and social problems if they do not bond with a caregiver in the first minutes, hours, or days after birth. In fact, there is ample time to build a positive parent-child relationship.

**bonding**
invalid claim that in humans the first few minutes and hours after birth are critical to mother–infant relationships

Nevertheless, this is a rare example of a false idea having good effects. As described earlier in the chapter, in developed countries the birth process had become highly medical by the 1950s and 1960s. Although bonding claims were false, the possibility that they were true led hospitals all over the world to reexamine their policies of sedating the mother and separating mother and child immediately after birth (Lamb, 1994). Subsequently, during the 1970s and after, hospital policies changed so that mother, child, and even father could all be in close contact after the birth. This may not be necessary for the baby's successful later development, but there is no reason not to allow it, and it does alleviate parents' anxieties and promotes feelings of warmth and confidence in caring for their newborn child (Bergström et al., 2009). More on the development of the parent-infant relationship will be presented in Chapter 9.

## Postpartum Depression

**LO 3.6.3 Describe the reasons for postpartum depression and its consequences for children.**

Although the birth of a child is often greeted with joy, some parents experience a difficult time emotionally in the early months of their baby's life. Low emotional states in mothers following birth may be due to rapid hormonal changes, as the high concentrations of estrogen and progesterone in the mother's body return to normal levels. However, **postpartum depression** is deeper and more enduring. Feelings of sadness and anxiety become so intense that they interfere with the ability to carry out simple daily tasks. Other symptoms include extreme changes in appetite and difficulty sleeping.

**postpartum depression**
in parents with a new baby, feelings of sadness and anxiety so intense as to interfere with the ability to carry out simple daily tasks

In the United States, postpartum depression often peaks about 4 weeks after childbirth—long after the mother's hormones would have returned to normal levels—and is estimated to occur in 9% to 16% of mothers within the first 6 months of delivery. Over half of all women who develop postpartum depression still suffer symptoms a year later (American Psychological Association, 2014; Clay & Seehusen, 2004). Fairly similar to the United States, prevalence rates for developed countries are estimated at around 7% to 13%. Recent research in developing countries indicates that rates vary widely, from 5% in Nepal to 50% in Guyana. As a whole, though, prevalence rates are higher in developing countries than in developed ones (Parsons et al., 2012). Map 3.5 shows the prevalence of maternal postpartum depression for 25 developing countries.

Why do some women and not others develop postpartum depression? Research in developed countries shows that women are at higher risk for postpartum depression if they have a history of any psychopathology, including previous episodes of postpartum depression (Parsons et al., 2012). This suggests that for postpartum depression, as for other forms of depression, some people may have a genetic vulnerability to becoming depressed when they experience intense life stresses. Women are also more likely to experience postpartum depression if they lack social support (Iles et al., 2011), or have a poor marital or partner relationship (Parsons et al., 2012). Thus, even if a mother has a genetic vulnerability to depression, it is unlikely to be expressed unless she also experiences a social and cultural context in which social support is lacking. For fathers, postpartum depression may result from the challenges of reconciling their personal and work-related needs with the demands of being a father (Genesoni & Tallandini, 2009; Ramchandani et al., 2005). Studies in the United States and the United Kingdom report that about 4% of fathers experience postpartum depression in the months following the birth of their child (Dennis, 2004; Ramchandani et al., 2005).

In both developed and developing countries, poverty and economic adversity are associated with maternal postpartum depression, and the higher rates of poverty in developing countries may be one reason for their overall higher postpartum depression rates. In developing countries, women with HIV/AIDS are also more likely to develop postpartum

**Map 3.5** Prevalence of Maternal Postpartum Depression in 25 Developing Countries

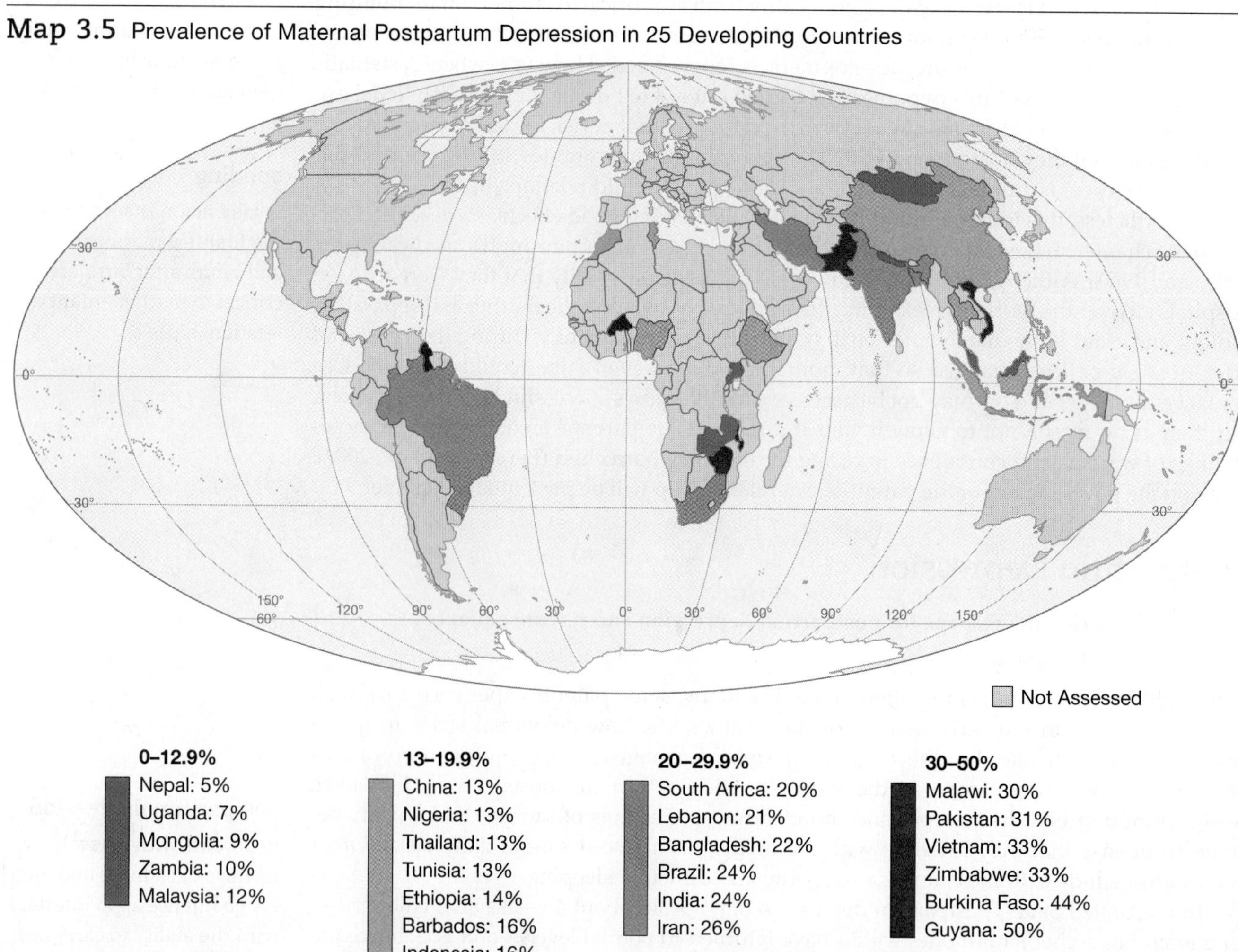

depression, as are women who give birth to a female child in countries where there is a premium on having sons (Parsons et al., 2012). As in developed countries, women who lack social support or who experience marital or family conflict are also more vulnerable to postpartum depression (Parsons et al., 2012).

In one study that included new mothers from 11 countries from four different continents, there was universal agreement that practical and emotional support from partners and family was important to overcoming postpartum depression. In developed countries, postpartum depression was also often seen as an illness requiring possible intervention of health professionals, and the United States was the only country where antidepressant medication was mentioned (Oates et al., 2004).

Women suffering from postpartum depression can benefit from psychotherapy, especially if paired with other supportive interventions such as partner support.

A review of studies, most of which were conducted in the United States, concluded that psychotherapy is often effective, especially if paired with other supportive interventions such as peer support, counseling by a health visitor, and partner support (Fitelson et al., 2011). Antidepressant medications may be helpful, but studies of their effectiveness have been limited. If used by breast-feeding mothers, certain antidepressants appear to be safer for nursing babies than others. Finally, there is insufficient evidence of the effectiveness of exercise, acupuncture, bright light therapy, and massage, although these interventions are low-risk and may have health benefits for the mother.

In terms of the impact of postpartum depression on child development, mothers' and fathers' postpartum depression is related to children's developmental problems in infancy and beyond. Almost all of this research has been carried out in developed countries (Parsons et al., 2012). Here, numerous studies of mothers with postpartum depression have found that their infants are more likely than other infants to be irritable, to have problems eating and sleeping, and to have difficulty forming attachments (Herrera et al., 2004; Martins & Gaffan, 2000). In later development, the children are at risk for being withdrawn or displaying antisocial behavior (Nylen et al., 2006). Children of fathers with postpartum depression have been found to have similar risks for their development (Kane & Garber, 2004; Ramchandani et al., 2005).

Of course, all of these studies are subject to the research design problem we discussed in Chapter 2, of passive and evocative genotype → environment effects. That is, the children in these studies received not only their environment from their parents but also their genes, and it is difficult to tell whether the relation between their problems and their parents' depression is due to genetics or environment (the problem of passive genotype → environment effects). Also, the studies usually assume that the mother's depression affected the child, but it could also be that the mothers became depressed in part because their infant was especially irritable and difficult (evocative genotype → environment effects). However, observational studies of mothers with postpartum depression have found that they talk to and look at their infants less than other mothers, and that they also touch them less and smile less often at them (Righetti-Veltema et al., 2002). This suggests that the behavior of depressed mothers is different in ways that may affect infants, even if passive and evocative genotype → environment effects are also involved.

## Education Focus: Getting a Better Start in Life: Improving the First Learning Environment

In the early 1970s, David Olds was working in an American inner-city day care. Struck by the difficulties and problems that already were present in the lives of young children from low-income families, he became convinced that the children and their families needed help much earlier and at home in order to get a better start in life. His goal became to change the children's first learning environment, and he began to organize a nurse home-visitation program for first-time, low-income mothers and their children (Nurse Family Partnership, 2014).

Several decades later, this program has become known as the Nurse-Family Partnership, and it is present in more than 40 states, the U.S. Virgin Islands, and several tribal communities.

This expansion was not a hasty one. Aiming to develop an effective program, Olds and his colleagues tested the program over many years in different locations (Denver, Colorado; Elmira, New York; Memphis, Tennessee). In this research, expectant mothers were randomly assigned to treatment or control groups.

Based on this research, the Nurse-Family Partnership today involves visits by registered professional nurses to the homes of low-income, first-time mothers that start by the 28th week of pregnancy. The visits take place approximately on a weekly or bi-weekly basis and continue until children are 2 years of age. The goal is to help mothers gain knowledge, confidence, and self-sufficiency in caring for their children, thereby creating a better home environment for their children. The home visitations focus on three key areas:

(1) Teaching expectant mothers about important health practices such as having a good diet and avoiding cigarettes, alcohol, and illegal substances; and assisting the women in attending regular prenatal care appointments with their healthcare providers.

(2) Teaching new mothers how to provide responsible and competent care for their infants and toddlers, including the avoidance of violent discipline.

(3) Teaching new mothers how to make plans for the financial self-sufficiency of the family, future pregnancies, and the continuation of their education and work.

One key underlying idea of the Nurse-Family Partnership is that in order for the teaching to be effective, it requires that nurses have in-depth knowledge of the mothers' everyday lives, and their social and cultural communities. As one nurse explained, "It's a different story when you work in the community. When you are in the home, you get a very comprehensive picture of the client. You know if they have heat, if they have electricity or food. It's a whole different story." Another nurse elaborated, "As I became more culturally responsive, it was just validating to see the relationship with the client develop for two and a half years and see the powerful outcome" (Farmer, 2014).

So what are the outcomes? Is the program effective? By now, many longitudinal studies have been conducted. A recent follow-up study with the primarily urban African American 12-year old children from Tennessee found that those who had had home visits had lower alcohol and drug use, fewer internalizing mental disorders (such as anxiety and depression), and higher math and reading scores, as compared to children in the control group. There was no difference between the two groups of children on externalizing disorders (such as aggression and breaking rules) (Kitzman et al., 2010).

Another recent study in a semirural community in New York that compared mostly white 19-year-old groups of children also found a number of ways in which those who had received home visits many years earlier were doing better. They had fewer children, fewer arrests, and needed Medicaid less. These group differences, however, were only found for girls (Eckenrode et al., 2001).

As a whole, changing the first learning environment of children from low-income families and providing knowledge and social support to first-time mothers are linked to remarkably long-term positive outcomes. As children grow older their social world expands, and it is important to think about the quality of these later environments too. In subsequent chapters, we will look at the long-term outcomes of programs that have focused on school-age children.

## Review Question

The current home visitations focus on three key areas. If you were to suggest a fourth key area addressing the children's cognitive or language development, what would it be and why?

## SUMMARY: Social and Emotional Aspects of Care for the Neonate and Mother

### LO 3.6.1 Describe neonates' types of crying and how crying patterns and soothing methods vary across cultures.

Three distinct kinds of crying signals have been identified: fussing, anger, and pain. Additionally, there is general or basic crying. Crying frequency rises steadily beginning at 3 weeks of age and reaches a peak by the end of the second month, then declines. This pattern is similar across cultures, but duration and intensity of crying are lower in cultures where babies are held or carried throughout much of the day and night. About 10% of Western babies have crying patterns of extreme duration, a condition known as colic.

### LO 3.6.2 Describe the extent to which human mothers "bond" with their neonates and the extent to which this claim has been exaggerated.

Some physicians have claimed on the basis of animal studies that the first few minutes and hours after birth are critical to mother–infant "bonding." This has now been shown to be false, but the claims had the beneficial effect of changing hospital policies to allow more contact between mothers, fathers, and neonates.

**LO 3.6.3 Describe the reasons for postpartum depression and its consequences for children.**

Many mothers experience mood fluctuations in the days following birth as their hormones return to normal levels, but some mothers experience an extended period of postpartum depression. Prevalence rates are higher in developing countries than in developed ones. Some fathers also experience postpartum depression. Mothers' and fathers' postpartum depression is related to children's developmental problems in infancy and beyond, including difficulty forming attachments and antisocial behavior.

## Apply Your Knowledge as a Professional

The topics covered in this chapter apply to a wide variety of career professions. Watch this video to learn how they apply to an instructor of maternity nursing.

**Journaling Question:** Imagine yourself as a first-time parent (mother or father) in a developing country. Write a narrative about one day in your life with your 4-month-old baby (daughter or son). How do you spend your time? How do you care for your child? Who are you with? What are your main worries? What gives you the most satisfaction?

Chapter 4

# Physical Development and Health

## Learning Objectives

### 4.1 Bodily Growth and Change

**4.1.1** Describe changes in weight and height from birth until adolescence, and explain how these changes are influenced by the environment and genetics.

**4.1.2** Identify the physical changes that begin with puberty.

**4.1.3** Identify influences on the timing of puberty and consequences of reaching puberty early or late.

**4.1.4** Distinguish between female and male puberty rituals worldwide.

### 4.2 Motor Development and Physical Functioning

**4.2.1** List the major changes in gross and fine motor development from infancy through middle childhood.

**4.2.2** Describe the development of handedness, and identify the consequences and cultural views of left-handedness.

**4.2.3** Describe the advances in physical functioning from middle childhood through emerging adulthood.

### 4.3 Health and Sleep

**4.3.1** Evaluate the risk factors for sudden infant death syndrome (SIDS), including the research evidence regarding cosleeping.

**4.3.2** Describe how the amount and pattern of sleep change from infancy through emerging adulthood.

### 4.4 Health and Nutrition

**4.4.1** Describe the weaning process and the nature of infants' first solid foods.

**4.4.2** Describe the harmful effects of nutritional deficiencies on growth.

**4.4.3** Explain the role of both genetics and cultural environment in childhood obesity.

### 4.5 Preventing Mortality: Diseases and Injuries

**4.5.1** List the major causes of mortality in the first 5 years of life, and explain important prevention efforts.

**4.5.2** Describe cultural approaches to protecting infants and young children from mortality.

**4.5.3** List the major causes of mortality from early childhood through emerging adulthood, and describe prevention efforts.

THE FIRST YEARS OF LIFE ARE CHARACTERIZED BY AMAZINGLY VIGOROUS GROWTH, but also exceptional vulnerability—especially for young children in developing countries. Across the world, we have gotten better at promoting health and staving off death. Today's children, adolescents, and emerging adults are bigger, stronger, and healthier than at any previous time in history. Still, developing countries continue to be plagued by poor nutrition and infectious diseases that have been a hallmark of most of human history. Developed countries, and to some extent developing countries, are also facing new health problems in children such as obesity.

In this chapter, we take a close look at bodily growth, motor development, and physical functioning from infancy through emerging adulthood—the point in life when the body is at its zenith of health, strength, and vigor. We also look at how physical health is related to sleep and nutrition, and at common causes of illness and death over the course of the first decades of life. You will see in the course of this chapter that physical development is intertwined with psychological development in myriad ways. Puberty, for example, is a biological event, but its emotional and social ramifications are profound. You will also see that physiology and culture are intertwined. Recent research, for example, suggests that there is a genetic tripwire for obesity that has been set off in contemporary American culture.

**Watch** CHAPTER INTRODUCTION: PHYSICAL DEVELOPMENT AND HEALTH

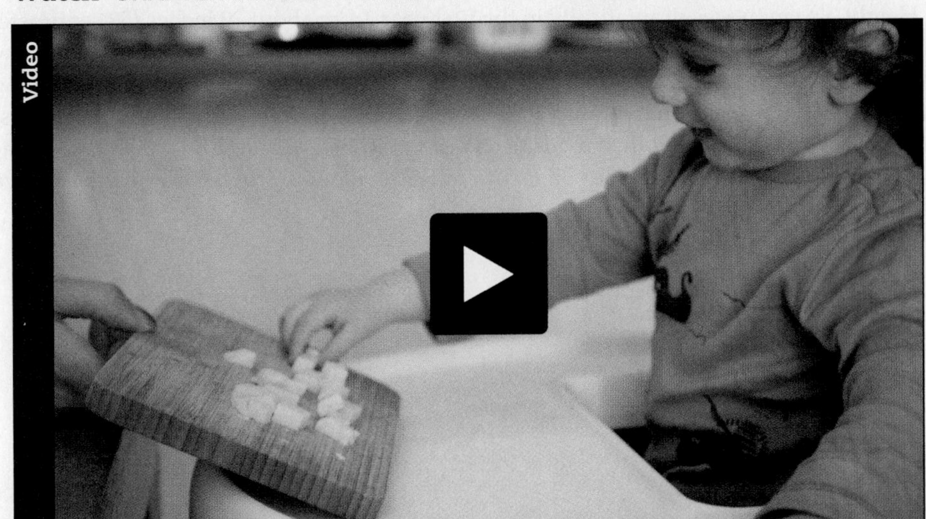

# 4.1 Bodily Growth and Change

During the first 2 years of life, babies gain weight and height at a remarkable rate. The growth rate slows through childhood and then a metamorphosis takes place in the second decade of life. It includes another swift growth spurt, the appearance of pubic and underarm hair, changes in body shape, breast development and menstruation in girls, the appearance of facial hair in boys, and much more. To adolescents and those around them, the changes can be exciting and joyful—but also annoying, surprising, and alarming.

**body mass index (BMI)**
measure of the ratio of weight to height

**cephalocaudal principle**
principle of biological development that growth begins at the top, with the head, and then proceeds downward to the rest of the body

**proximodistal principle**
principle of biological development that growth proceeds from the middle of the body outward

**puberty**
changes in physiology, anatomy, and physical functioning that develop a person into a mature adult biologically and prepare the body for sexual reproduction

## Gains in Weight and Height

**LO 4.1.1 Describe changes in weight and height from birth until adolescence, and explain how these changes are influenced by the environment and genetics.**

Babies gain weight at a faster rate in their first year than at any later time of life (Adolph & Berger, 2005; Murkoff & Mazel, 2014). Birth weight doubles by the time the infant is 5 months old and triples by the end of the first year, to about 22 pounds (10 kilograms) on average. If this rate of growth continued for the next 3 years, the average 4-year-old would weigh 600 pounds!

Babies especially accumulate fat in the early months, which helps them maintain a constant body temperature. At 6 months, a well-nourished baby looks on the plump side. Around their first birthday, however, they lose much of their "baby fat." This trend toward a lower ratio of fat to body weight continues until puberty (Fomon & Nelson, 2002). Likewise, the overall rate of weight gain slows down to a steadier pace by age 3 and will only accelerate again with puberty. The typical American 3-year-old weighs about 30 pounds (13.6 kg). From age 3 to puberty, children add 5 to 7 pounds (2.3–3.2 kg) per year.

Height also increases dramatically in the first year, from about 20 inches (50 centimeters) to about 30 inches (75 cm), at the rate of about an inch per month. Unlike weight, growth in height is uneven, occurring in spurts rather than steadily. Studies that have monitored height closely have found that infants, for example, may grow very little for several days or even weeks, then spurt a half inch in just a day or two (Lampl et al., 2001). By 3 years of age, the typical American child is about 37 inches tall (93 cm), and grows 2 to 3 inches per year (5–7 ½ cm) until puberty.

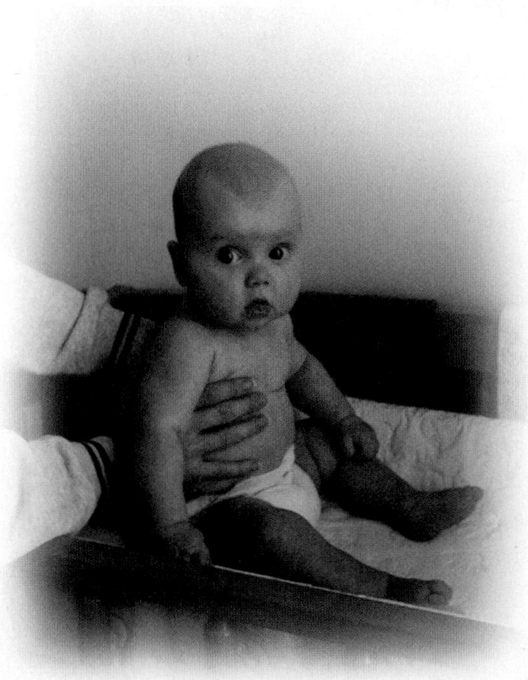

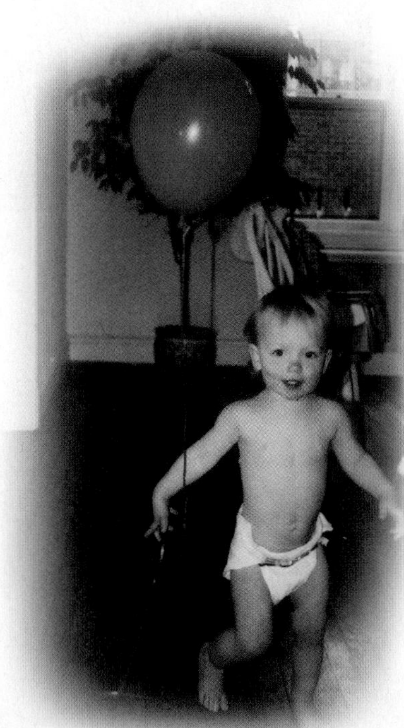

Toddlers lose a lot of their "baby fat" and often become leaner as they grow longer. This is our daughter Paris at 4 months and 18 months.

Figure 4.1 shows the average weight and height from ages 2 to 10 (Centers for Disease Control and Prevention [CDC], 2017). As you can see, girls and boys are similar in weight and height (CDC, 2017).

The ratio of weight to height is commonly measured in terms of a person's **body mass index (BMI)** (Guillaume & Lissau, 2002). Middle childhood is the time of life when boys and girls are most likely to be slim. Of all age groups in the entire life span, 6- to 10-year-olds have the lowest BMI. As we will see later, BMI is the measure used to assess whether or not a person's weight is within the normal range for their height.

Given roughly equal levels of nutrition and health care, individual differences in height and weight gains during childhood are due to genetics (Chambers et al., 2001). However, nutrition and health care make a big difference. Children in developed countries grow heavier and taller than children in developing countries. For the first 6 months of life, rates of growth are similar, because during the early months infants in most cultures rely mainly on breast milk or infant formula and eat little solid food. However, starting around 6 months of age, when they begin eating solid food as a larger part of their diet, children in developing countries receive less protein and begin to lag in their growth (World Health Organization [WHO], 2016). By the time they reach their first birthday, the weight and height of average children in developing countries are comparable to the bottom 5% of children in developed countries. This pattern continues through childhood into emerging adulthood, due to poorer nutrition and higher likelihood of childhood diseases.

As described in Chapter 1, economic differences tend to be large within developing countries. Wealthier people have more access to nutritional foods and better health care, so their children are taller and weigh more than poorer children of the same age (UNICEF, 2016).

Although children vary individually and across social groups on how much height and weight they gain, there are ontogenetic principles of growth shared by all children. In infancy, as during the prenatal period (see Chapter 2), growth tends to begin at the top, with the head, and then proceed downward to the rest of the body (Adolph & Berger, 2005). This is called the **cephalocaudal principle** (Latin for "head to tail"), and it is illustrated in Figure 4.2 (next page). In addition, growth proceeds from the middle of the body outward, which is the **proximodistal principle** (Latin for "near to far"). So, for example, the trunk and arms grow faster than the hands and fingers.

**Figure 4.1** Average Weight and Height for Females and Males, Ages 2–10

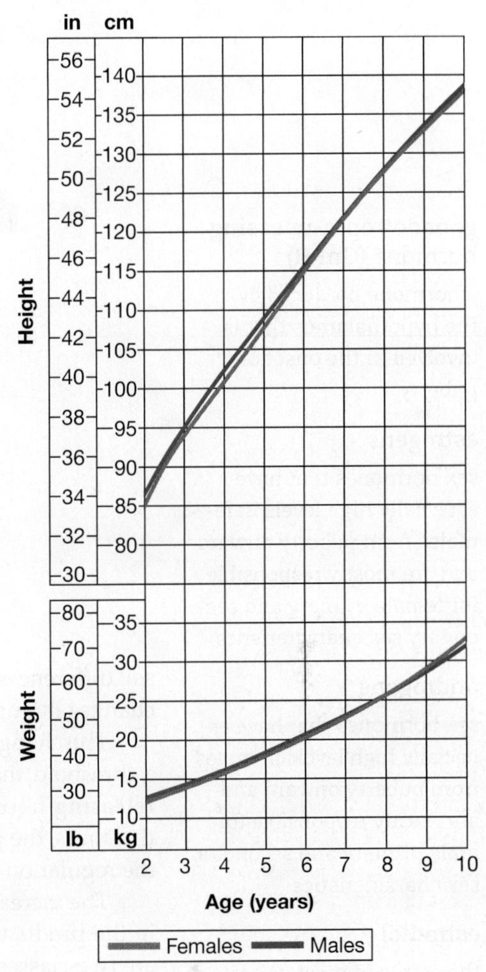


## The Physical Changes of Puberty: A Metamorphosis

**LO 4.1.2 Identify the physical changes that begin with puberty.**

The word *puberty* is derived from the Latin word *pubescere*, which means "to grow hairy." This fits—during puberty hair sprouts in a lot of places where it had not been before! But adolescents do a lot more during puberty than grow hairy. **Puberty** entails a metamorphosis that dramatically changes the adolescent's physical appearance and anatomy. By the time adolescents reach the end of their second decade of life, they look much different than before puberty, their bodies function much differently, and they are biologically prepared for sexual reproduction.

Puberty is also transformative in the sense that girls and boys become much more different in their physical development and characteristics than previously. Until puberty,

Middle childhood is the time of life when boys and girls have the lowest BMI.

**Figure 4.2** The Cephalocaudal Principle of Body Growth

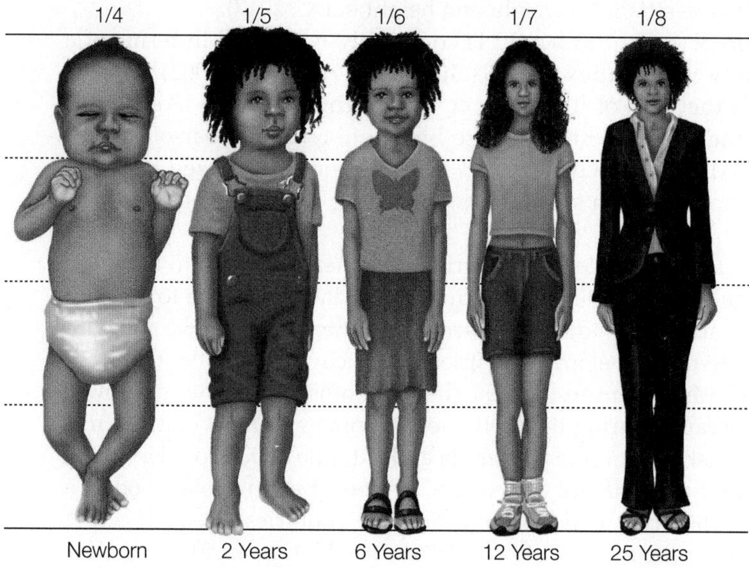


**gonadotropin-releasing hormone (GnRH)**
a hormone produced by the hypothalamus that is involved in the onset of puberty

**estrogens**
sex hormones that have especially high levels in females from puberty onward and are mostly responsible for female primary and secondary sex characteristics

**androgens**
sex hormones that have especially high levels in males from puberty onward and are mostly responsible for male primary and secondary sex characteristics

**estradiol**
the estrogen most important in pubertal development among girls

**testosterone**
the androgen most important in pubertal development among boys

sex differences in height, weight, muscle, fat, and body shape are small. With puberty, that changes in quite remarkable ways.

The changes of puberty are set in motion when the proportion of fat in the body reaches a threshold that stimulates the hypothalamus to increase its production of **gonadotropin-releasing hormone (GnRH)** (Shalatin & Philip, 2003). As we saw in Chapter 2, the hypothalamus, the peanut-sized structure located in the limbic system of the brain, is involved in the regulation of such fundamental functions as eating, drinking, and sexuality.

The increase in GnRH, in turn, sets off a series of hormonal events including an increase in the production of the sex hormones by the ovaries in girls and the testes in boys. There are two classes of sex hormones, the **estrogens** and the **androgens**. With respect to pubertal development, the most important estrogen is **estradiol** and the most important androgen is **testosterone** (Shirtcliff et al., 2009). Throughout childhood, the levels of estradiol and testosterone are about the same in boys and girls (Money, 1980). However, once puberty begins, the balance changes dramatically. By the mid-teens, estradiol production is about 8 times as high in girls as it was before puberty, but only about twice as high in boys (Susman & Rogol, 2004). In contrast, testosterone production in boys is about 20 times as high by the mid-teens as it was before puberty, but in girls it is only about 4 times as high.

Puberty is a metamorphosis. This is the same boy at ages 11 and 15.

One of the earliest signs of puberty for both girls and boys is the **adolescent growth spurt**. Figure 4.3 shows the typical pace of growth in height from the first year of life through age 17, including the adolescent growth spurt. At *peak height velocity*, when the adolescent growth spurt is at its maximum, girls grow at about 3.5 inches (9.0 cm) per year, and boys grow at about 4.1 inches (10.5 cm) (Huang et al., 2009; Tanner, 1971). For both girls and boys, the pace of growth at peak height velocity is the highest it has been since they were 2 years old.

During the adolescent growth spurt, some parts of the body grow faster than others. This **asynchronicity** in growth explains why some adolescents have a "gangly" look early in puberty. The extremities—feet, hands, and facial features—are the first to hit the growth spurt, followed by the arms and legs (Archibald et al., 2003). Also, some parts of the head grow more than others. The forehead becomes higher and wider, the mouth widens, the lips become fuller, and the chin, ears, and nose become more prominent (Mussen et al., 1990). The torso, chest, and shoulders are the last parts of the body to reach the growth spurt and therefore the last to reach the end of their growth.

In addition to the growth spurt, a spurt in muscle growth occurs during puberty, primarily because of the increase in testosterone (Son'kin, 2007; Tanner, 1971). Because boys experience greater increases in testosterone than girls do, they also experience greater increases in muscle growth. As Figure 4.4 shows, before puberty girls and boys are similar in their muscle mass. Levels of body fat also surge during puberty, but body fat increases more for girls than for boys, as Figure 4.5 shows. As a consequence of these sex differences in muscle and fat growth, by the end of puberty boys have a muscle-to-fat ratio of about 3:1, whereas the muscle-to-fat ratio for girls is 5:4 (Biro et al., 2010; Grumbach et al., 1974). Other sex

**Figure 4.3** Height Velocity for Average Females and Males

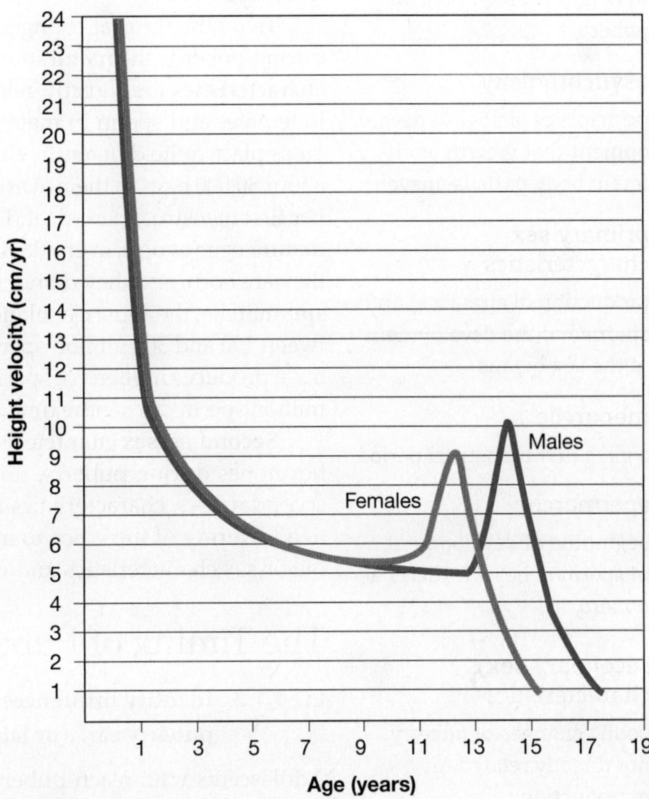


**Figure 4.4** Muscle Mass for Average Females and Males, Ages 4–18

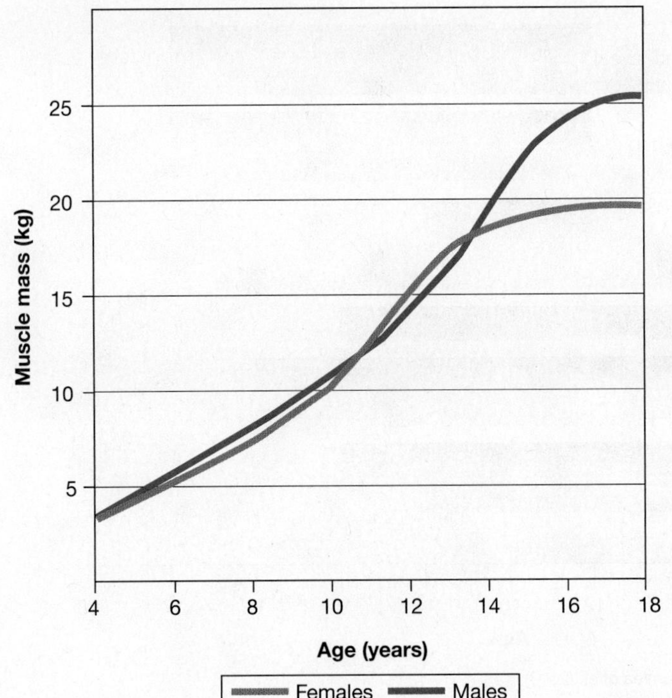


**Figure 4.5** Body Fat for Average Females and Males, Ages 4–18

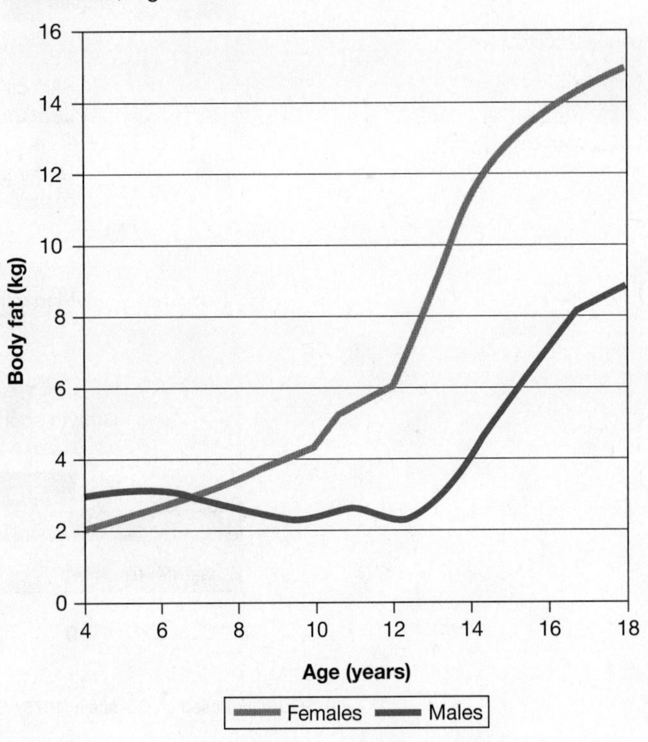

**adolescent growth spurt**
the rapid pace of growth in height characteristic of puberty

**asynchronicity**
principle of biological development that growth of different body parts is uneven

**primary sex characteristics**
production of eggs (ova) and sperm and the development of the sex organs

**menarche**
a girl's first menstrual period

**spermarche**
beginning of development of sperm in boys' testicles at puberty

**secondary sex characteristics**
bodily changes of puberty not directly related to reproduction

differences in body shape also develop during puberty. Hips and shoulders widen among both girls and boys, but hips widen more than shoulders in girls and shoulders widen more than hips in boys.

Two other crucial changes take place in the body in response to increased sex hormones during puberty, the maturation of the primary and secondary sex characteristics. **Primary sex characteristics** are directly related to reproduction: specifically, the production of eggs (ova) in females and sperm in males. As we saw in Chapter 2, the development of eggs and sperm takes place quite differently. Girls are born with all the eggs they will ever have, and they have about 80,000 eggs in their ovaries at the time they reach puberty. Once a girl reaches **menarche**, her first menstrual period, and begins having regular menstrual cycles, one egg develops into a mature egg (ovum), every 28 days or so. In contrast, males have no sperm in their testes when they are born, and they do not produce any until they reach puberty. However, beginning with **spermarche**, their first ejaculation, males produce sperm in astonishing quantities. There are between 100 and 300 million sperm in the typical male ejaculation, which means that the average male produces millions of sperm every day. If you are a man, you will probably produce over a million sperm during the time you read this chapter—even if you are a fast reader.

**Secondary sex characteristics** are the other bodily changes resulting from the rise in sex hormones during puberty, not including the changes related directly to reproduction. The secondary sex characteristics are many and varied, ranging from the growth of pubic hair to a lowering of the voice to increased production of skin oils and sweat. A summary of the major sex characteristics and when they develop is shown in Figure 4.6.

## The Timing of Puberty

**LO 4.1.3 Identify influences on the timing of puberty and consequences of reaching puberty early or late.**

Adolescents who reach puberty early or late, as compared to their peers, are sometimes at risk for problem behaviors. Research on the factors that influence the timing of puberty has flourished in recent years.

**Figure 4.6** Timing of Physical Changes of Puberty

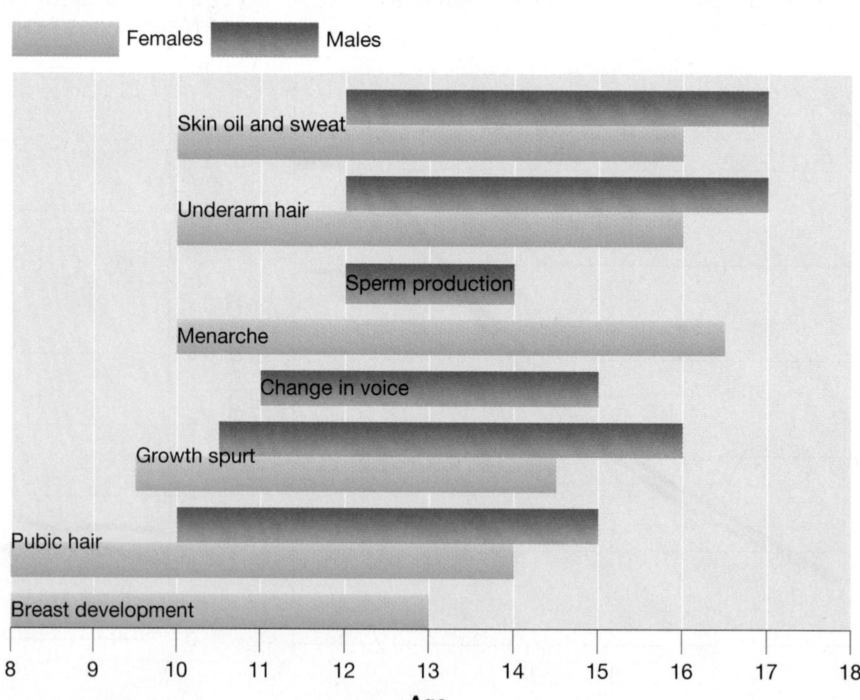


SOURCE: Based on Goldstein (1976); Chumlea et al. (2003).

**INFLUENCES ON PUBERTAL TIMING.** One influence on the timing of puberty is culture. Take another look at Figure 4.6. It is important to know that these age norms are for White American and British adolescents, who have been studied extensively in this area for many decades. Three studies, however, exemplify the variations that exist in other cultural groups. Among the Kikuyu of Kenya, boys show the first physical changes of puberty *before* their female peers, a reversal of the pattern in Figure 4.6 where girls generally begin puberty 2 years earlier than boys. In a study of Chinese girls, researchers found that pubic hair began to develop in most girls about 2 years after the development of breast buds, and only a few months before menarche, whereas for Western girls the development of pubic hair starts at the time of breast development and much earlier than menarche (Lee et al., 1963). Also, in an American study (Herman-Giddens et al., 1997, 2001.) nearly 50% of African American girls had begun to develop breasts or pubic hair or both at age 8, compared with just 15% of White girls. This was true even though African American and White girls were similar in their ages of menarche. Likewise, pubic hair and genital development began earlier for African American boys than for White boys. Studies such as these indicate that it is important to investigate further the influence of culture and ethnicity on the order, rates, and timing of pubertal events.

The age at which puberty begins is also influenced by the availability within a society of adequate nutrition and medical care (Alsaker & Flammer, 2006; Eveleth & Tanner, 1990). Evidence for this comes from historical records showing a steady decrease in the average age of menarche in Western countries from the mid-19th to the late-20th century, as seen in Figure 4.7. This downward pattern in the age of menarche, known as a **secular trend**, has occurred in every Western country for which records exist (Sørensen et al., 2012). Menarche is not a perfect indicator of the initiation of puberty—the first outward signs of puberty appear much earlier for most girls, and of course menarche does not apply to boys. However, menarche is a good indicator of when other events have begun in girls, and it is a reasonable assumption that if the downward trend in the age of puberty has occurred for girls, it has occurred for boys as well. Menarche is also the only aspect of pubertal development for which we have records going back so many decades. Scholars believe that the downward trend in the age of menarche is due to improvements in nutrition and medical care that have taken place during the past 150 years (Archibald et al., 2003; Bullough, 1981). As the inset to Figure 4.7 shows, age of menarche has leveled off since about 1970 as access to adequate nutrition and medical care has become widespread in developed countries. In developing countries, where nutrition may be limited and medical care is often rare or nonexistent, menarche takes place at an average age as high as 15. However, in countries that have undergone rapid economic development in recent decades, such as China and South Korea, a secular trend for pubertal events has also been documented (Cho et al., 2010; Hwang et al., 2003; Ji & Chen, 2008).

**secular trend**

average age of puberty decreasing over time

Another factor that influences the timing of puberty is genetics. A number of studies have shown that the more similar two people are genetically, the more similar they tend to be in the timing of their pubertal events, with identical twins the most similar of all (Anderson et al., 2007; Ge et al., 2007; Morris et al., 2011).

A systematic review of studies published between 1980 and 2013 suggests that there are a variety of other influences on the timing of puberty, including prenatal and early childhood factors (Yermachenko & Dvornyk, 2014). The review focused specifically on the age of menarche. Although the authors note that more research is needed to reach firm conclusions, they highlight the influences of:

- Weight gain by pregnant mothers that is either very low (less than 10 pounds) or very high (more than 40 pounds).
- Low birth weight, especially for White females.
- The absence of the biological father from the household, especially in early childhood.

**Figure 4.7** The Secular Trend in Age of Menarche

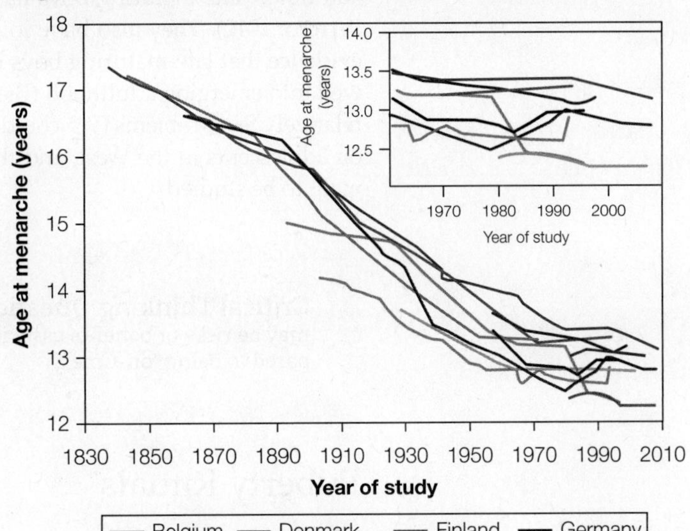


SOURCE: Sørensen et al. (2012).

Early-maturing girls are at high risk for problems, in part because they attract the interest of older boys.

**THE CONSEQUENCES OF PUBERTAL TIMING ON EMOTIONAL AND SOCIAL DEVELOPMENT.** How adolescents respond to reaching puberty depends in part on whether the timing is early or late, as compared to their peers. The results are complex. They differ depending on gender, and there is a difference between short- and long-term effects. Findings from a variety of Western countries concur that early-maturing girls are at risk for numerous problems, including depressed mood, negative body image, eating disorders, substance use, delinquency, aggressive behavior, school problems, and conflict with parents (Harden & Mendle, 2012; Westling et al., 2008). Early maturation is a problem for girls in part because it leads to a shorter and heavier appearance, which is a disadvantage in cultures that value female slimness. It can also be troublesome because their early physical development draws the attention of older boys, who then introduce them to an older group of friends and to substance use, delinquency, and early sexual activity (Graber et al., 2010; Skoog & Stattin, 2014; Westling et al., 2008). In an interview study with adolescents, Denise expressed this risk vividly when she explained:

> Since I've gotten more physically mature I get a lot of stares when I go out. Sometimes it feels nice or funny when I'm with my friends, especially when it's someone nice. But when it's some weirdo or when some older man says something like "Ooooooh," then it's scary and I want to say, "I'm only twelve, leave me alone" (Bell, 1998, p. 24).

Studies of the long-term effects of early maturation for girls are mixed, with some finding that the effects diminish by the late teens and others finding negative effects well into emerging adulthood (Graber, 2013; Posner, 2006; Weichold et al., 2003).

In contrast to girls, the effects of early maturation for boys are positive in some ways and negative in others (Mendle & Ferrero, 2012). Early-maturing boys tend to have more favorable body images and higher popularity than other boys (Graber et al., 2010; Weichold et al., 2003). The earlier development of facial hair, lowered voice, and other secondary sex characteristics may make early-maturing boys more attractive to girls. Early-maturing boys may also have a long-term advantage. One study that followed early-maturing adolescent boys 40 years later found that they had achieved greater success in their careers and had higher marital satisfaction than later-maturing boys (Taga et al., 2006). However, not everything about being an early-maturing boy is favorable. Like their female counterparts, early-maturing boys tend to become involved earlier in delinquency, sex, and substance use (Westling et al., 2008).

Late-maturing boys also show evidence of problems. Compared to boys who mature "on time," late-maturing boys have higher rates of alcohol use and delinquency (Mendle & Ferrero, 2012). They also have lower grades in school (Weichold et al., 2003). There is some evidence that late-maturing boys have elevated levels of substance use and deviant behavior well into emerging adulthood (Biehl et al., 2007; Graber et al., 2004). Late-maturing girls have relatively few problems (Weichold et al., 2003). It is important to note that this research focuses on adolescents in the West, and that adolescents' responses to puberty in other countries remain to be studied.

**Critical Thinking Question:** Can you think of other childhood events where there may be risks or benefits associated with being "off-time" (i.e., early or late), as compared to being "on-time"?

## Puberty Rituals

**LO 4.1.4 Distinguish between female and male puberty rituals worldwide.**

In contrast to the scarcity of research on adolescents' responses to puberty outside the West, there is extensive research on responses to puberty by the community as a whole among traditional cultures. Alice Schlegel and Herbert Barry (1991) analyzed information on adolescent development across 186 traditional cultures and reported that 68% had a **puberty ritual** for boys and 79% for girls. These rituals mark the departure from childhood and the entrance into adolescence. All children reaching puberty in traditional cultures are expected to go through the rituals, with no room for individual choice. When they successfully do so, they gain new status in the community (Schlegel & Barry, 2015).

Public circumcision for boys at puberty is still practiced in some African cultures. Here, three Masai adolescents from Tanzania celebrate their successful completion of the ritual.

**puberty ritual**
formal custom developed in many cultures to mark the departure from childhood and the entrance into adolescence

For girls, menarche is the pubertal event that is most often marked by ritual (Schlegel & Barry, 2015). In fact, in many cultures menarche initiates a monthly ritual related to menstruation that lasts throughout a woman's reproductive life. It is common, if not universal, for cultures to have strong beliefs concerning the power of menstrual blood. Menstrual blood is often believed to present a danger to the growth and life of crops, to the health of livestock, to the likelihood of success among hunters, and to the health and well-being of other people, particularly the menstruating woman's husband (Buckley & Gottlieb, 1988; Marván & Trujillo, 2010). Consequently, the behavior and movement of menstruating women are often restricted in many domains, including food preparation and consumption, social activities, religious practices, bathing, school attendance, and sexual activities (Crumbley, 2006; Mensch et al., 1998). Menarche is often believed to possess special power, perhaps because it is a girl's first menstruation, so the restrictions imposed may be even more extensive (Yeung et al., 2005).

Traditional puberty rituals for males do not focus on a particular biological event, but nevertheless share some common characteristics. Typically, they require the adolescent boy to display courage, strength, and endurance (Gilmore, 1990; Schlegel & Barry, 2015). Daily life in traditional cultures often demands these capacities from young men in warfare, hunting, fishing, and other tasks. In the past, rituals for boys were often violent. For example, among the Amhara of Ethiopia, boys were forced to take part in whipping contests in which they faced off and lacerated each other's faces and bodies (LeVine, 1966).

Because traditional cultures are changing rapidly in response to globalization, the puberty rituals are declining in frequency or disappearing altogether (Schlegel, 2010; Schlegel & Barry, 2015). However, public circumcision for boys is still maintained as a puberty ritual in many African cultures (Vincent, 2008). Female circumcision or cutting, which involves partial removal or alteration of the genitals, also remains common in Africa, with rates of over 70% in many countries and above 90% in Mali, Egypt, Somalia, and Djibouti (Baron & Denmark, 2006; Chibber et al., 2011). The most typical age of female circumcision is 7 to 10 years or just before puberty (UNFPA, 2015). The physical consequences of circumcision are much more severe for girls than for boys. Typically, a great deal of bleeding occurs, and the possibility of infection is high. Afterward many girls have chronic pain whenever they menstruate or urinate, and their risks of urinary infections and childbirth complications are heightened (Eldin, 2009). Critics have termed it *female genital mutilation* (FGM) and have waged an international campaign against it (Odeku et al., 2009). Nevertheless, it remains viewed in many African cultures as necessary in order for a young woman to be an acceptable marriage partner (Baron & Denmark, 2006).

**Critical Thinking Question:** Are there beliefs or behaviors in Western cultures in regard to adolescence that are comparable to those surrounding puberty rituals in traditional cultures, including beliefs about menarche and masculinity, restrictions on girls' social life, and cutting or other alterations of the body?

## SUMMARY: Bodily Growth and Change

**LO 4.1.1 Describe changes in weight and height from birth until adolescence, and explain how these changes are influenced by the environment and genetics.**

Children gain weight and height at a faster rate in their first year than at any later time of life. Middle childhood is when children typically have the lowest body mass index (BMI), or ratio of weight to height. All children's growth is influenced by two ontogenetic principles: the cephalocaudal (from top to bottom) and proximodistal (from middle of body and outward) principles. Genetics also influence individual differences between children, but nutrition and health care make a big difference. This is why children in developed countries grow heavier and taller than children in developing countries.

**LO 4.1.2 Identify the physical changes that begin with puberty.**

Puberty is set in motion when the proportion of fat in the body reaches a threshold that stimulates a series of hormonal changes. In turn, these lead to the adolescent growth spurt, muscle growth, and development of primary and secondary sex characteristics. As pubertal development proceeds, girls and boys become much more different in their physical development and characteristics than previously.

**LO 4.1.3 Identify influences on the timing of puberty and consequences of reaching puberty early or late.**

A variety of factors influence the timing of puberty, including culture, genetics, as well as prenatal and early childhood factors. The secular trend (the steady decrease in the average age of menarche in Western countries from the mid-19th to the late-20th centuries) also indicates that the availability within a society of adequate nutrition and medical care impacts the timing of puberty. Adolescents who reach puberty early or late, as compared to their peers, are sometimes at risk for problem behaviors such as delinquency and substance use. The risks, however, vary by gender.

**LO 4.1.4 Distinguish between female and male puberty rituals worldwide.**

Puberty rituals mark the departure from childhood and the entrance into adolescence. They are common in traditional cultures, and all children within these cultures are expected to go through the rituals. For girls, menarche is the pubertal event that is most often marked by ritual. For boys, puberty rituals do not focus on a particular biological event, but commonly require the display of courage, strength, and endurance.

# 4.2 Motor Development and Physical Functioning

One striking feature of human neonates is how little they are able to move around. Even if you hold neonates up, their heads flop to one side because their neck muscles are not yet strong enough to support their large heads. One striking fact about emerging adults is that on the whole they are faster and stronger than anyone else. If three people who were 10, 20, and 40 years old were sprinting a 400-meter race, who would you bet on? Nearly all top-performing athletes are in their 20s. We now turn to the remarkable changes from birth through emerging adulthood in gross and fine motor development and physical functioning.

## Gross and Fine Motor Development

**LO 4.2.1 List the major changes in gross and fine motor development from infancy through middle childhood.**

Even though neonates are limited in their motor abilities, they come into the world with reflexes such as stepping and grasping that facilitate their gross and fine motor development. Of course, experience is important too. Children's motor skills are shaped through guidance from others and independent practice.

**gross motor development**
development of motor abilities including balance and posture as well as whole-body movements such as crawling

**cerebellum**
structure at the base of the brain involved in balance and motor movements

**GROSS MOTOR DEVELOPMENT.** **Gross motor development** includes balance and posture as well as whole-body movements such as crawling, walking, and running. From infancy through early childhood, children gain a variety of new gross motor skills, such as the ability to hold their head up without support, cruise (walk while holding on to something), kick a ball, run, and ride a bicycle. Substantial myelination takes place in early childhood in the **cerebellum**, a structure at the base of the brain involved in balance and motor movements (see Chapter 2). Increased myelination enhances connections between the cerebellum and the cerebral cortex. This change underlies the child's increasing abilities to jump, throw a ball, climb a tree, and so on.

In the course of middle childhood and onward, these skills and new ones are improved upon. Children's *balance* improves, allowing them to ride a bike without training wheels. They become *stronger*, so that they can kick a ball farther. Their *coordination* advances so that they can perform movements in activities such as swimming and skating that require the synchronization of different body parts. They have greater *agility* so that they can move more quickly and precisely, for example when changing directions while playing soccer. Finally, their *reaction time* becomes faster, allowing them to respond rapidly to changing information, for example when hitting a tennis ball over the net (Kail, 2003). This improvement in reaction time in middle childhood for motor tasks is related to increasing myelination of the *corpus callosum* that connects the two hemispheres of the brain (Roeder et al., 2008). Table 4.1 lists milestones in gross motor development.

At 12–18 months many toddlers can barely walk, but by their third year they can run and jump.

Most developmental psychologists view the early development of gross motor skills as a dynamic combination of the genetic timetable, the maturation of the brain, support and assistance from adults for developing the skill, and the child's own efforts to practice the skill (Adolph & Berger, 2006; Thelen, 2001). Karen Adolph and colleagues (2003; 2013) have shown that infants and toddlers are primed to walk, but practice with walking leads to improvement in strength, balance, and perceptual judgment. For example, toddlers who are new to walking are much more likely to hazard onto steep and risky slopes than toddlers who have had more experience with walking.

**Table 4.1** Milestones in Gross Motor Development

| Age | Milestone |
|---|---|
| Infancy, 0–1 | • Holds head up without support<br>• Rolls over<br>• Sits without support<br>• Crawls<br>• Stands<br>• Cruises<br>• Walks (for some) |
| Toddlerhood, 1–3 | • Walks<br>• Runs<br>• Climbs<br>• Jumps up and down<br>• Kicks a ball<br>• Throws a small object<br>• Walks up and down stairs |
| Early Childhood, 3–6 | • Climbs stairs alternating feet and without support<br>• Increases running speed<br>• Runs with ability to stop or make sudden turns<br>• Rides bicycle with training wheels |
| Middle Childhood, 6–9 | • Rides bicycle without training wheels<br>• Increases running speed<br>• Increases kicking and throwing distance, accuracy, and force<br>• Increases coordination, as in playing a variety of sports |

**Watch** GROSS MOTOR DEVELOPMENT IN CHILDHOOD

Looking at infant gross motor development across cultures also provides a vivid example of how genetics and environment interact. In some cultures a common infant-care practice in the first few months of life is swaddling, as we saw in Chapter 3. If infants are strapped to their mothers' backs or swaddled for most of the day, they receive little practice in developing gross motor skills. These restrictive practices are partly to free the mother to work, but cultures that swaddle infants also believe that swaddling protects the infant from sickness and other threats to health (Gottlieb & DeLoache, 2017). In contrast, some cultures actively promote infants' gross motor development. For example, the Kipsigis people of Kenya begin encouraging gross motor skills from early on (Super & Harkness, 2015). Parents place infants in shallow holes and keep them upright with rolled blankets, months before they would be able to sit or stand on their own. Parents also encourage their infants to practice walking. Starting within the first month, they stimulate the stepping reflex (see Chapter 3) by holding infants up and bouncing their feet on the ground in an activity called "keguldó." By 6 months, in an activity called "kitwalse," adults start to slowly lead infants around while holding their hands. In a number of African cultures, such as the Kipsigis, that actively stimulate gross motor development, infants walk a few weeks earlier than children in the West (Adolph et al., 2010).

It appears that cultural practices can somewhat speed up or slow down the ontogenetic timetable for gross motor development, but the influence of the environment is relatively small and transient for this particular area of development. By age 6, there are no differences in gross motor development between children in the cultures that promote early motor achievement and cultures that do not. Watch the video *Gross Motor Development in Childhood* for an overview of key milestones.

**opposable thumb**
position of the thumb apart from the fingers, unique to humans, that makes possible fine motor movements

**fine motor development**
development of motor abilities involving finely tuned movements of the hands such as grasping and manipulating objects

**FINE MOTOR DEVELOPMENT.** One of the evolutionary developments that makes humans relatively anatomically distinctive among animals is the **opposable thumb**, that is, the position of our thumbs opposite our other four fingers. (Place your thumb against one of your other fingers and you will see what we mean.) The opposable thumb is the basis of **fine motor development**, the deft movements of our hands that enable us to make a tool, pick up a small object, or thread a needle.

Table 4.2 provides an overview of milestones in fine motor development. As you can see, infants learn to reach and grasp, including the acquisition of the "pincer

**Table 4.2** Milestones in Fine Motor Development

| Age | Milestone |
|---|---|
| Infancy, 0–1 | • Reaches for an object<br>• Grasps objects<br>• Transfers object from one hand to the other<br>• Uses spoon to feed self |
| Toddlerhood, 1–3 | • Holds a cup<br>• Scribbles with crayon<br>• Builds a block tower (gradually increasing the number of blocks)<br>• Turns the pages of a book<br>• Brushes own teeth |
| Early Childhood, 3–6 | • Draws recognizable objects<br>• Uses utensils such as chopsticks<br>• Writes first letters<br>• Writes short words<br>• Uses scissors |
| Middle Childhood, 6–9 | • Ties shoelaces<br>• Weaves rugs<br>• Writes in cursive |

grasp" at 9–12 months that allows them to hold a small object between their thumb and forefinger, such as a small piece of bread, a marble, or a crayon stub (Murkoff & Mazel, 2010). This allows them to begin feeding themselves small pieces of food, but the tendency to taste even the inedible remains at this age, so others have to be especially vigilant in monitoring what infants grasp and place in their mouths.

With age, a wide variety of fine motor skills are acquired. The myelination of regions of the brain that facilitates gross motor development in early and middle childhood also underlies the emergence of fine motor abilities. These abilities are also culturally shaped. Across cultures, children learn to draw and write. For example, by age 6 children are able to write the letters of their alphabet, their own names, and numbers from 1 to 10. In many developing countries, children become valuable as factory workers in middle childhood because of their abilities to perform intricate fine motor tasks such as weaving rugs (International Labor Organization [ILO], 2013). As children reach the end of middle childhood, their fine motor abilities have nearly reached adult maturity, whereas gross motor development will continue to advance for many years to come.

By about age 6, children are able to write letters or characters in their language.

## Cultural Approaches to Handedness

**LO 4.2.2 Describe the development of handedness, and identify the consequences and cultural views of left-handedness.**

The use of our fingers and hands is what defines fine motor development, but only about 1 of 100 persons is ambidextrous, or able to use both hands equally well (Rodriguez et al., 2010). The preference for one hand over the other appears prenatally. Fetuses show a definite preference for sucking the thumb of their right or left hand, with 90% preferring the right thumb (Hepper et al., 2005). The same 90% proportion of right-handers continues into childhood and throughout adulthood in most cultures (Hinojosa et al., 2003).

If handedness appears so early, that must mean it is determined genetically, right? Actually, the evidence is mixed on this issue. Adopted children are more likely to resemble their biological parents than their adoptive parents in their handedness, suggesting a genetic origin (Carter-Salzman, 1980). On the other hand (pun intended), identical twins are more likely than ordinary siblings to *differ* in handedness, even though identical twins share 100% of their genotype and other siblings only about 50% (Derom et al., 1996). This appears to be due to the fact that twins usually lie in opposite ways within the uterus, whereas most singletons lie toward the left. Lying toward one side allows for greater movement and hence greater development of the hand on the other side, so most twins end up with one being right-handed and one being left-handed, while most singletons end up right-handed. This suggests that the prenatal environment makes a difference.

Additionally, culture is a big part of the picture. Historically, many cultures have viewed left-handedness as dangerous and evil and have suppressed its development in children (Grimshaw & Wilson, 2013). In Western languages, the word *sinister* is derived from a Latin word meaning "on the left," and many paintings in Western art depict the devil as left-handed. In many Asian and Middle Eastern cultures, only the left hand is supposed to be used for wiping up after defecation, and all other activities are supposed to be done mainly with the right hand. In Africa, using the left hand is suppressed in many cultures from childhood onward, and the prevalence of left-handedness in some African countries is as low as 1%, far lower than the 10% figure in cultures where left-handedness is accepted (Provins, 1997).

Why do so many cultures regard left-handedness with such fear and contempt? Perhaps negative cultural beliefs about left-handedness developed because people noticed that left-handedness was associated with a greater likelihood of various problems. Left-handed infants are more likely to be born prematurely or to experience an unusually difficult birth, and there is evidence that brain damage prenatally or during birth can contribute to left-handedness (Powls et al., 1996). In early and middle childhood, left-handers are more likely to have problems learning to read and to have other verbal learning disabilities (Natsopoulos et al., 1998). This may have something to do with the fact that about one-fourth of left-handers process language in both hemispheres rather than primarily in the left hemisphere (Knecht et al., 2000). In adulthood, people who are left-handed have lower life expectancy and are more likely to die in accidents (Grimshaw & Wilson, 2013). A longitudinal study of ambidextrous children that followed them from childhood through adolescence similarly found that they were at heightened risk for learning and reading disabilities (Rodriguez et al., 2010).

However, this explanation is not entirely convincing because left-handedness is associated not only with greater likelihood of some types of problems but also with excellence and even genius in certain fields. Left-handed children are more likely to show exceptional verbal and math abilities (Bower, 1985; Flannery & Leiderman, 1995). Left-handers are especially likely to have strong visual-spatial abilities, and consequently they are more likely than right-handers to become architects or artists (Grimshaw & Wilson, 2013). Some of the greatest artists in the Western tradition have been left-handed, including Leonardo da Vinci, Michelangelo, and Pablo Picasso (Schacter & Ransil, 1996). It is worth keeping in mind that the majority of left-handers is in the normal range in their cognitive development and show neither unusual problems nor unusual gifts. Hence the widespread cultural prejudice against left-handers remains mysterious.

**Critical Thinking Question:** Do you have a hypothesis to account for the long-standing and widespread prejudice against left-handers?

## Physical Activity and Functioning

**LO 4.2.3 Describe the advances in physical functioning from middle childhood through emerging adulthood.**

Middle childhood is when children are most likely to be involved in organized sports.

If you look back at Tables 4.1 and 4.2, you can see that middle childhood is when a large number of gross and fine motor skills have been acquired, have become coordinated, and are increasing not so much in quantity as in quality. By this age, children can enjoy a wide range of formal and informal sports. All over the world, middle childhood is indeed a time of playing physically active games with siblings and friends, from tag to soccer, cricket, baseball, dancing, and handball. Most of the play is informal, and takes place on the street or in a park or in the school yard when a few kids gather and decide to start a game (Kirchner, 2000). However, middle childhood is also the time when children are most likely to be involved in organized sports. For example, Little League baseball is played in 75 countries around the world during the middle childhood years. In the United States, 66% of boys and 52% of girls are involved in organized sports at least once between the ages of 5 and 18 (Statistic Brain, 2014). Although boys are slightly more likely than girls to play on sports teams in middle childhood, the rate of participation among girls has risen worldwide in recent decades, especially in sports such as soccer, swimming, gymnastics, and basketball. Nevertheless, in the view of public health advocates, children do not get nearly as much gross motor activity as they should, contributing to high rates of obesity, as we will see shortly. Middle childhood may be a time of great advancements in motor abilities, but physically active games and sports compete today with the electronic allurements of TV and computer games (Anderson & Butcher, 2006). In Chapter 12, we will take an in-depth look at the positive and negative roles of media in the lives of today's children.

In the United States, the percentage of children involved in daily "physical education" programs in schools during middle childhood has decreased dramatically from 80% in 1969 to just 8% by 2005 (CDC, 2006). Health authorities recommend 60 minutes of physical activity a day for children ages 6 to 17, but few American children get that much.

While the potential for physical activity and functioning in middle childhood is high, physical functioning continues to increase into emerging adulthood. For example, physical stamina is often measured in terms of *maximal oxygen uptake*, or **$VO_{2max}$**, which reflects the ability of the body to take in oxygen during exercise and transport it to various organs. $VO_{2max}$ rises steadily through middle childhood and adolescence (Armstrong, 2006), and then peaks in the early 20s (Veldhuizen et al., 2014; Whaley, 2007). Similarly, **cardiac output**, the quantity of blood flow from the heart, peaks at age 25 (Lakatta, 1990; Parker et al., 2007). Reaction time is also faster in the early 20s than at any other time of life. Studies of grip

**$VO_{2\ max}$**
ability of the body to take in oxygen and transport it to various organs; also called maximum oxygen update

**cardiac output**
quantity of blood flow from the heart

## Education Focus: Physical Education: A Brain Tonic for Children

The benefits of physical activity go beyond physical health; they also extend to cognitive functioning. Based on extensive research, Charles Hillman, a professor of kinesiology and community health, has argued that it is shortsighted for school districts across the United States to decrease or eliminate physical education.

In one large study, Hillman and colleagues randomly assigned more than 200 children between the ages of 7 and 9 to either a 9-month afterschool physical activity (PA) program or a control-group (Hillman, 2014). The PA program took place after each school day for 2 hours. Children first engaged in moderate to vigorous physical activities for about an hour, then had about a 15-minute rest along with a healthy snack, and then spent another 45 minutes or so involved in organized games that provided an opportunity to refine motor skills. On average, the children in the PA group attended 81% of the sessions.

All children were given pre-tests before the start of the program and post-tests after the conclusion of the 9 months. Both groups increased in aerobic fitness from pre-test to post-test, illustrating the normal developmental increase in physical capacity that takes place in middle childhood. However, this increase was far more notable among the children who had been in the PA program. Furthermore, both groups increased in BMI, but here it was the control group that showed the greater increase. In short, compared to the control group children, the PA children got in better physical shape and gained less weight for their height.

The PA children also got in better cognitive shape than the control group. Hillman and colleagues focused on "executive function," which refers to the ability to solve cognitive problems without becoming distracted and to adjust one's strategy as the nature of a problem changes. On cognitive post-tests, the PA children scored higher on "attentional inhibition," which involved processing information quickly and accurately while not becoming distracted. They also scored higher on "cognitive flexibility," which involves analyzing information based on changing guidelines. The researchers also collected electroencephalogram (EEG) scans for the children (refer back to Chapter 1) and found that the two groups showed different electrophysiological activation patterns in their brains during the cognitive post-tests.

Hillman and colleagues conclude that their 9-month PA program increased physical and cognitive fitness in children. They argue that their "findings [are] important for educators and policy makers. Specifically, policies that reduce PA opportunities during the school day (e.g., recess), in an attempt to increase academic achievement may have unintended consequences. Indeed, the current data not only provide causal evidence for the beneficial effects of PA on cognitive and brain health, but they warrant modification of contemporary educational policies and practices, and indicate that youth should receive daily PA opportunities" (Hillman, 2014, p. 1070).

### Review Question

To what extent do you agree with Hillman and colleagues' conclusion about educational policies? If you were to suggest a set of changes to school policies and practices in regard to physical activity, what would they be?

**Figure 4.8** Number of Seconds Plank Position Held Among Children and Adolescents by Sex and Age

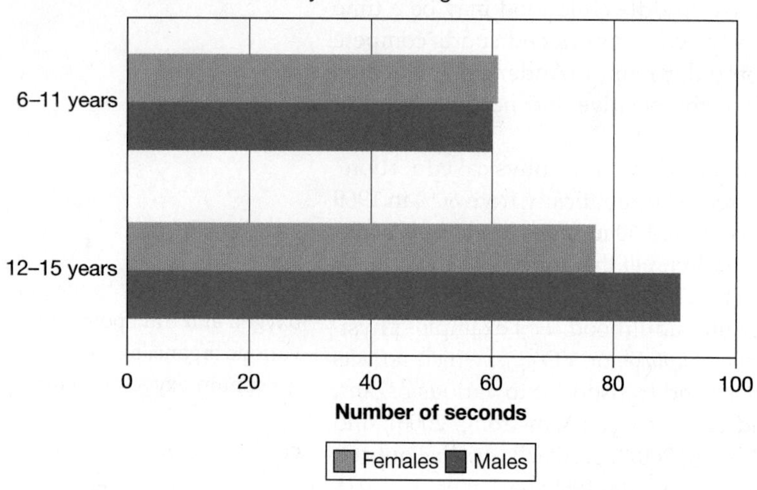


strength among men show the same pattern, with a peak in the 20s followed by a steady decline (Aldwin & Spiro, 2006). The strength of the bones increases during this time as well. Even after maximum height is attained in the late teens, the bones continue to grow in density, and peak bone mass is reached in the 20s (Zumwalt, 2008).

Several studies have been conducted to determine the ages when athletes produce their best performances (Ericsson, 1990; Schulz & Curnow, 1988; Stones & Kozma, 1996; Tanaka & Seals, 2003). The peak ages have been found to vary depending on the sport, with swimmers youngest (the late teens) and golfers oldest (the early 30s). However, for most sports the peak age of performance comes during the 20s. The capacity for peak physical performance, of course, requires being physically active and here the news is not as good. Longitudinal studies in the United States and Finland have found that physical activity, sports participation, and exercise decline from adolescence through emerging adulthood (Gordon-Larsen et al., 2004; Li et al., 2016; Telama et al., 2005). This is unfortunate because exercise in adolescence and emerging adulthood contributes to physical strength and endurance, and weight control (Centers for Disease Control and Prevention [CDC], 2015). Also, in one study, adolescents and emerging adults who went on a 30-minute run every morning during a 3-week period reported better mood, concentration, and sleep quality, compared to a control group (Kalak et al., 2012). As we will see shortly, too, there are behaviors pertaining to sleep and daily lifestyle that make emerging adults feel tired, weak, and depleted, despite their bodies' potential for optimal health.

The rise in $VO_{2max}$ from the teens into the 20s is smaller in females than males, with the difference between the sexes becoming larger with age. Sex difference in physical growth and functioning is quite small before puberty. You can see this if you go back and look at the figures for weight, height, muscle mass, and body fat. Before puberty, boys and girls are also about equal in strength and athletic performance, but during puberty boys surpass girls and this difference remains throughout adulthood (DeRose & Brooks-Gunn, 2006). A recent nationally representative study of American children and adolescents found no sex differences on measures of core, upper, and lower body strength among 6- to 11-year-olds, whereas boys were stronger than girls on all measures among 12- to 15–year-olds (Ervin et al., 2013). Figure 4.8 illustrates the difference for core muscle strength. (The plank position, used to measure core muscle strength, involves maintaining a fixed position similar to a push-up for the maximum possible time).

**Critical Thinking Question:** How might cultural expectations for physical activity in boys and girls relate to athletic participation and performance?

## SUMMARY: Motor Development and Physical Functioning

### LO 4.2.1 List the major changes in gross and fine motor development from infancy through middle childhood.

From infancy through middle childhood, children's gross motor skills improve steadily as they grow stronger and faster and more coordinated and agile. In some African cultures where adults actively stimulate gross motor development, infants walk a few weeks earlier than children in the West. The opposable thumb is the basis of fine motor development in humans, and a wide variety of fine motor abilities (grasping, drawing, writing) are acquired from infancy until the end of middle childhood when fine motor development has nearly reached adult maturity.

**LO 4.2.2 Describe the development of handedness, and identify the consequences and cultural views of left-handedness.**

The preference for one hand over the other appears prenatally, with 90% of fetuses preferring to suck their right thumb. Genetics and the prenatal environment influence handedness, as does culture. Left-handedness has been and continues to be viewed negatively in a variety of cultures. In some African countries, left-handedness is as low as 1%, far lower than the 10% figure in cultures where left-handedness is accepted.

**LO 4.2.3 Describe the advances in physical functioning from middle childhood through emerging adulthood.**

By middle childhood, children have become sufficiently strong and coordinated to take part in organized sports. Although the potential for physical activity and functioning in middle childhood is high, physical functioning continues to increase into emerging adulthood when stamina and reaction time peak. However, physical activity, sports participation, and exercise decline from adolescence through emerging adulthood.

# 4.3 Health and Sleep

At first glance, it may seem a bit odd that a chapter focused on physical growth, activity, and functioning should dwell on sleep—a mostly immobile state. But sleep, as we will see, is essential to good physical, cognitive, and emotional health. Here we will focus on both the quantity and quality of sleep from infancy through emerging adulthood. We begin, however, by addressing how the state of sleep poses a tragic risk to some infants in the form of sudden infant death syndrome (SIDS) and providing guidelines for how to diminish this risk.

## Sudden Infant Death Syndrome

**LO 4.3.1 Evaluate the risk factors for sudden infant death syndrome (SIDS), including the research evidence regarding cosleeping.**

When infants are 2–4 months of age, they are at highest risk for **sudden infant death syndrome (SIDS)**. Infants who die of SIDS do not have any apparent illness or disorder—they fall asleep and never wake up. SIDS is the leading cause of death for infants 1–12 months of age in developed countries (OECD, 2014). Infants of Asian descent are less likely to die of SIDS than those of European or African descent. In the United States, African American and Native American infants are at especially high risk, with rates 4–6 times higher than White Americans (Pickett et al., 2005). The higher rates of SIDS among African Americans and Native Americans are part of a larger pattern than begins with poorer prenatal care and continues with greater vulnerability in the first year of life.

**sudden infant death syndrome (SIDS)**
death within the first year of life due to unknown reasons, with no apparent illness or disorder

**RISK FACTORS.** Although deaths from SIDS have no clear cause, there are several factors known to put infants at risk, including: sleeping stomach-down or on the side instead of flat on the back; low birth weight and low Apgar score; having a mother who smoked during pregnancy, or being around smoke during infancy; soft bedding, including falling asleep on a sofa; sleeping in an overheated room, or wearing two or more layers of clothing during sleep (most SIDS deaths take place in autumn and winter) (AAP Task Force on Sudden Infant Death Syndrome, 2016; Kinney & Thach, 2009; Li et al., 2003; Rechtman et al., 2014).

One theory is that babies' vulnerability to SIDS at 2–4 months old reflects the transition from reflex behavior to intentional behavior (Lipsitt, 2003). For their first 2 months of life, when infants' breathing is blocked, a reflex causes them to shake their heads, bring their hands to their face, and push away the cause of the obstruction. After 2 months of age, once the reflex disappears, most babies are able to do this as intentional, learned behavior, but some are unable to make the transition, perhaps due in part to respiratory and muscular vulnerabilities. When these infants experience breathing difficulties during sleep, instead of being able to shake off the difficulty, they die.

One thing that is certain is that sleeping on the back instead of the stomach or side makes an enormous difference in lowering the risk of SIDS. In 1994, in response to

**Figure 4.9** The Impact of Prevention Campaigns on SIDS Rates

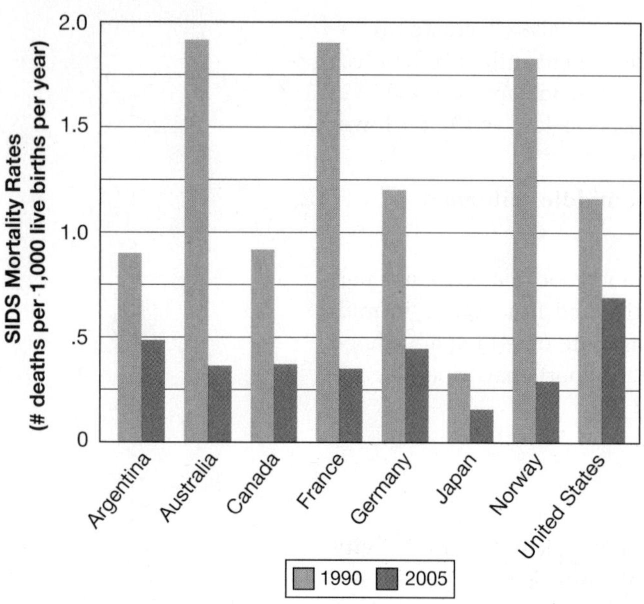


growing research evidence of the risks of stomach-sleeping, pediatricians in the United States launched a major "BACK to Sleep" campaign to inform parents and health professionals of the importance of putting infants to sleep on their backs. Over the next decade, the prevalence of stomach-sleeping among American infants declined from 70% to 20% and SIDS deaths declined by nearly one half (AAP Task Force on Sudden Infant Death Syndrome, 2016; National Center for Health Statistics, 2005). In response to similar campaigns in other countries, SIDS declined by 90% in the United Kingdom and by over 50% in many other developed countries (see Figure 4.9; National Sudden and Unexpected Infant/Child Death & Pregnancy Loss Resource Center, 2010).

**CULTURAL APPROACHES TO COSLEEPING.** Prominent pediatricians and health authorities in the United States warn against **cosleeping**, or bed-sharing, in which an infant or child sleeps in the same bed as the parents, arguing that it leads to excessive dependence on parents, can endanger the emotional health of children, or even lead to SIDS (American Academy of Pediatrics, 2016; American Academy of Pediatrics Task Force on Infant Positioning and SIDS [AAPTFIPS], 2000; AAP Task Force on Sudden Infant Death Syndrome, 2016; Spock & Needleman, 2004). However, this is one of many issues in this text where what is normal and seems healthy and "natural" in Western countries is actually extremely unusual worldwide.

**cosleeping**
cultural practice in which infants and sometimes older children sleep with one or both parents, also termed bed-sharing

**custom complex**
distinctive cultural pattern of behavior that reflects underlying cultural beliefs

Outside of the West, nearly all cultures have some form of cosleeping during infancy (Gottlieb & DeLoache, 2017; Small, 2005). This arrangement makes it easy for the infant to breast-feed when necessary during the night, without disturbing others and arousing the mother only slightly. In a study comparing sleeping arrangements among Guatemalan Maya and White Americans, all Mayan mothers coslept with their infants until the next child was born, whereupon the child would cosleep with the father or in a bed alongside the mother and the new baby (Morelli et al., 1992). The mothers explained that cosleeping helped promote a close parent–child attachment, highly valued in their collectivistic culture. The Mayan mothers were surprised and appalled when they learned that American infants typically sleep alone, and regarded this practice as cold and cruel. In contrast, few of the American mothers coslept with their infants, explaining that they wanted the child to become independent and that cosleeping would foster a degree of dependency that would be emotionally unhealthy.

In traditional cultures, typically a child sleeps beside the mother until the next child is born, which is usually when the child is 2–4 years old. While the toddler is ousted from that cozy spot beside the mother at night to make room for the new baby, this does not mean that toddlers sleep alone. Instead, they now sleep alongside older siblings, or perhaps the father (Owens, 2004). Throughout life, sleeping alone is rare in traditional cultures.

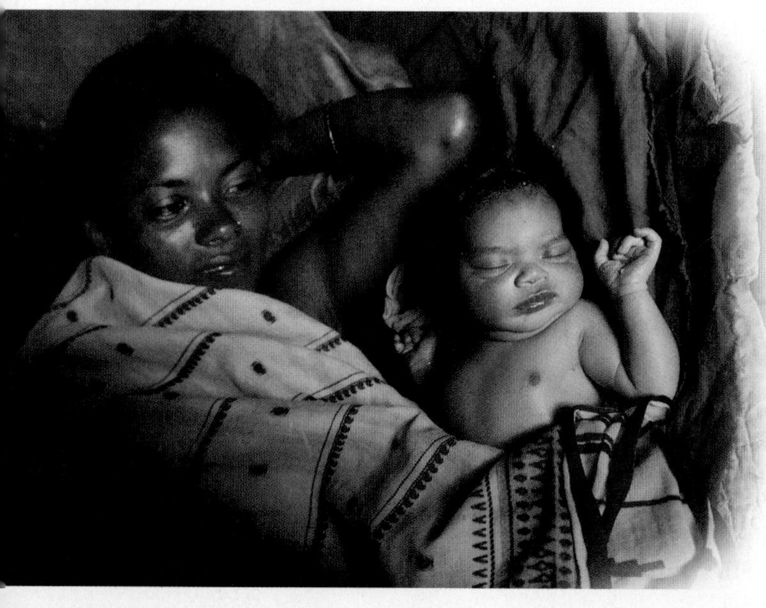

Cosleeping (or bed-sharing) is a common practice across traditional cultures. Mothers may view it not only as practical but also as fostering interdependence. This mother and baby are from India.

But it is not just in traditional cultures like the Guatemalan Maya that cosleeping is the norm. In Japan and South Korea, two of the most technologically advanced countries in the world, almost all infants cosleep with their mothers, and children continue to sleep by or near their mothers until puberty (Mindell et al., 2010). Like the Mayan mothers, Asian mothers justify their cosleeping practices on the basis of collectivistic values, explaining that this is one way for children to learn from a very early age that they are closely tied to others in bonds of interdependence and mutual obligation. Cultural customs regarding infant sleeping arrangements are a good example of a **custom complex**, that is, a distinctive cultural pattern of behavior that is based on underlying cultural beliefs. Cosleeping tends to reflect collectivistic beliefs, that members of the culture are closely bound to one another (Small, 1998). In contrast, having infants sleep alone tends to reflect an individualistic belief that each person should learn to be self-sufficient and not rely on others any more than necessary (Shweder et al., 1995). Parents in an individualistic culture may fear that cosleeping will make infants and children too dependent. However, children who cosleep with their parents in infancy are actually more self-reliant (e.g., able to dress themselves) and more socially independent (e.g., can make friends by themselves) than other children are (Keller & Goldberg, 2004). Watch the video *Cosleeping* for more information.

**Watch** COSLEEPING

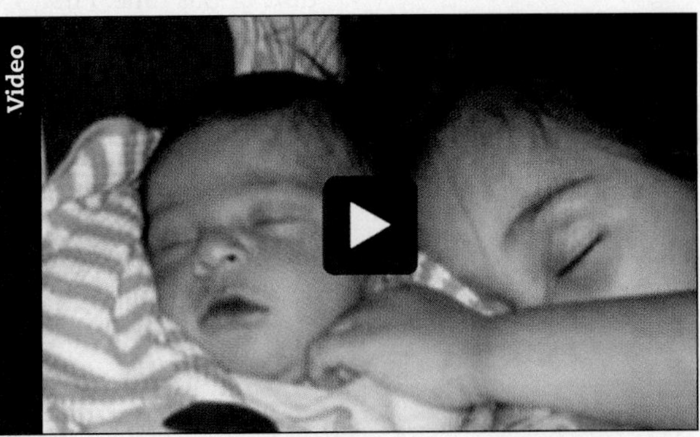


What about the danger of SIDS? Don't cultures where cosleeping is the norm have high rates of SIDS, if cosleeping is a risk factor for SIDS as most American pediatricians believe? On the contrary, SIDS is almost unknown in cultures where cosleeping is the norm (Hewlett & Roulette, 2014). In the United States, however, where most parents do not cosleep, rates of SIDS are among the highest in the world. There appear to be several reasons for this pattern (Bartick, 2014; McKenna & McDade, 2005). First, most parents and infants in cosleeping cultures sleep on relatively hard surfaces such as a mat on the floor or a futon, thus avoiding the soft bedding (such as sofas) that is sometimes implicated in SIDS. Second, infants who cosleep breast-feed more often and longer than infants who do not and these frequent episodes of arousal in the course of the night make SIDS less likely. Third, cosleeping mothers tend to lay their infants on their backs to make the mother's breast more easily accessible for breast feeding. Thus back-sleeping developed as a widespread cultural practice for practical reasons long before research showed that it lessened the risk of SIDS.

Some cultures within the United States have a long tradition of infant cosleeping. It is a common practice among African Americans and Latinos (Barajas et al., 2011; Milan et al., 2007). In the rural culture of the Appalachian Mountains, children typically sleep alongside their parents for the first 2 years of life (Abbott, 1992). In many developed countries, the prevalence of cosleeping in infancy has grown in recent years as research has shown that it causes no emotional harm and may even be protective against SIDS (Mindell et al., 2010; Willinger et al., 2003). Importantly, however, cosleeping infants may be at risk for SIDS if their parents are obese, or if parents consume alcohol or other drugs before sleeping and roll onto the baby without being roused. To extend another sensible warning: Don't drink and cosleep!

## Sleep Patterns

**LO 4.3.2 Describe how the amount and pattern of sleep change from infancy through emerging adulthood.**

Cultural norms and our inherent physiological need for sleep also come together to impact developmental sleep patterns, both in terms of how much we sleep and when. As described in Chapter 3, neonates sleep for 16–18 hours a day in periods of a few hours at a time. By 3–4 months old, infants sleep for longer periods, up to 6–7 hours in a row at night. By age 6 months, cultural practices influence how much infants sleep. American infants sleep about 14 hours a day at this age, including daytime naps (Murkoff et al., 2009). However, among the Kipsigis people of Kenya studied by Charles Super and Sara Harkness (1986, 2015), infants slept only about 12 hours a day at 6 months of age, perhaps because they spent much of the day strapped to their mothers or an older sibling, and so expended less energy than American infants do. Super and colleagues (1996) also studied infants in the Netherlands and compared their sleep patterns to American infants. The Dutch infants slept about 16 hours a day at 6 months, 2 hours more than the Americans, evidently due to Dutch cultural beliefs emphasizing rest and early bedtimes for young children.

By their first birthday, American toddlers sleep an average of 12 hours a day. The toddler not only sleeps less than the infant but also has more of a night-sleeping, day-waking arousal schedule. Most toddlers take only one nap during the day by the time they reach 18 months old, compared to the two or more naps a day typical of infants (Iglowstein et al., 2003). However, this does not mean that toddlers consistently sleep through the night—a fact to which many a bleary-eyed parent can attest. In fact, one study of toddlers in Israel, England, and Australia found that episodes of waking in the night increased in frequency from 1 to

2 years of age (Scher et al., 2004). There are two reasons why waking at night often increases during this time. First, 13 to 19 months of age is the time when the emergence of the molars, the large teeth in the back of the mouth, often causes eye-popping pain. Second, toddlers develop a more definite sense of themselves and others as they approach age 2, and if they sleep in a bed separate from their parents they become more aware of this separation and more intentional about relieving it by summoning a parent or going into the parents' room.

By early childhood, children typically sleep about 11 hours a day, and most have stopped napping by age 6. In both early and middle childhood, sleep is sometimes interrupted by fears, nightmares, sleep terrors (episodes of screaming, intense fear, and flailing), teeth grinding, and sleep walking (Mindell & Owens, 2003). Some of these interruptions are linked to the development of imagination that flourishes at this age. As parents, one of our most startling nighttime experiences occurred when our daughter, Paris, was just shy of her seventh birthday. About midnight, we suddenly heard something that sounded like running in the attic above our bedrooms. It seemed impossible, but as the noise continued we started to venture up the stairs to the attic, when Paris suddenly shot down past us—running and laughing. Now in pursuit, we tried to talk to her and ask her what was going on but she just laughed. It might sound funny (and in hindsight it is), but it was truly creepy. Finally we asked if she had to use the bathroom, and at that she zipped into the bathroom, then returned and jumped into bed, and was instantly fast asleep! We knew of sleep walking, but sleep running? Sleep laughing? As strange and unsettling as some of these nighttime experiences in early and middle childhood may be, they are normal and usually resolve themselves without the need for intervention.

In the course of middle childhood, not getting enough sleep becomes more common (Mindell & Owens, 2003), and by adolescence it is normative. Table 4.3 shows the amount of sleep recommended by medical authorities from infancy through adulthood. Although 9–10 hours of sleep may be ideal for adolescents, many studies have found that American adolescents report sleeping less than 8 hours on school nights (Carskadon, 2011) and 9 or more hours on weekends (Wahlstrom et al., 2014).

This pattern of sleeping a lot longer on weekends and holidays than on school (or work) days is also prevalent among American college students. Known as *delayed sleep phase syndrome* (Brown et al., 2002; Gradisar & Crowley, 2013; Jaquez et al., 2017), high school and college students tend to accumulate a *sleep debt* during the week as they sleep less than they need, then they try to make up their lost sleep when they have time off. College students' self-reports of their sleep patterns indicate that problems are common. In a national study of American college students, 43% reported sleep problems, such as insufficient sleep or difficulty falling asleep (Taylor et al., 2013). An international study of over 20,000 students in 26 countries found that 10% of students reported "severe or extreme" sleep problems (Peltzer & Pengpid, 2015). Sleep disturbances are in turn related to a wide variety of problems, such as depression and anxiety (Millman, 2005). Poor sleeping habits also cause cognitive deficits in attention, memory, and critical thinking (Regestein et al., 2010).

**morningness**
preference for going to bed early and waking up early

**eveningness**
preference for going to bed late and waking up late

One reason high school students, college students, and other emerging adults often have sleep problems is that the daily routines of their lives are set mostly by older adults who are likely to have different sleep preferences than they do. Sleep researchers have established that people vary in their **morningness** and **eveningness**, that is, their preference for either going to bed early and waking up early (morningness) or going to bed late and waking up late (eveningness). Furthermore, these preferences change with age, due to hormonal changes that are part of normal physiological development, specifically, levels of *growth hormone*. One massive study of over 55,000 Europeans from childhood through late adulthood concluded that children tend toward morningness, but in the course of adolescence and the early part of emerging adulthood, the balance shifts toward eveningness, with the peak of eveningness coming at about age 20–21 (slightly earlier for women than for men) (Roenneberg et al., 2007). Moreover, this shift in sleep pattern in human adolescents has also been found in other mammals at puberty (Hagenauer et al., 2009). After age 20–21, research with humans shows that the balance shifts again toward morningness for the remainder of the life span.

**Table 4.3** Amount of Recommended Sleep by Age

| Age | Recommended Amount of Sleep |
|---|---|
| Newborns | 16–18 hours a day |
| Preschool-aged children | 11–12 hours a day |
| Primary school-aged children | 10 hours or more a day |
| Adolescents | 9–10 hours a day |
| Adults | 7–8 hours a day |

SOURCE: Sleep Guidelines from the National Heart, Lung, and Blood Institute (2012).

What we have then is a case of a biological change in the circadian rhythm of adolescents and emerging adults colliding with societal expectations and norms for when to start school and work. In an attempt to better align with the biologically-based sleep patterns of adolescents, some American high school districts have delayed the start of the school day. A recent survey of more than 9,000 students in eight public high schools that have made this change found that the proportion of students who reported getting 8 or more hours of sleep rose steadily with a later school start. For example, 34% of students reported getting this much sleep in schools starting at 7:30 AM, whereas 60% did so when school started at 8:35 AM. Grades (for core subjects of English, math, science, and social studies), scores on state and national achievement tests, attendance rates, and reduced tardiness also showed significant improvement for schools that moved their start times to 8:35 AM or later (Wahlstrom et al., 2014).

Many college students report occasional problems with their sleep habits.

Certainly for college students, however, it is not just a lack of alignment between the start of classes and physiological sleep changes that contribute to sleep disturbances. It is also lifestyle factors, such as partying until late at night or waiting until the day before an exam to begin studying seriously. Have you ever stayed up all night long to study for an exam or to complete a paper due the next day? In one study of students at a 4-year liberal arts college, 60% had pulled at least one so-called "all-nighter" since coming to college (Thacher, 2008). Those who had pulled an all-nighter tended to have a greater preference for eveningness and had poorer overall academic achievement. Another study of all-nighters found that students who stayed up all night before exams self-rated their exam performance as better than students who slept 8 hours, but their actual performance turned out to be much worse (Pilcher & Waters, 1997).

**Critical Thinking Question:** How would you explain this dissonance between self-rated and actual exam performance among students who pulled all-nighters?

To promote *sleep hygiene*, sleep experts recommend the following practices (Brown et al., 2002; Horne, 2014):

- waking at the same time each day
- getting regular exercise
- avoiding late-afternoon naps
- limiting caffeine intake
- avoiding excessive alcohol intake
- turning off TV and digital devices well before going to sleep.

This may seem like commonsense advice, but the actual behavior of many college students contradicts these suggestions. Many drink coffee frequently during the day to stay alert, not realizing that frequent caffeine use will make it more difficult for them to sleep that night. Many believe that they can compensate for getting little sleep during the week by making it up during weekends and holidays, but it is precisely this delayed sleep phase syndrome that constitutes disrupted sleep. Many drink alcohol excessively, with sleep hygiene the last thing on their minds. And, of course, many of them find it difficult to turn off their digital devices, even at night (Rosen et al., 2016).

## SUMMARY: Health and Sleep

**LO 4.3.1 Evaluate the risk factors for sudden infant death syndrome (SIDS), including the research evidence regarding cosleeping.**

SIDS is most common at age 2–4 months. Sleeping on the back rather than the stomach or side greatly reduces the risk of SIDS. In cultures where infants sleep alongside their mothers on a firm surface, the risk of SIDS is very low. Historically and worldwide today, mother–infant cosleeping, or bed-sharing, is far more common than putting babies to sleep in a room of their own. Cosleeping infants may be at risk for SIDS if their parents are obese, or if parents consume alcohol or other drugs before sleeping and roll onto the baby without being roused.

**LO 4.3.2 Describe how the amount and pattern of sleep change from infancy through emerging adulthood.**

Sleep needs decline steadily in the course of childhood from about 16–18 hours in neonates, to 11 hours in early childhood, to 9–10 hours by adolescence. American adolescents and emerging adults, however, typically get less sleep than they need. One reason is that physiologically they tend toward eveningness (going to bed late and waking up late), but school requires waking up early.

# 4.4 Health and Nutrition

If you take a look at the list of bestselling advice and how-to books, you are likely to find that money and love are popular topics. But even more popular are books focusing on food and diet. Food is obviously a fundamental need. It is also a source of both deep-seated satisfaction and worry. What we eat, how much we eat, and with whom we eat have implications for physical growth and health. Here we pick up where we left off in Chapter 3 and look at the process of becoming weaned from breast milk and starting to eat solid foods. We then turn to malnutrition and obesity in childhood, and their lifelong implications.

## The Infant's Diet

**LO 4.4.1 Describe the weaning process and the nature of infants' first solid foods.**

Infants need a lot of food, and they need it often. In fact, during the first year of life nutritional energy needs are greater than at any other time of life, per pound of body weight (Vlaardingerbroek et al., 2009). Infants also need more fat in their diets than at any later point in life, to fuel the growth of their bodies and (especially) their brains. As described in Chapter 3, the best way to obtain good high-fat nutrition during infancy is through breast milk, especially in developing countries. As also noted in that chapter, cultures vary widely in whether and how long mothers breast-feed their children. However, based on what we know of human history and of practices today in traditional cultures, it is clear that breast-feeding for 2 to 3 years has been the most typical human custom, until recently (Small, 1998).

If breast-feeding takes place for only a few weeks or months during infancy, the transition from breast to bottle usually takes place fairly smoothly, especially if the bottle is introduced gradually (Murkoff & Mazel, 2016). However, the longer breast-feeding continues into toddlerhood, the more challenging **weaning** becomes when the mother decides the time has come for the child to stop drinking breast milk. The toddler is much more socially aware than the infant and much more capable of exercising intentional behavior. The toddler can also speak up, in a way the infant cannot, to make demands and protest prohibitions.

**weaning**
cessation of breast-feeding

Consequently, most traditional cultures have customary practices for weaning toddlers from the breast. Often, the approach is gentle and gradual at first, but becomes stronger if the toddler resists. Some cultures separate mother and toddler during weaning, so that the toddler will have no choice but to get used to life without breast-feeding. Among the Fulani people of West Africa, toddlers are sent to their grandmother's household during weaning (Johnson, 2000). In other cultures, mothers apply some substance to their breasts with an aversive flavor. For example, in Bali (an island that is part of Indonesia) parents feed their babies some solid food from the first few days of life and attempt gradual weaning beginning at about age 2. However, if the gradual approach does not work, mothers coat their breasts with bitter-tasting herbs (Deiner, 2000).

Apart from milk (from bottle or breast), infants also start eating some solid foods during the first year of life. Cultures vary widely in when they introduce solid food to infants, ranging from those that introduce it after just a few weeks of life to those that wait until the second half of the first year. Age 4–5 months is common, in part because that is an age when infants can sit up with support and also the age when they often begin to show an interest in what others are eating (Mayo Clinic, 2017; Small, 2005). At 4–5 months, infants still have a

People from different cultures eat all kinds of distinctive foods, and children usually enjoy whatever dishes adults provide for them. These children are from India, Japan, and Madagascar.

gag reflex that causes them to spit out any solid item that enters their mouths. Consequently, at first more food ends up on them than in them! The ability to chew and swallow does not develop until the second half of the first year (Napier & Meister, 2000). For this reason, infants' first "solid" foods worldwide are runny (such as thin rice cereal), or soft and smooth (such as pureed or prechewed bananas; Deiner, 2000).

As we saw in Chapter 3, neonates show a preference for the tastes and smells that were distinctive in the mother's diet in the days before birth (Schaal et al., 2000). With the introduction of solid foods, parental and cultural influences become pronounced. Children generally learn to like whatever foods the adults in their environment like and provide for them. In India kids eat rice with spicy sauces, in Japan kids eat sushi, in Mexico kids eat chili peppers. Nevertheless, a myth persists among many North American parents that kids in early childhood will only eat a small range of foods high in fat and sugar content, such as hamburgers, hot dogs, fried chicken, and macaroni and cheese (Zehle et al., 2007). This false belief then becomes a self-fulfilling prophecy, as children who eat foods high in sugar and fat lose their taste for healthier foods (Black et al., 2002). The assumption that young children like only foods high in fat and sugar also leads some parents to bribe their children to eat healthier foods—"If you eat three more bites of carrots, then you can have some ice cream"—which leads the children to view healthy foods as a trial and unhealthy foods as a reward (Birch et al., 2003). These cultural beliefs contribute to high rates of childhood obesity.

## Malnutrition

**LO 4.4.2 Describe the harmful effects of nutritional deficiencies on growth.**

In developing countries, malnutrition is the norm rather than the exception. Because infants have such great nutritional needs, and because their bodies are growing at a faster rate than at any later time of life, the effects of malnutrition in infancy are especially severe and enduring. Infants are capable of thriving mainly on breast milk, along with a little solid food after the early months, so malnutrition in infancy is usually due to the mother being unable or unwilling to breast-feed. Often the problem is that the mother is so ill or malnourished herself that she is unable to produce an adequate supply of breast milk. Or, she may have a disease that can be communicated through breast milk, such as tuberculosis or HIV, and she has been advised not to breast-feed. She may also have been misled to believe that infant formula is better for her baby than breast milk (see Chapter 3), so she has stopped breast-feeding and instead gives her infant the formula substitute, which may not be available in sufficient quantity. If the infant's mother has died—not unusual in the areas of the world where infant malnutrition is most common—there may be no one else who can breast-feed the baby or otherwise provide adequate nutrition.

The World Health Organization (WHO) estimates that about 80% of children in developing countries lack sufficient food or essential nutrients (World Health Organization [WHO], 2016). The three most common types of nutritional deficiencies are protein, iron, and iodine.

Lack of protein is experienced by about 25% of children under age 5 worldwide and can result in two fatal diseases: marasmus in infancy, and kwashiorkor in toddlerhood and early childhood. **Marasmus** is a disease in which the body wastes away due to insufficient

**marasmus**
disease in which the body wastes away from lack of nutrients

Toddlers who do not receive enough protein in their diets sometimes suffer from kwashiorkor. This boy is from Uganda.

protein and calories in general. The body stops growing, the muscles atrophy, the baby becomes increasingly lethargic, and eventually death results. Even among infants who survive, malnutrition impairs normal development for years to come (Galler et al., 2010; Nolan et al., 2002). However, studies in Guatemala and several other countries have found that nutritional supplements for infants in poor families have enduring beneficial effects on their physical, cognitive, and social development (Pollitt et al., 1996).

**Kwashiorkor**, a severe form of protein deficiency, leads to a range of symptoms such as lethargy, irritability, and thinning hair (Medline Plus, 2016). Often the body swells with water, especially the belly. Toddlers and children in early childhood with kwashiorkor may be getting enough calories in the form of starches such as rice, bread, or potatoes, but not enough protein. Kwashiorkor lowers the effectiveness of the immune system, making toddlers more vulnerable to disease, and over time can lead to coma followed by death. Improved protein intake can relieve the symptoms of kwashiorkor, but the damage to physical and cognitive development is likely to be permanent. For example, a study of 116 adult survivors of either kwashiorkor or marasmus in Jamaica found long-term diminished physical functioning (Tennant et al., 2014).

**kwashiorkor**

protein deficiency in childhood, leading to symptoms such as lethargy, irritability, thinning hair, and swollen body, which may be fatal if not treated

**anemia**

dietary deficiency of iron that causes problems such as fatigue, irritability, and attention difficulties

Iron deficiency, known as **anemia**, is experienced by the majority of children under age 5 in developing countries (Balarajan et al., 2012). Anemia causes fatigue, irritability, and difficulty sustaining attention, which in turn lead to problems in cognitive and social development (Black et al., 2011). Foods rich in iron include most meats, as well as vegetables such as potatoes, peas, and beets, and grains such as oatmeal and brown rice. Young children in developed countries may also experience anemia if they do not eat enough healthy foods (Brotanek et al., 2007). One national study of toddlers in the United States found that iron deficiency prevalence rates were about 7% overall and were twice as high among Latino toddlers (12%) as among White or African American toddlers (both 6%; Brotanek et al., 2007). Iron deficiency makes toddlers tired and irritable.

About one-third of the world's population has a dietary deficiency of iodine, especially in Africa and South Asia (Zimmermann et al., 2008). In young children a lack of iodine inhibits cognitive development, resulting in an estimated IQ (intelligence quotient) deficiency of 10 to 15 points, a substantial margin. Fortunately, adding iodine to a diet is simple—through iodized salt—and cheap, costing only a few cents per person per year.

Research indicates that there is a sensitive period for long-term effects of malnutrition from the second trimester of pregnancy through age 3 (Galler et al., 2005). Malnutrition that begins after age 3 does not appear to result in permanent cognitive or behavioral deficits. For example, a longitudinal study in Guatemala showed that children who were classified in early childhood as having "low nutrient levels" were less likely than children with "high nutrient levels" to explore new environments in middle childhood and to persist in a frustrating situation. They were also less energetic, more anxious, and showed less positive emotion (Barrett & Frank, 1987). A more recent study, in Ghana, reported similar results, with children who experienced mild-to-moderate malnutrition in their early years demonstrating lower levels of cognitive development in middle childhood on standardized tests and in teacher ratings, compared to children who were not malnourished (Appoh & Krekling, 2004). The malnourished children were also more likely to be rated by teachers as anxious, sad, and withdrawn (Appoh, 2004). Other studies in other countries have found similar results, with malnourished children scoring lower than better-nourished children on a wide range of cognitive and social measures by middle childhood (Grigorenko, 2003; Kitsao-Wekulo et al., 2013).

Nutritional deficiencies are not confined to developing countries but are also present in developed countries. Because young children in developed countries often eat too much of unhealthy foods and too little of healthy foods, many of them have specific nutritional deficiencies despite living in cultures where food is abundant. Calcium is the most common nutritional deficiency in the United States, with one-third of American 3-year-olds consuming less than the amount recommended by health authorities (Wagner & Greer, 2008). Calcium is especially important for the growth of bones and teeth, and is found in foods such as beans, peas, broccoli, and dairy products. Over the past 30 years, as children have consumed less milk and more soft drinks, calcium deficiencies in early childhood have become more common.

Within the United States, there are ethnic and immigrant group differences in the quality of early childhood diet. A study of more than seven hundred 3-year-olds found that African American and Latino children had lower intake of calcium, as compared to white children (de Hoog et al., 2014). The diets of African American and Latino children also included more soft drinks and fast food. These differences between the ethnic groups were only partially accounted for by white children growing up in households with higher socioeconomic status (SES). When the researchers used a statistical technique to hold SES constant across the groups, there were still differences. The study also showed that immigrant children whose mothers had been born outside of the United States had more healthful diets than children of native-born mothers. The immigrant children consumed less fast food and more nutritious foods such as beans and vegetables.

## Obesity

**LO 4.4.3 Explain the role of both genetics and cultural environment in childhood obesity.**

Apart from some risk of nutritional deficiencies, children in developed countries have a different kind of nutritional problem: too many calories. Being overweight or obese has become a major health problem in developed countries and is becoming a problem in developing countries as well (Cui et al., 2010; Werner & Bodin, 2007). A BMI above the 85th percentile for a child's age and sex is classified as **overweight**, and above the 95th percentile as **obese**. Across countries worldwide, rates of overweight and obese children are highest in the most affluent regions (North America and Europe) and lowest in the poorest regions (Africa and Southeast Asia). Rates of overweight and obese children, however, are increasing in countries that have become affluent in recent times such as China, Korea, and Saudi Arabia (Ahmad et al., 2010; OECD Obesity Update, 2014).

**overweight**

in children, defined as having a BMI exceeding 18

**obese**

in children, defined as having a BMI exceeding 21

In the United States, rates of overweight and obesity have risen sharply in recent decades. Figure 4.10 illustrates the increase in childhood obesity within the United States since the 1970s. Obesity is especially high in the least affluent ethnic minority groups, including African Americans and Latinos, as shown in Figure 4.11 (Ogden et al., 2014).

A variety of changes have contributed to the rise in childhood obesity (Ogden et al., 2014). The change in children's diet is very important. Over recent decades people have become less likely to prepare meals at home and more likely to buy meals away from home, especially "fast foods" like hamburgers, french fries, and pizza that are high in fat content, and then they wash it down with soft drinks high in sugar content. As we just saw, children growing up in African American and Latino families are particularly likely to consume fast food and soft drinks.

**Figure 4.10** The Rise in Childhood Obesity, United States, Children Ages 6–11

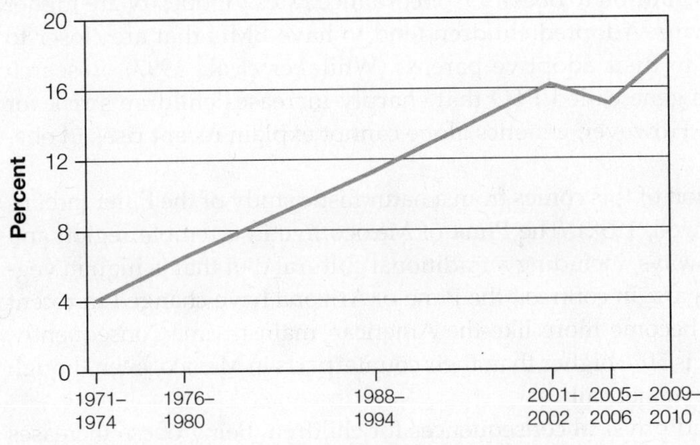


**Figure 4.11** Childhood Obesity Rates in the U.S., by Ethnicity

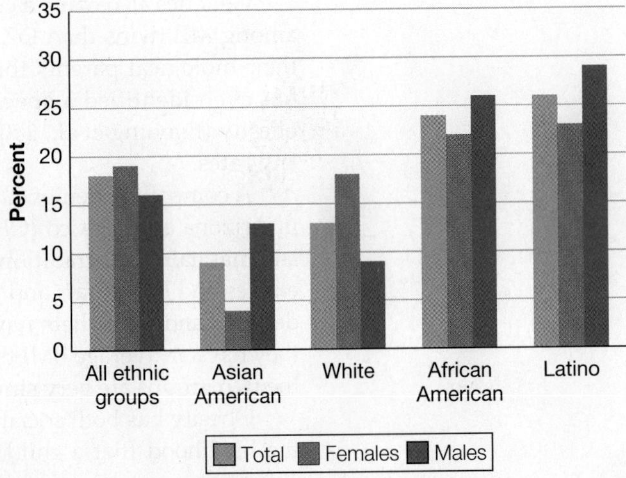


SOURCE: Ogden et al. (2014).

In recent decades, American children and youth have become much more likely to be overweight or obese. Fast food and soft drinks contribute to the problem.

The change in children's diet also reflects other social changes: Parents are less likely to prepare meals at home because they are more likely than in the past to be single parents or to be part of a dual-earner couple. Family meals have also declined, and these meals are associated with the consumption of healthier foods. A recent longitudinal study found that American adolescents who seldom or never ate dinner with their families were more likely to be overweight or obese 10 years later in emerging adulthood, as compared to adolescents who had commonly taken part in family meals (Berge et al., 2014). In developing countries, rates of overweight and obesity are rising in the populations in part because their diets are becoming more like the diets of people in developed countries (Gu et al., 2005; Popkin, 2010).

Another contributor is media. Most children in most developed countries watch at least 2 hours of television a day (Rideout, 2013). In a longitudinal study that followed a sample of American children from age 4 to 11, TV watching predicted gains in body fat (Proctor et al., 2003). Specifically, children who watched at least 3 hours of TV a day gained 40% more body fat over the course of the study than children who watched less than 1½ hours a day. Watching TV also exposes children to numerous advertisements for high-fat, high-sugar foods, which they then lobby their parents to buy (Kelly et al., 2010). Rates of overweight and obesity are especially high among African American and Latino children in part because those are also the children that tend to watch the most TV per day (Rideout, 2013).

Other studies have also shown that the more time children watch TV the less time they spend in physical exercise (Institute of Medicine of the National Academies, 2005; Williams, 2005). The allure of the Internet and electronic games gives children additional reasons to stay inside rather than getting outside and playing active physical games (Anderson & Butcher, 2006). As we saw earlier in this chapter, being physically active is important. Recall how in the study by Hillman and colleagues (Hillman, 2014), the children who had been randomly assigned to the physically active group got in better physical shape and gained less weight for their height, as compared to the control group.

Recent research has suggested that even changes to the prenatal environment may contribute to rising rates of obesity. Longitudinal research following children into middle childhood has found that prenatal exposure to antibiotics during the second and third trimesters increases the risk of obesity (Mueller et al., 2014). Since their discovery in 1948, antibiotics have been linked to weight gain in studies of both humans and animals (Kennedy, 2014). However, a causal mechanism still remains to be explained, and mothers who require antibiotics while pregnant should not avoid using them.

Genetics also make a contribution to obesity. Concordance rates for obesity are higher among MZ twins than DZ twins. Adopted children tend to have BMIs that are closer to their biological parents than to their adoptive parents (Whitaker et al., 1997). Research has even identified a specific gene called FTO that sharply increases children's risk for obesity (Frayling et al., 2007). However, genetics alone cannot explain recent rises in obesity rates.

A compelling demonstration of this comes from a naturalistic study of the Pima Indians in Arizona and Mexico (Gladwell, 1998). The Pima of Mexico live in a remote region and still maintain their traditional ways, including a traditional cultural diet that is high in vegetables and low in fats and sugars. In contrast, the Pima of Arizona have changed in recent decades and their diets have become more like the American mainstream. Consequently, they have an average BMI that is 50% higher than their counterparts in Mexico, even though the two groups are very similar genetically.

Obesity has both social and physical consequences for children. Being obese increases the likelihood that a child will be socially excluded and the object of ridicule by peers

(Janssen et al., 2004; Puhl et al., 2010). Other children tend to associate obesity with undesirable traits such as being lazy, sloppy, ugly, and stupid (Tiggemann & Anesbury, 2000). By middle childhood obesity is a risk factor for a variety of emotional and behavioral problems (Puhl et al., 2010).

Physically, the consequences of obesity are equally serious. Even in middle childhood, obesity can result in diabetes, which can eventually lead to problems such as blindness, kidney failure, and stroke (Hannon et al., 2005; Ramchandani, 2004). Obesity also proves hard to shake from childhood to adulthood. About 80% of obese children remain overweight as adults (Ogden et al., 2014; Oken & Lightdale, 2000). For adults, the range of health problems resulting from obesity is even greater—including high blood pressure, heart attack, and cancer—and more likely to be fatal (Ng, 2014).

What can be done to reverse the sharp increase in childhood obesity? One step is recognizing the problem. Perhaps because obese children tend to have obese parents, studies indicate that fewer than half of parents of obese children view their children as overweight (Jeffrey, 2004; Young-Hyman et al., 2003). Public policies have begun to address the problem of childhood obesity. In the United States, school lunches have been notoriously unhealthy for decades, but national standards have been revised to provide healthier school lunches that are lower in fats and sugars (Jalonick, 2010).

**Critical Thinking Question:** Suggest one other national policy to combat the problem of obesity, and explain why you chose that particular one.

## Cultural Focus: Is Contemporary American Culture Setting off a Genetic Tripwire for Obesity?

Although genetics alone cannot explain recent rises in obesity rates, there may in fact be an interaction of genetics and the environment. In 2007, researchers discovered that people who have a common variant of the gene FTO tend to be heavier than those who do not. This turns out, however, only to be the case for people born after World War II.

James Niels Rosenquist and colleagues (2015) recently made this discovery when they examined data from a long-term study in Massachusetts. In 1948, over 5,000 people were recruited for a study of their health. Many of their children were added to the study in 1971, and grandchildren as well by 2002. The study involved the collection of a variety of physiological and biological measurements, including participants' BMI and information on their genes. Rosenquist and colleagues found that people with the risky variant of FTO who were born before the early 1940s were not heavier than those without the genetic variant. But that changed after the early 1940s when those with the risky variant started to become comparatively heavier. And the more recently participants were born, the greater the risk for obesity.

In short, something in the environment appears to set off a genetic tripwire for obesity. Exactly what environmental factors are involved is not clear. It may involve the decline in physical activity. It may be the rise of the modern diet. When studies have compared people who eat fried foods and drink sugary beverages, those with the risky FTO variant gain more weight than those without it (Zimmer, 2014). For more information, watch the video *Obesity*.

**Watch OBESITY**

### Review Question

Think back to some of the basics of genetics that we covered in Chapter 2. Can you explain how the study by Rosenquist and colleagues relates to epigenetics, and the extent to which it addresses culture?

## Summary: Health and Nutrition

**LO 4.4.1 Describe the weaning process and the nature of infants' first solid foods.**

If breast-feeding takes place for only a few weeks or months during infancy, the transition from breast to bottle usually takes place fairly smoothly. When weaning takes place in the second or third year of life, toddlers often resist. Customs in traditional cultures for promoting weaning include sending the toddler to a relative's household for a while or coating the mother's breast with an unpleasant substance. Apart from milk (from bottle or breast), infants also start eating some solid foods during the first year of life, and they generally learn to like the types of foods that adults in their culture provide for them.

**LO 4.4.2 Describe the harmful effects of nutritional deficiencies on growth.**

In developing countries, malnutrition is the norm rather than the exception. The three most common types of nutritional deficiencies are protein, iron, and iodine. Malnutrition may lead to diseases such as marasmus and kwashiorkor, both of which can be fatal. Among infants and toddlers who survive, malnutrition impairs normal physical, cognitive, and social development for years to come. Due to an imbalance between healthy and unhealthy foods, some children in developed countries also are deficient in nutrients such as calcium.

**LO 4.4.3 Explain the role of both genetics and cultural environment in childhood obesity.**

Being overweight (BMI above 85th percentile) or obese (BMI above 95th percentile) has become a major health problem in developed countries and is becoming a problem in developing countries as well. With respect to environmental influences, obesity has been linked to prenatal (exposure to antibiotics) and postnatal (diet and media) factors. A specific gene called FTO sharply increases children's risk for obesity.

# 4.5 Preventing Mortality: Diseases and Injuries

The first years of life have always been a perilous period for the human species. Human females typically have a reproductive span of at least 20 years, from the late teens through the late 30s, and with regular sexual intercourse most would have at least three to seven children during that span. Yet, until recently in human history there was little increase in the total human population. This means that many children died before reaching reproductive age, and based on current patterns it seems likely that many of them died early in life. Even now, worldwide, the first few years of life have a much higher risk of death than any other period from age 5 through emerging adulthood (GDB 2013 Mortality and Causes Death Collaborators, 2014). You can see this in Figure 4.12. We now turn to the major causes of death in those first few years. Understanding these causes is important not only to be knowledgeable about the most serious threats to children's physical health and development, but also to be able to formulate prevention policies. As it turns it, there is uplifting news. In recent decades, prevention efforts have resulted in the major decline in mortality between 1990 and 2013 that is shown in Figure 4.12. In this section, we also discuss how different cultures have approached infant and early childhood mortality. Finally, we focus on the period from age 5 through the 20s when mortality is lower and the causes are different.

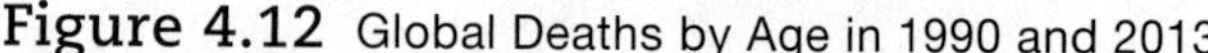

**Figure 4.12** Global Deaths by Age in 1990 and 2013

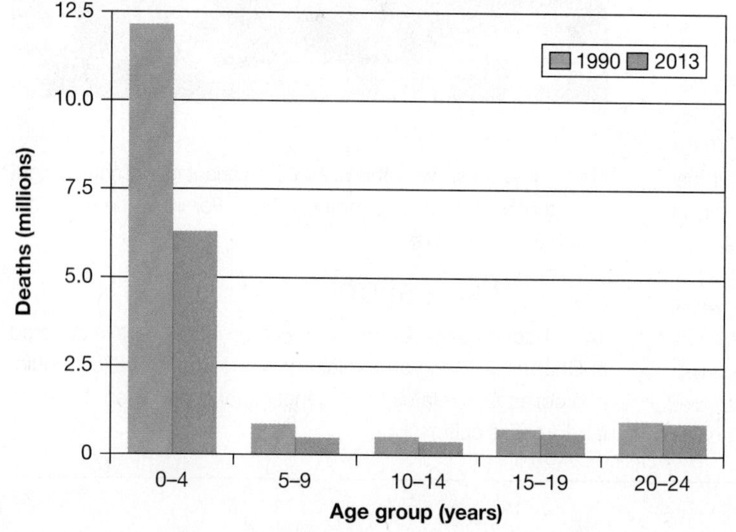

## Mortality Before Age 5

**LO 4.5.1 List the major causes of mortality in the first 5 years of life, and explain important prevention efforts.**

Most infant mortality takes place during the first month of life. In 2012, 44% of deaths before age 5 occurred during the neonatal period. Usually mortality during this period is due to severe birth defects or preterm birth complications, or is an indirect consequence of the death of the mother during childbirth (UNICEF, 2014). Neonatal mortality rates are much higher in developing than in developed countries. UNICEF (2015) has issued a list of recommendations to reduce neonatal mortality in developing countries. These include increasing the availability of trained midwives and access to hospitals in case of complications or emergencies (see also Chapter 3).

As you can see in Map 4.1, rates of mortality before age 5 are also much higher in developing countries than in developed countries (UNICEF, 2013). With regard to deaths beyond the first month but within the first 4 years, malnutrition is a major contributor. As described earlier, nutritional supplements to the diets of young children and families are highly beneficial.

Diseases are another major cause of mortality worldwide. Lower respiratory infections, primarily due to pneumococcus and *H. influenzae* Type B (types of bacteria), are a major cause of death (GDB 2013 Mortality and Causes Death Collaborators, 2014). Malaria, a blood disease spread by mosquitoes (see Chapter 2), is another major cause, mainly in Africa (Finkel, 2007). Diarrhea is also very dangerous early in life. Infants and young children with diarrhea lose fluids and eventually die from dehydration if untreated. Diarrhea may be caused by a range of digestive illnesses, and is often a consequence of bottle-feeding in unsanitary conditions, or mixing formula powder with unclean water.

Diarrhea can be cured easily through simple, inexpensive **oral rehydration therapy (ORT)**. ORT involves having infants with diarrhea drink a solution of salt and glucose mixed with (clean) water. Since 1980 the WHO has led an international effort to reduce infant deaths through providing ORT, and the effort has reduced the worldwide rate of infant deaths due to diarrhea from 4.5 million per year to less than 2 million (Boschi-Pinto et al., 2009). However, the reason the rate is still as high as 2 million per year is that even now, in the parts of the world where infant diarrhea is most common, this simple, inexpensive remedy is often unavailable.

**oral rehydration therapy (ORT)**
treatment for infant diarrhea that involves drinking a solution of salt and glucose mixed with clean water

**Map 4.1** Under-5 Mortality Rates Worldwide, 2013

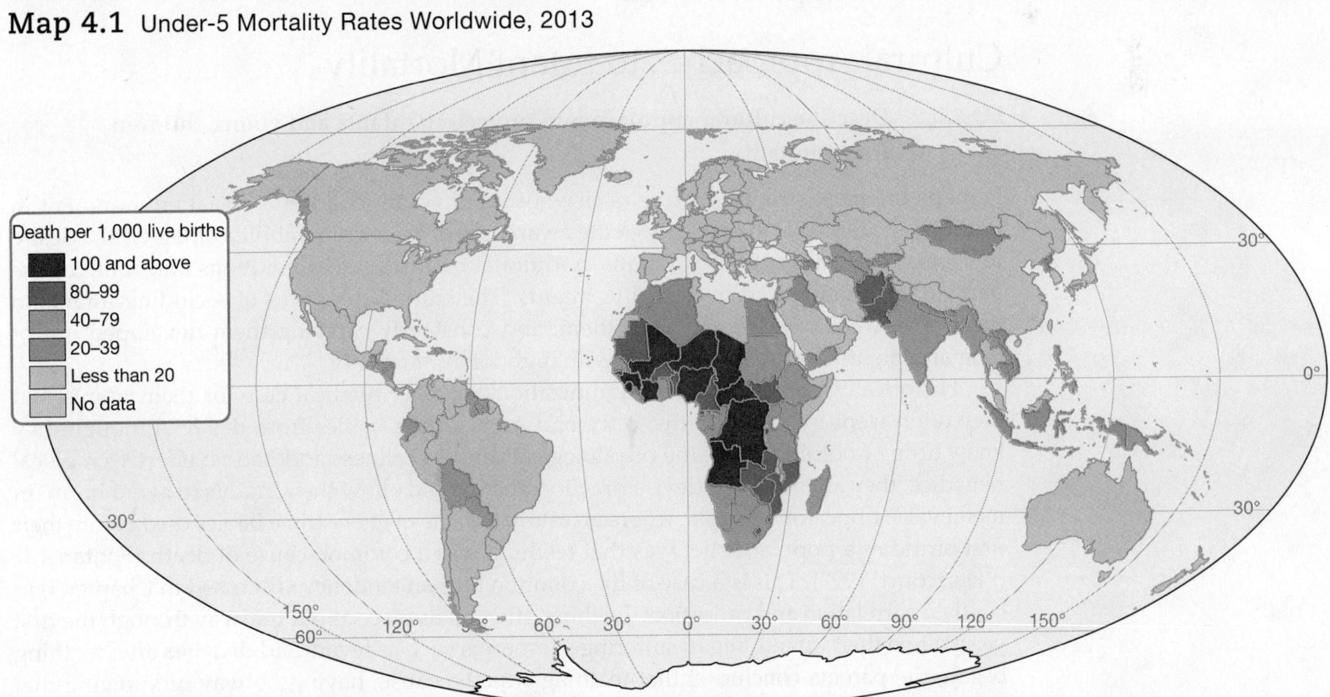

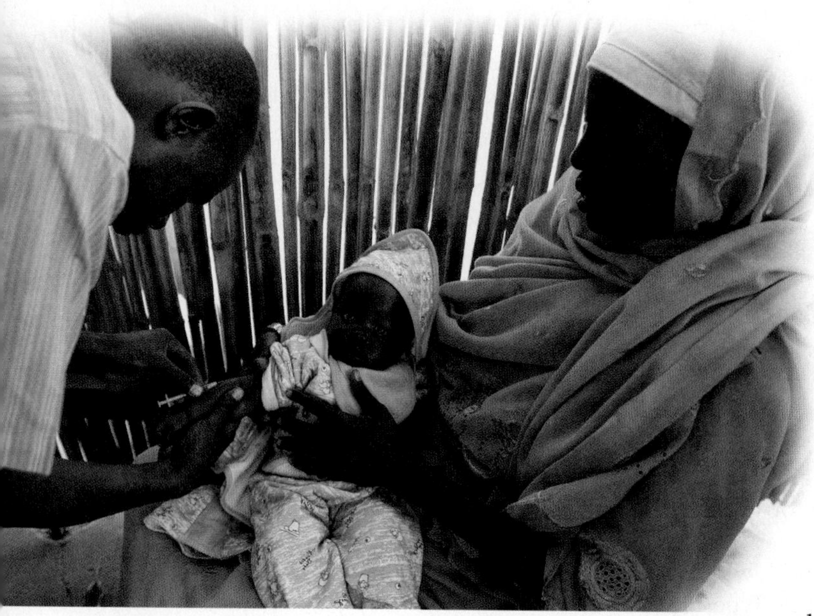

Increased prevalence of vaccinations in infancy has greatly reduced infant mortality worldwide. Here, an infant receives a vaccination in southern Sudan.

Although millions of infants and young children worldwide die yearly from lack of adequate nutrition and medical care, in the past half-century many diseases that formerly killed infants and young children have been reduced or even eliminated due to improved food production and vaccines that provide immunization. Immunization programs have eradicated smallpox, eliminated measles and polio in large regions of the world, and greatly reduced the prevalence of diphtheria, tetanus, and yellow fever (Population Reference Bureau, 2014). Typically, children receive vaccinations for these diseases in the first or second year of life. However, there is a great deal of variability worldwide in how likely children are to be vaccinated. As of 2013, coverage for the major infant vaccines was about 70% in Africa and South Asia, and over 90% in Europe and the Americas (UNICEF, 2013). In recent years, a major effort to provide immunization to all children has been made by the WHO, UNICEF, and private foundations, and the rate of immunization has been increasing, especially in Africa (UNICEF, 2013). Recently these agencies have also started a global effort to vaccinate against pneumococcus and *H. influenzae* Type B. So far, however, declines in lower respiratory deaths due to this immunization effort have primarily taken place in developed regions of the world and Latin America (GDB 2013 Mortality and Causes Death Collaborators, 2014).

Although rumors have circulated that some vaccinations may actually cause harm to children, for example by triggering autism or causing SIDS, scientific studies have found no basis for these claims (Centers for Disease Control and Prevention [CDC], 2010; Rodier, 2009). Unfortunately, some parents have been deceived by these claims and consequently refused to have their children vaccinated, which, ironically—and sadly—exposes their children and other people's children to the genuine danger of contracting infectious diseases.

Nonetheless, in developed countries, where most children receive vaccinations and have access to adequate food and medical care, life-threatening illnesses are rare. Minor illnesses are common in early childhood, with most children experiencing 7 to 10 per year (Kesson, 2007). Minor illnesses help build up the immune system, so that children experience them less frequently with age.

## Cultural Approaches to Infant Mortality

**LO 4.5.2 Describe cultural approaches to protecting infants and young children from mortality.**

Perhaps the most striking feature of newborn and young children's social environment in traditional cultures is the parents' acute awareness of their vulnerability, along with a desire to protect against mortality. In many traditional cultures, these emotions and motives are particularly pronounced in regard to infants. The cultural practices of secluding infants in their early weeks, cosleeping with them, and constantly carrying them developed out of long and painful human experience with high infant mortality.

Historically, parents had no immunizations or other medical care for their infants, but they often went to great lengths to try and protect their babies from death. Although they knew little or nothing about the physiological causes of illness and had no effective medical remedies, they attempted to devise practices that would allow their infants to avoid harm. In medieval Europe, for example, where an estimated one of every three babies died before their first birthday, a popular belief was that teething was a common cause of death (Fontanel & d'Hartcourt, 1997). This is a case of the common human tendency, discussed in Chapter 1, to conflate correlation and causation. Teething often takes place about midway through the first year. When their infants began suffering symptoms such as fevers and diarrhea after teething began, the parents concluded that teething was the cause, having no way of knowing that the real source of the symptoms was a disease such as malaria, typhus, or cholera. So, they addressed the illness by placing a charm or amulet around the child's neck, or by placing leeches on the baby's gums, sadly to no good effect (Reese, 2000).

Today, too, in cultures where medical remedies for infant illness are scarce, parents often resort to an assortment of practices intended to protect their babies from disease and death. Observations today in places with little access to medical care offer many poignant examples of the cultural practices that have developed to try to protect infants. For example, the people of Bali, in Indonesia, believe that infants should be treated like gods, since they have just arrived from the spirit world, where the gods dwell (Diener, 2000). Consequently, infants should be held constantly and should never touch the ground, out of respect for their godly status. If an infant dies, this is often interpreted as indicating that the infant was not shown the proper respect and so decided to return to the spirit world. The Fulani people of West Africa believe that a sharp knife should always be kept near the baby to ward off the witches and evil spirits that may try to take its soul (Johnson, 2000). Compliments to the baby should be avoided at all costs, as this may only make the baby seem more valuable and beautiful and so all the more attractive to the evil spirits. Instead, the Fulani people believe parents should give the infant an unattractive nickname like "Cow Turd," so that the evil spirits will think the baby is not worth taking. Finally, the Ifalaluk of Micronesia believe that neonates should be covered with cloths in the weeks after birth to encourage sweating, which they believe helps babies grow properly (Le, 2000). Babies should be washed three times a day, morning, noon, and afternoon, but not in the evening, because evil spirits are out then. Any time babies are outside they should be covered with a cloth so that they will not be spied by evil spirits.

Deaths worldwide among children age 5 and under have declined due to increased childhood vaccinations. Here, a Red Cross volunteer in El Salvador gives an oral vaccination to a young boy.

**Critical Thinking Question:** Can you think of beliefs and behaviors in your culture that reflect the deep-seated desire to keep infants and young children healthy and protected against mortality? For example, earlier we mentioned the erroneous belief that vaccinations may cause autism or SIDS.

## Mortality From Age 5 Through the 20s

**LO 4.5.3 List the major causes of mortality from early childhood through emerging adulthood, and describe prevention efforts.**

As we saw above, mortality rates worldwide drop sharply by age 5. Gradually there is also a change in the main cause of mortality. The risk from injuries starts to climb. Do you remember becoming injured in early or middle childhood? If you do, you are not alone. Most young children—and their parents—can count on spending a portion of their childhood nursing an injury; a minor "boo-boo" if they're lucky, but in some cases something far more serious. Young children have high activity levels and their motor development is advanced enough for them to be able to run, jump, and climb, but their cognitive development is not always advanced enough for them to anticipate situations that might be dangerous. In the United States each year, one-third of children under 10 become injured badly enough to receive medical attention (Field & Behrman, 2003). Boys are more likely than girls to become injured, in part because their play tends to be rougher and more physically active.

In the course of teenage years, injury rates continue to rise, and injuries account for a higher proportion of deaths in adolescents than in any other age group (Patton et al. 2014). Causes of injury and death include drowning, falls, and fire. Drowning, for example, is a notable cause of death in some south Asian countries such as Bangladesh. Interpersonal violence

is also an important cause of adolescent deaths in many Latin American countries and several countries in southern Africa (GDB 2013 Mortality and Causes Death Collaborators, 2014).

Road traffic accidents, however, are a major worldwide source of injuries and deaths from age 5 and through the 20s (National Highway Traffic Safety Administration [NHTSA], 2014; Safe Kids Worldwide, 2013). An organization called Safe Kids Worldwide (2013) is working to advocate safety measures for young children in both developed and developing countries. It currently has chapters in more than 20 countries, including China, Brazil, India, and Canada, and is expanding steadily. It addresses safety in a variety of areas, and traffic safety is a major focus including pedestrian safety, use of bicycle helmets, and use of seat belts in cars. Mortality rates due to traffic accidents are rapidly increasing in developing countries because of the growth of motorization. Pedestrians are most often affected, followed by car occupants and motorcyclists.

Traffic safety measures such as bike helmets and designated bike lanes are important to children's lives. Here, school children in Spain take part in a cycling awareness class.

In contrast to developing countries, deaths from traffic accidents are decreasing in developed countries. Nonetheless, the most serious threat to the lives and health of adolescents and emerging adults comes from automobile driving (Patton et al., 2009). In the United States, as you can see in Figure 4.13, young people ages 16 to 24 have the highest rates of automobile accidents, injuries, and fatalities of any age group (NHTSA, 2014). In other developed countries, a higher minimum driving age (usually 18) and less access to automobiles have made rates of accidents and fatalities among young people substantially lower than in the United States, but motor vehicle injuries are the leading cause of death during emerging adulthood in those countries as well (Pan et al., 2007; Twisk & Stacey, 2007).

What is responsible for these grim statistics? Is it young drivers' inexperience or their risky driving behavior? Inexperience certainly plays a large role. Rates of accidents and fatalities are extremely high in the early months of driving, but fall dramatically by 1 year after licensure (McKnight & Peck, 2002; Valentine et al., 2013). Studies that have attempted to disentangle experience and age in young drivers have generally concluded that inexperience is partly responsible for young drivers' accidents and fatalities. However, studies have also concluded that inexperience is not the only factor involved. Equally important is the way young people drive and the kinds of risks they take (Valentine et al., 2013). Compared to older drivers, young drivers (especially males) are more likely to drive at excessive speeds, follow other vehicles too closely, violate traffic signs and signals, take more risks in lane changing and passing other vehicles, allow too little time to merge, and fail to yield to pedestrians (Bina et al., 2006; Williams & Ferguson, 2002). They are also more likely than older drivers to report driving under the influence of alcohol. Drivers ages 21 to 24 involved in fatal accidents are more likely to have been intoxicated at the time of the accident than persons in any other age group (NHTSA, 2014). Nearly half of American college students report driving while intoxicated within the past year (Clapp et al., 2005; Glassman et al., 2010). Young people are also less likely than older drivers to wear seat belts, and in serious car crashes, occupants not wearing seat belts are twice as likely to be killed and three times as likely to be injured, compared to those wearing seat belts (NHTSA, 2014).

**Figure 4.13** Rates of Car Fatalities by Age

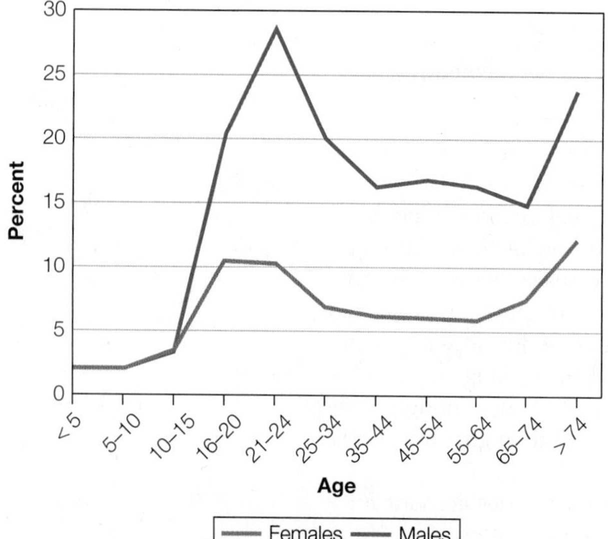


SOURCE: Based on NHTSA (2014).

What else leads to crashes among young drivers? Young drivers are more likely than older drivers to believe their friends would approve of risky driving behavior such as speeding, closely following another vehicle, and passing another car in risky circumstances (Chen et al., 2007; U.S. Department of Transportation, 1995). Driver characteristics matter, too. Personality characteristics such as sensation seeking and aggressiveness promote risky driving and subsequent crashes, and these characteristics tend to be highest in young male drivers (Shope & Bingham, 2008). In an interview study, 23-year-old Nick gave voice to his—and his friend's—taste for risky driving:

> I love to drive fast, but after awhile driving fast just wasn't doing it any more. So I started driving without the lights on [at night], going about ninety on country roads. I even got a friend to do it. We'd go cruising down country roads, turn off the lights, and just fly. It was incredible. We'd go as fast as we could, [and] at night, with no lights it feels like you're just flying (Arnett, 1996, p. 79).

What can be done to reduce the rates of automobile accidents and fatalities among young drivers? Parental involvement and monitoring of adolescents' driving behavior has been shown to be especially important in the early months of driving, and interventions to increase parental involvement can be effective (Simmons-Morton, 2007; Simons-Morton et al., 2002, 2006, 2008). However, by far the most effective approach is a program of restricted driving privileges called **graduated driver licensing (GDL)**. GDL is a government program in which young people obtain driving privileges gradually, contingent on a safe driving record, rather than all at once. GDL programs allow young people to obtain driving experience under conditions that limit the likelihood of crashes by restricting the circumstances under which novices can drive (Foss, 2007; Williams et al., 2012). Watch the video *Graduated Driver Licensing* to learn more.

**graduated driver licensing (GDL)**
government program in which young people obtain driving privileges gradually, contingent on a safe driving record, rather than all at once

## Research Focus: Graduated Driver Licensing

Graduated driver licensing (GDL) typically includes three stages. The learning license is the stage in which the young person obtains driving experience under the supervision of an experienced driver. For example, the GDL program in California requires young people to complete learning-license driver training of 50 hours under the supervision of a parent, of which 10 hours must take place at night.

The second stage is a period of restricted license driving. In this stage young drivers are allowed to drive unsupervised, but with tighter restrictions than those that apply to adults. The restrictions are based on research revealing the factors that are most likely to place young drivers at risk for crashes. For example, in some states GDL programs include driving curfews, which prohibit young drivers from driving late at night except for a specific purpose such as going to and from work. There are also prohibitions against driving with teenage passengers when no adults are present, requirements for seat belt use, and a "zero tolerance" rule for alcohol use. Recently, most American states have also passed laws against any cell phone use for novice drivers, including both calling and texting. In this restricted stage, any violations of these restrictions may result in a suspended license. It is only after the GDL period has passed—usually no more than 1 year—that a young person obtains a full license and enters the third stage of having the same driving privileges as adults.

What have research studies shown regarding the effectiveness of GDL programs? Numerous studies in the past decade have shown GDL programs to be the most effective way to reduce automobile accidents among young drivers. One summary review (or meta-analysis) of 21 studies conducted by Jean Shope (2007) concluded that GDL programs consistently reduce young drivers' crash risk by 20% to 40%.

**Watch** GRADUATED DRIVER LICENSING

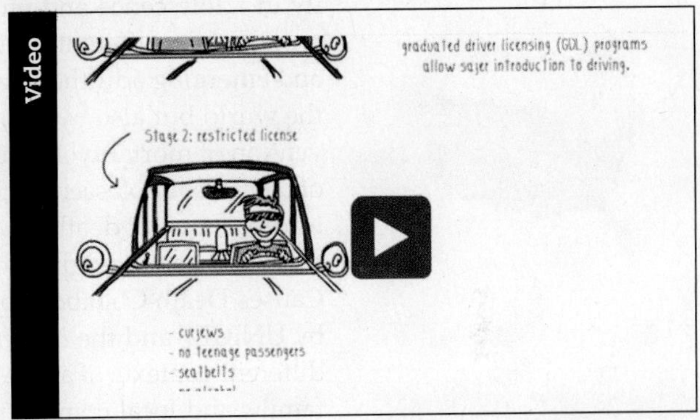


Driving curfews in particular have been found to reduce young people's crash involvement dramatically. Fatal crashes among 16-year-old drivers in the United States decreased by 40% in the past decade, and this improvement is attributed mainly to GDL programs. Legislators in many states have responded to this evidence by passing more of these programs. All 50 American states now have some kind of GDL program, a dramatic rise over the past 20 years. GDL programs have also been instituted in Canada and are becoming more common in European countries. Research indicates that these laws work in part by making it easier for parents to enforce restrictions on their adolescents' driving behavior. Across developed countries, automobile accidents remain the number-one cause of death in the teens and 20s, but effective GDL programs have dramatically reduced the number of deaths in recent decades.

## Review Questions

1. Which of the following is NOT one of the typical components of a GDL program?
   a. Driving curfew
   b. No more than 2 teenage passengers
   c. Mandatory seat belt use
   d. Zero tolerance for alcohol

2. Which of the following has been the consequence of widespread adoption of GDL programs?
   a. Injuries among teens have declined, but not fatalities
   b. Most teens have found ways to avoid the regulations
   c. Auto fatalities among 16-year-olds have sharply declined
   d. Girls' driving habits have changed but boys' have not

In addition to injuries and traffic accidents, HIV/AIDS is another common cause of adolescent mortality. More than 50% of adolescents with HIV/AIDS reside in sub-Saharan Africa and India (Children & Aids, 2016). HIV-related deaths have more than tripled since 2000, making it a leading cause of adolescent deaths worldwide (World Health Organization [WHO], 2016; UNAIDS, 2017). Whereas prevention efforts in developing countries have dramatically reduced mother–child transmission of HIV/AIDS in recent years (see Chapter 2), prevention and treatment efforts with adolescents have lagged. For example, 70% of 15- to 19-year-olds in sub-Saharan Africa have limited knowledge of HIV/AIDS (Children & Aids, 2016).

Recently, the need for prevention efforts to address mortality in adolescents and emerging adults has gained attention. While mortality in young children has been a major focus of prevention efforts for decades, the focus on adolescents and emerging adults is much more recent. UNICEF, for example, has expanded its focus on younger children to adolescents (Diers, 2013). Recently, the Executive Director of UNICEF wrote that "surely we do not want to save children in their first decade of life only to lose them in the second" (UNICEF, 2011, p. iii). The *Lancet*, a top medical journal, has also partnered with leading academic institutions to establish a commission on the health and well-being of adolescents and emerging adults (Patton et al., 2014).

A key part of the challenge, as we have seen in this chapter, is that the causes of mortality in adolescence and emerging adulthood differ vastly from early childhood, and hence require very different prevention efforts. Also, as we have seen in this chapter, adolescence and emerging adulthood are characterized not only by differentials in mortality by region of the world but also by sex. This adds a dimension that is not nearly as important to the prevention of mortality in young children. In Africa, for example, childbirth is the leading cause of death for adolescent girls (Diers, 2013). In developed countries, road traffic injuries are the leading cause of death among adolescent girls. Also, deaths from injuries and violence in adolescence and emerging adulthood affect males more than females (GDB 2013 Mortality and Causes Death Collaborators, 2014). To address these challenges, recent efforts such as those by UNICEF and the *Lancet* commission are beginning to focus on reaching across the many different contexts of adolescents' and emerging adults' everyday lives, such as school, work, family, and local communities (Patton et al., 2012). There is also an emphasis on including adolescents and emerging adults in the formulation of preventive policies.

**Critical Thinking Question:** In Chapter 1, we addressed how the contemporary field of child development spans from the prenatal period through emerging adulthood. Explain the extent to which worldwide health and mortality prevention initiatives fit with this broadened understanding of child development.

## SUMMARY: Preventing Mortality: Diseases and Injuries

**LO 4.5.1 List the major causes of mortality in the first 5 years of life, and explain important prevention efforts.**

Mortality rates are much higher in developing than developed countries. During the neonatal period, mortality is usually due to severe birth defects or preterm birth complications or is an indirect consequence of the death of the mother during childbirth. Prevention efforts involve the availability of trained midwives and access to hospitals in case of complications during birth. With regard to deaths beyond the first month but within the first 4 years, malnutrition is a major contributor. Nutritional supplements to the diets of young children and families are highly beneficial. Malaria, diarrhea, and respiratory infections are other major causes of mortality in young children.

**LO 4.5.2 Describe cultural approaches to protecting infants and young children from mortality.**

The cultural practices of secluding infants in their early weeks, cosleeping with them, and constantly carrying them developed out of long and painful human experience with high infant mortality.

**LO 4.5.3 List the major causes of mortality from early childhood through emerging adulthood, and describe prevention efforts.**

Mortality rates worldwide drop sharply by age 5. After this age, the biggest risks to children's lives come from injury, traffic accidents, and HIV/AIDS. Although mortality in young children has been a major focus of prevention efforts for decades, the focus on adolescents and emerging adults is much more recent. Some governments and nonprofit organizations have focused on road safety, including graduated driver licensing (GDL).

## Apply Your Knowledge as a Professional

The topics covered in this chapter apply to a wide variety of career professions. Watch this video to learn how they apply to a dance instructor.

**Journaling Question:** Consider the foods that you typically see on the "kids' menu" in restaurants. Write an analysis where you explicate how these menus reflect developmental and cultural beliefs about food. Then explain what your ideal "kids' menu" would look like, and why.

Chapter 5

# Cognition: Stages, Processes, and Social Learning

## Learning Objectives

### 5.1 Piaget's Theory of Cognitive Development

5.1.1 Describe the meaning of maturation, schemes, assimilation, and accommodation.

5.1.2 Describe the six sensorimotor substages.

5.1.3 Explain how object permanence, deferred imitation, and categorization develop over the course of the first 2 years.

5.1.4 Explain the features of Piaget's preoperational stage of cognitive development.

5.1.5 Explain the major cognitive advances that occur during Piaget's concrete operations stage.

5.1.6 Describe the features of hypothetical-deductive reasoning and the extent to which adolescents and emerging adults use formal operations.

5.1.7 Summarize the strengths and limitations of Piaget's theory.

### 5.2 Post-Piagetian Approaches

5.2.1 Describe how adolescents engage in abstract, complex, and metacognitive thinking, and explain the neurological underpinnings of these abilities.

5.2.2 Describe how pragmatism and dialectical thought allow emerging adults to become better at addressing real-life problems.

### 5.3 Information-Processing Approaches

5.3.1 Describe how attention, memory, and executive function change during infancy and early childhood, including how current research accounts for infantile amnesia.

5.3.2 Describe how attention, memory, and executive function change during middle childhood, and identify the characteristics of children who have ADHD.

5.3.3 Summarize the major changes in attention, memory, and executive function that take place in adolescence and emerging adulthood.

5.3.4 Summarize the strengths and limitations of information-processing approaches.

### 5.4 Social Cognition

5.4.1 Explain what "theory of mind" is and the evidence for when it develops during early childhood.

5.4.2 Define the imaginary audience and the personal fable, and explain how they reflect egocentrism in adolescence.

5.4.3 Summarize the strengths and limitations of research on social cognition.

### 5.5 Sociocultural Theories of Cognitive Development

5.5.1 Describe Vygotsky's sociocultural theory of cognitive development and contrast it with Piaget's theory.

5.5.2 Identify ways that cultural learning takes place from childhood through emerging adulthood.

5.5.3 Summarize the strengths and limitations of sociocultural theories of cognitive development.

THE FRENCH PHILOSOPHER RENÉ DESCARTES (1596–1650) FAMOUSLY DECLARED: "I THINK, THEREFORE I AM," THEREBY RENDERING COGNITION THE VERY BASIS AND PROOF OF HUMAN EXISTENCE. Developmental psychology, too, has a long and prolific tradition of examining fundamental concepts and processes pertaining to cognition, or thinking. As we will see, the focus on cognitive development goes back to Jean Piaget's stage theory from many decades ago, and is also characteristic of more recent research on information processing and social cognition. These lines of research have largely, if not exclusively, focused on the universals of cognitive development.

Many centuries before Descartes, Lao-Tzu (circa 6th–5th century BCE), the Chinese philosopher and originator of Taoism, proclaimed: "Stop thinking, and end your problems," suggesting a strikingly different understanding of cognition and the self. A focus on how cultural groups differ on cognitive development and their understandings of the meaning and value of cognition is the hallmark of sociocultural theories, including the work of Lev Vygotsky. In this chapter, we delve into research within the traditions of Piaget, information processing, social cognition, and Vygotsky. The diverse research traditions on children's cognitive development have generated fascinating insight into how children use their cognitive capabilities every day, from play to schoolwork to extracurricular activities to household chores.

**Watch CHAPTER INTRODUCTION: COGNITION: STAGES, PROCESSES, AND SOCIAL LEARNING**

**mental structure**
a way of thinking within a stage of development that is applied across all aspects of life

**cognitive-developmental approach**
focuses on how cognitive development takes place in a sequence of distinct stages, pioneered by Piaget and subsequently adopted by researchers addressing other areas of development

**maturation**
concept that an innate, biologically based program is the driving force behind development

**schemes**
cognitive structures for processing, organizing, and interpreting information

**assimilation**
cognitive process of altering new information to fit an existing scheme

# 5.1 Piaget's Theory of Cognitive Development

Unquestionably, the most influential theory of cognitive development from infancy through adolescence is the one developed by the Swiss psychologist Jean Piaget (1896–1980). Piaget's observations convinced him that children of different ages think differently and that changes in cognitive development proceed in distinct stages (Piaget, 1954).

## Basic Cognitive-Developmental Concepts

**LO 5.1.1 Describe the meaning of maturation, schemes, assimilation, and accommodation.**

Each stage of Piaget's theory involves a different way of thinking about the world. The idea of cognitive stages means that each person's cognitive abilities are organized into coherent **mental structures**; a person who thinks within a particular stage in one aspect of life should think within that stage in all other aspects of life as well, because all thinking is part of the same mental structure (Collins & Hartup, 2013; Keating, 1990). Because Piaget focused on how cognition changes with age, his approach (and the approach of those who have followed in his tradition) is known as the **cognitive-developmental approach**.

According to Piaget, the driving force behind development from one stage to the next is **maturation**, a biologically driven program of developmental change (Inhelder & Piaget, 1958; Piaget, 2002). Each of us has within our genotype a prescription for cognitive development that prepares us for certain changes at certain ages. A reasonably normal environment is necessary for cognitive development to occur, but the effect of the environment is limited. You cannot teach a 1-year-old something that only a 4-year-old can learn, no matter how sophisticated your teaching techniques are. By the time the 1-year-old reaches age 4, the biological processes of maturation will make it easy to understand the world as a typical child of 4 understands it, and no special teaching will be required.

Along with maturation, Piaget emphasized that cognitive development is driven by the child's efforts to understand and influence the surrounding environment (Demetriou & Raftopoulos, 2004; Piaget, 2002). Children actively examine the world and construct their understanding of it, rather than being merely the passive recipients of environmental influences.

Piaget emphasized you cannot teach a 1-year-old something that only a 4-year-old is capable of doing. Here, a young girl tells a story to her baby sister.

Piaget proposed that the child's construction of reality takes place through the use of **schemes**, which are cognitive structures for processing, organizing, and interpreting information. For infants, schemes are based on sensory and motor processes such as sucking and grasping. After infancy, however, schemes become symbolic and representational. This includes words, ideas, and concepts. For example, words such as *chair* and *dog* evoke cognitive structures that allow you to process, organize, and interpret information. That creature in the distance running full speed toward you on the sidewalk: Is it a dog? What kind of dog is it? Is it friendly or not? Do you know this dog? These questions may well form part of your scheme for dogs, and your answers to the questions will provide you with information to better know what to do.

The two processes involved in the use of schemes are **assimilation** and **accommodation**. Assimilation occurs when *new information is altered to fit an existing scheme.* In contrast, accommodation entails *changing the scheme to adapt to the new information.* Assimilation and accommodation usually take place together in varying degrees; they are "two sides of the same cognitive coin" (Flavell et al., 2002, p. 5). For example, an infant who has been breast-feeding may use mostly assimilation and a slight degree of accommodation when learning to suck from the nipple on a bottle, but if sucking on a brush handle or a parent's finger the infant would be able to use assimilation less and need to use accommodation more. Watch the video *Assimilation and Accommodation* for additional examples of each process in infants.

People of other ages, too, use both assimilation and accommodation whenever they are processing cognitive information. One example is right in front of you. In the course of reading this text, you will easily assimilate information that is related to what you already know. Other information, perhaps the information from cultures other than your own, will be different from the schemes you have developed from living in your culture and will require you to use accommodation in order to expand your knowledge and understanding of child development worldwide.

Based on his own research and collaborations with his colleague Barbel Inhelder, Piaget devised a theory of cognitive development to describe four stages that children's thinking passes through as they grow up (Inhelder & Piaget, 1958; Piaget, 1972). Table 5.1 provides an overview. We now turn to an in-depth examination of each stage.

**Watch** ASSIMILATION AND ACCOMMODATION

**accommodation**
cognitive process of changing a scheme to adapt to new information

## The Sensorimotor Stage: Six Substages

**LO 5.1.2 Describe the six sensorimotor substages.**

The first 2 years of life Piaget termed the **sensorimotor stage**. Cognitive development in this stage involves learning how to coordinate the activities of the senses (such as watching an object as it moves across your field of vision) with motor activities (such as reaching out to grasp the object). Piaget divided the sensorimotor stage into six substages (Piaget, 1952, 1954):

**sensorimotor stage**
in Piaget's theory, the first 2 years of cognitive development, which involves learning how to coordinate the activities of the senses with motor activities

***Substage 1: Simple reflexes (0–1 month).*** In this substage, cognitive activity is based mainly on the neonatal reflexes described in Chapter 3, such as sucking, rooting, and grasping. Reflexes are a type of scheme because they are a way of processing and organizing information. However, unlike most schemes, for which there is a balance of assimilation and accommodation, reflex schemes are weighted heavily toward assimilation because they do not adapt much in response to the environment.

***Substage 2: First habits and primary circular reactions (1–4 months).*** In these early months, infants' activities become based less on reflexes and more on the infants' purposeful behavior. Specifically, infants in this substage learn to repeat bodily movements that occurred initially by chance. For example, infants often like to suck on their hands and fingers in this substage. While moving their hands around randomly, fingers end up in their mouth and they begin sucking on them. Finding this sensation soothing or pleasurable, they repeat the movement, now intentionally. The movement is *primary* because it focuses on the infant's own body, and *circular* because, once it is discovered, it is repeated intentionally.

***Substage 3: Secondary circular reactions (4–8 months).*** Secondary circular reactions also entail the repetition of movements that originally occurred by chance. Unlike primary circular

**Table 5.1** Stages of Cognitive Development in Piaget's Theory

| Stage | Ages | Characteristics |
|---|---|---|
| **Sensorimotor** | 0–2 | Capable of coordinating the activities of the senses with motor activities |
| **Preoperational** | 2–7 | Capable of symbolic representation, such as in language, but with limited ability to use mental operations |
| **Concrete operations** | 7–11 | Capable of using mental operations, but only in concrete, immediate experience; difficulty thinking hypothetically |
| **Formal operations** | 11–15 and up | Capable of thinking logically and abstractly; capable of formulating hypotheses and testing them systematically; thinking is more complex, including ability to think about thinking (metacognition) |

reactions that focus on the infant's own body, secondary circular reactions involve activity in relation to the external world. For example, Piaget recorded how his daughter Lucienne accidentally kicked a mobile hanging over her crib. Delighted at the effect, she now repeated the behavior intentionally, over and over, each time squealing with laughter (Crain, 2000).

***Substage 4: Coordination of secondary circular reactions (8–12 months).*** In this substage, for the first time the baby's actions begin not as reflexes or accidents, but as intentional and goal-directed behaviors. Furthermore, rather than exercise one scheme at a time, the infant can now coordinate schemes. For example, at this age, Piaget's son Laurent was able to move an object (Piaget's hand) out of the way in order to reach another object (a matchbox), thus coordinating three schemes: moving something aside, reaching, and grasping.

***Substage 5: Tertiary Circular Reactions (12–18 months).*** Now, toddlers intentionally try out new behaviors to see what the effects will be. Like secondary circular reactions, tertiary circular reactions are circular because they are performed repeatedly; the difference is that now the toddler is intentionally aiming to do something novel in order to see what happens. To Piaget, this substage heralded the beginnings of human curiosity. For example, at 17 months, our twins became curious as to what would happen if you repeatedly stuffed the toilet with gobs of tissue and flushed. One day, when on their own in the upstairs bathroom, they flushed and flushed and flushed until the flushing system broke and water began overflowing. We were sitting downstairs when suddenly water whooshed out of the vents in the ceiling! We found the twins, standing in 3 inches of water, giggling with glee, absolutely delighted. We don't recall thinking of Piaget at that moment, but he would probably have been pleased. To Piaget, in this substage, toddlers become like little scientists, experimenting on the objects around them.

**mental representations**
Piaget's final substage of sensorimotor development in which toddlers first think about the range of possibilities and then select the action most likely to achieve the desired outcome

***Substage 6: Mental Representation (18—24 months).*** In this final substage of sensorimotor development, toddlers first think about possible actions and then select the one most likely to achieve the desired outcome, instead of trying out a range of actions as in tertiary circular reactions. Piaget gave the example of his daughter Lucienne, who sought to obtain a small chain from inside the matchbox where her father had placed it. First she turned the box upside down; then, she tried to jam her finger into it, but neither of these methods worked. She paused for a moment, holding the matchbox and considering it intently. Then, she opened and closed her mouth, and suddenly slid back the cover of the matchbox to reveal the chain (Crain, 2000). To Piaget, opening and closing her mouth showed that she was pondering potential solutions, then mimicking the solution that had occurred to her. In other words, Lucienne had formed a **mental representation** of the problem, and that prompted her sudden solution. Mental representation is a crucial milestone in cognitive development because it is the basis of the most important and most distinctly human cognitive abilities, including language. Words are mental representations of objects, people, actions, and ideas—a topic we will explore in Chapter 6.

As you can see, the sensorimotor substages chart how the neonate develops into an intentional and inquisitive toddler who explores the environment, not only physically, but also through mental representation.

Piaget emphasized how toddlers are intentional and inquisitive, exploring their environment physically and through mental representation. This toddler seems fascinated by the sea shore.

## The Sensorimotor Stage: Object Permanence, Deferred Imitation, and Categorization

**LO 5.1.3 Explain how object permanence, deferred imitation, and categorization develop over the course of the first 2 years.**

Piaget highlighted three key cognitive accomplishments that he considered necessary to reaching the conclusion of the sensorimotor stage: object permanence, deferred imitation, and categorization.

As we will see, recent research that has made use of advanced technology indicates that these abilities actually develop earlier than Piaget claimed.

**OBJECT PERMANENCE.** An important cognitive advance in infancy is the initial understanding of **object permanence**. This is the awareness that objects (including people) continue to exist even when we are not in direct sensory or motor contact with them. From his observations and simple experiments, Piaget concluded that infants have little understanding of object permanence for much of the first year of life (Piaget, 1952). When infants younger than 4 months drop an object, they do not look to see where it went. Piaget interpreted this as indicating that, to the infants, the object ceased to exist once they could no longer see or touch it. From 4 to 8 months, infants who drop an object will look briefly to see where it has gone, but only briefly, which Piaget interpreted as indicating that they are unsure whether the object still exists. If infants at this age are shown an interesting object—Piaget liked to use his pocket watch—and then that object is placed under a blanket, they will not lift up the blanket to look for it. It is only at 8–12 months that infants begin to show a developing awareness of object permanence, according to Piaget. Now, when shown an interesting object that then disappears under a blanket, the infants will pick up the blanket to find it.

**object permanence**
awareness that objects (including people) continue to exist even when we are not in direct sensory or motor contact with them

According to Piaget, however, an infant's grasp of object permanence at this age is still rudimentary. To show this, he made the task slightly more complicated. After an 8-month-old successfully solved the object-under-the-blanket task several times, Piaget introduced a second blanket next to the first, showed the infant the object, and this time placed it under the second blanket. Infants at this age then looked for the object—but not under the second blanket, where they had just seen it hidden. Instead, they searched under the first blanket, where they had found the object before! Piaget called this the *A-not-B error.* The infants were used to finding the object under blanket *A*, so they continued to look under blanket *A*, not blanket *B*, even after they had seen the object hidden under blanket *B*. To Piaget, this error indicated that the infants believed their own action—looking under blanket *A*—caused the object to reappear. They did not yet understand that the object continued to exist irrespective of their actions, so they did not yet fully grasp object permanence. According to Piaget, that would only happen by the sixth and last sensorimotor substage. In fact, even though the A-not-B error is less common in toddlerhood than in infancy, search errors still happen occasionally even into early childhood, up to ages 4 and 5 (Hood et al., 2003; Newcombe & Huttenlocher, 2006). The video *Object Permanence Across Cultures* shows how infants and toddlers respond to Piaget's tasks.

In recent decades, methods of testing infants' cognitive abilities, including object permanence, have become much more technologically advanced. Infants' motor development occurs along with their cognitive development, so when they fail to remove a blanket in order to look for a hidden object, could it be that they lack the necessary motor coordination rather than believe the object has disappeared? One line of research by Renee Baillargeon and colleagues has tested this hypothesis by using the "violation of expectations method." This method does not require an infant to engage in any fine or gross motor movement. Instead, it relies on

## Cultural Focus: Object Permanence Across Cultures

The knowledge of object permanence is something that all young children need to learn in order to function in the world. In this video, we see demonstrations of children at various ages being tested with Piaget's tasks to see if they grasp the concept of object permanence or not. The results with children from many different cultures indicate that this is a universal concept.

### Review Question

According to this video, object permanence is universal across cultures. Why would this be such an important concept for children to acquire?

**Watch** OBJECT PERMANENCE ACROSS CULTURES

Infants all over the world love the game "peek-a-boo," reflecting some understanding of object permanence.

technology that measures an infants' viewing patterns. The assumption is that infants will look longer at an event that violates their expectations. If they look longer at an event violating the rule of object permanence, this indicates some understanding of object permanence. For example, at age 5–6 months, infants will look longer when a toy they have seen hidden at one spot in a sandbox emerges from a different spot (Baillargeon, 2008; Newcombe & Huttenlocher, 2006). This seems to indicate an expectation that it should have emerged from the same spot, as a permanent object would. Even at 2–3 months, infants look longer at events involving objects that are physically impossible (Wang et al., 2005), showing a more advanced understanding of objects than Piaget would have predicted. There is by now a wealth of evidence that young infants perceive objects as permanent and whole (Johnson, 2013).

The argument that Piaget's measurement of object permanence at least in part reflects motor development also finds some support from cultural research. One study using Piaget's methods found that infants in Ivory Coast reached sensorimotor stage milestones earlier than Piaget had described (Dasen et al., 1978), probably because their parents encouraged them to develop motor skills.

Other cultural findings also support the argument that some understanding of object permanence develops earlier than Piaget claimed. Infants all over the world love the game "peek-a-boo," in which older children or adults cover their face with their hands or an object (such as a cloth), then suddenly reveal it. One study found that this game was played by adults and infants across a diverse range of cultures, including Brazil, Greece, India, Indonesia, Iran, South Africa, and South Korea (Fernald & O'Neill, 1993). Infants everywhere delighted in the game, and across cultures there were developmental changes. In the early months, infants responded only when the other person's face reappeared. Beginning at about 5 months, babies would begin to smile and laugh even before the other person reappeared, indicating that they were anticipating the event. In other words, they seemed to expect the person's face still to be there. They certainly were anticipating its reappearance. By 12 months old, as their motor and cognitive development had progressed further, infants would initiate the game themselves by holding a cloth up to the adult's face or putting it over their own.

It also turns out that object permanence is not distinctly human. Chimpanzees, dogs, and carrion crows, for example, have been shown to possess object permanence on various versions and extensions of Piaget's tasks (Call, 2001; Collier-Baker & Suddendorf, 2006; Hoffmann et al., 2011; Miller et al., 2009). Also, in both human infants and rhesus monkeys, successful performance on Piaget's A-not-B task is linked to activation in the frontal lobe of the brain (Baird et al., 2002; Diamond & Goldman-Rakic, 1989). Because understanding the permanence of the physical world is crucial to being able to function in that world, it is perhaps not surprising that humans and other animals would share this ability (Brownell & Kopp, 2007).

**deferred imitation**
ability to repeat actions observed at an earlier time

**DEFERRED IMITATION.** The ability to repeat actions observed at an earlier time is called **deferred imitation**. Piaget's favorite example involved his daughter Jacqueline, who witnessed another child exploding into an elaborate public tantrum and then repeated the tantrum herself at home the next day (Crain, 2000). Deferred imitation is a frequent part of toddlers' pretend play, as they observe the actions of other children or adults—making a meal, digging a hole, using a laptop—and then imitate those actions later in their play (Lillard, 2007). Deferred imitation is a crucial ability for learning because it means that when we observe something important to know, we can repeat it later ourselves.

Piaget proposed that deferred imitation begins around 18 months, but subsequent research has shown that it develops much earlier (Bauer, 2006). Deferred imitation of facial expressions has been reported as early as 6 weeks of age, when infants exposed to an unusual facial expression from an unfamiliar adult imitated it when the same adult appeared before them the next day (Meltzoff & Moore, 1994). At 6 months of age, infants can imitate a simple sequence of events a day later, such as taking off a puppet's glove and shaking it to ring a bell inside the glove (Barr et al., 2003).

However, if the delay is longer, toddlers are more proficient at deferred imitation than infants are. In a series of studies, children 9, 13, and 20 months old were shown two-step sequences of events, such as placing a car on a track to make a light go on, then pushing a rod to make the car run down a ramp (Bauer et al., 2000, 2001, 2003). After a 1-month interval, when shown the same materials, fewer than half of the 9-month-olds could imitate the steps they had seen previously, compared with about two-thirds of the 13-month-olds and nearly all the 20-month-olds. Other studies have shown that better deferred imitation among toddlers than infants may be due principally to brain maturation. Specifically, the *hippocampus*, the part of the brain especially important in long-term memory, is still in a highly immature state of development during infancy but matures substantially during toddlerhood (Bauer et al., 2010; Liston & Kagan, 2002).

Toddlers' play is often based on deferred imitation. Here, a toddler in Peru offers a bottle to her doll.

**CATEGORIZATION.** Like the complete attainment of object permanence and deferred imitation, **categorization** requires mental representation in Piaget's view (see Substage 6, discussed above). Once we are able to represent an image of a house mentally, for example, we can understand the category *house* and understand that different houses are all part of that category. These categories, in turn, become the basis for language, because each noun and verb represents a category (Waxman, 2003). The word *truck* represents the category *truck*, containing every possible variety of truck; the word *run* represents the category *run*, containing all varieties of running, and so on.

Here, too, recent experiments seem to indicate that Piaget underestimated children's early abilities. Infants and toddlers are able to do more than he had thought. Even infants as young as a few months old have been shown to have a rudimentary understanding of categories. As we have seen, infants tend to look longer at images that are new or unfamiliar, and their attention to images is often used in research to infer what they know and do not know. In one study, 3- and 4-month-old infants were shown a series of cat photos (Quinn et al., 1993). Next, the infants were shown two new photos, one of a cat and one of a dog. The infants looked longer at the dog photo, indicating that they had been using a category for "cat" and the dog photo did not fit.

**categorization**
process of sorting and organizing into groups and classes

However, research has generally confirmed Piaget's insight that categorization becomes more advanced during toddlerhood (Bornstein & Arterberry, 2010). For example, one study compared children who were 9, 12, and 18 months old (Gopnik et al., 1999). The children were given four different toy horses and four different pencils. At 9 months, they played with the objects, but made no effort to separate them into categories. At 12 months, some of the children would place the objects into categories and some would not. By 18 months, nearly all the children would systematically and deliberately separate the objects into a *horse* category and a *pencil* category.

By the time they are 2 years old, toddlers can go beyond the appearance of objects to categorize them on the basis of their functions or qualities. In a study demonstrating this ability, 2-year-olds were shown a machine and a collection of blocks that appeared to be identical (Gopnik et al., 1999). Then they were shown that two of the blocks made the machine light up when placed on it, whereas others did not. The researcher picked up one of the blocks that had made the machine light up and said, "This is a blicket. Can you show me the other blicket?" The 2-year-olds were able to choose the other block that had made the machine light go on, even though it looked the same as the blocks that had not had that effect. Although *blicket* was a nonsense word the toddlers had not heard before, they were still able to understand that the category *blicket* was defined by causing the machine to light up.

**Critical Thinking Question:** Explain how this experiment also provides a good demonstration of how categorization is the basis of language.

## The Preoperational Stage

**LO 5.1.4 Explain the features of Piaget's preoperational stage of cognitive development.**

In Piaget's theory, early childhood is a crucial turning point in children's cognitive development because this is when thinking becomes *representational* (Piaget, 1952). During the first 2 years of life, the sensorimotor stage, thinking takes place primarily in association with sensorimotor activities such as reaching and grasping. Gradually, toward the end of the sensorimotor period, in the second half of the second year, children begin to internalize the images of their sensorimotor activities, marking the beginning of representational thought.

However, it is during the latter part of toddlerhood and especially in early childhood that we become truly representational thinkers. Language requires the ability to represent the world symbolically, through words, and this is when language skills develop most dramatically (as we will see in Chapter 6). Once we can represent the world through language, we are freed from our momentary sensorimotor experience. With language, we can represent not only the present but the past and the future, not only the world as we see it before us but the world as we previously experienced it and the world as it will be—the coming cold or warm season, a decline in the availability of food or water, and so on. We can even represent the world as it has never been, through mentally combining ideas—flying monkeys, talking trees, and people who have superhuman powers. These are marvelous cognitive achievements.

Yet, early childhood fascinated Piaget not only for what children of this age are able to do cognitively, but also for the kinds of mistakes they make. In fact, Piaget termed the age period from 2 to 7 the **preoperational stage**, emphasizing that children of this age were not yet able to perform mental *operations*, that is, cognitive procedures that follow certain logical rules. Piaget specified a number of areas of preoperational cognitive mistakes that are characteristic of early childhood, including conservation, egocentrism, and classification.

**Conservation** is the principle that the amount of a physical substance remains the same even if its physical appearance changes. According to Piaget, children in early childhood lack this understanding. In his best-known demonstration of this mistake, Piaget showed young children two identical glasses holding equal amounts of water and asked them if the two amounts of water were equal. The children typically answered "yes;" they were capable of understanding that much. Then Piaget poured the contents from one of the glasses into a taller, thinner glass, and asked the children again if the two amounts of water were equal. Now, most of the children answered "no," failing to understand that the *amount* of water remained the same even though its *appearance* had changed. Piaget also demonstrated that children made this error with solid substances. Watch the video *Conservation Tasks* to see how children of different ages respond to Piaget's tasks involving both liquid and solid substances.

Piaget interpreted children's mistakes on conservation tasks as indicating two kinds of cognitive deficiencies. One is the lack of **reversibility**, the ability to reverse an action mentally. When the water is poured from the original glass to the taller glass in the conservation task, anyone who reverses that action mentally can see that the amount of water would be the same. Young children cannot perform the mental operation of reversibility, so they mistakenly believe the amount of water has changed. The other is **centration**, meaning that young children's thinking is *centered*, or focused, on one noticeable aspect of a cognitive problem to the exclusion of other important aspects. In the conservation-of-liquid task, they notice the change in height as the water is poured into the taller glass, but neglect to observe the change in width that takes place simultaneously.

Another cognitive limitation of the preoperational stage, in Piaget's view, is **egocentrism**, the inability to distinguish between your own perspective and another person's perspective. To demonstrate egocentrism, Piaget and his colleague Barbel Inhelder (1969) devised what they called the "three mountain task." In this task, shown in Figure 5.1, a child is shown a clay model of three mountains of varying sizes and with different features at each peak, such as snow, a pillar, and a cross. The child walks around the table to see what the mountains look like from each side, then sits down while the experimenter moves a doll to different points around the table. At each of the doll's locations, the child is shown a series of photographs and asked

**preoperational stage**
in Piaget's theory, cognitive stage from age 2 to 7 during which the child becomes capable of representing the world symbolically—for example, through the use of language—but is still limited in ability to use mental operations

**conservation**
mental ability to understand that the quantity of a substance or material remains the same even if its appearance changes

**reversibility**
ability to reverse an action mentally

**centration**
Piaget's term for young children's thinking as being centered, or focused, on one noticeable aspect of a cognitive problem to the exclusion of other important aspects

**egocentrism**
cognitive inability to distinguish between one's own perspective and another person's perspective

**Watch** CONSERVATION TASKS

which one indicates the doll's point of view. In the early years of the preoperational stage, children tend to pick the photo that matches their own perspective, not the doll's. Watch the video *Egocentrism Task* for another example of how to test for egocentrism.

**Figure 5.1** Piaget's Three Mountain Task

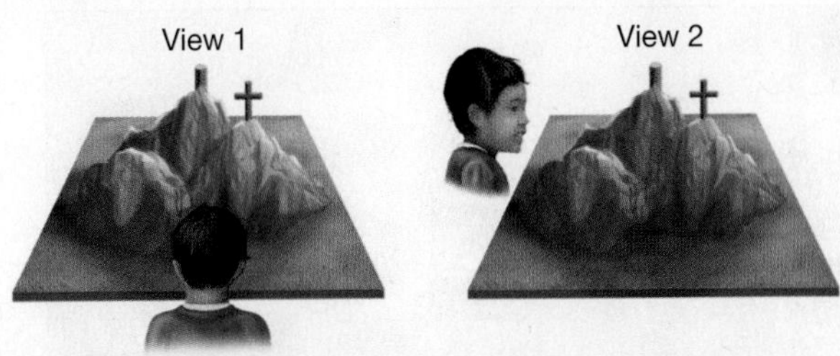


**Critical Thinking Question:** Do you see a relationship between centration and egocentrism? Explain.

**Watch** EGOCENTRISM TASK

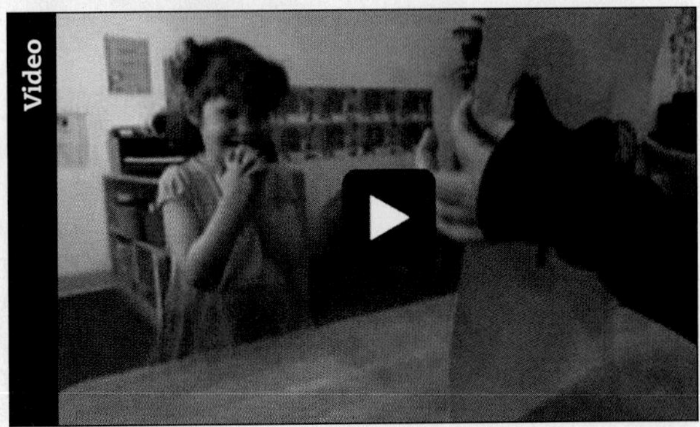


One aspect of egocentrism is **animism**, the tendency to attribute human thoughts and feelings to inanimate objects and forces. According to Piaget, when young children believe that the thunder is angry or the moon is following them, it reflects their animistic thinking. Attributing their own thoughts and feelings to inanimate things also reflects their egocentrism. Children's play with stuffed animals and dolls is a good example of animistic thinking. When they play with these toys, children frequently attribute human thoughts and feelings to them—often the thoughts and feelings they might have themselves.

In addition to their lack of conservation and their egocentrism, Piaget argued that preoperational children also lack the capacity for **classification**. This means that they have difficulty understanding that objects can be simultaneously part of more than one class or group. He demonstrated this by showing children a drawing of 4 blue flowers and 12 yellow flowers and asking, "Are there more yellow flowers, or more flowers?" In early childhood, children would typically answer "More yellow flowers," because they did not understand that yellow flowers could be both part of the class "yellow flowers" and part of the class "flowers."

**animism**
tendency to attribute human thoughts and feelings to inanimate objects and forces

**classification**
ability to understand that objects can be part of more than one class or group, for example, an object can be classified with red objects as well as with round objects

Here, as with conservation, the cognitive limitations of centration and lack of reversibility are at the root of the error, in Piaget's view. Young children center on the fact that the yellow flowers are yellow, which leads them to overlook the fact that the yellow flowers are also flowers. They also lack reversibility in that they cannot perform the mental operation of placing the yellow and blue flowers together into the "flowers" class, and then move them back into the "yellow flowers" and "blue flowers" classes, respectively.

Many studies over the past several decades have shown that children ages 2–7 years are cognitively capable of more than Piaget recognized. Regarding egocentrism, children are more likely to take someone else's point of view when the three mountains task is modified so that familiar objects are used (Newcombe & Huttenlocher, 2006). Studies using different methods also show that 2- to 7-year-old children are less egocentric than Piaget thought. For example, toddlers demonstrate the beginnings of an ability to take others' perspectives when they figure out what they can do to annoy a sibling (Dunn, 1988). On the more positive side, toddlers will also spontaneously help others achieve their goal (Warneken & Tomasello, 2006). By age 4, children switch to shorter, simpler sentences when talking to toddlers or babies, showing a distinctly un-egocentric ability to take the perspective of the younger children (Bryant & Barrett, 2007). In short, Piaget underestimated the cognitive capabilities of 2- to 7-year olds, just as he did for infants.

## The Concrete Operations Stage

**LO 5.1.5 Explain the major cognitive advances that occur during Piaget's concrete operations stage.**

If you grew up in a Western country, perhaps you believed in Santa Claus when you were a young child. According to one version of the story, on Christmas Eve, Santa Claus rides around the world on a sleigh borne by flying reindeer, stopping at every house to climb down the chimney and deliver toys to all the good girls and boys. Do you remember when you stopped believing it? For most children, the story starts to seem far-fetched once they get to

Watch SERIATION

be 7 or 8 years old (Sameroff & Haith, 1996). How could one person make it all the way around the world in one night, even with flying reindeer? How could a large man make it down a narrow chimney, dragging a sack full of toys? And what if you don't have a chimney? The loss of belief in this myth reflects gains in cognitive development, as children develop a more true-to-life understanding of the world.

Middle childhood is when children develop a better grasp of what the physical world is really like—of what is and is not possible. Piaget regarded 7- to 11-year-olds as being in the **concrete operations stage**. During this stage, children become systematic and logical thinkers. According to Piaget, the advances of concrete operations are evident in new abilities for performing tasks of conservation, classification, and seriation.

**concrete operations**
in Piaget's theory, cognitive stage from 7 to 11 during which children become capable of using systematic and logical mental operations

**seriation**
ability to arrange things in a logical order, such as shortest to longest, thinnest to thickest, or lightest to darkest

As described above, prior to age 7 children usually make mistakes when performing tasks requiring an understanding of conservation. Conservation is a key milestone of cognitive development because it enables the child to perceive regularities and principles in the natural world, which is the basis of being able to think logically about how the world works. A second important cognitive achievement of concrete operations is classification. To return to our earlier example involving the drawing of 4 blue flowers and 12 yellow flowers, children in the concrete operational stage become capable of differentiating yellow and blue flowers into two classes while simultaneously keeping in mind that both form part of the larger class of flowers. To a child in the concrete operational stage, it would be clear that there are more flowers than yellow flowers.

**Seriation**, the third achievement of concrete operations emphasized by Piaget, is the ability to arrange things in a logical order (e.g., shortest to longest, thinnest to thickest, lightest to darkest). Piaget found that preoperational children have an incomplete grasp of concepts such as *longer than* or *smaller than*. For example, when asked to arrange a set of sticks from shortest to longest, children in the preoperational age period would typically start with a short stick, then pick a long stick—but then pick another short stick, then another long stick, and so on. However, by age 7, most children can accurately arrange six to eight sticks by length. Watch the video *Seriation* for a demonstration of how children of different ages respond to a seriation task.

Piaget also found that during concrete operations, children developed the ability to seriate mentally. Take this problem, for example: If Brielle is taller than Anna, and Anna is taller than Lilia, is Brielle taller than Lilia? To get this right, the child has to be able to order the heights mentally from tallest to shortest: Brielle, Anna, Lilia. Piaget considered the achievement of this skill of performing mental operations to be a key part of learning to think logically and systematically.

Research has shown that children become capable of performing some concrete operations tasks at an earlier age than Piaget claimed (Marti & Rodriguez, 2012; Vilette, 2002). However, for Piaget it was not enough for a child to grasp *some* aspects of conservation, classification, and seriation in order to be considered a concrete operational thinker; the child had to have *complete* mastery of each task associated with the stage (Piaget, 1965). Thus, the difference between Piaget and his critics on this issue is more a matter of definition—"What qualifies a child as a concrete operational thinker?"—than of research findings.

Piaget also claimed that teaching children concrete operations would not work because their grasp of the principles of the stage has to occur naturally as part of their interaction with their environment (Piaget, 1965). Here, however, many studies show that with training and instruction, children under age 7 can learn to perform the tasks of concrete operations and also understand the underlying principles well enough to apply them to new tasks (Marti & Rodriguez, 2012; Parameswaran, 2003).

## The Formal Operations Stage

**formal operations**
in Piaget's theory, cognitive stage beginning at age 11 in which people learn to think systematically about possibilities and hypotheses

**LO 5.1.6 Describe the features of hypothetical-deductive reasoning and the extent to which adolescents and emerging adults use formal operations.**

According to Piaget (1972), the stage of **formal operations** begins at about age 11 and reaches completion somewhere between ages 15 and 20. Children in concrete operations can perform tasks that require logical and systematic thinking, but formal operations allow adolescents to reason about much more complex tasks and problems involving multiple variables. An example is **hypothetical-deductive reasoning**, which is the ability to think scientifically and apply the rigor of the scientific method to cognitive tasks. To demonstrate this new ability, let us look at one of the tasks Piaget used to test whether a child has progressed from concrete to formal operations: the *pendulum problem* (Inhelder & Piaget, 1958). In this task, illustrated in Figure 5.2, children and adolescents are shown a pendulum (consisting of a weight hanging from a string and then set in motion) and asked to figure out what determines the speed at which the pendulum sways from side to side. Is it the heaviness of the weight? The length of the string? The height from which the weight is dropped? The force with which it is dropped? They are given various weights and various lengths of string to use in their deliberations.

**Figure 5.2** Pendulum Problem

Children in concrete operations tend to approach the problem with random attempts, often changing more than one variable at a time. They may try the heaviest weight on the longest string dropped from medium height with medium force, then a medium weight on the smallest string dropped from medium height with less force. When the speed of the pendulum changes, it remains difficult for them to say what caused the change, because they altered more than one variable at a time. If they happen to arrive at the right answer—it's the length of the string—they find it difficult to explain why. This is crucial, for Piaget. Cognitive advances at each stage are reflected not just in the answers children devise for problems, but in their explanations for how they arrived at the solution.

**hypothetical-deductive reasoning**

Piaget's term for the process of applying scientific thinking to cognitive tasks

It is only with formal operations that we become able to find the right answer to a problem like this and explain why it is the right answer. Formal operational thinkers approach the pendulum problem by utilizing the kind of hypothetical thinking involved in a scientific experiment. They change one variable while holding the others constant and systematically test the different possibilities. Through this process, formal operational thinkers arrive at an answer that is not only correct but can also be explained.

Abundant research, however, indicates a great range of individual differences among adolescents and even emerging adults in the attainment of formal operations (Kuhn, 2008). Some adolescents and adults use formal operations over a wide range of situations; others use them selectively; still others appear to use them rarely or not at all. On any given Piagetian task of formal operations, the success rate among late adolescents and adults is only 40–60%, depending on the task and on individual factors such as educational background (Keating, 2012; Lawson & Wollman, 2003). Adolescents who have had courses in math and science are more likely than other adolescents to exhibit formal operational thought (Keating, 2004; Lawson & Wollman, 2003).

Even people who demonstrate the capacity for formal operations tend to use them selectively for problems and situations in which they have the most experience and knowledge (Miller, 2011). For example, an adolescent with experience working on cars may find it easy to apply principles of formal operations in that area, but have difficulty using them to perform classroom tasks.

Research in different cultures has also vividly shown the importance of experience to the use of formal operations. This research indicates that people in many cultures use reasoning that could be called *formal operational*, provided that they are using materials and completing tasks that are relevant to their daily lives (Matusov & Hayes, 2000). There is widespread support among scholars for the view that the stage of formal operations constitutes a universal human potential, but that potential takes on different forms across cultures, depending on the kinds of problems people encounter in their daily lives (Cole, 1996). For example, adolescent boys in the Inuit culture of

In what ways might hunting seals require formal operations?

the Canadian Arctic traditionally learn how to hunt seals (Condon, 1990; Grigorenko et al., 2004). To become successful, a boy would have to think through the components involved in a hunt and test his knowledge of hunting through experience. If he were unsuccessful on a particular outing, he would have to ask himself why. Was it because of the location he chose? The equipment he took along? The tracking method he used? Or were there other causes? On future hunts, he might systematically alter these factors to see if his success improved. This would be hypothetical-deductive reasoning, altering and testing different variables to arrive at a solution to a problem. In every culture, there is likely to be considerable variation in the extent to which adolescents and adults display formal operational thought, from persons who display it in a wide variety of circumstances, to persons who display it little or not at all.

**Critical Thinking Question:** The director of a science museum asks you to help set up exhibits that would be educational for middle school and high school students. Based on what you have learned from cognitive-developmental theory and research, what key guidelines would you provide?

## Evaluating Piaget's Theory

**LO 5.1.7 Summarize the strengths and limitations of Piaget's theory.**

Even today, over 70 years after he began formulating it, Piaget's theory of cognitive development remains influential. Like all good theories, it has inspired a wealth of research to test its assertions and implications. And, like even the best theories, it has been modified and altered on the basis of research. On the whole, Piaget:

1. Underestimated the cognitive abilities of younger children.
2. Overestimated the cognitive abilities of adolescents.
3. Arrived at overly broad theoretical and empirical claims based on the specific research methods that he devised.
4. Did not consider how learning, including cultural experience, can lead to the development of cognitive skills in a stage ahead of the child's age.
5. Overemphasized stages in the development of cognition, when research generally shows that mental operations change gradually over the course of childhood.
6. Overemphasized the logical and science-oriented side of cognition over its other everyday purposes.

One classic study illustrates this last point (Glick, 1975). An experimenter asked a Kpelle farmer in Africa to sort 20 objects like an orange, a potato, a hoe, and a knife into categories. To successfully solve this classification problem, the experimenter expected the farmer to divide the objects into categories such as foods and tools. Instead, the farmer divided them in more functional ways, for example, putting the knife with an orange and the hoe with potatoes. Asked to repeat the task, the farmer kept sorting the objects on a functional basis. When questioned, the farmer volunteered that that was the way a wise man would do it. The exasperated experimenter then asked, "How would a fool do it?" The farmer then made neat piles with foods in one, tools in another, and so forth (Rogoff, 1990).

While Piaget's theory has quite a lot of limitations, the sheer number is actually a testament to just how much research has been inspired by his and Inhelder's work. Certainly, too, many of their concepts and findings have stood the test of time.

## SUMMARY: Piaget's Theory of Cognitive Development

### LO 5.1.1 Describe the meaning of maturation, schemes, assimilation, and accommodation.

Maturation is the biologically based program of development. Piaget proposed that the child's construction of reality takes place through the use of schemes, which are cognitive structures for processing, organizing, and interpreting information. The two processes involved in the use of schemes are assimilation and accommodation. Assimilation occurs when new information is altered to fit an existing scheme. In contrast, accommodation entails changing the scheme to adapt to the new information.

### LO 5.1.2 Describe the six sensorimotor substages.

Substage 1 is based on neonatal reflexes; substage 2 entails repetition of movements focused on the infant's own body (thumb-sucking); substage 3 entails repetition of movements involving the external world (kicking an object); substage 4 involves goal-directed and relatively complex behaviors; substage 5 involves new, exploratory behaviors; and substage 6 requires mentally selecting among behaviors before deciding on the most useful one.

### LO 5.1.3 Explain how object permanence, deferred imitation, and categorization develop over the course of the first 2 years.

Piaget argued that only by about age 2 do toddlers attain a complete sense of object permanence. Newer research using the "violation of expectations method," however, shows that even young infants perceive objects as permanent and whole. Piaget proposed that deferred imitation, the ability to repeat actions observed at an earlier time, begins around 18 months. Subsequent research has shown that it develops as early as 6 weeks of age. Experiments also indicate that Piaget underestimated children's ability to categorize. Infants who are a few months old already have some understanding of categorization.

### LO 5.1.4 Explain the features of Piaget's preoperational stage of cognitive development.

Piaget viewed children in the preoperational stage (ages 2–7) as prone to a variety of errors, including lack of conservation and reversibility, centration, egocentrism, and animism. Research has shown that Piaget underestimated the cognitive abilities of early childhood.

### LO 5.1.5 Explain the major cognitive advances that occur during Piaget's concrete operations stage.

According to Piaget, children progress from the preoperational stage to the stage of concrete operations during middle childhood, as they learn to think more systematically about how the world works and avoid cognitive errors. Cognitive advances during this stage include the ability to understand conservation, improved classification skills, and the understanding of seriation.

### LO 5.1.6 Describe the features of hypothetical-deductive reasoning and the extent to which adolescents and emerging adults use formal operations.

Hypothetical-deductive reasoning entails the ability to test solutions to a problem systematically, altering one variable while holding the others constant. The pendulum problem is one way Piaget tested the attainment of formal operations. He proposed that when adolescents reach formal operations they use it for all cognitive activities; however, research has shown that adolescents and emerging adults tend to use formal operations in some areas of their lives but not in others.

### LO 5.1.7 Summarize the strengths and limitations of Piaget's theory.

Over 70 years after he began formulating it, Piaget's theory of cognitive development remains a source of inspiration to researchers. The theory also has a number of limitations, including classifying children too rigidly into stages while ignoring the importance of learning, culture, and everyday uses of cognition.

# 5.2 Post-Piagetian Approaches to Cognitive Development

One way that Piaget continues to influence the field is through the work of researchers who have taken his stages in new directions. Here we focus on two notable lines of post-Piagetian research. The first line has broadened the meaning of the formal operations stage, and the second has gone beyond formal operations to address postformal thinking.

**abstract thinking**
thinking pertaining to concepts and processes that cannot be experienced directly through the senses

**complex thinking**
thinking that takes into account multiple connections and interpretations, such as in the use of metaphor, satire, and sarcasm

## Broadening the Formal Operations Stage

**LO 5.2.1 Describe how adolescents engage in abstract, complex, and metacognitive thinking, and explain the neurological underpinnings of these abilities.**

Formal operations as primarily examined by Piaget focused on logical, systematic, and scientific thinking. Researchers, however, have proposed that formal operations can also encompass abstract thinking, complex thinking, and metacognition (Ginsburg & Opper, 1988; Keating, 2004). Piaget discussed these capacities, but, since then, other scholars have done considerable research on them as well. Recent research also suggests that these cognitive capacities are linked to brain development in adolescence and emerging adulthood.

Adolescents gain the capacity to understand and use abstract ideas, such as justice, freedom, and courage. Here, British adolescents express their political ideas at a public protest.

**ABSTRACT, COMPLEX, AND METACOGNITIVE THINKING.** **Abstract thinking** addresses concepts or processes that cannot be experienced directly through the senses. Some of the abstract concepts that you have read about in this text include culture, the West, socioeconomic status, development, and adolescence. You cannot actually see, hear, taste, or touch these things; they exist only as ideas. Researchers have found that adolescents become capable of engaging in discussions about politics, morality, and religion in ways they could not when they were younger. Unlike children, adolescents gain the capacity to understand and use abstract ideas involved in these discussions, such as justice, freedom, courage, goodness, and history (Eisenberg et al., 2011).

**Complex thinking** involves thinking about multiple dimensions and aspects of a situation or an idea. For example, metaphors are complex because they have more than one meaning—the literal, concrete meaning, as well as more subtle and symbolic meanings. Poems, plays, and novels are full of metaphors. Consider this famous passage from the beginning of Shakespeare's play Richard III. The Duke of Gloucester is greeting the Duke of York:

> Now is the winter of our discontent
> Made glorious summer by this sun of York;
> And all the clouds that lour'd upon our house
> In the deep bosom of the ocean buried.

On one level, the passage is literally about changing weather. But a deeper interpretation is that it is about a change in emotional states; Gloucester's mood has risen with York's arrival. Adolescents can grasp multiple meanings to a degree that children usually cannot (Gibbs et al., 2002; Sternberg & Nigro, 1980).

One study examined understandings of metaphors in adolescents and emerging adults (Duthie et al., 2008). The study used sayings such as "One bad apple spoils the whole barrel." Early adolescents tended to describe the meanings of the metaphors in concrete terms. For example, an 11-year-old explained: "There's a big barrel of apples and a woman picks up one that is rotten and there are worms in it and the worms go to all the other apples." In later adolescence and emerging adulthood, understanding of the metaphors became more abstract and more focused on their social meanings. For example, a 21-year-old observed that "One bad comment can spoil the entire conversation."

*Sarcasm* is another example of complex thinking. As with metaphors, more than one interpretation is possible. Adolescents become capable of understanding (and using) sarcasm in a way children cannot, and as a result sarcasm is more often part of adolescent conversations (Cameron et al., 2010; Creusere, 1999; Eder, 1995) and media popular among adolescents (Katz et al., 2004). One study examined how understanding of sarcasm changes from middle childhood through adolescence (Demorest et al., 1984). Participants were presented with stories and asked to judge whether a particular remark was sincere, deceptive, or sarcastic (for example, "That new haircut you got looks terrific"). Children aged 9 or younger had difficulty identifying sarcastic remarks. Adolescents aged 13 were better at it, but college students surpassed the 13-year-olds.

Another study examined adolescents' uses of humor, including sarcasm, in relation to difficult life circumstances (Cameron et al., 2010). The researchers video-recorded "A Day in the Life" of adolescents who were experiencing poverty, family conflict, and parental substance abuse. The adolescents used sarcasm for multiple purposes, such as talking about socially sensitive topics and situations, and reaffirming affiliations with friends. The researchers concluded that sarcastic humor is an aspect of adolescents' resilience that helps them navigate challenging social terrain.

**metacognition**
capacity to think about thinking

**Metacognition** is the ability to think about thinking. The quotes by Descartes and Lao-Tzu at the outset of this chapter are good examples. Research has shown that metacognition enables adolescents to learn and solve problems more efficiently (Klaczynski, 2006; Schneider & Lockl, 2008). In fact, one study indicates that instructing adolescents in metacognitive strategies improves their academic performance (Kramarski, 2004). While metacognition first emerges in adolescence, it continues to develop in emerging adulthood and beyond. One study compared adolescents and adults of various ages (Vukman, 2005). They were given several problems and asked to "think out loud" so that the researchers could record their metacognitive processes. Self-awareness of thinking processes rose from adolescence to emerging adulthood and again from emerging adulthood to midlife, before declining in later adulthood. Perhaps it is not mere coincidence that Descartes was 41 years old when he wrote "I think, therefore I am." (As to the age of Lao-Tzu when he declared his principle, we do not know.)

**COGNITION AND BRAIN DEVELOPMENT IN ADOLESCENCE AND EMERGING ADULTHOOD.** Research suggests that the abstract, complex, and metacognitive thinking capabilities that develop during adolescence are linked to neurological development (Casey et al., 2008; Giedd, 2008; Taber-Thomas & Perez-Edgar, 2015). Scientists have learned that a sharp increase in synaptic connections occurs around the time puberty begins, ages 10–12, a process called *synaptic exuberance* (see Chapter 2). Synaptic exuberance occurs in many parts of the brain during adolescence, but it is especially concentrated in the frontal lobes (Markant & Thomas, 2013). The frontal lobes are involved in most of the higher functions of the brain, such as planning ahead, solving problems, and making moral judgments. After synaptic exuberance peaks at about age 11 or 12, it is followed by a massive amount of synaptic pruning, in which the overproduction of synapses is whittled down considerably (refer back to Chapter 2, Figure 2.10). In fact, the average brain loses 7% to 10% of its volume through synaptic pruning between the ages of 12 and 20 (Giedd et al., 2012). Synaptic pruning allows the brain to work more efficiently, as brain pathways become more specialized. Research using functional magnetic resonance imaging (fMRI) measurements shows that synaptic pruning is especially rapid in highly intelligent adolescents (Shaw et al., 2006). Myelination, the blanketing of axons with fatty substance that makes brain functioning faster, also continues through the teens (Giedd, 2008; Sowell et al., 2002).

Researchers studying brain development in adolescence and emerging adulthood have also discovered growth of the cerebellum (Taber-Thomas & Perez-Edgar, 2015). This has been a surprise because the cerebellum is part of the lower brain (as we saw in Chapter 2) and has long been thought to be involved only in basic functions such as movement. Now, however, research shows that the cerebellum also is important for many higher functions, such as understanding humor, social skills, and decision-making.

## Postformal Thinking

**LO 5.2.2 Describe how pragmatism and dialectical thought allow emerging adults to become better at addressing real-life problems.**

Research indicates that cognitive development often continues in important ways during emerging adulthood. Some of this research builds on Piaget while also going beyond his theory by focusing on **postformal thinking** (Malott, 2011; Sinnott, 2014). Two of the most notable aspects of postformal thinking in emerging adulthood concern advances in pragmatism and dialectical thinking.

**postformal thinking**
according to some theorists, the stage of cognitive development that follows formal operations and includes advances in pragmatism and reflective judgment

**pragmatism**
adapting logical thinking to the practical constraints of real-life situations

**PRAGMATISM.** The adaptation of logical thinking to the practical constraints of real-life situations is called **pragmatism**. Several scholars have developed theories of postformal thinking emphasizing pragmatism (Basseches, 1984, 1989; Labouvie-Vief, 1998, 2006; Labouvie-Vief & Diehl, 2002; Sinnott, 2014). What the theories have in common is an emphasis that problems faced in normal adult life often contain complexities and inconsistencies that cannot be addressed with the logic of formal operations.

According to Gisela Labouvie-Vief (1982; 1990; 1998; 2006), cognitive development in emerging adulthood is distinguished from adolescent thinking by a greater recognition and incorporation of practical limitations to logical thinking. In this view, adolescents exaggerate the extent to which logical thinking will be effective in real life. In contrast, emerging adulthood brings a growing awareness of how social influences and factors specific to a given situation must be taken into account in approaching most of life's problems.

For example, in one study Labouvie-Vief (1990) presented adolescents and emerging adults with stories and asked them to predict what they thought would happen. One story described a man who was a heavy drinker, especially at parties. His wife had warned him that if he came home drunk one more time, she would leave him and take the children. Some time later, he went to an office party and came home drunk. What would she do? Labouvie-Vief found that adolescents tended to respond strictly in terms of the logic of formal operations: She said she would leave if he came home drunk once more; he came home drunk, therefore she will leave. In contrast, emerging adults considered many possible dimensions of the situation. Did he apologize and beg her not to leave? Did she really mean it when she said she would leave him? Has she considered the possible effects on the children? Rather than relying strictly on logic and assuming an outcome of definite right or wrong answers, the emerging adults tended to be postformal thinkers in the sense that they realized that the problems of real life often involve a great deal of complexity and ambiguity. However, Labouvie-Vief (2006) emphasizes that with postformal thinking, as with formal thinking, not everyone continues to move to higher levels of cognitive complexity, and many people continue to apply earlier, more concrete thinking in emerging adulthood and beyond.

**dialectical thought**
awareness that problems often have no clear solution and two opposing strategies or points of view may each have some merit

**DIALECTICAL THINKING.** Michael Basseches (1984, 1989) has proposed that **dialectical thought** develops in emerging adulthood. It involves an awareness that problems often have no clear solution and two opposing strategies or points of view may each have some merit (Basseches, 2005). For example, people may have to decide whether to quit a job they dislike without knowing whether their next job will be more satisfying.

Some cultures may promote dialectical thinking more than others (Spencer-Rodgers et al., 2010). One team of researchers conducted studies comparing Chinese and American college students (Peng & Nisbett, 1999). They found that the Chinese students were more likely than the Americans to prefer dialectical proverbs containing contradictions. In addition, when two apparently contradictory propositions were presented, the Americans tended to embrace one and reject the other, whereas the Chinese students were moderately accepting of both propositions, seeking to reconcile them. These results suggest that the Chinese engaged in more dialectical thinking.

**Critical Thinking Question:** Think back to the earlier example of the Kpelle farmer who thought it wisest to categorize objects based on their function. In your view, does his cognitive approach fit with post-Piagetian approaches to cognitive development?

### SUMMARY: Post-Piagetian Approaches

**LO 5.2.1 Describe how adolescents engage in abstract, complex, and metacognitive thinking, and explain the neurological underpinnings of these abilities.**

Adolescents become capable of understanding abstract ideas such as justice and courage. They can also think about ideas and situations in complex ways, taking multiple dimensions into account. Metacognition, the ability to think about thinking, first emerges in adolescence but continues to develop in emerging adulthood and beyond. Research suggests that the new cognitive capabilities that develop during adolescence are linked to changes in the frontal lobes and cerebellum.

**LO 5.2.2 Describe how pragmatism and dialectical thought allow emerging adults to become better at addressing real-life problems.**

Cognitive development often continues in important ways during emerging adulthood. This includes the adaptation of logical thinking to the practical constraints of real-life situations (pragmatism), and awareness that problems sometimes have no clear solution or may have more than one solution (dialectical thought). Some cultures may promote dialectical thinking more than others.

# 5.3 Information-Processing Approaches

The **information-processing approaches** to cognitive development are quite different from Piagetian and post-Piagetian theories. Rather than viewing cognitive development as *discontinuous*, that is, as separated into distinct stages, the information-processing approaches view cognitive change as *continuous*, meaning gradual and steady. The focus is on how mental capabilities and processes gradually change with age, for example, how memory becomes swifter, more accurate, and more capacious over the course of childhood. In this section, we review what is known about information processing from infancy through emerging adulthood.

**information-processing approaches**
focus on cognitive processes that exist at all ages, rather than on viewing cognitive development in terms of discontinuous stages

## Information Processing in Infancy and Early Childhood

**LO 5.3.1 Describe how attention, memory, and executive function change during infancy and early childhood, including how current research accounts for infantile amnesia.**

The original model for information-processing approaches was the computer (Hunt, 1989). Researchers tried to break human thinking into components, such as input, processing, and memory, similar to how the functions of a computer are differentiated. Recent models of information processing have moved away from a simple computer analogy, recognizing that the brain is more complex than any computer (Ashcraft, 2009). Rather than occur in step-by-step fashion as in a computer, in humans, the different components of thinking operate together, as Figure 5.3 (next page) illustrates. Information-processing researchers have studied attention and memory for many decades, and have more recently examined executive function as well (Carlson et al., 2013). Next, let's look at how these capabilities develop during infancy and early childhood.

**ATTENTION.** In infants, the study of attention has focused on **habituation**, which is the gradual decrease in attention to a stimulus after repeated presentations. For example, infants will look longer at a toy the first time it is presented than the fourth or fifth time. A complementary concept, **dishabituation**, is the revival of attention when a new stimulus is presented following several presentations of a previous stimulus. For example, if you show infants a picture of the same face several times in a row, then show a new face, they will generally dishabituate to the new face, that is, they will pay more attention to it than to the "old" face. Habituation and dishabituation can be studied by monitoring infants' looking behavior, but infants rarely lay still for long even if they are paying attention to something, so two other methods have been frequently used: heart rate and sucking rate. Heart rate declines when a new stimulus is presented and

**habituation**
gradual decrease in attention to a stimulus after repeated presentations

**dishabituation**
following habituation, the revival of attention when a new stimulus is presented

**Figure 5.3** Information-Processing Model

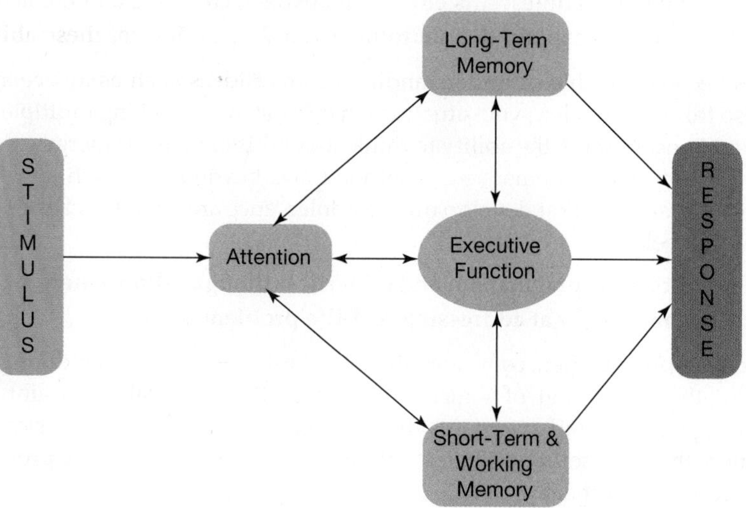


gradually rises as habituation takes place. Infants suck on a pacifier more frequently when a new stimulus is presented and gradually decline in their sucking rate with habituation.

**joint attention**

paying attention to the stimuli on which other people are focusing

During the course of the first year of life, it takes less and less time for habituation to occur. When presented with a visual stimulus, neonates may take several minutes before they show signs of habituating (as measured by changes to their looking time, heart rate, or sucking rate). By 4–5 months old, habituation in a similar experiment takes only about 10 seconds, and by 7–8 months only a few seconds (Domsch et al., 2010; Kavšek & Bornstein, 2010). This appears to occur because infants become more efficient at perceiving and processing a stimulus.

Even when they are a few months old, infants of the same age vary in their rates of habituation, and these individual differences tend to be stable over time. Some infants are more efficient than others at processing information; consequently, they habituate more quickly. Infants who habituate relatively slowly appear to do so not because they are especially good at sustaining their attention, but because they seem to get stuck on the stimulus and have difficulty disengaging from it. Speed of habituation predicts memory ability on other tasks in infancy, as well as later performance on intelligence tests (Courage et al., 2004; Rose et al., 2005).

Joint attention develops by the end of the first year.

In the second half of the first year, infants' patterns of attention become increasingly social. They begin to direct their attention to the stimuli that people around them are attending to, engaging in **joint attention**. By the end of the first year, infants often notice what important people around them are paying attention to and will look or point in the same direction. One experiment showed that 10-month-old infants were less likely to look or point in the direction an adult was faced if the adult's eyes were closed or blindfolded, indicating that the infants were aware of the adult's attentional patterns and matched their own to them (Brooks & Meltzoff, 2005.)

Joint attention is the basis not just of infants' information-processing development, but also of language and emotional communication (Friedlmeier et al., 2015; Goldin-Meadow & Alibali, 2013; Parish-Morris et al., 2013). This makes sense; one way infants and children learn new words is to observe what another person is doing or looking at when they use a word. Often this takes place during social interactions between infants and others, but it can also take place through infants observing where the attention of another person is directed. Not all cultures encourage verbal interactions with infants, and research shows that infants and young children in these cultures learn a great deal of their language by observing adults' language use and "listening in," that is, using joint attention to discern the meaning of words (Akhtar, 2005).

**MEMORY.** Infants' memory abilities expand greatly during the first year of life, both for short- and for long-term memory. **Short-term memory** refers to the capacity to retain information for a brief time. One reflection of the development of short-term memory is infants' improvement on Piaget's object permanence tasks. While Piaget regarded his tasks as assessing whether infants understand that an object that is out of sight still exists, other researchers have pointed out that the tasks may more accurately reflect memory development. Memory studies using these tasks show that the number of locations infants can remember and search to look for a hidden object increases sharply in the second half of the first year (Morra et al., 2008).

**short-term memory**
memory for information that is the current focus of attention

**Long-term memory**, knowledge that is accumulated and retained over time, also improves notably over the course of the first year. In one experiment, researchers tied a string to the foot of infants 2 to 6 months old and taught them to move a mobile hanging above their cribs by kicking their foot (Rovee-Collier, 1999). The 2-month-olds forgot the training within a week—they no longer kicked to make the mobile move when the string was tied to their legs—but the 6-month-olds remembered it for about 3 weeks, demonstrating better long-term memories.

**long-term memory**
memory for information that is committed to longer-term storage, so that it can be drawn upon after a period when attention has not been focused on it

Further experiments showed an interesting distinction between *recognition memory* and *recall memory* (Hildreth et al., 2003). After the mobile-kicking trick appeared to be lost from the infants' memories, the researchers gave the infants a hint by making the mobile move. The infants *recognized* this clue and began kicking again to make the mobile move, up to a month later, even though they had been unable to *recall* the memory before being prompted. The older the infant was, the more effective the prompting. From infancy onward, recognition memory comes easier to us than recall memory (Flavell et al., 2002).

**INFANTILE AMNESIA.** Clearly, infants and young children attend to information and learn a lot, so why is it that later in our development we forget a great deal of what happened in our early years? This loss of memory of information up to about age 4 is known as **infantile amnesia** (Insel, 2013). It is not that we forget everything. We retain language, habits, and general information learned before age 4. This is known as *semantic memory*. For example, by age 4 you probably knew that dogs bark and birds fly, and you never forgot. However, most if not all of our memories for unique events vanish. This is known as *episodic memory* (Tulving, 1983). If you attended preschool, for example, it is unlikely that you remember your teacher's name (unless you were reminded later in life). A specific kind of episodic memory is known as *autobiographical memory* and involves the recollection of specific personal experiences (Courage & Cowan, 2009). For example, if you played a special role in a preschool musical performance at age 3, you have probably forgotten.

**infantile amnesia**
loss of memory of information up to about age 4

Explanations for infantile amnesia, a term coined by Freud (1905/1953), have been varied. As you might imagine, based on what you read in Chapter 1, Freud erroneously attributed it to repression of childhood sexual desires. Some researchers have proposed that the retention of long-term memories requires language and a sense of self, which only become well-developed in the course of early childhood. However, some other animals also show "infantile amnesia," so this cannot be the main explanation. Memory researchers have proposed that the answer lies in the development of the hippocampus, part of the lower brain (Josselyn & Frankland, 2012). The hippocampus is immature at birth and adds neurons at a high rate in the early years of development. The addition of so many new neurons may interfere with the existing memory circuits, so that long-term memories cannot be formed until the production of neurons in the hippocampus declines in early childhood, as it becomes more fully developed (Insel, 2013).

Many questions remain in this area, for example, whether traumatic events in infancy and early childhood are remembered differently. In one study, children who had been hospitalized for a medical emergency at age 2–3 were interviewed 5 years later (Peterson & Whalen, 2001). Even the children who were only 2 years old at the time of the injury recalled the main features of their hospital experience accurately 5 years later, although 3-year-olds remembered more details of the experience. Interestingly, neurological research shows that stress leads to a decrease in the production of neurons. However, whether this is related to the finding that some memories involving early childhood trauma are retained rather than forgotten is a scientific question yet to be examined (Insel, 2013).

Some cultures promote greater attention to personal experiences and consequently children in these cultures have earlier autobiographical memories. Here, an American girl celebrates her 3rd birthday.

Culture also plays a role in autobiographical memories (Leichtman, 2011). In a study comparing adults' autobiographical memories, British and White American adults remembered more events prior to age 5 than Chinese adults did, and their earliest memory was 6 months earlier on average (Wang, 2013). The interpretation proposed by the authors was that the greater individualism of British and American cultures promotes greater attention to personal experiences and consequently more and earlier autobiographical memories.

**EXECUTIVE FUNCTION.** As we saw in Chapter 4, **executive function** refers to problem solving, and includes inhibitory control (or staying focused on the task at hand and not becoming distracted) and flexibility (or adjusting one's strategy as the nature of a task changes) (Carlson et al., 2013). One common task used to assess executive function is the *flanker task* (Eriksen & Eriksen, 1974). For example, looking at an array of fish on a computer screen, you would aim to quickly and accurately indicate whether the middle fish faces in the same or opposite direction as the flanking fish. Research shows that greater executive function is required for opposite-facing conditions (Hillman et al., 2014).

Another common measure of executive function is the *dimensional change card sort* (DCCS) (Zelazo et al., 2014). The cards for this task show images that combine two dimensions, such as a red circle and a blue square (Espy, 1997). Children are first asked to sort based on one dimension (e.g., color), and then to switch to the other (e.g., shape). The switch condition requires greater executive function, and indeed 3-year-olds continue to sort based on the first dimension when asked to switch to the second one. In contrast, most 5-year-olds are able to inhibit the inclination to continue doing what they had been doing and flexibly switch to the new requirement.The period from age 3 to about 6 years is when executive function emerges and rises quite steeply (Carlson et al., 2013).

To date, there has not been much research on executive function across cultures. However, one study comparing American and Chinese preschoolers found that the Chinese showed a 6-month developmental advantage (Sabbagh et al., 2006). In a follow-up to the study, researchers found that Chinese preschoolers especially seemed to excel on inhibitory control and **selective attention**, or the ability to focus on relevant information and disregard what is irrelevant (Lan et al., 2011). The researchers suggested that the emphasis on self-control and following directions in Chinese culture and preschools may contribute to the difference.

A study that compared Chinese-Canadian and European-Canadian 5-year-olds also found that the Chinese-Canadian children performed better on executive function, as measured by a *Go/No-Go task*. In this kind of task, stimuli (such as differently colored dots) are presented in a continuous stream and participants have to make one of two decisions for each stimulus. One decision requires participants to make a motor response, such as pressing a button if a dot on a computer screen is purple (the *Go* response). The other decision requires participants to withhold a response, such as not pressing the button if the dot is orange (*No-Go*). Accuracy and reaction time are measured for each response. Additionally, this study with 5-year-olds measured electroencephalogram (EEG) patterns and found differences between the two cultural groups (Lahat et al., 2010). The Chinese-Canadian children showed more activation in a part of the brain linked to reaction time. Consequently, Stephanie Carlson and colleagues (2013) have suggested that brain development in regard to executive function may not occur in the same way across cultures.

**executive function**
includes inhibitory control, or staying focused on the task at hand and not becoming distracted, and flexibility, or adjusting one's strategy as the nature of a task changes

**selective attention**
ability to focus attention on relevant information and disregard what is irrelevant

## Information Processing in Middle Childhood

**LO 5.3.2 Describe how attention, memory, and executive function change during middle childhood, and identify the characteristics of children who have ADHD.**

Ever try to play a board game with a 3-year-old? If you do, it had better be short and simple. But by middle childhood, children can play a wide variety of board games that adults enjoy, too. This is one reflection of how information processing improves during middle childhood.

**ATTENTION.** In middle childhood, children improve on selective attention (Goldberg et al., 2001; Janssen et al., 2014). For example, in one line of research, children of various ages were shown a series of cards, each containing one animal and one household item, and told to try to remember where the animal on each card was located (Hagen & Hale, 1973). Nothing was mentioned about the household items. Afterward, when asked about the location of the animals on each card, older children performed better than younger children. However, when asked how many of the household items they could remember, younger children performed better than older children. The older children were capable of focusing on the information they were told would be relevant—the location of the animals—and capable of ignoring the household items as irrelevant. In contrast, the younger children's poorer performance in identifying the locations of the animals was partly due to being distracted by the household items.

**ATTENTION DEFICIT/HYPERACTIVITY DISORDER.** Being able to maintain attention becomes especially important once children enter school at about age 6 or 7, because the school setting requires children to pay attention to their teachers' instructions. Children with especially notable difficulties in maintaining attention may be diagnosed with **attention-deficit/hyperactivity disorder (ADHD)**, which includes problems of inattention, hyperactivity, and impulsiveness. Children with ADHD have difficulty following instructions and waiting their turn. In the United States, it is estimated that 7% of children ages 4–10 are diagnosed with ADHD (National Resource Center on ADHD, 2014). Boys are over twice as likely as girls to have ADHD. A pediatrician usually makes the diagnosis after evaluating the child and consulting with parents and teachers. In the United States, nearly 9 of 10 children and adolescents diagnosed with ADHD receive Ritalin or other medications to suppress their hyperactivity and help them concentrate better. Medications are often effective in controlling the symptoms of ADHD, with 70% of children showing improvements in academic performance and peer relations (Prasad et al., 2013). However, there are concerns about side effects, including slower physical growth and higher risk of depression. Behavioral therapies are also effective, and the combination of medication and behavioral therapy is more effective than either treatment alone (American Academy of Pediatrics, 2011).

**attention-deficit/hyperactivity disorder (ADHD)**
diagnosis that includes problems of inattention, hyperactivity, and impulsiveness

Although most research on ADHD has taken place in the United States, one large study in Europe included over 1,500 children and adolescents (ages 6–18) in 10 countries (Rothenberger et al., 2006). In this Attention-deficit/hyperactivity Disorder Observational Research in Europe (ADORE) study, pediatricians and child psychiatrists collected observational data on children and adolescents at seven time points over 2 years, with data including diagnosis, treatment, and outcomes. Parents also participated, and their assessments showed high agreement with the assessments of the pediatricians and child psychiatrists. Like the American studies, ADORE found higher rates of ADHD among boys than among girls, but the ratios varied widely among countries, from 3:1 to 16:1 (Novik et al., 2006). Symptoms of ADHD were similar among boys and girls. However, girls were more likely to have additional emotional problems and to be bullied by their peers, and boys were more likely to have conduct problems. For both boys and girls, having ADHD resulted in frequent problems in their relations with peers, teachers, and parents (Coghill et al., 2006). Parents reported frequent stresses and strains due to children's ADHD behavior, including disruptions of family activities and worries about the future (Riley et al., 2006). In contrast to the American approach of relying heavily on medications, the European approaches to treatment were diverse: medications (25%), psychotherapy (19%), combination of medications and psychotherapy (25%), other therapy (10%), and no treatment (21%) (Preuss et al., 2006). Watch the video *A Boy Talks About Having ADHD* for more information.

**working memory**
the retention and processing of information for a brief time

**MEMORY.** In early childhood, memory is often fleeting, as any parent who has ever asked a 4-year-old what happened to those nice new mittens he wore out to play that morning can attest. Mittens? What mittens?

In middle childhood, the capacity of **working memory** enlarges. Working memory, like short-term memory, involves the capacity to retain information for a brief time. The difference is that the information in working memory is not simply retained, it is also processed in some way. For example, a standard way to test short-term memory involves listening to a string of digits (e.g., 3, 5, 1, 8, 9), and repeating them just as they were presented. To make this a working memory task, however, the requirement is to repeat them in the opposite order (i.e., 9, 8, 1, 5, 3).

**Watch** A BOY TALKS ABOUT HAVING ADHD

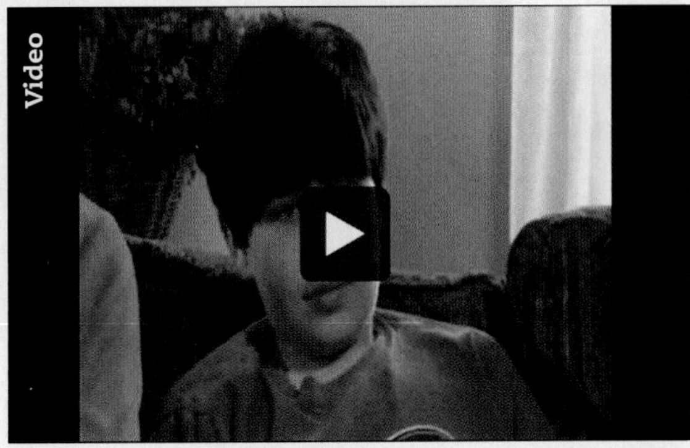

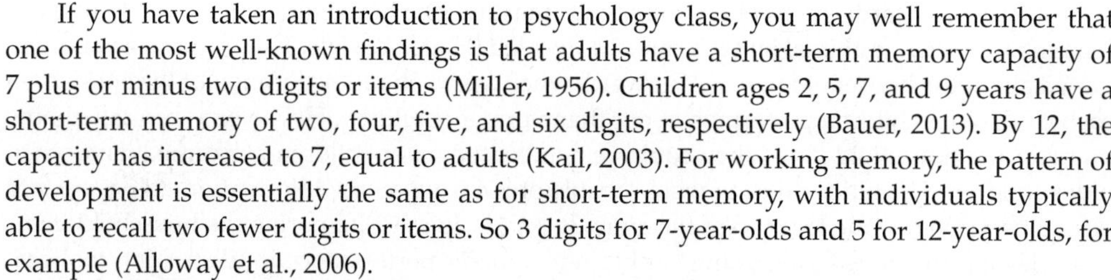

If you have taken an introduction to psychology class, you may well remember that one of the most well-known findings is that adults have a short-term memory capacity of 7 plus or minus two digits or items (Miller, 1956). Children ages 2, 5, 7, and 9 years have a short-term memory of two, four, five, and six digits, respectively (Bauer, 2013). By 12, the capacity has increased to 7, equal to adults (Kail, 2003). For working memory, the pattern of development is essentially the same as for short-term memory, with individuals typically able to recall two fewer digits or items. So 3 digits for 7-year-olds and 5 for 12-year-olds, for example (Alloway et al., 2006).

**mnemonics**
memory strategies, such as rehearsal, organization, and elaboration

**rehearsal**
mnemonic that involves repeating the same information over and over

Importantly, middle childhood is also the period when children first learn to use **mnemonics**, or memory strategies, such as rehearsal, organization, and elaboration. **Rehearsal**, which involves repeating the information over and over, is a simple but effective mnemonic. You probably use it yourself, perhaps when new acquaintances tell you their names for the first time. In a classic study, John Flavell and his colleagues (1966) showed how rehearsal emerges as a memory strategy in middle childhood. They outfitted children ages 5 and 10 with a space helmet with a dark visor and displayed seven pictures of familiar objects in front of them. Each child was told that the researcher was going to point to three objects that the child was to remember (in order), then pull down the space helmet visor so the child could not see for 15 seconds, and then lift the visor and ask the child to point to the three objects. During the 15-second delay, 85% of the 10-year-olds but only 10% of the 5-year-olds moved their lips or recited the names of the objects aloud, showing that they were using rehearsal. At each age, rehearsers recalled the objects much more accurately than non-rehearsers.

**organization**
mnemonic that involves mentally placing things into meaningful categories

**Organization**—placing things into meaningful categories—is another effective memory strategy that is used more commonly in the course of middle childhood (Schneider, 2002). Studies typically test this ability by giving people a list of items to remember, for example, shoes, zebra, baseball, cow, tennis racket, dress, raccoon, soccer goal, hat. Numerous studies have shown that if children are given a list of items to remember, they are more likely to group them into categories—such as clothes, animals, sports items—in middle childhood than in early childhood (Sang et al., 2002). Organization is a highly effective memory strategy, because each category serves as a *retrieval cue* for the items within the category, so that if the category can be remembered, all the items within the category are likely to be remembered as well (Schneider, 2002).

**elaboration**
mnemonic that involves transforming bits of information in a way that connects them and hence makes them easier to remember

A third mnemonic that emerges in middle childhood is **elaboration**, which involves transforming bits of information in a way that connects them and hence makes them easier to remember (Terry, 2003). One example is the English-language way of teaching children the lines of the treble clef in music, EGBDF: Every Good Boy Does Fine. Or, if you were going to the grocery store and wanted to remember to buy butter, lettuce, apples, and milk, you could arrange the first letter of each of the items into one word, *BLAM*. The word *BLAM* serves as a retrieval cue for the items represented by each letter of the word. While elaboration emerges in middle childhood, it is more common by adolescence (Bauer, 2013).

Why do young chess masters remember chess configurations better than older novices do?

Although children are more likely to use mnemonics in middle childhood than in early childhood, even in middle childhood and beyond, relatively few people use such memory strategies on a regular basis. Instead, they rely on more concrete, practical methods. In one study, children in kindergarten, first, third, and fifth grade were asked how they would remember to bring their ice skates to a party the next day (Kreutzer et al., 1975). In all three age groups, children came up with sensible approaches, such as putting the skates where they would be easy to see, writing themselves a note, and tying a string to their finger.

Apart from the use of mnemonics, another reason why memory improves from early childhood to middle childhood is that children's knowledge base expands, and the more you know, the easier it is to remember new information that is related to what you know. In a classic study illustrating this, 10-year-old chess masters and college student novice chess players were compared on their ability to remember configurations of pieces on a chess board (Chi, 1978). The 10-year-old chess masters performed far better than the college student novices, even though the college students were better at recalling a series of random numbers. In another study, 9- and 10-year-olds were separated into two groups, soccer "experts" and soccer "novices," and asked to try to remember lists of soccer items and non-soccer items (Schneider & Bjorklund, 1992). The soccer experts remembered more items on the soccer list than on the non-soccer list.

Middle childhood is not only a time of advances in memory abilities but also of advances in understanding how memory works, or **metamemory**. Even by age 5 or 6, most children have some grasp of metamemory (Kvavilashvili & Ford, 2014). They recognize that it is easier to remember something that happened yesterday than something that happened long ago. They understand that short lists are easier to remember than long lists, and that familiar items are more easily remembered than unfamiliar items. However, their appraisal of their own memory abilities tends to be inflated. When children in early childhood and middle childhood were shown a series of 10 pictures and asked if they could remember all of them, more than half of the younger children but only a few older children claimed they could (none of them actually could!) (Flavell et al., 1970). In the course of middle childhood, children develop more accurate assessments of their memory abilities (Schneider & Pressley, 1997).

**metamemory**
understanding of how memory works

**EXECUTIVE FUNCTION.** In the course of middle childhood, children also become better at **problem solving**, which involves the use and selection of strategies in order to arrive at a goal. One reason is that with age, children make use of more strategies. Thomas Coyle and David Bjorklund (1997) tested second-, third-, and fourth-grade children on a memory task, and found that the number of strategies they used to help them remember increased steadily with age, from 1.6 to 1.9 to 2.4.

**problem solving**
the ability to select and use strategies in order to arrive at a goal

Another reason there is improvement in problem solving in middle childhood is the use of more effective strategies. Robert Siegler (1995, 1996) has shown that at age 5, a child will typically use a variety of strategies to try to solve Piaget's conservation-of-numbers problem. As children get into middle childhood, they continue to use multiple strategies, but now select more effective ones. They are able to do so not only because they have more knowledge, but also because they adjust to new information in a more flexible way.

**Critical Thinking Question:** A company asks you to help them design a video game aimed at 8- and 9-year-old children. What key pieces of advice would you provide based on information-processing research findings?

# Information Processing in Adolescence and Emerging Adulthood

**LO 5.3.3 Summarize the major changes in attention, memory, and executive function that take place in adolescence and emerging adulthood.**

Would you let a 9-year-old drive a car? How about go on a trip abroad on his own? As much as children in middle childhood advance on information processing, there are still many cognitive challenges that they typically are not ready to handle. In the course of adolescence and emerging adulthood, however, major improvements have taken place. Executive function, for example, peaks in the mid-20s.

**ATTENTION.** Are you able to read a textbook while someone else in the same room is watching television? Can you have a conversation at a party where music and other conversations are blaring loudly all around you? As described above, these are tasks that require *selective attention*, the ability to focus on relevant information while screening out information that is irrelevant. Adolescents tend to be better than younger children at tasks that require selective attention, and emerging adults are generally better than adolescents (Sinha & Goel, 2012).

Adolescents are also more adept than younger children at tasks that require **divided attention**—reading a book and listening to music at the same time, for example.

**divided attention**
ability to focus on more than one task at a time

Adolescents are more adept than younger children at doing multiple tasks at once, but divided attention can hinder learning.

But even for adolescents, divided attention may result in less efficient learning than if attention were focused entirely on one thing. One study found that watching TV interfered with adolescents' homework performance, but listening to music did not (Pool et al., 2003).

**MEMORY.** Memory also improves in adolescence, especially long-term memory. Adolescents are more likely than younger children to use mnemonic devices, such as organizing information into coherent patterns (Schneider, 2010). Another reason long-term memory improves is that adolescents have accumulated yet more experience and more knowledge than younger children, and these advantages enhance the effectiveness of long-term memory (Keating, 2012). Having more knowledge helps you learn new information and store it in long-term memory.

The capacity of working memory also shows increases into adolescence (Conklin et al., 2007; Keage et al., 2008; Luciana et al., 2005). An experiment by Robert Sternberg and his colleagues demonstrates how increases in working memory take place between childhood and adolescence (Sternberg & Nigro, 1980). They presented analogies to 3rd-grade, 6th-grade, 9th-grade, and college students. For example, "Sun is to moon as asleep is to ...?" 1) Star, 2) Bed, 3) Awake, or 4) Night. There was improvement with age, especially between the younger (3rd- and 6th-grade) and older (9th-grade and college) students. Sternberg attributed the differences to working memory capacities. Analogies require you to keep the first set of words ("sun is to moon") and the nature of their relationship in your working memory continuously as you consider the other possible pairings ("asleep is to star... asleep is to bed...") and analyze their relationships as well. Adolescents become proficient at performing tasks like this very effectively. (Just in case you were wondering, the solution to the analogy is "awake").

Working memory is also closely related to **automaticity**, that is, how much cognitive effort a person needs to devote to process information (Case, 1997). If you are given computational problems such as 100 divided by 20, 60 minus 18, 7 times 9, you can probably do them quickly, without writing them down. This is partly because you have done problems like this so many times in the course of your life that they are almost automatic—much more than they would be for a preadolescent child. The more automatic a cognitive task is, the faster you are able to do it. Also, the more automatic a task is, the less working memory capacity it takes, leaving more room for other tasks.

**automaticity**
how much cognitive effort a person needs to devote to process information; the more automaticity, the less effort

Adolescents and emerging adults show greater automaticity of processing in a variety of respects, compared with preadolescent children. However, automaticity depends more on experience than on age alone. Again, this has been shown in studies of chess players. Expert chess players have been found to process the configurations on chessboards with a high degree of automaticity, enabling them to remember the configurations better and analyze them faster and more effectively than novices do (Bruer, 1993; Chase & Simon, 1973; Chi et al., 1982). Furthermore, expert chess players who are children or adolescents demonstrate greater automaticity in processing chess configurations than novice adults do, even though the adults outperform them on other cognitive tests (Chi et al., 1982).

**EXECUTIVE FUNCTION.** Adolescents and emerging adults advance in their executive function. In fact, studies that use tasks such as the flanker test and the DCCS (described above) indicate that performance peaks around age 25 years (Carlson et al., 2013). Figure 5.4 illustrates this developmental pattern between ages 9 and 49. Improvements in executive functioning allow adolescents and emerging adults to perform a large number of cognitive tasks that younger children cannot, such as driving an automobile or working as a clerk in a retail store.

Even so, there are distinct cultural differences in how children's capabilities are viewed and the responsibilities they are given. If you live in a developed country, you

**Figure 5.4** Executive Function Among 9- to 49-Year-Olds

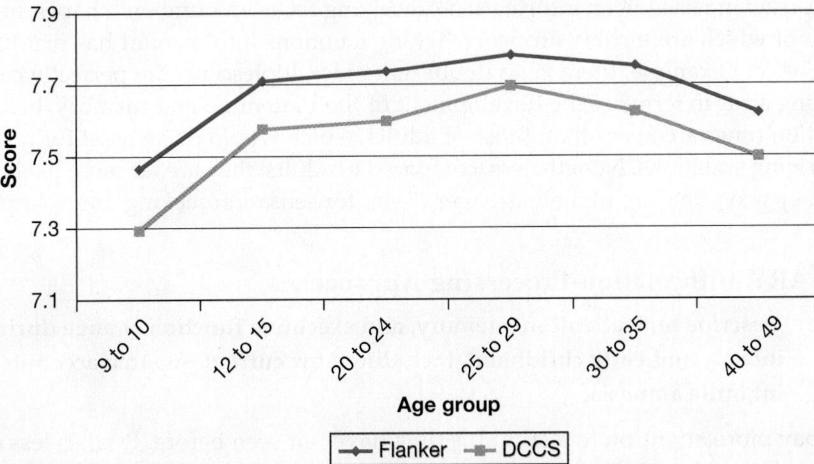


SOURCE: Zelazo et al. (2012).

probably would not hire a 7-year-old baby-sitter for your infant. Yet, in many cultures, by age 7, girls are given daily responsibility for infant care, and some of this work requires a substantial amount of executive function (Whiting & Edwards, 1988).

> **Critical Thinking Question:** Explain how driving an automobile is a good example of executive function.

# Evaluating Information-Processing Approaches

**LO 5.3.4 Summarize the strengths and limitations of information-processing approaches.**

Like Piaget's theory of cognitive development, information-processing approaches have generated large amounts of research. Information-processing researchers have excelled at providing detailed insight into various components of cognition and also to some extent the relation among components. They have also contributed to the tremendous growth of studies on executive function, a cognitive skill that highlights the relation among components such as attention and memory.

Critiques of information-processing approaches tend to home in on two issues.

1. What information-processing researchers often see as a strength—the detailed focus on components of cognitive processes—is actually a weakness, according to some critics. According to this critique, information-processing approaches are **reductionistic**, which means breaking up a phenomenon into separate parts to such an extent that the coherence and complexity of the phenomenon as a whole become lost. The analogy of a computer once favored by information-processing scholars is misguided because human beings are not computers. In humans, mental capabilities are integrated. Furthermore, computers have no capacity for self-reflection, and no awareness of how their cognitive processes are integrated, organized, and monitored. Computers—unlike Descartes, Lao-Tzu, and you—do not have metacognition.

**reductionistic**

breaking up a phenomenon into separate parts to such an extent that the meaning and coherence of the phenomenon as a whole become lost

2. Computers also lack emotions, and according to some scholars, emotions must be taken into account when considering cognitive functioning. Recent research on executive

function is starting to address "hot executive function," or problem solving in emotionally charged situations (Carlson et al., 2013). As we have seen, however, many of the tasks used in research on information processing focus on numbers, shapes, and fish—none of which are terribly arousing. Taking emotions into account has real-life implications. For example, there is no doubt that older adolescents are perfectly capable of driving a car in terms of the development of their attention and memory. In fact, their reaction times are faster than those of adults, which would be an asset for responding to driving situations. Nonetheless, compared to adults, they are far more likely to drive in risky ways because of their stronger desire for sensation seeking, for example.

### SUMMARY: Information-Processing Approaches

**LO 5.3.1 Describe how attention, memory, and executive function change during infancy and early childhood, including how current research accounts for infantile amnesia.**

Infants pay more attention to a stimulus they have not seen before. It takes less and less time for habituation to new stimuli to occur during the first year. Furthermore, infants also increasingly engage in joint attention with others during the first year. Their short- and long-term memory abilities also expand greatly. Nonetheless, infants and young children forget a great deal of what happened up to about age 4. This infantile amnesia appears to be influenced both by neurological changes in the hippocampus and cultural factors. The period from age 3 to 6 years is when executive function emerges and rises quite steeply.

**LO 5.3.2 Describe how attention, memory, and executive function change during middle childhood, and identify the characteristics of children who have ADHD.**

In middle childhood, children become more capable of focusing their attention on relevant information and disregarding what is irrelevant. Children with especially notable difficulties in maintaining attention may be diagnosed with attention-deficit/hyperactivity disorder (ADHD), which includes problems of inattention, hyperactivity, and impulsiveness. Middle childhood is the period when working memory enlarges, and children first learn to use memory strategies such as rehearsal, organization, and elaboration. They also become better at using efficient and multiple strategies to solve problems.

**LO 5.3.3 Summarize the major changes in attention, memory, and executive function that take place in adolescence and emerging adulthood.**

Information-processing abilities improve in adolescence, with the notable additions of selective attention and divided attention. Memory also improves in adolescence, especially long-term memory. Adolescents and emerging adults advance in their executive function, an ability that peaks in the mid-20s.

**LO 5.3.4 Summarize the strengths and limitations of information-processing approaches.**

Information-processing researchers have excelled at providing detailed insight into various components of cognition, and to some extent the relation among components such as executive function. Critiques argue that the approach is reductionistic, separating out mental capabilities that are integrated. Also, most information-processing research disregards how thinking often occurs in situations laden with emotions.

# 5.4 Social Cognition

**social cognition**
how people think about other people, social relationships, and social institutions

**Social cognition** is the term for the way we think about other people, social relationships, and social institutions (Evans, 2008). We will look closely at social relationships and institutions in later chapters, and focus here on the development of the ability to understand other people's cognitions and perspectives. Much of this research has focused on either young children or adolescents.

## Young Children's Social Cognition: Theory of Mind

**LO 5.4.1 Explain what "theory of mind" is and the evidence for when it develops during early childhood.**

**theory of mind**
ability to understand thinking processes in oneself and others

One popular area of research in recent years is **theory of mind**, or the ability to attribute mental states to self and others and to understand that others have beliefs, intentions, and perspectives that are different from one's own (Astington, 1993; Perner, 1991; Wellman, 1990). Understanding how others think is a challenge even for adults, but the beginnings of theory of mind appear very early.

Through behavior such as joint attention and the use of language vocalizations, infants and toddlers show that they understand that others have mental states (Tomasello & Rakoczy, 2003). By 12 months of age, for example, infants will point to an event or object that others are unaware of in order to draw their attention to it (Liszkowski et al., 2007). Between 12 and 18 months, toddlers will point an adult in the direction of something that the adult is searching for (Liszkowski et al., 2006), thereby showing an understanding of the adult's intentions. By age 2, as they begin to use language more, children show increasing recognition that others have thoughts and emotions that can be contrasted with their own (e.g., "That man is mad!" or "I like applesauce. Brother no like applesauce."). At age 2, children begin to use words that refer to mental processes, such as "think," "remember," and "pretend" (Flavell et al., 2002). By age 3, children know it is possible for them and others to imagine something that is not physically present (such as an ice cream cone). They can respond to an imaginary event as if it has really happened, and they realize that others can do the same (Andrews et al., 2003). This understanding becomes the basis of pretend play for many years to come.

A common set of measures for testing young children's theory of mind involve *false-belief tasks*. In one experiment testing understanding of false beliefs, children are shown a doll named Maxi who places chocolate in a cabinet and then leaves the room (Amsterlaw & Wellman, 2006). Next, another doll, his mother, enters the room and moves the chocolate to a different place. Children are then asked, "Where will Maxi look for the chocolate when he returns?" Most 3-year-old children answer erroneously that Maxi will look for the chocolate in the new place, where his mother stored it. In contrast, by age 4, most children recognize that Maxi will believe falsely that the chocolate is in the cabinet where he left it. The proportion of children who understand this correctly rises even higher by age 5. By age 6, nearly all children in developed countries solve false-belief tasks easily.

There have been few false-belief studies in developing countries, but some have found a delay in children's acquisition of false-belief reasoning. However, these studies rely on highly language-dependent tasks, like the story about Maxi and his mother. They also rely on children being willing to answer questions about others' mental states. These studies may not be ecologically valid (refer to Chapter 1) in the sense that there is misfit between the measurement approach and the everyday life of the people being studied. In one study, Daniel Haun and colleagues devised a nonverbal game that tested for false beliefs and found that 4- to 7-year-olds from Germany, Namibia, and Samoa showed identical levels of performance (Haun, 2015). Watch the video *Spontaneous Response Tasks and Theory of Mind* to see how another nonverbal method has changed what we know about the development of theory of mind.

### Research Focus: Spontaneous Response Tasks and Theory of Mind

We saw earlier in this chapter that the way young children are tested can lead to different conclusions about their cognitive development. Research by Renee Baillargeon and colleagues using the "violation of expectations method" suggests that children acquire object permanence earlier than what Piaget concluded based on the task of lifting a blanket off an object. Piaget's task requires the coordination of mental and motor abilities, whereas Baillargeon's measure relies solely on children's looking behavior.

The violation of expectations method is one of a variety of spontaneous-response tasks (Baillargeon et al., 2010). In spontaneous-response tasks, children's cognition is inferred from behaviors they spontaneously produce as they observe a scene unfold. Spontaneous-response tasks also include preferential looking (the place an infant prefers to look) and anticipatory looking (the place an infant looks in anticipation of an event) (Haun, 2015).

Baillargeon is among a number of researchers who have used anticipatory looking tasks to examine whether children

**Watch** SPONTANEOUS RESPONSE TASKS AND THEORY OF MIND

Video

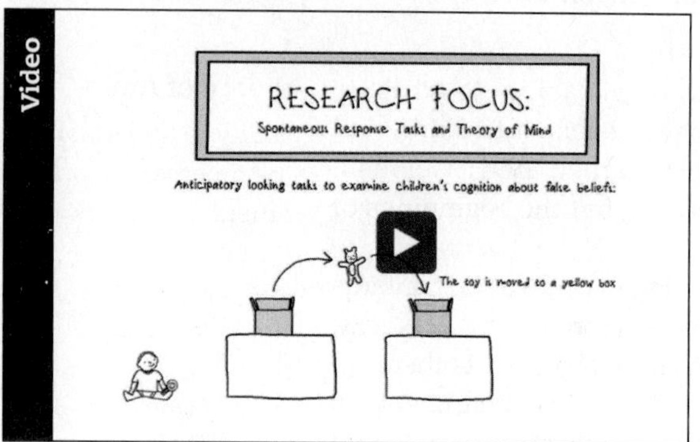


visually anticipate where a person with a false belief about the location of an object will search for the object. The researchers do not ask children to verbally explain where a person will look for an object. Instead, they simply measure where children look. For example, children will watch a person place a toy inside a green box. The person leaves and the toy is moved to a yellow box. When the person returns in search of the object, where will children look? If they have acquired false-belief reasoning, they should look at the green box where the person left the toy and believes—falsely—that it is still located. If children have not acquired false-belief reasoning, they should look at the yellow box where the toy is now located.

Where would you hypothesize that 15-month-old toddlers look? Based on standard verbal false-belief tasks, we would expect that children younger than about 4 years of age do not have false-belief understanding and hence look at the yellow box. But it turns out that 15-month-olds look toward the green box (Onishi & Baillargeon, 2005). Evidence from a number of other studies also suggests that children in the second year of life can attribute false beliefs to others.

Researchers, however, continue to differ as to the extent and depth to which children of different ages have acquired false-belief reasoning. Some have argued that spontaneous response tasks test for "implicit knowledge." In their view, explicit and full-fledged understanding of false beliefs only develops in early childhood (Perner & Roessler, 2012).

## Review Question

1. Spontaneous-response tasks can be useful to understand the cognitive development of infants and toddlers because:
   a. They rely solely on children's motor responses
   b. They support Piaget's conclusions about object permanence
   c. They rely solely on children's looking behavior
   d. They support previous conclusions about false beliefs that were based on children's verbal responses

Research on theory of mind continues to flourish. In the coming years, it is likely that some of the unresolved questions will be answered. What is currently clear is that insight into other people's minds can be a challenge. People's beliefs and intentions are multifaceted, and the extent to which people show what is on their mind depends on the situation. Here is an illustrative example from a conversation between a mother and a 5-year-old child on the New York City subway (Gilbert, 2015, p. A16):

Child: Why are they all so sad? (Referring to the people sitting across from her).

Mom: Oh, they're not sad. That's just their subway face.

## Adolescents' Social Cognition: The Imaginary Audience and the Personal Fable

**LO 5.4.2 Define the imaginary audience and the personal fable, and explain how they reflect egocentrism in adolescence.**

**adolescent egocentrism**
type of egocentrism in which adolescents have difficulty distinguishing their thinking about their own thoughts from their thinking about the thoughts of others

**imaginary audience**
belief that others are acutely aware of and attentive to one's appearance and behavior

Apart from the focus on young children, social cognition has also been studied quite extensively in adolescence. Interestingly, Piaget (1967) proposed that adolescents show a distinctive kind of **adolescent egocentrism**, where they conflate their thinking about themselves with what others are thinking about them. Piaget's idea was developed further by David Elkind (1967, 1985; Alberts et al., 2007). According to Elkind, adolescent egocentrism has two aspects: the imaginary audience and the personal fable.

Because they think about themselves so much and are so acutely aware of how they might appear to others, adolescents conclude that others must also be thinking about them a great deal. Because they exaggerate the extent to which others think about them, they imagine a rapt audience for their appearance and behavior. This is what Elkind called the **imaginary audience**. The imaginary audience makes adolescents much more self-conscious than they were in middle childhood. Do you remember waking up in 7th or 8th grade with a pimple on your forehead, or discovering a food stain on your sweater and wondering how long it had been there, or saying something in class that made everybody laugh (even though you didn't intend it to be funny)? Of course, experiences like these are not much fun as an adult, either. But they tend to be worse in adolescence, because the imaginary audience makes it seem as though "everybody" knows about your humiliation and will remember it for a long, long time. For today's adolescents, this tendency may be promoted by social media; several studies have found that using social media such as Facebook deepens their feelings of being the center of an imaginary audience (Cingel & Krcmar, 2014). Watch the video *The Imaginary Audience* for an example of an adolescent explaining her self-conscious experience.

**Watch** THE IMAGINARY AUDIENCE

The imaginary audience is not something that simply disappears when adolescence ends. Adults are egocentric, too, to some extent. Adults, too, imagine (and sometimes exaggerate) an audience for their behavior. It is just that this tendency is stronger in adolescence, when the capacity for distinguishing between our own perspective and the perspective of others is less developed (Alberts et al., 2007).

According to Elkind (1967, 1985), the belief in an imaginary audience that is highly conscious of how you think, look, and act leads to the belief that there must be something special, something unique, about you. Adolescents' belief in the uniqueness of their personal experiences and their personal destiny is known as the **personal fable**. The personal fable can be the source of adolescent anguish, when it makes them feel that "no one understands me" because no one can share their unique experience (Elkind, 1978). It can be the source of high hopes, too, as adolescents imagine their unique personal destiny leading to the fulfillment of dreams to be a rock musician, a professional athlete, a famous actor, or simply successful in the field of their choice. It can also contribute to risky behavior by adolescents whose sense of uniqueness leads them to believe that adverse consequences of behavior such as unprotected sex or drunk driving "won't happen to me." According to research by Elkind and his colleagues, personal fable scores increase from early to mid-adolescence and are correlated with participation in risky behaviors (Alberts et al., 2007).

**personal fable**
belief in one's personal uniqueness, often including a sense of invulnerability to the consequences of taking risks

**Critical Thinking Question:** Research on the imaginary audience and personal fable has mostly been conducted in the United States. To what extent would you expect these concepts to be prevalent in other cultures? Explain your reasoning.

Like the imaginary audience, the personal fable diminishes with age. For most of us, however, it never entirely disappears. Adults also like to think there is something special, if not unique, about their personal experiences and their personal destiny. But the personal fable tends to be stronger in adolescence than at later ages, because with age our experiences and conversations with others lead us to an awareness that our thoughts and feelings are not as exceptional as we once might have believed (Elkind, 1978; Martin & Sokol, 2011).

## Evaluating Research on Social Cognition

**LO 5.4.3 Summarize the strengths and limitations of research on social cognition.**

The research on social cognition adds an important dimension to cognitive development in that it recognizes that the human mind is a not a self-contained island. To a large extent, from infancy onward, we are profoundly attuned to what other people have in mind—what they are thinking and the nature of their intentions. Furthermore, the research on adolescent egocentrism shows how cognitive development and emotional development are connected, and it provides for psychological insight that can be helpful to adolescents and those around them.

Given the focus on the social side of life, it is perhaps surprising that the research on social cognition has paid limited attention to how people's social and cultural circumstances are highly varied.

The personal fable can lead adolescents to believe that negative consequences from taking risks "won't happen to me."

As we have seen, most of the research relies on methods, samples, and concepts that come from the United States and Europe. Some researchers are conducting research in non-Western societies and have devised more ecologically sensitive measures. Nevertheless, there is ample room for additional methods, research with diverse samples, and new theory in this area.

### SUMMARY: Social Cognition

**LO 5.4.1 Explain what "theory of mind" is and the evidence for when it develops during early childhood.**

Theory of mind is the ability to attribute mental states to self and others and to understand that others have beliefs, intentions, and perspectives that are different from one's own. False-belief tasks, a common set of measures for testing theory of mind, indicate that most 4-year-olds have attained theory of mind. However, research using other methods suggests that 1-year-olds have some understanding that other people can hold false beliefs.

**LO 5.4.2 Define the imaginary audience and the personal fable, and explain how they reflect egocentrism in adolescence.**

The imaginary audience is the exaggerated belief that others are paying intense attention to one's appearance and behavior. The personal fable is the belief that there is something special and unique about one's personal destiny. These beliefs result from adolescents' egocentrism. Because they think about themselves so much and are so acutely aware of how they might appear to others, adolescents conclude that others must also be thinking about them a great deal. Because they exaggerate the extent to which others think about them, they imagine a rapt audience for their appearance and behavior.

**LO 5.4.3 Summarize the strengths and limitations of research on social cognition.**

The research on social cognition recognizes that, from infancy and onward, we are profoundly attuned to what other people think and feel. Critics point out that research on social cognition has paid limited attention to how people's diverse social and cultural circumstances influence social cognition.

## 5.5 Sociocultural Theories of Cognitive Development

How is cultural learning taking place here?

Although they differ in many ways, the major perspectives on cognitive development discussed so far—cognitive-developmental, information processing, and social cognition—all primarily aim to discover principles of cognitive development that apply to all people in all times and all cultures (Cole, 1996; Rogoff, 2003). Sociocultural theories of cognitive development, in contrast, emphasize that human beings are social, and that social experiences are infused with cultural beliefs and norms. This approach is founded on the ideas of the Russian psychologist Lev Vygotsky (1896–1934). Vygotsky died of tuberculosis when he was just 37, and it took decades before his ideas about cognitive development were translated and recognized by scholars outside Russia. Only in recent decades has his work become widely influential among Western scholars. Even so, his influence is increasing as interest in understanding the cultural basis of development continues to grow (Gauvain & Nicolaides, 2015; Maynard & Martini, 2005).

### Basic Sociocultural Concepts

**LO 5.5.1 Describe Vygotsky's sociocultural theory of cognitive development and contrast it with Piaget's theory.**

Vygotsky's theory is often referred to as a *sociocultural theory,* because cognitive development is always both a social and a cultural process in his view (Daniels et al., 2007). It is social, because children learn through interactions with others and require assistance from others in order to learn what they need to know. It is cultural, because what children need to know and how they learn it is determined by the culture they live in. Vygotsky recognized that there are distinct cultural differences in the knowledge children must acquire—from agricultural skills in rural Asia, to caring for cattle in eastern Africa, to the verbal and scientific reasoning skills taught in Western schools. This is very different from Piaget's theory, which emphasizes the child's solitary interactions with the physical environment and views cognitive development as essentially the same across cultures.

Two of Vygotsky's most influential ideas are the zone of proximal development and scaffolding (Gauvain & Nicolaides, 2015). The **zone of proximal development** is the distance between skills or tasks that children can accomplish alone and those they are capable of performing if guided by an adult or a more competent peer. According to Vygotsky, children learn best if the instruction they are provided is within the zone of proximal development, so that they need assistance at first but gradually become capable of performing the task on their own. For example, children learning a musical instrument may be lost or overwhelmed if learning entirely on their own, but can make progress if guided by someone who already knows how to play the instrument. Watch the video *Zone of Proximal Development* for more information.

**zone of proximal development**
difference between skills or tasks that children can accomplish alone and those they are capable of performing if guided by an adult or a more competent peer

As they learn in the zone of proximal development and have conversations with those guiding them, children begin to speak to themselves in a self-guiding and self-directing way, first aloud, then internally. Vygotsky called this **private speech** (Winsler et al., 2009). As children become more competent in what they are learning, they internalize their private speech and gradually decrease its use. Toddlerhood and early childhood are crucial periods in Vygotsky's theory, because it is during these life stages that children are most likely to use private speech and transition from using it aloud to using it internally (Feigenbaum, 2002). However, private speech continues throughout life. In fact, Vygotsky believed that private speech was necessary to all higher-order cognitive functioning. In recent years, studies have shown that adolescents and adults use private speech when solving tasks of diverse kinds (Medina et al., 2009). In contrast to Vygotsky, Piaget regarded speaking aloud to oneself as a sign of egocentrism—something that young children do because they fail to consider whether others might be interested in or understand what they are saying (Piaget, 1923).

**private speech**
in Vygotsky's theory, self-guiding and self-directing comments children make to themselves as they learn in the zone of proximal development and have conversations with those guiding them; first spoken aloud, then internally

**Critical Thinking Question:** Do you ever talk aloud to yourself? If so, think about where, when, and what purposes it serves.

The second key idea in Vygotsky's theory is **scaffolding**, which is the nature of assistance provided to children in the zone of proximal development. For example, scaffolding might involve recruiting the child's interest, breaking a task into manageable units, keeping the child focused on the task, helping to manage risk and frustration in problem solving, and pointing out differences between what the child accomplished and a more ideal task solution. According to Vygotsky, scaffolding should gradually decrease as children become more competent at a task. When children begin learning a task, they require substantial instruction and involvement from an adult or more capable peer; but as they gain knowledge and skill, the teacher should gradually scale back the amount of direct instruction provided. For example, young children require their parents' help to get dressed. With age and experience, they become capable of doing more and more of it themselves, until eventually they can do it on their own. Scaffolding can occur at any age, whenever there is someone who is learning a skill or gaining knowledge from someone else.

**scaffolding**
degree of assistance provided to the learner in the zone of proximal development, gradually decreasing as the learner's skills develop

**Watch** ZONE OF PROXIMAL DEVELOPMENT

**Critical Thinking Question:** Give an example of the zone of proximal development and scaffolding involving adolescents or emerging adults.

## The Development of Cultural Ways of Thinking

**LO 5.5.2 Identify ways that cultural learning takes place from childhood through emerging adulthood.**

**guided participation**

interaction between two people in a culturally valued activity where the more experienced person guides the learning of the less experienced person

One scholar who has been important in extending Vygotsky's theory is Barbara Rogoff (1990; 1995; 1998; 2003). Her idea of **guided participation** refers to the interaction between two people (often an adult and a child) as they participate in a culturally valued activity. The guidance is "the direction offered by cultural and social values, as well as social partners" as learning takes place (Rogoff, 1995, p. 142). As an example of guided participation, Rogoff (2003) describes a toddler and caregiver in Taiwan "playing school" together. As part of the game, the caregiver teaches the toddler to stand up and bow down to the teacher at the beginning and end of class, thereby teaching not only the routine of the classroom but also the cultural value of respect for teachers' authority. The teaching in guided participation may also be indirect. For example, from her extensive research with the Mayan people of Guatemala, Rogoff (2003) describes how toddlers observe their mothers making tortillas and attempt to imitate them. Mothers give them a small piece of dough and help their efforts along by rolling the dough into a ball and starting the flattening process. Otherwise, the mothers do not provide explicit teaching, instead allowing toddlers to learn through observing and then attempting to imitate their mother's actions.

Sociocultural research with young children has also helped to highlight how the processes that promote cognitive development are culturally varied. In one research program, Mary Gauvain has focused on children's questioning. Developmental psychologists have claimed that toddlers and preschoolers are characterized by their fondness for asking "why?" Research with American 3- to 5-year-olds has shown that almost one-quarter of their information-seeking questions were aimed at obtaining explanations: "why do birds fly?" or "why is the moon so high up?" (Chouinard, 2007). In turn, this proclivity for explanation-seeking has been taken to be a fundamental and universal "mechanism" for cognitive development. Gauvain and colleagues (2013) analyzed almost 3,000 utterances from 96 children ages 3–5 years from four traditional cultures in Belize, Kenya, Nepal, and American Samoa. In contrast to the findings with American children, they found that only 4.5% of the utterances were "why" questions. The children were curious and did ask questions, but they mostly sought answers to questions such as "where are you going?" Gauvain argues that there is "no gulf in cognitive activity between them and Western children of the same age," but that research has to pay attention to the distinct cultural mechanisms or processes of cognitive development.

While there is cultural diversity in how children learn and what they learn from adults and peers, sociocultural research based on a wide range of cultures has demonstrated that between 5 and 7 years of age children experience a change in the roles and responsibilities that they are assigned, and this change has consequences for cognitive development (Gauvain & Nicolaides, 2015). Ages 5–7 is the time when children in many cultures are first given important responsibilities in the family for food preparation, child care, and animal care (LeVine & LeVine, 2016). To go back to the example given earlier, a 5-year-old can readily learn the skills involved in making tortillas, whereas a 2-year-old would not have the necessary learning abilities, motor skills, or impulse control (Rogoff, 2003). It is not only in traditional cultures that this shift in roles and responsibilities takes place at age 5–7. At this age, a child in an economically developed country might help his parents prepare a grocery shopping list, and in the course of this process learn culturally valued skills such as reading, using lists as tools for organization and planning, and calculating sums of money (Rogoff, 2003). Finally, the fact that formal schooling worldwide typically starts between ages 5–7 is another reflection of the cognitive shift at this age.

**Critical Thinking Question:** A Girl Scout troop wants to involve 8- to 9-year-olds in its annual sale of cookies to the public. Set up a step-by-step scaffolding sequence that would aid the girls in carrying out various aspects of the sale.

Guided participation, scaffolding, and the zone of proximal development continue to apply during adolescence, when the skills necessary for adult work are being learned. An example can be found in research on weaving skills among male adolescents in the Dioula culture in Ivory Coast, on the western coast of Africa (Tanon, 1994). An important part of the Dioula economy is making and selling large handmade cloths with elaborate designs. Boys grow up watching their fathers weave. The training by fathers of sons begins when boys are age 10–12 and continues for several years. Training takes place through scaffolding: The boy attempts a simple weaving pattern, the father corrects his mistakes, the boy tries again. When the boy gets it right, the father gives him a more complex pattern, thus raising the upper boundary of the zone of proximal development so that the boy continues to be challenged and his skills continue to improve. As the boy becomes more competent at weaving, the scaffolding provided by the father diminishes. Eventually the boy gets his own loom, but he continues to consult with his father for several years before he can weave entirely by himself. In other words, guided participation takes place over many years.

In Vygotsky's theory, children's cognitive development is always both social and cultural. Here, a father in the Middle Eastern country of Oman shows his son how to weave a basket.

As the example of the Dioula illustrates, in developing countries, the most necessary skills and knowledge are often those involved in making things the family can use or that other people will want to buy (Larson et al., 2010). Increasingly, the skills and knowledge of the global economy involve the ability to use information technology such as computers and the Internet. In most countries, the highest-paying jobs require these kinds of skills. These are skills that often take a long time to acquire, accounting for increasing proportions of people continuing their education into emerging adulthood. Guided participation is part of this learning process, but seldom does it take place primarily between parents and their children.

## Evaluating Sociocultural Theories of Cognitive Development

**LO 5.5.3 Summarize the strengths and limitations of sociocultural theories of cognitive development.**

Sociocultural theories have expanded the area of cognitive development in several ways. Because of their emphasis on the role of culture, they have spurred research in many parts of the world. In turn, this research has highlighted that cognition serves different functions within diverse communities. Also, because sociocultural theories underscore the social side of cognition, research has detailed ways that interactions between children and those around them promote development.

Guided participation is helpful in learning skills of the global economy, such as the ability to use complex technology.

Critics have pointed out that Vygotsky had little to say about the role of biology in cognitive development, and clearly his focus was on the ways that the social and cultural environment shapes and enhances children's cognitive abilities. Interestingly, contemporary cultural researchers often emphasize biology. Gauvain and Nicolaides (2015, p. 203), for example, have argued that "the sociocultural basis of cognitive development was crafted over the long period of human evolution.... Human biology and culture are the dual legacy or inheritance of our species. In other words, they co-evolved." They and other researchers also emphasize the plasticity of the human brain that makes us both adaptable to local environments, and capable of modifying and constructing the physical and social environment around us (Haun, 2015).

## Education Focus: Bringing Theories of Cognitive Development Into the Classroom

As we have seen, the cognitive-developmental, information-processing, social cognition, and sociocultural approaches have all contributed important findings on cognitive development. Those findings have also inspired educational ideas and practices. Here we review two central guiding educational implications for each approach:

**Cognitive-developmental:** (1) Learning needs to be "child-centered" in the sense that the materials have to be appropriate to the developmental stage of the child (Case, 1998; Piaget, 1972). In Piaget's view, children cannot be drastically propelled forward. Instead, they need to be met at their level of thinking and encouraged to retain what they understand correctly, while also helped to understand mistakes in their thinking. (2) Children's in-depth learning is promoted through experimenting on their environment, such as sorting candy of different colors to illustrate a mathematical or statistical principle (Kamii, 1989).

**Information Processing:** (1) Learning is enhanced by participation in activities such as card and board games that involve figuring out the most useful strategies (Siegler & Ramani, 2009). Strategies can also be modeled and explicitly verbalized by teachers as part of an activity (Meltzer et al., 2007). (2) Practice promotes automaticity, which in turn makes it possible to solve problems faster and to move on to more complex problems (Pressley, 2007).

**Social Cognition:** (1) Learning is enhanced by relatively natural and informal interactions in venues such as zoos and community centers that harness children's social skills. (2) Face-to-face individual tutoring is a particularly effective way of teaching, even as it has time and cost constraints (Meltzoff et al., 2009).

**Sociocultural:** (1) Learning is promoted by teachers who provide assistance in children's zone of proximal development. In other words, teachers need to assess where that level is and then scaffold appropriate new skills (Daniels, 2007). (2) Collaboration within and between groups of children encourages learning from one another and helps children to see how pooling their knowledge can lead to deeper and broader understanding (Brown, 1997; Takala, 2006).

### Review Question

Imagine that you are a first-grade teacher for a day. You are teaching your class how to read. Explain how you would combine the principles of at least two of the above approaches in putting together one lesson. That evening, you also have parent–teacher conferences. Explain how you would draw on the principles of at least two of the above approaches in meeting parents.

## SUMMARY: Sociocultural Theories of Cognitive Development

**LO 5.5.1 Describe Vygotsky's sociocultural theory of cognitive development and contrast it with Piaget's theory.**

Unlike Piaget and most other cognitive theorists and researchers, Vygotsky emphasized the cultural basis of cognitive development in childhood. He proposed concepts such as scaffolding and the zone of proximal development to describe how children obtain cultural knowledge from adults.

**LO 5.5.2 Identify ways that cultural learning takes place from childhood through emerging adulthood.**

A great deal of children's cultural learning takes place through observing and working alongside parents or siblings. Between 5 and 7 years of age, children in many traditional cultures are given important family responsibilities for food preparation, child care, and animal care. In the course of adolescence, they typically learn all the skills necessary for adult work in their community. However, the global economy involves the ability to use information technology. These skills are often acquired outside the family and often take a long time to acquire, accounting for increasing proportions of people continuing their education into emerging adulthood.

**LO 5.5.3 Summarize the strengths and limitations of sociocultural theories of cognitive development.**

Sociocultural theories have spurred research in many parts of the world and highlighted diversity in child development. Critics have pointed out that Vygotsky had little to say about the role of biology in cognitive development.

## Apply Your Knowledge as a Professional

The topics covered in this chapter apply to a wide variety of career professions. Watch this video to learn how they apply to a zoo director.

**Journaling Question:** David Bjorklund (2013, p. 464) has written that "the great bulk of cognitive…research has been conducted in laboratories or quiet rooms in children's schools, and the topics of study have often been divorced from children's everyday lives." Reflect on the extent to which you agree with this statement based on the research from this chapter. Also, based on your own experience, do you think there are some important settings and topics that cognitive development research has yet to include? Explain.

# Chapter 6
# Learning Languages

## Learning Objectives

### 6.1 Languages in Today's World

**6.1.1** Provide an overview of languages spoken in today's world.

**6.1.2** Describe the impact of globalization on the languages that children grow up to speak.

### 6.2 Evolutionary and Biological Bases of Language

**6.2.1** Summarize the evidence for the biological and evolutionary bases of language.

**6.2.2** Explain why the acquisition of language provides an evolutionary advantage.

### 6.3 Theories of Language Development

**6.3.1** Describe how behaviorist, innatist, and cognitive theories explain language development, including the extent to which they emphasize nature or nurture.

**6.3.2** Describe how interactionist/social and Bayesian theories explain the development of language, including the extent to which they emphasize nature or nurture.

### 6.4 First Sounds and Words

**6.4.1** Describe how young infants go from being universal listeners to being native listeners by age 1.

**6.4.2** List four kinds of approaches that infants use to recognize words.

**6.4.3** Explain how both babbling and gesturing involve turn-taking and word-learning.

**6.4.4** Describe cultural variations in the use of infant-directed speech and explain the extent to which infants benefit from it.

**6.4.5** Explain how social class is related to children's language development.

### 6.5 From First Words to Cultural Competence

**6.5.1** Describe the quantitative (how many) and qualitative (what kinds) characteristics of vocabulary growth from age 1 to early adolescence.

**6.5.2** Explain what telegraphic speech is and what it reveals about children's development of grammatical rules.

**6.5.3** Give examples of children's development of pragmatics from infancy through adolescence, and identify the extent to which these social rules are culturally based.

**6.5.4** Describe how children in middle childhood and adolescence create new language.

**6.5.5** Explain how becoming competent in a language relates to cultural styles of cognition.

### 6.6 Multilingualism

**6.6.1** Describe characteristics of multilingual development.

**6.6.2** Summarize benefits and risks of multilingualism.

**6.6.3** Define language brokering and explain its positive and negative sides.

ACROSS THE WORLD, PEOPLE SPEAK ABOUT 7,000 DIFFERENT LANGUAGES. Some languages are spoken by large numbers of people, others by small and diminishing communities. Babies come into the world primed to learn to speak any of the languages. In fact, they have an ability to detect differences among the sounds of all languages. By their first birthday, this ability will dramatically diminish as they become attuned to the specific language or languages spoken in their social world. Roughly around 1 year of age is also when children speak their first word, and in the course of the next few years, their skill at stringing together grammatically correct sentences and communicating in accordance with the cultural norms of their community develops with astonishing speed, especially between ages 2 and 3. In today's globalizing world, it is also increasingly common for children to grow up to be multilingual. In this chapter, we cover the unique human ability to go from zero words to fluency in one or more languages in the course of relatively few years. We also look at how children, adolescents, and emerging adults not only learn the languages of the adults in their community, but also take a lead role in creating new forms, including sign language and slang.

**Watch** CHAPTER INTRODUCTION: LEARNING LANGUAGES

# 6.1 Languages in Today's World

**language**
a system of sounds or gestures that people use to communicate with one another

All human communities have **language**, a system of sounds or gestures that people use to communicate with one another. At the same time, the vast and heterogeneous collection of languages that exist on a worldwide scale is a remarkable testament to cultural diversity. We start with a survey of the world's linguistic landscape that forms the backdrop for babies born today, including the impact of globalization.

## Humanity's Linguistic Diversity

**LO 6.1.1 Provide an overview of languages spoken in today's world.**

*Ethnologue*, an authoritative source on the state of the world's languages, estimates that the world has about 7,000 living languages (www.ethnologue.com). Only 11 of these are spoken by at least 100 million people: Arabic, Bengali, English, German, Hindi, Japanese, Lahnda, Mandarin, Portuguese, Russian, and Spanish. Approximately 85 languages are spoken by at least 10 million people, and about 300 languages by between 1 and 10 million. Each of the remaining 6,000-plus languages is spoken by fewer than 1 million people. Map 6.1 shows the primary locations of the 11 most commonly spoken languages. Many languages, including the most widespread ones, have a literary tradition, but hundreds of spoken languages do not and hence are more difficult to document (Rubenstein, 2017).

In some countries, a plethora of languages are spoken. For example, there are about 440 languages spoken in India, 29 of which are spoken by at least 1 million people. Indonesia, the world's fourth-most-populous country, is home to more than 700 languages (Rubenstein, 2017). In Africa as a whole, more than 2,000 languages and several thousand dialects have been documented (Ethnologue, 2017). These large numbers result from at least 5,000 years of minimal interaction among thousands of cultural groups inhabiting the African continent. Each group developed its own language, religion, and other cultural traditions.

Linguists expect that hundreds of languages will die out during this century and that only about 300 are entirely safe from extinction because they have a sufficient number of

**Map 6.1** Worldwide Distribution of the Most Common Languages

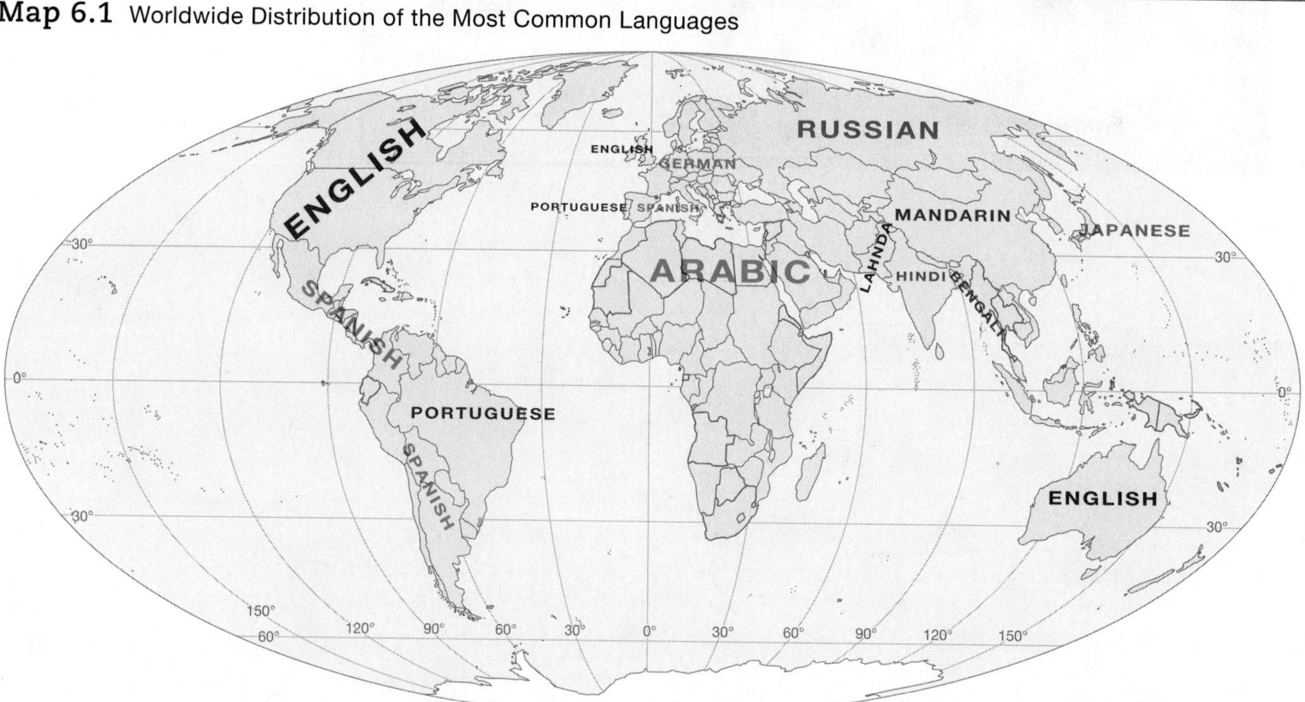

speakers, or they have been designated as official languages by governments (Rubenstein, 2017). To counteract extinction, movements have sprung up aimed at reviving and preserving languages. These preservation efforts take many forms. For example, there is now a movement to preserve Irish. In Western Ireland, English road signs were banned and replaced with Irish ones in 2005. A TV station now broadcasts exclusively in Irish (Rubenstein, 2017). Preservation efforts are typically geared toward children and adolescents, and sometimes the younger generation also plays an active part. For example, Irish singers, including many rock groups consisting of emerging adults, have begun performing in Irish (Malone, 2010).

Many Indian children learn several languages.

## The Impact of Globalization

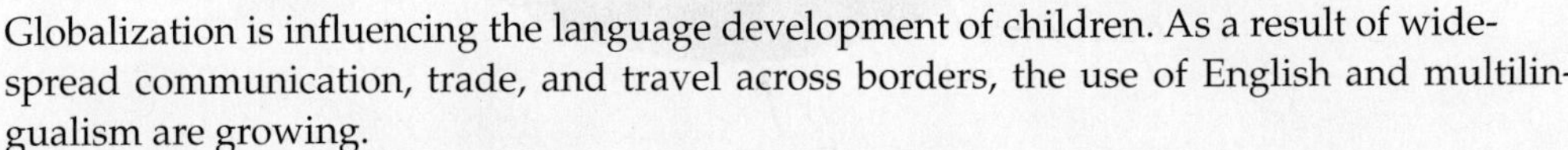

**LO 6.1.2 Describe the impact of globalization on the languages that children grow up to speak.**

Globalization is influencing the language development of children. As a result of widespread communication, trade, and travel across borders, the use of English and multilingualism are growing.

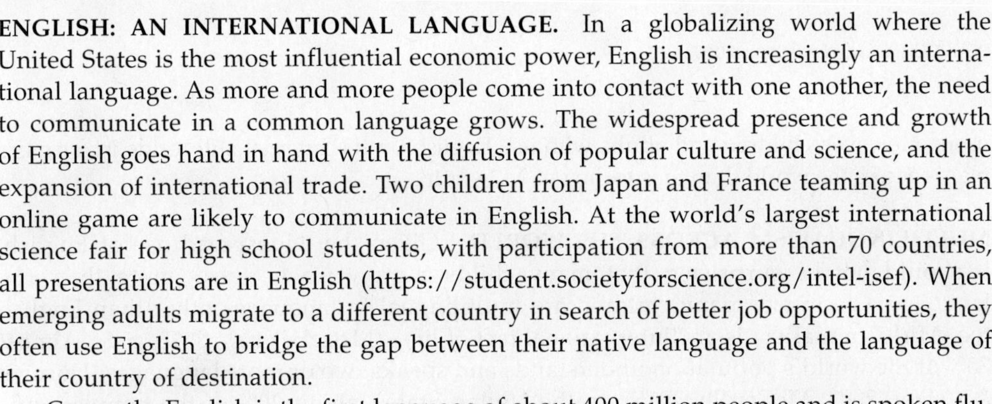

**ENGLISH: AN INTERNATIONAL LANGUAGE.** In a globalizing world where the United States is the most influential economic power, English is increasingly an international language. As more and more people come into contact with one another, the need to communicate in a common language grows. The widespread presence and growth of English goes hand in hand with the diffusion of popular culture and science, and the expansion of international trade. Two children from Japan and France teaming up in an online game are likely to communicate in English. At the world's largest international science fair for high school students, with participation from more than 70 countries, all presentations are in English (https://student.societyforscience.org/intel-isef). When emerging adults migrate to a different country in search of better job opportunities, they often use English to bridge the gap between their native language and the language of their country of destination.

Currently, English is the first language of about 400 million people and is spoken fluently by approximately 1 billion people (www.englishlanguageguide.com; Rubenstein, 2017). By the year 2050, the projection is that half of the world's population will be proficient English speakers. In part, this projection is based on the fact that children learn English in school in more and more countries. School systems increasingly seek to teach children English to enhance their ability to participate in the global economy. In China, for example, all children now begin learning English in primary school (Chang, 2008). In the European Union, more than 90% of students learn English in school. Also, students worldwide increasingly seek admission to universities in countries that teach in English (Rubenstein, 2017). As we will see later in this chapter, language is a vehicle to learn about the cultural beliefs and values of other people. To some extent, then, children across the world are increasingly learning a cultural worldview that goes with the English language.

The Internet has also strengthened the use of English, even if the initial supremacy of English on the Internet has diminished. English dominated the Internet in the 1990s. In 1998, 71% of people online used English. However, as shown in Figure 6.1 (next page), this is changing. In 2016, for example, just 26% of online users communicated in English. In contrast, Mandarin went from being the language of 2% of users in 1998 to 21% in 2016. The number of Mandarin-language users on the Internet is growing more rapidly than English-language

**Figure 6.1** Languages Used Online

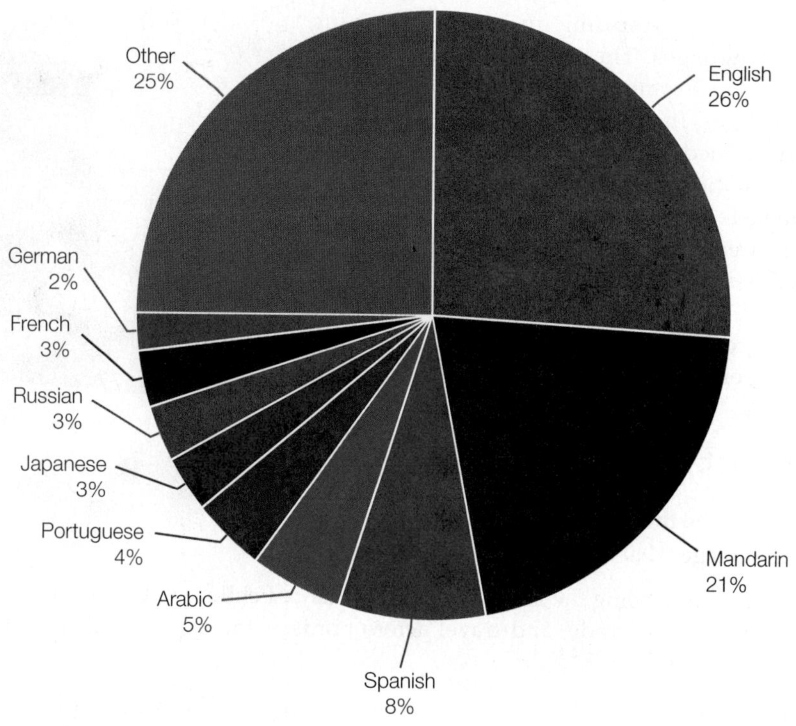


SOURCE: Internet World Stats (2016).

users. However, children and adults who use English on the Internet still reside in far more places across the world than those who use Mandarin.

**multilingualism**
the use of two or more languages

**MULTILINGUALISM ACROSS THE WORLD.** Given the widespread use of English, it should not be surprising that many children grow up to speak more than one language. Of course, many children are multilingual in languages other than English too. **Multilingualism** is an "international fact of life" (McCabe et al., 2013, p. 3). Almost 70% of the world's population understands and speaks two or more languages (Dörnyei & Csizér, 2002; McCardle, 2015). In the United States, about 20% of the population is multilingual (Grosjean, 2010). Not only is the multilingual proportion of the American population quite low from a worldwide standpoint, but it is also distinctive in other ways. As we will see later in this chapter, multilingual children in the United States are primarily recent immigrants, and many come from low-income families (McCabe et al., 2013).

English is the common language for students presenting at international science fairs.

Across the world, children generally grow up in a multilingual environment for one of two reasons. Some children live in a region where different languages have traditionally been spoken over a long period of time. An increasing number of children, however, are multilingual because they attend urban schools where students speak many different languages due to cross-national and urban migration (UNESCO, 2003).

A variety of school systems emphasize multilingual education. The official policy of the European Community is that schools should teach two foreign languages in addition to the students' native language. More than half of Europeans speak a second language, usually English. In Africa, 35 of 49 nations use one or more local languages for instruction during the first 2 or 3 years of primary school, with subsequent transition to a European language (McCardle, 2015). As we will explore in-depth later, multilingual children have some advantages compared to monolingual children on cognitive abilities and brain development.

### SUMMARY: Languages in Today's World

**LO 6.1.1 Provide an overview of languages spoken in today's world.**

The world has about 7,000 living languages. In many countries, more than one language is spoken and children grow up with knowledge of two or more languages. Linguists expect that hundreds of languages will die out during this century. To counteract extinction, preservation efforts geared to children and adolescents have sprung up.

**LO 6.1.2 Describe the impact of globalization on the languages that children grow up to speak.**

Globalization is influencing the language development of children. The use of English is growing worldwide, and the projection is that half of the world's population will be proficient English speakers by the year 2050. In part because of the spread of English, multilingualism is growing. Almost 70% of the world's population understands and speaks two or more languages.

# 6.2 Evolutionary and Biological Bases of Language

Of all the qualities that distinguish humans from other animals, language is certainly one of the most important. Other species of animals have their own ways of communicating, but language allows humans to communicate about a vastly broader range of topics. Using language, humans can communicate about not just what is observable in the present—as other animals might communicate about food or predators in their immediate environment—but also about an infinite range of things beyond the present moment. With language, we can communicate not just about things that exist, but also about things that might exist—things that we imagine. As linguist Derrick Bickerton remarks, "Only language could have broken through the prison of immediate experience in which every other creature is locked, releasing us into infinite freedoms of space and time" (Leakey, 1994, p. 119). Let's look now at the biological and evolutionary bases of language in humans.

## Language and Human Biology

**LO 6.2.1 Summarize the evidence for the biological and evolutionary bases of language.**

You may have heard that some primates have learned how to use language. Attempts to teach language to apes have a long history in the social sciences, going back over a half century. In the earliest attempts, researchers treated baby chimpanzees as closely as possible to how a human infant would be treated, having the chimpanzees live in the researcher's household as part of the family and making daily efforts to teach the chimps how to speak (Hayes & Hayes, 1951). Years of these efforts yielded nothing but the single word "mama"—and a badly disordered household. It turned out that chimpanzees, like other nonhuman primates, lack the vocal apparatus that makes human speech possible.

In the 1960s, researchers hit on the clever idea of teaching apes sign language (Gardner & Gardner, 1969). These attempts were much more successful. One famous chimpanzee, Washoe, learned to use about 100 signs, mostly involving requests for food (Small, 2001). She even learned to lie and to make jokes. However, she never learned to make original combinations of signs (with one possible exception, when she saw a duck for the first time and signed "water bird"). Mostly, Washoe and other primates who have

Chimpanzees can learn to use some sign language in a limited way, but they lack the infinite generativity of human language.

learned sign language simply mimic the signs they have been taught by their human teachers. They lack the most important and distinctive feature of human language: **infinite generativity**, which is the ability to take the word symbols of a spoken language or the gestures of a sign language and combine them in a virtually infinite number of new ways.

A variety of human biological characteristics indicate that humans, unlike other primates, have evolved to use language (Kenneally, 2007). Let's review three of those characteristics.

- *Vocal Apparatus.* Humans have a unique vocal apparatus. We are able to make a much wider range of sounds than other primates because, for us, the larynx is located lower in the throat, creating a large sound chamber, the pharynx, above the vocal cords. We also have a relatively small and mobile tongue that can push the air coming past the larynx in various ways to make different sounds, and lips that are flexible enough to stop and start the passage of air.
- *Brain Specialization.* Two areas in the left hemisphere of the human brain are specifically devoted to language functions (Nakano & Blumstein, 2004; Pizzamiglio et al., 2005). **Broca's area** in the left frontal lobe is specialized for language production, and **Wernicke's area** in the left temporal lobe is specialized for language comprehension (see Figure 6.2). If damage to one of these areas occurs in adulthood, the specialized language function of the area is also damaged; but if damage takes place in childhood, other areas of the brain can compensate—with compensation being greater the younger the brain injury takes place (Akshoomoff et al., 2002; Huttenlocher, 2002). In addition to Broca's and Wernicke's areas, many other regions of the brain contribute to language use (Dick et al., 2004). In fact, some linguists argue that the extraordinary size of the human brain in comparison to other species is due mainly to the evolution of language (Pinker, 2004).

**infinite generativity**
the ability to take the word symbols of a spoken language or the gestures of a sign language and combine them in a virtually infinite number of new ways

**Broca's area**
an area of the brain located in the left frontal lobe that is specialized for language production

**Wernicke's area**
an area of the brain in the left temporal lobe that is specialized for language comprehension

**Critical Thinking Question:** Relate the above findings pertaining to brain damage and language development to the "plasticity" of the brain described in Chapter 2.

- *Specific Genetic Systems.* Genes for language development have recently been identified (Gazzaniga, 2008; Pinker, 2004). Because Broca's and Wernicke's areas have long been known to be part of normal brain anatomy, the genetic basis of language was clear. However, identifying specific genes and genetic systems involved in language development strengthens our knowledge of how deeply language is embedded in human phylogenetic (species) development (Sun et al., 2006; Tomblin & Mueller, 2013).

## An Evolutionary Advantage

**LO 6.2.2 Explain why the acquisition of language provides an evolutionary advantage.**

Although modern humans are biologically equipped for language, our earliest ancestors were not. Early hominins (see Chapter 1) had a larynx similar in placement to modern nonhuman primates and so must have been incapable of spoken language (Leakey, 1994). The placement of the larynx became notably lower beginning nearly 2 million years ago, and the earliest *Homo sapiens*, 200,000 years ago, had a vocal apparatus not much different from yours.

Undoubtedly, the development of language gave humans a substantial evolutionary advantage (Small, 2001). Language would have made it easier to communicate about the location of food sources and about how to make tools, which would in turn enhance survival. If your clan could craft a better spear, you would have a better chance of killing the prey that would provide the necessary nourishment. If your group could construct a boat, you could potentially travel to new food sources if the local ones became depleted.

Many evolutionary biologists believe that language also conferred an evolutionary advantage because of its social function (Pagel, 2016). During the course of human evolution, the size of human groups gradually increased (Leakey, 1994), leading to a greater need for communication that would allow them to function effectively. Because language abilities improved the efficiency of group functioning, groups that excelled in language would have been more likely than other groups to survive and reproduce. Within groups, too, using language effectively would have conferred an advantage in obtaining mates, food, and status, so natural selection would have favored language abilities in the course of human evolutionary history (Pinker, 2004).

**Figure 6.2** Brain Lobes Showing Broca's Area and Wernicke's Area

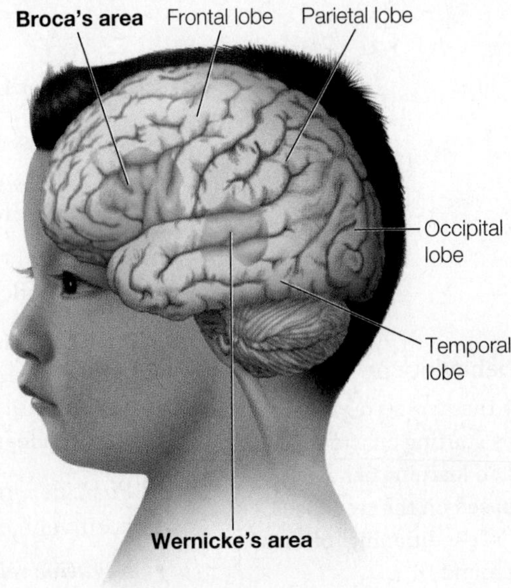


## SUMMARY: Evolutionary and Biological Bases of Language

**LO 6.2.1 Summarize the evidence for the biological and evolutionary bases of language.**

The larynx is lower in the throat of humans than in other primates, making spoken language possible. Also, humans have areas in the brain specifically devoted to language functions. Furthermore, genes for language development have been identified in humans.

**LO 6.2.2 Explain why the acquisition of language provides an evolutionary advantage.**

Language would have made it easier for early humans to communicate about the location of food sources and about how to make tools, which would in turn enhance survival. Many evolutionary biologists believe that language also conferred an evolutionary advantage because of its social function.

# 6.3 Theories of Language Development

Humans are biologically built for learning language but not for learning any *specific* language. None of the world's approximately 7,000 languages come prerecorded on our brains. Whatever language we learn must come from our social and cultural environment. This was first shown in a bizarre experiment devised by Frederick II (1194–1250), the Holy Roman Emperor. He wanted to find out what language infants would speak "naturally," if they were left to their own resources. He chose a group of neonates in an orphanage and instructed their caregivers never to speak in their presence. What language would the babies begin to speak spontaneously on their own? Would it be Latin, the language of scholars at that time? Would it be German, Frederick's own language, or (God forbid) French, the language of his chief rivals? The answer turned out to be, as you may have guessed, none of them. Tragically, all of the infants died. This is a poignant illustration of how we are poised for language to be part of the human social environment, and of how humans need language to develop properly.

Fast forward some 700 years. Over the course of the last century, developmental psychologists have continued to weigh the roles of nature and nurture in how language is acquired. The pendulum has swung back and forth between extremes, to a present-day focus on both our inherent predisposition for language and the importance of the social environment. We now turn to a review of the five major psychological theories of language development, from early to recent theories.

## Early Theories

**LO 6.3.1 Describe how behaviorist, innatist, and cognitive theories explain language development, including the extent to which they emphasize nature or nurture.**

Three early theories bring very different perspectives to language development, and continue to influence present-day research.

**behaviorism**

a theory that regards infants as starting out from scratch and learning behaviors based on the responses or "conditioning" of those around them

**BEHAVIORISM.** For language acquisition, as for the development of any other skill, **behaviorism** regards infants as starting out from scratch and learning behaviors based on the responses or "conditioning" of those around them (Skinner, 1957). According to this theory, children learn language based on:

- *Positive reinforcement:* when a caregiver encourages a child's behavior by responding positively to it, for example, with praise or a reward.
- *Negative reinforcement:* when a caregiver encourages a child's behavior by stopping or removing something negative, such as nagging or being grounded.
- *Imitation:* when a caregiver models a behavior for the child to learn and repeat.
- *Punishment:* when a caregiver discourages a child's behavior by imposing an unpleasant condition such as yelling or extra chores.

As you can see, the first three kinds of responses by a caregiver are aimed at promoting the onset or continuation of a child's behavior, whereas the last response is aimed at putting an end to it.

Here is an example of how imitation promotes language development. In our family, we have a Danish ritual where we start each dinner by raising our glasses, clinking, and saying "*skål*" (rhymes with "goal"). The two of us would do this when our twins were still too young to participate and could only watch from their highchairs. By the time they were 18 months old, however, they would take part. They would even initiate it, lifting up their cups, grunting until we noticed, and then smacking their plastic cups vigorously against our glasses as we all said *skål*. They liked to do this about 8,000 times per meal.

**Critical Thinking Question:** The skål example shows how language can be promoted through imitation. Can you think of examples of how a child might acquire language through each of the other three kinds of conditioning?

**innatist theory**

emphasizes that children are born with a **Language Acquisition Device (LAD)**

**grammar**

the rules for creating words and sentences

**Language Acquisition Device (LAD)**

a theorized innate mechanism that allows young children to perceive and quickly grasp the grammatical rules of the language around them

**INNATIST THEORY.** The **innatist theory** points out that learning from scratch cannot account for the speed with which children learn language, nor their generative ways of using it. A half-century ago, at a time when many behaviorists were arguing that language had no biological origin, Noam Chomsky (1957, 1969) pointed out that all children learn many of the complicated grammatical rules of their language already by 2 to 3 years of age. **Grammar** consists of the rules for creating words (such as adding *ing* to verbs in English) and sentences (such as the ordering of words, "Dad is diapering the baby" is right whereas "The baby is diapering dad" is not). Chomsky proposed that children are born with a **Language Acquisition Device (LAD)** such that they perceive and quickly grasp the grammatical rules of the language around them.

Toddlers' amazing mastery of grammar supports Chomsky's theory, not only in how well they use the rules of their language, but also in the mistakes they make. As they learn the grammar of their language, they make mistakes that reflect **overregularization**, which means applying grammatical rules even to words that are exceptions to the rule. Here are two examples from English that illustrate overregularization. First, creating the plural of most English nouns involves adding *s* to the singular form. However, there are irregular exceptions, such as *mice* as the plural of *mouse*, and *feet* as the plural of *foot*. Between ages 2 and 3, toddlers sometimes make mistakes with these kinds of words, saying things like *mouses* and *foots*. Second, the rule for the past tense of an English verb is to add *ed* to the end, but there are irregular exceptions, such as *went* as the past tense of *go* and *threw* as the past tense of *throw*. Toddlers sometimes make mistakes with these exceptions, saying things like "Mommy *goed* to the store" or "I *throwed* the ball." To innatists, overregularization is a telling mistake because no one in a child's environment (except perhaps another toddler) makes these kinds of mistakes. In other words, toddlers are spontaneously generating words they have never heard before, and they do so based on their grasp of grammatical principles. It is a testament to toddlers' language mastery that by 3 years of age, mistakes of this kind become rare (Bochner & Jones, 2003).

Common activities (such as toasting) and the words that go with them (such as "cheers") contribute to children's language development. Here, an Austrian family shares a meal and a toast.

**overregularization**
applying grammatical rules even to words that are exceptions to the rule

**cognitive theory**
regards language as a symbolic ability that develops in concert with thinking as a whole

To innatists, then, children are born with a distinctive understanding of universal principles of language that is triggered by exposure to language. Today, language researchers generally agree that language development is a biological potential that is nurtured by social interaction, although there is still a lively debate about the nature of the biological foundation of language and the kinds of social stimulation needed to develop it (Hoff, 2009).

**COGNITIVE THEORY.** The **cognitive theory**, first proposed by Piaget (1926), regards language as an ability that develops in concert with cognition as a whole. Unlike Chomsky's innatist theory, the focus is not on language as a distinctive psychological domain. Cognitive theorists regard language as part of symbolic thought, an ability that blooms between ages 1 and 3. As to the process of language acquisition, Piaget emphasized children's inherent maturation and their active engagement with the world—just as he did for cognitive development in general (Parish-Morris et al., 2013).

Remember the experiment from Chapter 5 in which toddlers were tested on their cognitive ability to categorize objects termed "blickets"? It provides a good example of how language acquisition and cognitive development go together. Two-year-olds were shown a machine and a collection of blocks that appeared to be identical (Gopnik et al., 1999). Then they were shown that two of the blocks made the machine light up when placed on it, whereas the remainder did not. The researcher picked up one of the two blocks and said, "This is a blicket. Can you show me the other blicket?" The 2-year-olds were able to choose the other block that had made the machine light go on. Not only were they able to understand that the category "blicket" was defined by causing the machine to light up, but they also mapped the new nonsense word onto the new category. Language researchers continue to examine and debate the extent to which language acquisition is part of cognitive development in general, or a fairly distinctive ability.

## Recent Theories

**LO 6.3.2 Describe how interactionist/social and Bayesian theories explain the development of language, including the extent to which they emphasize nature or nurture.**

Two recent theories of language development have taken research in interesting new directions, including attention to social context and infants' statistical prowess.

A toddler happily takes part in a "blicket" experiment.

**interactionist or social theories**

regard language as a tool that is largely learned and put to social and cultural uses

**Bayesian theories**

emphasize that children infer the meaning of words based on assessment of statistical probability

**INTERACTIONIST/SOCIAL THEORIES.** **Interactionist** or **social theories** regard language as a tool that is put to social and cultural purposes and is therefore to a large extent learned through interpersonal interactions (Nelson, 2007; Ratner & Bruner, 1978; Tomasello, 2003). These theorists recognize that there is an inherent preparedness for learning language but also emphasize that language develops in diverse social contexts, including with parents, peers, and media. Furthermore, these social contexts are often quite culturally distinctive, and consequently so are a variety of features of language development (Fitneva & Matsui, 2015).

For example, based on ethnographic research (see Chapter 1) among the Kaluli people of Papua New Guinea, Bambi Schieffelin (1986, 1990) found that caregivers quite commonly used linguistic expressions aimed at shaming children. When they thought children should know better, caregivers used name-calling, negative commands, rhetorical questions, and sarcastic comments. Schieffelin found that shaming started at about 6 months of age. By 14 months, caregivers would use expressions such as "Be ashamed! (*Sindiloma!*)" and "Aren't you ashamed?! (*Go:no:mo:sindilowaba?!*)" in order to teach children how to control their actions. By the age of 2, Kaluli children had learned such linguistic expressions themselves, and now used them with younger children. The early emergence of shaming in conversations and social interactions has also been found in other cultures, such as Taiwan (Fung, 1999).

**BAYESIAN THEORIES.** **Bayesian theories** argue that children infer the meaning of words based on assessment of statistical probability (Frank et al., 2009; Perfors et al., 2011). In every language, certain sounds are more likely to go together than others (Christiansen & Dale, 2001). Studies by Richard Aslin, Jenny Saffran, and their colleagues have shown that infants pick up on this (Aslin et al., 1998; Saffran et al., 1996).

In one study, for example, 8-month-old infants first listened to a 2-minute stream of made-up "words" consisting of three syllables (*bidaku, golabu, padoti, tupiro*). They were spoken without pauses, mimicking the way that words in ordinary speech often run together. The words were also presented in random order (e.g., *bidaku/golabu/bidaku/tupiro/tupiro/bidaku*). This meant that some of the consonant-vowel combinations co-occurred 100% of the time (e.g., *bida*), akin to the way that sounds are more likely to co-occur when they form part of an actual word. Other consonant-vowel combinations only co-occurred about 30% of the time (e.g., *kugo*), analogous to sounds that occasionally occur together during the transition between words but are unlikely to form part of a word.

Next, the infants were presented one-by-one with the made-up "words" they had previously heard as part of a continuous word stream, and new three-syllable "non-words." These non-words were created by combining the last syllable of one "word" with the first two of another "word" (e.g., *kugola*). Interestingly, the infants were able to distinguish the words from the non-words. They paid more attention to the unexpected non-words, as compared to the original "words." Evidently, in only 2 minutes, the babies had segmented the word stream into distinct words and habituated to them. In short, then, infants seem to be remarkable intuitive statisticians who learn to differentiate words from one another based on the probabilities that certain sounds go together. As we will see elsewhere in this text, infants compute probabilities related to other areas of development, too.

Clearly, the five early and recent theories of language development that we have reviewed are different. Moderate forms of each of the five theories can be compatible, however, and many current researchers use aspects of more than one theory. Also, each theory is stronger in accounting for some aspects of language development than others.

### SUMMARY: Theories of Language Development

**LO 6.3.1 Describe how behaviorist, innatist, and cognitive theories explain language development, including the extent to which they emphasize nature or nurture.**

According to behaviorism, infants start out without innate dispositions and learn language solely based on the responses of those around them. Innatist theory holds that children are born with a Language Acquisition Device (LAD) such that they perceive and quickly grasp the grammatical rules of the language around them. The cognitive theory regards language as an ability that develops in concert with cognition as a whole and involves both inherent maturation and children's active engagement with the world.

**LO 6.3.2 Describe how interactionist/social and Bayesian theories explain the development of language, including the extent to which they emphasize nature or nurture.**

Interactionist/social theories regard language as a tool that is put to social and cultural purposes and is therefore largely learned through interpersonal interactions, even as humans have an inherent preparedness for language acquisition. Bayesian theorists argue that children infer the meaning of words based on realization that certain sounds are more likely to go together than others.

# 6.4 First Sounds and Words

According to the traditional beliefs of the Beng people of Ivory Coast in Africa, in the spirit world all people understand all languages (Gottlieb, 2000). Babies have just come from the spirit world when they are born, so they understand whatever is said in any language. However, during the first year, memory of all other languages fades and babies come to understand only the language they hear around them. This is actually a pretty accurate summary of how babies' language development takes place in the course of the first year of life, as you will see next.

## Perception of Speech

**LO 6.4.1 Describe how young infants go from being universal listeners to being native listeners by age 1.**

Infants come into the world attentive and attuned to speech. Neonates display an innate interest in human faces (see Chapter 3). This visual bias naturally draws their attention to the source of spoken language. By 2 months, infants can match facial expressions with the sounds of specific vowels (Patterson & Werker, 2002). Infants' attention to where a person is looking, or **joint attention**, also aids in their vocabulary development, as we will discuss in more detail below (Brooks & Meltzoff, 2008).

**joint attention**
infants' attention to where a person is looking

Infants come primed to perceive not only people but also speech itself in a way that facilitates their language development. For example, neonates prefer to listen to natural speech over made-up nonsense speech, and by 3 months of age they prefer human speech to natural vocalizations by macaques and rhesus monkeys (Shultz & Vouloumanos, 2010; Vouloumanos et al., 2010). With respect to human speech, neonates also prefer their mother's native language to a foreign language, because they have become accustomed to it while still in the womb.

Remarkably, even in our early weeks we have the capacity to differentiate speech sounds. Neonates hear the difference between sounds such as *ba, pa,* and *ga* (Eimas et al., 1971). This ability to perceive speech sounds as belonging to discrete categories is also known as **categorical perception**. Categorical perception of consonant sounds (such as *b, p,* and *g*) is present at birth, and for vowels (such as *a, o,* and *e*) at about 6 months of age (Kuhl, 1979).

**categorical perception**
the ability to perceive speech sounds as belonging to discrete categories

At around 6 months of age, infants are what we might call universal listeners. They have the ability to perceive speech sounds in all of the world's languages. By 12 months, however, infants become native listeners, only hearing the segments of sound that are meaningful in

**Figure 6.3** Successful Differentiation of Foreign-Language Sounds, Infants 6 to 12 Months

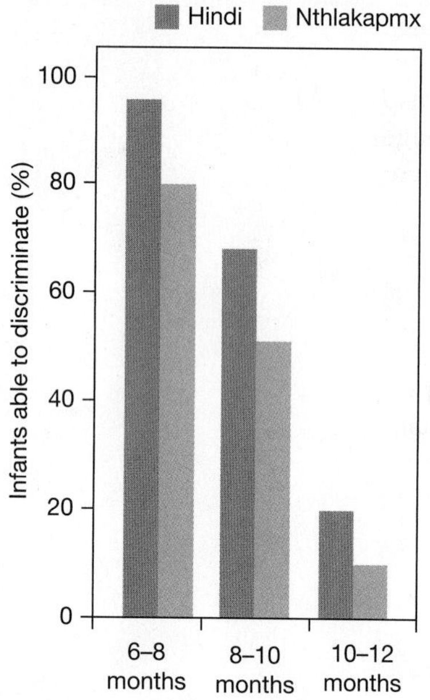


SOURCE: Based on Werker (1989).

the language spoken by those around them. This cultural specialization in speech perception has been shown in influential research by Janet Werker and colleagues. They compared 6- to 12-month-olds from English-speaking families on their ability to hear the differences between syllables and sounds in Hindi and Nthlakapmx (a language of a First Nations people in Canada). Figure 6.3 shows how at 6–8 months, the infants could hear essentially all sound distinctions, but this perceptive ability gradually declined and had by and large vanished by 10–12 months.

Although this vanishing ability might seem like a loss, it turns out to be a very important part of children becoming competent in their native language. One of the tasks involved in learning a language is discriminating correctly and efficiently among **phonemes**, or the smallest units of sound that distinguish one word from another. There are hundreds of different phonemes across the world's languages, but no one language differentiates all of them. English, for example, has about 44 phonemes. In English, the phonemes /l/ and /r/ are important in differentiating all kinds of words, such as lam and ram. In comparison, Japanese has about 22 phonemes, and /l/ and /r/ do not carry different meanings. So whereas a 6-month-old infant in Japan is able to hear the difference between these two phonemes, a 12-month old Japanese child with no exposure to English is not (Iverson et al., 2003). Longitudinal research has shown that 7 month-olds who were better at discriminating between native language phonemes had a larger vocabulary in their second year of life (Kuhl et al., 2005, 2008). By the time these children reached 5 years of age, they were also on the road to becoming better readers (Kuhl, 2011). Clearly, then, becoming a native listener is an import developmental milestone.

**phonemes**

the smallest units of sound that distinguish one word from another

It turns out that perceptual specialization takes place not only for spoken language, but similarly for sign language. In one study, 4-month old infants who had never been exposed to American Sign Language (ASL) were able to differentiate among highly similar ASL gestures. By 14 months, however, only those infants who were learning ASL retained this ability (Palmer et al., 2012).

**Critical Thinking Question:** What would you hypothesize about the development of infants and toddlers learning American Sign Language (ASL) in terms of their ability to differentiate basic gestures in ASL and Nicaraguan Sign Language (NSL)?

**prosody**

patterns of stress, rhythm, and intonation in a language

On the road to becoming native listeners and communicators, infants also pay attention to **prosody**, or patterns of stress, rhythm, and intonation in a language. As we saw in Chapter 3, neonates already attend to tone and music. In large part, languages sound different from one another because they differ in prosody. Many languages in the world also use variations in tone to express meaning. Tonal languages are extremely common in Africa, Central America, and East Asia. In these languages, tone is used to differentiate words that otherwise are identical in terms of their phonemes. In Mandarin, for example, different tones combine with a syllable such as *ma* to produce different words (i.e., *mā* = mom, *mǎ* = horse, and *mà* = scold). You can see how learning a tonal language poses quite the challenge (and potential for embarrassment) for a speaker of a non-tonal language. English is not a tonal language, but it does rely on stress-patterns, such as emphasizing certain syllables in a word (e.g., poTAto, not POtato or potaTO). Toward the end of their first year and into the beginning of their second one, English-learning infants rely on stress patterns to recognize words (Jusczyk et al., 1999; Nazzi et al., 2005).

## Recognition of Words

**LO 6.4.2 List four kinds of approaches that infants use to recognize words.**

As we have seen, infants are adept at recognizing phonemes, first across languages, then with increasing sophistication within their native language. But infants also have to figure out which phonemes combine to form words and which do not. As we saw above, infants

Gestures in combination with speech facilitate word learning.

turn out to be remarkable statisticians who learn to differentiate words from one another based on the probabilities that certain sounds go together. Interestingly, infants seem to track probabilities in other areas, too. For example, researchers have found that 7-month-olds also figure out which musical tones in a sequence of tones are likely to go together based on probability (Saffran et al., 1999).

Infants, however, are not just indiscriminate statisticians. While lots of phenomena in the world could be subject to statistical analyses, it turns out that infants pay special attention to the people around them. In a series of experiments, Patricia Kuhl and colleagues have shown that 9-month-old infants who are exposed to a foreign language quickly learn to differentiate phonemes and words in the new language. However, they only do so when the language is spoken in the context of interactions with a live human being rather than via television or an audiotape (Conboy & Kuhl, 2011; Kuhl et al., 2003). Kuhl suggests that at least in infancy, **social gating** is taking place, such that infants are more likely to use their statistical capabilities to differentiate new words in the context of social interactions. Research on *joint attention* also supports the importance of social interactions in vocabulary development. Longitudinal research shows that 10- to 11-month-old infants who more often follow a person's gaze to look at an object have larger vocabularies at 14, 18, and 24 months of age, compared to infants who engage is less joint attention (Brooks & Meltzoff, 2008).

**social gating**
infants' reliance on social interactions to help them differentiate units of sound

In addition to paying careful attention to probabilities and the people around them, infants also use their familiarity with one word to help differentiate other words in the stream of words that they hear. By 4.5 months, infants are attuned to the sound of their own name (Mandel et al., 1995). Researchers have shown that 6-month-olds use their recognition of familiar words to segment a novel word from a stream. Specifically, babies at this age seem to understand that the sounds that follow a familiar word constitute a different word. For example, if you say "Is Juanita hungry?" to a 6-month old, she may well figure out that *hungry* is a word.

Of course, recognizing that something is a word is good, but knowing what it means is better. **Semantics** is the study of meaning in language, including words and phrases. At about 5 months, infants understand the meaning of words that they hear frequently, such as their own name, *mommy*, *banana*, and *brother* (Mandel et al., 1995; Tincoff & Jusczyk, 1999). By 8 months, they understand phrases such as "don't touch" or "give kisses." Also, if you hold up your hand and say "high five," an 8-month old will know what to do (at least in the United States and other cultures where this phrase is used). In fact, gestures in combination with speech facilitate word learning (Goldin-Meadow & Alibali, 2013). This, then, is yet another way that babies come to understand words.

**semantics**
the study of meaning in language

Infants come to understand far more words than they can speak. Most infants can speak only one or a few words by their first birthday, but on average they understand about 50 words (Menyuk et al., 1995). At all ages, not just during our first year of life, language *comprehension* (the words we understand) exceeds language *production* (the words we use). This difference is especially striking and notable during infancy, however, when almost no words are spoken.

## Production of Sounds, Gestures, and First Words

**LO 6.4.3 Explain how both babbling and gesturing involve turn-taking and word-learning.**

Infants may not speak more than a word or two by their first birthday, but they have hardly been quiet for a year. Infants make all kinds of sounds. Infants cry, and the way they cry communicates different meanings, such as anger or pain. Very early on, babies also begin to make other sounds that will eventually develop into language (Waxman & Lidz, 2006). The video *The Development of Vocalizations* provides an overview of the progression of sounds and first words.

**cooing**
prelanguage "oo-ing" and "ah-ing," and gurgling sounds babies make beginning at about 2 months old

There is **cooing**, the "oo-ing" and "ah-ing" and gurgling sounds babies make beginning at about 2 months old. Often cooing takes place in interactions with others, but sometimes it takes place without interactions, as if babies are discovering their vocal apparatus and trying out the sounds it can make.

**babbling**
repetitive prelanguage consonant–vowel combinations such as "ba-ba-ba" or "do-do-do-do," made by infants universally beginning at about 4–6 months of age

Around 4–6 months of age, cooing develops into **babbling**, repetitive consonant–vowel combinations such as "ba-ba-ba" or "do-do-do-do." Our son Miles was an enthusiastic babbler. At 4 months old, he repeated the sounds "ah-gee" so often that for a while we called him "Mr. Ah-Gee." When we played a song for him on the piano at 6 months, he "sang" along with his repertoire of babble sounds—sounding a bit like a howling dog. Babbling appears to be universal among infants. In fact, babies the world over appear to babble with some of the same sounds initially, regardless of the language of their culture (Lee et al., 2010). Gradually, babies' babbling inventory expands, and they begin to babble in the sounds distinctive to their culture and cease to make sounds they have not heard used by the people around them. Deaf infants exposed to sign language have a form of babbling, too, using their hands instead of sounds (van Beinum, 2008). By the time infants are about 9 months old, untrained listeners can distinguish whether a recording of babbling is from an infant raised amidst Arabic, French, or Mandarin (Oller et al., 1997). Their babbling has taken on the sounds and prosody of their native language, before they even utter their first word. However, gaining complete mastery in producing all of the sounds of a native language is challenging and only reached by about 8 years of age (Ferguson et al., 1992).

**pragmatics**
knowledge of how language is used in social contexts

Apart from learning the sounds (phonemes and prosody) and meanings (semantics) of language, children also have to learn the **pragmatics**. In other words, they have to learn how language is used in social contexts. One key component of the pragmatic side of people's language use is *turn-taking*. It is not much of a conversation if one person does all the talking, or if everybody speaks all at once. Research has shown that babbling may initiate turn-taking between infants and caregivers. Also, when an adult responds to an infant's babbling by immediately labeling an object, the infant is more likely to learn the meaning of the word than if the labeling occurs in the absence of babbling (Goldstein et al., 2010). The babbling may signal that the baby is ready to have a conversation (of sorts) and to learn.

**Watch** THE DEVELOPMENT OF VOCALIZATIONS

One day, when our twins were 7 months old, we had them on our laps facing each other. They started to carry on what seemed like a long and happy conversation, each taking turns. Here's an excerpt:

> Miles: Ah-gee.
> Paris: Doo-doo-doo-da-da.
> Miles: Ah-boo.
> Paris: Boo-doo-doo-doo-da!

And so on. Infants also take part in non-verbal turn-taking early on. For example, by about 4 months, when a caregiver smiles, an infant might smile back expectantly, then the caregiver might tickle the infant, and the infant might laugh, leading the caregiver to laugh, and so on. Infants worldwide also enjoy "peek-a-boo," a game that involves turn-taking (see Chapter 5). Some researchers have argued that caregiver-infant games facilitate the important skill of conversational turn-taking (Bruner, 1977).

**Critical Thinking Question:** If you were taking care of a 7-month-old, what other games or activities might you start that would engage the infant in turn-taking?

By around 8–10 months, infants begin to use gestures to communicate (Goldin-Meadow, 2009). They may lift their arms up to indicate they wish to be picked up,or point to an object they would like to have brought to them, or hold out an object to offer it to someone else, or wave bye-bye. Using gestures is a way of evoking behavior from others (for example, being picked up after lifting their arms in request), and also a way of evoking verbal responses from others (such as a spoken "bye-bye" in response to the infant's gestured bye-bye), at a time when infants still cannot produce words of their own (Golinkoff, 1986). When caregivers translate their infant's gestures into words, those words are likely soon to become part of the infant's spoken vocabulary (Goldin-Meadow et al., 2007). This suggests that infants use their hands to tell their caregivers what to say. Both infant gesturing and babbling, then, engage caregivers in turn-taking and facilitate word learning.

Infants' first words usually are spoken a month or two before or after their first birthday. Typical first words include important people (*Mama, Dada*), familiar animals (*dog*), moving objects (*car*), foods (*milk*), and greetings or farewells (*hi, bye-bye*) (Waxman & Lidz, 2006). As infants start to produce words, the conversational possibilities multiply exponentially.

## Infant-Directed Speech

**LO 6.4.4 Describe cultural variations in the use of infant-directed speech and explain the extent to which infants benefit from it.**

Suppose you were to say to an adult, "Are you hungry?" How would you say it? Now imagine saying the same thing to an infant. Would you change how you said it? In many cultures, people speak in a special way to infants and toddlers, often called **infant-directed speech (IDS)** (Bryant & Barrett, 2007). In IDS, the pitch of the voice becomes higher than in normal speech, and the intonation is exaggerated. Grammar is simplified, and words and phrases are more likely to be repeated than in normal speech. Topics of IDS often pertain to objects ("Look at the birdie! See the birdie?") or emotional communication ("What a good girl! You ate your applesauce!").

**infant-directed speech (IDS)**
speaking in a specific way to infants and toddlers, including with raised pitch and exaggerated intonation.

Why do people often use IDS? One reason is that infants seem to like it. Even when IDS is in a language they do not understand, infants show a preference for it by the time they are 4 months old, as indicated by paying greater attention to IDS in an unfamiliar language than to non-IDS in the same language (Singh et al., 2009). The video *Infant-Directed Speech* provides examples of parents using IDS with their infants.

Watch **INFANT-DIRECTED SPEECH**

And why do infants like IDS? One theory is that infants prefer it because it is more emotionally charged than other speech (Trainor et al., 2000). Also, IDS helps infants unravel the mysteries of language at a time when it is still new to them. The exaggeration and repetition of words gives infants cues to their meaning (Soderstrom, 2007). By exaggerating the sounds used in making words, IDS provides infants with information about the building blocks of speech they will use in the language of their culture (Kuhl, 2004). The exaggerations of IDS also separate speech into specific phonemes, words, and phrases more clearly than normal speech does (Thiessen et al., 2005).

Research with infants and toddlers has shown that IDS has benefits. A recent longitudinal study using an experimental design (see Chapter 1) provides particularly convincing evidence because it goes beyond merely showing a correlation between caregiver language use and infant language learning. Toddlers were randomly sorted into groups who either heard IDS or regular speech. Findings showed that 21-month-olds with small vocabularies learned more new words when presented with IDS, compared to 21-month-olds with small vocabularies who listened to regular adult speech. In contrast, 21-month-olds with large vocabularies learned equally well from the two kinds of speech. By 27 months, all groups of toddlers with small and large vocabularies learned equally well from infant-directed and adult speech (Ma et al., 2011). The findings suggest that there may be a window of time when IDS is particularly beneficial to toddlers with relatively small vocabularies.

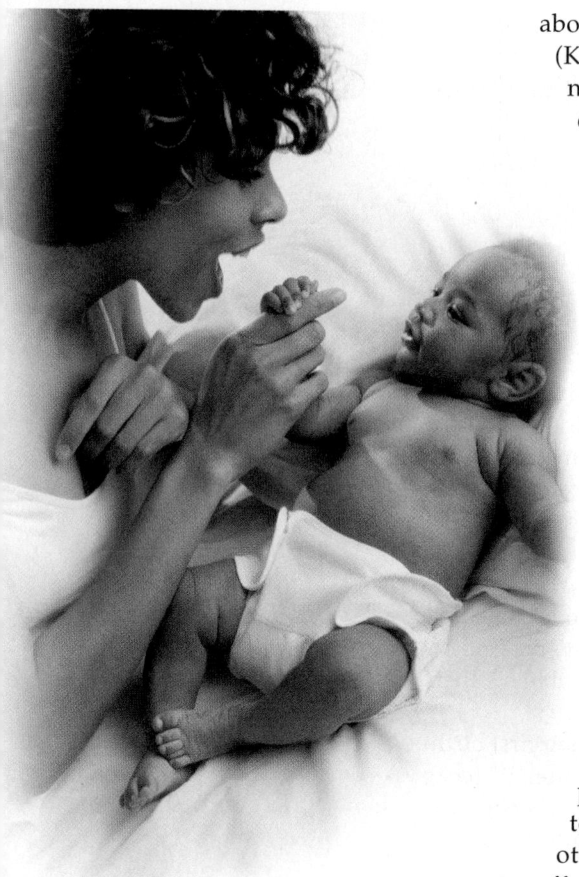

Adults in many cultures use infant-directed speech, including simplified grammar and repeated words.

IDS is common in Western cultures (Bryant & Barrett, 2007). Studies with Japanese and Korean caregivers have also found that IDS is common (Lee et al., 2010; Mazuka et al., 2008). Outside developed countries, however, there is more variability. Some traditional cultures use IDS, such as the Fulani of West Africa, who say single words and phrases to their infants from their very first days of life in an effort to stimulate their language development (Johnson, 2000). However, in other traditional cultures, parents do not use IDS and make no special effort to speak to infants. For example, the Ifaluk people of Micronesia believe there is no point in speaking to infants because they cannot understand what you say (Le, 2000). Similarly, Samoan caregivers do not use IDS (Ochs & Schieffelin, 1984). Nevertheless, despite receiving no IDS, children in traditional cultures learn their language fluently within a few years, just as children in cultures with IDS do.

Does this mean you do not need to speak to your own infants in your culture? Definitely not. Parents from some traditional cultures may not speak directly to their infants and toddlers very often, but these children are part of a language-rich environment all day long. They are surrounded by conversation from their mother, siblings, and other relatives. Instead of spending the day with one parent and perhaps a sibling, as infants do in cultures where IDS is common, infants and toddlers in traditional cultures typically have many adults and children around them in the course of the day. Families are bigger, extended family members live either in the same household or nearby, and interactions with other community members are common (Akhtar & Tomasello, 2000). Perhaps IDS developed because, in the small nuclear families that are typical of developed countries today, without IDS infants may have very little other language stimulation. The success of children in traditional cultures in learning their languages despite having no IDS shows that listening to others' conversations in a language-rich environment is also an effective way of acquiring a language (Akhtar, 2005).

Toddlers in traditional cultures often experience a language-rich environment. Here, a Mongolian family shares a meal and conversation.

## Cultural Focus: Cultural Views on Speaking to Infants and Toddlers

Because most research on language development is conducted in developed Western countries, an assumption of this research is that most infant and toddler language use takes place in a parent–child dyad—just the two of them. This assumption may be true for the families being studied in developed countries, but the social environment that most infants and toddlers experience worldwide is much different. Consequently their language environment differs as well.

When infants and toddlers are with their parents in developing and traditional countries, usually many other people are around as well, such as siblings, extended family members, and neighbors. In fact, toddlers in most cultures spend most of their days not with their parents, but in mixed-age groups of other children, including an older girl, often an older sister, who is mainly responsible for caring for them (Edwards et al., 2015). This makes for a language-rich environment. With so many people present, there is talking going on almost constantly. However, relatively little of this talk may be directed specifically at the toddler, because there are so many other people around and because others may not see it as necessary to speak directly to toddlers in order to stimulate their language development (Fitneva & Matsui, 2015).

In fact, the others in a toddler's social environment may even see it as bad parenting to speak often with toddlers. Among the Gusii of Kenya, parents speak to infants substantially less than American parents do (LeVine et al., 1994; Richman et al., 2010). The Gusii, like people in many traditional cultures, carry their infants around almost constantly and have a great deal of physical contact with them, including cosleeping at night, but they do not view it as necessary or useful to speak to infants. The Gusii people of Kenya worry that encouraging young children to speak is a mistake because it makes it more likely that they will grow up to be selfish and disobedient (LeVine et al., 1994). Their children learn the Gusii language as proficiently as American children learn English, but they learn it from being frequently in social groups where adults and older children are using language, not from having their language development stimulated directly in frequent daily interactions with their parents.

It is not only in rural cultures in developing countries that this view of infants' and toddlers' language development is found, but in developed countries that emphasize collectivistic rather than individualistic cultural beliefs. One study compared Japanese mothers and Canadian mothers in their interactions with their young children (Minami & McCabe, 1995). In Japanese culture, being talkative is considered impolite and undesirable, especially for males, because the Japanese believe it is better to blend in harmoniously with the group than to call attention to yourself (Henrich et al., 2010; Rothbaum et al., 2001). Consequently, the Japanese mothers in the study often discouraged their children from talking, especially their boys. In contrast, the Canadian mothers encouraged their children to talk more, by asking them questions and suggesting they provide more details. This approach was interpreted by the researchers as being based on a belief system favoring individualism and self-expression. The video *Cultural Views on Speaking to Infants and Toddlers* shows how parents from different cultural backgrounds communicate with their infants and toddlers and what parents do, if anything, to foster their child's language development.

**Watch** CULTURAL VIEWS ON SPEAKING TO INFANTS AND TODDLERS

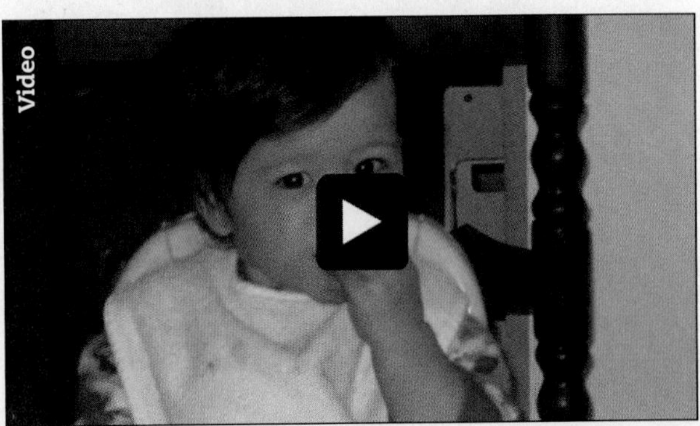


### Review Question

Discuss the three factors mentioned in the video that influence the language development of infants and toddlers. What are some additional factors that might also impact their language development?

## Reading to Infants and Toddlers

**LO 6.4.5 Explain how social class is related to children's language development.**

What kind of social environment do toddlers need to develop their language skills? In American research, as described above, the focus has been on how parents foster language development in young children. In the United States and other developed countries, parents often read to their infants and toddlers, explaining the meaning of the words as they go along (Fitneva & Matsui, 2015). This is a way of preparing children for an economic future in which the ability to comprehend and use large quantities of information will be crucial. Parents in the majority culture are more likely than parents in ethnic minority cultures

Preschool teachers who use a rich vocabulary facilitate children's reading.

to read to their toddlers, promoting an early advantage in verbal development that continues through the school years (Driessen et al., 2010).

Several studies have examined social-class differences in parents' language stimulation and how this is related to the pace of children's language development. The higher the social class of the parents, the more likely they are to read to their infants and toddlers (Fitneva & Matsui, 2015). Social class status is also correlated with how much parents speak to their young children. For example, one longitudinal study videotaped parent–child interactions in the homes of low-, middle-, and high-income families on several occasions, beginning when the children were 7 to 9 months old (Hart & Risley, 1999, 2003). There were striking differences in how many words were spoken to children of different income levels. Parents in high-income families talked the most to their children, averaging about 35 words a minute; parents in middle-income families talked to their children an average of about 20 words a minute; and parents of low-income families provided the least language stimulation, just 10 words per minute. By 30 months old there were substantial differences in the toddlers' vocabularies, averaging 766 words in the high-income families and just 357 words in the low-income families. A more recent study reached similar conclusions (Weisleder & Fernald, 2013).

Of course, there is a research design problem in studies like this, because parents provide not only their children's environment, but also their genes; this is known as passive genotype–environment effects (see Chapter 2). In studies of parents and children in biological families, genes and environment are *confounded*, which means they are closely related and difficult to separate.

However, in early childhood and beyond, the influence of teachers' language use on children's language development provides more definite evidence of an environmental effect, because teachers and children have no genetic relationship (Huttenlocher et al., 2002). Research has shown that children whose preschool teachers use a rich vocabulary have better reading comprehension by the fourth grade, as compared to children whose preschool teachers used a relatively limited vocabulary (Dickinson & Porche, 2011).

**Critical Thinking Question:** From this section on First Sounds and Words, can you identify one piece of support for each of the five theories of language development?

## SUMMARY: First Sounds and Words

**LO 6.4.1 Describe how young infants go from being universal listeners to being native listeners by age 1.**

At around 6 months of age, infants have the ability to perceive speech sounds in all of the world's languages. By 12 months, however, infants become native listeners, only hearing the segments of sound that are meaningful in the language spoken by those around them. This specialization takes place not only for spoken language, but also for sign language.

**LO 6.4.2 List four kinds of approaches that infants use to recognize words.**

(1) Infants are remarkable statisticians who learn to differentiate words from one another based on the probabilities that certain sounds go together. (2) Infants learn words through social interactions such as joint attention. (3) They also use their familiarity with one word to help differentiate other words in the stream of words that they hear. (4) Infants rely on people's gestures in combination with speech to facilitate word learning.

**LO 6.4.3 Explain how both babbling and gesturing involve turn-taking and word-learning.**

Infant babbling, repetitive consonant–vowel combinations such as "ba-ba-ba" or "doo-doo-da-da," is universal. When an adult responds to an infant's babbling by immediately labeling an object, the infant is more likely to learn the meaning of the word. By around 8–10 months, infants begin to use gestures to communicate. When caregivers respond by translating their infant's gestures into words, those words are likely soon to become part of the infant's spoken vocabulary.

**LO 6.4.4 Describe cultural variations in the use of infant-directed speech and explain the extent to which infants benefit from it.**

Many cultures use infant-directed speech (IDS), and babies appear to enjoy hearing it. Even in cultures that do not use IDS, however, children become adept users of language by the time they are a few years old. Research suggests that there may be a window of time when IDS is particularly beneficial to toddlers with relatively small vocabularies.

**LO 6.4.5 Explain how social class is related to children's language development.**

The higher the social class of the parents, the more likely they are to speak and read to their infants and toddlers. Young children who are in a language-rich environment, because of the approach of their parents or teachers, develop larger vocabularies and better reading comprehension.

# 6.5 From First Words to Cultural Competence

By the time they turn 1 year old, infants have laid an important foundation for language. They can comprehend many words, make sounds that match the tones and rhythm of their native language, and even engage in turn-taking conversations that involve sounds and gestures. Still, their language production is very limited—perhaps a word or two or three. The real explosion in language production comes between ages 1 and 2. Then, in the course of the next few years, children become amazingly adept at stringing together meaningful sentences and using their native language in ways that fit cultural expectations and styles of cognition. By adolescence, especially, there is also the invention of new linguistic forms, such as slang, that often challenge rather than conform to adult expectations. Let's examine these achievements.

## Adding Words

**LO 6.5.1 Describe the quantitative (how many) and qualitative (what kinds) characteristics of vocabulary growth from age 1 to early adolescence.**

For the first 6 months of toddlerhood, language develops at a steady but slow pace. Between 12 and 18 months, toddlers learn to speak 1 to 3 new words a week, reaching a total of 10 words by 15 months old and 50 words by about 18 months old, on average, in American studies (Bloom, 1998). There is a wide range of variability around these averages. Toddlers may speak their 10th word anywhere from 13 to 19 months old, and their 50th word anywhere from 14 to 24 months old, and still be considered within the normal range. Just as the timing of toddlers' first steps has no relation to later athletic ability, timing of speaking the 1st, 10th, or 50th word has no relation to later verbal ability.

The first 50 words tend to be words that are part of toddlers' daily routines (Waxman & Lidz, 2006), and include:

- important people (*Mama, Dada*),
- familiar animals (*dog, kitty*),
- body parts (*hair, tummy*),
- moving objects (*car, truck*),

- foods (*milk, cookie*),
- actions (*eat, bath*),
- household items (*cup, chair*),
- toys (*ball, bear*),
- greetings or farewells (*hi, bye-bye*).

**holophrases**
use of a single word to represent different forms of whole sentences

**overextension**
use of a single word to represent a variety of related objects

**underextension**
use of a general word to refer to a specific object

**fast mapping**
the ability to learn and remember the term for an object after only being told once

There are similarities across cultures in toddlers' earliest words. For example, one study found that the earliest words of three groups of toddlers learning Cantonese, Mandarin, and English included: *mommy, daddy, hi,* and *bye*. There were also differences, however, that hinted at diversity across the toddlers' daily lives. Both groups of Chinese toddlers, for example, were more likely than the American toddlers to refer to nonparental family members such as brother, sister, grandma, and grandpa. The American toddlers said the word *bottle*, whereas the Chinese toddlers did not. Only the Mandarin-using toddlers spoke the word *naughty* (Tardif et al., 2008).

Toddlers first learn words they need to use in practical ways to communicate with the people around them, usually as part of shared activities. Often, at this age, they speak in partial words, for example *bah* for bird, *meh* for milk, or *na-na* for banana.

From 12 to 18 months most toddlers use one word at a time, but a single word can have varied meanings. Toddlers' single words are called **holophrases**, meaning that for them a single word can be used to represent different forms of whole sentences (Flavell et al., 2002). For example, cup could mean "Fill my *cup* with juice," or "I dropped the *cup* on the floor," or "Hand me my *cup*, I can't reach it," or "Here, take this *cup*," depending on when and how and to whom it is said.

Another way toddlers make the most of their limited vocabulary is to have a single word represent a variety of related objects. This is called **overextension** (Bloom, 2000). For example, when the son of two language researchers learned the name of the furry family dog, Nunu, he applied it not only to the original Nunu, but to all dogs, as well as to other fuzzy objects such as slippers, and even to a salad with a large black olive that apparently reminded him of Nunu's nose (de Villiers & de Villiers, 1978).

Toddlers also exhibit **underextension**, applying a general word to a specific object (Woodward & Markman, 1998). An example would be a child who thinks that the word *kitty* only refers to the family's pet cat. Underextension often occurs in this way, with a toddler first applying a new word to a specific object, then learning later to apply it to a category of objects.

Toddlers exhibit overextension when they use a single word (such as "raspberry") to represent a variety of related objects (such as strawberries and other red berries).

Here, as at all ages, *production* (speaking) lags behind *comprehension* (understanding) in language development. Although toddlers do not reach the 50-word milestone in production until about 18 months old, they usually achieve 50-word comprehension by about 13 months old (Menyuk et al., 1995). During toddlerhood, comprehension is a better predictor of later verbal intelligence than production is (Reznick et al., 1997).

After learning to speak words at a slow rate for the first half of their second year, toddlers' word production suddenly takes off from 18 to 24 months. The pace of learning new words doubles, from one to three words per week to five or six words per week (Kopp, 2003). This is known as the *naming explosion* or *vocabulary spurt* (Bloom et al., 1985; Goldfield & Reznick, 1990). After just one time of being told what an object is called, toddlers this age will learn it and remember it, a process called **fast mapping** (Gopnik et al., 1999; Markman & Jaswal, 2004). Fast mapping is due not just to memory, but also to toddlers' ability to quickly infer the meaning of words based on how the word is used in a sentence and how it seems to be related to words they already know (Dixon et al., 2006). By their second birthday, toddlers have an average vocabulary of about 200 words (Dale & Goodman, 2005).

This rapid pace of learning and remembering words will continue for years, but it is especially striking at 18 to 24 months because this is when it begins (Ganger & Brent, 2004). Neurological research suggests that toddlers' brains are particularly attuned to language. The functional magnetic resonance imaging (fMRI) method is not often used with toddlers, perhaps because they are too wiggly and incapable of restraining their movements (Graham et al., 2015). However, one study solved this problem by assessing toddlers (21 months) and 3-year-olds as they slept and found that toddlers showed greater frontal lobe activity in response to speech than older children did, reflecting the brain's readiness for rapid language acquisition during the toddler period (Redcay et al., 2008). In toddlerhood, a gender difference also emerges. Girls' vocabulary increases faster than boys' vocabulary, initiating a difference in verbal abilities that will persist throughout childhood (Lovas, 2011).

Two notable words toddlers learn are *gone* and *no*. Using the word *gone* reflects their awareness of object permanence because it signifies that something has disappeared from view but still exists somewhere (Gopnik et al., 1999). Using the word *no* reflects their budding sense of self (*me, my*, and *mine* also begin to be used at this age). Saying *no* can be short for "You may want me to do to that, but I don't want to do it!" Of course, they also begin to hear "No!" more often around this age, as their mobility and curiosity leads them to behavior that the adults around them may regard as dangerous or destructive (Kopp, 2003). During this 18- to 24-month period, they also learn to name one or two colors, at least six body parts, and emotional states like "tired" and "mad" (Kopp, 2003).

As toddlers add more and more words, they generally use *open-class* words such as nouns, verbs, and adjectives (e.g., monkey, jump, high) far more frequently than *closed-class* words such as prepositions (e.g., in, on, to), pronouns (e.g., he, it, they), and conjunctions (e.g., and, but, or). This has been found for children learning American English, Dutch, French, Hebrew, Italian, Korean, and Spanish (Bornstein et al., 2004). Interestingly, open-class words are also much more likely than closed-class words to be added to languages (Kucera & Francis, 1967). Examples in recent years include words like *Internet* and *blogging*.

The kinds of open-class words children fast-map earliest depend partly on the language. Children learning Eastern languages such as Chinese, Japanese, and Korean tend to learn more verbs than nouns at first, because sentences often emphasize verbs and imply nouns without speaking them (Kim et al., 2000). In contrast, children learning English and other Western languages fast-map nouns earlier than verbs, because nouns are prominent in these languages. In both Eastern and Western languages, adjectives and modifiers (words such as large, narrow, pretty, and low) that modify the meaning of the main noun in a sentence are added more slowly than nouns and verbs (Mintz, 2005; Parish-Morris et al., 2013).

From ages 2 to 3, children continue to expand their speaking vocabulary at the same rapid pace that began at 18 to 24 months. They learn to use prepositions such as *under*, *over*, and *through*. They also use words that reflect a more complex understanding of categories. For example, they understand that a bear is not only a bear but also an animal (Kopp, 2003).

Although the vocabulary spurt that occurs from 18 months to 2 years stands out because toddlers go from saying very few words to swiftly using many different ones, vocabulary growth actually continues at a rapid pace during the rest of toddlerhood and beyond. Table 6.1 shows the average number of words used by children at different ages. At ages 5–7, when children enter formal school and begin reading, their vocabulary expands as never before as they pick up new words not just from conversations, but also from books and other written sources. As they reach the threshold of adolescence, this rapid expansion continues (Fitneva & Matsui, 2015). Part of this growth comes from an expanding ability to use the different forms that words can take. A child who knows how to use the word *calculate* will also now be able to generate words such as *calculated, calculation, miscalculate*, and *recalculating* (Anglin, 1993).

**morphology**
the rules for forming a word

**telegraphic speech**
phrases of about 2 to 4 words that strip away connecting words, such as *the* and *and*

**Table 6.1** Average Number of Spoken Words at Different Ages (in Years)

| Age | Number of Words |
|---|---|
| 1 | 1 |
| 1.5 | 50 |
| 2 | 200 |
| 3 | 1,000 |
| 5 | 2,500 |
| 6 | 10,000 |
| 11 | 40,000 |

NOTE: For each age there is a normal range.
SOURCE: Based on Bloom (1988).

## Forming Words and Sentences

**LO 6.5.2 Explain what telegraphic speech is and what it reveals about children's development of grammatical rules.**

That brings us to the developmental wonders of grammar, the rules for forming words and sentences. One aspect of grammar involves **morphology**, the rules for forming a word (such as adding *s* at the end of English nouns to change from the singular to the plural form). As we saw previously, toddlers grasp rules such as these very early, in fact, to the point where they overregularize (e.g., mouses).

Toward the end of the 18- to 24-month period, toddlers begin to combine spoken words for the first time. Their first word combinations are usually two words, in what is called **telegraphic speech** (Bloom, 1998; Brown, 1973; Edmonds, 2011). Like a telegram in the old days, telegraphic speech strips away closed-class words like *the* and *and*, getting right to the point with nouns, verbs, and adjectives. Telegraphic speech takes similar forms in a variety of languages, from English to German to Finnish to Samoan: "See doggie," "Big car," "More cookie," or "Mommy gone" (Bochner & Jones, 2003; Slobin, 1972).

**syntax**
an aspect of grammar that involves the grammatical rules for how to order words in a sentence

**syntactic bootstrapping**
using knowledge of syntax to figure out the meaning of novel words

An interesting feature of telegraphic speech is that it already shows an initial knowledge of **syntax**—an aspect of grammar that involves the grammatical rules for how to order words in a sentence. Toddlers say "See doggie," not "Doggie see"; they say "Mommy gone," not "Gone mommy." Between ages 2 and 3, toddlers continue to use telegraphic speech, but now in three- and four-word statements ("Ball under bed!") rather than two words. Increasingly, from ages 2 to 3, they begin to speak in short, complete sentences.

Toddlers also use their understanding of syntax to figure out the meaning of novel words, a strategy called **syntactic bootstrapping.** In one experiment, children heard sentences containing a made-up verb, such as "Look, the bunny is *gorping* the duck," while watching two screens showing a "bunny" and a "duck" (persons in costumes). The children would look longer at the screen where the bunny was acting on the duck, rather than the other way around, revealing that they were using the structure of the sentence and the word order to make sense of the novel word (Gertner et al., 2006). Research has shown that, by 19 months, toddlers use syntactic bootstrapping to determine the meaning of unfamiliar verbs (Yuan et al., 2012).

By the end of their third year toddlers have learned the main grammatical rules of their language, no matter how complex those rules may seem to someone who does not speak it. They know morphology and syntax. Consider this example (Slobin, 1972, 2014). In Turkish, the grammatical rules are different from English. In English, "The girl fed the dog" has quite a different meaning from "The dog fed the girl." The *subject* (girl) is supposed to go first, followed by the *verb* (fed), then the *object* (dog). However, in Turkish, the object is indicated not by the syntax, but by the morphology of attaching the suffix, *u*. So, "The girl fed the dog-u" means the same as "The dog-u fed the girl." Turkish toddlers use the *u* rule correctly by age 3, just as English-speaking children learn the correct ordering of words by this age.

Toddlers learn the rules of their language without much in the way of explicit instruction. Parents and other adults model grammatically correct speech. They will also restate a child's telegraphic speech into a complete sentence, for example, changing "more cookie" to "would you like another cookie?" Parents, however, generally ignore toddlers' grammatical mistakes (Brown & Hanlon, 1970), and seldom try to explain the rules of grammar. Without any formal training, young children grasp the grammatical rules of their language with few errors, simply by hearing and using the language in daily interactions. By age 4, it is estimated that children use correct grammar in 90% of their statements (Guasti, 2000; Pinker, 1994). As described earlier, the speed and self-sufficiency with which children grasp grammar was key to Chomsky (1969) proposing an innatist theory of language acquisition.

## Becoming an Adept Native Speaker

**LO 6.5.3 Give examples of children's development of pragmatics from infancy through adolescence, and identify the extent to which these social rules are culturally based.**

**sensitive period**
in the course of development, a period when the capacity for learning in a specific area is especially pronounced

By the time they turn 3 years of age, most children are remarkably skilled language users (Maratsos, 1998). They can communicate with others about a wide range of topics. They can speak about events that are happening in the present, as well as those in the past and future. Toddlers raised in homes where Mandarin is spoken have learned that different tones change the meaning of a word. French toddlers have learned how to make nasal sounds and say *Voilà*! and !Kung San toddlers in Botswana have learned how to click their tongues against various parts of their mouths to make the words of their language (Small, 2001). Although their pronunciation of words is not as precise as it will later become, by the time they reach age 4, most children use grammar and speak clearly enough to make themselves understood about nearly anything they wish. Clearly children's brains are built for learning language, and early childhood is a **sensitive period** for language development, when the capacity for learning grammar and vocabulary is especially pronounced (Pinker, 1994).

To become adept native language users, however, children must learn not only grammar and vocabulary, but also the social rules or *pragmatics* for using language in interaction with others. Acquiring the pragmatics of language use includes knowledge of when to speak, what to say and how to say it, who to listen to, and how to interpret statements where what is meant is different from what is said. Mastery of most of the pragmatics of a language is probably not reached until adolescence or emerging adulthood. For example, only half of the 10-year-olds in a study understood that a speaker who said "I had my favorite cake for dessert" in a sad voice was not happy. They attended to the meaning of the words, but not the tone of voice. In the same study, none of the 4-year-olds picked up on the sad voice, whereas all 18- to 22-year-olds did (Morton & Trehub, 2001).

How might the language used in this kind of play demonstrate a grasp of pragmatics?

Children begin learning pragmatics even before they begin speaking, through gestures, for example, when they wave "bye-bye" to someone when leaving. By the age of 2, they use the pragmatics of a basic conversation, including taking turns speaking (Pan & Snow, 1999). However, at this age they have not yet grasped the pragmatics of sustaining a conversation on one topic, and they tend to change topics rapidly as new things occur to them, without much awareness of the other person's perspective.

By age 4, children are more sensitive to the characteristics of their conversational partner and will adjust their speech accordingly. In one study using hand puppets, 4-year-olds used different kinds of speech when acting out different puppet roles (Anderson, 2000). When playing a socially dominant role such as teacher or doctor, they used commands frequently, whereas they spoke more politely when playing subordinate roles such as student or patient.

Sensitivity to the characteristics of others also influences preschoolers' uptake of new words. In one study, 4-year-olds watched one adult correctly label objects and another adult incorrectly label the same objects. Subsequently, when presented with unfamiliar objects, the children were more likely to apply the labels used by the previously correct adult (Koenig & Harris, 2005). Another study found that preschoolers preferred the labels for objects used by a speaker who claimed to be knowledgeable about the objects, as compared to a speaker who professed ignorance (Sabbagh & Shafman, 2009).

**Critical Thinking Question:** Can you relate the findings from these two studies to the concept of social gating described earlier?

The use of pragmatics represents not only social understanding but also cultural knowledge. All cultures have their own rules for what kinds of speech can be used in what kinds of situations. For example, some cultures require children to address adults with respectful titles, such as "Mr." for adult men and "Dr." for college professors. Many cultures have words that are classified as "bad words" that are not supposed to be spoken, especially by children. Many languages also have two versions of the word *you*, an informal version used when there is a close attachment (such as with family and close friends) and a formal version used with unfamiliar persons and persons with whom there is a professional but not personal relationship (such as employers). Knowing when and with whom to use each version of "you" requires extensive familiarity not just with the language but also with the cultural norms. Using them inappropriately is often considered impolite or even offensive.

Learning what to say and what not to say is part of developing an understanding of how to use the pragmatics of language in accordance with cultural views of politeness. Many studies across different cultures have found that children develop culturally specific rules of linguistic politeness between the ages of 2 and 5 years (Fitneva & Matsui, 2015). Middle-class mothers in the United States, for example, actively teach their children polite

Polite expressions and routines are common in Japan.

expressions and routines. They frequently instruct their children to say "please," "thank you," and "excuse me" (Gleason et al., 1984). A language such as Japanese involves an extensive repertoire of ways to communicate politely, including the length of sentences, the extent of formal word use, verb conjugation, and use of prefixes (Fitneva & Matsui, 2015). The extensive nature of the repertoire may be one reason why Japanese parents and preschool teachers explicitly teach polite expressions and routines to children, and why Japanese preschool children have been found to prompt peers with how to speak politely (Burdelski, 2012). Watch the video *Observing Everyday Storytelling* for a fascinating example of how pragmatics are reflected in the stories that parents tell in the presence of their toddlers.

## Research Focus: Observing Everyday Storytelling

Around age 5, children become capable of telling stories. Well before that age, they have also been listening to stories told by the people around them (Miller et al., 2014; Nelson, 1993). Stories are told across cultures and contribute to a language-rich environment. Interestingly, stories also hold both implicit and explicit cultural lessons for children about what to say and how to say it.

Peggy Miller (1996) has studied the stories that parents tell in the presence of their toddlers for many decades. Her observational research involves video-recording the natural, everyday behaviors of families in their home (see Chapter 1). Each family is assigned one researcher who comes for regular visits over the course of an extended period. For example, one study of six families in Taiwan and six families in the United States involved 2 years of observations (Miller et al., 1997, 2008).

In order to address the issue that families react to the presence of researchers by changing their behavior, each researcher first spends considerable time with the families, habituating them to their presence. Only video-recordings taken after the family seems comfortable and back to regular routines are used. Also, in an effort to capture true-to-life interactions, Miller's research team matched up researchers to share key demographic characteristics with the families being studied. For example, they assigned Taiwanese researchers to the six Taiwanese families, and American researchers to the American families. Once the families were comfortable with the researchers, the Taiwanese families referred to the researcher as kin, calling her "aunty," whereas the American families tended to treat the researchers as a first-name family friend.

Although the research in the two countries included only a small number of families, hundreds of stories were recorded and analyzed. Every story was coded independently by two researchers, and inter-rater reliability was calculated (see Chapter 1). The analyses showed that the content of stories—what was said—differed between Taiwanese and American families. Taiwanese families were more likely to tell stories about their children's transgressions, whereas American stories tended to highlight how the children were cute, smart, or unusual. Miller interprets the Taiwanese

**Watch** OBSERVING EVERYDAY STORYTELLING

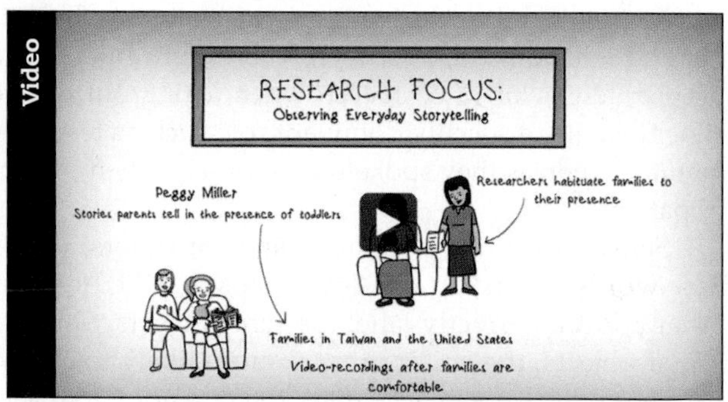


content as fitting the Chinese maxim that "the deeper the love, the greater the correction" (*Ai zhi shen, ze zhi qie*). In contrast, what was taken to be story-worthy among American families centered more on self-affirmation and entertainment. This does not mean that American families do not care about children's transgressions, but that these were not regarded as fitting story topics.

The structure of the stories–how things were said—also differed between the two cultures. Taiwanese adults often ended their stories by explicitly stating the moral of the story. For instance, one Taiwanese mother concluded a story by emphasizing that: "Saying dirty words is not good." American stories seldom ended this way. The structure of the Taiwanese stories, then, matched the content. Both elements conveyed the view that a parent has more knowledge than a child, and that the parent has a responsibility to impart this knowledge.

### Review Question

**1.** Taiwanese families called the researcher "aunty." This is an example of:

**a.** Infinite generativity
**b.** Pragmatics
**c.** Social gating
**d.** Overextension

By middle childhood, children not only master the art of telling stories, they also have become adept at humor. A substantial amount of humor in middle childhood involves violating the expectations set by pragmatics. For example, here is an old joke that made our son howl with laughter when he first learned it at age 8:

Person in restaurant: "Waiter, what's that fly doing in my soup?"

Waiter: "I believe he's doing the backstroke, sir."

For this to be funny, you have to understand pragmatics. Specifically, you have to understand that by asking, "What's that fly doing in my soup?" the diner means "What are you going to do about that disgusting fly?" The waiter, however, is either a bit slow on his pragmatics, or cleverly sarcastic. What makes it funny is that your understanding of pragmatics leads you to expect an answer to the pragmatic side of the question, not a literal reply about the behavior of the fly. Pragmatics are always culturally grounded, which is one reason why jokes seldom travel well between cultures.

## Creating New Language

**LO 6.5.4 Describe how children in middle childhood and adolescence create new language.**

With their adeptness at using the grammar, semantics, and pragmatics of their native language, adolescents also create new language (Stenström, 2014). **Slang**, an informal vocabulary and grammar that is different from that of the native language, is an example. Adolescence is a prime time for the creation of slang. Slang is often ephemeral, changing from one generation of adolescents to the next (Moore, 2004). Evidence for adolescent use of slang, however, goes back several centuries (Aulino & Bergami, 2009).

**slang**
an informal vocabulary and grammar that is different from that of the native language

The purposes of slang are many. Slang is used to create a vivid or original effect (Dumas & Lighter, 1978). Given the frequent inclusion of taboo and vulgar words, slang is also a way for adolescents to differentiate themselves from adults and even challenge adult norms. Slang can also be used to signify whether or not an adolescent is a member of a specific peer group (Eckert, 2004).

In ethnographic research from an American high school in Detroit during the 1980s and 1990s, for example, adolescents who self-identified as "burn-outs" used multiple negatives in 42% of their utterances (as in *I didn't do nothing*). These academically disinterested adolescents seemed to be emphatically setting themselves apart from teachers (who considered it improper grammar) and college-aspiring "jocks" (who mostly did not use this kind of slang) (Eckert, 1989). In a northern California high school in the 1990s, "geek" girls also aimed to distance themselves both from what they regarded as demeaning adult feminine norms and their peers' trivial concerns with popularity. Aiming to stand out as intelligent, they adopted a British pronunciation of certain words (Bucholtz, 1996).

Adolescence is a prime time for the creation and use of slang. Do you spy any slang in this graffiti?

Recent research has also focused on how globalization is leading adolescents from around the world to incorporate English into their slang. One study of a group of Japanese adolescent girls found that they often created a Japanese-English hybrid language, for example, saying "*ikemen getto suru*" (I wanna get a cool dude) (Miller, 2004). A study of Bulgarian 10th-grade adolescents also found frequent familiarity with and use of American English slang (Charkova, 2007). Common slang terms involved: swear words, terms for sexual activities and body parts, derogatory terms for men and women, and positive terms for men and women. The adolescents reported that they primarily learned the terms and expressions from movies, television, and song lyrics. They also reported gaining prestige among their peers from knowing English slang. As one Bulgarian 10th-grade boy explained (Charkova, 2007, p. 401):

> I want to learn English slang because when I tell my friends a new word or a phrase that they do not know, they look at me with respect and consider me an expert on a topic related to music, songs, movies, and so on.

Like the Japanese adolescent girls, the Bulgarian adolescents also often created a hybrid language interweaving Bulgarian and English (as in *Toi e istinski asshole*).

The involvement of children in creating a language has also been documented in very different ways. In the late 1970s and early 1980s, more than 400 deaf Nicaraguan children were brought together in two schools in the city of Managua (Senghas & Coppola, 2001). Prior to this time, the children had stayed home, communicating in simple signs with their hearing family members. The teachers in the new schools did not know any formal sign language and focused on teaching the children how to lip-read and speak Spanish. These efforts were not successful.

As the children came together on school grounds and buses, however, they began to develop a shared sign language. Each year, as new students entered the school, they would learn from the current students. Over time and several cohorts of students, a complex Nicaraguan Sign Language (NSL) was created, with its own gestures and grammar. Researchers argue that the creation of NSL shows how, in the absence of an existing mature language, children in middle childhood and adolescence can create and transmit a new language.

## Language and Cultural Cognition

**LO 6.5.5 Explain how becoming competent in a language relates to cultural styles of cognition.**

Given the fact that language use is thoroughly cultural in many ways, does that mean becoming an adept speaker of a particular language also shapes your thinking in cultural ways? Various political scientists and governments have certainly thought so because they have invented or mobilized words and phrases for political purposes. Examples include the ancient Greek notion of the "philosopher-king," and Marx's reinterpretations of terms such as "proletariat" and "bourgeoisie." George Orwell, author of the dystopian novel *1984*, who worried deeply about totalitarian regimes, wrote: "If thought corrupts language, language can also corrupt thought."

In psychology, interest in the question of the cognitive impact of language goes back close to a century. The *Sapir-Whorf hypothesis* holds that cognitive development is influenced by language development (Whorf, 1939/1956). If this hypothesis is taken to mean that language provides for culturally specific cognitive styles, then there is support across a number of different cognitive areas. For example, language impacts our numerical thinking. Pirahá (a language from the Amazon) does not have words for numbers larger than five. Adults who only speak Pirahá can easily perform cognitive tasks involving small quantities, but have difficulty with tasks involving larger quantities. Children, however, who speak both Pirahá and Portuguese, are able to handle both kinds of tasks, lending support to the conclusion that language impacts numerical thinking (Gordon, 2004).

Nicaraguan Sign Language (NSL) was created by deaf school children.

Language also influences spatial thinking. Spatial cognition may be differentiated along two broad types. An egocentric frame of reference is where the location of an object is determined in relation to the location of the self (e.g., "the cat is to the left of the house" from the perspective of the self). An allocentric frame of reference is where the object is located either in relation to another object (e.g., "the cat is by the front door of the house"), or based on cardinal-direction type systems (e.g., "the cat is on the west side of the house"). Some languages such as ≠Akhoe Hai || om (of Namibia) primarily use an allocentric frame of reference, whereas other languages such as Dutch and English provide an egocentric frame of reference. Research has found that children between 3 and 5 years of age commonly use allocentric spatial cognition. Older children and adults, however, vary depending on their language. For example, 8-year-olds and adults who speak ≠Akhoe Hai || om use allocentric reasoning, whereas Dutch 8-year-olds and adults used egocentric spatial reasoning (Haun et al., 2006). In short, something as basic as spatial cognition is shaped by the language that we learn to speak.

## SUMMARY: From First Words to Cultural Competence

**LO 6.5.1 Describe the quantitative (how many) and qualitative (what kinds) characteristics of vocabulary growth from age 1 to early adolescence.**

After learning to speak words at a slow rate for the first half of their second year, word production suddenly takes off and continues at a rapid pace into adolescence. Typically children speak 1 word at 1 year of age, 50 words at 2 years, about 2,500 words at 5 years, and some 40,000 words at 11 years. Toddlers first learn words they need to use in practical ways to communicate (milk, no). Then, nouns, verbs, and adjectives are added, followed by prepositions, pronouns, and conjunctions. Children and adolescents also gain the ability to use the different forms that words can take (calculate, calculating, recalculate).

**LO 6.5.2 Explain what telegraphic speech is and what it reveals about children's development of grammatical rules.**

Toward the end of the 18- to 24-month-period, toddlers begin using telegraphic speech, combining two or a few spoken words (mama no go). Toddlers' telegraphic speech already shows an initial knowledge of syntax, or the grammatical rules for how to order words in a sentence. By the end of the third year, toddlers have learned the main grammatical rules of their language, indicating an innate propensity.

**LO 6.5.3 Give examples of children's development of pragmatics from infancy through adolescence, and identify the extent to which these social rules are culturally based.**

To become adept native language users, children must learn not only grammar and vocabulary but also the social rules or pragmatics for using language in interaction with others. For example, 2-year-olds take turns speaking, 4-year-olds speak more politely to people in authority, and 8-year-olds are adept at humor. Pragmatics are culturally based; for example, some cultures require children to address adults with respectful titles, and humor seldom translates well from one language to another.

**LO 6.5.4 Describe how children in middle childhood and adolescence have created new language.**

By middle childhood and adolescence, children also create new language. Research has documented this for slang and Nicaraguan Sign Language (NSL).

**LO 6.5.5 Explain how becoming competent in a language relates to cultural styles of cognition.**

Language provides for culturally specific cognitive styles. Pirahá (a language from the Amazon) does not have words for numbers larger than five, and individuals who only speak Pirahá have difficulty with tasks involving larger quantities.

# 6.6 Multilingualism

As we have seen, children are marvelously well-suited to learning a language. But what happens when they try to learn two or three or more languages? Does becoming multilingual enhance their language development or impede it? How does multilingualism influence neurological, cognitive, and social development? Next we turn to research that addresses these questions. As you saw at the outset of this chapter, multilingualism is a fact of life for most children around the world.

## The Development of Multilingualism

**LO 6.6.1 Describe characteristics of multilingual development.**

When children learn two languages, they usually become adept at using both (Baker, 2011; Ishihara, 2014). They understand that they are learning more than one language (Meisel, 2011), and learning a second language does not interfere with mastering the first language (Lessow-Hurley, 2005). Children learning two languages from birth, in fact, become proficient at both languages with the same timing and in the same order as monolingual children (Albareda-Castellot et al., 2011).

In early childhood, multilingual children sometimes mix the syntax of the different languages. In Spanish, for example, dropping the subject in a sentence is grammatically correct, as in *no quiero ir* (I don't want to go). If a multilingual child applies this rule to English, it comes out as *no want go*, which is not correct. However, the intermixing of syntax has not been consistently found across groups of multilingual children (Lucas & Singer, 1975; Paradis & Genesee, 1996; Yip & Matthews, 2000). Also, by the time they reach middle childhood, children can easily keep their different languages separate.

Sometimes older children blend different languages on purpose. They import some words from one language when speaking in the other, to create "Spanglish" (a blend of Spanish and English) or "Chinglish" (Chinese and English) or "Franglais" (French and English), for example (Suárez-Orozco, 2004).

When children learn a second language after already becoming fluent in their first language, it takes longer to master the second language, usually 3–5 years (Baker, 2011; Hakuta, 1999). Even so, learning a second language comes much easier in early and middle childhood than it does at later ages. For example, in one study, adults who had immigrated to the United States from China or Korea at various ages were tested on their grammatical knowledge of English (Johnson & Newport, 1991). The participants who had arrived in the United States in early or middle childhood scored as well on the test as native English speakers, but beyond middle childhood, the older the age at immigration, the less the person's grammatical knowledge. Other studies have shown that beyond the age of about 12, it is difficult for people to learn to speak a new language without a noticeable accent (Birdsong, 2006). Clearly, children have a biological readiness for learning new languages that adults lack, but the decline in this ability is gradual and steady from childhood to adulthood.

**metalinguistic skills**
knowledge of the underlying structure of language

## Benefits and Risks of Multilingualism

**LO 6.6.2 Summarize benefits and risks of multilingualism.**

When children learn two languages, they usually become adept at using both.

Becoming multilingual has a variety of benefits. Children who speak two languages have better **metalinguistic skills** than monolingual children, meaning that they have greater awareness of the underlying structure of language (Schwartz et al., 2008). In one early study (Oren, 1981), researchers compared bilingual and monolingual children ages 4–5 on metalanguage skills by instructing them to use nonsense words for familiar objects (e.g., *dimp* for dog, *wug* for car) and by asking them questions about the implications of changing object labels (if we call a dog a cow, does it give milk?). The bilingual children were consistently better than the monolingual children in metalanguage understanding. Specifically, they were better at applying grammatical rules to nonsense words (one *wug*, two *wugs*) and at understanding that words are symbols for objects (calling a dog a cow won't make it give milk). Other studies have confirmed that bilingual children are better than monolingual children at detecting mistakes in grammar and meaning (Baker, 2011; Bialystok, 1993, 1997).

Multilingual children also score higher on more general measures of cognitive ability, indicating that becoming multilingual also has general cognitive benefits (Bialystok, 1999, 2001; Swanson et al., 2004). On tests of executive function, such as the Dimensional Change Card Sort task that involves both staying focused and switching strategies (see Chapter 5), multilingual preschoolers perform better than monolinguals (Bialystok & Martin, 2004). Similar results have been found for children in early and middle childhood (Carlson & Choi, 2009). Recent research aiming to detect just how early these differences on executive function emerge has documented that 3-year-old multilinguals show an advantage over monolinguals (Bialystok et al., 2010). What is even more amazing is that 7-month-old infants exposed to two languages do better than their monolingual peers on a visual task requiring staying focused and not becoming distracted (Kovacs & Mehler, 2009).

The differences between multilingual and monolingual children on executive function may be linked to the ways that their brains develop differently. Neurological research has shown that children exposed to two languages have denser brain tissue in areas related not only to language, but also attention and memory (Mechelli et al., 2004). This is especially the case for children who heard different languages before the age of 5 years.

Are there risks to growing up multilingual? The research does not suggest notable disadvantages per se. In the United States, however, multilingual children are often from immigrant families who are disproportionately low-income. They often enter preschool speaking a native language but have limited proficiency in English. Over the years, they often fail to keep pace with their monolingual, English-speaking peers (McCabe et al., 2013). The risk, however, comes not from growing up in a multilingual environment but from growing up poor. As we saw earlier, monolingual children from low-income families also struggle to keep up in their language development. Map 6.2 shows the percentage of people over age 5 in the U.S. who speak a language other than English at home.

**Map 6.2** Multilingualism in the United States

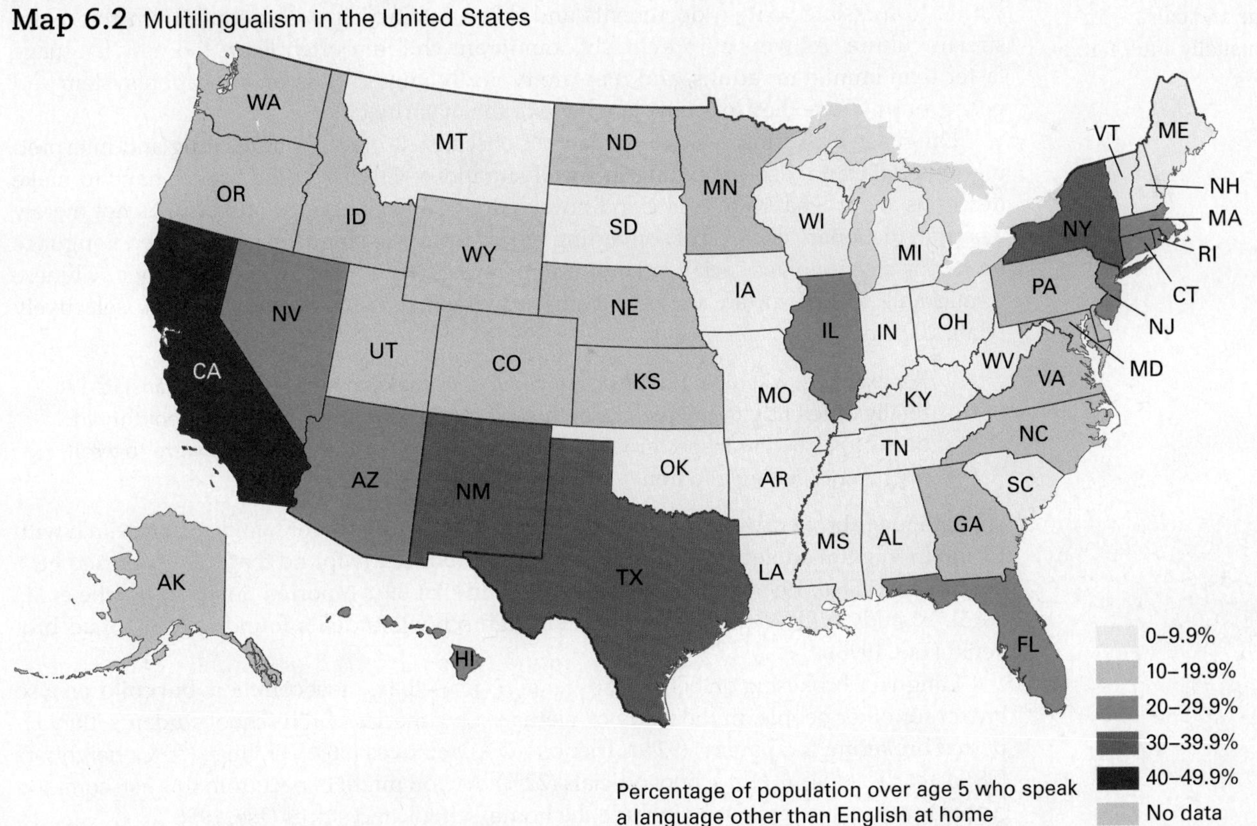

## Education Focus: Early Multilingual Education Across Contexts

On the basis of a comprehensive review of the research on multilingualism, a group of social scientists has issued policy guidelines for professional caregivers and teachers to ensure that multilingual children in the United States develop strong language skills. The report was endorsed by the American Academy of Pediatrics (McCabe et al., 2013). The report highlights six strategies:

(1) Avoid attributing children's language delays to multilingualism.

(2) Ensure that multilingual children have exposure to rich versions of both the first language and English across a variety of contexts.

(3) Provide support for development of the first language in the childcare environment.

(4) Support the first language by also visiting other contexts and places where it is spoken.

(5) Have the caregiver speak to the child in the language that comes most naturally to ensure a rich language environment.

(6) Develop programs that expose children to high-quality English at an early age. Such exposure may involve home visitation, center-based early childhood education programs, healthcare providers, and mass media.

### Review Question

The policy report focuses on ways to support multilingual development in immigrant children. Do you think there is need for new policies for professional caregivers and teachers to support multilingual development among American children from families in which only English is spoken? Explain.

## Language Brokering

**LO 6.6.3 Define language brokering and explain its positive and negative sides.**

**language brokering**
immigrant children translating and interpreting the language and culture for others, usually adult family members

As immigrant children in the United States and elsewhere reach middle childhood, they often engage in **language brokering**, that is, they bridge the linguistic gap between immigrant adults and the majority culture. For example, older family members with less fluency in the language of their new culture rely on preadolescents, adolescents, and emerging adults to translate written documents and when interacting with people from the mainstream culture. As we saw previously, immigrant children often learn the new language faster than immigrant adults, and they are typically immersed in an education system and peer groups where they learn the language of the majority culture.

Language brokering is a complex activity because it involves translating and interpreting materials, and also mediating in social situations. Children who broker have to make decisions about what to translate and how to do it. Thus, language brokering is not merely a neutral dictionary exercise of converting words from one language into another. Language brokering also involves social and cultural meanings. For example, in one study of Chinese immigrants to Britain, an adolescent girl explained that she would translate selectively (Hall, 2001, p. 2):

> For example, when the fire inspector came to our take-away shop, I just translated it totally differently to my parents because it would stop them worrying about it, and then I told the fire inspector what I thought the appropriate answers were to avoid my parents getting into trouble. You just get used to that situation.

Language brokering appears to be common among immigrant families. In research with Latino immigrant adolescents in the United States, one study found that 100% reported having brokered (Tse, 1995) and another study found that 89% reported doing so (Roche et al., 2015). A study with Vietnamese-American high school students found that 89% had brokered (Tse, 1996).

Language brokering on behalf of parents appears to be most common, but children also broker for other people. In the study of Vietnamese-American high school students, they reported brokering for: parents (92%), friends (63%), relatives (56%), siblings (50%), neighbors (38%), teachers (34%), and school officials (22%). As you might expect from this list, common places for language brokering include the home, school, and stores (Tse, 1996).

Are there positive or negative sides to language brokering? The answer appears to be some of both, but with recent evidence tipping the scales in the positive direction. Research suggests that there is more conflict between children and parents in families where a very high degree of brokering takes place, compared to families with less brokering (Kam & & Lazarevic, 2014).

As long as the need for brokering is not excessive, however, studies show that children regard brokering as normal (Cline et al., 2011; Degener, 2010), and as a way to feel helpful to their parents. On their part, parents often express a sense of gratitude (Morales et al., 2012). For both children and parents, then, the focus is on positive family interdependence (Dorner et al., 2008).

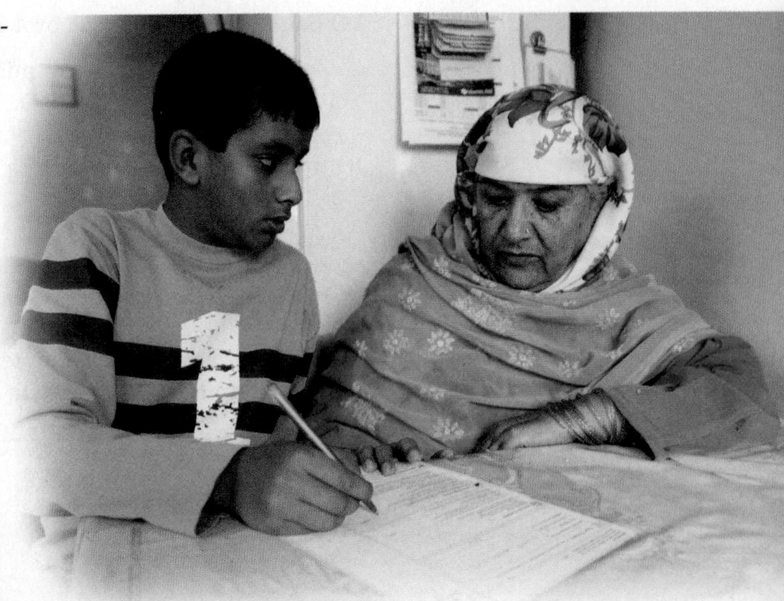

Language brokering is common among immigrant families and is often experienced as positive by both children and adults. Here, a boy helps his grandmother fill out forms in English which is not her first language.

Research has also shown that language brokers report that the activity helps them better learn both of the languages in question (De Ment et al., 2005). Studies in both Britain and the United States have suggested that brokering helps to increase the vocabulary of immigrant children (Halgunseth, 2003; Hall & Sham, 2007). A longitudinal study also found that adolescents who brokered extensively scored higher on reading tasks than adolescents who brokered infrequently (Dorner et al., 2007).

Finally, language brokering may also contribute to an enhanced sense of connection with two cultures. Among Vietnamese-American high school students, almost 40% reported that brokering helped them to know American culture better, and similarly, almost 40% stated that they knew Vietnamese culture better due to their language brokering (Tse, 1996). Among emerging adults from immigrant families in the United States, research has shown that frequent language brokers scored higher on both feeling acculturated to American ways of life and identifying with their heritage culture, compared to infrequent language brokers. The authors argue that language brokering may instill crucial ways of thinking that are useful in multicultural societies (Weisskirch et al., 2011).

Brokering, then, is an important linguistic, cognitive, and social skill in today's world—a world where multilingualism is an "international fact" (McCabe et al., 2013, p. 3). Language brokering is experienced in largely positive ways by children, even as there may also be a downside for some of them. We end this chapter with the words of Nadia, a 16-year-old Portuguese immigrant to Britain, capturing how she experiences both sides (de Abreu & Lambert, 2003, p. 207):

> I feel important! I feel useful because I can speak [both] languages. . . . It is also embarrassing for me because no one of my age does that with their parents. I mean, [my friend] Carmo does. The Portuguese all do. But the English do not. . . . It is to the contrary. Very often when they go to the doctor, their parents go with them, but I have to go with my parents. It is different.

## SUMMARY: Multilingualism

### LO 6.6.1 Describe characteristics of multilingual development.

When children learn two languages simultaneously, they understand that they are learning more than one language, and learning a second language does not interfere with mastering the first language. When children learn a second language after already becoming fluent in their first language, it takes longer to master the new language. Also, learning a second language comes much easier in early and middle childhood than it does at later ages.

### LO 6.6.2 Summarize benefits and risks of multilingualism.

Compared to monolingual children, multilingual children have greater awareness of the underlying structure of language and score higher on measures of cognitive ability. Research has not shown notable disadvantages of being multilingual.

**LO 6.6.3 Define language brokering and explain its positive and negative sides.**

As immigrant children reach middle childhood, they often engage in language brokering, that is, they bridge the linguistic gap between immigrant adults and the majority culture. As long as the need for language brokering is not excessive, it enhances children's vocabulary, their sense of being helpful to parents, and their affiliation with two cultures.

# Apply Your Knowledge as a Professional

The topics covered in this chapter apply to a wide variety of career professions. Watch this video to learn how they apply to an education coordinator at a language immersion school.

**Journaling Question:** Write a story about yourself that you could tell or perform in about 2 minutes. After writing it, explain why you used certain words, grammatical features, and organizational or structural features. Also, can you explain some of the pragmatics of your story?

# Chapter 7
# Emotions, Self, and Identity

## Learning Objectives

### 7.1 Temperament: Individual Differences in Emotion and Self-Regulation

**7.1.1** Define infant temperament and describe two ways of conceptualizing it.

**7.1.2** Explain how the idea of goodness-of-fit pertains to temperament on both a family level and a cultural level.

### 7.2 Emotions

**7.2.1** Review the key features of the evolutionary, differentiation, functionalist, and internalization theories of emotional development.

**7.2.2** Describe the development of primary emotions and emotion perception in infants.

**7.2.3** Describe how emotional development advances during toddlerhood, and identify the impact of culture on these changes.

**7.2.4** Identify the characteristics of Autism Spectrum Disorder and how it affects children's prospects as they grow to adulthood.

**7.2.5** Explain why self-regulation continues to improve in middle childhood.

**7.2.6** Summarize the results of the Experience Sampling Method studies with respect to adolescent emotionality.

**7.2.7** Identify the different types and rates of adolescent depression, and summarize the most effective treatments for depression and suicide ideation.

### 7.3 Self-Conceptualization

**7.3.1** Describe the emergence of self-recognition and self-reflection in infancy and toddlerhood.

**7.3.2** Explain how the self-concept changes from early childhood through middle childhood.

**7.3.3** Describe the complex self-conceptions that develop in adolescence.

### 7.4 Self-Esteem

**7.4.1** Explain how different ways of thinking about self-esteem are rooted in cultural beliefs.

**7.4.2** Summarize how global self-esteem and differentiated self-esteem change in the course of childhood and adolescence.

**7.4.3** Describe the prevalence, symptoms, and treatment of eating disorders.

### 7.5 Identity

**7.5.1** Review key features of Erikson's theory, and explain how Marcia extended the theory.

**7.5.2** Describe the various forms identity development can take during emerging adulthood.

**7.5.3** Describe how identity development varies across cultures, including the impact of globalization.

**7.5.4** Explain why ethnic identity development comes to the forefront in adolescence, and differentiate among ethnic identity statuses.

THE TWOS ARE NOT TERRIBLE EVERYWHERE, ADOLESCENTS ARE NOT VOLATILE EVERYWHERE, AND THE SELF IS NOT PRAISED EVERYWHERE. The development of emotions, self, and identity vary across cultures. Yet, there are also important commonalities. Across cultures, some infants are more even-tempered than others. Toddlers learn to regulate their emotions. Children develop a personal self, often describing themselves in terms of activities they enjoy and their ties to family and friends. We now take an in-depth look at the theories and research that have captured these similarities and differences in the development of emotions, self, and identity.

Watch **CHAPTER INTRODUCTION: EMOTIONS, SELF, AND IDENTITY**

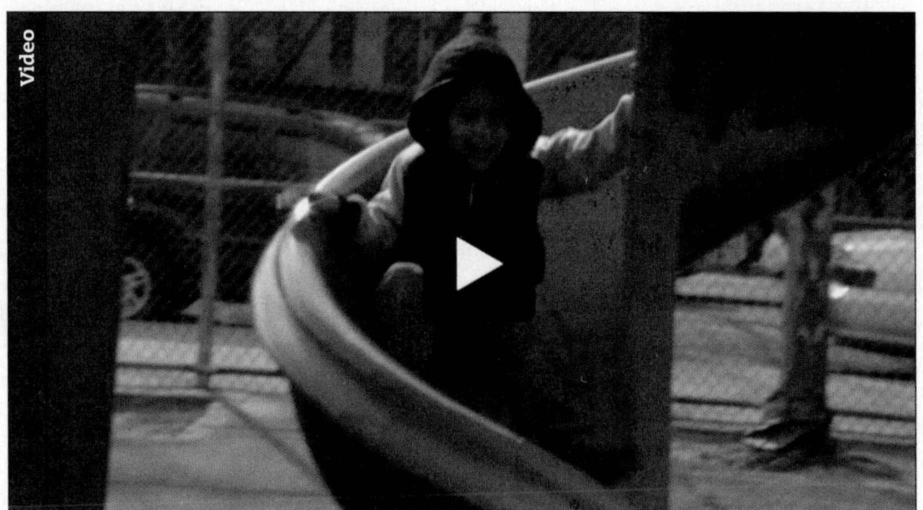

# 7.1 Temperament: Individual Differences in Emotion and Self-Regulation

Have you had any experience in caring for infants, perhaps as a babysitter, older sibling, or parent? If so, you have probably observed that they differ from early on in their emotional and behavioral responses to you and to the environment. Some infants will smile at you almost right away when they first meet you, whereas others will be fearful. Some infants will be fascinated by a toy, whereas others will quickly lose interest. When unhappy, some infants are easy to soothe, whereas others will cry and cry. Ask any parents of more than one child about these kinds of individual differences, and they will probably have tales to tell (Horwitz et al., 2010).

## The Raw Material of Personality

**LO 7.1.1 Define infant temperament and describe two ways of conceptualizing it.**

In the study of child development, individual differences in emotionality and the ability to regulate one's emotions are viewed as indicators of **temperament**. Temperament includes qualities such as activity level, positive affect, adaptability, attention span, and self-regulation. You can think of temperament as the biologically based raw material of personality (Fox et al., 2013; Goldsmith, 2009; Rothbart et al., 2000). Researchers on temperament believe that all infants are born with certain tendencies toward behavior and personality development, and that the environment then shapes those tendencies in the course of development.

**temperament**
innate responses to the physical and social environment, including qualities of positive affect, adaptability, activity level, attention span, and self-regulation

The idea of temperament is not new. The ancient Greeks had a notion of temperament as a person's typical mood and behavior resulting from the balance of the four humors in the body: blood, black bile, yellow bile, and phlegm (Shiner & DeYoung, 2013). The focus was on emotional and biological processes, a view in harmony with today's research. However, as you will see, developmental psychologists today focus on neurological foundations, not blood, bile, or phlegm. Let's look at influential psychological ways of conceptualizing temperament, then at some of the challenges involved in measuring and studying it.

**THOMAS AND CHESS.** Temperament was originally proposed as a psychological concept by Alexander Thomas and Stella Chess, who in 1956 began the New York Longitudinal Study (NYLS). Thomas and Chess wanted to see how infants' innate tendencies would be shaped into personality in the course of development through childhood and adolescence. Using parents' reports, among other measures, they assessed infant temperament by judging qualities such as activity level, adaptability, intensity of reactions, and quality of mood. On this basis, Thomas and Chess classified infants into three categories: easy, slow-to-warm-up, and difficult.

1. *Easy* babies (40% of the sample) were those whose moods were generally positive. They adapted well to new situations and were generally moderate rather than extreme in their emotional reactions.
2. *Slow-to-warm-up* babies (15%) were notably low in activity level, reacted negatively to new situations, and had fewer positive or negative emotional extremes than other babies.
3. *Difficult* babies (10%) did not adapt well to new situations, and their moods were intensely negative more frequently than other babies.

By following these babies into adulthood in their longitudinal study, Thomas and Chess were able to show that temperament in infancy predicted later development in some respects (Chess & Thomas, 1984; Ramos et al., 2005; Thomas et al., 1968). The difficult babies in their study were at high risk for problems in childhood, such as aggressive behavior, anxiety, and social withdrawal. Slow-to-warm-up babies rarely seemed to have problems in early childhood, but once they entered school they were sometimes fearful and had problems academically and with peers because of their relatively slow responsiveness.

Perhaps you noticed that the three categories in the classic Thomas and Chess study added up to only 65% of the infants they studied. The other 35% could not be classified as easy, slow-to-warm-up, or difficult. It is clearly a problem to exclude 35% of infants, so other temperament researchers have avoided categories, instead rating all infants on the basis of temperamental traits.

Are these babies with easy and difficult temperaments, or are they just momentarily happy and sad? Temperament is difficult to assess because infants' emotional states fluctuate so much.

**self-regulation**

ability to exercise control over one's emotions and reactions

**SELF-REGULATION AND BEHAVIORAL INHIBITION.** Mary Rothbart and her colleagues kept some of the Thomas and Chess temperament qualities, such as activity level and attention span, but also added a dimension of **self-regulation**, which is the ability to manage emotions and reactions (Rothbart, 2004; Rothbart et al., 2001). Table 7.1 provides a summary of the two conceptions of temperament. Rothbart's model informs much of the current research on temperament.

In Table 7.1, the first five qualities of temperament listed for Rothbart describe different kinds of *reactivity*, or infants' initial emotional and behavioral reactions to environmental stimuli. In addition to identifying differences in infant reactivity as an important aspect of temperament, Rothbart and colleagues point out that children also differ in how they regulate or manage their initial reactions. For example, instead of immediately starting to cry when something frightens them, infants may look to parents in order to gauge their

**Table 7.1** Two Conceptions of Infant Temperament

| Thomas and Chess | | Rothbart | |
|---|---|---|---|
| **Quality** | **Description** | **Quality** | **Description** |
| Activity level | Ratio of active time to inactive time | Activity level | Frequency and intensity of gross motor activity |
| Attention span | Length of time devoted to an activity before moving on to the next | Attention span/ Persistence | Duration of attention to a single activity |
| Intensity of reaction | Emotional expressiveness such as crying and laughing | Fearful distress | Fear/distress in response to novel or intense stimulation |
| Rhythmicity | Regularity of physical functions such as feeding and sleeping | Irritable distress | Expression of distress when frustrated |
| Distractibility | Extent to which new stimulation stops current behavior | Positive affect | Frequency of expression of happiness and other positive emotions |
| Approach/Withdrawal | Response to new object or person | Self-regulation | Ability to suppress an initial response to a situation and execute a more adaptive response |
| Adaptability | Adjustment to changes in routines | | |
| Threshold of responsiveness | Stimulation required to evoke a response | | |
| Quality of mood | General level of happy versus unhappy mood | | |

Based on: Rothbart et al. (2000); Thomas & Chess (1977).

response. In turn, they may rely on the parental response to modulate their own emotions. Redirecting attention and emotional control are key aspects of self-regulation. Rothbart suggests that self-regulation develops in the course of infancy and early childhood.

Rothbart and her colleagues have developed laboratory tasks and questionnaires to assess temperament from infancy through early childhood (Goldsmith & Rothbart, 1996; Rothbart, 1981; Rothbart et al., 2001). They have been moderately successful in predicting children's functioning from infant temperament (Rothbart & Bates, 2006).

One specific temperamental style that has been researched extensively is *behavioral inhibition*, or the tendency to withdraw and express fear in the face of stressful novel situations (Fox et al., 2005; Kagan et al., 1987). Based on longitudinal studies, Jerome Kagan, Nathan Fox, and their colleagues have found that infants and toddlers who were high on behavioral inhibition were more likely to be shy in childhood and adolescence than infants and toddlers who were low on behavioral inhibition. This line of research emphasizes biological underpinnings of behavioral inhibition. For example, Kagan argues that heightened activation of the amygdala, an almond-shaped mass in each temporal lobe of the brain, underlies the disposition toward behavioral inhibition (Fox et al., 2013; Kagan, 2001). Watch the video *Measuring Temperament* in the Research Focus feature to learn more about different measurement approaches to temperament.

## Research Focus: Measuring Temperament

All research on temperament faces measurement challenges because infants' emotional states change so frequently. When Thomas and Chess began studying temperament, they used parents' reports of infants' behavior as a key source for their temperament classifications. Even today, most studies of infant temperament are based on parents' reports.

There are some clear advantages to using parents' reports. After all, parents see their infants in many different situations on a daily basis over a long period of time. In contrast, a researcher who assesses temperament on the basis of the infants' performance on tasks administered in the laboratory sees the infant only on that one occasion. Because infants' states change so frequently, the researcher may assess infants as having a "difficult" temperament when in fact the infant is simply in a temporary state of distress—hungry, perhaps, or tired, or cold, or hot, or in need of a diaper change.

However, parents are not always accurate appraisers of their infants' behavior. For example, mothers who are depressed are more likely to rate their infants' temperament negatively; mothers' and fathers' ratings of their infants' temperament show only low to moderate levels of agreement; and parents tend to rate their twins or other siblings as less similar in temperament than researchers do, which suggests that parents may exaggerate the differences between their children.

What are options besides parents' reports? Thomas and Chess recommend that researchers observe infants' behavior in naturalistic settings (such as at home, or at the park) on several occasions, to avoid the problem of observing on just one occasion when the infant may have been in an unusually good or bad mood. Of course, this takes considerably more time and money than a simple parental questionnaire, and even a series of observations may not be as valid as the experiences parents accumulate over months of caring for their infants.

Another approach has been to have parents keep daily diaries of their infants' behavior (recording when they're sleeping, fussing, or crying). Reports using this method have been shown to correlate well with temperament ratings based on parental reports and performance on laboratory tasks.

**Watch** MEASURING TEMPERAMENT

Biological assessments of temperament are also useful since temperament is regarded as biologically based. One simple but effective biological measure of infant temperament is heart rate. Extremely shy children tend to have consistently high heart rates, and heart rates that show a greater increase in response to new stimulation such as new toys, new smells or new people, compared to other children. Other biological assessments of temperament have been developed, including measures of brain activity. Many current researchers argue in favor of multimethod assessments, including report-based, observational, and biological measures.

Although infant temperament can predict later development to some extent, predictions are more accurate when assessments of temperament are made after 2 years of age. Fussing, crying, and rapid changes in states are common in infancy across a wide range of infants. It is only after age 2 that children's moods and behavior settle into more stable patterns that predict later development. But can temperament still be assumed to be innate and biologically based once the environment has been experienced for 2 years or more?

## Review Questions

1. Although parents' reports are often used to evaluate infant temperament, a drawback of using parents' reports is that:
   a. Mothers' and fathers' reports are often inconsistent
   b. Parents tend to exaggerate the differences between their children
   c. Depressed mothers tend to rate their infants' temperaments more negatively
   d. All of the above

2. The most simple biological measure of temperament is:
   a. Blood pressure
   b. Heart rate
   c. Brain-wave intensity
   d. Hormonal stability

## Goodness-of-Fit

**LO 7.1.2 Explain how the idea of goodness-of-fit pertains to temperament on both a family level and a cultural level.**

**goodness-of-fit**
theoretical principle that children develop best if there is a good fit between the temperament of the child and environmental demands

All approaches to measuring temperament view it as the raw material of personality, which is then shaped by the environment. Thomas and Chess (1977) proposed the concept of **goodness-of-fit**, meaning that children develop best if there is a good fit between the temperament of the child and environmental demands. In their view, difficult and slow-to-warm-up babies need parents who are aware of their temperaments and willing to be especially patient and nurturing.

Subsequent studies have provided support for the idea of goodness-of-fit, finding that babies with negative temperamental qualities were able to learn to control their emotional reactions better by 3 years of age if their parents were understanding and tolerant (Warren & Simmens, 2005). Other research has shown that parents who respond to an infant's difficult temperament with anger and frustration are likely to find that the infant becomes a child who is defiant and disobedient, leading to further conflict and frustration for both parents and children (Calkins, 2002; 2012).

There may also be something like a cultural goodness-of-fit, given that different cultures have different views of the value of personality traits such as activity level and emotional expressiveness. In general, Asian babies have been found to be less active and irritable than babies in the United States and Canada, and appear to learn to regulate their emotionality earlier and more easily (Chen et al., 2005; Lewis et al., 1993, 2010). This temperamental difference may be, in part, the basis for differences later in childhood, such as Asian children being more likely to be shy. However, in contrast to the North American view of shyness as a problem to be overcome, in Asian cultures, shyness is viewed more positively. The children—and the adults—who listen rather than speak are respected and admired. Consequently, studies of Chinese children have shown that shyness is associated with academic success and being well liked by peers (Chen et al., 1995). Now that China is changing so rapidly, both culturally and economically, there is some evidence that shyness is becoming less valued and related to poor rather than favorable adjustment in childhood (Chen, 2011; Chen et al., 2005). We will take a closer look at this research in Chapter 10.

### SUMMARY: Temperament: Individual Differences in Emotion and Self-Regulation

**LO 7.1.1 Define infant temperament and describe two ways of conceptualizing it.**

Temperament includes qualities such as activity level, positive affect, adaptability, attention span, and self-regulation. Thomas and Chess conceptualized temperament by classifying infants as easy, difficult, and slow-to-warm-up. Mary Rothbart and colleagues focus on qualities such as activity level and attention span, used by previous researchers. They have also added the quality of self-regulation, which is the ability to manage emotions and reactions.

**LO 7.1.2 Explain how the idea of goodness-of-fit pertains to temperament on both a family level and a cultural level.**

Goodness-of-fit means that children develop best if there is a "good fit" between the temperament of the child and environmental demands. At the family level, research shows that infants with difficult temperaments benefit when parents respond with tolerance rather than anger. Goodness-of-fit varies culturally, given that different cultures have different views of the value of personality traits such as emotional expressiveness.

# 7.2 Emotions

Expressing and understanding emotions goes deep into our biological nature. As Charles Darwin observed in 1872 in *The Expression of Emotions in Man and Animals*, the strong similarity between emotional expressions in humans and other mammals indicates that human emotional expressions are part of a long evolutionary history. Tigers snarl, wolves growl, chimpanzees—and humans, too—bare their teeth and scream. The research on temperament focuses on individual differences in emotionality. Now, we turn to the development of emotions within and across cultures. We will look at theories of emotion development, and how emotions and self-regulation change from infancy through adolescence. We also focus on two major disruptions to normal emotional development: Autism Spectrum Disorder, which can be reliably diagnosed by toddlerhood, and depression, which emerges notably in adolescence.

## Theories of Emotion Development

**LO 7.2.1 Review the key features of the evolutionary, differentiation, functionalist, and internalization theories of emotional development.**

Not only did Darwin observe that humans share emotional characteristics with mammals, he also argued that emotional expressions are highly similar among humans in different cultures. Extending Darwin's perspective, contemporary **evolutionary theories** emphasize the existence of discrete emotions that are shared by all humans. Focusing on adults, Paul Ekman (2003) has found that people in various cultures can easily identify the facial expressions associated with emotions such as anger and surprise in photographs of people from outside their culture (Ekman, 2003). Focusing on infants and young children, Carroll Izard (1991) has similarly argued that infants across cultures express a common set of discrete emotions, including joy, anger, distress, disgust, and interest.

**evolutionary theories** emphasize the existence of discrete emotions that are innate and shared by all humans

In comparison to Ekman's and Izard's theories of discrete emotions, some researchers have argued that discrete emotions are not present at birth but only develop gradually. These **differentiation theories** emphasize, for example, that only in the course of the first

**differentiation theories** argue that discrete emotions are not present at birth but only develop gradually

Darwin observed that humans share emotional characteristics with mammals. Here, a cat, a human, and an orangutan all show some similar facial characteristics. What emotions might they share?

Emotions are not only biologically driven processes, but also shaped through interactions between infants and caregivers. There is cultural variation in how much mothers smile at and elicit smiles from their babies.

6 months of life do reflexive expressions gradually turn into distinct and recognizable emotions (Sroufe, 1996). Michael Lewis (2008, 2010) has also argued that certain emotions, such as shame and guilt, only emerge in the course of toddlerhood because they presuppose an understanding of self that develops during this time. From this theoretical perspective, by 3 years of age, children's emotions are quite differentiated, even as their emotional lives will continue to become more complex and elaborated.

**Functionalist theories** emphasize how emotions serve social functions. They signal desired goals both to self and others. As such, emotions are dependent on context. For example, a toddler may express some emotions more with certain people or in certain situations (Barrett & Campos, 1987; Camras & Fatani, 2008; Saarni et al., 2006). Whereas evolutionary and differentiation theories focus on the emergence and expression of emotions, functionalist theories address the individual and interpersonal purposes of emotions.

Recently, the socioculturally-based **internalization theory** has highlighted that children's emotion expression and the way they regulate their emotions in social contexts are guided by adults and cultural norms (Friedlmeier et al., 2015; Holodynski & Friedlmeier, 2006). In this view, emotions are not only biologically driven processes, but also shaped through interactions between infants and caregivers. Through these interactions, infants learn and internalize cultural norms about what it means to be an emotionally competent individual. As we will now see, each of the theoretical perspectives has contributed important findings on the development of emotions.

**functionalist theories**
emphasize how emotions serve social functions, for example, signaling desired goals both to self and others

**internalization theory**
focuses on how children's emotion expression and regulation in social contexts are guided by adults and cultural norms

**primary emotions**
most basic emotions, such as anger, sadness, fear, disgust, surprise, and happiness

**secondary emotions**
emotions that require social learning, such as embarrassment, shame, and guilt; also called sociomoral emotions

## Infancy: Primary Emotions and Emotion Perception

**LO 7.2.2 Describe the development of primary emotions and emotion perception in infants.**

From the first weeks of life, infants express emotions. Interestingly, they also already perceive others' emotions.

**PRIMARY EMOTIONS.** Studies of emotional development often distinguish between two broad classes of emotion (Lewis, 2008). **Primary emotions** are the most basic emotions, the ones we share with animals, such as anger, sadness, fear, disgust, surprise, and happiness. Primary emotions are all evident within the first year of life. **Secondary emotions** are emotions that require considerable social and cultural learning, such as embarrassment, shame, and guilt. They develop mostly between ages 1 and 2, as we will see below.

Three primary emotions are evident in the early weeks of life: distress, interest, and pleasure (Lewis, 2002, 2008). Distress is evident in crying, of course, and we have seen how infants' interest can be assessed from the first days of life by where they turn their attention. We have also seen, in Chapter 3, that neonates show a facial expression of pleasure when tasting a sweet substance. Gradually, in the first months of life, these three emotions become differentiated into other primary emotions: distress into anger, sadness, and fear; interest into surprise; and pleasure into happiness. Disgust also appears early, but unlike distress, interest, and pleasure, it does not develop more complex forms. Let's look at how each of the other primary emotions develops over the first year.

Anger is expressed early in the form of a distinctive anger cry, as described in Chapter 3, but as an emotional expression separate from crying, it shows development over the course of the first year of life (Dodge et al., 2006; Lewis, 2010). In one study of infants at 1, 4, and 7 months of age, raters observed babies' responses as their forearms were held down so that they could not move them for a few minutes, a condition none of them liked much (Oster et al., 1992). The 1-month-old infants showed clear distress, but raters (who did not know the hypotheses of the study) did not classify their distress responses as anger. The 4-month-old infants were also distressed, and about half of them showed their distress in facial expressions that could be clearly identified as anger. By 7 months, nearly all the infants showed a definite anger response. Another study also observed the clear expression of anger in 7-month-olds in response to having an attractive object taken away (Stenberg et al., 1983). As infants become capable of intentional behavior in the second half of the first year of life, their expressions of anger often occur when their intentions are thwarted (Izard & Ackerman, 2000).

Sadness is rare in the first year of life, except for infants with depressed mothers. When mothers are depressed, infants, too, show facial expressions of sadness by the time they are 2–3 months old (Herrera et al., 2004). Could this be a case of passive genotype → environment interactions? Perhaps both infants and mothers have a genetic predisposition toward sadness in such families. This is something to consider, but in one study nondepressed mothers were instructed to look depressed in a 3-minute interaction with their infants (Cohn & Tronick, 1983). The infants responded with distress, suggesting that sad infants with depressed mothers are responding to their mothers' sadness rather than being genetically predisposed to sad emotional expressions.

Fear develops by 6 months of age (Gartstein et al., 2010). By then, infants show facial expressions of fear, for example, in response to a toy that moves toward them suddenly and unexpectedly (Buss & Goldsmith, 1998). Fear also becomes social at this age, as infants begin to show *stranger anxiety* in response to unfamiliar adults (Grossman et al., 2005). Stranger anxiety is a sign that the infant has begun to develop attachments to familiar persons, a topic we will discuss in detail in Chapter 9.

Surprise, indicated by an open mouth and raised eyebrows, is first evident about halfway through the first year (Camras et al., 1996). It is most often elicited by something in the infant's perceptual world that violates expectations. For example, a toy such as a jack-in-the-box might elicit surprise, especially the first time the jack pops out.

Finally, the development of happiness is evident in changes in infants' smiles and laughter that take place during the early months. After a few weeks, infants begin to smile in response to certain kinds of sensory stimulation—after feeding, or while urinating, or when having their cheeks stroked (Murkoff & Mazel, 2014). However, it is not until the second or third month of life that the first **social smile** appears, an expression of happiness in response to interacting with others (Fogel et al., 2006). The first laughs occur about a month after the first smiles (Nwokah et al., 1999). Beginning around 4 months old, social interactions and sensory or perceptual events, such as tickling or kisses or games such as peek-a-boo can elicit both smiles and laughs (Fogel et al., 2006). By age 1, infants have several different kinds of smiles that they show in response to different people and in different situations (Bolzani et al., 2002).

**social smile**
expression of happiness in response to interacting with others, first appearing at age 2–3 months

Cultural research has suggested that the extent to which infants engage in social smiling depends on their caregivers (Super & Harkness, 2010). In one longitudinal study, the rate of social smiling was similar for German infants and Nso infants from Cameroon at 6 weeks. By 12 weeks, however, differences had emerged with German infants smiling more than Nso infants. As you can see in Figure 7.1, the mothers of the German infants also smiled much more at their infants than the Nso mothers did (Wörmann et al., 2012). The researchers point out that, while German mothers express care for their infants through smiling, Nso mothers express care through physical contact and body stimulation. These different cultural approaches to parenting seem to result in different emotional expressions at a very early point in infancy.

**Figure 7.1** Social Smiling among German and Nso Infant–Mother Dyads

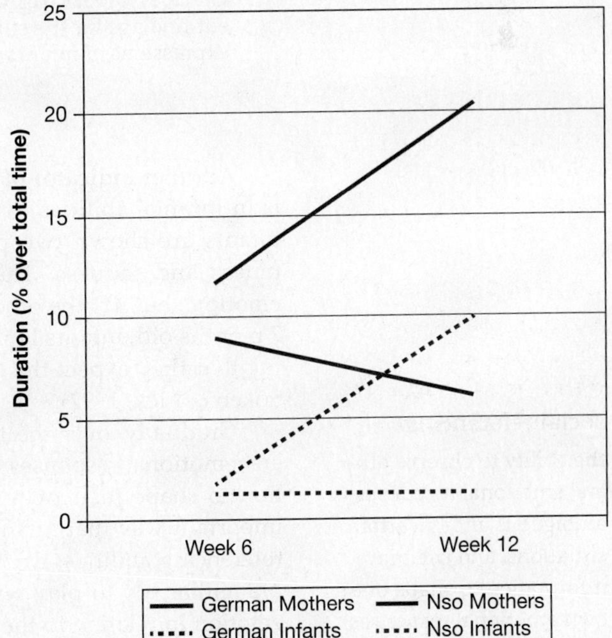


**Critical Thinking Question:** For the findings above on the emergence of primary emotions in infants, can you identify one piece of support for each of the four theories of emotion development: evolutionary, differentiation, functionalist, and internalization?

**emotional contagion**
in infants, crying in response to hearing another infant cry, evident at just a few days old

**EMOTION PERCEPTION.** Infants not only express emotions from the first days of life, they also perceive others' emotions. At just a few days old, neonates who hear another neonate cry often begin crying themselves, a phenomenon called **emotional contagion** (Geangu et al., 2010). This response shows that they recognize and respond to the cry as a signal of distress (Gazzaniga, 2008). Furthermore, they are more likely to cry in response to the cry of a fellow neonate than in response to an older infant's cry, a chimpanzee's cry, or a recording of their own cry, showing that they are remarkably perceptive at discriminating among cries.

At first, infants are better at perceiving emotions by hearing than by seeing. Remember, their auditory system is more developed than their visual system in the early weeks of life. When shown faces in the early weeks, neonates tend to look mainly at the boundaries and edges rather than at the internal features that are most likely to express emotion, such as mouth and eyes. By 2–3 months old, infants' eyesight has improved substantially and they can begin to discriminate among happy, sad, and angry faces (Haan & Matheson, 2009; Hunnius et al., 2011). To test this, researchers often use a *habituation method*, in which infants are presented with the same photograph of the same facial expression repeatedly until they no longer show any interest—that is, they become habituated. Then, they are shown the same face with a different facial expression. If they look longer at the new facial expression, this is taken to indicate that they have noticed the difference.

Another interesting way of showing that infants perceive emotions is to show no emotion at all. By age 2–3 months, when parents interacting with their infants are told by researchers to show no emotion for a time, the infants respond with distress (Adamson & Frick, 2003; Tronick, 2007). This method, known as the *still-face paradigm*, shows that infants quickly learn to expect certain emotional reactions from others, especially others who are familiar and important to them (Mesman et al., 2009).

More generally, infants' responses to the still-face paradigm demonstrate that, from early on, emotions are experienced through relations with others rather than originating only within the individual (Tronick, 2007). In the early weeks of life, infants have smiles that are stimulated by internal states and cries that may be due to being hungry, tired, or cold, but infants soon learn to discern others' emotions and adjust their own emotions in response. By the time they are just 2–3 months old, when infants vocalize or smile, they expect the people they know and trust to respond in familiar ways, as they have in the past, which is why the still-face paradigm disturbs infants so much.

**Critical Thinking Question:** Do you see any potential relation between the present findings for the still-face paradigm and the findings described above on the facial expressions of infants whose mothers are depressed? Explain.

Another indicator of the development of emotional perception during the first year is in infants' abilities to match auditory and visual emotion. In studies on this topic, infants are shown two photographs with markedly different emotions, such as happiness and sadness. Then, a vocal recording is played, matching one of the facial emotions but not the other, and the infants' attention is monitored. By the time they are 7 months old, infants look more at the face that matches the emotion of the voice, showing that they expect the two to go together (Kahana-Kalman & Walker-Andrews, 2001; Soken & Pick, 1992).

**social referencing**
the ability to observe others' emotional responses to ambiguous and uncertain situations, and use that information to shape one's own emotional responses

Gradually, over the first year of life, infants become more adept at observing others' emotional responses to ambiguous and uncertain situations and using that information to shape their own emotional responses. Known as **social referencing**, this is an important way that infants learn about the world around them. In studies testing social referencing abilities, typically a mother and infant in a laboratory situation are given an unfamiliar toy to play with, and the mother is instructed to show positive or negative emotion in relation to the toy. Subsequently, the infant will generally play with the toy if the mother showed positive emotion toward it, but avoid it if the mother's emotion was negative. This response appears by the time infants are about 9–10 months old (Schmitow & Stenberg, 2013). One recent study proposed social referencing to be the basis of the development of a sense of humor, which also first develops in the second half of the first year of life (Mireault et al., 2014). When parents smiled or laughed at an unexpected event, infants did, too.

## Toddlerhood: Secondary Emotions and Self-Regulation

**LO 7.2.3 Describe how emotional development advances during toddlerhood, and identify the impact of culture on these changes.**

In toddlerhood, secondary emotions—including guilt, shame, envy, and pride—are added to the primary ones (Cummings et al., 2010). All toddlers have a capacity for developing these secondary emotions, as indicated by the fact that they appear across a wide range of cultures and are accompanied by characteristic body postures. For example, toddlers who experience shame often lower their eyes, bow their heads, and cover their faces with their hands (Barrett & Nelson-Goens, 1997).

What evokes the secondary emotions, however, depends on what toddlers have learned about culturally based standards of right and wrong (Brownell & Kopp, 2007; Mascolo & Fischer, 2007). This is why the secondary emotions also are called **sociomoral emotions**. When toddlers experience guilt or envy, it is not just because they have made the cognitive comparison between what they have done and what others have expected of them. It is also because they have begun to learn to feel good when they measure up to the expected standard and bad when they do not. Thus, by age 2, most toddlers have begun to develop a conscience, an internalized set of moral standards that guides their emotions and behaviors (Jensen, 2015; Kochanska, 2002; Thompson, 2006).

**sociomoral emotions**
emotions evoked based on learned, culturally based standards of right and wrong; also called secondary emotions

Another important sociomoral emotion that first develops in toddlerhood is **empathy**, the ability to understand and respond helpfully to another person's distress. Even neonates have an early form of empathy, as indicated by crying when they hear the cry of another infant. Throughout the first year, infants respond to the distress of others with distress of their own. However, true empathy requires an understanding of the self as separate from others, so it develops along with self-awareness in toddlerhood (Gopnik et al., 1999). It is only in the second and especially the third year that toddlers have enough of a developed self to understand the distress of others and respond, not by becoming distressed themselves but by helping other persons relieve their distress (Brownell et al., 2009). In one study, toddlers responded to a researcher's feigned distress by offering a hug, a comforting remark, or a favorite stuffed animal or blanket (Hoffman, 2000). This demonstrates the beginning of **prosocial behavior**, which is behavior intended to help or benefit others (Svetlova et al., 2010).

**empathy**
ability to understand and respond helpfully to another person's distress

**prosocial behavior**
positive behavior toward others, including kindness, friendliness, and sharing

Although the triggers of the sociomoral emotions are learned from the social environment, there are probably some that are universal. Children everywhere seem to be taught not to hurt the people around them and not to damage or destroy things (Rogoff, 2003). However, even in toddlerhood there are cultural differences in how sociomoral emotions are shaped. Cultural differences are especially sharp regarding the emotions of pride and shame, that is, in how good a person should feel about individual accomplishments and how quickly, easily, and often shame should be evoked. In Western countries, especially in the United States, pride is often viewed positively (Bellah et al., 1985; Twenge, 2006). Children are praised and encouraged to feel good about themselves for accomplishments such as hitting a ball, dancing in a show, or learning something new. Everybody on the soccer team gets a trophy, win or lose. Shame, in contrast, is applied with hesitation, as parents and others worry that shame may harm the development of children's self-esteem. (We will return to the topic of self-esteem later in this chapter.)

In most non-Western cultures, however, pride is seen as a greater danger than shame. In Japanese and Chinese cultures, for example, children are taught from early on not to call attention to themselves and not to display pride in response to personal success (Akimoto & Sanbonmatsu, 1999; Miller, 2014). For example, in one study of mothers' and 2½-year-olds' conversations about misbehavior in Taiwan and the United States, American mothers

In Western countries, especially in the United States, pride is often viewed positively.

tended to frame the misbehavior as an emotionally positive learning experience—"Now you know not to do that next time, don't you?"—in order to preserve their toddlers' self-esteem. In contrast, Taiwanese mothers cultivated shame in their toddlers by emphasizing the negative consequences and negative feelings of others that resulted from the misbehavior. When a toddler tipped over a bowl of pudding, the mother warned: "Don't be like this. I don't like you being like this. You still have to behave yourself." To the Taiwanese mothers, teaching their toddlers shame was a way of teaching them to be considerate of others, and a way of preparing them to grow up in a collectivistic culture that emphasizes the value of consideration for others (Miller et al., 1997).

Apart from the development of new emotions in toddlerhood, there is also considerable advancement in the self-regulation of emotions. In the early months of life, infants tend to show how they feel. Happy or sad, hungry or mad, they let you know. Gradually, during the first year, infants develop the rudiments of emotional self-regulation. They learn to turn their attention away from unpleasant stimulation (Axia et al., 1999). The people around them soothe their distress, for example, by smiling or cuddling. In many cultures, frequent breast-feeding is used as an emotional regulator to quiet babies whenever they begin to fuss (Gottlieb & DeLoache, 2017; LeVine & LeVine, 2016).

During toddlerhood, self-regulation advances in four ways (Kopp, 1989; Miller, 2014; Thompson & Goodvin, 2007).

1. Toddlers develop *behaviors* that can help them regulate their emotions. For example, toddlers who are frightened may look or run to a trusted adult or older sibling, or cling to a comforting blanket or stuffed animal.
2. Toddlers use *language* to promote self-regulation. From about 18 months old, toddlers begin to use words to identify and talk about their emotions. Throughout toddlerhood and beyond, talking about feelings with others enhances children's understanding of their own and others' emotions, which in turn promotes their self-regulation (Bugental & Grusec, 2006; Parke & Buriel, 2006).
3. *External requirements* by others extend toddlers' capacities for emotional self-regulation. In toddlerhood, parents convey and enforce rules that require self-regulation: no hitting others no matter how angry you are, no jumping on the table no matter how happy you are, and so on (Calkins, 2012). Cultures vary in their requirements for emotional self-regulation, with collectivistic cultures such as China and Japan tending toward more demanding requirements than the more individualistic cultures of the West (Bornstein, 2006; Laible, 2004; Shweder et al., 2006).
4. Self-regulation in toddlerhood is promoted by the development of the *sociomoral emotions* (Brownell & Kopp, 2007). Becoming capable of guilt, shame, and embarrassment motivates toddlers to avoid these unpleasant emotional states. Because they may be admonished by others for expressing primary emotions too strongly (e.g., yelling angrily in a grocery store) or in the wrong context (e.g., laughing loudly in a quiet restaurant), they learn emotional self-regulation as part of an effort to win approval from others and avoid their disapproval.

If emotional self-regulation increases from infancy to toddlerhood, why is toddlerhood associated with tantrums? Why is age 2 popularly known in some cultures as the "terrible twos"? Perhaps it is that for toddlers, abilities for self-regulation increase, but so do expectations for emotional control. Consequently, when they have the brief but intense outburst of anger, crying, and distress that constitutes a tantrum, it is more noticed than the more frequent outbursts of infants (Calkins, 2012). Perhaps it is also that toddlers have a more developed sense of self, including the ability to protest with a tantrum when they don't get their way (Grolnick et al., 2006).

There is a cultural explanation as well. It is interesting to observe that in Western countries, such as the United Kingdom and the United States, it is widely accepted that toddlerhood tantrums are normal and even inevitable (Potegal & Davidson, 2003). One popular American advice book for parents of toddlers asserts that "Tantrums are a fact of toddler life, a behavior that's virtually universal ... turning little cherubs into little monsters" (Murkoff et al., 2003, p. 336). Yet outside the West, toddler tantrums are rarely mentioned, and toddlerhood is not seen as an age of "terrible" behavior. In African and Asian cultures, by the time toddlerhood is reached, children have already learned that they are expected to control their emotions and their behavior, and they exercise the control required of them (Holodynski, 2009; Miller, 2014; Miller et al., 2012). It appears that tantrums and the allegedly terrible twos are not "universal" after all, but a consequence of Western cultural beliefs in the value of self-expression, which children have already learned well by toddlerhood.

## Autism Spectrum Disorder

**LO 7.2.4 Identify the characteristics of Autism Spectrum Disorder and how it affects children's prospects as they grow to adulthood.**

In 1938, a well-known child psychiatrist received a visit from parents concerned about their little boy, Donald (Donovan & Zucker, 2010). According to the parents, even as a baby Donald had displayed "no apparent affection" (p. 85) for his parents, and still did not. He never cried when separated from them or wished to be comforted by them. Nor did he seem interested in other adults or children, appearing to "live within himself" (p. 85) with no need for social relations. Furthermore, Donald's use of language was peculiar. He was often unresponsive to his parents' instructions and requests and did not even react to his own name. Yet certain unusual words captivated him and he would repeat them over and over again: trumpet vine, business, chrysanthemum. He enjoyed repetition not only of words, but also of behaviors, such as spinning round objects.

**Autism Spectrum Disorder**

involves persistent deficits in social communication and interactions across contexts, as well as repetitive and restricted behavior

This description was the basis of the initial diagnosis of what is now known as **Autism Spectrum Disorder** (ASD), and the main features of the diagnosis are the same today as they were for Donald: (1) Persistent deficits in social communication and interactions across contexts, including lack of social-emotional reciprocity and understanding, and (2) repetitive and restricted behavior, such as insistence on predictable routines (American Psychiatric Association, 2013). Some children also have exceptional, isolated mental skills—Donald, for example, could multiply large numbers instantly in his head—but this is rare. The majority of children with ASD are low in intelligence and exhibit some degree of intellectual disability (Lord & Bishop, 2010). ASD may occur with or without language impairment.

Toddlers with ASD have deficits in their social and behavioral development. Here, a boy plays alone at a school for children with ASD in Beijing, China.

In the United States, 1 in 68 children fit the diagnostic criteria for ASD (Centers for Disease Control and Prevention [CDC], 2017). These rates are consistent across Asia, Europe, and North America, with some variation based on the diagnostic criteria used (CDC, 2017).

The origins of the disorder are unclear. It is believed to have a genetic basis, as evidence of abnormal brain development is present in the unusually large brains of children who will later develop ASD (Hadjikhani et al., 2004). The amygdala, especially, is abnormally large in toddlers with ASD (Schumann et al., 2009). Various environmental causes for ASD have been proposed, including dietary contributors and toddlerhood vaccines. Research has not supported

**Watch** AGAINST ODDS: CHILDREN WITH ASD

any role of diet or vaccines. However, a longitudinal study of almost 2,000 children followed from conception found that the risk of ASD rose in parallel with prenatal exposure to pollution. The association between ASD and pollution was stronger during the third trimester than during the first two trimesters (Raz et al., 2014).

Rates of ASD have increased in recent decades in developed countries, but there is no consensus on the reasons for the increase (CDC, 2017). It may be that disorders once diagnosed as schizophrenia or mental retardation are now diagnosed as ASD due to increased awareness of the disorder (Donovan & Zucker, 2010). Physicians in many countries now routinely screen toddlers for the disorder, whereas they did not in the past (CDC, 2017).

Usually the diagnosis of ASD is made during toddlerhood, between 18 and 30 months of age (American Psychiatric Association, 2013). However, studies analyzing home videos of infants later diagnosed with ASD indicate that signs of the disorder are already present in infancy (Dawson et al., 1998; Werner et al., 2000). Even at 8 to 10 months old, these infants show little or no evidence of normal social behaviors. They do not engage in joint attention with parents, or point to objects to show to others, or look at others, or respond to their own name. During infancy some of this behavior could be attributed to differences in temperament, but the diagnosis of ASD becomes more definite in toddlerhood.

What happens to children with ASD when they grow up? In the United States, 85% continue to live with parents, siblings, or other relatives (Donovan & Zucker, 2010). Some live in government-sponsored group homes, and in rare cases they are able to function at a high enough level to live alone, as Donald (now in his 70s) does. In some ways, ASD becomes more problematic in adulthood than in childhood, because the adults often lack emotional self-regulation as children with ASD do, but are bigger and can cause more disruption. They also develop sexual desires, without an understanding of the appropriate emotional and behavioral expression of those desires. There is no cure for ASD and few effective treatments, but with substantial help, many children and adults with ASD can learn some skills for daily living, such as wearing clean clothes, asking for directions (and then following them), and keeping track of money. Research shows that early intervention can improve the functioning of a child with ASD (CDC, 2015), making assessment in toddlerhood all the more important For more information, watch the video *Against Odds: Children With ASD.*

## Childhood: Self-Regulation and Contentment

**LO 7.2.5 Explain why self-regulation continues to improve in middle childhood.**

In the course of childhood, self-regulation of emotions continues to improve. Developing self-regulation is crucial to social relations because maintaining harmonious social relations often requires us to restrain our immediate impulses—to wait in line, to let others go first in a game or a conversation, or to take fewer pieces of candy than we really want. From ages 2 to 6, extremes of emotional expression such as temper tantrums, crying, and physical aggression decrease (Alink et al., 2006; Carlson, 2003; Carlson et al., 2013). By ages 7 to 10, during middle childhood, such outbursts become quite rare (Shipman et al., 2003).

In the brain, the development of the frontal cortex is linked to better self-regulation (Bell & Wolfe, 2007). The frontal lobes grow faster than the rest of the cerebral cortex during early childhood (Anderson & Jacobs, 2008; Markant & Thomas, 2013). Growth in the frontal lobes underlies the advances in emotional regulation, foresight, and planned behavior that take place during the preschool years (Carlson et al., 2013; Diamond, 2004).

Across cultures, early and middle childhood is also a time when demands for self-regulation increase (Geldhof et al., 2010; Whiting & Edwards, 1988). Beyond toddlerhood, children often move into new contexts: preschool followed by primary school, civic organizations (such as the Boy Scouts and Girl Scouts), sports teams, and music groups. All of these contexts require self-regulation and consideration of others. Children are expected to do what they are told (whether they feel like it or not), to wait their turn, and to cooperate with others. Expressions of emotional extremes are disruptive to the functioning of the group and are discouraged. Most children are capable of meeting these demands by middle childhood.

Another key reason why self-regulation increases is that children learn strategies for regulating their emotions (Grolnick et al., 2006). Experimental studies have identified the strategies that young children use when presented with an emotionally challenging situation, such as being given a disappointing prize after being led to expect a very attractive prize (Eisenberg & Fabes, 2006). Some of the most effective strategies are leaving the situation; talking to themselves; redirecting their attention to a different activity; and seeking comfort from an attachment figure. With age, children also learn how to conceal their emotions intentionally (Saarni, 1999). This allows them to show a socially acceptable emotion such as gratitude when, for example, they open a birthday present they didn't really want. In other words, children learn **emotion display rules**, the social norms for when, where, how, and to whom to express emotions (Saarni, 1999). In Asian cultures, children in middle childhood learn the concept of "face," which means showing to others the appropriate and expected emotion regardless of how you actually feel (Han, 2011). These strategies are part of what researchers call *effortful control*, when children focus their attention on managing their emotions (Cipriano & Stifter, 2010).

By middle childhood, most children cooperate peacefully with others and avoid emotional outbursts.

Effortful control is enhanced by understanding not only one's own emotions, but also others' emotions and perspective (Eisenberg & Fabes, 2006). In studies that show children cards depicting expressed emotions, by age 5 children are usually accurate in explaining the emotions of the situation (e.g., "She's happy because she got a present," or "He's sad because his mom scolded him"). They are also adept at understanding how emotional states are the basis of subsequent actions; for example, an angry child is more likely to hit someone (Kagan & Herschkowitz, 2005). Children's understanding of others' emotions is also reflected in increased capacity for empathy (Goldstein & Winner, 2012; Hoffman, 2000). By middle childhood, children also become better cognitively at perspective-taking, including the understanding that other people may display emotional expressions that do not indicate what they actually feel (Saarni, 1999).

**emotion display rules**
the social norms for when, where, how, and to whom to express emotions

Children vary in their success at achieving effortful control in childhood, depending both on their temperament and on the socialization provided by parents and others. Parents can help children develop effortful control by providing emotional and physical comfort when their children are upset, by suggesting possible strategies for managing emotions, and by modeling effortful control themselves (Katz & Windecker-Nelson, 2004).

Children who have problems of **undercontrol** have inadequately developed emotional self-regulation. These children are at risk for **externalizing problems**, such as aggression and conflict with others, in early childhood and beyond (Eisenberg et al., 2010). However, developing **overcontrol**, an excessive degree of self-regulation of emotions, is also problematic. This can lead to **internalizing problems**, such as anxiety and depression, in early childhood and beyond (Grolnick et al., 2006). Throughout life, internalizing problems are more common among females and externalizing problems are more common among males (Frick & Kimonis, 2008; Ollendick et al., 2008).

**undercontrol**
trait of having inadequate emotional self-regulation

**externalizing problems**
problems that involve others, such as aggression

**overcontrol**
trait of having excessive self-regulation of emotions

**internalizing problems**
problems that entail turning distress inward, toward the self, such as depression and anxiety

Successful self-regulation means developing a level of effortful control that is between the two extremes. However, different cultures have different views of what the optimal level of emotional control is (Chen et al., 2007). Behavior that looks like undercontrol in one culture could be valued as a healthy expression of assertiveness in another culture (LeVine & LeVine, 2016). Behavior that looks like overcontrol in one culture could be valued as the virtue of reticence in another culture (Chen, 2011; Rogoff, 2003).

By middle childhood, children have generally attained emotional self-regulation and most days are free of any negative emotional extremes. Middle childhood, in fact, is a time of remarkable contentment (Larson & Richards, 1994). At this age, children frequently report being "happy." Sure, they are sad or angry occasionally, but it is almost always due to something concrete and immediate such as getting scolded by a parent or losing a game, "events that pass quickly and are forgotten" (Larson & Richards, 1994, p. 85). With the entry into adolescence, that is about to change—at least in some cultures.

## Adolescence: Emotional Storm and Stress?

**LO 7.2.6 Summarize the results of the Experience Sampling Method studies with respect to adolescent emotionality.**

One of the most ancient and enduring observations of adolescence is that it is a time of heightened emotions (Arnett, 1999). Over 2,000 years ago, the Greek philosopher Aristotle observed that youth "are heated by Nature as drunken men by wine." About 250 years ago, the French philosopher Jean-Jacques Rousseau made a similar observation: "As the roaring of the waves precedes the tempest, so the murmur of rising passions announces the tumultuous change" of puberty and adolescence. Around the same time that Rousseau was writing, a type of German literature was developing that became known as *"sturm und drang"* literature—German for "storm and stress." In these stories, young people in their teens and early 20s experienced extreme emotions of angst, sadness, and romantic passion. As we saw in Chapter 1, early developmental psychologists such as G. Stanley Hall and Anna Freud also subscribed to the idea of emotional storm and stress in adolescence.

What does contemporary research tell us about the validity of these historical and popular views of adolescent emotionality? Probably the best source of data on this question is research using the Experience Sampling Method (ESM), which involves beeping people randomly during the day so that they can record their feelings, thoughts, and behavior. Each time they are beeped, participants rate the degree to which they currently feel happy to unhappy, cheerful to irritable, and friendly to angry, as well as how hurried, tired, and competitive they are feeling (Csikszentmihalyi & Larson, 1984; Larson & Csikszentmihalyi, 2014; Schneider, 2006). ESM studies have been conducted with participants in middle childhood, adolescence, and adulthood, so if we compare the patterns of emotions reported by the different groups, we can get a good sense of whether adolescence is a stage of more extremes of emotions.

The results indicate that adolescence in the United States is often a time of emotional volatility (Larson & Csikszentmihalyi, 2014; Larson et al., 1980; Larson & Richards, 1994). American adolescents report feeling "self-conscious" and "embarrassed" two to three times more often than their parents and are also more likely than their parents to feel awkward, lonely, nervous, and ignored. Adolescents are also moodier when compared to younger children. Comparing preadolescent fifth graders to adolescent eighth graders, Reed Larson and Maryse Richards (1994) describe the emotional "fall from grace" that occurs during that time, as the proportion of time experienced as "very happy" declines by 50%, and similar declines take place in reports of feeling "great," "proud," and "in control." The result is an overall deflation of childhood happiness as childhood ends and adolescence begins.

There is an emotional "fall from grace" from middle childhood into adolescence. Adolescents more often feel embarrassed, moody, or ignored.

How do emotional states change during the course of adolescence? Larson and Richards assessed their original ESM sample of 5th to 8th graders 4 years later, in 9th to 12th grades (Larson et al., 2002). As Figure 7.2 shows, they found that emotional states became steadily more negative with age.

What about other cultures? Is adolescent emotionality a uniquely American phenomenon, or does it take place in other cultures as well? There is somewhat limited evidence to answer this question. However, one study used ESM with adolescents and their parents in a city in urban India (Verma & Larson, 1999). The results indicated that, as in the United States, adolescents reported more extremes of emotion than their parents did. Some ethnographies from traditional cultures also describe adolescence as a time of mood disruptions (e.g., Davis & Davis, 1989).

Not all cultures experience the same levels of adolescent emotionality, however, and some evidently do not experience it at all. An analysis of adolescence in 186 traditional cultures worldwide (Schlegel & Barry, 1991, 2015) reported that most traditional cultures experience less emotional upheaval among adolescents compared to the West. A key difference between traditional cultures and the West is the degree of independence allowed by adults and expected by adolescents. In the majority cultures of the West, because of cultural values of individualism, it is taken for granted that adolescents should become independent from their parents during the course of adolescence (Jensen & Dost-Gözkan, 2015). Differences of opinion over the proper pace of this process are a source of conflict between adolescents and their parents, and contribute both to parents' perception of adolescence as difficult and to negative emotions on the part of adolescents. In contrast, independence for adolescents is less likely to be expected by adolescents and their parents in traditional cultures, so it is less likely to be a source of adolescent storm and stress (Kagitçibasi & Yalin, 2015).

**Figure 7.2** Change in Emotional States During Adolescence

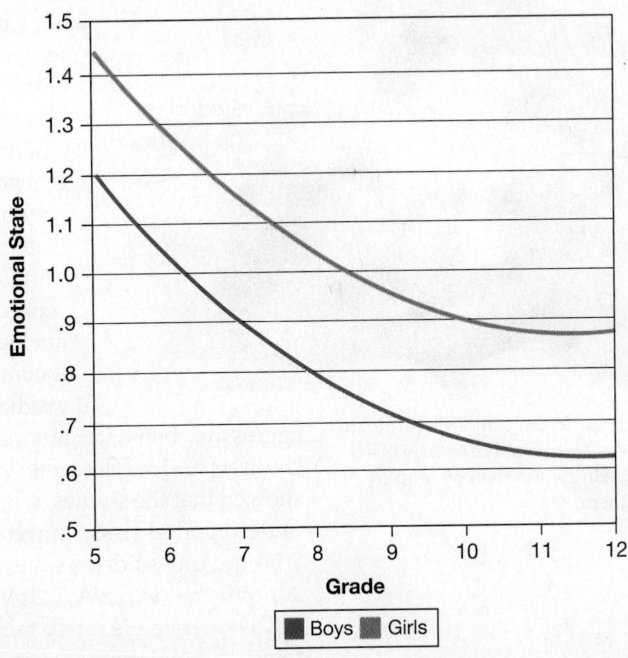


SOURCE: Based on Larson et al. (2002).

## Depression and Suicide in Adolescence and Emerging Adulthood

**LO 7.2.7 Identify the different types and rates of adolescent depression, and summarize the most effective treatments for depression and suicide ideation.**

Do you remember feeling sad at times during your teen years? As we have seen, many adolescents experience sadness and other negative emotions much more frequently than younger children or adults do. Psychologists make distinctions between different levels of depression. **Depressed mood** is a term for a temporary period of sadness, without any related symptoms. The most serious form of depression is **major depressive disorder** (MDD), which includes a more enduring period of sadness along with other symptoms such as frequent crying, fatigue, feelings of worthlessness, and feeling guilty, lonely, or worried. MDD may also include symptoms such as difficulty sleeping and changes in appetite (American Psychiatric Association [APA], 2013).

**depressed mood**
temporary period of sadness, without any other related symptoms of depression

**major depressive disorder**
clinical diagnosis pertaining to enduring period of sadness along with other symptoms such as frequent crying, fatigue, and feelings of worthlessness

Rates of MDD among adolescents range in various studies from 3% to 7% (Cheung et al., 2005; Thapar et al., 2012), which are fairly similar to the rates found in studies of adults (Kessler & Bromet, 2013). However, rates of depressed mood are substantially higher. For example, one longitudinal study found that the rate of depressed mood for Dutch adolescents at age 11 was 27% for girls and 21% for boys, rising by age 19 to 37% for girls and 23% for boys (Bennik et al., 2013). The most frequent causes of depressed mood tend to be common experiences among adolescents: conflict with family members or friends, disappointment or rejection in love, and poor performance in school (Costello et al., 2008; Larson & Richards, 1994).

**Critical Thinking Question:** Why do you think rates of depressed mood (and MDD) are higher among girls than boys?

One of the strongest risk factors for all types of depression in adolescence and beyond is being female (Thapar et al., 2012). A variety of explanations have been proposed. Some scholars have suggested that body image concerns provoke depression. There is substantial evidence that adolescent girls who have a poor body image are more likely than other girls to be depressed (Marcotte et al., 2002; Wichstrøm, 1999). Also, when faced with the beginning of a depressed mood, boys (and men) are more likely to distract themselves (and forget about it), whereas girls (and women) have a greater tendency to **ruminate** on their depressed feelings and thereby amplify them (Jose & Brown, 2008; Nolen-Hoeksema et al., 2008). Adolescent girls are also more likely than adolescent boys to devote their thoughts and feelings to their personal relationships, and these relationships can be a source of distress and sadness (Bakker et al., 2010; Conway et al., 2011).

**ruminate**
to think persistently about bad feelings and experiences

Some adolescent girls ruminate on their negative or depressed feelings and thereby amplify them.

For adolescents, as for adults, the two main types of treatment for depression are antidepressant medications and psychotherapy. Antidepressants such as Prozac are highly effective in treating adolescent depression (Bostic et al., 2005; Brent, 2004; Cohen et al., 2004; Thapar et al., 2012). A combination of medication and psychotherapy appears to be the most effective approach to treating adolescent depression. In one major study of 12- to 17-year-olds who had been diagnosed with MDD at 13 sites across the United States, 71% of the adolescents who received both Prozac and psychotherapy experienced an improvement in their symptoms (Treatment for Adolescents with Depression Study Team, 2004, 2007). Improvement rates for the other groups were 61% for Prozac alone, 43% for psychotherapy alone, and 35% for the placebo group. However, some research has raised concerns that use of antidepressants is associated with serious risks, including suicidal thoughts and behavior (Bridge et al., 2007). Findings documenting these risks have been mixed, but a recent review of 70 studies found a considerably higher risk of suicidal thoughts and aggressive behavior among children and adolescents treated with antidepressants than children and adolescents who received a placebo (Sharma et al., 2016). The review also showed that the studies, which were typically carried out by pharmaceutical companies, often underreported risks. Currently it is advised that children, adolescents, and emerging adults who are on antidepressant medications should be monitored closely (U.S. Food and Drug Administration [FDA], 2014; Thapar et al., 2012).

Depression is a risk factor for suicide. Suicide attempts are usually preceded by symptoms of depression (Asarnow et al., 2011; Pfeffer, 2006). However, young people's suicide attempts often occur as the symptoms of depression appear to be abating. At the depths of depression, young people are often too dispirited to engage in the planning required to commit suicide. As they improve slightly, they remain depressed, but now have enough energy and motivation to make a suicide attempt. Making a plan to commit suicide may also raise the mood of deeply depressed young people because they may believe suicide will mean an end to all the problems they feel are plaguing them.

Among American adolescents in grades 9 to 12 during 2013, 17% reported seriously considering suicide in the course of the previous 12 months (Kann et al., 2014). Furthermore, 3% had made a suicide attempt that required medical intervention. Suicide is the third most common cause of death among American teens ages 15 to 19, after automobile accidents and homicide (CDC, 2015). The current suicide rate among American teens is *four times* the suicide rate among teens in the 1950s (Oltmanns & Emery, 2010). The reason for this increase is not well understood. The suicide rate among emerging adults ages 20 to 24 also increased during this time and is nearly twice as high as among 15- to 19-year-olds (CDC, 2007; Suicide Awareness Voices of Education, 2016). Rates of suicide among young people are substantially higher in Canada, Japan, and the United States than in most other developed countries, as Figure 7.3 illustrates.

**Figure 7.3** Suicide Deaths Among 15- to 19-Year-Olds

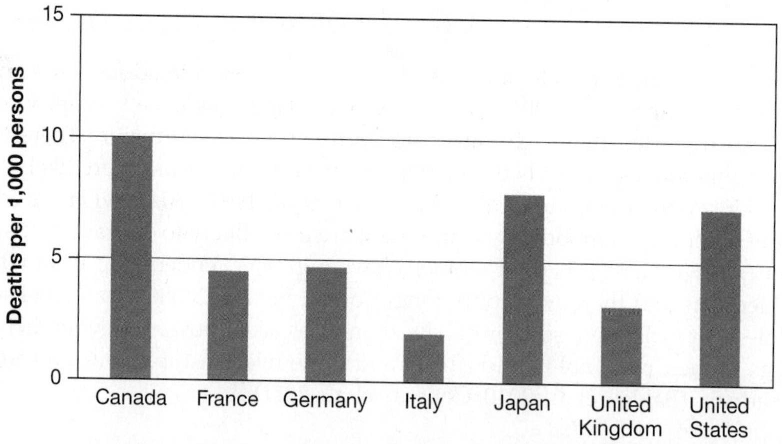

There are substantial ethnic differences in suicide rates. Rates of suicide in adolescence and emerging adulthood are higher among Whites than among Blacks and Latinos, and highest of all among Native Americans (CDC, 2015; Colucci & Martin, 2007). However, suicide rates rose alarmingly among young Black males in the 1990s and now nearly equal the rates for young White males (Balis & Postolache, 2008). The reasons for this increase are not known.

Sharp gender differences also exist in rates of suicide and suicide attempts. Females are about four times as likely as males to attempt suicide in adolescence and emerging adulthood, but males are about four times as likely as females actually to kill themselves (Oltmanns & Emery, 2010). These gender differences exist in adulthood as well. The higher rate of attempts among females is probably a consequence of their higher rates of depression (Langhinrichsen-Rohling et al., 2009). The reason for the higher rate of completed suicides among males seems mainly due to gender differences in the methods used. Males are more likely to use guns or hang themselves—far more deadly methods than the ingestion of poison or pills that is more common of female suicide attempts (CDC, 2007, 2017). In a study comparing suicide rates among young people in 34 countries (Johnson et al., 2000), rates were highest in countries where guns were most easily available.

Other than depression, what are the risk factors for suicide? One major factor for adolescents is *family disruption*. Across cultures, attempted and completed suicide has frequently been found to be related to a family life that is chaotic, disorganized, high in conflict, and low in warmth (Brent & Mann, 2006; Kuhlberg et al., 2010; Lee et al., 2006). Furthermore, an adolescent's suicide is often preceded by a period of months in which family problems have worsened (Brent, 2007). Adoption and twin studies indicate that families also contribute genetic vulnerability to suicide, via susceptibility to major depression and other mental illnesses (Brent & Mann, 2006).

In addition to family risk factors, suicidal adolescents often have substance abuse problems (Wong et al., 2013), perhaps as an attempt at self-medication for distress over family problems and depression. Also, suicidal adolescents have usually experienced problems in their relationships outside the family. Because they often come from families where they receive little in the way of emotional nurturance, suicidal adolescents may be more vulnerable to the effects of experiences such as school failure, loss of a boyfriend or girlfriend, or feelings of being rejected by peers (Herba et al., 2008).

Nevertheless, most adolescents who experience family disruption or substance use problems never attempt or commit suicide (Brent & Mann, 2006). In almost all cases, adolescent suicide takes place not in response to a single stressful or painful event, but only after a series of difficulties extending over months or even years (Asarnow et al., 2011). It is rare for suicidal adolescents to show no warning signs of emotional or behavioral problems prior to attempting suicide. Often, they have made efforts to address the problems in their lives, and the failure of these efforts has sent them on a downward spiral that deepened their hopelessness and led them to suicide. Table 7.2 identifies early warning signs

**Table 7.2** Early Warning Signs of Adolescent Suicide

| | |
|---|---|
| 1. | Direct suicide threats or comments such as "I wish I were dead"; "My family would be better off without me." |
| 2. | A previous suicide attempt, no matter how minor. Four out of five people who commit suicide have made at least one previous attempt. |
| 3. | Preoccupation with death in music, art, and personal writing. |
| 4. | Loss of a family member, pet, or boy/girlfriend. |
| 5. | Family disruptions such as unemployment, serious illness, relocation, or divorce. |
| 6. | Disturbances in sleeping and eating habits and in personal hygiene. |
| 7. | Declining grades and lack of interest in school or leisure activities that had previously been important. |
| 8. | Drastic changes in behavior patterns, such as a quiet, shy person becoming extremely gregarious. |
| 9. | Pervasive sense of gloom, helplessness, and hopelessness. |
| 10. | Withdrawal from family members and friends and feelings of alienation from significant others. |
| 11. | Giving away prized possessions and otherwise "getting my affairs in order." |
| 12. | Series of "accidents" or impulsive, risk-taking behaviors, for example, drug or alcohol abuse, disregard for personal safety, taking dangerous dares. |

SOURCES: Brent & Melhem (2007); Pfeffer (2006).

of adolescent suicide. As with MDD, the most effective treatments for suicidal adolescents combine antidepressant medications with psychotherapy (Donaldson et al., 2003; Emslie et al., 2002).

## SUMMARY: Emotions

### LO 7.2.1 Review the key features of the evolutionary, differentiation, functionalist, and internalization theories of emotional development.

Evolutionary theories emphasize that all humans share discrete emotions that are innate and present at birth. Differentiation theories agree that humans have discrete emotions, but note that several of these emotions only develop gradually rather than being present at birth. Functionalist theories emphasize how emotions serve social functions by signaling desired goals both to self and others. Internalization theories highlight that children's emotion expression and the way they regulate their emotions are guided by adults and cultural norms.

### LO 7.2.2 Describe the development of primary emotions and emotion perception in infants.

From the early weeks of life, infants experience three primary emotions: distress, interest, and pleasure. Gradually, over the course of the next year, these emotions develop into other primary emotions: anger, sadness, fear, surprise, happiness, and disgust. From the first days of life, infants also perceive others' emotions, responding with distress to the distress of others. Toward the end of the first year, in a process called social referencing, infants draw emotional cues from how others respond to ambiguous situations.

### LO 7.2.3 Describe how emotional development advances during toddlerhood, and identify the impact of culture on these changes.

Sociomoral emotions that develop in toddlerhood include guilt, shame, envy, pride, and empathy. They are called sociomoral emotions because they indicate that toddlers have begun to learn the moral standards of their culture. Toddlers in Western cultures have occasional tantrums, perhaps because they have a more developed sense of intentionality than infants do and so are more likely to protest when thwarted. However, tantrums are rare outside the West where cultures de-emphasize self-expression.

### LO 7.2.4 Identify the characteristics of Autism Spectrum Disorder and how it affects children's prospects as they grow to adulthood.

Autism Spectrum Disorder (ASD) is a developmental disorder marked by persistent deficits in social communication and interactions across contexts, and by repetitive and restricted behavior. A small minority of children with ASD have exceptional, isolated mental skills. Adults with ASD often live with family or in government-sponsored homes. Research shows that early intervention can improve the functioning of a child with ASD, making assessment in toddlerhood all the more important.

### LO 7.2.5 Explain why self-regulation continues to improve in middle childhood.

From ages 2 to 6, extremes of emotional expression such as temper tantrums, crying, and physical aggression decrease. By ages 7 to 10, during middle childhood, such outbursts become quite rare. Improved self-regulation is linked to the development of the frontal cortex. Across cultures, early and middle childhood is also a time when demands for self-regulation increase. Another key reason why self-regulation increases is that children learn strategies for regulating their emotions.

### LO 7.2.6 Summarize the results of the Experience Sampling Method studies with respect to adolescent emotionality.

Experience Sampling Method (ESM) studies show greater mood swings in adolescence than in middle childhood or adulthood. Also, emotional states became steadily more negative from 5th grade through 12th grade.

**LO 7.2.7 Identify the different types and rates of adolescent depression, and summarize the most effective treatments for depression and suicide ideation.**

Depressed mood involves a temporary period of sadness. Major depressive disorder (MDD) describes a more enduring period of sadness along with other symptoms such as frequent fatigue and feelings of worthlessness. Among adolescents, rates of depressed mood are approximately in the 20% to 35% range. MDD rates among adolescents range from about 3% to 7%. For adolescents, as for adults, the two main types of treatment for MDD and suicide ideation are antidepressant medications and psychotherapy. Research has raised concerns that use of antidepressants is associated with suicidal thoughts and behavior in adolescents.

# 7.3 Self-Conceptualization

As we have seen, the development of emotions is intertwined with the development of a sense of self. For example, sociomoral emotions such as pride and shame entail an evaluation of the self. Self-regulation involves a conscious management of one's emotions, including how one comes across to other people. Depression often goes together with a belief that aspects of the self are inadequate and, in the extreme, that the self as a whole is unworthy. For a long time, developmental psychologists have been interested in self-conceptualization. When do we know that the self is distinct from the external environment and from other people? How do we view and evaluate ourselves over the course of childhood?

## Infancy and Toddlerhood: The Birth of Self

**LO 7.3.1 Describe the emergence of self-recognition and self-reflection in infancy and toddlerhood.**

Even in the early weeks of life there is evidence that infants have the beginnings of a sense of self, a sense of being distinct from the objects and people around them. Infants recognize the smell of their mother's breast and the sound of her voice after just a few days of life, indicating an awareness of a difference between their own smells and sounds and those of others. In the first month, infants display a stronger rooting reflex in response to another person touching their cheek than in response to their own hand performing the same movement (Rochat & Hespos, 1997).

After a month or two, infants begin responding in interactions with others by smiling, moving, and vocalizing, thus showing an awareness of themselves and others as distinct social partners. Infants also expect others to behave in certain ways when they smile, move, and vocalize. For example, as we saw earlier in this chapter, infants become distressed in the still-face paradigm when someone does not respond to them but simply maintains a frozen facial expression. By 2 months, then, infants already have a sense of their own agency in relation to other people (Rochat, 2013). By the middle of the first year they also recognize and respond to their own name when others speak it, indicating the beginning of a name-based identity.

Around 9 months, infants start to engage with people in regard to the things that surround them (Rochat, 2013)—a milestone that some researchers have referred to as the "9-month miracle" (Tomasello, 1995). Now the focus is not just on the relationship between social partners, but increasingly on surrounding objects. For example, infants start pointing to objects. They engage in joint attention, following the gaze of someone else to see what they are looking at. By the time they turn 1, infants also search for hidden objects, and examine objects and put them in their mouths, all behaviors showing an awareness of the distinction between themselves and the external world (Harter, 2006; Thompson, 2006).

By the second half of their second year, toddlers show self-recognition and some self-reflection.

Although self-awareness begins to develop during infancy, it advances in important ways during toddlerhood. It is during the second and third years of life that

**self-recognition**
ability to recognize one's image in the mirror as one's self

**self-reflection**
capacity to think about one's self as one would think about other persons and objects

**self-concept**
person's view and evaluation of her- or himself

**social comparison**
how persons view themselves in relation to others with regard to status, abilities, or achievements

children first demonstrate **self-recognition**. This was demonstrated in a classic experiment in which toddlers were secretly dabbed on the nose with a red spot, then placed in front of a mirror (Lewis & Brooks-Gunn, 1979). Upon seeing the child with the red nose in the mirror, 9- and 12-month-old infants would reach out to touch the reflection as if it were someone else, but by 18 months most toddlers rubbed their own nose, recognizing the image as themselves.

Around the same time self-recognition first appears (as indicated in the red-nose test) toddlers also begin to use personal pronouns for the first time ("I," "me," "mine"), and they begin to refer to themselves by their own names (Lewis & Ramsay, 2004; Pipp et al., 1987). These developments show that by the second half of their second year, toddlers have the beginnings of **self-reflection**, or the capacity to think about themselves as they would think about other persons and objects.

Self-reflection enables toddlers to develop the sociomoral emotions. As toddlers become more self-aware, they learn that the people in their cultural environment have expectations for how to behave. They learn to feel negative emotions, such as embarrassment, when they do something defined as bad or wrong. They also learn to feel positive emotions, such as pride, when they do something good. In the course of toddlerhood, then, the self becomes an object of both reflection and evaluation.

## Early and Middle Childhood: The Self in the Present

**LO 7.3.2 Explain how the self-concept changes from early childhood through middle childhood.**

In middle childhood, children become more accurate in comparing themselves to others.

Our **self-concept**, that is, how we view and evaluate ourselves, changes during early and middle childhood from the external to the internal and from the physical to the psychological (Lerner et al., 2005; Marsh & Ayotte, 2003; Rosenberg, 1979). Up until the age of 7 or 8, most children describe themselves mainly in terms of external, concrete, physical characteristics. ("My name is Mona. I'm 7 years old. I have brown eyes and short black hair. I have two little brothers.") They may mention specific possessions ("I have a red bicycle.") and activities they enjoy ("I like to dance." "I like to play sports."). Three- to 4 year-olds tend to home in on relatively few of these concrete and observable characteristics, whereas 5- to 7-year-olds will speak of multiple characteristics, as in the case of 7-year-old Mona (Harter, 1999).

In the course of middle childhood, children add more internal, psychological, personality-related traits to their self-descriptions ("I'm shy." "I'm friendly." "I try to be helpful."). They may also mention characteristics that are *not me* ("I don't like drawing." "I'm not very good at jump-roping."). Toward the end of middle childhood their descriptions become more complex, as they recognize that they may be different on different occasions (Harter, 2003) ("Mostly I'm easy to get along with, but sometimes I lose my temper when I play soccer.").

Another important change in self-concept in middle childhood is that children engage in more accurate **social comparison**, in which they compare themselves to others (Guest, 2007). A 6-year-old might say, "I'm really good at math," whereas a 9-year-old might say, "I'm better than most kids at math, although there are a couple of kids in my class who are a little better." These social comparisons reflect advances in the cognitive ability of *seriation* (see Chapter 5). In the same way that children learn how to arrange sticks accurately from shortest to tallest in middle childhood, they also learn to rank themselves more accurately in abilities relative to other children. The age grading of schools also promotes social comparisons, as it places children in a setting where they spend most of a typical day around other children their age. Teachers compare them to one another by giving them grades, and they notice who is relatively good and not so good at reading, math, and so on.

## Adolescence: Possible Selves

**LO 7.3.3 Describe the complex self-conceptions that develop in adolescence.**

Adolescents are most likely to use a false self with dating partners.

Due to advances in cognitive development, self-conceptions in adolescence become more complex and more abstract. One aspect of the complexity of adolescents' self-conceptions is that they can distinguish between an **actual self** and **possible selves** (Markus & Nurius, 1986; Oyserman et al., 2015). The actual self is your self-conception, and possible selves are the different people you imagine you could become in the future depending on your choices and experiences. Scholars distinguish between two kinds of possible selves: an ideal self and a feared self (Chalk et al., 2005). The **ideal self** is the person the adolescent would like to be (for example, an adolescent may have an ideal of becoming highly popular with peers or highly successful in athletics or music). The **feared self** is the person the adolescent dreads becoming (for example, an adolescent might fear becoming an alcoholic or fear becoming like a disgraced relative). Both kinds of possible selves require adolescents to think abstractly. That is, possible selves exist only as abstractions, as *ideas* in the adolescent's mind.

The capacity for thinking about an actual, an ideal, and a feared self is a cognitive achievement, but this capacity may be troubling in some respects. If you can imagine an ideal self, you can also become aware of the discrepancy between your actual self and your ideal self—between what you are and what you wish you were. If the discrepancy is large enough, it can result in feelings of failure, inadequacy, and depression. Studies have found that the size of the discrepancy between the actual and ideal self is related to depressed mood in both adolescents and emerging adults (Moretti & Wiebe, 1999; Papadakis et al., 2006). Furthermore, the discrepancy between the actual and the ideal self is greater in mid-adolescence than in either early or late adolescence (Ferguson et al., 2010). This helps explain why rates of depressed mood rise from early adolescence to mid-adolescence.

One aspect related to the increasing complexity of self-conceptions is that adolescents become aware of times when they are exhibiting a **false self**, which is a self they present to others that does not represent what they are actually thinking and feeling (Harter et al., 1997; Weir & Jose, 2010). Research indicates that adolescents are most likely to put on their false selves with potential romantic partners and least likely with their close friends; parents are in between (Harter, 2006; Sippola et al., 2007). Most adolescents indicate that they sometimes dislike putting on a false self, but many also say that some degree of false self behavior is acceptable and even desirable, to impress someone or to conceal aspects of the self they do not want others to see. In recent years, Facebook and other social media have become places where adolescents can construct a false self (Michikyan et al., 2014).

**actual self**
person's perception of the self as it is, contrasted with the possible self

**possible self**
person's conceptions of the self as it potentially could be; may include both an ideal self and a feared self

**ideal self**
person one would like to be

**feared self**
person one imagines it is possible to become but dreads becoming

**false self**
self a person may present to others while realizing that it does not represent what he or she is actually thinking and feeling


## SUMMARY: Self-Conceptualization

**LO 7.3.1 Describe the emergence of self-recognition and self-reflection in infancy and toddlerhood.**

Even in the early weeks of life there is evidence that infants have the beginnings of a sense of self, a sense of being distinct from the objects and people around them. By 18 months, most toddlers demonstrate self-recognition. By this age, they also develop the beginnings of self-reflection, that is, the capacity to think about themselves as they would think about other persons and objects.

**LO 7.3.2 Explain how the self-concept changes from early childhood through middle childhood.**

Our self-concept, that is, how we view and evaluate ourselves, changes during early and middle childhood from the external to the internal and from the physical to the psychological. By middle childhood, children also engage in more accurate social comparison.

**LO 7.3.3 Describe the complex self-conceptions that develop in adolescence.**

One aspect of the complexity of adolescents' self-conceptions is that they can distinguish between an actual self and possible selves. The possible selves may be ideal or feared. Adolescents also recognize that they sometimes exhibit a false self, which is a self they present to others that does not represent what they are actually thinking and feeling.

# 7.4 Self-Esteem

As we have seen, children's self-concept includes not only how they view themselves, but also how they evaluate themselves, and these evaluations span the gamut from positive to negative. In American society in the past 50 years, a great deal has been written and said about self-esteem—a person's overall sense of worth and well-being. It was an American, the psychologist and philosopher William James, who first invented the term in the late 19th century. Here we will first look at the difference between the United States and other cultures in the emphasis upon self-esteem. We will then take an in-depth look at what research with American children has shown about the development of self-esteem.

## Culture and Self-Esteem

**LO 7.4.1 Explain how different ways of thinking about self-esteem are rooted in cultural beliefs.**

Even compared to people in other Western countries, Americans value high self-esteem to a greater extent, making the gap between Americans and people in non-Western countries especially great in this respect. For example, in traditional Japanese culture, self-criticism is a virtue and high self-esteem is a character problem (Heine et al., 1999). The belief in the value of high self-esteem is part of American individualism (Bellah et al., 1985; Rychlak, 2003).

Cultures that promote an *independent*, individualistic self also promote and encourage positive reflection about the self. In such cultures, it is seen as a good thing to think about yourself, to consider who you are as an independent person, and to think highly of yourself (within certain limits, of course—no culture values selfishness or egocentrism). Americans are especially known for their individualism and their focus on self-esteem (Cross & Gore, 2003; Henrich et al., 2010; Shweder et al., 2006).

Not all cultures look at the self in this way or value the self to the same extent. In collectivistic cultures, an *interdependent* conception of the self prevails (Markus & Kitayama 2010). In these cultures, the interests of the group—the family, the kinship group, the ethnic group, the nation, the religious institution—are supposed to come first, before the needs of the individual. This means that it is not necessarily a good thing, in these cultures, to think highly of yourself. People who think highly of themselves, who possess a high level of self-esteem, threaten the harmony of the group because they may be inclined to pursue their personal interests regardless of the interests of the groups to which they belong.

Cultural differences in the extent to which children express self-esteem emerge early. For example, research has found that Japanese preschoolers express less pride after successfully completing a task, compared to African American and European American preschoolers (Lewis et al., 2010). As children get older in cultures that value interdependence, they also sometimes try to play down their individual accomplishments. One study with Chinese and Taiwanese children found that they viewed lying about and concealing their own good deeds as increasingly positive from 7 to 11 years of age (Lee et al., 2001).

Cultural variations in views of self-esteem influence approaches to parenting. Parents in most places and times have been more worried that their children would become too selfish than have low self-esteem. As a result, parents have discouraged self-inflation as part of family socialization (Harkness et al., 2015; LeVine & LeVine, 2016). However, this kind of parenting works differently if it is part of a cultural norm rather than an exception within a culture. For example, children from Asian cultures are discouraged from valuing the self highly, yet they generally have high levels of academic performance and low levels of psychological problems (Markus & Kitayama, 2010). In contrast, children within the American majority culture who are exposed to parenting that is critical and negative show negative effects such as depression and poor academic performance (Bender et al., 2007; DeHart et al., 2006). It may be that children in Asian cultures learn to expect correction and criticism if they show signs of high self-esteem, and they see this as normal in comparison to other children, whereas American children learn to expect frequent praise, and hence suffer more if their parents are more critical than the parents of their peers (Rudy & Grusec, 2006).

It should be added that most cultures are neither purely independent nor interdependent in their conceptions of the self, but have elements of each (Kagitçibasi & Yalin, 2015). Also, with globalization, many cultures with a tradition of interdependence are changing toward a more independent view of the self (Arnett, 2011).

## The Development of Self-Esteem Among American Children

**LO 7.4.2 Summarize how global self-esteem and differentiated self-esteem change in the course of childhood and adolescence.**

"On the whole, I am satisfied with myself." "I feel that I have a number of good qualities." These are examples of questionnaire items that assess **global self-esteem**, or the extent to which a person generally feels positive about herself (Rosenberg, 1965). In contrast, "I find it pretty easy to make friends" and "I am happy with the way I look" are examples of items assessing **differentiated self-esteem**, how a person evaluates himself in specific domains such as social competence and physical appearance (Harter, 2012).

**global self-esteem**
the extent to which a person generally feels positive about her- or himself

**differentiated self-esteem**
how a person evaluates her- or himself in specific domains, such as social competence and physical appearance

**GLOBAL SELF-ESTEEM.** Research with 3- to 4-year-olds in the United States has found that they often have unrealistically positive self-evaluations (Harter, 1999). They sometimes call attention to their own accomplishments ("I am very strong. See? I can lift that chair!"). They also tend to inflate their own capacities.

Global self-esteem declines slightly in the transition from early childhood to middle childhood, as children enter a school environment in which social comparisons are a daily experience (Lerner et al., 2005; Wigfield et al., 1997). The decline is mild, and simply reflects children's more realistic appraisal of their abilities as they compare themselves to others and are rated by teachers. For the rest of middle childhood, overall self-esteem is high for most children, reflecting the generally positive emotional states mentioned earlier. In the United States, having low self-esteem in middle childhood is related to anxiety, depression, and antisocial behavior (Donnellan et al., 2005).

Several longitudinal studies show that self-esteem declines in early adolescence, then begins to rise again in late adolescence and into emerging adulthood (Erol & Orth, 2011; Harter, 2012; Orth & Robins, 2014). Figure 7.4 illustrates this low point in self-esteem in mid-adolescence. There are a number of reasons why self-esteem might follow this developmental pattern. The "imaginary audience" that we have discussed as part of cognitive development can make adolescents self-conscious in a way that decreases their self-esteem (Elkind, 1967, 1985). That is, as adolescents develop the capacity to imagine that others are especially conscious of how they look and what they say and how they act, they may suspect or fear that others are judging them harshly.

And they may be right. Adolescents in Western cultures tend to value the opinion of their peers highly, especially on day-to-day issues such as how they are dressed and what they say in social situations (Berndt, 1996). Also, adolescents have developed new cognitive capacities for sarcasm and ridicule, which tend to be dispensed freely toward any peer who seems odd or awkward or uncool (Cameron et al., 2010; Ichikawa et al., 2015). So, the combination of greater self-consciousness about evaluations by peers and peers' potentially harsh evaluations contributes to declines in global self-esteem in early adolescence. As peer evaluations become less important in late adolescence and emerging adulthood, self-esteem rises (Berndt, 1986; Bleidorn et al., 2016; Erol & Orth, 2011; Robins & Trzesniewski, 2005).

In a multicultural society like the United States, one might expect that the self-esteem of minorities would be influenced by low social status and negative social attitudes. One classic study in the 1940s found that when Black

**Figure 7.4** Global Self-Esteem, Ages 9 to 20

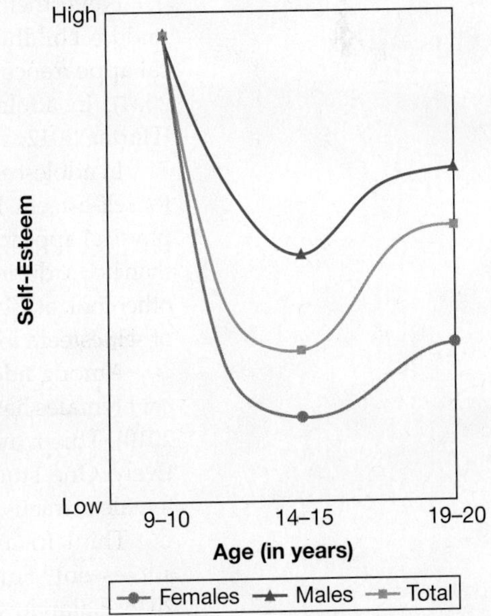


SOURCES: Adapted from Bleidorn et al. (2016), Erol & Orth (2011), Robins et al. (2002).

Black children and adolescents have relatively high self-esteem.

children and White children in middle childhood were given a choice of two dolls to play with, one Black and one White, even most of the Black children chose the White doll (Clark & Clark, 1947). Furthermore, children of both groups tended to choose the White doll as the "good" doll and the Black doll as the "bad" doll. Recent studies continue to show that children often view dark skin as "bad" and white skin as "good" (Byrd, 2012). In the past, these kinds of findings have been taken to imply that Blacks have lower self-esteem than Whites. However, a review of 261 studies involving more than half a million participants revealed that Black children and adolescents had higher self-esteem than White children and adolescents (Gray-Little & Hafdahl, 2000). In order to explain this finding, the authors suggest that self-esteem may depend more on comparisons with peers and other immediate social groups, not the larger society.

**DIFFERENTIATED SELF-ESTEEM.** In the course of middle childhood and adolescence self-esteem becomes more differentiated. In addition to global self-esteem, children and adolescents have self-concepts for several specific domains (Harter, 2012; Marsh & Ayotte, 2003). Susan Harter's (2012) Self-Perception Profile for Children assesses global self-worth, as well as self-worth for five specific domains: (1) Scholastic competence, (2) Social acceptance, (3) Athletic competence, (4) Behavioral conduct, and (5) Physical appearance. The measure is intended for children in third through sixth grade. Harter (1989) has also developed a measure for adolescents, the Self-Perception Profile for Adolescents, that adds three more domains (for a total of eight): (6) Job competence, (7) Romantic appeal, and (8) Close friendship.

**Critical Thinking Question:** In your view, are there any important domains missing for either children or adolescents?

The extent to which a specific domain is valued will influence how much it contributes to overall self-esteem. For example, a fifth grader may be no good at sports but also not care about sports, in which case low athletic self-concept would have no effect on global self-esteem. Some adolescents may view themselves as having low scholastic competence, but that would only influence their global self-esteem if it was important to them to do well in school.

Nevertheless, some domains of self-concept are more important than others. In both middle childhood and adolescence, research by Harter and others has found that physical appearance is most strongly related to global self-esteem (Harter, 2012; Klomsten et al., 2004). In adolescence, physical appearance is followed by social acceptance from peers (Harter, 2012; Shapka & Keating, 2005).

In adolescence, girls are more likely than boys to emphasize physical appearance as a basis for self-esteem. Because girls tend to evaluate their physical appearance negatively, and because physical appearance is at the heart of their global self-esteem, girls' self-esteem tends to be lower than boys' during adolescence (Robins & Trzesniewski, 2005; Shapka & Keating, 2005). Take another look at Figure 7.4 above. As you can see, it is only with the onset of adolescence that levels of self-esteem for girls and boys split, with girls' self-esteem dropping more than boys'.

Among adolescent girls, there are ethnic group differences. African American adolescent females have higher self-esteem than any other ethnic adolescent female group (Adams, 2010). This may be because they are less likely to evaluate their physical appearance negatively. One study found that Black adolescent girls often critique and reject the ideals of female attractiveness presented in teen magazines (Duke, 2002).

Think for a moment: how is your self-esteem today different from your self-esteem as an adolescent? For most people, self-esteem rises during emerging adulthood (Bleidorn et al., 2016; Galambos et al., 2006; McLean & Breen, 2015). There are a number of reasons for this. Physical appearance is important to adolescents' self-esteem, but most emerging adults have passed through the awkward changes of puberty and may be more comfortable with

## Education Focus: Praise, Motivation, and Academic Achievement

In the 1990s, the self-esteem movement called for parents and teachers to praise children in order to enhance their confidence, motivation, and academic achievement. A research program by Carol Dweck and her colleagues, however, has called into question the benefits of all-out, global praise. They argue that praise can be useful, but parents and teachers need to consider what exactly they are praising.

In an important series of six studies, Mueller and Dweck (1998) compared three groups of fifth graders who, upon completion of a task, were praised for: their intelligence (e.g., "You must be smart"), effort (e.g., "You must have worked hard"), and outcome (e.g., "You did well on this task"). Praising intelligence turned out to backfire. It led children subsequently to select safe, easy tasks rather than challenging ones they could learn from. Also, when presented with difficult tasks, children praised for their intelligence were more likely than the other groups to doubt their abilities, to report being unmotivated, to perform worse on the task, and to lie about their test scores. The group of children initially praised for their effort showed the most positive effects, with the children praised for their outcome falling in between. More recent research has obtained similar findings with preschoolers (Cimpian et al., 2007), seventh graders (Good et al., 2003), and college undergraduates (Aronson et al., 2002).

Dweck and her colleagues have also carried out experimental intervention studies. In one study, they followed seventh graders who took part in a program that emphasized that "you can grow your intelligence" over the course of 2 years. They found that their academic performance improved over time, as compared to seventh graders in a control group (Blackwell et al., 2007).

Dweck (2013, p.180) has concluded that "person praise" (such as for intelligence or being smart) has a cascade of unfortunate effects compared to "process praise" (such as for effort or problem-solving strategy). While person praise may be motivating as long as children are successful, it becomes a liability when children meet with more difficult materials and failures. At that point, the materials and failures may be experienced as a threat to their self-esteem, rather than as an opportunity to learn new skills. Dweck and her colleagues' advice to educators, parents, and researchers is: "As with criticism, it is better to separate 'the deed from the doer' by applying praise to children's strategies and work habits rather than to any particular trait" (Mueller & Dweck, 1998, p.50).

### Review Question

Do you see ways that this research program might apply not only to individuals, but also to groups within a society whose intellectual capabilities are subject to stereotypes?

how they look. Also, feeling accepted and approved by parents contributes to self-esteem, and from adolescence to emerging adulthood, relationships with parents generally improve, while conflict diminishes (Arnett, 2015; Fingerman & Yahurin, 2015; Galambos et al., 2006). Peers and friends are also important to self-esteem, and entering emerging adulthood means leaving the social pressure cooker of secondary school, where peer evaluations are a part of daily life and can be harsh (Gavin & Furman, 1989; Pascoe, 2007).

Also, reaching emerging adulthood usually means having more control over the social contexts of everyday life, which makes it possible for emerging adults to seek out the contexts they prefer and avoid the contexts they find disagreeable, in a way that adolescents cannot. For example, adolescents who dislike school and do poorly have little choice but to attend school, where poor grades may repeatedly undermine their self-esteem. However, emerging adults can leave school and instead engage in full-time work that they may find more gratifying and enjoyable, thus enhancing their self-esteem.

## Self-Esteem, Physical Appearance, and Eating Disorders

**LO 7.4.3 Describe the prevalence, symptoms, and treatment of eating disorders.**

As we have seen, physical appearance is the domain that most influences adolescents' self-esteem. For many adolescents, changes in the way they think about their bodies are accompanied by changes in the way they think about food. Girls, in particular, pay more attention to the food they eat once they reach adolescence, and worry more about eating too much and getting fat (Jones et al., 2014; Nichter, 2001). This is especially true in the United States. Currently, about 31% of American 10- to 17-year-olds are overweight or obese by medical standards (Kaiser Family Foundation, 2015). However, 60% of American adolescent girls and 30% of boys believe they weigh too much (Gray et al., 2011).

Fear of being or becoming overweight can lead adolescents to exhibit eating disordered behavior, including fasting for 24 hours or more, use of diet products, purging, and

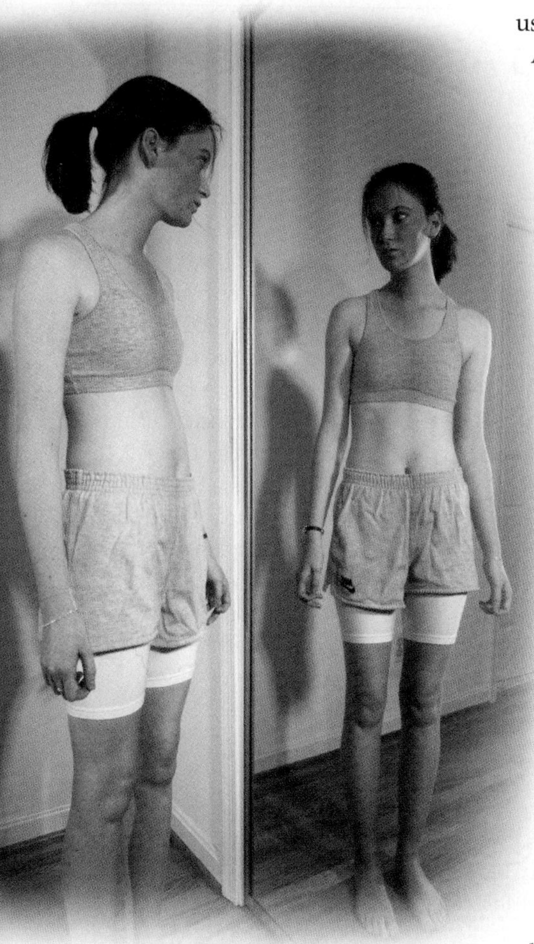

Young women with anorexia nervosa often see themselves as too fat even when they are so thin their lives are at risk.

use of laxatives to control weight. According to a national U.S. study, about 20% of American adolescent girls and 10% of boys in Grades 9–12 report engaging in eating disordered behavior in the past 30 days (Austin et al., 2008). Similar findings have been reported in other Western countries. In a national study of German 11- to 17-year-olds, 33% of girls and 15% of boys reported symptoms of eating disorders (Herpetz-Dahlmann et al., 2008). In Finland, a large study of 14- to 15-year-olds found eating disordered behavior among 24% of girls and 16% of boys (Hautala et al., 2008).

The two most common eating disorders are anorexia nervosa (intentional self-starvation) and bulimia (binge eating combined with purging). About 0.3% of American adolescents have anorexia nervosa and about 0.9% have bulimia (Swanson et al., 2011). Nearly all (90%) of eating disorders occur among females. Most cases of eating disorders have their onset among females in their teens and early 20s (Smink et al., 2012).

Anorexia is characterized by three primary symptoms (American Psychiatric Association, 2013):

1. eating less than needed to maintain a body weight that is at or above normal weight for height,
2. intense fear of weight gain, and
3. distorted body image with undue influence of body weight or shape on self-evaluation.

One of the most striking symptoms of anorexia is the cognitive distortion of body image (Striegel-Moore & Franko, 2006). Young women with anorexia sincerely believe themselves to be too fat, even when they have become so thin that their lives are threatened. Standing in front of a mirror with them and pointing out how emaciated they look does no good; the person with anorexia looks in the mirror and sees a fat person, no matter how thin she is. For more information, watch the video *Anorexia Nervosa: Tamora*.

Like those with anorexia, persons with bulimia have strong fears that their bodies will become big and fat (Campbell & Peebles, 2014). They engage in binge eating, which means eating a large amount of food in a short time. Then they purge themselves; that is, they use laxatives or induce vomiting to get rid of the food they have just eaten during a binge episode. People with bulimia often suffer damage to their teeth from repeated vomiting (because stomach acids erode tooth enamel). Unlike those with anorexia, persons with bulimia typically maintain a normal weight, because they have more or less normal eating patterns in between their episodes of bingeing and purging. Another difference from anorexia is that persons with bulimia do not regard their eating patterns as normal. They view themselves as having a problem and often despise themselves in the aftermath of their binge episodes.

Eating disorders are most common in cultures that emphasize slimness as part of the female physical ideal, especially Western countries (Piat et al., 2015). Presented with a cultural ideal that portrays the ideal female body as slim, at a time when their bodies are biologically tending to become more rounded, many adolescent girls feel distressed at the changes taking place in their body shape and attempt to resist or at least modify those changes. Girls who have an eating disorder are at higher risk for other internalizing disorders, such as depression and anxiety disorders (Rojo-Moreno et al., 2015). Eating disordered behavior is also related to substance use, especially cigarette smoking and binge drinking (Pisetsky et al., 2008).

**Watch** ANOREXIA NERVOSA: TAMORA

Within the United States, eating disorders are more common among White girls than among girls of other ethnic groups, probably due to a greater cultural value on female slimness (Campbell & Peebles, 2014). Although mainly a Western problem, eating disorders are increasing in parts of the world that are becoming more Westernized. We will examine the influence of Western media ideals, including female slimness, on adolescents around the globe in Chapter 12.

The success of treating anorexia and bulimia through hospitalization, medication, or psychotherapy is limited (Bulik et al., 2007; Grilo & Mitchell, 2010; Lock, 2015). About two-thirds of people treated for anorexia in hospital programs improve, but one-third remain chronically ill despite treatment (Lock, 2015; Steinhausen et al., 2003). Similarly, although treatments for bulimia are successful in about 50% of cases, there are repeated relapses in the other 50% of cases (Smink et al., 2012). Adolescents and emerging adults with a history of eating disorders often continue to show significant impairments in mental and physical health, self-image, and social functioning even after their eating disorder has faded (Berkman et al., 2007; Rojo-Moreno et al., 2015).

## SUMMARY: Self-Esteem

**LO 7.4.1 Explain how different ways of thinking about self-esteem are rooted in cutural beliefs.**

Compared to people in other Western countries, Americans value self-esteem to a greater extent, making the gap between Americans and people in non-Western countries especially great in this respect. Generally, cultures that promote an independent, individualistic self also promote and encourage positive reflection about the self. Cultures that promote an interdependent, collectivistic self are more likely to value self-restraint and self-criticism.

**LO 7.4.2 Summarize how global self-esteem and differentiated self-esteem change in the course of childhood and adolescence.**

Global self-esteem declines slightly in the transition from early childhood to middle childhood, as children enter a school environment in which social comparisons are a daily experience. In early adolescence, global self-esteem declines notably and then begins to rise again in late adolescence and into emerging adulthood. In the course of middle childhood and adolescence self-esteem becomes more differentiated. Children and adolescents evaluate their competence within specific domains, such as physical appearance and social acceptance.

**LO 7.4.3 Describe the prevalence, symptoms, and treatment of eating disorders.**

About 20% of American girls and 10% of boys in Grades 9–12 have engaged in eating disordered behavior in the past 30 days. The two most common eating disorders are anorexia nervosa and bulimia. About 0.3% of American adolescents have anorexia nervosa and about 0.9% have bulimia. Treatments for anorexia and bulimia include hospitalization, medication, and psychotherapy, but success rates are quite low.

# 7.5 Identity

Developing an identity involves thinking about who you are, what you believe in, and where you want your life to go. It involves exploring possibilities about love and work, culminating in commitments that set the foundation for adult life. In multicultural societies and a globalizing world, it also involves exploring ethnic and cultural affiliations.

For most of the history of research on identity, the focus was on adolescence. This focus was due mainly to the influence of the theories of Erik Erikson and James Marcia. Also, adolescence was formerly the life stage when the main choices in love and work were made. In societies that afford young people a stage of emerging adulthood, it is now generally accepted among scholars that this is the time when many of the most important steps in identity development take place (Côté, 2006; Lyckyx, 2006; McLean & Syed, 2016; Schacter, 2005; Schwartz et al., 2015).

## Erikson's and Marcia's Theories

**LO 7.5.1 Review key features of Erikson's theory, and explain how Marcia extended the theory.**

Both Erikson and Marcia regarded adolescence as a pivotal point in life. In their view, it is when we decide who we wish to become, even as our wishes may break with the expectations and traditions of those around us. Erikson expressed this idea eloquently and dramatically when he wrote: "In the period between puberty and adulthood, the resources of tradition fuse with new inner resources to create something new: A new person; and with this new person a new generation, and with that, a new era" (Erikson, 1958, p.20).

**psychosocial theory**

Erikson's theory that human development is driven by the need to become integrated into the social and cultural environment

**identity versus identity confusion**

in Erikson's theory, the crisis of adolescence, with two alternative paths, establishing a clear and definite identity, or experiencing identity confusion, which is a failure to form a stable and secure identity

**ERIKSON'S PSYCHOSOCIAL THEORY.** Erik Erikson proposed a **psychosocial theory** of development, in which the driving force behind development is the need to become integrated into the social and cultural environment. Across the life course, according to Erikson, a person moves through eight stages characterized by a distinctive developmental challenge or "crisis" that the person must resolve. Figure 7.5 provides a succinct summary of the names for the stages and the nature of the crisis at each stage. Erikson argued that a successful resolution of a crisis prepares the person well for the next stage of development. However, a person who has difficulty with the crisis in one stage enters the next stage at high risk for being unsuccessful at that crisis as well. The stages build on each other, for better and for worse.

Erikson's general theoretical ideas have endured quite well. Today, nearly all developmental psychologists would agree that development is lifelong, with important changes taking place at every phase of the life span (Baltes et al., 2006; Jensen, 2015; Lerner, 2006). Similarly, nearly all developmental psychologists today would agree with Erikson's recognition of the social and cultural basis of development. However, not all of Erikson's proposed life stages have been accepted as valid or valuable. It is mainly his ideas about identity in adolescence and generativity in midlife that have inspired substantial interest and attention among researchers (Clark, 2010). Here, we will address Erikson's ideas about adolescence.

In adolescence, according to Erikson, the crisis is **identity versus identity confusion**. The healthy path in adolescence involves establishing a clear and definite sense of who you are and how you fit into the world around you. The unhealthy alternative is identity confusion, which is a failure to form a stable and secure identity. Identity formation involves reflecting on what your traits, abilities, and interests are, then sifting through the range of life choices available in your culture, trying out various possibilities, and ultimately making commitments. The key areas in which identity is formed are love, work, and ideology (beliefs and values) (Erikson, 1968). In Erikson's view, a failure to establish commitments in these areas by the end of adolescence reflects identity confusion.

There are three elements essential to developing an identity, according to Erikson. First, adolescents evaluate their own abilities and interests. By this age, most people have a growing sense of what their strengths and weaknesses are and what they most and least enjoy doing. Second, adolescents reflect on the *identifications* they have accumulated in childhood (Erikson, 1968). Children *identify* with their parents and other loved ones as they grow up—that is, children love and admire them and want to be like them. Thus, adolescents create an identity in part by modeling themselves after parents, friends, and others they have loved in childhood, not simply by imitating them, but by integrating parts of their loved ones' behavior and attitudes into their own personality. Third, adolescents assess the opportunities available to them in their society. Many dream of a fabulous career in sports, music, or entertainment (Schneider, 2009), yet there are relatively few opportunities for people to make a living in these areas. Sometimes opportunities are restricted due to discrimination. Until fairly recently, women were discouraged or even barred from professions such as medicine and law. Today, ethnic minorities in many societies find that the doors to many professions are barred to them. In every society, adolescents need to take into account what they would like to do, what adults will allow them to do, and the extent to which they can overcome societal restrictions.

**Figure 7.5** Erikson's Eight Stages of Psychosocial Development

**Infancy:**
**Trust vs. Mistrust**
Main developmental challenge is to establish bond with trusted caregiver

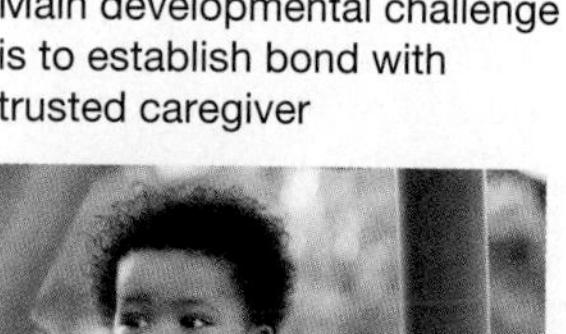

**Toddlerhood:**
**Autonomy vs. Shame and doubt**
Main developmental challenge is to develop a healthy sense of self as distinct from others

**Early Childhood:**
**Initiative vs. Guilt**
Main developmental challenge is to initiate activities in a purposeful way

**Middle Childhood:**
**Industry vs. Inferiority**
Main developmental challenge is to begin to learn knowledge and skills of culture

**Adolescence:**
**Identity vs. Identity confusion**
Main developmental challenge is to develop a secure and coherent identity

**Early Adulthood:**
**Intimacy vs. Isolation**
Main developmental challenge is to establish a committed, long-term love relationship

**Middle Adulthood:**
**Generativity vs. Stagnation**
Main developmental challenge is to care for others and contribute to well-being of the young

**Late Adulthood:**
**Ego integrity vs. Despair**
Main developmental challenge is to evaluate lifetime, accept it as it is

**MARCIA'S IDENTITY STATUSES.** Erikson's most influential interpreter has been James Marcia (Marcia, 1966, 1980, 1989, 1999, 2010; Marcia & Carpendale, 2004). Marcia constructed a measure called the Identity Status Interview that classified adolescents into one of four identity statuses: *diffusion, moratorium, foreclosure,* or *achievement*. This system of four categories, known as the **identity status model**, has also been used by scholars who have constructed questionnaires to investigate identity development rather than use Marcia's interview (e.g., Adams, 1999; Benson et al., 1992; Grotevant & Adams, 1984; Kroger, 2007).

Aspiring to advanced careers in science, technology, engineering, and math is becoming progressively more realistic for girls.

As shown in Table 7.3, each of these classifications involves a different combination of exploration and commitment. Erikson (1968) used the term *identity crisis* to describe the process through which young people construct their identity, but Marcia and other current scholars prefer the term *exploration* (Kroger, 2007; Marcia & Carpendale, 2004; Waterman, 2007). "Crisis" implies that the process inherently involves anguish and struggle, whereas "exploration" implies a more positive investigation of possibilities.

*Diffusion* is an identity status that combines no exploration with no commitment. For adolescents in a state of identity diffusion, no commitments have been made among the choices available to them. Furthermore, no exploration is taking place. The person in this status is not seriously attempting to sort through potential choices and make enduring commitments.

**identity status model**
Marcia's model for researching Erikson's theory of identity development, classifying identity development into four categories: diffusion, foreclosure, moratorium, or achievement

*Moratorium* involves exploration but no commitment. This is a status of actively trying out different personal, occupational, and ideological possibilities. Different possibilities are being sifted through, with some being discarded and some selected, in order for adolescents to be able to determine which of the available possibilities are best suited to them.

Adolescents who are in the *foreclosure* status have not experimented with a range of possibilities, but have nevertheless committed themselves to certain choices—commitment, but no exploration. This is often a result of their parents' strong influence. Marcia and most other scholars tend to see exploration as a necessary part of forming a healthy identity, and therefore see foreclosure as unhealthy.

Finally, the classification that combines exploration and commitment is *achievement*. Identity achievement is the status of young people who have made definite personal, occupational, and ideological choices. By definition, identity achievement is preceded by a moratorium in which exploration takes place. If commitment takes place without exploration, it is considered identity foreclosure rather than identity achievement.

## Identity in Emerging Adulthood

**LO 7.5.2 Describe the various forms identity development can take during emerging adulthood.**

Although Erikson designated adolescence as the stage of the identity crisis, and research using Marcia's model has mostly focused on adolescence, studies indicate that in developed countries it takes longer than scholars had expected to reach identity achievement. In fact,

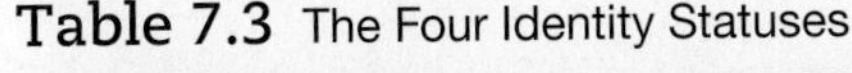

**Table 7.3** The Four Identity Statuses

| Exploration | Commitment: Yes | Commitment: No |
|---|---|---|
| **Yes** | Achievement | Moratorium |
| **No** | Foreclosure | Diffusion |

for most young people, identity achievement is reached—if at all—in emerging adulthood or beyond, rather than in adolescence. Studies comparing adolescents from ages 12 through 18 have found that, although the proportion of adolescents in the diffusion category decreases with age and the proportion of adolescents in the achievement category increases, even by early emerging adulthood, less than half are classified as having reached identity achievement (Kroger, 2003; Meeus et al., 1999; van Hoof, 1999; Waterman, 1999). An analysis pooling results across 124 studies of identity status between 1966 and 2005 found that only an average of 18% had achieved identity in adolescence (Kroger et al., 2010).

Studies of college students find that progress toward identity achievement also takes place during the college years, but mainly in the specific area of occupational identity rather than for identity more generally (Waterman, 1992). Some studies indicate that identity achievement may come faster for emerging adults who do not attend college, perhaps because the college environment tends to be a place where young people's ideas about themselves are challenged and they are encouraged to question previously held ideas (Lytle et al., 1997; Munro & Adams, 1977). However, for non-college emerging adults as well, the majority has not reached identity achievement by age 21 (Kroger et al., 2010; Waterman, 1999).

Even 50 years ago, Erikson observed that identity formation was taking longer and longer for young people in developed countries. He commented on the "prolonged adolescence" that was becoming increasingly common in such countries and how this was leading to a prolonged period of identity formation, "during which the young adult through free role experimentation may find a niche in some section of his society" (1968, p. 156). Considering the changes that have taken place since he made this observation in the 1960s, including much later ages of marriage and parenthood and longer education, Erikson's observation applies to far more young people today than it did then (Schwartz et al., 2014). Indeed, as described in Chapter 1, the conception of emerging adulthood as a distinct period of life is based to a considerable extent on the fact that, over recent decades, the late teens and early 20s have become a period of "free role experimentation" for an increasing proportion of young people (Arnett, 2000, 2015). The achievement of an adult identity comes later, compared with earlier generations, as many emerging adults use the years of their late teens and early to mid-20s for identity explorations in love, work, and ideology.

## Cultural Focus: The Features of Emerging Adulthood

Emerging adulthood, with its "free role experimentation," is not a universal period of human development, but a period that exists under certain conditions that have occurred only quite recently and only in some cultures. The main requirement for emerging adulthood to exist is a relatively high median age of entering marriage and parenthood. Postponing marriage and parenthood until the late 20s allows emerging adults to devote the late teens and the early to mid-20s to other activities, such as the identity explorations just described. So, emerging adulthood exists today mainly in developed countries, including those of Europe, the United States, Canada, Australia, and New Zealand, along with Asian countries such as Japan and South Korea (Arnett, 2011).

Currently in developing countries, there tends to be a split between urban and rural areas in whether emerging adulthood is experienced at all. Young people in urban areas of countries such as China and India are more likely to experience emerging adulthood, because they marry later, have children later, obtain more education, and have a greater range of occupational and recreational opportunities than young people in rural areas have (Nelson & Chen, 2007; Zhong & Arnett, 2014). In contrast, young people in rural areas of developing countries often receive minimal schooling, marry early, and have little choice of occupation aside from agricultural work. Watch the video *The Features of Emerging Adulthood* for more information.

**Watch** THE FEATURES OF EMERGING ADULTHOOD

### Review Question

Emerging adulthood is described as an "unstable" time of one's life. Based on this video, why would this be an accurate description?

## Identity and Variations Across Cultures

**LO 7.5.3 Describe how identity development varies across cultures, including the impact of globalization.**

Most of the research inspired by Erikson's theory has taken place among White middle-class adolescents in Europe and North America (Schwartz et al., 2014). What can we say about identity development among adolescents and emerging adults in other cultures? One observation is that although Erikson sought to ground his theory in historical and cultural context (Erikson, 1950, 1968; Kroger, 2002), his discussion of identity development nevertheless assumed an *independent* self that is allowed to make free choices in love, work, and ideology. The focus of Erikson's identity theory is on how young people develop an understanding of themselves as unique individuals. However, as we have discussed earlier in the chapter, this conception of the self is distinctively Western and is historically recent (Markus & Kitayama, 1991; Shweder et al., 2006). In most cultures, until recently, the self has been understood as *interdependent*, defined in relation to others, rather than as independent. Even today, Erikson's assertions of the prominence of identity issues in adolescence may apply more to modern Western adolescents than to adolescents in other cultures. For example, explorations in love are clearly limited or even nonexistent in cultures where dating is not allowed and marriages are either arranged by parents or strongly influenced by them. Explorations in work are limited in cultures where the economy is simple and offers only a limited range of choices.

Limitations on explorations in both love and work tend to be narrower for girls in developing countries than they are for boys. With regard to love, some degree of sexual experimentation is encouraged for adolescent boys in most cultures, but for girls sexual experimentation is more likely to be restricted or forbidden (Schlegel, 2010). With regard to work, in most traditional cultures today—and for most of human history in every culture—adolescent girls have been designated by their cultures for the roles of wife and mother, and these were essentially the only choices open to them.

**bicultural identity**
identity with two distinct facets, for example, one part based on the local culture and another part based on the global culture

In terms of ideology, too, a psychosocial moratorium has been the exception in human cultures rather than the standard. In most cultures, young people have been expected to grow up to believe what adults teach them to believe, without questioning it (Phinney & Baldelomar, 2011). It is only in recent history, and mainly in Western developed countries, that it has come to be seen as desirable for adolescents and emerging adults to think for themselves, decide on their own beliefs, and make their life choices independently (Bellah et al., 1985; Arnett, 1998).

Another identity issue that has important cultural dimensions is how globalization influences identity, especially for adolescents and emerging adults (Arnett, 2002, 2011). Because of globalization, more young people around the world now develop a **bicultural identity**, with one part of their identity rooted in their local culture, while another part stems from an awareness of their relation to the global culture (Rao et al., 2013). For example, India has a growing, vigorous high-tech economic sector, led largely by young people. However, even the better-educated young people, who have become full-fledged members of the global economy, still mostly prefer to have an arranged marriage, in accordance with Indian tradition (Chaudhary & Sharma, 2012). They also generally expect to care for their parents in old age, again in accordance with Indian tradition. Thus they have one identity for participating in the global economy and succeeding in the fast-paced world of high technology, and another identity, rooted in Indian tradition, that they maintain with respect to their families and their personal lives.

In most cultures through history, young people have been expected to believe what their parents believe, not to decide on their own beliefs. Here, a young Israeli man prays.

## Ethnic Identity

**LO 7.5.4 Explain why ethnic identity development comes to the forefront in adolescence, and differentiate among ethnic identity statuses.**

In addition to the complex identity issues that arise as a consequence of globalization, many people grow up as a member of an ethnic minority group. In fact, more people than ever have this experience, as worldwide immigration has climbed to unprecedented levels in recent decades (Berry et al., 2006; Phinney, 2006; Suárez-Orozco, 2015).

Like other identity issues, issues of ethnic identity come to the forefront in adolescence and continue to grow in importance into emerging adulthood (Pahl & Way, 2006; Syed & Mitchell, 2015). As part of their growing cognitive capacity for self-reflection, adolescents and emerging adults who are members of ethnic minority groups are likely to have a sharpened awareness of what it means for them to be a member of that group. Bicultural identities such as African American, Chinese Canadian, and Turkish Dutch take on a new meaning, as adolescents and emerging adults can now think about what these terms mean and how the term for their ethnic group applies to themselves. Also, as a consequence of their growing capacity to think about what others think about them, adolescents and emerging adults become more acutely aware of the prejudices and stereotypes about their ethnic group that others may hold.

For emerging adults, ethnic identity issues are likely to take on a greater prominence as they enter new social contexts such as college and the workplace, and as they meet a broader range of people from different ethnic backgrounds (Phinney, 2006). As children and adolescents, they may have been mostly around people of their own ethnic group, but emerging adulthood is likely to take them into new contexts with greater ethnic diversity, sharpening their awareness of their ethnic identity (Syed & Azmitia, 2010).

Because adolescents and emerging adults who are members of ethnic minority groups have to take into account ethnic identity issues, their identity development is likely to be more complex than for those who are part of the majority culture (Phinney, 2000, 2006; Syed & Mitchell, 2015). Consider identity development in the area of love. Love—along with dating and sex—is an area where cultural conflicts are especially likely to come up for adolescents and emerging adults who are members of ethnic minorities. For example, part of identity development in the American majority culture means trying out different possibilities in love by forming emotionally intimate relationships with different people and gaining sexual experience. However, this model is in sharp conflict with the values of certain American ethnic minority groups. In most Asian American groups, for example, recreational dating is disapproved and sexual experimentation before marriage is taboo—especially for females (Qin, 2009; Talbani & Hasanali, 2000). Young people in Asian American ethnic groups face a challenge in reconciling the values of their ethnic group on such issues with the values of the majority culture, to which they are inevitably exposed through school, the media, and peers.

How, then, does identity development take place for young people who are members of minority groups within Western societies? To what extent do they develop an identity that reflects the values of the majority culture, and to what extent do they retain the values of their minority group? One scholar who has done extensive work on these questions among American minorities is Jean Phinney (Phinney, 1990, 2000, 2006, 2010; Phinney & Devich-Navarro, 1997; Vedder & Phinney, 2014). On the basis of her research, Phinney has concluded that young people who are members of minority groups have four different ways of responding to their awareness of their ethnicity. As you can see in Table 7.4, these four ways are: biculturalism, assimilation, separation, and marginalization.

- *Biculturalism* involves developing a dual identity, one based in the ethnic group of origin and one based in the majority culture. Being bicultural means moving back and forth between the ethnic culture and the majority culture, and alternating identities as appropriate to the situation.

**Table 7.4** Four Ethnic Identity Statuses

| Identification with Majority Culture | Identification with Ethnic Group: High | Identification with Ethnic Group: Low |
|---|---|---|
| **High** | Biculturalism | Assimilation |
| **Low** | Separation | Marginalization |

SOURCE: Based on Phinney & Devich-Navarro (1997).

- *Assimilation* is the option that involves leaving behind the ways of one's ethnic group and adopting the values and way of life of the majority culture. This is the path that is reflected in the idea that a society is a "melting pot" that blends people of diverse origins into one national culture.
- *Separation* is the approach that involves associating only with members of one's own ethnic group and rejecting the ways of the majority culture.
- *Marginality* involves rejecting one's culture of origin but also feeling rejected by the majority culture. Some young people may feel little identification with the culture of their parents and grandparents, nor do they feel accepted and integrated into the larger society.

Biculturalism means developing a dual identity, one for the ethnic culture and one for the majority culture.

Which of these identity statuses is most common among ethnic minorities? Although ethnic identity is potentially most prominent in emerging adulthood (Phinney, 2006), most research thus far has taken place on adolescents. The bicultural status is the most common status among Mexican Americans and Asian Americans, as well as some European minority groups such as Turkish adolescents in the Netherlands (Neto, 2002; Phinney et al., 1994; Rotheram-Borus, 1990; Schwartz & Unger, 2010; Verkuyten, 2002). However, separation is the most common ethnic identity status among African American adolescents, and marginality is pervasive among Native American adolescents. Of course, each ethnic group is diverse and contains adolescents with a variety of different ethnic identity statuses. Adolescents tend to be more aware of their ethnic identity when they are in a context where they are in the minority. For example, in one study, Latino adolescents attending a predominately non-Latino school reported significantly higher levels of ethnic identity than adolescents in a predominately Latino or a balanced Latino/non-Latino school (Umaña-Taylor, 2005).

**Critical Thinking Question:** Can you explain how there might be a connection between the identity status of African American adolescents and the earlier finding that their self-esteem seems to be unrelated to societal attitudes about Blacks?

Is ethnic identity related to other aspects of development in adolescence and emerging adulthood? Generally, studies have found that adolescents who are bicultural or assimilated have higher self-esteem (e.g., Farver et al., 2002). However, for minority groups who are subject to negative societal views and discrimination, studies suggest that separation buffers against negative psychological outcomes and that ethnic pride enhances cognitive and emotional development (Quintana, 2007). Furthermore, several studies have found that having a strong ethnic identity is related to overall well-being, academic achievement, lower rates of risky behavior, and better relationships with parents (Giang & Wittig, 2006; Huang & Stormshak, 2011; St. Louis & Liem, 2005; Syed & Mitchell, 2015).

## SUMMARY: Identity

**LO 7.5.1 Review key features of Erikson's theory, and explain how Marcia extended the theory.**

According to Erikson, each of eight stages of life involves a crisis where a person may take either a healthy or unhealthy path. In adolescence, the crisis involves either successfully forming an identity or experiencing identity confusion. Building on Erikson's theory, Marcia constructed an interview measure that classifies adolescents into one of four identity atuses: diffusion, moratorium, foreclosure, or achievement.

**LO 7.5.2 Describe the various forms identity development can take during emerging adulthood.**

For most young people in developed countries, identity achievement is reached—if at all—in emerging adulthood or beyond, rather than in adolescence. Among college students, progress toward identity achievement mainly takes place in the specific area of occupational identity rather than for identity more generally.

**LO 7.5.3 Describe how identity development varies across cultures, including the impact of globalization.**

Even today, Erikson's assertions of the prominence of identity issues in adolescence may apply more to modern Western adolescents than to adolescents in traditional cultures who have limited self-determination in regard to love and work. Due to globalization, more adolescents and emerging adults around the world now develop a bicultural identity, with one part of their identity rooted in their local culture, while another part stems from an awareness of their relation to the global culture.

**LO 7.5.4 Explain why ethnic identity development comes to the forefront in adolescence, and differentiate among ethnic identity statuses.**

As part of their growing cognitive capacity for self-reflection, adolescents who are members of ethnic minority groups are likely to have a sharpened awareness of what it means for them to be a member of that group. They also become more acutely aware of prejudices and stereotypes about their ethnic group that others may hold. Phinney has differentiated four ways that members of minority groups respond to their awareness of their ethnicity: assimilation, marginality, separation, and biculturalism.

## Apply Your Knowledge as a Professional

The topics covered in this chapter apply to a wide variety of career professions. Watch this video to learn how they apply to a clinical psychologist.

**Journaling Question:** Who would you like to be 5 years from now? Write a letter to yourself describing where you hope to be in terms of such key matters as love, work, ideology, self-esteem, and emotional maturity. (You might consider saving the letter for revisiting in the future).

Chapter 8

# Gender: Biology, Socialization, and Cultural Change

## Learning Objectives

**8.1 Development of a Gendered Self**

8.1.1 Describe the development of gender identity, gender constancy, and gender roles.

8.1.2 Explain the development of gender stereotypes and how boys and girls differ in this regard.

8.1.3 Describe the gender-intensification hypothesis and the extent of support for it.

**8.2 Gender in Traditional Cultures**

8.2.1 Summarize common themes found in the socialization of adolescent girls in traditional cultures.

8.2.2 Describe the capabilities that adolescent boys in traditional cultures need to demonstrate in order to achieve manhood.

8.2.3 Explain why female and male physiology has a profound impact on gender roles in preindustrial societies, and describe how gender roles have changed in the last half-century.

**8.3 Gender Comparisons in Developed Countries**

8.3.1 Explain why meta-analyses are important for reaching conclusions about gender differences.

8.3.2 Review the two overarching conclusions about gender differences, and summarize specific gender differences revealed by meta-analyses.

8.3.3 Explain five important qualifications about gender differences revealed by meta-analyses.

**8.4 Reasons for Gender Differences: Theories and Research**

8.4.1 Explain the similarities and differences between biological and biosocial accounts of gender differences.

8.4.2 Describe the roles that parents, peers, media, and school play in gender socialization.

8.4.3 Explain how gender schemas lead to self-socialization.

8.4.4 Explain how gender inequity is related to gender differences.

**8.5 Beyond the Binary**

8.5.1 Describe the extent to which androgyny has been linked to positive outcomes.

8.5.2 Explain why gender nonconforming and transgender youth are starting to gain research attention.

8.5.3 Give an example of why intersectionality is important in understanding gender.

**8.6 Globalization and the Future of Gender**

8.6.1 Describe today's state of affairs for girls and women in regard to education, unpaid work, and physical violence.

8.6.2 Explain how economic changes in developing countries are changing gender roles.

IN ALL CULTURES, GENDER IS A FUNDAMENTAL ORGANIZING PRINCIPLE OF SOCIAL LIFE. All cultures distinguish different roles and expectations for females and males, although the strictness of those roles and expectations varies widely. Of course, many other animals, including all our mammal relatives and certainly our primate cousins, have female–male differences in their typical patterns of behavior and development. What makes humans distinctive is that, unlike other animals, culture shapes our expectations for how females and males are supposed to behave. Furthermore, cultural expectations for gender and the extent to which differences develop between the genders can change rapidly. In fact, as we will see in this chapter, revolutionary changes have taken place in developed countries in the last half-century and are beginning to occur in many developing countries.

**sex**
biological status of being female or male

**gender**
cultural categories of "female" and "male"

Before proceeding further, let's clarify the difference between *sex* and *gender.* While social scientists differ among themselves in their exact usage of the terms (Leaper, 2015), the term **sex** generally refers to the biological status of being female or male. This includes characteristics such as whether the 23rd pair of chromosomes is two Xs or an X and a Y, and whether the gonads are ovaries or testes (Hines, 2015). **Gender**, in contrast, refers to the cultural categories of "female" and "male" (Tobach, 2004). Use of the term *sex* implies that the characteristics of females and males have a biological basis. Use of the term *gender* implies that characteristics of females and males may be due to cultural and social beliefs, influences, and perceptions (Hines, 2015). For example, the fact that males are somewhat larger than females throughout most of life is a sex difference. However, the fact that girls in many cultures have longer hair than boys is a gender difference. The distinction between a sex difference and a gender difference is not always as clear as in these examples.

As we will see in this course of this chapter, the degree to which differences between females and males are biological or cultural is a subject of great importance and heated debate in the social sciences. Also, social scientists are increasingly focusing on the ways that individuals identify themselves in ways that go beyond the binary distinction between female and male.

**Watch** **CHAPTER INTRODUCTION: GENDER: BIOLOGY, SOCIALIZATION, AND CULTURAL CHANGE**

# 8.1 Development of a Gendered Self

Gender identity develops in toddlerhood. Here, a girl imitates her mother.

In a classic experimental study, adults were asked to play with a 10-month-old infant they did not know (Sidorowicz & Lunney, 1980). All adults played with the same infant. However, some were told it was a boy, some were told it was a girl, and some were given no information about the sex of the infant. There were three toys to play with: a doll, a rubber football, and a teething ring. When the adults believed the child was male, 50% of the men and 80% of the women played with the child using the football. When they believed the child was female, 89% of the men and 73% of the women used the doll in play.

From the moment of birth, people in all cultures communicate gender expectations to boys and girls by dressing them differently, talking to them differently, and playing with them differently (Hatfield et al., 2015). From infancy and toddlerhood, too, children begin to develop a gendered self. In this section, we will look at key steps in this development.

## Early Childhood

**LO 8.1.1 Describe the development of gender identity, gender constancy, and gender roles.**

By their first birthday, infants perceive differences between female and male faces. By age 2, toddlers associate female and male faces with gender-typed activities and objects (Poulin-Dubois & Serbin, 2006). Toddlers also begin to apply gender terms like *boy* and *girl, man* and *woman* to themselves and others (Campbell et al., 2004; Raag, 2003).

By age 3, toddlers have attained a **gender identity**, that is, they view themselves as female or male. Research shows that about 75% of children can tell you that they are a boy or girl at 2 1/2 years of age, and they can sort their photo and the photos of others into piles of females and males. By age 3, 95% of children can do this (Thompson, 1975).

In early childhood, gender issues intensify. By ages 3–4, children associate a variety of things with either females or males, including toys, games, clothes, household items, occupations, and even colors (Kapadia & Gala, 2015). Furthermore, preschoolers are often adamant and rigid in their understanding of maleness and femaleness, denying, for example, that it would be possible for a boy to wear a ponytail and still remain a boy, or for a girl to play roughly and still remain a girl (Blakemore, 2003)!

One reason for preschoolers' insistence on strict gender roles at this age may be cognitive. It is not until age 6 or 7 that children attain **gender constancy**, the understanding that femaleness and maleness are biological and will not change across situations (Ruble et al., 2006). Earlier, children may be so insistent about maintaining **gender roles**—the cultural expectations for behavior specific to females and males—because they believe that changing external features like clothes or hair styles could result in a change in gender (Halim et al., 2014). For more information, watch the video *Gender Development*.

**gender identity**
awareness of one's self as female or male

**gender constancy**
understanding that femaleness and maleness are biological and cannot change across situations

**gender roles**
cultural expectations for appearance and behavior specific to females and males

**stereotype**
belief that others possess certain characteristics simply as a result of being a member of a particular group

**Watch** GENDER DEVELOPMENT

## Middle Childhood

**LO 8.1.2 Explain the development of gender stereotypes and how boys and girls differ in this regard.**

In many ways, children's gender attitudes and behavior are stereotyped in middle childhood. A **stereotype** occurs when people believe that others possess certain characteristics simply as a result of being a member of a particular group. Gender stereotypes, then, attribute certain characteristics to others on the basis of whether they are female or male (Kite et al., 2008). In middle childhood, children increasingly view personality traits as associated with one gender or the other, rather than both. Traits such as "gentle"

Why are interactions between boys and girls often quasi-romantic and antagonistic in middle childhood?

and "dependent" become increasingly viewed as feminine, and traits such as "ambitious" and "dominant" become increasingly viewed as masculine (Best, 2001; Heyman & Legare, 2004). Both boys and girls also come to see occupations they associate with men, such as firefighter or engineer, as having higher status than occupations they associate with women, such as nurse or librarian, (Liben et al., 2001; Weisgram et al., 2010). Furthermore, children increasingly perceive some school subjects as boys' areas, such as math and science, and others as girls' areas, such as reading and art, (Guay et al., 2010).

Girls, however, are more flexible is their attitudes toward gender stereotypes and gender roles than boys. Girls are less likely than boys to give stereotyped answers to questions about what females and males can do and should do (Signorella et al., 1993). This divide between girls and boys has been shown in research conducted in developed countries. The research also shows that the divide has increased in recent decades. Girls, but not boys, have become more flexible about gender stereotypes and less disturbed by violations of gender roles (Leaper, 2015).

In terms of their gender self-perceptions, boys and girls also head in different directions in middle childhood (Banerjee, 2005; Kapadia & Gala, 2015). Boys increasingly describe themselves in terms of "masculine" traits. They become more likely to avoid activities that might be considered feminine, and their male peers become increasingly intolerant of anything that threatens to cross gender boundaries (Blakemore, 2003). In contrast, girls become more likely to attribute "masculine" characteristics such as "forceful" and "self-reliant" to themselves in the course of middle childhood. They do not become less likely to describe themselves as having "feminine" traits such as "warm" and "compassionate," but they add "masculine" traits to their self-perceptions. Similarly, they become more likely during middle childhood to aspire to future occupations usually associated with men, whereas boys become less likely to aspire to future occupations associated with women (Gaskins, 2015; Liben & Bigler, 2002).

Socially, children are quite gender-segregated in their play groups in middle childhood. Children begin to show a same-sex preference for playmates around 2 to 3 years of age, and by middle childhood this preference is pronounced (Leaper, 2015). When boys' and girls' play groups do interact in middle childhood, it tends to be in a manner that is at once quasi-romantic and antagonistic, such as playing a game where girls chase boys, or tossing mild insults at each other, like the one our daughter Paris came home chanting one day at age 7:

> GIRLS go to COllege to get more KNOWledge.
> BOYS go to JUpiter to get more STUpider.

Some researchers call this kind of gender play "borderwork" and see its function as clarifying gender boundaries during middle childhood (Thorne, 1993). It can also be seen as the first tentative step toward the romantic relations that will develop in adolescence.

## Adolescence

### LO 8.1.3 Describe the gender-intensification hypothesis and the extent of support for it.

**gender-intensification hypothesis**
hypothesis that psychological and behavioral differences between females and males become more pronounced at adolescence because of intensified socialization pressures to conform to culturally prescribed gender roles

Gender is an important part of the development of the self in adolescence. For example, as we saw in Chapter 7, adolescent girls experience more of a drop in their self-esteem than adolescent boys do. Physical appearance is central to adolescents' global self-esteem, and girls evaluate their physical appearance more negatively than do boys.

Gender is related not only to self-esteem, but also to many other aspects of self-development in adolescence. Psychologists John Hill and Mary Ellen Lynch (1983; Lynch, 1991) have proposed that adolescence is a particularly important time in gender socialization. According to their **gender-intensification hypothesis**, psychological and behavioral differences between females and males become more pronounced in the transition from childhood to adolescence because of intensified socialization pressures to conform to culturally prescribed gender roles. Hill and Lynch (1983) propose that it is this intensified socialization pressure, rather than the biological changes of puberty, that results in increased differences between females and males as adolescence progresses. Furthermore, they argue that the intensity of gender socialization in adolescence is greater for girls than for boys, and that this is reflected in a variety of ways in adolescent girls' development The video *Body Image in Adolescent Girls* illustrates how girls in the United States respond to gender intensification.

**Watch** BODY IMAGE IN ADOLESCENT GIRLS

Since Hill and Lynch (1983) proposed this hypothesis, other studies have supported it to some extent (Galambos, 2004; Perez-Brena et al., 2015; Priess & Lindberg, 2014). In one longitudinal study, boys and girls filled out a questionnaire on gender identity each year in sixth, seventh, and eighth grades (Galambos et al., 1990). Over this period, girls' self-descriptions became more "feminine" (e.g., gentle, affectionate), while boys' self-descriptions became more "masculine" (e.g., tough, aggressive). However, in contrast to Hill and Lynch's claim that gender intensification is strongest for girls, the pattern in this study was especially strong for boys. This is consistent with the research described in the previous section, showing that younger boys are more likely than younger girls to value strict gender roles.

It is possible that adolescent boys' emphasis on masculinity may change as they enter emerging adulthood, although research is limited. One study compared American males who were early adolescents, late adolescents, or college students (Lobel et al., 2004). Participants were given a description of either an average or outstanding male election candidate behaving gender-stereotypically or counter-stereotypically and were asked to indicate their personal election choice, to estimate the likelihood that others would choose each candidate, and to speculate how successful the candidate would be if elected. Adolescents were more likely than the emerging adult college students to favor the gender-stereotypical candidate. No differences were found between early and late adolescents. This suggests that the emphasis on male stereotypes may wane from adolescence to emerging adulthood. However, more research is needed on emerging adults' self-descriptions, and with emerging adults who are not in college.

**Critical Thinking Question:** What would you hypothesize about the self-descriptions of adolescents and emerging adults in the American majority culture? Explain whether or not you would expect an age difference in gender intensification.

Studies have shown that gender intensification is related not only to age and gender, but also to other factors. Family context turns out to be important. Researchers have found that increased conformity to gender roles during adolescence takes place primarily for adolescents whose parents value traditional gender roles (Crouter et al., 1995; Updegraff et al., 2014). Among emerging adults, too, longitudinal research has shown that those who adhere to traditional gender roles are more likely to have grown up in families where parents divided household work along traditional gender lines (Cunningham, 2001).

The findings described above on the development of the gendered self come largely from research conducted in North America. Gender intensification, however, is often considerably stronger in traditional cultures than in developed countries. Next, we take a closer look at gender in traditional cultures.

Some adolescent boys place an emphasis upon masculinity, and they may also experience social pressure to be masculine.

## SUMMARY: Development of a Gendered Self

**LO 8.1.1 Describe the development of gender identity, gender constancy, and gender roles.**

By age 3, toddlers have attained a gender identity, that is, they view themselves as female or male. It is not until age 6 or 7 that children attain gender constancy, which is the understanding that femaleness and maleness are biological and will not change across situations. Knowledge of gender roles, the cultural expectations for behavior specific to females and males, develops gradually in the course of childhood.

**LO 8.1.2 Explain the development of gender stereotypes and how boys and girls differ in this regard.**

In many ways, children's gender attitudes and behavior are stereotyped in middle childhood. Girls, however, are more flexible is their attitudes toward gender roles than boys. Also, in middle childhood, boys increasingly describe themselves exclusively in terms of masculine characteristics, while girls use both masculine and feminine self-descriptions.

**LO 8.1.3 Describe the gender-intensification hypothesis and the extent of support for it.**

According to the gender-intensification hypothesis, psychological and behavioral differences between females and males become more pronounced in the transition from childhood to adolescence because of intensified socialization pressures to conform to culturally prescribed gender roles. Also, according to this hypothesis, these pressures are greater for girls than for boys. Research provides evidence for gender intensification in early adolescence, but with boys generally showing more intensification than girls.

# 8.2 Gender in Traditional Cultures

For adolescents in traditional cultures, gender roles and expectations infuse virtually every aspect of life. Adolescent boys and girls in traditional cultures often have very different lives and spend little time in each others' presence. The expectations for their behavior as adolescents and for the kinds of work they will do as adults are sharply divided, and as a result, their daily lives do not often overlap (Schlegel & Hewlett, 2011). Furthermore, for both females and males, gender requirements tend to intensify at adolescence, allowing for very little deviation from the norm. We'll look first at the gender expectations for girls in traditional cultures, then at the gender expectations for boys.

## From Girl to Woman

**LO 8.2.1 Summarize common themes found in the socialization of adolescent girls in traditional cultures.**

Girls in traditional cultures typically work alongside their mothers from an early age. Usually by age 6 or 7, they help take care of younger siblings and cousins (Gottlieb & DeLoache, 2017; LeVine & LeVine, 2016; Whiting & Edwards, 1988). By 6 or 7 or even earlier, they also help their mothers obtain food, cook, make clothes, gather firewood, and perform all of the other activities that are part of running a household. By adolescence, girls typically work alongside their mothers as near-equal partners. The authority of mothers over their daughters is clear, but by adolescence daughters have learned the skills involved in child care and running a household so well that they can contribute an amount of work that is more or less equal to their mothers' work.

One important gender difference that occurs at adolescence in traditional cultures is that boys typically have less contact with their families and considerably more contact with their peers than they did before adolescence, whereas girls typically maintain a close relationship with their mothers and spend a great deal of time with them on a daily basis (Schlegel & Hewlett, 2011). This difference exists partly because girls are more likely to work alongside their mothers than boys are to work alongside their fathers. Even when adolescent boys do work with their fathers, they have less contact and intimacy with them than adolescent girls typically have with their mothers. This interdependence between mothers and daughters does not imply that girls remain suppressed in a dependent, childlike way. For example, Alice Schlegel (1973) described how among the Hopi, a Native American tribe, mother–daughter relationships are extremely close throughout life, yet adolescent girls are confident and assertive. Nevertheless, in the words of one team of scholars, "During adolescence, the world expands for boys and contracts for girls. Boys enjoy new privileges reserved for men; girls endure new restrictions observed for women" (Mensch et al., 1998, p. 2).

Another reason for the new restrictions placed on adolescent girls is that their budding sexuality is more tightly controlled than is the sexuality of boys (Larson et al., 2010; Regan et al., 2004). Typically, adolescent boys in traditional cultures are allowed and even expected to gain some sexual experience before marriage. Sometimes this is true of girls as well, but on the whole their sexuality is restrained. This double standard sets up a great deal of sexual and personal tension between adolescent girls and boys, with boys pressing for girls to relax their sexual resistance and girls fearful of the shame and disgrace that will fall on them (and not on the boy) if they should give in.

An excellent ethnographic example of gender-specific expectations for adolescent girls in traditional cultures comes from the work of Chiñas (1992), who studied adolescent girls and women in a Mexican village. As Chiñas describes it, prepubertal girls are often sent to the town plaza to shop for food at the outdoor market. In the course of performing this task, they become shrewd shoppers, adept at making change and performing mental addition and subtraction. However, in Mexican culture, virginity is demanded for girls before marriage. Consequently, once they reach puberty, girls are no longer allowed to go to the town plaza alone and are generally kept under close surveillance to reduce the likelihood of premarital sexual adventures. Furthermore, in the village studied by Chiñas, school is not a part of the adolescent girl's experience. If she has had the opportunity to go to school at all, it would have been only for a year or so at age 6 or 7, just long enough to become literate. Boys, in contrast, are much more likely to be allowed to attend school until age 12 or older.

In developing countries, the kinds of work children and adults do is often divided strictly by gender. Here, a girl in Mozambique helps prepare cassava, a local food.

Chiñas's description of the girls in this Mexican village illustrates common themes found in the socialization of adolescent girls in traditional cultures: early work responsibilities, limited education, close relationships with monitoring female adults, communal constraints on sexual behaviors, and preparation for marriage and gender-specific adult work.

## From Boy to Man

**LO 8.2.2 Describe the capabilities that adolescent boys in traditional cultures need to demonstrate in order to achieve manhood.**

The gender expectations for boys in traditional cultures, while similar to those for girls in some ways, are different in others. One striking difference is that for boys, manhood is something that has to be *achieved*, whereas girls are often thought to reach womanhood inevitably, mainly through biological changes (Leavitt, 1998; Lindsay & Miescher, 2003). It is true that girls are required to demonstrate various skills and character qualities before they can be said to have reached womanhood. However, in most traditional cultures, womanhood is seen as something that girls attain naturally during adolescence, and their readiness for womanhood is viewed as indisputably marked when they reach menarche. Adolescent boys have no comparable biological marker of readiness for manhood. For them, the attainment of manhood is often fraught with peril and carries a definite and formidable possibility of failure (Schlegel & Barry, 2015).

It is striking to observe how many cultures have a term for a male who is a failed man. In Spanish, for example, a failed man is termed *flojo* (a word that also means flabby, lazy, useless). Similar words exist in a wide variety of other languages (Gilmore, 1990). In contrast,

Learning to provide for a family economically is a traditional part of the male gender role. Here, an Egyptian father and son fish together on the Nile River.

although there are certainly many derogatory terms applied to women, none of them have connotations of failure at *being* a woman the way *flojo* and other terms mean failure at *being* a man.

So, what must an adolescent boy in traditional cultures do to achieve manhood and escape the stigma of being viewed as a failed man? The anthropologist David Gilmore (1990) analyzes this question across traditional cultures around the world in his book *Manhood in the Making: Cultural Concepts of Masculinity*. He concludes that in most cultures an adolescent boy must demonstrate three capacities before he can be considered a man: provide, protect, and procreate. He must *provide* in the sense that he must demonstrate that he has developed economically useful skills that will enable him to support the wife and children he is likely to have as an adult man. For example, if adult men mainly fish, the adolescent boy must demonstrate that he has learned the skills involved in fishing adequately enough to provide for a family.

Second, the adolescent boy must *protect*, in the sense that he must show that he can contribute to the protection of his family, kinship group, tribe, and other groups to which he belongs, from attacks by human enemies or animal predators. He learns this by acquiring the skills of warfare and the capacity to use weapons. As conflict between human groups has been a fact of life for most cultures throughout human history, this is a pervasive requirement.

Finally, he must learn to *procreate*, in the sense that he must gain some degree of sexual experience before marriage. An adolescent boy gains this experience not in order to demonstrate his sexual attractiveness, but so that he can prove that in marriage he will be able to perform well enough sexually to produce children. The importance of learning to procreate is reflected in the fact that sex is commonly a popular topic of conversation among adolescent boys. Among the Mehináku of Brazil, for example, adolescent boys and men joke and brag about sex, but they are also deeply concerned about potential failures because in their small community any failures to "perform" become public knowledge. Because impotence is so formidable, they use numerous magical rituals to prevent or cure it, such as rubbing the penis with various animal or plant products. As with providing and protecting, adolescent boys are under considerable pressure to show they can perform sexually, and they are ridiculed and ostracized if they cannot.

## Historical Changes and Recent Revolutions

**LO 8.2.3 Explain why female and male physiology has a profound impact on gender roles in preindustrial societies, and describe how gender roles have changed in the last half-century.**

Why are the expectations and roles so markedly different for females and males in traditional societies? These gender roles are rooted in two key biological differences that determine the kinds of work that men and women can perform in a preindustrial economy (Wood & Eagly, 2012):

1. Women's biological capacity for childbearing restricts their roles mainly to childbearing and childrearing. When they are unable to control their reproductive lives through contraception, women spend most of their late teens, 20s, and 30s either pregnant or nursing. Taking care of infants is energy-consuming. It is also time-consuming, and limits a woman's ability to spend uninterrupted time on lengthy tasks or training. Furthermore, taking care of infants restricts long-distance travel away from home, and means that activities that pose a danger to infants and young children are eschewed.

2. Men's greater physiological size, speed, and strength give them advantages in traditional work such as hunting, fishing, clearing land, plowing, and conducting warfare. Many of these activities are also too dangerous to be performed in the presence of infants and young children.

As economies become more developed and complex, however, brain matters more than brawn. Men's physical advantage does not apply to work that involves analyzing and processing information. In the past half-century, the United States and other developed countries have shifted from a manufacturing economy to a service economy requiring information and technology skills. Men continue to dominate blue-collar jobs that often require physical strength, such as construction and carpentry. Nonetheless, developed countries have undergone a technology revolution where education and knowledge have become far more important to employment prospects and success than physical prowess. Enrollment rates in tertiary education among 18- to 22-year-olds are now above 50% in every developed country (see Chapter 1).

Economic development also usually includes increased access to contraception; in turn, access to contraception makes women's adult roles less focused on childbearing and childrearing alone. The **sexual revolution**, sparked by the Federal Drug Administration's approval of the birth control pill for contraceptive use in 1960, also heralded less stringent standards of sexual morality after the 1960s and early 1970s—especially in Western countries. Young men and women no longer had to enter marriage to have a stable sexual relationship (Arnett, 2015). By now, most young people in Western developed societies have a series of sexual relationships before entering marriage, and there is widespread tolerance for premarital sex in the context of a committed, loving relationship.

**sexual revolution**
starting in the 1960s, social movement that challenged traditional codes of behavior related to sexuality and interpersonal relationships throughout the Western world

The **women's movement** of the 1960s and 1970s also vastly expanded the opportunities available to young women (Arnett, 2015). Young women of the 1950s and early 1960s were under a great deal of social pressure to find a husband. Being single was simply not a viable social status for a woman after her early 20s. Relatively few women attended college, and those who did were often there for the purpose of meeting their future husbands. The range of occupations open to young women was severely restricted—secretary, waitress, teacher, nurse, perhaps a few others. Even these occupations were supposed to be temporary for young women. What they were really supposed to be focusing on was finding a husband and having children.

**women's movement**
organized effort in the 20th century to obtain greater rights and opportunities for women

For young women in developed countries, this has changed in quite remarkable ways in the 21st century. In nearly every developed country, at every level of education from grade school through graduate school, girls now excel over boys in overall academic achievement. Young women's occupational possibilities are less restrained, and although men still dominate in engineering and some sciences, women are equal to men in obtaining law, business, and medical degrees. With many options open to them, and little pressure on them to marry in their early 20s, the lives of girls and women in developed countries today have changed almost beyond recognition from what they were some 50 years ago. Akin to boys and young men, the focus of girls and young women is on education followed by trying out various work options before making definite choices.

Take a look at Figure 8.1 (next page). It shows the results of the General Social Survey (GSS), an annual national survey of American adults, for views of the roles of men and women from 1977 to 2012. The figure shows a clear change toward more egalitarian gender attitudes in recent decades (Cotter et al., 2014). Compared to 1977, American adults today are less likely to believe men are better politicians, less likely to see women as the ones who should take care of the home, more likely to believe working mothers can have warm relationships with their children, and less likely to believe preschoolers would suffer if mothers work. However, the results of the GSS also show that

For girls and young women in developed countries, their educational and work opportunities have changed in quite remarkable ways in the 21st century.

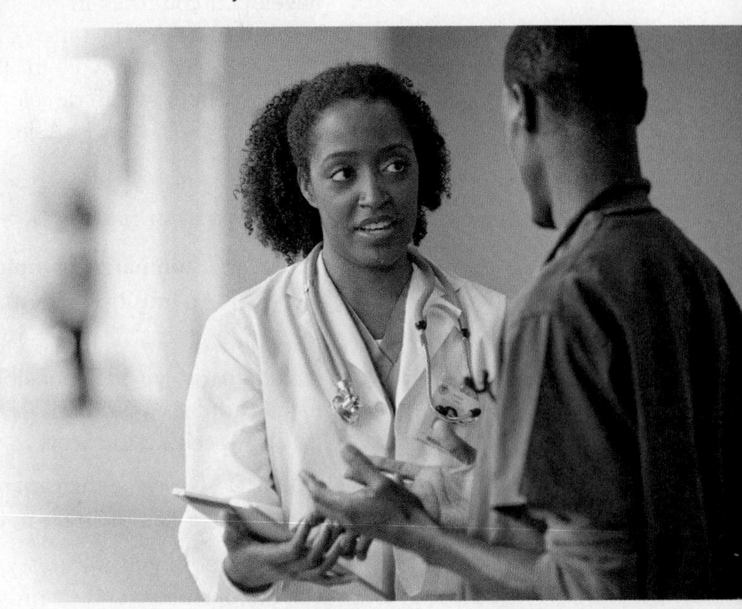

**Figure 8.1** Change in American Gender Attitudes, 1977–2012

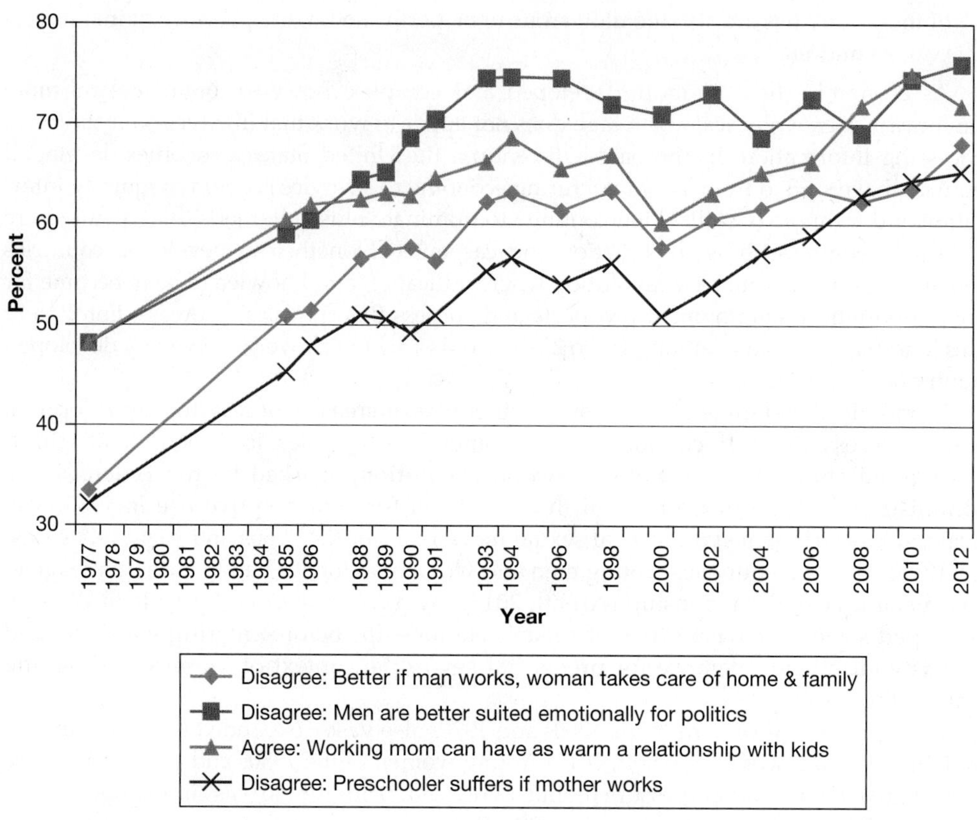


a considerable proportion of Americans—from about one-fourth to more than one-third, depending on the question—continue to harbor beliefs about gender roles not unlike the ones we have seen in traditional cultures: Men should hold the power and be out in the world doing things, and women should focus on caring for children and running the household. The GSS includes adults. Other surveys, however, show that adolescents in developing countries have less conservative perceptions of gender roles than adults do (Mensch et al., 1998; United Nations, 2010).

Gender expectations and roles, then, have undergone remarkable transformation in developed countries in the last five or so decades. The technology revolution, the sexual revolution, and the women's movement have changed expectations and roles for boys and girls, and men and women. That said, it is worth remembering that views on gender vary among people within developed countries (such as the United States), and between developed countries (such as Asian and Western countries).

## SUMMARY: Gender in Traditional Cultures

**LO 8.2.1 Summarize common themes found in the socialization of adolescent girls in traditional cultures.**

Common themes found in the socialization of adolescent girls in traditional cultures, include early work responsibilities, limited education, close relationships with monitoring female adults, communal constraints on sexual behaviors, and preparation for marriage and gender-specific adult work.

**LO 8.2.2 Describe the capabilities that adolescent boys in traditional cultures need to demonstrate in order to achieve manhood.**

In most traditional cultures, an adolescent boy must demonstrate three capacities before he can be considered a man: provide, protect, and procreate.

**LO 8.2.3 Explain why female and male physiology has a profound impact on gender roles in preindustrial societies, and describe how gender roles have changed in the last half-century.**

In preindustrial societies, women spend most of their late teens, 20s, and 30s either pregnant or nursing, which limits their mobility, and energy and time for nondomestic activities. For men, their greater physiological size, speed, and strength give them advantages in traditional work such as hunting, fishing, clearing land, plowing, and conducting warfare. As economies become more developed and complex, brain matters more than brawn. Today, in developed country, girls excel over boys at every level of education from grade school through graduate school.

# 8.3 Gender Comparisons in Developed Countries

Only 100 years ago, women were excluded from higher education and from virtually all professions. It was widely believed, even among scientists—who were all male—that women were biologically incapable of strenuous intellectual work. There has been no shortage of claims about how and why females and males are different, and runaway bestsellers such as *Men are from Mars, Women are from Venus* attest to our perennial interest in these questions.

In this section, we examine what current psychological research on cognition, emotions, and behavior shows about the extent of gender differences. In the following section, we will turn to the explanations that social scientists provide to account for the differences. (We promise that we will not be invoking the planets).

**meta-analysis**

a statistical technique that integrates the data from many studies into one comprehensive statistical analysis

**effect size**

the difference between two groups in a meta-analysis, represented by the letter *d*

**normal distribution, or bell curve**

typical distribution of characteristics of a population, resembling a bell curve in which most cases fall near the middle and the proportions decrease at the low and high extremes

## Analyzing Gender Differences

**LO 8.3.1 Explain why meta-analyses are important for reaching conclusions about gender differences.**

When we speak of gender differences, it is worth remembering that we are comparing one-half of the human species to the other—over 3.5 billion persons to the other 3.5 billion persons! Consequently, any one study showing a gender difference may be intriguing, but it does not make for strong conclusions. Instead, research on gender differences often uses a statistical technique called a meta-analysis. Let's take a closer look at this useful technique that helps us reach well-substantiated conclusions about gender differences: Watch the video *Meta-Analyses of Gender Differences* in the Research Focus feature.

## Research Focus: Meta-Analyses of Gender Differences

Child development researchers usually address research questions by conducting individual studies, such as an experiment or a survey. Sometimes, however, a researcher will approach a question by analyzing the findings that others have collected in a variety of studies. **Meta-analysis** is the name for the statistical technique that combines the data from many studies into one all-inclusive analysis. While often used to find out if females and males differ, a meta-analysis can be used on any topic for which numerous studies exist. Meta-analysis is used more often in research on gender than in most other areas, partly because so many studies have been published on gender differences (e.g., Friedman, 1989; Grabe et al., 2008; Maccoby & Jacklin, 1974).

The researcher who named this technique wrote that "the term is a bit grand, but it . . . refers to [an] analysis of analyses"

**Watch META-ANALYSES OF GENDER DIFFERENCES**

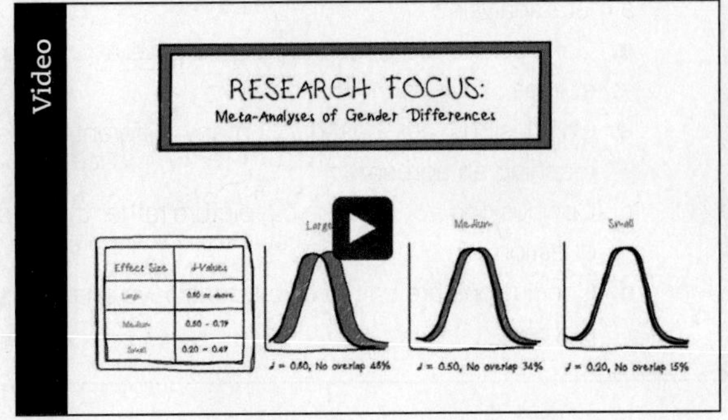

Effect Sizes and Corresponding *d* Values

| Effect Size | *d*-Values |
|---|---|
| Large | 0.80 or above |
| Medium | 0.50 – 0.79 |
| Small | 0.20 – 0.49 |

(Glass, 1976, p.3). A meta-analysis indicates whether a difference exists between groups, such as females and males. It also indicates the size of the difference. This is important because it helps us to know how meaningful a difference between groups is. The difference between groups is called the **effect size**, and it is usually represented by the letter *d* (Cohen, 1988). As you can see from the table, effect sizes can be large, medium, or small depending on the *d* values (Hines, 2015; Leaper, 2015).

So what does the effect size mean? The effect size reflects the extent to which there is no overlap between the distribution of scores for two groups. Scores for a group often fall into a **normal distribution**, or **bell curve**, in which most people are near the middle of the distribution and the proportion decreases at the low and high extremes. This is the case for wide variety of scores, such as height, academic achievement, and self-esteem.

As you can see in the following figures, an effect size or *d*-value of 0.8 means that a full 48% of scores between two groups do not overlap. This is the reason that 0.8 is a large effect size; there is a large difference between the two groups since almost half of all the people have scores that are so far apart. A *d*-value of 0.5, or medium effect, means that 34% of scores between groups do not overlap. And a *d*-value of 0.2 means that only 15% of scores do not overlap. This is why 0.2 is a small effect size. Only a small proportion of people in the two groups have scores that are entirely unalike.

Even when an effect size is large, there is still overlap between the two groups. For example, the effect size for the difference in height between men and women is very large. In Britain and the United States, the *d*-value is about 2.0 (Hines, 2015)! Yet, if you were to look around in a college classroom, you would still see quite a few men and women who were about the same height. Also, some women would be taller than some men, and some men would be shorter than some women.

In conclusion, meta-analyses are highly useful for reaching valid conclusions about group differences. This is certainly important in regard to gender because many claims of differences between females and males have been false, and any claim of differences between females and males involves a comparison of half of the human species to the other.

Distributions for Large, Medium, and Small Effect Sizes

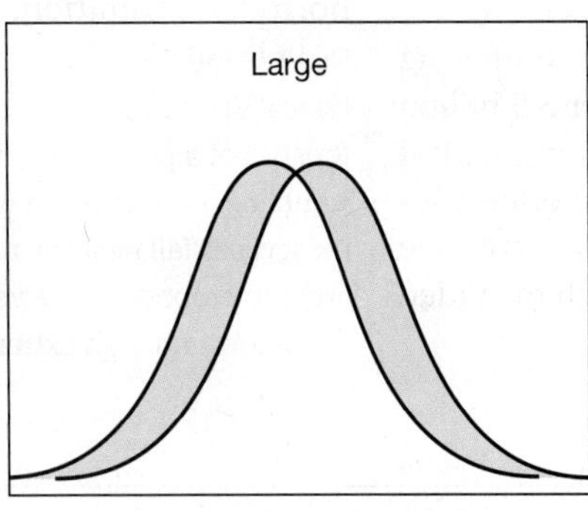

*d* = 0.80, No overlap 48%

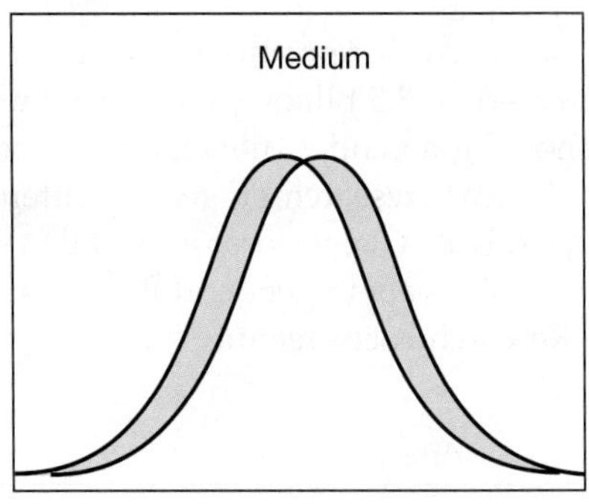

*d* = 0.50, No overlap 34%

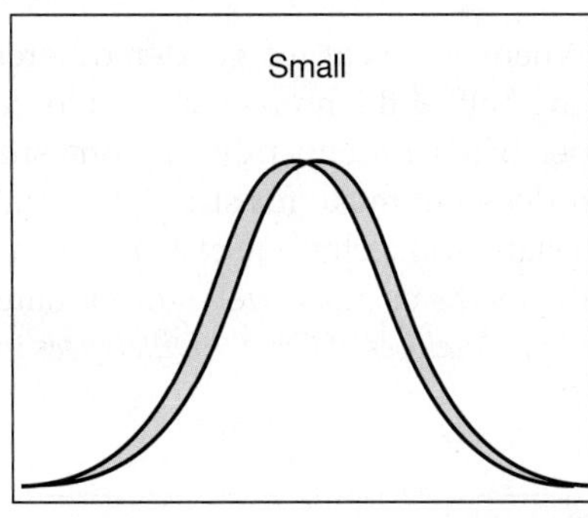

*d* = 0.20, No overlap 15%

## Review Questions

1. Which of the following statements most accurately describes a meta-analysis?
   **a.** Conclusions are based on a qualitative analysis of many studies
   **b.** Conclusions are based on many different researchers reaching an agreement
   **c.** Conclusions address the big picture rather than a specific question
   **d.** Conclusions are based on a quantitative analysis of many studies

2. Which of the following statements is true?
   **a.** A large effect size indicates that there is no overlap between two groups
   **b.** The effect size for the difference in height between men and women is small
   **c.** A large effect size means that the scores for two groups do not fall into a normal distribution
   **d.** A small effect size means that the vast majority of people in two groups are no different from another

## Differences Between Females and Males

**LO 8.3.2 Review the two overarching conclusions about gender differences, and summarize specific gender differences revealed by meta-analyses.**

Looking across meta-analyses testing for gender differences, there are two big "take-home" messages (Hyde, 2005; Zell et al., 2015):

1. There are more similarities than differences between females and males.
2. When there are gender differences, the effect size for many (but not all) of the differences are small.

To put it another way, the variability within each gender is much greater than the differences between the two genders, for most characteristics. Consequently, we should be careful not to let our perceptions of gender differences prejudge our estimations of the qualities or abilities of individual boys and girls or men and women.

Table 8.1 provides a synopsis of characteristics where large, medium, and small gender differences have been found in meta-analyses. (The table also includes a few

**Table 8.1** Gender Differences With Large, Medium, and Small Effect Sizes

| Effect Size | Psychological Characteristics | Gender Difference | Source of Evidence | Citation |
|---|---|---|---|---|
| **LARGE** | **Play** | | | |
| | Toy preference: Dolls, tea sets, dress-up clothes, etc. | Girls > Boys | Review | Hines (2015); Leaper (2015) |
| | Toy preference: Cars, action figures, sports equipment, etc. | Boys > Girls | Review | Hines (2015); Leaper (2015) |
| **MEDIUM** | **Sensorimotor** | | | |
| | Physical activity level | Boys > Girls | Meta-analysis | Else-Quest et al. (2006) |
| | Sensation seeking | Boys > Girls | Meta-analysis | Else-Quest et al. (2006) |
| | **Emotional & Interpersonal** | | | |
| | Self-control | Girls > Boys | Meta-analysis | Else-Quest et al. (2006) |
| | Self-disclosure in relationships | Girls > Boys | Review | Rose & Rudolph (2006) |
| **SMALL** | **Aggression** | | | |
| | Physical aggression | Boys > Girls | Meta-analysis | Card et al. (2008) |
| | Verbal aggression | Boys > Girls | Meta-analysis | Archer (2004) |
| | **Academic** | | | |
| | Grade point average: Overall | Girls > Boys | Meta-analysis | Voyer & Voyer (2014) |
| | Spacial ability: Mental rotation of 2- or 3-dimensional objects | Boys > Girls | Meta-analysis | Voyer et al. (1995) |
| | Spacial ability: Spatial perception of relations among objects | Boys > Girls[1] | Meta-analysis | Voyer et al. (1995) |
| | Mathematics achievement on standardized tests | Boys > Girls[1] | Meta-analysis | Lindberg et al. (2010) |
| | **Emotional & Interpersonal** | | | |
| | Collaborative speech: Responsiveness and acknowledgements | Girls > Boys | Meta-analysis | Leaper & Smith (2004) |
| | Directive speech | Boys > Girls | Meta-analysis | Leaper & Smith (2004) |
| | **Self-Concept** | | | |
| | Self-Esteem: Global | Boys > Girls | Meta-analysis | Kling et al. (1999) |
| | Self-Evaluation: Body image | Boys > Girls | Meta-analysis | Gentile et al. (2009) |
| | Self-Evaluation: Intelligence | Boys > Girls | Meta-analysis | Gentile et al. (2009); Syzmanow & Furnham (2011) |
| | Self-Evaluations: Athletic, mathematical, and spatial abilities | Boys > Girls | Meta-analysis | Gentile et al. (2009); Syzmanow & Furnham (2011) |
| | Self-Evaluations: Verbal abilities | Girls > Boys | Meta-analysis | Wilgenbusch & Merrell (1999) |

NOTE:
1. Adolescents, not younger children.

Boys surpass girls on physical aggression.

psychological characteristics where researchers did not conduct a meta-analysis, but reviewed several studies and indicated the mean or median effect size across the studies). As you can see, boys tend to be more physically active and aggressive than girls. This is reflected in play and toy preferences, and emotional and interpersonal behaviors. Boys also have higher self-evaluations in general and across more specific domains, as compared to girls. In terms of actual achievement, boys do better on some mathematical and spatial ability tests.

Girls tend to be more interpersonally and emotionally attuned, as compared to boys. They are better able to understand other people's communications. This attunement is also reflected in girls' greater self-disclosure in relationships. With respect to academic achievement, girls get better grades in school than boys.

## Qualifications About Differences Between Females and Males

**LO 8.3.3 Explain five important qualifications about gender differences revealed by meta-analyses.**

Meta-analyses provide far better information than one or a few individual studies, but there are five important qualifications about the information. The effect size of gender differences often depends on:

1. ***The Specifics of the Research.*** For example, a meta-analysis of studies on helping behaviors where people were being observed found a substantial gender difference ($d = 0.74$), with men being more helpful than women. For studies where the behaviors were not being watched, however, the gender difference vanished (Eagly & Crowley, 1986). In other words, we have to be clear about exactly what was measured when reaching conclusions about differences between females and males.
2. ***Age.*** For example, the gender difference on physical aggression is considerably larger in children than emerging adults (Hines, 2015). A finding that a gender difference exists at one point in the life course cannot be taken to mean that it exists at all points.
3. ***Culture.*** A meta-analysis examined gender differences on personality traits in 26 different cultures (Costa et al., 2001). Gender differences were larger in North America and Western Europe than in Africa and Asia. The authors suggest that people in individualistic cultures attribute their behaviors to personal characteristics, like personality traits, whereas people in collectivistic cultures are more likely to make attributions to their social roles. We need to keep in mind that differences between females and males in one culture may not exist elsewhere.
4. ***Historical Change.*** A meta-analysis of studies from 1962 to 2004 found that men used more directive speech (such as commands and critiques) than women in research conducted before 1985; but in studies published after 1985, this gender difference had disappeared (Leaper & Ayres, 2007). In fact, meta-analyses have found declines in gender differences on a considerable number of psychological characteristics over the course of the last half-century (Hyde & Linn, 1988; Leaper & Smith, 2004; Petersen & Hyde, 2010; Twenge, 2001).
5. ***Publication Bias.*** It is worth keeping in mind that journals are more likely to publish findings that indicate differences between groups than findings that do not (Ioannidis, 2005). Meta-analyses may therefore be skewed toward showing larger effect sizes for gender differences than is true in real life.

## SUMMARY: Gender Comparisons in Developed Countries

**LO 8.3.1 Explain why meta-analyses are important for reaching conclusions about gender differences.**

Meta-analysis is the name for the statistical technique that combines the data from many studies into one all-inclusive analysis. It indicates whether a difference exists between groups (e.g., females and males) and the size of the difference (*d*). Meta-analyses provide more valid results than any one study, especially when comparing one-half of the human species to the other.

**LO 8.3.2 Review the two overarching conclusions about gender differences, and summarize specific gender differences revealed by meta-analyses.**

There are two overarching conclusions: (1) there are more similarities than differences between females and males; (2) the effect sizes for many gender differences are small. As to specific gender differences, boys tend to be more physically active and aggressive than girls. They have higher self-evaluations and do better on some mathematical and spatial ability tests. Girls tend to be more interpersonally and emotionally attuned as compared to boys. Girls get better grades in school.

**LO 8.3.3 Explain five important qualifications about gender differences revealed by meta-analyses.**

Effect sizes for gender differences depend on who was studied: age (1), culture (2), and historical period (3). Effect sizes also vary depending on the research measurements used (4). Finally, meta-analyses may be skewed toward showing larger gender effect sizes than is true in real life because journals are more likely to publish findings that indicate differences between groups than findings that do not (5).

# 8.4 Reasons for Gender Differences: Theories and Research

Theories and research aiming to explain why there are differences between boys and girls, and men and women are plentiful. They run the gamut from a strong focus on biological factors to a robust emphasis on the role of socialization. Many researchers today draw across theories and emphasize the interaction of nature and nurture rather than the separation of the two. To understand the many theories and lines of research, it is helpful to differentiate them into four groups based on their core focus: biological and biosocial bases, socialization, cognition and motivation, and gender inequity. Next, we review the contributions of each.

## Biological and Biosocial Bases

**LO 8.4.1 Explain the similarities and differences between biological and biosocial accounts of gender differences.**

There are three elements to the biological basis of gender development: evolutionary, ethological, and hormonal. In the evolutionary view, females and males develop differently because over the course of many millennia of human evolution, different characteristics promoted survival for the two sexes (Buss, 2003, 2007). For males, aggressiveness and dominance promoted survival. Males with these characteristics were more likely than their peers to outfight other males for scarce resources and more likely to gain sexual access to females. Consequently, they were more likely to reproduce, and through the process of natural selection, gradually these characteristics became a standard part of a male human being. In this view, the aggressiveness, high levels of physical activity, sensation-seeking, and self-confidence of boys is rooted in a long evolutionary history.

For human females, in contrast, over the course of many millennia of evolution, survival was promoted by being nurturing, cooperative, and emotionally responsive to others. Females with these characteristics were more likely than their peers to attract males who would protect them and provide for them. They needed males to protect them because they would frequently be pregnant or caring for young children. Females with these qualities were also more likely to be effective at caring for children through the long period of vulnerability and dependency that is characteristic of the young of the human species. Consequently, their offspring were more likely to survive to reproductive age, and through natural selection, gradually these qualities became genetically, biologically based tendencies of the human female. In this view, the interpersonal and emotional responsiveness of girls is an outcome of a long evolutionary history.

**ethology**
study of animal behavior

**Ethology**, the study of animal behavior, also provides evidence of a biological basis of human gender differences. Differences that exist among female and male humans are also found among our closest primate and mammalian relatives (Diamond, 1992; Pinker, 2004). Like human males, the males in those species closely related to us are also more aggressive and dominant than females; and males who are highest in these qualities gain greater sexual access to females. Like human females, females in closely related species also are more nurturing and cooperative than males are, and they have primary responsibility for caring for the young. Like human children, the young of closely related species also play in same-sex groups. The similarity of sex-specific behavior across related species provides evidence for a biological basis for human gender differences.

**congenital adrenal hyperplasia (CAH)**
a genetic condition that involves overproduction of androgens during early prenatal development

Hormonal evidence also supports the biological basis of human gender differences. Throughout life, beginning even prenatally, female and male fetuses differ in their hormonal balances, with males having more androgens and females more estrogens. In fact, male fetuses must receive a burst of androgens in their third month of prenatal development in order to develop into males. These hormonal differences influence human development and behavior. The strongest evidence for this comes from studies of children who have hormonal abnormalities. Many studies have focused on girls with **congenital adrenal hyperplasia (CAH)**, a genetic condition that involves overproduction of androgens during early prenatal development. Girls with CAH are usually born with external genitalia that have both male and female features. In most cases the genitalia are ambiguous, and a female sex assignment takes place (Hines, 2015). In early childhood, girls with CAH are more likely than their female peers to show male-typical play behavior, including playing with "male" toys like trucks, a rough-and-tumble play style, and a preference for male playmates (Hines, 2004, 2011). Also, in two studies comparing girls with CAH to non-CAH female relatives, the girls with CAH were found to be more physically aggressive in childhood (Pasterski et al., 2007) and adolescence (Mathews et al., 2009).

Some studies have focused on girls whose mothers took hormones during pregnancy. They show that girls who were exposed to high levels of androgens engage in high levels of male-typical play (Ehrhardt & Money, 1967), whereas girls exposed to progestins (a female hormone) show high levels of female-typical play (Ehrhardt et al., 1977).

**Critical Thinking Question:** How is the case of children with hormonal abnormalities an example of a natural experiment? Do you see any limitations to the conclusions based on this research? Explain.

**biosocial construction model**
theory that emphasizes that evolution selected for human females and males to be flexible and adaptive to environmental variation and change, and that "gendered" behavior influences biology

Taken together, the evidence from evolutionary theory, ethological research, and research on hormonal abnormalities makes a compelling case for the biological basis of some gender differences in humans. The **biosocial construction model**, however, makes two important points about this evidence in arguing for the interaction of nature and nurture rather than a one-way influence of nature upon psychological development (Wood & Eagly, 2012).

The first point is that in the course of human history, especially in the last century, gender roles have changed dramatically. Recall that girls in developed countries now excel over boys at every level of education from grade school through graduate school. To give another example, women in developed countries now use as much directive speech as men. The list of dramatic changes in gender roles and diminished differences between the genders is long. Being born female or male is not nearly as determinative as evolutionary psychologists claim. This does not mean that evolution is irrelevant. According to the biosocial perspective, evolution selected for humans to be flexible and adaptive to environmental variation and change. For a very long time, under environmental conditions where brute strength rather than technological savvy was important, and where having many babies rather than limiting reproduction was important too, men protected women and men were dominant. Once those environmental conditions changed, however, so did female and male roles and psychological characteristics.

The second point highlighted by the biosocial construction model is that not only does biology influence behavior, but behavior also influences biology. Meta-analyses have shown that anticipation of athletic and other competitive behaviors cause men's testosterone to increase, apparently to energize and improve performance. Women's testosterone, too, rises with anticipation of sports participation. While men have up to 10 times the circulating levels of testosterone of women, this behavior-to-testosterone effect is similar in the sexes (Archer, 2006).

A number of studies have also shown that caring for infants and children is associated with hormonal changes (Wood & Eagly, 2012). One innovative study demonstrated that child care is associated with lower levels of testosterone in men. The study compared fathers to male peers who were not fathers in two neighboring Tanzanian groups with different approaches to child care. Among the Hadza, fathers are involved in child care on an everyday basis. They carry, bathe, feed, and soothe infants and children. Among the Datoga, child care is regarded as "women's work" and fathers have virtually no interaction with young children. As you can see in Figure 8.2, Hadza fathers had lower levels of testosterone than non-fathers. Among the Datoga, in contrast, fathers and non-fathers did not differ (Muller et al., 2009). What the study tells us is that fatherhood in and of itself does not influence testosterone levels, but taking care of infants and children seems to lower men's testosterone.

**Critical Thinking Question:** The study with Hadza and Datoga men from Tanzania was conducted at one point in time. Explain how a longitudinal design would strengthen the findings.

In sum, the biosocial construction model highlights that "gendered" behavior influences biology, differences between females and males are subject to considerable variation and change, and this human changeability may have been selected for in the course of evolution.

**Figure 8.2** Testosterone Levels in Hadza and Datoga Fathers and Non-Fathers

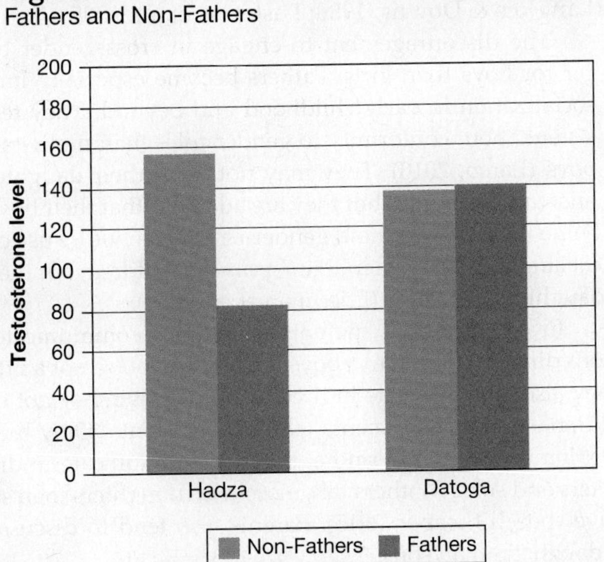

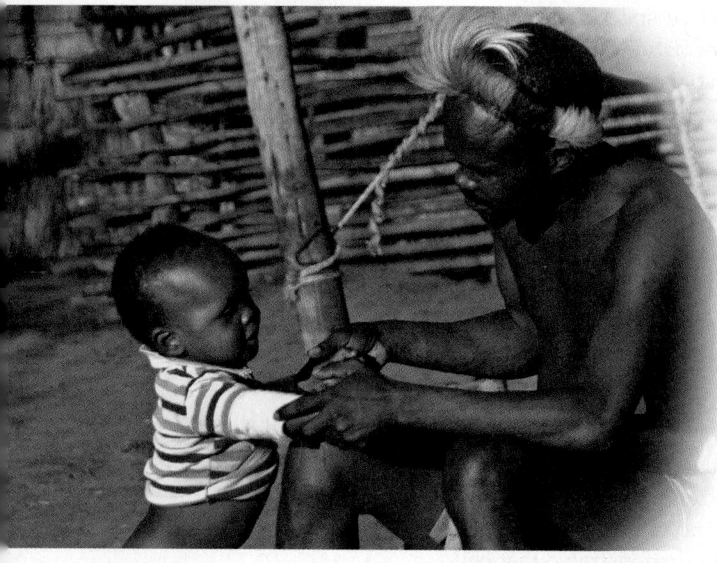

Among the Hadza, fathers are involved in child care on an everyday basis.

## Socialization

**LO 8.4.2 Describe the roles that parents, peers, media, and school play in gender socialization.**

**Social cognitive theory** emphasizes that gender differences are based on the behaviors that children learn from those around them. According to this theory, socialization takes place through three kinds of processes. First, children learn based on others' positive and negative feedback. For example, adolescent boys may tease or ridicule a male friend who signs up for after-school dance lessons. Second, children learn when they are given direct instruction in how to do things. An example would be the way girls' magazines provide guidelines for how to apply make-up. Third, children emulate the behaviors of role models. A mother who works as a physician may inspire her daughter to pursue an education in the natural sciences. Over time, according to social cognitive theory, children internalize the gender expectations and roles that surround them. Through socialization, the external norms become internal standards (Bandura, 1977; Bussey & Bandura, 2004).

**social cognitive theory**
emphasizes that gender differences are based on the behaviors that children learn from those around them

To demonstrate the importance of socialization, developmental psychologists identify how boys and girls are treated differently in ways that foster gender differences in psychological characteristics. Research has focused on parents, peers, media, and school.

**PARENTS.** In the early years, it is mainly parents who convey cultural gender messages (Kapadia & Gala, 2015; Ruble et al., 2006). They give their children names that are usually distinctively female or male. They dress boys differently from girls and provide them with different toys to play with (Bandura & Bussey, 2004). Toys are gender-specific *custom complexes*, representing distinctive cultural patterns of behavior that are based on underlying cultural beliefs (see Chapter 4). Toys for boys—such as guns, cars, and balls for playing sports—reflect the expectation that boys will be active, aggressive, and competitive. Toys for girls—such as dolls, jewelry, and playhouses—reflect the expectation that girls will be nurturing, cooperative, and attractive in appearance.

Gender socialization begins early in all cultures.

As we saw at the outset of this chapter, infants are given different toys based on gender beliefs. Parental socialization of toy choices seems to peak at about age 2 (Leaper, 2015; Lytton & Romney, 1991). Research shows that parents give more positive responses to girls than boys when they play with female-typed toys, and more positive responses to boys than girls when they play with male-typed toys. Parents also respond negatively to boys, but not girls, who play with gender-atypical toys (Langlois & Downs, 1980; Pasterski et al., 2005).

The discouragement to engage in cross-gender behaviors is stronger for boys than girls. Fathers become especially important to gender socialization in early childhood and beyond. They tend to be more insistent about conformity to gender roles than mothers are, especially for boys (Lamb, 2010). They may not want their daughters to play rough-and-tumble games, but they are adamant that their boys not be "wimps." Some mothers who hold gender-egalitarian views use counter-stereotypical language with their 3- to 7-year-old children, but they do so more with daughters than sons (Friedman et al., 2007).

In conversations, parents sometimes communicate gender expectations directly (parent to a boy: "Don't cry, you're not a little girl, are you?"). They also communicate indirectly, by approving or not contradicting their children's gender statements (child to a parent: "Only boys can be doctors, right Mommy?"). Furthermore, parents communicate in different ways with daughters and sons. Mothers talk more with daughters than sons, and use more supportive speech (Leaper, 2015). Parents also tend to discuss emotional issues more with daughters than sons.

Media, such as magazines aimed at adolescent girls, contribute to girls' gender stereotypes and concerns with their physical appearance.

Through their own behavior, language, and appearance, parents also model how females and males are supposed to be different in their culture (Bandura & Bussey, 2004). Parents who adhere to more traditional gender roles have children with more gender-typical behavior. One meta-analysis found that mother's employment is associated with children's more gender-egalitarian attitudes, and daughters' higher academic achievement (Goldberg et al., 2008).

**PEERS.** Children readily pick up cultural messages about gender roles and, by early childhood, they help enforce these roles with other children. Peers become a major source of gender socialization in early childhood and beyond. They reinforce each other for gender-appropriate behavior and reject peers who violate gender roles (Matlin, 2004; Ruble et al., 2006). One longitudinal study found that children who played with more same-sex peers showed a bigger increase in gender-typical behaviors by the end of a year, as compared to children who played with fewer same-sex peers (Martin & Fabes, 2001).

With peers, as with parents, the expectations are stricter for boys than for girls (Liben et al., 2013). Boys who cry easily or who like to play with girls and engage in girls' games are likely to be ostracized by other boys (David et al., 2004). Popular boys, more so than popular girls, are those who avoid cross-gender behavior (Blakemore et al., 2008).

**MEDIA.** Analyses of the content of media, including television, movies, magazines and videogames, show that they relentlessly promote gender stereotypes (Blakemore et al., 2008). Male characters are often aggressive and dominant, whereas female characters are victims. The physical appearance of girls and women is often highlighted, and they are often portrayed in hyper-sexualized ways. Analyses of magazines aimed at adolescent girls, for example, find that about 50% of the content focuses on physical appearance and how to be appealing to boys. This percentage actually understates the focus on physical appearance because it does not include the advertisements. Nearly half the space in magazines for adolescent girls is devoted to advertisements (Olson, 2007). Almost all of these ads are for clothes, cosmetics, and weight-loss programs. One summary of 47 studies found that the more girls were exposed to such magazines, the more they were dissatisfied with their own physical appearance (Murnen & Levine, 2007). A meta-analysis also found that exposure to media was associated with endorsement of gender stereotypes (Opplinger, 2007).

Social media also contribute to gender stereotypes and appearance concerns. Studies show that the more adolescent girls and young women use Facebook, the more likely they are to report dissatisfaction with their appearance and a "drive for thinness" (Tiggemann & Slater, 2013). It appears to be exposure to photographs on Facebook, in particular, that promotes unhappiness with appearance (Meier & Gray, 2014). When they view photos of their "friends" on Facebook, adolescent girls and young women often make appearance comparisons and draw negative conclusions about themselves (Fardouly & Vartanian, 2015).

While stereotypical gender images are common in media, there has been an increase over times in alternative images. These counter-stereotypical images are more common for female than male characters (Leaper, 2015).

**Critical Thinking Question:** Can you think of examples of female counter-stereotypical media images? How about for males?

**SCHOOL.** The school environment in many ways reflects and enforces the prevailing cultural views of gender. Do boys and girls attend different schools, or not? Do they sit intermixed in the classroom, or not? To what extent do they have the same or different subjects? Do teachers have the same achievement expectations for boys and girls, or not? How schools go about addressing these questions sends messages to children about gender.

## Education Focus: Gender in the Preschool and Primary School Classroom

School is a powerful socialization environment because children often spend many hours there. Children also often attend school for many years, starting in preschool, kindergarten, or first grade. Furthermore, teachers are very important role models. Children look to teachers for knowledge and approval.

The messages that the school context conveys to children about gender can be quite intentional, but sometimes the messages are more implicit. Two important natural experiments have examined the effects of explicit and implicit messages about gender on children.

In a study by Hilliard and Liben (2010), one group of American preschool teachers highlighted gender by referring to children by gender (such as "Good morning boys and girls"), and by organizing classroom activities based on gender (such as lining children up by sex, and posting separate boys' and girls' bulletin boards). This was the "high salience" condition. In the "low salience" condition, preschool teachers avoided making gender explicit.

The children were assessed at the outset of the study (the pretest) and after 2 weeks (the posttest). Among other things, the researchers observed the extent to which children played with same- and other-sex peers. As Figure 8.3 shows, there was no change over the course of the 2-week period for children in the low salience group. For the children in the high salience group, in contrast, there was a marked drop in play with other-sex peers. The researchers also had children rate how much they would like to play with each of their classmates. Similar to the findings for actual play, there was a drop in preference for playing with other-sex children in the high salience group, but not in the low salience group. Even when asked to rate how much they would like to play with unfamiliar children in photographs, the high salience group showed a decline in desire to play with other-sex children. Hilliard and Liben argue that "a clear implication of the findings . . . is that schools should make it as unacceptable to use gender-specific language and divisions as it is to use race-specific language and divisions" (p. 1796).

A second natural experiment was conducted by Karniol and Gal-Disegni (2009) on the impact of implicit gender stereotypes. Here the researchers compared Israeli first graders from two neighboring schools. The children in the schools were similar on demographic variables. In one school, however, first graders were taught how to read with the aid of a textbook that included a variety of gender-typed language, images, and examples. For example, boys were portrayed as playing with a ball and girls were shown playing with dolls. In the other school, first graders used a gender-neutral textbook. For example, females and males were portrayed as engaging in the same kinds of activities, whether preparing dinner, racing a bike, or buying flowers.

The children were assessed during the final month of the school year, and findings showed that the groups of children had come to differ. Children using the gender-neutral reader rated a larger number of behaviors as appropriate for both females and males, as compared to children using the gender-typed textbook. Children using the gender-neutral reader were also more likely to judge stereotypically female activities as appropriate for both females and males. The researcher conclude that: "To the extent that society has an interest in fostering more heterogeneous perceptions and the reduction of gender stereotypes, choices of [textbooks] and other educational materials should be guided by a deeper understanding of the impact of the implicit content of such materials on young children" (p. 418).

**Figure 8.3** Average Number of Peers Played With (Across 15-Second Observations)

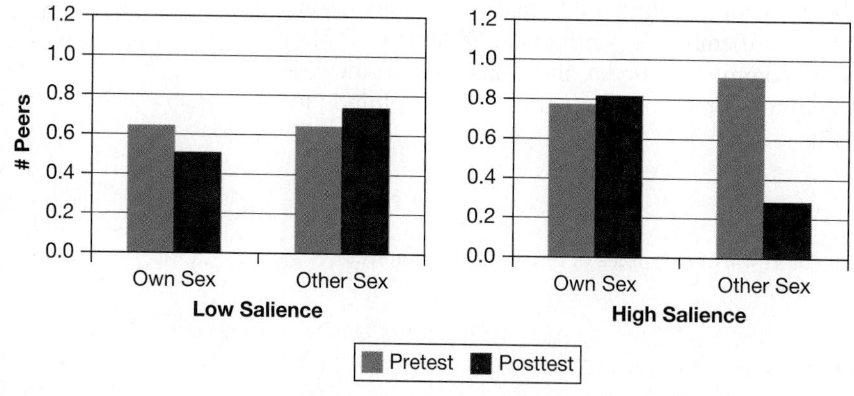


### Review Question

As authors, we made the decision to list groups alphabetically as much as possible in this text. If you look back in this chapter, you will see that we write: "boys and girls," "females and males," and "men and women." Similarly, if you glance across all chapters, you will see that we list other kinds of groups alphabetically, such as ethnic groups and nationalities. Why do you think we made that decision? Also, locate a recent issue of a reputable developmental journal (for example, *Child Development* or the *Journal of Research on Adolescence*) and review how groups are listed in articles? What did you find?

## Cognition and Motivation

**LO 8.4.3 Explain how gender schemas lead to self-socialization.**

As a result of gender socialization, from early childhood onward, children use **gender schemas** as a way of understanding and interpreting the world around them. Recall from Chapter 5 that *scheme* is Piaget's term for a cognitive structure for organizing and processing information. (*Scheme* and *schema* are used interchangeably in psychology.) A gender schema is a gender-based cognitive structure for organizing and processing information (Martin & Ruble, 2004).

Once children learn the gender roles of their culture, they may strive to conform to them. Here, girls in Cambodia attend a dance class.

According to **gender schema theory**, gender is one of our most important schemas from early childhood onward (Liben et al., 2014). By the time we reach the end of early childhood, on the basis of our socialization we have learned to categorize a wide range of activities, objects, and personality characteristics as "female" or "male." This includes not just the obvious—vaginas are female, penises are male—but many things that have no inherent "femaleness" or "maleness" but are nevertheless taught as possessing gender. Examples include the moon as "female" and the sun as "male" in traditional Chinese culture, or blue as a "boy color" and pink as a "girl color" (in Korea, pink is a "boy color," which illustrates how cultural these designations are).

Gender schemas influence how we interpret the behavior of others and what we expect from them (Frawley, 2008). In early childhood, children tend to believe that their own preferences are true for everyone in their gender (Liben et al., 2013). For example, a boy who dislikes peas may justify it by claiming "boys don't like peas." Children (and adults) also tend to encode, interpret, and remember in ways that reflect their gender schemas. In one study (Liben & Signorella, 1993), children who were shown pictures that violated typical gender roles (such as, a woman driving a truck) tended to remember them in accordance with their gender schemas (a man, not a woman, driving the truck). Throughout life, we tend to notice and remember information that fits within our gender schemas and ignore or dismiss information that is inconsistent with them (David et al., 2004).

Once young children possess gender schemas, they seek to maintain consistency between their schemas and their behavior, a process called **self-socialization**. The **gender self-socialization model** highlights that children actively internalize gender schemas as part of their identity (Tobin et al., 2010). Boys become quite insistent about doing things they regard as boy things and avoiding things that girls do; girls become equally intent on avoiding boy things and doing things they regard as appropriate for girls (Bandura & Bussey, 2004; Tobin et al., 2010). In this way, according to a prominent gender scholar, "cultural myths become self-fulfilling prophesies" (Bem, 1981, p. 355). By the end of early childhood, gender roles are enforced not only by socialization from others, but also by self-socialization, as children strive to conform to the gender expectations they perceive in the culture around them.

**gender schema**
gender-based cognitive structure for organizing and processing information, comprising expectations for females' and males' appearance and behavior

**gender schema theory**
emphasizes that children learn to categorize a wide range of activities, objects, and personality characteristics as "female" or "male"

**self-socialization**
process by which people seek to maintain consistency between their gender schemas and their behavior

**gender self-socialization model**
highlights that children actively internalize gender schemas as part of their identity

## Gender Inequity

**LO 8.4.4 Explain how gender inequity is related to gender differences.**

According to **social identity theory**, seeing oneself as a member of a social group, such as being female or male, leads to common biases. These biases include in-group favoritism, conformity to in-group norms, exaggeration of group contrasts, and out-group hostility (Tajfel & Turner, 1979). An important aspect of the differentiation between social groups is that members of higher-status groups tend to guard in-groups boundaries more strictly than members of lower-status groups (Liben et al., 2013). This may be why males exceed females in enforcing gender conformity. As we saw earlier, boys react more negatively to cross-gender behaviors in their male peers as compared to girls' responses to cross-gender behaviors in female peers. Also, fathers are more likely than mothers to discourage cross-gender behaviors in their sons.

**social identity theory**
emphasizes that seeing oneself as a member of a social group, such as being female or male, leads to common biases, including in-group favoritism

Fathers tend to promote conformity to gender roles more than mothers do.

While boys and men often lose status when behaving in "feminine" ways, girls and women sometimes gain status from adopting "masculine" attributes (Unger, 2007). This helps to explain the findings that boys in the course of childhood increasingly draw back from "feminine" activities and careers associated with women, whereas girls become more likely to embrace "masculine" self-perceptions and career aspirations.

What are the implications of gender inequity on gender differences? Research has compared nations that differ on men's and women's access to social power. For example, the United Nations Development Program (UNDP) has created a **Gender Empowerment Measure (GEM)** that combines assessments of the extent to which women are equal to men in earned income, as well as representation in national legislatures and executive business positions. Analyses show a correlation between GEM and the extent of psychological differences between men and women. Gender differences are larger in nations where women have less power, including on mathematics achievement, agreeableness, and physical aggression (Else-Quest & Grabe, 2012). Another way to put this is that as gender equity rises, gender differences diminish.

**Gender Empowerment Measure (GEM)**
assessments of the extent to which women are equal to men in earned income, as well as representation in national legislatures and executive business positions

As you can see, explaining differences between 3.5 billion females and 3.5 billion males is not simple, and perhaps for this reason a large number of accounts have been proffered. Biological, biosocial, socialization, cognitive, motivational, and gender inequity explanations have made contributions that help us gain a multi-faceted understanding.

## SUMMARY: Reasons for Gender Differences: Theories and Research

**LO 8.4.1 Explain the similarities and differences between biological and biosocial accounts of gender differences.**

The evidence from evolutionary theory, ethological research, and research on hormonal abnormalities makes a compelling case for the biological basis of some gender differences in humans. The biosocial construction model also sees biology as important, but it emphasizes the interaction of nature and nurture rather than a one-way influence of nature upon psychological development. According to the biosocial perspective, evolution selected for humans to be adaptive to environmental variation, rather than having fixed gender characteristics once and for all. Furthermore, even as biology influences behavior, behavior (such as child care) also influences biology.

**LO 8.4.2 Describe the roles that parents, peers, media, and school play in gender socialization.**

Social cognitive theory emphasizes that gender differences are based on the behaviors that children learn from those around them. Parents often encourage gender typical behavior (in dress and play) and discourage cross-gender behaviors. Children also reinforce each other for gender-appropriate behavior and reject peers who violate gender roles. Media commonly promote gender stereotypes. Schools typically reflect and enforce the prevailing cultural views of gender.

**LO 8.4.3 Explain how gender schemas lead to self-socialization.**

According to gender schema theory, gender is one of our most important schemas from early childhood onward. By the end of early childhood, on the basis of our socialization we have learned to categorize a wide range of activities, objects, and personality characteristics as "female" or "male." Once young children possess gender schemas, they seek to maintain consistency between their schemas and their behavior, a process called self-socialization.

**LO 8.4.4 Explain how gender inequity is related to gender differences.**

According to social identity theory, seeing oneself as a member of a social group, such as being female or male, leads to common biases. These biases include in-group favoritism, conformity to in-group norms, exaggeration of group contrasts, and out-group hostility. Also, members of higher-status groups tend to guard in-groups boundaries more strictly than members of lower-status groups. This may be why males (fathers, male peers) exceed females (mothers, female peers) in enforcing gender conformity.

# 8.5 Beyond the Binary

As a college student, you are probably well aware that colleges and universities in recent years are moving away from asking students to classify themselves into the binary categories of female and male. Alternatives are multiplying. Psychological research also increasingly addresses gender in ways that go beyond the binary.

## Androgyny

**LO 8.5.1 Describe the extent to which androgyny has been linked to positive outcomes.**

Must we think of people as being either feminine or masculine? If a girl possesses "feminine" traits, does that mean that she must be low on "masculine" traits, and vice versa for boys? Some scholars have argued that the healthiest human personalities contain both kinds of traits. **Androgyny** is the term for the combination of feminine and masculine traits in one person.

**androgyny**
a combination of "female" and "male" personality traits

The idea of androgyny first became popular in the 1970s (e.g., Bem, 1977; Spence & Helmreich, 1978). The women's movement of the 1960s and 1970s had led many people in the West to reconsider ideas about female and male roles. One outcome of this thinking was that it might be best to transcend the traditional opposition of feminine and masculine traits and instead promote the development of the best of each. In this view, there is no reason why a man could not be both independent ("masculine") and nurturing ("feminine"), or why a woman could not be both compassionate ("feminine") and ambitious ("masculine"). Androgynous persons would rate themselves highly on traits from both the "feminine" column and the "masculine" column in Table 8.2.

Advocates of androgyny have argued that being androgynous is better than being either masculine or feminine because androgynous persons have a greater repertoire of traits to draw on in their daily lives (Bem, 1977; Leszczynski & Strough, 2008). It might be better on some occasions to be gentle ("feminine") and on other occasions to be assertive ("masculine"). More generally, it might be best to be ambitious ("masculine") at work and affectionate ("feminine") at home. Advocates of androgyny point to research evidence that androgynous women are better at saying "no" to unreasonable requests (Kelly et al., 1981). In contrast,

**Table 8.2** Feminine and Masculine Traits

| Feminine | Masculine |
|---|---|
| Yielding | Self-reliant |
| Cheerful | Defends own beliefs |
| Shy | Independent |
| Affectionate | Athletic |
| Flatterable | Assertive |
| Loyal | Strong personality |
| Sensitive to others | Forceful |
| Understanding | Has leadership abilities |
| Compassionate | Willing to take risks |
| Eager to soothe hurt feelings | Makes decisions easily |
| Soft-spoken | Self-sufficient |
| Warm | Dominant |
| Tender | Willing to take a stand |
| Gullible | Aggressive |
| Childlike | Acts as a leader |
| Does not use harsh language | Individualistic |
| Loves children | Competitive |
| Gentle | Ambitious |

SOURCE: Bem (1974).

Child development research with gender and sexual minority youth is growing in parallel with changing societal norms—reflected in this parade in Massachusetts. Nonetheless, gender non-conforming youth are at risk for harassment and social ostracism.

highly feminine women have been found to be higher in anxiety and lower in self-esteem (Bem, 1975). One study found that androgynous men and women tend to have higher "emotional intelligence"—or insight into their own and others' feeling—than men and women who are more stereotypically masculine or feminine (Guastello & Guastello, 2003).

But what about children and adolescents? Is androgyny best for them? Some research has found that androgynous children and adolescents are more flexible and creative than other children and adolescents (Hemmer & Kleiber, 1981; Jönsson & Carlson, 2000). Research evidence also indicates that in adolescence, androgyny is more likely to be related to a positive self-image for girls than for boys. Androgynous girls generally have a more favorable self-image than girls who are either highly feminine or highly masculine. However, highly masculine boys have more favorable self-images than boys who are feminine or androgynous (Markstrom-Adams, 1989; Orr & Ben-Eliahu, 1993).

Why would this be the case? Probably because adolescents' views of themselves are a reflection of how they measure up to cultural expectations. As we have seen, people in the West have become more favorable toward females who are androgynous. It is regarded more favorably now than it was 50 years ago for females to be ambitious, independent, and athletic, and to possess other "masculine" traits.

It is revealing that not only self-image, but also peer acceptance is highest in adolescence among androgynous girls and masculine boys (Leszczynski & Strough, 2008; Massad, 1981). Among emerging adults, too, androgynous females and masculine males are viewed favorably by peers, whereas males who violate gender norms are viewed negatively (Sirin et al., 2004). For both adolescents and emerging adults, their evaluations of gender-related behavior reflect the expectations and values of their culture.

## Gender Minorities

**LO 8.5.2 Explain why gender nonconforming and transgender youth are starting to gain research attention.**

As described earlier, gender identity refers to a person's self-categorization as female or male. Psychological research is growing on children, adolescents, and emerging adults whose behaviors and self-identifications fall outside the norm. **Gender nonconforming** youth refers to youth who typically identify as either female or male, but whose behaviors are androgynous to a degree where it falls outside conventional norms (Diamond et al., 2015). As we saw above, some degree of androgyny has become increasingly acceptable and common, especially in girls. Scholars, however, are calling for more research on gender nonconforming youth because they are at risk for harassment and social ostracism. Also, researchers point out that there is a cultural association between gender nonconformity and homosexuality, but that studies of gender-nonconforming youth who are heterosexual are needed (Diamond et al., 2015). (We will discuss sexual minority youth in Chapter 10 when we address sexual development.)

**gender nonconforming**
persons who identify as either female or male, but whose behaviors are androgynous to a degree where it falls outside conventional norms

**Transgender** youth are those whose self-identification does not match their genetic sex. Historically, most research has been on transsexuals who typically report a fundamental mismatch between their gender and their sex, and who may address this misalignment through physical transformations ranging from wearing clothes characteristic of the other sex to sex reassignment surgery. The term *transgender*, however, has been created to encompass persons whose experiences are more ambiguous. For example, some transgender youth do not wish to self-identity with either gender. There is limited research on the processes of transgender identity development.

**transgender**
persons whose self-identification does not match their genetic sex

Research, however, indicates that transgender adolescent and emerging adults are at notable risk for verbal and physical aggression (Diamond et al., 2015). In one large-scale survey of more than 150,000 American college students, 24% of students who self-identified as transgender, genderqueer, nonconforming, or questioning reported experiencing sexual assault since entering college. Sexual assault was defined as "nonconsensual penetration or sexual touching involving physical force or incapacitation." The comparable figures for students self-identifying as female and male were 23% and 5%, respectively (Cantor et al., 2015). The overall response rate for this survey was quite low (19%), but the figures for sexual assault were similar across colleges that had low and high response rates.

**intersectionality**
describes how individuals have more than one social identity and that these various identities overlap

**marianismo**
in Latino cultures, an ideal that women should emulate the Virgin Mary, for example, by being submissive, self-denying, and pure

**machismo**
ideology of manhood, common in Latino cultures, which emphasizes males' dominance over females

## Intersectionality

**LO 8.5.3 Give an example of why intersectionality is important in understanding gender.**

Theory and research on **intersectionality** emphasize that individuals have more than one social identity and that these various identities overlap. Gender intersects, for example, with ethnicity and social class in important ways (Cole, 2009; Shields, 2008). If you go back and look at what you wrote about for the end-of-chapter journaling question for Chapter 1, this may be quite clear to you.

Gender roles in American minority cultures differ in important ways from gender roles in the majority culture. Among Asian and Latino communities in the United States, gender role expectations have in some ways been more traditional than within the majority culture, especially for girls. The Cultural Focus feature describes how this has been changing among Latinas.

## Cultural Focus: Gender Among Latinas

Gender roles intersect with ethnicity in the United States. Among Latinas and Latinos, gender roles have been highly traditional until recently, much along the lines of the traditional cultures described earlier in this chapter (Abreu et. al., 2000; Rivadeneyra & Ward, 2005; Vasquez & Fuentes, 1999). The role of women was concentrated on caring for children, taking care of the home, and providing emotional support for the husband. Historically, the Catholic Church has been influential in the Latino community, and women have been taught to emulate the Virgin Mary by being submissive and self-denying, an ideology known as **marianismo**. The role of men, in contrast, has been guided by the ideology of **machismo**, which emphasizes male dominance over females. Men have been expected to be the undisputed heads of household and to demand respect and obedience from their wives and children. The traditional aspects of manhood have been strong among Latinos—providing for a family, protecting the family from harm, and procreating a large family (Arciniega et al., 2008).

In recent years, however, evidence has emerged that gender expectations have begun to change in the Latino community, at least with respect to women's roles. Latina women are now employed at rates similar to Whites, and a Latina feminist movement has emerged (Denner & Guzmán, 2006; Taylor et al., 2007). This movement does not reject the traditional emphasis on the importance of the role of wife and mother, but seeks to value these roles while also expanding the roles available to Latinas. One study found that although Latina adolescents are aware of the traditional gender expectations of their culture, they often strive to negotiate a less traditional and more complex and personal form of the female gender role in their relationships with family, peers, and teachers (Denner & Dunbar, 2004). Watch the video *Gender Among Latinas* to hear how Latina adolescents speak about their views of gender.

**Watch** GENDER AMONG LATINAS

### Review Question

While gender roles and changes to those roles have distinctive characteristics in the Latino community, you have also seen in this chapter that on the whole expectations for American males have changed less than for American females. Some have argued that it is detrimental to American boys' and men's psychological well-being to be highly "masculine" because among other things it prevents them from expressing emotions, acknowledging psychological distress, forming close friendships, and seeking mental health treatment (Kindlon & Thompson, 1999; Pollack, 1998; Way, 2011). To what extent do you agree with this argument, and do you think it applies equally across ethnic groups within the United States? Explain.

Focusing on the intersection of gender, race, and residence, Richard Majors has described the "Cool Pose" as common to Black male adolescents and emerging adults in urban areas of the United States (Majors & Billson, 1992). The Cool Pose involves language and behavior intended to display toughness and detachment. It is demonstrated in creative, sometimes flamboyant performances in a variety of settings, from the classroom to the basketball court to the street. These performances are meant to convey pride and confidence. According to Majors (1989), this assertion of masculinity helps Black youth guard their self-esteem and dignity in the face of contemporary discrimination (Stevenson, 2004), and in the context of a history of slavery and denigration. However, Majors also argues that the Cool Pose can be damaging to the relationships of Black youth because it requires a refusal to express emotions or needs that they fear would make them vulnerable. Also, the Cool Pose has been linked to delinquency and crime in adolescents and emerging adults (Hall, 2009; Hall & Pizarro, 2011).

### SUMMARY: Beyond the Binary

**LO 8.5.1 Describe the extent to which androgyny has been linked to positive outcomes.**

Androgyny is the term for the combination of feminine and masculine traits in one person. Some research has found that androgynous children and adolescents are more flexible and creative than other children and adolescents. Also, androgynous girls have a more positive self-image than girls who are either highly feminine or highly masculine.

**LO 8.5.2 Explain why gender nonconforming and transgender youth are starting to gain research attention.**

Gender nonconforming youth refers to youth who typically identify as either female or male, but whose behaviors are androgynous to a degree that falls outside conventional norms. Transgender youth are those whose self-identification does not match their genetic sex. Both groups are at risk for social ostracism, harassment, and sexual assault.

**LO 8.5.3 Give an example of why intersectionality is important in understanding gender.**

Intersectionality means that individuals have more than one social identity, and that these various identities overlap. For example, researchers have described the "Cool Pose" as common to Black male adolescents and emerging adults in urban areas of the United States and have pointed out that it is associated with both benefits and risks.

# 8.6 Globalization and the Future of Gender

The social roles and psychological characteristics of girls and women have changed dramatically in most industrialized nations since the mid-20th century. The psychology of females has changed more than the psychology of males. Girls and women have adopted many of the attributes associated with boys and men, with little complementary tendency of boys and men to adopt female attributes. In developing countries, changes are also occurring in terms of opportunities and roles available to girls and women, but important gender gaps remain.

## Gender in Today's World: Education, Unpaid Work, and Physical Violence

**LO 8.6.1 Describe today's state of affairs for girls and women in regard to education, unpaid work, and physical violence.**

**Gender Parity Index (GPI)** assessment of the extent to which educational attainment is equal for boys and girls

The United Nations (UN) calculates the **Gender Parity Index (GPI)** to assess the extent to which educational attainment is equal for boys and girls. The GPI is calculated as a ratio of the value for females to that of males. A GPI value of 1.00 indicates parity between the sexes. Values below 1.00 indicate disparity in favor of boys, whereas values above 1.00 indicate disparity in favor of girls.

**Table 8.3** Gender Parity Index (GPI) in Primary and Secondary Education Enrollment

| | Gender Parity Index (GPI) | | | |
|---|---|---|---|---|
| | Primary | | Secondary | |
| | 1999 | 2007 | 1999 | 2007 |
| World | 0.93 | 0.97 | 0.92 | 0.96 |
| Africa | 0.89 | 0.93 | 0.88 | 0.87 |
| Asia | 0.93 | 0.97 | 0.87 | 0.95 |
| Europe | 0.99 | 1.00 | 1.03 | 1.01 |
| Latin America and the Caribbean | 0.98 | 1.00 | 1.06 | 1.07 |
| North America | 1.00 | 1.01 | 0.96 | 1.02 |
| Oceania | 0.98 | 0.97 | 0.99 | 0.99 |

SOURCE: United Nations (2010).

Table 8.3 shows the GPI for school enrollment rates in 1999 and 2007 for primary and secondary school in different regions of the world (United Nations, 2010). In 1999, as you can see in the table, there was a gender disparity in favor of boys for both primary and secondary education across almost all regions of the world. However, this gap between girls and boys has been closing in many regions of the world. By 2007, girls had reached parity with boys in Europe, Latin America and the Caribbean, and North America on primary school enrollment. On secondary school enrollment, girls had even come to surpass boys in those three regions of the world. However, girls continue to lag considerably behind boys in Africa and Asia, and this disparity accounts for the fact that on a worldwide scale fewer girls than boys are enrolled in primary and secondary school.

Now, take a look at Table 8.4 which shows the GPI for tertiary education in 1990 and 2007, both for the world as a whole, as well as for different regions (United Nations, 2010). As you can see, there are two main regions of the world where females lag behind males in enrollment: South and West Asia, and Sub-Saharan Africa. For all other regions and on a worldwide scale, however, females now surpass males among students who reach the tertiary level of education.

When it comes to **research and development (R&D)**, however, girls and women continue to lag behind in every region of the world. R&D comprise the creation of new knowledge through research and experimentation, and the use of this knowledge for new applications. R&D underlies many of the improvements to human welfare in the course of 20th century, including scientific and technological innovations. As you can see in Figure 8.4 (next page), there are far fewer female than male researchers across the regions of the world (United Nations, 2010).

**research and development (R&D)**
comprise the creation of new knowledge through research and experimentation, and the use of this knowledge for new applications

**Table 8.4** Gender Parity Index (GPI) in Tertiary Education Enrollment

| | Gender Parity Index (GPI) | |
|---|---|---|
| Region | 1990 | 2007 |
| World | 0.90 | 1.10 |
| Central and Eastern Europe | 1.20 | 1.30 |
| North America and Western Europe | 1.10 | 1.35 |
| Central Asia | 1.00 | 1.10 |
| Latin America and the Caribbean | 0.95 | 1.20 |
| East Asia and the Pacific | 0.65 | 1.00 |
| Arab States | 0.60 | 1.00 |
| South and West Asia | 0.50 | 0.75 |
| Sub-Saharan Africa | 0.45 | 0.65 |

SOURCE: United Nations (2010).

**Figure 8.4** Women's and Men's Share of the Total Number of Researchers

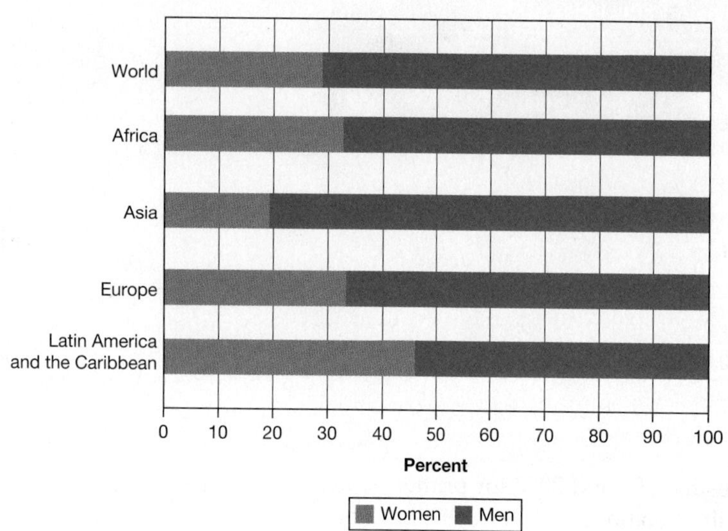


According to the United Nations, reasons for women's underrepresentation in R&D include the fact that they are less likely than men to obtain tertiary education in science, engineering, and technology. Also, women continue to have heavy household and family responsibilities, even as they work outside the home. Take a look at Figure 8.5, and you can see how women spend more hours than men every day on housework, caring for family members, and volunteer work. This gender gap ranges from about 1 hour in countries such as Denmark and Sweden to 5 hours in countries such as Iraq and Pakistan (United Nations, 2010). As we saw earlier in this chapter, the participation in household work and child care starts early for girls in traditional cultures. Also, families in traditional cultures often expect more domestic labor from daughters than sons, and allow sons to pursue more education than daughters.

Within the family, it is a worldwide phenomenon that many women suffer physical violence from their intimate partner. The proportion of women who experience such physical violence varies widely from country to country. For example, less than 10% of women report experiencing intimate partner violence during their lifetime in Albania and Canada. In countries such as Haiti, Lithuania, and Nicaragua, the figure is about 30%. The highest prevalence, at about 50%, is found in Ethiopia, Peru, and Zambia (United Nations, 2010). Consistently across countries, young females between ages 15 and 24 are the most likely to suffer physical violence from their intimate partner.

**Figure 8.5** Average Time Women and Men Spend on Housework, Caring for Family Members, and Volunteer Work

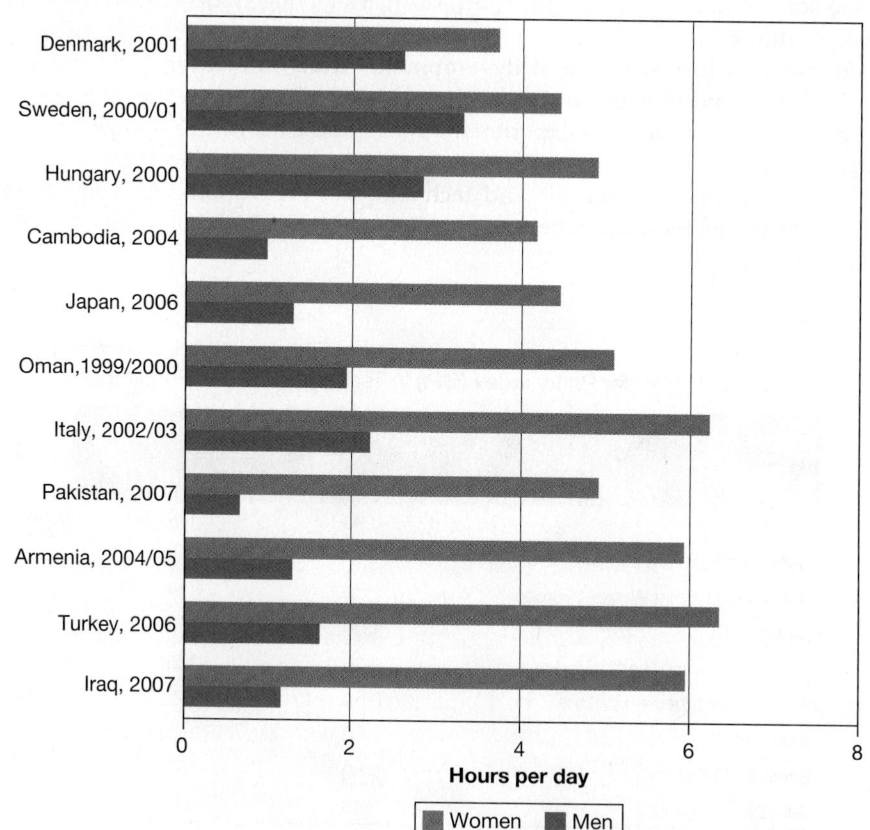

These snapshots in regards to education, unpaid labor, and domestic violence show that girls and women are at a disadvantage compared to boys and men across the world. The disparity, however, is far more pronounced in economically developing regions of the world. Also, gender disparities in educational attainment have been declining. In developed countries, girls now surpass boys in educational enrollment at every level.

## Gender in Tomorrow's World

**LO 8.6.2 Explain how economic changes in developing countries are changing gender roles.**

What would you predict in regards to gender parity and the everyday lives of girls and boys in tomorrow's world? Looking into the future is not easy. However, gender parity may increase and discrimination against girls may decrease as globalization proceeds and traditional cultures become increasingly industrialized and connected to the global economy.

The massive changes in women's roles over the past century in developed countries demonstrate the enormous influence that culture can have on the raw material of biology in human development. As cultures change, gender roles can change, even though the underlying biology of human development remains the same. Many female-male distinctions that were widely thought to be sex differences have turned out to be gender differences after all.

Because traditional cultures are likely to continue to move further in the direction of economic development, gender roles within these cultures are likely to become more egalitarian as well. Traditional gender roles are often rooted in biological differences—male physical strength and female reproductive capacity—that determine the kind of work that men and women can perform in a preindustrial economy. With economic development, however, brains matter more than brawn. As we have seen, the education gap between girls and boys has narrowed. Boys still get more education in most places, but girls exceed boys in some places. For all boys and girls, we might do well to heed the words of Malcolm X (1970): "Education is our passport to the future, for tomorrow belongs to the people who prepare for it today."

### SUMMARY: Globalization and the Future of Gender

**LO 8.6.1 Describe today's state of affairs for girls and women in regard to education, unpaid work, and physical violence.**

Even as girls still lag behind boys, the gap between girls and boys in educational attainment has been closing in the developing world. In the developed world, in contrast, girls now exceed boys in enrollment in primary, secondary, and tertiary educational institutions. Across the world, women spend more hours than men on unpaid work, such as child care. The proportion of women who suffer physical violence from their intimate partner varies widely from country to country (e.g., less than 10% in Albania and Canada, about 50% in Peru and Zambia).

**LO 8.6.2 Explain how economic changes in developing countries are changing gender roles.**

The massive changes in women's roles over the past century in developed countries demonstrate the enormous influence that culture can have on the raw material of biology in human development. Many female–male distinctions that were widely thought to be sex differences have turned out to be gender differences after all. Because traditional cultures are likely to continue to move further in the direction of economic development, gender roles within these cultures are likely to become more egalitarian as well.

# Apply Your Knowledge as a Professional

The topics covered in this chapter apply to a wide variety of career professions. Watch this video to learn how they apply to a professor of developmental psychology.

**Journaling Question:** There are quite a few stories and films that involve the premise of a person experiencing life as the "other" gender, for example, a man suddenly being able to hear what women are thinking. Imagine a day in your life as another gender (e.g., female, male, transgender). Reflect on your day, perhaps including key similarities and differences to your life so far.

Chapter 9

# Family Relationships: Foundations and Variations

## Learning Objectives

**9.1 The First Social Relationship: Two Theories**

9.1.1 Explain why Erikson emphasized that an infant's primary caregiver must provide love and care.

9.1.2 Review three key research findings that inspired Bowlby's attachment theory, and describe the essential features of the theory.

**9.2 Attachment to Parents**

9.2.1 Identify the four types of attachment quality, and explain their determinants and effects.

9.2.2 Explain the two major critiques of attachment theory and research.

9.2.3 Compare traditional cultures and developed countries on typical patterns of father involvement with infants and toddlers.

**9.3 The Parent–Child Relationship**

9.3.1 Describe the four types of parenting styles and their effects, and explain the cultural limitations of this research.

9.3.2 Describe the main cultural variations in how parents discipline young children, and explain how cultural context influences children's responses to discipline.

9.3.3 Explain how middle childhood represents a turning point in the parent–child relationship, and describe the extent of parent–child conflict in adolescence and emerging adulthood.

**9.4 Problems in the Parent–Child Relationship**

9.4.1 Distinguish among the causes and consequences of physical and sexual child abuse.

9.4.2 Distinguish running away from home in developed countries from becoming "street children" in developing countries.

9.4.3 Define resilience, and name the protective factors that are related to resilience in adolescence.

**9.5 Siblings and Grandparents**

9.5.1 Describe the family systems principles of disequilibrium and subsystems.

9.5.2 Identify the most common features of sibling relationships worldwide, and describe how children with no siblings differ from other children.

9.5.3 Delineate three key roles of grandparents.

**9.6 Changing Families**

9.6.1 Describe the consequences to children of parental divorce and remarriage.

9.6.2 Describe the consequences to children of growing up in single-parent families.

9.6.3 Describe the consequences to children of growing up in sexual minority families.

9.6.4 Describe the consequences to children of growing up in dual-earner families.

IN ALL THE WORLD'S CULTURES, FAMILY IS THE MAIN CONTEXT IN WHICH YOUNG CHILDREN DEVELOP. In more than 80% of the world's societies, mothers provide the primary care for infants (Edwards et al., 2015). More than any other individual, mothers carry, clean, feed, and interact with their infants. Rarely, however, are mothers the sole caregivers. Instead, they share responsibilities with family members, such as fathers, grandparents, and other children in the family. Across cultures, families take different forms and their approaches to the care of young children are varied. Also, in many parts of today's world where single, cohabiting, and married parents work outside the home, professional child care providers look after infants and young children.

When children are young, they rely on parents and other family members to provide love, support, protection, and comfort. As they get older, they increasingly contribute actively and positively to the family. As we all know, however, family life can be not only the source of our deepest attachments, but also our most bitter and painful conflicts. In the course of normal child development, conflicts with parents peak in adolescence. Sometimes family problems are outside normal boundaries, as in the case of child abuse, neglect, or abandonment. In this chapter, we look at all of these aspects of family life.

**Watch** CHAPTER INTRODUCTION: FAMILY RELATIONSHIPS: FOUNDATIONS AND VARIATIONS

# 9.1 The First Social Relationship: Two Theories

The two most influential theories of infants' social development are by Erik Erikson and John Bowlby. Infancy, however, was just one of eight developmental stages of interest to Erikson. Bowlby's attention was squarely on an infant's relationship with the primary caregiver, and his theory has inspired abundant amounts of research. As we will now see, both theorists placed tremendous importance on the infant's first social relationship.

## Erikson's First Stage

**LO 9.1.1 Explain why Erikson emphasized that an infant's primary caregiver must provide love and care.**

As described in Chapter 7, Erikson proposed that each of his eight life course stages involves a specific developmental challenge or "crisis." For infancy, the central crisis is **trust versus mistrust** (Erikson, 1950). Erikson recognized how dependent infants are on others for their survival, and this dependence is at the heart of the idea of trust versus mistrust. Because they require others to provide for their needs, infants must have someone who can be trusted to care for them and to be a reliable source of nourishment, warmth, love, and protection. In most cultures, this caregiver is the mother but it can also be a father, grandmother, older sister, or anyone else who provides love and care on a consistent basis. It is not the biological tie that is important but the emotional and social bond.

When infants have a caregiver who provides for them in these ways, they develop a basic trust in their social world. They come to believe that others will be trustworthy and that they themselves are worthy of love. However, if adequate love and care are lacking in the first year, infants may come to mistrust not only their first caregiver but also others in their social world. They learn that they cannot count on the goodwill of others, and they may shrink from social relations in a world that seems harsh and unfriendly. Thus, according to Erikson, basic trust or mistrust lasts long beyond infancy. Remember, in his theory each stage builds on previous stages, for better or worse. Developing trust in infancy provides a strong foundation for all future social development, whereas developing mistrust is likely to be problematic not only in infancy but in future life stages as well.

**trust versus mistrust**
the first stage in Erikson's theory where an infant needs a caregiver consistently to provide love and care in order to develop a lifelong sense of trust

**attachment theory**
Bowlby's theory of emotional and social development, focusing on the crucial importance of the infant's relationship with the primary caregiver

## Bowlby's Attachment Theory

**LO 9.1.2 Review three key research findings that inspired Bowlby's attachment theory, and describe the essential features of the theory.**

A similar theory of infant social development was proposed by the British scholar John Bowlby (1969). Like Erikson's theory, Bowlby's **attachment theory** focuses on the crucial importance of the infant's relationship with the primary caregiver. Like Erikson, Bowlby believed that the quality of this first important social relationship influenced social development not only in infancy but also later in development. Like Erikson, Bowlby viewed trust as the key issue in the infant's first attachment to another person. In Bowlby's terms, if the primary caregiver is *sensitive* and *responsive* in caring for the infant, the infant will learn that others, too, can be trusted in social relationships. However, if these qualities are lacking in the primary caregiver, the infant will come to expect—in infancy and beyond—that others, too, may not be reliable social partners.

Prior to Bowlby, the strong consensus in psychology was that human infants become attached to their mothers because mothers provide them with food. Hunger is a distressing physical state, especially for babies, who are growing rapidly and need to be fed often. Mothers relieve this distressing state and provide the pleasure of feeding. Over time, infants come to associate the mother with the relief of distress and the experience of pleasure.

Both Erikson and Bowlby viewed the first attachment relationship as the foundation for future emotional and social development.

This association becomes the basis for the love that infants feel for their mothers. However, around the middle of the 20th century, Bowlby (1969) began to observe that many research findings were inconsistent with this consensus.

Three findings were especially notable to Bowlby:

1. ***Institutionalized infants.*** French psychiatrist René Spitz (1945) reported that infants raised in institutions suffered in their physical and emotional development, even if they were fed well. Spitz studied infants who entered an orphanage when they were 3 to 12 months old. Despite adequate physical care, the babies lost weight and seemed listless and passive. Spitz attributed the infants' condition—which he called *anaclitic depression*—to the fact that one nurse had to care for seven infants and spent little time with each except for feeding them and changing their diapers. Anaclitic means "leaning upon," and Spitz chose this term because the infants had no one to lean upon. The infants showed no sign of developing positive feelings toward the nurse, even though the nurse provided them with nourishment. Other studies of institutionalized infants reported similar results (Rutter, 1996).
2. ***Rhesus monkeys.*** The second set of findings that called feeding into question as the basis of the infant–mother bond involved primates, specifically rhesus monkeys. In a classic study, Harry Harlow (1958) placed baby monkeys in a cage with two kinds of artificial "mothers." One of the mothers was made of wire mesh, the other of soft terry cloth. Harlow found that even when he placed a feeding bottle in the wire mother, the baby monkeys spent almost all their time by the cloth mother, going to the wire mother only to feed. Again, a simple link between feeding and emotional bonds was called into question.
3. ***Imprinting.*** The third set of findings noted by Bowlby proved the most important for his thinking. These findings came from the field of *ethology*, which, as we have noted, is the study of animal behavior. Ethologists reported that for some animals, the bond between newborns and their mothers was instantaneous and occurred immediately after birth. Konrad Lorenz (1965), a German ethologist, showed that newborn goslings would bond to the first moving object they saw after hatching and follow it closely, a phenomenon he called *imprinting* (see Chapter 3). To Lorenz and other ethologists, the foundation of the bond between the young of the species and their mothers was not nourishment but protection. Imprinting to the mother would cause the young to stay close to her and thereby be protected from harm.

**primary attachment figure**
person who is sought out when a child experiences some kind of distress or threat in the environment

**secure base**
role of primary attachment figure, allows child to explore world while seeking comfort when threats arise

Considering these three sets of findings, Bowlby concluded that the emotional tie between children and their mothers was based on children's need for protection and care for many years. Thus, as Bowlby described it, the *attachment* that develops between children and caring adults is an emotional bond that promotes the protection and survival of children during the years they are most vulnerable. The child's **primary attachment figure** is the person who is sought out when the child experiences some kind of distress or threat in the environment. This might be hunger, but also pain or an unfamiliar person or setting. Usually the primary attachment figure is a parent, most often the mother. However, the primary attachment figure could be anyone else who is most involved in the infant's care. According to Bowlby (1980), separation from the primary attachment figure is experienced by the child as especially threatening, and the loss of the primary attachment figure is a catastrophe for children's development.

Harlow's studies showed that attachments were not based on nourishment. As shown here, the monkeys preferred the cloth "mother" even though the wire "mother" provided nourishment.

Although children staying close to caring adults promotes survival, so does learning about the world around them. Consequently, under normal conditions, young children use their primary attachment figure as a **secure base** from which to explore the surrounding environment. If a threat appears in the environment, attachment behavior is activated and children seek direct physical contact with their attachment figure.

## Cultural Focus: Stranger Anxiety Across Cultures

Although infants can discriminate among the smells and voices of different people in their environment from early on, in their first months they can be held and cared for by a wide range of people, familiar as well as unfamiliar, without protesting. However, by about the middle of the first year of life, this begins to change. Gradually, they become more selective, developing stronger preferences for familiar others who have cared for them, and **stranger anxiety** emerges in response to being approached, held, or even smiled at by people they do not recognize and trust. Stranger anxiety exists in a wide range of cultures beginning at about age 6 months and grows stronger in the months that follow (Super & Harkness, 1986). So, if an infant or toddler turns away, frowns, or bursts into tears in response to your friendly overtures, don't take it personally!

According to Bowlby (1969), there is an evolutionary basis for the emergence of stranger anxiety at about age 6 months. This is the age when infants first become mobile. Learning to crawl allows them to begin to explore the environment, but it also carries the risk that they may crawl themselves into big trouble. Learning to stay close to familiar persons and avoid unfamiliar persons helps infants stay near those who will protect them and keep them safe. Consequently, stranger anxiety peaks at about 12 months of age as toddlers begin to walk. However, as you will see in the video *Stranger Anxiety Across Cultures*, there is cultural variation in the degree of stranger anxiety, depending on how much toddlers have experienced diverse caregivers.

**Watch** STRANGER ANXIETY ACROSS CULTURES

### Review Question

The video shows examples of both separation from the primary caregiver and stranger anxiety. Discuss the difference between pure separation anxiety and the impact that including a stranger can have on a child's reaction.

According to Bowlby, attachment develops gradually over the first 2 years of life, culminating in a *goal-corrected partnership* in which both persons use language to communicate about the child's needs and the primary attachment figure's responses. Over time, the child becomes steadily less dependent on the care and protection of the primary attachment figure. However, even into adulthood, people seek out their primary attachment figure for comfort during times of crisis.

**stranger anxiety**
fear in response to unfamiliar persons, usually evident in infants by age 6 months

## SUMMARY: The First Social Relationship: Two Theories

### LO 9.1.1 Explain why Erikson emphasized that an infant's primary caregiver must provide love and care.

Erikson proposed that each of his eight life course stages involves a specific developmental "crisis." For infancy, the central crisis is trust versus mistrust. Because infants require others to provide for their needs, they must have someone who is a reliable source of nourishment, warmth, love, and protection. When infants have a caregiver who provides for them in these ways, they develop a basic trust in their social world that will serve as a foundation for subsequent development.

### LO 9.1.2 Review three key research findings that inspired Bowlby's attachment theory, and describe the essential features of the theory.

When a primary caregiver is sensitive and responsive, according to Bowlby's attachment theory, the infant becomes attached to the caregiver and learns that others, too, can be trusted in social relationships. Three key findings influenced Bowlby: (1) the prevalence of anaclitic depression among institutionalized children who were well-fed, (2) baby rhesus monkeys' preference for a soft cloth "mother" over a wire "mother" with a feeding bottle, and (3) the fact that some species of baby animals imprint to their mother immediately following birth.

# 9.2 Attachment to Parents

Bowlby was a theorist, not a researcher, and he did not conduct studies to test his theory directly. The theory, however, has become one of the most influential in developmental psychology. It has inspired researchers to develop methods for evaluating the infant–caregiver relationship and to conduct a great number of studies (Cassidy & Shaver, 2008; Grossman et al., 2005; Morelli, 2015). While much of the research on attachment has focused on mothers, here we also address the role of fathers.

## Attachment Quality

**LO 9.2.1 Identify the four types of attachment quality, and explain their determinants and effects.**

Mary Ainsworth pioneered attachment research (Ainsworth & Bell, 1969; Ainsworth et al., 1978). She devised a procedure for differentiating the quality of toddlers' attachment to their primary attachment figures. In turn, researchers have examined the factors that determine the quality of attachment, and the effects of attachment quality on child development.

**Strange Situation**
laboratory assessment of attachment entailing a series of introductions, separations, and reunions involving the child, the mother, and an unfamiliar person

**FOUR TYPES OF ATTACHMENT.** Ainsworth followed Bowlby's theory in viewing the child's attachment as most evident in the response to separation from the primary attachment figure. To evoke children's attachment behavior, Ainsworth designed a laboratory procedure she called the **Strange Situation** (Ainsworth et al., 1978). The Strange Situation is a series of introductions, separations, and reunions involving the child, the mother, and an unfamiliar person. It was devised for toddlers, ages 12 to 24 months, because this is an age by which attachment has developed to a point where it can be assessed.

On the basis of toddlers' responses to the Strange Situation, four types of attachment were differentiated (Ainsworth et al., 1978; Ammaniti et al., 2005). Ainsworth proposed the first three, and later researchers added the fourth (Main & Solomon, 1990).

*Secure attachment.* Toddlers in this category use the mother as a secure base from which to explore, in the first part of the Strange Situation, when only the mother and toddler are present. Upon separation, securely attached toddlers usually cry or vocalize in protest, and they become especially distressed if an unfamiliar person approaches. When the mother returns, they greet her happily by smiling and going to her to be hugged and held.

*Insecure–avoidant attachment.* These toddlers show little or no interaction with the mother when she is present, and no response to the mother's departure or return. If these toddlers are picked up by the mother in the last episode of the Strange Situation, they may immediately seek to get down.

*Insecure–resistant attachment.* Toddlers classified as insecure–resistant are less likely than others to explore the toys when the mother is present, and they show greater distress when she leaves the room. When she returns, they show ambivalence, running to greet the mother in seeming relief but then pushing her away when she attempts to comfort or pick them up.

*Disorganized–disoriented attachment.* These toddlers show extremely unusual behavior in response to the Strange Situation (Ammaniti et al., 2005; Padrón et al., 2014; van IJzendoorn et al., 1999). They may seem dazed and detached when the mother leaves the room, but with outbursts of anger. When the mother returns they may seem fearful. Some freeze their movements suddenly in odd postures. This kind of attachment is especially shown by toddlers who display other signs of serious problems, such as Autism Spectrum Disorder (see Chapter 7) or Down syndrome (see Chapter 2), and those who have suffered severe abuse or neglect.

Although attachment classification is based on behavior throughout the Strange Situation, Ainsworth viewed the toddler's reunion behavior as the best indicator of the quality of attachment: What do the toddlers do when the mother reenters the room? Toddlers with secure attachments are delighted to see their mothers again after a separation and often seek physical contact with her. In contrast, toddlers with insecure attachments either respond little to her return (avoidant), seem both relieved and angry at her (resistant), or react fearfully (disorganized-disoriented).

**DETERMINANTS AND EFFECTS OF ATTACHMENT QUALITY.** Ainsworth's early research indicated that about two-thirds of toddlers had secure attachments to their mothers, with the remaining one-third either insecure–avoidant or insecure–resistant (Ainsworth et al., 1978). Many other studies of American and European children since then have found similar results (NICHD Early Child Care Research Network, 2006; van IJzendoorn & Sagi-Schwartz, 2008). Disorganized–disoriented attachment is rare.

But what determines the differences in the quality of toddlers' attachments to their mothers? In her early research, Ainsworth and her colleagues observed families in their homes, including the same mother–child pairs they later observed in the laboratory in the Strange Situation (Ainsworth, 1977). The home observations were extensive: every 3 weeks for 4 hours, from when the children were 3 weeks old to just past their first birthdays.

When considering the mother–child interactions in the home in relation to their behavior in the Strange Situation, Ainsworth concluded that the quality of attachment was based mainly on how sensitive and responsive the mother was. To be *sensitive* means to be good at judging what the child needs at any given time. For example, sensitive mothers could tell when their children had had enough to eat, whereas others seemed to stop feeding while the children were still hungry or tried to keep feeding them after they seemed full. To be *responsive* means to be quick to assist or soothe the children when they need it. For example, responsive mothers would hug or pick up or talk soothingly when their children were distressed, whereas others would let them cry for a while before going to their assistance.

**internal working model**
in attachment theory, the term for the cognitive framework, based on interactions in infancy with the primary caregiver, that shapes expectations and interactions in relationships to others throughout life

According to attachment theory, based on the degree of their mothers' sensitive and responsive behavior over the first year of life, children develop an **internal working model** of what to expect about her availability and supportiveness during times of need (Bowlby, 1969, 1980; Bretherton & Munholland, 1999). Children with secure attachments have developed an internal working model of the mother as someone they can rely on to provide help and protection. Children with insecure attachments are unsure that the mother will come through when they need her. They have an internal working model of her as someone who is unpredictable and cannot always be trusted. One reason the Strange Situation is first assessed in toddlerhood rather than infancy is that it is only by toddlerhood that children are cognitively mature enough to have developed an internal working model of their primary attachment figure (Ainsworth et al., 1978; Bowlby, 1969). From this perspective, then, the mother's behavior is the determinant of the child's attachment.

Is early attachment the basis of all future love relationships?

And what effects does attachment quality in toddlerhood have on later development? According to Bowlby (1969), the internal working model of the primary caregiver formed in infancy and toddlerhood is the foundational model for future relationships. In other words, the attachment to the primary caregiver established in the first 2 years shapes expectations and interactions in relationships with others throughout life, from friends to teachers to romantic partners to one's own future children. Securely attached children are able to love and trust others because they could love and trust their primary caregiver in their early years. Insecurely attached children display hostility, indifference, or overdependence on others in later relationships because they find it difficult to believe others will be worthy of their love and trust (Morelli, 2015).

Bowlby's claim is bold and intriguing. But how well does it hold up in research? A number of longitudinal studies on attachment have by now followed samples from toddlerhood through adolescence or emerging adulthood, and they provide mixed support for the predictions of attachment theory. Some longitudinal studies show a relationship between attachment quality assessed in toddlerhood and later emotional and social development, but other studies do not (Egeland & Carlson, 2004; Fraley et al., 2013). A recent meta-analysis that combined findings from 127 longitudinal studies of attachment concluded that the predictive power of toddler attachment classification weakened with time and had mostly faded by late adolescence and emerging adulthood (Pinquart et al., 2013). The current view is that attachment quality in infancy and toddlerhood establishes tendencies and expectations that may then be modified by later experiences in childhood, adolescence, and beyond. To put this in terms of the theory, the internal working model established early may be modified substantially by later experiences.

There is an exception, however. One of the four attachment styles is highly predictive of later problems (Ammaniti et al., 2005; van IJzendoorn et al., 1999; Vondra & Barnett, 1999). Can you predict which one? Toddlers with disorganized-disoriented attachment exhibit high hostility and aggression in early and middle childhood, and are likely to have cognitive problems as well (Weinfield et al., 2004). In adolescence and beyond, they are at higher risk for behavior problems and psychopathology (van IJzendoorn et al., 1999). However, this type of attachment is believed mainly to be due to abnormal neurological development. Only rarely, such as in the case of child abuse, is this type of attachment due to the behavior of the primary caregiver (Barnett et al., 1999; Graffi et al., 2015; Macfie et al., 2001).

## Critiques of Attachment Theory

**LO 9.2.2 Explain the two major critiques of attachment theory and research.**

Attachment theory has generated thousands of studies since Bowlby first articulated it over 40 years ago (Atkinson & Goldberg, 2004; Cassidy & Shaver, 2010; Sroufe et al., 2005). However, it has also generated critiques that point to its limitations. Two critiques are especially noteworthy: the child effect and the cultural variation critiques.

The "child effect" is one of the most common critiques of attachment theory. It argues that Bowlby's theory overstates the mother's influence and understates the child's influence on quality of attachment. Children are born with different temperaments (Bakermans-Kranenburg et al., 2004). If, in the Strange Situation, a toddler is highly anxious when the mother leaves the room, then behaves aggressively by pushing her away when she returns, it could be due to a difficult temperament, not the mother's failure to be sufficiently sensitive and responsive (van IJzendoorn et al., 2004). In other words, the mother is not the sole determinant of a child's attachment; the child too has an impact (Gentzler et al., 2014).

**Critical Thinking Question:** In Chapter 2, we reviewed three genotype-environment effects. Can you explain which one the "child effect" most closely resembles?

**reciprocal** or **bidirectional effects**

in relations between two persons, the principle that each of them affects the other

Related, in recent decades, researchers of human development have emphasized that parent–child relations are **reciprocal** or **bidirectional**. For example, mothers of toddlers with a disorganized–disoriented attachment classification have been found to behave differently in the Strange Situation than other mothers. They may fail to respond when their toddlers become distressed, and may hold them at arm's length when picking them up, rather than comforting them by holding them close (Lyons-Ruth et al., 1999; van IJzendoorn et al., 1999). These mothers sometimes appear confused, frustrated, or impatient. This could be a failure to be sensitive and responsive on the mother's part. It is also possible that the mothers are responding to the toddler's behavioral difficulties (Barnett et al., 1999). Most likely, however, the mothers and disorganized–disoriented toddlers are influencing each other in a negative bidirectional cycle (Lyons-Ruth et al., 1999; Symons, 2001). In short, child and mother codetermine each other's behaviors over time.

The second major critique of attachment theory and research points to cultural variation. In the decades of research since Bowlby proposed his theory, some researchers have concluded that children's attachments are "recognizably the same" across cultures (Cassidy & Shaver, 2010, p. xiii). However, other researchers have pointed to possible problems both with using the Strange Situation across cultures, and the Western view of human relationships woven into the theory.

Some aspects of attachment may be universal. In all cultures, infants and toddlers develop attachments to the people around them who provide loving, protective care (van IJzendoorn & Sagi-Schwartz, 2008). There is evidence that parents in many cultures have a common view of what constitutes a securely attached child. One study involved mothers of toddlers in six cultures: China, Colombia, Germany, Israel, Japan, and the United States (Posada et al., 1995). Across cultures, mothers described an "ideally secure" child in similar ways, as relying on the mother in times of need but also being willing to explore the surrounding world—in short, using her as a secure base from which to explore, much as described in attachment theory. Other studies involving multiple cultures have found that secure attachment is the most common classification in all cultures studied so far (van IJzendoorn & Sagi-Schwartz, 2008).

However, cultural variations have also been found (Morelli, 2015). One study compared Strange Situation results for toddlers in Japan, the United States, and several northern European countries (van IJzendoorn & Kroonenberg, 1988). In all countries, as you can see in Figure 9.1, the majority of toddlers were indeed found to be securely attached. However, the U.S. and northern European toddlers were more likely than Japanese toddlers to be classified as insecure–avoidant. In contrast, insecure–resistant attachment was especially common among the Japanese toddlers. These differences were attributed to toddlers reacting differently to the Strange Situation because of cultural differences in typical patterns of care. Specifically, a northern European and U.S. cultural emphasis on early independence were deemed to make insecure–avoidant attachment more likely. In contrast, Japanese mothers are rarely apart from their children and encourage a high degree of dependency in them. Consequently, their toddlers may have found the Strange Situation more stressful than the European or American toddlers did, making the insecure–resistant attachment classification more likely. As we discussed in Chapter 1, if a method means different things to different cultural groups, then it calls into question its ecological validity.

Cultural critics of attachment theory have also highlighted that the traditional, non-Western norm of maternal care emphasizes interdependence and collectivism to a greater extent than is found in attachment theory (Morelli, 2015; Rothbaum et al., 2000). Attachment theorists emphasize that sensitive and responsive maternal care should provide love and care while also encouraging self-expression and independence, but this is not an ideal found in all or even most cultures. In many traditional and non-Western cultures, where there is an emphasis on maintaining social harmony, the ideal for maternal care involves controlling a child's behavior, anticipating the child's needs, and curtailing strong emotional expression (Morelli, 2015). For example, Rothbaum and colleagues (2007) describe the Japanese concept

**Figure 9.1** Cultural Variations in the Strange Situation

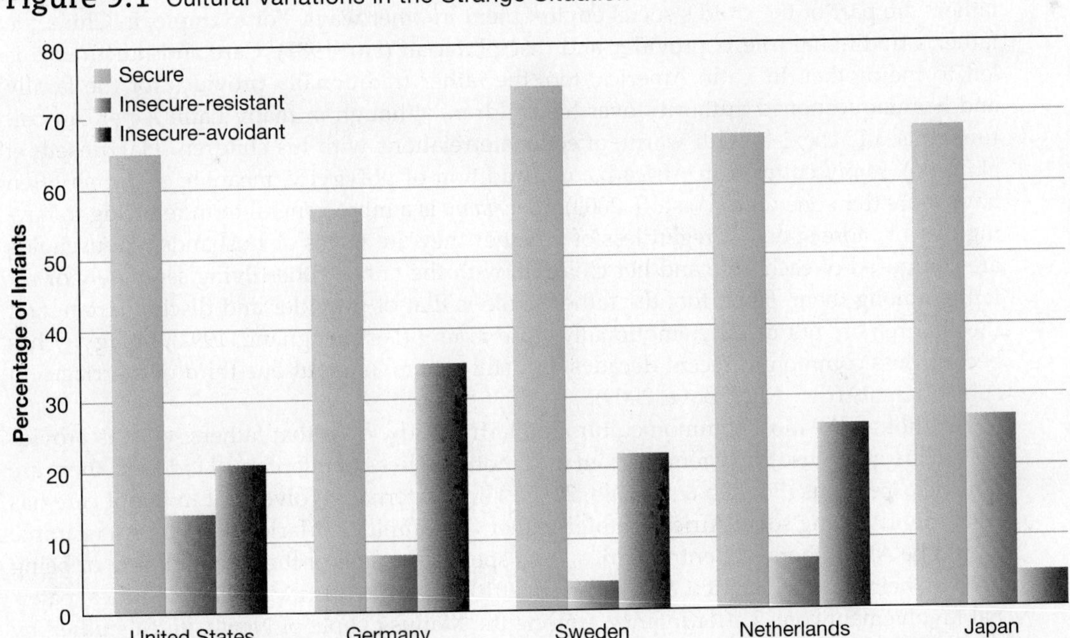


SOURCE: Data from IJzendoorn & Kroonenberg (1988).

Mothers and children in Japan often have very close relationships.

of *amae* (ah-may-uh), which is a very close, physical, indulgent relationship between the mother and her young child. This is the ideal in Japan, but to some attachment researchers it fits the description of the kind of mothering that promotes insecure–resistant attachment (George & Solomon, 1999). Also, attachment researchers describe how toddlers with secure attachments grow up to be children who are self-reliant, socially assertive, and have high self-esteem, but these traits are not viewed as virtues in all cultures (Rothbaum et al., 2000; Sullivan & Cottone, 2010).

## The Role of Fathers

**LO 9.2.3 Compare traditional cultures and developed countries on typical patterns of father involvement with infants and toddlers.**

Much of the theory and research on attachment has focused on mothers, although there is also research on fathers and other caregivers. The attention to mothers is reflective of the fact that mothers play a central role in the care of infants and toddlers in nearly all cultures (Shwalb & Shwalb, 2015). Fathers in traditional cultures are often excluded entirely from the birth process; in the weeks after birth, the mother and neonate are usually together constantly, whereas the father may or may not be involved in early care. There are two reasons that mothers have historically been the primary caretakers of infants and toddlers. The first is biological. Because breast milk has usually been the main form of nourishment for infants during the first half year, the mother tends to be the one who cares for the infant more than anyone else. Consequently, by toddlerhood mothers are usually the primary attachment figure (Bowlby, 1969; Cassidy & Shaver, 2010).

The second reason is cultural. In most cultures through nearly all of human history, female and male gender roles have been separate and distinct (Gilmore, 1990; Hatfield et al., 2015; Kapadia & Gala, 2015). In their adult roles, women have been expected to run the household and care for children, whereas men have been expected to protect and provide for the family. In their leisure time, women relax with children and other women, and men relax with other men. Consequently, in many cultures, historically, fathers have been on the periphery of the emotional lives of children.

Although paternal involvement in daily child care is quite rare in traditional cultures, fathers are part of the child's social environment in other ways. For example, in China the father's traditional role is provider and disciplinarian (Ho, 1987). Care and nurturance is left to the mother. In Latin America, too, the father traditionally provides for the family and has unquestioned authority over his children, although in many Latin American cultures this role coexists with warm, affectionate relations with his children (Halgunseth et al., 2006). Many cultures in Africa have a tradition of **polygyny**, meaning that men often have more than one wife (Westoff, 2003). (*Polygamy* is a more general term referring to having two or more spouses, regardless of whether they are wives or husbands.) Households are composed of each wife and her children, with the father either living separately or rotating among them. Here, too, the father's role is that of provider and disciplinarian, and the children are not usually emotionally close to him (Nsamengnang, 1992). Polygyny has become less common in recent decades, but still occurs in about one-third of marriages in sub-Saharan Africa (Riley Bove, 2009).

**polygyny**
cultural tradition in which men have more than one wife

Although the most common cultural pattern worldwide is that fathers serve as providers but are otherwise fairly remote from the emotional lives of infants and toddlers, there are notable exceptions (Shwalb & Shwalb, 2015). High paternal involvement in infant care has been found among some African hunter-gather communities (Marlowe, 2000). An example would be Aka fathers of Central Africa, who spend over half of their day holding or being nearby their infants (Hewlett & MacFarlan, 2010). In some traditional communities, paternal involvement comes after infancy. Among the Manus people of New Guinea studied by Margaret Mead (1930/2001), during the first year of life the infant and mother are together almost constantly, and the father is involved only occasionally. However, once the child enters toddlerhood and begins to walk, the father takes over most child care. The toddler sleeps with the father, plays with him, rides on his back, and goes along on his daily fishing expeditions. Later in childhood, if the parents quarrel and separate, the children often choose to stay with the father, indicating that by then he has become the primary attachment figure.

In some ways, the role of fathers in developed countries today is in line with the pattern historically and in traditional societies. Across developed countries, fathers interact less with their infants and toddlers than mothers do, and provide less care such as bathing, feeding, dressing, and soothing (Chuang et al., 2004; Lamb & Lewis, 2010; Shwalb & Shwalb, 2015). In the United States, about one-third of toddlers live with single mothers; nonresident fathers are less involved in toddler care than fathers who live in the household, although involvement is greater among nonresident fathers who are African American or Latino than among Whites (Cabrera et al., 2008). When fathers do interact with their infants and toddlers, it tends to be in play rather than care, especially in physical, highly stimulating, rough-and-tumble play (Lamb & Lewis, 2010; Paquette, 2004). Dad is the one throwing the kids in the air and catching them or wrestling with them, but usually he has not been the one feeding them applesauce, changing their diapers, or wiping their tears.

However, gender roles have become more flexible and egalitarian in developed countries, and there is a definite trend toward greater father involvement (Pleck, 2010). American fathers have been found to spend about 85% as much time as mothers do in caring for their young children, and Canadian fathers about 75% (Lamb, 2010). Fathers are more likely to provide near-equal care for young children when the mother and father work similar numbers of hours outside the home and when marital satisfaction is high (Lamb & Lewis, 2010; NICHD Early Child Care Network, 2000).

Fathers in developed countries do more child care than they did in the past, but still not as much as mothers do.

Some Scandinavian countries have also instituted policies to encourage father involvement in infant care and provide all parents with equal opportunity to balance work and infant care. In the Scandinavian countries, parental leave policies provide wage replacement of approximately 80%–100% (Haas & Hwang, 2013). To support fathers in taking advantage of these benefits, Norway and Sweden have achieved some success by experimenting with policies that extend the period of paid parental leave for families when both father and mother participate (Edwards et al., 2015). Like the examples of the Aka and Manus peoples, the findings of recent changes in fathers' care for young children in developed countries show that parenting is largely a learned rather than innate behavioral pattern that can change as a culture changes.

**child welfare institutions**
residential institutions that provide total care for children who are orphaned, abandoned, or otherwise separated from family

## Education Focus: Enhancing Attachment in Child Welfare Institutions

A deep insight of John Bowlby's theory of attachment was the recognition that infants and children need to have individuals in their lives who can be trusted to provide care—not just physical care, but also emotional care, and not just occasional care, but consistent care. A primary caregiver may be a mother, but it can also be a father, another family member, or someone from outside the family.

As we saw earlier, Bowlby partly based his theory of attachment on René Spitz's (1945) finding that infants raised in orphanages suffered in their physical and emotional development. Even if they were fed well, they lacked the crucial connection to a primary caregiver. Since Spitz, many other studies have also shown that young children raised in **child welfare institutions** become vulnerable to long-term problems, including malnutrition, behavioral disorders, and cognitive and language delays (Leiden Conference on the Development and Care of Children without Permanent Parents, 2012). In light of this, many Western countries have closed almost all child welfare institutions in favor of systems of adoption, foster care, kinship care, and small group homes. However, in countries in Africa, Asia, and Eastern Europe, child welfare institutions remain in existence in order to provide care for children who are orphaned, abandoned, or otherwise separated from a family.

Some developmental psychologists have demonstrated that training caregivers in child welfare institutions to make daily routines less "factory-like" and more "family-like" can be helpful (Edwards et al., 2015). In Russia, the St. Petersburg—USA

Orphanage Research Team (2008) found that institutionalized children showed improved physical and cognitive development when they were assigned primary caregivers who had been trained to respond in warm, sensitive, and responsive ways.

Another example comes from China, where Half the Sky Foundation, a nongovernmental organization that operates in partnership with the Chinese government, has launched programs that include training women, so-called "nannies," from the community to serve as primary caregivers for a group of two to four infants in local child welfare institutions (Cotton et al., 2007; Zheng et al., 2013). A nanny is together with her small group of infants a few hours each day in order to attend to their needs and build emotional bonds. Nannies also keep twice-weekly records of anecdotes and observations about their infants (Evans, 2003). These become "Memory Books" for the orphaned children.

### Review Question

Based on developmental psychology, explain why "Memory Books" may be helpful to infants as they get older. You may find it useful to draw on information from this and previous chapters.

### SUMMARY: Attachment to Parents

**LO 9.2.1 Identify the four types of attachment quality, and explain their determinants and effects.**

On the basis of toddlers' responses to the Strange Situation, four types of attachment have been differentiated: secure, insecure-avoidant, insecure-resistant, and disorganized-disoriented. According to attachment theorists, the optimal outcome of secure attachment depends on primary caregivers being sensitive and responsive to their infants. Research indicates that attachment quality in infancy and toddlerhood establishes tendencies and expectations that may be altered by later experiences. With the exception of disorganized–disoriented attachment, the predictive power of infant attachment classification has mostly faded by late adolescence and emerging adulthood.

**LO 9.2.2 Explain the two major critiques of attachment theory and research.**

(1) The "child effect" critique argues that Bowlby's theory overstates the primary caregiver's influence and understates the child's influence on quality of attachment. (2) The cultural critique argues that attachment theory is based on relatively individualistic values in that responsive maternal care involves love and care while also encouraging self-expression and independence. In many traditional and non-Western cultures, where there is an emphasis on maintaining social harmony, however, the ideal for maternal care involves controlling a child's behavior, anticipating the child's needs, and curtailing strong emotional expression.

**LO 9.2.3 Compare traditional cultures and developed countries on typical patterns of father involvement with infants and toddlers.**

In many traditional cultures, fathers are on the periphery of the emotional lives of children, and their role is primarily as provider and disciplinarian. In some ways, the role of fathers in developed countries today is in line with the pattern in traditional societies. Nonetheless, there is a definite trend toward greater father involvement in developed countries.

# 9.3 The Parent–Child Relationship

Everywhere, the parent–child relationship is important. How parents view their role and their approaches to discipline and punishment vary widely. In this section, we look at an influential model of parenting "styles" based on the American majority culture, and at alternative views of parenting based on research with families from American minority cultures and worldwide. We also look at how the relationship between parents and children changes with development.

## Parenting Styles

**LO 9.3.1 Describe the four types of parenting styles and their effects, and explain the cultural limitations of this research.**

Maybe you've heard the joke about the man who, before he had any children, had six theories about how they should be raised? Ten years later he had six children and no theories.

Well, jokes aside, most parents do have ideas about how best to raise children, even after they have had children for a while (Harkness et al., 2015; Tamis-LeMonda et al., 2008). In research, the investigation of this topic has often involved the study of **parenting styles**, that is, the practices that parents exhibit in relation to their children and their beliefs about those practices. This research originated in the United States and shows that different styles influence children in different ways. However, research also shows that the cultural context of parenting is crucial to child development.

**parenting styles**
practices that parents exhibit in relation to their children and their beliefs about those practices

**FOUR PARENTING STYLES.** For over 50 years, American scholars have engaged in research on this topic, and the results have been quite consistent (Bornstein & Bradley, 2014; Collins & Laursen, 2004; Maccoby & Martin, 1983). Virtually all of the prominent scholars who have studied parenting have described it in terms of two dimensions: demandingness and responsiveness (also known by terms such as *control* and *warmth*). Parental **demandingness** is the degree to which parents set rules and expectations for behavior and require their children to comply with them. Parental **responsiveness** is the degree to which parents are sensitive to their children's needs and express love, warmth, and concern.

**demandingness**
degree to which parents set rules and expectations for behavior and require their children to comply with them

**responsiveness**
degree to which parents are sensitive to their children's needs and express love, warmth, and concern for them

Various scholars have combined these two dimensions to describe different kinds of parenting styles. For many years, the best known and most widely used conception of parenting styles was the one articulated by Diana Baumrind (1968, 1971, 1991). Her research on middle-class White American families, along with the research of scholars inspired by her ideas, has identified four distinct parenting styles (Collins & Laursen, 2004; Maccoby & Martin, 1983; Steinberg, 2000).

As you can see in Table 9.1, **authoritative parents** are high in demandingness and high in responsiveness. They set clear rules and expectations for their children. Furthermore, they make clear what the consequences will be if their children do not comply, and they make those consequences stick if necessary. However, authoritative parents do not simply "lay down the law" and then enforce it rigidly. A distinctive feature of authoritative parents is that they *explain* the reasons for their rules and expectations, and willingly engage in discussion with their children over issues of discipline, sometimes leading to negotiation and compromise. For example, a child who wants to eat a whole bag of candy would not simply be told "No!" by an authoritative parent, but something like, "No, it wouldn't be healthy and it would be bad for your teeth." Authoritative parents are also loving and warm toward their children, and they respond to what their children need and desire.

**authoritative parents**
in classifications of parenting styles, parents who are high in demandingness and high in responsiveness

**Authoritarian parents** are high in demandingness but low in responsiveness. They require obedience from their children, and they punish disobedience without compromise. None of the verbal give-and-take common with authoritative parents is allowed by authoritarian parents. They expect their commands to be followed without dispute or dissent. To continue with the candy example, the authoritarian parent would respond to the child's request for a bag of candy simply by saying "No!" with no explanation. Also, authoritarian parents show little in the way of love or warmth toward their children. Their demandingness takes place without responsiveness, in a way that shows little emotional attachment and may even be hostile.

**authoritarian parents**
in classifications of parenting styles, parents who are high in demandingness but low in responsiveness

**Permissive parents** are low in demandingness and high in responsiveness. They have few clear expectations for their children's behavior, and they rarely discipline them. Instead, their emphasis is on responsiveness. They believe that children need love that is truly "unconditional." They may see discipline and control as having the potential to damage their children's healthy tendencies for developing creativity and expressing themselves however they wish. They provide their children with love and warmth and give them a great deal of freedom to do as they please.

**permissive parents**
in classifications of parenting styles, parents who are low in demandingness and high in responsiveness

**Table 9.1** Parenting Styles and the Two Dimensions of Parenting

| Responsiveness | Demandingness: High | Demandingness: Low |
|---|---|---|
| High | Authoritative | Permissive |
| Low | Authoritarian | Disengaged |

**disengaged parents**
in classifications of parenting styles, parents who are low in both demandingness and responsiveness

**Disengaged parents** are low in both demandingness and responsiveness. Their goal may be to minimize the amount of time and emotion they devote to parenting. Thus, they require little of their children and rarely bother to correct their behavior or place clear limits on what they are allowed to do. They also express little in the way of love or concern for their children. They may seem to have little emotional attachment to them.

**DETERMINANTS AND EFFECTS OF PARENTING STYLES.** A great deal of research has been conducted on how parenting styles influence children's development. A summary of the results is shown in Table 9.2. In general, authoritative parenting is associated with the most favorable outcomes, at least by American standards. Children who have authoritative parents tend to be independent, self-assured, creative, and socially skilled (Baumrind, 1991; Collins & Larsen, 2004; Steinberg, 2000; Williams et al., 2009). They also tend to do well in school and to get along well with their peers and with adults (Hastings et al., 2007; Spera, 2005). Authoritative parenting helps children develop characteristics such as optimism and self-regulation that in turn have positive effects on a wide range of behaviors (Jackson et al., 2005; Purdie et al., 2004).

All the other parenting styles are associated with some negative outcomes, although the type of negative outcome varies (Baumrind, 1991; Snyder et al., 2005). Children with authoritarian parents tend to be less self-assured, less creative, and less socially adept than other children. Boys with authoritarian parents are more often aggressive and unruly, whereas girls are more often anxious and unhappy (Bornstein & Bradley, 2014; Russell et al., 2003). Children with permissive parents tend to be immature and lack self-control. Because they lack self-control, they have difficulty getting along with peers and teachers (Linver et al., 2002). Children with disengaged parents tend to be impulsive. Partly as a consequence of their impulsiveness, and partly because disengaged parents do little to monitor their activities, children with disengaged parents tend to have higher rates of behavior problems (Pelaez et al., 2008).

Although parents undoubtedly affect their children profoundly by their parenting, the process is not nearly as simple as the cause-and-effect model just described. Sometimes discussions of parenting make it sound as though Parenting Style A automatically and inevitably produces Child Type X. However, enough research has taken place by now to indicate that the relationship between parenting styles and children's development is considerably more complex (Bornstein & Bradley, 2014; Lamb & Lewis, 2005; Parke & Buriel, 2006). Not only do parents affect their children, but children also affect their parents. Over time, parent and child codetermine each other's behaviors. As we saw for attachment, this principle is referred to by scholars as *reciprocal or bidirectional effects* between parents and children (Combs-Ronto et al., 2009).

Recall our discussion of evocative genotype → environment effects in Chapter 2. Children are not like billiard balls that head predictably in the direction they are propelled. They bring personalities and desires of their own to the parent–child relationship. Thus, children may evoke certain behaviors from their parents. An especially aggressive child may evoke authoritarian parenting; perhaps the parents find that authoritative explanations of the rules are simply ignored, and their responsiveness diminishes as a result of the child's repeated disobedience and disruptiveness. An especially mild-tempered child may evoke permissive parenting because parents may see no point in setting specific rules for a child who has no inclination to do anything wrong anyway.

Does this research discredit the claim that parenting styles influence children? No, but it does modify it. Parents certainly have beliefs about what is best for their children,

**Table 9.2** Outcomes Associated With Parenting Styles in White, Middle-Class Families

| Authoritative | Authoritarian | Permissive | Disengaged |
|---|---|---|---|
| Independent | Dependent | Irresponsible | Impulsive |
| Creative | Passive | Conforming | Behavior problems |
| Self-assured | Conforming | Immature | Early sex, drugs |
| Socially skilled | | | |

and they try to express those beliefs through their parenting behavior (Alwin, 1988; Harkness et al., 2015; Way et al., 2007). However, parents' actual behavior is affected not only by what they believe is best but also by how their children behave toward them and respond to their parenting. Being an authoritative parent is easier if your child responds to your demandingness and responsiveness with compliance and love, and not so easy if your love is rejected and your rules and the reasons you provide for them are rejected. Parents whose efforts to persuade their children through reasoning and discussion fall on deaf ears may be tempted either to demand compliance (and become more authoritarian) or to give up trying (and become permissive or disengaged).

How does the idea of reciprocal effects complicate claims of the effects of parenting styles?

**THE CULTURAL LIMITATIONS OF PARENTING STYLES.** So far we have looked at the parenting styles research based mainly on White, middle-class American families. What does research in other cultures indicate about parenting and its effects in early childhood?

One important observation is how rare the authoritative parenting style is in cultures outside the West (Bornstein & Bradley, 2014; Harkness et al., 2015). Remember, a distinctive feature of authoritative parents is that they do not rely on the authority of the parental role to ensure that children comply with their commands and instructions. They do not simply declare the rules and expect to be obeyed. On the contrary, authoritative parents explain the reasons for what they want children to do and engage in discussion over the guidelines for their children's behavior (Baumrind, 1971, 1991; Steinberg & Levine, 1997).

Outside of the West, however, this is an extremely rare way of parenting. In traditional cultures, parents expect that their authority will be obeyed, without question and without requiring an explanation (LeVine et al., 2008; LeVine & LeVine, 2016). This is true not only in nearly all developing countries but also in developed countries outside the West, most notably Asian countries such as Japan and South Korea (Tseng, 2004; Zhang & Fuligni, 2006). Asian cultures have a tradition of **filial piety**, meaning that children are expected to respect, obey, and revere their parents throughout life (Lieber et al., 2004). The role of parent carries greater inherent authority than it does in the West. Parents are not supposed to provide reasons for why they should be respected and obeyed. The simple fact that they are parents is viewed as sufficient justification for their authority.

**filial piety**
belief that children should respect, obey, and revere their parents throughout life; common in Asian cultures

In Latin American cultures, too, the authority of parents is viewed as paramount. The Latino cultural belief system places a premium on the idea of *respeto*, which emphasizes respect for and obedience to parents and elders, especially the father (Cabrera & García Coll, 2004; Halgunseth et al., 2006; Harwood et al., 2002). The role of the parent is considered to be enough to command authority, without requiring that the parents explain their rules to their children. Another pillar of Latino cultural beliefs is **familismo**, which emphasizes the love, closeness, and mutual obligations of Latino family life (Halgunseth et al., 2006; Harwood et al., 2002).

**familismo**
cultural belief among Latinos that emphasizes the love, closeness, and mutual obligations among family members

Does this mean that the typical parenting style in cultures outside the West is authoritarian? No, although scholars have sometimes come to this erroneous conclusion. It would be more accurate to state that the parenting-styles model is itself a cultural model, rooted in the American majority culture, and does not apply well across cultures. Of course, children everywhere need to have parents or other caregivers provide care for them in early childhood and beyond, and across cultures parents provide some combination of warmth and control. However, "responsiveness" is a distinctly American kind of warmth, emphasizing praise and physical affection, and "demandingness" is a distinctly American kind of control, emphasizing explanation and negotiation rather than the assertion of parental authority. Each culture has its own culturally based forms of warmth and control, but across cultures, warmth rarely takes the American form of praise, and control rarely takes the American form of explanation and negotiation (Harkness et al., 2015; Matsumoto & Yoo, 2006; Miller, 2004; Wang & Tamis-LeMonda, 2003).

Even within American society, the authoritative style is mainly dominant among White, middle-class families (Bornstein & Bradley, 2014). Most American minority cultures, including African Americans, Asian Americans, and Latinos, have been classified by researchers as "authoritarian," but this is inaccurate and results from applying to them a

A pillar of Latino cultural beliefs is familismo, or an emphasis on love, closeness, and mutual family obligation. Here, family members cook together at a gathering.

model that was based on the White majority culture (Chao & Tseng, 2002; Parmar et al., 2004, 2008). Each minority culture has its own distinctive form of warmth, but all tend to emphasize obeying parental authority rather than encouraging explanation and negotiation. Hence the White American middle-class model of parenting styles cannot really be applied to them.

Within cultures, parenting varies depending on the personalities of the parents, their goals for their children, and the characteristics of the children that evoke particular parenting responses. Overall, however, the dominant approach to parenting in a culture reflects certain things about the underlying cultural beliefs, such as the value of interdependence versus independence and the status of parental authority over children (Giles-Sims & Lockhart, 2005; Harkness et al., 2015; Hulei et al., 2006). The cultural beliefs about parenting are so crucial that what looks like the same parental behavior in two different cultures can have two very different effects, as we will see in the next section.

## Parental Use of Discipline

**LO 9.3.2 Describe the main cultural variations in how parents discipline young children, and explain how cultural context influences children's responses to discipline.**

All cultures require children to learn and follow cultural rules and expectations, and all cultures have some system of discipline for misbehavior. However, cultures vary widely in the nature of the discipline, and the consequences of discipline vary depending on the cultural beliefs that underlie the approach. Early childhood is when issues of discipline for disapproval of behavior first arise. It is common for cultures to be indulgent of infants and toddlers because they are seen as too young to exercise much judgment or self-control. However, by early childhood, children become more capable of emotional and behavioral self-regulation. When they disobey or defy others, they are believed to have enough understanding to know what they were doing and to be responsible for the consequences. For this reason, early childhood is usually when children are first disciplined for not following expectations or not doing what is required of them.

In Western cultures, the approach to discipline in early childhood tends to emphasize the authoritative style of explaining the consequences of misbehavior and the reasons for discipline (Huang et al., 2009; Tamis-LeMonda et al., 2008). ("Alex, if you don't stop banging that toy against the chair I'm going to take it away! Okay, now I'm going to take it away until you can learn to play with it nicely and not damage the furniture"). Western parents also tend to use a lot of praise for compliant and obedient behavior. ("Wow, Jordan, you did a great job setting the table"). This is notable because the use of praise is very rare in cultures outside the West (LeVine & LeVine, 2016; Whiting & Edwards, 1988). Discipline for misbehavior may involve taking away privileges or giving a **time out**, in which the child is required to sit still in a designated place for a brief period, usually only a few minutes (Morawska & Sanders, 2011). Little research has been conducted on the effectiveness of the time out under normal family circumstances, but it has been shown to be effective with young children who have behavioral problems (Everett et al., 2007; Fabiano et al., 2004).

**time out**

disciplinary strategy in which the child is required to sit still in a designated place for a brief period

In addition to using time out, parenting researchers recommend: (1) explaining the reasons for discipline; (2) being consistent so that the consequences will be predictable to the child (and hence avoidable); and (3) exercising discipline at the time of the misbehavior (not later on) so that the connection will be clear (Klass, 2008). One popular approach suggests that if a parent's request to a young child is ignored or disobeyed, the parent counts a warning: "One-two-*three*," and if the request is not obeyed by "three" the child is then put in time out, 1 minute for each year of their age (Phelan, 2010). We can tell you that, as parents, we found that counting worked like magic with our twins in early childhood; we almost never got to "three."

Different cultures have different approaches to discipline. Japan is an example of a culture where shame and withdrawal of love is the core of discipline in early childhood. Recall that *amae* is a Japanese word that describes the close attachment between mother and child (Rothbaum et al., 2007). During infancy, *amae* takes the form of an emotionally indulgent and physically close relationship between the Japanese mother and her baby. However, in toddlerhood and early childhood, a new element, shame and withdrawal of love, is added. Japanese mothers rarely respond to their children's misbehavior with loud reprimands or physical punishment. Instead, they express disappointment and withdraw their love temporarily. The child feels shame, which is a powerful inducement not to disobey again.

This system of early childhood socialization seems to work well in Japan. Japanese children have low rates of behavioral problems and high rates of academic achievement (Takahashi & Takeuchi, 2007). They grow up to be Japanese adults who have low rates of crime and social problems and high levels of economic productivity, making Japan one of the most stable and economically successful societies in the world.

However, the same parental behaviors appear to have a different, more negative effect in Western countries. Among American researchers, parenting that uses shame and withdrawal of love has been described using the term **psychological control** (Barber, 2002). In American studies, this kind of parenting has been found to be related to negative outcomes in early childhood and beyond, including anxious, withdrawn, and aggressive behavior, as well as problems with peers (Barber et al., 2005; Silk et al., 2003). In Finland, too, a longitudinal study that began in early childhood found psychological control to predict negative outcomes in later childhood and adolescence, especially when psychological control was combined with physical affection, as it is in *amae* (Aunola & Nurmi, 2004).

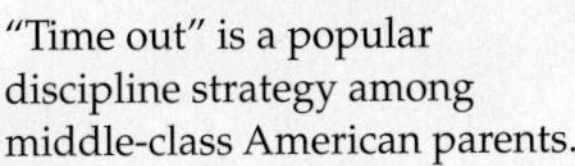

"Time out" is a popular discipline strategy among middle-class American parents.

What explains this difference? Why does *amae* appear to work well in Japan but not in the West? It is difficult to say since this question has not been researched directly. However, the answer may be some kind of interaction between the parents' behavior and the cultural belief system. In Japan, *amae* fits neatly into a larger system of cultural beliefs about duty and obligations to others, especially to family. In the West, psychological control contrasts and perhaps collides with cultural beliefs about the values of thinking and behaving independently. It may be this friction between parental practices and cultural beliefs that results in negative outcomes, not the parental practices in themselves.

**psychological control**
parenting strategy that uses shame and withdrawal of love to influence children's behavior

Research on physical punishment, also known as **corporal punishment**, suggests a similar kind of interaction between parenting practices and cultural beliefs. Physical punishment of young children is common in most parts of the world (Curran et al., 2001; LeVine & New, 2008). This approach to punishment has a long history. Most adults in most countries around the world remember experiencing physical punishment as children. Although most countries still allow parents to spank their young children, nearly all outlaw beatings and other harsh forms of physical punishment, which the historical record shows to have been quite common until about 100 years ago (Straus & Donnelly, 1994).

**corporal punishment**
physical punishment of children

Is physical punishment damaging to young children, or is it a form of instruction that teaches them to respect and obey adults? Here, as with *amae*, the answer appears to vary depending on the culture. Many studies conducted in the United States and Europe have found a correlation between physical punishment and a wide range of antisocial behaviors in children, including telling lies, fighting with peers, and disobeying parents (Alaggia & Vine, 2006; Kazdin & Benjet, 2003). Furthermore, several longitudinal studies have reported that physical punishment in early childhood increases the likelihood of bullying and delinquency in adolescence and aggressive behavior (including spousal abuse) in adulthood (Ferguson, 2013). On the basis of these studies, some scholars have concluded that physical punishment in early childhood increases children's compliance in the short run but damages their moral and mental health in the long run (Amato & Fowler, 2002; Gershoff, 2002).

Studies that cast a wider cultural net report considerably more complicated findings. In one longitudinal study, African American and White families were studied when the children were in early childhood and then 12 years later, when the children were in adolescence (Lansford et al., 2004). The White children showed the familiar pattern: physical punishment in early childhood predicted aggressive and antisocial behavior in adolescence. However, for African American children, physical punishment in early childhood was related to becoming less aggressive and antisocial in adolescence. Other studies have reported similar findings of the generally beneficial results of early childhood physical punishment among African Americans (Bluestone & Tamis-LeMonda, 1999; Brody & Flor, 1998; Steele et al., 2005). Similarly, studies of traditional cultures have found that many of the parents in these cultures use physical punishment on young children, and the children nevertheless grow up to be well-behaved, productive, mentally healthy adults (LeVine & LeVine, 2016; Whiting & Edwards, 1988).

Like the findings regarding *amae*, the findings on physical punishment show the crucial role of culture in how young children respond to their parents' behavior. In White American and European cultures, physical punishment is generally disapproved and not widely or frequently used (Bornstein & Bradley, 2014). In these cultures, physical punishment is likely to be combined with anger (Ferguson, 2013). In contrast, among African Americans, and in traditional cultures, the use of physical punishment in early childhood is widespread (Ispa & Halgunseth, 2004; Simons et al., 2013). Usually, it is mild in degree and is delivered not in an angry rage but calmly and sternly, as part of a "no-nonsense" parenting style (Brody & Flor, 1998). Physical punishment is often combined with parental warmth, so that children understand their parents' behavior not as a frightening and threatening loss of parental control but as a practice intended to teach them right from wrong and the importance of obeying their parents (Gunnoe & Mariner, 1997; Mosby et al., 1999). This seems to make the meaning and the consequences of physical punishment much different than it is in White American and European cultures.

## Parent–Child Coregulation and Conflict

**LO 9.3.3 Explain how middle childhood represents a turning point in the parent–child relationship, and describe the extent of parent–child conflict in adolescence and emerging adulthood.**

Young children in all cultures receive a great deal of parental care, supervision, and discipline. However, in middle childhood they become much more capable of going about their daily activities without constant monitoring and control by others. Sometimes, this newfound ability to make independent decisions leads to conflict with parents, especially in adolescence.

**coregulation**
relationship between parents and children in which parents provide broad guidelines for behavior but children are capable of a substantial amount of independent, self-directed behavior

**COREGULATION.** Middle childhood represents a key turning point in the parent–child relationship. From early childhood to middle childhood, parents and children move away from direct parental control and toward **coregulation**, in which parents provide broad guidelines for behavior but children are capable of a substantial amount of independent, self-directed behavior (Calkins, 2012; Maccoby, 1984; McHale et al., 2003). Parents continue to provide assistance and instruction, and they continue to know where their children are and what they are doing nearly all the time, but there is less need for direct, moment-to-moment monitoring. This pattern applies across cultures.

In developed countries, studies have shown that children spend substantially less time with their parents in middle childhood than in early childhood (Parke, 2004). Children respond more to parents' rules and reasoning, due to advances in cognitive development and self-regulation, and parents in turn use more explanation and less physical punishment (Collins et al., 2002; Parke, 2004). Parents begin to give their children simple daily chores such as making their own beds in the morning and setting the table for dinner.

In traditional cultures, parents and children also move toward coregulation in middle childhood. Children have learned family rules and routines by middle childhood and will often carry out their family duties without having to be told or urged by their parents (Gaskins, 2015). Also, children are allowed to play and explore further from home once they reach middle childhood (Whiting & Edwards, 1988). Boys are allowed more of this freedom than girls are, in part because girls are assigned more daily responsibilities in middle childhood. However, girls are also allowed more scope for independent activity in middle childhood. For example, in a Mexican village described by Beverly Chiñas (1992), when girls reach middle childhood, they are responsible for going to the village market each day to sell the tortillas they and their mothers have made that morning. By middle childhood they are capable of going to the market without an adult to monitor them, and they are also capable of making the monetary calculations required in selling the tortillas and providing change.

By middle childhood, in developed countries, parents expect their children to be self-directed and contribute to simple daily chores. Here, a girl makes her bed.

**CONFLICT.** Coregulation continues in the relationship between parents and adolescents, but now there is also sometimes conflict. Numerous studies have shown that adolescents and their parents agree on many of their beliefs and values, and typically they have a great deal of love and respect for one another (Kağitçibaşi & Yalin, 2015; Moore et al., 2002; Smetana, 2005). Nevertheless, studies in Western countries indicate that conflict with parents increases sharply in early adolescence, compared with middle childhood, and remains high for several years before declining in late adolescence (Dworkin & Larson, 2001; Kağitçibaşi & Yalin, 2015; Laursen et al., 1998; Van Doorn et al., 2011).

Figure 9.2 shows the increase in conflict from middle childhood to adolescence, from a longitudinal study that observed American mothers and sons in videotaped interactions on five occasions over 8 years (Granic et al., 2003). A Canadian study found that 40% of adolescents reported arguments with their parents at least once a week (Sears et al., 2007). Conflict in adolescence is especially frequent and intense between mothers and daughters (Collins & Laursen, 2004; Hofer et al., 2013). By mid-adolescence, conflict with parents tends to become somewhat less frequent but more intense before declining substantially in late adolescence (Fingerman & Yahirun, 2015).

**autonomy**

quality of being independent and self-sufficient, capable of thinking for one's self

There are several reasons why conflict with parents often rises during adolescence. First, adolescence entails reaching sexual maturity, which means that sexual issues may be a source of conflict in a way they would not have been in childhood. Early-maturing adolescents tend to have more conflict with parents than adolescents who mature "on time," perhaps because sexual issues arise earlier (Collins & Laursen, 2004; Graber, 2013). Second, advances in cognitive development make it possible for adolescents to rebut their parents' reasoning about rules and restrictions more effectively than they could have earlier. Third, and most importantly, in many cultures adolescence is a time of gaining greater independence from the family. Although parents and adolescents in these cultures usually share the same goal that the adolescent will eventually become a self-sufficient adult, they often disagree about the pace of adolescents' growing **autonomy** (Daddis & Smetana, 2005; Rote & Smetana, 2016). Parents may have concerns about adolescents' safety with respect to sexuality, automobile driving, and substance use, and restrict adolescents' behavior in an effort to protect them from risks (Arnett, 1999). Adolescents expect to be able to make their own decisions in these areas and resent their parents' restrictions, so conflict results.

**Figure 9.2** Parental Conflict in Adolescence

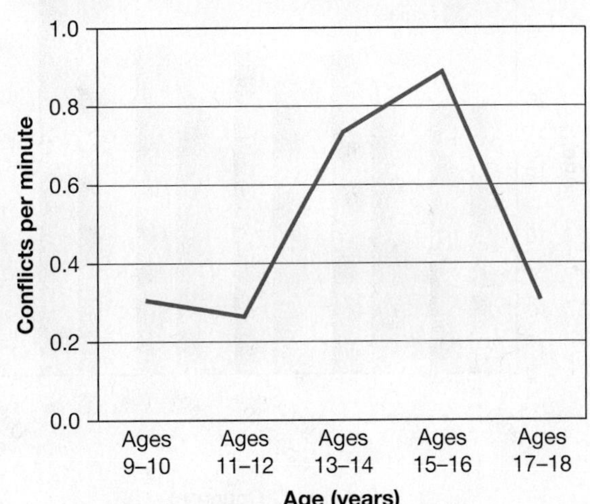


SOURCE: Based on Granic et al. (2003).

**Watch** ADOLESCENT CONFLICT WITH PARENTS ACROSS CULTURES

However, not all cultures value and encourage increased autonomy in adolescence. In traditional cultures, it is rare for parents and adolescents to engage in the kind of frequent conflicts typical of parent-adolescent relationships in Western cultures (Larson et al., 2010). The role of parent carries greater authority in traditional cultures than in the West, and this makes it less likely that adolescents in such cultures will express disagreements and resentments toward their parents (Phinney & Baldelomar, 2011).

Outside of the West, interdependence currently remains a higher value than independence, not only during adolescence but throughout adulthood (Markus & Kitayama, 2010; Phinney et al., 2005). Just as a dramatic increase in autonomy during adolescence prepares Western adolescents for adult life in an individualistic culture, learning to respect the authority of one's parents prepares adolescents in traditional cultures for an adult life in which interdependence is among the highest values and each person has a clearly designated position in a family hierarchy. Watch the video *Adolescent Conflict With Parents Across Cultures* for more information on cultural similarities and differences.

**Critical Thinking Question:** In the video *Adolescent Conflict With Parents Across Cultures*, the narrator in the video tells us that interdependence is valued in the Mexican village where one of the female teens is from. What are the economic reasons why interdependence might be more adaptive in this Mexican village than in the American family also shown in the video?

In most Western majority cultures, most young people move out of their parents' home sometime during emerging adulthood, and typically relationships between parents and emerging adults improve. In this case, at least, absence makes the heart grow fonder. Numerous studies have confirmed that emerging adults report fewer negative feelings and greater closeness toward their parents after moving out (Aquilino, 2006; Arnett & Schwab, 2012, 2013; Fingerman & Yahirun, 2015).

In the United States, although most emerging adults move out of their parents' home in their late teens, a substantial proportion (over one-third) stay home through their early 20s (Arnett & Schwab, 2012). Staying at home is more common among Asian Americans, Blacks, and Latinos than among White Americans (Fry, 2016). The reason for this is sometimes economic, especially for Latinos and African Americans, who have high rates of unemployment in emerging adulthood (U.S. Census Bureau, 2014). However, another important reason appears to be the greater emphasis on family closeness and interdependence in minority cultures, and less emphasis on independence as a value in itself. As one emerging adult, who lived with her Chinese American mother and Mexican American father during college, explained: "I loved living at home. I respect my parents a lot, so being home with them was actually one of the things I liked to do most.... Plus, it was free!" (Arnett, 2004, p. 54). In European countries, emerging adults tend to live with their parents longer than in the United States (Douglass, 2005, 2007; Kins et al., 2009). Figure 9.3 shows the the median age of leaving home in a selection of European countries, as compared to the United States (Iacovou, 2011). There are a number of practical reasons why European emerging adults stay home longer. European university students are more likely than American students to continue

**Figure 9.3** Median Age of Leaving Home in Europe Versus the United States

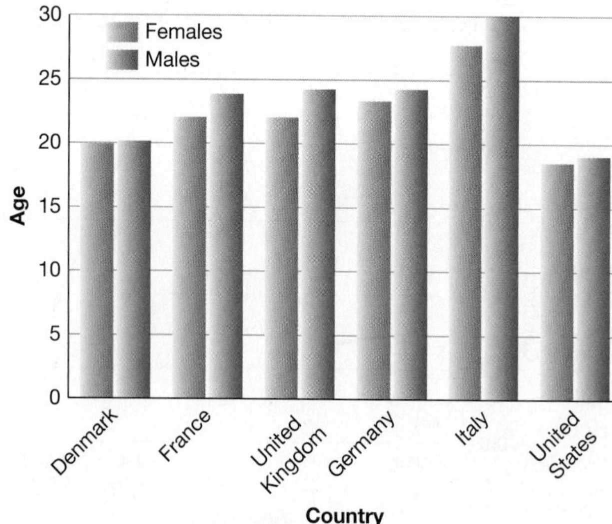


SOURCE: Data from Iacovou (2011).

to live at home while they attend university. European emerging adults who do not attend university may have difficulty finding or affording an apartment of their own. However, also important are European cultural values that emphasize mutual support within the family while also allowing young people substantial autonomy. Italy provides a good case in point (Chisholm & Hurrelmann, 1995; Krause, 2005). Ninety-four percent of Italians aged 15 to 24 live with their parents, the highest percentage in the European Union (EU) (Bonino & Cattelino, 2012). However, only 8% of them view their living arrangements as a problem—the lowest percentage among EU countries. Many European emerging adults remain at home contentedly through their early 20s, by choice rather than necessity.

In European countries, emerging adults tend to live with their parents longer than in the United States. Here, an emerging adult from Spain enjoys dinner with his parents.

There is more to the changes in relationships with parents from adolescence to emerging adulthood than simply the effects of moving out or staying home. Emerging adults also grow in their ability to understand their parents (Arnett, 2015). Adolescence is in some ways an egocentric period, and adolescents often have difficulty taking their parents' perspectives. They sometimes evaluate their parents harshly, magnifying their deficiencies and becoming easily irritated by their imperfections. Conflict with parents diminishes, as emerging adults mature and become more capable of understanding how their parents look at things. They come to see their parents as persons and begin to realize that their parents, like themselves, have a mix of qualities, merits as well as faults.

## SUMMARY: The Parent–Child Relationship

**LO 9.3.1 Describe the four types of parenting styles and their effects, and explain the cultural limitations of this research.**

Research has differentiated four parenting styles: authoritative, authoritarian, permissive, and disengaged. In general, authoritative parenting is associated with the most favorable outcomes for children, including independence, creativity, academic achievement, and sociability. Research on authoritative parenting is largely based on the American majority culture. Parents from American minority cultures and non-Western countries sometimes emphasize other values, including "familismo" and filial piety.

**LO 9.3.2 Describe the main cultural variations in how parents discipline young children, and explain how cultural context influences children's responses to discipline.**

In Western majority cultures the approach to discipline in early childhood tends to emphasize the authoritative approach of explaining the consequences of misbehavior and the reasons for discipline. Outside the West, the parental role has more authority and children are expected to be dutiful. Physical punishment and "psychological control" have quite different effects on children depending on culture.

**LO 9.3.3 Explain how middle childhood represents a turning point in the parent–child relationship, and describe the extent of parent–child conflict in adolescence and emerging adulthood.**

From early childhood to middle childhood, parents and children move away from direct parental control and toward coregulation, in which parents provide broad guidelines for behavior but children are capable of a substantial amount of independent, self-directed behavior. Coregulation continues in the relationship between parents and adolescents, but parent–child conflict rises significantly in early adolescence and remains high for several years before declining in late adolescence. As emerging adults mature and become more capable of understanding how their parents look at things, conflict diminishes further.

# 9.4 Problems in the Parent–Child Relationship

Although there are wide cultural variations in parenting styles and parents' approaches to discipline and punishment of children, today there is a widespread view across cultures that children should not be physically harmed and that parents have a responsibility to provide for their children's physical and emotional needs. However, there are all kinds of parents in the world, and in all cultures there are some who fail or are unable to meet these basic requirements. We now focus on child maltreatment, and on runaway and "street" children.

## Child Abuse and Neglect

**LO 9.4.1 Distinguish among the causes and consequences of physical and sexual child abuse.**

**child maltreatment**

neglect or abuse of children, including physical, emotional, or sexual abuse

**Child maltreatment** includes both the abuse and neglect of children, specifically:

- ***Physical abuse,*** which entails causing physical harm to a child, through hitting, kicking, biting, burning, or shaking the child;
- ***Sexual abuse,*** meaning any kind of sexual contact with a minor;
- ***Emotional abuse,*** including ridicule and humiliation as well as behavior causing emotional trauma to children, such as locking them in a dark closet; and
- ***Neglect,*** which is failure to meet children's basic needs of food, shelter, clothing, medical attention, and supervision.

Most research has focused on physical and sexual abuse. Next, we focus on each of these two kinds of child abuse.

**PHYSICAL ABUSE.** A variety of risk factors for physical abuse have been identified, involving characteristics of children as well as characteristics of parents. Young children are at risk for physical abuse if they are temperamentally difficult or if they are unusually aggressive or active and hence more difficult for parents to control (Li et al., 2010). However, studies indicate that physical abuse is more likely to be inflicted on adolescents than on younger children (Kilpatrick et al., 2000). Parental risk factors for physical abuse of children include poverty, unemployment, and single motherhood, all of which contribute to stress, which may in turn trigger abuse (Geeraert et al., 2004; Zielinski, 2009). Stepfathers are more likely to be abusive than biological fathers are, and child abuse is correlated with spouse abuse, suggesting that the abuser has a problem with anger management and self-control that is expressed in multiple ways (Asawa et al., 2008). Abusive parents often view their children as somehow deserving the abuse because of disobedience or because they are "no good" and will not respond to anything else (Bugental & Happaney, 2004). Parents who abuse their children were abused by their own parents in about one-third of cases (U.S. Department of Health & Human Services, 2016).

Physical abuse is destructive to young children in a wide variety of ways. It impairs emotional self-development, including self-regulation, empathy, and self-concept (Haugaard & Hazan, 2004). It is damaging to the development of friendships and social skills because abused children find it difficult to trust others (Elliott et al., 2005). It also interferes with school performance because abused children are often low in academic motivation and have behavior problems in the classroom (Boden et al., 2007). Furthermore, children who are abused are at risk for later emotional, social, and academic problems in adolescence and beyond (Fergusson et al., 2008, 2013; Herrenkohl et al., 2004).

What can be done to help abused children? In most cultures, there is some kind of system that removes children from their parents' care when the parents are abusive. In traditional cultures, the system tends to be informal. Children with abusive parents may go to live with relatives with whom they have a more positive, less conflictual relationship (LeVine et al., 2008). In Western countries, it is more often the formal legal system that intervenes in cases of child abuse. A state agency investigates reports of abuse, and if the report is verified the child is removed from the home.

The agency may then place the child in **foster care**, in which adults approved by the agency take over the care of the child (Pew Commission on Children in Foster Care, 2004). In the United States, about one-fourth of children in foster care are placed with relatives through the formal system (Child Welfare Information Gateway, 2013). In addition, three times as many children are estimated to live with nonparental relatives without the intervention of an agency, similar to the informal system of traditional cultures. Sometimes children in foster care return home after a period, sometimes they are adopted by their foster family, and sometimes they "age out" of foster care when they turn age 18 (Smith, 2011). Children in foster care are at high risk for academic, social, and behavioral problems, especially if they experience multiple foster-home placements (Crum, 2010; Plant & Siegel, 2008; Vig et al., 2005).

**foster care**
for maltreated children, approach in which adults approved by a state agency take over the care of the child

Programs have also been developed to prevent child maltreatment. In Chapter 3, we described one such program in the United States, the *Nurse–Family Partnership* (NFP). As you may recall, expectant mothers who have many of the risk factors for abuse receive regular home visits by a trained nurse until their children are 2 years old (Nurse Family Partnership, 2014; Olds, 2010). In a 15-year follow-up comparing families who participated in the NFP to other families with similar risks, the NFP group showed a 79% reduction in child abuse and neglect (Eckenrode et al., 2001).

**SEXUAL ABUSE.** Sexual abuse typically begins just before adolescence and then continues into adolescence. The causes of sexual abuse by parents are quite different from the causes of physical abuse. Physical abuse is more commonly inflicted on boys than on girls, whereas sexual abuse is usually inflicted on girls by their brothers, fathers, or stepfathers (Angold & Costello, 2006; Moore et al., 2010). Unlike physically abusive parents, sexually abusive fathers are usually not aggressive, but rather tend to be insecure and socially awkward around adults (Nevid et al., 2003). Because they feel inadequate in their relationships with adults—including, usually, their wives—they prefer to seek sexual satisfaction from children, who are easier for them to control (Haugaard, 1992). Sexual abuse usually results from motives such as these, rather than being an expression of affection that got out of control. On the contrary, fathers who abuse their adolescent daughters tend to have been detached and distant from them when they were younger. Sexual abuse is more likely to be committed by stepfathers than by fathers, perhaps because there is no biological incest taboo between stepfathers and their stepdaughters (Cyr et al., 2002; Seto et al., 2015).

The effects of sexual abuse tend to be even more profound and pervasive than the effects of physical abuse. Parental sexual abuse constitutes an ultimate breach of trust—rather than providing care and protection, the parent has exploited the child's need for nurturance and protection for the sake of his own needs. Consequently, many of the effects of parental sexual abuse are evident in the victim's social relationships. Adolescents who have been sexually abused tend to have difficulty trusting others and forming stable intimate relationships (Cherlin et al., 2004). During the period of sexual abuse and for many years afterward, many victims of sexual abuse experience depression, high anxiety, and social withdrawal (Bergen et al., 2003; Fergusson et al., 2013). Adolescent victims may react with one extreme or the other in their sexual behavior, becoming either highly avoidant of sexual contacts or highly promiscuous (Kendall-Tackett et al., 2001). Other consequences of sexual abuse include substance abuse, higher risk for a variety of psychological disorders, and suicidal thoughts and behavior (Bergen et al., 2003; Maikovich-Fong & Jaffee, 2010).

**Critical Thinking Question:** How would you explain the effects of sexual abuse in terms of attachment theory?

Although sexual abuse is among the most harmful things a parent can do to a child, one-third of sexually abused children demonstrate few or no symptoms as a result (Kendall-Tackett et al., 2001). Support from the mother after a father's or stepfather's sexual abuse has been disclosed as especially important to girls' recovery from sexual abuse; daughters cope far better if their mothers believe their account of the abuse and comfort and reassure them, rather than reject or blame them (Houck et al., 2010). Psychotherapy can also contribute to the girl's recovery (Mason, 2007).

## Runaway and "Street" Children

**LO 9.4.2 Distinguish running away from home in developed countries from becoming "street children" in developing countries.**

For some adolescents, family life becomes unbearable to them for one reason or another, and they run away from home. As one 15-year-old said: "I skipped out of school two days and my dad found out and he just gave it to me with his belt. I had bruises all over my hands and all over my legs. And my mother couldn't do anything about it and she was upset with me at the time, so that Friday I ran away" (Konopka, 1985, p. 78). It is estimated that about 1.6 to 2.8 million youth run away from home each year in the United States (Polly Klaas Foundation, 2015). About 80% to 90% of adolescents who leave home remain within 50 miles of home, often staying with a friend or relative, and return within a week (Whitbeck, 2009). Adolescents who stay away from home for weeks or months, or who never return at all, are at high risk for a wide variety of problems (Rosenthal & Rotheram-Borus, 2005).

Not surprisingly, adolescents who run away from home have often experienced high conflict with their parents, and many have experienced physical or sexual abuse from their parents (Chen et al., 2004; Thrane et al., 2006). Other family factors related to running away from home include low family income, parental alcoholism, and parental neglect (Whitbeck, 2009). Characteristics of the adolescent also matter. Adolescents who run away are more likely than other adolescents to have been involved in criminal activity, to use illegal drugs, and to have had problems at school (Mallett et al., 2005). They are also more likely to have had psychological difficulties such as depression and emotional isolation (Rohde et al., 2001), and they are more likely to be sexual minority youth (Diamond et al., 2015).

Although leaving home often represents an escape from a difficult family life, running away is likely to lead to other problems. Adolescents who run away from home tend be highly vulnerable to exploitation. Many of them report being robbed, physically assaulted, sexually assaulted, and malnourished (Pearson et al., 2017; Tyler et al., 2000, 2004; Whitbeck, 2009). In their desperation they may seek money through "survival sex," including trading sex for food or drugs, or becoming involved in prostitution or pornography (Al-Tayyib et al., 2014; Tyler et al., 2004). Depression and suicidal behavior are common among runaway adolescents (Lim et al., 2015; Rohde et al., 2001; Votta & Manion, 2004; Whitbeck et al., 2004).

Many urban areas have shelters for adolescent runaways. Typically, these shelters provide adolescents with food, protection, and counseling (Dekel et al., 2003). They may also assist adolescents in contacting their families, if the adolescents wish to do so and if it would be safe for them to go home. However, many of these shelters lack adequate funding and have difficulty providing services for all the runaway adolescents who come to them.

Adolescents who run away from home tend to be highly vulnerable to exploitation. Here, a runaway boy sleeps in an alley.

The United States is far from being the only country where youth can be found living on the streets of urban areas. "Street children," many of them adolescents, can be found in virtually every country in the world (Raffaelli & Iturbide, 2015). It is estimated that the total number of street children worldwide may be as high as 150 million (UNESCO, 2015). Many street children are homeless, but others roam the streets during the day and return to their families to sleep most nights. The main forces leading adolescents to the street vary in world regions, from family dysfunction in the West, to poverty in Asia and Latin America, to poverty, war, and family breakdown (due to AIDS) in Africa.

Street children across the world often exhibit remarkable resilience and manage to develop cognitive skills, make friends, and maintain supportive family relationships in the face of extremely difficult conditions (Raffaelli & Iturbide, 2015). However, they are at high risk for serious problems ranging from diseases to substance abuse to prostitution, especially girls, and their prospects for adult life are grim.

# Resilience

**LO 9.4.3 Define resilience, and name the protective factors that are related to resilience in adolescence.**

When children and adolescents develop problems, the source of the problems can often be traced to risk factors, such as poor family relationships, abusive or neglectful parenting, and poverty. However, there are also many children and adolescents who face dire conditions yet manage to adapt and function well. **Resilience** is the term for this phenomenon, defined as "good outcomes in spite of serious threats to adaptation and development" (Masten, 2001, p. 228). Sometimes "good outcomes" are measured as notable academic or social achievements, sometimes as psychological traits such as high well-being or self-esteem, and sometimes as the absence of notable problems. Children who are resilient are not necessarily high achievers who have some kind of extraordinary ability. More often they display what resilience researcher Ann Masten calls the "ordinary magic" of being able to function reasonably well despite being faced with unusually difficult circumstances (Masten, 2001, p. 227).

**resilience**
overcoming adverse environmental circumstances and achieving healthy development despite those circumstances

Resilience is promoted by **protective factors** that buffer against risk factors (Raffaelli & Iturbide, 2015). Some of the most important protective factors identified in resilience research are high intelligence, physical attractiveness, parenting that provides an effective balance of warmth and control, and a caring adult "mentor" outside the family. For example, high intelligence may allow an adolescent to perform well academically despite living in a disorderly household (Masten et al., 2006). Effective parenting may help a child have a positive self-image and avoid antisocial behavior despite growing up in poverty and living in a rough neighborhood (Brody & Flor, 1998). A mentor may foster high academic goals and good future planning in an adolescent whose family life is characterized by abuse or neglect (Rhodes & DuBois, 2008).

**protective factors**
characteristics of young people and their context that are related to lower likelihood of problems despite experiencing high-risk circumstances

One classic study followed a group of infants from birth through adolescence (Werner & Smith, 1982, 1992, 2001). It is known as the Kauai (ka-WHY-ee) study, after the Hawaiian island where the study took place. The Kauai study focused on a high-risk group of children who had four or more risk factors by age 2, such as problems in physical development, parents' marital conflict, parental drug abuse, low maternal education, and poverty. Out of this group, there was a resilient subgroup that showed good social and academic functioning and few behavior problems by ages 10–18. Compared with their less resilient peers, adolescents in the resilient group were found to benefit from several protective factors, including one well-functioning parent, higher intelligence, and higher physical attractiveness. More recent studies have supported the Kauai findings but also broadened the range of protective factors (Masten, 2007, 2014). Religiosity has also become recognized as an important protective factor (Howard et al., 2007; King & Boyatzis, 2015; Wallace et al., 2007).

## SUMMARY: Problems in the Parent–Child Relationship

**LO 9.4.1 Distinguish among the causes and consequences of physical and sexual child abuse.**

Risk factors for physical abuse include being an adolescent male and family poverty. Physical abuse is destructive to children, including their emotional, social, and academic development. Risk factors for sexual abuse include reaching puberty, being female, and having a male family member who is unusually insecure and socially awkward. During the period of sexual abuse and for many years afterward, many victims experience depression, high anxiety, and social withdrawal.

**LO 9.4.2 Distinguish running away from home in developed countries from becoming "street children" in developing countries.**

Adolescents who run away from home have often experienced high conflict with their parents, and many have experienced physical or sexual abuse from their parents. They are also more likely to be sexual minority youth. Many street children are homeless, but others roam the streets during the day and return to their families to sleep most nights. The main forces leading adolescents to the street vary in world regions, from family dysfunction in the West, to poverty in Asia and Latin America, to poverty, war, and family breakdown (due to AIDS) in Africa.

**LO 9.4.3 Define resilience, and name the protective factors that are related to resilience in adolescence.**

Resilience is the capacity to face dire conditions and yet manage to adapt and function well. Some of the most important protective factors are high intelligence, physical attractiveness, parenting that provides an effective balance of warmth and control, and a caring adult "mentor" outside the family. Religiosity can also be an important protective factor.

# 9.5 Siblings and Grandparents

When our twins were 8 years old, our daughter Paris had a long period where she would think of nice things to do for her brother Miles. One Saturday, she decided to make a special bath for him, and she ran a bath, lit some candles, and made him an original drink of multiple juices plus cream (yuck, but it's the thought that counts). "Wow," we said to Miles, observing this, "You're quite the little prince." "No," said Miles at his most earnest, "I'm a brother whose sister loves him."

So far, we have focused on the parent–child relationship, but families often consist of other members too, including siblings. As with parents and children, siblings also form attachments to one another. But as we will see, it is not all love and sweetness between siblings. There are other emotions too—some of them quite negative. In addition to siblings, we also focus on grandparents in this section.

## Family Systems Theory

**LO 9.5.1 Describe the family systems principles of disequilibrium and subsystems.**

**family systems approach**
an approach to understanding family functioning that emphasizes how each relationship within the family influences the family as a whole

**dyadic relationship**
a relationship between two persons

**disequilibrium**
in the family systems approach, this term describes a change that requires adjustments from family members

One useful framework for making sense of the complex ways family members interact with each other is the **family systems approach**. According to this approach, to understand family functioning one must understand how each relationship within the family influences the family as a whole (Goldenberg & Goldenberg, 2005; Minuchin, 1974, 2002). The family system is composed of a variety of subsystems. For example, in a family consisting of a mother, a father, and a child the subsystems would be mother and child, father and child, and mother and father. In families with more than one child, or with extended family members such as grandparents who are closely involved in the family, the family system becomes a more complex network of subsystems, consisting of each **dyadic relationship** (a relationship of two persons) as well as every possible combination of three or more persons.

The family systems approach is based on two key principles. One is that each subsystem influences every other subsystem in the family. For example, a high level of conflict between the parents affects not only the relationship between the two of them, but also the relationship that each of them has with a child (Bradford et al., 2004; Kan et al., 2008).

A second, related principle of the family systems approach is that a change in any family member or family subsystem results in a period of **disequilibrium** (or imbalance) until the family system adjusts to the change. Some disequilibriums are relatively uncommon or nonnormative, such as a child developing a psychological disorder. Other changes are normative such as the birth of a sibling. For both normative and nonnormative changes, adjustments in the family system are required to restore a new equilibrium.

**Critical Thinking Question:** What are some key similarities and differences between Family Systems Theory and Attachment Theory?

## Siblings

**LO 9.5.2 Identify the most common features of sibling relationships worldwide, and describe how children with no siblings differ from other children.**

Toddlers often react negatively to the birth of a younger sibling.

A gap of 2 to 4 years between siblings is common worldwide. Consequently, a substantial amount of research has focused on how toddlers and young children respond to the birth of a sibling. Overall, their reaction tends to be negative (Boer et al., 2013). Often, following the birth of a younger sibling, toddlers' attachment to the mother changes from secure to insecure, as they feel threatened by all the attention given to the new baby (Teti et al., 1996; Volling, 2012). Some toddlers display problems such as increased aggressiveness toward others, or become increasingly whiny, demanding, and disobedient (Hughes & Dunn, 2007). They may regress in their progress toward toilet training or self-feeding. Sometimes mothers become less patient and responsive with their toddlers, under the stress of caring for both a toddler and a new baby (Dunn & Kendrick, 1982).

What can parents do to ease the transition for toddlers? Studies indicate that if mothers pay special attention to the toddler before the new baby arrives and explain the feelings and needs of the baby after the birth, toddlers respond more positively to their new sibling (Boer et al., 2013; Howe et al., 2001; Hughes & Dunn, 2007).

What if the toddler is the younger sibling rather than the older sibling? Once younger siblings are no longer infants but toddlers, and develop the ability to talk, walk, and share in pretend play, older siblings show less resentment and become much more interested in playing with them (Hughes & Dunn, 2007). By their second year of life, toddlers often imitate their older siblings and look to them for cues on what to do and how to do it (Barr & Hayne, 2003).

In developed countries, studies show that toddlers have attachments to their older siblings (Shumaker et al., 2011). One study used an adaptation of the Strange Situation to examine American toddlers' attachments to siblings (Samuels, 1980). Two-year-old toddlers and their mothers were asked to come to the backyard of an unfamiliar home, sometimes with—and sometimes without—a 4-year-old sibling present. When no older sibling was present, the toddlers mostly responded to the mother's departure with distress and to her return with great relief, much as they do in the standard Strange Situation. However, when the older sibling was there along with the toddler, the toddler rarely showed distress when the mother left the backyard. The older sibling provided the emotional comfort and security of an attachment figure, making this outdoor Strange Situation less strange and intimidating.

Toddlers in traditional cultures most certainly also develop an attachment to the older siblings who care for them, but from the limited evidence available, it appears to be a secondary attachment rather than the primary attachment (Ainsworth, 1977; LeVine et al., 1994). That is, under most conditions toddlers are content to be under the care of older siblings, but in times of crisis they want the care and comfort of their mothers. By middle childhood, children in traditional cultures often have responsibility for caring for young siblings, and for many this responsibility continues into adolescence. This responsibility promotes attachments. Time together, and closeness, is especially high between siblings of the same gender, mainly because in traditional cultures, daily activities are often separated by gender.

Trust and care are not the only emotions between siblings. Conflict rises as toddlers become increasingly capable of asserting their own interests and desires. In one study that followed toddlers and their older siblings from when the toddlers were 14 months old to when they were 24 months old, home observations showed that conflict increased steadily during this period and became more physical (Dunn & Munn, 1985). In another study, 15- to 23-month-old toddlers showed remarkably advanced abilities for annoying their older siblings (Dunn, 1988). For example, one toddler left a fight with an older sibling to go and destroy an object the older sibling cherished; another toddler ran to find a toy spider and pushed it in his older sibling's face, knowing the older sibling was afraid of spiders!

Sibling conflict peaks in middle childhood (Cole & Kerns, 2001). In one study that recorded episodes of conflict between siblings, the average frequency of conflict was once every 20 minutes they were together (Kramer et al., 1999). The most common source of conflict is personal possessions (McGuire et al., 2000). Factors contributing to sibling conflict are family financial stress and parents' marital conflict (Jenkins et al., 2003). Sibling conflict is also especially high when one sibling perceives the other as receiving more affection and material resources from the parents (Dunn, 2004). When our daughter was 7 years old, she was selected to play the little mermaid in her school's play. She was very proud of this fact—maybe a little too proud. She lorded it over her brother a bit. When he would complain about something like her getting the first turn to do something or receiving what he perceived to be a bigger piece of cake than his, she would turn to him and say, "That's because I'm the Little Mermaid, Miles, and that's the lead role in the play!"

After the peak of sibling conflict in middle childhood, relationships with siblings become less emotionally intense in adolescence, mainly because adolescents gradually spend less time with their siblings (Cicirelli, 2013; Noller & Callan, 2015). There has been little research on sibling relationships in emerging adulthood (Aquilino, 2006; Scharf & Shulman, 2015). However, one study of adolescents and emerging adults in Israel found that emerging adults spent less time with their siblings than adolescents did, but also felt more emotional closeness and warmth toward them (Scharf et al., 2005). Emerging adults also reported less intense conflict and rivalry than adolescents. Qualitative analyses showed that emerging adults had a more mature perception of their relationship with their siblings than adolescents did, in the sense that they were better able to understand their siblings' needs and perspectives.

**only child**
child who has no siblings

Because of its "one-child policy," China today has many children without siblings.

On a worldwide scale, the normative pattern is for children to grow up with siblings. Over the past half-century as birthrates have fallen worldwide, however, growing up as an **only child** has become increasingly common. Let's take a moment to consider these children. In the United States, about 20% of children have no siblings. In some parts of Europe and Asia, birthrates are just 1.1–1.4 children per woman, meaning that there are more children who do not have a sibling than do have one (Population Reference Bureau, 2014).

Just as having siblings is a mixed blessing, having no siblings has mixed effects as well. In general, "only children" fare at least as well as children with siblings (Brody, 2004). Their self-esteem, social maturity, and intelligence tend to be somewhat higher than children with siblings, perhaps because they have more interactions with adults (Dunn, 2004). However, in American studies they are somewhat less successful in social relations with peers, perhaps because children with siblings gain peer-like practice in social relations (Kitzmann et al., 2002).

Only children have been especially common in China in recent decades. Beginning in 1978, in response to fears of overpopulation, the Chinese government instituted a "one-child policy," making it illegal for parents to have more than one child without special government approval. There were fears that this policy would create a generation of "little emperors and empresses" who were overindulged and selfish, but those fears appear to be unfounded. Like only children in the United States, only children in China demonstrate several advantages over children with siblings, including higher cognitive development, higher emotional security, and higher likeability (Jiao et al., 1996; Wang & Fong, 2009; Yang et al., 1995). Unlike their American counterparts, Chinese only children show no deficits in social skills or peer acceptance (Hart et al., 2003). China rescinded its one-child policy in 2015, due to concerns that if the birthrate remains low the population may become too heavily weighted toward older people who are no longer working. Demographers, however, predict that China's birthrate is unlikely to change much (Schiermeier, 2015).

## Grandparents

**LO 9.5.3 Delineate three key roles of grandparents.**

In addition to parents and siblings, grandparents often play an important role in children's development across many cultures. Due to increased longevity, psychologists are paying more attention to grandparenthood (Dunifon, 2013). In the United States, the involvement of grandparents is relatively low. One in 10 children lives in a family that includes a grandparent (Livingston & Parker, 2010; U.S. Census Bureau, 2014). Grandparents are the primary providers of child care for 30% of working mothers with children under age 5. In other countries—developed and developing—grandparents are more involved. In Chinese urban areas, for example, grandparents assist parents in providing care for 50%–70% of young children (Jingxiong et al., 2007). Cross-cultural studies have also shown that children in traditional cultures often grow up in a household that includes grandparents (Schlegel & Barry, 1991). Households that include not only parents and children, but also other adult relatives such as grandparents, are referred to as **extended families**. On a worldwide basis, extended families are most common in Asia, the Middle East, South America, and sub-Saharan Africa (Child Trends, 2014).

**extended families**
households that include not only parents and children, but also other adult relatives

The involvement of grandparents in families takes different forms (Baker & Silverstein, 2012). Three roles are as:

- ***Child savers***, who provide large amounts of care when parents are unavailable or incapable of providing care.
- ***Parent savers***, who provide some care in order to free up time for parents to devote to their jobs or education.
- ***Cultural custodians***, who provide care in order to transmit key cultural values, ethnic heritage, and family traditions. In Namibia, for example, many mothers in the urban capital arrange for infants as young as 6 months of age to go to the tribal homeland to live with grandparents in order for them to pass on traditional cultural values (Edwards et al., 2015).

**Critical Thinking Question:** Can you think of other key roles that grandparents play in their grandchildren's development?

While grandparents serve many positive functions in the lives of children, shared care by parents and grandparents is not always uncomplicated. Issues may arise when parents and grandparents hold differing childrearing beliefs and have different childrearing practices. Interviews with parents and grandparents in an urban city in China have shown that both sides express quite a lot of ambivalence (Goh, 2006). Some parents worry that grandparents perform chores that they think had best be left to the child, such as feeding oneself. Some grandparents fear that they and the parents give a child mixed messages.

### SUMMARY: Siblings and Grandparents

**LO 9.5.1 Describe the family systems principles of disequilibrium and subsystems.**

According to family systems theory, the subsystems comprise all of the relationships between the different members of a family. A change in any family member or family subsystem results in a period of disequilibrium (or imbalance) until the family system adjusts to the change.

**LO 9.5.2 Identify the most common features of sibling relationships worldwide, and describe how children with no siblings differ from other children.**

Sibling relationships are typically characterized by love and care, as well as conflict and rivalry. In general, "only children" fare at least as well as children with siblings. The effects of being an only child vary somewhat by culture.

**LO 9.5.3 Delineate three key roles of grandparents.**

Grandparents often play an important role in children's development across many cultures. Three key roles of grandparents are: child saver, parent saver, and cultural custodian.

# 9.6 Changing Families

Across cultures and across time, children have grown up in a wide variety of family environments. In this section, we focus on families that have become more common in the past 50 years. During this time, the most dramatic changes to family life have been the rise in: divorce and remarriage, single parenthood, sexual minority families, and dual-earner families. Let's examine the implications of each of these changes for child development.

## Divorce and Remarriage

**LO 9.6.1 Describe the consequences to children of parental divorce and remarriage.**

Rates of divorce have risen dramatically over the past half-century in Canada, northern Europe, and the United States. Currently, close to half of children in many of these countries experience their parents' divorce by the time they reach middle childhood. In contrast, divorce remains rare in southern Europe and in countries outside the West. Most adults who divorce remarry. Consequently, most children who experience their parents' divorce spend part of their childhood in a stepfamily.

**DIVORCE.** How do children respond to their parents' divorce? Overall, children respond negatively in a variety of ways, especially boys and especially in the first 2 years following divorce (Amato & Anthony, 2014). Children display increases in both externalizing problems (such as unruly behavior and conflict with mothers, siblings, peers, and teachers) and internalizing problems (such as depressed mood, anxieties, phobias, and sleep disturbances) (Clarke-Stewart & Brentano, 2006). Their school performance also declines (Amato & Boyd, 2013). If the divorce takes place during early childhood, children often blame themselves, but by middle childhood most children are less egocentric and more capable of understanding that their parents may have reasons for divorcing that have nothing to do with them (Hetherington & Kelly, 2002). Watch the video *Pam: A Divorced Mother of a Nine-Year-Old* to see how one mother describes the impact of divorce on her daughter.

In one renowned longitudinal study of divorces that took place when the children were in middle childhood, the researchers classified 25% of the children in divorced families as having severe emotional or behavioral problems, compared to 10% of children in two-parent, nondivorced families (Hetherington & Kelly, 2002). The low point for most children came 1 year after divorce. After that point, most children gradually improved in functioning, and by 2 years post-divorce, girls were mostly back to normal. However, boys' problems were still evident even 5 years after divorce.

**family process**
quality of the relationships between family members

**Watch** PAM: A DIVORCED MOTHER OF A NINE-YEAR-OLD

Not all children react negatively to divorce. Even if 25% have severe problems, that leaves 75% who do not. What factors influence how a divorce will affect children? Increasingly researchers have focused on **family process**, that is, the quality of the relationships between family members before, during, and after the divorce. In all families, whether divorced or not, parental conflict is linked to children's emotional and behavioral problems (Kelly & Emery, 2003). When parents divorce with minimal conflict, or when parents are able to keep their conflicts private, children show far fewer problems (Amato & Anthony, 2014). If divorce results in a transition from a high-conflict household to a low-conflict household, children's functioning often improves rather than deteriorates (Davies et al., 2002).

Another aspect of family process is children's relationship to the mother after divorce. Mothers often struggle in numerous ways following divorce (Wallerstein & Johnson-Reitz, 2004). In addition to the emotional stress of the divorce and conflict with ex-husbands, they often have full responsibility for household tasks and child care. There is increased financial stress, with the father's income no longer coming directly into the household. Most countries have laws requiring fathers to contribute to the care of their children after leaving the household, but despite these laws mothers often receive less than full child support from their ex-husbands (Statistics Canada, 2012; U.S. Census Bureau, 2011). Given this pile-up of stresses, it is not surprising that the mother's parenting often takes a turn for the worse in the aftermath of divorce, becoming less warm, less consistent, and more punitive (Hetherington & Kelly, 2002). Relationships between boys and their mothers are especially likely to go downhill after divorce. Mothers and boys sometimes become sucked into a **coercive cycle**, in which boys' lack of compliance evokes harsh responses from mothers, which in turn makes boys even more resistant to their mothers' control, evoking even harsher responses, and so on (Patterson, 2002). However, when the mother is able to maintain a healthy balance of warmth and control despite the stresses, her children's response to divorce is likely to be less severe (Leon, 2003).

Relationships between mothers and sons sometimes go downhill following divorce.

Family processes involving fathers are also important in the aftermath of divorce. In about 90% of cases (across countries) mothers retain custody of the children, so the father leaves the household and the children no longer see him on a daily basis. They may stay with him every weekend or every other weekend, and perhaps see him one evening during the week, in addition to talking to him on the phone. Now fathers must get used to taking care of the children on their own, without mothers present, and children must get used to two households that may have different sets of rules. For most children, contact with the father diminishes over time, and only 35%–40% of children in mother-custody families still have at least weekly contact with their fathers within a few years of the divorce (Kelly, 2003). When the father remarries, as most do, his contact with children from the first marriage declines steeply (Dunn, 2002). However, when fathers remain involved and loving, children have fewer post-divorce problems (Dunn et al., 2004; Finley & Schwartz, 2010).

In recent decades, **divorce mediation** has developed as a way of minimizing the damage to children that may take place due to heightened parental conflict during and after divorce (Emery et al., 2014; Sbarra & Emery, 2008). In divorce mediation, a professional mediator meets with divorcing parents to help them negotiate an agreement that both will find acceptable. Research has shown that mediation can settle a large percentage of cases otherwise headed for court, lead to better functioning in children following divorce, and lead to improved relationships between divorced parents and their children, even 12 years after the settlement (Emery et al., 2005).

**coercive cycle**
pattern in relations between parents and children in which children's disobedient behavior evokes harsh responses from parents, which in turn makes children even more resistant to parental control, evoking even harsher responses

**divorce mediation**
arrangement in which a professional mediator meets with divorcing parents to help them negotiate an agreement that both will find acceptable

**REMARRIAGE.** Because mothers retain custody of the children in about 90% of divorces, most stepfamilies involve the entrance of a stepfather into the family. You might expect that the entrance of a stepfather would be a positive development in most cases, given the problems that face mother-headed families following divorce. Low income is a problem, and when the stepfather comes into the family this usually means a rise in overall family income. Mothers' stress over handling all the household and child care responsibilities is a problem, and after a stepfather enters the family he can share some of the load. Mothers' emotional well-being is a problem, and her well-being is typically enhanced by remarriage, at least initially (Visher et al., 2003). If mothers' lives improve in all these ways, wouldn't their children's lives improve, too?

Unfortunately, no. Frequently, children take a turn for the worse once a stepfather enters the family. Compared to children in nondivorced families, children in stepfamilies have lower academic achievement, lower self-esteem, and greater behavioral problems (Coleman et al., 2000; Nicholson et al., 2008). According to one estimate, about 20% of children in stepfamilies have serious problems in at least one aspect of functioning in middle childhood, compared to 10% of their peers in nondivorced families (Hetherington & Kelly,

2002). Girls respond more negatively than boys to remarriage, a reversal of their responses to divorce (Bray, 1999). If the stepfather also has children of his own that he brings into the household, making a *blended family*, the outcomes for children are even worse than in other stepfamilies (Becker et al., 2013).

There are a number of reasons for children's negative responses to remarriage. First, remarriage represents another disruption that requires adjustment, usually at a point when the family had begun to stabilize following the earlier disruption of divorce (Hetherington & Stanley-Hagan, 2002). Second, stepfathers may be perceived by children as coming in between them and their mothers, especially by girls, who may have become closer to their mothers following divorce (Bray, 1999). Third, and perhaps most importantly, children may resent and resist their stepfathers' attempts to exercise authority and discipline (Robertson, 2008). Stepfathers may be attempting to support the mother in parenting and to fulfill the family role of father, but children may refuse to regard him as a "real" father and may in fact regard him as taking their biological father's rightful place (Weaver & Coleman, 2010). When asked to draw their families, many children in stepfamilies literally leave their stepfathers out of the picture (Stafford, 2004).

However, it is important to add that here, as elsewhere, family process counts for as much as family structure. Many stepfathers and stepchildren form harmonious, close relationships (Becker et al., 2013; Coleman et al., 2000). The likelihood of this outcome is enhanced if the stepfather is warm and open to his stepchildren and does not immediately try to assert authority (Visher et al., 2003). Also, the younger the children are, the more open they tend to be to accepting the stepfather (Jeynes, 2007). The likelihood of conflict between stepfathers and stepchildren increases with the children's age, from early childhood to middle childhood and again from middle childhood to adolescence (Hetherington & Kelly, 2002).

## Single Parenthood

**LO 9.6.2 Describe the consequences to children of growing up in single-parent families.**

Over the past 50 years, it has become increasingly common in some countries for children to be born to a single mother. The United States is one of the countries where the increase has been greatest, and currently over 40% of births are to single moms (CDC, 2017). Single motherhood has increased among both African Americans and Whites, but is highest among African Americans; over 70% of African American children are born to a single mother. Rates of single motherhood are also high in northern Europe (Ruggeri & Bird, 2014). However, it is more likely in northern Europe than in the United States for the father to be in the home as well, even though the mother and father may not be married.

What are the consequences of growing up in single-parent families? Because there is only one parent to carry out household responsibilities such as cooking and cleaning, children in single-parent households often contribute a great deal to the functioning of the family, much like children in traditional cultures. However, the most important consequence of growing up in a single-parent family is that it greatly increases the likelihood of growing up in poverty, and growing up in poverty, in turn, has a range of negative effects on children (Harvey & Fine, 2004). Poverty rates for single-mother households are especially high in the United States and Canada (about 48%). In comparison, the rates are much lower in Scandinavian countries (about 12%) (Legal Momentum, 2017). Research in the United States shows that compared to their peers in two-parent families, children in single-parent families generally are at higher risk for externalizing and internalizing behavior problems, and low school achievement (Breivik et al., 2009; Ricciuti, 2004).

Poverty is common in American single-parent families.

However, just as for children of divorced and remarried parents, family process is at least as important as family structure. Single-parent families are diverse, and many children who grow up in single-parent families function very well. When the mother makes enough money so the family is not in poverty, children in single-parent families function as well as children in two-parent families (Lipman et al., 2002). Many never-married single mothers have relationships with their children that are characterized by love and mutual support. Single-father families are relatively rare, but children with a single father are no different than their peers in middle childhood in regard to social and academic functioning (Amato, 2000).

It should also be noted that having a single parent does not always mean there is only one adult in the household. In many African American families, the grandmother acts as a "parent saver." She provides child care, household help, and financial support to the single mother (Crowther & Rodriguez, 2003). In about one-fourth of families with an African American single mother, the grandmother also lives in the household (Kelch-Oliver, 2011). In other words, it is an extended family household.

## Sexual Minority Families

**LO 9.6.3 Describe the consequences to children of growing up in sexual minority families.**

In the latest U.S. census, over 20% of gay couples and one-third of lesbian couples were living with children, a dramatic increase over the past 20 years (U.S. Bureau of the Census, 2010). In part this reflects a growing acceptance of **sexual minority families**. For example, same-sex couples are now allowed to jointly adopt children in some American states, many Western European countries, a number of South American countries, South Africa, New Zealand, and parts of Australia.

**sexual minority families**
a family headed by parents who self-identify as sexual or gender minorities

Reviews of studies of the children of gay and lesbian parents have found that they are similar to children with heterosexual parents on cognitive functioning, academic achievement, emotional development, social adjustment, and sexual and gender orientation (Anderssen et al., 2002; Goldberg, 2010; Patterson, 2006). More data are available for children from lesbian families, because the number of gay households with children has, until recently, been small. However, recent studies suggest that the psychological outcomes for children growing up with gay parents are no different from those of children growing up with lesbian and heterosexual parents (Farr et al., 2010; Goldberg, 2012). For more information, watch the video *A Family With Two Fathers*.

Children from sexual minority families, however, do face the issue of societal stigma. For example, an interview study with 10-year-old children from the National Lesbian Family Study (NLFS) found that 43% had experienced incidents where peers made disparaging comments (Gartrell et al., 2005). As one child put it, "It hurts my feelings.... If those kids knew somebody who was gay, they wouldn't say the things they do" (Gartrell et al., 2005, p. 522).

## Dual-Earner Families

**LO 9.6.4 Describe the consequences to children of growing up in dual-earner families.**

**dual-earner family**
a family in which both parents are employed

The last 50 years have seen the rise of **dual-earner families**. Employment among women with school-aged children has increased steadily, as shown in Figure 9.4 (next page). Part of the increase is related to the increase in rates of divorce and single parenthood discussed earlier, which have often left the mother as the only source of the family's income. Mothers in nondivorced families may also work to help the family maintain an adequate income (Schneider & Waite, 2005). Of course, noneconomic reasons are often involved as well. Many educational and occupational opportunities have opened up to women in the past 50 years that had been denied to them before. Research indicates that most employed mothers would continue to work even if they had enough money (Hochschild, 2001; Schneider & Waite, 2005). Women in professional careers as well as restaurant servers and

**Watch** A FAMILY WITH TWO FATHERS

**Figure 9.4** Proportion of Children With Mothers in the Labor Force, 1940–2010

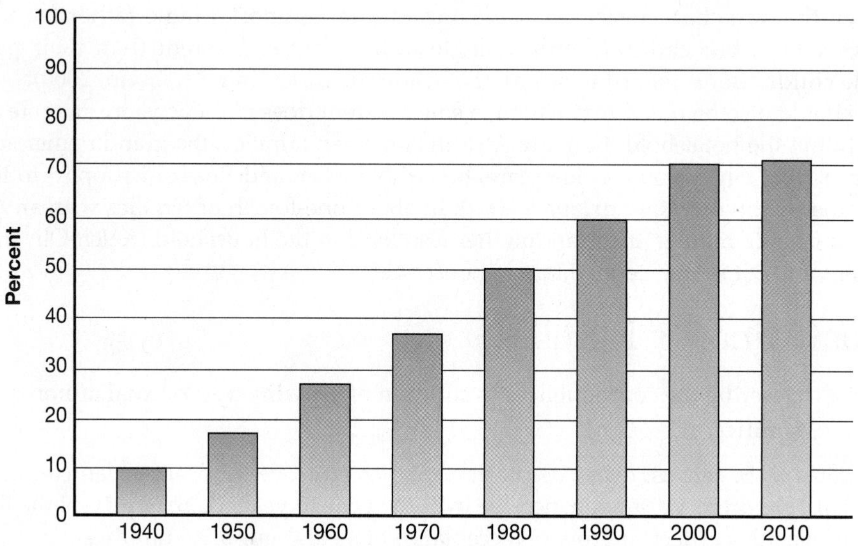


factory workers generally report that they are committed to their jobs, enjoy having a work role as well as family roles, and desire to continue to work.

For the most part, few substantial effects have been found on children from living in a dual-earner family as compared with a family where only one of the two parents is employed (Crouter & McHale, 2005; Dunn & O'Brien, 2013). However, girls from dual-earner families tend to be more confident and have higher career aspirations than girls whose mothers are not employed (Crouter & McHale, 2005). In contrast, several studies have found that adolescent boys in dual-earner families have more arguments with their mothers and siblings compared with boys whose mothers are not employed (Crouter & McHale, 2005; Montemayor, 1984). Apparently, these conflicts result from the greater household responsibilities required of adolescents when the mother is employed, and from the fact that boys resist these responsibilities more than girls do.

The number of hours worked by the parents is an important variable in some studies. Adolescents, both boys and girls, are at higher risk for various problems if both parents work full-time than if one parent works just part-time (Schneider & Waite, 2005). The risks are especially high for adolescents who are unsupervised by parents or other adults on a daily basis for several hours between the time school ends and the time a parent arrives home from work. These adolescents tend to have higher rates of social isolation, depression, and drug and alcohol use (Jacobson & Crockett, 2000; Voydanoff, 2004). Adolescents in dual-earner families are more likely to function well if parents maintain monitoring from a distance, for example, by having their children check in with them by phone (Waizenhofer et al., 2004). As for parenting in other families, when dual-earner parents maintain adequate levels of demandingness and responsiveness, their children generally function well.

Toddlers in high-quality childcare centers are as likely as children in home care to have secure attachments.

As we have just seen, the last several decades have seen a rise in dual-earner, single, and divorced parents. In turn, this has meant an increase in the number of young children who spend time in early child care. In developmental psychology, the impact on infants and toddlers of "other care" rather than "mother care" has been extensively researched. A common focus has been on the implications for attachment. So to conclude this chapter we return to the topic of attachment, but this time in relation to early child care. For an overview of findings, watch the video *Early Child Care and Its Consequences* in the Research Focus feature.

## Research Focus: Early Child Care and Its Consequences

The "NICHD Study of Early Child Care" began in 1991 with over 1,300 young children (from infancy through early childhood) at 10 sites around the United States. Children and their families were followed longitudinally for 7 years (NICHD Early Child Care Research Network, 2005). The sample was diverse in socioeconomic (SES) background, ethnicity, and geographical region. Multiple methods were used to assess the children and their families, including observations, interviews, questionnaires, and standardized tests.

Multiple aspects of the care children received were also assessed, including quantity, stability, quality, and type of care. A wide range of children's developmental domains were examined, including physical, social, emotional, cognitive, and language development.

There were many notable and illuminating findings in the study. About three-fourths of the children in the study began non-maternal child care by the age of 4 months. During infancy and toddlerhood most of this care was provided by relatives, but enrollment in childcare centers increased during toddlerhood, and beyond age 2 most children receiving nonmaternal care were in centers. Infants and toddlers averaged 33 hours a week in nonmaternal care. African American infants and toddlers experienced the highest number of hours per week of nonmaternal care and White infants and toddlers the lowest, with Latinos in between.

For infants and toddlers, the focus of the study was on how childcare arrangements might be related to attachment. The observations measured how sensitive and responsive caregivers were with the children, the two most important determinants of attachment quality according to attachment theory. As measured by the Strange Situation, attachments to mothers were no different for toddlers receiving nonmaternal care than for toddlers receiving only maternal care. However, insecure attachments were more likely if the nonmaternal care was low in quality, for more than 10 hours per week, or if mothers were low in sensitivity.

This was an impressively ambitious and comprehensive study, but even this study has limitations. Most notably, the children were not randomly assigned into childcare groups. The choices about the care they received and how many hours per week they were in care were made by their parents, not the researchers. Consequently, the outcomes of the children's childcare experiences were interwoven with many other variables, such as parents' income, education, and ethnicity. This is an example of how social scientists are rarely able to create an ideal experimental situation in their research, but must usually take human behavior as they find it and do their best to unravel the daunting complexity of real life.

**Watch** EARLY CHILD CARE AND ITS CONSEQUENCES

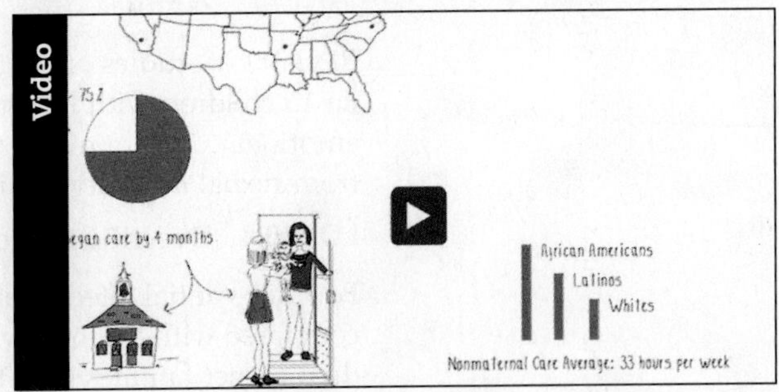


### Review Questions

1. Which of the following was NOT one of the research methods used in the study?
   - **a.** Questionnaires
   - **b.** Neurological exams
   - **c.** Interviews
   - **d.** Observations
2. Which of the following factors was related to insecure attachment in the toddlers?
   - **a.** Low-quality non-maternal care
   - **b.** Greater than 10 hours a week in non-maternal care
   - **c.** Low sensitivity in maternal care
   - **d.** All of the above

## SUMMARY: Changing Families

**LO 9.6.1 Describe the consequences to children of parental divorce and remarriage.**

About a quarter of children in divorced families show severe emotional or behavioral problems, and problems tend to peak about one year after the divorce. Divorce mediation has developed as a way of minimizing the damage to children that may take place due to heightened parental conflict during and after divorce. About 20% of children in stepfamilies have serious problems in at least one aspect of functioning.

**LO 9.6.2 Describe the consequences to children of growing up in single-parent families.**

Children in single-parent households often contribute a great deal to the functioning of the family. Growing up in a single-parent family in North America greatly increases the likelihood of growing up in poverty. In turn, growing up in poverty puts children at higher risk for externalizing and internalizing behavior problems, and low school achievement. When a single parent (usually a mother) makes enough money so the family is not in poverty, children in single-parent families function as well as children in two-parent families.

**LO 9.6.3 Describe the consequences to children of growing up in sexual minority families.**

Reviews of studies of the children of gay and lesbian parents have found that they are similar to children with heterosexual parents on cognitive functioning, academic achievement, emotional development, social adjustment, and sexual and gender orientation. Children from sexual minority families, however, face the issue of societal stigma.

**LO 9.6.4 Describe the consequences to children of growing up in dual-earner families.**

Few substantial effects have been found on children from living in a dual-earner family as compared with a family where only one of the two parents is employed. However, girls from dual-earner families tend to be more confident and have higher career aspirations than girls whose mothers are not employed. Adolescent boys in dual-earner families have more arguments with their mothers and siblings compared with boys whose mothers are not employed.

## Apply Your Knowledge as a Professional

The topics covered in this chapter apply to a wide variety of career professions. Watch this video to learn how they apply to a court-appointed child advocate.

**Journaling Question:** Think of an example of disequilibrium that occurred in your family during your childhood. How did the various family members adapt? You might find it helpful to draw on some of the concepts introduced in this chapter, such as attachment, parenting styles, and family processes.

# Chapter 10
# Peers, Friends, and Romantic Partners

## Learning Objectives

**10.1 Social Contexts Beyond the Family: Two Theories**

10.1.1 Explain how Mead's stages capture the broadening of children's social environment beyond the family.

10.1.2 Explain how Bronfenbrenner's ecological theory addresses social contexts beyond the family.

**10.2 Play with Peers and Friends**

10.2.1 Describe how styles of play change from toddlerhood through early childhood, including how play is shaped by gender, individual differences, and culture.

10.2.2 Describe how cognitive and physical development shape play in new ways in middle childhood and adolescence.

**10.3 Peers**

10.3.1 Review key characteristics that differentiate children's peer groups, and explain why crowds are common in American high schools.

10.3.2 Define the four main categories that differentiate children in terms of their popularity among peers, and explain why rejected-aggressive children benefit from intervention.

10.3.3 Describe different types of aggression among peers, including how aggression changes with age.

**10.4 Friends**

10.4.1 Describe similarities and differences in the meaning of friendship from toddlerhood through middle childhood.

10.4.2 Describe the characteristics of friendship in adolescence and emerging adulthood, including cliques.

10.4.3 Explain how culture plays a role in the importance and meaning of friendship.

**10.5 Problem Behaviors Among Friends**

10.5.1 Summarize key demographics of substance use, and explain why young people use substances.

10.5.2 Explain why age and crime are so strongly correlated, and describe the multisystemic approach to combating delinquency in adolescence.

**10.6 Romantic Partners**

10.6.1 Describe the extent to which romantic desires and relationships are shaped by culture, and outline the qualities emerging adults look for in a romantic partner.

10.6.2 Explain the role of culture and context in regard to premarital sex in adolescence and emerging adulthood.

10.6.3 Explain why emerging adulthood is the peak period for unintended pregnancies and sexually transmitted infections.

10.6.4 Explain how coming out among sexual minority adolescents is shaped by development and culture.

10.6.5 Review prevalence rates of sexual harassment and date rape.

"TO MAKE A FRIEND, CLOSE ONE EYE. TO KEEP A FRIEND, CLOSE THE OTHER EYE." This Jewish proverb wittily and wisely encapsulates many features of friendship. We value friends as people we can both have fun with and be serious with. We look for friends who understand us, in part based on common interests and experiences. We rely on friends to be gentle with us when we make mistakes and to support us and prop up our confidence when we are in doubt or afraid.

**friends**
persons with whom an individual has a valued, mutual relationship

**peers**
people who share some aspect of their status, such as being the same age

**Friends**, as you know, are people with whom you develop a valued, mutual relationship. **Peers** are persons who share some aspect of their status in common, such as age. So, in social science research on development, a child's peers are typically the same-age children who are part of the daily environment, such as the other children in the child's preschool class. Some of those peers may become the child's friends, others may not. Both friends and peers are important from toddlerhood and onward. Nonetheless, in many parts of the world, friends and peers take on notable importance during adolescence and emerging adulthood. These are periods in which the emotional center of young people's lives is shifting from their immediate families to persons outside the family.

**romantic partner**
person in regard to whom an individual feels some combination of love and sexual desire

In developed countries, experimentation with relationships involving love and sex is quite common in adolescence and emerging adulthood. Friends provide a bridge between the close attachments young people have to their family members and the close attachment they will eventually have to a **romantic partner**. Friends also sometimes become love interests, and sometimes sex spills into friendships. Eventually, most young people form a relationship outside the family in which they experience some combination of love, sexual desire, and commitment.

**Watch** CHAPTER INTRODUCTION: PEERS, FRIENDS, AND ROMANTIC PARTNERS

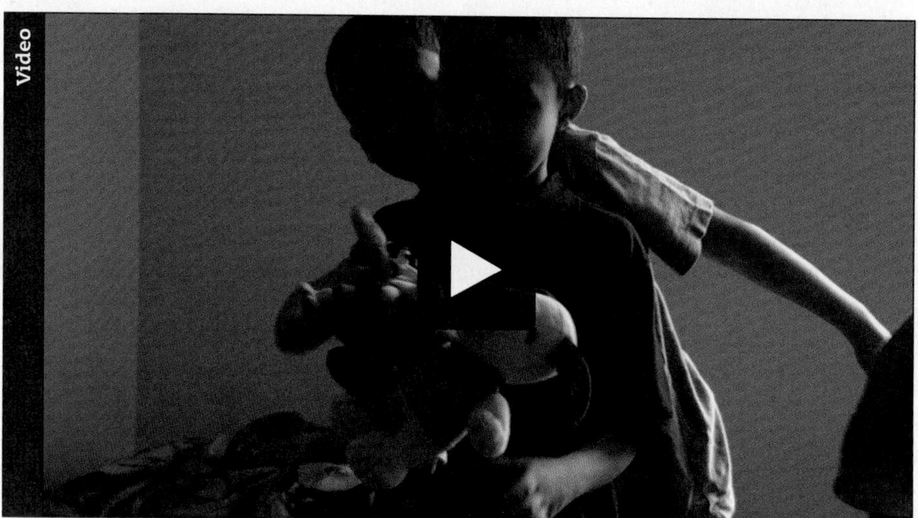

# 10.1 Social Contexts Beyond the Family: Two Theories

Parents and family are of vital importance in the lives of children. As we go through life, however, we also interact with many other people and social institutions. In a classic theory, the anthropologist Margaret Mead (1901–1978) captured this broadening of children's social circle beyond the immediate family to include peers, friends, and other members of the community. More recently, Urie Bronfenbrenner (1917–2005) proposed a theory that propelled the field of developmental psychology from its predominant focus on parents to consideration of the multiple social contexts that shape children's development. Let's take a close look at these two theories.

## Mead's Classifications of Childhood Social Stages

**LO 10.1.1 Explain how Mead's stages capture the broadening of children's social environment beyond the family.**

Margaret Mead (1935) proposed a general scheme many decades ago that still applies well to how most of the world's children experience the social changes of childhood. As you can see in Table 10.1, Mead designated children ages 0–2 with the term *lap child*, to denote their near-constant dependence on the care and monitoring of others. Toward the end of toddlerhood, children still need a considerable amount of care, but they no longer need to be constantly watched by others. For early childhood, Mead proposed two terms. The *knee child*, ages 3–4, is still cared for mainly by the mother but also spends time with other children. The *yard child*, ages 5–6, is given more scope to venture beyond the immediate family area and into the "yard," that is, into a social world where parents are nearby but not always directly present. Most time spent away from parents is in the company of daily peer companions. Mead used the term *school or community child* to describe 6- to 10-year-olds. Now, many hours of the day are spent with peers and friends, typically in school under the authority of teachers. In cultures with limited schooling, children often work alongside other children and adults.

Mead's scheme was the basis of an influential study of young children across cultures conducted by Beatrice Whiting and Carolyn Pope Edwards (1988). Whiting and Edwards studied 2–10 year old children in 12 different places around the world, including Africa, Asia, North America, and South America. Their goal was to see what kinds of similarities and differences exist in the social worlds of children across cultures.

They found substantial similarities worldwide in how cultures socialize young children and structure their social environments. As a child moves from the lap to the knee to the yard and finally into the school or broader community, there is a gradual lessening of dependence on the mother and a gradual move into the social orbit of peers and older children. Like lap children, knee children receive a great deal of nurturance from mothers and from older children. However, more is required of knee children than of lap children. Knee children are expected to stop breast-feeding and to have less bodily contact with the mother. Parents and older children expect knee children to perform minor chores, and to have basic manners such as waiting their turn and playing well with other children. Older children exercise more dominance over knee children than over lap children because knee children are perceived as better able to understand and follow commands.

**Table 10.1** Mead's Classifications of Childhood Social Stages

| Age | Term | Features |
|---|---|---|
| 0–2 | Lap child | Needs constant care; doted on by others |
| 3–4 | Knee child | Still cared for mainly by mothers, but spends more time with other children |
| 5–6 | Yard child | Spends more time with same-sex peers; sometimes unsupervised |
| 6–10 | School or Community child | Spends a large part of the day with peers, typically in school under the authority of teachers |

The "school or community" child, described by Mead, may spend most of the day in school in developed countries or working with other community members in traditional cultures.

Yard children are allowed more freedom than knee children. Yard children spend most of their time close to home, as knee children do, but 20% of the time they are outside of their immediate home area playing or doing errands (Whiting & Edwards, 1988). The yard child in many cultures has a substantial number of daily peer companions, about 10 or so in the cultures studied by Whiting and Edwards. However, most cultures share a view that children cannot reason very well until about age 6, and this limits how far a yard child can be away from home or supervision. Primary school starts around ages 6–8 in all cultures. With the start of school, children often spend much of the day with same-age peers and continue to do so for years to come.

The cultures studied by Mead and by Whiting and Edwards were mostly in developing countries, but many of the same patterns apply in developed countries. Across countries and cultures, the social world expands in early childhood to include more time and more interactions with peers and friends, as well as adults from outside the family.

## Bronfenbrenner's Ecological Theory

**LO 10.1.2 Explain how Bronfenbrenner's ecological theory addresses social contexts beyond the family.**

**ecological theory**
Bronfenbrenner's theory that child development is shaped by five interrelated systems in the social environment

An important recent theory of developmental psychology is Urie Bronfenbrenner's **ecological theory** (Bronfenbrenner, 1980, 2000, 2005; Bronfenbrenner & Morris, 1998). Unlike the scheme proposed by Mead, Bronfenbrenner's is not a stage theory. Like Mead, however, Bronfenbrenner focuses attention on the multiple influences that shape child development in the social environment. He presented his theory as a reaction to what he viewed as an overemphasis in developmental psychology on the immediate environment, especially the mother–child relationship. Mothers, fathers, and family are important, Bronfenbrenner acknowledged, but much more than this is involved in children's development.

Bronfenbrenner's theory has been successful at drawing research attention to the broader cultural environment that people experience as they develop, and to the ways the different levels of a person's environment interact. In later writings (Bronfenbrenner, 2000, 2005; Bronfenbrenner & Morris, 1998), Bronfenbrenner added a biological dimension to his framework (it is now sometimes called a *bioecological theory*), but the distinctive contribution of the theory remains its portrayal of the cultural environment.

According to Bronfenbrenner, as you can see in Figure 10.1, there are five key *systems* that play a part in child development:

1. The *microsystem* is Bronfenbrenner's term for the immediate environment, the settings where people experience their daily lives. Microsystems in most cultures include relationships with each parent, with siblings, and perhaps with extended family; with peers and friends; with teachers; and with other adults (such as coaches and religious leaders). Bronfenbrenner emphasizes that the child is an *active* agent in the microsystems.

**Figure 10.1** The Systems in Bronfenbrenner's Ecological Theory

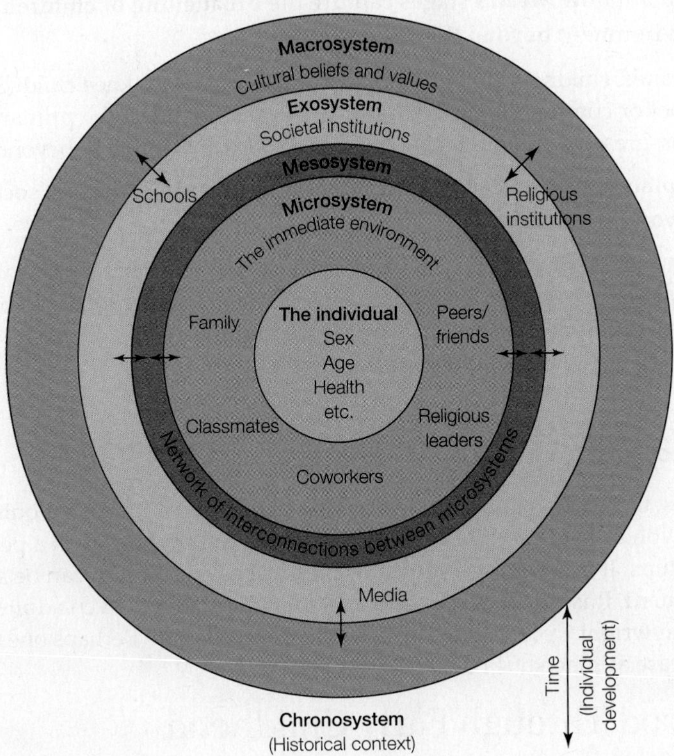


For example, children are affected by their friends but they also make choices about who to have as friends.

2. The *mesosystem* is the network of interconnections between the various microsystems. For example, a child who is experiencing abusive treatment from parents may become aggressive toward peers (Schwartz et al., 2001).
3. The *exosystem* refers to the societal institutions that have indirect but potentially important influences on development. In Bronfenbrenner's theory, these institutions include schools, media, and religious institutions. For example, in Asian countries such as China, competition to get into college is intense and depends chiefly on adolescents' performance on a national exam at the end of high school; consequently, there is limited time during the high school years to devote to close friendships (Liu et al., in press).
4. The *macrosystem* is the broad system of cultural beliefs and values, and the economic and governmental systems that are built on those beliefs and values. For example, in countries such as Iran and Saudi Arabia, cultural beliefs and values are based in the religion of Islam, as are economic and governmental systems. These beliefs and values, as we will see later in this chapter, have implications for the sexual norms and behaviors among adolescents and emerging adults.
5. Finally, the *chronosystem* refers to changes that occur in developmental circumstances over time, both with respect to individual development and to history. For example, with respect to individual development, dating is a much different experience at 14 than at 24; with respect to history, views of sexual minority youth in Western countries today are more tolerant than they were half a century ago.

Today, most developmental psychologists use the term *context* to refer to the environmental settings and relationships laid out by Bronfenbrenner. In this chapter we focus on peers, friends, and romantic partners. In the chapters to follow, we will turn to school and work, media, as well as civic and religious institutions. The impact of the ecological theory on developmental psychology is reflected in the fact that there is now a large body of research on all of these influential contexts.

### SUMMARY: Social Contexts Beyond the Family: Two Theories

**LO 10.1.1 Explain how Mead's stages capture the broadening of children's social environment beyond the family.**

Mead differentiated childhood into four phases: lap child (0–2), knee child (3–4), yard child (5–6), and school or community child (6–10). These phases reflect the primary setting of the child and the progressive broadening of children's social environment beyond the family.

**LO 10.1.2 Explain how Bronfenbrenner's ecological theory addresses social contexts beyond the family.**

Bronfenbrenner's ecological theory lays out five systems that play a part in child development: microsystem, mesosystem, exosystem, macrosystem, and chronosystem. Each of these systems involves different contexts, and the theory highlights how children develop in multiple contexts such as family, religion, media, and culture.

# 10.2 Play with Peers and Friends

In most cultures, toddlerhood is a time of forming the first social relations outside the family. This usually involves being part of a peer play group. Certainly, play is a pervasive part of social relationships. It is fun and serious. It is physical and mental. It can be spontaneous or carefully structured. It is for toddlers—and for older children and even adults, too. The Irish novelist and playwright Oscar Wilde (1854–1900) observed that "Perhaps one never seems so much at one's ease as when one has to play a part."

## Toddlerhood Through Early Childhood

**LO 10.2.1 Describe how styles of play change from toddlerhood through early childhood, including how play is shaped by gender, individual differences, and culture.**

Play is widespread across cultures, especially in the first years of life (Gaskins, 2015). In one study comparing 3-year-old children from Brazil, Kenya, and the United States, the children in all countries spent more time in play than in any other activity (Tudge et al., 2006). However, anthropologists have observed some cultures where play is rare even in the early years, such as the Kpelle of Liberia and the Maya of Guatemala (Gaskins, 2000, 2015). In general, the more work parents have to do, the earlier they involve children in work and the less time children have for play (Rogoff, 2003).

Nevertheless, in general, children in traditional cultures have some time for play. In traditional cultures, toddlerhood is when children first join play groups after having been cared for during infancy mainly by the mother. The play groups often include peers as well as siblings and cousins (Gaskins, 2015). These groups also usually include children of a variety of ages,

In traditional cultures, children play with one another but seldom with an adult—as is quite common in the West.

and often play is structured and directed by the older children. Unlike in the West, it is rare for children in traditional cultures to play with adults (LeVine et al., 2008; LeVine & LeVine, 2016).

In developed countries, too, peer relations expand in toddlerhood, often in the form of some kind of group child care (Rubin et al., 2006). Researchers observing toddlers in these settings have found that their peer play interactions are more advanced than early studies had reported (Dunfield & Kuhlmeier, 2013; Pálmadóttir & Johansson, 2015). One influential early study reported that toddlers engaged exclusively in *solitary play*, all by themselves, or *parallel play*, in which they would take part in the same activity but without acknowledging each other (Parten, 1932). However, more recent studies have found that toddlers engage not only in solitary and parallel play but also in *simple social play*, where they talk to each other, smile, and give and receive toys, and even in *cooperative pretend play*, involving a shared fantasy such as pretending to be animals (Howes, 1996; Hughes & Dunn, 2007). Watch the video *Play Styles in Toddlerhood* to see additional examples of each style.

**Watch** PLAY STYLES IN TODDLERHOOD

**Watch** PLAY STYLES IN EARLY CHILDHOOD

Furthermore, toddlers who know each other well tend to engage in more advanced forms of play than unacquainted toddlers do. In one study of toddlers attending the same child-care center, even young toddlers (16–17 months old) engaged in simple social play (Howes, 1985). By 24 months, half of the toddlers engaged in cooperative pretend play, as did all the toddlers between 30 and 36 months old. This is a striking contrast to studies of social relations among unacquainted toddlers, which had found mainly solitary and parallel play, with cooperative pretend play not appearing until at least age 3 (Howes, 1996; Hughes & Dunn, 2007).

In the course of early childhood, solitary play and parallel play decline somewhat, while simple social play and cooperative pretend play increase (Hughes & Dunn, 2007). Cooperative pretend play becomes more complex in the course of early childhood, as children's imaginations bloom and they become more creative and adept at using symbols, for example, using a stick to represent a sword and a blanket over two chairs to represent a castle (Dyer & Moneta, 2006). Like toddlers, most young children display a variety of types of play, engaging in cooperative play for a while and then making a transition to solitary play or parallel play (Robinson et al., 2003). For more information, watch the video *Play Styles in Early Childhood*.

Sex-segregation in play groups starts in early childhood and becomes more pronounced with age (Gaskins, 2015). In the 12-cultures study by Whiting and Edwards (1988), described earlier, children played in same-sex groups 30%–40% of the time at ages 2–3. By age 11, children played with same-sex peers over 90% of the time. American studies report similar results (Fabes et al., 2003). In one observational study, the percentage of time playing in same-sex groups was 45% for 4-year-old children and 73% for 6-year-old children (Martin & Fabes, 2001).

There are differences in play styles between boys' and girls' groups. Numerous studies have found that boys generally engage in high-activity, aggressive, competitive, "rough-and-tumble" play, whereas girls' play tends to be quieter, more cooperative, and more likely to involve fantasy and role playing (Ruble et al., 2006).

Physical aggression peaks in early childhood.

There are also individual differences between children in their approaches to peer play groups. Children vary in their levels of sociability from infancy onward, and by early childhood there are distinct differences among children in how successful they are at using the social skills required for play in a group setting. Preschool social life often rewards the bold, and children who are shy spend a lot of their preschool time watching others play without taking part themselves (Coplan et al., 2004; Rubin et al., 2002). However, for some children it simply takes time to become accustomed to the preschool social environment. The more preschool experience children have, the more successful they are at taking part in social play (Dyer & Moneta, 2006). Sometimes children observe other children's play as a prelude to entering the play themselves (Lindsey & Colwell, 2003). Also, some children simply enjoy playing by themselves. They may spend more time than others in solitary play, but this could be an indication of an unusually lively and creative imagination rather than a sign of being withdrawn or rejected (Coplan et al., 2004). Research has shown that children in different cultures differ on how they respond to shy peers and the extent to which they try to include peers who play alone. Watch the video *Shyness in China and Canada: Cultural Interpretations* for a fascinating example of this research.

## Research Focus: Shyness in China and Canada: Cultural Interpretations

There is cultural variation in how peers regard shyness in early childhood. In studies of young children in the West, shyness has long been associated with negative characteristics such as anxiety, insecurity, and social incompetence. Shy children have been found to experience problems in their relations with peers and to be prone to negative self-perceptions and depression. Shyness in young children has been viewed by Western researchers as a problem to be cured.

But what about in other cultures? Xinyin Chen hypothesized that shyness would have a different meaning in Chinese culture, and set out to compare the consequences of shyness among Chinese and Canadian children (Chen, 2016; Chen et al., 2005). In one study conducted by Chen and his colleagues, 4-year-old children in China and Canada were invited into a laboratory setting in groups of four and observed in two 15-minute free-play interactions. Shy children were identified as those who spent the most time in onlooker behavior (watching the activities of others) or unoccupied behavior (wandering around the room alone or sitting alone doing nothing). Through this process, 50 of 200 Chinese children and 45 of 180 Canadian children were classified as shy.

Although the proportion of shy children to non-shy children was identical in the two countries, the responses shy children received from their peers were very different. When shy Canadian children made attempts to interact with their peers, the peers often reacted negatively (for instance, saying "No!" or "I won't do it") and rarely reacted positively, with encouragement and support. In contrast, peers of shy children in China responded much more positively when shy children initiated contact, often inviting them to play or allowing them to join a game. Overall, peers in Canada tended to be antagonistic or nonresponsive toward shy children, whereas in China, peers of shy children were more often supportive and cooperative.

However, Chen and his colleagues have been conducting research in China for over 20 years now, and they have recorded striking shifts in the social implications of shyness for young Chinese children over that time. Recent decades have been a period of dramatic social change in China, as the country has moved rapidly from a state-controlled, Communist economy to a free-market economy. This transition has resulted in changes in values as well, with a decline in the traditional Chinese collectivistic values of duty, respect, and obligation, and a rise in individualistic values of self-assertion and independence.

**Watch** SHYNESS IN CHINA AND CANADA: CULTURAL INTERPRETATIONS

The change in values has been reflected in Chen's research on peers' responses to shy Chinese children. In the 1990 sample Chen studied, shyness was positively associated with a variety of favorable aspects of adjustment, including peer acceptance, leadership, and academic achievement. However, by the time Chen repeated the study in 2002, the correlation had flipped.

Now shyness was associated with negative adjustment, including peer rejection and depression. In just a 12-year period, the cultural meaning of shyness had reversed. As Chen observed, "the extensive change toward the capitalistic system in the economic reform and the introduction of Western ideologies may have led to the decline in the adaptive value of shyness."

### Review Question

1. Studies of young Chinese children in the 1990s and a decade later showed that over that time period:
   - **a.** Prevalence of shyness increased due to economic upheaval
   - **b.** Prevalence of aggressiveness increased during the transition to a market economy
   - **c.** Shyness became less culturally valued
   - **d.** Aggressiveness among girls rose substantially

**Critical Thinking Question:** Can you explain which of Bronfenbrenner's systems the research by Chen addresses? (You might find it helpful to take a look back at each of the five systems and ask yourself if it applies.)

## Middle Childhood Through Adolescence

**LO 10.2.2 Describe how cognitive and physical development shape play in new ways in middle childhood and adolescence.**

In most cultures, the proportion of same-gender play rises during early and middle childhood. Here, young girls in India play a clapping game together.

In middle childhood, simple social play remains popular (Manning, 1998). According to cross-cultural studies, simple social games such as tag and hide-and-seek are universally popular in middle childhood (Edwards, 2000). Some simple social games have a more local flavor. For example, in India, young girls play a game that involves clapping hands in time to a song. They clap against each other's hands in various patterns as they sing, going faster and faster as the song proceeds. The song goes through 11 verses that describe a girl's likely course through life, ending with turning into a spirit. Younger girls learn first by observing and listening as the older girls play, then by gradually taking part in the clapping song themselves.

Cooperative pretend play also continues to be popular in middle childhood. For example, children at this age pretend to be animals or heroes. All over the world, they also play pretend games where they imitate adult activities such as going to market, or herding cattle, or being the teacher in a classroom (Rogoff, 2003; Roopnarine et al., 1994).

Middle childhood, however, also brings new cognitive skills and with that, play becomes more complex and more rule-based. Children in early childhood may play with action figures, but in middle childhood there may be elaborate rules about the powers and limitations of the characters. For example, in the early 21st century, Japanese games involving Pokémon action figures became popular in middle childhood play worldwide, especially among boys (Ogletree et al., 2004; Simmons, 2014). These games involve characters with an elaborate range of powers and provide children with the enjoyment of competition and mastering complex information and rules. In early childhood the information about the characters would be too abundant and the rules too complex for children to follow, but by middle childhood this cognitive challenge is exciting and pleasurable. More recently, *Pokémon Go* has also captured the interest of adolescents and emerging adults. In this augmented-reality game, players use their mobile devices to battle, capture, and train Pokémon figures that "appear" in the real world. Players walk around in the real world and find the figures on their mobile devices. (In fact, the police in some cities have issued warnings to players to remain alert to traffic, not drive while playing, and not loiter on private property; Annear, 2016.)

Another type of fantasy play that begins in early childhood but sometimes becomes more elaborate in middle childhood and adolescence involves an imaginary companion or "friend." Researchers in the United States estimate that about 50% of children have an imaginary friend at some point in their lives (Lillard, 2015). Compared to their age mates without imaginary companions, these children have been found to have better narrative skills and more advanced social cognition, including theory of mind (Gleason, 2013; Lillard & Kavanaugh, 2014; Roby & Kidd, 2008; Taylor et al., 2004). One study that analyzed adolescents' diaries found that creative and socially well-adjusted adolescents were most likely to create an imaginary friend (Seiffge-Krenke, 1997). A longitudinal study also found that at-risk adolescents who had an imaginary friend were less likely to drop out of high school or be diagnosed with a psychiatric disorder, as compared to those without an imaginary friend (Taylor et al., 2010).

**Critical Thinking Question:** Explain whether you would expect children from traditional cultures to be less, equally, or more likely to have imaginary companions, as compared to the United States.

In middle childhood, card games and board games—that require counting, remembering, and planning—become popular. These games often remain common in adolescence (and beyond). These boys are from Mozambique.

Many other games become popular in middle childhood that are more cognitively challenging than the games younger children play, and these games often remain common in adolescence (and beyond). Card games and board games become popular, and often these games require children to count, remember, and plan strategies. Middle childhood is also a time when many children develop an interest in hobbies such as collecting certain types of objects (such as coins and dolls) or constructing and building things (such as with LEGO toys, a Danish invention that is popular around the world in middle childhood). These hobbies also provide enjoyable cognitive challenges of organizing and planning (McHale et al., 2001). Electronic games that involve substantial cognitive challenges also become popular in middle childhood (Olson et al., 2008).

Advances in physical development also spur new games in middle childhood. As children develop greater physical agility and skill in middle childhood, their games with rules include various sports that require greater physical abilities than their early childhood games did. In many countries, middle childhood is the time when children first join organized teams to play sports such as soccer, baseball, or basketball (see Chapter 4). Many children also play sports in games they organize themselves, often including discussions of the rules.

Anthropologists have also documented the interweaving of sexuality into play. Some of this sex play has been found in middle childhood and adolescence. One example is the people of the Trobriand Islands in the South Pacific. In Ford and Beach's (1951) description:

> Sexual life begins in earnest among the Trobrianders at six to eight years for girls, ten to twelve for boys. Both sexes receive explicit instruction from older companions whom they imitate in sex activities.... At any time a couple [of children] may retire to the bush, the bachelor's hut, an isolated yam house, or any other convenient place and there engage in prolonged sexual play with full approval of their parents. (pp. 188–191)

It should be noted that these descriptions are from the past. In recent decades, the Trobrianders have become less permissive in response to globalization and the censure of Christian missionaries (Hatfield & Rapson, 2005). Psychological research on sexuality in children, including sexual play in children, is almost non-existent (Diamond et al., 2015).

## SUMMARY: Play with Peers and Friends

**LO 10.2.1 Describe how styles of play change from toddlerhood through early childhood, including how play is shaped by gender, individual differences, and culture.**

Toddlers engage in solitary, parallel, simple social, and cooperative pretend play. In early childhood, the latter two styles of play become particularly popular. Sex-segregation in play groups starts in early childhood and becomes more pronounced with age. Children vary on their play preferences, with some enjoying solitary play. Children in collectivistic cultures are more encouraging of play with shy children than children in individualistic cultures.

**LO 10.2.2 Describe how cognitive and physical development shape play in new ways in middle childhood and adolescence.**

Middle childhood brings new cognitive skills and with that, play becomes more complex and more rule-based. As children develop greater physical agility and skill in middle childhood, their games with rules also include various sports that require greater physical abilities than their early childhood games did. Many of the types of play and games that emerge in middle childhood remain popular into adolescence.

# 10.3 Peers

Peers are important throughout life. They are the pool of people whom we draw on for a sense of affiliation and defining our identities. There are often status hierarchies within peer groups and between peer groups. On the one hand, these hierarchies may make us feel valued and important. On the other hand, they can be sources of victimization and bullying.

## Characteristics of Peer Groups

**LO 10.3.1 Review key characteristics that differentiate children's peer groups, and explain why crowds are common in American high schools.**

From toddlerhood through emerging adulthood, peer groups get carved out on the basis of a set of important characteristics. One characteristic is age. By age 3 or 4, most children in the West are in some kind of preschool setting for at least part of their typical week, and preschool classes are grouped by age. In developed countries, this grouping by age continues through high school and college. In traditional cultures, peer groups have more elastic age boundaries. Children often play in mixed-age groups that may include children in toddlerhood, early childhood, and middle childhood (LeVine and New, 2008). Also, children and adolescents often work alongside adults.

Gender is another defining characteristic of children's peer groups. Across cultures, relations with peers (and friends) tend to become more segregated by gender in the course of early childhood. Boys tend to have other boys as their peers, and the social world of girls is populated mostly by other females. The classroom in school is one place where boys and girls often are together, and it provides a mixed-gender context that runs counter to the segregation by sex often seen, for example, in play groups and on sports teams.

Social class, race, and ethnicity are also often important peer group characteristics. Depending on the extent of heterogeneity and restrictions of society, one or more of these factors may define children's peer groups. For example, an ethnographic study with girls in an Indian Himalayan village found that they seldom interacted across caste, let alone became friends across caste. In Hinduism, a person is born into a caste, and the caste system involves a complex social hierarchy. In the Himalayan village, restrictions on behaviors considered appropriate for different castes limited children's inter-caste relationships (Dyson, 2010).

**Critical Thinking Question:** Can you think of ways that social class, race, and ethnicity structure children's peer groups in this society?

Peer groups are also formed on the basis of common interests and reputation. A large number of studies have focused on **crowds** in American high schools. Adolescents grouped together as part of a crowd share broad interests, but they are not necessarily friends and do not necessarily spend much time together. Crowds also differ from one another in their reputations (Brown et al., 2008; Brown & Klute, 2003; Horn, 2003). A review of 44 studies on adolescent crowds concluded that five major types of crowds are found in many American schools (Sussman et al., 2007):

**crowds**
large, reputation-based groups of adolescents

- ***Elites*** (a.k.a. populars, preppies). The crowd recognized as having the highest social status in the school.
- ***Athletes*** (a.k.a. jocks). Sports-oriented students, usually members of at least one sports team.
- ***Academics*** (a.k.a. brains, nerds, geeks). Known for striving for good grades and for being socially inept.
- ***Deviants*** (a.k.a. druggies, burnouts). Alienated from the school social environment, suspected by other students of using illicit drugs and engaging in other risky activities.
- ***Others*** (a.k.a. normals, nobodies). Students who do not stand out in any particular way, neither positively nor negatively; mostly ignored by other students.

In the United States, high school students' clothing and demeanor sometimes differentiates them into crowds.

Even as members of a crowd may form friendships, the main function of crowds is not to provide a setting for adolescents' social interactions and close relationships. Crowds mainly serve the function of helping adolescents to locate themselves and others within the secondary school social structure (Brown & Klute, 2003). In other words, crowds help adolescents to define their own identities and the identities of others. Knowing that others think of you as a "brain" has implications for your identity; it means you are the kind of person who likes school, does well in school, and perhaps has more success in school than in social situations. Thinking of someone else as a "druggie" tells you something about that person (whether or not it is accurate); he or she uses drugs, of course, probably dresses unconventionally, and does not seem to care much about school.

Although the focus on crowds in adolescence reflects developmental characteristics such as identity formation, the cultural basis of crowds is also important. In developed countries, the fact that most adolescents remain in school at least until their late teens and the fact that these schools are almost always strictly age-graded makes crowd definition especially important. Spending so much time around peers on a daily basis elevates the importance of peers as social reference groups; that is, as groups that influence how adolescents think about how they compare to others (Brown et al., 2008). In the many cultures around the world where adolescents spend most of their time with family members or with groups of mixed ages, crowds have no relevance to their lives.

Crowds are also especially likely to exist in large secondary schools, where students are exposed to many other peers due to changing classes, extracurricular activities, and free time. In this particular context, a crowd structure is useful in helping adolescents make sense of a complex social context (Brown & Klute, 2003). In contrast to American high schools, Chinese high schools are often structured such that students are with the same peers throughout the day. They come to know their peers well, and relate to them on this basis rather than the crowd structure seen in American high schools, where students are exposed to many different peers throughout the day (French, 2015).

While the crowd structure is an important part of the social lives of American adolescents, its importance changes with development. Bradford Brown and David Kinney and their colleagues have described how crowds become more differentiated and more influential from early- to mid-adolescence, then less hierarchical and less influential from mid- to late-adolescence (Brown & Klute, 2003; Brown et al., 1994; Kinney, 1993, 1999; Sussman et al., 2007). During early- to mid-adolescence, identity issues are especially prominent, and the distinctive features of the crowd they belong to—the clothes they wear, the music they like best, the way they spend their leisure time, and so on—are ways for adolescents to define and declare their identities. By late adolescence, when their identities are better established, they no longer feel as great a need to rely on crowds for self-definition, and the importance of crowds diminishes. By that time, they may even see crowds as an impediment to their development as individuals. As they grow to adopt the individualism of the American majority culture, membership in any group—even a high-status one—may be seen as an infringement on their independence and uniqueness.

One reflection of this resistance to crowd identification is that adolescents do not always accept the crowd label attributed to them by their peers. According to one study (Brown, 1989), only 25% of the students classified by other students as jocks or druggies classified themselves that way, and only 15% of those classified as nobodies and loners by their peers also picked this classification for themselves. Thus, adolescents may readily sort their fellow students into distinct crowds, but be more likely to see themselves as the kind of person who is too distinctively individual to fit neatly into a crowd classification.

**Critical Thinking Question:** Why do you think adolescents resist identifying themselves as part of a particular crowd, even though they routinely apply crowd labels to others?

## Popularity Among Peers

**LO 10.3.2 Define the four main categories that differentiate children in terms of their popularity among peers, and explain why rejected-aggressive children benefit from intervention.**

When children are in a social environment with children of different ages, age is a key determinant of **social status**, in that older children tend to have more authority than younger children. Schools are usually **age graded**, which means that students at a given grade level tend to be the same age. When all children are about the same age, they find other ways of establishing who is high in social status and who is low. As we have seen, social status among same-age peers is partly ascribed based on group characteristics such as gender, social class, and crowd membership. Researchers have also focused on the extent to which individual children are popular among their peers.

**social status**
within a group, the degree of power, authority, and influence that each person has in the view of the others

**age graded**
social organization based on grouping persons of similar ages

**FOUR CATEGORIES OF SOCIAL STATUS.** Based on children's ratings of who they like or dislike among their peers, researchers have described four categories of social status (Cillessen & Mayeux, 2004; Rubin et al., 2013):

- *Popular children* are the ones who are most often rated as "liked" and rarely rated as "disliked."
- *Rejected children* are most often disliked and rarely liked by other children. Usually, rejected children are disliked mainly for being overly aggressive, but in about 10%–20% of cases, rejected children are shy and withdrawn (Hymel et al., 2004; Sandstrom & Zakriski, 2004). Boys are more likely than girls to be rejected.
- *Neglected children* are rarely mentioned as either liked or disliked; other children have trouble remembering who they are. Girls are more likely than boys to be neglected.
- *Controversial children* are liked by some children but disliked by others. They may be aggressive at times but friendly at other times.

About two-thirds of children in American samples fall into one of these categories in middle childhood, according to most studies (Wentzel, 2003). The rest are rated in mixed ways by other children and are classified by researchers as "average."

What characteristics determine a child's social status? Abundant research indicates that the strongest influence on popularity is **social skills** such as being friendly, helpful, cooperative, and considerate (Caravita & Cillessen, 2012; Chen et al., 2000). Children with social skills are good at perspective-taking; consequently they are good at understanding and responding to other children's needs and interests (Cassidy et al., 2003). Other important influences on popularity are intelligence, physical appearance, and (for boys) athletic ability (Dijkstra et al., 2013; McHale et al., 2003). Despite the stereotype of the "nerd" or "geek" as a kid who is unpopular for being smart, in general, intelligence enhances popularity in middle childhood. Some "nerds" and "geeks" are unpopular because they lack social skills, not because of their intelligence. In adolescence, it becomes a bit more complicated. As we just saw, "academics" are not at the top of the crowd hierarchy.

**social skills**
skills for successfully handling social relations and getting along well with others

Rejected children are usually more aggressive than other children, and their aggressiveness leads to conflicts (Coie, 2004). *Rejected-aggressive* children tend to be impulsive and have difficulty controlling their emotional reactions, which disrupts group activities, to the annoyance of their peers. In addition to this lack of self-control, their lack of social skills and social understanding leads to conflict with others. According to Kenneth Dodge (2008), who has done decades of research on this topic, rejected children often fail in their **social information processing (SIP)**.

**social information processing**
the interpretation of others' behavior and intentions in a social interaction

Rejected children are often disliked by other children. Usually rejected children are aggressive, but sometimes they are shy.

That is, they tend to interpret their peers' behavior as hostile even when it is not, and they tend to blame others when there is conflict.

For rejected children who are withdrawn rather than aggressive, the basis of their rejection is less clear. These *rejected-withdrawn* children may be shy and even fearful of other children, but these characteristics are also found often in neglected children. So what distinguishes rejected-withdrawn and neglected children? Rejected-withdrawn children are more likely to have internalizing problems such as low self-esteem and anxiety.

Neglected children, in contrast, are usually quite well-adjusted (Wentzel, 2003). They may not engage in social interactions with peers as frequently as other children do, but they usually have social skills equal to average children, are not unhappy, and report having friends.

Controversial children often have good social skills, as popular children do, but they are also high in aggressiveness, like rejected-aggressive children (DeRosier & Thomas, 2003). Their social skills make them popular with some children, and their aggressiveness makes them unpopular with others. They may be adept at forming alliances with some children and excluding others. Sometimes they defy adult authority in ways their peers admire but do not dare to emulate (Vaillancourt & Hymel, 2006).

**REJECTED-AGGRESSIVE CHILDREN.** Peer popularity has implications for children's development, especially for rejected-aggressive children. Because other children exclude them from their play and they have few or no friends, rejected-aggressive children often feel lonely and dislike going to school (Buhs & Ladd, 2001). Their aggressiveness and impulsiveness cause problems in their other social relationships, not just with peers, and they have higher rates of conflict with parents and teachers than other children do (Coie, 2004). According to longitudinal studies, being rejected by middle childhood is predictive of later conduct problems in adolescence and emerging adulthood, including delinquency, substance use, sexually risky behavior, and dropping out of school (Caravita & Cillessen, 2012; Dodge et al., 2003; Miller-Johnson et al., 2002; Prinstein & LaGreca, 2002). This is also known as a **developmental cascade** when a problem at one point in life surges into a series of problems over time (Bukowski et al., 2010).

**developmental cascade**
when a problem at one point in life surges into a series of problems over time

Being rejected may not per se cause later problems; rather, it may indicate that the aggressiveness that inspires rejection from peers in middle childhood often continues at later ages and causes problems that take other forms. Nevertheless, being rejected by peers makes it more difficult for children to develop the social skills that would allow them to overcome a tendency toward aggressiveness.

## Education Focus: School Intervention Programs for Rejected Children

Because rejected children are at risk for a downward spiral of problems in their social relationships, educators and psychologists have developed interventions to try to ameliorate their low social status. Some of these interventions focus on social skills, training rejected children how to initiate friendly interactions with their peers (Asher & Rose, 1997). Other programs focus on social information processing, and seek to teach rejected children to avoid jumping to the conclusion that their peers' intentions toward them are negative (Li et al., 2013). As part of the intervention, rejected children may be asked to role play hypothetical situations with peers or watch a videotape of peer interactions with an instructor and talk about why the peers in the video acted as they did (Ladd et al., 2004).

A number of programs have been designed for young children in an effort to halt or diminish aggressive behaviors before they become habitual, result in peer rejection, and set in motion a developmental cascade of problems. For example, the PATHS curriculum (Promoting Alternative Thinking Strategies) is implemented by teachers in order to reduce children's aggressive behaviors and improve their social competence. A longitudinal study followed almost 3,000 children who were taught based on the PATHS curriculum from first grade through third grade. Findings showed a reduction in aggressive behaviors and an increase in prosocial behaviors over time. Children who started out being rated as especially high on aggression were particularly likely to show improvement over the course of the 3-year period (Conduct Problems Prevention Research Group, 2010).

The Incredible Years is an example of another intervention aimed at children in early through middle childhood (Shernoff & Kratochwill, 2007; Webster-Stratton et al., 2001). This intervention has components designed for teachers (The Incredible Years Classroom Management Program) and parents (The Incredible Years Parenting Program). The programs aim at reducing children's disruptive conduct, improving their social competence, and strengthening collaboration between parents and teachers. One natural experiment randomly assigned at-risk kindergarteners to three different groups who received: no intervention, only the teacher intervention, or both teacher and parents interventions. The interventions lasted for 2 years. Aggression in the classroom went down for the two groups of children who received interventions, as compared to the children with no intervention. For the children who received both parent and teacher interventions, there was also improvement in children's emotion regulation and mothers' involvement in school (Reid et al., 2007).

Programs for aggressive and rejected children have often shown success in the short term, but it is unknown whether the gains from the programs are deep enough to result in enduring improvements (McCabe & Altamura, 2011). Some educators and psychologists have suggested that **integrated models** that pull together the most successful features of different programs may be the best way forward (Domitrovich et al., 2010). Such models focus on children's emotions, cognition, and behaviors. They also involve integration across different social contexts, such as schools, family, and peers.

## Review Question

Use the theories by Mead and Bronfenbrenner to explain why it might be beneficial to use intervention models with rejected children that integrate different social contexts. You might consider both developmental and cultural reasons.

## Aggression and Bullying Among Peers

**LO 10.3.3 Describe different types of aggression among peers, including how aggression changes with age.**

Early childhood is an important time for the development of aggression. As young children move more into the world of peers, they encounter more competition for resources—toys, play companions, adult attention, the last cookie—and this competition sometimes leads to conflict and aggression (Rubin & Pepler, 2013). An extreme form of peer aggression is bullying.

**TYPES OF AGGRESSION.** Scholars distinguish among several different types of aggression (Underwood, 2003). **Instrumental aggression** is involved when a child wants something (toys, food, attention) and uses aggressive behavior or words to get it. A child may also exhibit signs of anger and intend to inflict pain or harm on others. This is known as **hostile aggression**. Instrumental and hostile aggression can each be expressed in several ways. *Physical aggression* includes hitting, kicking, pushing, or striking with an object. *Verbal aggression* is the use of words to hurt others, through yelling at them, calling them names, or hostile teasing. **Relational aggression** (or *social aggression*) involves damaging another person's reputation among peers through social exclusion and malicious gossip.

Physical aggression among young children has been a target of a great deal of research. There is abundant evidence that physical aggression peaks in toddlerhood and early childhood (Alink et al., 2006). One prominent aggression researcher, Richard Tremblay (2002), summarized a wide range of longitudinal studies extending from infancy to adulthood, across many countries, and found a common pattern in which physical aggression peaks at 24 to 42 months—the second year of toddlerhood and the first year of early childhood—then declines. Boys are consistently more physically aggressive than girls, in early childhood and throughout the life span.

However, there is a great deal of variation around this average pattern. Not all boys are aggressive in early childhood, and not all boys and girls show a decline in aggression after age 3. One national study in the United States followed the course of physical aggression in a longitudinal study of children from age 2 to 9 (NICHD Early Childhood Research Network, 2004). The researchers identified five different "trajectory groups" with regard to aggression. The largest group declined steeply in physical aggression from age 2 to 9. However, there were also two "low trajectory" groups that never showed much physical aggression, one

**integrated models**
intervention programs for aggressive and rejected children that focus on their emotions, cognition, and behaviors, and that involve different social contexts such as schools, family, and peers

**instrumental aggression**
type of aggression when a child wants something and uses aggressive behavior or words to get it

**hostile aggression**
type of aggression that entails signs of anger and intent to inflict pain or harm on others

**relational aggression**
a form of nonphysical aggression that harms others by damaging their relationships, for example, by excluding them socially or spreading rumors about them

Verbal aggression becomes substituted for physical aggression across the years of early childhood. Here is an example of two young boys using both forms of aggression at once.

"moderate trajectory" group that remained moderate, and one "high trajectory" group that remained high.

In general, individual differences in physical aggression remain stable across time. That is, children who rarely display physical aggression in early childhood are unlikely to display it in middle childhood and adolescence, and children who are especially aggressive in early childhood tend to be more aggressive than their peers in later periods as well (Brame et al., 2001; Lansford et al., 2006; Schaeffer et al., 2003; Vaillancourt et al., 2003). However, longitudinal studies show that parents who are especially patient, sensitive, and involved can reduce high aggression in early childhood to moderate aggression by middle childhood (NICHD Early Childhood Research Network, 2004; Rubin & Pepler, 2013). Early childhood is a crucial time for moderating physical aggression, because high aggression at the end of early childhood is a strong predictor of later aggressive behavior in adolescence and adulthood (Loeber et al., 2005; Tremblay & Nagin, 2005).

Across cultures, aggression is frequently part of children's play in early and middle childhood, especially for boys (Edwards, 2005; Gaskins, 2015). Physical "rough-and-tumble" play such as wrestling is common among boys of the same age when they are brought together in school and playground settings (Scott & Panksepp, 2003). This aggressive play occurs in other mammals as well and is a way of establishing a dominance hierarchy (Hassett et al., 2008). Aggressive play establishes who is on top and who is not and in this way serves to avoid more serious aggression within the group.

In contrast to physical aggression, verbal aggression rises across early childhood, at least in the Western countries where this research has been done (Dodge et al., 2006; Underwood, 2003). As children become more adept at using words, they grow capable of applying their verbal abilities to a wide range of purposes, including aggression. Also, verbal aggression becomes substituted for physical aggression across the years of early childhood as children learn that adults regard physical aggression toward peers as unacceptable and as children become more capable of restraining their physically aggressive impulses (Tremblay, 2000, 2002; Tremblay & Nagin, 2005). Boys are slightly more likely than girls to engage in verbal aggression (Leaper, 2013).

Relational aggression also becomes more common in the course of early childhood (Crick et al., 2006). Like the increase in verbal aggression, the increase in relational aggression reflects children's growing cognitive and social understanding. They become more capable of understanding the complexities of social relationships and more aware of the ways that social weapons can be used to hurt others and gain social status. They learn that a punch on the shoulder does not hurt nearly as much, or last nearly as long, as the pain of being the only one not invited to a birthday party or being the subject of a nasty rumor (Murray-Close et al., 2007; Nelson et al., 2005). Relational aggression is slightly more common among girls than among boys, but the difference is minor—smaller than the gap between boys and girls in physical and verbal aggression (see Chapter 8).

**bullying**
in peer relations, the extremely aggressive assertion of power by one person over another

**BULLYING AND CYBERBULLYING.** An extreme form of peer aggression is **bullying**. Researchers define bullying as having three components (Olweus, 2000; Wolak et al., 2007): *hostile aggression* (physical or verbal); *repetition* (not just one incident, but a pattern over time); and *power imbalance* (the bully has higher peer status than the victim). The prevalence of bullying rises through middle childhood and peaks in early adolescence, then declines substantially by late adolescence (Pepler et al., 2006; Van Noorden et al., 2015). Bullying is an international phenomenon, observed in countries in Asia (Ando et al., 2005; Hokoda et al., 2006; Kanetsuna et al., 2006), Europe (Dijkstra et al., 2008; Eslea et al., 2004; Gini et al., 2008), and North America (Espelage & Swearer, 2004; Pepler et al., 2008; Volk et al., 2006). Estimates vary depending on age and country, but overall about 20% of children are victims of bullies at some point during middle childhood. Boys are more often bullies as well as victims (Berger, 2007). Boys bully using both physical and verbal aggression, but girls can be bullies, too, most often using verbal methods (Pepler et al., 2004; Rigby, 2004).

There are two general types of bullies. Some are rejected children who are bully-victims, that is, they are bullied by children who are higher in status and they in turn look for lower-status victims to bully (Kochenderfer-Ladd, 2003). Bully-victims often come from families where the parents are harsh or even physically abusive (Schwartz et al., 2001). Other bullies are controversial children who may have high peer status for their physical appearance, athletic abilities, or social skills, but who are also resented and feared for their bullying behavior toward some children (Vaillancourt et al., 2003). Bullies of both types tend to have a problem controlling their aggressive behavior toward others, not just toward peers, but also in their other relationships (Olweus, 2000). Bullies are also at higher risk than other children for depression (Fekkes et al., 2004; Ireland & Archer, 2004).

Many schools have activities aimed to raise awareness of bullying. Here, students paint a mural against bullying at a middle school in New York.

Victims of bullying are most often rejected-withdrawn children who are low in self-esteem and social skills (Champion et al., 2003). Because they have few friends, they often have no allies when bullies begin victimizing them (Goldbaum et al., 2003). They cry easily in response to bullying, which makes other children regard them as weak and vulnerable and deepens their rejection. Compared to other children, victims of bullying are more likely to be depressed, anxious, and lonely (Baldry & Farrington, 2004; Due et al., 2005; Rigby, 2004). Their low moods and loneliness may be partly a response to being bullied, but these are also characteristics that may make bullies regard them as easy targets.

A relatively recent variation on bullying is **cyberbullying** (also called *electronic bullying*), which involves bullying behavior via social media (such as Facebook), e-mail, or mobile phones (Kowalski et al., 2012; Thomas et al., 2015; Valkenberg & Peter, 2011). A Swedish study of 12- to 20-year-olds found an age pattern of cyberbullying similar to what has been found in studies of "traditional" bullying, with the highest rates in early adolescence and a decline through late adolescence and emerging adulthood (Slonje & Smith, 2008). In a study of nearly 4,000 adolescents in grades 6–8 in the United States, 11% reported being victims of a cyberbullying incident at least once in the past 2 months; 7% indicated that they had been cyberbullies as well as victims during this time period; and 4% reported committing a cyberbullying incident (Kowalski & Limber, 2007). Notably, half of the victims did not know the bully's identity, a key difference between cyberbullying and other bullying. However, cyberbullying usually involves only a single incident (Tokunaga, 2010), so it does not involve the repetition required in the standard definition of traditional bullying, and might be better termed *online harassment* (Thomas et al., 2015; Wolak et al., 2007).

**cyberbullying**
bullying via electronic means, mainly through the Internet

## SUMMARY: Peers

**LO 10.3.1 Review key characteristics that differentiate children's peer groups, and explain why crowds are common in American high schools.**

Peer groups are commonly defined by characteristics such as age, gender, social class, race, and ethnicity. Crowds in American high schools (e.g., elites, athletes) are formed on the basis of common interests and reputation. Crowds are also especially likely to exist in large secondary schools, where students are exposed to many other peers due to changing classes, extracurricular activities, and free time.

**LO 10.3.2 Define the four main categories that differentiate children in terms of their popularity among peers, and explain why rejected-aggressive children benefit from intervention.**

Based on children's ratings of who they like or dislike among their peers, researchers have described four categories of social status: popular (liked), rejected (disliked), neglected (neither liked nor disliked), and controversial (both liked and disliked). Rejected-aggressive children are often lonely and dislike going to school. They are at risk for experiencing a developmental cascade where minor problems become serious problems over time. For this reason, they benefit from early intervention.

**LO 10.3.3 Describe different types of aggression among peers, including how aggression changes with age.**

Aggression as a means to get something from another child is termed "instrumental." Aggression that comes out of anger is termed "hostile." Both types may be expressed physically (e.g., hitting), verbally (e.g., shouting), or relationally (e.g., gossiping). Physical aggression is most common in toddlerhood and among boys. Verbal and relational aggression rise across early childhood. Bullying and cyberbullying are extreme forms of peer aggression. Bullying is repetitive but cyberbullying usually involves a single incident.

# 10.4 Friends

According to ethologists, nonhuman primates have rudimentary friendships. Female baboons, for example, form stable and enduring bonds with others in their troop (Silk et al., 2010). In this light, it is not so surprising that friendships emerge very early in child development. With development, the importance we attribute to friendships, the amount of time we spend with friends, and what we most value about friends change. Also, depending on whether you grew up in Indonesia or the United States, for example, you would be likely to approach all of these aspects of friendship in different ways.

## Changes in Friendship in Childhood

**LO 10.4.1 Describe similarities and differences in the meaning of friendship from toddlerhood through middle childhood.**

Toddlers, as we have seen, are clearly capable of playing with each other in a variety of ways, but do they really form friendships? A substantial and growing body of research suggests they do (Goldman & Buysse, 2007). Their friendships appear to have many of the same features of friendships at other ages, such as companionship and mutual affection (Rubin et al., 2006). Even shortly after their first birthday, toddlers prefer some of their childcare or playgroup peers over others and seek them out as companions when they are together (Shonkoff & Phillips, 2000). Like older children and even adults, toddlers choose each other as friends based partly on similarities, such as activity level and social skills (Rubin et al., 2006). Toddlers who become friends develop favorite games they play when together (Howes, 1996). Toddler friends share emotions more frequently with each other than they do with nonfriends. They smile and laugh more, but also have more conflicts, although conflicts between toddler friends are milder and more quickly resolved than among nonfriends (Ross & Lollis, 1989). Friendships do change in quality with age, but even in toddlerhood many of the later features of friendship are evident.

Toddler friends smile and laugh more with each other than they do with nonfriends. Here, three boys in South Africa share a laugh.

By early childhood, children become more capable than toddlers of understanding and describing what a friendship entails. They regard a friend as someone you like and who likes you, and as someone who plays with you and shares toys with you (Hartup & Abecassis, 2004). By age 5 or 6, they also understand that friendship is characterized by mutual trust and support, and that a friend is someone you can rely on over time (Bagwell & Schmidt, 2013).

Friends rise in importance from early childhood to middle childhood, as decreased dependency on adults and greater freedom of movement allow children to visit and play with friends. Also, the entrance into formal schooling takes children away from the social context of the family and places them in a new context where they spend a substantial amount of most days around many other children of similar age. Daily contact between children makes it possible for them to develop close friendships.

The main basis of these friendships is similarity (Rubin et al., 2008). In middle childhood—as at all ages across the life course—people tend to prefer being around others who are like themselves, a principle called **selective association** (Popp et al., 2008). We have already seen how gender is an especially important basis of selective association in middle childhood. Boys tend to play with boys and girls with girls, more than at either younger or older ages. Other important criteria for selective association in middle childhood are sociability, aggression, and academic orientation (Hartup, 1996; Rubin et al., 2013). Sociable kids are attracted to each other as friends, as are shy kids; aggressive kids tend to form friendships with each other, as do kids who refrain from aggression; kids who care a lot about school tend to become friends, and so do kids who dislike school.

**selective association**
the principle that most people tend to choose friends who are similar to themselves

## Cultural Focus: Friendship and Play in Middle Childhood Across Cultures

Although selective association is an important basis of friendship at all ages, over the course of childhood, friendships change in other ways. An important change from early to middle childhood is in the relative balance of activities and trust (Rubin et al., 2008). Friendships in early childhood are based mainly on shared activities. Your friends are the kids who like to do the same things you like to do. Consequently, young children usually claim they have lots of friends, and their friends are more or less interchangeable. If you like to ride bikes, whoever is available to ride bikes with you is your friend. When they describe their friends, young children talk mainly about their shared activities (Damon, 1983; Rubin et al., 2013). In middle childhood, children continue to talk about shared activities, but they also talk about shared characteristics. In this video, *Friendship and Play in Middle Childhood Across Cultures*, children in three cultures talk about their friendships. For example, they describe who they like to play with and why.

**Watch** FRIENDSHIP AND PLAY IN MIDDLE CHILDHOOD ACROSS CULTURES

### Review Question

Many of those interviewed discuss how friendships in middle childhood are often same gender. Why do you think this sex-segregation takes place?

## Changes in Friendship in Adolescence and Emerging Adulthood

**LO 10.4.2 Describe the characteristics of friendship in adolescence and emerging adulthood, including cliques.**

In adolescence, selective association continues to be important in making and keeping friends. Adolescence is also a time when ethnic boundaries in friendships often become sharper. Research has shown this in Europe, Israel, and the United States (Titzmann et al., 2007). During childhood ethnicity is related to friendship, according to this research, but not strongly. However, as children enter adolescence, friendships become less interethnic, and by late adolescence they are generally ethnically segregated (Kao & Joyner, 2004). Why would this be so? One factor may be that as they grow into adolescence, young people become increasingly aware of interethnic tensions and conflict in their societies, and this awareness fosters mutual suspicion and mistrust. Similarly, as adolescents begin to form an ethnic identity, they may begin to see the divisions between ethnic groups as sharper than they had perceived them before. Some studies suggest that interethnic friendships among adolescents in the United States have become more common in recent times, but nonetheless same-ethnic friendships remain the norm (McBride Murry et al., 2015).

Friendship changes in other important ways in adolescence. As time spent with family decreases from middle childhood to adolescence, time spent with friends increases, in most cultures. Family ties remain important in the lives of adolescents, but friends spend more leisure time together than in childhood.

Adolescents in Western cultures tend to be happiest when with friends.

Friends also become increasingly influential in adolescents' emotional lives. Friends become the source of adolescents' happiest experiences, the people with whom they feel most comfortable, and the persons they feel they can talk to most openly (French, 2015; Richards et al., 2002). Studies in the United States using the Experience Sampling Method (ESM; see Chapter 7) find that adolescents share their happiest moments with friends. They are also generally much happier with friends than with family (Larson & Csikszentmihalyi, 2014). European studies show similar results. For example, a Dutch study found that 82% of adolescents named spending free time with friends as their favorite activity (Meeus, 2007).

One reason that adolescents enjoy their time with friends so much, according to Larson and Richards (1994), who have conducted many ESM studies, is that adolescents feel free and open with friends in a way they rarely do with parents or anyone else. There is room to let loose with adolescent exuberance. In one episode captured in an ESM study, a group of boys were hanging around in one of their backyards when they started spraying each other with a hose, taunting each other and laughing. In another episode, adolescent girls at a sleepover were found dancing on the pool table, laughing and hugging each other.

**cliques**

small groups of friends who know each other well, do things together, and form a regular social group

**intimacy**

the degree to which two people share personal knowledge, thoughts, and feelings

Small groups of friends who know each other really well, do things together, and form a regular social group are termed **cliques** by developmental psychologists (Brown & Braun, 2013). In adolescence, cliques are a counterpoint to the relative anonymity of peer crowds. Cliques are positive in many ways, but sometimes members of cliques come together to engage in risk behavior. Clique members also sometimes engage in "antagonistic interactions" where they evaluate each other and nonclique members in disparaging ways (Gavin &Furman, 1989). These interactions seem to be a way to establish a dominance hierarchy within the group, bring nonconformist members into line, and exclude nonclique members. Still, adolescent cliques are typically a venue for shared activities and fun, such as playing sports, listening to music, and playing electronic games.

In adolescence, there is also a new value placed on intimacy between friends, and herein lies a second reason that adolescents treasure their time with friends. **Intimacy** is the degree to which two people share personal knowledge, thoughts, and feelings. Adolescent friends confide hopes and fears, lend emotional support, and help each other understand what is going on with their parents, their teachers, and peers to a far greater degree than younger children do (Chan et al., 2015; Ravens-Sieberer et al., 2014). In an ESM study, one seventh-grade girl described her friend by saying (Larson & Richards, 1994, p. 92):

> She feels the same about the same things, and she understands what I mean.... And [even] if she doesn't, she'll say "Yeah, I understand what you're talking about."

Cliques are often formed around shared activities. Here, South African adolescents enjoy a game of soccer.

When adolescents are asked what they would want a friend to be like or how they can tell that someone is their friend, they tend to mention intimate features of the relationship (French, 2015; Radmacher & Azmitia, 2006). They state, for example, that a friend is someone who understands you, someone you can share your problems with, someone who will listen when you have something important to say (Bauminger et al., 2008; Way, 2004). Younger children are less likely to mention these kinds of features and more likely to stress shared activities—we both like to play basketball, we ride bikes together, we play computer games, and so on.

There are consistent gender differences in the intimacy of adolescent friendships, with girls tending to have more intimate friendships than boys do (Bauminger et al., 2008). Girls spend more time than boys talking to their friends, and they place a higher value on talking together as a component of their friendships (Furman & Rose, 2015; Legerski et al., 2015). Girls also rate their friendships as higher in affection, helpfulness, and nurturance, compared with boys' ratings of their friendships (Bokhorst et al., 2010). And girls are more likely than boys to say they trust and feel close to their friends (Shulman et al., 1997). In contrast, even in adolescence, boys are more likely to emphasize shared activities as the basis of friendship, such as sports or hobbies (Radmacher & Azmitia, 2006). Nevertheless, intimacy does become more important to boys' friendships in adolescence, even if not to the same extent as for girls. In one study of African American, Asian American, and Latino boys from poor and working-class families, Niobe Way (2004) reported themes of intimacy that involved sharing secrets, and disclosing feelings about family and friends.

Of course, adolescent friendships are not only about emotional support and good times. In the ESM studies, friends are also the source of adolescents' most negative emotions—anger, frustration, sadness, and anxiety. Adolescents' attachments to friends and their strong reliance on friends leave them vulnerable emotionally. They worry a great deal about whether their friends like them and about whether they are popular enough. Larson and Richards (1994) observed that "Triangles, misunderstandings, and conflicting alliances were a regular part of the social lives of the [adolescents] we studied" (p. 94). When adolescents explain why a close friendship has ended, they most often mention some form of breaking trust as the reason—failing to keep a secret, breaking promises, lying, or competing over a romantic partner (Youniss & Smollar, 1985).

Intimacy continues to be valued among emerging adult friends. The majority of emerging adults move away from home and so lose the daily social support they may have received from their parents and siblings (Barry et al., 2015). Even for the ones who return home or remain home, they may rely less on their parents for social support as they strive toward becoming self-sufficient and making their own decisions (Arnett, 2015). Consequently, they may turn more to friends than to parents for companionship and support. In one study (Radmacher & Azmitia, 2006), early adolescents (ages 12–13) and emerging adults (ages 18–20) described a time when they felt especially close to a friend. Emerging adults' accounts contained more self-disclosure and fewer shared activities, compared to early adolescents. Among the emerging adults (but not the early adolescents), there was a gender difference. Self-disclosure promoted emotional closeness for young women, whereas for young men shared activities were usually the basis of feeling emotional closeness.

What kinds of things do emerging adults do with their friends? Much of their time together involves visiting each other informally and going out together. Some drink alcohol or use drugs together. Emerging adults also participate in media-related activities together, such as watching TV or playing electronic games (Brown, 2006). Many enjoy playing sports or exercising together (Malebo et al., 2007).

## Cultural Variations in Friendship

**LO 10.4.3 Explain how culture plays a role in the importance and meaning of friendship.**

Across cultures, there are some striking differences in the amount of time children spend with friends, the importance attributed to friendships, why friends are valued, and how conflicts between friends are resolved. For example, adolescents in India tend to spend their leisure time with family rather than friends, not because they are required to do so but because of collectivistic Indian cultural values and because they enjoy their time with family (Chaudhary & Sharma, 2012; Larson et al., 2000). In Indonesia, too, there is a collectivistic pull toward family and peer groups, rather than an emphasis on intimate and exclusive friendships. Adolescent and emerging adult friendships in Indonesia are often low in intimacy and seldom long-lasting (French, 2015). In some developing countries, then, family and peers take precedence over cliques and intimate friendships.

Children and adolescents across many parts of the world see instrumental aid as key to friendship. Here, friends from the Palestinian Territories repair a bike together.

Adolescents from the American majority culture tend to deemphasize the value of **instrumental aid** in friendships. Perhaps because friendship is seen more as being about intimacy and affection, they do not speak much of helping out with things like homework, money, or other practical necessities. In an in-depth interview study with low-income, urban African American and Latino adolescents from the United States, however, Niobe Way (2006) found that sharing money and protecting friends from harm were key constituents of friendships. Chinese boys, too, emphasize the importance of aiding friends. For example, they value sharing their school work (Chen et al., 2004). On the whole, children and adolescents across many parts of the world, including Costa Rica, Cuba, and Indonesia, see instrumental aid as key to friendship (DeRosier & Kupersmidt, 1991; French et al., 2005; GonzáLez et al., 2004).

There are also cultural differences on the extent to which friendship involves mutual enhancement of self-esteem. For example, Canadian children have been found to exchange more compliments among friends, as compared to Chinese children (Chen et al., 2004). In a comparison of 11- and 14-year-olds from Indonesia and the United States, Doran French and his colleagues also found that the American adolescents rated their friendships higher on mutual enhancement of self-esteem (French et al., 2005).

**instrumental aid**
practical help, such as assistance with homework or expenses

> **Critical Thinking Question:** Can you explain how these results fit with the discussion of the cultural meaning of self-esteem from Chapter 7?

It is not uncommon for conflict to arise among friends. Conflict resolution, however, is based on socially shared scripts and these scripts differ across cultures (Kitayama & Markus, 1994). A prominent script for conflict resolution in North America is based on individual rights and the idea that conflict calls for self-assertion, negotiation, and compromise (Laursen et al., 2001). In contrast, Indonesians tend to avoid overt expression of conflict by avoiding provocations, refraining from interacting with others with whom they have conflict, relying on polite and ritual forms of interactions, and minimizing the expression of strong opinions and emotions (French, 2015). Research with 9- to 11-year-old American and Indonesian children asked them to describe their approaches to resolving conflict with friends. Indonesian children, more than American children, reported that they dealt with conflict by disengaging. They would avoid both the issue of the conflict and the friend in order to maintain social harmony (French et al., 2005). Furthermore, children who took this approach to conflict received higher teacher ratings on social status, suggesting that this behavior is regarded within Indonesian culture as valuable and competent. In another study, 9-year-old Canadian and Chinese children were placed in groups of four, where they had to deal with limited resources, such as the presence of only one toy. Chinese children were more likely to relinquish the toy in order to avoid conflict (French et al., 2011). While this was not a study of friends, it does suggest again that socially shared scripts for conflict management vary between cultures, impacting relations between friends and peers.

## SUMMARY: Friends

### LO 10.4.1 Describe similarities and differences in the meaning of friendship from toddlerhood through middle childhood.

Like older children and even adults, toddlers choose each other as friends based partly on similarities, such as activity level and social skills. Friends rise in importance from early childhood to middle childhood, as decreased dependency on adults and greater freedom of movement allow children to visit and play with friends.

**LO 10.4.2 Describe the characteristics of friendship in adolescence and emerging adulthood, including cliques.**

As time spent with family decreases from middle childhood to adolescence, time spent with friends increases, in most cultures. Friends also become increasingly influential in adolescents' emotional lives. Intimacy continues to be valued among emerging adult friends.

**LO 10.4.3 Explain how culture plays a role in the importance and meaning of friendship.**

In cultures that place a high value on family, friendship often comes second in children's lives. While intimacy is important to American friends, children in many other cultures also value friends for their instrumental aid. In resolving conflict among friends, children in some cultures (e.g., the U.S.) emphasize self-assertion and negotiation, while in other cultures (e.g., Indonesia), they minimize contact and expression of opinions.

# 10.5 Problem Behaviors Among Friends

Adolescents and emerging adults spend a lot of time with peers and friends. Much of that time is spent in supportive and positive ways. Yet, during adolescence and emerging adulthood, it is also the case that nearly all substance use and crime takes place among friends.

## Substance Use and Abuse

**LO 10.5.1 Summarize key demographics of substance use, and explain why young people use substances.**

Substance use varies by age, gender, ethnicity, and nationality. The purposes of substance use also vary.

**DEMOGRAPHICS OF SUBSTANCE USE.** In American society, substance use is rare before adolescence. Many types of substance use, however, are fairly common by the end of secondary school and reach a peak in emerging adulthood. According to national Monitoring the Future (MTF) data from 2013, the proportion of high school seniors who used substances within the past 30 days was 39% for alcohol, 26% for binge drinking (consuming five or more alcoholic drinks in a row), 23% for marijuana, and 16% for cigarettes (Johnston et al., 2014). Monitoring the Future surveys also show that substance use of all kinds tops off in the early 20s before declining in the late 20s. Figure 10.2 shows this pattern for binge drinking and marijuana use (Bachman et al., 2008). Other than alcohol, marijuana, and cigarette use, substance use is uncommon among American adolescents and emerging adults.

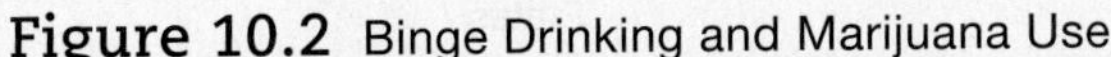

**Figure 10.2** Binge Drinking and Marijuana Use

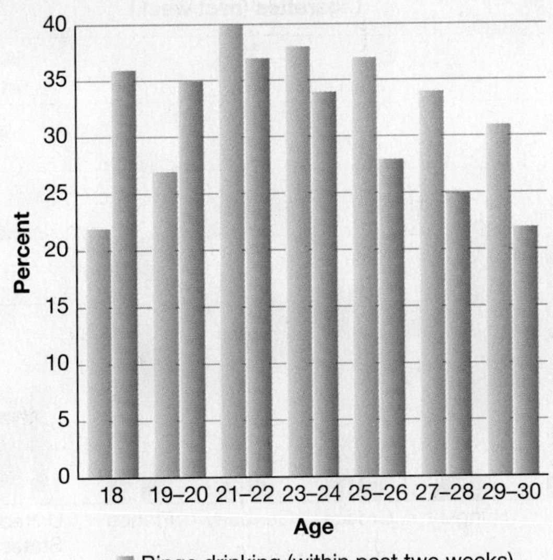


SOURCE: Based on Johnson et al. (2014).

In general, substance use in adolescence and emerging adulthood tends to be somewhat higher among men than among women. With respect to ethnicity or race, substance use is highest among Native Americans, followed by Whites and Latinos, with African American and Asian American adolescents and emerging adults lowest (Shih et al., 2010). Substance use, especially alcohol use, is also higher among college students than among emerging adults who do not attend college (Core Institute, 2013).

Rates of substance use in adolescence and emerging adulthood vary across Western countries. Figure 10.3 shows the proportion of 15-year-olds who had used alcohol and cigarettes within the past week in seven Western countries (WHO, 2016). Rates of cigarette smoking are lower among adolescents in the United States and Canada than in Europe, perhaps because governments in the United States and Canada have waged large-scale public health campaigns against smoking, whereas European countries have not (Johnston et al., 2014).

**Critical Thinking Question:** Can you think of other reasons to explain the differences among the Western countries shown in Figure 10.3?

**Figure 10.3** Substance Use in Western Countries Among 15-Year-Olds

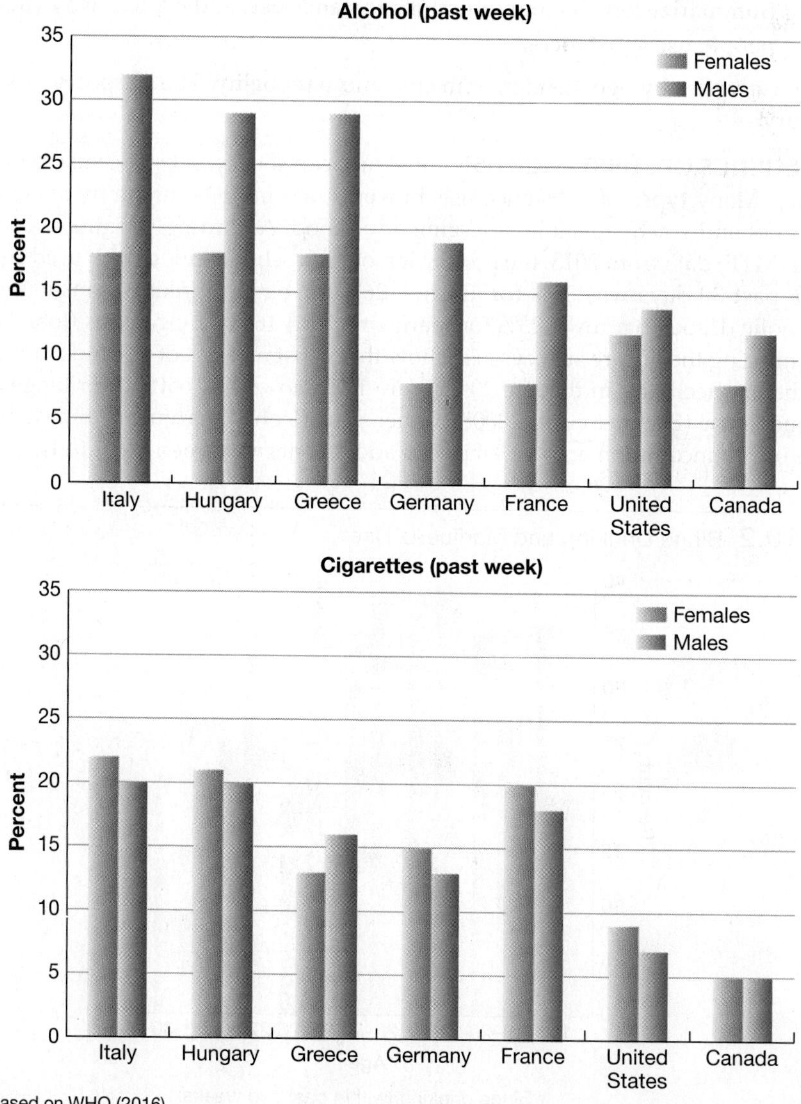


SOURCE: Based on WHO (2016).

Some evidence shows that substance use among emerging adults is also high in other Western countries. A Spanish study reported that among 18- to 24-year-olds, rates of binge drinking in the past 30 days were 31% for men and 18% for women (Valencia-Martín et al., 2007). A peak in binge drinking in emerging adulthood has been found in other European countries as well (Kuntsche et al., 2004). Among female college students in Scotland, most regarded binge drinking as "harmless fun" (Guise & Gill, 2007).

However, binge drinking and other types of substance use in adolescence and emerging adulthood are related to a wide variety of negative consequences, from unintended pregnancy to fatal car crashes, physical fights, vandalism, and sexual assault, in both Europe and the United States (Cantor et al., 2015; Jochman & Fromme, 2010; Plant et al., 2010).

**PURPOSES OF SUBSTANCE USE.** Why do young people use substances? Four purposes have been identified that can be classified as social, experimental, medicinal, and addictive (Weiner, 1992). The social and experimental purposes are the most common among young people. *Social substance use* involves the use of substances during social activities with one or more friends. Parties and dances are common settings for social substance use in adolescence and emerging adulthood. Young people who take part in *experimental substance use* try a substance once or perhaps a few times out of curiosity and then do not use it again. This kind of experimentation also commonly takes place at parties or gatherings of a few friends. Nearly all substance use among young people takes place as part of a group activity (Tyler &Johnson, 2006).

*Medicinal substance use* is undertaken to relieve an unpleasant emotional state such as sadness, anxiety, stress, or loneliness. Using substances for these purposes has been described as a kind of **self-medication** (Reimuller et al., 2011). Young people who use substances for self-medication tend to use them more frequently than those whose purposes are mainly social or experimental. Finally, *addictive substance use* takes place when a person has come to depend on regular use of substances to feel good physically or psychologically. People who are addicted to a substance experience withdrawal symptoms such as high anxiety and tremors when they stop taking the substance. People who are addicted are also the most frequent substance users. The four purposes for substance use described here indicate that young people may use substances in diverse ways, with diverse implications for their development.

**self-medication**
the use of substances for relieving unpleasant states such as sadness or stress

**unstructured socializing**
the term for young people spending time together with no specific event as the center of their activity

We now have an understanding of the purposes of substance use, but what explains the cresting of substance use in late adolescence and the first part of emerging adulthood? Wayne Osgood points to the high degree of opportunity for substance use during this age period, as a result of spending a high proportion of time in unstructured socializing (Osgood, 2009; Osgood et al., 1996, 2005). Osgood uses the term **unstructured socializing** to include behaviors such as riding around in a car for fun, going to parties, visiting friends informally, and going out with friends. Unstructured socializing is highest in the late teens and early 20s, and adolescents and emerging adults who are highest in unstructured socializing are also highest in substance use (Hoeben et al., 2016; Osgood et al., 1996, 2005). Rates of most types of substance use are especially high among emerging adults who are college students because they have so many opportunities for unstructured socializing with friends and peers.

Osgood and others have found the relationship between unstructured socializing and substance use also extends to risk behaviors such as dangerous driving, delinquency, and crime (Haynie & Osgood, 2005; Maimon & Browning, 2010). Furthermore, the relationship between unstructured socializing and risk behavior holds for both genders, a variety of ethnic groups, and across a wide range of developed and developing countries. Research also shows that substance use and other types of risk behavior decline in the mid- to late 20s, as role transitions such as marriage, parenthood, and full-time work cause a sharp decline in unstructured socializing (Johnston et al., 2014; Patrick et al., 2011).

Parties and dances are common settings for social and experimental substance use in adolescence and emerging adulthood.

**Critical Thinking Question:** Can you think of any other reasons, apart from the decline in unstructured socializing, as to why substance use starts to decline in the early- and mid-20s?

## Delinquency and Crime

**LO 10.5.2 Explain why age and crime are so strongly correlated, and describe the multisystemic approach to combating delinquency in adolescence.**

**delinquency**
violations of the law committed by juveniles

Crimes, of course, are acts that violate the law. When violations of the law are committed by persons defined by the legal system as juveniles, these violations are considered acts of **delinquency**. Legal systems in most countries define juveniles as persons who are under 18 years of age. Rates of crime begin rising in the mid-teens and peak at about age 18, then decline steadily. The great majority of crimes are committed by young people—mostly males—who are between the ages of 12 and 25 (Craig & Piquero, 2014). In the West, this finding is remarkably consistent over a period of greater than 150 years. Figure 10.4 shows the relationship between age and crime at two points, one in the 1840s and one relatively recent. At any point before, after, or in between these times, in most countries, the pattern would look very similar (Craig & Piquero, 2014; Wilson & Herrnstein, 1985). Adolescents and emerging adults are not only more likely than children or adults to commit crimes, but also more likely to be the victims of crimes.

What explains the strong and consistent relationship between age and crime? One theory suggests the key is that adolescents and emerging adults combine increased independence from parents and other adult authorities with increased time with peers and increased orientation toward peers (Wilson & Herrnstein, 1985). A consistent finding of research on crime is that crimes committed by young people in their teens and early 20s usually take place in a group of friends or peers, in contrast to the solitary crimes typical of adult offenders (Dishion & Dodge, 2005). Crime is an activity that in some adolescent cliques is encouraged and admired (Dishion et al., 1999).

**Figure 10.4** Age–Crime Relationship in (a) 1842 and (b) 1992

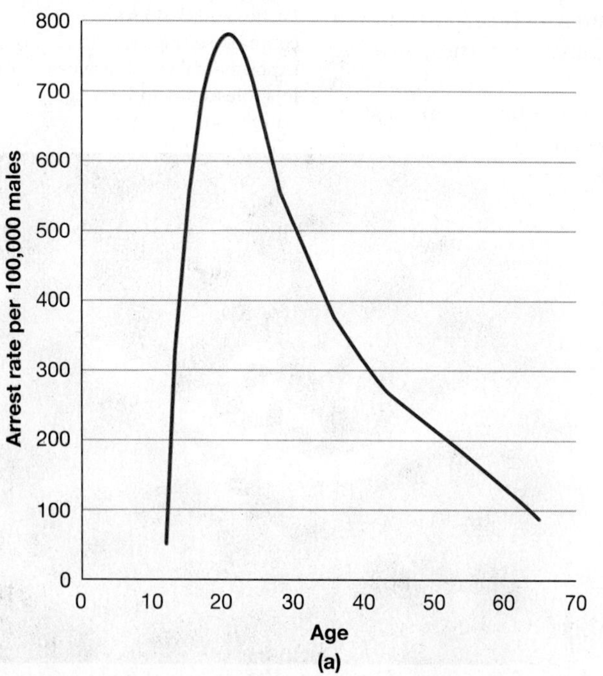


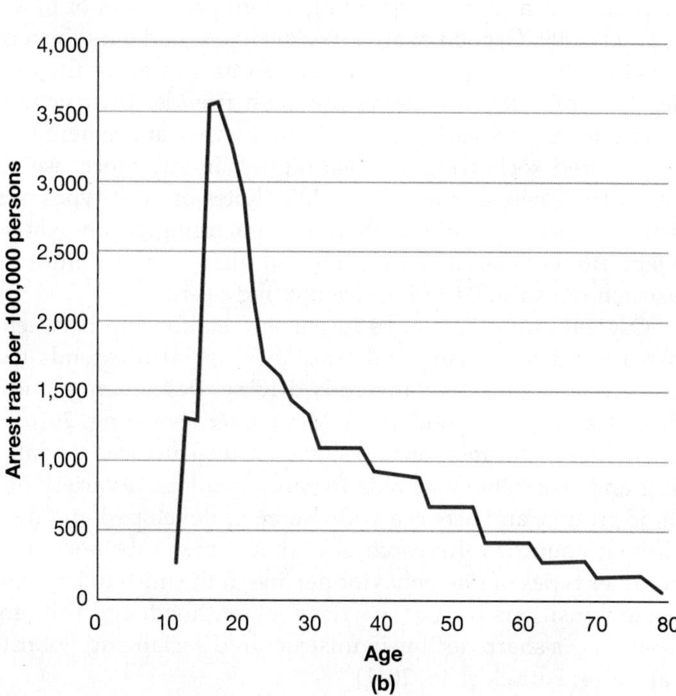


SOURCES: Gottfredson & Hirschi (1990), Osgood (2009).

This theory, however, does not explain why it is mainly boys who commit crimes, and why girls rarely do even though they also become more independent from parents and more peer-oriented in adolescence. Most surveys find that over three-fourths of adolescent boys commit at least one criminal act sometime before the age of 20 (Loeber & Burke, 2011; Moffitt, 2003). However, there are obvious differences between committing one or two acts of minor crime—vandalism or underage drinking, for example—and committing crimes frequently over a long period, including more serious crimes such as rape and physical assault. Ten percent of young men commit over two-thirds of all offenses (Craig & Piquero, 2014). What are the differences between adolescents who commit an occasional minor violation of the law and adolescents who are at risk for serious, long-term criminal behavior?

Terrie Moffitt (2003, 2007) has proposed a provocative theory in which she distinguishes between *life-course-persistent* delinquency (LCPD) and *adolescence-limited* delinquency (ALD). In Moffitt's view, these are two distinct types of delinquency, each with different motivations and different sources. However, the two types may be hard to distinguish from one another in adolescence, when criminal offenses are more common than in childhood or adulthood. The way to tell them apart, according to Moffitt, is to look at behavior before adolescence.

**Life-course-persistent delinquents (LCPDs)** show a pattern of problems from birth onward. Moffitt believes their problems originate in neuropsychological deficits that are evident in a difficult temperament in infancy and a high likelihood of attention-deficit/hyperactivity disorder (ADHD) and learning disabilities in childhood; all of these are more common among boys than girls. Children with these problems are also more likely than other children to grow up in a high-risk environment (such as low-income family), with parents who have a variety of problems of their own. Consequently, children's neurological deficits tend to be made worse rather than better by their environments. When they reach adolescence, children with the combination of neurological deficits and a high-risk environment are highly prone to engage in criminal activity. Furthermore, they tend to continue their criminal activity long after adolescence has ended, well into adulthood.

**life-course-persistent delinquents (LCPDs)**
in Moffitt's theory, adolescents who show a history of related problems both prior to and following adolescence

The **adolescence-limited delinquents (ALDs)** follow a much different pattern. They show no signs of problems in infancy or childhood, and few of them engage in any criminal activity after their mid-20s. It is just during adolescence—actually, adolescence and emerging adulthood, ages 12 to 25—that they have a period of occasional criminal activity, breaking the law with behavior such as vandalism, theft, and use of illegal drugs.

**adolescence-limited delinquents (ALDs)**
in Moffitt's theory, delinquents who engage in criminal acts in adolescence and/or emerging adulthood but show no evidence of problems before or after these periods

As we have seen in earlier chapters, the brain is still a long way from maturity during adolescence. Does the immaturity of the brain help explain why rates of delinquency and some other types of risky behavior are higher in adolescence than at younger ages? One prominent theory, the maturational gap model, hypothesizes that subcortical regions of the brain involved in the rewarding aspects of risky behavior may mature earlier than the prefrontal brain regions involved in cognitive control and decision making (Casey et al., 2008; Galvan, 2010; Somerville et al., 2010). According to the theory, depicted in Figure 10.5, this neurological mismatch means that, in adolescence, the fun and excitement of behaviors such as dangerous driving and vandalism outweigh recognition of the risks. The theory proposes that there is no maturational gap before adolescence, when both of the brain regions in question are immature, or after adolescence, when the regions are mature. Whereas this theory may have some application to risk behavior and crime in adolescence, it does not account for the fact that rates of many types of risk behavior and crime continue to rise into the early 20s (Males, 2010). Also, boys and girls are highly similar in brain development during adolescence, yet boys commit far more crimes. Furthermore, criminal activity among adolescents is much higher in some cultures than in others, even though it can be presumed that brain development follows a similar path across cultures.

**Figure 10.5** Maturational Gap Model

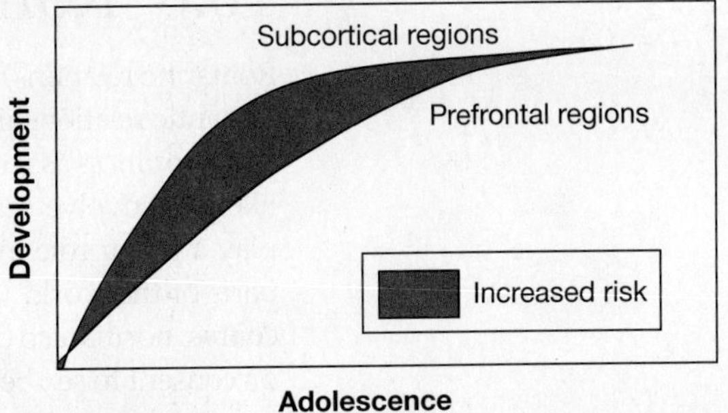


Delinquency has often proven to be resistant to change in adolescence, but one successful approach has been to intervene across several contexts, including the home, the school, and the neighborhood. This is known as the *multisystemic approach* (Borduin et al., 2003; Henggeler, 2011). Programs based on this approach include parent training, job

Figure 10.6 Multisystemic Approach to Delinquency

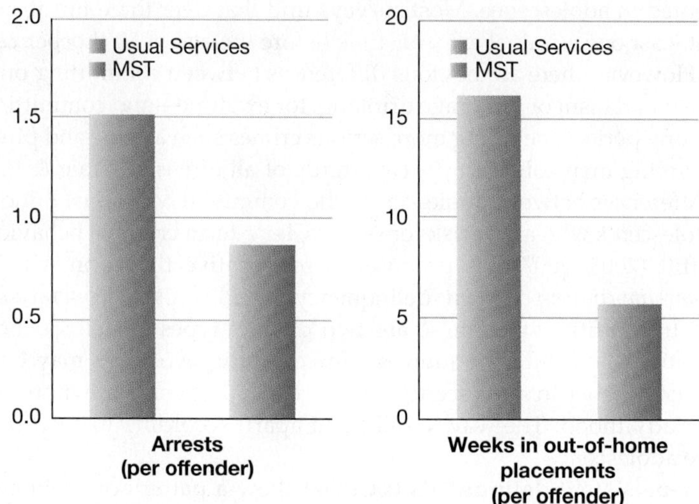


SOURCE: Data from Alexander (2001).

training and vocational counseling, and the development of neighborhood activities such as youth centers and athletic leagues. The goal is to direct the energy of delinquents into socially structured and constructive activities. The multisystemic approach has now been adopted by youth agencies all over the world (Henggeler, 2011; Schoenwald et al., 2008). As Figure 10.6 illustrates, programs using this approach have been shown to be effective in reducing arrests and out-of-home placements among delinquents (Henggeler et al., 2007; Ogden & Amlund Hagen, 2006). Furthermore, multisystemic programs have been found to be cheaper than other programs, primarily because they reduce the amount of time that delinquent adolescents spend in foster homes and detention centers (Alexander, 2001).

## Summary: Problem Behaviors Among Friends

**LO 10.5.1 Summarize key demographics of substance use, and explain why young people use substances.**

Alcohol and marijuana use are fairly common by the end of secondary school and reach a peak in emerging adulthood. Substance use varies by gender, ethnicity, and college attendance. Young people use substances for social, experimental, medicinal, and addictive purposes. The social and experimental uses are most common in adolescence and emerging adulthood.

**LO 10.5.2 Explain why age and crime are so strongly correlated, and describe the multisystemic approach to combating delinquency in adolescence.**

The great majority of crimes are committed by young people—mostly males—who are between the ages of 12 and 25. Explanations for the relationship between age and crime have pointed to peer influence, neurological underpinnings, and culture. One successful approach to crime prevention among youth, the multisystemic approach, involves intervention across contexts, including home, school, and neighborhood.

# 10.6 Romantic Partners

Romantic relationships in adolescence and emerging adulthood often begin as friendships. But romantic relationships tend to involve more intense emotions, including positive feelings of love and happiness as well as feelings of anxiety and discomfort. Romantic relationships are also more likely to involve sexual activity, although friendships sometimes involve sex. Cultural norms play a major role in whether or not sex is accepted as part of romantic relationships. In many parts of the world, chastity prior to marriage—especially in girls and women—is expected. Of course, norms also change. For example, many countries in the West are seeing changes in views on consent to sex between romantic partners, and in views of sexual minorities.

## Falling in Love, Finding a Soul Mate

**LO 10.6.1 Describe the extent to which romantic desires and relationships are shaped by culture, and outline the qualities emerging adults look for in a romantic partner.**

The prevalence of involvement in romantic relationships increases gradually over the course of adolescence. According to a study in the United States called the National Study of Adolescent Health, the percentage of adolescents reporting a current romantic relationship rises from 17% in 7th grade to 32% in 9th grade to 44% in 11th grade (Furman & Hand, 2006). By 11th grade, 80% of adolescents had experienced a romantic relationship at some point, even if they did not have one currently. Adolescents with an Asian cultural background tend to have their first romantic relationship later than adolescents with an African American, European, or Latino cultural background, because of Asian cultural beliefs that discourage early involvement in romantic relationships and encourage minimal or no sexual involvement before marriage (Connolly & McIsaac, 2011; Trinh et al., 2014).

Romantic experiences are associated with both positive and negative outcomes in adolescence (Furman et al., 2007; Furman & Rose, 2015). Adolescents who have a romantic relationship tend to be more popular and have a more positive self-image (La Greca & Harrison, 2005). However, this association with positive qualities depends partly on the age of the adolescents. For early adolescent girls, a serious love relationship tends to be related to negative outcomes such as depressed mood (Graber et al., 1997; Hayward et al., 1997; Kaltiala-Heino et al., 2003). An important reason for their depression appears to be that early adolescent girls in a serious relationship often find themselves under their boyfriends' pressure to participate in sexual activity before they feel ready (Young & d'Arcy, 2005). Also, for both boys and girls between 14 and 16, greater romantic experience is associated with greater substance use and more delinquent behavior (Furman et al., 2009).

It is not only in the United States that adolescents experience romantic love. On the contrary, feelings of passion appear to be virtually universal among young people. One study investigated this issue systematically by analyzing the *Standard Cross-Cultural Sample*, a collection of data provided by anthropologists on traditional cultures representing six distinct geographical regions around the world (Jankowiak & Fischer, 1992). The researchers concluded that there was evidence that young people fell passionately in love in 185 of the 186 cultures studied! Across cultures, young lovers experienced the delight and despair of passionate love, told stories about famous lovers, and sang love songs.

In the West, most adolescents have a romantic partner at some point in their teens.

However, this does not mean that young people in all cultures are allowed to act on their feelings of love. On the contrary, the idea that romantic love should be the basis of marriage is only about 300 years old in the West and is even newer in most of the rest of the world (Hatfield et al., 2015, 2016). In most cultures throughout most of history, marriages have been arranged by the family, with little regard for the passionate desires of their children. Parents and other adult kin have often held the authority and responsibility to arrange the marriages of their young people, sometimes with the young persons' consent, sometimes without it. Economic considerations have often been of primary importance.

Some cultures with a tradition of arranged marriage are beginning to change in their marriage expectations through the influence of globalization. India, for example, has a history of arranged marriage dating back 6,000 years (Prakasa & Rao, 1979). Today, however, nearly 40% of young Indians say they intend to choose their own mates (Chaudhary & Sharma, 2007; Netting, 2010). A similar pattern is taking place in many other cultures with a tradition of arranged marriage (Ahluwalia et al., 2009). Increasingly, young people in these cultures believe that they should be free to choose their mate or at least to have a significant role in whom their parents choose for them.

A revealing study compared three groups of female college students who had different degrees of exposure to globalization and Western values (Dhariwal & Connolly, 2013). The "traditional" group, with the least exposure to globalization, consisted of Indian students who attended single-sex colleges that focused on home economics. Students in the in-between, "transitional" group attended Indian co-educational colleges that focused on technology, science, and the humanities. The "diaspora" group, with the most exposure to globalization, consisted of Canadian Indian students from Toronto. The young women in all three groups were similar in the extent to which they had romantic desires and thought about romantic issues. However, romantic behaviors such as dating and autonomy from parents in selecting partners increased with exposure to globalization.

So, what are young people looking for in a romantic partner? Emerging adults around the world mention a wide variety of ideal qualities (Gibbons & Stiles, 2004; Hatfield & Rapson, 2005). Sometimes these are qualities of the individual: intelligent, attractive, or funny. But most often they mention interpersonal qualities, qualities a person brings to a relationship, such as kind, caring, loving, and trustworthy. Emerging adults hope to find a "soul mate" who will treat them well and who will be capable of an intimate, mutually loving, durable relationship.

Indeed, in romantic relationships as in friendships, intimacy becomes more important in emerging adulthood than it had been in adolescence (Shulman & Connolly, 2015). One study investigated views of the functions of love relationships among early adolescents (6th grade), late adolescents (11th grade), and college students (Roscoe et al., 1987). The early and late adolescents both considered recreation to be the most important function, followed by intimacy, and then status. For the college students, in contrast, intimacy ranked highest, followed by companionship, with recreation a bit lower, and status much lower. A more recent study reported similar results (Montgomery, 2005).

Just as with selective association among friends, romantic partners are typically alike in many ways (Shulman & Connolly, 2015). A long line of studies has established that emerging adults, like people of other ages, tend to have romantic relationships with people who are similar to themselves in characteristics such as personality, intelligence, social class, ethnic background, religious beliefs, and physical attractiveness (Furman & Simon, 2008; Markey & Markey, 2007). As Gloria, a 22-year-old Latina, explained in an interview (Arnett, 2004, p. 99):

> [The person I marry] would have to be someone who was of the same religion that I was and also the same ethnicity as me. And sometimes when I say that, people take it that I'm prejudiced or something. But it's not necessarily that, because I have a lot of traditions and customs that I grew up with and I want someone who understands the same traditions and everything. So I've always looked for someone who was Latino. And I've always looked for someone who was Catholic because I'm Catholic.

## Sexuality in Adolescence and Emerging Adulthood

**LO 10.6.2 Explain the role of culture and context in regard to premarital sex in adolescence and emerging adulthood.**

Cultures vary enormously in how they view adolescent and premarital sexuality. The best framework for understanding this variation among countries remains a book that is now over 60 years old, *Patterns of Sexual Behavior*, by Clellan Ford and Frank Beach (1951). These two anthropologists compiled information about sexuality from over 200 cultures. On the basis of their analysis, they described three types of cultural approaches to adolescent sexuality: permissive, semirestrictive, and restrictive.

- ***Permissive cultures*** tolerate and even encourage adolescent sexuality. Most of the countries of northern Europe today would fall into this category. Adolescents in these countries usually begin an active sexual life in their late teens, and parents often allow them to have a boyfriend or girlfriend spend the night (Trost, 2012).
- ***Semirestrictive cultures*** have prohibitions on premarital adolescent sex. However, in these cultures the formal prohibitions are not strongly enforced and are easily evaded. Adults in these cultures tend to ignore evidence of premarital sexual behavior as long as young people are fairly discreet. Most developed countries today would fall into this category, including Canada, most of Europe, and the United States (Regnerus & Uecker, 2011).

- ***Restrictive cultures*** place strong prohibitions on adolescent sexual activity before marriage. The prohibition on premarital sex is enforced through strong social norms and by keeping boys and girls separated through adolescence. Young people in Asia and South America tend to disapprove strongly of premarital sex, reflecting the view they have been taught by their cultures (Regan et al., 2004; Trinh et al., 2014).

In some countries, the restrictiveness of the taboo on premarital sex includes the threat of physical punishment and public shaming. A number of Middle Eastern countries take this approach, including Algeria, Saudi Arabia, and Syria. Premarital female virginity is a matter of not only the girl's honor but the honor of her family, and if she is known to lose her virginity before marriage, the males of her family may punish her, beat her, or even kill her (Dorjee et al., 2013). Although many cultures also value male premarital chastity, no culture punishes male premarital sex with such severity.

Premarital sexual relations in emerging adulthood most commonly take place in the context of a close romantic relationship (Regnerus & Uecker, 2011). However, various studies indicate that about one-fourth of sexual episodes among American emerging adults take place outside of a romantic partnership (Claxton & van Dulmen, 2015). Within American ethnic groups, African American emerging adults are most likely to report casual sexual experiences, and Asian American emerging adults least likely (Regnerus & Uecker, 2011). Male emerging adults are more likely than females to have sexual attitudes that favor recreational sex (Knox et al., 2001).

Premarital sex in emerging adulthood is accepted in some cultures and forbidden in others.

Frequently, casual sexual episodes are fueled by alcohol. In various studies, from one-fourth to one-half of emerging adults report having consumed alcohol before their most recent sexual encounter (Lefkowitz & Gillen, 2006), and emerging adults who drink often are more likely than others to have had multiple sexual partners (Regnerus & Uecker, 2011). The college environment is especially conducive to casual sex since it brings together so many emerging adults in a common setting that includes frequent social events that involve alcohol use.

## Contraceptive Use, Pregnancy, and Sexually Transmitted Infections

**LO 10.6.3 Explain why emerging adulthood is the peak period for unintended pregnancies and sexually transmitted infections.**

Although cultures vary in how they view adolescent sex, premarital pregnancy in adolescence is viewed as undesirable nearly everywhere in the world. Two types of countries have low rates of premarital pregnancy: those that are permissive about adolescent sex and those that are restrictive. Northern European countries such as Denmark, the Netherlands, and Sweden have low rates of adolescent pregnancy because they are permissive about adolescent sex (Avery & Lazdane, 2008). There are explicit safe-sex campaigns in the media. Adolescents have easy access to all types of contraception. Parents accept that their children will become sexually active by their late teens (Trost, 2012).

At the other end of the spectrum, restrictive countries such as Japan, South Korea, and Morocco strictly forbid adolescent sex (Davis & Davis, 2012; Dorjee et al., 2013; Hatfield & Rapson, 2005). Adolescents in these countries are strongly discouraged even from dating until they are well into emerging adulthood and are seriously looking for a marriage partner. It is rare for an adolescent boy and girl even to spend time alone together, much less have sex. Some adolescents follow the call of nature anyway and violate the taboo, but violations are rare because the taboo is so strong and the shame of being exposed for breaking it is so great.

The United States has a higher rate of teenage pregnancy than any other developed country, as Figure 10.7 (next page) illustrates. The main reason American adolescents have high rates of teenage pregnancy may be that there is no clear cultural message regarding adolescent sexuality (Males, 2010). The semirestrictive view of adolescent sexuality prevails: Adolescent sex is not strictly forbidden, but neither is it widely accepted. As a consequence, most American adolescents have sexual intercourse at some time before they reach the end of their teens, but often those who are sexually active are not comfortable enough with their sexuality to acknowledge that they are having sex and to prepare for it responsibly by obtaining and using contraception. However, rates of teen pregnancy in the United States have

**Figure 10.7** Teenage Pregnancy Rates in Developed Countries

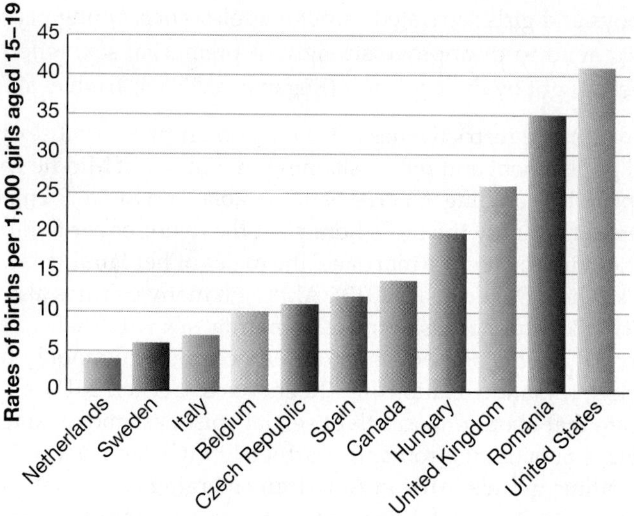


declined steeply in the past two decades, especially among African Americans (Males, 2011; U.S. Dept. of Health and Human Services, 2016). This may be because the threat of HIV/AIDS has made it more acceptable in the United States to talk to adolescents about sex and contraception and to provide them with sex education through the schools. Watch the video *Teen Pregnancy* for more information.

Most American emerging adults are quite responsible about contraceptive use, although certainly not all of them. Only about 10% of sexually active emerging adults report never using contraception, but an additional 35% of them report inconsistent or ineffective contraceptive use (Regnerus & Uecker, 2011).

Emerging adults in Western countries may view sex as a normal and enjoyable part of life, but that does not mean it is unproblematic. The long period between the initiation of sexual activity in adolescence and the entry into marriage in young adulthood typically includes sex with a series of romantic partners as well as occasional episodes of hooking up. In the course of these years, unintended pregnancies are not unusual. Although responsible contraceptive use is the norm, inconsistent and ineffective contraceptive use is common enough to make emerging adulthood the age period when both abortion and nonmarital childbirth are most common, across many countries (Claxton & van Dulmen, 2015; Hymowitz et al., 2013).

Emerging adulthood is also the peak period for **sexually transmitted infections (STIs)**, which are infections transmitted through sexual contact, including chlamydia, human papilloma virus (HPV), herpes simplex virus 2 (HSV-2), and HIV/AIDS. One-half of STIs in the United States occur in people who are ages 15–24 (Centers for Disease Control and Prevention [CDC], 2013). Rates of STIs are higher in emerging adulthood than in any other life stage, in both the United States and Europe (CDC, 2015; Uuskula et al., 2010).

**sexually transmitted infection (STI)**
infection transmitted through sexual contact

Why are emerging adults particularly at risk for STIs? Although few emerging adults have sex with numerous partners, hooking up occasionally with a temporary partner is quite common (Claxton & van Dulmen, 2015). Even if sex takes place in a committed relationship, most youthful love relationships do not endure for long and partners eventually break up and move on. In this way, young people gain experience with love and sex and see what it is like to be involved with different people. But having sex with a variety of people, even within a series of relationships, carries with it a substantial risk for STIs.

**Watch** TEEN PREGNANCY

The symptoms and consequences of STIs vary widely, from the merely annoying (pubic lice or "crabs") to the deadly (HIV/AIDS). Some STIs, such as chlamydia and HPV, increase the risk of infertility for women (Mills et al., 2006). Fortunately, chlamydia can be treated effectively with antibiotics. Also, a vaccine for HPV is now

**Map 10.1** HIV Population Worldwide, By Region

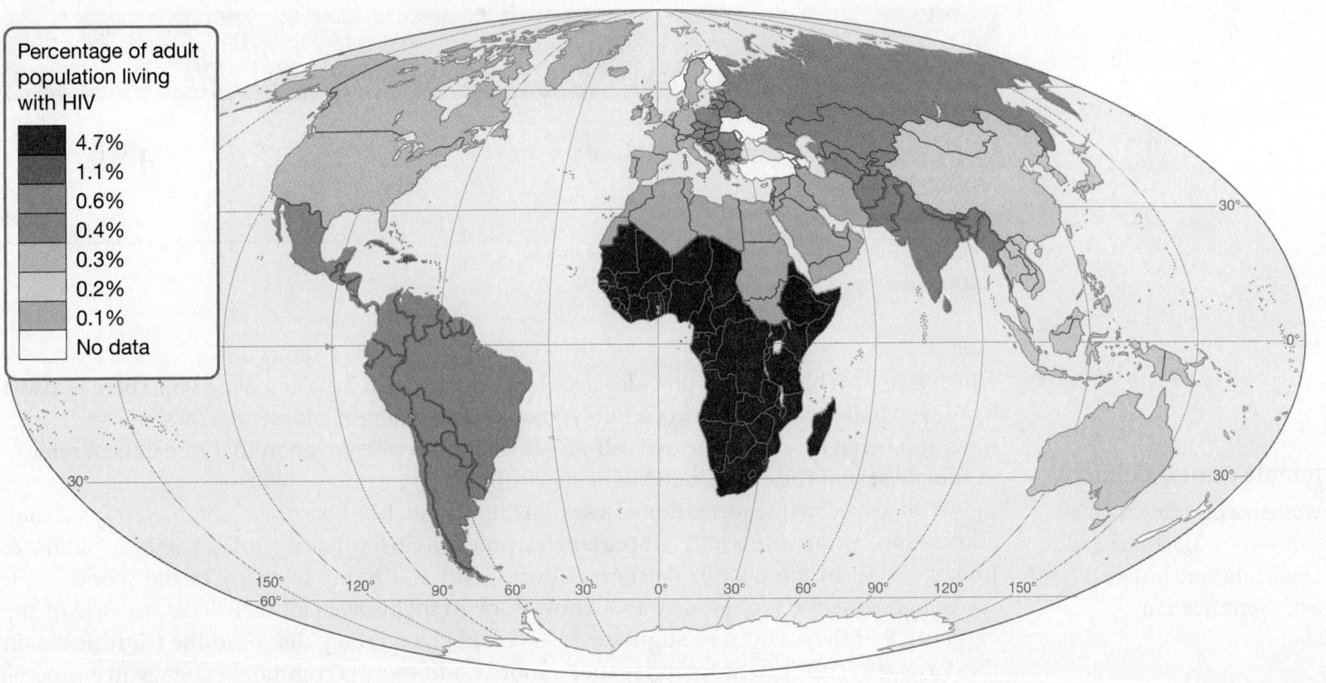

Percentage of adult population living with HIV

4.7%
1.1%
0.6%
0.4%
0.3%
0.2%
0.1%
No data

available, and public health advocates in many Western countries are highly recommending that adolescents be vaccinated before they become sexually active (Kahn, 2007; Woodhall et al., 2007). Herpes simplex 2 cannot be cured, but medications can relieve the symptoms and speed up the healing process when an episode occurs (King, 2005).

HIV/AIDS has been most devastating in southern Africa, where 10 of every 11 new HIV infections worldwide take place (see Map 10.1). Incidence of new HIV infections has decreased among young people worldwide in the past decade, due to a decline in risky sexual practices such as having multiple sexual partners (UNAIDS, 2010).

AIDS was once viewed as nearly impossible to treat effectively, but in recent years effective drug treatments for slowing the progress of AIDS have been developed. The cost of these drug treatments was initially extremely high, but has since declined, and the drugs are widely available even in developing countries, mainly through international aid organizations (UNAIDS, 2010). Prevention programs to reduce HIV risk among emerging adults have now been conducted in many developing countries and have been successful in changing young people's behavior to reduce their HIV risk (Ngongo et al., 2012).

## Sexual Minority Youth

**LO 10.6.4 Explain how coming out among sexual minority adolescents is shaped by development and culture.**

So far we have primarily focused on romantic partnerships and sexuality in terms of relations between females and males. Adolescence is when most people first become fully aware of their **sexual orientation**, meaning their tendencies of sexual attraction. Over the last few decades, research on the experiences of sexual minority youth has increased dramatically (Diamond et al., 2015). A national longitudinal study in the United States included several questions about same-sex and other-sex attractions and sexual behavior (Savin-Williams & Ream, 2007). Questionnaire data were collected at ages 16, 17, and 22. As shown in Table 10.2 (next page), at each age considerably more adolescents and emerging adults experienced same-sex romantic attractions than engaged in same-sex sexual behavior. At age 22, more emerging adults reported same-sex romantic attractions than reported same-sex sexual behavior or a lesbian, gay, or bisexual (LGB) identity, especially among women. Other studies have reported slightly higher levels of LGB attractions, sexual behavior, and sexual identity, but there is a consistent pattern across studies that prevalence of same-sex attractions is higher than same-sex behavior,

**sexual orientation**
a person's tendencies of sexual attraction

**Table 10.2** Same-Sex Romantic Attractions, Sexual Behavior, and Sexual Identity

| | Females | | | Males | | |
|---|---|---|---|---|---|---|
| **Sexual Domain** | **Age 16** | **Age 17** | **Age 22** | **Age 16** | **Age 17** | **Age 22** |
| Same-sex romantic attractions | 5% | 4% | 13% | 7% | 5% | 5% |
| Same-sex sexual behavior | 1% | 1% | 4% | 1% | 1% | 3% |
| Sexual identity: lesbian or gay | | | 1% | | | 2% |
| Sexual identity: bisexual | | | 3% | | | 1% |

NOTE: The question about sexual identity was asked only at age 22.

SOURCE: Savin-Williams & Ream (2007).

which is in turn higher than prevalence of LGB identity (Savin-Williams, 2005). There is also a consistent pattern that emerging adult women exceed emerging adult men on same-sex attractions and behaviors, and bisexual self-identification—a phenomenon that researchers refer to as **female sexual fluidity** (Diamond et al., 2015).

**female sexual fluidity**

women exceeding men on same-sex attractions and behaviors, and bisexual self-identification

With respect to the formation of a sexual identity such as bisexual, lesbian, or transsexual, adolescence is an especially important period (Savin-Williams, 2011; Savin-Williams & Joyner, 2014). In the past in Western cultures, and still today in many of the world's cultures, many people would keep this knowledge to themselves all their lives because of the certainty that they would be stigmatized and ostracized if they disclosed the truth. Today in most Western cultures, however, sexual minority adolescents commonly engage in a process of **coming out**, which involves a person's recognizing his or her own sexual identity and then disclosing the truth to friends, family, and others (Flowers & Buston, 2001; Potoczniak et al., 2009). Self-awareness usually begins in early adolescence, with disclosure to others coming in late adolescence or emerging adulthood (Floyd & Bakeman, 2006). Usually adolescents first disclose their sexual identity to a friend (Savin-Williams, 1998, 2001), with disclosure to others then following later. According to one longitudinal study, the coming-out process takes longer for African Americans and Latinos than for Whites, perhaps because of stronger disapproval in these cultures (Rosario et al., 2004).

**coming out**

for sexual minority individuals, the process of acknowledging their sexual identity and then disclosing the truth to their friends, family, and others

Given the pervasive hatred and fear of sexual minorities that exist in many societies (Baker, 2002), coming to the realization of a sexual minority identity can be traumatic for many adolescents. Sexual minority adolescents are often the target of bullying (Kosciw et al., 2012; Mishna et al., 2009). Many parents respond with dismay or even anger when they learn that their adolescents identify as sexual minorities (Baiocco et al., 2015). Also, if parents reject adolescents after their children come out, the consequences are dire. One study found that sexual minority adolescents who experience parental rejection were 8 times more likely to report having attempted suicide, 6 times more likely to report high levels of depression, 3 times more likely to use illegal drugs, and 3 times more likely to have had unprotected sex than sexual minority adolescents whose parents were more accepting of their sexual orientation (Ryan, 2009).

Among sexual minority youth in the U.S., the average of coming out has declined to about 16. Young women exceed men on same-sex attractions, same-sex behaviors, and bisexual self-identification.

Nevertheless, in recent years there has been a noticeable change in Western attitudes toward sexual minorities, constituting "a dramatic cultural shift" toward more favorable and tolerant perceptions, according to Ritch Savin-Williams (2005), a prominent researcher on sexual minority adolescents. Savin-Williams notes changes in popular culture, such as favorable portrayals in television, movies, and popular songs. Notably, the average age of coming out has declined in recent decades, from 21 in the 1970s to 16 in the present, perhaps because of growing acceptance (Savin-Williams & Joyner, 2014). There has also been a broadening of sexual minority identifications (including identities such as Queer, Intersex, and Asexual), perhaps again reflecting growing tolerance. Another sign that people are becoming more accepting of variations in sexual orientation is the legalization of same-sex marriage in Canada, New Zealand, South Africa, the United States, several countries in Latin America, many European countries, and parts of Australia.

## Sexual Harassment and Date Rape

**LO 10.6.5 Review prevalence rates of sexual harassment and date rape.**

Sexual interactions among adolescents and emerging adults are not always enjoyable or even voluntary. Two of the serious problems that arise in sexual interactions are sexual harassment and date rape. During adolescence, **sexual harassment** is a pervasive part of peer interactions. Sexual harassment is usually defined as including a wide range of behaviors, from mild harassment such as name-calling, jokes, and leering looks to severe harassment involving unwanted touching or sexual contact (Connolly & Goldberg, 1999; Uggen & Blackstone, 2004). In the United States, laws vary from state to state, but behaviors that are sometimes part of a pattern of sexual harassment are considered crimes. These behaviors can include threats and stalking. Rates of sexual harassment in adolescence are strikingly high (Leaper & Brown, 2008). Research indicates that the incidence of sexual harassment increases from grades 5 through 9, with about half of ninth graders reporting that they have been victims of sexual harassment from their peers (Connolly & Goldberg, 1999; Petersen & Hyde, 2009). Early-maturing girls are especially likely to be targeted for sexual harassment—from both boys and girls (Goldstein et al., 2007; Petersen & Hyde, 2009).

**sexual harassment**
a wide range of threatening or aggressive behaviors related to sexuality, from mild harassment such as name-calling, jokes, and leering looks to severe harassment involving unwanted touching or sexual contact

Sexual and romantic joking and teasing are a common part of adolescents' peer interactions, making it difficult to tell where the border is between harmless joking and harmful harassment. Indeed, the majority of adolescents who report being sexually harassed also report sexually harassing others (Lee et al., 1996). Teachers and other school personnel who witness adolescents' interactions may be reluctant to intervene, unsure of what should qualify as harassment. However, being the victim of persistent harassment can be extremely unpleasant for adolescents and can result in anxiety and depression as well as declining school performance (Connolly & Goldberg, 1999; Gruber & Fineran, 2008).

**Date rape**, a crime punishable by law, takes place when a person, usually a woman, is forced by a romantic partner, date, or acquaintance to have sexual relations against her will. Studies indicate that 15% of adolescent girls and 25% of emerging adult women (ages 18 to 24) in the United States have experienced date rape (Cantor et al., 2015; Michael et al., 1995; Vicary et al., 1995). Rates are highest of all for girls who have sex at an early age: nearly three-fourths of girls who have intercourse before age 14 report having had intercourse against their will (Alan Guttmacher Institute, 2002).

**date rape**
an act of sexual aggression in which a person is forced by a romantic partner, date, or acquaintance to have sexual relations against her or his will

Alcohol is a major risk factor in date rape on college campuses (Carey et al., 2015; King, 2005). Being intoxicated makes women less effective in communicating unwillingness to have sex and makes men more likely to ignore or overpower a woman's resistance. When men are intoxicated, they are more likely to mistake women's behavior, such as talking to them or dancing with them, as indicating sexual interest (Maurer & Robinson, 2008). Rape of an intoxicated or incapacitated victim is a crime, according to the U.S. Department of Justice.

Even when sober, young men and women often describe date rape incidents differently (Black & Gold, 2008; Miller & Benson, 1999). In their accounts of such incidents, young men often deny they forced sex on the woman and say they interpreted the way the young woman dressed or offered affection as cues that she wanted sex. In contrast, young women describing the same incident deny that their dress or behavior was intended to be sexually alluring and say that the men were coercive and ignored their verbal or nonverbal resistance to sex.

In order to address these issues, sex education programs are increasingly emphasizing the necessity of **affirmative consent**. Partners must stop sexual activity not only if one person indicates "no," verbally or nonverbally, but may only proceed in response to mutual and unequivocal agreement. In other words, the "no means no" mantra of a generation ago is being superseded by "yes means yes." California, for example, has passed a law that high school students must be educated about affirmative consent and that colleges use affirmative consent as the standard in campus disciplinary actions involving sexual assault (Medina, 2015). Critics argue that it is unclear how these laws will work out in the court of law. Nonetheless, they reflect changing sexual norms in American society, and an effort to address the alarming statistics on date rape among adolescents and emerging adults.

**affirmative consent**
unequivocal, verbal agreement to sexual activity

## SUMMARY: Romantic Partners

**LO 10.6.1 Describe the extent to which romantic desires and relationships are shaped by culture, and outline the qualities emerging adults look for in a romantic partner.**

Feelings of romantic desire are virtually universal among young people; however, cultural acceptance of romantic relationships varies within and across countries. In most cultures throughout most of history, marriages have been arranged by the family on the basis of economic considerations. Globalization, however, means that increasingly, emerging adults worldwide hope to find mutual trust and intimacy in a romantic partner.

**LO 10.6.2 Explain the role of culture and context in regard to premarital sex in adolescence and emerging adulthood.**

Cultures vary enormously in how they view adolescent and premarital sexuality. Three types of cultural approaches are: permissive (tolerant or encouraging), semirestrictive (formal prohibitions are easily evaded), and restrictive (prohibitions are strongly enforced).

**LO 10.6.3 Explain why emerging adulthood is the peak period for unintended pregnancies and sexually transmitted infections.**

The long period between the initiation of sexual activity in adolescence and the entry into marriage in young adulthood typically includes sex with a series of romantic partners as well as occasional episodes of hooking up. Inconsistent and ineffective contraceptive use is common enough to make emerging adulthood the age period when abortion, nonmarital childbirth, and sexually transmitted infections (STIs) are most common.

**LO 10.6.4 Explain how coming out among sexual minority adolescents is shaped by development and culture.**

Today in most Western cultures, sexual minority adolescents commonly engage in a process of coming out, which involves a person's recognizing her or his own sexual identity and then disclosing it to friends, family, and others. The average age of coming out has declined from 21 in the 1970s to 16 in the present, perhaps because of growing acceptance.

**LO 10.6.5 Review prevalence rates of sexual harassment and date rape.**

About 50% of American ninth graders report that they have been victims of sexual harassment from their peers. About 15% of adolescent girls and 25% of emerging adult women have experienced date rape. Alcohol is a major risk factor in date rape on college campuses.

# Apply Your Knowledge as a Professional

The topics covered in this chapter apply to a wide variety of career professions. Watch this video to learn how they apply to the founder and CEO of a residential facility for teenage mothers.

**Journaling Question:** Here is a letter that was submitted by a 16-year-old to an advice columnist: "Ok, so me and this guy have been talking for about 2 1/2 months now, and we're still not dating, but we already had sex, and we really like each other, but the thing is prom has just passed, and I went to an after party and got really drunk, and the next day found out that I made out with another guy. Well, I felt really bad, so I told the guy I liked that I kissed another dude, and he got really upset and said he didn't know if he wanted to be with me. What should I do?? –Ashley." Write a reply to Ashley where you draw on information from this chapter.

# Chapter 11
# School and Work: Developing Cultural Skills

## Learning Objectives

**11.1 Preschool**

**11.1.1** Identify the features that are most important in preschool quality, and explain how they reflect cultural values.

**11.1.2** Describe the outcomes of early intervention programs for children from low-income families.

**11.2 From Primary Education to Tertiary Education**

**11.2.1** Describe how enrollment in primary school has changed over time in developed and developing countries, and how cultures vary on the value attributed to education.

**11.2.2** Describe how reading and math skills develop from early childhood to middle childhood and the variations in approaches to teaching these skills.

**11.2.3** Compare the secondary education systems and academic performance of developed countries and developing countries.

**11.2.4** Compare the tertiary education systems and college experiences among developed countries, and review the long-term benefits of tertiary education.

**11.3 School and Other Contexts**

**11.3.1** Explain how children's school achievement is influenced by their relationships with parents and friends.

**11.3.2** Explain different ways that social class is related to school achievement.

**11.3.3** Explain different ways that ethnicity is related to school achievement.

**11.3.4** Describe the influence of "Americanization" on immigrant children's attitude toward school.

**11.4 Intelligence Tests and School Readiness**

**11.4.1** Describe the main features of the Wechsler Intelligence Scale for Children (WISC-V).

**11.4.2** Explain the influence of both genetics and the environment on IQ scores, including the Flynn effect.

**11.4.3** Describe the Bayley Scales of Infant Development (BSID-III) for measuring infant development, and explain how habituation assessments are used to predict later intelligence.

**11.4.4** Compare Gardner's and Sternberg's approaches to conceptualizing intelligence.

**11.4.5** Describe cultural variations on conceptions of intelligence.

**11.5 Work**

**11.5.1** Describe the kinds of work children do in middle childhood, and explain why work patterns differ between developed and developing countries.

**11.5.2** Summarize the typical forms of adolescent work in developing countries and developed countries, and name the features of apprenticeships in Europe.

**11.5.3** Describe the transition from school to full-time work, and explain who among emerging adults are most impacted by unemployment.

ONE HUNDRED AND FIFTY YEARS AGO, FEW CHILDREN IN ANY COUNTRY RECEIVED SCHOOLING OUTSIDE OF THE HOME. In most of the world today, in contrast, the daily lives of children are oriented around school. As the economic development of societies is increasingly based on information and technology, children need to learn skills such as reading, writing, and math to prepare for adult work. In this chapter, we look at the school context, from preschool education through tertiary education. We also examine intelligence tests and how they were developed to assess children's readiness for school. Finally we turn to work, including how the nature of work differs for children and adolescents in developing and developed countries.

**Watch** CHAPTER INTRODUCTION: SCHOOL AND WORK: DEVELOPING CULTURAL SKILLS

# 11.1 Preschool

Traditionally in many cultures, formal schooling has started at about age 7. This is the age at which children have been viewed as first capable of learning the skills of reading, writing, and math. However, because the need to learn how to use words and numbers is so strong in the modern, information-based economy, many countries now begin schooling earlier than ever. In developed countries about three-fourths of 3- to 5-year-old children are enrolled in group child care, preschool, or kindergarten (OECD, 2013). In developing countries, percentages are lower but rising. In the United States, about half of American states now fund some type of preschool programs for 4-year-old children, usually focusing on children from low-income families. Nevertheless, preschool participation in the United States lags behind nearly all other developed countries (OECD, 2013). For example, almost all 4-year-olds are enrolled in preschool in countries such as Japan, Sweden, and the United Kingdom. In the United States, just below 70% of 4-year-olds are enrolled.

## Preschool Quality and Cultural Goals

**LO 11.1.1 Identify the features that are most important in preschool quality, and explain how they reflect cultural values.**

What are the cognitive and social effects of attending preschool? For the most part, attending preschool is beneficial for young children. Cognitive benefits of attending preschool include higher verbal and math skills, and stronger performance on measures of memory and listening comprehension (Clarke-Stewart & Allhusen, 2002; Yoshikawa et al., 2013). In other words, children who have attended preschool perform better on tests of school readiness than children of similar backgrounds who did not attend preschool. Children from low-income backgrounds benefit even more cognitively from preschool than children from middle-class families do (Love et al., 2013; Yoshikawa et al., 2013).

There are also social benefits to attending preschool. Children who attend preschool are generally more independent and socially confident than children who remain home (National Institute of Child Health and Human Development [NICHD] Early Child Care Research Network, 2006). However, there appear to be social costs as well. Children attending preschool have been observed to be less compliant, less respectful toward adults, and more aggressive than other children (Jennings & Reingle, 2012). Furthermore, these negative social effects may endure long past preschool age. In one large national longitudinal study in the United States, children who attended preschool for more than 10 hours per week were more disruptive in class once they entered school, in follow-ups extending through 6th grade (NICHD Early Child Care Research Network, 2006).

Well-run, well-funded preschools offer cognitive and social benefits for young children.

Yet these findings concerning the overall positive or negative outcomes associated with preschool can be misleading. Preschool programs vary vastly in quality, and many studies have found that the quality of preschool child care is more important than the simple fact of whether or not children are in preschool (Clarke-Stewart & Allhusen, 2002; Maccoby & Lewis, 2003; NICHD Early Child Care Research Network, 2006). Culture also matters. A recent national study in Norway found no relation between hours in preschool and aggression (Zachrisson et al., 2013). Preschools in Norway are uniformly of high quality, and Norwegian children are used to being with other children in nonparental childcare from age 1.

What factors should parents consider when searching for a high-quality preschool experience for their children? There is a broad consensus among scholars of early childhood development that the most important features include the following (Lavzer & Goodson, 2006; National

Association for the Education of Young Children [NAEYC], 2010; Vandell et al., 2005; Yoshikawa et al., 2013):

- ***Teacher education and training.*** Unlike teachers at higher grade levels, preschool teachers often are not required to have education or credentials specific to early childhood education. Preschool teachers who have training in early childhood education provide a better social and cognitive environment.
- ***Class size and child-to-teacher ratio.*** Experts recommend no more than 20 children in a classroom, and a ratio of children to preschool teachers no higher than five to ten 3-year-olds per teacher or seven to ten 4-year-olds per teacher.
- ***Age-appropriate materials and activities.*** In early childhood, children learn more through active engagement with materials rather than through formal lessons or rote learning.
- ***Teacher–child interactions.*** Teachers should spend most of their time interacting with the children rather than with each other. They should circulate among the children, asking questions, offering suggestions, and assisting them when necessary.

Notice that the criteria for high-quality preschools do not include intense academic instruction. Here again there is a broad consensus among early childhood scholars that preschool teaching should be based on *developmentally appropriate educational practice* (NAEYC, 2010). At the preschool age, this means that learning should involve exploring and discovering through relatively unstructured, hands-on experiences—learning about the physical world through playing in a water or sand area, for example, or learning new words through songs and nursery rhymes.

One of the preschool programs best known for high quality and developmentally appropriate practice is the Montessori program. Research by developmental psychologist Angeline Lillard has demonstrated the effectiveness of the Montessori approach (Lillard, 2008; Lillard & Else-Quest, 2006). Lillard compared two groups of 3- to 6-year-old children. One group of children had attended a Montessori preschool, and the other group attended other types of preschools. All the children in the non-Montessori group had originally applied to Montessori schools but were not able to enter due to space limitations, with admission determined by a random lottery. This was a crucial aspect of the study design; do you see why? If the researchers had simply compared children in Montessori schools with children in non-Montessori schools, any differences would have been difficult to interpret, because there may have been many other differences between the families of children in the two types of schools. For example, children in Montessori schools may have higher-SES parents. Because the families of children in the non-Montessori schools had also applied to get their children into the Montessori schools, and selection among families was via random lottery, it can be assumed that the backgrounds of the children in the two groups were similar.

The children who attended Montessori preschools were more advanced in both cognitive and social development than the children who attended other preschools. Cognitively, the Montessori children scored higher on tests of reading and math skills than the other children. Socially, in playground observations, the Montessori children engaged more in cooperative play and less in rough, chaotic play such as wrestling. In sum, the Montessori approach appears to provide children with a setting that encourages self-initiated and active learning, thereby enhancing cognitive and social development.

Although attending preschool has become a typical experience among children in developed countries, there is great variation in how countries structure preschool and what they wish young children to learn. In most countries, parents hope for social benefits from preschool, but countries vary in their expectations for cognitive and academic benefits. In some countries, such as China and the United States, learning basic academic skills is one of the primary goals of having children attend preschool (LeVine & LeVine, 2016; Tobin et al., 2009). In other countries, such as Japan and most European countries, learning academic skills is a low priority in preschool (Hayashi et al., 2009). Rather, preschool is mainly a time for learning social skills such as how to function as a member of a group.

Japan is of particular interest in this area, because Japanese students have long been at or near the top of international comparisons in reading, math, and science from middle childhood through high school (NCES, 2014). You might expect, then, that one reason for this success is

Japanese preschools emphasize group play and cooperation.

that they begin academic instruction earlier than in other countries, but just the opposite turns out to be true. In one study of Japanese and American parents and preschool teachers, only 2% of the Japanese listed "to give children a good start academically" as one of the top three reasons for young children to attend preschool (Tobin et al., 2009). In contrast, over half the Americans named this as one of the top three reasons. There was a similarly sharp contrast in response to the item "to give children the experience of being a member of the group." Sixty percent of Japanese parents and teachers endorsed this reason for preschool, compared to just 20% of the Americans.

Preschools in Japan teach nothing about reading and numbers. Instead, the focus is on group play, so that children will learn the values of cooperation and sharing. Preschool children wear identical uniforms, with different colors to indicate their classroom membership. They each have the same equipment, which they keep in identical drawers. Through being introduced to these cultural practices in preschool, children also learn collectivistic Japanese values.

## Early Intervention Programs

**LO 11.1.2 Describe the outcomes of early intervention programs for children from low-income families.**

**early intervention program**
program directed at young children from low-SES families who are at risk for later problems

One type of preschool experience that focuses intensively on cognitive development is the **early intervention program**. These are programs directed at young children from low-income families—children at risk for later school problems. The goal of early intervention programs is to give these children extra cognitive stimulation in early childhood so that they will have a better opportunity to succeed once they enter school.

By far the largest early intervention program in the United States is Project Head Start. The program began in 1965 and is still going strong, with about 1 million American children enrolled each year (Head Start, 2015). The program provides 1 or 2 years of preschool for children ages 4-6, and it also includes other services. Children in the program receive free meals and health care. Parents receive health care as well as job-training services. Parents are also directly involved in the Head Start program, serving on councils that make policies for the centers and sometimes serving as teachers in the classroom. Canada has a similar program focusing on First Nations children, who are often at risk for later school problems.

Do these programs work? The answer is not simple. The main goal of Head Start originally was to raise the intelligence of children from low-income backgrounds so that their academic performance would be enhanced once they entered school. Children who participate in Head Start show a boost on intelligence tests and academic achievement compared to children from similar backgrounds who do not take part, so in this respect, yes, the program works. However, a consistent pattern in Head Start and many other early intervention programs is that the intelligence test and achievement gains fade within 2 or 3 years of entering elementary school (Barnett & Hustedt, 2005; Yoshikawa et al., 2013). This is not surprising in view of the fact that children in the program typically enter poorly funded, low-quality public schools after their Head Start experience. Nevertheless, the unexpected fading of initial gains has fallen short of the original goals of the program.

However, there have been some favorable results from the Head Start program, too (Brooks-Gunn, 2003; Resnick, 2010). Children who have participated in Head Start are less likely to be placed in special education or to repeat a grade. It should be kept in mind that Head Start is a program with a million children in tens of thousands of programs that inevitably vary in quality (Resnick, 2010; Zigler & Styfco, 2004).

Where Head Start was designed to serve children ages 4–6 and give them a "head start" in school readiness, in the 1990s, a new program, Early Head Start (EHS), was initiated for low-income families and their children from infancy up to age 3 (Raikes et al., 2010).

**Figure 11.1** Major Findings of the High Scope Preschool Study

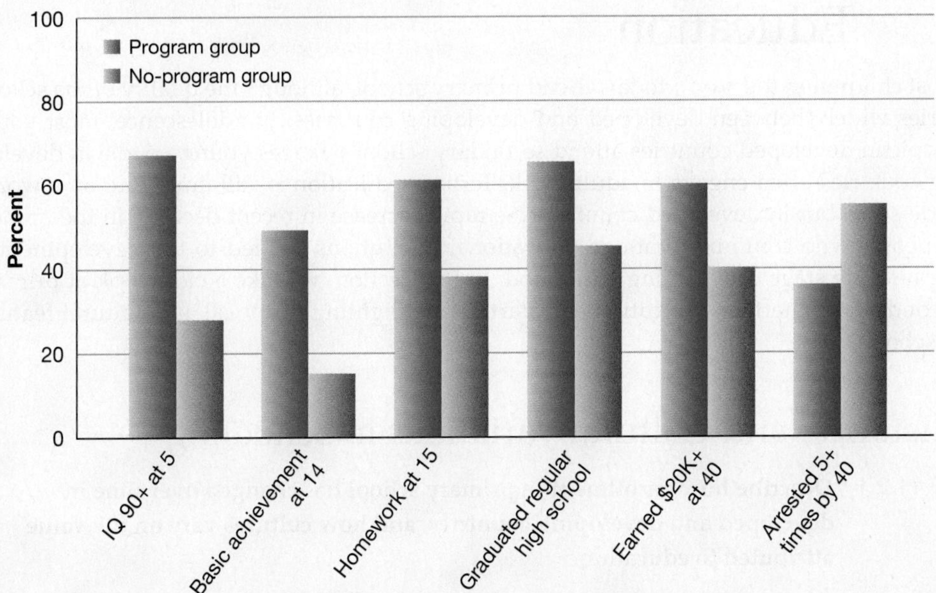


The goal of this program was to see if beginning the intervention at an earlier age would lead to greater effects on cognitive and social development. Research has shown that by age 5 the EHS children exhibited better attention and fewer behavioral problems than a control group of children from similar families (Love et al., 2013). EHS moms benefitted, too, in their mental health and likelihood of employment. However, for children, being in EHS did not affect their early school achievement unless it was followed by preschool programs at age 3–4.

Some small-scale, intensive early intervention programs have shown a broader range of enduring effects. One of the best known is the High Scope Preschool Project, a full-day, 2-year preschool program for children from low-income families (Schweinhart et al., 2004). The High Scope children showed the familiar pattern of an initial gain on intelligence tests and academic achievement followed by a decline, but demonstrated many other benefits of the program, compared to a control group. In adolescence, girls were less likely to become pregnant and boys were less likely to be arrested, and both boys and girls were more likely to graduate from high school and attend college. At age 27, the High Scope participants were more likely to be married and to own their home, less likely to have spent time in prison, and their monthly income was higher. At age 40, High Scope participants still displayed benefits of the program in a wide range of areas, including income and family stability. As you can see in Figure 11.1, this program shows that an intensive, high-quality early intervention program can have profound and lasting benefits.

## SUMMARY: Preschool

### LO 11.1.1 Identify the features that are most important in preschool quality, and explain how they reflect cultural values.

Children generally benefit from attending preschool, especially when program quality is high. Key dimensions of high-quality preschool programs include education and training of teachers, class size and child-to-teacher ratio, age-appropriate materials and activities, and quality of teacher–child interactions. American and Chinese preschools often include academic preparation, but preschools in Japan focus more on group play in order to reinforce cooperation and sharing.

### LO 11.1.2 Describe the outcomes of early intervention programs for children from low-income families.

Early intervention programs have often resulted in a rise in IQ that fades after a few years. Some early interventions have demonstrated positive social and behavioral outcomes not only in childhood, but also lasting well into adulthood.

# 11.2 From Primary Education to Tertiary Education

Most children in the world today attend primary school, although the quality of the schools varies widely between developed and developing countries. In adolescence, most young people in developed countries attend secondary school whereas young people in developing countries often engage in adult work. Tertiary education is still quite rare on a worldwide scale, but in developed countries the rapid increase in recent decades in the number of people who continue to attend educational institutions has led to the development of the new life stage of emerging adulthood. In this section, we take a close look at primary, secondary, and tertiary education. We start by highlighting historical and cultural features of school.

## Historical and Cultural Variations in Schooling

**LO 11.2.1 Describe how enrollment in primary school has changed over time in developed and developing countries, and how cultures vary on the value attributed to education.**

For people who have grown up in a place where primary school is a routine part of children's development, it is easy to assume that this has always been the case. Indeed, many developmental psychologists refer to children in middle childhood as "school-age children," as if going to school is a natural, universal, and inevitable part of children's development once they reach the age of 6 or 7. However, attending school has been a typical part of children's lives in most countries only for less than 200 years. In the United States, for example, it is estimated that prior to 1800 only about half of children attended school, and even for those who did, it lasted only a few years (Rogoff et al., 2005). Enrollment increased steadily over the 19th century, as industrialization created jobs that required literacy and people migrated from farms to urban areas. By 1900, most children completed several years of schooling. The school year remained quite short in the late 19th century, taking place mostly during the winter months, when children's labor was not needed on the farm. In 1870, the average child enrolled in school attended for only 78 days per year. Classrooms often mixed children of a wide range of ages.

In 1870, the average American child enrolled in school attended for only 78 days per year. Classrooms often mixed children of a wide range of ages.

Today, going to school has become a typical part of middle childhood, but it still is not universal, as Figure 11.2 shows (UNICEF, 2014). In most developing countries, about 18% of children ages 6–10 do not attend primary school, and in sub-Saharan Africa, 23% of boys and 21% of girls ages 6–10 do not attend. However, in all developing countries, primary school enrollment has risen steeply in recent decades.

In many developing countries, the change to a school-oriented daily life in middle childhood has been swift (Gaskins, 2015). For example, in Guatemala, Barbara Rogoff has been conducting ethnographic research in the same village for over 30 years. Over the course of just one generation, children's experiences were transformed (Rogoff et al., 2005). For example, as you can see in Table 11.1, not a single village girl today has learned weaving, even though nearly all of their mothers weaved as girls. For boys, the percentage who helped care for younger children dropped from 53% to 7% in just one generation. The percentage of boys helping with farm work also dropped from the parents' generation to the current generation. Because they now spend most of the day in school, girls no longer learn weaving, and boys are no longer available for farm work.

The change in children's focus from work to school was reflected in the change in their aspirations. In the parents' generation, few expected as children to continue education past Grade 6; for today's children, about three-fourths expect to go beyond Grade 6, and over half expect to go beyond Grade 12. Both boys and girls today envision a wider range of future occupations than their parents could have imagined, including accountant, teacher, pastor, and doctor.

A great deal of research examining cultural variations in schooling has compared the United States and Asian countries such as China, Japan, and South Korea. These Asian countries have cultural traditions emphasizing the importance and value of education going back over 2 millennia, and the traditions remain strong today (Li, 2011). High standards are applied to all children, as people in these countries believe that educational success is derived mainly from hard work and any child who tries hard enough can succeed (Stevenson et al., 2000; Sun et al., 2013). The same beliefs are characteristic of Asian American families (Fuligni et al., 2005). In contrast, most other Americans tend to believe that educational success is due mainly to innate ability. When a child does poorly, they tend to believe there is not much that can be done. Another difference is that Asian children tend to view academic striving as something they do not just for themselves but as a moral obligation to their families (Sun et al., 2013). In contrast, American children tend to view academic achievement as a mark of individual success.

**Figure 11.2** Primary School Attendance in World Regions

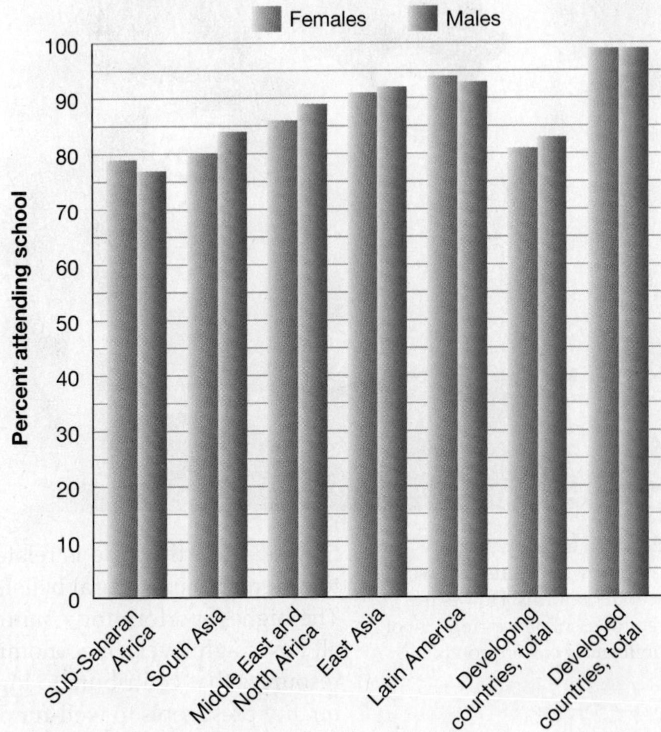


SOURCE: Data from UNICEF (2014).

Several features of Asian schools reflect collectivistic cultural beliefs emphasizing obedience and cooperation. Children are required to wear uniforms, underscoring diminished individuality and emphasizing conformity to the group. Children are also required to help maintain the cleanliness and order of the school, emphasizing the collectivistic cultural value of contributing to the well-being of the community. Here is an example of how a Japanese adolescent explained the obligation to maintain school property:

> When I see something broken, I try to fix it … [because] when we have guests visiting the school, I wouldn't want them to see the school property broken and think: "This school property looks great on the outside, but not on the inside." (Shimizu, 2001, p. 468)

Furthermore, children in Asian schools often work in groups, with students who have mastered a concept instructing those who have yet to grasp it (Shapiro & Azuma, 2004). In contrast, children in American schools typically do not wear uniforms (except in some private schools), are not required to help with school maintenance, and spend more time working alone (Stevenson & Zusho, 2002).

**Table 11.1** From Work to School in One Generation: Guatemalan Parents and Children

| | Parents % | Children % |
|---|---|---|
| Girls learn weaving | 87 | 0 |
| Expect to do farm work as adults (boys) | 77 | 22 |
| Boys do farm work | 57 | 36 |
| Boys learn to care for younger children | 53 | 7 |
| Expect to weave as adults (girls) | 43 | 15 |
| Expect education beyond Grade 6 (boys) | 7 | 71 |
| Expect education beyond Grade 6 (girls) | 3 | 76 |

SOURCE: Based on Rogoff et al. (2005).

Children in many Asian countries are required to wear school uniforms. How is the requirement of wearing school uniforms a custom complex?

There are other important differences between Asian countries and the United States in the structure of the school day and year. Asian children spend more time on a typical school day learning academic subjects than American children do; Americans spend only about half as much of their school time in academic activities as children in China and Japan do, and spend more school time in art, music, and sports (Shapiro & Azuma, 2004). Both the school day and the school year are longer in Asian countries. The school year in the United States is 180 days, compared to 220 in South Korea and 245 in China (Luckie, 2010).

How are these differences in school socialization and structure related to children's academic performance? In recent years, several excellent cross-national studies of academic performance have been conducted at regular intervals, including the Progress in International Reading Literacy Study (PIRLS) and the Trends in International Mathematics and Science Study (TIMSS). On the basis of these results, it appears that academic performance in fourth grade is related mainly to countries' economic development rather than to differences in cultural beliefs and (consequently) in educational practices (NCES, 2016). The highest-performing countries have widely varying educational approaches, but they all have high levels of economic development. As a result, they are most able to afford the resources that contribute to high academic performance, from good prenatal care to high-quality preschools to well-funded primary schools.

Within countries as well, the economic background of the family makes a great difference in children's academic performance. This is especially true in the United States, where schools are funded mostly on the basis of local property taxes rather than by the national government. As a result, the rich get richer, and the poor get poorer: schools in the poorest areas have the least amount of resources to provide for children coming from poor families, whereas schools in the most affluent areas have the most resources, and the children attending those schools, who are mainly from affluent families, reap the benefits. Not surprisingly, given this system, children from low-income families generally score worse than children from high-income families on tests of academic achievement (NCES, 2016). Similarly, the wealthiest American states have the highest school achievement test scores, and the poorest states have the lowest scores.

**Critical Thinking Question:** In your view, to what extent should academic subjects such as math and English be balanced with courses such as music, art, and physical education? Explain your view.

## Primary Education: Learning Reading and Mathematics

**LO 11.2.2 Describe how reading and math skills develop from early childhood to middle childhood and the variations in approaches to teaching these skills.**

In most cultures, primary school is when children first learn how to read and how to do math. However, there are variations in the timing and methods of teaching these skills, both within and between cultures.

**READING.** Children learn language with remarkable proficiency without being explicitly taught or instructed, just from being around others who use the language and interacting with them. However, when they enter primary school, children must learn a whole new way of processing language, via reading. For most children, learning to read takes direct instruction.

Learning to read is a relatively new development in human history. Until about 200 years ago, most people were illiterate all their lives. For example, in the United States in 1800, only about half of army recruits were even able to sign their own names on enlistment documents (Rogoff et al., 2005). Because most human economic activity involved simple agriculture or hunting or fishing, learning to read was unnecessary for most people. They could learn what they needed to know from observing others and working alongside them. Today, of course, in a globalized, information-based economy, learning to read is an essential skill for most economic activity, across cultures. Consequently, children almost everywhere learn to read, usually beginning around age 6 or 7, when they enter school.

Think for a moment about the cognitive skills reading requires, so that you can appreciate how complex and challenging it is. In order to read, you have to recognize that letters are symbols of sounds, and then match a speech sound to each letter or letter combination. You have to know the meanings of whole words—one or two at first, then dozens, then hundreds, and eventually many thousands. As you read a sentence, you have to keep the meanings of individual words or combinations of words in working memory while you continue to read the rest of the sentence. At the end of the sentence, you must put all the word and phrase meanings together into a coherent meaning for the sentence as a whole. Then you have to combine sentences into paragraphs and derive meanings of paragraphs from the relations between the sentences; then combine paragraphs for still larger meanings; and so on.

By now this process no doubt comes quite naturally to you, after so many years of reading. We perform the complex cognitive tasks of reading automatically after reading for some years, without thinking about the components that go into it. But what is the best way to teach children who are first learning to read? Two major approaches have emerged in educational research over the years:

- The **phonics approach** advocates teaching children by breaking down words into their component sounds, called *phonics*, then putting the phonics together into words (de Joyce & Feez, 2016; Gray et al., 2007). Reading in this approach involves learning gradually more complex units: phonics, then single words, then short sentences, then somewhat longer sentences, and so on. After mastering their phonics and being able to read simple words and sentences, children begin to read longer materials such as poems and stories.
- The **whole-language approach** emphasizes the meaning of written language in whole passages, rather than breaking down each word into its smallest components (de Joyce & Feez, 2016; Donat, 2006). This approach advocates teaching children to read using complete written material, such as poems, stories, and lists of related items. Children are encouraged to guess at the meaning of words they do not know, based on the context of the word within the written material. In this view, if the material is coherent and interesting, children will be motivated to learn and remember the meanings of words they do not already know.

Which approach works best? Each side has advocates, but evidence is substantial that the phonics approach is more effective at teaching children who are first learning to read (Beck & Beck, 2013). Children who have fallen behind in their reading progress using other methods improve substantially when taught with the phonics approach (Shaywitz et al., 2004; Xue & Meisels, 2004). However, once children have begun to read, they can also benefit from supplementing phonics instruction with the whole-language approach, with its emphasis on the larger meanings of written language and on using material from school subjects such as history and science to teach reading as well (Pressley & Allington, 2014).

Although learning to read is cognitively challenging, most children become able readers by Grade 3. However, some children find learning to read unusually difficult. One condition that interferes with learning to read is **dyslexia**, which includes difficulty sounding out letters, difficulty learning to spell words, and a tendency to misperceive the order of letters in words (Mayo Clinic, 2017). Children with dyslexia are not necessarily any less intelligent than other children; their cognitive problem is specific to the skill of reading. The causes of dyslexia are not known, but boys are about three times as likely as girls to have the disability, suggesting a genetic link to the Y chromosome (Hensler et al., 2010). Dyslexia is one of the most common types of **learning disabilities**, which are cognitive disorders that impede the development of learning a specific skill. Other learning disabilities involve difficulty with writing (or dysgraphia) and math (or dyscalculia).

**phonics approach**
method of teaching reading that advocates breaking down words into their component sounds, called phonics, then putting the phonics together into words

**whole-language approach**
method of teaching reading in which the emphasis is on the meaning of written language in whole passages, rather than breaking down words into their smallest components

**dyslexia**
learning disability that includes difficulty sounding out letters, difficulty learning to spell words, and a tendency to misperceive the order of letters in words

**learning disability**
in schools, a diagnosis made when a child or adolescent has normal intelligence but has difficulty in one or more academic areas and the difficulty cannot be attributed to any other disorder

Street children may learn math from the transactions involving the objects they sell. Here, a boy sells candy in a park in Rio de Janeiro, Brazil.

**MATHEMATICS.** There has been far more research on the development of reading than on the development of math skills (Berch & Mazzocco, 2007). Nevertheless, some interesting aspects of math development have been discovered. One is that even some nonhuman animals have a primitive awareness of **numeracy**, which means understanding the meaning of numbers, just as *literacy* means understanding the meaning of written words (Posner & Rothbart, 2007). Rats can be taught to discriminate between a two-tone and an eight-tone sequence, even when the sequences are matched in total duration. Monkeys can learn that the numbers 0 through 9 represent different quantities of rewards. In human infants, the beginning of numeracy appears surprisingly early. When infants are just 6 weeks old, if they are shown a toy behind a screen and see a second toy added, they look longer and appear more surprised if the screen is lowered to reveal one or three toys rather than the two toys they expected.

From toddlerhood through middle childhood, the development of math skills follows a path parallel to the development of language and reading skills (Doherty & Landells, 2006). Children begin to count around age 2, the same age at which their language development accelerates dramatically. They first become able to do simple addition and subtraction around age 5, about the same age they often learn to read their first words. In the course of middle childhood, as they become more adept readers, they typically advance in their math skills, moving from addition and subtraction to multiplication and division, and increasing their speed of processing in response to math problems (Posner & Rothbart, 2007). Children who have problems learning to read frequently have problems mastering early math skills as well.

Cultures vary in their timing and approach to teaching math skills to children, with consequences for the pace of children's learning. One study compared 5-year-old children in China, Finland, and England (Aunio et al., 2008). The children in China scored highest, with children in Finland second, and the English children third. The authors related these variations to cultural differences in how math is taught and promoted. Children in China learn math beginning in preschool, and there is a strong cultural emphasis on math as an important basis of future learning and success. In contrast, English preschools usually make little attempt to teach children math skills, in the belief that they are not ready to learn math until they enter formal schooling.

**numeracy**
understanding of the meaning of numbers

Most children learn math skills within school, but sometimes math skills can be learned effectively in a practical setting. In one study, Geoffrey Saxe (2002) found that Brazilian street children who sold candy worked out complex calculations of prices and profits. Some had

## Cultural Focus: Primary School Across Cultures

Attending primary school has become a near-universal experience. However, in some countries there are many children who attend for only a few years, because their families desperately need their labor for economic survival.

All primary schools teach children reading, writing, and math, but there are many variations in how children are taught and in what is expected of them, as you will see in this video.

Until recently, boys were more likely than girls to attend primary school. School attendance requires school fees in many countries, and some poor families would use their extremely limited resources for the boys' education. Girls were often kept home because it was believed that boys' education would be of greater benefit to the family. However, in recent years this gender difference has disappeared, and boys and girls are now equally likely to obtain primary education (UNICEF, 2014). In this video, *Primary School Across Cultures*, a Mexican girl observes that in her village, girls are more likely than boys to attend school, because boys are more often required to work to help the family.

**Watch** PRIMARY SCHOOL ACROSS CULTURES

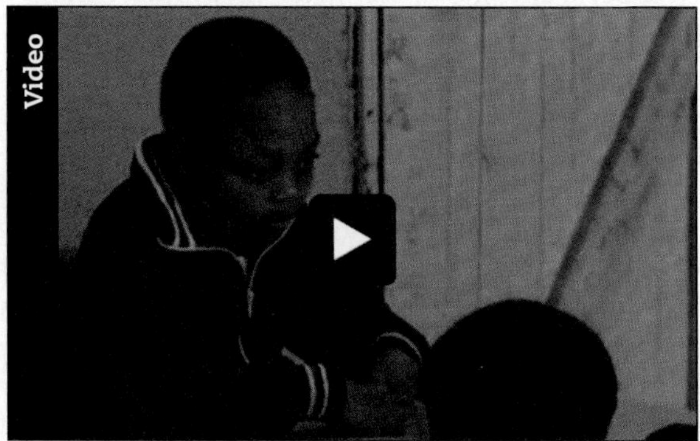


### Review Question

What common educational themes do you see among the individuals in this video?

attended school and some had not, and the ones who had been to school were more advanced in some math skills but not in the skills necessary for them to succeed in their candy selling.

## Secondary Education

**LO 11.2.3 Compare the secondary education systems and academic performance of developed countries and developing countries.**

Virtually all adolescents in developed countries are enrolled in **secondary schools** (middle schools and high schools). However, world regions vary in how likely adolescents are to attend secondary school. There is an especially sharp contrast between developed and developing countries, as you can see in Map 11.1. In many developing countries, only about 50% of adolescents attend secondary school (UNESCO, 2014).

**secondary schools**
the schools attended by adolescents, usually including a lower secondary school and an upper secondary school

A number of common themes recur in accounts of secondary education in developing countries (Lloyd, 2005; Lloyd et al., 2008; Masino & Niño-Zarazúa, 2016). All developing countries have seen rising rates of enrollment in recent decades (UNESCO, 2014). But that's about where the good news ends. Many of the schools are poorly funded and overcrowded. Many countries have too few teachers, and the teachers are insufficiently trained. Often families have to pay for secondary education, a cost they find difficult to afford, and families may have to pay for books and other educational supplies as well. There tends to be one education for the elite and a much inferior education for everyone else.

Given the underfunded and overcrowded nature of secondary schools in developing countries, it is not surprising that international studies comparing adolescents on academic performance find that affluent developed countries tend to perform better than developing countries. Figure 11.3 (next page) shows the recent performance of adolescents in various countries around the world on eighth-grade achievement tests. The pattern of results is similar across reading and math.

In developed countries, enrollment in secondary education is essentially universal. However, if you are a member of an ethnic minority in a developed country and your family has a low income, your chances of finishing secondary school may be substantially lower than in the majority culture (NCES, 2014). In the United States, high school graduation rates vary widely by ethnic group, as Figure 11.4 (next page) shows (NCES, 2014).

The transition from primary to secondary school is often challenging for adolescents in developed countries. It usually means moving from a small, personalized classroom setting with one or two teachers to a larger setting where a student has five or six or more teachers.

**Map 11.1** Secondary School Enrollment Worldwide

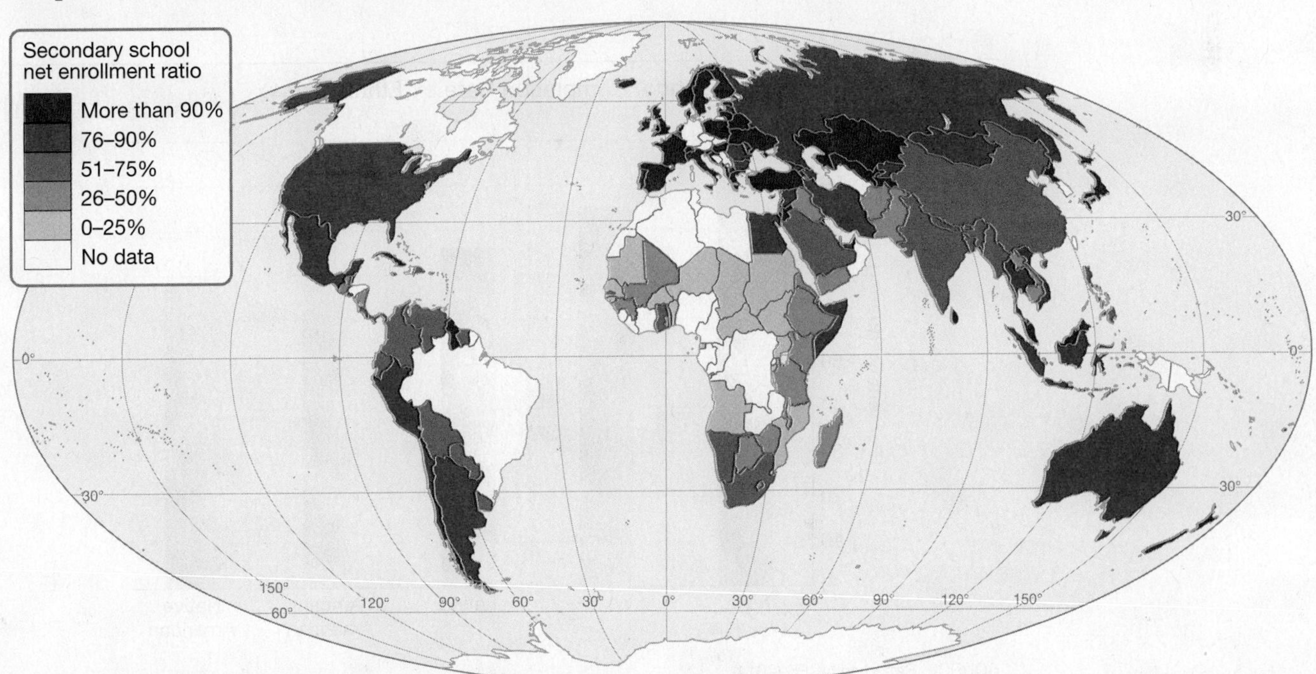

**Figure 11.3** International Performance in Reading and Math, Eighth Grade

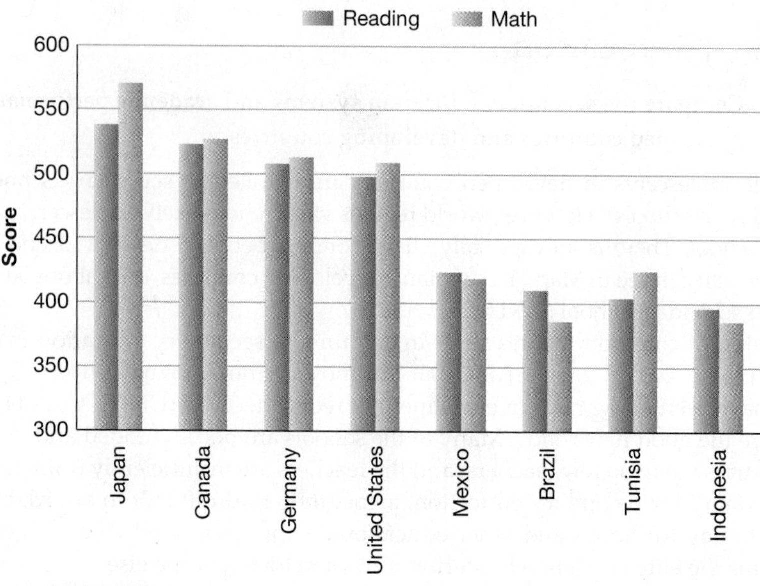


SOURCE: Based on NCES (2014).

It also means moving into a setting where the academic work is at a higher level and grades are suddenly viewed as a more serious measure of academic attainment than they may have been in primary school.

These changes in school experience can add to early adolescents' anxieties and school-related stress. A longitudinal study of over 1,500 American adolescents found a steady decline from the beginning of sixth grade to the end of eighth grade in students' perceptions of teacher support, autonomy in the classroom, and clarity of school rules and regulations (Way et al., 2007). These declines were in turn related to declines in psychological well-being and increases in behavior problems. However, there were also benefits from the transition to secondary school. One study found that seventh-grade adolescents made more positive than negative comments about the transition to middle school, with positive comments about topics such as peer relationships (more people to "hang around" with), academics (greater diversity of classes available), and independence (Berndt & Mekos, 1995).

**Figure 11.4** U.S. High School Completion Rate by Ethnic Group

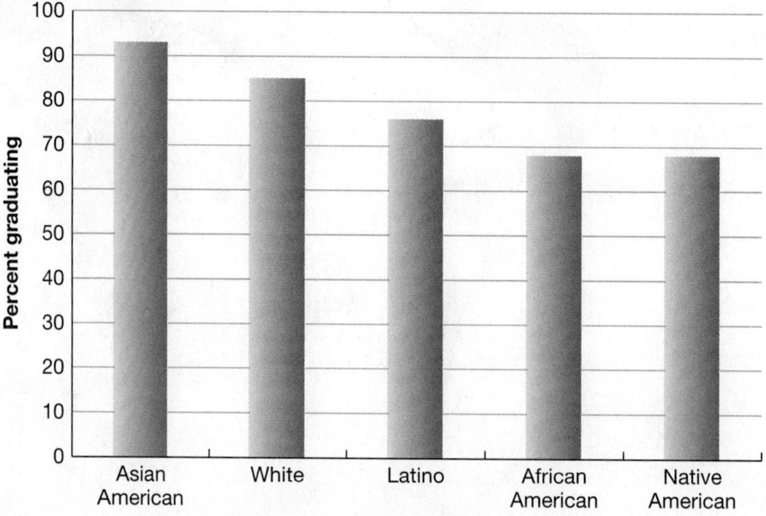


SOURCE: Based on NCES (2014).

## Education Focus: School Climate

Most scholars in education agree that the kinds of interactions that students and teachers have in the secondary school classroom are critical to student academic engagement and psychological well-being. **School climate** is the term for the quality of these interactions (Brand et al., 2003; Jia et al., 2009; Rutter, 1983; Way et al., 2007). It refers to how teachers interact with students, their expectations and standards for students, and their methods for regulating students' conduct.

The term *school climate* was coined by Michael Rutter (1983; Rutter et al., 1979), a British psychiatrist who has done extensive research on adolescents and schools. Rutter and his colleagues studied several thousand young adolescents in British secondary schools. The results indicated that students were better off in schools where teachers tended to be supportive and involved with students but also applied firm discipline when necessary and held high expectations for students' conduct and academic performance. Specifically, students in schools with this kind of school climate had higher attendance and achievement test scores and lower rates of delinquency compared with students in the schools where the school climate was not as favorable. This was true even after taking into account statistically the differences in the students' intelligence and socioeconomic background. So, it was not simply that the students in the better schools also came from more advantaged backgrounds. The schools themselves made a substantial difference in students' performance, based on differences in school climate.

These findings have been supported in many other studies in different countries (Anderson et al., 2004; Coleman & Hoffer, 1987; Coleman et al.,1982; Guthrie, 2008; Kutsyuruba et al., 2015; Loukas & Robinson, 2004; Newmann, 1992; O'Malley et al., 2015; Sirin & Rogers-Sirin, 2005; Wang et al., 2014). One study of over 100,000 students in over 100 American middle schools found that school climate was favorably related to academic, behavioral, and socioemotional outcomes (Brand et al., 2003). A study of Chinese and American adolescents reported that in both countries, a positive school climate (as measured by support from teachers and other students) was positively related to grades and negatively related to depressive symptoms (Jia et al., 2009).

### Review Question

Imagine that you have just become the principal of a secondary school. What could you do to assess the school climate in your school? How would you go about improving it if it were less than satisfactory?

There is a great deal of diversity in the kinds of secondary schools that adolescents attend. The United States is unusual in having only one institution—the "comprehensive" school—as the source of secondary education. Canada and Japan also have comprehensive secondary schools as the norm, but most other countries have several different kinds of schools that adolescents may attend. European countries usually have three types of secondary schools (Hamilton & Hamilton, 2006; Marshall & Butler, 2015). About half of adolescents attend a *college-preparatory school* that offers a variety of academic courses. The goal is general education rather than training for any specific profession. About one-fourth of adolescents attend a *vocational school*, where they learn the skills involved in a specific occupation such as plumbing or auto mechanics. Some European countries also have a third type of secondary school, a *professional school*, devoted to teacher training, the arts, or some other specific purpose. About one-fourth of European adolescents usually attend this type of school.

**school climate**

the quality of interactions between teachers and students, including how teachers interact with students, their expectations and standards for students, and their methods for regulating students' conduct

One consequence of the European system is that adolescents must decide at a relatively early age what direction to pursue for their education and occupation. At age 15 or 16, adolescents choose which type of secondary school they will enter—a decision that is likely to

European countries usually have three types of secondary schools: college-preparatory, vocational, and professional schools.

have an enormous impact on the rest of their lives. Usually the decision is made by adolescents in conference with their parents and teachers, based on adolescents' interests as well as on their school performance. Adolescents who attend a vocational school sometimes attend university simultaneously. Also, adolescents sometimes change schools after a year or two, but these switches are rare.

## Tertiary Education

**LO 11.2.4 Compare the tertiary education systems and college experiences among developed countries, and review the long-term benefits of tertiary education.**

**tertiary education**
education or training beyond secondary school

As Map 11.2 shows, a majority of emerging adults across a wide range of developed countries now obtain **tertiary education**, which includes any kind of education or training program beyond secondary school. This has been a remarkably rapid historical change. One hundred years ago, few young people—less than 10%—obtained tertiary education in any developed country; in fact, the majority did not even attend secondary school. Those who did attend college or university were mostly men. Historically, as we saw in Chapter 2, women were deemed to be cognitively inferior to men and therefore not worthy of higher education. A hundred years later, tertiary education is now a normative experience, and in most countries women are more likely than men to obtain it (Arnett, 2015).

Countries vary widely in how they structure tertiary education. Colleges in the United States, Canada, and Japan begin with 2 years of general education with no requirement of declaring a specialization or "major," which allows for the exploration of topics that may be unrelated to any occupational future. You may be a business major and nevertheless enjoy courses on literature or art or philosophy that lead you to explore a variety of ideas about what it means to be human. You may be a psychology major and yet find it interesting to explore ideas in courses on astronomy or chemistry.

Tertiary education is perhaps most relaxed and undemanding in Japan. This is in sharp contrast to Japanese secondary schools, which are exceptionally demanding with fierce competition to get into the best universities (Fackler, 2007). To prepare for entrance exams to universities, Japanese adolescents are pressed by parents and teachers to apply

**Map 11.2** Worldwide Enrollment in Tertiary Education

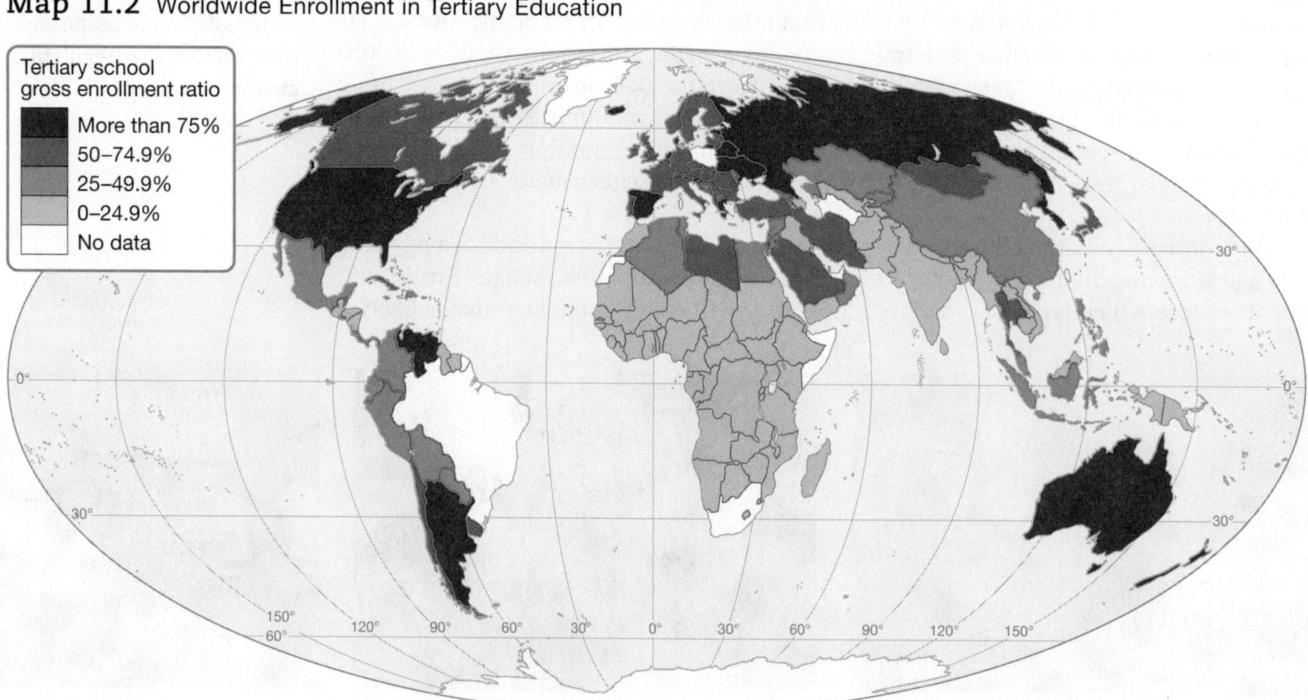

themselves seriously at school and in their homework. In addition, from middle childhood through adolescence many students attend "cram schools" after school or receive instruction from private tutors (Takahashi & Takeuchi, 2007). Beyond college and university, the Japanese workplace is also notoriously demanding, requiring long hours and mandatory after-hours socializing. For the Japanese, their time of leisure and fun comes during their college years. Once they enter college, grades matter little and standards for performance are relaxed. Instead, they have "four years of university-sanctioned leisure to think and explore" (Fackler, 2007;Rohlen, 1983, p. 168). Japanese college students spend a great deal of time walking around the city and hanging out together. Average homework time for Japanese college students is half the homework time of middle school or high school students (Takahashi & Takeuchi, 2007). For most Japanese, this brief period in emerging adulthood is the only time in their lives, from childhood until retirement, that they are allowed to enjoy extensive hours of leisure.

In Europe, the tertiary education system is structured quite differently than in the United States, Canada, and Japan. Rather than beginning with 2 years of general education, European students study in only one topic area from the time they enter university. Traditionally, university education in Europe often lasted 6 or more years because it culminated in a degree that was similar to American advanced degrees (master's or doctoral degree). However, the European system has changed recently to match the American system, with separate bachelor's, master's, and doctoral degrees. This was done to shorten the time European emerging adults spend in university and to promote the development of coordinated programs between European and American universities. It also reflects the growing globalization of education.

Is tertiary education worth the time and money it requires? It is certainly a substantial investment. Participation in tertiary education requires a great deal of money per year, paid mainly by emerging adults and their parents in the United States, and mainly by the government in other developed countries. Furthermore, the years in which emerging adults are focused on obtaining tertiary education are also years when most of them are not contributing to full-time economic activity. Not only are governments paying some or all of the costs of financing emerging adults' tertiary education, they are also losing the economic activity and tax revenue emerging adults would be contributing if their time and energy were devoted to full-time work.

Nevertheless, the benefits of tertiary education are great. For societies, an educated population is a key to economic growth in a world economy that is increasingly based on information, technology, and services. This is why countries are willing to make such a large investment in the tertiary education of their emerging adults. For emerging adults themselves, the benefits are also clear. Emerging adults who obtain tertiary education tend to have considerably higher earnings, occupational status, and career attainment over the long run, compared to those who do not attend college (NCES, 2011; Pascarella, 2006; Schneider & Stevenson, 1999). Over a lifetime of working, Americans with a college degree or more make an estimated one million dollars more than those who only obtain a high school education or less, as Figure 11.5 (next page) shows (Pew Research Center, 2014).

What kinds of academic and non-academic benefits do you think these students from the Massachusetts Institute of Technology derive from their college experience?

Tertiary education has multiple benefits in addition to increased earnings. Ernest Pascarella and Patrick Terenzini (1991; Pascarella, 2005, 2006) have conducted research in the United States on this topic for many years. They find a variety of intellectual benefits from attending college, in areas such as general verbal and quantitative skills, oral and written communication skills, and critical thinking. These benefits hold up even after taking into account factors such as age, gender, precollege abilities, and family social class background. Pascarella and Terenzini also find that in the course of the college years, students place less emphasis on college as a way to a better job and more emphasis on learning for the sake of enhancing their intellectual and personal growth.

**Figure 11.5** "The College Bonus" Showing Economic Benefits of Tertiary Education

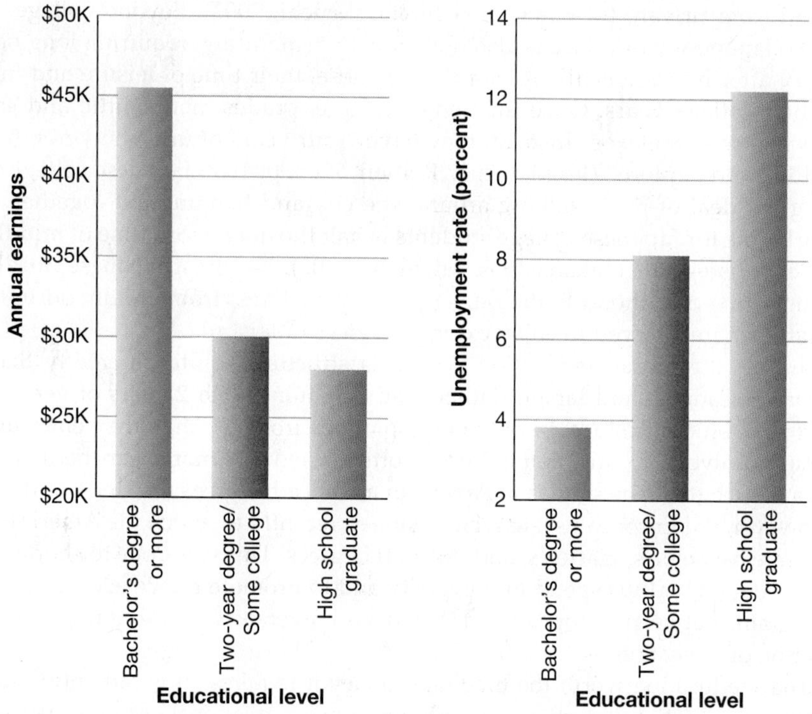

SOURCE: Based on Pew Research Center (2014).

In addition to the academic benefits, Pascarella and Terenzini describe a long list of nonacademic benefits. In the course of the college years, students develop clearer aesthetic and intellectual values. They gain a more distinct identity and become more confident socially. They become less dogmatic, less authoritarian, and less ethnocentric in their political and social views. Their self-concepts and psychological well-being improve. As with the academic benefits, these nonacademic benefits hold up even after taking into account characteristics such as age, gender, and family social class background.

## SUMMARY: From Primary Education to Tertiary Education

**LO 11.2.1 Describe how enrollment in primary school has changed over time in developed and developing countries, and how cultures vary on the value attributed to education.**

Attending school has been a typical part of children's lives in most countries for less than 200 years. Today, primary school attendance is universal in developed countries. In most developing countries, about 18% of children ages 6–10 do not attend school. Compared to the United States, Asian countries place more of an emphasis on academic achievement through hard work.

**LO 11.2.2 Describe how reading and math skills develop from early childhood to middle childhood and the variations in approaches to teaching these skills.**

When they enter primary school, children must learn a new way of processing language, via reading, and for most children, learning to read takes direct instruction. Phonics appears to be the most effective approach at teaching children who are first learning to read. Once children have begun to read, they can also benefit from the whole-language approach. Most children learn math skills within school, but sometimes math skills can be learned effectively in a practical setting.

**LO 11.2.3 Compare the secondary education systems and academic performance of developed countries and developing countries.**

Virtually all adolescents in developed countries are enrolled in secondary schools (comprehensive or specialized). In many developing countries, only about 50% of adolescents attend secondary schools, and schools are commonly underfunded and overcrowded. Adolescents from affluent developed countries perform better on academic tests than adolescents from developing countries.

**LO 11.2.4 Compare the tertiary education systems and college experiences among developed countries, and review the long-term benefits of tertiary education.**

Developed countries vary widely in how they structure tertiary education. European students study in only one topic area from the time they enter university. In contrast, students in Canada, Japan, and the United States typically do not need to declare a college major for the first 2 years. For societies, an educated population is a key to economic growth in a world economy. For emerging adults themselves, tertiary education correlates with higher SES, and academic and social benefits.

# 11.3 School and Other Contexts

How children do in school is related not only to characteristics of the school, such as school climate and educational approaches, but also to the relationship between school and other contexts. In this section we look at how children's school achievement is related to family, friends, social class, ethnicity, and immigrant generation.

## Family and Friends

**LO 11.3.1 Explain how children's school achievement is influenced by their relationships with parents and friends.**

Children whose parents and friends have high expectations for educational achievement tend to do well in school. However, being surrounded by high-achieving peers is not necessarily positive.

**PARENTING STYLE.** One way parents influence children's academic performance is through their expectations for achievement. Children whose parents expect them to do well tend to live up to those expectations, as reflected in their grades; children whose parents have lower expectations for their school performance tend to perform less well (Juang & Silbereisen, 2002; Simons-Morton & Chen, 2009). Parents who have high expectations also tend to be more involved in their children's education, attending school programs and keeping track of their children's performance. This involvement contributes to children's school success.

Parents' involvement in their children's education tends to reflect their overall parenting style (Juang & Silbereisen, 2002; Steinberg, 1996). In general, authoritative parenting has the most favorable associations with children's highest levels of engagement in school and the highest levels of school success (Spera, 2005). Authoritative parents contribute to children's school success directly by being more involved than other parents in their adolescents' education (Paulson, 1994). Such parents also have a variety of favorable indirect effects on their children's school performance. Children with authoritative parents are more likely than other adolescents to develop personal qualities such as self-reliance, persistence, and responsibility, which in turn lead to favorable school performance (Steinberg, 1996).

Children with authoritarian, permissive, or neglectful parents all tend to perform worse in school than children with authoritative parents (Spera, 2005). Adolescents' academic achievement tends to be worst when they have neglectful parents (low levels of both demandingness and responsiveness). Of course, here as with other parenting research (see Chapter 9), the direction of effects is not clear and the results should be interpreted carefully. It could be that authoritative parenting helps children do well in school, or it could be that children who do well in school are easier to parent with an admirable combination of demandingness and responsiveness.

**FRIENDS AND PEERS.** In school, as in other areas, the influences of parents and friends are often intertwined (Simons-Morton & Chen, 2009). On the one hand, parents influence children's choices of friends, which can in turn influence school performance. On the other hand, having friends who denigrate school tends to be related to lower school success, even for children with authoritative parents.

Friends with high educational achievements and aspirations tend to give each other support and encouragement for doing well in school. Here, two friends study together.

Friends with high educational achievements and aspirations tend to give each other support and encouragement for doing well in school. This is true even taking into account selective association (the fact that children tend to choose friends who are similar to themselves). When low-achieving children have high-achieving friends, over time the high achievers tend to have a positive influence, so that the low achievers' grades improve (Epstein, 1983; Zedd et al., 2002). Low-achieving adolescents with high-achieving friends are also more likely to plan to attend college, compared with low achievers whose friends are not high achievers.

However, the influence of having high-achieving *friends* appears to be different from the influence of being in a school of high-achieving *peers*. (Remember the distinction made in Chapter 10 between friends and peers.) Children in schools where their peers have lower average levels of school achievement tend to have better academic self-concepts and higher expectations for academic attainment than children surrounded by high-achieving classmates (Zedd et al., 2002). Educational researchers call this the "big fish in a little pond effect" (Marsh & Hau, 2003; Thijs et al., 2010). If classmates mostly seem to be doing fair or poor in their schoolwork, the slightly above-average child is likely to feel pretty good about how school is going—like a "big fish," in other words. However, in a school of high achievers, the same child may well feel inferior to others in academic abilities and prospects. One study of over 100,000 adolescents in 26 countries found that the "big fish" effect existed in all 26 countries: adolescents in less selective schools had a significantly higher academic self-concept than adolescents in more selective schools (Marsh & Hau, 2003).

## Social Class

**LO 11.3.2 Explain different ways that social class is related to school achievement.**

Social class or socioeconomic status (SES) is strongly related to academic achievement. Numerous studies have found a positive association between family SES and children's grades and achievement test scores, as well as between family SES and the highest level of education that adolescents or emerging adults ultimately attain. These social class differences appear early in development. Even before entering school, middle-class children score higher than working-class and lower-class children on tests of basic academic skills. By middle childhood, these class differences are clearly established, and class differences in academic achievement remain strong through high school (Kelly, 2004). Middle-class emerging adults are also more likely than emerging adults from lower social classes to attend college following high school (Albrecht & Albrecht, 2011).

What makes social class so important in predicting academic achievement? Parents' behavior varies by social class in ways that are related to adolescents' academic achievement. Middle-class parents are more likely than lower-class parents to have an authoritative parenting style that contributes to their children's school success (Annunziata et al., 2006; Dornbusch et al., 1987; Steinberg, 1996).

Social class represents many other family characteristics that contribute to achievement. Middle-class parents tend to have higher intelligence than lower-class parents, and they pass this advantage on to their children through both genes and environment; in turn, intelligence is related to academic achievement (Firkowska-Mankiewicz, 2011). Middle-class children also tend to receive better nutrition and health care than lower-class children, beginning prenatally and continuing through adolescence; for lower-class children, health problems may interfere with their ability to perform academically (Reichman, 2005).

Lower-class families also tend to be subject to more stresses than middle-class families. This is true both of major stresses (such as losing a job) as well as day-to-day minor stresses (such as the car breaking down), and these stresses are negatively related to children's school performance. One longitudinal study found that family stressors predicted academic problems among American adolescents of Chinese, European, and Mexican backgrounds (Flook & Fuligni, 2008).

The major and minor stresses experienced by lower-class families can interfere with academic achievement. Here, a girl from a poor household does homework in the family's main room.

## Ethnicity

**LO 11.3.3 Explain different ways that ethnicity is related to school achievement.**

Sharp differences exist between different American ethnic groups in educational achievement. Asian American adolescents have the best academic performance of any ethnic group in American society, followed by Whites, with the performance of Latino, African American, and Native American adolescents below Whites (Qin et al., 2008). These differences already exist in early primary school, but they become more pronounced in adolescence.

What explains these differences? To some extent, the explanation lies in ethnic group differences on the factors we have already discussed as important in school success, such as social class, parenting practices, and friends' influences. With regard to social class, African Americans, Latinos, and Native Americans are more likely than Asian Americans or Whites to live in poverty, and living in poverty is negatively associated with academic performance, regardless of ethnicity (Murphy et al., 2010). The role of poverty is also seen among Asian Americans. Poverty rates are high among Cambodian, Hmong, and Laotian families in the United States, and 35–40% of adolescents from these Asian American groups do not complete high school (The White House Initiative on Asian Americans and Pacific Islanders, 2016).

We have seen the importance of parental expectations in adolescents' educational achievement, and ethnic differences exist here as well. Although the majority of parents in all ethnic groups say they value education highly, the emphasis on education is especially strong in Asian cultures (Lee & Larson, 2000; Li, 2011). Asian American parents tend to have higher educational expectations than parents in other ethnic groups (Mistry et al., 2009).

Ethnic differences can also be seen in friends' attitudes toward education. The differences correspond to ethnic differences in academic achievement; Asian Americans are most likely to have academically oriented friends, African Americans and Latinos least likely, with Whites somewhere in between (Yu & Patterson, 2010). Specifically, Asian American adolescents are most likely to study with friends, most likely to say their friends think it is important to do well in school, and most likely to say they work harder on schoolwork to keep up with their friends. Although the influence of friends on school performance is usually positive for Asian Americans, for adolescents in other ethnic groups the influence is more likely to be negative (Goza & Ryabov, 2009).

Although differences pertaining to social class, parenting, and the influence of friends help explain ethnic differences in adolescents' academic achievement, many scholars have argued that other forces are at work as well, forces related specifically to prejudice and discrimination against certain ethnic groups in American society. In particular, some scholars have argued that the relatively low achievement of African American and Latino adolescents is due substantially to these children's perception that even if they excel educationally, their prospects for occupational success will be limited due to prejudice against them (Chavous et al., 2008; Thompson & Gregory, 2011). Some scholars have asserted that such prejudice leads many Black adolescents to view striving for educational achievement as "acting White" (Neal-Barnett et al., 2010; Ogbu, 2003). Studies have found that minority adolescents who believe that their opportunities are unfairly limited by ethnic discrimination have lower achievement than their minority peers who do not believe this (Thompson & Gregory, 2011; Wood & Clay, 1996). Educational expectations decline from eighth grade through high school for many Black adolescents, especially those from lower SES families, perhaps reflecting a growing perception of limited opportunities after high school (Trusty et al., 1999).

However, other studies have reported that African American and Latino students were equal to White and Asian students in their perceptions of the potential value of academic achievement for promoting future career success (Figueira-McDonough, 1998; Whaley & Noel, 2011). Where the adolescents in these studies differed was in their perceptions of the consequences of *not* succeeding academically. African American and Latino students generally agreed that doing well in school helps in finding later employment, but they also tended to believe that they could succeed in a career even if they did not obtain a high level of academic achievement, whereas White and Asian American students—especially Asian American students—tended to believe that failing to succeed academically would have more serious negative consequences. Thus, contrary to the view that African American and Latino adolescents are inhibited from academic achievement by a pessimistic view of the value of academic success, this research indicates that these adolescents may have less motivation to strive academically because they are optimistic about their chances of succeeding in the future even without excelling academically.

How does achieving well in school impact African Americans in the workplace? African American women who obtain a four-year college degree earn about 20% more than White women with the same education (*Chronicle of Higher Education*, 2005). African American men with a college degree, however, earn slightly less than White men with the same education (NCES, 2016).

## Immigrant Generation

**LO 11.3.4 Describe the influence of "Americanization" on immigrant children's attitude toward school.**

For children whose families have immigrated to the United States in recent generations, one consistent finding is that their school performance is related to how long their families have been in the United States. One could reasonably expect that the longer a child's family has been in the United States, the better the child would do in school, because English would be more likely spoken fluently at home, the child would be more familiar with the expectations of American schools, the parents would be more comfortable communicating with teachers and other school personnel, and so on.

However, research shows *just the opposite*. Research with adolescents has shown that the more generations Asian American and Latino families have been in the United States, the *worse* the adolescents tend to do in school (Fuligni et al., 2009). This is known as the **immigrant paradox** (Garcia Coll & Marks, 2012; Hofferth & Moon, 2016). The main reason seems to be that the longer the family has been in the United States, the more "Americanized" the adolescent is likely to become—that is, the more likely the adolescent is to value part-time work and socializing with friends over striving for academic excellence. For example, in one study, first-generation Chinese immigrant adolescents were highly motivated to work hard in school and valued demanding teachers, whereas those who were second-generation—that is, born in the United States, not in China—valued more entertaining teachers and did not want to work as hard for school success (Kaufman, 2004). Becoming American means becoming more likely to have adopted the American cultural values that both good times and academic achievement are important in adolescence.

**immigrant paradox**
the paradox that immigrant adolescents' academic achievement worsens across each successive generation living in the United States

### SUMMARY: School and Other Contexts

**LO 11.3.1 Explain how children's school achievement is influenced by their relationships with parents and friends.**

Children with authoritative parents tend to perform better in school than children with authoritarian, permissive, or neglectful parents. Children whose parents and friends have high expectations for educational achievement tend to do well in school.

**LO 11.3.2 Explain different ways that social class is related to school achievement.**

Family SES is positively correlated with academic achievement, including children's grades and highest level of educational attainment. Higher SES is related to many other characteristics that contribute to academic achievement, including authoritative parenting, better health care, and lower exposure to stresses.

**LO 11.3.3 Explain different ways that ethnicity is related to school achievement.**

Asian American adolescents have the best academic performance of any ethnic group in American society, followed by Whites, with the performance of Latino, African American, and Native American adolescents below Whites. However, ethnicity intersects with SES, parenting practices, friends' influences, and discrimination.

**LO 11.3.4 Describe the influence of "Americanization" on immigrant children's attitude toward school.**

Research with adolescents has shown that the more generations Asian American and Latino families have been in the United States, the worse the adolescents tend to do in school. This is known as the immigrant paradox. With "Americanization," adolescent immigrants become more likely to value part-time work and socializing with friends over solely striving for academic excellence.

# 11.4 Intelligence Tests and School Readiness

As we saw in Chapter 1, the first intelligence test was designed by Alfred Binet and Theodore Simon in order to identify children who would have difficulty learning in school and would need special instruction. As school attendance for children between 6 and 14 became mandatory in France, the government commissioned Binet to design a test for assessing children's cognitive abilities. The *Binet-Simon Scale* was introduced in 1905 (Binet, 1911; Binet & Simon, 1905). The updated and current version of the test is known as the **Stanford-Binet** (Bain & Allin, 2005).

In contemporary psychology, the evaluation of cognitive abilities with intelligence tests is known as the **psychometric approach**. Definitions of intelligence vary, but it is generally understood to be a person's capacity for acquiring knowledge, reasoning, and solving problems (Sternberg, 2004). At any given age, there are *individual differences* among children in their cognitive functioning. Within any group of same-age children, some will perform relatively high in their cognitive functioning and some relatively low. Even in infancy, toddlerhood, and early childhood, individual differences in cognitive development are evident, as children reach various cognitive milestones at different times, such as saying their first word. However, individual differences become more evident and more important in middle childhood, when children enter formal schooling and begin to be tested and evaluated on a regular basis.

Let us begin this section by looking at the characteristics of the most widely used intelligence test, the Wechsler Intelligence Scale for Children. Then we will address the interplay of environmental and genetic influences on intelligence. Following that we will consider alternative views of intelligence, including variations across cultures. As we will see, views of intelligence in part depend on how central schooling is to the economy and value system of a culture.

**Stanford-Binet**
widely used IQ test developed by Alfred Binet and Theodore Simon and revised by scholars at Stanford University

**psychometric approach**
the evaluation of cognitive abilities with intelligence tests

**Wechsler Intelligence Scale for Children (WISC)**
intelligence test for children aged 6 to 16

**Wechsler Preschool and Primary Scale of Intelligence (WPPSI)**
intelligence test for children aged 3 to 7

**Wechsler Adult Intelligence Scale (WAIS)**
intelligence test for persons aged 16 and older

## The Wechsler Intelligence Scale for Children

**LO 11.4.1 Describe the main features of the Wechsler Intelligence Scale for Children (WISC-V).**

The most widely used intelligence tests are the Wechsler scales. Here we will focus on the **Wechsler Intelligence Scale for Children (WISC)** for children ages 6 to 16 (Wechsler, 2014). There are also the **Wechsler Preschool and Primary Scale of Intelligence (WPPSI)** for children ages 3 to 7, and the **Wechsler Adult Intelligence Scale (WAIS)** for persons ages 16 and older.

The WISC-V (the fifth edition) assesses a child's cognitive ability on five indexes:

1. Verbal Comprehension Index
2. Visual Spatial Index
3. Fluid Reasoning Index
4. Processing Speed Index
5. Working Memory Index

To give a few examples of the kinds of tasks included, the Verbal Comprehension Index includes a Vocabulary task that asks a child to define different words (e.g., what is a diamond?). The Processing Speed Index includes a task called Symbol Search where the child has to indicate as quickly as possible whether or not a symbol (e.g., Δ) is present in a list of symbols (e.g., ◊ □ ⌂ Δ). The Working Memory Index includes a Digit Span task that requires the child to repeat a series of numbers (e.g., 5, 1, 8, 2).

The results provide a **Full Scale Intelligence Quotient**, or IQ, which is calculated relative to the performance of other people of the same age, with 100 as the **median** score. Instead of administering the full WISC-V, a subset of tasks may be used as part of assessing specific learning disabilities, such as dyslexia. For more information, watch the video *The Wechsler Intelligence Scale for Children: Creating a Measurement* in the Research Focus feature.

**Full Scale Intelligence Quotient**
IQ score calculated relative to the performance of other people of the same age, with 100 as the median score

**median**
in a distribution of scores, the point at which half of the population scores above and half below

## Research Focus: The Wechsler Intelligence Scale for Children: Creating a Measurement

A great deal of research has gone into the development of the Wechsler Intelligence Scale for Children, also known as the WISC (Hartman, 2009; Kaufman & Lichtenberger, 2006). One goal of this research was to establish **age norms**. This means that an individual child's test score is determined by comparing it to the "norm," or typical scores, for a large sample of children his or her age. The median score, that is, the point at which half of the sample scores above and half of the sample scores below, is assigned the value of 100. Other scores are determined according to how high or low they are in relation to the median.

A second goal in the development of the WISC was to establish **test-retest reliability**. This involves examining whether persons' scores on one occasion are similar to their scores on another occasion. The WISC has high test-retest reliability, and reliability improves as children get older (Psychological Corporation, 2000). For most people, little change in intelligence scores, or IQ scores, takes place after about age 10.

Of course, that does not mean that your mental abilities never advance after age 10! Keep in mind that a test score is relative. It indicates how you compare with other people your age. People who score higher than their peers at age 10 are also likely to score above average at age 14, 18, 24, and so on; people whose scores are below average at age 10 are also likely to score below average as they become older, relative to other people of the same age. So, after age 10, a child's mental abilities certainly continue to develop but the child's IQ score on the WISC is likely to stay about the same—from month to month, and year to year.

A third goal in the development of the WISC has been to establish validity. The validity of a measurement is the extent to which it assesses what it claims to assess. For the WISC as for other IQ tests, the validity question is whether they really measure intelligence? Questions about validity are much harder to answer than questions about reliability, and the validity of intelligence tests remains hotly debated among scholars and the public. In general, intelligence tests such as the WISC have reasonably good **predictive validity**. One study of children in 46 countries found that IQ scores and school achievement scores were highly correlated (Lynn & Mikk, 2007). Also, high IQ scores in adolescence predict high educational attainment in emerging adulthood, as well as occupational success in young adulthood and beyond (Firkowska-Mankiewicz, 2011).

The WISC was first created in 1949. Over time, it has been updated with the goal of making it representative of the cognitive abilities of diverse populations. For example, efforts have been made in recent editions to eliminate items that were biased against females and ethnic minorities. Over time, the WISC has also been translated into different languages, and age norms have been established for nations such as Brazil, France, India, and Japan.

**Watch** THE WECHSLER INTELLIGENCE SCALE FOR CHILDREN: CREATING A MEASUREMENT

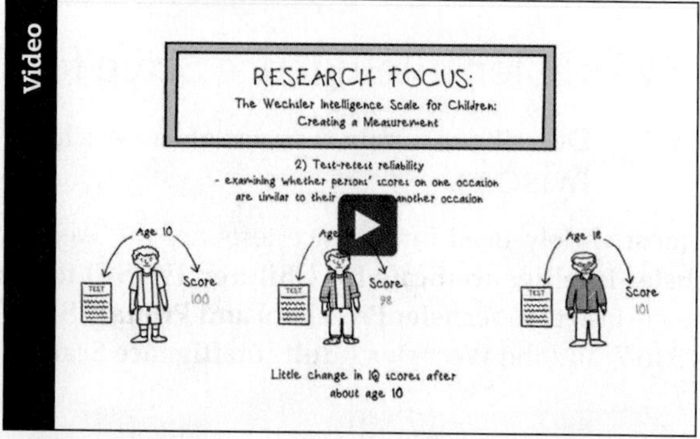

## Review Questions

1. Which of the following was NOT an important goal in the development of the Wechsler scales?
   **a.** Establishing reliability
   **b.** Establishing rank ordering
   **c.** Establishing age norms
   **d.** Establishing validity

2. Which of the following is true about the Wechsler scales?
   **a.** Earlier scales included items biased toward minorities
   **b.** Age norms are the same across countries
   **c.** IQ scores do not predict occupational success
   **d.** IQ scores do not predict academic achievement

Some scholars have distinguished between fluid and crystallized intelligence (Horn, 1982; Kaufman et al., 2009). **Fluid intelligence** refers to mental abilities that involve speed of analyzing, processing, and reacting to information, which is the kind of ability tapped by a processing speed task. IQ tests indicate that this kind of intelligence peaks in emerging adulthood. **Crystallized intelligence**, in contrast, refers to accumulated knowledge and enhanced judgment based on experience. Tasks involving verbal comprehension assess this kind of intelligence, and absolute scores on these subtests tend to improve through the 20s and 30s (Li, 2007).

# Influences on Intelligence

**LO 11.4.2 Explain the influence of both genetics and the environment on IQ scores, including the Flynn effect.**

IQ scores for a population-based sample usually fall into a **normal distribution**, or bell curve, in which most people are near the middle of the distribution and the proportions decrease at the low and high extremes, as shown in Figure 11.6. Persons with IQs below 70 are classified as having **intellectual disability**, and those with IQs above 130 are classified as **gifted**. But what determines whether a person's score is low, high, or somewhere in the middle? Is intelligence mainly an inherited trait, or is it shaped mainly by the environment?

**GENETICS AND ENVIRONMENT.** Social scientists increasingly regard the old nature–nurture debates as sterile and obsolete (see Chapter 2). Nearly all accept that both genetics and environment are involved in development, including the development of intelligence. A variety of new findings presented in the past 30 years provide insights into how genetics and environments interact and how both contribute to intelligence. Most of these studies use the natural experiments of adoption studies or twin studies in order to avoid the problem of passive genotype → environment effects. When parents provide both genetics and environment, as they do in most families, it is very difficult to judge the relative contribution of each. Adoption and twin studies help unravel that tangle.

One important conclusion from adoption and twin studies is that the more two people in a family are alike genetically, the higher the correlation in their IQs (Brant et al., 2009). As

**Figure 11.6** Bell Curve for Intelligence

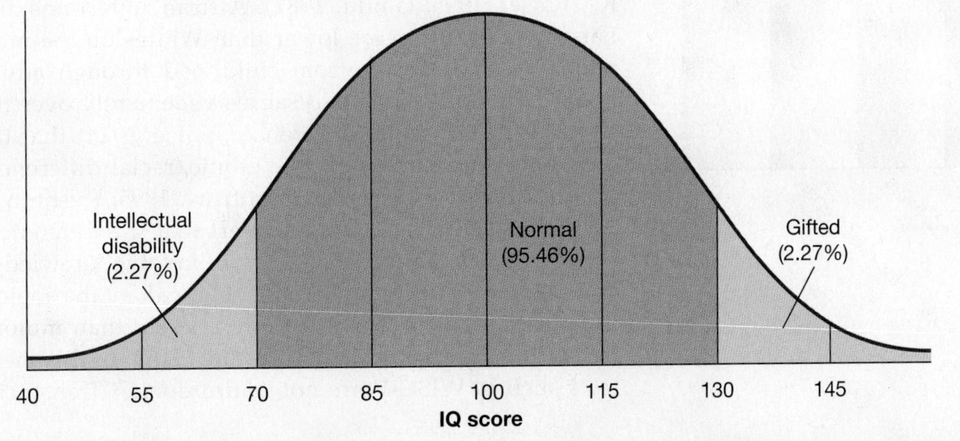


**age norms**
technique for developing a psychological test in which a typical score for each age is established by testing a large random sample of people from a variety of geographical areas and social class backgrounds

**test-retest reliability**
type of reliability that examines whether or not persons' scores on one occasion are similar to their scores on another occasion

**predictive validity**
in longitudinal research, the ability of a variable at Time 1 to predict the outcome of a variable at Time 2

**fluid intelligence**
mental abilities that involve speed of analyzing, processing, and reacting to information

**crystallized intelligence**
accumulated knowledge and enhanced judgment based on experience

**normal distribution**
typical distribution of characteristics of a population, resembling a bell curve in which most cases fall near the middle and the proportions decrease at the low and high extremes

**intellectual disability**
level of cognitive abilities of persons who score below 70 on IQ tests

**gifted**
level of cognitive abilities of persons who score above 130 on IQ tests

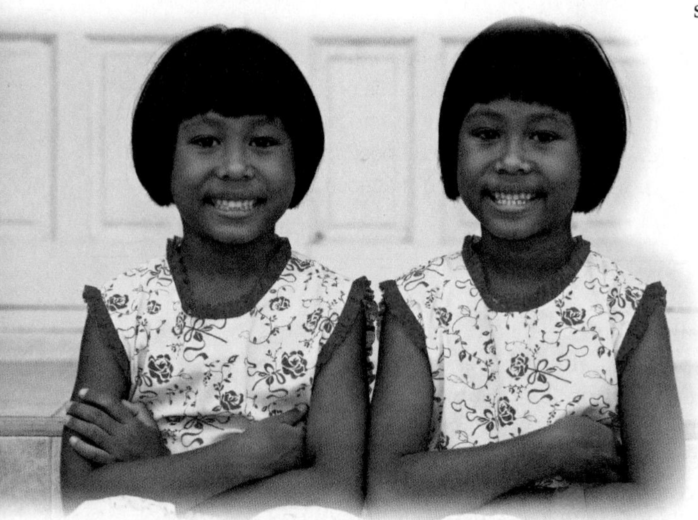

Identical twins have similar IQs, even when reared apart. Here, 6-year-old MZ twin sisters in Thailand smile for the camera.

shown in Figure 11.7, adopted siblings, who have none of their genotype in common, have a relatively low correlation for IQ, about 0.24. The environmental influence is apparent—ordinarily, the correlation between two genetically unrelated children would be zero—but limited. Parents and their biological children, who share half of their genotype in common, are correlated for IQ at about 0.40, slightly higher if they live together than if they live apart. The correlation for biological siblings is higher, about 0.50, and slightly higher still for DZ twins. Biological siblings and DZ twins share the same proportion of their genotype in common as parents and biological children do (again, about half), so the greater IQ similarity in DZ twins must be due to greater environmental similarity, from the womb onward. The highest IQ correlation of all, about 0.85, is among MZ twins, who have exactly the same genotype. Even when they are adopted by separate families and raised apart, the correlation in IQ scores of MZ twins is about 0.75 (Brant et al., 2009).

The results of these studies leave little doubt that genetics contribute strongly to IQ scores. It is especially striking that the correlation in IQ is much lower for adopted siblings, who have grown up in the same family and neighborhood and attended the same schools, than it is for MZ twins who have been raised separately and have never even known each other.

However, other adoption studies show that both environment and genetics have a strong influence on intelligence. In one study, researchers recruited a sample of adopted children whose biological mothers were at two extremes, either IQ under 95 or above 120 (remember, 100 is the median population IQ) (Loehlin et al., 1997). All the children had been adopted at birth by parents who were above average in education and income. When tested in middle childhood, children in both groups were above average in IQ. If we can assume that the high-education, high-income adoptive parents provided a healthy, stable, stimulating environment, this shows a strong influence of the environment for the children whose biological mothers all had IQs less than 95. On average they were above 100, due to the advantages of an environment provided by high-education, high-income parents. However, the children whose biological mothers had IQs above 120 were significantly higher in IQ than the children whose biological mothers had IQs less than 95, even though children in both groups had an advantaged environment, which showed the substantial influence of genetics.

**transracial adoption**
the adoption of children of one race by parents of a different race

**Figure 11.7** IQ and Genetics

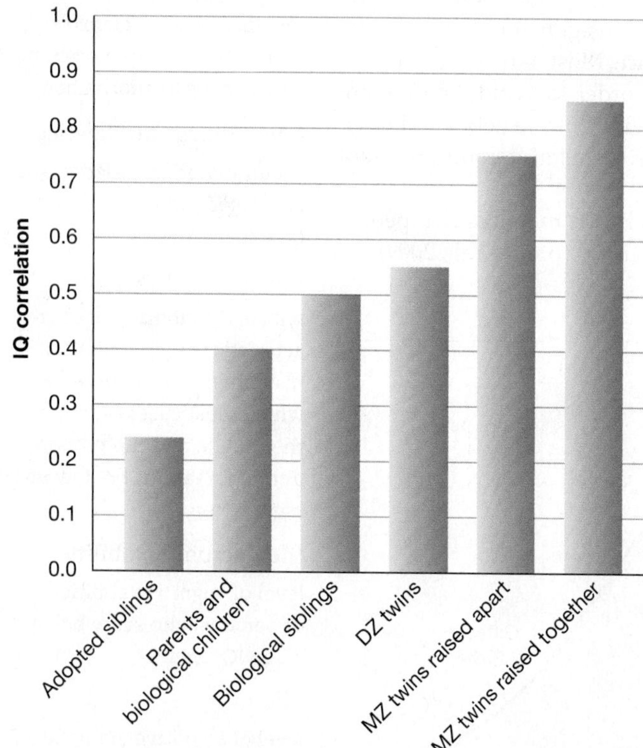


SOURCE: Data from Brant et al. (2009).

A particular line of adoption research concerns **transracial adoption**, specifically involving Black children who have been adopted by White parents (Burrow & Finley, 2004). One of the most bitter controversies surrounding intelligence tests concerns racial differences in IQ (Fraser, 1995; Gould, 1981). African Americans and Latinos generally score lower than Whites on the most widely used IQ tests, from childhood through adulthood. However, scholars disagree vehemently over the source of these group differences. Some assert that the differences are due to genetic ethnic/racial differences in intelligence (Herrnstein & Murray, 1995; Rushton & Arthur Jensen, 2005). Others assert that the differences simply reflect the fact that IQ tests involve knowledge and a style of communication obtained in the majority culture, which Whites are more likely than minorities to have grown up in (Anderson, 2007). In this view, tests such as WISC-V are not "culture-fair." Transracial adoption represents an extraordinary natural experiment, in that it involves raising African American children in the White-dominated majority culture. And what do these studies find? In general, they indicate that when Black children are raised in adoptive White families, their IQs are as high or higher than the average IQ for Whites (Weinberg et al., 1992). Their IQ scores decline somewhat in adolescence but nevertheless remain relatively high (Burrow & Finley, 2004). This indicates that overall differences in IQ between Whites and African Americans are due to cultural and social class differences rather than genetics.

Taken together, the adoption and twin IQ studies show that both genetics and environment contribute to the development of individual differences in intelligence. Specifically, every child has a genetically based *reaction range* for intelligence, meaning a range of possible developmental paths. With a healthy, stimulating environment, children reach the top of their reaction range for intelligence; with a poor, unhealthy, or chaotic environment, children are likely to develop a level of intelligence toward the bottom of the reaction range. There is both an upper and a lower limit to the reaction range. Even with an optimal environment, children with relatively low intellectual abilities are unlikely to develop superior intelligence; even with a subnormal environment, children with relatively high intellectual abilities are unlikely to end up well below average in IQ.

Recent research has revealed new insights into the intricate relations between genetics and environment in the development of intelligence. Specifically, research indicates that the influence of the environment on IQ is stronger for poor children than for children of affluent families (Nesbitt, 2009; Turkheimer et al., 2009). The less stimulating the environment, the less genetics influence IQ, because children's potentials are suppressed in an unstimulating environment. In contrast, an affluent environment generally allows children to receive the cognitive stimulation necessary to reach the top of their reaction range for IQ.

**FLYNN EFFECT.** One other highly important finding that attests to the importance of environmental influences on intelligence is that the median IQ score in Western countries rose dramatically in the course of the 20th century, a phenomenon known as the **Flynn effect**, named for the scholar who first noted it, James Flynn (1999, 2012). From 1932 to 1997 the median IQ score among children in the United States rose by 20 points (Howard, 2001). This is a huge difference. It means that a child whose IQ was average in 1932 would be way below average by today's standard. It means that half of children today would have scored at least 120 by 1932 scoring, placing them in the "superior intelligence" range, and about one-fourth of children today would be considered by 1932 standards to have "very superior intelligence"—a classification actually held by only 3% of children in 1932 (Horton, 2001). As shown in Figure 11.8, similar results have been found in other countries as well (Flynn, 1999, 2012).

**Flynn effect**

steep rise in the median IQ score in Western countries during the 20th century, named after James Flynn, who first identified it

What explains the Flynn effect? The root causes must be environmental, rather than genetic; the genes of the human population could not have changed so dramatically in such a short time. But what about the environment improved so much in the course of the 20th century that would explain such a dramatic rise in median IQ scores? Several possibilities have been identified (Rodgers & Wanstrom, 2007; Trahan et al., 2014). Prenatal care is better now than in the early 20th century, and better prenatal care leads to better intellectual development, including higher IQs. Families are generally smaller now than in the early 20th century, and in general the fewer children in a family, the higher their IQs. Far more children attend preschool now than was true in 1932, and preschool enhances young children's intellectual development. It has even been suggested that the invention of television may be one of the sources of the Flynn effect. Although television and other media are often blamed for societal ills, there is good evidence that watching educational television enhances young children's intellectual development (Scantlin, 2007).

**Figure 11.8** Flynn Effect

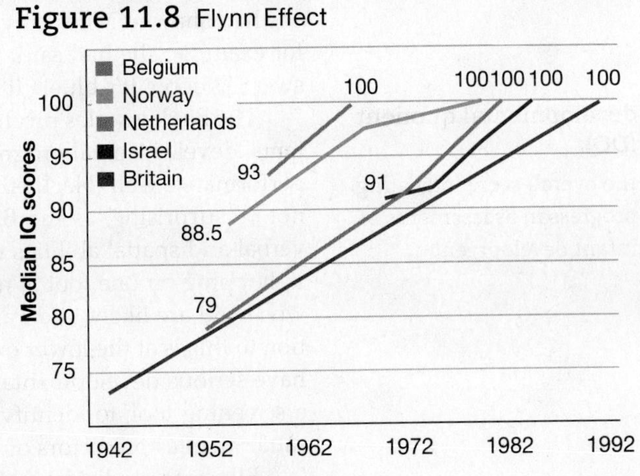


SOURCE: Based on Flynn (1999).

**Figure 11.9** Inverse Relation Between IQ and Disease

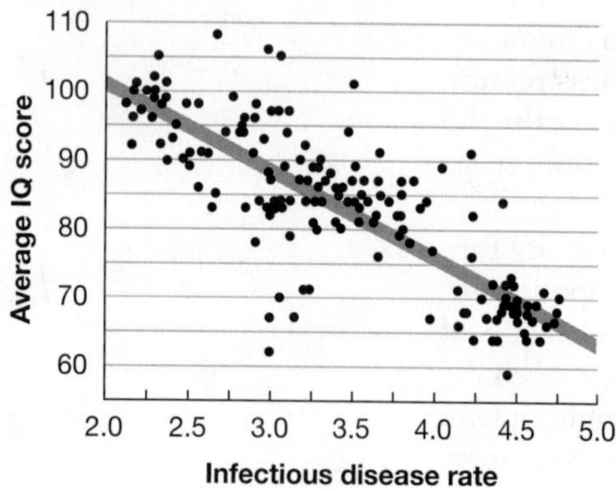


SOURCE: Based on Eppig et al. (2010).

One persuasive explanation recently proposed is the decline of infectious diseases (Eppig et al., 2010). Christopher Eppig and his colleagues note that the brain requires a great deal of the body's physical energy—87% in newborns, nearly half in 5-year-olds, and 25% in adults. Infectious diseases compete for this energy by activating the body's immune system and interfering with the body's processing of food during years when the brain is growing and developing rapidly. If this explanation is true, there should be an inverse relationship between IQ and infectious disease rates. As shown in Figure 11.9, this pattern was evident in the researchers' analysis of data from 113 countries. The higher a country's infectious disease burden, the lower the country's median IQ. Thus, the Flynn effect may well be influenced by the elimination of major infectious diseases in developed countries. A Flynn effect of the future may be awaiting developing countries as they reduce and eliminate infectious diseases.

## Assessing Cognitive Ability in Infants

**LO 11.4.3 Describe the Bayley Scales of Infant Development (BSID-III) for measuring infant development, and explain how habituation assessments are used to predict later intelligence.**

Scales for assessing cognitive ability and development in infants have been developed, in part with the goal of predicting later intelligence. Nancy Bayley produced the **Bayley Scales of Infant Development (BSID-III)**, now in their third edition (Bayley, 2005). The BSID-III can assess development from age 3 months to age 3½ years. There are three main scales:

**Bayley Scales of Infant Development**
assessment of infant development from age 3 months to 3½ years

1. **Cognitive Scale.** This scale measures mental abilities such as attention and exploration. For example, at 6 months it assesses whether the baby looks at pictures in a book; at 23–25 months it assesses whether a child can match similar pictures.
2. **Language Scale.** This scale measures use and understanding of language. For example, at 17–19 months it assesses whether the child can identify objects in a picture, and at 38–42 months it assesses whether the child can name four colors.
3. **Motor Scale.** This scale measures fine and gross motor abilities, such as sitting alone for 30 seconds at 6 months, or hopping twice on one foot at 38–42 months.

Testing young children is not always straightforward. When our son was 3 years old, his preschool teacher tested him by asking him to name the colors of differently colored crayons. She reported with some concern that Miles consistently had mixed up his colors, stating that the red crayon was "blue," the green crayon was "yellow," and so on. As his parents, we were quite certain that he knew the names for these colors, and we suggested that he might be playing a game. The next day, when we came to pick up Miles, his teacher reported that she had showed Miles crayons that she consistently mislabeled. Holding up a blue crayon, for example, she had said: "see, this one is yellow, isn't it?" Now, Miles gave the right answer: "Noooo! It's blue!" It seems they were finally taking the same test.

**developmental quotient (DQ)**
the overall score indicating progress in assessments of infant development

The Bayley scales produce a **developmental quotient (DQ)** as an overall measure of infants' developmental progress. However, the Bayley scales do not predict later IQ or school performance well (Hack et al., 2005). If you look closely at the examples above, this should not be surprising, as the Bayley scales measure quite different kinds of abilities than the verbal and spatial abilities that later IQ tests measure and school work requires. (Let's face it, hopping on one foot is not likely to be predictive of school performance or any kind of work you are likely to do as an adult, unless you become a ballet dancer.) The only exception to this is at the lower extreme. An infant who scores very low on the Bayley scales may have serious developmental problems. Consequently, the Bayley scales are used mainly as a screening tool, to identify infants with serious problems in need of immediate attention, rather than as predictors of later development for children within the normal range.

Efforts to predict later intelligence using information-processing approaches have shown greater promise. The focus of these approaches has been on habituation. Infants vary in how long it takes them to habituate to a new stimulus, such as a sight or a sound. Some are "short-lookers" who habituate quickly, others are "long-lookers" who take more time and more presentations of the stimulus before they habituate. The shorter the habituation time, the more efficient the infant's information-processing abilities. They look for a shorter length of time because it takes them less time to take in and process information about the stimulus.

Longitudinal studies have found that short-lookers in infancy tend to have higher IQ scores later in development than long-lookers do (Cuevas & Bell, 2014; Kavšek, 2004; Rose et al., 2005). In one study, short-lookers in infancy had higher IQs and higher educational achievement when they were followed up 20 years later, in emerging adulthood (Fagan et al., 2007). Habituation assessments in infancy are also useful for identifying infants who have developmental problems (Kavšek & Bornstein, 2010). Furthermore, habituation assessments tend to be more reliable than assessments of DQ using the Bayley scales, that is, they are more likely to be consistent when measured across more than one occasion (Cuevas & Bell, 2014; Kavšek, 2004). The most recent version of the Bayley scales now includes a measure of habituation (Bayley, 2005), which may improve reliability and predictive validity above previous versions of the scale.

Is musical ability a type of intelligence?

## Alternative Views of Intelligence

**LO 11.4.4 Compare Gardner's and Sternberg's approaches to conceptualizing intelligence.**

IQ testing has dominated research on children's intellectual development for about a century. However, in recent decades, alternative theories of intelligence have been proposed. These theories have sought to present a conception of intelligence that is much broader than the traditional one. Two of the most influential alternative theories of intelligence have been presented by Howard Gardner and Robert Sternberg.

As Table 11.2 shows, Gardner's (1983, 2004) **theory of multiple intelligences** includes eight types of intelligence. In Gardner's view, intelligence tests only evaluate two of them: *linguistic* and *logical–mathematical* intelligences. The other intelligences are *spatial* (the ability to think three-dimensionally); *musical; bodily–kinesthetic* (the kind that athletes and dancers excel in); *naturalist* (ability for understanding natural phenomena); *interpersonal* (ability for understanding and interacting with others); and *intrapersonal* (self-understanding). As evidence for the existence of these different types of intelligence, Gardner argues that each involves distinct cognitive skills, that each can be destroyed by damage to a particular part of the brain, and that each appears in extremes in geniuses as well as in *idiots savant* (the French term for people who are low in general intelligence but possess an extraordinary ability in one specialized area).

**theory of multiple intelligences**
Gardner's theory that there are eight separate types of intelligence

Gardner argues that schools should give more attention to the development of all eight kinds of intelligence and design programs that would be tailored to each child's individual profile of intelligences. He has proposed methods for assessing different

**Table 11.2** Gardner's Theory of Multiple Intelligences

| Type of Intelligence | Description |
|---|---|
| Linguistic | Ability to use language |
| Musical | Ability to compose and/or perform music |
| Logical/mathematical | Ability to think logically and to solve mathematical problems |
| Spatial | Ability to understand how objects are oriented in space |
| Bodily-kinesthetic | Speed, agility, and gross motor control |
| Interpersonal | Sensitivity to others and understanding motivation of others |
| Intrapersonal | Understanding of one's emotions and how they guide actions |
| Naturalist | Ability to recognize the patterns found in nature |

intelligences, such as measuring musical intelligence by having people attempt to sing a song, play an instrument, or orchestrate a melody (Gardner, 1999, 2011). However, thus far, neither Gardner nor anyone else has developed reliable and valid methods for analyzing the intelligences he proposes. Gardner (2011) is continuing to develop his theory and methods to assess it.

**triarchic theory of intelligence**
Sternberg's theory that there are three distinct but related forms of intelligence

Sternberg's (1983, 1988, 2002, 2003, 2005) **triarchic theory of intelligence** includes three distinct but related forms of intelligence. *Analytical intelligence* is Sternberg's term for the kind of intelligence that IQ tests measure, which involves acquiring, storing, analyzing, and retrieving information. *Creative intelligence* involves the ability to combine information in original ways to produce new insights, ideas, and problem-solving strategies. *Practical intelligence* is the ability to apply information to the kinds of problems faced in everyday life, including the capacity to evaluate social situations. Sternberg has conducted extensive research to develop tests of intelligence that measure the three types of intelligence he proposes. These tests involve solving problems, applying knowledge, and developing creative strategies. Sternberg's research on Americans has demonstrated that each person has a different profile on the three intelligences that can be assessed (Sternberg, 2005, 2007). He proposes that the three components are universal and contribute to intelligent performance in all cultures (Sternberg, 2005), but so far the theory has been tested little outside the United States. Neither Sternberg's nor Gardner's tests are widely used among psychologists, in part because they take longer to administer and score than standard IQ tests do.

The underlying issue in judging alternative theories of intelligence is the question of how intelligence should be defined. If intelligence is defined as the mental abilities required to succeed in school, the traditional approach to conceptualizing and measuring intelligence is generally successful. However, if one wishes to define intelligence more broadly, as the entire range of human mental abilities, the traditional approach may be seen as too narrow, and an approach such as Gardner's or Sternberg's may be preferred.

## Cultural Views of Intelligence

**LO 11.4.5 Describe cultural variations on conceptions of intelligence.**

Although the body of research showing a relation between IQ and educational achievement is large, nearly all of it is concentrated in developed countries, and some scholars have asserted that people in non-Western cultures may have quite different ideas about what constitutes intelligence. Foremost among the scholars promoting a broader, more culturally based view of intelligence is Robert Sternberg (Sternberg, 2004, 2007, 2010; Sternberg & Grigorenko, 2004). For a discussion of his research across cultures, watch the video *Robert Sternberg on Cultural Influences on Intelligence.*

Analyses of cultural views of intelligence find a great deal of variety (Hein et al., 2015). Among Chinese adults, for example, intelligence includes features such as humility, self-knowledge, and freedom from conventional standards of judgment (Sternberg & Grigorenko, 2004). Studies in various African cultures show a common theme where intelligence includes skills that help promote group harmony and social responsibilities. For example, adults in Zambia emphasize cooperativeness and obedience as qualities of intelligence (Serpell, 2011). In Kenya, adults include responsible participation in family and social life as important aspects of intelligence (Super & Harkness, 1993). In Zimbabwe, the word for intelligence, *ngware*, literally means to be prudent and cautious, especially in social relations (Sternberg & Grigorenko, 2004). In both Asian and African cultures, a common theme in conceptions of intelligence is that it includes social elements as well as cognitive elements such as knowledge (Sternberg, 2007).

**Watch** ROBERT STERNBERG ON CULTURAL INFLUENCES ON INTELLIGENCE

Sternberg (2004, 2010) has also argued that intelligence includes practical aspects, applied to the problems and challenges of everyday life. One study led by Elena Grigorenko demonstrated this among the Yup'ik, a Native Alaskan culture whose daily life is based mainly on hunting and fishing. Grigorenko and colleagues (2004) began by interviewing adults and elders in Yup'ik culture about the knowledge required for performance in the situations encountered in everyday life. From these interviews, the researchers developed a test of Yup'ik practical intelligence, covering topics such as how to hunt and fish, where to find edible berries, and knowledge of the weather. Adolescents in the study were given this test of practical intelligence as well as standard IQ tests. The researchers also interviewed adolescents, adults, and elders about the qualities most valued among the Yup'ik people, then asked the adults and elders to rate the adolescents on these qualities.

The results indicated that there was a correlation between the adolescents' performance on the test of practical intelligence and the likelihood that they would be nominated by the adults and elders for possessing the valued Yup'ik qualities. Furthermore, performance on the practical intelligence test was more likely than performance on the standard IQ test to predict which adolescents would be nominated. The researchers interpreted this finding as demonstrating that practical intelligence is a key component of intelligence that is culture-specific and is not adequately assessed by standard IQ tests.

According to Grigorenko and Sternberg, knowledge of hunting and fishing is a component of intelligence in some cultures. Here, a Yup'ik hunter takes aim at a whale.

**Critical Thinking Question:** If Binet (see also Chapter 1) had been commissioned by Yup'ik elders to develop a test for identifying children who would have difficulty being successful in their community, to what extent would you expect items and topics to be similar and different from his test for the French government?

## SUMMARY: Intelligence Tests and School Readiness

**LO 11.4.1 Describe the main features of the Wechsler Intelligence Scale for Children (WISC-V).**

The WISC-V for children ages 6 to 16 assesses cognitive ability on five indexes: Verbal Comprehension, Visual Spatial, Fluid Reasoning, Processing Speed, and Working Memory. The results provide a Full Scale Intelligence Quotient, which is calculated relative to the performance of other people of the same age, with 100 as the median score.

**LO 11.4.2 Explain the influence of both genetics and the environment on IQ scores, including the Flynn effect.**

Studies with twins and adopted children show that both genetics and environment contribute to intelligence. Every child has a genetically based reaction range for intelligence. The healthier and more stimulating a child's environment, the more likely that the child will reach the top of the reaction range. The Flynn effect describes the fact that average IQ scores have risen substantially over the 20th century in developed countries, and demonstrates the impact of the environment on intelligence.

**LO 11.4.3 Describe the Bayley Scales of Infant Development (BSID-III) for measuring infant development, and explain how habituation assessments are used to predict later intelligence.**

The BSID-III is widely used to measure infants' development, but scores do not predict later cognitive development except for infants with serious deficits. Efforts to predict later intelligence using information-processing approaches have shown greater promise. These assessments measure habituation by distinguishing between "short-lookers" and "long-lookers," with short-lookers higher in later intelligence.

**LO 11.4.4 Compare Gardner's and Sternberg's approaches to conceptualizing intelligence.**

Gardner's theory of multiple intelligences includes eight types of intelligence (e.g., interpersonal, musical, kinesthetic). Sternberg's triarchic theory of intelligence includes three forms of intelligence: analytical, creative, and practical. Both theories represent efforts at defining intelligence more broadly than traditional intelligence tests.

**LO 11.4.5 Describe cultural variations on conceptions of intelligence.**

Analyses of cultural views of intelligence find a great deal of variety. For example, some cultures included self-knowledge (China), cooperativeness and obedience (Zambia), prudence (Zimbabwe), and practical knowledge (Yup'ik).

# 11.5 Work

We end this chapter by focusing on work. In some parts of the world, children and adolescents receive very little schooling because their families need for them to work to contribute to the family income. With globalization, on the one hand, children's labor is exploited. On the other, there is also more international pressure to end child labor and to lengthen the amount of schooling that children and adolescents complete. In developed countries, a lengthening of schooling has also taken place. In recent times, tertiary education has become important to finding stable and meaningful employment.

## Child Labor

**LO 11.5.1 Describe the kinds of work children do in middle childhood, and explain why work patterns differ between developed and developing countries.**

Across cultures, by the time children reach 6 or 7 years of age, they are regarded as more capable than they were in early childhood. This is why primary school often starts at this age, and it is also why children are often given important work responsibilities starting at this age (Gaskins, 2015; Rogoff, 2003). In developing countries, the work that children do in middle childhood is a serious and sometimes perilous contribution to the family. In most developed countries, it is illegal to employ children in middle childhood (United Nations Development Programme [UNDP], 2010). However, in a large proportion of the world, middle childhood is the time when productive work begins.

Children in developing countries often work long hours in poor conditions by middle childhood. Here, a young boy works in a factory in Bangladesh.

Children who do not attend school are usually working, often for their families on a farm or family business, but sometimes in industrial settings. With the globalization of the world economy, many large companies have moved much of their manufacturing operations to developing countries, where labor costs are cheaper. Cheapest of all is the labor of children. Before middle childhood, children are too immature and lacking in self-regulation to be useful in manufacturing. Their gross and fine motor skills are limited, their attention wanders too much, and they are too erratic in their behavior and their emotions. However, by age 6 or 7, children have the motor skills, the cognitive skills, and the emotional and behavioral self-regulation to be excellent workers at many jobs.

The International Labor Organization (ILO) has estimated that about 73 million children ages 5–11 are employed worldwide—about 9% of the total population of children in that age group—and 95% of working children are in developing countries (International Labor Organization [ILO], 2013). A substantial proportion of children work in Asia, Latin America, and the Middle East/North Africa, but the greatest number of child workers is found in sub-Saharan Africa. Agricultural work is the most common form of child employment, usually on commercial farms or plantations, often working alongside parents but for only one-third to one-half the pay (ILO, 2013). Children can quickly master the skills needed to plant, tend, and harvest agricultural products.

**Watch** A BOY IN CONGO SELLS CAKES

In addition, many children in these countries work in factories and shops where they perform labor such as weaving carpets, sewing clothes, gluing shoes, curing leather, and polishing gems. The working conditions are often miserable—crowded garment factories where the doors are locked and children (and adults) work 14-hour shifts; small, poorly lit huts where they sit at a loom weaving carpets for hours on end; glass factories where the temperatures are unbearably hot and children carry rods of molten glass from one station to another (ILO, 2004). Other children work in cities in a wide variety of jobs, including in domestic service, at grocery shops, in tea stalls, and delivering messages and packages. To gain a sense of one child's experience with such work, watch the video *A Boy in Congo Sells Cakes.*

If children's work is so often difficult and dangerous, why do parents allow their children to work, and why do governments not outlaw child labor? For parents, the simple answer is that they need the money. Billions of people worldwide are very poor (see Chapter 1). Poor families in developing countries often depend on children's contributions to the family income for basic necessities such as food and clothing. As for governments, nearly all countries do have laws prohibiting child labor, but some developing countries do not enforce them, because of bribes from the companies employing the children or because they do not wish to incur the wrath of parents who need their children's income (Chaudary & Sharma, 2007).

Although the exploitation of children's labor in developing countries is widespread and often harsh, there are signs of positive change. According to the International Labor Organization, the number of child laborers ages 5–11 is rapidly declining (ILO, 2013). This decline has taken place because the issue of child and adolescent labor has received increased attention from the world media, governments, and international organizations such as the ILO and the United Nations Children's Fund (UNICEF). Furthermore, legislative action has been taken in many developing countries to raise the number of years children are legally required to attend school and to enforce the often ignored laws against employing children younger than their mid-teens. Amid such signs of progress, it remains the case that millions of children work in unhealthy conditions all around the world (ILO, 2013).

## Adolescent Work

**LO 11.5.2 Summarize the typical forms of adolescent work in developing countries and developed countries, and name the features of apprenticeships in Europe.**

Adolescents in developing countries often do the same types of difficult, dangerous, and poorly paid work as younger children do, but one type of work that usually begins in adolescence is prostitution. Estimates of the number of adolescent sex workers in developing countries vary, but it is widely agreed that adolescent prostitution is a pervasive problem, especially in Asia, particularly Thailand (Basu & Chau, 2007; ILO, 2002). Of course, adolescent sex workers exist in developed countries as well, but the problem is much more widespread in developing countries. Many of these adolescent girls are deceived or forced into **commercial sexual exploitation** (Jiminez et al., 2015). Some are kidnapped and taken to a separate country.

**commercial sexual exploitation**
forced sex work by children and adolescents

A large proportion of the customers in Asian brothels are Western tourists, leading the United States and several European countries to pass laws permitting prosecution of their citizens for sexually exploiting young adolescents in other countries.

Estimates of the number of adolescent sex workers in developing countries vary, but it is widely agreed that adolescent prostitution is a pervasive problem, especially in Asia.

For adolescents in developed countries, part-time work is common, but it is seldom dangerous or difficult. About 80% of adolescents in the United States and Canada hold at least one part-time job by the end of high school (Staff et al., 2014). Very little of the money they earn goes to their family's living expenses or saving for their future education, although adolescents in ethnic minority groups are more likely to contribute to their families (Fuligni, 2011). For the most part, the money goes toward purchases for themselves, here and now: clothes, music, car payments and gas, concert tickets, movies, eating out—and alcohol, cigarettes, and other drugs (Mortimer, 2013).

The work done by adolescents in developed countries does little to prepare them for the kind of work they are likely to do as adults. For example, the majority of jobs held by American and Canadian adolescents in high school involve restaurant work or retail sales (Mortimer, 2013; Staff et al., 2004). Consequently, few adolescents see their high school jobs as the basis for a future career, although they do see more general benefits such as learning responsibility, how to manage money, social skills, and how to organize their time (Mortimer, 2013; Mortimer et al., 2008).

While adolescents may learn some general skills from their part-time work, this has to be balanced against the effects of working too many hours. Beyond 10 hours a week, the more adolescents work, the lower their grades, the less time they spend on homework, the more they cut class, the more they cheat on their schoolwork, the less committed they are to school, and the lower their educational aspirations (Marsh & Kleitman, 2005; Staff et al., 2015). Similarly, reports of psychological symptoms jump sharply for adolescents working more than 10 hours a week and continue to rise among adolescents working 20 hours a week or more (Mortimer, 2013; Staff et al., 2015). Canadian research reports that when adolescents take on demanding jobs, they reduce their sleep by an hour per night and eliminate nearly all sports activities (Sears et al., 2007). Adolescents who work are also more likely to use alcohol, cigarettes, and other drugs, especially if they work more than 10 hours a week (Bachman et al., 2003; Longest & Shanahan, 2007; Wu et al., 2003). A national study of adolescents in Finland also found numerous negative effects of working more than 20 hours a week (Kuouvonen & Kivivuori, 2001).

**apprenticeship**

an arrangement, common in Europe, in which an adolescent "novice" serves under contract to a "master" who has substantial experience in a profession, and through working under the master, learns the skills required to enter the profession

Although most employment in adolescence in the United States and Canada has little relation to later careers, many European countries have a long tradition of apprenticeships that provides excellent preparation for adult occupations. In an **apprenticeship**, an adolescent "novice" serves under contract to a "master" who has substantial experience in a profession, and through working under the master the novice learns the skills required (Hamilton & Hamilton, 2006; Newman & Winston, 2016; Vazsonyi & Snider, 2008). Although apprenticeships originally began centuries ago in craft professions such as carpentry and blacksmithing, today they are undertaken to prepare for a wide range of professions, from auto mechanics and carpenters to police officers, computer technicians, and childcare workers (Fuller et al., 2005). Apprenticeships are especially common in central and northern Europe. For example, over 60% of adolescents in Germany and Switzerland participate in apprenticeships (Dolphin & Lanning, 2011).

Apprenticeships are common in Europe. These adolescents are apprenticing at a German power plant company.

Apprenticeship programs require close coordination between schools and employers, so that what adolescents learn at school will complement and reinforce what is being learned in their apprenticeship. This means

that schools consult employers with respect to the skills required in the workplace, and employers make opportunities available for adolescent apprentices. In Europe, the employers see this as worth their trouble because apprenticeships provide them with a reliable supply of well-qualified entry-level employees (Dustmann & Schoenberg, 2008).

**Watch** LOOKING FOR IDENTITY-BASED WORK

## Making the Transition to Adult Work

**LO 11.5.3 Describe the transition from school to full-time work, and explain who among emerging adults are most impacted by unemployment.**

As we have seen, adolescents in developed countries often work part time, but few of them see their part-time jobs as the beginning of the kind of work they expect to do as adults. Most emerging adults, in contrast, are looking for a job that will turn into a career—something that will not only bring in a paycheck, but also provide personal fulfillment (Arnett, 2015; Taylor, 2005). Work in emerging adulthood focuses on identity questions: What do I really want to *do*? What am I best at? What do I enjoy the most? How do my abilities and desires fit in with the kinds of opportunities that are available to me? In asking themselves what kind of work they want to do, emerging adults are also asking themselves what kind of person they are. In the course of emerging adulthood, as they try out various jobs, emerging adults begin to answer their identity questions, and they develop a better sense of what work suits them best. Watch the video *Looking for Identity-Based Work* to hear how emerging adults describe their work aspirations.

For most American emerging adults, the road to a stable, long-term job is long, with many brief, low-paying, dreary jobs along the way. *Exploration* would be a bit too lofty a word to describe their work history during their late teens and early 20s. Often it is not nearly as systematic, organized, and focused as "exploration" implies. *Meandering* might be a more accurate word, or maybe *drifting* or even *floundering* (Hamilton & Hamilton, 2006).

Although at least half of young people in developed countries now obtain tertiary education in some form, a substantial proportion of emerging adults enter the workplace after secondary school. What are the work prospects like for these emerging adults, and how successfully are they able to make the transition from school to the workplace? For the most part, they struggle to find work that pays enough to live on, much less the identity-based work that is the ideal for many emerging adults. Because the economy in developed countries has shifted from manufacturing to information, technology, and services over the past half-century, tertiary education is more important than ever in obtaining jobs that pay well. Those who lack the training, knowledge, and credentials conferred by tertiary education are at a great disadvantage in the modern economy. Their rates of unemployment are about three times as high as for people who have obtained a college degree (OECD, 2014).

**unemployment**
work status of persons who are not in school, are not working, and are looking for a job

In both Europe and the United States, the overall unemployment rate for emerging adults is consistently at least *twice as high* as for adults beyond age 25 (OECD, 2014). **Unemployment** applies only to people who are not in school, are not working, and are looking for a job. In both Europe and the United States, unemployment has been found to be associated with higher risk for depression, especially for emerging adults who lack strong parental support (Bjarnason & Sigurdardottir, 2003; Hämäläinen et al., 2005; Mossakowski, 2009).

**Figure 11.10** Unemployment Rates Among Americans, Ages 16–24

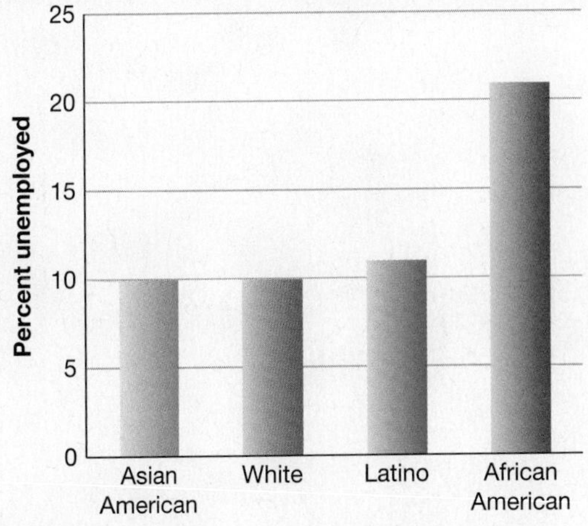


SOURCE: Based on Bureau of Labor Statistics (2016).

Figure 11.10 shows the unemployment rates for American young people in their late teens and early 20s. As you can see from the figure, unemployment is especially concentrated among Blacks and Latinos. Also, unemployment is extremely high among young people who drop out of high school. Over half of high school dropouts ages 18 to 21 are unemployed (NCES, 2014).

What explains the high rates of unemployment among minority groups? This was not always the case. Consider that in 1954, the teenage unemployment rate for Blacks was only slightly higher than for Whites—16.5% for Blacks, lower than it is today, and 12% for Whites (Quillian, 2003). To a large extent, the explanation for the change lies in shifting employment patterns in the American economy. As we have seen, young African Americans and Latinos tend to obtain less education than young Whites or Asian Americans (Hamilton & Hamilton, 2006; NCES, 2014). Without educational credentials, gaining access to jobs in the new information- and technology-based economy is difficult.

## SUMMARY: Work

**LO 11.5.1 Describe the kinds of work children do in middle childhood, and explain why work patterns differ between developed and developing countries.**

About 70 million children (5–11 years) in developing countries perform paid work by the time they reach middle childhood, in a wide variety of jobs ranging from agricultural work to factory work. Children in developing countries work more than children in developed countries in middle childhood because their contribution to the family income is needed.

**LO 11.5.2 Summarize the typical forms of adolescent work in developing countries and developed countries, and name the features of apprenticeships in Europe.**

Adolescents' work is often hard and perilous in developing countries, and in some countries adolescent girls are forced into prostitution. In developed countries, working more than 10 hours per week interferes with adolescents' school performance, sleep, and physical and psychological health. In some European countries, apprenticeships are available in which adolescents spend part of their time in school and part of their time in the workplace receiving direct occupational training.

**LO 11.5.3 Describe the transition from school to full-time work, and explain who among emerging adults are most impacted by unemployment.**

Emerging adults tend to seek identity-based work that fits their abilities and interests. In developed countries the best jobs require tertiary education, and emerging adults often struggle in the job market because they lack basic skills as well as educational credentials. Across developed countries, unemployment peaks in emerging adulthood. In the United States, unemployment is especially high among African Americans and Latinos, because they are more likely to lack educational credentials.

# Apply Your Knowledge as a Professional

The topics covered in this chapter apply to a wide variety of career professions. Watch this video to learn how they apply to a director of career services at a college.

**Journaling Question:** Think back on your teachers since the start of preschool or primary school. Think of one who was inspiring to you. Describe how and why this teacher was a source of inspiration.

Chapter 12

# Media: Uses, Risks, and Benefits

## Learning Objectives

### 12.1 Media Prevalence

12.1.1 Describe the worldwide diffusion of media.

12.1.2 Describe children's daily media consumption patterns.

### 12.2 Media and Other Contexts of Socialization

12.2.1 Specify the two distinctive socialization goals of media.

12.2.2 Describe how parents use media for socialization purposes.

12.2.3 List three overarching goals in schools' uses of media.

12.2.4 Compare government policies on children's access to media.

### 12.3 Theories of Media Influence

12.3.1 Explain how Cultivation Theory and Social Learning Theory share the same basic premise.

12.3.2 Explain the two key principles of the Uses and Gratifications Approach, and the role of identity in the Media Practice Model.

### 12.4 Uses of Media

12.4.1 Describe children's emotional uses of media.

12.4.2 Describe children's cognitive uses of media.

12.4.3 Describe children's social uses of media.

### 12.5 Risks of Media

12.5.1 Describe the risks of media in regard to obesity, tobacco use, and body image.

12.5.2 Explain the extent to which media causes aggressive behaviors and attitudes.

12.5.3 Describe how media contribute to sexual stereotypes and victimization.

### 12.6 Benefits of Media

12.6.1 Describe the cognitive benefits of educational media programs and cross-platform learning.

12.6.2 Describe the benefits to emotional development from media.

12.6.3 Describe the benefits to social development from media.

### 12.7 Globalization and Media

12.7.1 Describe how the worldwide diffusion of media impacts children's values pertaining to gender roles, individual choice in love and work, and independence.

12.7.2 Compare the concepts of bicultural and hybrid identity, and explain how each is related to global media.

CHILDREN ARE COMING OF AGE AT A TIME WHEN MEDIA ARE SPREADING ACROSS THE GLOBE AT AN INCREASING PACE. In developed countries, most children use media before their first birthday. With this early and pervasive presence in the lives of children, media have become a key context of socialization. Children continue to learn from parents, friends, and school teachers, to name a few, but they also learn a lot from media. In this chapter, we look at how socialization through media is related to socialization from other sources.

Another important question is this: what do children learn from media? Some theories emphasize the one-way view that media influence children, whereas others emphasize the interactionist view that children actively make choices about how they use media on the basis of their developmental motivations and needs. We will review these theories, as well as what research findings based on these theories show about children's motivations for media use, and the risks and benefits of media. While research has tended to focus on risks and negative effects, the balance is shifting, with more recent research addressing benefits. We end the chapter by considering the role that media play in the globalization of children. Are children from every corner of the world becoming similar through the influence of global media, or not? Do children in developing countries face particular developmental challenges reconciling a mostly Western media culture with their local cultures, or not?

**Watch** CHAPTER INTRODUCTION: MEDIA: USES, RISKS, AND BENEFITS

Video

# 12.1 Media Prevalence

In the space of a generation, media have become prevalent in people's everyday lives—reaching young and old across the globe. There are important variations in media consumption, across world regions and age groups. The prevalence of media is higher in developed than developing countries, and children are more accustomed to ever-changing media technologies than adults.

## The Worldwide Prevalence of Media

**LO 12.1.1 Describe the worldwide diffusion of media.**

A few years ago, two developmental researchers visited an Arab family in the Negev desert of Israel. A stone's throw from the family's new, marble-floored house was a subterranean cave that had been the home of their ancestors. Jaber, the father, who had grown up in the cave, invited the researchers to sit on handwoven mats on the dirt floor. As his wife and teenage son joined bearing afternoon tea and traditional bread, Jaber recounted how he had been the first family member to go to school, but left at 16 to marry and work in construction in a nearby city. Having earned more money than his father could have ever dreamed of earning from farming, Jaber returned to build his new home.

As the cooler evening came on, everyone went to the family room in the new house. The conversation continued, but a sizeable TV in the middle of the room competed for attention, broadcasting a show in Arabic, featuring turban-clad men reenacting nomadic desert life. Retreating to the corner of the room, Ahmad, the teenage son, booted up a computer and logged onto Facebook to respond to a series of blinking chat messages. By now, lost to the events of the family room, Ahmad had joined the global cyber world and was contentedly clicking away (Manago et al., 2015). In the space of a generation, Jaber's life changed radically from his father's. In the space of another generation, Ahmad is in the whirl of a different revolution—a worldwide one driven by media.

**diffusion**
the spread of products or people across space

**Diffusion** is the spread of products or people across space. Maps 12.1–3 show the number of televisions per 1,000 inhabitants across the world in 1954, 1970, and 2005. As you can see, TV has diffused across the entire globe from North America and Europe in the course of about 50 years. As of now, TV is the most prevalent form of electronic media in the world.

TV is one example of what is sometimes termed "old media." Other examples include books, magazines, radio, and movies. "New media" such as the Internet and mobile phones have appeared more recently, and their worldwide diffusion is occurring much more rapidly than TV's did. Maps 12.4–6 (next page) show the number of Internet users per 1,000 inhabitants in 1995, 2000, and 2014. What is striking is the fact that the worldwide diffusion that took half a century for TV has occurred in about two decades for the Internet. While still too early to tell for certain, it seems that 21st-century social media such as Facebook, Twitter, and YouTube are diffusing at an even faster pace (Rubenstein, 2017).

While electronic media increasingly are accessible to children across the globe, it is important to remember that a "digital divide" nonetheless exists between countries. More children in developed countries have access to media than in developing countries, and they have access to more kinds of media. The primary reason for lack of access in developing countries is lack of income. In some places, factors such as lack of electricity and mobile phone service also play a role (James, 2010; Rubenstein, 2017).

Media have become a prominent part of the everyday lives of children, especially in developed countries.

## Media Prevalence in Children's Lives

**LO 12.1.2 Describe children's daily media consumption patterns.**

As media are prevalent across cultures, they are also prevalent beginning early on in development. Surveys make clear just how common media have become in the lives of children in a developed country like the United States.

Do you remember how old you were when you first watched TV? Used a computer? Played a game on a handheld device? A national sample

**Maps 12.1–12.3** Diffusion of TV

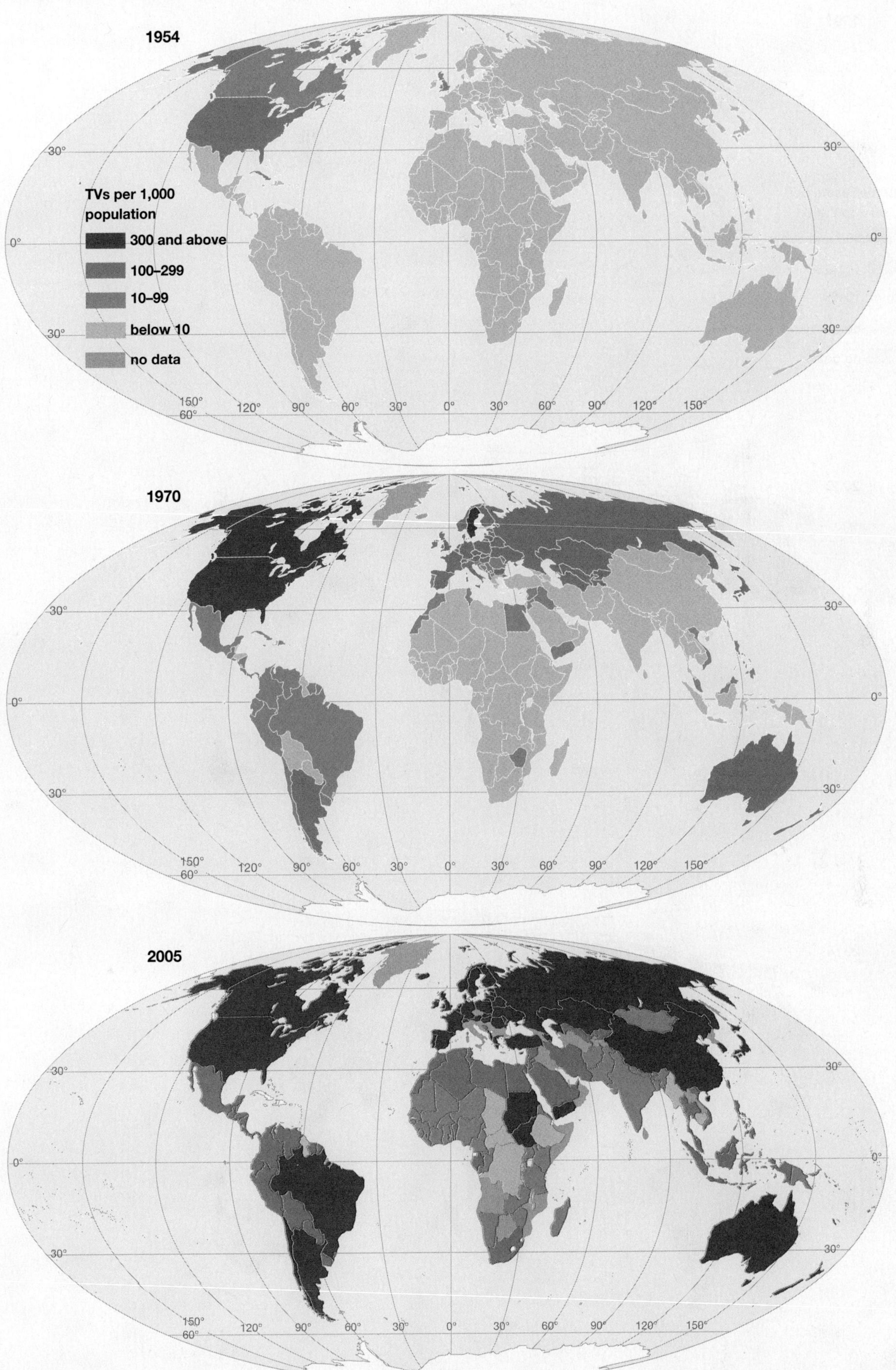

**Maps 12.4–12.6** Diffusion of the Internet

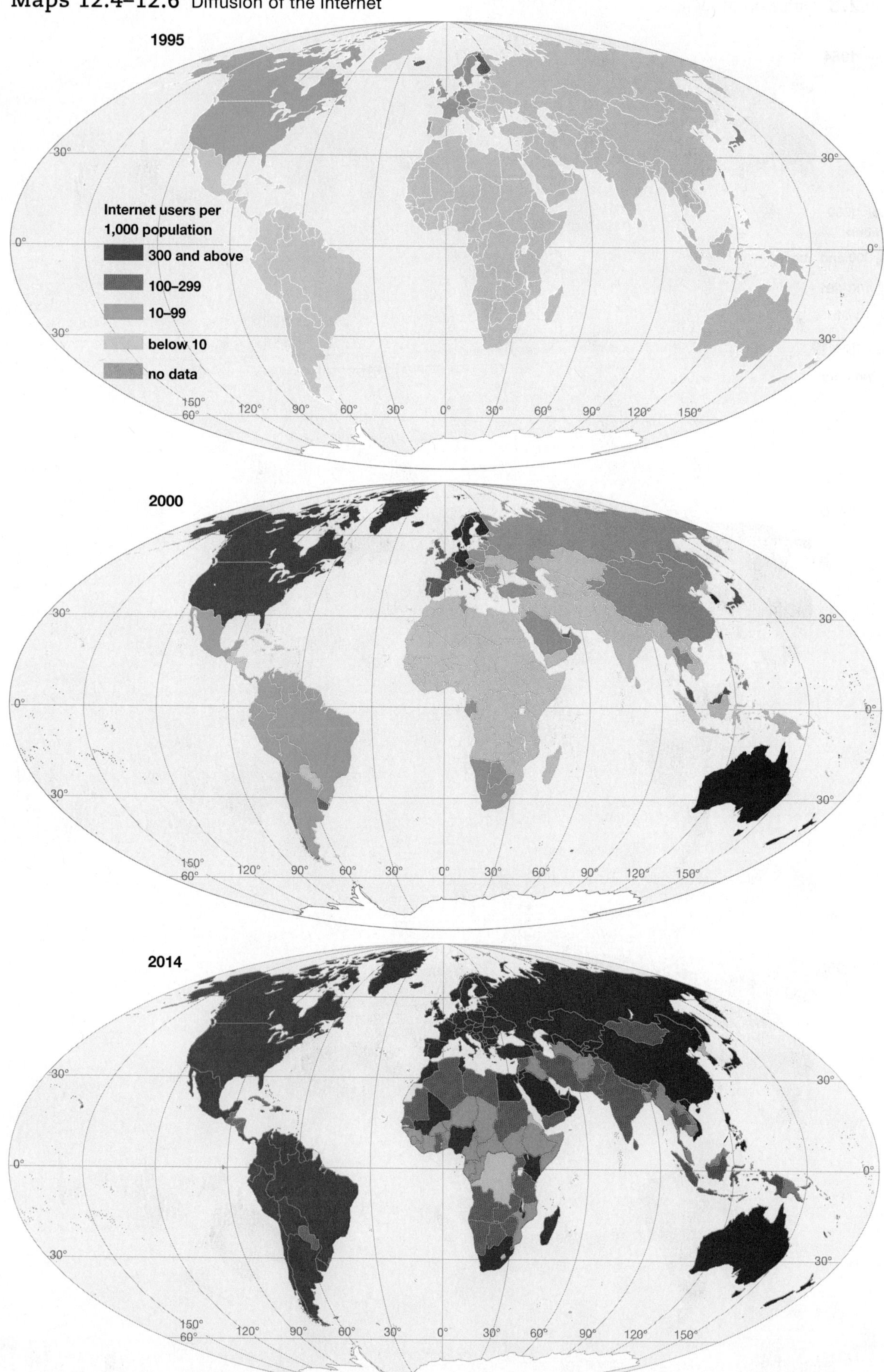

of American families were asked how old their children where when they first used different kinds of media in the household (Rideout, 2013). Results showed that:

- 89% had watched TV by 9 months.
- 85% had watched DVDs or videotapes by 11 months.
- 59% had used a computer by 3 ½ years.
- 51% had played a game on a console by 3 years and 11 months.
- 44% had played a game on a handheld device by 3 years and 11 months.

With this early an introduction to media, it is not entirely surprising to find that children spend a lot of their waking hours involved with media. Figure 12.1 shows the amount of time that American children and adolescents spend in a typical day with different kinds of media (Rideout, 2013; Rideout et al., 2010).

**media multitasking**
simultaneous use of more than one media form, such as playing an electronic game on a mobile device while watching TV

As you can see, TV is very popular at every age. American 8- to 18-year-olds spend an average of about 4 ½ hours watching TV in a typical day. As a point of comparison, European and Japanese adolescents watch TV for an average of 2 to 3 hours a day (Rey-Lopez et al., 2010; Stevenson & Zusho, 2002). But as Figure 12.1 shows, there is more to children's and adolescents' media lives than TV, and it all adds up. Eleven- to 14-year-olds, for example, have been found to pack in almost 12 hours of media exposure in a typical day. That is a lot of hours!

Part of the explanation for the frequent daily use of media is multitasking. In other words, a media activity is combined with other activities. For example, the TV might be on while eating dinner, doing homework, or socializing with friends. The TV might also be on while texting or using a computer. Also, mobile devices allow children to be connected to the Internet essentially everywhere and at all times. According to a recent survey, 92% of 13- to 17-year-olds connect to the Internet daily, and 24% say they are connected "almost constantly" (Lenhart, 2015). When people use more than one medium at a time, researchers refer to it as **media multitasking** (Rideout et al., 2010). For more information, watch the video *Media Use by Children Across Cultures*.

**Watch** MEDIA USE BY CHILDREN ACROSS CULTURES

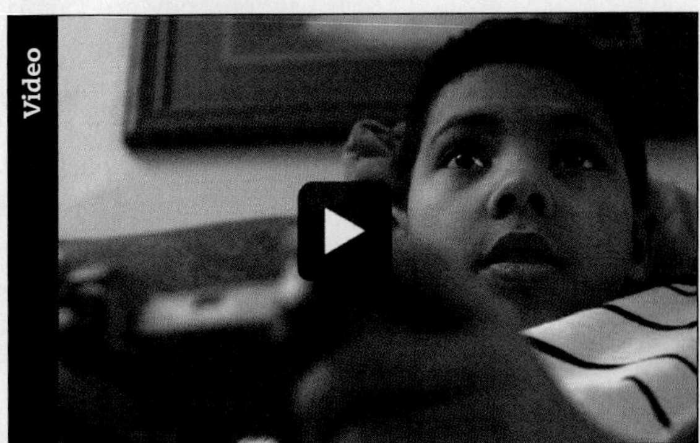


Take another look at Figure 12.1. It also shows that media use by and large rises over the course of childhood. Listening to music, for example, rises steadily from half an hour in a typical day for

**Figure 12.1** Daily Use of Media

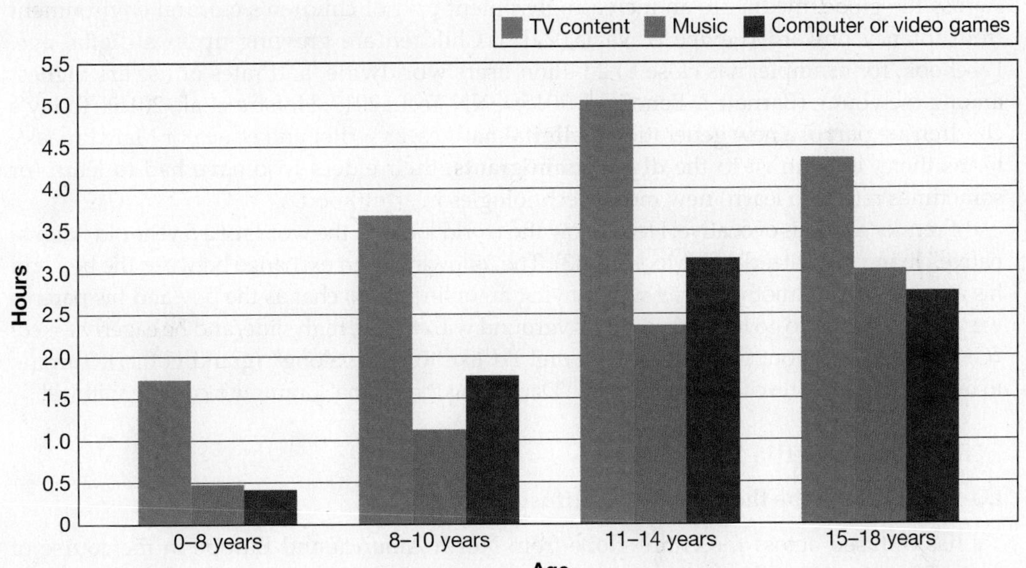

Emerging adults worldwide use the Internet. Here, digital media users from United Arab Emirates, the United States, and Japan.

0- to 8-year-olds to 3 hours for 15- to 18-year-olds. The figure does not include emerging adults, and there is surprisingly little research on emerging adults' uses of television and music. This may be due to an assumption that the effects of these media are more profound for children and adolescents. It has been hypothesized, however, that emerging adults use media even more than adolescents do because they spend more of their time alone (Arnett, 2004; Brown, 2006). A recent survey lends some support, showing that in the United States 93% of emerging adults own a digital device that allows them to access the Internet no matter where they are, compared to 75% of adolescents (Lenhart et al., 2010). In fact, high Internet use by emerging adults has been found worldwide. Across 17 countries in the Americas, Asia, Europe, and the Middle East, over 80% of 18- to 24-year-olds used the Internet in all but one country. For 10 of the countries, it was over 90% (World Internet Project, 2012).

As noted earlier, there is a digital divide between developed and developing countries that is largely based on income. Income also matters within countries, but it is not simply a matter of less money resulting in less access. On the one hand, American children ages 0 to 8 years from families with incomes below $30,000 have markedly less access than those with incomes above $75,000 to a home computer (48% vs. 91%), smartphone (27% vs. 57%), and video iPod or similar device (10% vs. 34%) (Rideout, 2013). On the other hand, children from lower-income families are more likely than children from higher-income families to have a TV in their bedroom (64% vs. 20%), and spend more time on media in a typical day (3 hours and 34 minutes vs. 2 hours and 47 minutes) (Rideout, 2013). Media use also varies by ethnicity. For children under 9 years of age, the average number of hours per day spent with media is 4 ½ for African Americans, 3 ½ for Latinos, and almost 3 for Whites.

Despite diversity across and within countries in access to media, there is a big picture. Across the globe, media are an increasingly potent part of children's cultural environment from infancy onward (Levine & Vaala, 2013). Children are growing up in a digital age. Facebook, for example, has close to 2 billion users worldwide, and rates of use are highest among the young (Barnett & Benefield, 2015; CNN Tech, 2017; Hofstra et al., 2016). Today's children are part of a new generation of **digital natives**, as writer and educator Marc Prensky terms them, in contrast to the **digital immigrants**, their elders who have had to learn (or sometimes refuse to learn) new media technologies in adulthood.

**digital natives**
today's generation of children who have grown up with digital media since infancy

**digital immigrants**
persons belonging to generations who have only used digital media upon reaching adulthood

Prensky's term is evocative. Here's how the world looks in the words of a 5 year-old "digital native" living in Switzerland (Moore, 2013). The following is an exchange between the boy and his American grandmother. They were having an online video chat as the boy and his parents were getting ready to go to his favorite playground with a long, high slide, and he eagerly asked: "Gramma, would you like to come?" "Sure! I'd like to come along" (grandmother). Turning to his father, the boy excitedly exclaimed: "Dad, bring the phone! Gramma's coming with us!"

## SUMMARY: Media Prevalence

### LO 12.1.1 Describe the worldwide diffusion of media.

TV has diffused across the entire globe from North America and Europe in the course of about 50 years. "New media" such as the Internet and mobile phones have appeared more recently, and their worldwide diffusion is occurring much more rapidly than TV's. A "digital divide" nonetheless exists between countries. More children in developed countries have access to media than in developing countries, and they have access to more kinds of media.

**LO 12.1.2 Describe children's daily media consumption patterns.**

American children are exposed to media from infancy onward. By and large, media use rises over the course of childhood. By middle childhood and early adolescence, children spend many hours on media in a typical day, including media multitasking. Today's children are part of a new generation of "digital natives."

# 12.2 Media and Other Contexts of Socialization

What does the prevalence of media imply for children's development? Essentially it amounts to the emergence of a new context of socialization. In this section, we look first at the distinctive socialization goals of media, and then at the intersection of media with other contexts. Specifically, we will focus on parents, schools, and governments.

## Media's Socialization Goals

**LO 12.2.1 Specify the two distinctive socialization goals of media.**

Media have some characteristics that distinguish them from other socialization contexts. One important characteristic is that media form part of an enterprise whose main purpose is economic success. The main goal is to sell. This makes media different from other socialization agents in children's environment, such as family members, teachers, neighbors, law enforcement agents, and religious authorities. Typically, these other socializers have an interest in encouraging children to accept the attitudes, beliefs, and values of adults in order to preserve social order and pass the culture on from one generation to the next. In contrast, media are driven not by a desire to promote successful socialization but by the uses children themselves can make of media (Goel & Stelter, 2013). Because the media are largely market-driven, media providers aim to furnish children, adolescents, and emerging adults with what they want—or can be persuaded to want. This does not mean that media providers can simply market any product. They have to be attuned to the wishes and values of other adult socializers such as parents, and the limits imposed by governments.

A second important characteristic of media is that they tend toward individualism, especially in societies that have freedom of speech and where the media are relatively uncontrolled and uncensored by government agencies. Given its commercial goal, the media enterprise aims to cover as many of children's media uses and desires as possible. Consequently, there is an increasing diversity of media offerings available in many countries. This provides children with a broad array of potential models and influences. In turn, this is likely to promote a wide range of individual differences in values, beliefs, interests, and personality characteristics as children, adolescents, and emerging adults are able to choose among the media offerings (Manago et al., 2015). They can tune in, log on, and launch into the media that resonate most strongly with their own particular inclinations.

Because the central purpose of most media is economic success, they aim to provide children, adolescents, and emerging adults with what they want—or can be persuaded to want.

> **Critical Thinking Question:** Revisit Bronfenbrenner's ecological theory from Chapter 10. As we saw, the theory describes the multiple "systems" of the cultural environment that shape human development. First, decide which system media form part of. Next, give an example of how media intersect with one of the other systems.

As we have seen, media have distinctive socialization goals. However, different contexts of socialization also intersect with one another in shaping children's development (Bronfenbrenner, 2000, 2005; Bronfenbrenner & Morris, 1998). Next, we will look more closely at media and their relation to parents, schools, and governments.

## Parents' Use of Media

**LO 12.2.2 Describe how parents use media for socialization purposes.**

From early on, parents make use of media as a babysitter. Among American parents of 0- to 8-year-old children, 15% say they "often" use media to keep their child occupied while they do chores, and 42% say they "sometimes" do. Just having a media device in the household is linked to higher use of it as a babysitter. For example, the percentage of parents who sometimes or often let their child use a handheld video game player while they are out of the house to run errands is 17% among all parents, but a whopping 72% among those who own such a device (Rideout, 2013). As parents of twins, we have to admit that we occasionally leaned on the "electronic nanny" in order to get things done in the house—although we would never recommend leaving a young child alone.

Some parents have aimed to use media not merely as a babysitter for their young children but even to enhance cognitive development—a sort of electronic super nanny. In the early 1990s, a study was published claiming that listening to the music of Mozart enhanced cognitive functioning (Rauscher et al., 1993). The study was conducted with university students, not babies, the "effect" lasted only 10 minutes, and subsequent studies failed to replicate even a 10-minute effect (Rauscher, 2003). Nevertheless, the study received worldwide attention and inspired the creation of a vast range of educational media products claiming to promote infants' cognitive development. Do they work? The answer appears to be no. Many studies have concluded that educational media products have no effect on infants' cognitive development. In fact, one study of 8- to 16-month-olds found that for every hour of "educational" DVDs viewed per day, the DVD viewers understood 6 to 8 *fewer* words than babies who watched no DVDs (Guernsey, 2007). The authors interpreted this surprising finding as due to the fact that the DVD viewers may have spent less time interacting with the people around them. That is, they were watching DVDs instead of interacting socially, and the DVD watching did not compensate for the deficit in social interaction. Another study found similar results (DeLoache et al., 2010). Fortunately, national studies have found that only 10% of babies in the United States use educational media products (Rideout, 2013). Watch the video *Media Use in Infancy* for more information.

As children get older, parents use media to keep in contact when their children are out of the household. For example, parents and adolescents use mobile phones to communicate when the adolescents are away from home. In fact, the number of American 8- to 18-year-olds who owned a mobile phone rose dramatically from 39% in 2005 to 66% in 2010 (Rideout et al., 2010). Also, in a typical day almost half of this age group sends text messages on a mobile phone. Among 8- to 18-year-olds, the rates of mobile phone ownership and text messaging rise steadily with age. For example, almost all 18-year-olds own a mobile phone (Pew, 2015). Research also shows that parents use social networking sites to maintain contact with their children when they move away to college (Padilla-Walker et al., 2010). New media are also used by parents of international students. For example, Chinese parents of children studying abroad have been found to rely on e-mail and Skype to stay in touch and maintain filial piety—a highly valued socialization goal of many Asian cultures (Kline & Liu, 2005).

**Watch** MEDIA USE IN INFANCY

While parents put media to use for their own socialization purposes, researchers also argue that, by adolescence, media goes "over the heads" of parents and other socializing adults in the adolescent's environment (Brown et al., 2014; Strasburger, 2006; Taillon, 2004). Parents are often unaware of the media their adolescents are using or hesitant to place restrictions, and most American adolescents easily gain access to whatever media they like (Funk et al., 1999; Roberts et al., 2005). If you think back to Marc Prensky's observation at the outset of this chapter that adults are "digital immigrants," it helps to explain the difficulty and reluctance that parents have in keeping up with their adolescents' media use. Parents may try to impose restrictions on the music, television shows, movies, and electronic games their adolescents consume, but these restrictions are unlikely to be successful if an adolescent is determined to avoid them. The limited time that parents and adolescents spend in each other's company also makes it difficult for parents to enforce such restrictions (Larson & Richards, 1994). In any case, most American parents do not attempt to impose restrictions. In one national study, less than half of adolescents reported that their parents had rules about the amount of time they spent watching television or about the content of the TV programs they watched (Rideout et al., 2010). The percentages concerning computer and Internet use were similarly low.

Parents of international students use new media to stay in touch. This family from Beijing video chats during the Chinese New Year.

## Schools' Use of Media

**LO 12.2.3 List three overarching goals in schools' uses of media.**

Virtually all schools in developed countries make use of both old and new media. As we will see later in this chapter, some developing countries—including some of the poorest ones such as Ethiopia—also aim to introduce media into schools. In the United States, the Secretary of Education announced the establishment of the Digital Promise at a White House event in 2011. The bipartisan, nonprofit initiative, overseen by prominent leaders in education and technology, aims to promote digital technologies with the potential to transform teaching and learning (The White House, 2011).

What are the overarching socialization goals when schools use media in today's world? A recent analysis (Levine & Vaala, 2013) indicates that the goals center on:

- Engagement, or having students feel and remain engaged and interested in school.
- Academic learning, including literacy and STEM (Science, Technology, Engineering, Math) skills.
- Development of 21st-century skills, including critical thinking and collaborative learning.

## Education Focus: Panwapa: An International Multimedia Educational Program

Sesame Workshop, formerly known as the Children's Television Workshop, is an American nonprofit organization behind the production of several educational children's programs that have run on public broadcasting around the world. Its current mission is to provide educational learning resources through television, articles, and other media. A variety of liaisons exist between Sesame Workshop and the U.S. Department of Education and the Corporation for Public Broadcasting (PBS). In 2008, Sesame Workshop launched "Panwapa," a multimedia, international project distributed in five languages. Designed for children 4 to 7 years old, the educational goals of Panwapa are to promote positive attitudes, skills, and behaviors for 21st-century global citizenship.

As part of the design and launch process, a study was conducted to assess the influence of Panwapa (Fisch et al., 2010). A total of 1,277 children, ages 4 to 7 years, from China, Egypt, Mexico, and the United States were divided into three groups. In each country, the "All Materials" group played hands-on games based on print instructions, watched Muppet videos, and engaged in online activities on the Panwapa website. The "No Web" group was similar to the first, except it did not have website access. The third (control) group did not use any Panwapa materials. There was a pre-test before the introduction of Panwapa, and then a post-test after 4 weeks of activities. The study also included interviews with 100 parents and teachers to learn more about their views of and engagement with the educational project.

The findings showed that a majority of all children in the "All Materials" and "No Web" groups understood and retained educational content, even when asked about Panwapa materials from early in the 4 weeks. But there were also differences between the groups. The children in the "All Materials" group learned more than the "No Web" group. They did better on naming different languages, naming different countries and finding them on a globe, as well as understanding that inequities in access to resources exist across different countries or cultures.

The findings also indicated that learning does not occur in a cultural vacuum. There were differences between children from the different countries, suggesting that culture and experience matter. For example, children from the United States showed the greatest improvement in understanding economic inequities. The researchers suggest that this may be because children sometimes learned more when they had had less exposure to an issue in their day-to-day lives.

Finally, some of the responses from teachers and parents were illuminating. Chinese educational practice places an emphasis on hands-on learning, and Chinese elders tended to prefer physical to virtual Panwapa games. In the interviews, one Chinese teacher said: "It's better to make things with paper, so that children's ability to use their hands can improve. Materials like paper are [better] for protecting their eyes." Teachers and parents in the other three countries did not express these beliefs about physical development and learning in preschoolers. Across all the cultures, adults seemed to think that learning about other cultures is valuable. One Egyptian teacher emphasized the global citizenship message of Panwapa: "The materials create the cooperation spirit inside the child. They teach him that we are all similar.... There is no difference between Egyptians and anyone else."

## Review Question

Why do you think the researchers decided to interview both teachers and parents in assessing Panwapa?

# Government Policies on Media

**LO 12.2.4 Compare government policies on children's access to media.**

Governments vary in the extent to which they place limits on the media and its content. Three countries dominate the TV industry and export of programs: Japan, the United Kingdom, and the United States (Rubenstein, 2017). In developing countries, many satellite and cable providers block program networks such as MTV and censor programs regarded by their governments as unacceptable. Typically, these governments are concerned with what they regard as American and Western cultural and economic imperialism. Substituted programs typically emphasize local history and values—such as the Arab broadcast on Ahmad's family's TV that you read about earlier. Governments also try to place limits on Internet content (Rubenstein, 2017). Map 12.7 shows variation across countries in level of restrictions on Internet content. Some countries, for example, curtail access to social and political content.

**Map 12.7** Level of Restrictions on Internet Content

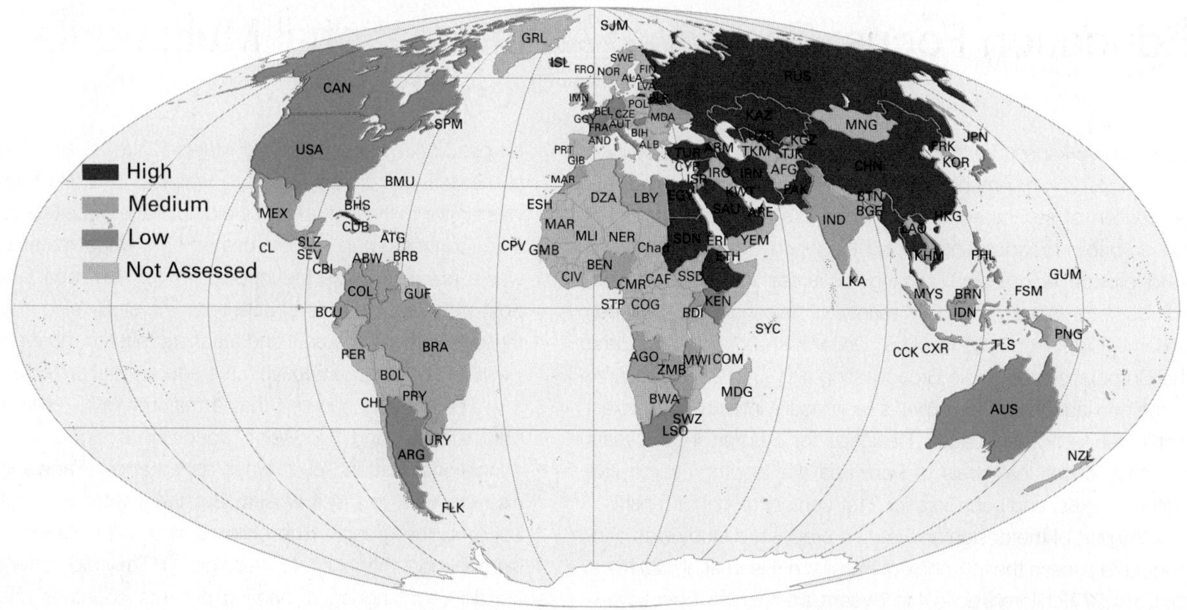

Most Western societies value free speech highly, so a diverse range of media content is allowed. However, the United States takes this principle further than European countries do. For example, Germany has a legal prohibition against music lyrics that express hatred or advocate violence toward minorities. In Norway, one person in the government reviews all movies before they are allowed to be shown in theaters and prohibits the showing of movies judged to be too violent. Neither of these prohibitions would be likely to survive a legal challenge in the United States because of the protection of free speech in the First Amendment of the Constitution. Nevertheless, the principle of free speech does not mean that all media must be accessible to all persons regardless of age. Age restrictions on access to media are allowable under the First Amendment, and the United States has rating systems for movies, music, television, and computer games that are designed to indicate to children, adolescents, and their parents which media may be unsuitable for persons under a certain age (Funk et al., 1999; Lambe, 2006).

The U.S. provides advisories, such as on this CD, to indicate to children, adolescents, and their parents which media may be unsuitable for persons under a certain age.

Whatever the extent of government restrictions on media access and content, technology continues to change in a way that pushes toward broad access for children. For example, governments have quite a hard time controlling TV satellite technology and Internet communications. Individual social media, such as blogs, mobile phone messages, and Twitter are even harder to control.

## SUMMARY: Media and Other Contexts of Socialization

**LO 12.2.1 Specify the two distinctive socialization goals of media.**

Media form part of an enterprise whose main purpose is economic success. This makes media different from other socialization agents in children's environment, such as family members, teachers, neighbors, law enforcement agents, and religious authorities. A second important characteristic of media is that they tend toward broad socialization, aiming to cover as many of children's media uses and desires as possible.

**LO 12.2.2 Describe how parents use media for socialization purposes.**

From early on, parents make use of media as a babysitter. As children get older, parents use media to keep in contact when their children are out of the household. While parents put media to use for their own socialization purposes, researchers also argue that, by adolescence, media goes "over the heads" of parents and other socializing adults in the adolescent's environment.

**LO 12.2.3 List three overarching goals in schools' uses of media.**

Virtually all schools in developed countries make use of both old and new media. The overarching socialization goals center on aiding students' academic learning, engagement with school, and development of 21st-century skills (such as critical thinking and collaborative learning).

**LO 12.2.4 Compare government policies on children's access to media.**

Governments vary in the extent to which they place limits on the media and its content, and hence the extent to which they try to curtail the individualistic and commercial aspects of media. Most Western societies value free speech highly, so a diverse range of media content is allowed.

# 12.3 Theories of Media Influence

We have seen how media are a prominent source of socialization, and how they intersect with other important socialization contexts such as parents and schools. An important question that follows is what children learn from media—good or bad. There are three prominent theories that address how media influence young people. Both Cultivation Theory and Social Learning Theory emphasize the effects of media on children. In contrast, the Uses and

Gratifications Approach highlights how children make choices about their use of media. Let's take a closer look at these theories.

## Cultivation Theory and Social Learning Theory

**LO 12.3.1 Explain how Cultivation Theory and Social Learning Theory share the same basic premise.**

**Cultivation Theory**

argues that media gradually shape or "cultivate" a person's worldview

**Cultivation Theory** argues that media gradually shape or "cultivate" a person's worldview, so that over time it comes to resemble the worldview most frequently presented by media. Research based on Cultivation Theory has especially focused on TV (Appel, 2008; Gerbner et al., 1994; Tan et al., 2003). For example, adolescent girls who are frequent viewers of soap operas have been found to be more likely than other girls to believe that single mothers have relatively easy lives because this is how single mothers are often depicted on these shows (Larson, 1996).

One aspect of Cultivation Theory is known as *Mean World Syndrome* (Gerbner et al., 1994). In Mean World Syndrome, the more people watch TV, the more they are likely to believe that the world is a dangerous place, that crime rates are high and rising, and that they themselves are at risk for being a victim of a crime (Riddle et al., 2011). According to Cultivation Theory, they believe this because television often depicts crime and violence on dramas and news shows, which leads viewers to cultivate a view of the world as mean, violent, and dangerous.

**Social Learning Theory**

argues that media shape children's behaviors

Like Cultivation Theory, **Social Learning Theory** focuses on the effects of media on children (Bandura, 1994; Jennings & Akers, 2011). Social Learning Theory, however, addresses children's behavior rather than their worldview. According to this theory, children will be more likely to imitate behaviors they see frequently performed by models who are rewarded or at least not punished. In a famous experiment known as the "Bobo doll" study, children watched an adult "model" kicking and punching a clownlike doll ("Bobo") (Bandura et al., 1961). Later, the children imitated the adult's aggressive behavior almost exactly.

Since this experiment from the early 1960s, researchers have conducted hundreds of media studies using Social Learning Theory, with the guiding framework that children will imitate media models (Huston et al., 2007). For example, studies have found that heavier exposure to sexual content on TV is related to earlier initiation of sexual intercourse among adolescents, and this has been interpreted as indicating that the adolescents modeled their sexual behavior after the TV characters (Martino et al., 2005). Many of the studies using Social Learning Theory have concerned the relationship between television and aggression.

Both Cultivation Theory and Social Learning Theory depict the media consumer as relatively passive and easily manipulated. In research using these theories, correlations between media use and attitudes or behaviors are routinely interpreted as causation, because it is assumed that media have effects and the consumer is a recipient of those effects. In short, both Cultivation Theory and Social Learning Theory emphasize the one-way view that media influence children.

## Uses and Gratifications Approach

**Uses and Gratifications Approach**

emphasizes that children differ in numerous ways that lead them to make different choices about which media to consume and that even children consuming the same media product will respond to it in a variety of ways, depending on their individual characteristics

**LO 12.3.2 Explain the two key principles of the Uses and Gratifications Approach, and the role of identity in the Media Practice Model.**

The **Uses and Gratifications Approach**, in contrast to Cultivation Theory and Social Learning Theory, emphasizes the interactionist view that children actively make choices about how they use media on the basis of their developmental motivations and needs. This theory views people as active rather than passive media consumers (Pierce, 2006; Rosengren, 1974; Rubin, 1993; Ruggiero, 2000; Slater, 2007; von Salisch et al., 2006).

The Uses and Gratifications Approach is based on two key principles. The first is that people differ in numerous ways that lead them to make different choices about which media to consume. For example, not all children and adolescents like violent TV shows;

**Figure 12.2** The Media Practice Model

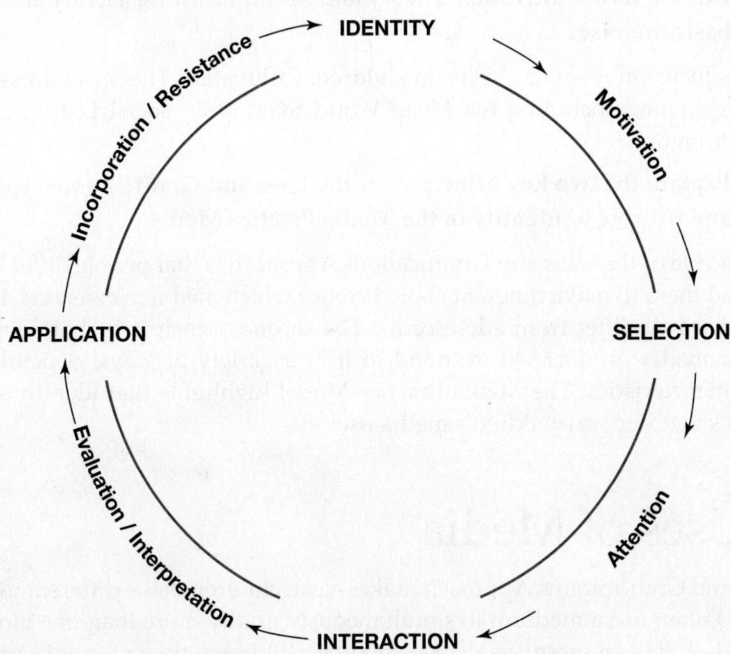


the Uses and Gratifications Approach assumes that those who like such shows differ from those who do not, prior to any effect that watching violent shows may have (Krcmar & Kean, 2005). The second principle is that people consuming the same media product will respond to it in a variety of ways, depending on their individual characteristics. For example, some girls may read teen magazines and respond by feeling extremely insecure about the way they look compared with the models in the magazine, whereas other girls may read the same magazines and be relatively unaffected (Brown et al., 2002). In short, the Uses and Gratifications Approach emphasizes that how media influences a child depends on the needs and motives that the child has for seeking out certain media in the first place.

Media researchers Jane Brown and Jane Steele and their colleagues have elaborated on the Uses and Gratifications Approach to incorporate the important developmental concept of identity. They call their theory the *Media Practice Model*. While their research focuses on adolescents (Brown, 2006; Brown et al., 2002; Steele, 2006), the model could also be applied to pre-teens and emerging adults. As you can see in Figure 12.2, the model proposes that each adolescent's identity motivates the *selection* of media products. Paying attention to certain media products leads to *interaction* with those products, meaning that the products are evaluated and interpreted. Then adolescents engage in *application* of the media content they have chosen. They may incorporate this content into their identities—for example, girls who respond to thin models by seeking to be thin themselves. Or they may resist the content—for example, girls who respond to thin models by rejecting them as a false ideal. Their developing identity then motivates new media selections, and so on.

**Critical Thinking Question:** What is your favorite movie and what is a movie that you truly dislike? Apply the concepts of selection, interaction, application, and identity from the Media Practice Model to your uses of these movies and other related media products.

### SUMMARY: Theories of Media Influence

**LO 12.3.1 Explain how Cultivation Theory and Social Learning Theory share the same basic premise.**

Both theories focus on media's effects on children. Cultivation Theory addresses effects on children's worldview, including the Mean World Syndrome. Social Learning Theory addresses effects on behavior.

**LO 12.3.2 Explain the two key principles of the Uses and Gratifications Approach, and the role of identity in the Media Practice Model.**

One key principle of the Uses and Gratifications Approach is that people differ in numerous ways that lead them to make different choices about which media to consume. For example, young children will differ from adolescents. The second principle is that people consuming the same media product will respond to it in a variety of ways, depending on their individual characteristics. The Media Practice Model highlights that identity is one of the characteristics that impacts children's media use.

# 12.4 Uses of Media

As the Uses and Gratifications Approach makes clear, children make different uses of media. Children also often use a medium to simultaneously gratify more than one motive or need (Stevens et al., 2008). In recent years, research on children's uses of media has flourished (Blumberg & Fisch, 2013; Olson, 2010; Revelle, 2013). In this next section, we will review emotional, cognitive, and social uses that come up frequently across this research.

## Emotional Uses

**LO 12.4.1 Describe children's emotional uses of media.**

All humans, from infancy and onward, experience emotions such as happiness, surprise, and anger. Research shows that we use media to elicit and regulate these kinds of emotions.

**sensation seeking**
a personality characteristic defined by the extent to which a person enjoys novelty and intensity of sensation

**ENTERTAINMENT.** Entertainment is one universal use of media. In a survey of 12- to 14-year-old American adolescents, 70% strongly agreed that they play electronic games because "it's just fun" (Olson, 2010). It was the top reason for playing electronic games. Children, adolescents, and emerging adults, like people of other ages, often make use of media as an enjoyable part of their leisure lives—even if they vary on what games, TV shows, music, and so on they find entertaining (Brake, 1985; Nabi & Krcmar, 2004). Young children often enjoy watching their favorite TV shows and movies over and over—a déjà vu approach to electronic media that mirrors the common childhood experience of re-reading cherished books (Stetler, 2013). Music often accompanies young people's leisure, from driving around in a car, to hanging out with friends, to secluding themselves in the privacy of their bedrooms for contemplation (Larson, 1995). The most common motivation stated by adolescents for listening to music is "to have fun" (Tarrant et al., 2000). Children of all ages—a fitting expression here—use media for the entertainment purposes of fun, amusement, and recreation.

Children use media for a variety of purposes, including entertainment.

**SENSATION SEEKING.** Another notable use of media is sensation seeking. **Sensation seeking** is a personality characteristic defined by the extent to which a person enjoys *novelty* and *intensity* of sensation. Adolescence and emerging adulthood tend to be the time of life when sensation seeking peeks (Zuckerman, 2007), and certain media provide the intense and novel sensations that appeal to many young people. Overall, sensation seeking is related to higher media consumption in adolescence, especially TV, music, and electronic games (Lachlan, 2006; Roberts et al., 2005; Stoolmiller et al., 2010; Zuckerman, 2006). One of the top reasons that 12- to 14-year-olds play electronic games is because "it's exciting" (Olson, 2010).

Many media products appeal to adults as well as young people, but some appeal almost exclusively to young people, at least partly because of the high-sensation quality of the stimulation. The audience for action films is composed mostly of males in adolescence and emerging adulthood because this is the segment of the population that is highest in sensation seeking, and consequently most likely to be drawn to films that portray scenes involving explosions, car chases and crashes, gunfire, and suspense (Hoffner & Levine, 2005; Stoolmiller et al., 2010). Adolescent boys also dominate the audiences for the high-sensation musical forms of hip hop, heavy metal, and hard rock (Arnett, 1996; Nater et al., 2005; Rawlings et al., 2000).

Music is a media form that may especially lend itself to high-sensation intensity. Most popular music is created by people who are adolescents and emerging adults or just beyond (with geriatric exceptions such as the Rolling Stones), and the sensory stimulation of most popular music is much higher than for television (think of the volume level of the last hip hop or alternative rock concert you may have attended). Adolescents' emotional arousal when listening to music tends to be high, at least partly because of the high sensory and emotional intensity of music (Larson, 1995; Rawlings & Leow, 2008).

**COPING.** Another media use that seems mostly to emerge in adolescence is coping. Young people use media to relieve and dispel negative emotions. One study has shown that preteen children do not speak of playing electronic games as a way to relieve stress and anger, whereas adolescents and emerging adults do (Funk et al., 2006). In a focus group, an adolescent boy explained that "getting wrapped up in a violent game, it's good. 'Cause if you're mad, when you come home, you can take your anger out on the people in the game" (Olson, 2010, p. 182).

Several studies indicate that "Listen to music" and "Watch TV" also are common coping strategies among adolescents who feel angry, anxious, or unhappy (Kurdek, 1987; Oliver, 2006). Music may be particularly important in this respect (Saarikallio & Erkkilä, 2007). Adolescents often listen to music in the privacy of their bedrooms while pondering the themes of the songs in relation to their own lives, as part of the process of emotional self-regulation (Larson, 1995). In early adolescence, when the number of problems at home, at school, and with friends increases, time spent listening to music also increases (Roberts et al., 2005).

Certain types of music, such as hip hop or heavy metal, may appeal especially to young people who use music for coping. Adolescent fans of heavy metal report that they listen to the music especially when they are angry and that it typically has the effect of purging their anger and calming them down (Arnett, 1991, 1996; Scheel & Westefeld, 1999). Listen how similar 21-year-old Ben, an avid heavy metal fan, sounds to the adolescent game player above: "Sometimes I'm upset and I like to put on heavy metal. It kind of releases the aggression I feel. I can just drive along [in the car] and turn it up. It puts me in a better mood. It's a way to release some of your pressures, instead of going out and starting a fight with somebody, or taking it out on your parents or your cat or something like that" (Arnett, 1996, p. 82).

Young people also sometimes use television for coping purposes. Adolescents often turn to television as a way of turning off the stressful emotions that have accumulated during the day (Larson, 1995; Ohannessian, 2009). Adolescents also may choose media materials for specific coping purposes. In the aftermath of the 1991 Persian Gulf War, a study indicated that Israeli adolescents used information obtained through the media to help them cope with the stress of the war (Zeidner, 1993).

Adolescents often listen to music to ponder the themes of the songs in relation to their own lives and for the purpose of emotional coping.

**Critical Thinking Question:** The use of media to cope with negative moods seems to become especially prominent by adolescence. How would you explain that? Also, do you think that younger children might sometimes use media to cope? If so, what negative emotions do you think they would be trying to relieve and dispel, and what types of media would they use for this purpose?

Media can be useful to obtain information that is not readily available in one's community. Here, Sioux children are using the Internet.

## Cognitive Uses

**LO 12.4.2 Describe children's cognitive uses of media.**

As we just saw, media can provide information. Sometimes information may be sought out for coping purposes, but often the purpose is to gain new knowledge.

**INFORMATION.** Children use media to obtain information, including information that would be difficult or impossible to obtain within one's immediate environment. A survey of American Indian and Alaska Native (AI/AN) teenagers from rural communities found that three-quarters had access to the Internet, and that one of the most common uses included "to get news about" health topics (76%), sports and entertainment (68%), AI/AN events (63%), and current events or politics (49%) (Craig Rushing & Stephens, 2011). The researchers point out that for these youth, who live in poor and rural communities, media are important sources of information. In fact, findings from the study are being used to design a multimedia, culturally appropriate health program for AI/AN youth.

Media scholars have also proposed that the media function as a **super peer** for adolescents, meaning that adolescents often look to media for information (especially concerning sexuality) that their parents may be unwilling to provide, in the same way they might look to a friend (Brown et al., 2014; Strasburger, 2006). These scholars point out that adolescents indeed gain information from media, but also warn that media may be misleading (for example, leading to overestimates of the number of teens who have sex).

**super peer**
one of the functions of media for adolescents, meaning that adolescents often look to media for information (especially concerning sexuality) that their parents may be unwilling to provide, in the same way they might look to a friend

**COGNITIVE ENGAGEMENT.** Cognitive engagement is another important developmental use of media. Among 12- to 14-year-olds, 45% say that they play electronic games because of the "challenge of figuring things out" (Olson, 2010). Media certainly differ on the extent to which children feel challenged when using them. In a British study that included children, some compared video games favorably with TV. For example, one boy said, "It's like watching TV but there is a sense of achievement" (Cragg et al., 2007, p. 39). Many video games provide feedback to players about the efficacy of their game actions, for example, through praise and increased level of difficulty. Many games also "scaffold" play, to use Vygotsky's concept (from Chapter 5), by providing assistance with hints and clues (Liao et al., 2011). Some researchers are working on understanding what features make electronic games intrinsically motivating, and the extent to which those features could be useful in the classroom to encourage students to persist with cognitively challenging tasks (Dickey, 2005; Gee, 2007; Revelle, 2013).

## Social Uses

**LO 12.4.3 Describe children's social uses of media.**

Media play an important part in children's social development. Children use media to socialize with peers, for civic and political purposes, and as part of identity formation.

**SOCIALIZING WITH PEERS AND FRIENDS.** Children, adolescents, and emerging adults use media for socializing with peers. Media provide opportunities to compete with others, teach others, make friends, spend time with friends, and keep in contact with friends. One survey found that 45% of 12- to 14-year-olds use electronic games because they "like to compete with others and win" (Olson, 2010). In the study, boys were significantly more likely to strongly agree with this use of media, as compared to girls. In focus groups, young adolescent boys also say that electronic games are a frequent conversation topic among their peers. Asked what boys at his school would talk about if they were not talking about games, a boy replied: "I don't know. Probably like girls, or something like that.... I don't even know, 'cause the most they talk about is girls and games—the two Gs" (Olson, 2010, p. 180).

It is not all competition, though. Girls and boys who play electronic games also cooperate and teach each other (Olson, 2010). In fact, according to our teenage son Miles, some electronic games increase in difficulty as you play to the point that they are best tackled by two or more children working together.

The proliferation of mobile phones and social-networking websites like Facebook shows another side of how media are used for socializing with peers. Mobile phones are used by young people not only for calling but also for text messaging. As we saw earlier, 66% of American 8- to 18-year-olds own a mobile phone (Rideout et al., 2010). In the United States, the highest rate of mobile phone ownership of any age group (over 90%) is among 18- to 29-year-olds (Lenhart, 2015; Lenhart et al., 2010; Pew, 2015). In Sweden, over 90% of 18- to 24-year-olds own one (Axelsson, 2010).

Among 18- to 29-year-olds in the United States, 80% use social-networking websites, the same rate as for teens and nearly twice the rate of persons age 30 and older (Pew, 2012). All over the world, as you can see in Table 12.1, 18- to 29-year-olds are far more likely than their elders to use social networking (Pew, 2012). The sites are used mainly to make new friends and to keep in touch with current and old friends (Ellison et al., 2007; Raacke & Bonds-Raacke, 2008).

**Table 12.1** Use of Social Networking (%)

| | 18–29 | 30+ |
|---|---|---|
| Lithuania | 84 | 27 |
| Spain | 81 | 35 |
| Israel | 80 | 43 |
| United States | 80 | 44 |
| Britain | 78 | 37 |
| China | 58 | 20 |
| Turkey | 52 | 17 |
| Indonesia | 26 | 4 |

SOURCE: Adapted from Pew Research Center (2012).

**CIVIC INVOLVEMENT.** By adolescence and emerging adulthood, media are sometimes used for civic and political purposes. As described earlier in this chapter, governments are finding it challenging to control a variety of new media technology. In 2011, for example, protesters against undemocratic governments in Egypt, Libya, Tunisia, and other countries in North Africa and Southwest Asia used mobile phones, Twitter, and other social media to coordinate their activities and promote their political causes (Rubenstein, 2017). Many of these media-using protesters were adolescents and emerging adults.

Another study also documented how ethnic minority adolescents in the United States use Facebook to create groups interested in civic involvement relating to race relations (Tynes et al., 2010). From the vantage point of the Uses and Gratifications Approach, it has also been argued that some Black adolescents in urban America use hip hop as an expression of their frustration and rage in the face of the difficult conditions in which they live. Young people's political uses of hip hop have also been documented in other parts of the world (Mitchell, 2001). From this vantage point, hip hop represents a protest.

**IDENTITY FORMATION.** "I like it in *YM* and *Seventeen* magazines how they have like your horoscope and what you're like—. . . if you're an 'earth person' or a 'water person,' something like that. They tell you what you are" (Currie, 1999, p. 154). Fourteen-year-old Lauren helps us to see that media can provide materials that children, adolescents, and emerging adults use toward the construction of an identity (Boehke et al., 2002; Brown et al., 2014). Part of identity formation is thinking about the kind of person you would like to become. Media provides ideal selves to emulate and feared selves to avoid. The use of media for this purpose is reflected in children's electronic game playing where they construct game characters, for example, selecting among a variety of physical features and magic powers for their character (Blascovich & Bailenson, 2011). It is also reflected in the pictures and posters adolescents put up in their rooms, which are often of media stars from entertainment and sports (Brown et al., 2002).

The use of media for identity development is reflected in children's electronic game playing where they construct game characters. Here, a boy is engrossed in Pokemon Go.

An important aspect of identity formation, and one for which adolescents may especially make use of media, is gender role identity (Chan et al., 2011; Hust, 2006; Steele & Brown, 1995). Adolescents take ideals of what it means to be a woman or a man partly from the media. Adolescents use the information provided in media to learn sexual and romantic scripts (Brown et al., 2002; Eggermont, 2006)—for example, how to approach a potential romantic partner for the first time, what to do on a date, and even how to kiss. One study of adolescents' messages in Internet chat rooms found that the exchange of identity information allowed participants to "pair off" with partners of their choice, despite the disembodied nature of chat participants (Subrahmanyam et al., 2004). The authors concluded that the virtual world of teen chat may offer a safer environment for exploring emerging sexuality than the real world. For both girls and boys, gender, sexuality, and relationships are central to the kind of identity exploration and identity formation for which adolescents use media (Brown et al., 2014; Ward, 1995).

Magazines are a medium where gender roles are an especially common theme, particularly in magazines for adolescent girls. The most popular magazines for teenage girls devote most of their space to advertisements and articles that focus on physical appearance, heterosexual relationships, and sexuality (Joshi et al., 2011; Kim, 2006). In contrast, the magazines most popular among adolescent boys are devoted to computer games, sports, humor, and cars—with little or no mention of how to improve physical appearance or how to form relationships with girls or any topic related to sexuality (Taylor, 2006). This gender difference in magazines changes in emerging adulthood. Magazines for young women, like the magazines for adolescent girls, continue to emphasize physical appearance, sexuality, and heterosexual relationships, but magazines for young men such as *Maxim* and *GQ* also contain substantial content on these topics, unlike the magazines popular among adolescent boys.

To sum up, the uses that children, adolescents, and emerging adults make of media are numerous. As we have seen, these uses depend on individual development, social class,

## Cultural Focus: "Teenagers" in Kathmandu, Nepal

Few places in the world have been more remote and more isolated from the West historically than Nepal, which is located between southwest China and northeast India. Not only is Nepal thousands of miles from the nearest Western country, but until 1951 the government made a special effort to isolate its citizens, banning all communications (travel, trade, books, movies, etc.) between Nepal and "the outside." Since then, Nepal, and especially its largest city, Kathmandu, has been undergoing a rapid transition into the world of global trade, Western tourism, and electronic mass media. Ethnographic research by the anthropologist Mark Liechty (1995, 2010) provides a vivid look at how adolescents and emerging adults in Kathmandu are responding to the diffusion of Western media.

According to Liechty and his colleagues, a variety of imported media are highly popular with young people in Kathmandu. Movies and videos from both India and the United States find a broad audience of young people. American and Indian television shows are also popular, and televisions and computers are a standard feature of middle-class homes. There is an avid audience among the young for Western music, including rock, heavy metal, and rap. Sometimes young people combine local culture with imported Western styles; Liechty gives the example of a local rock band that had recorded an original Nepali-language album in the style of the Beatles. However, many urban young people reject older traditions such as Nepali folk songs.

A locally produced magazine called *Teens* embodies the appeal of Western media to young people in Kathmandu. In addition to features such as comic strips, Nepali folk tales, puzzles, and games, each issue contains pages of profiles devoted to Western pop music heroes, including biographical data and lyrics to popular songs. Each issue also includes a list of the top 10 English-language albums of the month and a list of recent English video releases. A substantial proportion of the magazine is devoted to fashion, much as in American teen magazines, and the fashions shown are Western.

Nepalese people use the terms *"teen"* and *"teenager"* in English, even when speaking Nepali, to refer to young people

**Watch** "TEENAGERS" IN KATHMANDU, NEPAL

who are oriented toward Western tastes, especially Western media. Not all Nepalese young people are "teenagers," even if they are in their teen years—the term is not an age category, but a social category that refers to young people who are pursuing a Western identity and style based on what they have learned through media. However, some adults use "*teenager*" with less favorable connotations to refer to young people who are disobedient, antisocial, and potentially violent. Their use of the term in this way reflects their view that Western media can have corrupting effects on many of their young people.

To many young people in Kathmandu, being a "teenager" is something they covet and strive for. They associate it with leisure, affluence, and expanded opportunities. These teenagers use media to help them make sense of their own lives, growing up as they are in a rapidly changing society, and as material for imagining a broad range of possible selves. Watch the video *"Teenagers" in Kathmandu, Nepal* to hear how Nepali adolescents speak of media.

### Review Question

Of the various uses of media that we have reviewed, which ones would you say are used by "teenagers" in Kathmandu?

ethnicity, gender, personality, and culture. The type of media also matters. TV, music, electronic games, social-networking websites, magazines, and the Internet vary on why they are appealing.

## SUMMARY: Uses of Media

**LO 12.4.1 Describe children's emotional uses of media.**

Children use media for the entertainment purposes of fun, amusement, and recreation. Sensation seeking (the desire for novel and intense experiences) is another emotional use of media. Adolescence and emerging adulthood tend to be the time when sensation seeking peeks. Another media use that seems mostly to emerge in adolescence is coping. Young people use media to relieve and dispel negative emotions.

**LO 12.4.2 Describe children's cognitive uses of media.**

Children use media to obtain information, including information that would be difficult or impossible to obtain within one's immediate environment. Cognitive engagement is another important developmental use of media. In other words, some children enjoy media such as electronic games because they are challenging and provide a sense of achievement.

**LO 12.4.3 Describe children's social uses of media.**

Children, adolescents, and emerging adults use media for socializing with peers. Media provide opportunities to compete with others, teach others, make friends, spend time with friends, and keep in contact with friends. By adolescence and emerging adulthood, media are also sometimes used for civic and political purposes. Yet another social use of media is related to identity development. Media provides ideal selves to emulate and feared selves to avoid.

# 12.5 Risks of Media

As we have just seen, children make a variety of different uses of media. It is a valuable contribution of the Uses and Gratifications Approach to highlight that children are not passive automatons. They do not simply come to their media experiences in a happenstance way, but rather they actively use media to fulfill needs and motives. Nonetheless, media also come with risks and benefits that are above and beyond the uses that children are making of those media. For example, you might watch TV because it is entertaining, but meanwhile TV advertisements might induce a craving for high-fat, low-nutrient foods. Over time, that constitutes an unintended risk. Also, time watching TV is time not spent doing other beneficial activities such as reading or getting physical exercise or playing an instrument (unless you are fabulous at multitasking). Time taken away from more beneficial activities by media is known as the **displacement effect** (Weber, 2006). Cultivation Theory and Social Learning Theory remind us that media may influence our thoughts, emotions, and behaviors in ways that we do not always realize or bargain for. In this section, we will focus on what research tells us about the risks of media in three key areas: physical health, aggression, and sexuality.

**displacement effect**
in media research, term for how media use occupies time that could have been spent on other activities

## Physical Health

**LO 12.5.1 Describe the risks of media in regard to obesity, tobacco use, and body image.**

Media pose a risk to children's physical health in a number of ways. Children who watch a lot of TV do not exercise as much as children who watch less TV or no TV at all. The American Academy of Pediatrics recommends that children younger than 18 months not spend any time with television or other entertainment media, and children between 18 months and 5 years be limited to no more than 1 hour of high-quality entertainment media per day (American Academy of Pediatrics, 2016). One key basis for this recommendation is the displacement effect—that children would benefit more from play and being physically active.

Furthermore, children who watch a lot of TV are more likely to consume the junk food and sugary drinks that are advertised. In the United States, the average child sees about 40,000 TV commercials each year, mostly for cereal, candy, fast food, and toys (Scheibe, 2007). Young

Product placements in media contribute to children's exposure to unhealthy products. Here, a scene from the 2015 movie, *Growing Up Smith*.

children are especially susceptible to advertising, as they are less aware of the commercial intent than older children are. Most do not perceive a distinction between a program and an advertisement until about age 5 (Jennings, 2007). After a review of the literature, an American National Academies Committee concluded that food and beverage advertising is correlated with being overweight, and that there are causal links to children's food preferences, food choices, and short-term food consumption (McGinnis et al., 2006). Because most of the products children all over the world see advertised are unhealthy foods, concern has grown that TV advertising is one influence behind the growing international epidemic of obesity in children (Bergstrom, 2007; Ferguson & Iturbide, 2015).

It is not only younger children who are susceptible to advertising. Most media used by adolescents—TV, radio, magazines, Internet sites, and so on—contain advertising in some form. Some media such as movies and music videos have advertisements in a subtle form called "product placements," which means that companies pay to have their products used by actors and performers. For many years, the most controversial form of advertising with respect to adolescents was cigarette advertising. Advertising cigarettes on television or radio has been illegal in the United States since 1971, but after that ban took effect cigarette companies poured money into other forms of advertising and promotion, such as billboards, movie product placements, and sponsorship of sporting events and concerts (Cummings, 2002; Morgenstern et al., 2013).

Critics of cigarette advertising argue that it is targeted especially toward adolescents (Biener & Siegel, 2000; Cummings, 2002; Ling & Glantz, 2002; Pollay, 1997, 2006). They point out that 90% of smokers begin smoking by age 18 (Cummings, 2002), and brand loyalty is very strong once established. In lawsuits against the tobacco companies, the companies have been forced to release literally tons of internal documents, many of which provide stark evidence that for decades these companies have discussed the psychological characteristics of adolescents and have been acutely aware of the importance of adolescents as the perpetually new market for cigarettes (Cummings, 2002; Ling & Glantz, 2002). The documents contain such statements as "Today's teenager is tomorrow's potential regular customer," and "The base of our business is the high school student" (Pollay, 1997).

Several studies have established a relationship between cigarette advertising campaigns and adolescent smoking. One study, for example, traced tobacco companies' advertising expenditures in relation to rates of smoking among adolescents (ages 12 to 18) and adults over the period from 1979 to 1993 (Pollay et al., 1996). The researchers concluded that the effect of advertising on brand choice was three times as strong for adolescents as for adults. The "Joe Camel" campaign provides an example of this effect. Between 1988, when the "Joe" character was introduced, and 1993, Camel's market share among 12- to 17-year-olds rose from less than 1% to 13%, and the proportion of adolescents who smoked increased. Another study examined trends in smoking initiation from 1944 to 1988 (Pierce et al., 1994). It showed that for girls ages 14 to 17, a sharp rise in smoking initiation coincided with the introduction of three brands targeted at females—Virginia Slims, Silva Thins, and Eve—between 1967 and 1973. No such increase occurred during this period for girls ages 10 to 13 or 18 to 20, or for males. The ad campaigns were evidently particularly effective among (and targeted to?) adolescent girls ages 14 to 17—the age range when smoking initiation is most likely to take place.

Tobacco companies are now targeting developing countries, where smoking is increasing as wealth increases. Here, Cambodian youth ride by billboards.

In the past two decades, as a consequence of lawsuits and government policies, tobacco advertising in developed countries has decreased dramatically and cigarette smoking among young people has also declined (Johnston et al., 2015). Anti-tobacco advertising has also proven to be effective in decreasing the likelihood that adolescents will begin smoking (Terry-McElrath et al., 2007; Rhodes et al., 2009). However, recently tobacco companies have increased their online advertising (Richardson et al., 2013), especially for electronic cigarettes, for which health effects are still uncertain. Also, tobacco companies are now targeting developing countries, where smoking is increasing as wealth increases (Ho et al., 2007; Kostova & Blecher, 2013).

The media export of physical risks from the West to developing countries has also been found in regard to body image and eating disorders, especially among girls. Although mainly a Western problem, eating disorders are increasing in parts of the world that are becoming more Westernized. For example, on the island nation of Fiji, traditionally the ideal body type for women was rounded and curvy. However, television was first introduced in 1995, mostly with programming from the United States and other Western countries, and subsequently the incidence of eating disorders rose substantially (Becker et al., 2007). Interviews with adolescent girls on Fiji showed that they admired the Western television characters and wanted to look like them, and that this goal in turn led to higher incidence of negative body image, preoccupation with weight, and purging behavior to control weight (Becker, 2004). In developed countries, media have also been tied to these physical risks. Among 15-year-old girls in Australia, Internet use has been associated with negative body image (Tiggemann & Miller, 2010). American girls who read magazines such as *Seventeen*, which contain numerous ads and articles featuring thin models, are especially likely to strive to be thin themselves and to engage in eating disordered behavior (Utter et al., 2003).

## Aggression: Behaviors and Attitudes

**LO 12.5.2 Explain the extent to which media causes aggressive behaviors and attitudes.**

Many people have concerns about the effects of television, especially on children and especially with respect to aggression. Content analyses have found that children's programs are even more violent than programs for adults. One study found that two-thirds of all children's programs contained violence, and about half the violence took place in cartoons (Aikat, 2007). Violence was portrayed as funny about two-thirds of the time. In most cases, the victims were not shown experiencing pain and the perpetrator of the violence was not punished. The effects of media violence on children, however, vary by age.

**EARLY AND MIDDLE CHILDHOOD.** What are the effects of witnessing so much TV violence on young children's development? More than five decades of research, including more than 300 studies using a variety of methods, has led to a strong consensus among scholars that watching TV violence increases children's aggression (Bushman & Chandler, 2007). The more aggressive children already are, the more they like to watch TV violence, but TV violence inspires aggressive thoughts and behavior even in children who are not usually aggressive (Bushman & Huesmann, 2012). Experimental studies indicate that causation is involved, not just correlation. For example, in one early study, children in an American preschool were randomly assigned to two groups (Steur et al., 1971). Over 11 days, one group watched violent cartoons, whereas the other group saw the same cartoons with the violence removed. During playground observations following this 11-day experiment, children who had seen the violent cartoons were more likely than children in the nonviolent cartoon group to kick and hit their peers.

Young children ages 3 to 6 years are believed to be especially vulnerable to the effects of TV violence (Bushman & Chandler, 2007). They are more likely than younger or older children to model their behavior after the behavior of others, including TV characters. Also, they are less likely than older children to have a clear understanding of the boundary between fantasy and reality, and so more likely to believe that what they witness on TV is real.

There is also evidence, however, that TV violence can have effects in middle childhood. An interesting study using a natural experiment compared different Canadian communities. The children in "Notel" (the name given by the researchers) were studied before and after the introduction of television into the community (MacBeth, 2006). Aggressive behavior among children in Notel was compared with the behavior of children in two comparable communities, one with only one television channel ("Unitel") and one with multiple TV channels ("Multitel"). Researchers obtained several ratings of aggressiveness in each community, including teachers' ratings, self-reports, and observers' ratings of children's verbal and physical aggressiveness. At the beginning of the study, aggressive behavior was lower among children in Notel than among children in Unitel or Multitel. However, aggressive behavior increased significantly among children in Notel, so that Notel children were equal to their Unitel and Multitel peers 2 years after the introduction of TV.

Another well-known study also supports the risk of violent television in middle childhood. This longitudinal study began when participants were 8 years old and continued until they reached age 30 (Bushman & Huesmann, 2012; Coyne, 2006; Huesmann et al., 1984). Researchers assessed television-viewing patterns and aggressive behavior at ages 8, 19, and 30 and, not surprisingly, found a correlation between aggressiveness and watching violent TV at age 8. They also found correlations between watching violent TV at age 8 and aggressive behavior in boys at age 19 and age 30. The 30-year-old men who had watched violent TV at age 8 were more likely to be arrested, more likely to have traffic violations, and more likely to abuse their children. Importantly, this relation was found even controlling for boys' initial levels of aggressiveness at age 8. So, it was not simply that aggressive persons were especially likely to watch violent television at all three ages, but that 8 year-olds who watched high levels of TV violence were more likely to behave aggressively at later ages than 8 year-olds who had watched lower levels of TV violence. The relationship between watching violent TV and later aggressive behavior did not occur for girls.

**ADOLESCENCE.** When it comes to adolescents, the evidence for TV violence causing aggressive behaviors is thin. Unfortunately, most of the studies on adolescents and television violence are correlational studies, which ask adolescents about the television programs they watch and about their aggressive behavior. As we have often noted, correlational studies do not show causality, and these studies merely indicate the expected finding that aggressive adolescents prefer aggressive television programs (Selah-Shayovits, 2006). They cannot answer the crucial question: "Does watching violence on TV cause adolescents to become more aggressive, or are adolescents who are more aggressive simply more likely to enjoy watching violence on TV?"

**field studies**
studies in which people's behavior is observed in a natural setting

In an effort to address this question, researchers have conducted numerous **field studies** on the effects of television on adolescent aggression. Typically, adolescents (usually boys) in a natural setting such as a residential school or summer camp are separated into two groups. One group is shown TV or movies with violent themes whereas the other views TV or movies with nonviolent themes. Then, the behavior of the boys in the two groups is recorded and compared. However, the findings of these studies are weak and inconsistent, and overall do not support the claim that viewing violent media causes adolescents to be more aggressive (Browne & Hamilton-Giachritsis, 2005; Freedman, 1988).

Even Rowell Huesmann, one of the most prominent proponents of the argument that televised violence causes aggression in children, states that "we do not need to be as concerned about adults' or even teenagers' exposure to media violence as much as we do with children's exposure. Media violence may have short-term effects on adults, but the real long-term effects seem to occur only with children" (Huesmann et al., 2003, p. 219).

This is not to dismiss the potential of televised violence for provoking violence in some adolescents under some circumstances, especially for adolescents who are already at risk for violence due to factors in their personalities and social environments (Browne & Hamilton-Giachritsis, 2005; Huesmann et al., 2003; Kronenberger et al., 2005). It is probably true that, for a subset of adolescents, media violence becomes a model for their own aggressiveness. Occasionally there are horrific cases where adolescents (most often boys) enact violence in a way that seems to draw on media portrayals.

Focusing on a different form of aggressive behavior, scholars have also looked at television watching and interpersonal aggression, which includes behavior such as gossip, verbal insults, and excluding others from the peer group. In one study, over 300 adolescents ages 11 to 14 listed their five favorite television programs (Coyne & Archer, 2005). Researchers analyzed these programs for the amount of interpersonal aggression they contained. The adolescents who indicated that they watched programs containing interpersonal aggression were also rated by their peers as being high on this kind of aggression. This study suffers from the common correlation-causation problem. In a recent longitudinal study by one of the researchers, however, watching interpersonal aggression predicted later interpersonal aggression among adolescents, whereas interpersonal aggression did *not* predict future watching of televised interpersonal aggression (Coyne, 2016). This longitudinal study provides stronger evidence of causality than correlational studies.

In sum, the evidence for TV causing aggressive behaviors in adolescents remains spotty. The evidence is stronger that television violence influences *attitudes* toward violence among adolescents, making them more accepting of violent behavior and less empathic toward the victims of violence (Bushman, 2016; Murray, 2008; Paradise, 2006). With electronic games as with television, current findings also indicate that violent content may rarely provoke violent behavior, but more often influence social attitudes. For example, playing violent electronic games has been found to lower empathy and raise acceptance of interpersonal aggression (Anderson, 2004; Funk, 2005; Funk et al., 2002; Lull & Bushman, 2016).

Media can convey sexual stereotypes. Female characters in electronic games, such as Lara Croft, often have unrealistic body proportions.

## Sexual Stereotypes and Victimization

**LO 12.5.3 Describe how media contribute to sexual stereotypes and victimization.**

Sex is second only to violence as a topic of public concern with respect to the possible effects of media. With sexuality as with aggressiveness, it is difficult to establish causality, but most scholars in this area agree that, through TV programs and other media, children, adolescents, and emerging adults learn cultural beliefs about how female and male roles differ in sexual interactions and what is considered physically attractive in males and females (Pardun et al., 2005; Rivadeneyra & Ward, 2005).

While media can be very useful as sources of information about health and sexuality, media also convey sexual stereotypes. Female characters in electronic games, for example, often have unrealistic body proportions (Olson, 2010). Content analyses of television shows also find that they portray strong gender stereotypes, with the message that "boys will be boys and girls better be prepared," that is, that boys seek sex actively and aggressively and girls act as "sexual gatekeepers" who are supposed to attract boys' sexual interest but also resist their advances (Fox & Potocki, 2016; Hust et al., 2008; Kim et al., 2007; Kirsch & Murnen, 2015; Tolman et al., 2007).

Movies also provide sexual scripts, but in a more explicit way than TV does (Freeman, 2006; Hust et al., 2008; Pardun, 2002; Steele, 2002). As one prominent researcher in this area has observed, "What television suggests, movies and videos do" (Greenberg, 1994, p. 180). With pornographic movies easily accessible on the Internet, more children, adolescents, and emerging adults may be exposed to them and have their sexuality shaped by them. A study of Dutch adolescents concluded that boys who watched sexually explicit online movies were more likely than other boys to view women as sex objects (Peter & Valkenburg, 2007). There was no effect for exposure to pornographic magazines, only movies.

Online chat rooms are also sometimes frequented by adult sexual predators (Atkinson & Newton, 2010). In a study of "on-line victimization" among American adolescents ages 10 to 17 who were regular Internet users, 25% reported that they had been subjected to unwanted sexual exposure online (defined as pictures of naked people or people having sex), usually through surfing the Web (Finkelhor et al., 2000). Also, 20% had received a sexual solicitation, defined as a request for sex or sexual information.

> **Critical Thinking Question:** What are some key advertisement features that you would recommend to an American metropolitan city launching a public health campaign to counteract negative body images in teenage girls? Draw on your knowledge of how children and adolescents relate to media. Also, give consideration to how teenagers vary on factors such as ethnicity and social class.

### Summary: Risks of Media

**LO 12.5.1 Describe the risks of media in regard to obesity, tobacco use, and body image.**

Children's use of media is correlated with less exercise, consumption of more junk food and sugary drinks, smoking initiation, and negative body image.

**LO 12.5.2 Explain the extent to which media causes aggressive behaviors and attitudes.**

The more aggressive children already are, the more they like to watch TV violence, but TV violence inspires aggressive thoughts and behavior even in children who are not usually aggressive.

When it comes to adolescents, the evidence for TV violence causing aggressive behaviors is thin. Nonetheless, media violence may be a model for aggressiveness for a subset of adolescents.

**LO 12.5.3 Describe how media contribute to sexual stereotypes and victimization.**

While media can be very useful as sources of information about health and sexuality, media also convey sexual stereotypes including views of girls and women as sexual objects and gatekeepers. Online chat rooms are also sometimes frequented by adult sexual predators who expose children to sexual content, and solicit sex or sexual information from children.

# 12.6 Benefits of Media

For many decades the overwhelming focus was on the risks of media, but recent research is paying more attention to benefits. Since the role of media is increasing in the lives of children all over the world, it is important to know what the benefits are and how they might be promoted by parents, educators, and policy makers. We will focus on cognitive, emotional, and social benefits.

**Critical Thinking Question:** Why do you think the primary developmental research focus has been on the risks rather than benefits of media?

## Cognitive Benefits

**LO 12.6.1 Describe the cognitive benefits of educational media programs and cross-platform learning.**

**video deficit effect**
refers to children younger than 2 years learning better from watching behaviors by an actual person than a virtual person

Media offers cognitive benefits, but those benefits become more pronounced after age 2 and also depend on the content of the media (Kirkorian et al., 2008). Very young children sometimes learn best by interacting with people, not screens. The **video deficit effect** refers to children younger than 2 learning better from watching behaviors by an actual person than a virtual person. For example, experiments have compared 2-year-olds who watch either an actual adult in a room or a virtual adult on a video hide a toy. Findings show that those who have observed the actual person have a much easier time finding the toy afterward (Troseth, 2003; Troseth & DeLoache, 1998). The video deficit effect has also been found for other cognitive skills such as learning vocabulary (Krcmar et al., 2007) and deferred imitation (Hayne et al., 2003).

However, it turns out that the content of the media matters. One study had parents report toddlers' TV-viewing patterns every 3 months from age 6 to 30 months, then assessed the toddlers' language development at 30 months (Linebarger & Walker, 2005). Watching educationally oriented programs such as *Dora the Explorer* resulted in greater vocabularies and higher expressive language scores than watching other programs did. Other studies have found that TV can inspire imaginative play among toddlers (Weber, 2006). As parents, we remember this well from when our twins were toddlers. They would watch a TV show or a video and then invent their own elaborate games pretending to be characters they had watched, such as the *Teletubbies* or *Peter Pan*. We even bought them Teletubbies dolls to facilitate the games.

Some educational TV programs are highly popular among young children. Perhaps most notable is the *Sesame Street* program, which is broadcast in 120 countries worldwide (Truglio, 2007). The content of the program is based on developmental psychology knowledge of what will be most appealing to young children and most effective at teaching them the academic skills that will prepare them for school (Bergstrom, 2007). Content is adapted to the culture in which the program is shown, for example addressing the stigma of AIDS in South Africa and promoting cross-cultural respect and understanding among children in the Middle East (Fisch et al., 2010; Truglio, 2007).

*Sesame Street* and other programs have shown impressive positive effects on young children's development. In one study, viewing *Sesame Street* at ages 2 and 3 years predicted higher scores at age 5 on tests of language development and math skills, even controlling for parents' education and income (Scantlin, 2007). In another longitudinal study, children who viewed

*Sesame Street* at age 5 had higher grades in English, math, and science at ages 15 and 19 than children in the comparison group (Anderson et al., 2001). Studies of *Sesame Street* and other educational programs have shown the programs to have other positive effects as well, such as promoting imaginative play (Scantlin, 2007).

Increasingly, educational media projects incorporate different kinds of media. As we saw earlier, the Sesame Workshop launched *Panwapa*, a multimedia program, in 2008 (see the *Education Focus* box in this chapter). This has led to an interest in **cross-platform learning** (Fisch et al., in press), or how multiple media relate to learning. Studies are few, but some experiments have found more benefits to literacy and mathematical problem solving from use of multiple rather than one or no media (Fisch et al., in press; Piotrowski et al., 2013). But more may not always be better. Future research is needed on how many and which combinations of media are most effective (Fisch, 2013).

Television shows with prosocial themes can inspire prosocial behavior in toddlers.

**cross-platform learning**
use of multiple rather than one or no media for learning purposes

Children and adolescents in developed countries also commonly use media for school and homework. Research indicates that children who use computers produce written assignments that are longer and of higher quality than when they write by hand. Use of the computer and the Internet has also been linked to higher academic achievement (Attewell, 2001; Judge et al., 2006). The Internet is perhaps the greatest invention in human history for providing access to information. With a few clicks or taps of the finger, people are able to find a staggering array of information sources on virtually any topic. The Internet has tremendous potential to enhance education in childhood and adolescence, which is why schools have been so zealous about becoming connected to it.

Of course, we all know that not all uses of the Internet are positive. Although the Internet can be a great information resource for school projects, one concern is that older children, adolescents, and emerging adults use the Internet for academic cheating by downloading prewritten materials and papers (Jones et al., 2008; Mastin et al., 2009). Another concern is that too much time on the Internet compromises academic performance. One study of college students in the United Kingdom found a negative correlation between grade performance and hours per week spent online, perhaps indicating a displacement effect (Englander et al., 2010). Another study of Chinese college students in eight universities found that heavy Internet use (more than 15 hours a week) was related to poorer academic performance (Huang et al., 2009). It is important to keep in mind that these two studies show correlation, not causation.

## Emotional Benefits

**LO 12.6.2 Describe the benefits to emotional development from media.**

We have seen that the content of media, such as TV shows, matters for cognitive development. The same is true for emotional development. In one American study, a group of 2-year-olds was shown the TV show *Barney and Friends*, featuring a large, purple, talking dinosaur who encourages behavior such as kindness and sharing. This group was then compared in free play to another group of 2-year-olds who had not seen the show (Singer & Singer, 1998). The toddlers in the *Barney* group showed more prosocial behavior, such as sharing, and less aggressiveness. Studies of *Sesame Street* and other educational programs have also shown them to promote prosocial behavior such as cooperation (Bergstrom, 2007). In a national study, 70% of parents of children under age 3 reported that their toddlers had imitated positive behavior they had seen on television, such as sharing or helping, whereas only 27% had imitated aggressive behavior such as hitting or kicking (Rideout & Hamel, 2006).

Studies in Japan, Singapore, and the United States have likewise indicated that playing electronic games with prosocial content, such as helping others, is tied to subsequent prosocial behavior on the part of children, adolescents, and emerging adults (Gentile et al., 2009). Because most of these studies involved experimental and longitudinal designs, they help to document causation. Since the content of media is important, it is also important to know that the majority of adolescents' favorite electronic games involve violence. A content analysis of nearly 400 of the most popular electronic games found that 94% contained violence (Busching et al., 2015; Haninger & Thompson, 2004). One study asked boys themselves about the effects of playing violent electronic games (Olson et al., 2008). The interviews showed that the boys (ages 12–14) said that playing the games helped them get rid of negative feelings, such as anger and stress. This suggests that there was a **cathartic effect** where negative feelings were purged.

**cathartic effect**
experiences, including media experiences, that provide relief from negative emotions

Studies of adolescent and emerging adult fans of heavy metal music have also shown this. In one interview study, metal fans consistently said they listen to the music especially when they are angry; this is not surprising, in view of the violent, angry quality of the music and lyrics. However, they also consistently reported that the music has the effect of calming them down (Arnett, 1991, 1996; see also Scheel & Westefeld, 1999). This cathartic effect of heavy metal music has also been demonstrated experimentally (Wooten, 1992). Heavy metal music and violent electronic games, however, are unlikely to have a beneficial cathartic effect on everyone. Instead, the effect may well depend on the needs and characteristics of particular adolescents and emerging adults.

## Benefits to Social Development

**LO 12.6.3 Describe the benefits to social development from media.**

Media also appears to be beneficial to social development, including identity formation and relations with friends. This may especially be the case for new media.

**IDENTITY DEVELOPMENT.** The Internet provides adolescents with an opportunity to practice social communication and engage in "identity play," in which they actively choose how to represent themselves in terms of gender, personality, and conversational style (Theil, 2006). Adolescents who have particular interests or needs not shared by their peers may be able to find like-minded adolescents online. For example, a variety of websites offer resources for sexual and gender minority youth.

Social-networking profiles are also an arena for identity presentation (Davis, 2010; Mazur & Kozarian, 2010). Users of social-networking websites construct a profile describing themselves, containing information about topics such as their family, their romantic partner (if they have one), and their interests (Magnuson & Dundes, 2008). Most profiles also include a photo (Hinduja & Patchin, 2008). Many users have a blog linked to their profile, where they record their thoughts and feelings and experiences. Page design, images, and links are expressions of self that enable users to communicate a style and personality (Stern, 2002; Zhao et al., 2008). Analyses of blog content report that half of all teenage bloggers discussed sexual identity, love relationships, and real or desired girlfriends and boyfriends (Huffaker & Calvert, 2005).

**Critical Thinking Question:** How are "imaginary play" in children's media experience and "identity play" in adolescents' and emerging adults' media experience similar and different?

Social-networking profiles are an arena for identity presentation which can have a variety of benefits. Do you think there are any potential risks?

**RELATIONSHIPS WITH FRIENDS.** For both adolescents and emerging adults, the concern has been raised that use of the Internet may promote social isolation (Nie & Erbring, 2000; Turkle, 2011). However, research has shown that for most adolescents and emerging adults, the Internet and other new media are more likely to relieve social isolation and promote social connections. One national survey in the United States indicated that three of four online adolescent social network users have posted at least one comment to a friend's blog (Lenhart & Madden, 2007). Because blogs are often interconnected, they may facilitate the fulfillment of adolescents' and emerging adults' needs for conversation, social bonding, and relationship building and maintenance, with both their close friends and a larger group of acquaintances (Bortree, 2005; Lenhart & Madden, 2005).

Another national survey of American adolescents (ages 13–17) also found mostly positive effects of social media (Common Sense Media, 2012).

Adolescents reported that using social media makes them feel more confident and outgoing, and less shy. Over half (52%) also said that using social media has helped their friendships; only 4% said it has hurt. A majority of adolescents reported that social media use allows them to communicate with friends they do not see regularly, to get to know other students at their school better, and to connect with people with whom they share a common interest. This is not to say that using new media has nothing but positive effects. In the survey, nearly half (45%) of adolescents said they get frustrated with friends for texting or social networking when they are out together.

**Watch** MEDIA USE IN EMERGING ADULTHOOD ACROSS CULTURES

A review of research also concluded that Internet use both stimulated and enhanced self-disclosure among friends and acquaintances (Valkenburg & Peter, 2009). About one in three adolescents were able to self-disclose better online than in face-to-face situations. Also, adolescent boys benefitted more from online communication with existing friends than girls did. A recent study with adolescents from Bermuda found that the use of social-networking sites heightened their sense of peer belonging and made it easier for them to express themselves (Davis, 2012).

A study that followed American adolescents for 3 years after high school also found that e-mail and social networking helped them maintain their high school friendships even after they had moved away in emerging adulthood (Theil, 2006). Of course, some people do become dependent on the Internet to an extent that reduces their direct social contacts (Griffiths, 2006), but for most adolescents and emerging adults the Internet has beneficial effects on their relations with friends and peers. For more information, watch the video *Media Use in Emerging Adulthood Across Cultures*.

### SUMMARY: Benefits of Media

**LO 12.6.1 Describe the cognitive benefits of educational media programs and cross-platform learning.**

Media offers cognitive benefits, but those benefits become more pronounced after age 2 and also depend on the content of the media. For example, educationally-oriented TV programs contribute to language development and imaginative play. Studies of cross-platform learning, or how multiple media relate to learning, suggest benefits to literacy and mathematical problem solving.

**LO 12.6.2 Describe the benefits to emotional development from media.**

Prosocial media content can inspire cooperative and helping behaviors. Interestingly, however, some children and adolescents also seem to experience a cathartic effect of media content involving anger or violence. In other words, they gain relief from negative emotions that they were feeling.

**LO 12.6.3 Describe the benefits to social development from media.**

Media appear to be beneficial to identity formation. For example, social-networking profiles are an arena for experimenting with identity presentation. For most adolescents and emerging adults, the Internet and other new media also relieve social isolation and promote social connections.

## 12.7 Globalization and Media

There are interesting similarities and differences in the media uses of children across cultures. Some of the similarities reflect globalization of childhood and adolescence (Jensen, 2008, 2016). As we saw at the outset of this chapter, media have diffused all over the globe. This also means that young people, on every continent, are increasingly familiar with the same television shows, the same movies, the same video games, the same social-networking sites, and the same musical recordings and performers (Banaag, 2010; Taillon, 2004). For example, in a study of adolescents in Botswana, two-thirds reported watching American television programs on a weekly basis (Lloyd & Mendez, 2001). Children, adolescents, and emerging adults with access to the Internet can use it to make contacts with young people in other parts of the world, although, as we also saw at the outset, there is a "digital divide" between developing and developed countries.

Nevertheless, social and economic change has been extremely rapid in the past 50 years in developing countries. Today's children often have parents and grandparents who grew up in a time when their country had far less economic and technological contact with the West. While these adults are more familiar with and more attached to their native traditions, such as their indigenous musical forms and songs, the children are growing up with Western media, which compete for their attention even if they also learn the songs and arts of their own culture.

## Cultural Values

**LO 12.7.1 Describe how the worldwide diffusion of media impacts children's values pertaining to gender roles, individual choice in love and work, and independence.**

Several ethnographies provide examples of the role of the media in promoting globalization in the lives of children and adolescents. Among Moroccan adolescents studied by Davis and Davis (1989, 1995, 2007, 2012), this influence is especially notable with respect to gender roles. In the past, Moroccan culture, like many traditional cultures, had strictly defined gender roles. Marriages were arranged by parents and were made on the basis of practical family considerations rather than romantic love. Female—but not male—virginity at marriage was considered essential, and adolescent girls were forbidden to spend time in the company of adolescent boys. These gender differences continue to be part of Moroccan culture today, particularly in rural areas. They are also reflected in boys having more access to media (Davis & Davis, 2007).

For both adolescent girls and boys, however, exposure to media is changing the way they think about gender relations and gender roles. The TV programs, songs, and movies they are exposed to are produced not only in Morocco and other Islamic countries, but also include many from France (Morocco was once a French colony) and the United States. From these various sources, Moroccan adolescents are seeing portrayals of gender roles quite different from what they see among their parents, grandparents, and other adults around them. In the media that the adolescents use, romance and passion are central to male–female relationships. Love is the central basis for entering marriage, and the idea of accepting a marriage arranged by parents is either ignored or portrayed as something to be resisted. Young women are usually portrayed not in traditional roles but in professional occupations and as being in control of their lives and unashamed of their sexuality.

The reach of Western media is worldwide. Here, a girl in Jordan watches a film.

In many places, young people are using all this new information to construct a conception of gender roles quite different from the traditional conceptions in their culture (Obermeyer, 2000). Altogether it amounts to an influence toward globalization and toward the individualism of the West, as media are "used by adolescents in a period of rapid social change to reimagine many aspects of their lives, including a desire for more autonomy, for more variety in heterosexual interactions, and for more choice of a job and of a mate" (Davis & Davis, 1995, p. 578).

Another example of media and globalization comes from Richard Condon's (1988, 1995) fascinating study of the Inuit of the Canadian Arctic. Condon's ethnography is of particular interest with respect to media because he first observed Inuit adolescents in 1978, just before television first became available in 1980, and subsequently returned there for further observations several times during the 1980s. Between his first and subsequent visits, he observed striking changes in adolescents' behavior with respect to romantic relationships and competition in sports. Condon and many of the Inuit he interviewed attributed the changes to the introduction of television.

With respect to sports, before TV arrived, Inuit adolescents rarely played sports, and when they did they were reluctant to appear like they were trying hard to win over other players because of Inuit cultural traditions that discourage competition and encourage cooperation. All of this changed after the introduction of television. Baseball, football, and hockey games quickly became among the most popular TV programs, especially among adolescents, and participation in these sports (especially hockey) became a central part of the recreational activities of adolescent boys, with adolescent girls often coming to watch. Furthermore, adolescent boys became intensely competitive in the games they played, no longer shy about trying hard to win and talking loudly about their superior talent when they did win—clearly emulating the players they watched on TV. It is rare to see such an unambiguous example of the effects of media on adolescent attitudes and behaviors.

The other area in which the influence of television was observed by Condon was male–female relationships. Before the introduction of television, adolescents' dating and sexual behavior was furtive and secretive. Couples rarely displayed affection for one another in public; in fact, couples rarely even acknowledged any special relationship when they were around others. Condon described one adolescent boy whom he had known closely for a year before the boy confided that he had a girlfriend he had been dating for the past 4 years—and even then, the boy refused to reveal her name! However, all this changed after a couple of years of exposure to TV. Teenage couples were frequently seen together in public, holding hands or hugging. At community dances, young couples no longer ignored each other, staying at opposite ends of the dance hall, but sat together as couples and danced as couples. Condon's ethnographic research shows the influence of television on Inuit children. For another remarkable example of how children's values and sense of self can change with the introduction of media, watch the video *Ethiopian Children Receive Laptops* in the Research Focus feature.

## Research Focus: Ethiopian Children Receive Laptops

Nina Hansen, a Dutch researcher, and her colleagues have conducted a series of field experiments in Ethiopia in order to understand how the introduction of Western media influences children's cognitive and social development (Hansen et al., 2012; Hansen & Postmes, in press). In 2008, the Ethiopian government in collaboration with aid agencies decided to introduce laptops to 6,000 children in rural and urban schools. Hansen was motivated to do the research because, as she writes: "At some historical junctures, cultural changes occur that are both profound and long-lasting, to the point of changing the very societal structure and human psychology, itself" (Hansen, 2012, p. 222). As Hansen observes, media are powerful drivers of changes to human development and culture.

Ethiopia is one of the least developed countries in the world. In 2008, when the laptop program was started, 0.7% of the population owned a PC and 0.4% had access to the Internet. The comparable figures for the United States at that time were 81% and 74% (World Bank, 2009). With respect to values, Ethiopian culture emphasizes collectivism and respect for elders. Children, then, typically do not own much—let alone anything as valuable as a laptop. They also are not accustomed to making independent decisions.

Why might the introduction of a laptop into an Ethiopian child's life matter? First, according to Hansen and colleagues, the use of a laptop introduces new information. Second, the use of a laptop requires new knowledge and action that would be foreign to parents and other elders. Third, possessing something as valuable as a laptop represents a radical change from the economic status quo and also a potential upheaval of

**Watch** ETHIOPIAN CHILDREN RECEIVE LAPTOPS

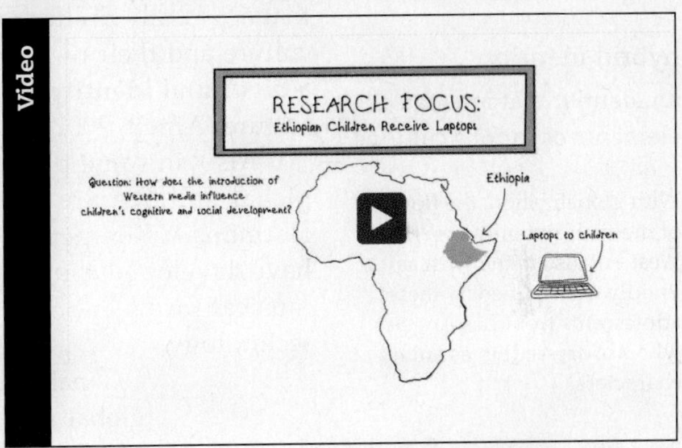


the social hierarchy. Such a possession clearly distinguishes a child from others.

In one of the studies by Hansen and colleagues (2012), 169 children in grades 7 and 8 were divided into three groups with approximately even numbers of girls and boys. There was a group where children had a fully functioning laptop, a group where the laptop stopped functioning (due to circumstances such as broken parts), and a group with no laptop. The goal was to determine if the children would come to differ on their sense of self or identity and cultural values.

After one year, the three groups were compared. With respect to identity, the three groups remained similar on interdependence, or valuing what others think of oneself. With respect to cultural values, the three groups remained similar on collectivism.

But the group with the functioning laptop also became different, in comparison to the other two groups. This group was significantly higher on independence, or valuing being unique and different from others. Also, the group with the functioning laptop was significantly higher on individualistic values emphasizing individual decision-making, achievement, and leadership.

The authors conclude that their results show that it is not the mere ownership of a laptop that matters, but rather that the use of a laptop changes identity development and cultural values.

In recent years, the African Union has committed to providing more laptops to primary school children throughout Africa.

## Review Questions

1. Hansen's research can best be described as an example of:
   - **a.** An ethnography
   - **b.** A survey
   - **c.** A natural experiment
   - **d.** A cross-sectional study
2. Results showed that after one year, the group with the functioning laptop differed from the other two groups in the following way:
   - **a.** It was higher on interdependence
   - **b.** It was higher on independence
   - **c.** It was higher on collectivism
   - **d.** It was higher on egocentrism

# Bicultural and Hybrid Identities

**LO 12.7.2 Compare the concepts of bicultural and hybrid identity, and explain how each is related to global media.**

**bicultural identity**
identity with two distinct facets, for example one for the local culture and one for the global culture

**hybrid identity**
an identity that integrates elements of various cultures

Does the globalization of media mean that Western (especially American) media will obliterate all the other media of the world and establish a homogeneous global culture dominated by the United States? It is difficult to say. As we saw at the start of this chapter, governments in some countries place restrictions on Western media and programs. Also, what seems to be happening in most places so far is that local media are coexisting with Western media. For example, young people watch Western television shows, but they also view shows in their own language produced in their own country, and perhaps shows from other countries as well. They go to American movies, but they also attend movies that are locally produced. They listen to British music, but also to the music of their own culture and their own artistic traditions. The globalization of media appears to promote a **bicultural identity**, with one rooted in the local culture and one attached to the global culture (Arnett, 2002).

Also, in some places, **hybrid identities** and cultural values arise where local and global cultures are merged to produce something new altogether (Hermans, 2015; Hermans & Kempen, 1998). For example, in Britain, immigrant musicians from India have developed a musical style dubbed "Indipop," a combination of traditional Indian musical forms and instruments with British and American popular music forms and technology.

With globalization, the flow of media is not only *from* the West but also *to* the West as vividly exemplified by these adolescents from Los Angeles who are dressed up as anime characters.

Finally, it is worth pointing out that it is not only Western media that have global reach. For example, the Japanese graphic novels known as "manga" and graphic videos known as "anime" have become popular worldwide (Coyne et al., 2015). In turn, they have inspired children and adolescents from many countries to become interested in aspects of Japanese culture and society (Bendazzi, 2016).

## SUMMARY: Globalization and Media

**LO 12.7.1 Describe how the worldwide diffusion of media impacts children's values pertaining to gender roles, individual choice in love and work, and independence.**

Media bring new values into the lives of children and adolescents from traditional cultures. This often includes relatively egalitarian gender roles and an emphasis on individual choice in romantic relationships and work.

**LO 12.7.2 Compare the concepts of bicultural and hybrid identity, and explain how each is related to global media.**

The globalization of media appears to promote a bicultural identity, with one rooted in the local culture and one attached to the global culture. Also, in some places, hybrid identities and cultural values arise where local and global cultures are merged to produce something new altogether, such as "Indipop" (traditional Indian musical forms and instruments merged with British and American popular music forms and technology).

## Apply Your Knowledge as a Professional

The topics covered in this chapter apply to a wide variety of career professions. Watch this video to learn how they apply to a media literacy teacher at a primary school.

**Journaling Question:** To what extent are you a digital native or a digital immigrant: cognitively, emotionally, and socially?

Chapter 13

# Meaning Systems: Moral, Religious, and Civic Development

## Learning Objectives

### 13.1 Moral Development: Emotions and Socialization

13.1.1 Describe the emergence of guilt, shame, and empathy, and evidence for the roles of nature and nurture in their development.

13.1.2 Describe different ways that the socialization of morality takes place, including the extent to which children and adolescents take active part in socialization.

### 13.2 Moral Development: Reasoning and Identity

13.2.1 Describe Piaget's and Kohlberg's stages of moral development and the evidence supporting the cognitive-developmental approach.

13.2.2 Describe the distinction made by domain theory between moral and non-moral reasoning and the extent to which findings support the theory.

13.2.3 Differentiate the two orientations proposed by Gilligan, and explain the main contributions of her theory.

13.2.4 Describe the cultural-developmental approach to moral reasoning and the extent of evidence for the approach.

13.2.5 Describe the extent to which moral identity involves consideration for others and self.

### 13.3 Religious and Spiritual Development

13.3.1 Explain how conceptions of supernatural entities depend on age and religion.

13.3.2 Describe the role of family, peers, and ethnic group on religious beliefs and behaviors.

13.3.3 Explain the extent to which religion serves a protective and positive role in development.

13.3.4 Describe the general religious beliefs of American adolescents and emerging adults, and explain the rise of secularism among those age groups in developed countries.

### 13.4 Civic Development

13.4.1 Summarize the characteristics of adolescents who engage in community service and the ways community service promotes positive development.

13.4.2 Describe the three major American government institutions through which emerging adults are involved in community service.

13.4.3 Describe the political thinking and participation of adolescents and emerging adults.

### 13.5 Political Conflict and Extremism

13.5.1 Review the consequences of children's and adolescents' exposure to and participation in war-time experiences, and describe interventions for youth traumatized by war.

13.5.2 Explain the nature of political extremism in emerging adulthood.

### 13.6 Values in Today's and Tomorrow's World

13.6.1 Explain the evidence for the rise of individualism in recent times.

13.6.2 Describe the extent to which children across the world are likely to have increased exposure to diversity in tomorrow's world.

ARISTOTLE, THE ANCIENT GREEK PHILOSOPHER, WAS BRILLIANT IN MANY WAYS. A prolific writer, he contributed groundbreaking knowledge to a very long list of areas, including ethics, politics, mathematics, physics, and biology. Yet he believed that dictatorship was superior to democracy, that some humans were born to be slaves, and that women were inferior to men in virtually every respect. Like all of us, Aristotle held beliefs characteristic of his time and place.

Certainly, when and where we are born influence our moral, religious, and political beliefs. At the same time, however, moral, religious, and civic development also show some common patterns from birth through adolescence and emerging adulthood. In this chapter, we examine these developmental patterns while also paying attention to the importance of culture and globalization.

**Watch** CHAPTER INTRODUCTION: MEANING SYSTEMS: MORAL, RELIGIOUS, AND CIVIC DEVELOPMENT

# 13.1 Moral Development: Emotions and Socialization

Chances are that when Aristotle was a toddler his sociomoral emotions—such as guilt, shame, and empathy—were not all that different from yours during your own toddlerhood. How soon do you think sociomoral emotions and behaviors start to take on a distinctive cultural stamp? In this section, we look at the early emergence of sociomoral emotions, including the extent to which those emotions are shaped by nature and nurture. Then, we turn to a closer examination of the many ways that morality is socialized.

**guilt**
feeling of responsibility and remorse for perceived wrong-doing by the self

**shame**
feeling of responsibility and remorse for perceived wrong-doing by self or others, with a focus on interpersonal consequences

## Sociomoral Emotions

**LO 13.1.1 Describe the emergence of guilt, shame, and empathy, and evidence for the roles of nature and nurture in their development.**

Toddlerhood is when the sociomoral emotions first appear (see Chapter 7). Three sociomoral emotions that psychologists have investigated in depth are guilt, shame, and empathy.

GUILT. By age 2, toddlers express **guilt**, the feeling of responsibility and remorse for perceived wrong-doing. In an experimental study where children were led to believe that they had damaged a valuable object, 22-month-olds exhibited signs of guilt. They looked down, squirmed, covered their faces with their hands, or started crying (Kochanska et al., 2002). Longitudinal research following up on this experiment has shown that the children who displayed more guilt at 22 and 45 months were more likely to avoid wrong-doing at 4½ years of age. For example, they refrained from touching a prohibited object and from cheating on a task (Kochanska et al., 2008). By 5½ years of age, these children were also less likely to engage in hurtful and problematic social behaviors (Kochanska et al., 2010).

By age 2, toddlers express guilt. Unrolling the bathroom tissue can be fun—until you're found out.

The development of guilt is related to both nature and nurture. Feeling guilty is linked to temperament, which is biologically based. Children with fearful temperaments are more likely to exhibit guilt (Kochanska et al., 2002). Many studies indicate that a nurturing relationship between mother and child also contributes (Killen & Smetana, 2015; Padilla-Walker & Memmott-Elison, in press; Thompson, 2012). Secure attachment is associated with the development of guilt and conscience (Kochanska & Aksan, 2006). Also, a study of conversations between American mothers and 4-year-olds about the children's past misbehaviors found that the mothers who most frequently discussed other people's feelings had children with the highest levels of guilt and conscience development (Laible & Thompson, 2000).

Furthermore, research has indicated that the fit between a child's temperament and parenting is important. Fearful children seem to benefit from having mothers who take a gentle approach to discipline and who reason with the child. Gentle discipline, however, is unrelated to the development of guilt and conscience in toddlers with a fearless temperament. For these toddlers, having a secure attachment to the mother seems to matter more (Kochanska & Aksan, 2004; Kochanska et al., 2011).

**Critical Thinking Question:** Can you elaborate on how these findings pertaining to fearful and fearless toddlers relate to the concept of goodness-of-fit introduced in Chapter 7?

SHAME. Like guilt, **shame** involves the feeling of responsibility and remorse for perceived wrong-doing. Shame, however, is more oriented toward interpersonal relationships. Shame involves a sense that others will think poorly of you because of what you did. Shame may also be felt not only in regard to wrong-doing done by you, but also by others with whom you have a relationship. In short, shame is often a group concern, rather than an individual one. Much of the research on the emergence and development of shame has been conducted in traditional and non-Western cultures. Among the Kaluli people of Papua New Guinea, 2-year-olds feel shame and use shaming language with other children, such as "aren't you ashamed?!" (Schieffelin, 1986, 1990). Research with Chinese families from Taiwan also shows the presence of shame by toddlerhood. Two-and-a-half-year-olds exhibit signs of shame, and 4-year-olds will join in shaming other people (Fung, 1999; Miller et al., 2012).

Extensive research with Taiwanese families indicates that parents teach their toddlers shame as a way of preparing the children to live in a collectivistic culture that emphasizes the value of consideration for others (Chao & Tseng, 2002; Miller et al., 1997, 2012). One study found that caregivers of young children were most likely to induce shame in response to three kinds of transgressions: (1) behaviors that threatened interpersonal harmony such as unruliness, (2) behaviors that violated property rules such as taking an object that belonged to someone else, and (3) unhealthy or unhygienic behaviors such as eating sloppily (Fung, 1999).

Whereas shaming may seem like an authoritarian approach to parenting, research indicates that shaming need not be harsh nor entail the absence of warmth and love. Analyses of conversations between caregivers and young children in Taiwan show that caregivers often accompany shaming with thoughtful reasoning about what is morally right and wrong, and that shaming is often keyed in ironic or playful ways (Fung, 1999; Miller et al., 2012). The primary goal of shame is not to make the child feel bad, but rather to use shame as a way to socialize morality in a collectivistic culture.

**EMPATHY.** A third sociomoral emotion that is important to moral development in early childhood is **empathy**, the ability to understand and respond helpfully to another person's distress. Empathy involves feeling emotions that are similar to or consistent with another person's situation (Hoffman, 2000). For example, you may feel distressed when witnessing someone in pain. Toddlers and even infants show signs of empathy, but the capacity for empathy develops further in early childhood (Eisenberg & Valiente, 2004). Children become better at perspective-taking, and being able to understand how others think and feel makes them more empathic. Empathy contributes to the moral understanding of principles such as avoiding harm and being fair, because through empathy children understand how their behavior would make another person feel. Empathy also promotes prosocial behavior such as being helpful (Carlo & Pierotti, in press; Eisenberg et al., 2010).

**empathy**
ability to understand and respond helpfully to another person's distress

Researchers have become interested in just how early empathy and helpful behaviors emerge in infancy and toddlerhood, and what this tells us about the importance of nature and nurture in moral development. A series of laboratory studies have shown that toddlers between the ages of 14 and 18 months will help an adult in need. The toddlers will pick up an object that the adult "accidentally" drops, open the door of a cabinet for an adult whose hands are full, and solve a problem for an adult who looks distressed or confused. The experiments also show that the toddlers clearly assess the emotions and needs of the adults because they do not, for example, help out an adult who intentionally throws down an object (Warneken & Tomasello, 2006, 2007).

Remarkably, even infants seem attuned to helpfulness. Infants who watch a video where a character climbing a hill either receives help from another character (the "helper") or is prevented from climbing by another character (the "hinderer") show a preference for the "helper." They look longer at this prosocial figure (Hamlin et al., 2007; Hamlin & Wynn, 2011).

To some developmental psychologists, the early presence of empathy and preference for helpfulness in infants and toddlers indicate that babies are born with a moral sense. Paul Bloom, who has contributed to the research on infants' reactions to helpfulness and hindering, has written that "babies are moral animals, equipped by evolution with empathy and compassion, [and] the capacity to judge the actions of others" (Bloom, 2013, p. 218). Michael Tomasello has also argued that early prosocial tendencies are universal and based in the evolutionary human heritage of interdependence and group-mindedness (Vaish & Tomasello, 2014). In other words, humans need to live in groups in order to survive and thrive, and therefore prosocial tendencies have been selected for in the course of human evolution.

Moral socialization, however, is not absent in infancy. A recent study in the United States examined the extent to which parents encourage and reinforce helping behaviors in 11- to 24-month-olds (Dahl, 2015). Researchers videotaped 2½ hours of family time in homes with infants and toddlers. Almost 90% of the children engaged in helping behaviors such as handing an object to a family member, sweeping the floor, or setting the table. Almost 70% of all helping by children was encouraged by a family member. For example, an adult might ask "can you give me the ball?" Also, almost 60% of the helping behaviors were reinforced by adults. For example, adults praised helpful behavior or said "Thank you!"

Interestingly, reinforcement was higher for younger than older children. The research suggests that reinforcement, such as praising and thanking, are important ways of keeping infants engaged in helping at a time when their abilities to help are just emerging. In contrast, as toddlers become reliable helpers, family members may restrict their approval only to situations where it still seems necessary and productive. While the study does not refute that infants may come into the world with natural tendencies toward empathy and helpfulness, it highlights that the socialization of empathy and helping starts early in development. Infants helped in the home from around their first birthday, and family members encouraged and reinforced the young children's helping.

Children in many traditional cultures also are expected to help from very early on (LeVine & LeVine, 2016; Whiting & Edwards, 1988). In traditional African agricultural communities, where mothers have a very high workload, they assign chores to their toddlers. The children in these communities are often encouraged to compete by working harder, and children take it as a sign of approval when their mothers assign them more chores.

Further evidence for the role of socialization is that there are cultural differences in young children's helpfulness. Children in collectivistic cultures such as Brazil and Guatemala have been shown to engage in more helpful and prosocial behaviors, as compared to children in the United States (Carlo et al., 2011; Mosier & Rogoff, 2003). In cultures that are relatively collectivistic, a high value is placed on empathy, consideration of others, and helpfulness. This has also been found within some ethnic cultures in the United States. African American children have been found to engage in more prosocial behaviors than Latino children, who, in turn, display more prosocial behaviors than white children (Armenta et al., 2011; Knight et al., 1993; Spivak & Howes, 2011).

There are also more subtle differences between cultures in regard to empathy and helpful behaviors. For example, one study found that Kenyan children on the whole were more prosocial than American children. At the same time, Kenyan children were particularly helpful toward family members and relatives, whereas American children were more helpful toward strangers (de Guzman et al., 2008).

In traditional African communities where mothers have a very high workload, toddlers help with chores. This child from a village in Mozambique is getting clean water from a well.

We see, then, that the sociomoral emotions of guilt, shame, and empathy clearly emerge very early in childhood, along with accompanying behaviors such as helping others and avoiding damaging other people's property. Guilt, shame, and empathy may have an evolutionary basis. Even by toddlerhood, however, these emotions and accompanying behaviors are shaped by cultural standards. Toddlers feel guilt and shame when they violate the expected standards for behavior in their social environment. Young children in different cultures vary on how much they help others, and whom they help. Tomasello, who argues that early prosocial tendencies are based in evolution, also emphasizes that "all of these tendencies are modified significantly by socialization and culture such that they might eventually look quite distinct across different groups and individuals" (Vaish & Tomasello, 2014, p. 294).

## Socialization of Morality

**LO 13.1.2 Describe different ways that the socialization of morality takes place, including the extent to which children and adolescents take active part in socialization.**

Young children do not inherently know the rules and expectations of their culture and must learn them, sometimes by unknowingly violating them and then observing the consequences in the responses of their parents and others. For example, one day when our twins were about 4 years old, they got into the laundry room in the basement and took cups of liquid detergent and spread it all over the basement furniture—sofa, table, loveseat, CD player—all of which were ruined! We don't think they had any intention or awareness of doing something wrong. More likely, they thought they were being helpful, since we had encouraged them to add cups of detergent to the washing machine when doing laundry. After we found out what they had done, they knew from our distressed response they should not do it again. And they never did.

Socialization, the process by which people acquire the behaviors and beliefs of the culture they live in, is important to the acquisition of moral rules and expectations (Grusec & Hastings, 2007; Grusec et al., 2014). A good example of cultural learning of morality can be found in the research of Richard Shweder, who has compared children, adolescents, and adults in India and the United States (2009; Shweder et al., 1990). Shweder found that there are some similarities in moral views in early childhood in India and the United States, but also many differences. At age 5, children in both countries have learned that it is wrong to take others' property ("steal flowers from a neighbor's garden") or to inflict harm intentionally ("kick a dog sleeping on the side of the road"). However, young children also already view many issues with a different moral perspective depending on whether they live in India or the United States. Young children in the United States view it as acceptable to eat beef, but young children in India view it as wrong. Young children in India view it as acceptable for more of a father's inheritance to go to his son than to his daughter, but young children in the United States view it as wrong. Young children in both cultures have the ability to understand their culture's moral rules, even though the moral rules they have learned by early childhood are quite different.

How do children learn moral rules so early in life? There are several ways. Sometimes moral rules are taught quite explicitly. The Ten Commandments of the Jewish and Christian religions are a good example. In one study, researchers recorded conversations between children and parents from religiously devout families in the United States (Fasoli, in press). Findings showed that the parents regularly invoked moral guidelines based in religious writings and encouraged their children to do so, too. For example, one mother–daughter dyad discussed why someone should put off an outing to the movies in order to visit a friend who had just been hospitalized (Hickman & Fasoli, 2015, pp. 161–162).

Child: She could see that movie anytime. This is the only time she can [go to the hospital]. She can't just take a time machine and go back.

Mother: Who is she thinking about if she goes to the hospital?

Child: Her friend.

Mother: And who is she thinking about if she goes to the movie?

Child: Herself.

Mother: And what does God ask us to do?

Child: Do unto others as you would have them do unto you.

Mother: Mmm. Or to serve others, right?

Sometimes morality is taught through stories. Barbara Rogoff (2003) gives examples of storytelling as moral instruction in a variety of cultures, including Canadian First Nations people, Native Americans, and the Xhosa people of South Africa. Among the Xhosa (pronounced ZO-sa), the elders usually tell the stories, but the stories have been told many times before, and even young children soon learn them and participate in the narrative.

Moral lessons are often communicated through stories. Here, a village elder tells children stories in Tanzania.

Young children also learn morality through custom complexes (see Chapter 4). Remember, the essence of the custom complex is that every customary practice of a culture contains not just the practice itself but the underlying cultural beliefs, often including moral beliefs. Shweder (Shweder et al., 1990) gives an example of this kind of moral learning in India. Like people in many cultures, Indians have a tradition of believing that a woman's menstrual blood has potentially dangerous powers. Consequently, a menstruating woman is not supposed to cook food or sleep in the same bed as her husband. Shweder found that Indian children, by the end of early childhood, have learned not just that a menstruating woman does not cook food or sleep with her husband (the cultural practice) but that it would be *wrong* for her to do so (the moral belief).

A variation on the custom complex can be found in American research on *modeling*. Research extending over several decades has shown that young children tend to model their behavior after the behavior of others they observe (Bandura, 1977; Bussey & Bandura, 2004). Most of this research has been experimental, involving situations where children observe other children or adults behaving aggressively or kindly, selfishly or generously; then children's own behavior in a similar experimental situation is observed. Children are especially likely to model their behavior after another person if the other person's behavior is rewarded. Also, they are more likely to model their behavior after adults who are warm and responsive or who are viewed as having authority or prestige. According to modeling theory, after observing multiple occasions of others' behavior being rewarded or punished, children conclude that the rewarded behavior is morally desirable and the punished behavior is forbidden (Bandura, 2002). So, by observing behavior (and its consequences), they learn their culture's principles of moral conduct. As in the custom complex, culturally patterned behavior implies underlying moral beliefs.

Children are not only the recipients of moral socialization, they also contribute to the socialization of others—thereby further strengthening their own commitment to the moral rules and expectations.

It is not only the case that children are the recipients of moral socialization; they also contribute to the socialization of others—thereby further strengthening their own commitment to the moral rules and expectations. Recall that toddlers and preschoolers will use shaming language with other children, and young children take part in the telling of stories with moral implications. Experimental research with 3-year-olds has shown that they protest when they watch a puppet destroy a drawing intended for another puppet ("you can't do that!"). The children also told adults about the destructive puppet, and they behaved more prosocially toward the wronged puppet (Vaish et al., 2011). In another laboratory experiment, 5-year-olds had to choose how to distribute flowers to two persons who each had damaged an object. The children gave more flowers to the person who displayed guilt, as compared to the one who did not (Vaish et al., 2011).

Research in traditional cultures has shown that, by adolescence, groups of boys will use sarcasm and ridicule to bring nonconformist community members into line and reinforce conformity to moral standards (Schlegel & Barry, 1991, 2015). The adolescents' uses of sarcasm and ridicule are directed not just toward other children and adolescents, but also toward adults. The Mbuti Pygmies of Africa, for example, consider it improper to be argumentative. Persons who violate this prohibition are likely to find themselves awakened very early the next morning by a group of adolescent boys making loud noises, climbing on their hut and pounding on the roof, tearing off leaves and sticks. Among the Hopi in the American

Southwest, when a man is known to be visiting a woman at night while her husband is away, the adolescent boys of the village publicize and punish the adultery by leaving a trail of ashes during the night between his house and hers for everyone to see the next morning. Thus, in some culturally approved circumstances, young people are given permission to do what under other circumstances would be seen by adults as intolerable, even criminal behavior (Schlegel & Barry, 1991). Allowing young people to use sarcasm and ridicule can be a socially constructive way to enforce community standards and save the adults the trouble of doing so.

**Critical Thinking Question:** Do you think adolescents use sarcasm or ridicule in your society as a way of socializing moral rules and expectations? If so, what is an example and who is the recipient of the socialization (children, adolescents, or adults)?

Teaching moral rules is a large part of socializing children. But, of course, children and adolescents do not always comply with socialization messages. They also negotiate, argue, and evade (Grusec et al., 2000; Smetana, 2011). We experienced this firsthand when we bought a nice leather chair for our living room when our twins turned 4 years old. We were thinking that by now, they were old enough to know they should be gentle with a nice piece of furniture. Wrong! Within 2 weeks, they had put several large scratches in it. When confronted, they confessed at first, but then retracted their confession and looked for an alibi. "We didn't do it" claimed Paris, lawyer for the defense. "Well, then who did?!" we demanded. She cast her eyes down, as if it were painful for her to reveal the true offender. "Santa Claus," she explained.

### SUMMARY: Moral Development: Emotions and Socialization

**LO 13.1.1 Describe the emergence of guilt, shame, and empathy, and evidence for the roles of nature and nurture in their development.**

By age 2, toddlers express both guilt and shame. Empathy and helping behaviors are also present in toddlers. Even infants show a preference for helping over hindering when observing the behaviors of others. The early emergence of these sociomoral emotions points to an evolutionary basis, although research also shows how they are shaped by parents and culture.

**LO 13.1.2 Describe different ways that the socialization of morality takes place, including the extent to which children and adolescents take active part in socialization.**

Socialization is important to the acquisition of moral rules and expectations. Adults aim to convey moral lessons in a variety of ways, including by means of explicit teachings, storytelling, and modeling of behaviors. Children also contribute to the socialization of others—thereby further strengthening their own commitment to the moral rules and expectations.

## 13.2 Moral Development: Reasoning and Identity

Children's reasoning about moral issues has been a subject of extensive and fascinating research in developmental psychology. What kinds of explanations do children give for why something is right or wrong, and the extent to which someone should be punished or rewarded? Next we turn to four theories that have contributed important insights on the development of moral reasoning: the cognitive-developmental, domain, justice and care orientations, and cultural-developmental approaches. After that, we look at research on moral identity, or one's commitment to moral ideals in thought and behavior.

# The Cognitive-Developmental Approach

**LO 13.2.1 Describe Piaget's and Kohlberg's stages of moral development and the evidence supporting the cognitive-developmental approach.**

**heteronomous morality**
Piaget's term for the period of moral development from about ages 4 to 7, in which moral rules are viewed as having a sacred, fixed quality, handed down from figures of authority

**autonomous morality**
Piaget's term for the period of moral development starting at about ages 10 to 12, involving a growing realization that moral rules can be changed if people decide they should be changed

**hypothetical dilemmas**
research measure created by Kohlberg where participants are asked to reason about situations in which a choice has to be made between two or more alternatives

According to the cognitive-developmental approach, moral development occurs in a series of stages that are universal and grounded in cognitive development. The approach originated with Jean Piaget (1932), whose research, in turn, was a key source of inspiration to Lawrence Kohlberg.

**PIAGET'S STAGES OF MORAL DEVELOPMENT.** In his explorations of children's moral thinking, Piaget asked Swiss children about hypothetical situations involving stealing, lying, and punishment, among other things. In one set of stories, he asked children to explain who was "naughtier": a boy who broke one cup while trying to take some jam from a cupboard without asking, or a boy who accidentally broke 15 cups when opening a door.

Based on children's responses, Piaget concluded that there are two stages of moral development in childhood. **Heteronomous morality** corresponds to the preoperational stage of cognitive development (see Chapter 5), from about age 4 to age 7. In this stage, children focus on the consequences of behaviors (15 broken cups is worse than 1 cup), favor severe punishment for any wrong-doing ("I'd give him a damn good box on the ear!" Piaget, 1932, p. 211), and see moral rules as given once and for all by figures of authority (especially parents).

**Autonomous morality** is reached at the beginning of adolescence, with the onset of formal cognitive operations at about age 10 to 12. In this stage, the focus is on people's intentions (it is worse to break something while doing wrong than simply by accident) and tailoring punishment to fit with a variety of aspects of a situation (such as intentions and degree of harm done). The hallmark of autonomous morality is a growing realization that moral rules can be changed if people decide they should be changed. Through a democratic process, people can present their different viewpoints, negotiate, and jointly arrive at new moral rules. (From age 7 to age 10 there is a transitional stage between heteronomous and autonomous moral thinking, with some properties of each.)

Piaget's focus on the democratic nature of deciding on moral rules in the autonomous stage went hand-in-hand with his belief that moral development is promoted by interactions with peers. In Piaget's view, peers' equal status requires them to discuss their disagreements, negotiate with one another, and come to a consensus. According to Piaget, parents are much less effective than peers in promoting children's moral development because parents' greater power and authority make it difficult for children to argue and negotiate with them as equals.

According to Piaget and Kohlberg, children's moral development is promoted by interactions with similar-age peers. Here, adolescents engage in a classroom debate.

**KOHLBERG'S THEORY OF MORAL DEVELOPMENT.** In the 1950s, inspired by Piaget, Kohlberg initiated a research program examining moral development from a cognitive perspective. It would be difficult to overstate the magnitude of Kohlberg's influence (Jensen, 2015). Not only was he highly productive himself and in his collaborations with colleagues, but he also inspired many others to investigate moral development according to the theory he proposed (Gibbs et al., 2007). As we will see, some of his former students also created entirely new theories of moral development.

Kohlberg wanted to find out if moral reasoning develops in a predictable sequence of stages. To help answer this question, he interviewed children and adolescents about **hypothetical dilemmas**. Many of the dilemmas pit the value of life against the value of property, or the value of one person's life against the value of several people's lives. In the best-known dilemma, Heinz, who lives in a German village, has a dying wife who might be cured by a particular medicine. Heinz, however, cannot afford it, and the town pharmacist will not lower his high price or extend credit. As a research participant, one has to decide whether Heinz should steal the drug, and even more importantly, why or why not.

Based on his research and readings of philosophy, Kohlberg concluded that moral reasoning occurs in a sequence of three levels. Each level includes two stages, for a total of six.

- *Pre-Conventional Level.* At this level, a child reasons strictly in terms of ego-centered considerations. At Stage 1, the child focuses on avoidance of punishment and obtainment of rewards. At Stage 2, the child homes in on satisfaction of self-interests. In one of Kohlberg's studies, for example, a boy in Stage 2 argued that Heinz "should steal because he needs his wife to cook for him" (Kohlberg, 1981, p. 115).

**Pre-Conventional Level**
Kohlberg's term for the lowest level of moral development focused on ego-centered considerations

- *Conventional Level.* A person's reasoning shifts to group-centered considerations. At Stage 3, the focus is on adhering to the norms and expectations of family and other groups to which one belongs. At Stage 4, maintaining social order and upholding the laws of society are key considerations. An adolescent interviewed by Kohlberg reasoned from a Stage 4 standpoint when he explained that: "The pharmacist still has his legal rights, regardless of his unfairness" (1958, p. 396).

**Conventional Level**
Kohlberg's term for the intermediate level of moral development focused on group-centered considerations

- *Post-Conventional Level.* Moral reasoning at this level goes beyond both the self and one's society. At Stage 5, the emphasis is on reaching decisions democratically and finding solutions that entail the greatest good for the greatest number of people. At Stage 6, a person invokes universal principles pertaining to justice and individual rights. For example, a philosopher interviewed by Kohlberg spoke in terms of Stage 6, arguing that "all property has only relative value and only persons can have unconditional value. The decision [that Heinz should steal the drug is] a principled one. [It can] be made from a disinterested point of view that is consistent with the decision of any rational agent in a similar situation" (Kohlberg, 1981, p. 163).

**Post-Conventional Level**
Kohlberg's term for the highest level of moral development focused on universal moral principles

Kohlberg began his research by studying the moral reasoning of 72 boys ages 10, 13, and 16 from middle-class and working-class families in the Chicago area (Kohlberg, 1958). He and his colleagues followed this initial group of adolescent boys over the next 20 years (Colby et al., 1983), interviewing them every 3 or 4 years. Over the years, many other studies were carried out by Kohlberg and other researchers.

Findings across this large body of studies have supported some, but not all, of Kohlberg's theoretical proposals (e.g., Colby & Kohlberg, 1987; Colby et al., 1983; Gibbs et al., 2007; Kohlberg, 1984, 1986; Snarey, 1985; Walker, 1989). Here are the key findings:

1. Younger children often use the concepts from Stages 1 and 2, and in the course of adolescence, the concepts from Stage 3 become common.
2. The first three stages are common across diverse cultures. Stages 4 and 5 are less common. In one comprehensive review of 44 cross-cultural studies, 66% of studies found no reasoning at Stages 4 or 5. In the 34% of studies where these two stages did occur, they were rare (Snarey, 1985). Stage 6 is so rare that it was removed from the cognitive-developmental scoring manual by the early 1980s.
3. Reasoning in terms of Stages 4 and 5 mostly occurs among Western or Westernized middle and upper-middle-class adolescents and adults residing in urban areas.

Like Piaget, Kohlberg emphasized that peer groups provide a good venue for children and adolescents to enhance their moral development. In his view, egalitarian relations and having equal voice are important. Thus, Kohlberg and his colleagues started school programs where children discuss hypothetical dilemmas. They also worked with schools to institute "just communities" where every student and teacher is given one vote to decide on school policies (Higgins, 1991; Power et al., 2007).

**Critical Thinking Question:** List several ways in which Kohlberg's method and theory are similar to Piaget's.

## The Domain Approach

**LO 13.2.2 Describe the distinction made by domain theory between moral and non-moral reasoning and the extent to which findings support the theory.**

**moral domain**

in domain theory, reasoning pertaining to fairness, harm to other individuals, and individual rights

**conventional/societal domain**

in domain theory, reasoning pertaining to communal and religious norms, interests, and authorities

**personal/psychological domain**

in domain theory, reasoning pertaining to the welfare of the self

Kohlberg wanted to find out if moral reasoning develops in a predictable sequence of stages. In the latter half of the 1970s, Elliot Turiel—a former student of Kohlberg's—and his colleagues proposed taking a step back from Kohlberg's question of how moral reasoning develops to the question of what is moral in the first place (e.g., Nucci & Turiel, 1978). Turiel and his colleagues wanted to find out whether children differentiate moral from non-moral issues. To address this question, Turiel and his colleagues have often presented children and adolescents with hypothetical situations. For example, in one situation a child pushes a peer off a swing, and in another, a child calls a grandfather by his first name.

Turiel and his colleagues have concluded that three domains can be differentiated, even if occasional overlap occurs (e.g., Nucci, 1981, 1985; Nucci & Turiel, 1993; Smetana, 1983; Turiel, 1983; Turiel et al., 1987). The domains involve different kinds of reasoning, and different kinds of issues. One is the **moral domain**. The other two, termed the **conventional/societal domain** and the **personal/psychological domain**, are non-moral (Killen & Smetana, 2014).

According to the domain approach, children, adolescents, and adults reason about moral issues with reference to fairness, harm to other individuals, and individual rights. They also think moral rules apply to everyone and that the rules cannot be changed. Conventional/societal reasoning, in contrast, focuses on communal and religious norms, interests, and authorities. Personal/psychological reasoning focuses on the welfare of the self. Also, conventional/societal and personal/psychological rules can be changed.

Based on these three modes of reasoning, according to domain theorists, examples of moral issues include stealing and aggressive acts (pushing someone off a swing).

Conventional/societal issues involve a wide variety of acts such as those pertaining to forms of address (calling a grandfather by first name), attire (wearing a head scarf), sexual customs (premarital sex), food habits (eating pork), and familial arrangements (divorce). Personal/psychological issues include one's choice of friends and recreational activities.

Domain theorists argue that the features of the three domains are innate, and that a young child, through independent observation and exposure to diverse behaviors, will conclude that harm to another individual or unequal treatment of two similar individuals, for example, is of moral consequence. Meanwhile, the child will also conclude that other kinds of issues are not moral.

According to domain theorists, moral issues include stealing and aggressive acts. Here, two siblings from South Africa fight over a toy.

Research testing and using the domain theory have revealed the following key findings:

1. Children—even as young as 3 years of age—differentiate hypothetical moral situations where an innocent child is pushed, hit, or robbed from conventional/societal situations where children eat food with their fingers or fail to follow the rules of a game. By and large, children respond to these hypothetical situations in terms of the reasoning predicted by the domain approach (Ardila-Rey & Killen, 2001; Killen & Sueyoshi, 1995; Nucci et al., 1996; Yau & Smetana, 2003). In other words, contrary to Kohlberg's theory,

even very young children are capable of reasoning in terms of fairness and avoidance of harm to other individuals. They are not exclusively self-centered in their moral reasoning.

2. Clear-cut distinctions between the three domains have mostly been found for a select set of hypothetical situations (such as pushing a child versus eating food with one's fingers). In many other situations, people blend reasoning from the domains (Killen & Smetana, 2014).
3. Age groups differ on how they reason about hypothetical situations. For example, in the United States, parents of adolescents frequently view issues pertaining to dress, hair-style, and choice of friends as conventional/societal matters about which they should have a say. In contrast, adolescents regard these issues as being within their personal/psychological domain (Smetana, 2005, 2008). Especially in early adolescence, parents and adolescents often disagree about these issues.
4. Contrary to the theory, children and adults from diverse cultures regard many situations and reasons that are excluded from the moral domain by Turiel and his colleagues as moral. For example, situations pertaining to respect (such as honoring a deathbed promise), sexuality (such as premarital sex), and avoiding disgusting behaviors (such as eating certain foods) are viewed as moral in many parts of the world. Also, many children and adults consider reasons pertaining to social order, interpersonal duties, spirituality, religion, and personal interests to be moral (Haidt et al., 1993; Jensen & McKenzie, 2016; Miller & Bersoff, 1994; Miller et al., 1990; Nisan, 1987; Vainio, 2015; Vasquez et al., 2001).

Although the distinctions between the three domains are not clear-cut and universal as the theory claimed, the domain approach has raised the important question of how distinctions between moral and non-moral reasoning develop.

## The Justice and Care Orientations Approach

**LO 13.2.3 Differentiate the two orientations proposed by Gilligan, and explain the main contributions of her theory.**

Did you happen to notice that Kohlberg's original research sample included only males? Later, when he began to study females as well, he initially found that adolescent females tended to reason at a lower moral level than males of the same age. To Carol Gilligan, a former student of Kohlberg's, this led to the question of whether girls indeed are less developed, or if they speak in a different moral "voice"—one that has been misinterpreted or gone unheard (Gilligan, 1982, 2008). It also raised the question of whether the cognitive-developmental approach inappropriately downgraded the moral reasoning of girls and women.

On the basis of interviews with American children, adolescents, and adults, Gilligan came to the conclusion that there are two kinds of moral orientations. One is a **justice orientation**, focused on how to negotiate among competing rights in an impartial manner. This orientation, according to Gilligan, is characteristic of male development—and of Piaget's and Kohlberg's approaches. In comparison, the **care orientation** is more characteristic of female development. Here the concern is with tending to the needs of self and those with whom one has relationships. Revisiting the Heinz dilemma, Gilligan noted how some girls in her research did not regard it as a conflict between the value of property and the value of life—as intended by Kohlberg. Instead, they interpreted the dilemma as a matter of how to maintain good relationships between the persons involved. To Gilligan, this care orientation is different from the justice orientation, but it deserves to be heard and valued.

**justice orientation**
Gilligan's term for a type of moral orientation that places a premium on abstract principles of justice, equality, and fairness

**care orientation**
Gilligan's term for a type of moral orientation that involves focusing on relationships with others as the basis for moral reasoning

Gilligan's ideas have inspired a great deal of attention and research since she first articulated them in the early 1980s. What does the research tell us?

1. Contrary to Gilligan's claim, meta-analyses of research using Kohlberg's cognitive-developmental approach do not show differences between females and males on their level of moral reasoning (Walker, 1984, 1989).

According to Gilligan, the development of care had been overlooked and downgraded in the field of moral psychology.

2. A meta-analysis of research using the two orientations approach showed a small gender difference, with females using the care orientation more than males (Jaffee & Hyde, 2000). The gender difference in use of the justice orientation was negligible. In other words, there was a difference, but it is not of much consequence.

3. Females and males tend to emphasize somewhat different moral concerns (Galotti et al., 1991; Jaffee & Hyde, 2000; Skoe & Gooden, 1993). For example, when adolescents are asked to recall *real-life moral experiences* that they have had, girls are more likely than boys to report experiences that involve interpersonal relationships.

The justice and care orientations approach, then, has contributed to directing attention toward people's real-life moral experiences, as compared to hypothetical moral dilemmas and situations. Gilligan herself interviewed pregnant young women who were contemplating whether to have an abortion. Also, this approach entails a relatively broad view of moral reasoning. Unlike the cognitive-developmental and domain approaches, it does not primarily emphasize fairness, justice, and individual rights. It also includes moral reasoning centered on care and interpersonal relationships.

**Critical Thinking Question:** Almost all of the research on the two orientations has been conducted in the United States. To what extent do you think that gender differences on moral concerns and reasoning might depend on culture? Do you think that gender differences might be stronger in some cultures than others?

## The Cultural-Developmental Approach

**LO 13.2.4 Describe the cultural-developmental approach to moral reasoning and the extent of evidence for the approach.**

**Ethic of Autonomy**
within the cultural-developmental approach, moral reasoning pertaining to an individual's rights, interests, and well-being

**Ethic of Community**
within the cultural-developmental approach, moral reasoning pertaining to duties to others, and promoting the interests and welfare of groups

**Ethic of Divinity**
within the cultural-developmental approach, moral reasoning pertaining to religious rules, spiritual degradation, and moral purity

While the two orientations approach added breadth to the kinds of moral reasons studied by developmental psychologists, Richard Shweder and his colleagues have suggested casting a still wider net—one that catches the moral reasons used by people from many different cultures. Based on his research with children and adults in India and the United States, as well as a review of research from Western and non-Western cultures, Shweder and his colleagues proposed a distinction between three kinds of ethics (Jensen, 1995; Shweder et al., 1990; Shweder et al., 1997).

The three ethics entail different conceptions of the moral self and different moral reasons (Jensen, 2015). The **Ethic of Autonomy** defines the self as an autonomous individual who is free to make choices, being restricted primarily by concerns with inflicting harm on other individuals and encroaching on their rights. Moral reasoning within this ethic centers on an individual's rights, interests, and well-being, and on equality between individuals. The **Ethic of Community** defines the moral self through membership in social groups such as family and nation and responsibilities that ensue from this membership. Moral reasoning within this ethic includes a focus on a person's duties to others, and promoting the interests and welfare of groups to which the person belongs. The **Ethic of Divinity** defines the self as a spiritual entity. Here, moral reasoning centers on religious rules, injunctions, and lessons found in sacred texts (e.g., Hindu scriptures, the Koran) and the striving on the part of a person to avoid spiritual degradation and come closer to moral purity. Unlike the cognitive-developmental approach, the three ethics are not stages. A child or adult may draw on one or more of the ethics when faced with a moral issue.

Research has shown the presence of the three ethics across diverse countries, including Brazil, Finland, India, Japan, Thailand, and New Zealand (Arnett et al., 2001; Guerra & Giner-Sorolla, 2010, 2015; Haidt et al., 1993; Hickman & Fasoli, 2015; Jensen & McKenzie, 2016; Kapadia & Bhangaokar, 2015; Padilla-Walker & Nelson, 2015; Pandya & Bhangaokar, 2015; Rozin et al., 1999; Vasquez et al., 2001). Research has also indicated differences between countries, social classes, and religious groups. Findings suggest that American children and adolescents use Ethic of Autonomy reasoning more than children and adolescents in countries such as Brazil and India. With respect to class, research suggests that middle- and upper-middle-class children and adolescents reason more in terms of Autonomy and less in terms of Community, as compared to children and adolescents of lower economic classes. Research has also indicated a difference between religious groups. Children and adolescents from conservative religious communities reason less in terms of Autonomy and more in terms of Divinity than children and adolescents from liberal religious communities.

Research with the cultural-developmental approach has shown cultural and developmental variation in use of the Ethics of Autonomy, Community, and Divinity. Here, a family in Mumbai, India worship an idol of the elephant god Ganesh.

These findings show the role of culture across and within countries. But what about development? The cultural-developmental approach charts developmental trajectories for each of the three ethics from childhood through adulthood (Jensen, 2008, 2015). As shown in Figure 13.1, the proposal is that Ethic of Autonomy reasoning emerges early in childhood and stays relatively stable across adolescence and into adulthood. Ethic of Community reasoning is expected to rise across the life course. Turning to the Ethic of Divinity, the expectation is that its use will often be low among children but rise in adolescence and become similar to adult use. These trajectories are based on research with the three ethics, and on a large set of findings from other lines of research in psychology and anthropology.

Unlike stage theories of moral development, however, the trajectories for the three ethics are not one-size-fits-all. Instead, they are proposed as *templates*. What this means is that they describe general patterns of development that are bound to be shaped by culture. For example, in collectivistic cultures where social harmony is highly valued, Ethic of Community reasoning is likely to emerge particularly early in childhood and rise along an especially steep slope to reach a high level in adulthood. In more individualistic cultures, Ethic of Community reasoning may be less common throughout childhood and adolescence, as children learn that the rights of the individual are more important than the interests of the group.

**Critical Thinking Question:** Can you explain how the cultural findings described earlier for shame, empathy, and helpfulness fit with this prediction for the development of the Ethic of Community?

**Figure 13.1** The Cultural-Developmental Template of Moral Reasoning

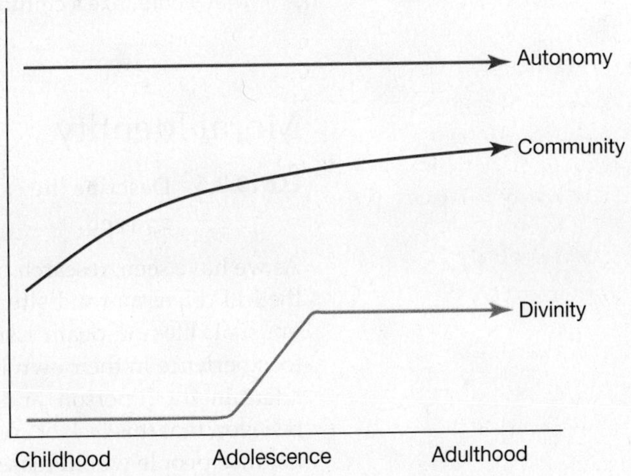


Research with the cultural-developmental approach has involved questionnaires and interviews about hypothetical situations and people's real-life moral experiences. Some key findings include:

1. Adolescents from India and Thailand—two relatively collectivistic cultures—frequently reason in terms of the Ethic of Community, and use of this ethic is even higher among their parents and other adults (Kapadia & Bhangaokar, 2015; McKenzie & Jensen, in press).

**Figure 13.2** Moral Reasoning Among Children, Adolescents, and Adults From Conservative and Liberal Religious Communities

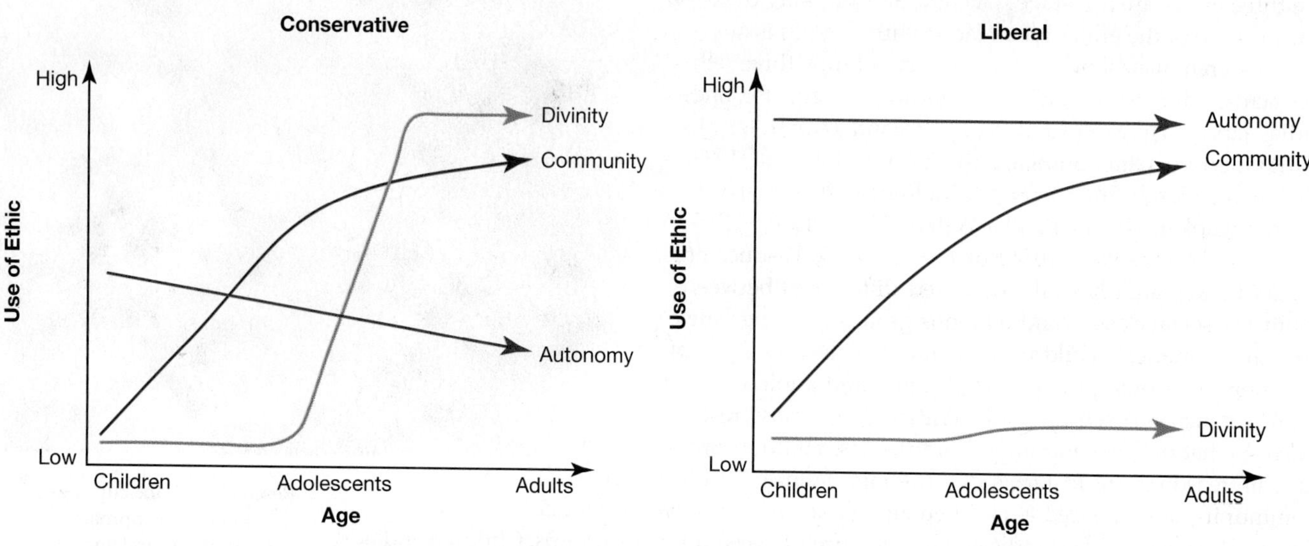


2. Research with children, adolescents, and adults from conservative and liberal religious communities has found that their development follows the general cultural-developmental trajectories while also being shaped by their religious cultures, as predicted. The findings are illustrated in Figure 13.2 (Hickman & Fasoli, 2015; Jensen, 2008; Jensen & McKenzie, 2016; McKenzie & Jensen, in press; Vainio, 2015).
3. In societies where there is a period of emerging adulthood, researchers have predicted a temporary upswing in Ethic of Autonomy reasoning. The hallmarks of emerging adulthood—independent decision making, financial self-sufficiency, and accepting responsibility for oneself—all center on Ethic of Autonomy considerations. Emerging adults have indeed been found to reason more in terms of Autonomy than the other two kinds of ethics in Brazil, Denmark, Israel, New Zealand, the United Kingdom, and the United States (Arnett & Jensen, 2015; Arnett et al., 2001; Guerra & Giner-Sorolla, 2015).

The cultural-developmental approach has helped to call attention to the intersection of moral development and culture. Due to its focus on culture, it has also facilitated research with diverse groups both within and across countries. However, the approach is still relatively new and more research is needed to further test it. For example, longitudinal research with children from different cultural communities would be useful.

**Critical Thinking Question:** Can you think of a research question and study that would take a cultural-developmental approach to morality? Explain.

# Moral Identity

**LO 13.2.5 Describe the extent to which moral identity involves consideration for others and self.**

As we have seen, research on moral reasoning has often asked children to respond to hypothetical dilemmas and situations. Many of Kohlberg's hypothetical dilemmas centered on unusual, life-and-death issues that most people—especially children—would be unlikely to experience in their own lives, such as stealing in order to save a life, the mercy killing of a terminally ill person, and a soldier's sacrifice of his life for his fellow soldiers. Kohlberg believed that this lack of connection to everyday experience was a strength of his dilemmas because people would reason about them without preconceptions or preexisting tendencies based on experience (Walker et al., 1999). By responding to hypothetical dilemmas, people would reveal the underlying cognitive basis of their moral reasoning.

But what does reasoning about such dilemmas actually tell us about the commitment of children and adolescents to moral ideals in their everyday lives? What does it tell us about their everyday behavior? The fact that the dilemmas are hypothetical does not mean they are unrelated to behavior. Children, adolescents, and emerging adults who rate low on Kohlberg's stages are also more likely to engage in antisocial and aggressive behaviors, more likely to engage in cheating, and less likely to assist others in need of help (Arsenio et al., 2009; Hart et al., 2003; Olthof, 2010). In other words, they are indeed self-centered in both moral reasoning and behavior.

However, this still does not tell us about a person's commitment to positive moral ideals in thought and behavior, or what researchers term **moral identity** (Blasi, 2004; Colby & Damon, 1992; Hardy & Carlo, 2011; Hardy et al., in press). Since adolescence is a key time for identity formation in general, it is not surprising that research addressing moral identity also has focused on adolescence (Hardy et al., 2013). This research has shown that adolescence is an important time in life for the acquisition of a sense of responsibility (Nunner-Winkler, 2007), the emergence of substantial consideration for others (Carlo, 2006; Youniss et al., 1997), and consistently feeling positive emotions when making decisions benefitting others rather than the self (Malti et al., 2012).

**moral identity**
a person's commitment to positive moral ideals in thought and behavior

Researchers generally agree that having a moral identity entails a commitment to causes larger than the self (Damon & Malin, in press; Narvaez & Lapsley, 2009), but Lawrence Walker has highlighted that moral identity development is more likely to be successful if self-interest lines up with, or at least does not run counter to, these larger causes (Frimer & Walker, 2009; Walker, 2013). Walker has found that when adolescents (and adults) describe their real-life moral decisions, including those where they think they behaved in a morally right and good way, they still often give consideration to personal costs (such as losing one's job) and benefits (such as having a fun experience).

## SUMMARY: Moral Development: Reasoning and Identity

**LO 13.2.1 Describe Piaget's and Kohlberg's stages of moral development and the evidence supporting the cognitive-developmental approach.**

Piaget differentiated two stages of moral development, heteronomy and autonomy. Kohlberg's theory includes three levels, each consisting of two stages (for a total of six). Younger children often use the concepts from Stages 1 and 2, and in the course of adolescence, the concepts from Stage 3 become common. Stages 4–6, however, are rare and not universal.

**LO 13.2.2 Describe the distinction made by domain theory between moral and non-moral reasoning and the extent to which findings support the theory.**

Domain theory differentiates three domains termed: moral, conventional/societal, and personal/psychological. Clear-cut distinctions between the three domains have mostly been found for a select set of hypothetical situations. Contrary to the theory, children and adults from diverse cultures regard many situations and reasons that are excluded from the moral domain as moral.

**LO 13.2.3 Differentiate the two orientations proposed by Gilligan, and explain the main contributions of her theory.**

Gilligan differentiates two orientations: justice and care. This theory contributes a relatively broad view of moral reasoning. Unlike the cognitive-developmental and domain approaches, it does not primarily define morality in terms of fairness, justice, and individual rights. It also includes moral reasoning centered on care and interpersonal relationships—which is slightly more common among females than males.

**LO 13.2.4 Describe the cultural-developmental approach to moral reasoning and the extent of evidence for the approach.**

The cultural-developmental approach describes how three kinds of ethics—Autonomy, Community, and Divinity—are shaped both by development and culture. Due to its focus on the entire life course and culture, the approach has facilitated research with diverse age groups both within and across countries. Studies have supported hypotheses based on this new approach, but more research is warranted.

**LO 13.2.5 Describe the extent to which moral identity involves consideration for others and self.**

Researchers use the term moral identity to describe a person's commitment to positive moral ideals in thought and behavior. Adolescence is an important time for development of moral identity. Moral identity development may be more likely to be successful if self-interest lines up with, or at least does not run counter to, the commitment to causes that are larger than the self.

# 13.3 Religious and Spiritual Development

Virtually all cultures have religious and spiritual beliefs of some kind. Now we turn to the development of these beliefs. For example, how do children and adolescents think about the supernatural? We also look at the socialization of religious beliefs and behaviors. As we will see, religion often serves a positive and protective function in development, especially in early adolescence and then again after middle adolescence. However, this does not mean that religion is of primary importance in the lives of adolescents and emerging adults. In developed countries, many adolescents and emerging adults take an individualized or secular approach to religion.

## Conceptions of Supernatural Entities

**LO 13.3.1 Explain how conceptions of supernatural entities depend on age and religion.**

As with moral development, there has been a lot of research examining the cognitive characteristics of children's religious beliefs. Until a few decades ago, most of this research examined how children think about God, and asked children to describe God in interviews or depict God in drawings (Bassett et al., 1990; Elkind, 1970; Goldman, 1965; Harms, 1944; Nye & Carlson, 1984). This research found that children up until the age of about 10 or 11 primarily view God in concrete ways (a man with a white beard), whereas adolescents have much more abstract images (God is everywhere). As you can see, these findings correspond to Piaget's division between the stages of concrete operations and formal operations (see Chapter 5).

Newer research, some of which uses different methods, has shown that differences among children, adolescents, and adults on their conceptions of supernatural entities are not nearly as clear-cut. Young children have beliefs about God that are abstract (Wigger et al., 2013). In one experiment using a false-belief task (see Chapter 5), children were asked to state what their mom and God would think was inside a closed cracker box that actually contained rocks. By age 6, most children stated that mom would think it contained crackers whereas God would think it contained rocks (Barrett et al., 2001). A study with Yukatek Maya children from Southeastern Mexico obtained similar findings (Knight et al., 2004). The children in these experiments seem to think that God is all-knowing, which is an abstract conception.

Similarly, adolescents (and adults) have beliefs about God that are fairly concrete. For example, one study compared children (7–12), adolescents (13–18), and adults (36–57) on their images of God and the Devil (Jensen, 2009). Detailed analyses of interviews showed that while the children's descriptions of God included concrete images (God is male), so did the images of the adolescents and adults. Children did speak more in terms of physical characteristics than adolescents and adults when describing the Devil (a cruel smile). When it came to describing God, however, children were not different from adolescents and adults in discussing physical characteristics.

Children's religious background also matters. For example, a study found that children from Mennonite, Mormon, and Lutheran families drew pictures of God with more concrete features (God as a person), as compared to children of Jewish background (Pitts, 1976). Another study showed that Hindu children, more than Jewish, Roman Catholic, and Baptist children, described a many-sided God (Heller, 1986). The Hindu children said they felt close to God while also portraying God as an abstract form of energy. In these studies, children's drawings and statements reflect the different images of God that distinguish their religions.

All in all, children from some religious backgrounds may be more concrete in their conceptions of some religious entities (such as the Devil), as compared to adolescents and adults. To many children, adolescents, and adults, however, it seems that God is both concrete and abstract.

## Socialization of Religious Beliefs and Behaviors

**LO 13.3.2 Describe the role of family, peers, and ethnic group on religious beliefs and behaviors.**

The finding that children from families with different religious backgrounds, such as Hinduism, Judaism, and Christianity, vary in their conceptions of God speaks to the role of socialization of religious beliefs. Recall the conversation earlier in the chapter between the mother and daughter about putting off an outing to the movies in order to visit a friend who had just been hospitalized (Hickman & Fasoli, 2015). When the mother said, "And what does God ask us to do?" she was clearly encouraging her daughter to think in terms of God, and to see God as a supreme moral exemplar.

Religious socialization within the family is important and takes a variety of forms. A study of Christian families found that parents, especially mothers, spoke with their 3- to 12-year-old children about religious and spiritual issues about 3 times per week. Children were active participants, either initiating or terminating about 50% of the conversations (Boyatzis & Janicki, 2003). Family prayer is another way that parents socialize religious beliefs and behaviors in their children (King & Boyatzis, 2015; King et al., 2002). In the United States, family prayer is common in African-American Protestant, conservative Protestant, and Mormon families (Ozorak, 1989). In all of these communities, religion is highly valued. Also notable is that, when parents disagree with each other about religious beliefs, their adolescent children are less likely to be religious (Copen & Silverstein, 2007; Smith & Denton, 2005). Presumably, in these families, there are no or few unified religious messages that are conveyed to the adolescents and that they are encouraged to share.

The quality of the relationship between children and parents seems to influence the outcome of socialization. Adolescents with secure attachments to parents are more likely to share their parents' faith and conceptions of God (Hertel & Donahue, 1995). More generally, studies suggest that parents who are warm and supportive have adolescents who are more accepting of their parents' religious and spiritual views (Hardy et al., 2011; King & Furrow, 2004).

By adolescence, peer socialization also becomes important. Adolescents' participation in religious activities is predicted not only by parental behaviors, but also by their peers' religiosity (Regnerus et al., 2004). The impact of adolescent peers has also been shown in a longitudinal study where peers' church attendance during high school was one of the strongest predictors of religiosity during emerging adulthood (Gunnoe & Moore, 2002). It seems likely that adolescents are socialized and shaped by their peers, but they may also select peers who are similar to themselves on religious beliefs and behaviors.

Ethnic background also plays an important role in adolescents' religiosity. African American adolescents are more religious than adolescents of other ethnicities (Smith & Denton, 2005). For example, 47% of African American 12th graders report that religion plays a very important role in their lives, compared to 28% of Latinos and 24% of European Americans (Child Trends, 2014). Latino adolescents are somewhat more religious than European Americans (King & Boyatsis, 2015). One study that examined stories told by Latino college students found that they talked about their families as sources of religious and spiritual beliefs, behaviors, and support (Knight et al., 2004). Asian American adolescents tend to be less religious than youth from other ethnic groups (Smith & Denton, 2005).

Family prayer is one way that parents socialize religious beliefs and behaviors in their children. This family from San Angelo, Texas says a blessing before dinner.

## Religion as a Protective Factor

**LO 13.3.3 Explain the extent to which religion serves a protective and positive role in development.**

Religion contributes to positive youth development (Lerner et al., 2008, 2015). A meta-analysis examined the extent to which spirituality and religiosity are associated with psychological outcomes such as risk behavior, depression, well-being, and self-esteem (Yonker et al., 2012). The analysis pooled 75 studies. The studies were conducted between 1990 and 2010, and included a total of more than 66,000 adolescents and emerging adults. Spirituality and religiosity was associated with lower levels of risk behavior and depression, and higher levels of well-being and self-esteem. These findings indeed suggest that religion protects youth against negative outcomes and contributes to positive youth development. However, none of the associations was very strong. On the whole, then, these findings suggest that spirituality and religiosity play a positive but modest role in the development of adolescents and emerging adults.

Research suggests that the positive role of religiosity depends on age and ethnicity. With respect to age, an important longitudinal study that included a national representative sample of American adolescents between 12 and 18 years found that the association between religiosity and risk behavior varied over the course of adolescence (Regnerus & Elder, 2003). Religiosity served as a protective factor in early adolescence, ceased to be related to risk behavior in middle adolescence, and then reemerged as a strong protective factor in late adolescence. Another longitudinal study of a national U.S. sample of adolescents and emerging adults similarly found that weekly religious involvement in adolescence predicted having "minimal" problems in emerging adulthood (Terzian et al., 2014). Specifically, religiosity protected against heavy alcohol and marijuana use, illicit drug use, criminal behavior, and financial hardship. Another national study found that religious belief and participation among American emerging adults were related not only to lower rates of risk behavior but to higher rates of well-being (Smith & Snell, 2010).

## Cultural Focus: Religion in the Lives of African American Adolescents

Religion serves a protective and positive role in the lives of African American adolescents. As described above, African American adolescents are considerably more religious than adolescents of other ethnic backgrounds (Child Trends, 2014). Alongside the family, the church is a strong social influence within the African American community (Mattis et al., 2006). African American adolescents have diverse religious affiliations, including Catholicism and Islam, but are mainly Protestant (King & Boyatzis, 2015).

The relatively high rate of religiosity among African American adolescents helps explain why they have low rates of alcohol and drug use (Stevens-Watkins & Rostosky, 2010). Also, Aerika Brittian and Margaret Beale Spencer (2012) have found that religious and ethnic identity correlate with less risk behavior for African American adolescents. Another study, comparing African American and European American emerging adults, reported that African Americans were more likely to cope with stress by relying on their religious beliefs, and in turn they experienced fewer anxiety symptoms than European American emerging adults (Chapman & Steger, 2010). High religiosity in African American adolescents is also related to better academic performance and better study habits (Abar et al., 2009; Regnerus & Elder, 2003). For more information, watch the video *Religion in the Lives of African American Adolescents*.

**Watch** RELIGION IN THE LIVES OF AFRICAN AMERICAN ADOLESCENTS

### Review Question

Can you give other examples of how religion is or has been important to the African American community and sense of identity?

## Individualized and Secular Approaches to Religion

**LO 13.3.4 Describe the general religious beliefs of American adolescents and emerging adults, and explain the rise of secularism among those age groups in developed countries.**

Americans are more religious than people in virtually any other developed country, and this is reflected in the lives of American adolescents. A landmark study of American adolescents' religious beliefs, called the National Survey of Youth and Religion (NSYR), involved over 3,000 adolescents ages 13 to 17 in every part of the United States, from all major ethnic groups, and included qualitative interviews with 267 of the adolescents. Table 13.1 shows how, for a substantial proportion of American adolescents, religion plays an important part in their lives (Smith & Denton, 2005).

Although religion is important to many American adolescents, the directors of the NSYR concluded that it has a lower priority for most of them than many other parts of their lives do, including school, friendships, media, and work. As sociologists Christian Smith and Melinda Denton (2005, p. 161) put it, "For most U.S. teenagers, [religion has] quite a small place at the end of the table for a short period of time each week (if that)."

Furthermore, the religious beliefs of American adolescents do not tend to follow traditional religious doctrines. Instead, they tend to embrace a general set of beliefs that Smith and Denton (2005) call "Moralistic Therapeutic Deism," with the following features:

- A God exists who created and orders the world and watches over human life on earth.
- God wants people to be good, nice, and fair to each other, as taught in the Bible and by most world religions.
- The central goal of life is to be happy and to feel good about oneself.
- God does not need to be particularly involved in one's life except when needed to resolve a problem.
- Good people go to heaven when they die.

For most American adolescents today, religion is not about adhering to specific religious doctrines or taking part in the practices of a religious community. American adolescents are increasingly likely to say that they are "spiritual, but not religious" (Smith & Denton, 2005). Spirituality is understood to involve a person's individual quest for meaning and happiness.

The National Study on Youth and Religion (NYSR) is longitudinal, and it has now examined the 13- to 17-year-olds in the original study at ages 18–23 (Smith & Snell, 2010). Just as in adolescence, religious beliefs in emerging adulthood were highly individualized. Few emerging adults accepted a standard religious doctrine; instead, they took pieces of beliefs that they had learned from their parents and many other sources and puzzled them together into their own individual creations. Consequently, religious denomination did not hold much meaning for most of them. They could state they were "Catholic" or "Presbyterian"

**Table 13.1** Religion Among American Adolescents

| Beliefs and Behaviors | Percentage of Adolescents |
|---|---|
| Believe in God or a universal spirit | 84% |
| Pray at least once a week | 65% |
| Believe in the existence of angels | 63% |
| Attend religious services at least twice a month | 52% |
| Religion important in daily life | 51% |
| Involved in a church youth group | 38% |

SOURCE: Based on Smith & Denton (2005).

or "Jewish" without actually believing much of what is stated in the traditional doctrine of that faith and without participating in it. This individualized approach to religion led to great religious diversity in emerging adulthood. It is exemplified by 24-year-old Jared, who explained (Arnett, 2004, p. 171):

> My parents put me through Sunday School, and I was baptized and stuff. But I like the theory that all these religions, Mohammed and Buddha and Jesus, all the patterns there are very similar. And I believe that there's a spirit, an energy. Not necessarily a guy or something like that, but maybe just a power force. Like in Star Wars—the Force. The thing that makes it possible to live.

In American studies, religiosity generally declines from adolescence through emerging adulthood. Both religious participation and religious beliefs decline throughout the teens and are lower in the late teens and early 20s than at any other period of the life span (Pew Research Center, 2012). For example, one-third of emerging adults in a recent national poll did not consider themselves to be a member of any religious denomination or organization. People in this category are known to researchers on religion as the "**nones**," because, when asked what religion they are, they respond with some version of "none"—atheist, agnostic, spiritual but not religious, or just not religious.

**nones**
people who identify as atheist, agnostic, spiritual but not religious, or just not religious

In general, adolescents and emerging adults in developed countries are less religious than their counterparts in developing countries. Developed countries tend to be highly **secular**—based on nonreligious beliefs and values. In every developed country, religion has gradually faded in its influence over the past two centuries (Bellah et al., 1985; Watson, 2014). Religious beliefs and practices are especially low among adolescents and emerging adults in Europe. For example, in Belgium, only 8% of 18-year-olds attend religious services at least once a month (Goossens & Luyckx, 2007). In Spain, traditionally a highly Catholic country, only 18% of adolescents attend church regularly (Gibbons & Stiles, 2004). A recent interview study in Denmark, one of the least religious countries in the world (International Social Survey Programme, 2012), found that almost 80% of emerging adults described themselves as either agnostic, atheist, or as having no religious beliefs (Arnett & Jensen, 2015).

**secular**
based on nonreligious beliefs and values

Traditionally, religion has provided answers to questions about the meaning of life and death. How do secular adolescents and emerging adults think about these questions? In the interview study in Denmark, the emerging adults were asked what they believe happens after death (Arnett & Jensen, 2015). Despite unbelief being the norm, 62% of the Danish emerging adults nonetheless believed in some form of afterlife. They were vague about what form it might take. To some, it seemed illogical that death should be the end of existence ("I find it difficult to accept that it's just over and done"). For others, it was emotionally unpalatable to believe that there is no life after death ("I can't tolerate the idea that if someone in your family dies, there's nothing more"). Still others stated a belief in a soul that goes on in some form ("Our soul can't just disappear. It lives on, in one place or another, but I don't know how").

One-third of emerging adults in a recent U.S. poll on religiosity were "nones"—atheist, agnostic, spiritual but not religious, or just not religious.

The absence of religion in the worldviews of today's Danish emerging adults can be explained partly on the basis of their society's affluence and stability. Cross-national studies have found that, although within many countries religiosity is associated with well-being and serves a protective function against risk behavior, the countries that are the most prosperous and well-functioning also tend to be the least religious (Diener et al., 2011). Yet even for the Danish emerging adults who have had all the advantages of coming of age in a wealthy and stable society, the majority believed in some kind of life after death. From the point of view of developmental psychology, secularism—which is rising the world over—merits future research.

## SUMMARY: Religious and Spiritual Development

**LO 13.3.1 Explain how conceptions of supernatural entities depend on age and religion.**

Children, like adults, have both concrete and abstract conceptions of supernatural entities. Children's drawings and verbal statements reflect the different images of God that distinguish their religions.

**LO 13.3.2 Describe the role of family, peers, and ethnic group on religious beliefs and behaviors.**

Religious socialization takes a variety of forms, including conversation and prayer. Warm and supportive parents have adolescents who are more accepting of their religious and spiritual views. Adolescents' participation in religious activities is also predicted by their peers' religiosity. African American adolescents are more religious than adolescents of other ethnicities.

**LO 13.3.3 Explain the extent to which religion serves a protective and positive role in development.**

Spirituality and religiosity in adolescence is associated with lower levels of risk behavior and depression, and higher levels of well-being and self-esteem. The association is strongest before and after middle adolescence.

**LO 13.3.4 Describe the general religious beliefs of American adolescents and emerging adults, and explain the rise of secularism among those age groups in developed countries.**

American adolescents are more religious than adolescents in virtually any other developed country. Their beliefs, however, do not tend to follow traditional religious doctrines. Instead, their beliefs are "spiritual" and individualized. Secularism is also growing among American adolescents and emerging adults, and is prominent in much of Europe.

# 13.4 Civic Development

On the afternoon of October 9, 2012, 15-year-old Malala Yousafzai boarded her school bus in northwestern Pakistan. A man asked for her by name, then pointed a pistol and shot her in the head. Since early adolescence, Malala had advocated for education for girls and women, and her efforts had attracted attention and supporters. To the Taliban, with which the shooter identified, this was a deadly offense. Despite her grave injuries, Malala survived. She continues to work for girls' education and for religious tolerance. In 2014, she became the youngest-ever recipient of the Nobel Peace Prize.

Malala's story is unique, but her willingness to devote time and passion to a civic cause is shared by other youth. **Civic development** refers to the ways that youth "engage in collective actions that contribute to their local communities, nation-states, and global societies" (Flanagan et al., 2015, p. 471). Civic activities take different forms. Researchers often distinguish between **community service**, unpaid volunteer work through school and voluntary associations that serves others, and **political involvement**, unpaid activities aimed at political goals (Putnam, 2000; Sherrod et al., 2002). Furthermore, a distinction is often made between *conventional political involvement*, such as voting or joining a political party, and *political activism*, such as taking part in demonstrations or boycotts. In this section we look at both community and political engagement. Most of the research on civic development has focused on adolescents and emerging adults, and that too will be our focus.

**civic development**
pertaining to involvement in collective actions that contribute to local communities, nation-states, or global societies

**community service**
volunteer work provided as a contribution to the community, without monetary compensation

**political involvement**
unpaid activities aimed at political goals

## Community Service in Adolescence

**LO 13.4.1 Summarize the characteristics of adolescents who engage in community service and the ways community service promotes positive development.**

According to national surveys, high proportions of American high school seniors report taking part in community service within the last 12 months. Between the mid-1970s

**Table 13.2** The Most Common Volunteer Activities by 16- to 18-Year-Old High School Students

| Volunteer Activity | Percentage of High School Volunteers |
|---|---|
| Fundraise or sell items to raise money | 29% |
| Collect, prepare, distribute, or serve food | 25% |
| Engage in general labor, supply transportation for people | 23% |
| Mentor youth | 21% |
| Tutor or teach | 19% |
| Engage in music, performance, or other artistic activities | 16% |
| Collect, make, or distribute clothing, crafts, or goods other than food | 15% |
| Coach, referee, supervise sports team | 11% |
| Be an usher, greeter, or minister | 10% |

SOURCE: Based on Marcelo (2007).

and 1990, about 68% reported doing so. Since the early 1990s and through the present, the number has gradually risen to encompass about 75% of high school seniors (HERI, 2012, 2017; Marcelo, 2007). This service covers a wide variety of activities, such as serving meals to the homeless, cleaning up parks and playgrounds, and tutoring fellow students. Table 13.2 list the most common volunteer activities by high school students. For an example of adolescents engaging in the most common volunteer activity of fundraising, watch the video *Teen Girls Bake Cookies to Help Neighbor*.

Often, community service takes place under the guidance of a community organization, such as a religious group, 4-H, the Boy or Girl Scouts, or Boys and Girls Club. Also, local, state, and federal governments have made numerous efforts to promote community service among adolescents. Nearly 30% of American high schools require some type of community service before graduation (HERI, 2017; McNeil & Helwig, 2015).

Research on adolescents and community service has focused on two main questions: What are the distinctive characteristics of adolescents who do volunteer work? And what effects does volunteer work have on adolescents who take part in it?

A meta-analysis of 49 studies concluded that community service has a variety of positive influences on adolescents' personal, academic, and social development (Goethem et al., 2015). Adolescents who volunteer tend to have a high sense of personal competence, and they tend to have higher educational goals and performance than other adolescents (Johnson et al., 1998; Pancer et al., 2007). They tend to have high ideals and to perceive a higher degree of similarity between their "actual selves" and their "ideal selves" than other adolescents do (Hart & Fegley, 1995; McIntosh et al., 2005). Adolescents who participate in community service often report that one or both parents do so as well (Pancer et al., 2007). By their participation, parents provide both a model for community service and concrete opportunities for adolescents to participate (Yates & Youniss, 1996). Adolescents who are high on religiosity are also more likely to volunteer than their less religious peers (Kerestes et al., 2004; King & Furrow, 2004; King et al., 2014).

**Watch** TEEN GIRLS BAKE COOKIES TO HELP NEIGHBOR

For most adolescents, community service is motivated by both collectivistic and individualistic values. Often, of course, they are motivated by collectivistic values such as wanting to help others or a concern for those who have been less fortunate than themselves. However, perhaps less obviously, studies have found that individualistic values are equal to collectivistic values as a motivation for adolescents' community service. In addition to wanting to help others, adolescents also volunteer because it gives them a sense of personal satisfaction and they enjoy doing the work.

**Critical Thinking Question:** Can you explain how the role of individualistic reasons for doing community service parallels findings on adolescents' moral reasoning about their real-life moral decisions?

With regard to the effects of community service, scholars have observed that such service is often part of adolescents' political socialization. Through their participation, adolescents become more concerned about social issues and develop an understanding of themselves as members of their society (McIntosh et al., 2005; Metz et al., 2003; Pancer et al., 2007; Reinders & Youniss, 2006). In one example of this effect, James Youniss and Miranda Yates (1997, 2000) studied adolescents who were volunteering in a soup kitchen for homeless people. Through the course of a year of service, the adolescents began to reassess themselves, not only reflecting on their fortunate lives in comparison to the people they were working with, but also seeing themselves as potential actors in working for the reforms needed to address the problem of homelessness. Furthermore, the adolescents began to raise questions about characteristics of the American political system in relation to homelessness, such as policies regarding affordable housing and job training. Thus, their participation made them more conscious of themselves as American citizens, more critical of political policies, and more aware of their own responsibility in addressing social problems in American society.

**Critical Thinking Question:** Do you think adolescent political socialization is likely to result from all types of community service? Explain.

Studies have also examined the long-term effects of taking part in volunteer work in adolescence. In general, these studies indicate that people who take part in volunteer work in adolescence are also more likely to be active in political activities and volunteer organizations as adults (Flanagan, 2015; Hart et al., 2007; Sherrod et al., 2002). Of course, these studies do not show that community service in adolescence causes people to volunteer in adulthood as well. As we have seen, adolescent volunteers already differ from their peers in ways that explain their greater participation in community service in adolescence and beyond.

Nevertheless, the study by Youniss and Yates (1997, 2000) and other studies (e.g., Johnson et al., 1998; McIntosh et al., 2005; Metz et al., 2003) indicate that community service does have a variety of favorable effects on the young people who take part in it. One longitudinal study found that, among adolescents who were required to perform community service in high school, those who indicated that they would have served voluntarily showed no changes resulting from their participation (Metz & Youniss, 2005). However, those who indicated that they would not have volunteered to serve without the requirement showed an increase on measures of civic attitudes and behaviors, such as interest in political and social issues and interest in participating in civic organizations. This indicates positive effects of community service even on—in fact, especially on—adolescents who might not have been inclined to serve.

Community service, such as working in a soup kitchen, can spur adolescents' political socialization.

## Education Focus: Schools as Civic Institutions

While high schools may promote community service through a service requirement, high schools also are sites for civic development in other ways. Constance Flanagan has argued that school is a mediating institution in civil society. Every nation or state has a set of rules and obligations that it expects its citizens to follow, and—according to Flanagan—school is a key context through which adolescents acquire those rules and obligations (Flanagan et al., 2015).

Across nations, schools typically encourage students' identification with the dominant civil culture through three common sets of practices:

(1) Explicit positive narratives about the nation's history,

(2) Ethnocentric biases in the curriculum,

(3) Use of symbols (such as a national flag) and practices (such as a pledge of allegiance) of civil culture.

Whereas these practices reinforce the social order and allegiance to the nation, Flanagan points out that schools can also be "free spaces" where students challenge the ways things are and change the status quo. This concept emerged in the context of the American civil rights movement in the 1960s (Evans & Boyte, 1992). One of the originators of the concept has described how a cafeteria at Duke University provided a space for students freely to debate and question the culture and structures of segregation (Boyte, 2016).

### Review Question

Can you give one example of how your college experience fits with each of the three mediating practices proposed by Flanagan and also one example of how your college provides a "free space"?

## Community Service in Emerging Adulthood

**LO 13.4.2 Describe the three major American government institutions through which emerging adults are involved in community service.**

Like many adolescents, many emerging adults do volunteer work, such as working with children and collecting and distributing food, clothing, and other resources to the poor. During emerging adulthood, community service in American society also occurs through three major government institutions: the Peace Corps, AmeriCorps, and the military. For each of these the minimum age requirement for an individual to volunteer is 18 years old.

**Peace Corps**
an international service program in which Americans provide service to a community in a foreign country for 2 years

The **Peace Corps** is an organization that sends American volunteers all around the world to assist people in other nations by providing knowledge and skills in areas such as medical care, housing, sanitation, and food production. The organization began in 1961, when President John F. Kennedy exhorted young college graduates to give 2 years of their time in service to those in other nations who lacked the basic necessities of life. The Peace Corps is open to adults of any age, but the main participants have been emerging adults (Peace Corps, 2011).

From its beginnings, the Peace Corps grew rapidly, to a peak of 15,000 volunteers in 1966. All together, over 220,000 people have served as of 2015 (Peace Corps, 2016). Currently, almost 10,000 volunteers are in the field in more than 60 countries, with almost half serving on the African continent. They are a highly educated group: 95% have undergraduate degrees (Peace Corps, 2012). Also, 63% are women. In recent years, the Peace Corps has aimed to recruit more minority volunteers, and it reports that 28% were minorities in 2015 (Peace Corps, 2016).

Volunteers serve in a variety of areas, including education, environment, business, agriculture, and health. Across these areas, 50% report working with youth (Peace Corps, 2011). During their service, volunteers receive a monthly living allowance only high enough to enable them to live at the level of others in their community—not much, in other words. However, after the completion of their 2 years of service, they receive a bonus to assist them in making the transition back to American society.

As benefits of serving in the Peace Corps, the organization points to the enhancement of career prospects from obtaining overseas experience, gaining knowledge of different cultures, and learning the language of the host country (Peace Corps, 2016). Although returning Peace Corps volunteers have written numerous personal accounts, few systematic studies have been conducted on the volunteers' experience and how it affects them. However, in 2000 the first comprehensive survey of returning volunteers was published (Peace Corps, 2000).

Another more recent survey was published in 2011. Among the findings was that 67% of volunteers indicated they would "definitely" make the same decision to join if they had it to do again (Peace Corps, 2011). The top reasons for volunteering were to: help others (88%), gain international experience (86%), and attain personal growth (83%).

In comparison to the Peace Corps, the **AmeriCorps** program is newer, with the first group of volunteers serving in 1994. AmeriCorps has been larger than the Peace Corps from its inception. Over 20,000 volunteered in 1994, and by 2016 over 900,000 volunteers had served (AmeriCorps, 2016). Nearly all volunteers are 18 to 24 years old. About 70% are female. With respect to ethnicity, about 25% are African American, 13% Latino, and 50% White. Most volunteers have attained a high school degree, and about 30% have a college degree.

**AmeriCorps**
the national service program in the United States in which young people serve in a community organization for up to 2 years for minimal pay

The AmeriCorps agency does not administer a volunteer program, but instead sponsors volunteers to work in local community organizations, doing such work as tutoring children and adults, rehabilitating housing for low-income families, immunizing children against diseases, and helping persons with disabilities and elderly persons to maintain independent living. In return for their service, volunteers receive a small living allowance, health insurance, and an education award for each year served (1 or 2 years) to be applied toward college expenses, existing student loans, or an approved vocational training program (AmeriCorps, 2016). Surveys indicate that the top reasons for joining AmeriCorps are to: help others (77%), acquire skills useful for school or jobs (75%), and gain educational scholarship (70%) (Corporation for National & Community Service, 2007).

Evaluations of the AmeriCorps program have shown the benefits that it provides both to emerging adults and to their communities (Simon & Wang, 2002). An assessment of a random sample of volunteers before and after their participation in the program showed that 76% gained significantly in all five "life skills areas" examined: communication, interpersonal, analytical problem solving, understanding organizations, and using information technology (Aguirre International, 1999). A longitudinal study reported that, 8 years after their service in the program, AmeriCorps volunteers were higher than the comparison group (who expressed interest in AmeriCorps but did not enroll) on understanding of community problems, engagement in civic activity such as attending meetings of community organizations, and overall life satisfaction (Corporation for National and Community Service, 2008).

Military service is another type of service experienced by many emerging adults. Several times during the 20th century—during World Wars I and II, the Korean War, and most of the Vietnam War—all young men in the United States were required to serve in the military, but since the early 1970s volunteers have staffed the military. Half of all active-duty military personnel are 25 years of age or younger (Department of Defense, 2014). About 85% of all volunteers are men. African Americans and Latinos are more likely than Whites to enlist. About 31% of active-duty military personnel are minorities.

Emerging adults who volunteer for military service are more likely than other emerging adults to come from low-SES family backgrounds (Bachman et al., 2000; Burdette et al., 2009). Whereas most have graduated from high school (93%), only about 6% have a college degree. Recruits tend to have average grades in high school and low college aspirations. Motivations for enlistment include patriotism, but also the belief that military service will promote the development of personal qualities such as maturity, responsibility, and discipline. Furthermore, volunteers are motivated by the prospect of receiving money, educational support, and job training (Griffith & Perry, 1993; Teachman, 2007).

How does serving in the military influence the development of emerging adults? The answer to this question is mixed. Most veterans of World War II and the Vietnam War believed that military service broadened them intellectually and made them more self-reliant, but many of them had difficulty making the transition to civilian employment after their service. Vietnam veterans were more likely than nonveterans to have problems with alcohol abuse, especially if they had witnessed intense combat (Bookwala et al., 1994; MacLean & Elder, 2007). For more recent veterans, since the establishment of the all-volunteer military, the effects of military service have been found to be positive in many ways (Teachman & Tedrow, 2008; Whyman et al., 2011). Veterans report that their service benefited them in multiple ways, including self-confidence, self-discipline, leadership skills, and ability to work with others. Benefits have been found to be especially strong for African Americans and Latinos, who often receive educational and job-training opportunities in the military that would not be readily available to them in the civilian world.

However, in addition to these positives, a survey of recent veterans found that 44% said their adjustment to civilian life was difficult, and 37% believed they suffered from post-traumatic stress (whether or not they had been formally diagnosed) (Pew Research Center, 2011). Also, the death of about 7,000 American soldiers in Iraq and Afghanistan—mostly emerging adults—is a sobering reminder that, for emerging adults who join the military, their expanded educational and occupational opportunities come with serious risks attached.

## Political Involvement in Adolescence and Emerging Adulthood

**LO 13.4.3 Describe the political thinking and participation of adolescents and emerging adults.**

Studies of the development of political thinking in adolescence have described how political thinking becomes increasingly abstract and complex, progressing from simple views of preadolescence to a more coherent, abstract ideology of late adolescence (Torney-Purta, 1990; 2004). Also, authoritarianism declines in adolescence (Flanagan & Botcheva, 1999). For example, tolerance of opposing or offensive political views increases from childhood to adolescence and peaks in late adolescence (Flanagan, 2004). Recent studies on political development have also touted the promise of the Internet as a source of international knowledge, which could promote tolerance and perspective taking in adolescents' political views (Bakker & de Vrees, 2011; Quintelier & Vissers, 2008).

Little research has been done on political thinking in emerging adulthood, but in Europe as well as in Canada and the United States, the political participation of emerging adults is strikingly low by conventional measures such as voting rates and involvement in political parties (Barrio et al., 2007; Botcheva et al., 2007; Meeus, 2007; Núñez & Flanagan, 2015; Sears et al., 2007). Emerging adults tend to have lower political participation not only in comparison to adults, but also in comparison to previous generations of young people. They tend to be skeptical of the motivations of politicians and to see the activities of political parties as irrelevant to their lives. One study of young people in eight European countries found that low levels of trust in political authorities and political systems were consistent from adolescence through emerging adulthood (Hooghe & Wilkenfeld, 2008).

Often frustrated by conventional political processes, adolescents and emerging adults may choose to engage in political activism. Here, a demonstrator takes part in a rally in London on climate change.

However, the rejection of conventional politics should not be construed as a lack of interest in improving the state of their communities, their societies, and the world. On the contrary, emerging adults in many countries are more likely than older adults to be involved in organizations devoted to particular issues, such as environmental protection and efforts against war and racism (Goossens & Luyckx, 2007; Meeus, 2007; Núñez & Flanagan, 2015). In one nationwide survey of first-year college students in the United States, only 28% said they were interested in politics, but 45% had participated in a political demonstration (Kellogg, 2001). Emerging adults have also been prominent in historic political activism. For example, when the collapse of communism began in eastern Europe in 1989, it was initiated by emerging adults through strikes, demonstrations, and the formation of new, youth-oriented political parties (Botcheva et al., 2007; Flanagan & Botcheva, 1999; Macek, 2012). Also, the 2010–2012 Arab Spring movements in the Middle East and North Africa involved emerging adults more than any other age group (Barber, 2013). Often frustrated by conventional political processes, then, emerging adults choose instead to engage in political activism, and to direct their energies toward specific areas of importance to them, where they believe they are more likely to see genuine progress. Watch the video *Beyond Deficiency: Civic Development in Immigrant Youth* in the Research Focus feature for more information on unconventional activism.

## Research Focus: Beyond Deficiency: Civic Development in Immigrant Youth

In 1996, Cynthia García Coll and her colleagues authored a landmark article in which they called for attention to minority children and their developmental competencies (Coll et al., 1996; Marks et al., 2015). The late 1990s were generally years during which many developmental scholars called for a broadening of developmental psychology, away from one-size-fits-all theories based on the majority culture and toward more attention to the overlooked and distinctive competencies of minority groups. García Coll and her colleagues argued that measured against the standards of the majority, children of minority social class, culture, ethnicity, or race were often found to be deficient. They urged developmental psychologists to move beyond these deficiency models. Specifically, they encouraged new theory and research that start by taking into account "social position" variables (such as class), and that aim to uncover developmental competencies.

Research on civic development has seen changes according to the approach urged by García Coll and colleagues. Traditionally, research on civic involvement focused on voting and support for political parties. By these measures, there is little reason to pay attention to children or adolescents since they cannot vote. Indeed, for a long time, there was very little research on civic development. Essentially, the mainstream models pertained to politics and adults. However, research on citizenship can include not only voting and involvement with political parties but also more general involvement with others in the community, such as community service (Sherrod et al. 2002, 2010; Torney-Purta et al., 2007).

Recently, researchers have further highlighted how minority youth may opt for different kinds of civic involvement than majority youth, and how they may make use of a different set of competencies. For example, research with immigrant youth in the United States shows that they are less likely than native-born youth to be involved in conventional political activities (such as displaying political campaign signs), but more likely to be involved in political activism (such as participating in a protest march) (Jensen, 2010, 2015; Jensen & Flanagan, 2008; Jensen & Laplante, 2015; Stepick et al., 2008).

**Watch** **BEYOND DEFICIENCY: CIVIC DEVELOPMENT IN IMMIGRANT YOUTH**

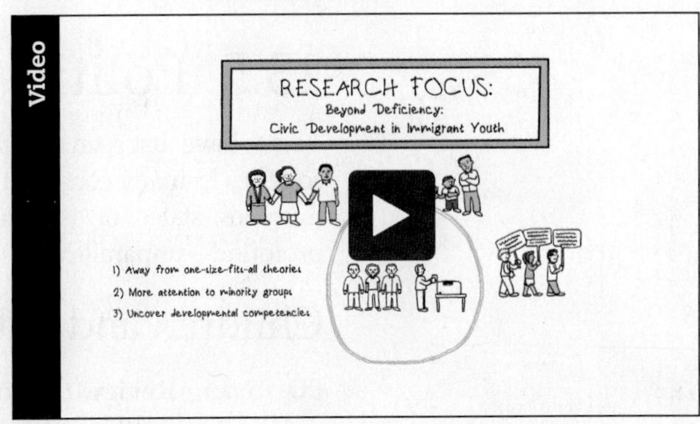


Immigrant youth are also more likely to be involved in civic activities where they put to use their multilingual and bicultural skills, such as translating documents. Furthermore, immigrant youth—who often come from cultures oriented to interdependence—emphasize that they take part in civic activities on the basis of collectivistic motives.

The civic development of immigrant youth, then, is not deficient but different. It involves distinctive behaviors, motives, and skills that contribute to positive civic development.

### Review Question

**1.** As compared to native-born youth, which of the following is true in regard to immigrant youths' civic involvement:

**a.** It tends to be more unconventional
**b.** It is often motivated by collectivism
**c.** It draws on cognitive skills distinctive to immigrants
**d.** All of the above

## SUMMARY: Civic Development

**LO 13.4.1 Summarize the characteristics of adolescents who engage in community service and the ways community service promotes positive development.**

Adolescents who engage in community service tend to be high on personal competence, academic achievement, identity development, and religiosity. Community service contributes to adolescents' political socialization.

**LO 13.4.2 Describe the three major American government institutions through which emerging adults are involved in community service.**

Like many adolescents, many emerging adults do volunteer work. During emerging adulthood, community service in American society also occurs through three major government institutions: the Peace Corps, AmeriCorps, and the military.

**LO 13.4.3 Describe the political thinking and participation of adolescents and emerging adults.**

During adolescence, political thinking becomes more abstract and complex, and less authoritarian. Emerging adults tend to have lower voting rates and involvement in political parties than adults. However, they are more likely than adults to be involved in political organizations and activism devoted to particular issues, such as environmental protection and efforts against war and racism.

# 13.5 Political Conflict and Extremism

As we have just seen, civic behaviors contribute to local communities, nation-states, and global societies in many constructive ways that are positive both for youth and for others. When communities, states, or societies engage in warfare or terrorism, however, the risks to youth are profound—unparalleled even. In this section, we address this dark side of human social behavior.

## Children and Adolescents in War

**LO 13.5.1 Review the consequences of children's and adolescents' exposure to and participation in war-time experiences, and describe interventions for youth traumatized by war.**

Over the past decades, millions of children and adolescents in parts of Africa, Asia, the Middle East, and other areas of the world have been affected by war.

**EXPOSURE TO WAR AND CHILD SOLDIERS.** During war, children risk exposure to extremely traumatic experiences. For example, a study of more than 300 children who were internally displaced after conflict began in Sudan in 2003 found that they commonly witnessed torture (75%) and rape (40%), were threatened with death (50%), experienced the death of a sibling (more than 40%) or parent (24%), or were forced to injure or kill a family member (22%) (Morgos et al., 2008).

When children and adolescents are forced to become child soldiers, their exposure to and participation in horrendous behaviors escalate. A rare study in northern Uganda compared the experiences of former child soldiers to other youth (Moscardino et al., 2012). The child soldiers had been abducted when they were between 5 and 17 years old, and held for an average of 2 years. The average age of abduction was 12. As shown in Table 13.3, the former child soldiers had much higher rates of traumatic experiences than the never-abducted youth. Nearly half had killed someone, and over three-fourths had been beaten. For an interview with a former child soldier, watch the video *Exposure to War and Child Soldiers*.

Reviews of studies of child soldiers and children exposed to war-time experiences have shown the following patterns in terms of the consequences (Masten et al., 2015):

1. Older children have greater exposure and more trauma symptoms.
2. Girls show more anxiety and depression, whereas boys show more aggressive and disruptive behaviors.
3. Severe and prolonged exposure results in worse and longer lasting effects.
4. Loss of parenting poses considerable risk.
5. Girls who experience rape sometimes receive little or no support from their communities afterward and are often stigmatized.

**Watch EXPOSURE TO WAR AND CHILD SOLDIERS**

Research has found that adolescents sometimes voluntarily join violent conflicts and wars, thereby endangering themselves psychologically and physically. Voluntary participation by adolescents has especially been seen in areas with lengthy histories of political conflict, such as in the Middle East and Northern Ireland (Barber, 2009a; Cummings et al., 2012; Dimitry, 2012). Adolescents who join report gaining a sense of identity and agency through engagement (Barber, 2009b). They sometimes come to see their engagement as part of a larger purpose.

**Table 13.3** Traumatic Experiences of Child Soldiers and Never-Abducted Children in Uganda

| | Child Soldiers | Never-Abducted Children |
|---|---|---|
| Injured | 80 | 52 |
| Been beaten | 78 | 52 |
| Had to fight | 76 | 22 |
| Had to punish other children | 76 | 16 |
| Witnessed killing | 69 | 31 |
| Had to drink urine | 51 | 10 |
| Killed someone | 47 | 7 |
| Forced to engage in sexual contact | 45 | 19 |

SOURCE: Based on Moscardino et al. (2012).

Child soldiers, even those coerced into service, also sometimes redefine themselves as leaders in an important cause. Adults may exploit youths' yearning for a sense of control and meaning, for example, by rewarding child soldiers who fall into line with the goals of the group. A longitudinal study in Mozambique found that children who had spent 6 or fewer months as child soldiers described themselves as "victims," whereas those who had spent a year or longer described themselves as "members" of the Mozambique National Resistance (Boothby et al., 2009). As one child explained, "I first served as his personal servant. Then he made me chief of a group of other boys. I had power" (Boothby et al., 2009, p. 244).

**INTERVENTION AND PREVENTION.** Many studies have emphasized the importance of normalizing the everyday life for youth who have been exposed to or taken part in political violence and war (Masten & Narayan, 2012). This includes restoring family routines, resuming school, having opportunities for play and socializing with peers, and engagement with cultural and religious practices (Franks, 2011; Masten & Osofsky, 2010).

An example of an approach to normalizing life for children, their families, and communities comes from Mozambique. Child soldiers who had been part of the Mozambique National Resistance took part in "cleansing ceremonies" that absolved them of shame and blame for what they may have done during the war, and that were followed by the resumption of school or work (Boothby et al., 2009). In the words of one former child soldier, the ceremony represents a chance to be "like everyone else" (Boothby et al., 2009, p. 248).

Certain kinds of therapeutic interventions have also shown promise (Masten et al., 2015). Narrative Exposure Therapy (NET) involves youth recounting autobiographical narratives of their experiences while also receiving individual therapy for post-traumatic stress symptoms. Interpersonal Therapy in Group format (IPT-G) involves group activities, including play exercises.

Focusing on prevention, UNICEF provides "Peace Education" materials and activities for children, aimed at reducing conflict and promoting understanding among children and adolescents who live in regions with political conflict. UNICEF defines peace education as "the process of promoting the knowledge, skills, attitudes and values needed to bring about behavior change that will enable children, youth and adults to prevent conflict and violence, both overt and structural; to resolve conflict peacefully; and to create the conditions conducive to peace, whether at an interpersonal, intergroup, national or international level" (UNICEF, 2016). Initiatives include providing teaching materials for schools, encouraging families to keep their children in school, and having children take part in sports events that incorporate peace messages.

A 12-year-old boy soldier in the Democratic Republic of Congo.

## Extremism in Emerging Adulthood

**LO 13.5.2 Explain the nature of political extremism in emerging adulthood.**

Emerging adulthood is a time of life where voluntary involvement in revolutionary movements and terrorism is particularly pronounced. The leaders of politically extreme groups are usually middle aged or older, but many of their most zealous followers are often emerging adults. There are many recent historical examples. The "Cultural Revolution" that took place in China from 1966 to 1975 and involved massive destruction and violence toward anyone deemed to be a threat to the "purity" of Chinese communism was instigated by Chairman Mao and his wife Jiang Ching, but carried out almost entirely by fervent Chinese emerging adults (MacFarquhar & Schoenhals, 2006). Terrorist attacks by Muslim extremists against Western targets—most notably the attacks of September 11, 2001—have been planned by older men but executed almost entirely by emerging adult men (Sen & Samad, 2007).

Why are emerging adults especially likely to be involved in extreme and violent movements? One reason is that they have fewer social ties and obligations than people in other age groups (Arnett, 2015). Children and adolescents can often, if not always, be restrained from involvement by their parents. Young, middle, and older adults can be deterred from involvement by their commitments to others who depend on them, especially a spouse and children. However, emerging adulthood is a time when social commitments and social control are at their low point. Emerging adults have more freedom than people at other age periods, and this freedom allows some of them to become involved in violent movements.

Another possibility is that their involvement is identity related. Although identity issues are important in adolescence, they may become even more prominent in some respects during emerging adulthood. One aspect of identity exploration is ideology or worldview (Arnett, 2015; Erikson, 1968). Emerging adulthood is a time when people are looking for an ideological framework for explaining the world, and some emerging adults may be attracted to the definite answers provided by extreme political movements. Embracing an extreme political ideology may relieve the discomfort that can accompany the uncertainty and doubt of ideological explorations. Still, these explanations beg the question: Since only a small minority of emerging adults are involved in these extreme movements, why them and not the others?

### SUMMARY: Political Conflict and Extremism

**LO 13.5.1 Review the consequences of children's and adolescents' exposure to and participation in war-time experiences, and describe interventions for youth traumatized by war.**

During war, children risk exposure to extremely traumatic experiences, including murder, torture, and rape. When children and adolescents are forced to become child soldiers, their exposure to and participation in horrendous behaviors escalate. Many studies have emphasized the importance of normalizing the everyday life for youth who have been exposed to or taken part in political violence and war.

**LO 13.5.2 Explain the nature of political extremism in emerging adulthood.**

Emerging adulthood is a time of life where voluntary involvement in revolutionary movements and terrorism is particularly pronounced. One explanation may be that they have fewer social ties and obligations than people in other age groups. For some emerging adults, extremism may also resolve struggles with identity development.

## 13.6 Values in Today's and Tomorrow's World

This chapter has described the moral, religious, and civic values that emerge in children's development in today's world. What might those values look like in tomorrow's world? What changes are on the horizon that will impact child development? We end this chapter and text by pointing to two changes that we anticipate, and by then opening up to you—the reader—to think about this very question too.

## Individualism on the Rise

**LO 13.6.1 Explain the evidence for the rise of individualism in recent times.**

As we have seen in this text, all cultures value interdependence and collectivism. Generally, these values are more pronounced in traditional rural communities than in urban communities, more pronounced in developing than developed countries, and more pronounced in Eastern than Western countries.

We would expect collectivism to remain valued in all cultures, but also to see a rising emphasis on individualism. Even in the United States—a place long associated with esteem for the individual—there has been a marked rise in individualistic values. In the 1920s, Helen and Robert Lynd described life in a typical American community they called "Middletown" (Lynd & Lynd, 1929). The Lynds studied many aspects of life in Middletown (actually Muncie, Indiana), including women's beliefs about the values they considered most important to promote in their children. Fifty years later, another group of researchers returned to Middletown and asked the residents many of the same questions (Caplow et al., 2004). As you can see from Table 13.4, the results indicate that the child-rearing beliefs of the American majority culture changed dramatically over the 20th century (Alwin, 1988; Caplow et al., 2004). Values such as loyalty to church and obedience declined in importance, whereas values such as independence and tolerance became central to parents' child-rearing beliefs. Other studies have confirmed this rise in individualism in the American majority culture during the 20th century (Alwin et al., 1994; Cohn, 1999; Twenge, 2006).

Many examples exist of how individualism is on the rise, even in traditional cultures. For example, the Aborigines of Australia were nomadic hunters and gatherers until about 70 years ago (Burbank, 1988, 1994). They moved their small communities from one place to another according to the seasons and the availability of food such as fish and sea turtles. They had few possessions. A key part of traditional childhood socialization among the Aborigines involves the teaching of a set of beliefs and values known as the Law. The Law includes an explanation of how the world began, instructions for how various ritual ceremonies should be performed, and moral precepts for how interpersonal relations should be conducted. For example, there are complex rules about who may have sex with whom, and who may marry whom. Also, it is viewed as best if marriages are arranged by the parents. The values expressed in the Law are collectivistic. Children and adolescents are taught that they have obligations to others as part of the Law and that they must allow others to make important decisions that affect them, such as whom they shall marry.

Traditionally, socialization of the Law includes an elaborate and extended series of three public ceremonies, with each ceremony representing a stage in the transition from boyhood to manhood. Although both boys and girls learn the Law, only boys participate in the public ceremonies. In the ceremonies, various aspects of the Law are taught. The whole community attends. However, like so many other traditional cultures, globalization has had an enormous impact on the Aborigines (Robinson, 1997; Silburn et al., 2007). The ceremonies still exist, and boys still take part. But the rituals have been dramatically shortened and simplified. Furthermore, today's adolescents are showing increasing resistance to learning and adhering to the traditional beliefs and values, such as having an arranged marriage. To many of them, the Law seems irrelevant to the world they live in, which is no longer a world of nomadic hunting and gathering but of schools, a complex economy, and modern media.

**Table 13.4** Child-Rearing Values of Women in Middletown, 1928 and 1978

| | 1928 | 1978 |
|---|---|---|
| Loyalty to church | 50 | 22 |
| Strict obedience | 45 | 17 |
| Good manners | 31 | 23 |
| Independence | 25 | 76 |
| Tolerance | 6 | 47 |

NOTE: The table indicates the percentage of women in 1928 and 1978 who listed each of the indicated values as one of the three most important for their children to learn, out of a list of 15 values.

SOURCE: Based on Alwin (1988).

Aborigine children and adolescents now develop values based not just on the Law, but also on their other experiences, and these experiences have made their values more individualistic.

In tomorrow's world, then, children are likely to have more exposure than ever to individualistic values. How this will affect them and their relationships with others remains to be seen.

We expect children in tomorrow's world will grow up in virtually daily contact with people of diverse cultural backgrounds.

## Exposure to Diversity

**LO 13.6.2 Describe the extent to which children across the world are likely to have increased exposure to diversity in tomorrow's world.**

As we have seen throughout this text, children are coming of age in a globalizing world, where languages, people, ideas, and identities are swirling across cultures. Movement across cultures is not new, but the current extent and speed of the movement are (Friedman, 2000; Giddens, 2000; Hermans, 2015). There are still traditional cultures in the world, but it is increasingly rare for people from a culture not to have exposure to and interactions with other people far beyond their own borders.

We would expect that in tomorrow's world, children will grow up with virtually daily contact with people of diverse cultural backgrounds. With urbanization, diverse children meet in school—and urbanization is increasing worldwide. With immigration, diverse children live in the same neighborhood—and immigration, too, is rising rapidly. With the continued growth of global media, children learn about cultures outside their own, and have virtual interactions with children from those cultures.

With globalization, then, there will be a rise in the different values to which a developing child will have exposure. This would seem to hold the potential for development of a certain measure of tolerance for diverse values, but it also seems inevitable that not all values will be compatible. Perhaps then, in tomorrow's world, children will have to make more choices about the values that resonate with them the most.

### SUMMARY: Values in Today's and Tomorrow's World

**LO 13.6.1 Explain the evidence for the rise of individualism in recent times.**

The rise of individualism is seen across many societies, including in child-rearing values, diminishment of traditional coming-of-age ceremonies, and adolescents' desire for more independence.

**LO 13.6.2 Describe the extent to which children across the world are likely to have increased exposure to diversity in tomorrow's world.**

Due to globalization and urbanization, children increasingly grow up with daily contact with people of diverse cultural backgrounds. This would seem to hold the potential for development of a certain measure of tolerance for diverse values, but it also seems inevitable that not all values will be compatible. Perhaps then, in tomorrow's world, children will have to make more choices about the values that resonate with them the most.

# Apply Your Knowledge as a Professional

The topics covered in this chapter apply to a wide variety of career professions. Watch this video to learn how they apply to an emerging leaders program manager at a nonprofit organization.

**Journaling Question:** We end this chapter and text with predictions about two ways that values might change for children growing up in tomorrow's world. First, reflect on whether or not you agree with the two expected changes. Then, reflect on one kind of change in values that you would expect to take place in the future.

## Apply Your Knowledge as a Professional

# Glossary

**abstract thinking** thinking pertaining to concepts and processes that cannot be experienced directly through the senses

**accommodation** cognitive process of changing a scheme to adapt to new information

**active genotype → environment effects** in the theory of genotype → environment effects, the type that results when people seek out environments that correspond to their genotypic characteristics

**actual self** person's perception of the self as it is, contrasted with the possible self

**adolescence-limited delinquents (ALDs)** in Moffitt's theory, delinquents who engage in criminal acts in adolescence and/or emerging adulthood but show no evidence of problems before or after these periods

**adolescent egocentrism** type of egocentrism in which adolescents have difficulty distinguishing their thinking about their own thoughts from their thinking about the thoughts of others

**adolescent growth spurt** the rapid pace of growth in height characteristic of puberty

**affirmative consent** unequivocal, verbal agreement to sexual activity

**age graded** social organization based on grouping persons of similar ages

**age norms** technique for developing a psychological test, in which a typical score for each age is established by testing a large random sample of people from a variety of geographical areas and social class backgrounds

**AIDS (acquired immune deficiency syndrome)** sexually transmitted infection caused by HIV, resulting in damage to the immune system

**allele** on a pair of chromosomes, each of two forms of a gene

**AmeriCorps** the national service program in the United States in which young people serve in a community organization for up to 2 years for minimal pay

**amniocentesis** prenatal procedure in which a needle is used to withdraw amniotic fluid containing fetal cells from the placenta, allowing possible prenatal problems to be detected

**amnion** fluid-filled membrane that surrounds and protects the developing organism in the womb

**androgens** sex hormones that have especially high levels in males from puberty onward and are mostly responsible for male primary and secondary sex characteristics

**androgyny** a combination of "female" and "male" personality traits

**anemia** dietary deficiency of iron that causes problems such as fatigue, irritability, and attention difficulties

**animism** tendency to attribute human thoughts and feelings to inanimate objects and forces

**anoxia** deprivation of oxygen during birth process and soon after that can result in serious neurological damage within minutes

**Apgar scale** neonatal assessment scale with five subtests: Appearance (color), Pulse (heart rate), Grimace (reflex irritability), Activity (muscle tone), and Respiration (breathing)

**apprenticeship** an arrangement, common in Europe, in which an adolescent "novice" serves under contract to a "master" who has substantial experience in a profession, and through working under the master, learns the skills required to enter the profession

**artificial insemination** procedure of injecting sperm directly into the uterus

**assimilation** cognitive process of altering new information to fit an existing scheme

**assisted reproductive technologies (ART)** methods for overcoming infertility that include artificial insemination, fertility drugs, and IVF

**asynchronicity** principle of biological development that growth of different body parts is uneven

**attachment theory** Bowlby's theory of emotional and social development, focusing on the crucial importance of the infant's relationship with the primary caregiver

**attention-deficit/hyperactivity disorder (ADHD)** diagnosis that includes problems of inattention, hyperactivity, and impulsiveness

**authoritarian parents** in classifications of parenting styles, parents who are high in demandingness but low in responsiveness

**authoritative parents** in classifications of parenting styles, parents who are high in demandingness and high in responsiveness

**Autism Spectrum Disorder (ASD)** involves persistent deficits in social communication and interactions across contexts, as well as repetitive and restricted behavior

**automaticity** how much cognitive effort a person needs to devote to process information; the more automaticity, the less effort

**autonomous morality** Piaget's term for the period of moral development starting at about ages 10 to 12, involving a growing realization that moral rules can be changed if people decide they should be changed

**autonomy** quality of being independent and self-sufficient, capable of thinking for one's self

**axon** part of a neuron that transmits electric impulses and releases neurotransmitters

**babbling** repetitive prelanguage consonant–vowel combinations such as "ba-ba-ba" or "do-do-do-do," made by infants universally beginning at about 4–6 months of age

**Bayesian theories** emphasize that children infer the meaning of words based on assessment of statistical probability

**Bayley Scales of Infant Development** assessment of infant development from age 3 months to 3½ years

**behavior genetics** field in the study of human development that aims to identify the extent to which genes influence behavior, primarily by comparing persons who share different amounts of their genes

**behaviorism** a theory that regards infants as starting out from scratch and learning behaviors based on the responses or "conditioning" of those around them

**bicultural identity** identity with two distinct facets, for example one part based on the local culture and another part based on the global culture

**biological measurements** includes measures of genetic, hormonal, and brain activity

**biosocial construction model** theory that emphasizes that evolution selected for human females and males to be flexible and adaptive to environmental variation and change, and that "gendered" behavior influences biology

**blastocyst** ball of about 100 cells formed by about 1 week following conception

**body mass index (BMI)** measure of the ratio of weight to height

**bonding** invalid claim that in humans the first few minutes and hours after birth are critical to mother–infant relationships

**Brazelton Neonatal Behavioral Assessment Scale (NBAS)** 27-item scale of neonatal functioning with overall ratings "worrisome," "normal," and "superior"

**breech presentation** positioning of the fetus so that feet or buttocks, rather than the head, would come first out of the birth canal

**Broca's area** an area of the brain located in the left frontal lobe that is specialized for language production

**bullying** in peer relations, the extremely aggressive assertion of power by one person over another

**cardiac output** quantity of blood flow from the heart

**care orientation** Gilligan's term for a type of moral orientation that involves focusing on relationships with others as the basis for moral reasoning

**case study** the detailed examination of a particular person, group, or situation over time

**categorical perception** the ability to perceive speech sounds as belonging to discrete categories

**categorization** process of sorting and organizing into groups and classes

**cathartic effect** experiences, including media experiences, that provide relief from negative emotions

**centration** Piaget's term for young children's thinking as being centered, or focused, on one noticeable aspect of a cognitive problem to the exclusion of other important aspects

**cephalocaudal principle** principle of biological development that growth begins at the top, with the head, and then proceeds downward to the rest of the body

**cerebellum** structure at the base of the brain involved in balance and motor movements

**cerebral cortex** outer portion of the brain, containing four regions with distinct functions

**cesarean deliver, or c-section** type of birth in which mother's abdomen is cut open and fetus is retrieved directly from the uterus

**child development** the ways individuals grow and change until adulthood

**child maltreatment** neglect or abuse of children, including physical, emotional, or sexual abuse

**child study movement** European and American movements around the turn of the 20th century that advocated scientific research on child and adolescent development, and the improvement of conditions for children and adolescents in the family, school, and workplace

**child welfare institutions** residential institutions that provide total care for children who are orphaned, abandoned, or otherwise separated from family

**chorionic villus sampling (CVS)** prenatal technique for diagnosing genetic problems, involving taking a sample of cells at 5–10 weeks gestation by inserting a tube into the uterus

**chromosome** structure in the nucleus of cells, containing genes, which are paired, except in reproductive cells

**civic development** pertaining to involvement in collective actions that contribute to local communities, nation-states, or global societies

**civilization** form of human social life, beginning about 5,000 years ago, that includes cities, writing, occupational specialization, and states

**classification** ability to understand that objects can be part of more than one class or group, for example, an object can be classified with red objects as well as with round objects

**cliques** small groups of friends who know each other well, do things together, and form a regular social group

**coercive cycle** pattern in relations between parents and children in which children's disobedient behavior evokes harsh responses from parents, which in turn makes children even more resistant to parental control, evoking even harsher responses

**cognitive theory** regards language as a symbolic ability that develops in concert with thinking as a whole

**cognitive-developmental approach** focuses on how cognitive development takes place in a sequence of distinct stages, pioneered by Piaget and subsequently adopted by researchers addressing other areas of development

**cohort effect** in scientific research, an explanation of group differences among people of different ages based on the fact that they grew up in different *cohorts* or historical periods

**colic** infant crying pattern in which the crying goes on for more than 3 hours a day over more than 3 days at a time for more than 3 weeks

**collectivistic** cultural values such as obedience and group harmony

**colostrum** thick, yellowish liquid produced by mammalian mothers during the first days following birth, extremely rich in protein and antibodies that strengthen the baby's immune system

**coming out** for sexual minority individuals, the process of acknowledging their sexual identity and then disclosing the truth to their friends, family, and others

**commercial sexual exploitation** forced sex work by children and adolescents

**community service** volunteer work provided as a contribution to the community, without monetary compensation

**complex thinking** thinking that takes into account multiple connections and interpretations, such as in the use of metaphor, satire, and sarcasm

**concordance rate** degree of similarity in phenotype among pairs of family members, expressed as a percentage

**concrete operations** in Piaget's theory, cognitive stage from 7 to 11 during which children become capable of using systematic and logical mental operations

**congenital adrenal hyperplasia (CAH)** a genetic condition that involves overproduction of androgens during early prenatal development

**conservation** mental ability to understand that the quantity of a substance or material remains the same even if its appearance changes

**contexts** settings and circumstances that contribute to variations in pathways of human development, including SES, gender, and ethnicity, as well as family, school, community, and media

**Conventional Level** Kohlberg's term for the intermediate level of moral development focused on group-centered considerations

**conventional/societal domain** in domain theory, reasoning pertaining to communal and religious norms, interests, and authorities

**cooing** prelanguage "oo-ing" and "ah-ing," and gurgling sounds babies make beginning at about 2 months old

**corporal punishment** physical punishment of children

**corregulation** relationship between parents and children in which parents provide broad guidelines for behavior but children are capable of a substantial amount of independent, self-directed behavior

**correlation** statistical relationship between two variables such that knowing one of the variables makes it possible to predict the other. A statistical value of 0 indicates no correlation. Values of 1 and −1 indicate the strongest possible positive and negative correlations

**correlational design** data collected on naturally occurring variables on a single occasion

**cosleeping** cultural practice in which infants and sometimes older children sleep with one or both parents, also termed bed-sharing

**cross-platform learning** use of multiple rather than one or no media for learning purposes

**cross-sectional design** data with people of different ages are collected at a single point in time

**crossing over** at the outset of meiosis, the exchange of genetic material between paired chromosomes

**crowds** large, reputation-based groups of adolescents

**crystallized intelligence** accumulated knowledge and enhanced judgment based on experience

**Cultivation Theory** argues that media gradually shape or "cultivate" a person's worldview

**cultural-developmental approach** the study of development within and across cultures in order to understand both what is universal and what is culturally distinctive

**culture** the total pattern of a group's customs, beliefs, art, and technology

**custom complex** distinctive cultural pattern of behavior that reflects underlying cultural beliefs

**cyberbullying** bullying via electronic means, mainly through the Internet

**date rape** an act of sexual aggression in which a person is forced by a romantic partner, date, or acquaintance to have sexual relations against her or his will

**deferred imitation** ability to repeat actions observed at an earlier time

**delinquency** violations of the law committed by juveniles

**delivery** second stage of the birth process, during which the fetus is pushed out of the cervix and through the birth canal

**demandingness** degree to which parents set rules and expectations for behavior and require their children to comply with them

**dendrites** arrays of short neural fibers that receive neurotransmitters

**dependent variable** in an experiment, the outcome that is measured to calculate the results of the experiment by comparing the experimental group to the control group

**depressed mood** temporary period of sadness, without any other related symptoms of depression

**depth perception** ability to discern the relative distance of objects in the environment

**developed countries** world's most economically developed and affluent countries, with the highest median levels of income and education

**developing countries** countries that have lower levels of income and education than developed countries but are experiencing rapid economic growth

**developmental cascade** when a problem at one point in life surges into a series of problems over time

**developmental quotient (DQ)** the overall score indicating progress in assessments of infant development

**dialectical thought** awareness that problems often have no clear solution and two opposing strategies or points of view may each have some merit

**differentiated self-esteem** how a person evaluates her- or himself in specific domains, such as social competence and physical appearance

**differentiation theories** argue that discrete emotions are not present at birth but only develop gradually

**diffusion** the spread of products or people across space

**digital immigrants** persons belonging to generations who have only used digital media upon reaching adulthood

**digital natives** today's generation of children who have grown up with digital media since infancy

**disengaged parents** in classifications of parenting styles, parents who are low in both demandingness and responsiveness

**disequilibrium** in the family systems approach, this term describes a change that requires adjustments from family members

**dishabituation** following habituation, the revival of attention when a new stimulus is presented

**displacement effect** in media research, term for how media use occupies time that could have been spent on other activities

**divided attention** ability to focus on more than one task at a time

**divorce mediation** arrangement in which a professional mediator meets with divorcing parents to help them negotiate an agreement that both will find acceptable

**dizygotic (DZ) twins** twins who result from two eggs that each are fertilized by a sperm; also called fraternal twins

**DNA (deoxyribonucleic acid)** long strand of cell material that stores and transfers genetic information in all life forms

**dominant-recessive inheritance** pattern of inheritance in which a pair of chromosomes contains one dominant and one recessive gene, but only the dominant gene is expressed in the phenotype

**Down syndrome** genetic disorder due to carrying an extra chromosome on the 21st pair

**dual-earner family** a family in which both parents are employed

**dyadic relationship** a relationship between two persons

**dyslexia** learning disability that includes difficulty sounding out letters, difficulty learning to spell words, and a tendency to misperceive the order of letters in words

**early intervention program** program directed at young children from low-SES families who are at risk for later problems

**ecological theory** Bronfenbrenner's theory that child development is shaped by five interrelated systems in the social environment

**ecological validity** the extent to which there is a fit between the measurement approach and the everyday life of the people being studied

**ectoderm** in the embryonic period, the outer of the three cell layers, which will become the skin, hair, nails, sensory organs, and nervous system

**effect size** the difference between two groups in a meta-analysis, represented by the letter *d*

**egocentrism** cognitive inability to distinguish between one's own perspective and another person's perspective

**elaboration** mnemonic that involves transforming bits of information in a way that connects them and hence makes them easier to remember

**electroencephalogram (EEG)** device that measures the electrical activity of the cerebral cortex, allowing researchers to measure overall activity of the cerebral cortex as well as activation of specific parts of it

**electronic fetal monitoring (EFM)** method that tracks the fetus's heartbeat, either externally through the mother's abdomen or directly by running a wire through the cervix and placing a sensor on the fetus's scalp

**embryonic period** weeks 3–8 of prenatal development

**emerging adulthood** new life stage in developed countries, lasting from the late teens through the mid-twenties, in which people are gradually making their way toward taking on adult responsibilities in love and work

**emotion display rules** the social norms for when, where, how, and to whom to express emotions

**emotional contagion** in infants, crying in response to hearing another infant cry, evident at just a few days old

**empathy** ability to understand and respond helpfully to another person's distress

**endoderm** in the embryonic period, the inner layer of cells, which will become the digestive system and the respiratory system

**epidural** during birth process, injection of an anesthetic drug into the spinal fluid to help the mother manage the pain while also remaining alert

**epigenetics** the study of how genetic activity responds to environmental influences

**episiotomy** incision to make the vaginal opening larger during birth process

**estradiol** the estrogen most important in pubertal development among girls

**estrogens** sex hormones that have especially high levels in females from puberty onward and are mostly responsible for female primary and secondary sex characteristics

**Ethic of Autonomy** within the cultural-developmental approach, moral reasoning pertaining to an individual's rights, interests, and well-being

**Ethic of Community** within the cultural-developmental approach, moral reasoning pertaining to duties to others, and promoting the interests and welfare of groups

**Ethic of Divinity** within the cultural-developmental approach, moral reasoning pertaining to religious rules, spiritual degradation, and moral purity

**ethnicity** group identity that may include components such as cultural origin, cultural traditions, race, religion, and language

**ethnographic research** research design that involves spending extensive time among the people being studied

**ethology** study of animal behavior

**eveningness** preference for going to bed late and waking up late

**evocative genotype → environment effects** in the theory of genotype → environment effects, the type that results when a person's inherited characteristics evoke responses from others in the environment

**evolutionary psychology** branch of psychology that examines how patterns of human functioning and behavior have resulted from adaptations to evolutionary conditions

**evolutionary theories** emphasize the existence of discrete emotions that are innate and shared by all humans

**executive function** includes inhibitory control, or staying focused on the task at hand and not becoming distracted, and flexibility, or adjusting one's strategy as the nature of a task changes

**experimental design** entails comparing an *experimental group* that receives a treatment of some kind to a *control group* that receives no treatment

**extended families** households that include not only parents and children, but also other adult relatives

**externalizing problems** problems that involve others, such as aggression

**false self** self a person may present to others while realizing that it does not represent what he or she is actually thinking and feeling

**familismo** cultural belief among Latinos that emphasizes the love, closeness, and mutual obligations among family members

**family process** quality of the relationships between family members

**family systems approach** an approach to understanding family functioning that emphasizes how each relationship within the family influences the family as a whole

**fast mapping** the ability to learn and remember the term for an object after only being told once

**feared self** person one imagines it is possible to become but dreads becoming

**female sexual fluidity** women exceeding men on same-sex attractions and behaviors, and bisexual self-identification

**fetal alcohol spectrum disorder (FASD)** set of problems that occur as a consequence of high maternal alcohol use during pregnancy, including facial deformities, heart problems, misshapen limbs, and a variety of cognitive problems

**fetal period** in prenatal development, the period from Week 9 until birth

**field studies** studies in which people's behavior is observed in a natural setting

**filial piety** belief that children should respect, obey, and revere their parents throughout life; common in Asian cultures

**fine motor development** development of motor abilities involving finely tuned movements of the hands such as grasping and manipulating objects

**fluid intelligence** mental abilities that involve speed of analyzing, processing, and reacting to information

**Flynn effect** steep rise in the median IQ score in Western countries during the 20th century, named after James Flynn, who first identified it

**follicle** during the female reproductive cycle, the ovum plus other cells that surround the ovum and provide nutrients

**fontanels** soft spots on the skull between loosely joined pieces of the skull that shift during the birth process to assist passage through the birth canal

**formal operations** in Piaget's theory, cognitive stage beginning at age 11 in which people learn to think systematically about possibilities and hypotheses

**foster care** for maltreated children, approach in which adults approved by a state agency take over the care of the child

**friends** persons with whom an individual has a valued, mutual relationship

**Full Scale Intelligence Quotient** IQ score calculated relative to the performance of other people of the same age, with 100 as the median score

**functional magnetic resonance imaging (fMRI)** method of monitoring brain activity in which a person lies inside a machine that uses a magnetic field to record changes in blood flow and oxygen use in the brain in response to different kinds of stimulation

**functionalistic theories** emphasize how emotions serve social functions, for example, signaling desired goals both to self and others

**gametes** cells, distinctive to each sex, that are involved in reproduction (egg cells in the ovaries of the female and sperm in the testes of the male)

**gender** cultural categories of "female" and "male"

**gender constancy** understanding that femaleness and maleness are biological and cannot change across situations

**Gender Empowerment Measure (GEM)** assessments of the extent to which women are equal to men in earned income, as well as representation in national legislatures and executive business positions

**gender identity** awareness of one's self as female or male

**gender intensification hypothesis** hypothesis that psychological and behavioral differences between females and males become more pronounced at adolescence because of intensified socialization pressures to conform to culturally prescribed gender roles

**gender nonconforming** persons who identify as either female or male, but whose behaviors are androgynous to a degree where it falls outside conventional norms

**Gender Parity Index (GPI)** assessment of the extent to which educational attainment is equal for boys and girls

**gender roles** cultural expectations for appearance and behavior specific to females and males

**gender schema** gender-based cognitive structure for organizing and processing information, comprising expectations for females' and males' appearance and behavior

**gender schema theory** emphasizes that children learn to categorize a wide range of activities, objects, and personality characteristics as "female" or "male."

**gender self-socialization model** highlights that children actively internalize gender schemas as part of their identity

**genes** basic units of hereditary information

**genetic mutation** a permanent alteration of a DNA sequence that makes up a gene

**genotype** organism's unique genetic inheritance

**germinal period** first 2 weeks after conception

**gestation** in prenatal development, elapsed time since conception

**gifted** level of cognitive abilities of persons who score above 130 on IQ tests

**global self-esteem** the extent to which a person generally feels positive about her- or himself

**globalization** increasing worldwide technological and economic integration, which is making different parts of the world increasingly connected

**gonadotropin-releasing hormone (GnRH)** a hormone produced by the hypothalamus that is involved in the onset of puberty

**goodness-of-fit** theoretical principle that children develop best if there is a good fit between the temperament of the child and environmental demands

**graduated driver licensing (GDL)** government program in which young people obtain driving privileges gradually, contingent on a safe driving record, rather than all at once

**grammar** the rules for creating words and sentences

**gross motor development** development of motor abilities including balance and posture as well as whole-body movements such as crawling

**guided participation** interaction between two people in a culturally valued activity where the more experienced person guides the learning of the less experienced person

**guilt** feeling of responsibility and remorse for perceived wrongdoing by the self

**habituation** gradual decrease in attention to a stimulus after repeated presentations

**heritability** statistical estimate of the extent to which genes are responsible for the differences among persons within a specific population, with values ranging from 0 to 1.00

**heteronomous morality** Piaget's term for the period of moral development from about ages 4 to 7, in which moral rules are viewed as having a sacred, fixed quality, handed down from figures of authority

**holophrases** use of a single word to represent different forms of whole sentences

***Homo sapiens*** species of modern humans

**hostile aggression** type of aggression that entails signs of anger and intent to inflict pain or harm on others

**human genome** the sum total of hereditary information

**hybrid identity** an identity that integrates elements of various cultures

**hypothesis** a researcher's idea about one possible answer to the question proposed for investigation

**hypothetical dilemmas** research measure created by Kohlberg where participants are asked to reason about situations in which a choice has to be made between two or more alternatives

**hypothetical-deductive reasoning** Piaget's term for the process of applying scientific thinking to cognitive tasks

**ideal self** person one would like to be

**identity status model** Marcia's model for researching Erikson's theory of identity development, classifying identity development into four categories: diffusion, foreclosure, moratorium, or achievement

**identity versus identity confusion** in Erikson's theory, the crisis of adolescence, with two alternative paths, establishing a clear and definite identity, or experiencing identity confusion, which is a failure to form a stable and secure identity

**idiographic** research aimed at providing knowledge of how individuals are unique

**imaginary audience** belief that others are acutely aware of and attentive to one's appearance and behavior

**immigrant paradox** the paradox that immigrant adolescents' academic achievement worsens across each successive generation living the United States

**implantation** occurs at the end of the germinal period when the blastocyst becomes firmly embedded into the lining of the uterus

**imprinting** instant and enduring bond to the first moving object seen after birth; common in birds

**in vitro fertilization (IVF)** form of infertility treatment that involves using drugs to stimulate the growth of multiple follicles in the ovaries, removing the follicles and combining them with sperm, then transferring the most promising zygotes to the uterus

**incomplete dominance** form of dominant–recessive inheritance in which the phenotype is influenced primarily by the dominant gene but also to some extent by the recessive gene

**independent variable** in an experiment, the variable that is different for the experimental group than for the control group

**individualistic** cultural values such as independence and self-expression

**infant-directed speech (IDS)** speaking in a specific way to infants and toddlers, including with raised pitch and exaggerated intonation

**infantile amnesia** loss of memory of information up to about age 4

**infertility** inability to attain pregnancy after at least a year of regular sexual intercourse

**infinite generativity** the ability to take the word symbols of a spoken language or the gestures of a sign language and combine them in a virtually infinite number of new ways

**information-processing approaches** focus on cognitive processes that exist at all ages, rather than on viewing cognitive development in terms of discontinuous stages

**informed consent** standard procedure in social scientific studies that entails informing potential participants of what their participation would involve, including any possible risks

**innatist theory** emphasizes that children are born with a Language Acquisition Device (LAD)

**instrumental aggression** type of aggression when a child wants something and uses aggressive behavior or words to get it

**instrumental aid** practical help, such as assistance with homework or expenses

**integrated models** intervention programs for aggressive and rejected children that focus on their emotions, cognition, and behaviors, and that involve different social contexts such as schools, family, and peers

**intellectual disability** level of cognitive abilities of persons who score below 70 on IQ tests

**interactionist or social theories** regard language as a tool that is largely learned and put to social and cultural uses

**intermodal perception** integration and coordination of information from two or more various senses

**internal working model** in attachment theory, the term for the cognitive framework, based on interactions in infancy with the primary caregiver, that shapes expectations and interactions in relationships to others throughout life

**internalization theory** focuses on how children's emotion expression and regulation in social contexts are guided by adults and cultural norms

**internalizing problems** problems that entail turning distress inward, toward the self, such as depression and anxiety

**intersectionality** describes how individuals have more than one social identity and that these various identities overlap

**interventions** programs intended to change the attitudes and/or behavior of the participants

**interviews** spoken questions where participants typically are free to provide their own answers

**intimacy** the degree to which two people share personal knowledge, thoughts, and feelings

**joint attention** paying attention to the stimuli on which other people are focusing

**justice orientation** Gilligan's terms for a type of moral orientation that places a premium on abstract principles of justice, equality, and fairness

**kangaroo care** recommended care for preterm and low-birth-weight neonates, in which mothers or fathers are advised to place the baby skin-to-skin on their chests for 2–3 hours a day for the early weeks of life

**kwashiorkor** protein deficiency in childhood, leading to symptoms such as lethargy, irritability, thinning hair, and swollen body, which may be fatal if not treated

**labor** first and longest stage of the birth process

**language** a system of sounds or gestures that people use to communicate with one another

**language acquisition device (LAD)** a theorized innate mechanism that allows young children to perceive and quickly grasp the grammatical rules of the language around them

**language brokering** immigrant children translating and interpreting the language and culture for others, usually adult family members

**lanugo** downy hair that helps the vernix stick to the skin of the developing fetus

**lateralization** specialization of functions in the two hemispheres of the brain

**learning disability** in schools, a diagnosis made when a child or adolescent has normal intelligence but has difficulty in one or more academic areas and the difficulty cannot be attributed to any other disorder

**let-down reflex** in females, a reflex that causes milk to be released to the tip of the nipples in response to the sound of an infant's cry, seeing its open mouth, or even thinking about breast-feeding

**life-course-persistent delinquents (LCPDs)** in Moffitt's theory, adolescents who show a history of related problems both prior to and following adolescence

**long-term memory** memory for information that is committed to longer-term storage, so that it can be drawn upon after a period when attention has not been focused on it

**longitudinal design** the same persons are followed over time and data are collected on two or more occasions

**low birth weight** term for neonates weighing less than 2,500 grams (5.8 lb)

**machismo** ideology of manhood, common in Latino cultures, which emphasizes males' dominance over females

**major depressive disorder** clinical diagnosis pertaining to enduring period of sadness along with other symptoms such as frequent crying, fatigue, and feelings of worthlessness

**majority culture** within a country, the cultural group that sets most of the norms and standards and holds most of the positions of political, economic, intellectual, and media power

**mammary glands** in females, the glands that produce milk to nourish babies

**marasmus** disease in which the body wastes away from lack of nutrients

**marianismo** in Latino cultures, an ideal that women should emulate the Virgin Mary, for example, by being submissive, self-denying, and pure

**maternal blood screening** examines different substances in a blood sample from the mother, such as proteins, hormones, and genetic fragments of DNA from the fetus

**maturation** concept that an innate, biologically based program is the driving force behind development

**media multitasking** simultaneous use of more than one media form, such as playing an electronic game on a mobile device while watching TV

**median** in a distribution of scores, the point at which half of the population scores above and half below

**meiosis** process by which gametes are generated, through separation and duplication of chromosome pairs, ending in four new gametes from the original cell, each with half the number of chromosomes of the original cell

**menarche** a girl's first menstrual period

**mental representations** Piaget's final stage of sensorimotor development in which toddlers first think about the range of possibilities and then select the action most likely to achieve the desired outcome

**mental structure** a way of thinking within a stage of development that is applied across all aspects of life

**mesoderm** in the embryonic period, the middle of the three cell layers, which will become the muscles, bones, reproductive system, and circulatory system

**meta-analysis** a statistical technique that integrates the data from many studies into one comprehensive statistical analysis

**metacognition** capacity to think about thinking

**metalinguistic skills** knowledge of the underlying structure of language

**metamemory** understanding of how memory works

**mitosis** process of cell replication in which the chromosomes duplicate themselves and the cell divides into two cells, each with the same number of chromosomes as the original cell

**mnemonics** memory strategies, such as rehearsal, organization, and elaboration

**monozygotic (MZ) twins** twins who result from one fertilized egg splitting in two and who, except in extraordinarily rare cases, have exactly the same genotype; also called identical twins

**moral domain** in domain theory, reasoning pertaining to fairness, harm to other individuals, and individual rights

**moral identity** a person's commitment to positive moral ideals in thought and behavior

**morningness** preference for going to bed early and waking up early

**Moro reflex** reflex in response to a sensation of falling backward or to a loud sound, in which the neonate arches its back, flings out its arms, and then brings its arms quickly together in an embrace

**morphology** the rules for forming a word

**multifactorial** involving a combination of genetic and environmental factors

**multilingualism** the use of two or more languages

**myelination** process of the growth of the myelin sheath around the axon of a neuron

**natural childbirth** approach to childbirth that avoids medical technologies and interventions

**natural experiment** a situation that occurs naturally but that provides interesting scientific information to the perceptive observer

**natural selection** evolutionary process in which the offspring best adapted to their environment survive to produce offspring of their own

**nature-nurture debate** debate among scholars as to whether human development is influenced mainly by genes (nature) or environment (nurture)

**neonatal jaundice** yellowish pallor common in the first few days of life due to immaturity of the liver

**neonatal period** the first 28 days of a newborn child's life

**neural tube** in the embryonic period, the part of the ectoderm that will become the spinal cord and brain

**neurogenesis** the production of neurons

**neuron** cell of the nervous system

**nomothetic** research aimed at providing universal knowledge

**nones** people who identify as atheist, agnostic, spiritual but not religious, or just not religious

**normal distribution or bell curve** typical distribution of characteristics of a population, resembling a bell curve in which most cases fall near the middle and the proportions decrease at the low and high extremes

**numeracy** understanding of the meaning of numbers

**obese** in children, defined as having a BMI exceeding 21

**object permanence** awareness that objects (including people) continue to exist even when we are not in direct sensory or motor contact with them

**observations** observations and recording of people's behaviors either on video or through written records

**obstetrics** field of medicine that focuses on prenatal care and birth

**only child** child who has no siblings

**opposable thumb** position of the thumb apart from the fingers, unique to humans, that makes possible fine motor movements

**oral rehydration therapy (ORT)** treatment for infant diarrhea that involves drinking a solution of salt and glucose mixed with clean water

**organization** mnemonic that involves mentally placing things into meaningful categories

**overcontrol** trait of having excessive self-regulation of emotions

**overextension** use of a single word to represent a variety of related objects

**overregularization** applying grammatical rules even to words that are exceptions to the rule

**overweight** in children, defined as having a BMI exceeding 18

**oxytocin** hormone released by pituitary gland that causes labor to begin

**parenting styles** practices that parents exhibit in relation to their children and their beliefs about those practices

**passive genotype → environment effects** in the theory of genotype → environment effects, the type that results from the fact that in a biological family, parents provide both genes and environment to their children

**Peace Corps** an international service program in which Americans provide service to a community in a foreign country for 2 years

**peer-review** in scientific research, the system of having other scientists review a manuscript to judge its merits and worthiness for publication

**peers** people who share some aspect of their status, such as being the same age

**perception** refers to how sensations are understood or interpreted

**permissive parents** in classifications of parenting styles, parents who are low in demandingness and high in responsiveness

**personal fable** belief in one's personal uniqueness, often including a sense of invulnerability to the consequences of taking risks

**personal/psychological domain** in domain theory, reasoning pertaining to the welfare of the self

**phenotype** organism's actual characteristics, derived from its genotype

**phonemes** the smallest units of sound that distinguish one word from another

**phonics approach** method of teaching reading that advocates breaking down words into their component sounds, called phonics, then putting the phonics together into words

**placenta** structure connecting mother and the developing organism that among other things channels nutrients to the organism, and blocks mother's bacteria and wastes from reaching the organism

**plasticity** the responsiveness of brain development to environmental circumstances

**political involvement** unpaid activities aimed at political goals

**polygenic inheritance** expression of phenotypic characteristics due to the interaction of multiple genes

**polygyny** cultural tradition in which men have more than one wife

**population** the entire group of people of interest in a study, and that the sample aims to represent

**possible self** person's conceptions of the self as it potentially could be; may include both an ideal self and a feared self

**Post-Conventional Level** Kohlberg's term for the highest level of moral development focused on universal moral principles

**postformal thinking** according to some theorists, the stage of cognitive development that follows formal operations and includes advances in pragmatism and reflective judgment

**postpartum depression** in parents with a new baby, feelings of sadness and anxiety so intense as to interfere with the ability to carry out simple daily tasks

**pragmatics** knowledge of how language is used in social contexts

**pragmatism** adapting logical thinking to the practical constraints of real-life situations

**Pre-Conventional Level** Kohlberg's term for the lowest level of moral development focused on ego-centered considerations

**predictive validity** in longitudinal research, the ability of a variable at Time 1 to predict the outcome of a variable at Time 2

**preoperational stage** in Piaget's theory, cognitive stage from age 2 to 7 during which the child becomes capable of representing the world symbolically—for example, through the use of language—but is still very limited in ability to use mental operations

**preterm** babies born at 37 weeks gestation or less

**primary attachment figure** the person who is sought out when a child experiences some kind of distress or threat in the environment

**primary emotions** most basic emotions, such as anger, sadness, fear, disgust, surprise, and happiness

**primary sex characteristics** production of eggs (ova) and sperm and the development of the sex organs

**private speech** in Vygotsky's theory, self-guiding and self-directing comments children make to themselves as they learn in the zone of proximal development and have conversations with those guiding them; first spoken aloud, then internally

**problem solving** the ability to select and use strategies in order to arrive at a goal

**procedure** the step-by-step order in which a study is conducted and data are collected. For example, researchers must obtain participants' consent before data collection can begin

**prosocial behavior** positive behavior toward others, including kindness, friendliness, and sharing

**prosody** patterns of stress, rhythm, and intonation in a language

**protective factors** characteristics of young people and their context that are related to lower likelihood of problems despite experiencing high-risk circumstances

**proximodistal principle** principle of biological development that growth proceeds from the middle of the body outward

**psychological control** parenting strategy that uses shame and withdrawal of love to influence children's behavior

**psychometric approach** the evaluation of cognitive abilities with intelligence tests

**psychosexual theory** Freud's theory proposing that sexual desire is the driving force behind psychological development

**psychosocial theory** Erikson's theory that human development is driven by the need to become integrated into the social and cultural environment

**puberty** changes in physiology, anatomy, and physical functioning that develop a person into a mature adult biologically and prepare the body for sexual reproduction

**puberty ritual** formal custom developed in many cultures to mark the departure from childhood and the entrance into adolescence

**qualitative** data that is collected in non-numerical form, usually in interviews or observations

**quantitative** data that is collected in numerical form, usually on questionnaires

**questionnaire** written questions where participants typically select among answers chosen by the researcher

**rapid eye movement (REM) sleep** phase of the sleep cycle in which a person's eyes move back and forth rapidly under the eyelids; persons in REM sleep experience other physiological changes as well

**reaction range** range of possible developmental paths established by genes; environment determines where development takes place within that range

**reciprocal or bidirectional effects** in relations between two persons, the principle that each of them affects the other

**reductionistic** breaking up a phenomenon into separate parts to such an extent that the meaning and coherence of the phenomenon as a whole become lost

**reflex** automatic response to certain kinds of stimulation

**rehearsal** mnemonic that involves repeating the same information over and over

**relational aggression** a form of nonphysical aggression that harms others by damaging their relationships, for example, by excluding them socially or spreading rumors about them

**reliability** the extent to which a measurement generates consistent results

**research and development (R&D)** comprise the creation of new knowledge through research and experimentation, and the use of this knowledge for new applications

**research design** the master plan for when, where, and with whom to collect the data for a study

**research measurement** the approach to collecting data. Examples of common measurements in the field of child development are observations and interviews.

**resilience** overcoming adverse environmental circumstances and achieving healthy development despite those circumstances

**responsiveness** degree to which parents are sensitive to their children's needs and express love, warmth, and concern for them

**reversibility** ability to reverse an action mentally

**romantic partner** person in regard to whom an individual feels some combination of love and sexual desire

**rooting reflex** reflex in response to a sensation of falling backward or to a loud sound, in which the neonate arches its back, flings out its arms, and then brings its arms quickly together in an embrace

**ruminate** to think persistently about bad feelings and experiences

**sample** the people included in a given study, who are intended to represent the population of interest

**scaffolding** degree of assistance provided to the learner in the zone of proximal development, gradually decreasing as the learner's skills develop

**schemes** cognitive structures for processing, organizing, and interpreting information

**school climate** the quality of interactions between teachers and students, including how teachers interact with students, their expectations and standards for students, and their methods for regulating students' conduct

**scientific method** process of scientific investigations, involving a series of steps from identifying a research question through forming a hypothesis, selecting measurements and designs, collecting and analyzing data, and drawing conclusions

**secondary emotions** emotions that require social learning, such as embarrassment, shame, and guilt; also called sociomoral emotions

**secondary school** the schools attended by adolescents, usually including a lower secondary school and an upper secondary school

**secondary sex characteristics** bodily changes of puberty not directly related to reproduction

**secular** based on nonreligious beliefs and values

**secular trend** average age of puberty decreasing over time

**secure base** role of primary attachment figure, allows child to explore world while seeking comfort when threats arise

**selective association** the principle that most people tend to choose friends who are similar to themselves

**selective attention** ability to focus attention on relevant information and disregard what is irrelevant

**self-concept** person's view and evaluation of her- or himself

**self-medication** the use of substances for relieving unpleasant states such as sadness or stress

**self-recognition** ability to recognize one's image in the mirror as one's self

**self-reflection** capacity to think about one's self as one would think about other persons and objects

**self-regulation** ability to exercise control over one's emotions and reactions

**self-socialization** process by which people seek to maintain consistency between their gender schemas and their behavior

**semantics** the study of meaning in language

**sensation** the ability to feel stimulation through the physical senses, such as the ears and eyes

**sensation seeking** a personality characteristic defined by the extent to which a person enjoys novelty and intensity of sensation

**sensitive period** in the course of development, a period when the capacity for learning in a specific area is especially pronounced

**sensorimotor stage** in Piaget's theory, the first 2 years of cognitive development, which involve learning how to coordinate the activities of the senses with motor activities

**seriation** ability to arrange things in a logical order, such as shortest to longest, thinnest to thickest, or lightest to darkest

**sex** biological status of being female or male

**sex chromosomes** chromosomes that determine whether an organism is female (XX) or male (XY)

**sexual harassment** a wide range of threatening or aggressive behaviors related to sexuality, from mild harassment such as name-calling, jokes, and leering looks to severe harassment involving unwanted touching or sexual contact

**sexual minority family** a family headed by parent(s) who self-identify as sexual or gender minorities

**sexual orientation** a person's tendencies of sexual attraction

**sexual revolution** starting in the 1960s, social movement that challenged traditional codes of behavior related to sexuality and interpersonal relationships throughout the Western world

**sexually transmitted infection (STI)** infection transmitted through sexual contact

**shame** feeling of responsibility and remorse for perceived wrong-doing by self or others, with a focus on interpersonal consequences

**shape constancy** the perception that the shape of an object is the same, even if it might look different from different angles

**short-term memory** memory for information that is the current focus of attention

**size constancy** the perception that two objects are the same size, even if it might look like one is smaller than the other because it is farther away

**slang** an informal vocabulary and grammar that is different from that of the native language

**small for date** term applied to neonates who weigh less than 90% of other neonates who were born at the same gestational age

**social cognition** how people think about other people, social relationships, and social institutions

**social cognitive theory** emphasizes that gender differences are based on the behaviors that children learn from those around them

**social comparison** how persons view themselves in relation to others with regard to status, abilities, or achievements

**social gating** infants' reliance on social interactions to help them differentiate units of sound

**social identity theory** emphasizes that seeing oneself as a member of a social group, such as being female or male, leads to common biases, including in-group favoritism

**social information processing** the interpretation of others' behavior and intentions in a social interaction

**Social Learning Theory** argues that media shape children's behaviors

**social referencing** the ability to observe others' emotional responses to ambiguous and uncertain situations, and use that information to shape one's own emotional responses

**social skills** skills for successfully handling social relations and getting along well with others

**social smile** expression of happiness in response to interacting with others, first appearing at age 2–3 months

**social status** within a group, the degree of power, authority, and influence that each person has in the view of the others

**sociocultural** research aimed at providing knowledge of particular cultural and social groups

**socioeconomic status (SES)** person's social class, including educational level, income level, and occupational status

**sociomoral emotions** emotions evoked based on learned, culturally based standards of right and wrong; also called secondary emotions

**sound localization** ability to tell where a sound is coming from

**spermarche** beginning of development of sperm in boys' testicles at puberty

**Stanford-Binet** widely used IQ test developed by Alfred Binet and Theodore Simon and revised by scholars at Stanford University

**states of arousal** ways of being awake and asleep

**stereotype** belief that others possess certain characteristics simply as a result of being a member of a particular group

**Strange Situation** laboratory assessment of attachment entailing a series of introductions, separations, and reunions involving the child, the mother, and an unfamiliar person

**stranger anxiety** fear in response to unfamiliar persons, usually evident in infants by age 6 months

**sudden infant death syndrome (SIDS)** death within the first year of life due to unknown reasons, with no apparent illness or disorder

**super peer** one of the functions of media for adolescents, meaning that adolescents often look to media for information (especially concerning sexuality) that their parents may be unwilling to provide, in the same way they might look to a friend

**surfactant** substance in lungs that promotes breathing and keeps the air sacs in the lungs from collapsing

**swaddling** practice of infant care that involves wrapping an infant tightly in cloths or blankets

**synaptic exuberance** also called *synaptogenesis*, refers to a period when there is a tremendous spurt in new synaptic connections

**synaptic pruning** process whereby dendritic connections that are unused whither away

**syntactic bootstrapping** using knowledge of syntax to figure out the meaning of novel words

**syntax** an aspect of grammar that involves the grammatical rules for how to order words in a sentence

**techniques of prenatal monitoring** include ultrasound, maternal blood screening, amniocentesis, and chorionic villus sampling (CVS), which provide the ability to monitor the growth and health of the fetus and detect prenatal problems

**telegraphic speech** phrases of about 2 to 4 words that strip away connecting words, such as *the* and *and*

**temperament** innate responses to the physical and social environment, including qualities of positive affect, adaptability, activity level, attention span, and self-regulation

**teratogen** behavior, environment, or bodily condition that can have damaging influence on prenatal development

**tertiary education** education or training beyond secondary school

**test-retest reliability** type of reliability that examines whether or not persons' scores on one occasion are similar to their scores on another occasion

**testosterone** the androgen most important in pubertal development among boys

**theory** framework that presents a set of interconnected ideas in an original way and inspires further research

**theory of genotype → environment effects** theory proposing that genes influence the kind of environment we experience

**theory of mind** ability to understand thinking processes in oneself and others

**theory of multiple intelligences** Gardner's theory that there are eight separate types of intelligence

**time out** disciplinary strategy in which the child is required to sit still in a designated place for a brief period

**total fertility rate (TFR)** in a population, the number of births per woman

**traditional cultures** people in the rural areas of developing countries, who tend to adhere more closely to the historical traditions of their culture than people in urban areas do

**transgender** persons whose self-identification does not match their genetic sex

**transracial adoption** the adoption of children of one race by parents of a different race

**triarchic theory of intelligence** Sternberg's theory that there are three distinct but related forms of intelligence

**trimester** prenatal development is divided into three 3-month periods

**trust versus mistrust** the first stage in Erikson's theory where an infant requires a caregiver consistently to provide love and care in order to develop a lifelong sense of trust

**ultrasound** machine that uses sound waves to produce images of the fetus during pregnancy

**umbilical cord** structure connecting the placenta to the mother's uterus

**undercontrol** trait of having inadequate emotional self-regulation

**underextension** use of a general word to refer to a specific object

**unemployment** work status of persons who are not in school, are not working, and are looking for a job

**unstructured socializing** the term for young people spending time together with no specific event as the center of their activity

**Uses and Gratifications Approach** emphasizes that children differ in numerous ways that lead them to make different choices about which media to consume and that even children consuming the same media product will respond to it in a variety of ways, depending on their individual characteristics

**validity** the extent to which a measurement assesses what it claims to measure

**vernix** at birth, babies are covered with this oily, cheesy substance, which protects their skin from chapping in the womb

**video deficit effect** refers to children younger than 2 years learning better from watching behaviors by an actual person than a virtual person

**visual acuity** clarity of vision

**$VO_{2max}$** ability of the body to take in oxygen and transport it to various organs; also called maximum oxygen update

**weaning** cessation of breast-feeding

**Wechsler Adult Intelligence Scale (WAIS)** intelligence test for persons aged 16 and older

**Wechsler Intelligence Scale for Children (WISC)** intelligence test for children aged 6 to 16

**Wechsler Preschool and Primary Scale of Intelligence (WPPSI)** intelligence test for children aged 3 to 7

**Wernicke's area** an area of the brain in the left temporal lobe that is specialized for language comprehension

**wet nursing** cultural practice, common in human history, of hiring a lactating woman other than the mother to feed the infant

**whole-language approach** method of teaching reading in which the emphasis is on the meaning of written language in whole passages, rather than breaking down words into their smallest components

**women's movement** organized effort in the 20th century to obtain greater rights and opportunities for women

**working memory** the retention and processing of information for a brief time

**X-linked inheritance pattern** pattern of inheritance in which a recessive characteristic is expressed because it is carried on the male's X chromosome

**zone of proximal development** difference between skills or tasks that children can accomplish alone and those they are capable of performing if guided by an adult or a more competent peer

**zygote** following fertilization, the new cell formed from the union of sperm and ovum

# References


A special report on the human genome. (2010). *The Economist*. Retrieved from http://www.economist.com/node/16349358

Abar, B., Carter, K. L., & Winsler, A. (2009). The effects of maternal parenting style and religious commitment on self-regulation, academic achievement, and risk behavior among African-American parochial college students. *Journal of Adolescence, 32*(2), 259–273. doi:10.1016/j.adolescence.2008.03.008

Abbott, S. (1992). Holding on and pushing away: Comparative perspectives on an eastern Kentucky child-rearing practice. *Ethos, 20*, 33–65.

Abitz, M., Nielsen, R. D., Jones, E. G., Laursen, H., Graem, N., & Pakkenberg, B. (2007). Excess of neurons in the human newborn mediodorsal thalamus compared with that of the adult. *Cerebral Cortex, 17*(11), 2573–2578. doi:10.1093/cercor/bhl163

Abramovitz, R., Freedman, J. L., Henry, K., & Van Brunschot, M. (1995). Children's capacity to agree to psychological research: Knowledge of risks and benefits and voluntariness. *Ethics and Behavior, 5*, 25–48.

Abrejo, F. G., Shaikh, B. T., & Rizvi, N. (2009). And they kill me, only because I am a girl … a review of sex-selective abortions in South Asia. *European Journal of Contraception and Reproductive Health Care, 14*, 10–16.

Abreu, J. M., Goodyear, R. K., Campos, A., & Newcomb, M. D. (2000). Ethnic belonging and traditional masculine ideology among African Americans, European Americans, and Latinos. *Psychology of Men & Masculinity, 1*, 75–86.

Adams, G. R. (1999). *The objective measure of ego identity status: A manual on test theory and construction.* Guelph, Ontario, Canada: Author.

Adams, P. E. (2010). Understanding the different realities, experience, and use of self-esteem between Black and White adolescent girls. *Journal of Black Psychology, 36*(3), 255–276. doi:10.1177/0095798410361454

Adamson, L., & Frick, J. (2003). The still face: A history of a shared experimental paradigm. *Infancy, 4*, 451–473.

Addis, M. (2011). *Invisible men: Men's inner lives and the consequences of silence.* New York, NY: Macmillian.

Adolph, K. E., & Berger, S. E. (2005). Physical and motor development. In M. H. Bornstein & M. E. Lamb (Eds.), *Developmental science: An advanced textbook* (5th ed., pp. 223–281). Mahwah, NJ: Lawrence Erlbaum.

Adolph, K. E., & Berger, S. E. (2006). Motor development. In W. Damon & R. Lerner (Series Eds.), & D. Kuhn & R. Sieglery (Vol. Eds.), *Handbook of child psychology: Vol. 2. Cognition, perception and language* (6th ed., pp. 161–213). New York, NY: Wiley.

Adolph, K. E., Karasik, L. B., & Tamis-LeMonda C. S. (2010). Motor skill. In M. H. Bornstein (Ed.), *Handbook of cultural developmental science* (pp. 61–88). New York, NY: Psychology Press.

Adolph, K. E., & Robinson, S. R. (2013). The road to walking: What learning to walk tells us about development. In P. D. Zelazo (Ed.), *Oxford handbook of developmental psychology: Vol. 1: Body and mind* (pp. 403–446). New York, NY: Oxford University Press.

Adolph, K. E., Vereijken, B., & Shrout, P. E. (2003). What changes in infant walking and why. *Child Development, 74*(2), 475–497. doi:10.1111/1467-8624.7402011

Aguirre International. (1999). *Making a difference: Impact of AmeriCorps state/national direct on members and communities, 1994–95 and 1995–96.* San Mateo, CA: Author.

Ahluwalia, M. K., Suzuki, L. A., & Mir, M. (2009). Dating, partnerships, and arranged marriages. In N. Tewari & A. N. Alvarez, *Asian American psychology: Current perspectives* (pp. 273–294). New York, NY: Lawrence Erlbaum Associates.

Ahmad, Q. I., Ahmad, C. B., & Ahmad, S. M. (2010). Childhood obesity. *Indian Journal of Endocrinology and Metabolism, 14*(1): 19–25. PMCID: PMC3063535

Aikat, D. (2007). Violence, extent and responses to violence. In J. J. Arnett (Ed.), *Encyclopedia of children, adolescents, and the media* (Vol. 2, pp. 852–854). Thousand Oaks, CA: Sage.

Ainsworth, M. D. S., Behar, M. C., Waters, E., & Wall, S. (1978). *Patterns of attachment: A psychological study of the strange situation.* Oxford, UK: Erlbaum.

Ainsworth, M. D. S., & Bell, S. M. (1969). Some contemporary patterns of mother–infant interaction in the feeding situation. In A. Ambrose (Ed.), *Stimulation in early infancy* (pp. 133–170). London, UK: Academic Press.

Ainsworth, M. S. (1977). Infant development and mother–infant interaction among Ganda and American families. In P. H. Leiderman, S. R. Tulkin, & A. Rosenfeld (Eds.), *Culture and infancy: Variations in the human experience* (pp. 119–149). New York, NY: Academic Press.

Akhtar, N. (2005). Is joint attention necessary for early language learning? In B. D. Homer & C. S. Tamis-LeMonda (Eds.), *The development of social cognition and communication* (pp. 165–179). Mahwah, NJ: Lawrence Erlbaum.

Akhtar, N., & Tomasello, M. (2000). The social nature of words and word learning. In R. M. Golinkoff, K. Hirsh-Pasek, L. Bloom, L. B. Smith, A. L. Woodward, & N. Akhtar (Eds.), *Becoming a word learner: A debate on lexical acquisition* (pp. 115–135). New York, NY: Oxford University Press.

Akimoto, S. A., & Sanbonmatsu, D. M. (1999). Differences in self-effacing behavior between European and Japanese Americans: Effect on competence evaluations. *Journal of Cross-Cultural Psychology, 30*, 159–177.

Akshoomoff, N. A., Feroleto, C. C., Doyle, R. E., & Stiles, J. (2002). The impact of early unilateral brain injury on perceptual organization and visual memory. *Neuropsychologia, 40*, 539–561.

Alaggia, R., & Vine, C. (Eds.). (2006). *Cruel but not unusual: Violence in Canadian families.* Waterloo, Ontario, Canada: Wilfrid Laurier University Press.

Alan Guttmacher Institute (AGI) (2001). *Teenage sexual and reproductive behavior in developed countries: Can more progress be made?* New York, NY: Author. Available: www.agi-usa.org.

Albareda-Castellot, B., Pons, F., & Sebastián-Gallés, N. (2011). The acquisition of phonetic categories in bilingual infants: New data from an anticipatory eye movement paradigm. *Developmental Science, 14*(2), 395–401. doi:10.1111/j.1467-7687.2010.00989.x

Alberts, A., Elkind, D., & Ginsberg, S. (2007) The personal fable and risk-taking in early adolescence. *Journal of Youth and Adolescence, 36*(1), 71–76.

Albrecht, C. M., & Albrecht, D. E. (2011). Social status, adolescent behavior, and educational attainment. *Sociological Spectrum, 31*(1), 114–137.

Aldridge, M. A., Stillman, R. D., & Bower, T. G. R. (2001). Newborn categorization of vowel-like sounds. *Developmental Science, 4*, 220–232.

Aldwin, C. M., & Spiro, A. III (2006). *Health, behavior, and optimal aging: A life span developmental perspective.* San Diego, CA: Academic Press.

Alexander, B. (2001, June). Radical idea serves youth, saves money. *Youth Today*, pp. 1, 42–44.

Alexander, G. M., & Hines, M. (2002). Sex differences in response to children's toys in nonhuman primates. *Evolution and Human Behavior, 23*, 467–479.

Alink, L. R. A., Mesman, J., van Zeijl, J., Stolk, M. N., Juffer, F., Koot, H. M.,… van IJzendoorn, M. H. (2006). The early childhood aggression curve: Development of physical aggression in 10- to 50-month-old children. *Child Development, 77*, 954–966.

Alloway, T. P., Gathercole, S. E., & Pickering, S. J. (2006). Verbal and visuospatial short-term and working memory in children: Are they separable? *Child Development, 77*(6), 1698–1716. doi:10.1111/j.1467-8624.2006.00968.x

Alsaker, F., & Flammer, A. (2006). Pubertal development. In S. Jackson & L. Goosens (Eds.), *Handbook of adolescent development: European perspectives* (pp. 30–50). New York, NY: Psychology Press.

Alvarez, M. (2004). Caregiving and early infant crying in a Danish community. *Journal of Developmental and Behavioral Pediatrics, 25*, 91–98.

Alwin, D. F. (1988). From obedience to autonomy: Changes in traits desired in children, 1928–1978. *Public Opinion Quarterly, 52*, 33–52.

Alwin, D. F., Xu, X., & Carson, T. (1994, October). *Childrearing goals and child discipline.* Paper presented at the Public World of Childhood Project workshop on Children Harmed and Harmful, Chicago.

Al-Tayyib, A. A., Rice, E., Rhoades, H., & Riggs, P. (2014). Association between prescription drug misuse and injection among runaway and homeless youth. *Drug and Alcohol Dependence, 134*, 406–409.

Amato, P. R. (2000). Diversity within single-parent families. In D. H. Demo, K. R. Allen, & M. A. Fine (Eds.), *Handbook of family diversity* (pp. 149–172). New York, NY: Oxford University Press.

Amato, P. R., & Anthony, C. J. (2014). Estimating the effects of parental divorce and death with fixed effects models. *Journal of Marriage and Family, 76*(2), 370–386.

Amato, P. R., & Boyd, L. M. (2013). Children and divorce in world perspective. In A. Abela & J. Walker (Eds.), *Contemporary Issues in Family Studies: Global Perspectives on Partnerships, Parenting and Support in a Changing World* (pp. 227–243). Chichester, UK: Wiley-Blackwell.

Amato, P. R., & Fowler, F. (2002). Parenting practices, child adjustment, and family diversity. *Journal of Marriage and the Family, 64*, 703–716.

American Academy of Pediatrics. (2011). ADHD: Clinical practice guidelines for the diagnosis, evaluation, and treatment of Attention-Deficit/ Hyperactivity Disorder in children and adolescents. *Pediatrics, 128*, 1–16.

American Academy of Pediatrics. (2013). *Media and children*. Retrieved from http://www.aap.org/en-us/advocacy-and-policy/aap-health-initiatives/pages/media-and-children.aspx

American Academy of Pediatrics. (2016). American Academy of Pediatrics announces new recommendations for children's media use. Retrieved from https://www.aap.org/en-us/about-the-aap/aap-press-room/pages/american-academy-of-pediatrics-announces-new-recommendations-for-childrens-media-use.aspx

American Academy of Pediatrics. (2016). American Academy of Pediatrics announces new safe sleep recommendations to protect against SIDS, sleep-related infant deaths. Retrieved from https:// www.aap.org/en-us/about-the-aap/aap-press-room/pages/american-academy-of-pediatrics-announces-new-safe-sleep-recommendations-to-protect-against-sids.aspx

American Academy of Pediatrics Task Force on Infant Positioning and SIDS (AAPTFIPS). (2000). Changing concepts of sudden infant death syndrome. *Pediatrics, 105*, 650–656.

American Dental Association. (2006). Tooth eruption: The permanent teeth. *Journal of the American Dental Association, 137*. Retrieved from http://www.ada.org/~/media/ada/publications/files/patient_58.ashx

American Psychiatric Association. (2013). *Diagnostic and statistical manual of mental disorders* (5th ed.). Arlington, VA: Author.

American Psychological Association. (2014). *Postpartum depression fact sheet*. Retrieved from http://www.apa.org/pi/women/programs/depression/postpartum.aspx

Americorps. (2016). About CNCS. Retrieved from http://www.nationalservice.gov/about

Ammaniti, M., Speranza, A. M., & Fedele, S. (2005). Attachment in infancy and in early and late childhood. In K. Kearns & R. A. Richardson (Eds.), *Attachment in middle childhood* (pp. 115–136). New York, NY Guilford Press.

Amsterlaw, J., & Wellman, H. (2006). Theories of mind in transition: A microgenetic study of the development of false belief understanding. *Journal of Cognition and Development, 7*, 139–172.

Anders, T. F., & Taylor, T. (1994). Babies and their sleep environment. *Children's Environments, 11*, 123–134.

Anderson, A., Hamilton, R. J., & Hattie, J. (2004). Classroom climate and motivated behavior in secondary schools. *Learning Environments Research, 7*, 211–225.

Anderson, C. A. (2004). An update on the effects of playing violent video games. *Journal of Adolescence, 27*, 113–122.

Anderson, C. A., Gentile, D. A., & Buckley, K. E. (2007). *Violent video game effects on children and adolescents: Theory, research, and public policy*. New York, NY: Oxford University Press.

Anderson, D. R., Huston, A. C., Schmitt, K., Linebarger, D. L., & Wright, J. C. (2001). Early childhood viewing and adolescent behavior: The recontact study. *Monographs of the Society for Research in Child Development, 66*(1), I–VIII, 1–147.

Anderson, E. (2000). Exploring register knowledge: The value of "controlled improvisation." In L. Menn & N. B. Ratner (Eds.), *Methods for studying language production* (pp. 225–248). Mahwah, NJ: Erlbaum.

Anderson, M. (2007). Biology and intelligence—The race/IQ controversy. In S. Della Sala (Ed.), *Tall tales about the mind & brain: Separating fact from fiction* (pp. 123–147). New York, NY: Oxford University Press.

Anderson, P., & Butcher, K. (2006). Childhood obesity: Trends and potential causes. *The Future of Children, 16*, 19–45.

Anderson, V., & Jacobs, R. (Eds.). (2008). *Executive functions and the frontal lobes: A lifespan perspective*. Philadelphia, PA: Taylor & Francis.

Anderssen, N., Amlie, C., & Ytterøy, E. A. (2002). Outcomes for children with lesbian or gay parents. A review of studies from 1978 to 2000. *Scandinavian Journal of Psychology, 43*(4), 335–351. doi:10.1111/1467-9450.00302

Ando, M., Asakura, T., & Simons-Morton, B. (2005). Psychosocial influences in physical, verbal and indirect bullying among Japanese early adolescents. *Journal of Early Adolescence, 25*, 268–297.

Andrews, G., Halford, G., & Bunch, K. (2003). Theory of mind and relational complexity. *Child Development, 74*, 1476–1499.

Anglin, J. M. (1993). Vocabulary development: A morphological analysis. *Monographs of the Society for Research in Child Development, 58*(10), i, iii, v–vi, 1–186.

Angold, A., & Costello, E. J. (2006). Puberty and depression. *Child and Adolescent Psychiatric Clinics of North America, 15*(4), 919–937.

Annear, S. (2016, July 12). Don't let your Pokémon game lead you into danger. *The Boston Globe*. Retrieved from https://www.bostonglobe.com/metro/2016/07/12/police-dont-let-your-pokemon-game-lead-you-into-danger/CwnnOp6KhLuliyBqnG866H/story.html

Annunziata, D., Hogue, A., Faw, L., & Liddle, H. A. (2006). Family functioning and school success in at-risk, inner-city adolescents. *Journal of Youth and Adolescence, 35*(1), 105–113.

Apgar, V. (1953, July–August). A proposal for a new method of evaluation of the newborn infant. *Current Researches in Anesthesia and Analgesia*, 260–267.

Appel, M. (2008) Fictional narratives cultivate just-world beliefs. *Journal of Communication, 58*(1), 62–83.

Appoh, L. Y. (2004). Consequences of early malnutrition for subsequent social and emotional behaviour of children in Ghana. *Journal of Psychology in Africa; South of the Sahara, the Caribbean, and Afro-Latin America, 14*, 87–94.

Appoh, L. Y., & Krekling, S. (2004). Effects of early childhood malnutrition on cognitive performance of Ghanaian children. *Journal of Psychology in Africa; South of the Sahara, the Caribbean, and Afro-Latin America, 14*, 1–7.

Aquilino, W. S. (2006). Family relationships and support systems in emerging adulthood. In J. J. Arnett & J. Tanner (Eds.), *Coming of age in the 21st century: The lives and contexts of emerging adults* (pp. 193–218). Washington, DC: American Psychological Association.

Arcangeli, T., Thilaganathan, B., Hooper, R., Khan, K. S., & Bhide, A. (2012). Neurodevelopmental delay in small babies at term: A systematic review. *Ultrasound in Obstetrics & Gynecology, 40*, 267–275.

Archer, J. (2006). Testosterone and human aggression: An evaluation of the challenge hypothesis. *Neuroscience & Biobehavioral Reviews, 30*, 319–345.

Archibald, A. B., Graber, J. A., & Brooks-Gunn, J. (2003). Pubertal processes and physiological growth in adolescence. In G. Adams & M. Berzonsky (Eds.), *Blackwell handbook of adolescence*. Malden, MA: Blackwell.

Arciniega, G. M., Anderson, T. C., Tovar-Blank, Z. G., & Tracey, T. J. G. (2008). Toward a fuller conception of machismo: Development of a traditional machismo and caballerismo scale. *Journal of Counseling Psychology, 55*(1), 19–33.

Ardila-Rey, A., & Killen, M. (2001). Middle class Columbian children's evaluations of personal, moral, and socio-conventional interactions in the classroom. *International Journal of Behavioral Development, 25*, 246–255.

Arditi-Babchuk, H., Eidelman, A. I., & Feldman, R. (2009). Rapid eye movement (REM) in premature neonates and developmental outcome at 6 months. *Infant Behavior & Development, 32*, 27–32.

Armenta, B. E., Knight, G. P., Carlo, G., & Jacobson, R. P. (2011). The relation between ethnic group attachment and prosocial tendencies: The mediating role of cultural values. *European Journal of Social Psychology, 41*, 107–115.

Armstrong, N. (2006). Aerobic fitness of children and adolescents. *Journal of Pediatrics, 82*(6), 406–408. doi:10.2223/JPED.1571

Arnett, J. (1991). Adolescents and heavy metal music: From the mouths of metalheads. *Youth & society, 23*, 76–98.

Arnett, J. J. (1996). *Metalheads: Heavy metal music and adolescent alienation*. Boulder, CO: Westview Press.

Arnett, J. J. (1998). Learning to stand alone: The contemporary American transition to adulthood in cultural and historical context. *Human Development, 41*, 295–315.

Arnett, J. J. (1999). Adolescent storm and stress, reconsidered. *American Psychologist, 54*, 317–326.

Arnett, J. J. (2000). Emerging adulthood: A theory of development from the late teens through the twenties. *American Psychologist, 55*, 469–480.

Arnett, J. J. (2002). The psychology of globalization. *American Psychologist, 57*, 774–783.

Arnett, J. J. (2004). *Emerging adulthood: The winding road from the late teens through the twenties*. New York, NY: Oxford University Press.

Arnett, J. J. (2005). The Vitality Criterion: A new standard of publication for *Journal of Adolescent Research*. *Journal of Adolescent Research, 20*, 3–7.

Arnett, J. J. (2006). G. Stanley Hall's *Adolescence: Brilliance and nonsense*. *History of Psychology, 9*, 186–197.

Arnett, J. J. (2008). The neglected 95%: Why American psychology needs to become less American. *American Psychologist, 63*, 602–614.

Arnett, J. J. (2011). Emerging adulthood(s): The cultural psychology of a new life stage. In L. A. Jensen (Ed.), *Bridging cultural and developmental approaches to psychology: New syntheses in theory, research, and policy* (pp. 255–275). New York, NY: Oxford University Press.

Arnett, J. J. (2015). The cultural psychology of emerging adulthood. In L. A. Jensen (Ed.), *Oxford handbook of human development and culture* (pp. 487–501). New York, NY: Oxford University Press.

Arnett, J. J. (2015). *Emerging adulthood: The winding road from the late teens through the twenties* (2nd ed.). New York, NY: Oxford University Press.

Arnett, J. J., & Jensen, L. A. (2015). "There's more between heaven and earth": Danish emerging adults' religious beliefs and values. *Journal of Adolescent Research, 30*(6), 661–682. doi:10.1177/0743558415602555

Arnett, J. J., Ramos, K. D., & Jensen, L. A. (2001). Ideologies in emerging adulthood: Balancing the ethics of autonomy and community. *Journal of Adult Development, 8*, 69–79.

Arnett, J. J., & Schwab, J. (2012). *The Clark University poll of emerging adults: Thriving, struggling, and hopeful.* Worcester, MA: Clark University. Retrieved from http://www.clarku.edu/clark-poll-emerging-adults/

Arnett, J. J., & Schwab, J. (2013). *Parents and their grown kids: Harmony, support, and (occasional) conflict.* Worcester, MA: Clark University. Retrieved from http://www.clarku.edu/clark-poll-emerging-adults/

Arnett, J. J., & Taber, S. (1994). Adolescence terminable and interminable: When does adolescence end? *Journal of Youth & Adolescence, 23*, 517–537.

Aronson, J., Fried, C. B., & Good, C. (2002). Reducing the effects of stereotype threat on African American college students by shaping theories of intelligence. *Journal of Experimental Social Psychology, 38*, 113–125.

Aronson, P. J., Mortimer, J. T., Zierman, C., & Hacker, M. (1996). Generational differences in early work experiences and evaluations. In T. J. Mortimer & D. M. Finch (Eds.), *Adolescents, work, and family: An intergenerational developmental analysis* (pp. 25–62). Thousand Oaks, CA: Sage.

Arsenio, W. F., Adams, E., & Gold, J. (2009). Social information processing, moral reasoning, and emotion attributions: Relations with adolescents' reactive and proactive aggression. *Child development, 80*, 1739–1755.

Asakawa, K., & Csikszentmihalyi, M. (1999). The quality of experience of Asian American adolescents in activities related to future goals. *Journal of Youth & Adolescence, 27*, 141–163.

Asarnow, J. R., Porta, G., Spirito, A., Emslie, G., & Clarke, G. (2011). Suicide attempts and nonsuicidal self-injury in the treatment of resistant depression in adolescents: Findings from the TORDIA study. *Journal of the American Academy of Child & Adolescent Psychiatry, 50*(8), 772–781.

Asawa, L. E., Hansen, D. J., & Flood, M. F. (2008). Early childhood intervention programs: Opportunities and challenges for preventing child maltreatment. *Education and Treatment of Children, 31*, 73–110.

Ashcraft, M. H. (2009). *Cognition.* Upper Saddle River, NJ: Prentice Hall.

Asher, S. R., & Rose, A. J. (1997). Promoting children's social–emotional adjustment with peers. In P. Salovey & D. J. Sluyter (Eds.), *Emotional development and emotional intelligence* (pp. 193–195). New York, NY: Basic Books.

Aslin, R. N., Jusczyk, P. W., & Pisoni, D. B. (1998). Speech and auditory processing during infancy: Constraints on and precursors to language. In W. Damon (Ed.), *Handbook of child psychology* (pp. 147–198) (5th ed., Vol. 2). New York, NY: Wiley.

Aslin, R. N., Saffran, J. R., & Newport, E. L. (1998). Computation of conditional probability statistics by 8-month-old infants. *Psychological Science, 9*(4), 321–324. doi:10.1111/1467-9280.00063

Astington, J. W. (1993). *The child's discovery of the mind.* Cambridge, MA: Harvard University Press.

Atkinson, C., & Newton, D. (2010). Online behaviours of adolescents: Victims, perpetrators and web 2.0. *Journal of Sexual Aggression, 16*(1), 107–120.

Atkinson, J. (2000). *The developing visual brain.* Oxford, UK: Oxford University Press.

Atkinson, J., & Braddick, O. (2013). Visual development. In P. E. Nathan & P. D. Zelazo (Eds.), *The Oxford handbook of developmental psychology, Volume 1: Body and mind* (pp. 271–309). New York, NY: Oxford University Press.

Atkinson, L., & Goldberg, S. (Eds.). (2004). *Attachment issues in psychopathology and intervention.* Mahwah, NJ: Erlbaum.

Attewell, P. (2001). The first and second digital divides. *Sociology of Education, 74*, 252–259.

Aulino, B., & Bergami, R. (2009). Italian-Canadian, Italian-Australian and Italian Adolescent Speech: A contemporary analysis. *Journal of the Worldwide Forum on Education and Culture, 1*(1), 30–40.

Aunio, P., Aubrey, C., Godfrey, R., Pan, Y., & Liu, Y. (2008). Children's early numeracy in England, Finland and People's Republic of China. *International Journal of Early Years Education, 16*, 203–221.

Aunola, K., & Nurmi, J.-E. (2004). Maternal affection moderates the impact of psychological control on a child's mathematical performance. *Developmental Psychology, 40*, 965–978.

Austin, S. B., Ziyadeh, N. J., Forman, S., Prokop, L. A., Keliher, A., Jacobs, D. (2008). Screening high school students for eating disorders: Results of a national initiative. *Preventing Chronic Disease, 5.* Retrieved from http://www.cdc.gov/pcd/issues/2008/oct/07_0164.htm

Avery, L., & Lazdane, G. (2008). What do we know about sexual and reproductive health among adolescents in Europe? *European Journal of Contraception and Reproductive Health, 13*, 58–70.

Axelsson, A.-S. (2010). Perpetual and personal: Swedish youth adults and their use of mobile phones. *New Media & Society, 12*, 35–54.

Axia, G., Bonichini, S., & Benini, F. (1999). Attention and reaction to distress in infancy: A longitudinal study. *Developmental Psychology, 35*, 500–504.

Bachman, J. G., O'Malley, P. M., Schulenberg, J. E., Johnston, L. D., Freedman-Doan, P., & Messersmith, E. E. (2008). *The education-drug use connection: How successes and failures in school relate to adolescent smoking, drinking, drug use, and delinquency.* New York, NY: Lawrence Erlbaum.

Bachman, J. G., Safron, D. J., Sy, S. R., & Schulenberg, J. E. (2003). Wishing to work: New perspectives on how adolescents' part-time work intensity is linked to educational engagement, substance use, and other problem behaviors. *International Journal of Behavioral Development, 27*, 301–315.

Bachman, J. G., Segal, D. R., Freedman-Doan, P., & O'Malley, P. M. (2000). Who chooses military service? Correlates of propensity and enlistment in the U.S. Armed Forces. *Military Psychology, 12*, 1–30.

Baer, J. S., Sampson, P. D., Barr, H. M., Connor, P. D., & Streissguth, A. P. (2003). A 21-year longitudinal analysis of the effects of prenatal alcohol exposure on young adult drinking. *Archives of General Psychiatry, 60*, 377–385.

Bagwell, C. L., & Schmidt, M. E. (2013). *Friendships in childhood and adolescence.* New York, NY: Guilford Press.

Baillargeon, R. (2008). Innate ideas revisited: For a principle of persistence in infants' physical reasoning. *Perspectives on Psychological Science, 3*(1), 2–13.

Baillargeon, R., Scott, R. M., & He, Z. (2010). False-belief understanding in infants. *Trends in Cognitive Sciences, 14*(3), 110–118. doi:10.1016/j.tics.2009.12.006

Bain, S. K., & Allin, J. D. (2005). Stanford-Binet intelligence scales, fifth edition. *Journal of Psychoeducational Assessment, 23*, 87–95.

Baiocco, R., Fontanesi, L., Santamaria, F., Ioverno, S., Marasco, B., Baumgartner, E., … Laghi, F. (2015). Negative parental responses to coming out and family functioning in a sample of lesbian and gay young adults. *Journal of Child and Family Studies, 24*, 1490–1500.

Baird, A. A., Kagan, J., Gaudette, T., Walz, K. A., Hershlag, N., & Boas, D. A. (2002). Frontal lobe activation during object permanence: Data from near-infrared spectroscopy. *NeuroImage, 16*, 1120–1126.

Baker, J. M. (2002). *How homophobia hurts children: Nurturing diversity at home, at school, and in the community.* New York, NY: Haworth Press.

Baker, C. (2011). *Foundations of bilingual education and bilingualism* (5th ed.). New York, NY: Multilingual Matters.

Baker, L., & Silverstein, M. (2012). The well-being of grandparents caring for grandchildren in China and the United States. In S. Arber & V. Timonen (Eds.), *Contemporary grandparenting: Changing family relationships in global contexts* (pp. 51–70). Bristol, UK: The Policy Press.

Bakermans-Kranenburg, M. J., van Uzendoorn, M. H., Bokhorst, C. L., & Schuengel, C. (2004). The importance of shared environment in infant–father attachment: A behavioral genetic study of the attachment q-sort. *Journal of Family Psychology, 18*, 545–549.

Bakker, M. P., Ormel, J., Verhulst, F. C., & Oldehinkel, A. J. (2010). Peer stressors and gender differences in adolescents' mental health: The TRAILS study. *Journal of Adolescent Health, 46*(5), 444–450.

Bakker, T. P., & de Vreese, C. H. (2011). Good news for the future? Young people, Internet use, and political participation. *Communication Research, 38*(4), 451–470. doi:10.1177/0093650210381738

Balarajan, Y., Ramakrishnan, U., Özaltin, E., Shankar, A. H., & Subramanian, S. V. (2012). Anaemia in low-income and middle-income countries. *The Lancet, 378*, 2123–2135.

Baldry, A. C., & Farrington, D. P. (2004). Evaluation of an intervention program for the reduction of bullying and victimization in schools. *Aggressive Behavior, 30*, 1–15.

Balen, F. V., & Inhorn, M. C. (2002). Interpreting infertility: A view from the social sciences. In M. C. Inhorn & F. V. Balen (Eds.), *Infertility around the globe: New thinking on childlessness, gender, and reproductive technologies* (pp. 3–32). Berkeley, CA: University of California Press.

Balis, T., & Postolache, T. T. (2008). Ethnic differences in adolescent suicide in the United States. *International Journal of Child Health and Human Development, 1*(3), 281–296.

Balodis, I. M., Wynne-Edwards, K. E., & Olmstead, M. C. (2011). The stress-response-dampening effects of placebo. *Hormones and Behavior, 59*, 465–472.

Baltes, P. B., Lindenberger, U., & Staudinger, U. M. (2006). Life span theory in developmental psychology. In W. Damon & R. M. Lerner (Eds.), *Handbook of child psychology* (Vol. 1., pp. 569–664). New York, NY: Wiley.

Banaag, C. G., Jr. (2010). Industrialization: Its impact on child and adolescent mental health. In M. E. Garralda & J. P. Raynaud (Eds.), *Increasing awareness of child and adolescent mental health* (pp. 71–92). Lanham, MD: Jason Aronson.

Bandura, A. (1977). *Social learning theory.* Englewood Cliffs, NJ: Prentice-Hall.

Bandura, A. (1994). Social cognitive theory of mass communication. In J. Bryant & D. Zillman (Eds.), *Media effects: Advances in theory and research* (pp. 61–90). Hillsdale, NJ: Erlbaum.

Bandura, A. (2002). Social cognitive theory in cultural context. *Applied Psychology: An International Review, 51*, 269–290.

Bandura, A., & Bussey, K. (2004). On broadening the cognitive, motivational, and sociostructural scope of theorizing about genderdevelopment and functioning: Comments on Martin, Buble and Szkrybalo (2002). *Psychological Bulletin*, 130, 691–701.

Bandura, A., Ross, D., & Ross, S. A. (1961). The transmission of aggression through imitation of aggressive models. *Journal of Abnormal and Social Psychology, 63*, 575–582.

Banerjee, R. (2005). Gender identity and the development of gender roles. In S. Ding & K. Littleton (Eds.), *Children's personal and social development* (pp. 142–179). Malden, MA: Blackwell.

Barajas, R. G., Martin, A., Brooks-Gunn, J., & Hale, L. (2011). Mother-child bed-sharing in toddlerhood and cognitive and behavioral outcomes. *Pediatrics, 128*(2), e339–e347.

Barber, B. K. (2002). *Intrusive parenting: How psychological control affects children and adolescents.* Washington, DC: American Psychological Association.

Barber, B. K. (Ed.). (2009). *Adolescents and war: How youth deal with political violence.* New York, NY: Oxford University Press.

Barber, B. K. (2009). Making sense and no sense of war: Issues of identity and meaning in adolescents' experience with political conflict. In B. K. Barber (Ed.), *Adolescents and war: How youth deal with political violence.* New York, NY: Oxford University Press.

Barber, B. K. (2013). Annual research review: The experience of youth with political conflict–challenging notions of resilience and encouraging research refinement. *Journal of Child Psychology and Psychiatry, 54*(4), 461–473.

Barber, B. K., Stolz, H. E., & Olsen, J. A. (2005). Parental support, psychological control, and behavioral control: Assessing relevance across time, culture, and method: IV. Assessing relevance across time: U.S. analyses and results. *Monographs of the Society for Research in Child Development, 70*(4), 1–137.

Barnett, D., Ganiban, J., & Cicchetti, D. (1999). Maltreatment, negative expressivity, and the development of type D attachments from 12 to 24 months of age. *Monographs of the Society for Research in Child Development, 64*, 97–118.

Barnett, G. A., & Benefield, G. A. (2015). Predicting international Facebook ties through cultural homophily and other factors. *New Media & Society, 19*, 217–239. doi:10.1177/1461444815604421

Barnett, W. S., & Hustedt, J. T. (2005). Head Start's lasting benefits. *Infants and Young Children, 18*, 16–24.

Baron, E. M., & Denmark, F. L. (2006). An exploration of female genital mutilation. In F. L. Denmark, H. H. Krauss, E. Halpern, & J. A. Sechzer (Eds.), *Violence and exploitation against women and girls* (pp. 339–355). Malden, MA: Blackwell.

Barr, H. M., & Streissguth, A. P. (2001). Identifying maternal self-reported alcohol use associated with Fetal Alcohol Spectrum Disorders. *Alcoholism: Clinical and Experimental Research, 25*, 283–287.

Barr, R., & Hayne, H. (2003). It's not what you know, it's who you know: Older siblings facilitate imitation during infancy. *Child Development, 70*, 1067–1081.

Barr, R., Marrott, H., & Rovee-Collier, C. (2003). The role of sensory preconditioning in memory retrieval by preverbal infants. *Learning and Behavior, 31*, 111–123.

Barr, R. G. (2009). The phenomena of early infant crying and colic. Paper presented at the Centre for Community and Child Health, Melbourne, Australia, March 2.

Barr, R. G., & Gunnar, M. (2000). Colic: The "transient responsivity" hypothesis. In R. G. Barr, B. Hopkins, & J. A. Green (Eds.), *Crying as a sign, a symptom, and a signal* (pp. 41–66). Cambridge, UK: Cambridge University Press.

Barrett, D. E., & Frank, D. A. (1987). *The effects of undernutrition on children's behavior.* New York, NY: Gordon & Breach.

Barrett, J. L., Richert, R. A., & Driesenga, A. (2001). God's beliefs versus mother's: The development of nonhuman agent concepts. *Child Development, 72*, 50–65.

Barrett, K. C., & Campos, J. J. (1987). Perspectives on emotional development: II. A functionalist approach to emotions. In J. Osofsky (Ed.), *Handbook of Infant Development* (2nd ed., pp. 555–578). New York, NY: Wiley.

Barrett, K. C., & Nelson-Goens, G. C. (1997). Emotion communication and the development of the social emotions. *New Directions for Child Development, 77*, 69–88.

Barrio, C., Morena, A., & Linaza, J. L. (2007). Spain. In J. J. Arnett, R. Ahmed, B. Nsamenang, T. S. Saraswathi, & R. Silbereisen (Eds.), *International encyclopedia of adolescence* (pp. 906–924). New York, NY: Routledge.

Barry, C. M., Madsen, S. D., & Grace, A. (2015). Friendships in emerging adulthood. In J. J. Arnett (Ed.), *Oxford handbook of emerging adulthood* (pp. 215–229). New York, NY: Oxford University Press.

Bartick, M. (2014, December 19). Pediatric politics: How dire warnings against infant bed sharing "backfired." Retrieved from http://commonhealth.wbur.org/2014/12/dire-warnings-against-infant-bed-sharing-backfired

Bartoshuk, L. M., & Beauchamp, G. K. (1994). Chemical senses. *Annual Review of Psychology, 45*, 419–449.

Basseches, M. (1984). *Dialectical thinking and adult development.* Norwood, NJ: Ablex.

Basseches, M. A. (1989). Dialectical thinking as an organized whole: Comments on Irwin and Kramer. In M.L. Commons, J. D. Sinnott, F. A. Richards, & C. Armon (Eds.), *Adult development, Vol. 1: Comparisons and applications of developmental models* (pp. 161–178). New York: Praeger.

Basseches, M. (2005). The development of dialectical thinking as an approach to integration. *Integral Review, 1*(1), 47–63.

Bassett, R. L., Miller, S., Anstey, K., & Crafts, K. (1990). Picturing God: A nonverbal measure of God concept for conservative Protestants. *Journal of Psychology and Christianity 9*(1), 73–81.

Basu, A. K., & Chau, N. H. (2007). An exploration of the worst forms of child labor: Is redemption a viable option? In K. A. Appiah & M. Bunzl (Eds.), *Buying freedom: The ethics of economics of slave redemption* (pp. 37–76). Princeton, NJ: Princeton University Press.

Bates, B., & Turner, A. N. (2003). Imagery and symbolism in the birth practices of traditional cultures. In L. Dundes (Ed.), *The manner born: Birth rites in cross-cultural perspective* (pp. 85–97). Walnut Creek, CA: AltaMira Press.

Batzer, F. R., & Ravitsky, V. (2009). Preimplantation genetic diagnosis: Ethical considerations. In V. Ravitsky, A. Fiester, & A. L. Caplan (Eds.), *The Penn Center guide to bioethics* (pp. 339–354). New York, NY: Springer.

Bauer, P. J. (2006). Event memory. In W. Damon & R. Lerner (Eds.), *Handbook of child psychology: Vol. 2. Cognition, perception and language* (6th ed., pp. 373–425). New York, NY: Wiley.

Bauer, P. J. (2013). Memory. In P. D. Zelazo (Ed.), *The Oxford handbook of developmental psychology: Volume 1: Body and mind* (pp. 505–541). New York, NY: Oxford University Press.

Bauer, P. J., San Souci, P., & Pathman, T. (2010). Infant memory. *Wiley Interdisciplinary Reviews: Cognitive Science, 1*, 267–277.

Bauer, P. J., Wenner, J. A., Dropik, P. I., & Wewerka, S. S. (2000). Parameters of remembering and forgetting in the transition from infancy to early childhood. *Monographs of the Society for Research in Child Development, 65*, 1–204.

Bauer, P. J., Wiebe, S. A., Carver, L. J., Waters, J. M., & Nelson, C. A. (2003). Developments in long-term explicit memory late in the first year of life: Behavioral and electrophysiological indices. *Psychological Science, 14*, 629–635.

Bauer, P. J., Wiebe, S. A., Waters, J. M., & Banston, S. K. (2001). Reexposure breeds recall: Effects of experience on 9-month-olds' ordered recall. *Journal of Experimental Child Psychology, 80*, 174–200.

Bauminger, N., Finzi-Dottan, R., Chason, S., & Har-Even, D. (2008). Intimacy in adolescent friendship: The roles of attachment, coherence and self-disclosure. *Journal of Social and Personal Relationships, 25*(3), 409–428.

Baumrind, D. (1968). Authoritative vs. authoritarian parental control. *Adolescence, 3*, 255–272.

Baumrind, D. (1971). Current patterns of parental authority. *Developmental Psychology Monograph, 4* (No. 1, Pt. 2), 1–103.

Baumrind, D. (1991). The influence of parenting style on adolescent competence and drug use. *Journal of Early Adolescence, 11*, 56–95.

Baumrind, D. (1993). The average expectable environment is not enough: A response to Scarr. *Child Development, 64*, 1299–1317.

Bayley, N. (2005). *Bayley Scales of Infant and Toddler Development, Third Edition* (Bayley-III). San Antonio, TX: Harcourt Assessment.

Beck, I. L., & Beck, M. E. (2013). *Making sense of phonics: The hows and whys.* New York, NY: Guilford.

Becker, A. E. (2004). Television, disordered eating, and young women in Fiji: Negotiating body image and identity during rapid social change. *Culture, Medicine & Psychiatry, 28*, 533–559.

Becker, A. E., Fay, K., Gilman, S. E., & Striegel-Moore, R. (2007). Facets of acculturation and their diverse relations to body shape concern in Fiji. *International Journal of Eating Disorders, 40*, 42–50.

Becker, O. A., Salzburger, V., Lois, N., & Nauck, B. (2013). What narrows the stepgap? Closeness between parents and adult (step) children in Germany. *Journal of Marriage and Family, 75*(5), 1130–1148.

Bel, A., & Bel, B. (2007). Birth attendants: Between the devil and the deep blue sea. In B. Bel, J. Brouwer, B. T. Das, V. Parthasarathi, & G. Poitevin (Eds.), *Communication processes 2: The social and the symbolic* (pp. 353–385). Thousand Oaks, CA: Sage.

Bell, M. A. (1998). Frontal lobe function during infancy: Implications for the development of cognition and attention. In J. E. Richards (Ed.), *Cognitive neuroscience of attention: A developmental perspective* (pp. 327–362). Mahwah, NJ: Erlbaum.

Bell, M. A., & Wolfe, C. D. (2007). The cognitive neuroscience of early socioemotional development. In C. A. Brownell & C. B. Kopp (Eds.), *Socioemotional development in the toddler years: Transitions and transformations* (pp. 345–369). New York, NY: Guilford Press.

Bell, S. M., & Ainsworth, M. D. S. (1972). Infant crying and maternal responsiveness. *Child Development, 43*, 1171–1190.

Bellah, R. N., Madsen, R., Sullivan, W. M., Swidler, A., & Tipton, S. M. (1985). *Habits of the heart: Individualism and commitment in American life*. New York, NY: Harper & Row.

Belluck, P. (2015, December 31). A study of risks and benefits is welcomed by all sides in a growing debate. *The New York Times*, pp. A10 & A14.

Bem, S. L. (1974). The measurement of psychological androgyny. *Journal of Clinical and Consuling Psychology*, 42, 155–162.

Bem, S. L. (1975). Sex role adaptability: One consequence of psychological androgyny. *Journal of Personality and Social Psychology, 31*, 634–643.

Bem, S. L. (1977). On the utility of alternative procedures for assessing psychological androgyny. *Journal of Consulting and Clinical Psychology, 45*, 196–205.

Bem, S. L. (1981). Gender schema theory: A cognitive account of sex-typing. *Psychological Review, 88*, 354–364.

Bendazzi, G. (2016). *Animation: A world history*. Boca Raton, FL: CRC Press/Taylor & Francis Group.

Bender, H. L., Allen, J. P., McElhaney, K. B., Antonishak, J., Moore, C. M., Kelly, H. O., & Davis, S. M. (2007). Use of harsh physical discipline and developmental outcomes in adolescence. *Development and Psychopathology, 19*, 227–242.

Bennik, E. C., Nederhof, E., Ormel, J., & Oldehinkel, A. J. (2013). Anhedonia and depressed mood in adolescence: Course, stability, and reciprocal relation in the TRAILS study. *European Child & Adolescent Psychiatry*, 1–8.

Benson, M., Harris, P., & Rogers, C. (1992). Identity consequences of attachment to mothers and fathers among late adolescents. *Journal of Research on Adolescents, 2*, 187–204.

Berch, D., & Mazzocco, M. (2007). Why is math so hard for some children? *The nature and origins of mathematical learning difficulties and disabilities*. Baltimore, MD: Paul H. Brookes.

Berge, J. M., Wall, M., Hsueh, T.-F., Fulkerson, J. A., Larson, N., & Neumark-Sztainer, D. (2014). The protective role of family meals for youth obesity: 10-year longitudinal associations. *The Journal of Pediatrics, 166*, 206–301. doi.org/10.1016/j.jpeds.2014.08.030

Bergen, H. A., Martin, G., Richardson, A. S., Allison, S., & Roeger, L. (2003). Sexual abuse and suicidal behavior: A model constructed from a larger community sample of adolescents. *Journal of the American Academy of Child & Adolescent Psychiatry, 42*, 1301–1309.

Berger, K. S. (2007). Update on bullying at school: Science forgotten? *Developmental Review, 27*, 90–126.

Bergstrom, A. (2007). Food advertising, international. In J. J. Arnett (Ed.), *Encyclopedia of children, adolescents, and the media* (pp. 347–348). Thousand Oaks, CA: Sage.

Bergstrom, A. (2007). Cartoons, educational. In J. J. Arnett (Ed.), *Encyclopedia of children, adolescents, and the media* (pp. 137–140). Thousand Oaks, CA: Sage.

Bergström, M., Kieler, H., & Waldenström, U. (2009). Effects of natural childbirth preparation versus standard antenatal education on epidural rates, experience of childbirth and parental stress in mothers and fathers: A randomised controlled multicentre trial. *BJOG: An International Journal of Obstetrics & Gynaecology, 116*, 1167–1176.

Berkman, N. D., Lohr, K. N., & Bulik, C. M. (2007). Outcomes of eating disorders: A systematic review of the literature. *International Journal of Eating Disorders, 40*(4), 293–309.

Berlyne, D. B. (1958). The influence of the albedo and complexity of stimuli on visual fixation in the human infant. *British Journal of Psychology, 49*(4), 315–318. doi:10.1111/j.2044-8295.1958.tb00669.x

Berndt, T. J. (1986). Children's comments about their friendships. In M. Perlmutter (Ed.), Minnesota symposia on child psychology, Vol. 18. *Cognitive perspectives on children's social and emotional development* (pp. 189–212). Hillsdale, NJ: Erlbaum.

Berndt, T. J. (1996). Transitions in friendship and friends' influence. In J. A. Graber, J. Brooks-Gunn, & A. C. Petersen (Eds.), *Transitions through adolescence: Interpersonal domains and context* (pp. 57–84). Mahwah, NJ: Erlbaum.

Berndt, T. J., & Mekos, D. (1995). Adolescents' perceptions of the stressful and desirable aspects of the transition to junior high school. *Journal of Research on Adolescence, 5*, 123–142.

Berney, T. (2009). Ageing in Down Syndrome. In G. O'Brien, & L. Rosenbloom (Eds.), *Developmental disability and ageing* (pp. 31–38). London, UK: Mac Keith Press.

Berry, J. W., Phinney, J. S., Sam, D. L., & Vedder, P. (Eds.). (2006). *Immigrant youth in cultural transition: Acculturation, identity, and adaptation across national contexts*. Mahwah, NJ: Lawrence Erlbaum.

Berry, R. J., Li, Z., Erickson, J. D., Li, S., Moore, C. A., Wang, H., ... Correa, A. (1999). Prevention of neural-tube defects with folic acid in China. *New England Journal of Medicine, 341*, 1485–1490.

Bertenthal, B. I., & Campos, J. J. (1984). A reexamination of fear and its determinants on the visual cliff. *Psychophysiology, 21*(4), 413–417. doi:10.1111/j.1469-8986.1984.tb00218.x

Best, D. L. (2001). Gender concepts: Convergence in cross-cultural research and methodologies. *Cross-cultural Research: The Journal of Comparative Social Science, 35*, 23–43.

Better Health Channel. (2017). *Maternal serum screening*. Retrieved from http://www.betterhealth.vic.gov.au/BHCV2/bhcarticles.nsf/pages/Maternal_serum_screening

Bialystok, E. (1993). Metalinguistic awareness: The development of children's representations in language. In C. Pratt & A. Garton (Eds.), *Systems of representation in children* (pp. 211–233). London, UK: Wiley.

Bialystok, E. (1997). Effects of bilingualism and biliteracy on children's emerging concepts of print. *Developmental Psychology*, 33, 429–440.

Bialystok, E. (1999). Cognitive complexity and attentional control in the bilingual mind. *Child Development*, 70, 636–644.

Bialystok, E. (2001). *Bilingualism in development: Language, literacy, and cognition*. New York, NY: Cambridge University Press.

Bialystok, E., Barac, R., Blaye, A., & Poulin-Dubois, D. (2010). Word mapping and executive functioning in young monolingual and bilingual children. *Journal of Cognition and Development, 11*(4), 485–508. doi:10.1080/15248372.2010.516420

Bialystok, E., & Martin, M. M. (2004). Attention and inhibition in bilingual children: Evidence from the dimensional change card sort task. *Developmental Science, 7*(3), 325–339. doi:10.1111/j.1467-7687.2004.00351.x

Biehl, M. C., Natsuaki, M. N., & Ge, X. (2007). The influence of pubertal timing on alcohol use and heavy drinking trajectories. *Journal of Youth and Adolescence, 36*(2), 153–167.

Biener, L., & Siegel, M. (2000). Tobacco marketing and adolescent smoking: More support for a causal inference. *American Journal of Public Health, 90*, 407–411.

Bina, M., Graziano, F., & Bonino, S. (2006). Risky driving and lifestyles in adolescence. *Accident Analysis & Prevention, 38*, 472–481.

Binet, A. (1911). Methods nouvelle sur la measure du niveau intel- lectual des anormaux. *L'Anne Psychologique, 17*, 145–201.

Binet, A., & Simon, T. (1905). Methods nouvelles pour le diagnostic du niveau intellectual des anormaux. *L'Anne Psychologique, 11*, 191–244.

Birch, L. L., Fisher, J. O., & Davison, K. K. (2003). Learning to overeat: Maternal use of restrictive feeding practices promotes girls' eating in the absence of hunger. *American Journal of Clinical Nutrition, 78*, 215–220.

Birdsong, D. (2006). Age and second language acquisition and processing: A selective overview. *Language Learning, 56* (Suppl. s1), 9–49.

Biro, F. M., Huang, B., Morrison, J. A., Horn, P. S., & Daniels, S. R. (2010). Body mass index and waist-to-height changes during teen years in girls are influenced by childhood body mass index. *Journal of Adolescent Health, 46*(3), 245–250.

Bjarnason, T., & Sigurdardottir, T. J. (2003). Psychological distress during unemployment and beyond: Social support and material deprivation among youth in six Northern European countries. *Social Science & Medicine, 56*, 973–985.

Bjorklund, D. F. (2007). *Why youth is not wasted on the young*. Malden, MA: Blackwell Publishing.

Bjorklund, D. F. (2013). Cognitive development: An overview. In P. D. Zelazo (Ed.), *Oxford handbook of developmental psychology: Vol. 1: Body and mind* (pp. 447–476). New York, NY: Oxford University Press.

Black, K. A., & Gold, D. J. (2008). Gender differences and socioeconomic status biases in judgments about blame in date rape scenarios. *Violence and Victims*, 23(1), 115–128.

Black, M. M., Quigg, A. M., Hurley, K. M., & Pepper, M. R. (2011). Iron deficiency and iron-deficiency anemia in the first two years of life: Strategies to prevent loss of developmental potential. *Nutrition Reviews*, 69, S64–S70.

Black, R. E., Williams, S. M., Jones, I. E., & Goulding, A. (2002). Children who avoid drinking cow milk have lower dietary calcium intakes and poor bone health. *American Journal of Clinical Nutrition, 76*, 675–680.

Black, S. E., Devereux, P. J., & Salvanes, K. G. (2007). From the cradle to the labor market? The effects of birth weight on adult outcomes. *The Quarterly Journal of Economics, 122*, 409–439. https://doi.org/10.1162/qjec.122.1.409

Blackwell, L. S., Trzesniewski, K. H., & Dweck, C. S. (2007). Implicit theories of intelligence predict achievement across an adolescent transition: A longitudinal study and an intervention. *Child development, 78*(1), 246–263.

Blair, J. M., Hanson, D. L., Jones, H., & Dwokin, M. S. (2004). Trends in pregnancy rates among women with human immunodeficiency virus. *Obstetrics and Gynecology, 103*, 663–668.

Blakemore, J. E. O. (2003). Children's beliefs about violating gender norms: Boys shouldn't look like girls, and girls shouldn't act like boys. *Sex Roles, 48*, 411–419.

Blakemore, J. E. O., Berenbaum, S. A., & Liben, L. S. (2008). *Gender development*. New York, NY: Psychology Press.

Blascovich, J., & Bailenson, J. (2011). *Infinite reality: Avatars, eternal life, new worlds, and the dawn of the virtual revolution*. New York, NY: HarperCollins.

Blasi, A. (2004). Neither personality nor cognition: An alternative approach to the nature of the self. In C. Lightfoot, C. Lalonde, & M. Chandler (Eds.), *Changing conceptions of psychological life* (pp. 3–25). Mahwah, NJ: Erlbaum.

Bleidorn, W., Arslan, R. C., Denissen, J. J., Rentfrow, P. J., Gebauer, J. E., Potter, J., & Gosling, S. D. (2016). Age and gender differences in self-esteem—A cross-cultural window. *Journal of Personality and Social Psychology, 111*, 396.

Bloom, L. (1998). Language acquisition in its developmental context. In W. Damon (Ed.), & D. Kuhn & R. S. Siegler (Vol. Eds.), *Handbook of child psychology* (5th ed.): *Vol. 2. Cognition, perception and language* (pp. 309–370). New York, NY: Wiley.

Bloom, L., Lifter, K., & Broughton, J. (1985). The convergence of early cognition and language in the second year of life: Problems in conceptualization and measurement. In M. Barrett (Ed.), *Single word speech* (pp. 149–181). New York, NY: Wiley.

Bloom, L. (1998). Language acquisition in its developmental context. In W. Damon (Ed.), & D. Kuhn & R. S. Siegler (Vol. Eds.), *Handbook of child psychology, vol. 2: Cognition, perception and language* (pp. 309–370). New York, NY: Wiley.

Bloom, P. (2000). *How children learn the meanings of words*. Cambridge, MA: MIT Press.

Bloom, P. (2013). *Just babies: The origins of good and evil*. New York, NY: Crown Publishers.

Bluestone, C., & Tamis-LeMonda C. S. (1999). Correlates of parenting styles in predominately working- and middle-class African American mothers. *Journal of Marriage and the Family, 61*, 881–893.

Blumberg, F. C., & Fisch, S. M. (2013). Introduction: Digital games as a context for cognitive development, learning, and developmental research. *New Directions for Child and Adolescent Research, 139*, 1–9.

Blumenthal, J., Jeffries, N. O., Castellanos, F. X., Liu, H., Zidjdenbos, A., Paus, T.,…Giedd, J. N. (1999). Brain development during childhood and adolescence: A longitudinal MRI study. *Nature Neuroscience, 10*, 861–863.

Bochner, S., & Jones, J. (2003). Augmentative and alternative forms of communication as stepping stones to speech. In S. Bochner & J. Jones (Eds.), *Child language development: Learning to talk* (2nd ed., pp. 143–156). London, UK: Whurr Publishers.

Boden, J. M., Horwood, L. J., & Fergusson, D. M. (2007). Exposure to childhood sexual and physical abuse and subsequent educational achievement outcomes. *Child Abuse and Neglect, 31*, 1101–1114.

Boehke, K., Muench, T., & Hoffman, D. (2002). Development through media use? A German study on the use of radio in adolescence. *International Journal of Behavioral Development*, 26, 193–201.

Boer, F., Goedhardt, A. W., & Treffers, P. D. A. (2013). Siblings and their parents. In F. Boer, J. Dunn, & J. F. Dunn (Eds.), *Children's sibling relationships: Developmental and clinical issues* (pp. 41–54). New York, NY: Wiley.

Bokhorst, C. L., Sumpter, S. R., & Westenberg, P. M. (2010). Social support from parents, friends, classmates, and teachers in children and adolescents aged 9 to 18 years: Who is perceived as most supportive. *Social Development, 19*(2), 417–426. doi:10.1111/j.1467-9507.2009.00540.x

Bolzani, L. H., Messinger, D. S., Yale, M., & Dondi, M. (2002). Smiling in infancy. In M. H. Abel (Ed.), *An empirical reflection on the smile* (pp. 111–136). Lewiston, NY: Edwin Mellen Press.

Bonino, S., & Cattelino, E. (2012). Italy. In J. J. Arnett (Ed.), *Adolescent psychology around the world* (pp. 290–305). New York, NY: Taylor & Francis.

Bookwala, J., Frieze, I. H., & Grote, N. (1994). The long-term effects of military service on quality of life: The Vietnam experience. *Journal of Applied Social Psychology, 24*, 529–545.

Booth, D. A., Higgs, S., Schneider, J., & Klinkenberg, I. (2010). Learned liking versus inborn delight: Can sweetness give sensual pleasure or is it just motivating? *Psychological Science, 21*, 1656–1663.

Boothby, N., Crawford, J., & Mamade, A. (2009). Mozambican child soldier life outcome study. In B. K. Barber (Ed.), *Adolescents and war: How youth deal with political violence* (pp. 238–255). New York, NY: Oxford University Press.

Borduin, C. M., Schaeffer, C. M., & Ronis, S. T. (2003). Multisystemic treatment of serious antisocial behavior in adolescents. In C. A. Essau (Ed.), *Conduct and oppositional defiant disorders: Epidermiology, risk factors, and treatment* (pp. 299–318). Mahwah, NJ: Lawrence Erlbaum.

Borgaonkar, D. S. (1997). *Chromosomal variation in man: A catalog of chromosomal variants and anomalies* (8th ed.). New York, NY: Wiley.

Bornstein, M. H. (2006). Parenting science and practice. In W. Damon & R. Lerner (Eds.), & K. A. Renninger & L. E. Sigel (Vol. Eds.), *Handbook of child psychology: Vol. 4. Child psychology in practice* (6th ed., pp. 893–949). New York, NY: Wiley.

Bornstein, M. H. (2010). *Handbook of cultural developmental science*. New York, NY: Psychology Press.

Bornstein, M. H., & Arterberry, M. E. (2010). The development of object categorization in young children: Hierarchical inclusiveness, age, perceptual attribute, and group versus individual analyses. *Developmental Psychology, 46*, 350–365. doi:10.1037/a0018411

Bornstein, M. H., & Bradley, R. H. (2014). *Socioeconomic status, parenting, and child development*. New York, NY: Routledge.

Bornstein, M. H., Cote, L. R., Maital, S., Painter, K., Park, S. Y., Pascual, L., … Vyt, A. (2004). Cross-linguistic analysis of vocabulary in young children: Spanish, Dutch, French, Hebrew, Italian, Korean, and American English. *Child Development, 75*(4), 1115–1139. doi:10.1111/j.1467-8624.2004.00729.x

Bortolus, R., Parazzini, F., Chatenoud, L., Benzi, G., Bianchi, M. M., & Marini, A. (1999). The epidemiology of multiple births. *Human Reproduction Update, 5*, 179–187.

Bortree, D. S. (2005). Presentation of self on the web: An ethnographic study of teenage girls' weblogs. *Education, Communication and Information Journal, 5*, 25–39.

Boschi-Pinto, C., Lanata, C. F., & Black, R. E. (2009). The global burden of childhood diarrhea. *Maternal and Child Health, 3*, 225–243.

Bostic, J. Q., Rubin, D. H., Prince, J., & Schlozman, S. (2005). Treatment of depression in children and adolescents. *Journal of Psychiatric Practice, 11*, 141–154.

Botcheva, L., Kalchev, P., & Ledierman, P. H. (2007). Bulgaria. In J. J. Arnett, R. Ahmed, B. Nsamenang, T. S. Saraswathi, & R. Silbereisen (Eds.), *International encyclopedia of adolescence* (pp. 108–120). New York, NY: Routledge.

Bouchard, T. J., & McGue, M. (2003). Genetic and environmental influences on human psychological differences. *Journal of Neurobiology, 54*, 4–45.

Bower, B. (1985). The left hand of math and verbal talent. *Science News, 127*, 263.

Bowers, W. A., Evans, K., LeGrange, D., & Andersen, A. E. (2003). Treatment of adolescent eating disorders. In M. A. Reinecke & F. M. Dattilio (Eds.), *Cognitive therapy with children and adolescents: A casebook for clinical practice* (2nd ed., pp. 247–280). New York, NY: Guilford Press.

Bowlby, J. (1969). *Attachment and loss, Vol. 1: Attachment*. New York, NY: Basic Books.

Bowlby, J. (1980). *Attachment and loss, Vol. 3: Loss, sadness, and depression*. New York, NY: Basic Books.

Boyatzis, C. J., & Janicki, D. L. (2003). Parent-child communication about religion: Survey and diary data on unilateral transmission and bi-directional reciprocity styles. *Review of Religious Research, 44*, 252–270.

Boyte, H. (2016, February 2). Free spaces in schools and colleges. *The Huffington Post*. Retrieved from http://www.huffingtonpost.com/harry-boyte/free-spaces-in-schools-and_b_9138744.html

Bradford, K., Barber, B. K., Olsen, J. A., Maughan, S. L., Erickson, L. D., Ward, D., et al. (2004). A multi-national study of interparental conflict, parenting, and adolescent functioning: South Africa, Bangladesh, China, India, Bosnia, Germany, Palestine, Columbia, and the United States. *Marriage & Family Review, 35*, 107–137.

Brake, M. (1985). *Comparative youth culture: The sociology of youth cultures and youth subcultures in America, Britain, and Canada*. London, UK: Routledge and Kegan Paul.

Brambati, B., & Tului, L. (2005). Chorionic villus sampling and amniocentesis. *Current Opinion in Obstetrics and Gynecology, 17*, 197–201.

Brame, B., Nagin, D. S., & Tremblay, R. E. (2001). Developmental trajectories of physical aggression from school entry to late adolescence. *Journal of Child Psychology and Psychiatry, 42*, 503–512.

Brand, S., Felner, R., Shim, M., Seitsinger, A., & Dumas, T. (2003). Middle school improvement and reform: Development and validation of a school level assessment of climate, cultural pluralism, and school safety. *Journal of Educational Psychology, 95*, 570–588.

Brant, A. M., Haberstick, B. C., Corley, R. P., Wadsworth, S. J., DeFries, J. C., & Hewitt, J. K. (2009). The development etiology of high IQ. *Behavior Genetics, 39*, 393–405.

Bray, J. H. (1999). From marriage to remarriage and beyond: Findings from the Developmental Issues in Stepfamilies Research Project. In E. M. Hetherington (Ed.), *Coping with divorce, single parenting, and remarriage: A risk and resiliency perspective* (pp. 295–319). Mahwah, NJ: Erlbaum.

Brazelton, T. B., Koslowski, B., & Tronick, E. (1976). Neonatal behavior among urban Zambians and Americans. *Journal of the American Academy of Child Psychiatry, 15*, 97–107.

Breger, L. (2000). *Freud: Darkness in the midst of vision*. New York, NY: Wiley & Sons.

Breivik, K., Olweus, D., & Endresen, I. (2009). Does the quality of parent–child relationships mediate the increased risk for antisocial behavior and substance use among adolescents in single-mother and single-father families? *Journal of Divorce & Remarriage, 50*(6), 400–426.

Brent, D. (2007). Antidepressants and suicidal behavior: Cause or cure? *The American Journal of Psychiatry, 164*(7), 989–991.

Brent, D. A. (2004). Antidepressants and pediatric depression: The risk of doing nothing. *New England Journal of Medicine, 35*, 1598–1601.

Brent, D. A., & Mann, J. J. (2006). Familial pathways to suicidal behavior: Understanding and preventing suicide among adolescents. *New England Journal of Medicine, 355*(26), 2719–2721.

Bretherton, I., & Munholland, K. (1999). Internal working models in attachment relationships: A construct revisited. In J. Cassidy & P. R. Shaver (Eds.), *Handbook of attachment: Theory, research, and clinical applications* (pp. 89–111). New York, NY: Guilford Press.

Bridge, J. A., Yengar, S., Salary, C. B., Barbe, R. P., Birmaher, B., Pincus, H. A., … Brent, D. A. (2007). Clinical response and risk for reported suicidal ideation and suicide attempts in pediatric antidepressant treatment: A meta-analysis of randomized controlled trials. *JAMA, 63*, 332–339.

Briggs, C. L. (2003). *Learning how to ask*. Cambridge, UK: Cambridge University Press.

Brittian, A. S., & Spencer, M. B. (2012). Assessing the relationship between ethnic and religious identity among and between diverse American youth. In A. E. Alberts Warren, R. M. Lerner, & E. Phelps (Eds.), *Thriving and spirituality among youth: Research perspectives and future possibilities* (pp. 205–230). Hoboken, NJ: John Wiley & Sons, Inc. doi:10.1002/9781118092699.ch10

Brody, G. H. (2004). Siblings' direct and indirect contributions to child development. *Current Directions in Psychological Science, 13*(3), 124–126.

Brody, G. H., & Flor, D. L. (1998). Maternal resources, parenting practices, and child competence in rural, single-parent African American families. *Child Development, 69*(3), 803–816.

Brody, J. (2013, October 7). Breakthroughs in prenatal screening. *The New York Times*. Retrieved from http://well.blogs.nytimes.com/2013/10/07/breakthroughs-in-prenatal-screening/?_r=0

Bronfenbrenner, U. (1980). *The ecology of human development*. Cambridge, MA: Harvard University Press.

Bronfenbrenner, U. (2000). Ecological theory. In A. Kazdin (Ed.), *Encyclopedia of psychology* (pp. 1018–1054). Washington, DC: American Psychological Association.

Bronfenbrenner, U. (Ed.). (2005). *Making human beings human: Bioecological perspectives on human development*. Thousand Oaks, CA: Sage.

Bronfenbrenner, U., & Morris, P. A. (1998). The ecology of developmental processes. In W. Damon (Series Ed.) and R. Lerner (Vol. Ed.), *Handbook of child psychology, Vol. 1: Theoretical models of human development* (pp. 993–1028). New York, NY: Wiley.

Brooks, R., & Meltzoff, A. N. (2005). The development of gaze following and its relation to language. *Developmental Science, 8*, 535–543.

Brooks, R., & Meltzoff, A. N. (2008). Infant gaze following and pointing predict accelerated vocabulary growth through two years of age: A longitudinal, growth curve modeling study. *Journal of Child Language, 35*(1), 207–220. doi:http://dx.doi.org/10.1017/S030500090700829X

Brooks-Gunn, J. (2003). Do you believe in magic? What we can expect from early childhood intervention programs. *Social Policy Report of the Society for Research in Child Development, 17*, 3–14.

Brotanek, J. M., Gosz, J., & Weitzman, M. (2007). Iron deficiency in early childhood in the United States: Risk factors and racial/ethnic disparities. *Pediatrics, 120*, 568–575.

Brown, A. L. (1997). Transforming schools into communities of thinking and learning about serious matters. *American Psychologist, 52*(4), 399–413. doi:10.1037/0003-066X.52.4.399

Brown, A. S., & Susser, E. S. (2002). In utero infection and adult schizophrenia. *Mental Retardation and Developmental Disabilities Research Reviews, 8*, 51–57.

Brown, B. B. (1989). The role of peer groups in adolescents' adjustment to secondary school. In T. J. Berndt & G. W. Ladd (Eds.), *Peer relationships in child development* (pp. 188–215). New York, NY: Wiley.

Brown, B. B., Bakken, J. P., Ameringer, S. W., & Mahon, S. D. (2008). A comprehensive conceptualization of the peer influence process in adolescence. In M. J. Prinstein & K. A. Dodge (Eds.), *Understanding peer influence in children and adolescents: Duke series in child development and public policy* (pp. 72–93). New York, NY: Guilford Press.

Brown, B. B., & Braun, M. T. (2013). Peer relations. In C. Proctor & P. A. Linley (Eds.), *Research, applications, and interventions for children and adolescents* (pp. 149–164). Amsterdam, Netherlands: Springer.

Brown, B. B., & Klute, C. (2003). Friendships, cliques, and crowds. In R. G. Adams & D. M. Berzonsky (Eds.), *Blackwell handbook of adolescence* (pp. 330–348). Malden, MA: Blackwell.

Brown, B. B., Mory, M., & Kinney, D. A. (1994). Casting adolescent crowds in relational perspective: Caricature, channel, and context. In R. Montemayor, G. R. Adams, & T. P. Gullotta (Eds.), *Advances in adolescent development: Vol. 6. Personal relationships during adolescence* (pp. 123–167). Newbury Park, CA: Sage.

Brown, F. C., Buboltz Jr, W. C., & Soper, B. (2002). Relationship of sleep hygiene awareness, sleep hygiene practices, and sleep quality in university students. *Behavioral Medicine*, 28, 33–38.

Brown, J. D. (2006). Emerging adults in a media-saturated world. In J. J. Arnett & J. Tanner (Eds.), *Coming of age in the 21st century: The lives and contexts of emerging adults* (pp. 279–299). Washington, DC: American Psychological Association.

Brown, J. D., El-Toukhy, S., & Ortiz, R. (2014). Growing up sexually in a digital world. In A. B. Jordan & D. Romer (Eds.), *Media and the well-being of children and adolescents* (pp. 90–108). New York, NY: Oxford University Press.

Brown, J. D., Steele, J., & Walsh-Childers, K. (Eds.). (2002). *Sexual teens, sexual media*. Mahwah, NJ: Erlbaum.

Brown, J. D., Steele, J. R., & Walsh-Childers, K. (2002). Introduction and overview. In J. D. Brown, J. R Steele, & K. Walsh-Childers (Eds.), *Sexual teens, sexual media: Investigating media's influence on adolescent sexuality* (pp. 1–24). Mahwah, NJ: Erlbaum.

Brown, R. (1973). *A first language: The early stages*. Cambridge, MA: Harvard University Press.

Brown, R., & Hanlon, C. (1970). Derivational complexity and order of acquisition in child speech. In J. R. Hayes (Ed.), *Cognition and the Development of Language* (Vol. 8, pp. 11–53). New York, NY: Wiley.

Browne, K. D., & Hamilton-Giachritsis, C. (2005). The influence of violent media on children and adolescents: A public health approach. *Lancet, 356*, 702–710.

Brownell, C. A., & Kopp, C. B. (2007). *Socioemotional development in the toddler years*. New York, NY: Guilford.

Brownell, C. A., Svetloca, M., & Nicols, S. (2009). To share or not to share: When do toddlers respond to another's needs? *Infancy, 14*(1), 11–130.

Bruer, J. T. (1993). The mind's journey from novice to expert. *American Educator, 17*, 6–15, 38–46.

Bruner, J. S. (1977). Early social interaction and language acquisition. In H. R. Schaffer (Ed.), *Studies in mother–infant interaction* (pp. 271–289). London, UK: Academic Press.

Bryant, G. A., & Barrett, H. C. (2007). Recognizing intentions in infant-directed speech: Evidence for universals. *Psychological Science, 18*, 746–751.

Bryder, L. (2009). From breast to bottle: A history of modern infant feeding. *Endeavour, 33*, 54–59.

Buboltz, W. C., Soper, B., Brown, F., & Jenkins, S. (2002). Treatment approaches for sleep difficulties in college students. *Counseling Psychology Quarterly, 15*, 229–237.

Bucholtz, M. (1996). Geek the girl: Language, femininity, and female nerds. In N. Warner, J. Ahler, L. Bilmes, M. Oliver, S. Wertheim, & M. Chen (Eds.), *Gender and belief systems* (pp. 119–131). Gender and Belief Systems: Proceedings of the Fourth Berkeley Women and Language Conference, Berkeley Women and Language Group. Berkeley, CA: Berkeley Women and Language Group.

Buckley, T., & Gottlieb, A. (1988). *Blood magic: The anthropology of menstruation*. Berkeley, CA: University of California Press.

Bugental, D. B., & Grusec, J. E. (2006). Socialization processes. In N. Eisenberg, W. Damon, & R. M. Lerner (Eds.), *Handbook of child psychology: Vol. 3. Social, emotional, and personality development* (6th ed., pp. 366–428, xxiv, 1128). Hoboken, NJ: John Wiley & Sons.

Bugental, D. B., & Happaney, K. (2004). Predicting infant maltreatment in low-income families: The interactive effects of maternal attributions and child status at birth. *Developmental Psychology, 40*, 234–243.

Buhs, E. S., & Ladd, G. W. (2001). Peer rejection as antecedent of young children's school adjustment: An examination of mediating processes. *Developmental Psychology, 37*, 550–560.

Bukowski, W. M., Laursen, B., & Hoza, B. (2010). The snowball effect: Friendship moderates escalations in depressed affect among avoidant and excluded children. *Development and Psychopathology*, 22(4), 749–757. doi:http://dx.doi.org/10.1017/S095457941000043X

Bulik, C. M., Berkman, N. D., Brownley, K. A., Sedway, J. A., & Lohr, K. N. (2007). Anorexia nervosa treatment: A systematic review of randomized controlled trials. *International Journal of Eating Disorders, 40*(4), 310–320.

Bullough, V. L. (1981). Comments on Mosher's "Three dimensions of depth involvement in human sexual response." *Journal of Sex Research, 17*, 177–178.

Burbank, V. (1994). Australian Aborigines: An adolescent mother and her family. In M. Ember, C. Ember, & D. Levinson (Eds.), *Portraits of culture: Ethnographic originals* (pp. 103–126). Upper Saddle River, NJ: Prentice Hall.

Burbank, V. K. (1988). *Aboriginal adolescence: Maidenhood in an Australian community*. New Brunswick, NJ: Rutgers University Press.

Burdelski, M. (2012). Language socialization and politeness routines. In A. Duranti, E. Ochs, & B. B. Schieffelin (Eds.), *The handbook of language socialization* (pp. 275–295). Malden, MA: Blackwell.

Burdette, A. M., Wang, V., Elder, G. H., Hill, T. D., & Benson, J. (2009). Serving God and country? Religious involvement and military service among young adult men. *Journal for the Scientific Study of Religion, 48*(4), 794–804.

Burnham, M., Goodlin-Jones, B., & Gaylor, E. (2002). Nighttime sleep–wake patterns and self-soothing from birth to one year of age: A longitudinal intervention study. *Journal of Child Psychology & Psychiatry & Allied Disciplines, 43*, 713–725.

Burrow, A. L., & Finley, G. E. (2004). Transracial, same-race adoptions, and the need for multiple measures of adolescent adjustment. *American Journal of Orthopsychiatry, 74*, 577–583.

Busching, R., Gentile, D. A., Krahé, B., Möller, I., Khoo, A., Walsh, D. A., & Anderson, C. A. (2015). Testing the reliability and validity of different measures of violent video game use in the United States, Singapore, and Germany. *Psychology of Popular Media Culture, 4*, 97.

Bushman, B. J. (2016). Violent media and hostile appraisals: A meta-analytic review. *Aggressive Behavior, 42*, 605–613.

Bushman, B. J., & Chandler, J. J. (2007). Violence, effects of. In J. J. Arnett (Ed.), *Encyclopedia of children, adolescents, and the media* (Vol. 2, pp. 847–850). Thousand Oaks, CA: Sage.

Bushman, B. J., & Huesmann, L. R. (2001). Effects of televised violence on aggression. In D. G. Singer & J. L. Singer (Eds.), *Handbook of children and the media* (pp. 223–254). Thousand Oaks, CA: Sage.

Bushman, B. J., & Huesmann, L. R. (2012). Effects of violent media on aggression. In D. G. Singer & J. L. Singer. Handbook of children and the media (pp. 231–248). Thousand Oaks: Sage.

Buss, D. M. (2003). *The evolution of desire: Strategies of human mating* (Revised Ed.). New York, NY: Basic Books.

Buss, D. M. (2007). The evolution of human mating. *Acta Psychologica Sinica*, 39, 502–512.

Buss, K. A., & Goldsmith, H. H. (1998). Fear and anger regulation in infancy: Effects on the temporal dynamics of affective expression. *Child Development, 69*, 359–374.

Buss, R. R., Sun, W., & Oppenheim, R. W. (2006). Adaptive roles of programmed cell death during nervous system development. *Annual Review of Neuroscience, 29*, 1–35. doi:10.1146/annurev.neuro.29.051605.112800

Bussey, K., & Bandura, A. (2004). Social cognitive theory of gender development and functioning. In A. H. Eagly, A. Beall, & R. Sternberg (Eds.), *The psychology of gender* (2nd ed., pp. 92–119). New York, NY: Guilford Press.

Byrd, C. M. (2012). The measurement of racial/ethnic identity in children: A critical review. *Journal of Black Psychology, 38*(1), 3–31.

Cabrera, N. J., & Garcia Coll, C. (2004). Latino fathers: Uncharted territory in need of much exploration. In M. E. Lamb (Ed.), *The role of the father in child development* (4th ed., pp. 98–120). Hoboken, NJ: Wiley.

Cabrera, N. J., Ryan, R. M., Mitchell, S. J., Shannon, J. D., & Tamis-LeMonda C. T. (2008). Low-income nonresident father involvement with their toddlers: Variation by fathers' race and ethnicity. *Journal of Family Psychology, 22*(4), 643–651. doi:10.1037/0893-3200.22.3.643

Caetano, R., Ramisetty-Mikler, S., Floyd, L. R., & McGrath, C. (2006). The epidemiology of drinking among women of child-bearing age. *Alcoholism: Clinical and Experimental Research, 30*, 1023–1030.

Calkins, S. (2012). Caregiving as coregulation: Psychobiological processes and child functioning. In A. Booth, S. M. McHale, & N. Landale (Eds.), *Biosocial foundations of family processes* (pp. 49–59). New York, NY: Springer.

Calkins, S. D. (2002). Does aversive behavior during toddlerhood matter? The effects of difficult temperament on maternal perceptions and behavior. *Child Development, 67*, 523–540.

Call, J. (2001). Object permanence in orangutans, chimpanzees, and children. *Journal of Comparative Psychology, 115*, 159–171.

Cameron, E. L., Fox, J. D., Anderson, M. S., & Cameron, C. A. (2010). Resilient youths use humor to enhance socioemotional functioning during a day in the life. *Journal of Adolescent Research, 25*(5), 716–742.

Cameron, J. L. (2001). Effects of sex hormones on brain development. In C. A. Nelson & M. Luciana (Eds.), *Handbook of developmental cognitive neuroscience* (pp. 59–78). Cambridge, MA: MIT Press.

Campbell, A., Shirley, L., & Candy, J. (2004). A longitudinal study of gender-related cognition and behavior. *Developmental Science, 7*, 1–9.

Campbell, K., & Peebles, R. (2014). Eating disorders in children and adolescents: State of the art review. *Pediatrics, 134*, 582–592. doi:10.1542/peds.2014-0194

Campos, J. J., Langer, A., & Krowitz, A. (1970). Cardiac responses on the visual cliff in prelocomotor human infants. *Science, 170*, 196–197.

Camras, L. A., & Fatani, S. S. (2008). The development of facial expressions: Current perspectives. In M. Lewis, J. Haviland-Jones, & L. F. Barrett (Eds.), *Handbook of emotions* (3rd ed., pp. 291–303). New York, NY: Guilford Press.

Camras, L. A., Lambrecht, L., & Michel, G. F. (1996). Infant "surprise" expressions as coordinative motor structures. *Journal of Nonverbal Behavior, 20*, 183–195.

Cantor, D., Fisher, B., Chibnall, S., Townsend, R., Lee, H., Bruce, C., & Thomas, G. (2015, September 21). *Report on the AAU campus climate survey on sexual assault and sexual misconduct*. Retrieved from http://sexualassaulttaskforce.harvard.edu/files/taskforce/files/final_report_harvard_9.21.15.pdf

Caplow, T., Bahr, H. M., & Call, V. R. A. (2004). The Middletown replications: 75 years of change in adolescent attitudes, 1924–1999. *Public Opinion Quarterly, 68*(2), 287–313.

Caravita, S., & Cillessen, A. H. (2012). Agentic or communal? Associations between interpersonal goals, popularity, and bullying in middle childhood and early adolescence. *Social development, 21*(2), 376–395.

Carey, B. (2014, February 27). Mental health risks seen for children of older fathers. *The New York Times*, p. A6.

Carey, K. B., Durney, S. E., Shepardson, R. L., & Carey, M. P. (2015). Incapacitated and forcible rape of college women: Prevalence across the first year. *Journal of Adolescent Health*, 56, 678–680.

Carlo, G. (2006). Care-based and altruistically-based morality. In M. Killen & J. Smetana (Eds.), *Handbook of moral development* (pp. 551–580). Mahwah, NJ: Erlbaum.

Carlo, G., Knight, G. P., McGinley, M., & Hayes, R. (2011). The roles of parental inductions, moral emotions, and moral cognitions in prosocial tendencies among Mexican American and European American early adolescents. *The Journal of Early Adolescence, 31*(6), 757–781. doi:10.1177/0272431610373100

Carlo, G., & Pierotti, S. (in press). The development of prosocial motives. In L. A. Jensen (Ed.), *Oxford handbook of moral development: An interdisciplinary perspective*. New York, NY: Oxford University Press.

Carlo, W. A. (2016). Prematurity and intrauterine growth restrictions. In Kliegman et al. (Eds.), *Nelson textbook of pediatrics* (pp. 821–829). Philadelphia, PA: Elsevier, Inc.

Carlson, S. M. (2003). Executive function in context: Development, measurement, theory and experience. *Monographs of the Society for Research in Child Development, 68*(3), 138–151.

Carlson, S. M., & Choi, H. P. (2009). Bilingual and bicultural: Executive function in Korean and American children. In K. G. Millett (Chair), *Cognitive Effects of Bilingualism: A Look at Executive Function and Theory of Mind*. Paper symposium presented at the biennial meeting of the Society for Research in Child Development, Denver, CO.

Carlson, S. M., Zelazo, P. D., & Faja, S. (2013). Executive function. In P. D. Zelazo (Ed.), *The Oxford handbook of developmental psychology, Volume 1: Body and mind* (pp. 706–743). New York, NY: Oxford University Press.

Carr, J. (2002). Down syndrome. In P. Howlin & O. Udwin (Eds.), *Outcomes in neurodevelopmental and genetic disorders* (pp. 169–197). New York, NY: Cambridge University Press.

Carroll, J. L., & Wolpe, P. R. (2005). *Sexuality now: Embracing diversity*. Belmont, CA: Wadsworth.

Carskadon, M. A. (2011). Sleep in adolescents: The perfect storm. *Pediatric Clinics of North America, 58*, 637–647. doi:10.1016/j.pcl.2011.03.003

Carter, K. C., & Carter, B. R. (2005). *Childbed fever. A scientific biography of Ignaz Semmelweis*. Edison, NJ: Transaction.

Carter-Saltzman, L. (1980). Biological and sociocultural effects on handedness: Comparison between biological and adoptive families. *Science, 209*, 1263–1265.

Case, R. (1997). The development of conceptual structures. In D. Kuhn & R. S. Siegler (Eds.), *Handbook of child psychology* (pp. 745–800) (5th ed., Vol. 2). New York, NY: John Wiley & Sons.

Case, R. (1998). The development of conceptual structures. In W. Damon (Series Ed.) & D. Kuhn & R. S. Siegler (Vol. Eds.), *Handbook of child psychology: Vol. 2: Cognition, perception, and language* (5th ed., pp. 745–800). New York, NY: Wiley.

Case, R. (1999). Conceptual development in the child and the field: A personal view of the Piagetian legacy. In E. K. Skolnick, K. Nelson, S. A. Gelman, & P. H. Miller (Eds.), *Conceptual development* (pp. 23–51). Mahwah, NJ: Erlbaum.

Casey, B. J., Getz, S., & Galvan, A. (2008). The adolescent brain. *Developmental Review, 28*(1), 62–77.

Casey, B. M., McIntire, D. D., & Leveno, K. J. (2001). The continuing value of the Apgar score for the assessment of newborn infants. *New England Journal of Medicine, 344*, 467–471.

Casey Foundation. (2010). *2010 Kids Count data book.* Baltimore, MD: Annie E. Casey Foundation.

Cassidy, J., & Shaver, P. R. (2008). *Handbook of attachment: Theory, research, and clinical applications.* New York, NY: Guilford.

Cassidy, J., & Shaver, P. R. (2010). *Handbook of attachment: Theory, research, and clinical applications.* New York, NY: Guilford.

Cassidy, K. W., Werner, R. S., Rourke, M., Zubernis, L. S., & Balaraman, G. (2003). The relationship between psychological understanding and positive social behaviors. *Social Development, 12*, 198–221.

Cassidy, T. (2006). *Birth: The surprising history of how we are born.* New York, NY: Atlantic Monthly Press.

Cassidy, T. (2008). *Taking great pains: An abridged history of pain relief in childbirth.* Retrieved from http://wondertime.go.com/learning/article/childbirth-pain-relief.html

Cavallini, A., Fazzi, E., & Viviani, V. (2002). Visual acuity in the first two years of life in healthy term newborns: An experience with the Teller Acuity Cards. *Functional neurology: New trends in adaptive & behavioral disorders, 17*, 87–92.

Centers for Disease Control and Prevention (CDC). (2002). Infant mortality and low birth weight among black and white infants: United States, 1980–2000. *Morbidity & Mortality Weekly Report*, 51, 589–592.

Centers for Disease Control and Prevention (CDC) (2006). School health policies and programs study (SHPPS). *Journal of School Health*. 2007; 27(8).

Centers for Disease Control and Prevention (CDC). (2007). Suicide trends among youths and young adults ages 10–24 years—United States, 1990–2004. *Morbidity and Mortality Weekly Report, 56*(35), 905–908.

Centers for Disease Control and Prevention (CDC). (2010). Sudden infant death syndrome (SIDS) and infant vaccines. Retrieved from http://www.cdc.gov/vaccinesafety/Concerns/sids_faq.html

Centers for Disease Control and Prevention (CDC). (2011). Heart disease is the number one cause of death. Retrieved from http://www.cdc.gov/features/heartmonth/

Centers for Disease Control and Prevention (CDC). (2013). Progress in increasing breastfeeding and reducing racial/ethnic differences. *MMWR, 62*(5), 77–80.

Centers for Disease Control and Prevention (CDC). (2013). *Sexually Transmitted Disease Surveillance 2012.* Atlanta, GA: U.S. Department of Health and Human Services.

Centers for Disease Control and Prevention (CDC). (2014). Breastfeeding report card. Retrieved from http://www.cdc.gov/breastfeeding/pdf/2013breastfeedingreportcard.pdf

Centers for Disease Control and Prevention (CDC). (2015). Physical activity facts. Retrieved from http://www.cdc.gov/healthyschools/physicalactivity/facts.htm

Centers for Disease Control and Prevention (CDC). (2015). Sexually transmitted diseases: Adolescents and young adults. Retrieved from https://www.cdc.gov/std/life-stages-populations/adolescents-youngadults.htm

Centers for Disease Control and Prevention (CDC). (2015). Suicide prevention. Retrieved May 25, 2015, from http://www.cdc.gov/violenceprevention/pub/youth_suicide.html

Centers for Disease Control and Prevention (CDC). (2017). Autism spectrum disorder (ASD). Retrieved from https://www.cdc.gov/ncbddd/autism/data.html

Centers for Disease Control and Prevention (CDC). (2017). Fetal alcohol spectrum disorders (FASD). Retrieved from https://www.cdc.gov/ncbddd/fasd/facts.html

Centers for Disease Control and Prevention (CDC). (2017). Over 23,000 infants died in the United States in 2014. The loss of a baby takes a serious toll on the health and well-being of families, as well as the nation. Retrieved from https://www.cdc.gov/reproductivehealth/maternalinfanthealth/infantmortality.htm

Centers for Disease Control and Prevention (CDC). (2017). Preconception health and health care. Retrieved from https://www.cdc.gov/preconception/women.html

Centers for Disease Control and Prevention (CDC). (2017). Suicide prevention. Retrieved from https://www.cdc.gov/violenceprevention/suicide/

Centers for Disease Control and Prevention (CDC). (2017). *2 to 20 years: Boys stature weight-for-age percentiles.* Retrieved from https://www.cdc.gov/growthcharts/data/set1clinical/cj41l021.pdf

Centers for Disease Control and Prevention (CDC). (2017). *2 to 20 years: Girls stature weight-for-age percentiles.* Retrieved from https:// www.cdc.gov/growthcharts/data/set2clinical/cj41c072.pdf

Centers for Disease Control and Prevention (CDC). (2017). Unmarried childbearing. Retrieved from https://www.cdc.gov/nchs/fastats/unmarried-childbearing.htm

Centers for Disease Control and Prevention (CDC). (2017). Weight gain during pregnancy. Retrieved from https://www.cdc.gov/reproductivehealth/maternalinfanthealth/pregnancy-weight-gain.htm

Centers for Disease Control and Prevention, National Center for Injury Prevention and Control, Division of Violence Prevention. (2015). *Suicide: Facts at a glance*. Retrieved from https://www.cdc.gov/violenceprevention/pdf/suicide-datasheet-a.pdf

Chalk, L. M., Meara, N. M., Day, J. D., & Davis, K. L. (2005). Occupational possible selves: Fears and aspirations of college women. *Journal of Career Assessment, 13*(2), 188–203.

Chambers, M. L., Hewitt, J. K., Schmitz, S., Corley, R. P., & Fulker, D. W. (2001). Height, weight, and body mass index. In R. N. Emde & J. K. Hewitt (Eds.), *Infancy to early childhood: Genetic and environmental influences on developmental change* (pp. 292–306). New York, NY: Oxford University Press.

Champion, K. M., Vernberg, E. M., & Shipman, K. (2003). Non-bullying victims of bullies: Aggression, social skills, and friendship characteristics. *Journal of Applied Developmental Psychology, 24*, 535–551.

Chan, C. G., & Elder, G. H., Jr. (2000). Matrilineal advantage in grandchild–grandparent relations. *Gerontologist, 40*, 179–190.

Chan, H. Y., Brown, B. B., & Von Bank, H. (2015). Adolescent disclosure of information about peers: The mediating role of perceptions of parents' right to know. *Journal of Youth and Adolescence, 44*, 1048–1065.

Chan, K., Tufte, B., Cappello, G., & Williams, R. B. (2011). Tween girls' perception of gender roles and gender identities: A qualitative study. *Young Consumers, 12*(1), 66–81.

Chang, L. (2008). *Factory girls: From village to city in a changing China.* New York, NY: Spiegel & Grau.

Chao, R., & Tseng, V. (2002). Parenting of Asians. In M. H. Bornstein (Ed.), *Handbook of parenting, Vol. 4: Social conditions and applied parenting* (pp. 59–93). Mahwah, NJ: Erlbaum.

Chapman, L. K., & Steger, M. F. (2010). Race and religion: Differential prediction of anxiety symptoms by religious coping in African American and European American young adults. *Depression and Anxiety, 27*(3), 316–322.

Charkova, K. D. (2007). A language without borders: English slang and Bulgarian learners of English. *Language Learning, 57*(3), 369–416. doi:10.1111/j.1467-9922.2007.00420.x

Charpak, N., Ruiz-Pelaez, J. G., & Figueroa, Z. (2005). Influence of feeding patterns and other factors on early somatic growth of healthy, preterm infants in home-based kangaroo mother care: A cohort study. *Journal of Pediatric Gastroenterology and Nutrition, 41*, 430–437.

Chase, W. G., & Simon, H. A. (1973). Perception in chess. *Cognitive Psychology, 4*, 55–81.

Chaudhary, N., & Sharma, N. (2007). India. In J. J. Arnett (Ed.), *International encyclopedia of adolescence* (pp. 442–459). New York, NY: Routledge.

Chaudhary, N., & Sharma, P. (2012). India. In J. J. Arnett (Ed.), *Adolescent psychology around the world.* New York, NY: Taylor & Francis.

Chavous, T. M., Rivas-Drake, D., Smalls, C., Griffin, T., & Cogburn, C. (2008). Gender matters, too: The influences of school racial discrimination and racial identity on academic engagement outcomes among African American adolescents. *Developmental Psychology, 44*(3), 637–654.

Chen, X. (2011). Culture, peer relationships, and human development. In L. A. Jensen (Ed.), *Bridging cultural and developmental approaches to psychology* (pp. 92–111). New York, NY: Oxford University Press.

Chen, X. (2016). Socioemotional Development across Cultures. In Minnesota Symposium on Child Psychology, Volume 38: *Culture and Developmental Systems.* Hoboken, NJ: John Wiley & Sons.

Chen, X., Rubin, K. H., & Li, Z. Y. (1995). Social functioning and adjustment in Chinese children: A longitudinal study. *Developmental Psychology, 31*, 531.

Chen, X., Cen, G., Li, D., & He, Y. (2005). Social functioning and adjustment in Chinese children: The imprint of historical time. *Child Development, 76*, 182–195.

Chen, X., Li, D., Li, Z. Y., Li, B. S., & Liu, M. (2000). Sociable and prosocial dimensions of social competence in Chinese children: Common and unique contributions to social, academic, and psychological adjustment. *Developmental Psychology*, 36, 302–314.

Chen, X., Tyler, K. A., Whitbeck, L. B., & Hoyt, D. R. (2004). Early sexual abuse, street adversity, and drug use among female homeless and runaway adolescents in the Midwest. *Journal of Drug Issues, 34*, 1–21.

Chen, X., Wang, L., & DeSouza, A. (2007). Temperament, socioemotional functioning, and peer relationships in Chinese and North American children. In X. Chen, D. C. French, & B. H. Schneider (Eds.), *Peer relationships in cultural context* (pp. 123–146). New York, NY: Cambridge University Press.

Cherlin, A. J., Burton, L. M., Tera, R., & Purvin, D. M. (2004). The influence of physical and sexual abuse on marriage and cohabitation. *American Sociological Review, 69*, 768–789.

Chess, S., & Thomas, A. (1984). *Origins and evolution of behavior disorders*. New York, NY: Brunner/Mazel.

Cheung, A. H., Emslie, G. J., & Mayes, T. (2005). Review of the efficacy and safety of antidepressants in youth depression. *Journal of Child Psychology & Psychiatry, 46*, 735–754.

Chi, M. T. (1978). Knowledge structures and memory development. In R. S. Siegler (Ed.), *Children's thinking: What develops?* (pp. 73–96). Hillsdale, NJ: Erlbaum.

Chi, M. T. H., Glaser, R., & Rees, E. (1982). Expertise in problem solving. In R. J. Sternberg (Ed.), *Advances in the psychology of human intelligence* (pp. 7–75). Hillsdale, NJ: Erlbaum.

Chibber, R., El-saleh, E., & El harmi, J. (2011). Female circumcision: Obstetrical and psychological sequelae continues unabated in the 21st century. *Journal of Maternal-Fetal and Neonatal Medicine, 24*(6), 833–836.

Child Health USA. (2014). Preterm birth and low birth weight. Retrieved from https://mchb.hrsa.gov/chusa14/health-status-behaviors/infants/preterm-birth-low-birth-weight.html

Child Trends. (2014). *Low and very low birth weight infants*. Child Trends Data Bank. Retrieved from http://www.childtrends.org/?indicators=low-and-very-low-birth-weight-infants

Child Trends. (2014, September). *Religiosity among youth: Indicators on children and youth*. Retrieved from http://www.childtrends.org/wp-content/uploads/2012/05/35_Religiosity.pdf

Child Welfare Information Gateway. (2013). *Foster care statistics*. Retrieved from https://www.childwelfare.gov/pubs/factsheets/foster.pdf#page=1&view=Key Findings

Children and AIDS. (2016). *Situation: What we know on children, adolescents, and AIDS*. Retrieved from http://www.childrenandaids.org/situation

Chiñas, B. (1992). *The Isthmus Zapotecs: A matrifocal culture of Mexico*. New York, NY: Harcourt Brace Jovanovich College Publishers.

Chisholm, L., & Hurrelmann, K. (1995). Adolescence in modern Europe: Pluralized transition patterns and their implications for personal and social risks. *Journal of Adolescence, 18*, 129–158.

Cho, G. J., Park, H. T., Shin, J. H., Hur, J. Y., Kim, Y. T., Kim, S. H., … Kim, T. (2010). Age at menarche in a Korean population: Secular trends and influencing factors. *European Journal of Pediatrics, 169*(1), 89–94. doi:10.1007/s00431-009-0993-1

Chomsky, N. (1957). *Syntactic structures*. The Hague, Netherlands: Mouton.

Chomsky, N. (1969). *Aspects of the theory of syntax*. Cambridge, MA: MIT Press.

Chouinard, M. M. (2007). Children's questions: A mechanism for cognitive development. *Monographs of the Society for Research in Child Development, 72*(1), vii–ix, 1–112.

Christiansen, M., & Dale, R. (2001). *Integrating distributional, prosodic and phonological information in a connectionist model of language acquisition*. Carbondale, IL: Southern Illinois University.

Chronicle of Higher Education. (2005). Census data show value of a college education. Retrieved April 14, 2005, from http://chronicle.com/daily/2005/03/2005032903n.htm

Chuang, M. E., Lamb, C. P., & Hwang, C. P. (2004). Internal reliability, temporal stability, and correlates of individual differences in parental involvement: A 15-year longitudinal study in Sweden. In R. D. Day & M. E. Lamb (Eds.), *Conceptualizing and measuring father involvement* (pp. 129–148). Mahwah, NJ: Erlbaum.

Cicirelli, V. G. (2013). *Sibling relationships across the life span*. Berlin, Germany: Springer Science & Business Media.

Cillessen, A. H. N., & Mayeux, L. (2004). From censure to reinforcement: Developmental changes in the association between aggression and social status. *Child Development, 75*, 147–163.

Cimpian, A., Arce, H. M. C., Markman, E. M., & Dweck, C. S. (2007). Subtle linguistic cues affect children's motivation. *Psychological Science, 18*, 314–316.

Cingel, D. P., & Krcmar, M. (2014). Understanding the experience of imaginary audience in a social media environment: Implications for adolescent development. *Journal of Media Psychology: Theories, Methods, and Applications, 26*, 155.

Cipriano, E. A., & Stifter, C. A. (2010). Predicting preschool effortful control from toddler temperament and parenting behaviour. *Journal of Applied Developmental Psychology, 31*, 221–230.

Clapp, J. D., Johnson, M., Voas, R. B., Lange, J. E., Shillington, A., & Russell, C. (2005). Reducing DUI among US college students: Results of an environmental prevention trial. *Addiction, 100*(3), 327–334.

Clark, J. J. (2010). Life as a source of theory: Erik Erikson's contributions, boundaries, and marginalities. In T. W. Miller (Ed.), *Handbook of stressful transitions across the lifespan* (pp. 59–83). New York, NY: Springer.

Clark, K. B., & Clark, M. P. (1947). Racial identification and preference in Negro children. *Readings in Social Psychology*, 602–611.

Clarke-Stewart, A., & Brentano, C. (2006). *Divorce: Causes and consequences*. New Haven, CT: Yale University Press.

Clarke-Stewart, K., & Allhusen, V. (2002). Nonparental caregiving. In M. Bornstein (Ed.), *Handbook of parenting: Vol. 3: Being and becoming a parent* (2nd ed., pp. 215–252). Mahwah, NJ: Lawrence Erlbaum Associates.

Class, Q. A., Lichtenstein, P., Långström, N., & D'Onofrio, B. M. (2011). Timing of prenatal maternal exposure to severe life events and adverse pregnancy outcomes: A population study of 2.6 million pregnancies. *Psychosomatic Medicine, 73*(3), 234–241. doi:10.1097/PSY.0b013e31820a62ce

Claxton, S. E., & van Dulmen, M. H. (2015). Casual sexual relationships and experiences. In J. J. Arnett (Ed.), *Oxford handbook of emerging adulthood* (pp. 245–261). New York, NY: Oxford University Press.

Clay, E. C., & Seehusen, D. A. (2004). A review of postpartum depression for the primary care physician. *Southern Medical Journal, 97*(2), 157–161. doi:10.1097/01.SMJ.0000091029.34773.33

Cline, T., Crafter, S., O'Dell, L., & de Abreau, G. (2011). Young people's representations of language brokering. *Journal of Multilingual and Multicultural Development, 32*, 207–220. doi:10.1080/01434632.2011.558901

CNN Tech. (2017). Facebook is closing in on 2 billion users. Retrieved from http://money.cnn.com/2017/02/01/technology/facebook-earnings/

Coghill, D., Spiel, G., Baldursson, G., Döpfner, M., Lorenzo, M. J., Ralston, S. J., … ADORE Study Group. (2006). Which factors impact on clinician-rated impairment in children with ADHD? *European Child & Adolescent Psychiatry, 15*(Suppl. 1), I30–I37.

Cohen, D., Gerardin, P., Mazet, P., Purper-Ouakil, D., & Flament, M. F. (2004). Pharmacological treatment of adolescent major depression. *Journal of Child and Adolescent Psychopharmacology, 14*(1), 19–31.

Cohen, J. (1988). *Statistical power analysis for the behavioral sciences*. Hillsdale. NJ: Lawrence Erlbaum Associates.

Cohn, D. (1999, November 24). Parents prize less a child's obedience. *Washington Post*, p. A8.

Cohn, J. F., & Tronick, E. Z. (1983). Three-month-old infants' reaction to stimulated maternal depression. *Child Development, 23*, 185–193.

Coie, J. (2004). The impact of negative social experiences on the development of antisocial behavior. In J. B. Kupersmidt & K. A. Dodge (Eds.), *Children's peer relations: From the development to intervention* (pp. 243–267). Washington, DC: American Psychological Association.

Colby, A., & Damon, W. (1992). *Some do care: Contemporary lives of moral commitment*. New York, NY: Free Press.

Colby, A., & Kohlberg, L. (1987). *The measurement of moral judgment*. New York, NY: Cambridge University Press.

Colby, A., Kohlberg, L., Gibbs, J., & Lieberman, M. (1983). A longitudinal study of moral judgment. *Monographs of the Society for Research in Child Development, 48*(1–2), 1–96.

Cole, A., & Kerns, K. A. (2001). Perceptions of sibling qualities and activities in early adolescents. *Journal of Early Adolescence, 21*, 204–226.

Cole, E. R. (2009). Intersectionality and research in psychology. *American Psychologist, 64*, 170.

Cole, M. (1996). *Cultural psychology: A once and future discipline*. Cambridge, MA: Harvard University Press.

Cole, P. M., Teti, L. O., & Zahn-Waxler, C. (2003). Mutual emotion regulation and the stability of conduct problems between preschool and early school age. *Development and Psychopathology, 15*, 1–18.

Coleman, J., & Hoffer, T. (1987). *Public and private high schools: The impact of communities*. New York, NY: Basic Books.

Coleman, J., Hoffer, T., & Kilgore, S. (1982). *High school achievement: Public, Catholic and other private schools compared*. New York, NY: Basic Books.

Coleman, M., Ganong, L., & Fine, M. (2000). Reinvestigating remarriage: Another decade of progress. *Journal of Marriage and the Family, 62*, 1288–1307.

Coll, C. G., Lamberty, G., Jenkins, R., McAdoo, H. P., Crnic, K., Wasik, B. H., & Garcia, H. V. (1996). An integrative model for the study of developmental competencies in minority children. *Child Development*, 1891–1914. doi:http://www.jstor.org/stable/1131600

Collier-Baker, E., & Suddendorf, T. (2006). Do chimpanzees and 2-year-old children understand double invisible displacement? *Journal of Comparative Psychology, 120*, 89–97.

Collins, W. A., & Hartup, W. W. (2013). History of research in developmental psychology. In Zelazo, P. D. (Ed.), *The Oxford handbook of developmental psychology: Volume 1: Body and mind* (pp. 13–34). New York, NY: Oxford University Press.

Collins, W. A., & Laursen, B. (2004). Parent–adolescent relationships and influences. In R. M. Lerner & L. Steinberg (Eds.), *Handbook of adolescent psychology* (2nd ed., pp. 331–361).

Collins, W. A., Maccoby, E. E., Steinberg, L., Hetherington, E. M., & Bornstein, M. H. (2000). Contemporary research on parenting: The case for nature and nurture. *American Psychologist, 55*, 218–232.

Collins, W. A., Madsen, S. D., & Susman-Stillman, A. (2002). Parenting during middle childhood. In M. H. Bornstein (Ed.), *Handbook of parenting: Vol. 1* (2nd ed., pp. 73–101). Mahwah, NJ: Erlbaum.

Colombo, J., & Mitchell, D. W. (2009). Infant visual habituation. *Neurobiology of Learning and Memory, 92*, 225–234.

Colucci, E., & Martin, G. (2007). Ethnocultural aspects of suicide in young people: A systematic literature review. Part 1: Rates and methods of youth suicide. *Suicide and Life-Threatening Behavior, 37*(2), 197–221.

Combs-Ronto, L. A., Olson, S. L., Lunkenheimer, E. S., & Sameroff, A. J. (2009). Interactions between maternal parenting and children's early disruptive behaviour: Bidirectional associations across the transition from preschool to school entry. *Journal of Abnormal Child Psychology, 37*, 1151–1163.

Common Sense Media. (2012). Teens on social media: Many benefits to digital life, but downsides, too. Retrieved from https://www.commonsensemedia.org/about-us/news/press-releases/teens-on-social-media-many-benefits-to-digital-life-but-downsides-too

Compas, B. E., Ey, S., & Grant, K. E. (1993). Taxonomy, assessment, and diagnosis of depression during adolescence. *Psychological Bulletin, 114*, 323–344.

Conboy, B. T., & Kuhl, P. K. (2011). Impact of second-language experience in infancy: Brain measures of first- and second-language speech perception. *Developmental Science, 14*(2), 242–248. doi:10.1111/j.1467-7687.2010.00973.x

Condon, R. (1990). The rise of adolescence: Change and life stage dilemmas in the central Canadian arctic. *Human Organization, 49*(3), 266–279.

Condon, R. G. (1988). *Inuit youth: Growth and change in the Canadian Arctic*. New Brunswick, NJ: Rutgers University Press.

Condon, R. G. (1995). The rise of the leisure class: Adolescence and recreational acculturation in the Canadian Arctic. *Ethos, 23*, 47–68.

Conduct Problem Prevention Research Group. (2010). The effects of a multiyear universal social–emotional learning program: The role of student and school characteristics. *Journal of Consulting and Clinical Psychology, 78*, 156–168.

Conklin, H. M., Luciana, M., Hooper, C. J., & Yarger, R. S. (2007). Working memory performance in typically developing children and adolescents: Behavioral evidence of protracted frontal lobe development. *Developmental Neuropsychology, 31*(1), 103–128.

Connolly, J., & Goldberg, A. (1999). Romantic relationships in adolescence: The role of friends and peers in their emergence and development. In W. Furman, B. B. Brown, & C. Feiring (Eds.), The development of romantic relationships in adolescence (pp. 266–290). New York: Cambridge University Press.

Connolly, J., & McIsaac, C. (2011). Romantic relationships in adolescence. In M. K. Underwood & J. H. Rosen (Eds.), *Social development: Relationships in infancy, childhood, and adolescence* (pp. 180–206). New York, NY: Guilford.

Conway, C. C., Rancourt, D., Adelman, C. B., Burk, W. J., & Prinstein, M. J. (2011). Depression socialization within friendship groups at the transition to adolescence: The roles of gender and group centrality as moderators of peer influence. *Journal of Abnormal Psychology, 120*(4), 857–867.

Cook, M., & Birch, R. (1984). Infant perception of the shapes of tilted plane forms. *Infant Behavior and Development, 7*(4), 389–402. doi:10.1016/S0163-6383(84)80001-6

Copen, C., & Silverstein, M. (2007). The transmission of religious beliefs across generations: Do grandparents matter? *Journal of Comparative Family Studies, 38*(4), 497–510.

Coplan, R. J., Prakash, K., O'Neil, K., & Arner, M. (2004). Do you "want" to play? Distinguishing between conflicted shyness and social disinterest in early childhood. *Developmental Psychology, 40*, 244–258.

Core Institute. (2013). Executive summary, Core Alcohol and Drug Survey-Long Form. Retrieved from http://core.siu.edu/_common/documents/report0911.pdf

Cornelius, M. D., Day, N. L., De Genna, N. M., Goldschmidt, L., Leech, S. L., & Willford, J. A. (2011). Effects of prenatal cigarette smoke exposure on neurobehavioral outcomes in 10-year-old children of adolescent mothers. *Neurotoxicology and Teratology, 33*, 137–144.

Corporation for National and Community Service. (2008). Still serving: Measuring the impact of AmeriCorps on alumni. Retrieved from https://www.nationalservice.gov/pdf/08_0513_longstudy_executive.pdf

Corporation for National and Community Service, Office of Research and Policy Development. (2007). *The health benefits of volunteering: A review of recent research.* Washington, DC: Author.

Cosminsky, S. (2003). Cross-cultural perspectives on midwifery. In L. Dundes (Ed.), *The manner born: Birth rites in cross-cultural perspective* (pp. 69–84). Walnut Creek, CA: AltaMira Press.

Costa, P., Jr., Terracciano, A., & McCrae, R. R. (2001). Gender differences in personality traits across cultures: Robust and surprising findings. *Journal of Personality and Social Psychology, 81*(2), 322. doi:http://dx.doi.org/10.1037/0022-3514.81.2.322

Costello, D. M., Swendsen, J., Rose, J. S., & Dierker, L. C. (2008). Risk and protective factors associated with trajectories of depressed mood from adolescence to early adulthood. *Journal of Consulting and Clinical Psychology, 76*(2), 173–183.

Cote, J. (2006). Emerging adulthood as an institutionalized moratorium: Risks and benefits to identity formation. In J. J. Arnett & J. L. Tanner (Eds.), *Emerging adults in America: Coming of age in the 21st century* (pp. 85–116). Washington, DC: American Psychological Association Press.

Cotter, D. A, Hermsen, J. M., & Vanneman, R. (2014). Brief: *Back on track? The stall and rebound in support of women's new roles in work and politics*, 1977–2012. Paper presented at Council on Contemporary Families Gender Rebound Symposium, July, Miami.

Cotton, J. N., Edwards, C. P., Zhao, W., & Gelabert, J. M. (2007). Nurturing care for China's orphaned children. *Young Children, 62*(6), 58–62. doi:http://journal.naeyc.org/btj/200711/pdf/BTJEdwards.pdf

Coughlin, C. R. (2009). Prenatal choices: Genetic counseling for variable genetic diseases. In V. Ravitsky, A. Fiester, & A. L. Caplan (Eds.), *The Penn Center guide to bioethics* (pp. 415–424). New York, NY: Springer.

Courage, M., & Cowan, N. (Eds.). (2009). *The development of memory in infancy and childhood* (2nd ed.). New York, NY: Psychology Press.

Courage, M. L., Howe, M. L., & Squires, S. E. (2004). Individual differences in 3.5 month olds' visual attention: What do they predict at 1 year? *Infant Behavior and Development, 127*, 19–30.

Coyle, T. R., & Bjorklund, D. F. (1997). Age difference in, and consequences of, multiple and variable-strategy use on a multitrial sort-recall task. *Developmental Psychology, 33*, 372–380.

Coyne, S. (2006). Violence, longitudinal studies. In J. J. Arnett (Ed.), *Encyclopedia of children, adolescents, and the media* (pp. 859–860). Thousand Oaks, CA: Sage.

Coyne, S. M. (2016). Effects of viewing relational aggression on television on aggressive behavior in adolescents: A three-year longitudinal study. *Developmental Psychology, 52*, 284.

Coyne, S. M., & Archer, J. (2005). The relationship between indirect and physical aggression on television and in real life. *Social Development, 14*, 324–338.

Coyne, S.M., Padilla-Walker, L.M., & Howard, E. (2015). Media uses in emerging adulthood. In J.J. Arnett (Ed.), *Oxford handbook of emerging adulthood*. New York, NY: Oxford University Press.

Cozby, P. C., & Bates, S. C. (2015). *Methods in behavioral research*. New York, NY: McGraw-Hill Education.

Cragg, A., Taylor, C., & Toombs, B. (2007). *Video games: Research to improve understanding of what players enjoy about video games, and to explain their preferences for particular games.* London, UK: British Board of Film Classification. Retrieved from http://www.bbfc.co.uk

Craig, J. M., & Piquero, A. R. (2014). Crime and punishment in emerging adulthood. In J. J. Arnett (Ed.), *Oxford handbook of emerging adulthood* (pp. 543–558). New York, NY: Oxford University Press.

Craig Rushing, S., & Stephens, D. (2011). Use of media technologies by Native American teens and young adults in the Pacific Northwest: Exploring their utilitiy for designing culturally appropriate technology-based health interventions. *Journal of Primary Prevention, 32*, 135–145.

Crain, W. (2000). *Theories of development: Concepts and applications.* Upper Saddle River, NJ: Prentice Hall.

Crawford, C., & Krebs, D. (2008). *Foundations of evolutionary psychology*. New York, NY: Lawrence Erlbaum.

Creusere, M. A. (1999). Theories of adults' understanding and use of irony and sarcasm: Applications to and evidence from research with children. *Developmental Review, 19*, 213–262.

Crick, N. R., Ostrov, J. M., Burr, J. E., Cullerton-Sen, C., Jansen-Yeh, E., & Ralston, P. (2006). A longitudinal study of relational and physical aggression in preschool. *Journal of Applied Developmental Psychology, 27*, 254–268.

Crncec, R., Matthey, S., & Nemeth, D. (2010). Infant sleep problems and emotional health: A review of two behavioural approaches. *Journal of Reproductive and Infant Psychology, 28*, 44–54.

Cross, S. E., & Gore, J. S. (2003). Cultural models of the self. In E. S. Cross, S. J. Gore, & R. M. Leary (Eds.), *Handbook of self and identity* (pp. 536–564). New York, NY: Guilford Press.

Crouter, A. C., Manke, B. A., & McHale, S. M. (1995). The family context of gender intensification in early adolescence. *Child Development, 66*, 317–329.

Crouter, A. C., & McHale, S. M. (2005). The long arm of the job revisited: Parenting in dual-earner families. In T. Luster & L. Okagaki (Eds.), *Parenting: An ecological perspective* (2nd ed., pp. 275–296). Mahwah, NJ: Lawrence Erlbaum.

Crow, J. F. (2003). There's something curious about parental–age effects. *Science, 301*, 606–607.

Crowther, M., & Rodriguez, R. (2003). A stress and coping model of custodial grandparenting among African Americans. In B. Hayslip & I. Patrick (Eds.), *Working with custodial grandparents* (pp. 145–162). New York, NY: Springer.

Crum, W. (2010). Foster parent parenting characteristics that lead to increased placement stability or disruption. *Children and Youth Services Review, 32*, 185–190.

Crumbley, D. H. (2006). "Power in the blood": Menstrual taboos and women's power in an African Instituted Church. In R. M. Griffith & B. D. Savage, *Women and religion in the African diaspora: Knowledge, power, and performance* (pp. 81–97). Baltimore, MD: Johns Hopkins University Press.

Csibra, G., Davis, G., Spratling, M. W., & Johnson, M. H. (2000). Gamma oscillations and object processing in the infant brain. *Science, 290*, 1582–1585.

Csikszentmihalyi, M., & Larson, R. W. (1984). *Being adolescent: Conflict and growth in the teenage years.* New York, NY: Basic Books.

Cuevas, K., & Bell, M. A. (2014). Infant attention and early childhood executive function. *Child Development, 85*, 397–404. doi:10.1111/cdev.12126

Cui, Z., Huxley, R., Wu, Y., & Dibley, M. J. (2010) Temporal trends in overweight and obesity of children and adolescents from nine Provinces in China from 1991–2006. *International Journal of Pediatric Obesity, 5*, 365–374.

Cummings, E. M., George, M. R., & Kouros, C. D. (2010). Emotional development. In I. B. Weiner & W. B. Craighead (Eds.), *Corsini encyclopedia of psychology* (pp. 1–2). New York, NY: Wiley.

Cummings, E. M., Merrilees, C. E., Schermerhorn, A. C., Goeke-Morey, M. C., Shirlow, P., & Cairns, E. (2012). Political violence and child adjustment: Longitudinal tests of sectarian antisocial behavior, family conflict, and insecurity as explanatory pathways. *Child Development, 83*(2), 461–468. doi:10.1111/j.1467-8624.2011.01720.x

Cummings, K. M. (2002). Marketing to America's youth: Evidence from corporate documents. *Tobacco Control, 11*(Suppl. 1), i5–i17.

Cunningham, M. (2001). Parental influences on the gendered division of housework. *American Sociological Review, 66*, 184–203. doi:http://www.jstor.org/stable/2657414

Curran, K., DuCette, J., Eisenstein, J., & Hyman, I. A. (2001, August). *Statistical analysis of the cross-cultural data: The third year.* Paper presented at the meeting of the American Psychological Association, San Francisco, CA.

Currie, D. (1999). *Girl talk: Adolescent magazines and their readers.* Toronto, Canada: University of Toronto Press.

Currie, J., & Walker, R. (2011). Traffic congestion and infant health: Evidence from E-ZPass. *American Economic Journal: Applied Economics, 3*, 65–90.

Cyr, M., Wright, J., McDuff, P., & Perron, A. (2002). Intrafamilial sexual abuse: Brother-sister incest does not differ from father-daughter and stepfather-stepdaughter incest. *Child Abuse & Neglect, 26*, 957–973.

Daddis, C., & Smetana, J. (2005). Middle-class African American families' expectations for adolescents' behavioural autonomy. *International Journal of Behavioral Development, 29*, 371–381.

Dahl, A. (2015). The developing social context of infant helping in two US samples. *Child Development, 86*(4), 1080–1093. doi:10.1111/cdev.12361

Dale, P. S., & Goodman, J. C. (2005). Commonality and individual differences in vocabulary growth. In M. Tomasello & D. I. Slobin (Eds.), *Beyond nature–nurture: Essays in honor of Elizabeth Bates* (pp. 41–78). Mahwah, NJ: Erlbaum.

Damon, W. (1983). *Social and personality development.* New York, NY: Norton.

Damon, W., & Malin, H. (in press). The development of purpose: An international perspective. In L. A. Jensen (Ed.). *Oxford handbook of moral development: An interdisciplinary perspective.* New York, NY: Oxford University Press.

Daniels, H. (2007). Pedagogy. In H. Daniels, J. Wertsch, & M. Cole (Eds.), *The Cambridge companion to Vygotsky* (pp. 307–331). New York, NY: Cambridge University Press.

Daniels, H., Cole, M., & Wertsch, J. V. (Eds.). (2007). *The Cambridge companion to Vygotsky.* London, UK: Cambridge University Press.

Daniels, P., Godfrey, F. N., & Mayberry, R. (2006). Barriers to prenatal care among Black women of low socioeconomic status. *American Journal of Health Behavior, 30*, 188–198.

Darwin, C. (1872). *The expression of the emotions in man and animals.* New York, NY: D. Appleton.

Darwin, C. (1907) *On the origin of species.* New York: The Collier Press.

Dasen, P., Inhelder, B., Lavalle, M., & Retschitzki, J. (1978). *Naissance de l'intelligence chez l'enfant Baoule de Cote d'Ivorie.* Berne, Germany: Hans Huber.

Davenport, M. (1979). *Mozart.* New York, NY: Avon.

David, B., Grace, D., & Ryan, M. K. (2004). The gender wars: A self-categorization perspective on the development of gender identity. In M. Bennett & S. Fabio (Eds.), *The development of the social self* (pp. 135–157). East Sussex, England: Psychology Press.

Davies, P. T., Harold, G. T., Goeke-Morey, M. C., & Cummings, E. M. (2002). Child emotional security and interparental conflict. *Monography of the Society for Research in Child Development, 67*(3), i–v, vii–viii, 1–115.

Davis, D. W. (2003). Cognitive outcomes in school-age children born prematurely. *Neonatal Network, 22*, 27–38.

Davis, K. (2010). Coming of age online: The developmental underpinnings of girls' blogs. *Journal of Adolescent Research, 25*, 145–171.

Davis, K. (2012). Friendship 2.0: Adolescents' experiences of belonging and self-disclosure online. *Journal of Adolescence, 35*, 1527–1536.

Davis, K. F., Parker, K. P., & Montgomery, G. L. (2004). Sleep in infants and young children. Part I: Normal sleep. *Journal of Pediatric Health Care, 18*, 65–71.

Davis, S., & Davis, D. (2012). Morocco. In J. J. Arnett (Ed.), *Adolescent Psychology Around the World* (pp. 47–60). New York, NY: Taylor & Francis.

Davis, S. S., & Davis, D. A. (1989). *Adolescence in a Moroccan town.* New Brunswick, NJ: Rutgers.

Davis, S. S., & Davis, D. A. (1995). "The mosque and the satellite": Media and adolescence in a Moroccan town. *Journal of Youth & Adolescence, 24*, 577–594.

Davis, S. S., & Davis, D. A. (2007). Morocco. In J. J. Arnett, R. Ahmed, B. Nsamenang, T. S. Saraswathi, & R. Silbereisen (Eds.), *International encyclopedia of adolescence* (pp. 645–655). New York, NY: Routledge.

Dawson, G., Meltzoff, A. N., Osterling, J., Rinaldi, J., & Brown, E. (1998). Children with autism fail to orient to naturally occurring social stimuli. *Journal of Autism & Developmental Disorders, 28*, 479–485.

de Abreu, G., & Lambert, H. (2003). *The education of Portuguese students in England and Channel Island schools.* Final report of research project commissioned by Ministério de Educacão, Portugal.

de Guzman, M. R. T., Carlo, G., & Edwards, C. P. (2008). Prosocial behaviors in context: Examining the role of children's social companions. *International Journal of Behavioral Development, 32*(6), 522–530. doi:10.1177/0165025408095557

de Hoog, M. L., Kleinman, K. P., Gillman, M. W., Vrijkotte, T. G., van Eijsden, M., & Taveras, E. M. (2014). Racial/ethnic and immigrant differences in early childhood diet quality. *Public Health Nutrition, 17*(06), 1308–1317. doi:http://dx.doi.org/10.1017/S1368980013001183

de Joyce, H. S., & Feez, S. (2016). *Exploring literacies.* London, UK: Palgrave Macmillan.

De Ment, T. L., Buriel, R., & Villanueva, C. M. (2005). Children as language brokers: A narrative of the recollections of college students. In R. Hoosain & F. Salili (Eds.), *Language in multicultural education* (pp. 255–272). Charlotte, NC: Information Age.

de Villarreal, L. E. M., Arredondo, P., Hernández, R., & Villarreal, J. Z. (2006). Weekly administration of folic acid and epidemiology of neural tube defects. *Maternal and Child Health Journal, 10*, 397–401.

de Villiers, P. A., & de Villiers, J. G. (1978). *Language acquisition.* Cambridge, MA: Harvard University Press.

de Vonderweid, U., & Leonessa, M. (2009). Family centered neonatal care. *Early Human Development, 85*, S37–S38.

De Waal, F. (2009). *The age of empathy: Nature's lessons for a kinder society.* New York, NY: Three Rivers Press.

De Weerd, A. W., & van den Bossche, A. S. (2003). The development of sleep during the first months of life. *Sleep Medicine Reviews, 7*, 179–191.

DeCasper, A. J., & Spence, M. J. (1986). Prenatal maternal speech influences newborns' perception of speech sounds. *Infant Behavior and Development, 9*, 133–150.

Degener, J. L. (2010). Sometimes my mother does not understand, then I need to translate: Child and youth language brokering in Berlin-Neuköln (Germany). *mediAzioni, 10*, 346–367.

Degler, C. (1991). *In Search of Human Nature.* New York, NY: Oxford University Press.

DeHart, T., Pelham, B., & Tennen, H. (2006). What lies beneath: Parenting style and implicit self–esteem. *Journal of Experimental Social Psychology, 42*, 1–17.

Dekel, R., Peled, E., & Spiro, S. E. (2003). Shelters for houseless youth: A follow-up evaluation. *Journal of Adolescence, 26*, 201–212.

DeLoache, J., & Gottlieb, A. (2000). *A world of babies: Imagined childcare guides for seven societies.* New York, NY: Cambridge University Press.

DeLoache, J. S., Chiong, C., Sherman, K., Islam, N., Vanderborght, M., Troseth, G. L., . . . O'Doherty, K. (2010). Do babies learn from baby media? *Psychological Science, 21*, 1570–1574.

DeMeo, J. (2006). *Saharasia: The 4000 bce origins of child abuse, sex-repression, warfare and social violence, in the deserts of the old world* (Revised 2nd ed.). El Cerrito, CA: Natural Energy Works.

Demetriou, A., & Raftopoulos, A. (Eds.). (2004). *Cognitive developmental change: Theories, models and measurement.* New York, NY: Cambridge University Press.

Demorest, A., Meyer, C., Phelps, E., Gardner, H., & Winner, E. (1984). Words speak louder than actions: Understanding deliberately false remarks. *Child Development, 55*, 1527–1534.

Denner, J., & Dunbar, N. (2004). Negotiating femininity: Power and strategies of Mexican American girls. *Sex Roles, 50*, 301–314.

Denner, J., & Guzmán, B. L. (Eds.). (2006). *Latina girls: Voices of adolescent strength in the United States.* New York: New York University Press.

Dennis, C. L. (2004). Can we identify mothers at risk for postpartum depression in the immediate postpartum period using the Edinburgh Postnatal Depression Scale? *Journal of Affective Disorders, 78*, 163–169.

DeParle, J. (2010, June 27). A world on the move. *The New York Times*, pp. WK1, 4.

Deputy, N. P., Sharma, A. J., & Kim, S. Y. (November 6, 2015). Gestational weight gain—United States, 2012 and 2013. *Centers for Disease Control and Prevention: Morbidity and Mortality Weekly Report, 64*(43), 1215–1220. Retrieved from http://www.cdc.gov/mmwr/preview/mmwrhtml/mm6443a3.htm. doi:10.15585/mmwr.mm6443a3

Derom, C., Thiery, E., Vlientinck, R., Loos, R., & Derom, R. (1996). Handedness in twins according to zygosity and chorion type: A preliminary report. *Behavior Genetics, 26*, 407–408.

DeRose, L. M., & Brooks-Gunn, J. (2006). Transition into adolescence: The role of pubertal processes. In L. Balter & C. S. Tamis-LeMonda (Eds.), *Child psychology: A handbook of contemporary issues* (2nd ed., pp. 385–414). New York, NY: Psychology Press.

DeRosier, M. E., & Kupersmidt, J. B. (1991). Costa Rican children's perceptions of their social networks. *Developmental Psychology, 27*(4), 656–662. doi:http://dx.doi.org/10.1037/0012-1649.27.4.656

DeRosier, M. E., & Thomas, J. M. (2003). Strengthening sociometric prediction: Scientific advances in the assessment of children's peer relations. *Child Development, 75*, 1379–1392.

Dhariwal, A., & Connolly, J. (2013). Romantic experiences of homeland and diaspora South Asian youth: Westernizing processes of media and friends. *Journal of Research on Adolescence, 23*(1), 45–56. doi:10.1111/j.1532-7795.2012.00803.x

Diamond, A. (2004). Normal development of prefrontal cortex from birth to young adulthood: Cognitive functions, anatomy, and biochemistry. In D. T. Stuff & R. T. Knight (Eds.), *Principles of frontal lobe function* (pp. 466–503). New York, NY: Oxford University Press.

Diamond, A., & Goldman-Rakic, P. S. (1989). Comparison of human infants and rhesus monkeys on Piaget's A-not-B task: Evidence for dependence on dorsolateral prefrontal cortex. *Experimental Brain Research, 74*, 24–40.

Diamond, J. (1992). *The third chimpanzee: The evolution and future of the human animal.* New York, NY: Harper Perennial.

Diamond, L. M., Bonner, S. B., & Dickenson, J. (2015). The development of sexuality. In R. M. Lerner (Series Ed.), M. E. Lamb (Vol. Ed.), *Handbook of child psychology and developmental science, Vol. 3: Socioemotional processes* (7th ed., pp. 888–931). New York, NY: Wiley.

Dick, F., Dronkers, N. F., Pizzamiglio, L., Saygin, A. P., Small, S. L., & Wilson, S. (2004). Language and the brain. In M. Tomasello & D. I. Slobin (Eds.), *Beyond nature–nurture: Essays in honor of Elizabeth Bates* (pp. 237–260). Mahwah, NH: Erlbaum.

Dickey, M. (2005) Engaging by design: How engagement strategies in popular computer and video games can inform instructional design. *Educational Technology Research and Development, 53*, 67–83

Dickinson, D. K., & Porche, M. V. (2011). Relation between language experiences in preschool classrooms and children's kindergarten and fourth-grade language and reading abilities. *Child Development, 82*(3), 870–886. doi:10.1111/j.1467-7687.00140

Diener, E., Tay, L., & Myers, D. G. (2011). The religion paradox: If religion makes people happy, why are so many dropping out? *Journal of Personality and Social Psychology, 101*, 1278.

Diener, M. (2000). Gifts from gods: A Balinese guide to early child rearing. In J. DeLoache & A. Gottlieb (Eds.), *A world of babies: Imagined childcare guides for seven societies* (pp. 91–116). New York, NY: Cambridge University Press.

Diers, J. (2013). Why the world needs to get serious about adolescents: A view from UNICEF. *Journal of Research on Adolescence, 23*(2), 214–222. doi:10.1111/jora.12042

Dieter, J. N., Field, T., Hernandez-Reif, M., Emory, E. K., & Redzepi, M. (2003). Stable preterm infants gain more weight and sleep less after five days of massage therapy. *Journal of Pediatric Psychology, 28*(6), 403–411.

Dijkstra, J. K., Cillessen, A. H., & Borch, C. (2013). Popularity and adolescent friendship networks: Selection and influence dynamics. *Developmental Psychology, 49*(7), 1242.

Dijkstra, J. K., Lindenberg, S., & Veenstra, R. (2008). Beyond the class norm: Bullying behavior of popular adolescents and its relation to peer acceptance and rejection. *Journal of Abnormal Child Psychology, 36*(8), 1289–1299.

Dimitry, L. (2012). A systematic review on the mental health of children and adolescents in areas of armed conflict in the Middle East. *Child: Care, Health and Development, 38*(2), 153–161. doi:10.1111/j.1365-2214.2011.01246.x

DiPietro, J. A., Hilton, S. C., Hawkins, M., Costigan, K. A., & Pressman, E. K. (2002). Maternal stress and affect influence fetal neurobehavioral development. *Developmental psychology, 38*, 659.

Dishion, T. J., & Dodge, K. A. (2005). Peer contagion in interventions for children and adolescents: Moving towards an understanding of the ecology and dynamics of change. *Journal of Abnormal Child Psychology, 33*, 395–400.

Dishion, T. J., McCord, J., & Poulin, F. (1999). When interventions harm: Groups and problem behavior. *American Psychologist, 54*, 755–764.

Dixon, W. E., Jr., Salley, B. J., & Clements, A. D. (2006). Temperament, distraction, and learning in toddlerhood. *Infant Behavior and Development, 29*(3), 342–357.

Dodge, K. A. (2007). The nature–nurture debate and public policy. In G. W. Ladd (Ed.), *Appraising the human developmental sciences: Essays in honor of Merrill-Palmer Quarterly* (pp. 262–271). Detroit, MI: Wayne State University Press.

Dodge, K. A. (2008). Framing public policy and prevention of chronic violence in American youths. *American Psychologist*, 63, 573–590.

Dodge, K. A., Coie, J. D., & Lynam, D. (2006). Aggression and antisocial behavior in youth. In W. Damon & R. Lerner (Eds.), & N. Eisenberg (Vol. Ed.), *Handbook of child psychology: Vol. 3. Social, emotional and personality development* (6th ed., pp. 719–788). New York, NY: Wiley.

Dodge, K. A., Lansford, J. E., Burks, V. S., Bates, J. E., Pettit, G. S., Fontaine, R. P., & Price, J. M. (2003). Peer rejection and social information-processing factors in the development of aggressive behavior problems in children. *Child Development, 74*, 374–393.

Doherty, I., & Landells, J. (2006). Literacy and numeracy. In J. Clegg & J. Ginsborg (Eds.), *Language and social disadvantage: Theory into practice* (pp. 44–58). Hoboken, NJ: John Wiley & Sons.

Dolphin, T., & Lanning, T. (Eds.). (2011). *Rethinking apprenticeships.* London, UK: Institute for Public Policy Research.

Domitrovich, C. E., Bradshaw, C. P., Greenberg, M. T., Embry, D., Poduska, J. M., & Ialongo, N. S. (2010). Integrated models of school-based prevention: Logic and theory. *Psychology in the Schools, 47*(1), 71–88. doi:10.1002/pits.20452

Domsch, H., Lohaus, A., & Thomas, H. (2010). Infant attention, heart rate, and looking time during habituation/dishabituation. *Infant Behavior & Development, 33*, 321–329.

Donaldson, D., Spirito, A., & Overholser, J. (2003). In A. Spirito & J. C. Overholser (Eds.), *Evaluating and treating adolescent suicide attempters: From research to practice* (pp. 295–321). San Diego, CA: Academic Press.

Donat, D. (2006). Reading their way: A balanced approach that increases achievement. *Reading & Writing Quarterly: Overcoming Learning Difficulties, 22*, 305–323.

Donnellan, M. B., Trzesniewski, K. H., Robins, R. W., Moffitt, T. E., & Caspi, A. (2005). Low self-esteem is related to aggression, antisocial behavior, and delinquency. *Psychological Science, 16*, 328–335.

D'Onofrio, B. M., Rickert, M. E., Frans, E., Kuja-Halkola, R., Almqvist, C., Sjölander, A., ... Lichtenstein, P. (2013). Paternal age at childbearing and offspring psychiatric and academic morbidity. *JAMA Psychiatry, 71*(4), 432–438. doi:10.1001/jamapsychiatry.2013.4525

Donovan, J., & Zucker, C. (2010, October). Autism's first child. *The Atlantic*, pp. 78–90.

Dorjee, T., Baig, N., & Ting-Toomey, S. (2013). A social ecological perspective on understanding "honor killing": An intercultural moral dilemma. *Journal of Intercultural Communication Research, 42*(1), 1–21.

Dornbusch, S. M., Ritter, P., Liederman, P., Roberts, D., & Fraleigh, M. (1987). The relation of parenting style to adolescent school performance. *Child Development, 58*, 1244–1257.

Dorner, L. M., Orellana, M. F., & Jiménez, R. (2008). "It's one of those things that you do to help the family": Language brokering and the development of immigrant adolescents. *Journal of Adolescent Research, 23*(5), 515–543. doi:10.1177/0743558408317563

Dorner, L. M., Orellana, M. F., & Li-Grining, C. P. (2007). "I helped my mom," and it helped me: Translating the skills of language brokers into improved standardized test scores. *American Journal of Education, 113*(3), 451–478. doi:10.1086/512740

Dörnyei, Z., & Csizér, K. (2002). Some dynamics of language attitudes and motivation: Results of a longitudinal nationwide survey. *Applied Linguistics, 23*, 421–462. doi:10.1093/applin/23.4.421

Douglass, C. B. (2005). *Barren states: The population "implosion" in Europe.* New York, NY: Berg.

Douglass, C. B. (2007). From duty to desire: Emerging adulthood in Europe and its consequences. *Child Development Perspectives, 1*, 101–108.

Doyle, L. W., Faber, B., Callanan, C., Ford, G. W., & Davis, N. M. (2004). Extremely low birth weight and body size in early adulthood. *Archives of Disorders in Childhood, 89*, 347–350.

Driessen, R., Leyendecker, B., Schölmerich, A., & Harwood, R. (2010). Everyday experiences of 18- to 36-month-old children from migrant families: The influence of host culture and migration experience. *Early Child Development and Care, 180*, 1143–1163.

DuBois, D., Felner, R., Brand, S., Phillip, R., & Lease, A. (1996). Early adolescent self-esteem: A developmental–ecological framework and assessment strategy. *Journal of Research on Adolescence, 6*, 543–579.

Due, P., Holstein, B. E., Lunch, J., Diderichsen, F., Gabhain, S. N., Scheidt, P., & Currie, C. (2005). The health behavior in school-aged children bullying working group. *European Journal of Public Health, 15*(2), 128–132.

Duke, L. (2002). Get real! Cultural relevance and resistance to the mediated feminine ideal. *Psychology & Marketing, 19*, 211–233.

Dumas, B., & Lighter, J. (1978). Is *slang* a word for linguists? *American Speech, 53*, 5–17.

Dunfield, K. A., & Kuhlmeier, V. A. (2013). Evidence for partner choice in toddlers: Considering the breadth of other-oriented behaviours. *Behavioral and Brain Sciences*, 36, 88–89.

Dunifon, R. (2013). The influence of grandparents on the lives of children and adolescents. *Child Development Perspectives, 7*(1), 55–60. doi:10.1111/cdep.12016

Dunn, J. (1988). *The beginnings of social understanding*. Cambridge, MA: Harvard University Press.

Dunn, J. (2002). The adjustment of children in stepfamilies: Lessons from community studies. *Child and Adolescent Mental Health, 7*, 154–161.

Dunn, J. (2004). Sibling relationships. In P. K. Smith & C. H. Hart (Eds.), *Handbook of childhood social development* (pp. 223–237). Malden, MA: Blackwell.

Dunn, J., Cheng, H., O'Connor, T. G., & Bridges, L. (2004). Children's perspectives on their relationships with their nonresident fathers: Influences, outcomes and implications. *Journal of Child Psychology and Psychiatry, 45*, 553–566.

Dunn, J., & Kendrick, C. (1982). *Siblings: Love, envy, and understanding*. London, UK: Grant McIntyre.

Dunn, J., & Munn, P. (1985). Becoming a family member: Family conflict and the development of social understanding in the second year. *Child Development, 56*, 480–492.

Dunn, M. G., & O'Brien, K. M. (2013). Work–family enrichment among dual-earner couples: Can work improve our family life? *Journal of Counseling Psychology, 60*(4), 634–640. doi:10.1037/a0033538

Dustmann, C., & Schoenberg, U. (2008). Why does the German apprenticeship system work? In K. U. Mayer & H. Solga (Eds.), *Skill information: Interdisciplinary and cross-national perspective* (pp. 85–108). New York, NY: Cambridge University Press.

Duthie, J. K., Nippold, M. A., Billow, J. L., & Mansfield, T. C. (2008). Mental imagery of concrete proverbs: A developmental study of children, adolescents and adults. *Applied Psycholinguistics, 29*(1), 151–173.

Dweck, C. (2013). Social development. In P. D. Zelazo (Ed.), *The Oxford handbook of developmental psychology: Volume 2: Self and other* (pp. 167–190). New York, NY: Oxford University Press.

Dworkin, J. B., & Larson, R. (2001). Age trends in the experience of family discord in single-mother families across adolescence. *Journal of Adolescence, 24*, 529–534.

Dyer, S., & Moneta, G. (2006). Frequency of parallel, associative and cooperative play in British children of different socioeconomic status. *Social Behavior and Personality, 34*, 587–592.

Dyson, J. (2010). Friendship in practice: Girls' work in the Indian Himalayas. *American Ethnologist, 37*, 482–498.

Eagly, A. H., & Crowley, M. (1986). Gender and helping behavior: A meta-analytic review of the social psychological literature. *Psychological Bulletin, 100*(3), 283. doi:http://dx.doi.org/10.1037/0033-2909.100.3.283

Eberhart-Phillips, J. E., Frederick, P. D., & Baron, R. C. (1993). Measles in pregnancy: A descriptive study of 58 cases. *Obstetrics and Gynecology, 82*, 797–801.

Ebstyne King, P., Clardy, C. E., & Ramos, J. S. (2014). Adolescent spiritual exemplars: Exploring spirituality in the lives of diverse youth. *Journal of Adolescent Research, 29*, 186–212.

Eckenrode, J., Zielinski, D., Smith, E., Marcynyszyn, L. A., Henderson, C. R., Jr., & Kitzman, H. (2001). Child maltreatment and the early onset of problem behaviors: Can a program of nurse home visitation break the link? *Development and Psychopathology, 13*, 873–890.

Eckert, P. (1989). *Jocks and burnouts: Social categories and identity in the high school*. New York, NY: Teachers College Press.

Eckert, P. (2004). Adolescent language. In E. Finegan & J. R. Rickford (Eds.), *Language in the USA: Themes for the twenty-first century* (pp. 361–374). Cambridge, UK: Cambridge University Press.

*The Economist*. (2017, January 21). Sex selection: Boy trouble.

Eder, D. (1995). *School talk: Gender and adolescent culture*. New Brunswick, NJ: Rutgers University Press.

Edmonds, L. (2011). Telegraphic speech. In J. Kreutzer, J. DeLuca, & B. Kaplan (Eds.), *Encyclopedia of clinical neuropsychology* (pp. 2477–2479). New York, NY: Springer.

Edwards, C. P. (2000). Children's play in cross-cultural perspective: A new look at the Six Cultures study. *Cross-Cultural Research: The Journal of Comparative Social Science, 34*, 318–338.

Edwards, C. P. (2005). Children's play in cross-cultural perspective: A new look at the "six cultures" study. In F. F. McMahon, D. E. Lytle, & B. Sutton-Smith (Eds.), *Play: An interdisciplinary synthesis* (pp. 81–96). Lanham, MD: University Press of America.

Edwards, C. P., Ren, L., & Brown, J. (2015). Early contexts of learning: Family and community socialization during infancy and toddlerhood. In L. A. Jensen (Ed.), *The Oxford handbook of human development and culture: An interdisciplinary perspective* (pp. 165–181). New York, NY: Oxford University Press.

Egeland, B., & Carlson, E. A. (2004). Attachment and psychopathology. In L. Atkinson & S. Goldberg (Eds.), *Attachment issues in psychopathology and intervention* (pp. 27–48). Mahwah, NJ: Erlbaum.

Eggermont, S. (2006). Television viewing and adolescents' judgment of sexual request scripts: A latent growth curve analysis in early and middle adolescence. *Sex Roles, 55*(7–8), 457–468.

Ehrenberg, H. M., Dierker, L., Milluzzi, C., & Mercer, B. M. (2003). Low maternal weight, failure to thrive in pregnancy, and adverse pregnancy outcomes. *American Journal of Obstetrics and Gynecology, 189*, 1726–1730.

Ehrenreich, B. (2010). *Witches, midwives, and nurses: A history of women healers*. New York, NY: Feminist Press.

Ehrhardt, A. A., Grisanti, G. C., & Meyer-Bahlburg, H. F. (1977). Prenatal exposure to medroxyprogesterone acetate (MPA) in girls. *Psychoneuroendocrinology, 2*(4), 391–398. doi:10.1016/0306-4530(77)90010-5

Ehrhardt, A. A., & Money, J. (1967). Progestin-induced hermaphroditism: IQ and psychosexual identity in a study of ten girls. *Journal of Sex Research, 3*(1), 83–100. doi:10.1080/00224496709550517

Eiden, R. D., & Reifman, A. (1996). Effects of Brazelton demonstrations on later parenting: A meta-analysis. *Journal of Pediatric Psychology, 21*, 857–868.

Eimas, P. D., Siqueland, E. R., Jusczyk, P., & Vigorito, J. (1971). Speech perception in infants. *Science, 171*(3968), 303–306. doi:10.1126/science.171.3968.303

Eisenberg, N., Castellani, V., Panerai, L., Eggum, N. D., Cohen, A. B., Pastorelli, C., & Caprara, G. V. (2011). Trajectories of religious coping from adolescence into early adulthood: Their form and relations to externalizing problems and prosocial behavior. *Journal of Personality, 79*(4), 841–873.

Eisenberg, N., Eggum, N. D., & Edwards, A. (2010). Empathy-related responding and moral development. In W. F. Arsenio & E. A. Lermerise (Eds.), *Emotions, aggression, and morality in children: Bridging development and psychopathology* (pp. 115–135). Washington, DC: American Psychological Association.

Eisenberg, N., & Fabes, R. A. (2006). Emotion regulation and children's socioemotional competence. In L. Balter & C. S. Tamis-LeMonda (Eds.), *Child psychology: A handbook of contemporary issues* (2nd ed., pp. 357–381). New York, NY: Psychology Press.

Eisenberg, N., Spinrad, T. L., & Eggum, N. D. (2010). Emotion-related self-regulation and its relation to children's maladjustment. *Annual review of clinical psychology, 6*, 495–525.

Eisenberg, N., & Valiente, C. (2004). Empathy-related responding: Moral, social and socialization correlates. In A. G. Miller (Ed.), *Social psychology of good and evil* (pp. 386–415). New York, NY: Guilford Press.

Ekman, P. (2003). *Emotions revealed*. New York, NY: Times Books.

Eldin, A. S. (2009). Female mutilation. In P. S. Chandra, H. Herrman, J. Fisher, M. Kastrup, U. Niaz, M. B. Rondón, & A. Okasha (Eds.), *Contemporary topics in women's mental health: Global perspectives in a changing society* (pp. 485–498). Hoboken, NJ: Wiley & Sons.

Elkind, D. (1967). Egocentrism in adolescence. *Child Development, 38*, 1025–1034.

Elkind, D. (1970). The origins of religion in the child. *Review of Religious Research, 12*, 35–42.

Elkind, D. (1978). Understanding the young adolescent. *Adolescence, 13*, 127–134.

Elkind, D. (1985). Egocentrism redux. *Developmental Review, 5*, 218–226.

Elliott, G. C., Cunningham, S. M., Linder, M., Colangelo, M., & Gross, M. (2005). Child physical abuse and self-perceived social isolation among adolescents. *Journal of Interpersonal Violence, 20*, 1663–1684.

Ellison, N. C., Steinfield, C., & Lampe, C. (2007). The benefits of Facebook "friends": Social capital and college students' use of online social network sites. *Journal of Computer-Mediated Communication, 12*(4), 1143–1168.

Else-Quest, N. M., & Grabe, S. (2012). The political is personal: Measurement and application of nation-level indicators of gender equity in psychological research. *Psychology of Women Quarterly, 36*(2), 131–144. doi:10.1177/0361684312441448

Else-Quest, N. M., Hyde, J. S., Goldsmith, H. H., & Van Hulle, C. A. (2006). Gender differences in temperament: A meta-analysis. *Psychological Bulletin*, 132, 33–72.

Ember, C. R., Ember, M., & Peregrine, P. N. (2011). *Anthropology* (13th ed.). New York, NY: Pearson.

Emery, R. E., Rowen, J., & Dinescu, D. (2014). New roles for family therapists in the courts: An overview with a focus on custody dispute resolution. *Family Process, 53*(3), 500–515. doi:10.1111/famp.12077

Emery, R. E., Sbarra, D., & Grover, T. (2005). Divorce mediation: Research and reflections. *Family Court Review, 43*, 22–37.

Emslie, G. J., Heiligenstein, J. H., & Wagner, K. D. (2002). Fluoxetine for acute treatment of depression in children and adolescents: A placebo-controlled randomized clinical trial. *Journal of the American Academy of Child & Adolescent Psychiatry, 41*, 1205–1214.

Englander, F., Terregrossa, R. A., & Wang, Z. (2010). Internet use among college students: Tool or toy? *Educational Review, 62*, 85–96.

Eppig, C., Fincher, C. L., & Thornhill, R. (2010). Parasite prevalence and the worldwide distribution of cognitive ability. *Proceedings of the Royal Society B, 277*, 3801–3808.

Epstein, J. (1983). Selecting friends in contrasting secondary school environments. In J. Epstein & N. Karweit (Eds.), *Friends in school* (pp. 73–92). New York, NY: Academic Press.

Ericsson, K. A. (1990). Peak performance and age: An examination of peak performance in sports. In P. Baltes & M. M. Baltes (Eds.), *Successful aging* (pp. 164–196). Cambridge, MA: Cambridge University Press.

Eriksen, B. A., & Eriksen, C. W. (1974). Effects of noise letters upon the identification of a target letter in a nonsearch task. *Perception & Psychophysics, 16*(1), 143–149. doi:10.3758/BF03203267

Erikson, E. H. (1950). *Childhood and society*. New York, NY: Norton.

Erikson, E. H. (1958). *Young man Luther*. New York, NY: Norton.

Erikson, E. H. (1959). Identity and the life cycle. Psychological Issues, 1, 1–171.

Erikson, E. H. (1968). *Identity: Youth and crisis*. New York, NY: Norton.

Eriksson, C., Hamberg, K., & Salander, P. (2007). Men's experiences of intense fear related to childbirth investigated in a Swedish qualitative study. *Journal of Men's Health & Gender, 4*, 409–418.

Erlandsson, K., & Lindgren, H. (2009). From belonging to belonging through a blessed moment of love for a child—The birth of a child from the fathers' perspective. *Journal of Men's Health, 6*, 338–344.

Erol, R. Y., & Orth, U. (2011). Self-esteem development from age 14 to 30 years: A longitudinal study. *Journal of Personality and Social Psychology, 101*, 607–619.

Ervin, R. B., Wang, C. Y., Fryar, C. D., Miller, I. M., & Ogden, C. L. (2013). Measures of muscular strength in US children and adolescents, 2012. *NCHS Data Brief, 139*, 1–8.

Eslea, M., Menesini, E., Morita, Y., O'Moore, M., Mora-Nerchan, J. A., Pereira, B., & Smith, P. K. (2004). Friendship and loneliness among bullies and victims: Data from seven countries. *Aggressive Behavior, 30*, 71–83.

Espelage, D. L., & Swearer, S. M. (2004). *Bullying in American schools*. Mahwah, NJ: Lawrence Erlbaum.

Espy, K. A. (1997). The Shape School: Assessing executive function in preschool children. *Developmental Neuropsychology, 13*(4), 495–499. doi:10.1080/87565649709540690

Espy, K. A., Fang, H., Johnson, C., Stopp, C., Wiebe, S. A., & Respass, J. (2011). Prenatal tobacco exposure: Developmental outcomes in the neonatal period. *Developmental Psychology, 47*, 153–169.

Ethnologue. (2017). Summary by world area. Retrieved from https:// www.ethnologue.com/ statistics

Evans, J. St. B. T. (2008). Dual-processing accounts of reasoning, judgment, and social cognition. *Annual Review of Psychology, 59*, 255–278.

Evans, K. (Ed.). (2003). *For the children: The Half the Sky Foundation's guide to infant nurture and preschool education in China's social welfare institutions*. Retrieved from www.halfthesky.org

Evans, S. M., & Boyte, H. C. (1992). *Free spaces: The sources of democratic change in America*. Chicago, IL: University of Chicago Press.

Eveleth, P. B., & Tanner, J. M. (1990). *Worldwide variation in human growth*. Cambridge, MA: Cambridge University Press.

Everett, G. E., Olmi, D. J., Edwards, R. P., Tingstrom, D. H., Sterling-Turner, H. E. & Christ, T. J. (2007). An empirical investigation of time-out with and without escape extinction to treat escape-maintained noncompliance. *Behavior Modification, 31*, 412–434.

Ezkurdia, I., Juan, D., Rodriguez, J. M., Frankish, A., Diekhans, M., Harrow, J., … Tress, M. L. (2014). Multiple evidence strands suggest that there may be as few as 19,000 human protein-coding genes. *Human Molecular Genetics, 23*, 5866–5878.

Fabes, R. A., Martin, C. L., & Hanish, L. D. (2003). Young children's play qualities in same-, other-, and mixed-sex peer groups. *Child Development, 74*, 921–932.

Fabiano, G. A., Pelham, W. E., Jr., Manos, M. J., Gnagy, E. M., Chronis, A. M., Onvango, A. N.,…Swain, S. (2004). An evaluation of three time-out procedures for children with attention deficit/hyperactivity disorder. *Behavior Therapy, 35*, 449–469.

Fackler, M. (2007, June 22). As Japan ages, universities struggle to fill classrooms. *The New York Times*, p. A3.

Fagan, J. F., Holland, C. R., & Wheeler, K. (2007). The prediction, from infancy, of adult IQ and achievement. *Intelligence, 35*, 225–231.

Fantz, R. L. (1961). The origin of form perception. *Scientific American, 204*(5), 66–72. doi:http:// dx.doi.org/10.1038/scientificamerican0561-66

Fardouly, J., & Vartanian, L. R. (2015). Negative comparisons about one's appearance mediate the relationship between Facebook usage and body image concerns. *Body Image, 12*, 82–88.

Farmer, R. (2014, April 25). *The Nurse-Family Partnership program*. Retrieved from http://minoritynurse.com/article/nurse-family-partnership-program

Farr, R. H., Forssell, S. L., & Patterson, C. J. (2010). Parenting and child development in adoptive families: Does parental sexual orientation matter? *Applied Developmental Science, 14*(3), 164–178. doi:10.1080/10888691.2010.500958

Farver, J. A., Bhadha, B. R., & Narang, S. K. (2002). Acculturation and psychological functioning in Asian Indian adolescents. *Social Development, 11*, 11–29.

Fasoli, A. D. (in press). From autonomy to divinity: The cultural socialization of moral reasoning in an evangelical Christian community. *Child Development.*

Fearon, P., O'Connell, P., Frangou, S., Aquino, P., Nosarti, C., Allin, M.,…Murray, R. (2004). Brain volumes in adult survivors of very low birth weight: A sibling–controlled study. Q *Pediatrics, 114*, 367–371.

Feigenbaum, P. (2002). Private speech: Cornerstone of Vygotsky's theory of the development of higher psychological processes. In D. Robbins & A. Stetsenko (Eds.), *Voices within Vygotsky's non-classical psychology: Past, present, future* (pp. 161–174). New York, NY: Nova Science.

Fekkes, M., Pijpers, F. I., & Verloove-Vanhorick, S. P. (2004). Bullying behavior and associations with psychosomatic complaints and depression in victims. *Journal of Pediatrics*, 144, 17–22.

Feldman, R., Weller, A., Sirota, L., & Eidelman, A. I. (2003). Testing a family intervention hypothesis: The contribution of mother–infant skin-to-skin (kangaroo care) to family interaction, proximity, and touch. *Journal of Family Psychology, 17*, 94–107.

Feldman-Salverlsberg, P. (2002). Is infertility an unrecognized public health and population problem? The view from the Cameroon grassfields. In M. C. Inhorn & F. van Balen (Eds.), *Infertility around the globe: New thinking on childlessness, gender, and reproductive technologies* (pp. 215–231). Berkeley, CA: University of California Press.

Ferber, S. G., Kuint, J., Weller, A., Feldman, S. D., Arbel, E., & Kohelet, D. (2002). Massage therapy by mothers and trained professionals enhances weight gain in preterm infants. *Early Human Development, 67*, 37–45.

Ferguson, C. A., Menn, L., & Stoel-Gammon, C. (Eds.). (1992). *Phonological development: Models, research, implications*. Timonium, MD: York Press.

Ferguson, C. J. (2013). Spanking, corporal punishment and negative long-term outcomes: A meta-analytic review of longitudinal studies. *Clinical Psychology Review, 33*(1), 196–208.

Ferguson, G. M., Hafen, C. A., & Laursen, B. (2010). Adolescent psychological and academic adjustment as a function of discrepancies between actual and ideal self-perceptions. *Journal of Youth and Adolescence, 39*, 1485–1497.

Ferguson, G. M., & Iturbide, M. I. (2015). Family, food, and culture: Mothers' perspectives on Americanization in Jamaica. *Caribbean Journal of Psychology, 7*(1), 43–63.

Fergusson, D. M., Boden, J. M., & Horwood, L. J. (2008). Exposure to childhood sexual and physical abuse and adjustment in early adulthood. *Child Abuse and Neglect, 32*, 607–619.

Fergusson, D. M., McLeod, G. F., & Horwood, L. J. (2013). Childhood sexual abuse and adult developmental outcomes: Findings from a 30-year longitudinal study in New Zealand. *Child Abuse & Neglect, 37*, 664–674.

Fernald, A., & O'Neill, D. K. (1993). Peekaboo across cultures: How mothers and infants play with voices, faces, and expectations. In K. MacDonald (Ed.), *Parent–child play* (pp. 259–285). Albany, NY: State University of New York Press.

Field, M. J., & Behrman, R. E. (Eds.). (2003). *When children die.* Washington, DC: National Academies Press.

Field, T. (2010). Pregnancy and labor massage. *Expert Reviews in Obstetrics & Gynecology, 5*, 177–181.

Field, T. (2014). Massage therapy research review. *Contemporary Therapies in Clinical Practice, 20*, 224–229. http://dx.doi.org/10.1016/j.ctcp.2014.07.002

Field, T., Diego, M., & Hernandez-Reif, M. (2010). Preterm infant massage therapy: A review. *Infant Behavior and Development, 33*, 115–124.

Field, T., Hernandez-Reif, M., & Diego, M. (2006). Newborns of depressed mothers who received moderate versus light pressure massage during therapy. *Infant Behavior and Development, 29*, 54–58.

Field, T. M. (1998). Massage therapy effects. *American Psychologist, 53*, 1270–1281.

Field, T. M. (2001). Massage therapy facilitates weight gain in preterm infants. *Current Directions in Psychological Science, 10*, 51–55.

Field, T. M. (2004). Massage therapy effects on depressed pregnant women. *Journal of Psychosomatic Obstetrics and Gynaecology, 25*, 115–122.

Figueira-McDonough, J. (1998). Environment and interpretation: Voices of young people in poor inner-city neighborhoods. *Youth & Society, 30*, 123–163.

Fildes, V. (1995). The culture and biology of breastfeeding: An historical review of Western Europe. In P. Stuart-Macadam & K. A. Dettwyler (Eds.), *Breastfeeding: Biocultural perspectives* (pp. 101–131). Hawthorne, NY: Aldein de Gruyter.

Fingerman, K. L., & Yahirun, J. J. (2015). Emerging adulthood in the context of family. In J. J. Arnett (Ed.), *The Oxford handbook of emerging adulthood* (pp. 163–176). New York, NY: Oxford University Press.

Fingerman, K. L., & Yahirun, J. J. (2015). Family relationships. In J. J. Arnett (Ed.), *Oxford handbook of emerging adulthood* (pp. 163–176). New York, NY: Oxford University Press.

Finkel, M. (2007, July). Bedlam in the blood: Malaria. *National Geographic*, pp. 32–67.

Finkelhor, D., Mitchell, K. J., & Wolak, J. (2000). *Online victimization: A report on the nation's youth.* Durham, NH: Crimes Against Children Research Center. Retrieved from http://www.unh.edu/ccrc/VictimizationOnlineSurvey.pdf

Finley, G. E., & Schwartz, S. J. (2010). The divided world of the child: Divorce and long-term psychosocial adjustment. *Family Court Review, 48*, 516–527.

Finn, C. A. (2001). Reproductive ageing and the menopause. *International Journal of Developmental Biology, 45*, 613–617.

Firkowska-Mankiewicz, A. (2011). Adult careers: Does childhood IQ predict later life outcome? *Journal of Policy and Practice in Intellectual Disabilities, 8*(1), 1–9.

Fisch, H., Hyun, G., Golden, R., Hensle, T. W., Olsson, C. A., & Liberson, G. L. (2003). The influence of paternal age on Down syndrome. *Journal of Urology, 169*, 2275–2278.

Fisch, S. M. (2013). Cross-platform learning: On the nature of children's learning from multiple media platforms. In F. C. Blumberg & S. M. Fisch (Eds.), *Digital games: A context for cognitive development. New Directions for Child and Adolescent Development, 139*, 59–70.

Fisch, S. M, Lesh, R., Motoki, E., Crespo, S., & Melfi, V. (in press). Cross-platform learning: How do children learn from multiple media? In F. C. Blumberg (Ed.), *Learning by playing: Frontiers of video gaming education* (pp. 207–219). New York, NY: Oxford University Press.

Fisch, S. M., Yeh, H., Zhou, Z., Jin, C., Hamed, M., Khadr, Z., … Guha, M. L. (2010). Crossing borders: Learning from educational media in four countries. *Televizion, 23*, 42–45.

Fisher, C. B. (2003). A goodness–of–fit ethic for child assent to nonbeneficial research. *The American Journal of Bioethics, 3*, 27–28.

Fitelson, E., Kim, S., Baker, A. S., & Leight, K. (2011). Treatment of postpartum depression: Clinical, psychological and pharmacological options. *International Journal of Women's Health, 3*, 1–14. doi:10.2147/IJWH.S6938

Fitneva, S., & Matsui, T. (2015). The emergence and development of language across cultures. In L. A. Jensen (Ed.), *The Oxford handbook of human development and culture: An interdisciplinary perspective* (pp. 111–126). New York, NY: Oxford University Press.

Flaherty, E. G., Stirling, J., & The Committee on Child Abuse and Neglect. (2010). The pediatrician's role in child maltreatment prevention. *Pediatrics, 126*, 833–841.

Flanagan, C., & Botcheva, L. (1999). Adolescents' preference for their homeland and other countries. In F. D. Alsaker & A. Flammer (Eds.), *The adolescent experience: European and American adolescents in the 1990s* (pp. 131–144). Mahwah, NJ: Erlbaum.

Flanagan, C., Lin, C., Luisi-Mills, H., Sambo, A., & Hu, M. (2015). Adolescent civic development across cultures. In L. A. Jensen (Ed.), *Oxford handbook of human development and culture* (pp. 471–486). New York, NY: Oxford University Press.

Flanagan, C. A. (2004). Volunteerism, leadership, political socialization, and civic engagement. In R. M. Lerner & L. Steinberg (Eds.), *Handbook of adolescent psychology* (2nd ed., pp. 721–745). Hoboken, NJ: John Wiley & Sons Inc.

Flannery, K. A., & Liederman, J. (1995). Is there really a syndrome involving the co-occurrence of neurodevelopmental disorder, talent, non–right handedness and immune disorder among children? *Cortex, 31*, 503–515.

Flavell, J. H., Beach, D. R., & Chinsky, J. M. (1966). Spontaneous verbal rehearsal in a memory task as a function of age. *Child Development, 37*, 283–299.

Flavell, J. H., Friedrichs, A., & Hoyt, J. (1970). Developmental changes in memorization process. *Cognitive Psychology, 1*, 324–340.

Flavell, J. H., Miller, P. A., & Miller, S. A. (1993). *Cognitive development* (3rd ed.). Englewood Cliffs, NJ: Prentice-Hall.

Flavell, J. H., Miller, P. A., & Miller, S. A. (2002). *Cognitive development* (4th ed.). Upper Saddle River, NJ: Prentice-Hall.

Fleming, T. P. (2006). The periconceptional and embryonic period. In P. Gluckman, & M. Hanson (Eds.), *Developmental origins of health and disease* (pp. 51–61). New York, NY: Cambridge University Press.

Flook, L., & Fuligni, A. J. (2008). Family and school spillover in adolescents' daily lives. *Child Development, 79*(3), 776–787.

Flowers, P., & Buston, K. (2001). "I was terrified of being different": Exploring gay men's accounts of growing up in a heterosexist society. *Journal of Adolescence*, 24, 51–66.

Floyd, F., & Bakeman, R. (2006). Coming-out across the life course: Implications of age and historical context. Archives of Sexual Behavior, 35, 287–297.

Flynn, J. R. (1999). The discovery of IQ gains over time. *American Psychologist, 54*, 5–20.

Flynn, J. R. (2012). Are we getting smarter? Rising IQ in the twenty-first century. Cambridge, UK: Cambridge University Press.

Fogel, A., Hsu, H., Nelson-Goens, G. C., Shapiro, A. F., & Secrist, C. (2006). Effects of normal and perturbed social play on the duration and amplitude of different types of infant smiles. *Developmental Psychology, 42*, 459–473.

Fomon, S. J., & Nelson, S. E. (2002). Body composition of the male and female reference infants. *Annual Review of Nutrition, 22*, 1–17.

Fontanel, B., & d'Harcourt, C. (1997). *Babies: History, art and folklore.* New York, NY: Harry N. Abrams.

Ford, C., & Beach, F. (1951). *Patterns of sexual behavior.* New York, NY: Harper & Row.

Ford, C. S. (1945). *A comparative study of human reproduction.* New Haven, CT: Yale University Press.

Foss, R. D. (2007). Improving graduated driver licensing systems: A conceptual approach and its implications. *Journal of Safety Research, 38*(2), 185–192.

Fox, J., & Potocki, B. (2016). Lifetime video game consumption, interpersonal aggression, hostile sexism, and rape myth acceptance: A cultivation perspective. *Journal of interpersonal violence, 31*, 1912–1931.

Fox, N. A., Henderson, H. A., Marshall, P. J., Nichols, K. E., & Ghera, M. M. (2005). Behavioral inhibition: Linking biology and behavior within a developmental framework. *Annual Review of Psychology, 56*, 235–262. doi:10.1146/annurev.psych.55.090902.141532

Fox, N. A., Reeb-Sutherland, B. C., & Degnan, K. (2013). Personality and emotional development. In P. D. Zelazo (Ed.), *The Oxford handbook of developmental psychology: Volume 2: Self and other* (pp. 15–44). New York, NY: Oxford University Press.

Fraley, R. C., Roisman, G. I., Booth-LaForce, C., Owen, M. T., & Holland, A. S. (2013). Interpersonal and genetic origins of adult attachment styles: A longitudinal study from infancy to early adulthood. *Journal of Personality and Social Psychology, 104*, 817–838. doi:10.1037/a0031435

Frank, M. C., Goodman, N. D., & Tenenbaum, J. B. (2009). Using speakers' referential intentions to model early cross-situational word learning. *Psychological Science, 20*, 578–585. doi:10.1111/j.1467-9280.2009.02335.x

Frankman, E. A., Wang, L., Bunker, C. H., & Lowder, J. L. (2009). Episiotomy in the United States: Has anything changed? *American Journal of Obstetrics and Gynecology, 537*, e1–e7.

Franks, B. A. (2011). Moving targets: A developmental framework for understanding children's changes following disasters. *Journal of Applied Developmental Psychology, 32*, 58–69. doi:10.1016/j.appdev.2010.12.004

Fransen, M., Meertens, R., & Schrander-Stumpel, C. (2006). Communication and risk presentation in genetic counseling: Development of a checklist. *Patient Education and Counseling, 61*, 126–133.

Fraser, S. (1995). *The bell curve wars: Race, intelligence, and the future of America*. New York, NY: Basic Books.

Frawley, T. J. (2008). Gender schema and prejudicial recall: How children misremember, fabricate, and distort gendered picture book information. *Journal of Research in Childhood Education, 22*, 291–303.

Frayling, T. M., Timpson, N. J., Weedon, M. N., Zeggini, E., Freathy, R. M., Lindgren, C. M.,... McCarthy, M. I. (2007). A common variant in the *FTO* gene is associated with body mass index and predisposes children and adult obesity. *Science, 316*, 889–894.

Freedman, D. S., Khan, L. K., Serdula, M. K., Ogden, C. L., & Dietz, W. H. (2006). Racial and ethnic differences in secular trends for childhood BMI, weight, and height. *Obesity*, 301–308.

Freedman, J. L. (1988). Television violence and aggression: What the evidence shows. *Applied Social Psychology Annual, 8*, 144–162.

Freeman, S. K. (2006). Facts of life and more: Adolescent sex and sexuality education. In C. Cocca (Ed.), *Adolescent sexuality: A historical handbook and guide. Children and youth: History and culture* (pp. 45–63). Westport, CT: Praeger Publishers/Greenwood Publishing Group.

French, D. (2015). Cultural templates of adolescent friendships. In L. A. Jensen (Ed.), *Oxford handbook of human development and culture: An interdisciplinary perspective* (pp. 425–437). New York, NY: Oxford University Press.

French, D. C., Chen, X., Chung, J., Li, M., Chen, H., & Li, D. (2011). Four children and one toy: Chinese and Canadian children faced with potential conflict over a limited resource. *Child Development, 82*(3), 830–841. doi:10.1111/j.1467-8624.2011.01581.x

French, D. C., Pidada, S., & Victor, A. (2005). Friendships of Indonesian and United States youth. *International Journal of Behavioral Development, 29*(4), 304–313. doi:10.1177/01650250544000080

Freud, A. (1946). *The ego and the mechanisms of defense*. New York, NY: International Universities Press.

Freud, A. (1958). Adolescence. *Psychoanalytic Study of the Child, 15*, 255–278. New York, NY: International Universities Press, Inc.

Freud, A. (1968). Adolescence. In A. E. Winder & D. Angus (Eds.), *Adolescence: Contemporary studies* (pp. 13–24). New York, NY: American Book.

Freud, A. (1969). Adolescence as a developmental disturbance. In G. Caplan & S. Lebovici (Eds.), *Adolescence: Psychosocial perspectives* (pp. 5–10). New York, NY: Basic Books.

Freud, S. (1901/1953). *The interpretations of dreams*. London, UK: Hogarth.

Freud, S. (1905/1953). Three essays on the theory of sexuality. In J. Strachey (Ed.), *The standard edition of the complete psychological works of Sigmund Freud* (Vol. 7; pp. 13–243). London, UK: Hogarth Press.

Freud, S. (1905/1953). *Three essays on the theory of sexuality*. London, UK: Hogarth.

Frick, P. J., & Kimonis, E. R. (2008). Externalizing disorders of childhood. In J. E. Maddux & B. A. Winstead (Eds.), *Psychopathology: Foundations for a contemporary understanding* (2nd ed., pp. 349–374). New York, NY: Routledge/Taylor & Francis Group.

Friedlmeier, W., Corapci, F., & Benga, O. (2015). Early emotional development in cultural perspective. In L. A. Jensen (Ed.), *Oxford handbook of human development and culture: An interdisciplinary perspective* (pp. 127–148). New York, NY: Oxford University Press.

Friedman, A. M., Ananth, C. V., Prendergast, E., D'Alton, M. E., & Wright, J. D. (2015). Variation in and factors associated with use of episiotomy. *JAMA, 313*(2), 197–199. doi:10.1001/jama.2014.14774

Friedman, C. K., Leaper, C., & Bigler, R. S. (2007). Do mothers' gender-related attitudes or comments predict young children's gender beliefs? *Parenting: Science and Practice, 7*, 357–366.

Friedman, H. S., & Martin, L. R. (2011). *The longevity project*. New York, NY: Penguin.

Friedman, L. (1989). Mathematics and the gender gap: A meta-analysis of recent studies on sex differences in mathematical tasks. *Review of Educational Research, 59*, 185–213.

Friedman, T. L. (2000). *The Lexus and the olive tree: Understanding globalization*. New York, NY: Picador.

Frimer, J. A., & Walker, L. J. (2009). Reconciling the self and morality: An empirical model of moral centrality development. *Developmental psychology, 45*, 1669–1681.

Fry, R. (2016). For first time in modern era, living with parents edges out other living arrangements for 18–34-year-olds. Washington, DC: Pew Research Center.

Fuligni, A., Tseng, V., & Lam, M. (2005). Ethnic identity and the academic adjustment of adolescents from Mexican, Chinese, and European backgrounds. *Developmental Psychology, 41*(5), 799–811.

Fuligni, A. J. (2011). Social identity, motivation, and well being among adolescents from Asian and Latin American backgrounds. In G. Carlo, L. J. Crockett, & M. A. Carranza (Eds.), *Health disparities in youth and families: Research and applications* (pp. 97–120). New York, NY: Springer.

Fuligni, A. J., Hughes, D. L., & Way, N. (2009). Ethnicity and immigration. In R. M. Lerner & L. Steinberg (Eds.), *Contextual influences on adolescent development, Vol 2: Contextual influences on adolescent development* (3rd ed., pp. 527–569). Hoboken, NJ: John Wiley & Sons Inc.

Fuller, A., Beck, V., & Unwin, L. (2005). The gendered nature of apprenticeship: Employers' and young peoples' perspectives. *Education & Training, 47*(4–5), 298–311.

Fung, H. (1999). Becoming a moral child: The socialization of shame among young Chinese children. *Ethos, 27*, 180–209. doi:10.1525/eth.1999.27.2.180

Funk, J. B. (2005). Children's exposure to violent video games and desensitization to violence. *Child & Adolescent Psychiatric Clinics of North America, 14*, 387–404.

Funk, J. B., Chan, M., Brouwer, J., & Curtiss, K. (2006). A biopsychosocial analysis of the video game-playing experiences of children and adults in the United States. *SIMILE: Studies in Media & Information Literacy Education, 6*, 79.

Funk, J. B., Flores, B., Buchman, D. D., & Germann, J. N. (1999). Rating electronic video games: Violence is in the eye of the beholder. *Youth & Society, 30*, 283–312.

Funk, J. B., Hagan, J., Schimming, J., Bullock, W. A., Buchman, D. D., & Myers, M. (2002). Aggression and psychopathology in adolescents with a preference for violent electronic games. *Aggressive Behavior, 28*, 134–144.

Furman, W., & Hand, L. S. (2006). The slippery nature of romantic relationships: Issues in definition and differentiation. In A. C. Crouter & A. Booth (Eds.), *Romance and sex in adolescence and emerging adulthood: Risks and opportunities* (pp. 171–178). Mahwah, NJ: Lawrence Erlbaum.

Furman, W., Ho, M. J., & Low, S. M. (2007). The rocky road of adolescent romantic experience: Dating and adjustment. In R. C. M. E. Engels, M. Kerr, & H. Stattin (Eds.), *Friends, lovers and groups: Key relationships in adolescence. Hot topics in developmental research* (pp. 61–80). New York, NY: John Wiley & Sons Ltd.

Furman, W., Low, S., & Ho, M. J. (2009). Romantic experience and psychosocial adjustment in early adolescence. *Journal of Consulting and Clinical Psychology, 38*(1), 75–90.

Furman, W., & Rose, A. J. (2015). Friendships, romantic relationships, and peer relationships. In R. M. Lerner (Series Ed.), M. E. Lamb (Vol. Ed.), *Handbook of child psychology and developmental science, Vol. 3: Socioemotional processes* (7th ed., pp. 932–974). New York, NY: Wiley.

Furman, W., & Simon, V. A. (2008). Homophily in adolescent romantic relationships. In M. J. Prinstein & K. A. Dodge (Eds.), *Understanding peer influence in children and adolescents* (pp. 203–224). New York, NY: Guilford.

Futagi, Y., Toribe, Y., & Suzuki, Y. (2009). Neurological assessment of early infants. *Current Pediatric Reviews, 5*, 65–70.

Gaddis, A., & Brooks-Gunn, J. (1985). The male experience of pubertal change. *Journal of Youth and Adolescence, 14*, 61–69.

Galambos, N., Almeida, D., & Petersen, A. (1990). Masculinity, femininity, and sex role attitudes in early adolescence: Exploring gender intensification. *Child Development, 61*, 1905–1914.

Galambos, N. L. (2004). Gender and gender role development in adolescence. In R. Lerner & L. Steinberg (Eds.), *Handbook of adolescent psychology* (pp. 233–262). New York, NY: Wiley.

Galambos, N. L., Barker, E. T., & Krahn, H. J. (2006). Depression, anger, and self-esteem in emerging adulthood: Seven-year trajectories. *Developmental Psychology, 42*, 350–365.

Gale, C. R., Godfrey, K. M., Law, C. M., Martyn, C. N., & O'Callaghan, F. J. (2004). Critical periods of brain growth and cognitive function in children. *Brain: A Journal of Neurology, 127*, 321–329.

Gall, S. (Ed.). (1996). *Multiple pregnancy and delivery*. St. Louis, MO: Mosby.

Galler, J. R., Bryce, C. P., Waber, D., Hock, R. S., Exner, N., Eaglesfield, D.,... Harrison, R. (2010). Early childhood malnutrition predicts depressive symptoms at ages 11–17. *Journal of Child Psychology and Psychiatry, 51*, 789–798.

Galler, J. R., Waber, D., Harrison, R., & Ramsey, F. (2005). Behavioral effects of childhood malnutrition. *The American Journal of Psychiatry, 162*, 1760–1761.

Galotti, K., Kozberg, S., & Farmer, M. (1991). Gender and developmental differences in adolescents' conceptions of moral reasoning. *Journal of Youth and Adolescence, 20*, 13–30.

Galvan, A. (2010). Adolescent development of the reward system. *Frontiers in Human Neuroscience, 4*(6), 1–9. doi:http://dx.doi.org/10.3389/neuro.09.006.2010

Ganger, J., & Brent, M. R. (2004). Reexamining the vocabulary spurt. *Developmental Psychology, 40*, 621–632.

Garcia Coll, G. E., & Marks, A. K. E. (Eds.). (2012). *The immigrant paradox in children and adolescents: Is becoming American a developmental risk?* Washington, DC: American Psychological Association. doi:10.1037/13094-000

García Coll, C. G., Lamberty, G., Jenkins, R., McAdoo, H. P., Crnic, K., Wasik, B. H., & Garcia, H. V. (1996). An integrative model for the study of developmental competencies in minority children. *Child Development, 67*(5), 1891–1914. doi:http://www.jstor.org/stable/1131600

Gardner, H. (1983). *Frames of mind.* New York, NY: Basic Books.

Gardner, H . (1999). Who owns intelligence? *Atlantic Monthly, 283,* 67–76.

Gardner, H. (2004). *Frames of mind: The theory of multiple intelligences.* New York, NY: Basic Books.

Gardner, H. (2011). Multiple intelligences: The first thirty years. *Harvard Graduate School of Education.*

Gardner, R. A., & Gardner, B. T. (1969). Teaching sign language to a chimpanzee. *Science, 165*(3894), 664–672.

Gartrell, N., Deck, A., Rodas, C., Peyser, H., & Banks, A. (2005). The national lesbian family study: 4. Interviews with the 10-year-old children. *American Journal of Orthopsychiatry, 75*(4), 518–524. doi:10.1037/0002-9432.75.4.518

Gartstein, M. A., Slobodskaya, H. R., Zylicz, P. O., Gosztyla, D., & Nakagawa, A. (2010). A cross-cultural evaluation of temperament: Japan, USA, Poland and Russia. *International Journal of Psychology and Psychological Therapy, 10,* 55–75.

Gaskins, S. (2000). Children's daily activities in a Mayan village: A culturally grounded description. *Cross-Cultural Research, 34,* 375–389.

Gaskins, S. (2015). Childhood practices across cultures: Play and household work. In L. A. Jensen (Ed.), *Oxford handbook of human development and culture: An interdisciplinary perspective* (pp. 185–197). New York, NY: Oxford University Press.

Gauvain, M., Munroe, R. L., & Beebe, H. (2013). Children's questions in cross-cultural perspective: A four-culture study. *Journal of Cross-Cultural Psychology, 44,* 148–165.

Gauvain, M., & Nicolaides, C. (2015). Cognition in childhood across cultures. In L. A. Jensen (Ed.), *Oxford handbook of human development and culture: An interdisciplinary perspective* (pp. 198–213). New York, NY: Oxford University Press.

Gavin, A. R., Hill, K. G., Hawkins, J. D., & Maas, C. (2011). The role of maternal early-life and later-life risk factors on offspring low birth weight: Findings from a three-generational study. *Journal of Adolescent Health, 49,* 166–171.

Gavin, L., & Furman, W. (1989). Age differences in adolescents' perceptions of their peer groups. *Developmental Psychology, 25,* 827–834.

Gazzaniga, M. (2008). *Human: The science behind what makes us unique.* New York, NY: Ecco.

GBD 2013 Mortality and Causes of Death Collaborators. (2014). Global, regional, and national age-sex specific all-cause and cause-specific mortality for 240 causes of death, 1990–2013: A systematic analysis for the Global Burden of Disease Study 2013. *Lancet, 385,* 117–171. doi:10.1016/S0140-6736(14)61682-2

Ge, X., Natsuaki, M. N., Neiderhiser, J. M., & Reiss, D. (2007). Genetic and environmental influences on pubertal timing: Results from two national sibling studies. *Journal of Research on Adolescence, 17*(4), 767–788.

Geangu, E., Benga, O., Stahl, D., & Striano, T. (2010). Contagious crying beyond the first days of life. *Infant Behavior & Development, 33,* 279–288.

Geary, D. C. (2010). *Male, female: The evolution of human sex differences* (2nd ed.). Washington, DC: American Psychological Association.

Gee, J. P. (2007). *What videogames have to teach us about learning and literacy.* New York, NY: Palgrave Macmillan.

Geeraert, L., Van den Noortgate, W., Grietens, H., & Onghena, P. (2004). The effects of early prevention programs for families with young children at risk for physical child abuse and neglect: A meta-analysis. *Child Maltreatment, 9,* 277–291.

Geldhof, G. J., Little, T. D., & Columbo, J. (2010). Self-regulation across the lifespan. In M. E. Lamb & A. M. Freund (Eds.), *Handbook of Lifespan Development (Social and Emotional Development,* Vol. 2, pp. 116–157). Hoboken, NJ: Wiley.

Genesoni, L., & Tallandini, M. A. (2009). Men's psychological transition to fatherhood: An analysis of the literature, 1989–2008. *Birth: Issues in Perinatal Care, 36,* 305–318.

Gentile, B., Grabe, S., Dolan-Pascoe, B., Twenge, J. M., Wells, B. E., & Maitino, A. (2009). Gender differences in domain-specific self-esteem: A meta-analysis. *Review of General Psychology, 13*(1), 34–45.

Gentzler, A. L., Ramsey, M. A., Yuen Yi, C., Palmer, C. A., & Morey, J. N. (2014). Young adolescents' emotional and regulatory responses to positive life events: Investigating temperament, attachment, and event characteristics. *The Journal of Positive Psychology, 9,* 108–121.

George, C., & Solomon, J. (1999). Attachment and caregiving: The caregiving behavioural system. In J. Cassidy & P. R. Shaver (Eds.), *Handbook of attachment: Theory, research, and clinical applications* (pp. 649–670). New York, NY: Guilford Press.

Gerbner, G., Gross, L., Morgan, M., & Signorelli, N. (1994). Growing up with television: The cultivation perspective. In J. Bryant & D. Zillman (Eds.), *Media effects: Advances in theory and research* (pp. 17–41). Hillsdale, NJ: Erlbaum.

Gergen, K. (2011). The acculturated brain. *Theory and Psychology, 20,* 1–20.

Gershoff, E. T. (2002). Corporal punishment by parents and associated child behaviors and experiences: A meta-analytic and theoretical review. *Psychological Bulletin, 128,* 539–579.

Gertner, Y., Fisher, C., & Eisengart, J. (2006). Learning words and rules: Abstract knowledge of word order in early sentence comprehension. *Psychological Science, 17*(8), 684–691. doi:10.1111/j.1467-9280.2006.01767.x

Gewirtz, J. (1977). Maternal responding and the conditioning of infant crying: Directions of influence within the attachment–acquisition process. In B. C. Etzel, J. M. LeBlanc, & D. M. Baer (Eds.), *New developments in behavioral research* (pp. 31–57). Hillsdale, NJ: Lawrence Erlbaum.

Giang, M. T., & Wittig, M. A. (2006). Implications of adolescents' acculturation strategies for personal and collective self-esteem. *Cultural Diversity and Ethnic Minority Psychology, 12*(4), 725–739.

Gibbons, A. (2016, January 4). Grisly find suggests humans inhabited Arctic 45,000 years ago. *Science Magazine.* Retrieved from http://www.sciencemag.org/news/2016/01/grisly-find-suggests-humans-inhabited-arctic-45000-years-ago

Gibbons, J. L., & Stiles, D. A. (2004). *The thoughts of youth: An international perspective on adolescents' ideal persons.* Greenwich, CT: IAP Information Age.

Gibbs, J. C., Basinger, K. S., Grime, R. L., & Snarey, J. R. (2007). Moral judgment development across cultures: Revisiting Kohlberg's universality claims. *Developmental Review, 27*(4), 443–500.

Gibbs, R., Jr., Leggitt, J., & Turner, E. (2002). What's special about figurative language in emotional communication? In S. R. Fussell (Ed.), *The verbal communication of emotion* (pp. 125–149). Mahwah, NJ: Erlbaum.

Gibson, E. J. (1988). Exploratory behavior in the development of perceiving, acting, and the acquiring of knowledge. *Annual Review of Psychology, 39*(1), 1–42. doi:annurev.ps.39.020188.000245

Gibson, E. J., & Walk, R. D. (1960). The "visual cliff." *Scientific American, 202,* 64–71.

Giddens, A. (2000). *Runaway world: How globalization is reshaping our lives.* New York, NY: Routledge.

Giedd, J. N. (2008). The teen brain: Insights from neuroimaging. *Journal of Adolescent Health, 42*(4), 335–343.

Giedd, J. N., Raznahan, A., Mills, K. L., & Lenroot, R. K. (2012). Review: Magnetic resonance imaging of male/female differences in human adolescent brain anatomy. *Biology of Sex Differences, 3*(1), 19.

Gilbert, S. (2015, April 13). "Dear diary." *The New York Times,* p. A16.

Giles-Sims, J., & Lockhart, C. (2005). Culturally shaped patterns of disciplining children. *Journal of Family Issues, 26,* 196–218.

Gilligan, C. (1982). *In a different voice.* Cambridge, MA: Harvard University Press.

Gilligan, C. (2008). Exit-voice dilemmas in adolescent development. In D. L. Browning (Ed.), *Adolescent identities: A collection of readings* (pp. 141–156). New York, NY: Analytic Press/Taylor & Francis Group.

Gilmore, D. (1990). *Manhood in the making: Cultural concepts of masculinity.* New Haven, CT: Yale University Press.

Gini, G., Albierto, P., Benelli, B., & Altoe, G. (2008). Determinants of adolescents' active defending and passive bystanding behavior in bullying. *Journal of Adolescence, 31*(1), 93–105.

Ginsburg, H. P., & Opper, S. (1988). *Piaget's theory of intellectual development* (3rd ed.). Englewood Cliffs, NJ: Prentice Hall

Giscombe, C. L., & Lobel, M. (2005). Explaining disproportionately high rates of adverse birth outcomes among African Americans: The impact of stress, racism, and related factors in pregnancy. *Psychological Bulletin, 131,* 662–683.

Gladwell, M. (1998, February 2). The Pima paradox. *The New Yorker,* pp. 44–57.

Glass, G. V. (1976). Primary, secondary, and meta-analysis of research. *Educational Researcher,* 5, 3–8.

Glassman, T. J., Dodd, V., Miller, E. M., & Braun, R. E. (2010). Preventing high-risk drinking among college students: A social marketing case study. *Social Marketing Quarterly, 16,* 92–110.

Gleason, J. B., Perlmann, R. Y., & Greif, E. B. (1984). What's the magic word: Learning language through politeness routines. *Discourse Processes, 7*(4), 493–503. doi:10.1080/01638538409544603

Gleason, T. R. (2013). Imaginary relationships. In M. Taylor (Ed.), *The Oxford handbook of the imagination* (pp. 251–271). New York, NY: Oxford University Press.

Glick, J. (1975). Cognitive development in cross-cultural perspective. *Review of Child Development Research, 4,* 595–654.

Goddard, H. H. (1911). Two thousand normal children measured by the Binet measuring scale of intelligence. *Pedagogical Seminary, 18*, 232–259.

Goel, V., & Stelter, B. (2013, October 2). Social networks in a battle for the second screen. *The New York Times.*

Goethem, A., Hoof, A., Orobio de Castro, B., Van Aken, M., & Hart, D. (2015). The role of reflection in the effects of community service on adolescent development: A meta-analysis. *Child Development, 85*, 2114–2130.

Goh, E. C. (2006). Raising the precious single child in urban China—An intergenerational joint mission between parents and grandparents. *Journal of Intergenerational Relationships, 4*, 6–28.

Goldbaum, S., Craig, W. M., Pepler, D., & Connolly, J. (2003). Developmental trajectories of victimization: Identifying risk and protective factors. *Journal of Applied School Psychology, 19*, 139–156.

Goldberg, A. E. (2010). *Lesbian and gay parents and their children.* Washington, DC: American Psychological Association.

Goldberg, A. E. (2012). *Gay dads: Transitions to adoptive fatherhood.* New York, NY: New York University Press.

Goldberg, M. C., Maurer, D., & Lewis, T. L. (2001). Developmental changes in attention: The effects of endogenous cueing and of distracters. *Developmental Science, 4*, 209–219.

Goldberg, W. A., Prause, J., Lucas-Thompson, R., & Himsel, A. (2008). Maternal employment and children's achievement in context: A meta-analysis of four decades of research. *Psychological Bulletin, 134*, 77–108. http://dx.doi.org/10.1037/0033-2909.134.1.77

Goldenberg, H., & Goldenberg, I. (2005). Family therapy. In R. J. Corsini & D. Wedding (Eds.), *Current psychotherapies* (7th ed., pp. 372–404). Belmont, CA: Thomson Brooks/Cole Publishing.

Goldfield, B. A., & Reznick, J. S. (1990). Early lexical acquisition: Rate, content and the vocabulary spurt. *Journal of Child Language, 17*, 171–183.

Goldin-Meadow, S. (2009). Using the hands to study how children learn language. In J. Colombo, L. Freund, & P. McCardle (Eds.), *Infant pathways to language: Methods, models, and research disorders* (pp. 195–210). New York, NY: Psychology Press.

Goldin-Meadow, S., & Alibali, M. W. (2013). Gesture's role in speaking, learning, and creating language. *Annual Review of Psychology, 64*, 257–283. doi:10.1146/annurev-psych-113011-143802

Goldin-Meadow, S., Goodrich, W., Sauer, E., & Iverson, J. (2007). Young children use their hands to tell their mothers what to say. *Developmental Science, 10*(6), 778–785. doi:10.1111/j.1467-7687.2007.00636.x

Goldman, B. D., & Buysse, V. (2007). Friendships in very young children. In O. Saracho & B. Spodek (Eds.), *Contemporary perspectives on socialization and social development in early childhood education* (pp. 165–192). New York, NY: IAP.

Goldman, R. (1965). *Religious thinking from childhood to adolescence.* London, UK: Routledge and Kegan Paul.

Goldsmith, H. H. (2009). Genetics of emotional development. In R. J. Davidson, K. R. Scherer, & H. H. Goldsmith (Eds.), *Handbook of affective sciences* (pp. 300–319). New York, NY: Oxford University Press.

Goldsmith, H. H., & Rothbart, M. K. (1996). *The laboratory temperament assessment battery (Lab-TAB): Locomotor Version 3.0.* Madison, WI: University of Wisconsin–Madison.

Goldstein, M. H., Schwade, J., Briesch, J., & Syal, S. (2010). Learning while babbling: Prelinguistic object-directed vocalizations indicate a readiness to learn. *Infancy, 15*(4), 362–391. doi:10.1111/j.1532-7078.2009.00020.x

Goldstein, S. E., Malanchuk, O., Davis-Kean, P. E., & Eccles, J. S. (2007). Risk factors of sexual harassment by peers: A longitudinal investigation of African American and European American adolescents. *Journal of Research on Adolescence,* 17(2), 285–300.

Goldstein, T. R., & Winner, E. (2012). Enhancing empathy and theory of mind. *Journal of Cognition and Development, 13*(1), 19–37.

Golinkoff, R. M. (1986). "I beg your pardon?": The preverbal negotiation of failed messages. *Journal of Child Language, 13*(03), 455–476. doi:http://dx.doi.org/10.1017/S0305000900006826

González, Y. S., Moreno, D. S., & Schneider, B. H. (2004). Friendship expectations of early adolescents in Cuba and Canada. *Journal of Cross-Cultural Psychology, 35*, 436–445.

Good, C., Aronson, J., & Inzlicht, M. (2003). Improving adolescents' standardized test performance: An intervention to reduce the effects of stereotype threat. *Journal of Applied Developmental Psychology, 24*, 645–662.

Goodnow, J. J., & Lawrence, J. A. (2015). Children and cultural context. In R. M. Lerner (Series Ed.), M. H. Bornstein & T. Leventhal (Vol. Eds.), *Handbook of child psychology and developmental science, Volume 4: Ecological settings and processes* (7th ed., pp. 746–786). New York, NY: Wiley.

Goodwin, C. J. (2009). *Research in psychology: Methods and design.* New York, NY: Wiley.

Goossens, L., & Luyckx, K. (2007). Belgium. In J. J. Arnett, U. Gielen, R. Ahmed, B. Nsamenang, T. S. Saraswathi, & R. Silbereisen (Eds.), *International encyclopedia of adolescence* (pp. 64–76). New York, NY: Routledge.

Gopnik, A., Meltzoff, A. N., & Kuhl, P. K. (1999). *The scientist in the crib: Minds, brains, and how children learn.* New York, NY: William Morrow.

Gordon, P. (2004). Numerical cognition without words: Evidence from Amazonia. *Science, 306*(5695), 496–499. doi:10.1126/science.1094492

Gordon-Larsen, P., Nelson, M. C., & Popkin, B. M. (2004). Longitudinal physical activity and sedentary behavior trends: Adolescence to adulthood. *American Journal of Preventative Medicine, 27*, 277–283.

Gottesman, I. I. (2004). Postscript: Eyewitness to maturation. In L. E. DiLalla (Ed.), *Behavior genetics principles* (pp. 217–223). Washington, DC: American Psychological Association.

Gottlieb, A. (2000). Luring your child into this life: A Beng path for infant care. In J. DeLoache & A. Gottlieb (Eds.), *A world of babies: Imagined childcare guides for seven societies* (pp. 55–89). New York, NY: Cambridge University Press.

Gottlieb, A., & DeLoache, J. (2017). *A world of babies.* New York, NY: Cambridge University Press.

Gottlieb, G. (2004). Normally occurring environmental and behavioral influences on gene activity. In C. G. Coll, E. L. Bearer, & R. M. Lerner (Eds.), *Nature and nature: The complex interplay of genetic and environmental influences on human behavior and development* (pp. 85–106). Mahwah, NJ: Erlbaum.

Gottlieb, G. (2007). Probabilistic epigenesis. *Developmental Science, 10*, 1–11.

Gottlieb, G., & Lickliter, R. (2007) Probabilistic epigenesis. *Developmental Science, 10*, 1–11.

Gould, S. J. (1981). *The mismeasure of man.* New York, NY: Norton.

Goza, F., & Ryabov, I. (2009). Adolescents' educational outcomes: Racial and ethnic variations in peer network importance. *Journal of Youth and Adolescence, 38*, 1264–1279.

Grabe, S., Ward, L. M., & Hyde, J. S. (2008). The role of the media in body image concerns among women: A meta-analysis of experimental and correlational studies. *Psychological Bulletin, 134*(3), 460–476.

Graber, J. A. (2013). Pubertal timing and the development of psychopathology in adolescence and beyond. *Hormones and Behavior, 64*, 262–269.

Graber, J. A., Lewinsohn, P. M., Seeley, J. R., & Brooks-Gunn, J. (1997). Is psychopathology associated with the timing of pubertal development? *Journal of the American Academy of Child and Adolescent Psychiatry, 36*, 1768–1776.

Graber, J. A., Nichols, T. R., & Brooks-Gunn, J. (2010). Putting pubertal timing in developmental context: Implications for prevention. *Developmental Psychobiology, 52*, 254–262.

Graber, J. A., Seeley, J. R., Brooks-Gunn, J., & Lewinsohn, P. M. (2004). Is pubertal timing associated with psychopathology in young adulthood? *Journal of the American Academy of Child & Adolescent Psychiatry, 43*, 718–726.

Gradisar, M., & Crowley, S. J. (2013). Delayed sleep phase disorder in youth. *Current Opinion in Psychiatry, 26*, 580.

Graffi, J., Moss, E., Jolicoeur-Martineau, A., Moss, G., Lecompte, V., Pascuzzo, K., … Sassi, R. (2015). Preschool children without 7-repeat DRD4 Gene more likely to develop disorganized attachment style. *Birth, 23*, 27.

Graham, A. M., Pfeifer, J. H., Fisher, P. A., Lin, W., Gao, W., & Fair, D. A. (2015). The potential of infant fMRI research and the study of early life stress as a promising exemplar. *Developmental Cognitive Neuroscience, 12*, 12–39.

Graham, M. J., Larsen, U., & Xu, X. (1999). Secular trend in age of menarche in China: A case study of two rural counties in Anhui province. *Journal of Biosocial Science, 31*, 257–267.

Granic, I., Dishion, T. J., & Hollenstein, T. (2003). The family ecology of adolescence: A dynamic systems perspective on normative development. In G. R. Adams & M. D. Berzonsky (Eds.), *Blackwell handbook of adolescence* (pp. 60–91). Malden, MA: Blackwell.

Gray, C., Ferguson, J., Behan, S., Dunbar, C., Dunn, J., & Mitchell, D. (2007). Developing young readers through the linguistic phonics approach. *International Journal of Early Years Education, 15*, 15–33.

Gray, W. N., Simon, S. L., Janicke, D. M., & Dumont-Driscoll, M. (2011). Moderators of weight-based stigmatization among youth who are overweight and non-overweight: The role of gender, race, and body dissatisfaction. *Journal of Developmental & Behavioral Pediatrics, 32*(2), 110–116.

Gray-Little, B., & Hafdahl, A. R. (2000). Factors influencing racial comparisons of self-esteem: A quantitative review. *Psychological Bulletin, 126*(1), 26–54. doi:10.1037//0033-2909.126.1.26

Greenberg, B. S. (1994). Content trends in media sex. In D. Zillman, J. Bryant, & A. C. Huston (Eds.), *Media, children and the family: Social scientific, psychodynamic, and clinical perspectives* (pp. 165–182). Hillsdale, NJ: Erlbaum.

Greenberger, E., & Steinberg, L. (1986). *When teenagers work: The psychological social costs of adolescent employment.* New York, NY: Basic Books.

Greenfield, P. M. (2005). Paradigms of cultural thought. In K. J. Holyoak, & R. G. Morrison (Eds.), *The Cambridge handbook of thinking and reasoning* (pp. 663–682). New York, NY: Cambridge University Press.

Greenough, W. T., & Black, J. E. (1992). Induction of brain structure by experience: Substrates for cognitive development. In M. R. Gunnar & C. A. Nelson (Eds.), *Minnesota Symposia on Child Development: Vol. 24. Developmental Behavioral Neuroscience* (pp. 155–200). Hillsdale, NJ: Erlbaum.

Griffith, J., & Perry, S. (1993). Wanting to soldier: Enlistment motivations of Army Reserve recruits before and after Operation Desert Storm. *Military Psychology, 5*, 127–139.

Griffiths, M. (2006). Internet use, addiction. In J. J. Arnett (Ed.), *Encyclopedia of children, adolescents, and the media* (pp. 431–432). Thousand Oaks, CA: Sage.

Grigorenko, E. (2003). Intraindividual fluctuations in intellectual functioning: Selected links between nutrition and the mind. In R. Sternberg & J. Lautrey (Eds.), *Models of intelligence: International perspectives* (pp. 91–115). Washington, DC: American Psychological Association.

Grigorenko, E. L., Lipka, J., Meier, E., Mohatt, G., Sternberg, R. J., & Yanez, E. (2004). Academic and practical intelligence: A case study of the Yup'ik in Alaska. *Learning and Individual Differences, 14*, 183–207.

Grilo, C. M., & Mitchell, J. E. (Eds.). (2010). *The treatment of eating disorders: A clinical handbook.* New York, NY: Guilford.

Grimshaw, G. S., & Wilson, M. S. (2013). A sinister plot? Facts, beliefs, and stereotypes about the left-handed personality. *Laterality: Asymmetries of Body, Brain and Cognition, 18*, 135–151.

Grolnick, W. S., McMenamy, J. M., & Kurowski, C. O. (2006). Emotional self-regulation in infancy and toddlerhood. In L. Balter & C. S. Tamis-LeMonda (Eds.), *Child psychology: A book of contemporary issues* (pp. 3–25). New York, NY: Psychology Press.

Grosjean, F. (2010) *Bilingual: Life and reality.* Cambridge, MA: Harvard University Press.

Grossman, K. E., Grossman, K., & Waters, E. (Eds.). (2005). *Attachment from infancy to adulthood: The major longitudinal studies.* New York, NY: Guilford.

Grotevant, H. D., & Adams, G. R. (1984). Development of an objective measure to assess ego identity in adolescence: Validation and replication. *Journal of Youth and Adolescence, 13*, 419–438.

Gruber, J. E., & Fineran, S. (2008). Comparing the impact of bullying and sexual harassment victimization on the mental and physical health of adolescents. *Sex Roles*, 59(1–2), 1–13.

Grumbach, M., Roth, J., Kaplan, S., & Kelch, R. (1974). Hypothalamic-pituitary regulation of puberty in man: Evidence and concepts derived from clinical research. In M. Grumbach, G. Grave, & F. Mayer (Eds.), *Control of the onset of puberty* (pp. 115–166). New York, NY: Wiley.

Grusec, J., Chaparro, M. P., Johnston, M., & Sherman, A. (2014). The development of moral behavior from a socialization perspective. In M. Killen & J. G. Smetana (Eds.), *Handbook of moral development* (2nd ed., pp. 113–134). New York, NY: Psychology Press.

Grusec, J. E., Goodnow, J. J., & Kuczynski, L. (2000). New directions in analyses of parenting contributions to children's acquisition of values. *Child Development, 71*(1), 205–211. doi:10.1111/1467-8624.00135

Grusec, J. E., & Hastings, P. D. (Eds.). (2007). *Handbook of socialization: Theory and research.* New York, NY: Guilford Press.

Gu, D., Reynolds, K., Wu, N., Chen, J., Duan, X., Reynolds, R. F., … InterASIA Collaborative Group. (2005). Prevalence of the metabolic syndrome and overweight among adults in China. *Lancet, 365*, 1398–1405.

Guastello, D. D., & Guastello, S. J. (2003). Androgyny, gender role behavior, and emotional intelligence among college students and their parents. *Sex Roles, 49*, 663–673.

Guasti, M. T. (2000). An excursion into interrogatives in early English and Italian. In M. A. Friedemann & L. Rizzi (Eds.), *The acquisition of syntax* (pp. 105–128). Harlow, UK: Longman.

Guay, F., Chanal, J., Ratelle, C. F., Marsh, H. W., Larose, S., & Boivin, M. (2010). Intrinsic, identified, and controlled types of motivation for school subjects in young elementary school children. *British Journal of Educational Psychology, 80*, 711–735.

Guernsey, L. (2007). *Into the minds of babes: How screen time affects children from birth to age 5.* New York, NY: Perseus.

Guerra, V. M., & Giner-Sorolla, R. (2010). Community, Autonomy, and Divinity Scale (CADS): Development of a theory-based moral codes scale. *Journal of Cross-Cultural Psychology, 41*, 35–50.

Guerra, V. M., & Giner-Sorolla, R. (2015). Investigating the three ethics in emerging adulthood: A study in five countries. In L. A. Jensen (Ed.), *Moral development in a global world: Research from a cultural-developmental perspective* (pp. 117–140). New York, NY: Cambridge University Press.

Guest, A. M. (2007). Cultures of childhood and psychosocial characteristics: Self-esteem and social comparison in two distinct communities. *Ethos, 35*, 1–32.

Guillaume, M., & Lissau, I. (2002). Epidemiology. In W. Burniat, T. Cole, I. Lissau, & E. M. E. Poskitt (Eds.), *Child and adolescent obesity: Causes and consequences, prevention and management* (pp. 28–49). Cambridge, MA: Cambridge University Press.

Guise, J. M. F., & Gill, J. S. (2007). "Binge drinking? It's good, it's harmless fun": A discourse analysis of accounts of female undergraduate drinking in Scotland. *Health Education Research, 22*(6), 895–906.

Gunnoe, M. L., & Mariner, C. L. (1997). Toward a developmental–contextual model of the effects of parental spanking on children's aggression. *Archives of Pediatrics and Adolescent Medicine, 151*, 768–775.

Gunnoe, M. L., & Moore, K. A. (2002). Predictors of religiosity among youth aged 17–22: A longitudinal study of the National Survey of Children. *Journal for the Scientific Study of Religion, 41*, 613–622.

Guthrie, J. T. (2008). Reading motivation and engagement in middle and high school: Appraisal and intervention. In J. T. Guthrie (Ed.), *Engaging adolescents in reading* (pp. 1–16). Thousand Oaks, CA: Corwin Press.

Haan, M. D., & Matheson, A. (2009). The development and neural bases of processing emotion in faces and voices. In M. D. H. & M. R. Gunnar, *Handbook of developmental social neuroscience* (pp. 107–121). New York, NY: Guilford.

Haas, L. L., & Hwang, C. P. (2013). Fatherhood and social policy in Scandinavia. In D. W. Schwalb, B. J. Schwalb, & M. E. Lamb (Eds.), *Fathers in cultural context* (pp. 303–331). New York, NY: Routledge.

Hack, M., Taylor, G., Drotar, D., Schluchter, M., Cartar, L., Wilson-Costello, D.,… Morrow, M. (2005). Poor predictive validity of the Bayley Scales of Infant Development for cognitive function of extremely low birth weight children at school age. *Pediatrics, 116*, 333–341.

Hadjikhani, N., Chabris, C. F., Joseph, R. M., Clark, J., McGrath, L., Aharon, L.,… Harris, G. J. (2004). Early visual cortex organization in autism: An fMRI study. *Neuroreport: For Rapid Communication of Neuroscience Research, 15*, 267–270.

Haffner, W. H. J. (2007). Development before birth. In M. L. Batshaw, L. Pellegrino, & N. J. Roizen (Eds.), *Children with disabilities* (pp. 23–33). Baltimore, MD: Paul H. Brookes.

Hagen, J., & Hale, G. (1973). The development of attention in children. In A. Pick (Ed.), *Minnesota symposium on child psychology* (Vol. 7, pp. 117–140). Minneapolis, MN: University of Minnesota Press.

Hagenauer, M. H., Perryman, J. I., Lee, T. M., & Carskadon, M. A. (2009). Adolescent changes in the homeostatic and circadian regulation of sleep. *Developmental Neuroscience, 31*, 276–284. doi:10.1159/000216538

Haidt, J., Koller, S. H., & Dias, M. G. (1993). Affect, culture, and morality, or is it wrong to eat your dog? *Journal of Personality and Social Psychology, 65*, 613–628.

Hakuta, K. (1999). The debate on bilingual education. *Developmental and Behavioral Pediatrics, 20*, 36–37.

Halgunseth, L. (2003). Language brokering: Positive developmental outcomes. In M. Coleman & L. Ganong (Eds.), *Points and counterpoints: Controversial relationship and family issues in the 21st century: An anthology* (pp. 154–157). Los Angeles, CA: Roxbury.

Halgunseth, L. C., Ispa, J. M., & Rudy, D. (2006). Parental control in Latino families: An integrated review of the literature. *Child Development, 77*(5), 1282–1297.

Halim, M. L., Ruble, D. N., Tamis-LeMonda C. S., Zosuls, K. M., Lurye, L. E., & Greulich, F. K. (2014). Pink frilly dresses and the avoidance of all things "girly": Children's appearance rigidity and cognitive theories of gender development. *Developmental Psychology, 50*(4), 1091. doi:http://dx.doi.org/10.1037/a0034906

Hall, B., Chesters, J., & Robinson, A. (2011). Infantile colic: A systematic review of medical and conventional therapies. *Journal of Paediatrics and Child Health, 48*, 128–137. doi:10.1111/j.1440-1754.2011.02061.x

Hall, G. S. (1904). Adolescence: Its psychology and its relation to physiology, anthropology, sociology, sex, crime, religion, and education (Vols. 1 & 2). Englewood Cliffs, NJ: Prentice-Hall.

Hall, N. (2001, August). *The child in the middle: Agency and diplomacy in language brokering events.* Paper presented at the European Society for Translation Studies Conference, Copenhagen.

Hall, N., & Sham, S. (2007). Language brokering as young people's work: Evidence from Chinese adolescents in England. *Language and Education, 21*(1), 16–30. doi:10.2167/le645.0

Hall, R. E. (2009). Cool pose, Black manhood, and juvenile delinquency. *Journal of Human Behavior in the Social Environment, 19*(15), 531–539.

Hall R. E ., & Pizarro J. M. (2011). Cool pose: Black male homicide and the social implications of manhood. *Journal of Social Service Research, 37*, 86–98.

Halpern, D. F. (2000). *Sex differences in cognitive abilities* (3rd ed.). Mahwah, NJ: Lawrence Erlbaum.

Hämäläinen, J., Poikolainen, K., Isometsa, E., Kaprio, J., Heikkinen, M., Lindermman, S., & Aro, H. (2005). Major depressive episode related to long unemployment and frequent alcohol intoxication. *Nordic Journal of Psychiatry, 59*(6), 486–491.

Hamilton, B. E., Martin, J. A., Osterman, M. J. K., Curtin, S. C., & Mathews, T. J. (2015). Births: Final

Data for 2014. *National Vital Statistics Reports, 64*, No. 12. Hyattsville, MD: National Center for Health Statistics.

Hamilton, S., & Hamilton, M. A. (2006). School, work, and emerging adulthood. In J. J. Arnett & J. L. Tanner (Eds.), *Coming of age in the 21st century: The lives and contexts of emerging adults* (pp. 257–277). Washington, DC: American Psychological Association.

Hamilton, S. F., & Hamilton, M. A. (2000). Research, intervention, and social change: Improving adolescents' career opportunities. In L. J. Crockett & R. K. Silbereisen (Eds.), *Negotiating adolescence in times of social change* (pp. 267–283). New York, NY: Cambridge University Press.

Hamlin, J. K., & Wynn, K. (2011). Young infants prefer prosocial to antisocial others. *Cognitive Development, 26*(1), 30–39. doi:10.1016/j.cogdev.2010.09.001

Hamlin, J. K., Wynn, K., & Bloom, P. (2007). Social evaluation by preverbal infants. *Nature, 450*(7169), 557–559. doi:10.1038/nature06288

Han, C. (2011). Embitterment in Asia: Losing face, inequality, and alienation under historical and modern perspectives. In M. Linden & A. Maercker (Eds.), *Embitterment: Societal, psychological, and clinical perspectives* (pp. 168–176). New York, NY: Springer.

Haninger, K., & Thompson, K. M. (2004). Content and ratings of teen rated video games. *JAMA: Journal of the American Medical Association, 291*, 856–865.

Hannon, T. S., Rao, G., & Arslanian, S. A. (2005). Childhood obesity and Type 2 diabetes mellitus. *Pediatrics, 116*, 473–480.

Hansen, N., Koudenburg, N., Hiersemann, R., Tellegen, P. J., Kocsev, M., & Postmes, T. (2012). Laptop usage affects abstract reasoning of children in the developing world. *Computers & Education, 59*, 989–1000.

Hansen, N., & Postmes, T. (in press). Broadening the scope of societal change research: Psychological, cultural, and political impacts of development aid. *Journal of Social and Political Psychology, 1*, 273–292.

Hansen, N., Postmes, T., van der Vinne, N., & van Thiel, W. (2012). Information and communication technology and cultural change: How ICT changes self-construal and values. *Social Psychology, 43*, 222–231.

Harden, K. P., & Mendle, J. (2012). Gene-environment interplay in the association between pubertal timing and delinquency in adolescent girls. *Journal of Abnormal Psychology, 121*(1), 73.

Hardy, S. A., & Carlo, G. (2011). Moral identity: What is it, how does it develop, and is it linked to moral action? *Child Development Perspectives, 5*, 212–218.

Hardy, S. A., Krettenauer, T., & Hunt, N. (in press). Moral identity development. In L. A. Jensen (Ed.). *Oxford handbook of moral development: An interdisciplinary perspective*. New York, NY: Oxford University Press.

Hardy, S. A., Pratt, M. W., Pancer, S. M., Olsen, J. A., & Lawford, H. L. (2011). Community and religious involvement as contexts of identity change across late adolescence and emerging adulthood. *International Journal of Behavioral Development, 35*(2), 125–135.

Hardy, S. A., Walker, L. J., Olsen, J. A., Woodbury, R. D., & Hickman, J. R. (2013). Moral identity as moral ideal self: Links to adolescent outcomes. *Developmental Psychology, 50*, 45–57.

Harkness, S., Mavridis, C. J., Liu, J. J., & Super, C. (2015). Parental ethnotheories and the development of family relationships in early and middle childhood. In L. A. Jensen (Ed.), *Oxford handbook of human development and culture: An interdisciplinary perspective* (pp. 271–291). New York, NY: Oxford University Press.

Harlow, H. F. (1958). The nature of love. *American Psychologist, 13*, 673–685.

Harms, E. (1944). The development of religious experience in children. *American Journal of Sociology, 50*, 112–122. doi:http://www.jstor.org/stable/2770961

Harnad, S. (2012). *Lateralization in the nervous system*. New York, NY: Academic Press.

Harrison, D. M. (2008). Oral sucrose for pain management in infants: Myths and misconceptions. *Journal of Neonatal Nursing, 14*(2), 39–46. doi:10.1016/j.jnn.2007.12.002

Hart, B., & Risley, T. R. (1999). *The social world of children learning to talk*. Baltimore, MD: Paul H. Brookes.

Hart, B., & Risley, T. R. (2003). The early catastrophe: The 30 million word gap by age 3. *American Educator, 27*(1), 4–9.

Hart, C. H., Newell, L. D., & Olsen, S. F. (2003). Parenting skills and social-communicative competence in childhood. In J. O. Greene & B. R. Burleson (Eds.), *Handbook of communication and social interaction skills* (pp. 753–797). Mahwah, NJ: Erlbaum.

Hart, D., Donnelly, T. M., Touniss, J., & Atkins, R. (2007). High school community service as a predictor of adult voting and volunteering. *American Educational Research Journal, 44*(1), 197–219.

Hart, D., & Fegley, S. (1995). Prosocial behavior and caring in adolescence: Relations to self-understanding and social judgment. *Child Development, 66*, 1346–1359.

Harter, S. (1989). Causes, correlates, and the functional role of global self-worth: A life-span perspective. In J. Kolligian & R. Sternberg (Eds.), *Perceptions of competence and incompetence across the life span*. New Haven, CT: Yale University Press.

Harter, S. (1999). *The construction of the self: A developmental perspective*. New York, NY: Guilford.

Harter, S. (2003). The development of self-representations during childhood and adolescence. In M. R. Leary & J. P. Tangney (Eds.), *Handbook of self and identity* (pp. 610–642). New York, NY: Guilford.

Harter, S. (2006). The development of self-esteem. In M. H. Kernis (Ed.), *Self-esteem issues and answers: A sourcebook of current perspectives* (pp. 144–150). New York, NY: Psychology Press.

Harter, S. (2006). The self. In W. Damon & R. Lerner (Eds.), & N. Eisenberg (Vol. Ed.), *Handbook of child psychology: Vol. 3. Social, emotional and personality development* (6th ed., pp. 505–570). New York, NY: Wiley.

Harter, S. (2012). *The construction of the self: Developmental and sociocultural foundations*. New York, NY: Guilford.

Harter, S., Waters, P. L., & Whitesell, N. R. (1997). Lack of voice as a manifestation of false-self behavior among adolescents: The school setting as a stage upon which the drama of authenticity is enacted. *Educational Psychologist, 32*, 153–173.

Hartman, D. E. (2009). Test review: Wechsler Adult Intelligence Scale IV (WAIS IV): Return of the gold standard. *Applied Neuropsychology, 16*(1), 85–87.

Hartup, W. W. (1996). The company they keep: Friendships and their developmental significance. *Child Development, 67*, 1–13.

Hartup, W. W., & Abecassis, M. (2004). Friends and enemies. In P. K. Smith & C. H. Hart (Eds.), *Blackwell handbook of childhood social development* (pp. 285–306). Malden, MA: Blackwell.

Harvey, J. H., & Fine, M. A. (2004). *Children of divorce: Stories of loss and growth*. Mahwah, NJ: Lawrence Erlbaum Associates.

Harwood, R., Leyendecker, B., Carlson, V., Asencio, M., & Miller, A. (2002). Parenting among Latino families in the U.S. In M. H. Bornstein (Ed.), *Handbook of parenting, Vol. 4. Social conditions and applied parenting* (2nd ed., pp. 21–46). Mahwah, NJ: Erlbaum.

Hassett, J. M., Siebert, E. R., & Wallen, K. (2008). Sex differences in rhesus monkey toy preference parallel those of children. *Hormones and Behavior, 54*, 359–364.

Hassold, T. J., & Patterson, D. (Eds.). (1999). *Down syndrome: A promising future, together*. New York, NY: Wiley-Liss.

Hastings, P. D., McShane, K. E., Parker, R., & Ladha, F. (2007). Ready to make nice: Parental socialization of young sons' and daughters' prosocial behaviors with peers. *The Journal of Genetic Psychology: Research and Theory on Human Development, 168*, 177–200.

Hatfield, E., Feybesse, C., Narine, V., & Rapson, R. L. (2016). Passionate love: Inspired by angels or demons? In K. Aumer (Ed.), *The psychology of love and hate in intimate relationships* (pp. 65–82). New York, NY: Springer.

Hatfield, E., Mo, Y. M., & Rapson, R. L. (2015). Love, sex, and marriage across cultures. In L. A. Jensen (Ed.), *The Oxford handbook of human development and culture* (pp. 570–585). New York, NY: Oxford University Press.

Hatfield, E., & Rapson, R. L. (2005). *Love and sex: Cross-cultural perspectives* (2nd ed.). Boston, MA: Allyn & Bacon.

Haugaard, J. J. (1992). Epidemiology and family violence involving children. In R. I. Ammerman & M. Hersen (Eds.), *Assessment of family violence* (pp. 89–120). New York, NY: Wiley.

Haugaard, J. L., & Hazan, C. (2004). Recognizing and treating uncommon behavioral and emotional disorders in children and adolescents who have been severely maltreated: Reactive attachment disorder. *Child Maltreatment, 9*, 154–160.

Haun, D. B., Rapold, C. J., Call, J., Janzen, G., & Levinson, S. C. (2006). Cognitive cladistics and cultural override in Hominid spatial cognition. *Proceedings of the National Academy of Sciences, 103*(46), 17568–17573. doi:10.1073/pnas.0607999103

Haun, D. B. M. (2015). Comparative and developmental cognitive anthropology: Studying the origins of cultural variability in cognitive function. In L. A. Jensen (Ed.), *Oxford handbook of human development and culture: An interdisciplinary perspective* (pp. 94–110). Oxford, UK: Oxford University Press.

Hautala, L. A., Junnila, J., Helenius, H., Vaananen, A.-M., Liuksila, P.-R., Raiha, H., … Saarijarvi, S. (2008). Towards understanding gender differences in disordered eating among adolescents. *Journal of Clinical Nursing, 17*(13), 1803–1813.

Hayashi, A., Karasawa, M., & Tobin, J. (2009). The Japanese preschool's pedagogy of feeling: Cultural strategies for supporting young children's emotional development. *Ethos, 37*, 32–49.

Hayes, K. J., & Hayes, C. (1951). The intellectual development of a home-raised chimpanzee. *Proceedings of the American Philosophical Society*, 105–109. doi:http://www.jstor.org/stable/3143327

Hayne, H., Herbert, J., & Simcock, G. (2003). Imitation from television by 24- and 30-month-olds. *Developmental Science, 6*, 254–261.

Haynie, D. L., & Osgood, D. W. (2005). Reconsidering peers and delinquency: How do peers matter? *Social Forces, 84*, 1109–1130.

Hayward, C., Killen, J. D., Wilson, D. M., & Hammer, L. D. (1997). Psychiatric risk associated with early puberty in adolescent girls. *Journal of the American Academy of Child and Adolescent Psychiatry, 36*, 255–262.

Head Start. (2015). Head Start Program Facts Fiscal Year 2015. Retrieved from https://eclkc.ohs.acf.hhs.gov/hslc/data/factsheets/2015-hs-program-factsheet.html

Hein, S., Reich, J., & Grigorenko, E. L. (2015). Cultural manifestation of intelligence in formal and informal learning environments during childhood. In L. A. Jensen (Ed.), *The Oxford handbook of human development and culture: An interdisciplinary perspective* (pp. 214–229). New York, NY: Oxford University Press.

Heine, S. H., Lehman, D. R., Markus, H. R., & Kitayama, S. (1999). Is there a universal need for positive self-regard? *Psychological Review, 106*, 766–794.

Heller, D. (1986). *The children's God*. Chicago, IL: University of Chicago Press.

Hemmer, J. D., & Kleiber, D. A. (1981). Tomboys and sissies: Androgynous children? *Sex Roles, 7*, 1205–1211.

Henggeler, S. W. (2011). Efficacy studies to large-scale transport: The development and validation of multisystemic therapy programs. *Annual Review of Clinical Psychology, 7*, 351–381.

Henggeler, S. W., Sheidow, A. J., & Lee, T. (2007). Multisystemic treatment of serious clinical problems in youths and their families. In D. W. Springer & A. R. Roberts (Eds.), *Handbook of forensic mental health with victims and offenders: Assessment, treatments, and research* (pp. 315–345). New York, NY: Springer.

Henrich, J., Heine, S. J., & Norenzayan, A. (2010). Beyond WEIRD: Towards a broad-based behavioral science. *Behavioral and Brain Sciences, 33*, 111–135.

Henrichs, J., Schenk, J. J., Barendregt, C. S., Schmidt, H. G., Steegers, E. A. P., Hofman, A., … Tiemeier, H. (2010). Fetal growth from mid- to late pregnancy is associated with infant development: The Generation R study. *Developmental Medicine & Child Neurology, 52*, 644–651.

Hensler, B. A., Schatschneider, C., Taylor, J., & Wagner, R. K. (2010). Behavioral genetic approach to the study of dyslexia. *Journal of Developmental and Behavioral Pediatrics, 31*, 525–532.

Hepper, P. G., Wells, D. L., & Lynch, C. (2005). Prenatal thumb sucking is related to postnatal handedness. *Neuropsychologia, 43*, 313–315.

Herba, C. M., Ferdinand, R. F., Stijnen, T., Veenstra, R., Oldehinkel, A. J., Ormel, J., & Verhulst, F. C. (2008). Victimisation and suicide ideation in the trails study: Specific vulnerabilities of victims. *Journal of Child Psychology and Psychiatry, 49*(8), 867–876.

Herculano-Houzel, S. (2009). The human brain in numbers: A linearly scaled-up primate brain. *Frontiers in Human Neuroscience, 3*. doi:10.3389/neuro.09.031.2009

HERI. (2012). The American freshman: National norms fall 2012. Retrieved from: https://www.heri.ucla.edu/monographs/TheAmericanFreshman2012-Expanded.pdf

HERI. (2017). The American freshman: Fifty-year trends 1966–2015. Retrieved from: https://heri.ucla.edu/

Herman-Giddens, M., Slora, E., Wasserman, R., Bourdony, C., Bhapkar, M., Koch, G., & Hasemeier, C. (1997). Secondary sexual characteristics and menses in young girls seen in office practice: A study from the Pediatric Research in Office Settings Network. *Pediatrics, 88*, 505–512.

Herman-Giddens, M., Wang, L., & Koch, G. (2001). Secondary sexual characteristics in boys. *Archives of Pediatrics and Adolescent Medicine, 155*, 1022–1028.

Hermans, H. (2015). Human development in today's globalizing world: Implications for self and identity. In L. A. Jensen (Ed.), *Oxford handbook of human development and culture* (pp. 28–42). New York, NY: Oxford University Press.

Hermans, H. J. M. (2015). Human development in today's globalizing world: Implications for self and identity. In L. A. Jensen (Ed.), *Oxford handbook of human development and culture: An interdisciplinary perspective* (pp. 28–42). New York, NY: Oxford University Press.

Hermans, H. J. M., & Kempen, H. J. G. (1998). Moving cultures: The perilous problems of cultural dichotomies in a globalizing society. *American Psychologist, 53*, 1111–1120.

Herpetz-Dahlmann, B., Wille, N., Holling, J., Vloet, T. D., & Ravens-Sieberer, U. [BELLA study group (Germany)]. (2008). Disordered eating behavior and attitudes, associated psychopathology and health-related quality of life: Results of the BELLA study. *European Child & Adolescent Psychiatry, 17*(Suppl. 1), 82–91.

Herrenkohl, T. I., Mason, W. A., Kosterman, R., Lengua, L. J., Hawkins, J. D., & Abbott, R. D. (2004). Pathways from physical childhood abuse to partner violence in young adulthood. *Violence and Victims, 19*, 123–136.

Herrera, E., Reissland, N., & Shepherd, J. (2004). Maternal touch and maternal child-directed speech: Effects of depressed mood in the postnatal period. *Journal of Affective Disorders, 81*, 29–39.

Herrnstein, R. J., & Murray, C. (1995). *The bell curve: Intelligence and class structure in American life*. New York, NY: Simon & Schuster.

Hertel, B. R., & Donahue, M. J. (1995). Parental influences on God images among children: Testing Durkheim's metaphoric parallelism. *Journal for the Scientific Study of Religion, 34*, 186–199. doi:10.2307/1386764

Hetherington, E. M., Henderson, S., & Reiss, D. (1999). Adolescent siblings in stepfamilies: Family functioning and adolescent adjustment. *Monographs of the Society for Research in Child Development, 64*(4).

Hetherington, E. M., & Kelly, J. (2002) *For better or worse: Divorce reconsidered*. New York, NY: Norton.

Hetherington, E. M., & Stanley-Hagan, M. (2002). Parenting in divorced and remarried families. In M. H. Bornstein (Ed.), *Handbook of parenting, Vol. 3: Being and becoming a parent* (2nd ed., pp. 287–315). Mahwah, NJ: Erlbaum.

Hewlett, B. S., & Macfarlan, S. J. (2010). Fathers' roles in hunter-gatherer and other small-scale cultures. *The Role of the Father in Child Development, 413*, 434.

Hewlett, B. S., & Roulette, J. W. (2014). Cosleeping beyond infancy: Culture, ecology, and evolutionary biology of bed-sharing among Aka foragers and Ngandu farmers in central Africa. In D. Narvaez et al., (Eds.), *Ancestral landscapes in human evolution: Culture, childrearing, and social well-being* (pp. 129–163). New York, NY: Oxford University Press.

Heyman, G. D., & Legare, C. H. (2004). Children's beliefs about gender differences in the academic and social domains. *Sex Roles, 50*, 227–239.

Hickman, J. R. & Fasoli, A. D. (2015). The dynamics of ethical co-occurrence in Hmong and American evangelical families: New directions for The Ethics research. In L. A. Jensen (Ed.), *Moral development in a global world: Research from a cultural-developmental perspective* (pp. 141–169). New York, NY: Cambridge University Press.

Higgins, A. (1991). The Just Community approach to moral education: Evolution of the idea and recent findings. In W. M. Kurtines & J. L. Gerwitz (Eds.), *Handbook of moral behavior and development, Vol. 3: Application* (pp. 111–141.) Hillsdale, NJ: Lawrence Erlbaum Associates.

Hildreth, K., Sweeney, B., & Rovee-Collier, C. (2003). Differential memory-preserving effects of reminders at 6 months. *Journal of Experimental Child Psychology, 84*, 41–62.

Hill, J., & Lynch, M. (1983). The intensification of gender-related role expectations during early adolescence. In J. Brooks-Gunn & A. Petersen (Eds.), *Girls at puberty: Biological and psychosocial perspectives* (pp. 201–228). New York, NY: Plenum.

Hille, E. T., Weisglas-Kuperus, N., Van Goudoever, J. B., Jacobusse, G. W., Ens-Dokkum, M. H., de Groot, L., … Kollée, L. A. (2007). Functional outcomes and participation in young adulthood for very preterm and very low birth weight infants: The Dutch project on preterm and small for gestational age infants at 19 years of age. *Pediatrics, 120*(3), e587–e595. doi:10.1542/peds.2006-2407

Hilliard, L. J., & Liben, L. S. (2010). Differing levels of gender salience in preschool classrooms: Effects on children's gender attitudes and intergroup bias. *Child Development, 81*(6), 1787–1798. doi:10.1111/j.1467-8624.2010.01510.x

Hillman, C. H. (Ed.). (2014). *The relation of childhood physical activity to brain health, cognition, and scholastic achievement*. Boston, MA: Wiley.

Hillman, C. H., Pontifex, M. B., Castelli, D. M., Khan, N. A., Raine, L. B., Scudder, M. R., … Kamijo, K. (2014). Effects of the FITKids randomized controlled trial on executive control and brain function. *Pediatrics, 134*(4), e1063–e1071. doi:10.1542/peds.2013-3219

Hinduja, S., & Patchin, J. W. (2008). Personal information of adolescents on the Internet: A quantitative content analysis of MySpace. *Journal of Adolescence, 31*(1), 125–146.

Hines, M. (2004). *Brain gender*. New York, NY: Oxford University Press.

Hines, M. (2011). Gender development and the human brain. *Annual Review of Neuroscience, 34*, 67–86. doi:10.1146/annurev-neuro-061010-113654

Hines, M. (2011). Prenatal endocrine influences on sexual orientation and on sexually differentiated childhood behavior. *Frontiers in Neuroendocrinology, 32*, 170–182.

Hines, M. (2015). Gendered development. In R. M. Lerner (Series Ed.), M. E. Lamb (Vol. Ed.), *Handbook of child psychology and developmental science* (7th ed.), *Vol. 3: Socioemotional processes* (pp. 842–887). New York, NY: Wiley.

Hinojosa, T., Sheu, C.-F., & Michael, G. F. (2003). Infant hand-use preference for grasping objects contributes to the development of a hand-use preference for manipulating objects. *Developmental Psychobiology, 43*, 328–334.

Hiscock, H., & Jordan, B. (2004). Problem crying in infancy. *Medical Journal of Australia, 181*, 507–512.

Hjelmstedt, A., Andersson, L., Skoog-Svanberg, A., Bergh, T., Boivin, J., & Collins, A. (1999). Gender differences in psychological reactions to infertility among couples seeking IVF- and ICSI-treatment. *Acta Obstet Gynecol Scand, 78*, 42–48.

Ho, D. Y. F. (1987). Fatherhood in Chinese culture. In M. E. Lamb (Ed.), *The father's role: Cross-cultural perspectives* (pp. 227–245). Hillsdale, NJ: Erlbaum.

Ho, M. G., Shi, Y., Ma, S., & Novotny, T. R. (2007). Perceptions of tobacco advertising and marketing that might lead to smoking initiation among Chinese high school girls. *Tobacco Control: An International Journal, 16*(5), 359–360.

Hochschild, A. R. (2001). Emotion work, feeling rules, and social structure. In A. Branaman (Ed.), *Self and society: Blackwell readers in sociology* (pp. 138–155). Malden, MA: Blackwell.

Hodapp, R. M., Burke, M. M., & Urdano, R. C. (2012). What's age got to do with it? Implications of maternal age on families of offspring with Down syndrome. In R. M. Hodapp (Ed.), *International review of research in developmental disabilities* (pp. 111–143). New York, NY: Academic Press.

Hodnett, E. D., Gates, S., Hofmeyr, G. J., & Sakala, C. (2007). Continuous support for women during childbirth. *Cochrane Database of Systematic Reviews, 3*.

Hoeben, E. M., Meldrum, R. C., & Young, J. T. (2016). The role of peer delinquency and unstructured socializing in explaining delinquency and substance use: A state-of-the-art review. *Journal of Criminal Justice, 47*, 108–122.

Hofer, C., Eisenberg, N., Spinrad, T. L., Morris, A. S., Gershoff, E., Valiente, C., … Eggum, N. D. (2013). Mother–adolescent conflict: Stability, change, and relations with externalizing and internalizing behavior problems. *Social Development, 22*, 259–279.

Hoff, E. (2009). *Language development*. Belmont, CA: Wadsworth.

Hofferth, S. L., & Moon, U. J. (2016). How do they do it? The immigrant paradox in the transition to adulthood. *Social Science Research, 57*, 177–194.

Hoffman, M. L. (2000). *Empathy and moral development*. New York, NY: Cambridge University Press.

Hoffmann, A., Rüttler, V., & Nieder, A. (2011). Ontogeny of object permanence and object tracking in the carrion crow, Corvus corone. *Animal Behaviour, 82*(2), 359–367.

Hoffner, C. A., & Levine, K. J. (2005). Enjoyment of mediated fright and violence: A meta analysis. *Media Psychology, 7*(2), 207–237.

Hofman, P. L., Regan, F., Jackson, W. E., Jefferies, C., Knight, D. B., Robinson, E. M., & Cutfield, W. S. (2004). Premature birth and later insulin resistance. *New England Journal of Medicine, 351*, 2179–2186.

Hofmeyr, G. J. (2002). Interventions to help external cephalic version for breech presentation at term. *Cochrane Database of Systematic Reviews, 2*, CD000184.

Hofstra, B., Corten, R., & van Tubergen, F. (2016). Who was first on Facebook? Determinants of early adoption among adolescents. *New Media & Society, 18*, 2340–2358. doi:10.1177/1461444815584592

Hogan, M. C., Foreman, K. J., Naghavi, M., Ahn, S. Y., Wang, M., Makela, S. M.,…Murray, C. J. L. (2010). Maternal mortality for 181 countries, 1980–2008: A systematic analysis of progress toward Millennium Development Goal 5. *The Lancet, 375*, 1–15.

Hoh, J., & Ott, J. (2003). Mathematical multi-locus approaches to localizing complex human trait genes. *Nature Reviews Genetics, 4*, 701–709.

Hokoda, A., Lu, H.-H. A., & Angeles, M. (2006). School bullying in Taiwanese adolescents. *Journal of Emotional Abuse, 6*(4), 69–90.

Holodynski, M. (2009). Milestones and mechanisms of emotional development. In B. Rottger-Rossler & H. J. Markowitsch (Eds.), *Emotions as bio-cultural processes* (pp. 139–163). New York, NY: Springer US.

Holodynski, M., & Friedlmeier, W. (2006). *Development of emotions and their regulation: A socioculturally based internalization model*. Boston, MA: Kluwer Academic.

Holsti, L., & Grunau, R. E. (2010). Considerations for using sucrose to reduce procedural pain in preterm infants. *Pediatrics, 125*, 1042–1049.

Honein, M. A., Paulozzi, L. J., Mathews, T. J., Erickson, J. D., & Wong, L. C. (2001). Impact of folic acid fortification of the U.S. food supply on the occurrence of neural tube defects. *The Journal of the American Medical Association, 285*, 2981–2986.

Hood, B., Cole-Davies, V., & Dias, M. (2003). Looking and search measures of object knowledge in preschool children. *Developmental Psychology, 39*, 61–70.

Hooghe, M., & Wilkenfeld, B. (2008). The stability of political attitudes and behaviors a cross adolescence and early adulthood: A comparison of survey data on adolescents and young adults in eight countries. *Journal of Youth and Adolescence, 37*(2), 155–167.

Horn, J. L. (1982). The aging of human abilities. In B. B. Wolman (Ed.), *Handbook of developmental psychology* (pp. 847–870). Englewood Cliffs, NJ: Prentice-Hall.

Horn, K., Dino, G., Kalsekar, I., & Mody, R. (2005). The impact of *Not on Tobacco* on teen smoking cessation: End-program evaluation results, 1998–2003. *Journal of Adolescent Research, 20*, 640–661.

Horn, S. (2003). Adolescents' reasoning about exclusion from social groups. *Developmental Psychology, 39*, 71–84.

Horne, J. (2014). Sleep hygeine: Exercise and other 'do's and don'ts'. *Sleep Medicine, 15*, 731–732.

Horton, D. M. (2001). The disappearing bell curve. *Journal of Secondary Gifted Education, 12*, 185–188.

Horwitz, B. N., Neiderhiser, J. M., Ganiban, J. M., Spotts, E. L., Lichtenstein, P., & Reiss, D. (2010). Genetic and environmental influences on global family conflict. *Journal of Family Psychology, 24*, 217.

Houck, C. D., Nugent, N. R., Lescano, C. M., Peters, A., & Brown, L. K. (2010). Sexual abuse and sexual risk behavior: Beyond the impact of psychiatric problems. *Journal of Pediatric Psychology, 35*(5), 473–483.

Howard, K. S., Carothers, S. S., Smith, L. E., & Akai, C. E. (2007). Overcoming the odds: Protective factors in the lives of children. In J. G. Borkowski, J. R. Farris, T. L. Whitman, S. S. Carothers, K. Weed, et al. (Eds.), *Risk and resilience: Adolescent mothers and their children grow up* (pp. 205–232). Mahwah, NJ: Lawrence Erlbaum.

Howard, R. W. (2001). Searching the real world for signs of rising population intelligence. *Personality & Individual Differences, 30*, 1039–1058.

Howe, N., Aquan-Assee, J., & Bukowski, W. M. (2001). Predicting sibling relations over time: Synchrony between maternal management styles and sibling relationship quality. *Merrill-Palmer Quarterly, 47*, 121–141.

Howes, C. (1985). Sharing fantasy: Social pretend play in toddlers. *Child Development, 56*, 1253–1258.

Howes, C. (1996). The earliest friendships. In W. M. Bukowski, A. F. Newcomb, & W. W. Hartup (Eds.), *The company they keep: Friendship in childhood and adolescence* (pp. 66–86). Boston, MA: Cambridge University Press.

Hoza, B., Kaiser, N., & Hurt, E. (2008). Evidence-based treatments for attention deficit/hyperactivity disorder (ADHD). In R. G. Steele, D. T. Elkin, & M. C. Roberts (Eds.), *Handbook of evidence-based therapies for children and adolescents: Bridging science and practice. Issues in clinical child psychology* (pp. 197–219). New York, NY: Springer.

Huang, B., Biro, F. M., & Dorn, L. D. (2009). Determination of relative timing of pubertal maturation through ordinal logistic modeling: Evaluation of growth and timing parameters. *Journal of Adolescent Health, 45*(4), 383–388.

Huang, C. Y., & Stormshak, E. A. (2011). A longitudinal examination of early adolescence ethnic identity trajectories. *Cultural Diversity and Ethnic Minority Psychology, 17*(3), 261–270. doi:10.1037/a0023882

Huang, R. L., Lu, Z., Liu, J. J., You, Y. M., Pan, Z. Q., Wei, Z.,…Wang, Z. Z. (2009). Features and predictors of problematic Internet use in Chinese college students. *Behaviour & Information Technology, 28*, 485–490.

Hublin, J. J. (2005). Evolution of the human brain and compara- tive paleoanthropology. In S. Dehaene, J.-R. Duhamel, M. D. Hauser, & G. Rizzolatti (Eds.), *From monkey brain to human brain: A Fyssen Foundation symposium* (pp. 57–71). Cambridge, MA: The MIT Press.

Huesmann, L. R., Eron, L. D., Lefkowitz, M. M., & Walder, L. O. (1984). Stability of aggression over time and generations. *Developmental Psychology, 20*, 1120–1134.

Huesmann, L. R., Moise-Titus, J., Podolski, C., & Eron, L. D. (2003). Longitudinal relations between children's exposure to TV violence and their aggressiveness in young adulthood, 1977–1992. *Developmental Psychology, 39*, 201–221.

Huffaker, D. A., & Calbert, S. L. (2005). Gender, identity, and language use in teenage blogs. *Journal of Computer-Mediated Communication, 10*(2). Retrieved January 22, 2008, from http://www.jcmc.indiana.edu/vol10/issue2/huffaker.html

Hughes, C., & Dunn, J. (2007). Children's relationships with other children. In C. A. Brownell & C. B. Kopp (Eds.), *Socioemotional development in the toddler years* (pp. 177–200). New York, NY: Guilford.

Hulei, E., Zevenbergen, A., & Jacobs, S. (2006). Discipline behaviors of Chinese American and European American mothers. *Journal of Psychology: Interdisciplinary and Applied, 140*, 459–475.

Hulme, C., & Snowling, M. J. (2004). Reading development and dyslexia. San Diego, CA: Singular.

Hunnius, S., de Wit, T. C. J., Vrins, S., & von Hofsten, C. (2011). Facing threat: Infants' and adults' visual scanning of faces with neutral, happy, sad, angry, and fearful emotional expressions. *Cognition and Emotion, 25*, 193–205.

Hunt, E. (1989). Cognitive science: Definition, status, and questions. *Annual Review of Psychology, 40*, 603–629.

Hunziker, U. A., & Barr, R. G. (1986). Increased carrying reduces infant crying: A randomized controlled trial. *Pediatrics, 77*, 641–648.

Hust, S. (2006). Gender identity development. In J. J. Arnett (Ed.), *Encyclopedia of children, adolescents, and the media*. Thousand Oaks, CA: Sage.

Hust, S. J. T., Brown, J. D., & L'Engle, K. L. (2008). Boys will be boys and girls better be prepared: An analysis of the rare sexual health messages in young adolescents' media. *Mass Communication and Society, 11*(1), 3–23.

Huston, A. C., Bickham, D. S., Lee, J. H., & Wright, J. C. (2007). From attention to comprehension: How children watch and learn from television. In N. Pecora, J. P. Murray, & E. A. Wartella (Eds.), *Children and television: Fifty years of research* (pp. 41–63). Mahwah, NJ: Lawrence Erlbaum Associates Publishers.

Huttenlocher, P. R. (2002). *Neural plasticity: The effects of environment on the development of the cerebral cortex.* Cambridge, MA: Harvard University Press.

Hwang, J. Y., Shin, C., Frongillo, E. A., Shin, K. R., & Jo, I. (2003). Secular trend in age at menarche for South Korean women born between 1920 and 1986: The Ansan Study. *Annals of Human Biology, 30*(4), 434–442. doi:10.1080/0301446031000111393

Hyde, J. S. (2005). The gender similarities hypothesis. *American Psychologist, 60*, 581.

Hyde, J. S., & Linn, M. C. (1988). Gender differences in verbal ability: A meta-analysis. *Psychological Bulletin, 104*(1), 53. doi:http://dx.doi.org/10.1037/0033-2909.104.1.53

Hymel, S., McDougall, P., & Renshaw, P. (2004). Peer acceptance/rejection. In P. K. Smith & C. H. Hart (Eds.), *Blackwell handbook of childhood social development* (pp. 265–284). Malden, MA: Blackwell.

Hymowitz, K., Carroll, J. S., Wilcox, W. B., & Kaye, K. (2013). *Knot yet: The benefits and costs of delayed marriage in America.* Charlottesville, VA: National Marriage Project.

Iacovou, M. (2011). *Leaving home: Independence, togetherness, and income in Europe.* New York, NY: United Nations Population Division. Retrieved from http://www.un.org/en/development/desa/population/publications/pdf/expert/2011-10_Iacovou_Expert-paper.pdf

Ichikawa, H., Toyoda, Y., Takeuchi, M., Tashiro, M., & Suzuki, M. (2015). Do personal attributes and an understanding of sarcasm and metaphor explain problematic experiences on the Internet? A survey for the development of information literacy education tools. *Transactions on Networks and Communications, 3*, 158.

Iglowstein, I., Jenni, O. G., Molinari, L., & Largo, R. H. (2003). Sleep duration from infancy to adolescence: Reference values and generational trends. *Pediatrics, 111*, 302–307.

Iles, J., Slade, P., & Spiby, H. (2011). Posttraumatic stress symptoms and postpartum depression in couples after childbirth: The role of partner support and attachment. *Journal of Anxiety Disorders, 25*, 520–530.

Iliodromiti, S., Mackay, D. F., Smith, G. C. S., Pell, J. P., & Nelson, S. M. (2014). Apgar score and the risk of cause-specific infant mortality: A population-based cohort study. *The Lancet, 384*, 1749–1755.

Inhelder, B., & Piaget, J. (1958). *The growth of logical thinking from childhood to adolescence.* New York, NY: Basic Books.

Insel, T. (2010). Rethinking schizophrenia. *Nature, 468*, 187–193.

Insel, T. (2013, August 19). *Director's Blog: Infantile Amnesia.* Retrieved from http://www.nimh.nih.gov/about/director/2013/infantile-amnesia.shtml

Institute of Medicine of the National Academies. (2005). *Preventing childhood obesity: Health in the balance.* Washington, DC: Author.

International Labor Organization (ILO). (2002). *A future without child labour.* New York, NY: Author.

International Labor Organization (ILO). (2004). *Investing in every child. An economic study of the costs and benefits of eliminating child labour.* New York, NY: Author.

International Labor Organization (ILO). (2013). *Marking progress against child labour: Global estimates and trends 2000–2012.* Geneva, Switzerland: Author.

International Social Survey Programme (ISSP). (2012). *Religion III, variable report.* Unter Sachsenhausen, Germany: Leibniz. Institute for Social Sciences.

Ioannidis, J. P. (2005). Why most published research findings are false. *PLoS Medicine, 2*(8), 696–701. doi:10.1371/journal.pmed.0020124

Ip, S., Chung, M., Raman, G., Chew, P., Magula, N., DeVine, D.,... Lau, J. (2007). *Breastfeeding and maternal and infant health outcomes in developed countries. Evidence Report/Technology Assessment No. 153.* Rockville, MD: Agency for Healthcare Research and Quality.

Ireland, J. L., & Archer, N. (2004). Association between measures of aggression and bullying among juvenile young offenders. *Aggressive Behavior, 30*, 29–42.

Irner, T. B. (2012). Substance exposure in utero and developmental consequences in adolescence: A systematic review. *Child Neuropsychology, 18*, 521–549. http://dx.doi.org/10.1080/09297049.2011.628309

Ishihara, N. (2014). Is it rude language? Children learning pragmatics through visual narrative. *TESL Canada Journal, 30*(7), 135.

Ispa, J. M., & Halgunseth, L. C. (2004). Talking about corporal punishment: Nine low-income African American mothers' perspectives. *Early Childhood Research Quarterly, 19*, 463–484.

Iverson, R., Kuhl, P. K., Akahane-Yamada, R., Diesch, E., Tohkura, Y., & Kettermann, A. (2003). A perceptual interference account of acquisition difficulties for non-native phonemes. *Cognition, 87*, B47–B57.

Izard, C. E. (1991). *The psychology of emotions.* New York, NY: Plenum Press.

Izard, C. E., & Ackerman, B. P. (2000). Motivational, organizational, and regulatory functions of discrete emotions. In M. Lewis & J. M. Haviland-Jones (Eds.), *Handbook of emotions* (2nd ed., pp. 253–264). New York, NY: Guilford.

Jaakkola, J. J., & Gissler, M. (2004). Maternal smoking in pregnancy, fetal development, and childhood asthma. *American Journal of Public Health, 94*, 136–140.

Jackson, L. M., Pratt, M. W., Hunsberger, B., & Pancer, S. M. (2005). Optimism as a mediator of the relation between perceived parental authoritativeness and adjustment among adolescents: Finding the sunny side of the street. *Social Development, 14*, 273–304.

Jacobson, K. C., & Crockett, L. J. (2000). Parental monitoring and adolescent adjustment: An ecological perspective. *Journal of Research on Adolescence, 10*, 65–98.

Jaffee, S., & Hyde, J. S. (2000). Gender differences in moral orientation: A meta-analysis. *Psychological Bulletin, 126*(5), 703. doi:10.1037/0033-2909.126.5.703

Jalonick, M. C. (2010, December 13). Obama signs historic school lunch nutrition bill. Retrieved from http://www.salon.com/food/feature/2010/12/13/us_obama_child_nutrition

James, C., Hadley, D. W., Holtzman, N. A., & Winkelstein, J. A. (2006). How does the mode of inheritance of a genetic condition influence families? A study of guilt, blame, stigma, and understanding of inheritance and reproductive risks in families with X-linked and autosomal recessive diseases. *Genetics in Medicine, 8*, 234–242.

James, J. (2010). Mechanisms of access to the Internet in rural areas of developing countries. *Telematics and informatics, 27*, 370–376.

Jankowiak, W. R., & Fischer, E. F. (1992). A cross-cultural perspective on romantic love. *Ethology, 31*, 149–155.

Janssen, I., Katzmarzyk, P. T., Ross, R., Leon, A. S., Skinner, J. S., Rao, D. C., Wilmore, J. H.,... Bouchard, C. (2004). Fitness alters the associations of BMI and waist circumference with total and abdominal fat. *Obesity Research, 12*, 525–537.

Janssen, M., Chinapaw, M. J. M., Rauh, S. P., Toussaint, H. M., van Mechelen, W., & Verhagen, E. A. L. M. (2014). A short physical activity break from cognitive tasks increases selective attention in primary school children aged 10–11. *Mental Health and Physical Activity, 7*, 129–134.

Jaquez, S. D., Thakre, T. P., & Krishna, J. (2017). Delayed Sleep Phase Syndrome. In S. V. Kathare & R. Q. Scott (Eds.), *Sleep disorders in adolescents* (pp. 7–25). New York, NY: Springer.

Jeffrey, J. (2004, November). Parents often blind to their kids' weight. *British Medical Journal Online.* Retrieved from content.health.msn.com/content/article/97/104292.htm

Jenkins, J. M., Rabash, J., & O'Connor, T. G. (2003). The role of the shared family context in differential parenting. *Developmental Psychology, 39*, 99–113.

Jennings, N. (2007). Advertising, viewer age and. In J. J. Arnett (Ed.), *Encyclopedia of children, adolescents, and the media* (pp. 55–57). Thousand Oaks, CA: Sage.

Jennings, W., & Akers, R. L. (2011). Social learning theory. In C. D. Bryant (Ed.), *The Routledge handbook of deviant behavior* (pp. 106–113). New York, NY: Routledge/Taylor & Francis Group.

Jennings, W. G., & Reingle, J. M. (2012). On the number and shape of developmental/life-course violence, aggression, and delinquency trajectories: A state-of-the-art review. *Journal of Criminal Justice, 40*, 472–489.

Jensen, L. A. (1995). Habits of the heart revisited: Autonomy, community, and divinity in adults' moral language. *Qualitative Sociology, 18*, 71–86.

Jensen, L. A. (2008). Coming of age in a multicultural world: Globalization and adolescent cultural identity formation. In D. L. Browning (Ed.), *Adolescent identities: A collection of readings* (pp. 3–17). New York, NY: Analytic Press.

Jensen, L. A. (2008). Through two lenses: A cultural-developmental approach to moral psychology. *Developmental Review, 28*, 289–315.

Jensen, L. A. (2009). Conceptions of God and the devil across the lifespan: A cultural-developmental study of religious liberals and conservatives. *Journal for the Scientific Study of Religion, 48*(1), 121–145. doi:10.1111/j.1468-5906.2009.01433.x

Jensen, L. A. (2010). Immigrant youth in the United States: Coming of age among diverse civic cultures. In L.R. Sherrod, J. Torney-Purta, & C. A. Flanagan (Eds.), *Handbook of research on civic engagement in youth* (pp. 425–443). Hoboken, NJ: Wiley.

Jensen, L. A. (Ed.). (2011). *Bridging cultural and developmental psychology.* New York, NY: Oxford University Press.

Jensen, L. A. (2011). The cultural-developmental theory of moral psychology: A new synthesis. In L. A. Jensen (Ed.), *Bridging cultural and developmental psychology: New syntheses in theory, research and policy* (pp. 3–25). New York, NY: Oxford University Press.

Jensen, L. A. (2015). Cultural-developmental scholarship for a global world: An introduction. In L. A. Jensen (Ed.), *Oxford handbook of human development and culture: An interdisciplinary perspective* (pp. 3–13). New York, NY: Oxford University Press.

Jensen, L. A. (2015). *Moral development in a global world: Research from a cultural-developmental perspective.* New York, NY: Cambridge University Press.

Jensen, L. A. (2015). Moral reasoning: Developmental emergence and life course pathways among cultures. In Jensen, L. A. (Ed.), *The Oxford handbook of human development and culture: An interdisciplinary perspective* (pp. 230–254). New York, NY: Oxford University Press.

Jensen, L. A. (2015). *Oxford handbook of human development and culture: An interdisciplinary perspective.* New York, NY: Oxford University Press.

Jensen, L. A. (Ed.). (2016). *The Oxford handbook of human development and culture: An interdisciplinary perspective.* New York, NY: Oxford University Press.

Jensen, L. A., Arnett, J. J., & McKenzie, J. (2012). Globalization and cultural identity development in adolescence and emerging adulthood. In S. J. Schwartz, K. Luyckx, & V. L. Vignoles (Eds.), *Handbook of identity theory and research* (pp. 285–301). New York, NY: Springer Publishing Company.

Jensen, L. A., & Dost-Gözkan, A. (2015). Adolescent–parent relations in Asian Indian and Salvadoran immigrant families: A cultural–developmental analysis of autonomy, authority, conflict, and cohesion. *Journal of Research on Adolescence, 25,* 340–351.

Jensen, L. A., & Flanagan, C. A. (Eds.). (2008). Immigrant civic engagement: New translations. *Applied Developmental Science, 12,* 55–57.

Jensen, L. A., & LaPlante, J. (2015). Civic involvement. In C. Suárez-Orozco, M. M. Abo-Zena, & A. K. Marks (Eds.), *Transitions: The development of children of immigrants* (pp. 276–296). New York, NY: New York University Press.

Jensen, L. A., & McKenzie, J. (2016). The moral reasoning of U.S. evangelical and mainline Protestant children, adolescents, and adults: A cultural-developmental study. *Child Development, 87,* 446–464.

Jensen, T. K., Jørgensen, N., Punab, M., Haugen, T. B., Suominen, J., Zilaitiene, B., … Skakkebaek, N. E. (2004). Association of in utero exposure to maternal smoking with reduced semen quality and testis size in adulthood: A cross-sectional study of 1,770 young men from the general population in five European countries. *American Journal of Epidemiology, 159*(1), 49–58. doi:10.1093/aje/kwh002

Jequier, A. (2011). *Male infertility: A clinical guide.* New York, NY: Cambridge University Press.

Jessor, R., Colby, A., & Shweder, R. A. (1996). *Ethnography and human development: Context and meaning in social inquiry.* Chicago, IL: University of Chicago Press.

Jeynes, W. H. (2007). The impact of parental remarriage on children: A meta-analysis. *Marriage & Family Review, 40*(4), 75–102.

Ji, C., & Chen, T. J. (2008). Secular changes in stature and body mass index for Chinese youth in sixteen major cities, 1950s–2005. *American Journal of Human Biology, 20,* 530–537. doi:10.1002/ajhb.20770

Jia, Y., Way, N., Ling, G., Yoshikawa, H., Chen, X., Hughes, D., … Lu, Z. (2009). The influence of student perceptions of school climate on socioemotional and academic adjustment: A comparison of Chinese and American adolescents. *Child Development, 80*(5), 1514–1530.

Jiao, S., Ji, G., & Jing, Q. (1996). Cognitive development of Chinese urban only children and children with siblings. *Child Development, 67,* 387–395.

Jimenez, M., Jackson, A. M., & Deye, K. (2015). Aspects of abuse: Commercial sexual exploitation of children. *Current Problems in Pediatric and Adolescent Health Care, 45,* 80–85.

Jingxiong, J., Rosenqvist, U., Huishan, W., Greiner, T., Guangli, L., & Sarkadi, A. (2007). Influence of grandparents on eating behaviors of young children in Chinese three-generation families. *Appetite, 48,* 377–383.

Jochman, K. A., & Fromme, K. (2010). Maturing out of substance use: The other side of etiology. In L. Scheier (Ed.), *Handbook of drug use etiology: Theory, methods, and empirical findings* (pp. 565–578). Washington, DC: American Psychological Association.

Johnson, D. J., Jaeger, E., Randolph, S. M., Cauce, A. M., Ward, J., & National Institute of Child Health and Human Development: Early Child Care Research Network. (2003). Studying the effects of early child care experiences on the development of children of color in the United States: Toward a more inclusive research agenda. *Child Development, 74,* 1227–1244.

Johnson, D. M. (2005). Mind, brain, and the upper Paleolithic. In C. E. Erneling & D. M. Johnson (Eds.), *The mind as a scientific object: Between brain and culture* (pp. 499–510). New York, NY: Oxford University Press.

Johnson, G. R., Krug, E. G., & Potter, L. B. (2000). Suicide among adolescents and young adults: A cross-national comparison of 34 countries. *Suicide & Life-Threatening Behavior, 30,* 74–82.

Johnson, J. S., & Newport, E. L. (1991). Critical period effects on universal properties of language: The status of subjacency in the acquisition of a second language. *Cognition, 39,* 215–258.

Johnson, M. C. (2000). The view from the Wuro: A guide to child rearing for Fulani parents. In J. DeLoache & A. Gottlieb (Eds.), *A world of babies: Imagined childcare guides for seven societies* (pp. 171–198). New York, NY: Cambridge University Press.

Johnson, M. D. (2016). *Human biology: Concepts and current issues.* New York, NY: Pearson.

Johnson, M. K., Beebe, T., Mortimer, J. T., & Snyder, M. (1998). Volunteerism in adolescence: A process perspective. *Journal of Research on Adolescence, 8*(3), 309–332.

Johnston, L. D., O'Malley, P. M., Miech, R. A., Bachman, J. G., & Schulenberg, J. E. (2014). *Monitoring the future: National results on drug use: 1975–2013: Overview, key findings on adolescent drug use.* Ann Arbor, MI: Institute for Social Research, The University of Michigan.

Johnston, L. D., O'Malley, P. M., Miech, R. A., Bachman, J. G., & Schulenberg, J. E. (2015). *Monitoring the Future: 2015 Overview: Key Findings on Adolescent Drug Use.* Ann Arbor, MI: The University of Michigan Institute for Social Research.

Jones, E., & Kay, M. A. (2003). The cultural anthropology of the placenta. In L. Dundes (Ed.), *The manner born: Birth rites in cross-cultural perspective* (pp. 101–116). Walnut Creek, CA: AltaMira Press.

Jones, K. O., Reid, J., & Bartlett, R. (2008). E-learning and e-cheating. *Communication & Cognition, 41*(1–2), 61–70.

Jones, M. D., Crowther, J. H., & Ciesla, J. A. (2014). A naturalistic study of fat talk and its behavioral and affective consequences. *Body Image, 11,* 337–345. doi:10.1016/j.bodyim.2014.05.007

Jones, R. E., & Lopez, K. H. (2014). *Human reproductive biology* (4th ed.). Waltham, MA: Academic Press.

Jonson, S. P. (2013). Object perception. In Zelazo, P. D. (Ed.), *The Oxford handbook of developmental psychology: Volume 1: Body and mind* (pp. 371–379). New York, NY: Oxford University Press.

Jönsson, P., & Carlson, I. (2000). Androgyny and creativity: A study of the relationship between a balanced sex-role and creative functioning. *Scandinavian Journal of Psychology, 41,* 269–274.

Jordan, B. (1994). *Birth in four cultures.* Long Grove, IL: Westland.

Jose, P. E., & Brown, I. (2008). When does the gender difference in rumination begin? Gender and age differences in the use of rumination by adolescents. *Journal of Youth and Adolescence, 37*(2), 180–192.

Joshi, S. P., Peter, J., & Valkenburg, P. M. (2011). Scripts of sexual desire and danger in US and Dutch teen girl magazines: A cross-national content analysis. *Sex Roles, 64*(7–8), 463–474.

Josselyn, S. A., & Frankland, P. W. (2012). Infantile amnesia: A neurogenic hypothesis. *Learning & Memory, 19*(9), 423–433.

Juang, L. P., & Silbereisen, R. K. (2002). The relationship between adolescent academic capability beliefs, parenting and school grades. *Journal of Adolescence, 25,* 3–18.

Judge, S., Puckett, K., & Bell, S. (2006). Closing the digital divide: Update from the early childhood longitudinal study. *Journal of Education Research, 100,* 52–60.

Jusczyk, P. W., Houston, D. M., & Newsome, M. (1999). The beginnings of word segmentation in English-learning infants. *Cognitive Psychology, 39*(3), 159–207. doi:10.1006/cogp.1999.0716

Kagan, J. (2001). Temperamental contributions to affective and behavioral profiles in childhood. In S. G. Hoffman & P. M. Dibartolo (Eds.), *From social anxiety to social phobia: Multiple perspectives* (pp. 216–234). Needham Heights, MA: Allyn & Bacon.

Kagan, J., & Herschkowitz, E. C. (2005). *Young mind in a growing brain.* Mahwah, NJ: Erlbaum.

Kagan, J., Reznick, J. S., & Snidman, N. (1987). The physiology and psychology of behavioral inhibition in children. *Child Development, 58,* 1459–1473. doi:10.2307/1130685

Kağitçibaşi, C., & Yalin, C. (2015). Family in adolescence: Relatedness and autonomy across cultures. In L. A. Jensen (Ed.), *Oxford handbook of human development and culture: An interdisciplinary perspective* (pp. 410–424). New York, NY: Oxford University Press.

Kahana-Kalman, R., & Walker-Andrews, A. S. (2001). The role of person familiarity in young infants' perception of emotional expressions. *Child Development,* 72, 352–369.

Kahn, J. A. (2007). Maximizing the potential public health impact of HPV vaccines: A focus on parents. *Journal of Adolescent Health, 20,* 101–103.

Kail, R. V. (2003). Information processing and memory. In M. H. Bornstein, L. Davidson, C. L. M. Keyes, K. A. Moore, & the Center for Child Well-Being (Eds.), *Well-being: Positive development across the life course* (pp. 269–280). Mahwah, NJ: Erlbaum.

Kaiser Family Foundation. (2015). Percent of children (ages 10–17) who are overweight or obese. Retrieved from http://kff.org/other/state-indicator/overweightobese-children

Kalak, N., Gerber, M., Kirov, R., Mikoteit, T., Yordanova, J., Pühse, U., … & Brand, S. (2012). Daily morning running for 3 weeks improved sleep and psychological functioning in healthy adolescents compared with controls. *Journal of Adolescent Health, 51*(6), 615–622. doi:10.1016/j.jadohealth.2012.02.020

Kaltiala-Heino, R., Kosunen, E., & Rimpelä, M. (2003). Pubertal timing, sexual behaviour and self-reported depression in middle adolescence. *Journal of Adolescence, 26*, 531–545.

Kam, J. A., & Lazarevic, V. (2014). Communicating for one's family: An interdisciplinary review of language and cultural brokering in immigrant families. *Communication Yearbook, 38*, 25–54.

Kamii, C. (1989). *Young children continue to reinvent arithmetic*. New York, NY: Teachers College Press.

Kan, M. L., McHale, S. M., & Crouter, A. C. (2008). Interparental incongruence in differential treatment of adolescent siblings: Links with marital quality. *Journal of Marriage and Family, 70*(2), 466–479.

Kane, P., & Garber, J. (2004). The relations among depression in fathers, children's psychopathology, and father–child conflict: A meta-analysis. *Child Psychology Review, 24*, 339–360.

Kanetsuna, T., Smith, P., & Morita, Y. (2006). Coping with bullying at school: Children's recommended strategies and attitudes to school-based intervention in England and Japan. *Aggressive Behavior, 32*, 570–580.

Kann, L., Kinchen, S., Shanklin, S. L., Flint, K. H., Kawkins, J., Harris, W. A., … Whittle, L. (2014). Youth risk behavior surveillance—United States, 2013. *MMWR Surveillance Summary, 63* (Suppl. 4), 1–168.

Kantrowitz, B., & Wingert, P. (1999, October 18). The truth about teens. *Newsweek*, pp. 62–72.

Kao, G., & Joyner, K. (2004). Do race and ethnicity matter among friends? Activities among interracial, interethnic, and intraethnic adolescent friends. *Sociological Quarterly, 45*, 557–573.

Kapadia, S., & Bhangaokar, R. (2015). An Indian moral worldview: Developmental patterns in adolescents and adults. In L. A. Jensen (Ed.), *Moral development in a global world: Research from a cultural-developmental perspective* (pp. 69–91). New York, NY: Cambridge University Press.

Kapadia, S., & Gala, J. (2015). Gender across cultures: Sex and socialization in childhood. In L. A. Jensen (Ed.), *Oxford handbook of human development and culture: An interdisciplinary perspective* (pp. 307–326). New York, NY: Oxford University Press.

Kaplan, B. J., Crawford, S. G., Field, C. J., Simpson, J., & Steven, A. (2007). Vitamins, minerals, and mood. *Psychological Bulletin, 133*, 747–760.

Kaplan, S., Heiligenstein, J., West, S., Busner, J., Hardor, D., Dittmann, R.,… Wernicke, J. E. (2004). Efficacy and safety of atomoxetine in childhood attention deficit/hyperactivity disorder with comorbidity oppositional defiant disorder. *Journal of Attention Disorders, 8*, 45–52.

Karlsson, J. L. (2006). Specific genes for intelligence. In L. V. Wesley (Ed.), *Intelligence: New research* (pp. 23–46). Hauppauge, NY: Nova Science.

Karniol, R., & Gal-Disegni, M. (2009). The impact of gender-fair versus gender-stereotyped basal readers on 1st-grade children's gender stereotypes: A natural experiment. *Journal of Research in Childhood Education, 23*(4), 411–420. doi:10.1080/02568540909594670

Katz, A. N., Blasko, D. G., & Kazmerski, V. A. (2004). Saying what you don't mean: Social influences on sarcastic language processing. *Current Directions in Psychological Science, 13*, 186–189.

Katz, L. F., & Windecker-Nelson, B. (2004). Parental meta-emotion philosophy in families with conduct-problem children: Links with peer relations. *Journal of Abnormal Child Psychology, 32*, 385–398.

Kaufman, A. S., Kaufman, J. C., Liu, X., & Johnson, C. K. (2009). How do educational attainment and gender relate to fluid intelligence, crystallized intelligence, and academic skills at ages 22–90 years? *Archives of Clinical Neuropsychology, 24*(2), 153–163.

Kaufman, A. S., & Lichtenberger, E. O. (2006). *Assessing adolescent and adult intelligence* (3rd ed.). Hoboken, NJ: John Wiley & Sons.

Kaufman, J. (2004). The interplay between social and cultural determinants of school effort and success: An investigation of Chinese-immigrant and second-generation Chinese students' perceptions toward school. *Social Science Quarterly, 85*, 1275–1298.

Kavšek, M. (2004). Predicting later IQ from infant visual habituation and dishabituation: A meta-analysis. *Journal of Applied Developmental Psychology, 25*, 369–393.

Kavšek, M., & Bornstein, M. H. (2010). Visual habituation and dishabituation in preterm infants: A review and meta-analysis. *Research in Developmental Disabilities, 31*, 951–975.

Kazdin, A. E., & Benjet, C. (2003). Spanking children: Evidence and issues. *Current Directions in Psychological Science, 12*, 99–103.

Keage, H. A. D., Clark, C. R., Hermens, D. F., Williams, L. M., Kohn, M. R., Clarke, S., … Gordon, E. (2008). Putative biomarker of working memory systems development during childhood and adolescence. *Neuroreport: For Rapid Communication of Neuroscience Research, 19*(2), 197–201.

Keating, D. (1990). Adolescent thinking. In S. Feldman & G. Elliott (Eds.), *At the threshold: The developing adolescent* (pp. 54–89). Cambridge, MA: Harvard University Press.

Keating, D. (2004). Cognitive and brain development. In L. Steinberg & R. M. Lerner (Eds.), *Handbook of adolescent psychology* (2nd ed., pp. 45–84). New York, NY: Wiley.

Keating, D. P. (2012). Cognitive and brain development in adolescence. *Enfance, 3*, 267–279.

Kelch-Oliver, K. (2011). The experiences of African American grandmothers in grandparent–headed families. *The Family Journal, 19*, 73–82.

Keller, M. A., & Goldberg, W. A. (2004). Co–sleeping: Help or hindrance for young children's independence? *Infant and Child Development, 13*, 369–388.

Kellman, P. J., & Arterberry, M. E. (2006). Infant visual perception. In W. Damon & R. Lerner (Eds.), & D. Kuhn & R. Siegler (Vol. Eds.), *Handbook of child psychology: Vol. 2. Cognition, perception, and language* (6th ed., pp. 109–160). New York, NY: Wiley.

Kellogg, A. (2001, January). Looking inward, freshmen care less about politics and more about money. *Chronicle of Higher Education*, pp. A47–A49.

Kelly, B., Halford, J. C. G., Boyland, E. J., Chapman, K., Bautista-Castaño, I., Berg, C., … Sumbebell, C. (2010). Television food advertising to children: A global perspective. *American Journal of Public Health, 100*, 1730–1736.

Kelly, J. A., O'Brien, G. G., & Hosford, R. (1981). Sex roles and social skills: Considerations for interpersonal judgment. *Psychology of Women Quarterly, 5*, 758–766.

Kelly, J. B. (2003). Changing perspectives on children's adjustment following divorce: A view from the United States. *Childhood: A Global Journal of Child Research, 10*, 237–254.

Kelly, J. B., & Emery, R. E. (2003). Children's adjustment following divorce: Risk and resilience perspectives. *Family Relations, 52*, 352–362.

Kelly, S. (2004). Do increased levels of parental involvement account for social class differences in track placements? *Social Science Research, 33*, 626–659.

Kendall-Tackett, K. A., Williams, L. M., & Finkelhor, D. (2001). Impact of sexual abuse on children: A review and synthesis of recent empirical studies. In R. Bull (Ed.), *Children and the law: The essential readings* (pp. 31–76). Malden, MA: Blackwell.

Kenneally, C. (2007). *The first words: The search for the origins of language*. New York, NY: Viking.

Kennedy, P. (2014, March 8). The fat drug: How humankind unwittingly joined an experiment on antibiotics and weight gain. *The New York Times*, pp. 1, 6.

Kent, M. M., & Haub, C. (2005). Global demographic divide. *Population bulletin, 6*, 1–24.

Kerber, L. K. (1997). *Toward an intellectual history of women*. Chapel Hill, NC: University of North Carolina Press.

Kerestes, M., Youniss, J., & Metz, E. (2004). Longitudinal patterns of religious perspective and civic integration. *Applied Developmental Science, 8*(1), 39–46.

Kessler, R. C., & Bromet, E. J. (2013). The epidemiology of depression across cultures. *Annual Review of Public Health, 34*, 119–138. doi:10.1146/annurev-publhealth-031912-114409

Kesson, A. M. (2007). Respiratory virus infections. *Paediatric Respiratory Reviews, 8*, 240–248.

Kett, J. (1977). *Rites of passage: Adolescence in America, 1790 to the present*. New York, NY: Basic Books.

Killen, M., & Smetana, J. (2014). Morality: Origins and development. In L. Lamb & C. Garcia Coll (Eds.), *Handbook of child psychology, Vol. 3, Social and emotional development* (7th ed.). New York, NY: Wiley/Blackwell Publishers.

Killen, M., & Smetana, J. G. (2015). Origins and development of morality. In M. Lamb & C. Garcia Coll (Eds.), *Handbook of child psychology, Vol. 3: Social and emotional development* (7th ed., pp. 701–749). New York, NY: Wiley/Blackwell Publishers.

Killen, M., & Sueyoshi, L. (1995). Conflict resolution in Japanese social interactions. *Early Education and Development, 6*, 317–334.

Kilpatrick, D. G., Acierno, R., Saunders, B., Resnick, H. S., Best, C. L., & Schnurr, P. P. (2000). Risk factors for adolescent substance abuse and dependence: Data from a national sample. *Journal of Consulting & Clinical Psychology, 68*, 19–30.

Kim, J. (2006). Magazines for adolescent girls. In J. J. Arnett (Ed.), *Encyclopedia of children, adolescents, and the media* (pp. 482–485). Thousand Oaks, CA: Sage.

Kim, J. L., Sorsoli, C. L., Collins, K., Zylbergold, B. A., Schooler, D., & Tolman, D. L. (2007). From sex to sexuality: Exposing the heterosexual script on primetime network television. *Journal of Sex Research, 44*(2), 145–157.

Kim, M., McGregor, K. K., & Thompson, C. K. (2000). Early lexical development in English- and Korean-speaking children: Language-general and language-specific patterns. *Journal of Child Language, 27*, 225–254.

Kindlon, D., & Thompson, M. (1999). *Raising Cain: Protecting the emotional life of boys*. New York, NY: Ballantine Books.

King, B. M. (2005). *Human sexuality today* (5th ed.). Upper Saddle River, NJ: Prentice Hall.

King, P. E., & Boyatzis, C. J. (2015). Religious and spiritual development. In M. E. Lamb (Volume Ed.) & R. M. Lerner (Ed.-in-Chief), *Handbook of child psychology and developmental science, Vol. 3: Socioemotional processes* (pp. 975–1021). Hoboken, NJ: Wiley.

King, P. E., & Furrow, J. L. (2004). Religion as a resource for positive youth development: Religion, social capital, and moral outcomes. *Developmental Psychology, 40*, 703–713. doi:10.1037/0012-1649.40.5.703

King, P. E., Furrow, J. L., & Roth, N. (2002). The influence of families and peers on adolescent religiousness. *Journal of Psychology and Christianity, 21*, 109–120.

King, P. E., Clardy, C. E., & Ramos, J. S. (2014). Adolescent spiritual exemplars: Exploring spirituality in the lives of diverse youth. *Journal of Adolescent Research, 29*, 186–212.

Kinney, D. (1993). From nerds to normals: The recovery of identity among adolescents from middle school to high school. *Sociology of Education, 66*, 21–40.

Kinney, D. A. (1999). From "headbangers" to "hippies": Delineating adolescents' active attempts to form an alternative peer culture. *New Directions for Child Development, 84*, 21–35.

Kinney, H. C., & Thach, B. T. (2009). Medical progress: The sudden infant death syndrome. *The New England Journal of Medicine, 361*, 795–805.

Kins, E., Beyers, W., Soenens, B., & Vansteenkiste, M. (2009). Patterns of home leaving and subjective well-being in emerging adulthood: The role of motivational processes and parental autonomy support. *Developmental Psychology, 45*(5), 1416–1429.

Kirchner, G. (2000). *Children's games from around the world.* Boston, MA: Allyn & Bacon.

Kirkorian, H. L., Wartella, E. A., & Anderson, D. R. (2008). Media and young children's learning. *The Future of Children, 18*(1), 39–61.

Kirsch, A. C., & Murnen, S. K. (2015). "Hot" girls and "cool dudes": Examining the prevalence of the heterosexual script in American children's television media. *Psychology of Popular Media Culture, 4*, 18.

Kisilevsky, B. S., Hains, S. M., Lee, K., Xic, X., Huang, H., Ye, H. H., … Wang, Z. (2003). Effects of experience on fetal voice recognition. *Psychological Science, 14*, 220–224.

Kitayama, S., & Markus, H. R. (1994). Introduction to cultural psychology and emotion research. In S. Kitayama & H. R. Markus (Eds.), *Emotion and culture: Empirical studies of mutual influence* (pp. 1–22). Washington, DC: American Psychological Association.

Kite, M. E., Deaux, K., & Hines, E. (2008). Gender stereotypes. In F. L. Denmark & M. A. Paludi (Eds.), *Psychology of women: A handbook of issues and theories* (2nd ed., pp. 205–236). Westport, CT: Praeger.

Kitsao-Wekulo, P., Holding, P., Taylor, G. H., Abubakar, A., Kvalsvig, J., & Connolly, K. (2013). Nutrition as an important mediator of the impact of background variables on outcomes in middle childhood. *Frontiers in Human Neuroscience, 7*, 713.

Kitzman, H. J., Olds, D. L., Cole, R. E., Hanks, C. A., Anson, E. A., Arcoleo, K. J., … Holmberg, J. R. (2010). Enduring effects of prenatal and infancy home visiting by nurses on children: Follow-up of a randomized trial among children at age 12 years. *Archives of Pediatrics & Adolescent Medicine, 164*(5), 412–418. doi:10.1001/archpediatrics.2010.76

Kitzmann, K. M., Cohen, R., & Lockwood, R. L. (2002). Are only children missing out? Comparison of the peer-related social competence of only children and siblings. *Journal of Social and Personal Relationships, 19*, 299–316.

Klaczynski, P. A. (2006). Learning, belief biases, and metacognition. *Journal of Cognition and Development, 7*(3), 295–300.

Klass, C. S. (2008). *The home visitor's guidebook: Promoting optimal parent and child development* (3rd ed.). Baltimore, MD: Paul H. Brookes.

Klaus, M. H., & Kennell, J. H. (1976). *Maternal–infant bonding: The impact of early separation or loss on family development.* St. Louis, MO: Mosby.

Kline, S. L., & Liu, F. (2005). The influence of comparative media use on acculturation, acculturative stress, and family relationships of Chinese international students. *International Journal of Intercultural Relations, 29*, 367–390.

Klomsten, A. T., Skaalvik, E. M., & Espnes, G. A. (2004). Physical self-concept and sports: Do gender differences exist? *Sex Roles, 50*, 119–127.

Knecht, S., Drager, B., Deppe, M., Bobe, L., Lohmann, H., Floel, A.,…Henningsen, H. (2000). Handedness and hemispheric language dominance in healthy humans. *Brain, 135*, 2512–2518.

Knect, S., Jansen, A., Frank, A., van Randenborgh, J., Sommer, J., Kanowski, M., & Heinze, H. J. (2003). How atypical is atypical language dominance? *Neuroimage, 18*, 917–927.

Knight, G. P., Cota, M. K., & Bernal, M. E. (1993). The socialization of cooperative, competitive, and individualistic preferences among Mexican American children: The mediating role of ethnic identity. *Hispanic Journal of Behavioral Sciences, 15*, 291–309.

Knight, M., Author, N., Bently, C., & Dixon, I. (2004). The power of Black and Latina/o counterstories: Urban families and college-going processes. *Anthropology and Education, 35*, 99–120. doi:10.1525/aeq.2004.35.1.99

Knox, D., Sturdivant, L., & Zusman, M. E. (2001). College student attitudes toward sexual intimacy. *College Student Journal, 35*, 241–243.

Kochanska, G. (2002). Mutually responsive orientation between mothers and their young children: A context for the early development of conscience. *Current Directions in Psychological Science, 11*, 191–195.

Kochanska, G., & Aksan, N. (2004). Development of mutual responsiveness between parents and their young children. *Child development, 75*, 1657–1676.

Kochanska, G., & Aksan, N. (2006). Children's conscience and self-regulation. *Journal of Personality, 74*, 1587–1618.

Kochanska, G., Barry, R. A., Aksan, N., & Boldt, L. J. (2008). A developmental model of maternal and child contributions to disruptive conduct: The first six years. *Journal of Child Psychology and Psychiatry, 49*(11), 1220–1227. doi:10.1111/j.1469-7610.2008.01932.x

Kochanska, G., Gross, J. N., Lin, M. H., & Nichols, K. E. (2002). Guilt in young children: Development, determinants, and relations with a broader system of standards. *Child Development, 73*(2), 461–482. doi:10.1111/1467-8624.00418

Kochanska, G., Kim, S., Barry, R. A., & Philibert, R. A. (2011). Children's genotypes interact with maternal responsive care in predicting children's competence: Diathesis–stress or differential susceptibility? *Development and Psychopathology, 23*(02), 605–616. doi:10.1017/S0954579411000071

Kochanska, G., Koenig, J. L., Barry, R. A., Kim, S., & Yoon, J. E. (2010). Children's conscience during toddler and preschool years, moral self, and a competent, adaptive developmental trajectory. *Developmental Psychology, 46*(5), 1320. doi:10.1037/a0020381

Kochenderfer-Ladd, B. (2003). Identification of aggressive and asocial victims and the stability of their peer victimization. *Merrill-Palmer Quarterly, 49*, 401–425.

Koenig, M. A., & Harris, P. L. (2005). Preschoolers mistrust ignorant and inaccurate speakers. *Child Development, 76*(6), 1261–1277. doi:http://www.jstor.org/stable/3696632

Kohlberg, L. (1958). *The development of modes of moral thinking and choice in the years 10 to 16.* Unpublished doctoral dissertation. University of Chicago.

Kohlberg, L. (1981). *Essays on moral development, Vol. 1: The philosophy of moral development.* New York, NY: Harper & Row.

Kohlberg, L. (1986). A current statement on some theoretical issues. In S. Modgit & C. Modgl (Eds.), *Lawrence Kohlberg* (pp. 485–546). Philadelphia, PA: Falmer.

Konopka, G. (1985). *Young girls: A portrait of adolescence.* New York, NY: Harrington Park Press.

Kopp, C. B. (1989). Regulation of distress and negative emotions: A developmental view. *Developmental Psychology, 25*, 343–354.

Kopp, C. B. (2003). *Baby steps: A guide to your child's social, physical, mental, and emotional development in the first two years.* New York, NY: Owl.

Korkman, M., Kettunen, S., & Autti-Rämö, I. (2003). Neurocognitive impairment in early adolescence following prenatal alcohol exposure of varying duration. *Child Neuropsychology, 9*(2), 117–128.

Kosciw, J. G., Greytak, E. A., Bartkiewicz, M. J., Boesen, M. J., & Palmer, N. A. (2012). The 2011 National School Climate Survey: The Experiences of Lesbian, Gay, Bisexual and Transgender Youth in Our Nation's Schools. New York, NY: Gay, Lesbian and Straight Education Network (GLSEN).

Kosciw, J. G., Palmer, N. A., & Kull, R. M. (2015). Reflecting resiliency: Openness about sexual orientation and/or gender identity and its relationship to well-being and educational outcomes for LGBT students. *American Journal of Community Psychology, 55*, 167–178.

Kostandy, R. R., Ludington-Hoe, S. M., Cong, X., Abouelfettoh, A., Bronson, C., Stankus, A., & Jarrell, J. R. (2008). Kangaroo care (skin contact) reduces crying response to pain in preterm neonates: Pilot results. *Pain Management Nursing, 9*, 55–65.

Kostonvic, I., & Vasung, L. (2009). Insights from in vitro magnetic resonance imaging of cerebral development. *Seminars in Perina- tology, 33*, 220–233.

Kostova, D., & Blecher, E. (2013). Does advertising matter? Estimating the impact of cigarette advertising on smoking among youth in developing countries. *Contemporary Economic Policy, 31*, 537–548.

Kovacs, A. M., & Mehler, J. (2009). Cognitive gains in 7-month-old bi- lingual infants. *Proceedings of the National Academy of Sciences USA, 106*, 6556–6560.

Kowalski, R. M., & Limber, S. P. (2007). Electronic bullying among middle school students. *Journal of Adolescent Health, 41*(6), S22–S30.

Kowalski, R. M., Limber, S., Limber, S. P., & Agatston, P. W. (2012). *Cyberbullying: Bullying in the digital age.* New York, NY: John Wiley & Sons.

Kramarski, B. (2004). Making sense of graphs: Does metacognitive instruction make a difference on students' mathematical conceptions and alternative conceptions? *Learning and Instruction, 14*, 593–619.

Kramer, L., Perozynski, L., & Chung, T. (1999). Parental responses to sibling conflict: The effects of development and parent gender. *Child Development, 70*, 1401–1414.

Krause, E. L. (2005). "Toys and perfumes": Imploding Italy's population paradox and motherly myths. In C. B. Douglass (Ed.), *Barren states: The population "implosion" in Europe* (pp. 159–182). New York, NY: Berg.

Krcmar, M., Grela, B., & Linn, K. (2007). Can toddlers learn vocabulary from television? An experimental approach. *Media Psychology, 10*, 41–63.

Krcmar, M., & Kean, L. G. (2005). Uses and gratifications of media violence: Personality correlates of viewing and liking violent genres. *Media Psychology, 7*(4), 399–420.

Kreutzer, M., Leonard, C., & Flavell, J. H. (1975). An interview study of children's knowledge about memory. *Monographs of the Society for Research in Child Development, 40*(1, Serial No. 159).

Kroger, J. (2002). Commentary on "Feminist perspectives on Erikson's theory: Their relevance for contemporary identity development research." *Identity, 2*, 257–266.

Kroger, J. (2003). Identity development during adolescence. In G. Adams & M. Berzonsky (Eds.), *Blackwell handbook of adolescence* (pp. 205–225). Malden, MA: Blackwell.

Kroger, J. (2007). *Identity development: Adolescence through adulthood* (2nd ed.). Thousand Oaks, CA: Sage.

Kroger, J., Martinussen, M., & Marcia, J. E. (2010). Identity status change during adolescence and young adulthood: A meta-analysis. *Journal of Adolescence, 33*(5), 683–698.

Kronenberger, W. G., Mathews, V. P., Dunn, D. W., Wang, Y., Wood, E. A., Giauque, A. L., … Li, T. Q. (2005). Media violence exposure and executive functioning in aggressive and control adolescents. *Journal of Clinical Psychology, 61*, 725–737.

Kucera, H., & Francis, W. N. (1967). *Computational analysis of present-day American English.* Providence, RI: Brown University Press.

Kuhl, P. K. (1979). Speech perception in early infancy: Perceptual constancy for spectrally dissimilar vowel categories. *The Journal of the Acoustical Society of America, 66*(6), 1668–1679. doi:http://dx.doi.org/10.1121/1.383639

Kuhl, P. K. (2004). Early language acquisition: Cracking the speech code. *Nature Reviews Neuroscience, 5*, 831–843.

Kuhl, P. K. (2011). Early language learning and literacy: Neuroscience implications for education. *Mind, Brain, and Education, 5*(3), 128–142. doi:10.1111/j.1751-228X.2011.01121.x

Kuhl, P. K., Conboy, B. T., Coffrey-Corina, S., Padden, D., Rivera-Gaxiola, M., & Nelson, T. (2008). Early phonetic perception as a gateway to language: New data and native language magnet theory expanded (NLM-e). *Philosophical Transactions of the Royal Society B, 363*, 979–1000.

Kuhl, P. K., Conboy, B. T., Padden, D., Nelson, T., & Pruitt, J. (2005). Early speech perception and later language development: Implications for the "Critical Period." *Language Learning and Development, 1*(3–4), 237–264. doi:10.1080/15475441.2005.9671948

Kuhl, P. K., Tsao, F. M., & Liu, H. M. (2003). Foreign-language experience in infancy: Effects of short-term exposure and social interaction on phonetic learning. *Proceedings of the National Academy of Sciences, 100*(15), 9096–9101. doi:10.1073/pnas.1532872100

Kuhlberg, J. A., Peña, J. B., & Zayas, L. H. (2010). Familism, parent-adolescent conflict, self-esteem, internalizing behaviors and suicide attempts among adolescent Latinas. *Child Psychiatry and Human Development, 41*, 425–440.

Kuhn, D. (2008). Formal operations from a twenty-first century perspective. *Human Development, 51*, 48–55.

Kuntsche, E., Rehm, J., & Gmel, G. (2004). Characteristics of binge drinkers in Europe. *Social Science & Medicine, 59*(1), 113–127.

Kuouvonen, A., & Kivivuori, J. (2001). Part-time jobs, delinquency and victimization among Finnish adolescents. *Journal of Scandinavian Studies in Criminology and Crime Prevention, 2*(2), 191–212.

Kurdek, L. (1987). Gender differences in the psychological symptomatology and coping strategies of young adolescents. *Journal of Early Adolescence, 7*, 395–410.

Kutsyuruba, B., Klinger, D. A., & Hussain, A. (2015). Context and implications document for: Relationships among school climate, school safety, and student achievement and well-being: A review of the literature. *Review of Education, 3*, 136–137.

Kvavilashvili, L., & Ford, R. M. (2014). Metamemory prediction accuracy for simple prospective and retrospective memory tasks in 5-year-old children. *Journal of Experimental Psychology, 127*, 65–81.

Labouvie-Vief, G. (1982). Dynamic development and mature autonomy: A theoretical prologue. *Human Development, 25*, 161–191.

Labouvie-Vief, G. (1990). Modes of knowledge and the organization of development. In M. L. Commons, J. D. Sinnott, F. A. Richards, & C. Armon (Eds.), *Models and methods in the study of adolescent and adult thought* (pp. 43–62). New York, NY: Praeger.

Labouvie-Vief, G. (1998). Cognitive-emotional integration in adulthood. In K. W. Schaie & M. P. Lawton (Eds.), *Annual review of gerontology and geriatrics, Vol. 17: Focus on emotion and adult development* (pp. 206–237). New York, NY: Springer.

Labouvie-Vief, G. (2006). Emerging structures of adult thought. In J. J. Arnett & J. Tanner (Eds.), *Emerging adults in America: Coming of age in the 21st century* (pp. 59–84). Washington, DC: American Psychological Association.

Labouvie-Vief, G., & Diehl, M. (2002). Cognitive complexity and cognitive-affective integration: Related or separate domains of adult development? *Psychology and Aging, 15*, 490–594.

Lachlan, K. (2006). Sensation seeking. In J. J. Arnett (Ed.), *Encyclopedia of children, adolescents, and the media* (pp. 748–749). Thousand Oaks, CA: Sage.

Ladd, G. W., Buhs, E., & Troop, W. (2004). School adjustment and social skills training. In P. K. Smith & C. H. Hart (Eds.), *Blackwell handbook of childhood social development* (pp. 394–416). Malden, MA: Blackwell.

La Greca, A. M., & Harrison, H. M. (2005). Adolescent peer relations, friendships, and romantic relationships: Do they predict social anxiety and depression? *Journal of Clinical Child and Adolescent Psychology, 34*(1), 49–61.

Lahat, A., Todd, R. M., Mahy, C. E. V., Lau, K., & Zelazo, P. D. (2010). Neurophysiological correlates of executive function: A comparison of European-Canadian and Chinese-Canadian 5-year-old children. *Frontiers in Human Neuroscience, 3*, 72.

Laible, D. (2004). Mother–child discourse in two contexts: Links with child temperament, attachment security and socioemotional competence. *Developmental Psychology, 40*, 979–992.

Laible, D. J., & Thompson, R. A. (2000). Mother–child discourse, attachment security, shared positive affect, and early conscience development. *Child Development, 71*(5), 1424–1440. doi:10.1111/1467-8624.00237

Lakatta, E. G. (1990). Heart and circulation. In E. L. Schneider & J. W. Rowe (Eds.), *Handbook of the biology of aging* (3rd ed., pp. 181–217). San Diego, CA: Academic Press.

Lamb, M. E. (1994). Infant care practices and the application of knowledge. In C. B. Fisher & R. M. Lerner (Eds.), *Applied developmental psychology* (pp. 23–45). New York, NY: McGraw-Hill.

Lamb, M. E. (2010). *The role of the father in child development.* New York, NY: Wiley.

Lamb, M. E., & Lewis, C. (2005). The role of parent–child relationships in child development. In M. H. Bornstein & M. E. Lamb (Eds.), *Developmental psychology* (5th ed., pp. 429–468). Mahwah, NJ: Erlbaum.

Lamb, M. E., & Lewis, C. (2010). The role and significance of father-child relationships in two-parent families. In M. E. Lamb (Ed.), *The role of the father in child development* (pp. 94–153). New York, NY: Wiley.

Lambe, J. (2006). Regulation, industry self-regulation. In J. J. Arnett (Ed.), *Encyclopedia of children, adolescents, and the media* (pp. 706–707). Thousand Oaks, CA: Sage.

Lampl, M., Johnson, M. L., & Frongillo, E. A., Jr. (2001). Mixed distribution analysis identifies saltation and stasis growth. *Annals of Human Biology, 28*, 403–411.

Lan, X., Legare, C. H., Ponitz, C. C., Li, S., & Morrison, F. J. (2011). Investigating the links between the subcomponents of executive function and academic achievement: A cross-cultural analysis of Chinese and American preschoolers. *Journal of Experimental Child Psychology, 108*, 677–692.

Lancy, D. F. (2008). *The anthropology of childhood: Cherubs, chattel, changelings.* New York, NY: Cambridge University Press.

Lane, B. (2009). Epidural rates in the U.S. and around the world: How many mothers choose to use an epidural to provide pain relief? Retrieved from http://www.suite101.com/content/epidural-for-labor-a168170

Langhinrichsen-Rohling, J., Palarea, R. E., Cohen, J., & Rohlin, M. L. (2002). Breaking up is hard to do: Unwanted pursuit behaviors following the dissolution of a romantic relationship. In K. E. Davis & I. H. Frieze (Eds.), *Stalking: Perspectives on victims and perpetrators* (pp. 212–236). New York, NY: Springer.

Langhinrichsen-Rohling, J., Friend, J., & Powell, A. (2009). Adolescentsuicide, gender, and culture: A rate and risk factor analysis. *Aggression and Violent Behavior*, 14(5), 402–414.

Langlois, J. H., & Downs, A. C. (1980). Mothers, fathers, and peers as socialization agents of sex-typed play behaviors in young children. *Child Development, 51*, 1237–1247. doi:10.2307/1129566

Lansford, J. E., Deater-Deckard, K., Dodge, K. A., Bates, J. E., & Pettit, G. S. (2004). Ethnic differences in the link between physical discipline and later adolescent externalizing behaviors. *Journal of Child Psychology and Psychiatry, 45*, 801–812.

Lansford, J. E., Malone, P. S., Dodge, K. A., Crozier, J. C., Pettit, G. S., & Bates, J. E. (2006). A 12-year prospective study of patterns of social information processing problems and externalizing behaviors. *Journal of Abnormal Child Psychology, 34*, 715–724.

Larson, M. (1996). Sex roles and soap operas: What adolescents learn about single motherhood. *Sex Roles, 35*, 97–121.

Larson, R. (1995). Secrets in the bedroom: Adolescents' private use of media. *Journal of Youth & Adolescence, 24*, 535–550.

Larson, R., & Csikszentmihalyi, M. (2014). The Experience Sampling Method. In M. Csikszentmihalyi, *Flow and positive psychology* (pp. 21–34). New York, NY: Springer.

Larson, R., Moneta, G., Richards, M. H., & Wilson, S. (2002). Continuity, stability, and change in daily emotional experience across adolescence. *Child Development, 73*, 1151–1165.

Larson, R., & Richards, M. H. (1994). *Divergent realities: The emotional lives of mothers, fathers, and adolescents*. New York, NY: Basic Books.

Larson, R., Verman, S., & Dwokin, J. (2000, March). Adolescence without family disengagement: The daily family lives of Indian middle-class teenagers. Paper presented at the biennial meeting of the Society for Research on Adolescence, Chicago, IL.

Larson, R. W., Csikszentmihalyi, M., & Graef, R. (1980). Mood variability and the psycho-social adjustment of adolescents. *Journal of Youth & Adolescence, 9*, 469–490.

Larson, R. W., Wilson, S., & Rickman, A. (2010). Globalization, societal change, and adolescence across the world. In R. Lerner & L. Steinberg (Eds.), *Handbook of adolescent psychology* (3rd ed., pp. 590–622). Hoboken, NJ: John Wiley & Sons.

Lauersen, N. H., & Bouchez, C. (2000). *Getting pregnant: What you need to know right now.* New York, NY: Fireside.

Laursen, B., Coy, K. C., & Collins, W. A. (1998). Reconsidering changes in parent–child conflict across adolescence: A meta-analysis. *Child Development, 69*, 817–832.

Laursen, B., Finkelstein, B. D., & Betts, N. T. (2001). A developmental meta-analysis of peer conflict resolution. *Developmental Review, 21*(4), 423–449. doi:10.1006/drev.2000.0531

Lavzer, J. L., & Goodson, B. D. (2006). The "quality" of early care and education settings: Definitional and measurement issues. *Evaluation Review, 30*, 556–576.

Lawson, A. E., & Wollman, W. T. (2003). Encouraging the transition from concrete to formal operations: An experiment. *Journal of Research in Science Teaching, 40*(Suppl.), S33–S50.

Le, H. N. (2000). Never leave your little one alone: Raising an Ifaluk child. In J. DeLoache & A. Gottlieb (Eds.), *A world of babies: Imagined childcare guides for seven societies* (pp. 199–222). New York, NY: Cambridge University Press.

Leakey, R. (1994). *The origins of humankind.* New York, NY: Basic Books.

Leaper, C. (2013). Gender development during childhood. In P. D. Zelazo (Ed.), *The Oxford handbook of developmental psychology*: Volume 2: Self and other (pp. 326–377). New York, NY: Oxford University Press.

Leaper, C. (2015). Gender and social-cognitive development. In R. M. Lerner (Series Ed.), L. S. Liben & U. Muller (Vol. Eds.), *Handbook of child psychology and developmental science* (7th ed., pp. 806–853), *Vol. 2: Cognitive processes.* New York, NY: Wiley.

Leaper, C., Anderson, K. J., & Sanders, P. (1998). Moderators of gender effects on parents' talk to their children: A meta-analysis. *Developmental Psychology, 34*(1), 3–27.

Leaper, C., & Ayres, M. M. (2007). A meta-analytic review of gender variations in adults' language use: Talkativeness, affiliative speech, and assertive speech. *Personality and Social Psychology Review, 11*(4), 328–363. doi:10.1177/1088868307302221

Leaper, C., & Brown, C. S. (2008). Perceived experiences with sexism among adolescent girls. *Child Development, 79*, 685–704.

Leaper, C., & Smith, T. E. (2004). A meta-analytic review of gender variations in children's language use: Talkativeness, affiliative speech, and assertive speech. *Developmental Psychology, 40*, 993–1027.

Leavitt, S. C. (1998). The Bikhet mystique: Masculine identity and patterns of rebellion among Bumbita adolescent males. In G. Herdt & S. C. Leavitt (Eds.), *Adolescence in Pacific Island societies* (pp. 173–194). Pittsburgh, PA: University of Pittsburgh Press.

Lee, J. C., & Staff, J. (2007). When work matters: The varying impact of work intensity on high school dropouts. *Sociology of Education, 80*(2), 158–178.

Lee, K., Xu, F., Fu, G., Cameron, C. A., & Chen, S. (2001). Taiwan and Mainland Chinese and Canadian children's categorization and evaluation of lie- and truth-telling: A modesty effect. *British Journal of Developmental Psychology, 19*(4), 525–542. doi:10.1348/026151001166236

Lee, M., & Larson, R. (2000). The Korean "examination hell": Long hours of studying, distress, and depression. *Journal of Youth & Adolescence, 29*, 249–271.

Lee, M. M. C., Chang, K. S. F., & Chan, M. M. C. (1963). Sexual maturation of Chinese girls in Hong Kong. *Pediatrics, 32*, 389–398.

Lee, M. T. Y., Wong, B. P., Chow, B. W.-Y., & McBride-Chang, C. (2006). Predictors of suicide ideation and depression in Hong Kong adolescents: Perceptions of academic and family climates. *Suicide and Life-Threatening Behavior, 36*(1), 82–96.

Lee, S. A. S., Davis, B., & MacNeilage, P. (2010). Universal production patterns and ambient language influences in babbling: A cross-linguistic study of Korean- and English-learning infants. *Journal of Child Language, 37*, 293–318.

Lee, V., Croninger, R., Linn, E., & Chen, X. (1996). The culture of harassment in secondary schools. *American Educational Research Journal*, 33, 383–417.

Lefkowitz, E. S., & Gillen, M. M. (2006). "Sex is just a normal part of life": Sexuality in emerging adulthood. In J. J. Arnett & J. L. Tanner (Eds.), *Emerging adults in America: Coming of age in the 21st century* (pp. 235–255). Washington, DC: American Psychological Association.

Legal Momentum. (2017). Poverty rates for single mothers are higher in the U.S. than in other high income countries. Retrieved from http://www.ncdsv.org/images/LM_PovertyRatesSingleMothersHigherUS_6-2011.pdf

Legerski, J. P., Biggs, B. K., Greenhoot, A. F., & Sampilo, M. L. (2015). Emotion talk and friend responses among early adolescent same-sex friend dyads. *Social Development, 24*, 20–38.

Lehtinen, M., Paavonen, J., & Apter, D. (2006). Preventing common sexually transmitted infections in adolescents: Time for rethinking. *The European Journal of Contraception and Reproductive Health Care, 11*, 247–249.

Leichtman, M. (2011). A global window on memory development. In L. Jenson (Ed.), *Bridging cultural and developmental approaches to psychology: New syntheses in theory, research, and policy* (pp. 49–70). New York, NY: Oxford University Press.

Leiden Conference on the Development and Care of Children without Permanent Parents. (2012). The development and care of institutionally reared children. *Child Development Perspectives, 6*, 174–180.

Lenhart, A. (2015). *A majority of American teens report access to a computer, game console, smartphone and a tablet* (Teens, Social Media & Technology Overview 2015). Washington, DC: Pew Research Center.

Lenhart, A., & Madden, M. (2005). *Teen content creators and consumers.* Retrieved June 1, 2008, from http://www.pewinternet.org/pdfs/PIP_Teens_Content_Creation.pdf

Lenhart, A., & Madden, M. (2007, January 7). *Social networking websites and teens: An overview.* Retrieved January 3, 2008, from http://www.pewinternet.org/PPF/R/198/report_display.asp

Lenhart, A., Purcell, K., Smith, A., & Zickuhr, K. (2010). *Social media and mobile Internet use among teens and young adults.* Washington, DC: Pew Research Center.

Leon, K. (2003). Risk and protective factors in young children's adjustment to parental divorce: A review of the research. *Family Relations, 52*, 258–270.

Leonard, L. (2002). Problematizing fertility: "Scientific" accounts and Chadian women's narratives. In M. C. Inhorn & F. van Balen (Eds.), *Infertility around the globe: New thinking on childlessness, gender, and reproductive technologies* (pp. 193–213). Berkeley, CA: University of California Press.

Lerner, R. M. (2006). Developmental science, developmental systems, and contemporary theories of human development. In R. M. Lerner & W. Damon (Eds.), *Handbook of child psychology* (6th ed., pp. 1–17), *Vol 1: Theoretical models of human development.* Hoboken, NJ: John Wiley & Sons.

Lerner, R. M., Lerner, J. V., Bowers, E. P., & Geldhof, G. J. (2015). Positive youth development and relational-developmental systems. In W. F. Overton, P. C. M. Molenaar (Vol. Eds.) & R. M. Lerner (Ed.-in-Chief), *Handbook of child psychology and developmental science, Vol. 1: Theory and method* (pp. 607–651). Hoboken, NJ: Wiley.

Lerner, R. M., Roeser, R. W., & Phelps, E. (Eds.). (2008). *Positive youth development and spirituality: From theory to research.* West Conshohocken, PA: Templeton Foundation Press.

Lerner, R. M., Theokas, C., & Jelicic, H. (2005). Youth as active agents in their own positive development: A developmental systems perspective. In W. Greve, L. Rothermund, & D. Wentura, *The adaptive self: Personal continuity and intentional self-development* (pp. 31–47). Göttingen, Germany: Hogrefe & Huber.

Lessow-Hurley, J. (2005). *The foundations of dual language instruction* (4th ed.). Boston, MA: Allyn & Bacon.

Leszczynski, J. P., & Strough, J. (2008). The contextual specificity of masculinity and femininity in early adolescence. *Social Development, 17*(3), 719–736.

LeVine, D. N. (1966). The concept of masculinity in Ethiopian culture. *International Journal of Social Psychiatry, 12*, 17–23.

Levine, M. H., & Vaala, S. E. (2013). Games for learning: Vast wasteland or a digital promise. In F. C. Blumberg & S. M. Fisch (Eds.), *Digital games: A context for cognitive development. New Directions for Child and Adolescent Development, 139*, 71–82.

LeVine, R. A., Dixon, S., LeVine, S., Richman, A., Leiderman, P. H., Keefer, C. H., & Brazelton, T. B. (1994). *Childcare and culture: Lessons from Africa.* New York, NY: Cambridge University Press.

LeVine, R. A., Dixon, S., LeVine, S. E., Richman, A., Keefer, C., Liederman, P. H., & Brazelton, T. B. (2008). The comparative study of parenting. In R. A. LeVine & R. S. New, *Anthropology and child development: A cross–cultural reader* (pp. 55–65). Malden, MA: Blackwell Publishing.

LeVine, R. A., & LeVine, S. (2016). *Do parents matter? Why Japanese babies sleep soundly, Mexican siblings don't fight, and American families should just relax.* Philadelphia, PA: PublicAffairs.

LeVine, R. A., & New, R. S. (Eds.). (2008). *Anthropology and child development: A cross-cultural reader.* Malden, MA: Blackwell.

Levitin, D. (2007). *This is your brain on music.* New York, NY: Plume.

Lewis, M. (2002). Early emotional development. In A. Slater & M. Lewis (Eds.), *Introduction to infant development* (pp. 216–232). New York, NY: Oxford University Press.

Lewis, M. (2008). The emergence of human emotions. In L. F. Barrett, J. M. Haviland-Jones, & M. Lewis (Eds.), *Handbook of emotions* (3rd ed., pp. 304–319). New York, NY: Guilford Press.

Lewis, M. (2010). The development of anger. In M. Potegal, G. Stemmler, & C. Spielberger (Eds.), *International handbook of anger: Constituent and concomitant biological, psychological, and social processes* (pp. 177–191). New York, NY: Springer.

Lewis, M., & Brooks-Gunn, J. (1979). *Social cognition and the acquisition of self.* New York, NY: Plenum.

Lewis, M., & Ramsay, D. S. (1999). Effect of maternal soothing and infant stress response. *Child Development, 70*, 11–20.

Lewis, M., & Ramsay, D. S. (2004). Development of self-recognition, personal pronoun use, and pretend play during the 2nd year. *Child Development, 75*, 1821–1831.

Lewis, M., Ramsay, D. S., & Kawakami, K. (1993). Differences between Japanese infants and Caucasian American infants in behavioral and cortisol response to inoculation. *Child Development, 64*, 1722–1731.

Lewis, M., Takai-Kawakami, K., Kawakami, K., & Sullivan, M. W. (2010). Cultural differences in emotional responses to success and failure. *International Journal of Behavioral Development, 34*, 53–61.

Lewis, R. (2015). *Human genetics: Concepts and applications.* New York, NY: McGraw-Hill.

Lewkowitz, D. J., & Lickliter, R. (2013). *The development of intersensory perception.* New York, NY: Psychology Press.

Levi-Strauss, C. (1967). *The scope of anthropology*, . (Trans. S. O. Paul
and R. A. Paul). London, UK: Jonathan Cape.

Li, D. K., Petitti, D. B., Willinger, M., et al. (2003). Infant sleeping position and the risk of sudden infant death syndrome in California, 1997–2000. *American Journal of Epidemiology*, 157, 446–455.

Li, F., Godinet, M. T., & Arnsberger, P. (2010). Protective factors among families with children at risk of maltreatment: Follow up to early school years. *Children and Youth Services Review, 33*, 139–148.

Li, J. (2011). Cultural frames of children's learning beliefs. In L. A. Jensen (Ed.), *Bridging cultural and developmental approaches to psychology: New syntheses in theory, research, and policy* (pp. 26–48). New York, NY: Oxford University Press.

Li, J., Fraser, M. W., & Wike, T. L. (2013). Promoting social competence and preventing childhood aggression: A framework for applying social information processing theory in intervention research. *Aggression and Violent Behavior, 18*(3), 357–364.

Li, K., Liu, D., Haynie, D., Gee, B., Chaurasia, A., Seo, D. C., … & Simons-Morton, B. G. (2016). Individual, social, and environmental influences on the transitions in physical activity among emerging adults. *BMC Public Health*, *16*, 682.

Li, S.-C. (2007). Biocultural co-construction of developmental plasticity across the lifespan. In S. Kitayama & D. Cohen (Eds.), *Handbook of cultural psychology* (pp. 528–544). New York, NY: Guilford Press.

Liao, C. C., Chen, Z.-H., Cheng, H. N., Chen, F.-C., & Chan, T.-W. (2011). My mini-pet: A handheld pet-nurturing game to engage students in arithmetic practices. *Journal of Computer Assisted Learning, 27*, 76–89.

Liben, L. S., & Bigler, R. S. (2002). The developmental course of gender differentiation: Conceptualizing, measuring, and evaluating constructs and pathways. *Monographs of the Society for Research in Child Development, 6*(4, Series. No. 271).

Liben, L. S., Bigler, R. S., & Hilliard, L. J. (2013). Gender development. *Societal Contexts of Child Development: Pathways of Influence and Implications for Practice and Policy,* 3.

Liben, L. S., Bigler, R. S., & Hilliard, L. J. (2014). Gender development. In E.T. Gershoff, R. S. Mistry, & D. A. Crosby (Eds.), *Societal contexts of child development: Pathways of influence and implications for practice and policy* (pp. 3–18). New York, NY: Oxford University Press.

Liben, L. S., Bigler, R. S., & Krogh, H. R. (2001). Pink and blue collar jobs: Children's adjustments of job status and job aspirations in relation to sex of worker. *Journal of Experimental Child Psychology, 79*, 346–363.

Liben, L. S., & Signorella, M. L. (1993). Gender-schematic processing in children: The role of initial interpretation of stimuli. *Developmental Psychology, 29*, 141–149.

Lickliter, R., & Honeycutt, H. (2015). Biology, development, and human systems. *Handbook of Child Psychology and Developmental Science, 1*(5), 1–46.

Lieber, E., Nihira, K., & Mink, I. T. (2004). Filial piety, modernization, and the challenges of raising children for Chinese immigrants: Quantitative and qualitative evidence. *Ethos, 32*, 324–347.

Liechty, M. (1995). Media, markets, and modernization: Youth identities and the experience of modernity in Kathmandu, Nepal. In V. Amit-Talai & H. Wulff (Eds.), *Youth cultures: A cross-cultural perspective* (pp. 166–201). New York, NY: Routledge.

Liechty, M. (2010) *Out here in Kathmandu: Modernity on the global periphery*. Kathmandu, Nepal: Martin Chautari Press.

Lillard, A. S. (2007). Pretend play in toddlers. In C. A. Brownell & C. B. Kopp (Eds.), *Socioemotional development in the toddler years* (pp. 149–176). New York, NY: Guilford.

Lillard, A. S. (2008). *Montessori: The science behind the genius.* New York, NY: Oxford University Press.

Lillard, A. S. (2015). The development of play. In R. M. Lerner (Series Ed.), L. S. Liben & U. Müller (Vol. Eds.), *Handbook of child psychology and developmental science* (7th ed., pp. 425–468), *Vol. 2: Cognitive processes.* New York, NY: Wiley.

Lillard, A. S., & Else-Quest, N. (2006). Evaluating Montessori education. *Science, 313*, 1893–1894.

Lillard, A. S., & Kavanaugh, R. D. (2014). The contribution of symbolic skills to the development of an explicit theory of mind. *Child Development, 85*(4), 1535–1551. doi:10.1111/cdev.12227

Lim, C., Rice, E., & Rhoades, H. (2015). Depressive symptoms and their association with adverse environmental factors and substance use in runaway and homeless youths. *Journal of Research on Adolescence, 26*, 403–417.

Lindsay, L. A., & Miescher, S. F. (Eds.). (2003). *Men and masculinities in modern Africa.* Portsmouth, NH: Heinemann.

Lindsey, E., & Colwell, M. (2003). Preschooler's emotional competence: Links to pretend and physical play. *Child Study Journal, 33*, 39–52.

Linebarger, D. L., & Walker, D. (2005). Infants' and toddlers' television viewing and language outcomes. *American Behavioral Scientist, 48*(5), 624–645.

Ling, P. M., & Glantz, S. A. (2002). Why and how the tobacco industry sells cigarettes to young adults: Evidence from industry documents. *American Journal of Public Health, 92*, 908–916.

Linver, M. R., Brooks-Gunn, J., & Kohen, D. E. (2002). Family processes as pathways from income to young children's development. *Developmental Psychology, 38*, 719–734.

Lipman, E. L., Boyle, M. H., Dooley, M. D., & Offord, D. R. (2002). Child well-being in single-mother families. *Journal of the American Academy of Child and Adolescent Psychiatry, 41*, 75–82.

Lipsitt, L. P. (2003). Crib death: A biobehavioral phenomenon? *Psychological Science, 12*, 164–170.

Liston, C., & Kagan, J. (2002). Brain development: Memory enhancement in early childhood. *Nature, 419*(6910), 896–896.

Liszkowski, U., Carpenter, M., Striano, T., & Tomasello, M. (2006). 12- and 18-month-olds point to provide information for others. *Journal of Cognition and Development, 7*(2), 173–187. doi:10.1207/s15327647jcd0702_2

Liszkowski, U., Carpenter, M., & Tomasello, M. (2007). Pointing out new news, old news, and absent referents at 12 months of age. *Developmental Science, 10*(2), F1–F7. doi:10.1111/j.1467-7687.2006.00552.x

Litovsky, R. Y., & Ashmead, D. H. (1997). Development of binaural and spatial hearing in infants and children. In R. H. Gilkey & T. R. Anderson (Eds.), *Binaural and spatial hearing in real and virtual environments* (pp. 571–592). Mahwah, NJ: Erlbaum.

Liu, J., Li, D., Purwono, U., Chen, X., & French, D. (in press). Loneliness of Indonesian and Chinese adolescents as predicted by relationships with parents and friends. *Merrill-Palmer Quarterly, 61*, 362–382.

Livingston, G., & Parker, K. (2010, September 9). Since the start of the great recession, more children raised by grandparents. Retrieved from http://pewresearch.org/pubs/1724/sharp-increase-children-with-grandparent-caregivers

Lloyd, B. T., & Mendez, J. L. (2001). Botswana adolescents interpretation of American music videos: So that's what that means! *Journal of Black Psychology, 27*, 464–476.

Lloyd, C. (Ed.). (2005). *Growing up global: The changing transitions to adulthood in developing countries.* Washington, DC: National Research Council and Institute of Medicine.

Lloyd, C. B., Grant, M., & Ritchie, A. (2008). Gender differences in time use among adolescents in developing countries: Implications of rising school enrollment rates. *Journal of Research on Adolescence, 18*, 99–120.

Lobel, T. E., Nov-Krispin, N., Schiller, D., Lobel, O., & Feldman, A. (2004). Perceptions of social status, sexual orientation, and value dissimilarity. Gender discriminatory behavior during adolescence and young adulthood: A developmental analysis. *Journal of Youth & Adolescence, 33*, 535–546.

Lock, J. (2015). An update on evidence-based psychosocial treatments for eating disorders in children and adolescents. *Journal of Clinical Child & Adolescent Psychology, 44*, 707–721. doi:10.1080/15374416.2014.971458

Loeber, R., & Burke, J. D. (2011). Developmental pathways in juvenile externalizing and internalizing problems. *Journal of Research on Adolescence, 21*, 34–46.

Loeber, R., Lacourse, E., & Homish, D. L. (2005). Homicide, violence, and developmental trajectories. In R. E. Tremblay, W. W. Hartup, & J. Archer (Eds.), *Developmental origins of aggression* (pp. 202–222). New York, NY: Guilford Press.

Loehlin, J. C., Horn, J. M., & Willerman, L. (1997). Heredity, environment, and IQ in the Texas Adoption Project. In R. J. Sternberg & E. L. Grigrenko (Eds.), *Intelligence, heredity, and environment* (pp. 105–125). New York, NY: Cambridge University Press.

Lohaus, A., Keller, H., Ball, J., Voelker, S., & Elben, C. (2004). Maternal sensitivity in interactions with three- and 12-month-old infants: Stability, structural composition, and developmental consequences. *Infant and Child Development, 13*, 235–252.

Longest, K. C., & Shanahan, M. J. (2007). Adolescent work intensity and substance use: The mediational and moderational roles of parenting. *Journal of Marriage & Family, 69*(3), 703–720.

Lord, C., & Bishop, S. L. (2010). Autism spectrum disorders. *Social Policy Report, 24*(2), 3–16.

Lorenz, K. (1957). Companionship in bird life. In C. Scholler (Ed.), *Instinctive behavior: The development of a modern concept* (pp. 83–128). New York, NY: International Universities Press.

Lorenz, K. Z. (1965). *Evolution and the modification of behavior.* Chicago, IL: University of Chicago Press.

Loukas, A., & Robinson, S. (2004). Examining the moderating role of perceived school climate in early adolescent adjustment. *Journal of Research on Adolescence, 14*, 209–233.

Lovas, G. S. (2011). Gender and patterns of language development in mother-toddler and father-toddler dyads. *First Language, 31*(1), 83–108.

Love, J. M., Chazan-Cohen, R., Raikes, H., & Brooks-Gunn, J. (2013). What makes a difference: Early Head Start evaluation findings in a developmental context. *Monographs of the Society for Research in Child Development, 78*(1), vii–viii.

Lucas, M. S., & Singer, H. (1975). Dialect in relation to oral reading achievement: Recoding, encoding, or merely a code? *Journal of Literacy Research, 7*(2), 137–148. doi:10.1080/10862967509547130

Luciana, M., Conklin, H. M., Hooper, C. J., & Yarger, R. S. (2005). The development of nonverbal working memory and executive control processes in adolescents. *Child Development, 76*, 697–712.

Luckie, M. (2010). School year around the world. Retrieved from http://californiawatch.org/k-12/how-long-school-year compare-california-world

Ludington-Hoe, S. M. (2013). Kangaroo care as neonatal therapy. *Newborn and Infant Nursing Reviews, 13*, 73. doi:10.1053/j.nainr.2013.03.004

Lull, R. B., & Bushman, B. J. (2016). Immersed in violence: Presence mediates the effect of 3D violent video gameplay on angry feelings. *Psychology of Popular Media Culture, 5*, 133.

Lyckyx, K. (2006). *Identity formation in emerging adulthood: Developmental trajectories, antecedents, and consequences.* Dissertation, Catholic University, Leuven, Belgium.

Lynch, M. E. (1991). Gender intensification. In R. M. Lerner, A. C. Petersen, & J. Brooks-Gunn (Eds.), *Encyclopedia of adolescence* (Vol. 1, pp. 395–397). New York, NY: Garland.

Lynd, R. S., & Lynd, H. M. (1929). *Middletown: A study in modern American culture.* New York, NY: Harvest Books.

Lynn, R., & Mikk, J. (2007). National differences in intelligence and educational attainment. *Intelligence, 35*, 115–121.

Lynne, S. D., Graber, J. A., Nichols, T. R., Brooks-Gunn, J., & Botvin, G. J. (2007). Links between pubertal timing, peer influences, and externalizing behaviors among urban students followed through middle school. *Journal of Adolescent Health, 40*, e7–e13.

Lyon, E. (2007). *The big book of birth.* New York, NY: Plume.

Lyons-Ruth, K., Bronfman, E., & Parsons, E. (1999). Maternal frightened, frightening, or atypical behavior and disorganized infant attachment patterns. *Monographs of the Society for Research in Child Development, 64*(3, Serial No. 258), 67–96.

Lytle, L. J., Bakken, L., & Romig, C. (1997). Adolescent female identity development. *Sex Roles, 37*, 175–185.

Lytton, H., & Romney, D. M. (1991). Parents' differential socialization of boys and girls: A meta-analysis. *Psychological Bulletin, 109*(2), 267. doi:http://dx.doi.org/10.1037/0033-2909.109.2.267

Ma, W., Golinkoff, R. M., Houston, D. M., & Hirsh-Pasek, K. (2011). Word learning in infant- and adult-directed speech. *Language Learning and Development, 7*(3), 209–225. doi:10.1080/15475441.2011.579839

MacBeth, T. (2006). Notel, Unitel, Multitel study. In J. J. Arnett (Ed.), *Encyclopedia of children, adolescents, and the media* (pp. 627–630). Thousand Oaks, CA: Sage.

Maccoby, E., & Martin, J. (1983). Socialization in the context of the family: Parent–child interaction. In P. H. Mussen (Ed.) & E. M. Hetherington (Vol. Ed.), *Handbook of child psychology. Vol. 4: Socialization, personality, and social development* (4th ed., pp. 1–101). New York, NY: Wiley.

Maccoby, E. E. (1984). Socialization and developmental change. *Child Development, 55*, 317–328.

Maccoby, E. E., & Jacklin, C. N. (1974). *The psychology of sex differences.* Stanford, CA: Stanford University Press.

Maccoby, E. E., & Lewis, C. C. (2003). Less day care or different day care? *Child Development, 76*, 1069–1075.

MacDorman, M. F., Matthews, T. J., Mohangoo, A. D., & Zeitlin, J. (2014). International comparisons of infant mortality and related factors: United States and Europe, 2010. *National vital statistics reports: from the Centers for Disease Control and Prevention, National Center for Health Statistics, National Vital Statistics System, 63*(5), 1–6. PMID:25252091

MacDorman, M. F., Menacker, F., & Declercq, E. (2010). Trends and characteristics of home and other out-of-hospital births in the United States, 1990–2006. *National Vital Statistics Reports, 58*, 1–14, 16.

Macek, P. (2012). Czech Republic. In J. J. Arnett (Ed.), *Adolescent psychology around the world* (pp. 243–256). New York, NY: Taylor & Francis.

MacFarquhar, R., & Schoenhals, J. (2006). *Mao's last revolution.* Cambridge, MA: Harvard University Press.

Macfie, J., Cicchetti, D., & Toth, S. L. (2001). The development of dissociation in maltreated preschool-aged children. *Development and Psychopathology, 13*, 233–254.

Machado, A., & Silva, F. J. (2007). Toward a richer view of the scientific method: The role of conceptual analysis. *American Psychologist, 62*, 671–681.

Machin, G. (2009). Familial monozygotic twinning: A report of seven pedigrees. *American Journal of Medical Genetics, 151C*, 152–154. doi:10.1002/ajmg.c.30211

MacLean, A., & Elder, G. H., Jr. (2007). Military service in the life course. *Annual Review of Sociology, 33*, 175–196.

Madlon-Kay, D. J. (2002). Maternal assessment of neonatal jaundice after hospital discharge. *The Journal of Family Practice, 51*, 445–448.

Magnuson, M. J., & Dundes, L. (2008). Gender differences in "social portraits" reflected in MySpace profiles. *CyberPsychology & Behavior, 11*(2), 239–241.

Maheshwari, A., Hamilton, M., & Bhattacharya, S. (2008). Effect of female age on the diagnostic categories of infertility. *Human Reproduction, 23*, 538–542.

Maikovich-Fong, A. K., & Jaffee, S. R. (2010). Sex differences in childhood sexual abuse characteristics and victims' emotional and behavioral problems: Findings from a national sample of youth. *Child Abuse & Neglect, 34*(6), 429–437.

Maimon, D., & Browning, C. R. (2010). Unstructured socializing, collective efficacy, and violent behavior among urban youth. *Criminology: An Interdisciplinary Journal, 48*, 443–474.

Main, M., & Solomon, J. (1990). Procedures for identifying infants as disorganized/disoriented during the Ainsworth Strange Situation. In M. T. Greenberg, D. Cicchetti, & E. M. Cummings (Eds.), *Attachment in the preschool years: Theory, research, and intervention* (pp. 121–160). Chicago, IL: University of Chicago Press.

Majors, R. (1989). Cool pose: The proud signature of black survival. In M. S. Kimmel & M. A. Messner (Eds.), *Men's lives* (pp. 83–87). New York: Macmillan.

Majors, R., & Billson, J. M. (1992). *Cool pose.* New York, NY: Lexington.

Malcolm X. (1970). *By any means necessary: Speeches, interviews, and a letter by Malcolm X.* New York, NY: Pathfinder Press.

Malebo, A., van Eeden, C., & Wissing, M. P. (2007). Sport participation, psychological well-being, and psychosocial development in a group of young black adults. *South African Journal of Psychology, 37*, 188–206.

Males, M. (2010). Is jumping off the roof always a bad idea? A rejoinder on risk taking and the adolescent brain. *Journal of Adolescent Research, 25*, 48–63.

Males, M. A. (2010). *Teenage sex and pregnancy: Modern myths, unsexy realities*. Santa Barbara, CS: ABC-CLIO, LLC.

Mallett, S., Rosenthal, D., & Keys, D. (2005). Young people, drug use and family conflict: Pathways into homelessness. *Journal of Adolescence, 28*, 185–199.

Malone, A. (2010, March 8). Minority language report: Meet the bands singing in Irish, Manx, and Breton. *The Guardian*. Retrieved from http://www.theguardian.com/music/musicblog/2010/mar/08/minority-language-report

Malott, C. S. (2011). What is postformal psychology? Toward a theory of critical complexity. In C. S. Malott (Ed.), *Critical pedagogy and cognition* (pp. 97–111). Amsterdam, Netherlands: Springer.

Malti, T., Keller, M., & Buckmann, M. (2012). Do moral choices make us feel good? The development of adolescents' emotions following moral decision making. *Journal of Adolescent Research, 23*, 389–397.

Manago, A. M., Guan, S.-S. A., & Greenfield, P. M. (2015). New media, social change, and human development. In L. A. Jensen (Ed.), *The Oxford handbook of human development and culture: An interdisciplinary perspective* (pp. 519–534). New York, NY: Oxford University Press.

Mandel, D. R., Lusczyk, P. W., & Pisoni, D. B. (1995). Infants' recognition of the sound patterns of their own names. *Psychological Science, 6*, 314–317.

Mange, E. J., & Mange, A. P. (1998). *Basic human genetics* (2nd ed.). Sunderland, MA: Sinauer Associates.

Manning, M. L. (1998). Play development from ages eight to twelve. In D. P. Fromberg & D. Bergen, *Play from birth to twelve and beyond* (pp. 154–161). London, UK: Garland Publishing.

Maratsos, M. (1998). The acquisition of grammar. In W. Damon (Ed.), & D. Kuhn & R. S. Siegler (Vol. Eds.), *Handbook of child psychology: Vol. 2. Cognition, perception and language* (5th ed., pp. 421–466). New York, NY: Wiley.

Marcelo, K. B. (2007, July). *Volunteering among high school students*. Retrieved from http://www.civicyouth.org/PopUps/FactSheets/FS07_High_School_Volunteering.pdf

Marcia, J. (1966). Development and validation of ego identity status. *Journal of Personality and Social Psychology, 3*, 551–558.

Marcia, J. (1980). Identity in adolescence. In J. Adelson (Ed.), *Handbook of adolescent psychology* (pp. 159–187). New York, NY: Wiley.

Marcia, J. (1989). Identity and intervention. *Journal of Adolescence, 12*, 401–410.

Marcia, J. E. (1999). Representational thought in ego identity, psychotherapy, and psychosocial developmental theory. In I. E. Siegel (Ed.), *Development of mental representation: Theories and applications* (pp. 391–414). Mahwah, NJ: Erlbaum.

Marcia, J. E. (2010). Life transitions and stress in the context of psychosocial development. In T. W. Miller (Ed.), *Handbook of stressful transitions across the lifespan* (pp. 19–34). New York, NY: Springer.

Marcia, J. E., & Carpendale, J. (2004). Identity: Does thinking make it so? In C. Lightfoot & M. Chandler (Eds.), *Changing conceptions of psychological life* (pp. 113–126). Mahwah, NJ: Erlbaum.

Marcotte, D., Fortin, L., Potvin, P., & Papillon, M. (2002). Gender differences in depressive symptoms during adolescence: Role of gender-typed characteristics, self-esteem, body image, stressful life events, and pubertal status. *Journal of Emotional and Behavioral Disorders, 10*, 29–42.

Markant, J. C., & Thomas, K. M. (2013). Postnatal brain development. In Zelazo, P. D. (Ed.), *The Oxford handbook of developmental psychology: Volume 1: Body and mind* (pp. 129–163). New York, NY: Oxford University Press.

Markey, P. M., & Markey, C. N. (2007). Romantic ideals, romantic obtainment, and relationship experiences: The complementarity of interpersonal traits among romantic partners. *Journal of Social and Personal Relationships, 24*, 517–533.

Markman, E. M., & Jaswal, V. K. (2004). Acquiring and using a grammatical form class: Lessons from the proper-count distinction. *Weaving a Lexicon*, 371–409.

Marks, A. K., Ejesi, K., McCullough, M. B., & García Coll, C. (2015). Developmental implications of discrimination. In M. E. Lamb (Volume Ed.) & R. M. Lerner (Ed.-in-Chief), *Handbook of child psychology and developmental science, Vol. 3: Socioemotional processes* (pp. 324–365). Hoboken, NJ: Wiley.

Markstrom-Adams, C. (1989). Androgyny and its relation to adolescent psychological well-being: A review of the literature. *Sex Roles, 21*, 469–473.

Markus, H., & Kitayama, S. (1991). Culture and the self: Implications for cognition, emotion, and motivation. *Psychological Review, 98*, 224–253.

Markus, H., & Nurius, R. (1986). Possible selves. *American Psychologist, 41*, 954–969.

Markus, H. R., & Kitayama, S. (2003). Culture, self, and the reality of the social. *Psychological Inquiry, 14*, 277–283.

Markus, H. R., & Kitayama, S. (2010). Cultures and selves: A cycle of mutual constitution. *Perspectives on Psychological Science, 5*(4), 420–430.

Marlier, L., Schaal, B., & Soussignan, R. (1998). Neonatal responsiveness to the odor of amniotic and lacteal fluids: A test of perinatal chemosensory continuity. *Child Development, 69*, 611–623.

Marlow, N., Wolke, D., Bracewell, M. A., & Samara, M. (2005). Neurologic and developmental disability at six years of age after extremely preterm births. *New England Journal of Medicine, 352*, 9–19.

Marlowe, F. (2000). Paternal investment and the human mating system. *Behavioural Processes, 51*, 45–61.

Marsh, H. W., & Ayotte, V. (2003). Do multiple dimensions of self-concept become more differentiated with age? The differential distinctiveness hypothesis. *Journal of Educational Psychology, 95*, 687–706.

Marsh, H. W., & Hau, K. T. (2003). Big fish little pond effect on academic self-concept: A cross-cultural (26-country) test of the negative effects of academically selective schools. *American Psychologist, 58*, 364–376.

Marsh, H. W., & Kleitman, S. (2005). Consequences of employment during high school: Character building, subversion of academic goals, or a threshold? *American Educational Research Journal, 42*, 331–369.

Marsh, M., & Ronner, W. (1996). *The empty cradle: Infertility in America from colonial times to the present.* Baltimore, MD: Johns Hopkins University Press.

Marshall, B. K. (1972). Universal social dilemmas and Japanese educational history: The writing of R. P. Dore. *History of Education Quarterly, 12*(1), 97–106.

Marshall, E. A., & Butler, K. (2015). School-to-work transitions in emerging adults. In J. J. Arnett (Ed.), *The Oxford handbook of emerging adulthood* (pp. 316–333). New York, NY: Oxford University Press.

Marti, E., & Rodriguez, C. (Eds.). (2012). *After Piaget*. New York, NY: Transaction Publishers.

Martin, A., Brooks-Gunn, J., Klebanov, P., Buka, S., & McCormick, M. (2008). Long-term maternal effects of early childhood intervention: Findings from the Infant Health and Development Program (IHDP). *Journal of Applied Developmental Psychology, 29*, 101–117.

Martin, C. K., & Fabes, R. A. (2001). The stability and consequences of young children's same-sex peer interactions. *Developmental Psychology, 37*, 431–446.

Martin, C. L., & Ruble, D. (2004). Children's search for gender cues: Cognitive perspectives on gender development. *Current Directions in Psychological Science, 13*(2), 67–70.

Martin, J., & Sokol, B. (2011). Generalized others and imaginary audiences: A neo-Meadian approach to adolescent egocentrism. *New Ideas in Psychology, 29*(3), 364–375.

Martin, J. A., Hamilton, B. E., Sutton, P. D., Ventura, S. J., Menacker, F., & Munson, M. L. (2003). Births: Final data for 2002. *National Vital Statistics Reports, 52*(10). Hyattsville, MD: National Center for Health Statistics.

Martin, J. A., Hamilton, B. E., Sutton, P. D., Ventura, S. J., Menacker, F., & Munson, M. L. (2005). Births: Final data for 2003. *National Vital Statistics Reports, 54*, 1–116.

Martin, J. A., Park, M. M., & Sutton, P. D. (2002). Births: Preliminary data for 2001. *National Vital Statistics Reports, 50*(10). Hyattsville, MD: National Center for Health Statistics.

Martin, P., & Midgley, E. (2010). *Immigration in America, 2010.* Washington, DC: Population Reference Bureau.

Martino, S. C., Collins, R. L., Kanouse, D. E., Elliott, M., & Berry, S. H. (2005). Social cognitive processes mediating the relationship between exposure to television's sexual content and adolescents' sexual behavior. *Journal of Personality and Social Psychology, 89*(6), 914–924.

Martins, C., & Gaffan, E. A. (2000). Effects of maternal depression on patterns of infant-mother attachment: A meta-analytics investigation. *Journal of Child Psychology and Psychiatry, 41*, 737–746.

Marván, M. L., & Trujillo, P. (2010). Menstrual socialization, beliefs, and attitudes concerning menstruation in rural and urban Mexican women. *Health Care for Women International, 31*, 53–67.

Mascarenhas, M. N., Flaxman, S. R., Boerma, T., Vanderpoel, S., & Stevens, G. A. (2012). National, regional, and global trends in infertility prevalence since 1990: A systematic analysis of 277 health surveys. *PLoS Med, 9*(12), 1–12. doi:10.1371/journal.pmed.1001356

Mascolo, M. F., & Fischer, K. W. (2007). The codevelopment of self and sociomoral emotions during the toddler years. In C. A. Brownell & C. B. Kopp (Eds.), *Socioemotional development in the toddler years* (pp. 66–99). New York, NY: Guilford.

Masino, S., & Niño-Zarazúa, M. (2016). What works to improve the quality of student learning in developing countries? *International Journal of Educational Development, 48*, 53–65.

Mason, R. (2007). Working with abused children and adolescents. In T. Ronen, & A freeman (Eds.), *Cognitive behavior therapy in clinical social work practice* (pp. 235–260). New York: Springer Publishing Co.

Massad, C. (1981). Sex role identity and adjustment during adolescence. *Child Development, 52*, 1290–1298.

Masten, A. S. (2001). Ordinary magic: Resilience processes in development. *American Psychologist, 56*(3), 227–238.

Masten, A. S. (2007). Competence, resilience, and development in adolescence: Clues for prevention science. In D. Romer & E. F. Walker (Eds.), *Adolescent psychopathology and the developing brain: Integrating brain and prevention science* (pp. 31–52). New York, NY: Oxford University Press.

Masten, A. S. (2014). Global perspectives on resilience in children and youth. *Child Development, 85*(1), 6–20.

Masten, A. S., & Narayan, A. J. (2012). Child development in the context of disaster, war, and terrorism: Pathways of risk and resilience. *Annual Review of Psychology, 63*, 227–257. doi:10.1146/annurev-psych-120710-100356

Masten, A. S., Narayan, A. J., Silverman, W. K., & Osofsky, J. D. (2015). Children in war and disaster. In M. H. Bornstein, T. Leventhal (Vol.Eds.), & R. M. Lerner (Ed.-in-Chief), *Handbook of child psychology and developmental science, Vol. 4: Ecological settings and processes* (pp. 704–745). Hoboken, NJ: Wiley.

Masten, A. S., Obradovic, J., & Burt, K. B. (2006). Resilience in embracing emerging adulthood: Developmental perspectives on continuity and transformation. In J. J. Arnett & J. L. Tanner (Eds.), *Emerging adults in America: Coming of age in the 21st century* (pp. 173–190). Washington, DC: American Psychological Association.

Masten, A. S., & Osofsky, J. D. (2010). Disasters and their impact on child development: Introduction to the special section. *Child Development, 81*(4), 1029–1039. doi:10.1111/j.1467-8624.2010.01452.x

Mastin, D. F., Peszka, J., & Lilly, D. R. (2009). Online academic integrity. *Teaching of Psychology, 36*(3), 174–178.

Mathews, G. A., Fane, B. A., Conway, G. S., Brook, C. G., & Hines, M. (2009). Personality and congenital adrenal hyperplasia: Possible effects of prenatal androgen exposure. *Hormones and Behavior, 55*(2), 285–291. doi:10.1016/j.yhbeh.2008.11.007

Matlin, M. W. (2004). *The psychology of women* (5th ed.). Belmont, CA: Wadsworth.

Matsumoto, D., & Yoo, S. H. (2006). Toward a new generation of cross-cultural research. *Perspectives on Psychological Science, 1*, 234–250.

Mattis, J. S., Ahluwalia, M. K., Cowie, S. E., & Kirkland-Harris, A. M. (2006). Ethnicity, culture, and spiritual development. In E. C. D. Roehlkepartain, P. E. King, L. Wagner, & P. L. Benson (Eds.), *The handbook of spiritual development in childhood and adolescence* (pp. 283–296). Thousand Oaks, CA: Sage.

Mattson, S. N., Roesch, S. C., Fagerlund, Å., Autti-Rämö, I., Jones, K. L., May, P. A., … CIFASD. (2010). Toward a neurobehavioral profile of fetal alcohol spectrum disorders. *Alcoholism: Clinical and Experimental Research, 34*, 1640–1650.

Matusov, E., & Hayes, R. (2000). Sociocultural critique of Piaget and Vygotsky. *New Ideas in Psychology, 18*, 215–239.

Maurer, T. W., & Robinson, D. W. (2008). Effects of attire, alcohol, and gender on perceptions of date rape. *Sex Roles*, 58, 423–434.

Maynard, A. E., & Martini, M. I. (Eds.). (2005). *Learning in cultural context: Family, peers, and school.* New York, NY: Kluwer.

Mayo Clinic. (2017). Dyslexia. Retrieved from http://www.mayoclinic.org/diseases-conditions/dyslexia/basics/definition/con-20021904

Mayo Clinic. (2017). Infant and toddler health. Retrieved from http://www.mayoclinic.org/healthy-lifestyle/infant-and-toddler-health/in-depth/healthy-baby/art-20046200

Mayo Clinic Staff. (2017). Labor pain: Weigh your options for relief. Retrieved from http://www.mayoclinic.org/healthy-lifestyle/labor-and-delivery/in-depth/labor-pain/art-20044845?pg=1

Mayo Clinic Staff (2011). *Stages of labor: Baby, it's time!* Retrieved from http://www.mayoclinic.com/health/stages-of-labor/PR00106/NSECTIONGROUP=2

Mayo Clinic Staff. (2017). *Labor and delivery, postpartum care.* Retrieved from http://www.mayoclinic.org/healthy-lifestyle/labor-and-delivery/in-depth/stages-of-labor/art-20046545

Mazuka, R., Kondo, T., & Hayashi, A. (2008). Japanese mothers' use of specialized vocabulary in infant-directed speech: Infant-directed vocabulary in Japanese. In N. Masataka (Ed.), *The origins of language: Unraveling evolutionary forces* (pp. 39–58). New York, NY: Springer.

Mazur, E., & Kozarian, L. (2010). Self-presentation and interaction in blogs of adolescents and young emerging adults. *Journal of Adolescent Research, 25*, 124–144.

McBride Murry, V., Hill, N. E., Witherspoon, D., Berkel, C., & Bartz, D. (2015). Children in diverse contexts. In R. M. Lerner (Series Ed.), M. H. Bornstein & T. Leventhal (Vol. Eds.), *Handbook of child psychology and developmental science, Volume 4: Ecological Setting and Processes* (7th ed., pp. 416–454). New York, NY: Wiley. doi:10.1002/9781118963418.childpsy411

McCabe, A., Tamis-LeMonda C., Bornstein, M., Brockmeyer Cates, C., Golinkoff, R., Guerra, A. W., … Song, L. (2013). Multilingual children: Beyond myths and towards best practices. *Social Policy Report, 27*(4), 1–19. Retrieved from www.srcd.org/publications/social-policy-report

McCabe, P. C., & Altamura, M. (2011). Empirically valid strategies to improve social and emotional competence of preschool children. *Psychology in the Schools, 48*(5), 513–540. doi:10.1002/pits.20570

McCardle, P. (2015). Bilingualism: Research and policy. In E. L. Grigorenko (Ed.), *The global context for new directions for child and adolescent development. New Directions for Child and Adolescent Development, 2015*(147), 41–48. doi:10.1002/cad.20088

McCarthy, G., & Maughan, B. (2010). Negative childhood experiences and adult love relationships: The role of internal working models of attachment. *Attachment & Human Development, 12*(5), 445–461.

McCartney, K., & Berry, D. (2009). Whether the environment matters more for children in poverty. In K. McCartney and R. A. Weinberg (Eds.), *Experience and development: A festschrift in honor of Sandra Wood Scarr* (pp. 99–124). New York, NY: Psychology Press.

McClure, V. S. (2000). *Infant massage—Revised Edition: A handbook for loving parents.* New York, NY: Bantam.

McDowell, M. A., Brody, D. J., & Hughes, J. P. (2007). Has age at menarche changed? Results from the National Health and Nutrition Examination Survey (NHANES) 1999–2004. *Journal of Adolescent Health, 40*, 227–231.

McFalls, J. A. (2007). Population: A lively introduction. *Population Bulletin, 62*, 1–31.

McGinnis, J. M., Gootman, J. A., & Kraak, V. I. (Eds.), and the Committee on Food Marketing and the Diet of Children and Youth. (2006). *Food marketing to children and youth: Threat or opportunity?* Washington, DC: The National Academies Press.

McGue, M., & Christensen, K. (2002). The heritability of level and rate-of-change in cognitive functioning in Danish twins aged 70 years and older. *Experimental Aging Research, 28*, 435–451.

McGuire, S., Manke, B., Eftekhari, A., & Dunn, J. (2000). Children's perceptions of sibling conflict during middle childhood: Issues and sibling (Dis) similarity. *Social Development, 9*, 173–190.

McHale, S., Dariotis, J., & Kauh, T. (2003). Social development and social relationships in middle childhood. In R. Lerner & M. Easterbrooks (Eds.), *Handbook of psychology: Developmental psychology* (Vol. 6., pp. 241–265). New York, NY: John Wiley & Sons.

McHale, S. M., Crouter, A. C., & Tucker, C. J. (2001). Free-time activities in middle childhood: Links with adjustment in early adolescence. *Child Development, 72*, 1764–1778.

McHale, S. M, Crouter, A. C., & Whiteman, S. D. (2003). The family contexts of gender development in childhood and adolescence. *Social Development, 12*(1), 125–148.

McIntosh, H., Metz, E., & Youniss, J. (2005). Community service and identity formation in adolescents. In J. L. Mahoney, R. W. Larson, & J. S., Eccles (Eds.), *Organized activities as contexts of development: Extracurricular activities, after-school and community programs* (pp. 331–351). Mahwah, NJ: Lawrence Erlbaum.

McKenna, J. J., & McDade, T. (2005). Why babies should never sleep alone: A review of the co-sleeping controversy in relation to SIDS, bed-sharing, and breastfeeding. *Paediatric Respiratory Reviews, 6*, 134–152.

McKenzie, J., & Jensen, L. A. (in press). Charting the moral life courses: A theory of moral development in US evangelical and mainline Protestant cultures. *Culture & Psychology*. doi:10.1177/1354067X16656578

McKinsey Global Institute. (2010). *Lions on the move: The progress and potential of Africa's economies.* Washington, DC: Author.

McKnight, A. J., & Peck, R. C. (2002). Graduated licensing: What works? *Injury Prevention, 8*(Suppl. 2), ii32–ii38.

McLean, K. C., & Breen, A. V. (2015). Selves in a world of stories during emerging adulthood. In J. J. Arnett (Ed.), *Oxford handbook of emerging adulthood* (pp. 385–400). New York, NY: Oxford University Press.

McLean, K. C., & Syed, M. (2016). Personal, master, and alternative narratives: An integrative framework for understanding identity development in context. *Human Development, 58*(6), 318–349.

McLuhan, M. (1960). *The Gutenberg galaxy.* Toronto, Canada: University of Toronto Press.

McNamara, F., & Sullivan, C. E. (2000). Obstructive sleep apnea in infants. *Journal of Pediatrics, 136*, 318–323.

McNeil, J., & Helwig, C. C. (2015). Balancing social responsibility and personal autonomy: Adolescents' reasoning about community service programs. *The Journal of Genetic Psychology, 176*, 349–368.

Mead, M. (1930/2001). *Growing up in New Guinea.* New York, NY: Anchor.

Mead, M. (1935). *Sex and temperament in three primitive societies.* New York, NY: William Morrow.

Mechelli, A., Crinion, J. T., Noppeney, U., O'Doherty, J., Ashburner, J., Frackowiak, R. S., & Price, C. J. (2004). Neurolinguistics: Structural plasticity in the bilingual brain. *Nature, 431*(7010), 757–757. doi:10.1038/431757a

Medina, J. (2015, October 15). Sex ed lesson: "yes means yes," but it's tricky. *New York Times*, p. A1.

Medina, J., Ojeda-Aciego, M., & Ruiz-Calviño, J. (2009). Formal concept analysis via multi-adjoint concept lattices. *Fuzzy Sets and Systems, 160*(2), 130–144.

Medline. (2008). Kwashiorkor. *Medline Plus medical encyclopedia.* Retrieved from http://www.nlm.nih.gov/MEDLINEPLUS/ency/article/001604.htm

Medline Plus. (2016). *Cesarean Section.* Retrieved from https://www.nlm.nih.gov/medlineplus/cesareansection.html

MedlinePlus. (2016). *Kwashiorkor.* Retrieved from https://medlineplus.gov/ency/article/001604.htm

Meeus, W. (2007). Netherlands. In J. J. Arnett, R. Ahmed, B. Nsamenang, T. S. Saraswathi, & R. Silbereisen (Eds.), *International encyclopedia of adolescence* (pp. 666–680). New York, NY: Routledge.

Meeus, W., Iedema, J., Helsen, M., & Vollebergh, W. (1999). Patterns of adolescent identity development: Review of literature and longitudinal analysis. *Developmental Review, 19*, 419–461.

Meier, E. P., & Gray, J. (2014). Facebook photo activity associated with body image disturbance in adolescent girls. *Cyberpsychology, Behavior, and Social Networking, 17*, 199–206.

Meisel, M. J. (2011). *First and second language acquisitions: Parallels and differences.* New York, NY: Cambridge University Press.

Meltzer, L., Pollica, L. S., & Barzillai, M. (2007). Executive function in the classroom: Embedding strategy instruction into daily teaching practices. In L. Meltzer (Ed.), *Executive function in education: From theory to practice* (pp. 165–193). New York, NY: Guilford Press.

Meltzoff, A. N., Kuhl, P. K., Movellan, J., & Sejnowski, T. J. (2009). Foundations for a new science of learning. *Science, 325*, 284–288

Meltzoff, A. N., & Moore, M. K. (1994). Imitation, memory, and the representation of persons. *Infant Behavior and Development, 17*, 83–99.

Mendle, J., & Ferrero, J. (2012). Detrimental psychological outcomes associated with pubertal timing in adolescent boys. *Developmental Review, 32*(1), 49–66.

Menella, J. (2000, June). The psychology of eating. Paper presented at the annual meeting of the American Psychological Society, Miami, FL.

Mennella, J. A., Jagnow, C. P., & Beauchamp, G. K. (2001). Prenatal and postnatal flavor learning by human infants. *Pediatrics, 107*, e88. doi:10.1542/peds/107/6/e88

Mensch, B. S., Bruce, J., & Greene, M. E. (1998). *The uncharted passage: Girls' adolescence in the developing world.* New York, NY: Population Council.

Menyuk, P., Liebergott, J., & Schultz, M. (1995). *Early language development in full-term and premature infants.* Hillsdale, NJ: Erlbaum.

Meredith, M. (2011). *Born in Africa: The quest for the origins of human life.* New York, NY: PublicAffairs.

Merewood, A., Mehta, S. D., Chamberlain, L. B., Phillipp, B. L., & Bauchner, H. (2005). Breastfeeding rates in U.S. baby-friendly hospitals: Results of a national survey. *Pediatrics, 116*, 628–634.

Merten, S., Dratva, J., & Achermann-Liebrich, U. (2005). Do baby-friendly hospitals influence breastfeeding duration on a national level? *Pediatrics, 116*, c702–c708.

Merz, E., & Abramowicz, J. (2012). 3D/4D ultrasound in prenatal diagnosis: Is it time for routine use? *Clinical Obstetrics & Gynecology, 55*, 336–351.

Mesman, J., van IJzendoorn, M. H., & Bakermans-Kranenburg, M. J. (2009). The many faces of the Still-Face Paradigm: A review and meta-analysis. *Developmental Review, 29*, 120–162.

Messinger, D. S., & Lester, B. M. (2008). Prenatal substance exposure and human development. In A. Fogel, B. J. King, & S. G. Shanker (Eds.), *Human development in the 21st century: Visionary policy ideas from systems scientists* (pp. 225–232). Bethesda, MD: Council on Human Development.

Metz, E., McLellan, J., & Youniss, J. (2003). Types of voluntary service and adolescents' civic development. *Journal of Adolescent Research, 18*, 188–203.

Metz, E. C., & Youniss, J. (2005). Longitudinal gains in civic development through school-based required services. *Political Psychology, 26*, 413–437.

Meyer, L. E., & Erler, T. (2011). Swaddling: A traditional care method rediscovered. *World Journal of Pediatrics*, *7*, 155–160.

Michael, R. T., Gagnon, J. H., Laumann, E. O., & Kolata, G. (1995). *Sex in America: A definitive study.* New York, NY: Warner Books.

Michikyan, M., Dennis, J., & Subrahmanyam, K. (2015). Can you guess who I am? Real, ideal, and false self-presentation on Facebook among emerging adults. *Emerging Adulthood, 3*, 55–64.

Milan, S., Snow, S., & Belay, S. (2007). The context of preschool children's sleep: Racial/ethnic differences in sleep locations, routines, and concerns. *Journal of Family Psychology, 21*, 20–28.

Miller, B. C., & Benson, B. (1999). Romantic and sexual relationship development during adolescence. In W. Furman, B. B. Brown, & C. Feiring (Eds.), *The development of romantic relationships in adolescence. Cambridge studies in social and emotional development* (pp. 99–121). New York: Cambridge University Press.

Miller, G. A. (1956). The magical number seven, plus or minus two: Some limits on our capacity for processing information. *Psychological Review, 63*, 81–97.

Miller, H. C., Gipson, C. D., Vaughan, A., Rayburn-Reeves, R., & Zentall, T. R. (2009). Object permanence in dogs: Invisible displacement in a rotation task. *Psychonomic Bulletin & Review, 16*, 150–155.

Miller, J. G. (2004). The cultural deep structure of psychological theories of social development. In R. J. Sternberg & E. L. Grigorenko (Eds.), *Culture and competence: Contexts of life success* (pp. 111–138). Washington, DC: American Psychological Association.

Miller, J. G., & Bersoff, D. M. (1994). Cultural influences on the moral status of reciprocity and the discounting of endogenous motivation. *Personality and Social Psychology Bulletin, 20*, 592–602.

Miller, J. G., Bersoff, D. M., & Harwood, R. L. (1990). Perceptions of social responsibility in India and in the United States: Moral imperatives or personal decisions? *Journal of Personality and Social Psychology, 58*, 33–47.

Miller, J. G., Goyal, M., & Wice, M. (2015). Ethical considerations in research on human development and culture. In L. A. Jensen (Ed.), *The Oxford handbook of human development and culture: An interdisciplnary perspective* (pp. 14–27). New York, NY: Oxford University Press.

Miller, L. (2004). Those naughty teenage girls: Japanese kogals, slang, and media assessments. *Journal of Linguistic Anthropology, 14*(2), 225–247. doi:10.1525/jlin.2004.14.2.225

Miller, P. (2011). Piaget's theory. In U. Goswami (Ed.), *The Wiley-Blackwell handbook of childhood cognitive development* (pp. 649–672). Hoboken, NJ: John Wiley & Sons, Inc.

Miller, P. J. (1996). Instantiating culture through discourse practices: Some personal reflections on socialization and how to study it. In Jessor, R., Colby, A., & Shweder, R. A. (Eds.), *Ethnography and human development* (pp. 183–204). Chicago, IL: University of Chicago Press.

Miller, P. J. (2014). Placing discursive practices front and center: A sociocultural approach to the study of early socialization. In C. Wainryb & H. E. Recchia (Eds.), *Talking about right and wrong: Parent-child conversations as contexts for moral development* (pp. 416–447). New York, NY: Cambridge University Press.

Miller, P. J., Chen, E. C. H., & Olivarez, M. (2014). Narrative making and remaking in the early years: Prelude to the personal narrative. *New Directions for Child and Adolescent Development, 2014*(145), 15–27. doi:10.1002/cad.20064

Miller, P. J., Fung, H., Lin, S., Chen, E. C.-H., & Boldt, B. R. (2012). How socialization happens on the ground: Narrative practices as alternate socializing pathways in Taiwanese and European-American families. *Monographs of the Society for Research in Child Development, 77*, 1–140.

Miller, P. J., Wiley, A. R., Fung, H., & Liang, C. H. (1997). Personal storytelling as a medium of socialization in Chinese and American families. *Child Development, 68*(3), 557–568. doi:10.1111/j.1467-8624.1997.tb01958.x

Miller, P. J., Wiley, A. R., Fung, H., & Liang, C.-H. (2008). Personal storytelling as a medium of socialization in Chinese and American families. In M. Gauvain & M. Cole (Eds.), *Readings on the development of children* (pp. 205–216). New York, NY: Worth Publishers.

Miller, T. R., Finkelstein, A. E., Zaloshnja, E., & Hendrie, D. (2012). The cost of child and adolescent injuries and savings from prevention. In K. Liller (Ed.), *Injury prevention for children and adolescents* (pp. 21–81). Washington, DC: American Public Health Association.

Miller-Johnson, S., Costanzo, P. R., Cole, J. D., Rose, M. R., & Browne, D. C. (2003). Peer social structure and risk-taking behaviour among African American early adolescents. *Journal of Youth & Adolescence*, 32, 375–384.

Millman, R. P. (2005). Excessive sleepiness in adolescents and young adults: Causes, consequences, and treatment strategies. *Pediatrics, 115*, 1774–1786.

Mills, N., Daker-White, G., Graham, A., Campbell, R., & The Chlamydia Screening Studies (ClaSS) Group. (2006). Population screening for *Chlamydia trachomatis* infection in the UK: A qualitative study of the experiences of those screened. *Family Practice, 23*, 550–557.

Minami, M., & McCabe, A. (1995). Rice balls and bear hunts: Japanese and North American family narrative patterns. *Journal of Child Language, 22*, 423–445.

Mindell, J. A., & Owens, J. O. (2003). Sleep problems in pediatric practice: Clinical issues for the pediatric nurse practitioner. *Journal of Pediatric Health Care, 17*, 324–331.

Mindell, J. A., Sadeh, A., Kohyama, J., & How, T. H. (2010). Parental behaviors and sleep outcomes in infants and toddlers: A cross cultural comparison. *Sleep Medicine, 11*, 393–399.

Mintz, T. H. (2005). Linguistic and conceptual influences on adjective acquisition in 24- and 36-month-olds. *Developmental Psychology, 41*, 17–29.

Minuchin, P. (2002). Looking toward the horizon: Present and future in the study of family systems. In J. P. McHale & W. S. Grolinick (Eds.), *Retrospect and prospect in the study of families* (pp. 259–278). Mahwah, NJ: Erlbaum.

Minuchin, S. (1974). *Families and family therapy*. Cambridge, MA: Harvard University Press.

Mireault, G. C., Crockenberg, S. C., Sparrow, J. E., Pettinato, C. A., Woodward, K. C., & Malza, K. (2014). Social looking, social referencing, and humor perception in 6- and 12-month-old infants. *Infant Behavior and Development, 37*, 536–545.

Mishna, F., Newman, P. A., Daley, A., & Solomon, S. (2009). Bullying of lesbian and gay youth: A qualitative investigation. *British Journal of Social Work*, 39, 1598–1614.

Mistry, R. S., Benner, A. D., Tan, C. S., & Kim, S. Y. (2009). Family economic stress and academic well-being among Chinese-American youth: The influence of adolescents' perceptions of economic strain. *Journal of Family Psychology, 23*(3), 279–290.

Mitchell, A., & Boss, B. J. (2002). Adverse effects of pain on the nervous systems of newborns and young children: A review of the literature. *Journal of Neuroscience and Nursing, 34*, 228–235.

Mitchell, T. (2001). *Global noise: Rap and hip hop outside the USA*. Middletown, CT; Wesleyan University Press.

Modell, J., & Goodman, M. (1990). Historical perspectives. In S. S. Feldman & G. Elliott (Eds.), *At the threshold: The developing adolescent* (pp. 34–51). Cambridge, MA: Harvard University Press.

Moffitt, T. E. (2003). Life-course-persistent and adolescence-limited antisocial behavior: A 10-year research review and a research agenda. In B. B. Lahey & T. E. Moffitt (Eds.), *Causes of conduct disorder and juvenile delinquency* (pp. 49–75). New York, NY: Guilford.

Moffitt, T. E. (2006). Life-course-persistent versus adolescence-limited antisocial behavior. In D. J. Cohen & D. Cicchetti (Eds.), *Developmental psychopathology, Vol. 3: Risk, order, and adaptation* (2nd ed., pp. 570–598). Hoboken, NJ: Wiley.

Moffitt, T. E. (2007). A review of research on the taxonomy of life-course persistent versus adolescence-limited antisocial behavior. In D. J. Flannery, A. T. Vazsonyi, & I. D. Waldman (Eds.), *The Cambridge handbook of violent behavior and aggression* (pp. 49–74). New York, NY: Cambridge University Press.

Molina, G., Weiser, T. G., Lipsitz, S. R., Esquivel, M. M., Uribe-Leitz, T., Azad, T., … & Haynes, A. B. (2015). Relationship between cesarean delivery rate and maternal and neonatal mortality. *JAMA, 314*, 2263–2270.

Money, J. (1980). *Love and love sickness: The science of sex, gender difference, and pair-bonding*. Baltimore, MD: Johns Hopkins University Press.

Montagu, D., Yamey, G., Visconti, A., Harding, A., & Yoong, J. (2011). Where do poor women in developing countries give birth? A multi-country analysis of demographic and health survey data. *PloS One, 6*(2), e17155. doi:10.1371/journal.pone.0017155

Montemayor, R. (1984). Maternal employment and adolescents' relations with parents, siblings, and peers. *Journal of Youth and Adolescence, 13*, 543–557.

Montgomery, M. J. (2005). Psychosocial intimacy and identity: From early adolescence to emerging adulthood. *Journal of Adolescent Research, 20*, 346–374.

Moon, C., Cooper, R. P., & Fifer, W. P. (1993). Two-day-olds prefer their native language. *Infant Behavior and Development, 16*, 495–500.

Moore, A. S. (2013, October 6). Tales from the city. *The Boston Globe Magazine*, p. 4.

Moore, E. E., Romaniuk, H., Olsson, C. A., Jayasinghe, Y., Carlin, J. B., & Patton, G. C. (2010). The prevalence of childhood sexual abuse and adolescent unwanted sexual contact among boys and girls living in Victoria, Australia. *Child Abuse & Neglect, 34*(5), 379–385.

Moore, K. A., Chalk, R., Scarpa, J., & Vandivere, S. (2002, August). Family strengths: Often overlooked, but real. *Child Trends Research Brief*, 1–8.

Moore, K. L., Persaud, T. V. N., & Torchia, M. G. (2015). *Before we are born: Essentials of embryology and birth defects*. Philadelphia, PA: Saunders.

Moore, R. L. (2004). We're cool, mom and dad are swell: Basic slang and generational shifts in values. *American Speech, 79*(1), 59–86.

Morales, A., Yakushko, O. F., & Castro, A. J. (2012). Language brokering among Mexican-Immigrant families in the Midwest: A multiple case study. *The Counseling Psychologist, 40*(4), 520–553. doi:10.1177/0011000011417312

Morawska, A., & Sanders, M. (2011). Parental use of time out revisited: A useful or harmful parenting strategy? *Journal of Child and Family Studies, 20*, 1–8.

Morelli, G. (2015). The evolution of attachment theory and cultures of human attachment in infancy and early childhood. In L. A. Jensen (Ed.), *Oxford handbook of human development and culture* (pp. 149–164). New York, NY: Oxford University Press.

Morelli, G., Rogoff, B., Oppenheim, D., & Goldsmith, D. (1992). Cultural variation in infants' sleeping arrangements: Question of independence. *Developmental Psychology, 39*, 604–613.

Morelli, G., & Rothbaum, F. (2007). Situating the child in context: Attachment relationships and self-regulation in different cultures. In S. Kitayama & D. Cohen (Eds.), *Handbook of cultural psychology* (pp. 500–527). New York, NY: Guilford Press.

Moretti, M. M., & Wiebe, V. J. (1999). Self-discrepancy in adolescence: Own and parental standpoints on the self. *Merrill-Palmer Quarterly, 45*, 624–649.

Morgan, M. A., Cragan, J. D., Goldenberg, R. L., Rasmussen, S. A., & Schulkin, J. (2010). Management of prescription and nonprescription drug use during pregnancy. *Journal of Maternal–Fetal and Neonatal Medicine, 23*, 813–819.

Morgenstern, M., Sargent, J. D., Engels, R. C., Scholte, R. H., Florek, E., Hunt, K., ... & Hanewinkel, R. (2013). Smoking in movies and adolescent smoking initiation: longitudinal study in six European countries. *American Journal of Preventive Medicine*, 44, 339–344.

Morgos, D., Worden, J. W., & Gupta, L. (2008). Psychosocial effects of war experiences among displaced children in southern Darfur. *OMEGA-Journal of Death and Dying, 56*(3), 229–253. doi:10.2190/OM.56.3.b

Morra, S., Gobbo, C., Marini, Z., & Sheese, R. (2008). *Cognitive development: Neo–Piagetian perspectives*. New York, NY: Taylor & Francis.

Morris, D. H., Jones, M. E., Schoemaker, M. J., Ashworth, A., & Swerdlow, A. J. (2011). Familial concordance for age at menarche: Analyses from the Breakthrough Generations Study. *Paediatric and Perinatal Epidemiology, 25*(3), 306–311. doi:10.1111/j.1365-3016.2010.01183.x

Mortimer, J. (2013). Work and its positive and negative effects on youth's psychosocial development. *Health and Safety of Young Workers*, 66–79.

Mortimer, J. T. (2003). *Working and growing up in America*. Cambridge, MA: Harvard University Press.

Mortimer, J. T., Vuolo, M., Staff, J., Wakefield, S., & Xie, W. (2008). Tracing the timing of "career" acquisition in a contemporary youth cohort. *Work and Occupations, 35*(1), 44–84.

Morton, J. B., & Trehub, S. E. (2001). Children's understanding of emotion in speech. *Child Development, 72*(3), 834–843. doi:10.1111/1467-8624.00318

Mosby, L., Rawls, A. W., Meehan, A. J., Mays, E., & Pettinari, C. J. (1999). Troubles in interracial talk about discipline: An examination of African American child rearing narratives. *Journal of Comparative Family Studies, 30*, 489–521.

Moscardino, U., Scrimin, S., Cadei, F., & Altoè, G. (2012). Mental health among former child soldiers and never-abducted children in northern Uganda. *The Scientific World Journal, 2012*, 1–7. doi:10.1100/2012/367545

Mosier, C. E., & Rogoff, B. (2003). Privileged treatment of toddlers: Cultural aspects of individual choice and responsibility. *Developmental Psychology, 39*(6), 1047–1060. doi:10.1037/0012-1649.39.6.1047

Mossakowski, K. N. (2009). The influence of past unemployment duration on symptoms of depression among young women and men in the United States. *American Journal of Public Health, 99*(10), 1826–1832.

Motola, M., Sinisalo, P., & Guichard, J. (1998). Social habits and future plans. In J. Nurmi (Ed.), *Adolescents, cultures, and conflicts* (pp. 43–73). New York, NY: Garland.

Mueller, C. M., & Dweck, C. S. (1998). Praise for intelligence can undermine children's motivation and performance. *Journal of Personality and Social Psychology, 75*, 33.

Mueller, N. T., Whyatt, R., Hoepner, L., Oberfield, S., Dominguez-Bello, M. G., Widen, E. M., … Rundle, A. (2014). Prenatal exposure to antibiotics, cesarean section and risk of childhood obesity. *International Journal of Obesity*. doi:10.1038/ijo.2014.180

Mugford, M. (2006). Cost effectiveness of prevention and treatment of neonatal respiratory distress (RDS) with exogenous surfactant: What has changed in the last three decades? *Early Human Development, 82*, 105–115.

Muller, F., Rebiff, M., Taillandier, A., Qury, J. F., & Mornet, E. (2000). Parental origin of the extra chromosome in prenatally diagnosed fetal trisomy. *Human Genetics, 106*, 340–344.

Muller, M. N., Marlowe, F. W., Bugumba, R., & Ellison, P. T. (2009). Testosterone and paternal care in East African foragers and pastoralists. *Proceedings of the Royal Society of London B: Biological Sciences, 276*(1655), 347–354. doi:10.1098/rspb.2008.1028

Munro, G., & Adams, G. R. (1977). Ego-identity formation in college students and working youth. *Developmental Psychology, 13*, 523–524.

Muret-Wagstaff, S., & Moore, S. G. (1989). The Hmong in America: Infant behavior and rearing practices. In J. K. Nugent, B. M. Lester, & T. B. Brazelton (Eds.), *Biology, culture, and development* (Vol. 1, pp. 319–339). Norwood, NJ: Ablex.

Murkoff, H., Eisenberg, A., & Hathaway, S. (2009). *What to expect the first year.* New York, NY: Workman.

Murkoff, H., & Mazel, S. (2008). *What to expect when you're expecting.* New York, NY: Workman.

Murkoff, H., & Mazel, S. (2010). *What to Expect When You're Expecting, 4th Edition.* New York: Simon and Schuster.

Murkoff, H., & Mazel, S. (2014). *What to expect the first year* (3rd ed.). New York, NY: Workman.

Murkoff, H., & Mazel, S. (2016). *What to expect when you're expecting.* New York, NY: Workman.

Murkoff, H. E., Eisenberg, A., Mazel, S., & Hathaway, S. E. (2003). *What to expect the first year* (2nd ed.). New York, NY: Workman.

Murnen, S. K., & Levine, M. P. (2007). *Do fashion magazines promote body dissatisfaction in girls and women?* Paper presented at the annual meeting of the American Psychological Association, San Francisco, CA.

Murphy, P. K., Buehl, M. M., Zeruth, J. A., Edwards, M. N., Long, J. F., & Monoi, S. (2010). Examining the influence of epistemic beliefs and goal orientations on the academic performance of adolescent students enrolled in high-poverty, high-minority schools. In L. Bendixen & F. C. Feucht (Eds.), *Personal epistemology in the classroom: Theory, research, and implications for practice* (pp. 328–367). New York, NY: Cambridge University Press.

Murray, J. P. (2008). Media violence: The effects are both real and strong. *American Behavioral Scientist, 51*(8), 1212–1230.

Murray-Close, D., Ostrov, J., & Crick, N. (2007). A short-term longitudinal study of growth and relational aggression during middle childhood: Associations with gender, friendship, intimacy, and internalizing problems. *Development and Psychopathology, 19*, 187–203.

Mussen, P. H., Conger, J. J., Kagan, J., & Huston, A. (1990). *Child development and personality* (7th ed.). New York, NY: Harper & Row.

Nabi, R. L., & Krcmar, M. (2004). Conceptualizing media enjoyment as attitude: Implications for mass media effects research. *Communication Theory, 14*, 288–310.

NAEYC. (2010). 2010 NAEYC Standards for Initial and Advanced Early Childhood Professional Preparation Programs. Washington, DC: NAEYC/ National Association for the Education of Young Children.

Nakano, H., & Blumstein, S. E. (2004). Deficits in thematic processes in Broca's and Wernicke's aphasia. *Brain and Language, 88*, 96–107.

Napier, K., & Meister, K. (2000). *Growing healthy kids: A parents' guide to infant and child nutrition.* New York, NY: American Council on Science and Health.

Narayanan, U., & Warren, S. T. (2006). Neurobiology of related disorders: Fragile X syndrome. In S. O. Moldin & J. L. R. Rubenstein, *Understanding autism: From basic neuroscience to treatment* (pp. 113–131). Washington, DC: Taylor Francis.

Narvaez, D., & Lapsley, D. K. (2009). *Personality, identity, and character: Explorations in moral psychology.* New York, NY: Cambridge University Press.

Nater, U. M., Krebs, M., & Ehlert, U. (2005). Sensation seeking, music preference, and psycho-physiological reactivity to music. *Musicae Scientiae, 9*(2), 239–254.

National Center for Biotechnology Information. (2017). Prenatal genetic counseling. Retrieved from https://www.ncbi.nlm.nih.gov/books/ NBK115507/

National Center for Education Statistics (NCES). (2011). *The condition of education, 2011.* Washington, DC: U.S. Department of Education.

National Center for Education Statistics (NCES). (2012). *The condition of education, 2012.* Washington, DC: U.S. Department of Education.

National Center for Education Statistics (NCES). (2014). *The condition of education, 2014.* Washington, DC: U.S. Department of Education.

National Center for Education Statistics (NCES). (2016). *The Condition of Education 2016.* Retrieved from https://nces.ed.gov/pubs2016/2016144.pdf

National Center for Health Statistics. (2005). *Health, United States, 2005. With chartbook on trends in the health of Americans.* Hyattsville, MD: Author.

National Highway Traffic Safety Administration (2014). Traffic safety facts. Washington, DC: U.S. Department of Transportation.

National Human Genome Research Institute. (2012). 2012 National DNA day. Retrieved from http://www.genome.gov/DNADay/q.cfm?aid=2&year=2012

National Human Genome Research Institute. (2017). NIH to expand critical catalog for genomics research. Retrieved from https:// www. genome. gov/27567592/2017-release-nih-to-expand-critical-catalog-for-genomics-research/2017-release-nih-to-expand-critical-catalog-for-genomics-research/

National Resource Center on ADHD (2014). *Statistical prevalence of ADHD.* Retrieved from http://www.help4adhd.org/about/statistics

National Sudden and Unexpected Infant/Child Death & Pregnancy Loss Resource Center. (2010). *Statistics overview.* Retrieved from http://sidcenter.org/Statistics.html

National Women's Health Information Center. (2011). *Infertility.* Retrieved from http://www.womenshealth.gov/faq/infertility.cfm#f

Natsopoulos, D., Kiosseoglou, G., Xeroxmeritou, A., & Alevriadou, A. (1998). Do the hands talk on the mind's behalf? Differences in language between left- and right-handed children. *Brain and Language, 64*, 182–214.

Nazzi, T., Dilley, L. C., Jusczyk, A. M., Shattuck-Hufnagel, S., & Jusczyk, P. W. (2005). English-learning infants' segmentation of verbs from fluent speech. *Language and Speech, 48*(3), 279–298. doi:10.1177/00238309050480030201

Neal-Barnett, A., Stadulis, R., Singer, N., Murray, M., & Demmings, J. (2010). Assessing the effects of experiencing the acting White accusation. *The Urban Review, 42*(2), 102–122.

Neberich, W., Penke, L., Lenhart, J., & Asendorph, J. B. (2010). Family of origin, age at menarche, and reproductive strategies: A test of four evolutionary–developmental models. *European Journal of Developmental Psychology, 7*, 153–177.

Nelson, D. A., Robinson, C. C., & Hart, C. H. (2005). Relational and physical aggression of preschool-age children: Peer status linkages across informants. *Early Education and Development, 16*, 115–139.

Nelson, K. (1993). The psychological and social origins of autobiographical memory. *Psychological Science, 4*(1), 7–14. doi:10.1111/j.1467-9280.1993.tb00548.x

Nelson, K. (2007). Becoming a language user: Entering a symbolic world. In C. B. Brownell & C. B. Kopp (Eds.), *Socioemotional development in the toddler years: Transitions and transformations* (pp. 221–240). New York, NY: Guilford Press.

Nelson, L. J., & Chen, X. (2007). Emerging adulthood in China: The role of social and cultural factors. *Child Development Perspectives, 1*, 86–91.

Nesbitt, R. E. (2009). *Intelligence and how to get it: Why schools and cultures matter.* New York, NY: Norton.

Neto, F. (2002). Acculturation strategies among adolescents from immigrant families in Portugal. *International Journal of Intercultural Relations, 26*, 17–38.

Netting, N. (2010). Marital ideoscapes in 21st-century India: Creative combinations of love and responsibility. *Journal of Family Issues, 31*, 707–726.

Nevid, J. S., Rathus, S. A., & Greene, B. (2003). *Abnormal psychology in a changing world.* Upper Saddle River, NJ: Prentice Hall.

Newcombe, N., & Huttenlocher, J. (2006). Development of spatial cognition. In W. Damon & R. Lerner (Eds.), & D. Kuhn & R. Siegler (Vol. Eds.), *Handbook of child psychology: Vol. 2. Cognition, perception and language* (6th ed., pp. 734–776). New York, NY: Wiley.

Newman, K. S., & Winston, H. (2016). *Reskilling America: Learning to labor in the twenty-first century.* New York, NY: Metropolitan Books.

Newmann, F. (1992). Higher-order thinking and prospects for classroom thoughtfulness. In F. Newmann (Ed.), *Student engagement and achievement in American high schools.* New York, NY: Teachers College Press.

Newton, N., & Newton, M. (2003). Childbirth in cross–cultural perspective. In L. Dundes (Ed.), *The manner born: Birth rites in cross–cultural perspective* (pp. 9–32). Walnut Creek, CA: AltaMira.

Ng, M., Fleming, T., Robinson, M., Thomson, B., Graetz, N., Margono, C., … Gakidou, E. (2014). Global, regional, and national prevalence of overweight and obesity in children and adults during 1980–2013: A systematic analysis of the Global Burden of Disease Study 2013. *The Lancet, 309.* doi:10.1016/S0140-6736(14)60460-8

Ngongo, P. B., Priddy, F., Park, H., Becker, J., Bender, B., Fast, P., … & Mebrahtu, T. (2012). Developing standards of care for HIV prevention research in developing countries—A case study of 10 research centers in Eastern and Southern Africa. *AIDS Care, 24*(10), 1277–1289.

NICHD Early Child Care Research Network. (2000). Factors associated with fathers' caregiving activities and sensitivity with young children. *Developmental Psychology, 14*, 200–219.

NICHD Early Child Care Research Network. (2004). Trajectories of physical aggression from toddlerhood to middle childhood. *Monographs of the Society for Research in Child Development, 69* (Serial No. 278), vii–129.

NICHD Early Child Care Research Network. (2005). Early child care and children's development in the primary grades: Results from the NICHD Study of Early Child Care. *American Educational Research Journal, 43*, 537–570.

NICHD Early Child Care Research Network. (2006). *Child care and child development: Results from the NICHD study of early child care and youth development.* New York, NY: Guilford.

NICHD Early Child Care Research Network. (2006). Infant-mother attachment classification: Risk and protection in relation to changing maternal caregiving quality. *Developmental Psychology, 42*, 38–58.

Nicholson, J. M., Sanders, M. R., Halford, W. K., Phillips, M., & Whitton, S. W. (2008). The prevention and treatment of children's adjustment problems in stepfamilies. In J. Pryor (Ed.), *The international handbook of stepfamilies: Policy and practice in legal, research, and clinical environments* (pp. 485–521). Hoboken, NJ: John Wiley & Sons.

Nichter, M. (2001). *Fat talk: What girls and their parents say about dieting.* Cambridge, MA: Harvard University Press.

Nie, N. H., & Erbring, L. (2000). *Internet and society: A preliminary report.* Palo Alto, CA: Stanford Institute for the Quantitative Study of Society. Retrieved from http://www.stanford.edu/group/siqss/Press_Release/Preliminary_ Report.pdf

Nisan, M. (1987). Moral norms and social conventions: A cross-cultural study. *Developmental Psychology, 23*, 719–725.

Noia, G., Cesari, E., Ligato, M. S., Visconti, D., Tintoni, M., Mappa, I., . . . Caruso, A. (2008). Pain in the fetus. *Neonatal Pain, 2*, 45–55.

Nolan, K., Schell, L. M., Stark, A. D., & Gomez, M. I. (2002). Longitudinal study of energy and nutrient intakes for infants from low-income, urban families. *Public Health Nutrition, 5*, 405–412.

Nolen-Hoeksema, S., Wisco, B. E., & Lyubomirsky, S. (2008). Rethinking rumination. *Perspectives on Psychological Science, 3*(5), 400–424.

Noller, P., & Callan, V. (2015). *The adolescent in the family.* New York, NY: Routledge.

Norman, R. L. (2014). Reproductive changes in the female lifespan. In J. J. Robert-McComb, R. Norman, & M. Zumwalt (Eds.), *The active female* (pp. 25–31). New York, NY: Springer.

Novik, T. S., Hervas, A., Ralston, S. J., Dalsgaard, S., Rodrigues Pereira, R., Lorenzo, M. J., & ADORE Study Group. (2006). Influence of gender on attention deficit/hyperactivity disorder in Europe—ADORE. *European Child & Adolescent Psychiatry, 15*(Suppl. 1), 5–24.

Nsamengnang, B. A. (1992). Perceptions of parenting among the Nso of Cameroon. In B. Hewlett (Ed.), *Father–child relations: Cultural and biosocial contexts* (pp. 321–344). New York, NY: De Gruyter.

Nucci, L. (1981). The development of personal concepts: A domain distinct from moral and societal concepts. *Child Development, 52*, 118–121.

Nucci, L., Camino, C., & Sapiro, C. M. (1996). Social class effects on northeastern Brazilian children's conceptions of areas of personal choice and social regulation. *Child Development, 67*, 1223–1242.

Nucci, L., & Turiel, E. (1993). God's word, religious rules, and their relation to Christian and Jewish children's concepts of morality. *Child Development, 64*, 1475–1491.

Nucci, L. P. (1985). Children's conceptions of morality, societal convention, and religious prescription. In C. G. Harding (Ed.), *Moral dilemmas: Philosophical and psychological issues in the development of moral reasoning* (pp. 137–174). Chicago, IL: Precedent Publishing.

Nucci, L. P., & Turiel, E. (1978). Social interactions and the development of social concepts in preschool children. *Child development*, 400–407.

Nugent, K., & Brazelton, T. B. (2000). Preventive infant mental health: Uses of the Brazelton scale. In J. D. Osofsky & H. E. Fitzgerald (Eds.), *WAIMH handbook of infant mental health* (Vol. 2) (pp. 159–202). New York, NY: Wiley.

Nugent, K. J., Petrauskas, B. J., & Brazelton, T. B. (Eds.). (2009). *The newborn as a person: Enabling healthy infant development worldwide.* Hoboken, NJ: John Wiley & Sons.

Nuland, S. B. (2003). *The doctor's plague: Germs, childbed fever, and the strange story of Ignac Semmelweis.* New York, NY: Norton.

Núñez, J., & Flanagan, C. (2015). Political beliefs and civic engagement in emerging adulthood. In J. J. Arnett (Ed.), *Oxford handbook of emerging adulthood* (pp. 481–497). New York, NY: Oxford University Press.

Nunner-Winkler, G. (2007). Development of moral motivation from early childhood to early adulthood. *Journal of Moral Education, 36*, 399–414.

Nurse Family Partnership. (2014). *From a desire to help people, to a plan that truly does.* Retrieved from http://www.nursefamilypartnership.org/about/program-history

Nwokah, E. E., Hsu, H., Davies, P., & Fogel, A. (1999). The integration of laughter and speech in vocal communication: A dynamic systems perspective. *Journal of Speech and Hearing Research, 42*, 880–894.

Nye, W. C., & Carlson, J. S. (1984). The development of the concept of God in children. *The Journal of Genetic Psychology, 145*(1), 137–142. doi:10.1080/00221325.1984.10532259

Nylen, K., Moran, T., Franklin, C., & O'Hara, M. (2006). Maternal depression: A review of relevant treatment approaches for mothers and infants. *Infant Mental Health Journal, 27*, 327–343.

Oates, M. R., Cox, J. L., Neema, S., Asten, P., Glangeaud-Freudenthal, N., Figueiredo, B., . . . TCS–PND Group. (2004). Postnatal depression across countries and cultures: A qualitative study. *British Journal of Psychiatry, 184*, s10–s16.

Obermeyer, C. M. (2000). Sexuality in Morocco: Changing context and contested domain. *Culture, Health and Sexuality, 2*, 239–254.

Ochs, E., & Schieffelin, B. (1984). Language acquisition and socialization: Three developmental stories. In R. A. Shweder & R. A. LeVine (Eds.), *Culture theory: Mind, self, and emotion* (pp. 276–320). Cambridge, UK: Cambridge University Press.

Odeku, K., Rembe, S., & Anwo, J. (2009). Female genital mutilation: A human rights perspective. *Journal of Psychology in Africa, 19*(1), 55–62.

Ogbu, J. U. (2003). *Black American students in an affluent suburb: A study of academic disengagement.* Mahwah, NJ: Lawrence Erlbaum.

Ogden, C. L., Carroll, M. D., Kit, B. K., & Flegal, K. M. (2014). Prevalence of childhood and adult obesity. *JAMA, 311*, 806–814.

Ogden, T., & Amlund Hagen, K. (2006). Multisystemic treatment of serious behavior problems in youth: Sustainability of therapy effectiveness two years after intake. *Child and Adolescent Mental Health, 11*(3), 142–149.

Ogletree, S. M., Martinez, C. N., Turner, T. R., & Mason, M. (2004). Pokémon: Exploring the role of gender. *Sex Roles, 50*(11–12), 851–859.

Ohannessian, C. M. (2009). Media use and adolescent psychological adjustment: An examination of gender differences. *Journal of Child and Family Studies, 18*(5), 582–593.

Ohgi, S., Arisawa, K., Takahashi, T., Kusomoto, T., Goto, Y., & Saito, A .T. (2003). Neonatal behavioral assessment scale as a predictor of later developmental disabilities of low birth-weight and/or premature infants. *Brain Development, 25*, 313–321.

Oken, E., & Lightdale, J. R. (2000). Updates in pediatric nutrition. *Current Opinion in Pediatrics, 12*, 282–290.

Olds, D. L. (2010). The nurse–family partnership: From trials to practice. In A. J. Reynolds, A. J. Rolnick, M. M. Englund, & J. A. Temple (Eds.), *Childhood programs and practices in the first decade of life: A human capital integration* (pp. 49–75). New York, NY: Cambridge University Press.

Oliver, M. B. (2006). Mood management theory. In J. J. Arnett (Ed.), *Encyclopedia of children, adolescents, and the media* (pp. 539–540). Thousand Oaks, CA: Sage.

Ollendick, T. H., Shortt, A. L., & Sander, J. B. (2008). Internalizing disorders in children and adolescents. In J. E. Maddux & B. A. Winstead (Eds.), *Psychopathology: Foundations for a contemporary understanding* (2nd ed., pp. 375–399). New York, NY: Routledge.

Oller, D. K., Eilers, R. E., Urbano, R., & Cobo-Lewis, A. B. (1997). Development of precursors to speech in infants exposed to two languages. *Journal of Child Language, 24*, 407–425.

Olson, C. K. (2010). Children's motivations for video game play in the context of normal development. *Review of General Psychology, 14*, 180–187.

Olson, C. K., Kutner, L. A., & Warner, D. E. (2008). The role of violent video game content in adolescent development: Boys' perspectives. *Journal of Adolescent Research, 23*, 55–75.

Olson, E. (2007, May 28). OMG! Cute boys, kissing tips and lots of pics, as magazines find a niche. *New York Times*, p. 156.

Olthof, T. (2010). Conscience in the classroom: Early adolescents' moral emotions, moral judgments, and moral identity as predictors of their interpersonal behavior. In W. Koops, D. Brugman, T. J. Ferguson, & A. F. Sanders (Eds.), *The development and structure of conscience* (pp. 327–341). New York, NY: Psychology Press.

Oltmanns, T. F., & Emery, R. E. (2010). *Abnormal psychology* (6th ed.). Upper Saddle River, NJ: Prentice Hall.

Olweus, D. (2000). Bullying. In A. E. Kazdin (Ed.), *Encyclopedia of psychology* (Vol. 1, pp. 487–489). Washington, DC: American Psychological Association.

O'Malley, M., Voight, A., Renshaw, T. L., & Eklund, K. (2015). School climate, family structure, and academic achievement: A study of moderation effects. *School Psychology Quarterly, 30*, 142.

Onishi, K. H., & Baillargeon, R. (2005). Do 15-month-old infants understand false beliefs? *Science, 308*(5719), 255–258. doi:10.1126/science.1107621

Opplinger, P. A. (2007). Effects of gender stereotyping on socialization. In R. W. Preiss, B. M. Gayle, M. Burrell, M. Allen, & J. Bryant (Eds.), *Mass media effects research: Advances through meta-analysis* (pp. 199–214). New York, NY: Routledge.

Oren, D. L. (1981). Cognitive advantages of bilingual children related to labeling ability. *The Journal of Educational Research, 74*(3), 163–169.

Organisation for Economic and Cooperative Development (OECD). (2014). Education at a Glance 2014: OECD Indicators. Retrieved from http://www.oecd.org/edu/Education-at-a-Glance-2014.pdf

Organization for Economic Cooperation and Development (OECD). (2009). *Health at a glance 2009: OECD indicators.* Author.

Organization for Economic Cooperation and Development (OECD). (2013). *Education at a glance: Indicators and annexes.* Retrieved from http://www.oecd.org/edu/educationataglance2013-indicatorsandannexes.htm#ChapterC

Organization for Economic Cooperation and Development (OECD). (2014). Infant mortality. Family database, Social Policy Division. Retrieved from www.oecd.org/social/family/database

Organization for Economic Cooperation and Development (OECD). (2014). Obesity update. Retrieved from http://www.oecd.org/health/Obesity-Update-2014.pdf

Organization for Economic Cooperation and Development (OECD). (2014). OECD Statextracts: Labor Force Statistics by sex and age. Retrieved from http://stats.oecd.org/Index.aspx?DatasetCode=LFS_SEXAGE_I_R

Organization for Economic Cooperation and Development (OECD). (2017). List of OECD member countries: Ratification on the convention of the OECD. Retrieved from http://www.oecd.org/about/membersandpartners/list-oecd-member-countries.htm

Orr, E., & Ben-Eliahu, E. (1993). Gender differences in idiosyncratic sex-typed self-images and self-esteem. *Sex Roles, 29,* 271–296.

Orth, U., & Robins, R. W. (2014). The development of self-esteem. *Current Directions in Psychological Science, 23,* 3811–3817.

Osgood, D. W. (2009). *Illegal behavior: A presentation to the Committee on the Science of Adolescence of the National Academies.* Washington, DC: National Academies Press.

Osgood, D. W., Anderson, A. L., & Shaffer, J. N. (2005). Unstructured leisure in the afterschool hours. In L. J. Mahoney, R. W. Larson, & J. S. Eccles (Eds.), *Organized activities as contexts of development: Extracurricular activities, after-school and community programs* (pp. 45–64). Mahwah, NJ: Lawrence Erlbaum.

Osgood, D. W., Wilson, J. K., Bachman, J. G., O'Malley, P. M., & Johnston, L. D. (1996). Routine activities and individual deviant behavior. *American Sociological Review, 61,* 635–655.

Oster, H., Hegley, D., & Nagel, L. (1992). Adult judgments and fine-grained analysis of infant facial expressions: Testing the validity of a priori coding formulas. *Developmental Psychology, 28,* 1115–1131.

Out, D., Pieper, S., Bakermans-Kranenburg, M. J., Zeskind, P. S., & van IJzendoorn, M. H. (2010). Intended sensitive and harsh caregiving responses to infant crying: The role of cry pitch and perceived urgency in an adult twin sample. *Child Abuse & Neglect, 34,* 863–873.

Owens, J. A. (2004). Sleep in children: Cross-cultural perspectives. *Sleep and Biological Rhythms, 2*(3), 165–173.

Oyserman, D., Destin, M., & Novin, S. (2015). The context-sensitive future self: Possible selves motivate in context, not otherwise. *Self and Identity, 14,* 173–188.

Oyserman, D., & Fryberg, S. (2006). The possible selves of diverse adolescents: Content and function across gender, race and national origin. In C. Dunkel & J. Kerpelman (Eds.), *Possible selves: Theory, research and applications* (pp. 17–39). Hauppauge, NY: Nova Science.

Ozorak, E. W. (1989). Social and cognitive influences on the development of religious beliefs and commitment in adolescence. *Journal for the Scientific Study of Religion, 28,* 448–463. doi:10.2307/1386576

Padilla-Walker, L., & Memmott-Elison, M. (in press). Family and moral development. In L. A. Jensen (Ed.), *Oxford handbook of moral development: An interdisciplinary perspective.* New York, NY: Oxford University Press.

Padilla-Walker, L., & Nelson, L. (2017). *Flourishing in emerging adulthood: Positive development during the third decade of life.* New York, NY: Oxford University Press.

Padilla-Walker, L. M., & Nelson, L. J. (2015). Moral worldviews of religious emerging adults: Three patterns of negotiation between development and culture. In L. A. Jensen (Ed.), *Moral development in a global world: Research from a cultural-developmental perspective* (pp.92–116). New York, NY: Cambridge University Press.

Padilla-Walker, L. M., Nelson, L. J., Carroll, J. S., & Jensen, A. C. (2010). More than a just a game: Video game and Internet use during emerging adulthood. *Journal of Youth and Adolescence, 39,* 103–113.

Padrón, E., Carlson, E. A., & Sroufe, L. A. (2014). Frightened versus not frightened disorganized infant attachment: Newborn characteristics and maternal caregiving. *American Journal of Orthopsychiatry, 84,* 201–208.

Pagel, M. (2016, April). Language: Why us and only us? [Review of the book The social evolution of human nature: From biology to language, by H. Smit]. *Trends in Ecology & Evolution, 21*(4), 258–259. doi:10.1016/j.tree.2016.1.009

Pahl, K., & Way, N. (2006). Longitudinal trajectories of ethnic identity among urban black and Latino adolescents. *Child Development, 77*(5), 1403–1415.

Pálmadóttir, H., & Johansson, E. M. (2015). Young children's communication and expression of values during play sessions in preschool. *Early Years, 35,* 289–302.

Palmer, S. B., Fais, L., Golinkoff, R. M., & Werker, J. F. (2012). Perceptual narrowing of linguistic sign occurs in the 1st year of life. *Child Development, 83*(2), 543–553. doi:10.1111/j.1467-8624.2011.01715.x

Pan, B. A., & Snow, C. E. (1999). The development of conversation and discourse skills. In M. Barrett (Ed.), *The development of language* (pp. 229–249). Hove, UK: Psychology Press.

Pan, S. Y., Desmueles, M., Morrison, H., Semenciw, R., Ugnat, A.-M., Thompson, W., & Mao, Y. (2007). Adolescent injury deaths and hospitalization in Canada: Magnitude and temporal trends (1979–2003). *Journal of Adolescent Health, 41,* 84–92.

Pancer, S. M., Pratt, M., Hunsberger, B., & Alisat, S. (2007). Community and political involvement in adolescence: What distinguishes the activists from the uninvolved? *Journal of Community Psychology, 35*(6), 741–759.

Pandya, N., & Bhangaokar, R. (2015). Divinity in the development of Indian children. In L. A. Jensen (Ed.), *Moral development in a global world: Research from a cultural-developmental perspective* (pp. 20–45). New York, NY: Cambridge University Press.

Pankow, L. J. (2008). Genetic theory. In B. A. Thyer, K. M. Sowers, & C. N. Dulmus (Eds.), *Comprehensive handbook of social work and social welfare: Vol. 2. Human behavior in the social environment* (pp. 327–353). Hoboken, NJ: John Wiley & Sons.

Papadakis, A. A., Prince, R. P., Jones, N. P., & Strauman, T. J. (2006). Self-regulation, rumination, and vulnerability to depression in adolescent girls. *Development and Psychopathology, 18*(3), 815–829.

Paquette, D. (2004). Theorizing the father–child relationship: Mechanisms and developmental outcomes. *Human Development, 47,* 193–219.

Paradis, J., & Genesee, F. (1996). Syntactic acquisition in bilingual children. *Studies in Second Language Acquisition, 18*(01), 1–25. doi:10.1017/S0272263100014662

Paradise, A. (2006). Television violence, susceptibility. In J. J. Arnett (Ed.), *Encyclopedia of children, adolescents, and the media* (pp. 825–826). Thousand Oaks, CA: Sage.

Parameswaran, G. (2003). Age, gender, and training in children's performance of Piaget's horizontality task. *Educational Studies, 29,* 307–319.

Pardun, C. J. (2002). Romancing the script: Identifying the romantic agenda in top-grossing movies. In J. D. Brown, J. R. Steele, & K. Walsh-Childers (Eds.), *Sexual teens, sexual media: Investigating media's influence on adolescent sexuality* (pp. 211–225). Mahwah, NJ: Erlbaum.

Pardun, C. J., L'Engle, K. L., & Brown, J. D. (2005). Linking exposure to outcomes: Early adolescents' consumption of sexual content in six media. *Mass Communication & Society, 8,* 75–91.

Parish-Morris, J., Hirsch-Pasek, K., Golinkoff, R. M., & Hirch-Pasek. (2013). From coo to code: A brief story of language development. In P.D. Zelazo (Ed.), *The Oxford handbook of developmental psychology: Volume 1: Body and mind* (pp. 867–908). New York, NY: Oxford University Press.

Parke, R. D. (2004). Development in the family. *Annual Review of Psychology, 55,* 363–399.

Parke, R. D., & Buriel, R. (2006). Socialization in the family: Ethnic and ecological perspectives. In W. Damon & R. Lerner (Eds.), & N. Eisenberg (Vol. Ed.), *Handbook of child psychology: Vol. 3. Social, emotional and personality development* (6th ed., pp. 429–504). New York, NY: Wiley.

Parker, E. D., Schmitz, K. H., Jacobs, D. R., Jr., Dengel, D. R., & Schreiner, P. J. (2007). Physical activity in young adults and incident hypertension over 15 years of follow-up: The CARDIA study. *American Journal of Public Health, 97,* 703–709.

Parmar, P., Harkness, S., & Super, C. M. (2004). Asian and Euro-American parents' ethnotheories of play and learning: Effects on preschool children's home routines and school behaviour. *International Journal of Behavioral Development, 28*(2), 97–104. doi:10.1080/01650250344000307

Parmar, P., Harkness, S., & Super, C. M. (2008). Teacher or playmate? Asian immigrant and Euro-American parents' participation in their young children's daily activities. *Social Behavior and Personality: An International Journal, 36*(2), 163–176.

Parsons, C. E., Young, K. S., Rochat, T. J., Kringelbach, M. L., & Stein, A. (2012). Postnatal depression and its effects on child development: A review of evidence from low- and middle-income countries. *British Medical Bulletin, 101,* 57–79. doi:10.1093/bmb/ldr047

Parten, M. (1932). Social play among preschool children. *Journal of Abnormal Social Psychology, 27,* 243–269.

Pascalis, O., & Kelly, D. J. (2009). The origins of face processing in humans: Phylogeny and ontogeny. *Perspectives on Psychological Science, 4,* 200–209.

Pascarella, E., & Terenzini, P. (1991). *How college affects students: Findings and insights from twenty years of research.* San Francisco, CA: Jossey-Bass.

Pascarella, E. T. (2005). Cognitive impacts of the first year of college. In R. S. Feldman (Ed.), *Improving the first year of college: Research and practice* (pp. 111–140). Mahwah, NJ: Lawrence Erlbaum.

Pascarella, E. T. (2006). How college affects students: Ten directions for future research. *Journal of College Student Development, 47*(5), 508–520.

Pascoe, C. J. (2007). *Dude, you're a fag: Masculinity and sexuality in high school.* Berkeley, CA: University of California Press.

Pashigian, M. J. (2002). Conceiving the happy family: Infertility and marital politics in northern Vietnam. In M.C. Inhorn & F. van Balen (Eds.), *Infertility around the globe: New thinking on childlessness, gender, and reproductive technologies* (pp. 134–150). Berkeley, CA: University of California Press.

Pasterski, V., Hindmarsh, P., Geffner, M., Brook, C., Brain, C., & Hines, M. (2007). Increased aggression and activity level in 3- to 11-year-old girls with congenital adrenal hyperplasia (CAH). *Hormones and Behavior, 52*(3), 368–374. doi:10.1016/j.yhbeh.2007.05.015

Pasterski, V. L., Geffner, M. E., Brain, C., Hindmarsh, P., Brook, C., & Hines, M. (2005). Prenatal hormones and postnatal socialization by parents as determinants of male-typical toy play in girls with congenital adrenal hyperplasia. *Child Development, 76*(1), 264–278. doi:10.1111/j.1467-8624.2005.00843.x

Patel, Z. P., & Niederberger, C. S. (2011). Male Factor Assessment in Infertility. *Medical Clinics of North America, 95*, 223–234.

Patrick, M. E., Schulenberg, J. E., O'Malley, P. M., Johnston, L. D., & Bachman, J. G. (2011). Adolescents' reported reasons for alcohol and marijuana use as predictors of substance use and problems in adulthood. *Journal of Studies on Alcohol and Drugs, 72*(1), 106.

Patterson, C. J. (2006). Children of lesbian and gay parents. *Current Directions in Psychological Science, 15*(5), 241–244. doi:10.1111/j.1467-8721.2006.00444.x

Patterson, G. R. (2002). The early development of coercive family process. In J. B Reid, G. R. Patterson, & J. Snyder (Eds.), *Antisocial behavior in children and adolescents: A developmental analysis and model for intervention* (pp. 25–44). Washington, DC: American Psychological Association.

Patterson, M. L., & Werker, J. F. (2002). Infants' ability to match dynamic phonetic and gender information in the face and voice. *Journal of Experimental Child Psychology, 81*, 93–115.

Patton, G. C., Coffey, C., Cappa, C., Currie, D., Riley, L., Gore, F., … Ferguson, J. (2012). Health of the world's adolescents: A synthesis of internationally comparable data. *The Lancet, 379*(9826), 1665–1675. doi:10.1016/S0140-6736(12)60203-7

Patton, G. C., Coffey, C., Sawyer, S. M., Viner, R. M., Haller, D. M., Bose, K., … Mathews, C. D. (2009). Global patterns of mortality in young people: A systematic analysis of population health data. *Lancet, 374*, 881–892.

Patton, G. C., Ross, D. A., Santelli, J. S., Sawyer, S. M., Viner, R. M., & Kleinert, S. (2014). Next steps for adolescent health: A Lancet Commission. *The Lancet, 383*(9915), 385–386. doi:http://dx.doi.org/10.1016/S0140-6736(14)60039-8

Paulson, S. E. (1994, February). Parenting style or parental involvement: Which is more important for adolescent achievement? Paper presented at the meeting of the Society for Research on Adolescence, San Diego, CA.

Peace Corps. (2000). *Two years of services a lifetime of benefits.* Retrieved on March 24, 2003, from www.peacecorps.gov/volunteer/benefits.html

Peace Corps. (2011, October). Peace Corps 2011 annual volunteer survey results. Retrieved from http://files.peacecorps.gov/multimedia/pdf/policies/2011_Annual_Volunteer_Survey.pdf

Peace Corps. (2012). About the Peace Corps. Retrieved on January 15, 2012, from http://www.peacecorps.gov/index.cfm?shell=learn.whyvol

Peace Corps. (2016). Fast facts. Retrieved from http:// www. peacecorps.gov/about/fastfacts

Pearson, J., Thrane, L., & Wilkinson, L. (2017). Consequences of runaway and thrownaway experiences for sexual minority health during the transition to adulthood. *Journal of LGBT Youth, 14*, 145–171.

Peirano, P., Algarin, C., & Uauy, R. (2003). Sleep–wake states and their regulatory mechanism throughout early human development. *Journal of Pediatrics, 143*(Suppl.), S70–S79.

Pelaez, M., Field, T., Pickens, J. N., & Hart, S. (2008). Disengaged and authoritarian parenting behavior of depressed mothers with their toddlers. *Infant Behavior and Development, 31*, 145–148.

Peltzer, K., & Pengpid, S. (2015). Nocturnal sleep problems among university students from 26 countries. *Sleep and Breathing, 19*, 499–508.

Peng, K., & Nisbett, R. E. (1999). Culture, dialectics, and reasoning about contradiction. *American Psychologist, 54*, 741–754.

Pennington, B. F., Moon, J., Edgin, J., Stedron, J., & Nadel, L. (2003). The neuropsychology of Down syndrome: Evidence for hippocampal dysfunction. *Child Development, 74*, 75–93.

Pepler, D., Craig, W., Yuile, A., & Connolly, J. (2004). Girls who bully: A developmental and relational perspective. In M. Putallaz & K. L. Bierman (Eds.), *Aggression, antisocial behavior, and violence among girls: A developmental perspective* (pp. 90–109). New York, NY: Guilford.

Pepler, D. J., Craig, W. M., Connolly, J. A., Yuile, A., McMaster, L., & Jiang, D. (2006). A developmental perspective on bullying. *Aggressive Behavior, 32*(4), 376–384.

Pepler, D. J., Jiang, D., Craig, W. M., & Connolly, J. A. (2008). Developmental trajectories of bullying and associated factors. *Child Development, 79*(2), 325–338.

Perez-Brena, N. J., Wheeler, L. A., Updegraff, K. A., & Schaefer, D. R. (2015). Mexican-American adolescents' gender-typed characteristics: The role of sibling and friend characteristics. *Archives of Sexual Behavior, 44*, 1255–1268.

Perfors, A., Tenenbaum, J. B., Griffiths, T. L., & Xu, F. (2011). A tutorial introduction to Bayesian models of cognitive development. *Cognition, 120*, 302–321. doi:10.1016/j.cognition.2010.11.015

Perner, J. (1991). *Understanding the representational mind.* Cambridge, MA: The MIT Press.

Perner, J., & Roessler, J. (2012). From infants' to children's appreciation of belief. *Trends in Cognitive Sciences, 16*(10), 519–525. doi:10.1016/j.tics.2012.08.004

Peter, J., & Valkenburg, P. M. (2007). Adolescents' exposure to a sexualized media environment and their notions of women as sex objects. *Sex Roles, 56*(5–6), 381–395.

Petersen, J. L., & Hyde, J. S. (2009). A longitudinal investigation of peer sexual harassment victimization in adolescence. *Journal of Adolescence*, 32, 1173–1188.

Petersen, J. L., & Hyde, J. S. (2010). A meta-analytic review of research on gender differences in sexuality, 1993–2007. *Psychological Bulletin, 136*, 21–38

Peterson, C., & Whalen, N. (2001). Five years later: Children's memory for medical emergencies. *Applied Cognitive Psychology, 15*, S7–S24.

Pew. (2015). The demographics of device ownership. Retrieved from http://www.pewinternet.org/2015/10/29/the-demographics-of-device-ownership/

Pew Commission on Children in Foster Care. (2004). Safety, permanence and well-being for children in foster care. Retrieved from: http://pewfostercare.org/research/docs/FinalReport.pdf

Pew Research Center. (2011, October 5). War and sacrifice in the post-9/11 era: The military-civilian gap. Retrieved from http://www.pewsocialtrends.org/2011/10/05/war-and-sacrifice-in-the-post-911-era/

Pew Research Center. (2012). *"Nones" on the rise: One in five adults has no religious affiliation.* Washington, DC: Author.

Pew Research Center. (2012, February 29). Global Digital Communication: Texting, Social Networking Popular Worldwide. Retrieved from http://www.pewglobal.org/2011/12/20/global-digital-communication-texting-social-networking-popular-worldwide/

Pew Research Center. (2014). The rising cost of not going to college. Retrieved from http://www.pewsocialtrends.org/2014/02/11/the-rising-cost-of-not-going-to-college/

Pfeffer, C. R. (2006). Suicide in children and adolescents. In D. J. Stein, D. J. Kupfer, & A. F. Schatzberg (Eds.), *The American Psychiatric Publishing textbook of mood disorders* (pp. 497–507). Arlington, VA: American Psychiatric Publishing.

Phelan, T. W. (2010). *1-2-3 magic: Effective discipline for children 2-12.* New York, NY: Child Management.

Phinney, J. S. (1990). Ethnic identity in adolescents and adults: A review of research. *Psychological Bulletin, 108*, 499–514.

Phinney, J. S. (2000, March). *Identity formation among U.S. ethnic adolescents from collectivist cultures.* Paper presented at the biennial meeting of the Society of Research on Adolescence, Chicago, IL.

Phinney, J. S. (2006). Ethnic identity in emerging adulthood. In J. J. Arnett & J. L. Tanner (Eds.), *Emerging adults in America: Coming of age in the 21st century* (pp. 117–134). Washington, DC: American Psychological Association.

Phinney, J. S. (2010). Multigroup Ethnic Identity Measure (MEIM). In C. S. Clauss-Ehlers (Ed.), *Encyclopedia of Cross-Cultural School Psychology* (pp. 642–643). New York, NY: Springer US.

Phinney, J. S., & Baldelomar, O. A. (2011). Identity development in multiple cultural contexts. In L. A. Jensen (Ed.), *Bridging cultural and developmental psychology: New syntheses in theory, research and policy* (pp. 161–186). New York, NY: Oxford University Press.

Phinney, J. S., & Devich-Navarro, M. (1997). Variation in bicultural identification among African American and Mexican American adolescents. *Journal of Research on Adolescence, 7*, 3–32.

Phinney, J. S., DuPont, S., Espinosa, A., Revill, J., & Sanders, K. (1994). Ethnic identity and American identification among ethnic minority adolescents. In A. M. Bouvy, F. J. R. van de Vijver, P. Boski, & P. Schmitz (Eds.), *Journeys into cross-cultural psychology* (pp. 167–183). Amsterdam, Netherlands: Garland Science.

Phinney, J. S., Kim-Jo, T., Osorio, S., & Vilhjalmsdottir, P. (2005). Autonomy and relatedness in adolescent-parent disagreements: Ethnic and developmental factors. *Journal of Adolescent Research, 20*(1), 8–39.

Piaget, J. (1923). *The language and thought of the child.* New York, NY: Harcourt Brace & Company.

Piaget, J. (1932). *The moral judgment of the child.* New York, NY: Harcourt Brace Jovanovich.

Piaget, J. (1936/1952). *The origins of intelligence in children.* New York, NY: Norton.

Piaget, J. (1954). *The construction of reality in the child.* New York, NY: Basic Books.

Piaget, J. (1965). *The moral judgment of the child.* New York, NY: Free Press.

Piaget, J. (1967). *Six psychological studies.* New York, NY: Random House.

Piaget, J. (1972). Intellectual evolution from adolescence to adulthood. *Human Development, 15,* 1–12.

Piaget, J. (1972). *Psychology and epistemology: Towards a theory of knowledge* (P. A. Wells, Trans.). Harmondsworth, UK: Penguin.

Piaget, J. (2002). The epigenetic system and the development of cognitive functions. In R. O. Gilmore, M. H. Johnson, & Y. Munakata (Eds.), *Brain development and cognition: A reader* (2nd ed., pp. 29–35). Malden, MA: Blackwell.

Piaget, J., & Inhelder, B. (1969). *The child's conception of space* (F. J. Langdon & J. L. Lunger, Trans.). New York, NY: W. W. Norton.

Piat, M., Pearson, A., Sabetti, J., Steiger, H., Israel, M., & Lal, S. (2015). International training programs on eating disorders for professionals, caregivers, and the general public: A scoping review. *Journal of Eating Disorders, 3,* 1–8. doi:10.1186/s40337-015-0066-y

Pickett, K. E., Luo, Y., & Lauderdale, D. S. (2005). Widening social inequalities in risk for sudden infant death syndrome. *American Journal of Public Health, 95*(11), 1976.

Pierce, J. P., Lee, L., & Gilpin, E. A. (1994). Smoking initiation by adolescent girls, 1944 through 1988: An association with targeted advertising. *JAMA: Journal of the American Medical Association, 271,* 608–611.

Pierce, K. (2006). Uses and gratifications theory. In J. J. Arnett (Ed.), *Encyclopedia of children, adolescents, and the media* (pp. 841–843). Thousand Oaks, CA: Sage.

Pilcher, J. J., & Walters, A. S. (1997). How sleep deprivation affects psychological variables related to college students' cognitive performance. *Journal of American College Health, 46,* 121–126.

Pinker, S. (1994). *The language instinct.* New York, NY: Williams Morrow.

Pinker, S. (2004). *The blank slate: The modern denial of human nature.* New York, NY: Penguin.

Pinquart, M., Feussner, C., & Ahnert, L. (2013). Meta-analytic evidence for stability in attachments from infancy to early adulthood. *Attachment & Human Development, 15*(2), 189–218. doi:10.1080/14616734.2013.746257

Piotrowski, J. T., Jennings, N. A., & Linebarger, D. L. (2013). Extending the lessons of educational television with young American children. *Journal of Children and Media, 7,* 216–234.

Pipp, S., Fischer, K. W., & Jennings, S. (1987). Acquisition of self- and mother knowledge in infancy. *Developmental Psychology, 23,* 86–96.

Pisetsky, E. M., Chao, Y. M., Dierker, L. C., May, A. M., & Striegel-Moore, R. H. (2008). Disordered eating and substance use in high school students: Results from the Youth Risk Behavior Surveillance System. *International Journal of Eating Disorders, 41*(5), 464–470.

Pitts, V. P. (1976). Drawing the invisible: Children's conceptualization of God. *Character Potential, 8,* 12–24.

Pizzamiglio, A. P., Saygin, S. L., Small, S., & Wilson, S. (2005). Language and the brain. In M. Tomasello & D. A. Slobin (Eds.), *Beyond nature-nurture* (pp. 237–260). Mahwah, NJ: Erlbaum.

Plant, M., Miller, P., Plant, M., Gmel, G., Kuntsche, S., Bergmark, K.,... Vidal, A. (2010). The social consequences of binge drinking among 24- to 32-year-olds in six European countries. *Substance Use & Misuse, 45,* 528–542.

Plant, R. W., & Siegel, L. (2008). Children in foster care: Prevention and treatment of mental health problems. In T. P. Gullotta & G. M. Blau (Eds.), *Family influences on childhood behavior and development: Evidence-based prevention and treatment approaches* (pp. 209–230). New York, NY: Routledge.

Pleck, J. H. (2010). Paternal involvement: Revised conceptualization and theoretical linkages to child outcomes. In M. E. Lamb (Ed.), *The role of the father in child development* (pp. 58–93). New York, NY: Wiley.

Plomin, R. (2009). The nature of nurture. In K. McCartney and R. A. Weinberg (Eds.), *Experience and development: A festschrift in honor of Sandra Wood Scarr* (pp. 61–80). New York, NY: Psychology Press.

Plotkin, S. A., Katz, M., & Cordero, J. F. (1999). The eradication of rubella. *JAMA: Journal of the American Medical Association, 306,* 343–450.

Pollack, W. (1998). *Real boys: Rescuing our sons from the myths of boyhood.* New York, NY: Henry Holt.

Pollay, R. W. (1997). Hacks, flacks, and counterattacks: Cigarette advertising, sponsored research, and controversies. *Journal of Social Issues, 53,* 53–74.

Pollay, R. W. (2006). Cigarette advertising, history. In J. J. Arnett (Ed.), *Encyclopedia of children, adolescents, and the media* (pp. 175–178). Thousand Oaks, CA: Sage.

Pollay, R. W., Siddarth, S., Siegel, M., Haddix, A., Merritt, R. K., Giovino, G. A., et al. (1996). The last straw? Cigarette advertising and realized market shares among youths and adults, 1979–1993. *Journal of Marketing, 60,* 1–16.

Pollitt, E., Golub, M., Gorman, K., Gratham-McGregor, S., Levitsky, D., Schurch, B.,... Wachs, T. (1996). A reconceptualization of the effects of undernutrition on children's biological, psychosocial, and behavioral development. *Social Policy Report, 10,* 1–28.

Polly Klaas Foundation. (2015). The truth about runaway teens. Retrieved from http://www.pollyklaas.org/enews-archive/2013-enews/article-web-pages/the-truth-about-runaways.html

Pool, M. M., Koolstra, C. M., & van der Voort, T. H. A. (2003). The impact of background radio and television on high school students' homework performance. *Journal of Communication, 53,* 74–87.

Popkin, B. M. (2010). Recent dynamics suggest selected countries catching up to US obesity. *The American Journal of Clinical Nutrition, 91*(1), 284S–288S.

Popp, D., Lauren, B., Kerr, M., Stattin, H., & Burk, W. K. (2008). Modeling homophily over time with an actor-partner independence model. *Developmental Psychology, 44*(4), 1028–1039.

Popp, M. S. (2005). *Teaching language and literacy in elementary classrooms.* Mahwah, NJ: Erlbaum.

Population Reference Bureau. (2013). World population data sheet 2013. Retrieved from http://www.prb.org/pdf13/2013-population-data-sheet_eng.pdf

Population Reference Bureau. (2014). *World population data sheet, 2014.* Washington, DC: Author.

Porath, M., Korp, L., Wendrich, D., Dlugay, V., Roth, B., & Kribs, A. (2011). Surfactant in spontaneous breathing with nCPAP: Neurodevelopmental outcome at early school age of infants = 27 weeks. *Acta Paediatrica, 100,* 352–359.

Porges, S. W., & Lispitt, L. P. (1993). Neonatal responsivity to gustatory stimulation: The gustatory–vagal hypothesis. *Infant Behavior & Development, 16,* 487–494.

Porter, R. H., & Rieser, J. J. (2005). Retention of olfactory memories by newborn infants. In R. T. Mason, P. M. LeMaster, & D. Müller-Schwarze (Eds.), *Chemical signals in vertebrates* (pp. 300–307). New York, NY: Springer.

Posada, G., Gao, Y., Wu, F., Posada, R., Tascon, M., Schoelmerich, A.,... Synnevaag, B. (1995). The secure-base phenomenon across cultures: Children's behavior, mothers' preferences, and experts' concepts. *Monographs of the Society for Research in Child Development, 60,* 27–48.

Posner, M. I., & Rothbart, M. K. (2007). Numeracy. In M. I. Posner & M. K. Rothbart, *Educating the human brain* (pp. 173–187). Washington, DC: American Psychological Association.

Posner, R. B. (2006). Early menarche: A review of research on trends in timing, racial differences, etiology and psychosocial consequences. *Sex Roles, 54*(5–6), 315–322.

Potegal, M., & Davison, R. J. (2003). Temper tantrums in young children, 1: Behavioral composition. *Journal of Developmental & Behavioral Pediatrics, 24,* 140–147.

Potoczniak, D., Crosbie-Burnett, M., & Saltzburg, N. (2009). Experiences regarding coming out to parents among African American, Hispanic, and White gay, lesbian, bisexual, transgender, and questioning adolescents. *Journal of Gay & Lesbian Social Services: Issues in Practice, Policy & Research,* 21(2–3), 189–205.

Poulin-Dubois, D., & Serbin, L. (2006). La connaissance des catégories de genre et des stéréotypes sexués chez le jeune enfant. *Enfance, 58,* 283–292.

Power, F. C., Nuzzi, R. J., & Narvaez, D. (2007). *Moral education: A handbook.* Westport, CT: Greenwood Publishing Group.

Powls, A., Botting, N., Cooke, R. W. I., & Marlow, N. (1996). Handedness in very-low birth-weight (VLBW) children at 12 years of age: Relation to perinatal and outcome variables. *Developmental Medicine and Child Neurology, 38,* 594–602.

Prakasa, V. V., & Rao, V. N. (1979). Arranged marriages: An assessment of the attitudes of college students in India. In G. Kurian (Ed.), *Cross-cultural perspectives on mate selection and marriage* (pp. 11–31). Westport, CT: Greenwood Press.

Prasad, V., Brogan, E., Mulvaney, C., Grainge, M., Stanton, W., & Sayal, K. (2013). How effective are drug treatments for children with ADHD at improving on-task behaviour and academic achievement in the school classroom? A systematic review and meta-analysis. *European Child & Adolescent Psychiatry, 22*(4), 203–216.

Pressley, M. (2007). Achieving best practices. In L. B. Gambrell, L. M. Morrow, & M. Pressley (Eds.), *Best practices in literacy instruction* (pp. 397-404). New York, NY: Guilford.

Pressley, M., & Allington, R. L. (2014). *Reading instruction that works: The case for balanced teaching*. New York, NY: Guilford Publications.

Pressley, M., Wharton-McDonald, R., Raphael, L. M., Bogner, K., & Roehrig, A. (2002). Exemplary first-grade teaching. In B. M. Taylor & P. D. Pearson (Eds.), *Teaching reading: Effective schools, accomplished teachers* (pp. 73–88). Mahwah, NJ: Erlbaum.

Preuss, U., Ralston, S. J., Baldursson, G., Falissard, B., Lorenzo, M. J., Rodrigues Pereira, R.,... ADORE Study Group. (2006). Study design, baseline patient characteristics and intervention in a cross-cultural framework: Results from the ADORE study. *European Child & Adolescent Psychiatry, 15*(Suppl. 1), 4–19.

Price Waterhouse Coopers. (2011). The accelerating shift of global economic power: Challenges and opportunities. Retrieved from http://www.pwc.com/en_GX/gx/world-2050/pdf/world-in-2050-jan-2011.pdf

Priess, H. A., & Lindberg, S. A. (2014). Gender intensification. In R. Levesque (Ed.), *Encyclopedia of adolescence* (pp. 1135–1142). New York, NY: Springer.

Prinstein, M. J., & La Greca, A. M. (2002). Peer crowd affiliation and internalizing distress in childhood and adolescence: A longitudinal follow-back study. *Journal of Research on Adolescence, 12*, 325–351.

Proctor, M. H., Moore, L. L., Gao, D., Cupples, L. A., Bradlee, M. L., Hood, M. Y., & Ellison, R. C. (2003). Television viewing and change in body fat from preschool to early adolescence: The Framingham Children's Study. *International Journal of Obesity, 27*, 827–833.

Provins, K. A. (1997). Handedness and speech: A critical reappraisal of the role of genetic and environmental factors in the cerebral lateralization of function. *Psychological Review, 104*, 554–571.

Psychological Corporation. (2000). *Technical/product information*. Retrieved from www.psychcorp.com

Puhl, R. M., Heuer, C. A., & Brownell, K. D. (2010). Stigma and social consequences of obesity. In P. G. Kopelman, I. D. Caterson, & W. H. Dietz (Eds.), *Clinical obesity in adults and children* (pp. 25–40). New York, NY: Wiley.

Purdie, N., Carroll, A., & Roche, L. (2004). Parenting and adolescent self-regulation. *Journal of Adolescence, 27*, 663–676.

Putnam, R. (2000). *Bowling alone: The collapse and revival of American community*. New York, NY: Simon & Schuster.

Qin, D. B. (2009). Being "good" or being "popular": Gender and ethnic identity negotiations of Chinese immigrant adolescents. *Journal of Adolescent Research, 24*(1), 37–66.

Qin, D. B., Way, N., & Mukherjee, P. (2008). The other side of the model minority story: The familial and peer challenges faced by Chinese American adolescents. *Youth and Society, 39*(4), 480–506.

Quillian, L. (2003). The decline of male employment in low income Black neighborhoods, 1950–1990. *Social Science Research, 32*, 220–250.

Quinn, J. M. (2013). Dizygotic twin. *Encyclopædia Britannica*. Retrieved from https://www.britannica.com/science/dizygotic-twin

Quinn, P. C., Eimas, P. D., & Rosenkranz, S. L. (1993). Evidence for representations of perceptually similar natural categories by 3-month-old and 4-month-old infants. *Perception, 22*, 463–475.

Quintana, S. M. (2007). Racial and ethnic identity: Developmental perspectives and research. *Journal of Counseling Psychology*, 54, 259–270.

Quintelier, E., & Vissers, S. (2008). The effect of Internet use on political participation: An analysis of survey results for 16-year-olds in Belgium. *Social Science Computer Review, 26*(4), 411–427.

Raacke, J., & Bonds-Raacke, J. (2008). MySpace and Facebook: Applying the uses and gratifications theory to exploring friend-networking sites. *CyberPsychology & Behavior, 11*(2), 169–174.

Raag, T. (2003). Racism, gender identities and young children: Social relations in a multi-ethnic, inner-city primary school. *Archives of Sexual Behavior, 32*, 392–393.

Radmacher, K., & Azmitia, M. (2006). Are there gendered pathways to intimacy in early adolescents' and emerging adults' friendships? *Journal of Adolescent Research, 21*(4), 415–448.

Raffaelli, M., & Iturbide, M. (2015). Adolescent risks and resiliences across cultures. In L. A. Jensen (Ed.), *The Oxford handbook of human development and culture* (pp. 342–354). New York, NY: Oxford University Press.

Rah, J. H., Shamim, A. A., Arju, U. T., Labrique, A. B., Rashid, M., & Christian, P. (2009). Age of onset, nutritional determinants, and seasonal variations in menarche in rural Bangladesh. *Journal of Health, Population, and Nutrition, 27*(6), 802–807.

Raikes, H. H., Chazan-Cohen, R., Love, J. M., & Brooks-Gunn, J. (2010). Early Head Start impacts at age 3 and a description of the age 5 follow-up study. In A. J. Reynolds, A. J. Rolnick, & M. M. Englund (Eds.), *Childhood programs and practices in the first decade of life: A human capital integration* (pp. 99–118). New York, NY: Cambridge University Press.

Ramchandani, N. (2004). Diabetes in children: A burgeoning health problem among overweight young Americans. *American Journal of Nursing, 104*, 65–68.

Ramchandani, P., Stein, A., Evans, J., O'Connor, T. G., & the ALSPAC Study Team. (2005). Paternal depression in the postnatal period and child development: A prospective population study. *Lancet, 365*, 2201–2205.

Ramos, M. C., Guerin, D. W., Gottfried, A. W., Bathurst, K., & Oliver, P. H. (2005). Family conflict and children's behavior problems: The moderating role of child temperament. *Structural Equation Modeling, 12*, 278–298.

Rao, M. A., Berry, R., Gonsalves, A., Hastak, Y., Shah, M., & Roeser, R. W. (2013). Globalization and the identity remix among urban adolescents in India. *Journal of Research on Adolescence, 23*(1), 9–24. doi:10.1111/jora.12002

Rao, R., & Georgieff, M. K. (2001). Neonatal iron nutrition. *Seminars in Neonatology, 6*, 425–435.

Ratner, N., & Bruner, J. (1978). Games, social exchange and the acquisition of language. *Journal of Child Language*, 5(03), 391–401. doi:http://dx.doi.org/10.1017/S0305000900002063

Rauscher, F. H. (2003). Can music instruction affect children's cognitive development? *ERIC Digest, EDO-PS-03-12*.

Rauscher, F. H., Shaw, G. L., & Ky, K. N. (1993). Listening to Mozart enhances spatial-temporal reasoning: Towards a neurophysiological basis. *Neuroscience Letters, 185*, 44–47.

Ravens-Sieberer, U., Herdman, M., Devine, J., Otto, C., Bullinger, M., Rose, M., & Klasen, F. (2014). The European KIDSCREEN approach to measure quality of life and well-being in children: Development, current application, and future advances. *Quality of Life Research, 23*(3), 791–803.

Ravn, M. N. (2005). A matter of free choice? Some structural and cultural influences on the decision to have or not to have children in Norway. In C. B. Douglas (Ed.), *Barren states: The population "implosion" in Europe* (pp. 29–47). New York, NY: Berg.

Rawlings, D., Barrantes, V. N., & Furnham, A. (2000). Personality and aesthetic preference in Spain and England: Two studies relating sensation seeking and openness to experience to liking for paintings and music. *European Journal of Personality, 14*, 553–576.

Rawlings, D., & Leow, S. H. (2008). Investigating the role of psychoticism and sensation seeking in predicting emotional reactions to music. *Psychology of Music, 36*(3), 269–287.

Raz, R., Roberts, A. L., Lyall, K., Hart, J. E., Just, A. C., Laden, F., & Weisskopf, M. G. (2014). Autism spectrum disorder and particulate matter air pollution before, during, and after pregnancy: A nested case–control analysis within the Nurses' Health Study II cohort. *Environmental Health Perspectives, 123*(3), 264–270 doi:10.1289/ehp.1408133.

Rechtman, L. R., Colvin, J. D., Blair, P. S., & Moon, R. Y. (2014). Sofas and infant mortality. *Pediatrics, 134*(5), e1293–e1300. doi:10.1542/peds.2014-1543

Redcay, E., Haist, F., & Courchesne, E. (2008). Functional neuroimaging of speech perception during a pivotal period in language acquisition. *Developmental Science, 11*(2), 237–252.

Reddy, U. M., & Mennuti, M. T. (2006). Incorporating first-trimester Down syndrome studies into prenatal screening. *Obstetrics and Gynecology, 107*, 167–173.

Redshaw, M. E. (1997). Mothers of babies requiring special care: Attitudes and experiences. *Journal of Reproductive & Infant Psychology, 15*, 109–120.

Reese, D. (2000). A parenting manual, with words of advice for Puritan mothers. In J. DeLoache & A. Gottlieb (Eds.), *A world of babies: Imagined childcare guides for seven societies* (pp. 29–54). New York, NY: Cambridge University Press.

Reeves, G., & Schweitzer, J. (2004). Pharmacological management of attention deficit hyperactivity disorder. *Expert Opinions in Pharmacotherapy, 5*, 1313–1320.

Regan, P. C., Durvasula, R., Howell, L., Ureno, O., & Rea, M. (2004). Gender, ethnicity, and the developmental timing of the first sexual and romantic experiences. *Social Behavior & Personality, 32*, 667–676.

Regestein, Q., Natarajan, V., Pavlova, M., Kawasaki, S., Gleason, R., & Koff, E. (2010). Sleep debt and depression in female college students. *Psychiatry Research, 176*(1), 34–39.

Regev, R. H., Lusky, A., Dolfin, T., Litmanovitz, I., Arnon, S., Reichman, B., & Israel Neonatal Network. (2003). Excess mortality and morbidity among small-for-gestational-age premature infants: A population-based study. *The Journal of Pediatrics, 143*(2), 186–191

Regnerus, M., & Uecker, J. (2011). *Premarital sex in America: How young Americans meet, mate, and think about marrying*. New York, NY: Oxford University Press.

Regnerus, M. D., & Elder, G. H., jr. (2003). Staying on track in school: Religious influences in high- and low-risk settings. *Journal for the Scientific Study of Religion, 42*, 633–649. doi:10.1046/j.1468-5906.2003.00208.x

Regnerus, M. D., Smith, C., & Smith, B. (2004). Social context in the development of adolescent religiosity. *Applied Developmental Science, 8*(1), 27–38. doi:10.1207/S1532480XADS0801_4

Reichman, N. E. (2005). Low birth weight and school readiness. *The Future of Children, 15*(1), 91–116.

Reid, C. (2004). Kangaroo care. *Neonatal Network, 23*, 53.

Reid, M. J., Webster-Stratton, C., & Hammond, M. (2007). Enhancing a classroom social competence and problem-solving curriculum by offering parent training to families of moderate- to high-risk elementary school children. *Journal of Clinical Child and Adolescent Psychology, 36*(4), 605–620. doi:10.1080/15374410701662741

Reimuller, A., Shadur, J., & Hussong, A. M. (2011). Parental social support as a moderator of self-medication in adolescents. *Addictive Behaviors, 36*, 203–208.

Reinders, H., & Youniss, J. (2006). School-based required community service and civic development in adolescents. *Applied Developmental Science, 10*(1), 2–12.

Resnick, G. (2010). Project Head Start: Quality and links to child outcomes. In A. J. Reynolds, A. J. Rolnick, M. M. Englund, & J. A. Temple (Eds.), *Childhood programs and practices in the first decade of life: A human capital integration* (pp. 121–156). New York, NY: Cambridge University Press.

RESOLVE: The National Infertility Association. (2016). Insurance coverage of infertility treatments. Retrieved from http://www.resolve.org/about/insurance-coverage-of-infertility-treatments.html

Revelle, G. (2013). Applying developmental theory and research to the creation of educational games. In F. C. Blumberg & S. M. Fisch (Eds.), *Digital games: A context for cognitive development. New Directions for Child and Adolescent Research, 139*, 31–40.

Rey-López, J. P., Vicente-Rodriguez, G., Ortega, F. B., Ruiz, J. R., Martinez-Gómez, D., De Henauw, S., … HELENA Study Group. (2010). Sedentary patterns and media availability in European adolescents: The HELENA study. *HELENA Study Group; Preventive Medicine: An International Journal Devoted to Practice and Theory, 51*(1), 50–55.

Reznick, J. S., Corley, R., & Robinson, J. (1997). A longitudinal study of intelligence in the second year. *Monographs of the Society for Research in Child Development, 62*, 1–154.

Rhodes, J. E., & DuBois, D. L. (2008). Mentoring relationships and programs for youth. *Current Directions in Psychological Science, 17*(4), 254–258.

Rhodes, N., Roskos-Ewoldsen, D., Eno, C. A., & Monahan, J. L. (2009). The content of cigarette counter-advertising: Are perceived functions of smoking addressed? *Journal of Health Communication, 14*(7), 658–673.

Ricciuti, H. N. (2004). Single parenthood, achievement, and problem behavior in White, Black, and Hispanic children. *Journal of Educational Research, 97*, 196–206.

Richards, M. H., Crowe, P. A., Larson, R., & Swarr, A. (2002). Developmental patterns and gender differences in the experience of peer companionship in adolescence. *Child Development, 69*, 154–163.

Richardson, A., Ganz, O., Stalgaitis, C., Abrams, D., & Vallone, D. (2013). Noncombustible tobacco product advertising: How companies are selling the new face of tobacco. *Nicotine & Tobacco Research, 16*(5), 606–614.

Richman, A. L., Miller, P. M., & LeVine, R. A. (2010). Cultural and educational variations in maternal responsiveness. In R. A. LeVine (Ed.), *Psychological anthropology: A reader on self in culture* (pp. 181–192). Malden, MA: Wiley-Blackwell.

Riddle, K., Potter, W. J., Metzger, M. J., Nabi, R. L., & Linz, D. G. (2011). Beyond cultivation: Exploring the effects of frequency, recency, and vivid autobiographical memories for violent media. *Media Psychology, 14*(2), 168–191.

Rideout, V. (2013). *Zero to eight: Children's use of media in America, 2013*. Washington, DC: Common Sense Media.

Rideout, V. J., Foehr, U. G., & Roberts, D. F. (2010). *Generation $M^2$: Media in the lives of 8- to 18-year-olds*. Menlo Park, CA: The Henry J. Kaiser Family Foundation.

Rideout, V. J., & Hamel, E. (2006). *The media family: Electronic media in the lives of infants, toddlers, preschoolers, and their parents*. Menlo Park, CA: The Henry J. Kaiser Family Foundation.

Ridley, M. (2010). *The rational optimist: How prosperity evolves*. New York, NY: Harper.

Rigby, K. (2002). Bullying in childhood. In P. K. Smith & C. H. Hart (Eds.), *Blackwell handbook of childhood social development* (pp. 549–568). Malden, MA: Blackwell.

Rigby, K. (2004). Bullying in childhood. In P. K. Smith & C. H. Hart (Eds.), *Blackwell handbook of childhood social development*. Malden, MA: Blackwell.

Righetti, P. L., Dell'Avanzo, M., Grigio, M., & Nicolini, U. (2005). Maternal/paternal antenatal attachment and fourth-dimensional ultrasound technique: A preliminary report. *British Journal of Psychology, 96*, 129–137.

Righetti-Veltema, M., Conne-Perreard, E., Bousquest, A., & Manzano, J. (2002). Postpartum depression and mother–infant relationship at 3 months old. *Journal of Affective Disorders, 70*, 291–306.

Riley, A. W., Lyman, L. M., Spiel, G., Döpfner, M., Lorenzo, M. J., Ralston, S. J., & ADORE Study Group. (2006). The Family Strain Index (FSI). Reliability, validity, and factor structure of a brief questionnaire for families of children with ADHD. *European Child & Adolescent Psychiatry, 15*(Suppl. 1), 72–78.

Riley Bove, C. V. (2009). Polygyny and women's health in sub-Saharan Africa. *Social Science & Medicine, 68*, 21–29.

Rivadeneyra, R., & Ward, L. M. (2005). From Ally McBeal to Sábado Gigante: Contributions of television viewing to the gender role attitudes of Latino adolescents. *Journal of Adolescent Research, 20*, 453–475.

Roberto, C. A., Steinglass, J., Mayer, L. E. S., Attia, E., & Walsh, B. T. (2008). The clinical significance of amenorrhea as a diagnostic criterion for anorexia nervosa. *International Journal of Eating Disorders, 41*, 559–563.

Roberts, D. F., Foehr, U. G., & Rideout, V. (2005). *Generation M: Media in the lives of 8–18-year-olds*. Washington, DC: The Henry J. Kaiser Family Foundation.

Robertson, J. (2008). Stepfathers in families. In J. Pryor (Ed.), *The international handbook of stepfamilies: Policy and practice in legal, research, and clinical environments* (pp. 125–150). Hoboken, NJ: John Wiley & Sons.

Robins, R. W., Gosling, S. D., & Craik, K. H. (1999). An empirical analysis of trends in psychology. *American Psychologist, 54*, 117–128.

Robins, R. W., & Trzesniewski, K. H. (2005). Self-esteem development across the lifespan. *Current Directions in Psychological Science, 14*(3), 158–162.

Robinson, C. C., Anderson, G. T., Porter, C. L., Hart, C. H., & Wouden-Miller, M. (2003). Sequential transition patterns of preschoolers' social interactions during child-initiated play: Is parallel-aware play a bi-directional bridge to other play states? *Early Childhood Research Quarterly, 18*, 3–21.

Robinson, G. (1997). Families, generations and self: Conflict, loyalty and recognition in an Australian aboriginal society. *Ethos, 25*(3), 303–332.

Roby, A. C., & Kidd, E. (2008). The referential communication skills of children with imaginary companions. *Developmental Science, 11*(4), 531–540. doi:10.1111/j.1467-7687.2008.00699.x

Rochat, P. (2013). Self-conceptualization in development. In P. D. Zelazo (Ed.), *The Oxford handbook of developmental psychology: Volume 2: Self and other* (pp. 378–397). New York, NY: Oxford University Press.

Rochat, P., & Hespos, S. J. (1997). Differential rooting responses by neonates: Evidence for an early sense of self. *Early Development and Parenting, 6*, 105–112.

Roche, K. M., Lambert, S. F., Ghazarian, S. R., & Little, T. D. (2015). Adolescent language brokering in diverse contexts: Associations with parenting and parent–youth relationships in a new immigrant destination area. *Journal of Youth and Adolescence, 44*(1), 77–89. doi:10.1007/s10964-014-0154-3

Rodgers, J. L., & Wanstrom, L. (2007). Identification of a Flynn Effect in the NLSY: Moving from the center to the boundaries. *Intelligence, 35*, 187–196.

Rodier, P. M. (2009). *Science under attack: Vaccines and autism*. Berkeley, CA: University of California Press.

Rodriguez, A., Kaakinen, M., Moilanen, I., Taanila, A., McGough, J. J., Loo, S., & Järvelin, M. R. (2010). Mixed-handedness is linked to mental health problems in children and adolescents. *Pediatrics, 125*(2), e340–e348. doi:10.1542/peds.2009-1165

Roeder, M. B., Mahone, E. M., Larson, J. G., Mostofsky, S., Cutting, L. E., Goldberg, M. C., & Denckla, M. B. (2008). Left–right differences on timed motor examination in children. *Child Neuropsychology, 14*, 249–262.

Roenneberg, T., Kuehnle, T., Juda, M., Kantermann, T., Allebrandt, K., Gordijn, M., & Merrow, M. (2007). Epidemiology of the human circadian clock. *Sleep Medicine Reviews, 11*, 429–438.

Rogoff, B. (1990). *Apprenticeship in thinking: Cognitive development in social context*. New York, NY: Oxford University Press.

Rogoff, B. (1995). Observing sociocultural activities on three planes: Participatory appropriation, guided participation, and apprenticeship. In J. V. Wertsch, P. del Rio, & A. Alvarez (Eds.), *Sociocultural studies of the mind* (pp. 273–294). New York, NY: Cambridge University Press.

Rogoff, B. (1998). Cognition as a collaborative process. In D. Kuhn & R. S. Siegler (Eds.), *Handbook of child psychology: Vol. 2. Cognition, perception, and language* (5th ed., pp. 679–744). New York, NY: Wiley.

Rogoff, B. (2003). *The cultural nature of human development*. New York, NY: Oxford University Press.

Rogoff, B., Correa-Chávez, M., & Cotuc, M. N. (2005). A cultural/historical view of schooling in human development. In D. B. Pillemer & S. H. White (Eds.), *Developmental psychology and social change: Research, history and policy* (pp. 225–263). New York, NY: Cambridge University Press.

Rohde, P., Noell, J., Ochs, L., & Seeley, J. R. (2001). Depression, suicidal ideation, and STD-related risk in homeless older adolescents. *Journal of Adolescence, 24*, 447–460.

Rohlen, T. P. (1983). *Japan's high schools*. Berkeley, CA: University of California Press.

Rojo-Moreno, L., Arribas, P., Plumed, J., Gimeno, N., García-Blanco, A., Vaz-Leal, F., … Livianos, L. (2015). Prevalence and comorbidity of eating disorders among a community sample of adolescents: 2-year follow-up. *Psychiatry Research, 227*, 52–57. doi:10.1016/j.psychres.2015.02.015

Rokade, S., & Mane, A. (2008). A study of age at menarche, the secular trend and factors associated with it. *The Internet Journal of Biological Anthropology*, 3. Retrieved from http://ispub.com/IJBA/3/2/7469

Roopnarine, J. L., Hossain, Z., Gill, P., & Brophy, H. (1994). Play in the East Indian context. In J. L. Roopnarine, J. E. Johnson, & F. H. Hooper (Eds.), *Children's play in diverse cultures* (pp. 9–30). Albany, NY: State University of New York Press.

Ropospi. (2011). African Union and OLPC commit to educational transformation work throughout Africa. Retrieved from http://blog.laptop.org/2011/02/16/afracan-union-olpc-mou/

Rosario, M., Schrimshaw, E. W., & Hunter, J. (2004). Ethnic/racial differences in the comingout process of lesbian, gay, and bisexual youths: A comparions of sexual indentity development over time. *Cultural Diversity & Ethnic Minorities*, 10, 215–228.

Roscoe, B., Dian, M. S., & Brooks, R. H. (1987). Early, middle, and late adolescents' views on dating and factors influencing partner selection. *Adolescence, 22*, 59–68.

Rose, A. J., & Rudolph, K. D. (2006). A review of sex differences in peer relationship processes: potential trade-offs for the emotional and behavioral development of girls and boys. *Psychological Bulletin*, 132, 98–131.

Rose, S. A., Feldman, J. F., Jankowski, J. J., & Van Rossem, R. (2005). Pathways from prematurity and infant abilities to later cognition. *Child Development, 76*, 1172–1184.

Rosen, L., Carrier, L. M., Miller, A., Rokkum, J., & Ruiz, A. (2016). Sleeping with technology: Cognitive, affective, and technology usage predictors of sleep problems among college students. *Sleep Health*, 2, 49–56.

Rosenberg, M. (1965). *Society and the adolescent self-image*. Princeton, NJ: Princeton University Press.

Rosenberg, M. (1979). *Conceiving the self*. New York, NY: Basic Books.

Rosengren, K. E. (1974). Uses and gratifications: A paradigm outlined. In J. G. Bumler & E. Katz (Eds.), *The uses of mass communications: Current perspectives of gratifications research* (pp. 269–286). Beverly Hills, CA: Sage.

Rosenquist, J. N., Lehrer, S. F., O'Malley, A. J., Zaslavsky, A. M., Smoller, J. W., & Christakis, N. A. (2015). Cohort of birth modifies the association between FTO genotype and BMI. *Proceedings of the National Academy of Sciences, 112*(2), 354–359. doi:10.1073/pnas.1411893111

Rosenthal, D., & Rotheram-Borus, M. J. (2005). Young people and homelessness. *Journal of Adolescence, 28*, 167–169.

Rosnow, R. L., & Rosenthal, R. L. (2005). *Beginning behavioral research* (5th ed.). Upper Saddle River, NJ: Prentice Hall.

Ross, H. S., & Lollis, S. P. (1989). A social relations analysis of toddler peer relationships. *Child Development, 60*, 1082–1091.

Rote, W. M., & Smetana, J. G. (2016). Patterns and predictors of mother–adolescent discrepancies across family constructs. *Journal of Youth and Adolescence, 45*, 2064–2079.

Rothbart, M. K. (1981). Measurement of temperament in infancy. *Child Development, 52*, 569–578. doi:10.2307/1129176

Rothbart, M. K. (2004). Emotion-related regulation: Sharpening the definition. *Child Development, 75*, 334–339.

Rothbart, M. K., Ahadi, S. A., & Evans, D. E. (2000). Temperament and personality: Origins and outcome. *Journal of Personality and Social Psychology, 78*, 122–135.

Rothbart, M. K., Ahadi, S. A., Hershey, K. L., & Fisher, P. (2001). Investigations of temperament at three to seven years: The Children's Behavior Questionnaire. *Child Development, 72*(5), 1394–1408. doi:10.1111/1467-8624.00355

Rothbart, M. K., & Bates, J. E. (2006). Temperament. In W. Damon & R. Lerner (Series Eds.), & N. Eisenberg (Vol. Ed.), *Handbook of child psychology: Vol. 3. Social, emotional, and personality development* (6th ed., pp. 99–166). New York, NY: Wiley.

Rothbaum, F., Kakinuma, M., Nagaoka, R., & Azuma, H. (2007). Attachment and *amae*: Parent–child closeness in the United States & Japan. *Journal of Cross-Cultural Psychology, 38*, 465–486.

Rothbaum, F., & Morelli, G. (2005). Attachment and culture: Bridging relativism and universalism. In W. Friedlmeier, P. Chakkarath, & B. Schwarz (Eds.), *Culture and human development: The importance of cross-cultural research to the social sciences* (pp. 99–124). Lisse, The Netherlands: Swets & Zeitlinger.

Rothbaum, F., Weisz, J., Pott, M., Miyake, K., & Morelli, G. (2000). Attachment and culture: Security in the United States and Japan. *American Psychologist, 55*, 1093–1104.

Rothbaum, F., Weisz, J., Pott, M., Miyake, K., & Morelli, G. (2001). Deeper into attachment and culture. *American Psychologist, 56*, 827–829.

Rothenberger, A., Coghill, D., Dopfner, M., Falissard, B., & Stenhausen, H. C. (2006). Naturalistic observational studies in the framework of ADHD health care. *European Child and Adolescent Psychiatry, 15*(Suppl. 1), 1–3.

Rotheram-Borus, M. J. (1990). Adolescents' reference group choices, self-esteem, and adjustment. *Journal of Personality and Social Psychology, 59*, 1075–1081.

Rovee-Collier, C. K. (1999). The development of infant memory. *Current Directions in Psychological Science, 8*, 80–85.

Rozin, P. (2006). Domain denigration and process preference in academic psychology. *Perspectives on Psychological Science, 1*, 365–376.

Rozin, P., Lowery, L., Imada, S., & Haidt, J. 1999. The CAD triad hypothesis: A mapping between three moral emotions (contempt, anger, disgust) and three moral codes (community, autonomy, divinity). *Journal of Personality and Social Psychology, 76*, 574–586.

Rubenstein, J. M. (2017). *The cultural landscape: An introduction to human geography* (12th ed.). New York, NY: Pearson.

Rubin, A. M. (1993). Uses, gratifications, and media effects research. In J. Bryant & D. Zillman (Eds.), *Perspectives on media effects*. Hillsdale, NJ: Erlbaum.

Rubin, K., Fredstrom, B., & Bowker, J. (2008). Future directions in friendship in childhood and early adolescence. *Social Development, 17*(4), 1085–1096.

Rubin, K. H., Bowker, J. C., McDonald, K. L., & Menzer, M. (2013). Peer relationships in childhood. In P. D. Zelazo (Ed.), *The Oxford handbook of developmental psychology: Volume 2: Self and other* (pp. 242–274). New York, NY: Oxford University Press.

Rubin, K. H., Bukowski, W., & Parker, J. G. (2006). Peer interactions, relationships and groups. In W. Damon & R. Lerner (Eds.), & N. Eisenberg (Vol. Ed.), *Handbook of child psychology: Vol. 3. Social, emotional and personality development* (6th ed., pp. 571–645). New York, NY: Wiley.

Rubin, K. H., Burgess, K. B., & Hastings, P. D. (2002). Stability and social-behavioral consequences of toddlers' inhibited temperament and parenting behaviors. *Child Development, 73*, 483–495.

Rubin, K. H., & Pepler, D. J. (Eds.). (2013). *The development and treatment of childhood aggression*. New York, NY: Psychology Press.

Ruble, D. N., Martin, C. L., & Berenbaum, S. (2006). Gender development. In W. Damon & R. M. Lerner (Series Eds.), & N. Eisenberg (Vol. Ed.), *Handbook of child psychology: Vol. 3. Social, emotional and personality development* (6th ed., pp. 858–932). Hoboken, NJ: Wiley.

Rucker, J. H., & McGuffin, P. (2010). Polygenic heterogeneity: A complex model of genetic inheritance in psychiatric disorders. *Biological Psychiatry, 68*, 312–313.

Rückinger, S., Beyerlein, A., Jacobsen, G., von Kries, R., & Vik, T. (2010). Growth in utero and body mass index at age 5 years in children of smoking and non-smoking mothers. *Early Human Development, 86*, 773–777.

Rudy, D., & Grusec, J. (2006). Authoritarian parenting in individualist and collectivist groups: Associations with maternal emotion and cognition and children's self-esteem. *Journal of Family Psychology, 43*, 302–319.

Ruggeri, K., & Bird, C. E. (2014). *Single parents and employment in Europe*. Cambridge, UK: Rand Europe.

Ruggiero, T. E. (2000). Uses and gratifications theory in the 21st century. *Mass Communication & Society, 3*, 3–37.

Rushton, J. P., & Jensen, A. R. (2005). Thirty years of research on race differences in cognitive ability. *Psychology, Public Policy, and Law, 11* (2), 235–294.

Russell, A., Hart, C. H., Robinson, C. C., & Olsen, S. F. (2003). Children's sociable and aggressive behavior with peers: A comparison of the U.S. and Australia, and contributions of temperament and parenting styles. *International Journal of Behavioral Development, 27*, 74–86.

Rutter, M. (1983). School effects on pupil progress: Research findings and policy implications. *Child Development, 54*, 1–29.

Rutter, M. (1996). Maternal deprivation. In M. H. Bornstein (Ed.), *Handbook of parenting: Vol. 4. Applied and practical parenting* (pp. 3–31). Mahwah, NJ: Erlbaum.

Rutter, M. (2002). The interplay of nature, nurture, and developmental influences: The challenge ahead for mental health. *Archives of General Psychiatry, 59*(11), 996–1000.

Rutter, M., Maughan, B., Mortimore, P., & Ouston, J. (1979). *Fifteen thousand hours: Secondary schools and their effects on children*. Cambridge, MA: Harvard University Press.

Ryan, C., Huebner, D., Diaz, R. M., & Sanchez, J. (2009). Family rejection as a predictor of negative health outcomes in white and Latino lesbian, gay and bisexual young adults. *Pediatrics*, 123, 346–352.

Ryan, A. S., Zhou, W., & Arensberg, M. B. (2006). The effects of employment status on breastfeeding in the United States. *Women's Health Issues, 16*, 243–251.

Rychlak, J. F. (2003). The self takes over. In J. F. Rychlak, *The human image in postmodern America* (pp. 69–82). Washington, DC: American Psychological Association.

Saarikallio, S., & Erkkilä, J. (2007). The role of music in adolescents' mood regulation. *Psychology of Music, 35*(1), 88–109.

Saarni, C. (1999). *The development of emotional competence.* New York, NY: Guilford.

Saarni, C., Campos, J. J., Camras, L. A., & Witherington, D. (2006). Emotional development: Action, communication, and understanding. In W. Damon & R. M. Lerner (Eds.), *Handbook of child psychology, Vol. 3* (pp. 226–299). Hoboken, NJ: John Wiley and Sons, Inc.

Sabbagh, M. A., & Shafman, D. (2009). How children block learning from ignorant speakers. *Cognition, 112*(3), 415–422. doi:10.1016/j.cognition.2009.06.005

Sabbagh, M. A., Xu, F., Carlson, S. M., Moses, L. J., & Lee, K. (2006). The development of executive functioning and theory of mind: A comparison of Chinese and U.S. preschoolers. *Psychological Science, 17*, 74–81.

Safe Kids Worldwide. (2013). *Unintentional childhood injury-related deaths.* Retrieved from http://www.safekidsgainesvillehall.org/unintentional-childhood-injury-related-deaths

Saffran, J. R., Aslin, R. N., & Newport, E. L. (1996). Statistical learning by 8-month-old infants. *Science, 274*(5294), 1926–1928. doi:10.1126/science.274.5294.1926

Saffran, J. R., Johnson, E. K., Aslin, R. N., & Newport, E. L. (1999). Statistical learning of tone sequences by human infants and adults. *Cognition, 70*(1), 27–52. doi:10.1016/S0010-0277(98)00075-4

Salkind, N. (2011). *Exploring research.* Upper Saddle River, NJ: Pearson.

Sameroff, A. J., & Haith, M. M. (1996). *The five to seven year shift: The age of reason and responsibility.* Chicago, IL: University of Chicago Press.

Samuels, H. R. (1980). The effect of an older sibling on infant locomotor exploration of a new environment, *Child Development, 51*, 607–609.

Sandstrom, M. J., & Zakriski, A. L. (2004). Understanding the experience of peer rejection. In J. B. Kupersmidt & K. A. Dodge (Eds.), *Children's peer relations: From development to intervention.* Washington, DC: American Psychological Association.

Sang, B., Miao, X., & Deng, C. (2002). The development of gifted and nongifted young children in metamemory knowledge. *Psychological Science (China), 25*, 406–424.

Sansavani, A., Bertoncini, J., & Giovanelli, G. (1997). Newborns discriminate the rhythm of multisyllabic stressed words. *Developmental Psychology, 33*, 3–11.

Savelsbergh, G. J. P., Ledebt, A., Smorenburg, A. R. P. & Deconinck, F. J. A. (2013). Upper limb activity in children with unilateral spastic cerebral palsy: The role of vision in movement strategies. *Developmental Medicine and Child Neurology, 55*, 38–42. doi:10.1111/dmcn.12305

Savin-Williams, R. (1998). *"–and then I became gay"*: Young men's stories. Hove, United Kingdom: Psychology Press.

Savin-Williams, R. (2001). *Mom, dad, I'm gay.* Washington, DC: American Psychological Association.

Savin-Williams, R. (2005). *The new gay teenager.* Cambridge, MA: Harvard University Press.

Savin-Williams, R. C. (2011). Identity development among sexual-minority youth. In S. J. Schwartz, K Luyckx, & V. L. Vignoles (Eds.), *Handbook of identity theory and research* (pp. 671–689). New York: Springer.

Savin-Williams, R. C., & Joyner, K. (2014). The politicization of gay youth health: Response to Li, Katz-Wise, and Calzo (2014). *Archives of Sexual Behavior, 43*, 1027.

Savin-Williams, R. C., & Ream, G. L. (2007). Prevalence and stability of sexual orientation components during adolescence and young adulthood. *Archives of Sexual Behavior, 36*(3), 385–394.

Sawnani, H., Jackson, T., Murphy, T., Beckerman, R., & Simakajornboon, N. (2004). The effect of maternal smoking on respiratory and arousal patterns in preterm infants during sleep. *American Journal of Respiratory and Critical Care Medicine, 169*, 733–738.

Sax, L., & Kautz, K. J. (2003). Who first suggests the diagnosis of attention deficit/hyperactivity disorder? *Annals of Family Medicine, 1*, 171–174.

Saxe, G. B. (2002). Candy selling and math learning. In C. Desforges & R. Fox (Eds.), *Teaching and learning: The essential readings* (pp. 86–106). Malden, MA: Blackwell.

Sbarra, D. A., & Emery, R. E. (2008). Deeper into divorce: Using actor-partner analyses to explore systemic differences in coparenting conflict following custody dispute resolution. *Journal of Family Psychology, 22*(1), 144–152.

Scantlin, R. (2007). Educational television, effects of. In J. J. Arnett (Ed.), *Encyclopedia of children, adolescents, and the media* (pp. 255–258). Thousand Oaks, CA: Sage.

Scarr, S. (1993). Biological and cultural diversity: The legacy of Darwin for development. *Child Development, 64*, 1333–1353.

Scarr, S., & McCartney, K. (1983). How people make their own environments: A theory of genotype environment effects. *Child Development, 54*, 424–435.

Schaal, B., Marlier, L., & Soussignan, R. (2000). Human fetuses learn odours from their pregnant mother's diet. *Chemical Senses, 25*, 729–737.

Schachter, E. P. (2005). Erikson meets the postmodern: Can classic identity theory rise to the challenge? *Identity, 5*, 137–160.

Schachter, S. C., & Ransil, B. J. (1996). Handedness distributions in nine professional groups. *Perceptual and Motor Skills, 82*, 51–63.

Schaeffer, C., Petras, H., & Ialongo, B. (2003). Modeling growth in boys' aggressive behavior across elementary school: Links to later criminal involvement, conduct disorder, and antisocial personality disorder. *Developmental Psychology, 39*, 1020–1035.

Scharf, M., & Shulman, S. (2015). Closeness, distance, and rapprochement in sibling relationships. In J. J. Arnett (Ed.), *The Oxford handbook of emerging adulthood* (pp. 190–202). New York, NY: Oxford University Press.

Scharf, M., Shulman, S., & Avigad-Spitz, L. (2005). Sibling relationships in emerging adulthood and in adolescence. *Journal of Adolescent Research, 20*, 64–90.

Scheel, K. R., & Westefeld, J. S. (1999). Heavy metal music and adolescent suicidality: An empirical investigation. *Adolescence, 34*(134), 253–273.

Scheibe, C. (2007). Advertising on children's programs. In J. J. Arnett (Ed.), *Encyclopedia of children, adolescents, and the media* (pp. 59–60). Thousand Oaks, CA: Sage.

Scher, A., Epstein, R., & Tirosh, E. (2004). Stability and changes in sleep regulation: A longitudinal study from 3 months to 3 years. *International Journal of Behavioral Development, 28*, 268–274.

Schieffelin, B. B. (1986). The acquisition of Kaluli. In D. Slobin (Ed.), *The cross-linguistic study of language acquisition* (pp. 525–593). Hillsdale, NJ: Erlbaum.

Schieffelin, B. B. (1986). Teasing and shaming in Kahili children's interactions. In B. B. Schieffelin & E. Ochs (Eds.), *Language socialization across cultures* (pp. 165–181). New York, NY: Cambridge University Press.

Schieffelin, B. B. (1990). *The give and take of everyday life: Language socialization of Kaluli children.* New York, NY: Cambridge University Press.

Schiermeier, Q. (2015, October 29). China's birth rate won't be dramatically affected by end of one-child policy. *Nature News.* Retrieved from http://www.nature.com/news/china-s-birth-rate-wont-be-dramatically-affected-by-end-of-one-child-policy-1.18687

Schlegel, A. (1973). The adolescent socialization of the Hopi girl. *Ethnology, 4*, 449–462.

Schlegel, A. (2010). Adolescent ties to adult communities: The intersection of culture and development. In L. Jensen (Ed.), *Bridging cultural and developmental approaches to psychology* (pp. 138–159). New York, NY: Oxford University Press.

Schlegel, A., & Barry, H. (1991). *Adolescence: An anthropological inquiry.* New York, NY: Free Press.

Schlegel, A., & Barry, H. (2015). Leaving childhood: The nature and meaning of adolescent transition rituals. In L. A. Jensen (Ed.), *The Oxford handbook of human development and culture* (pp. 327–340). New York, NY: Oxford University Press.

Schlegel, A., & Barry, H. III. (2015). The nature and meaning of adolescent transition rituals. In L. A. Jensen (Ed.), *Oxford handbook of human development and culture: An interdisciplinary perspective.* New York, NY: Oxford University Press.

Schlegel, A., & Hewlett, B. L. (2011). Contributions of anthropology to the study of adolescence. *Journal of Research on Adolescence, 21*(1), 281–289.

Schmidt, L., Holstein, B., Christensen, U., & Boivin, J. (2005). Does infertility cause marital benefit? An epidemiological study of 2250 men and women in fertility treatment. *Patient Education and Counseling, 59*, 244–251.

Schmitow, C., & Stenberg, G. (2013). Social referencing in 10-month-old infants. *European Journal of Developmental Psychology, 10*, 533–545. doi:10.1080/17405629.2013.763473

Schneider, B. (2006). In the moment: The benefits of the Experience Sampling Method. In M. Pitt-Catsouphes, E. E. Kossek, & S. Sweet (Eds.), *The work and family handbook: Multi-disciplinary perspectives, methods, and approaches* (pp. 469–488). Mahwah, NJ: Erlbaum.

Schneider, B. (2009). Challenges of transitioning into adulthood. In I. Schoon & R. K. Silbereisen (Eds.), *Transitions from school to work: Globalization, individualization, and patterns of diversity* (pp. 265–290). New York, NY: Cambridge University Press.

Schneider, B., & Stevenson, D. (1999). *The ambitious generation: America's teenagers, motivated but directionless.* New Haven, CT: Yale University Press.

Schneider, B., & Waite, L. J. (Eds.). (2005). *Being together, working apart: Dual-career families and the work-life balance.* New York: Cambridge University Press.

Schneider, W. (2002). Memory development in childhood. In U. Goswami (Ed.), *Blackwell handbook of childhood cognitive development* (pp. 236–256). Malden, MA: Blackwell.

Schneider, W. (2010). Metacognition and memory development in childhood and adolescence. In H. S. Waters & W. Schneider (Eds.), *Metacognition, strategy use, and instruction* (pp. 54–81). New York, NY: Guilford.

Schneider, W., & Bjorklund, D. F. (1992). Expertise, aptitude, and strategic remembering. *Child Development, 63*, 461–473.

Schneider, W., & Lockl, K. (2008). Procedural metacognition in children: Evidence for developmental trends. In J. Dunlosky & R. A. Bjork (Eds.), *Handbook of metamemory and memory* (pp. 391–409). New York, NY: Psychology Press.

Schneider, W., & Pressley, M. (1997). *Memory development between two and twenty* (2nd ed.). Mahwah, NJ: Erlbaum.

Schoenwald, S. K., Heiblum, N., Saldana, L., & Henggeler, S. W. (2008). The international implementation of multisystemic therapy. *Evaluation & the Health Professions, 31*, 211–225.

Schoolcraft, W. (2010). *If at first you don't conceive: A complete guide to infertility from one of the nation's leading clinics.* New York, NY: Rodale Books.

Schott, J. M., & Rossor, M. N. (2003). The grasp and other primitive reflexes. *Journal of Neurological and Neurosurgical Psychiatry, 74*, 558–560.

Schulz, R., & Curnow, C. (1988). Peak performance and age among superathletes: Track and field, swimming, baseball, tennis, and golf. *Journal of Gerontology, 43*(5), P113–P120.

Schulze, P. A., & Carlisle, S. A. (2010). What research does and doesn't say about breastfeeding: A critical review. *Early Child Development and Care, 180*, 703–718.

Schumann, C. M., Carter Barnes, C., Lord, C., & Courchesne, E. (2009). Amygdala enlargement in toddlers with autism related to severity of social and communication impairments. *Biological Psychiatry, 66*(10), 942–949. doi:10.1016/j.biopsych.2009.07.007

Schwartz, D., Proctor, L. J., & Chien, D. H. (2001). The aggressive victim of bullying: Emotional and behavioral dysregulation as a pathway to victimization by peers. In J. Juonen & S. Graham (Eds.), *Peer harassment in school: The plight of the vulnerable and victimized* (pp. 147–174). New York, NY: Guilford.

Schwartz, M., Share, D. L., Leikin, M., & Kozminsky, E. (2008). On the benefits of bi-literacy: Just a head start in reading or specific orthographic insights? *Reading and Writing, 21*, 905–927.

Schwartz, S. J., Syed, M., Yip, T., Knight, G. P., Umana-Taylor, A. J., Rivas-Drake, D., & Lee, R. M. (2014). Methodological issues in ethnic and racial identity research within ethnic minority populations: Theoretical precision, measurement issues, and research designs. *Child Development, 85*(1), 58–76.

Schwartz, S. J., & Unger, J. B. (2010). Biculturalism and context: What is biculturalism, and when is it adaptive? *Human Development, 53*(1), 26–32. doi:10.1159/000268137

Schwartz, S. J., Zamboanga, B. L., Luyckx, K, Meca, A., & Ritchie, R. (2015). Identity development in emerging adulthood. In J. J. Arnett (Ed.), *Oxford handbook of emerging adulthood* (pp. 401–420). New York, NY: Oxford University Press.

Schwartz, S. J., Zamboanga, B. L., Luyckx, K., Mecca, A., & Ritchie, R. A. (2013). Identity in emerging adulthood: Reviewing the field and looking forward. *Emerging Adulthood, 1*, 96–113.

Schweinhart, L. J., Montie, J., Xiang, Z., Barnett, W. S., & Belfield, C. R. (2004). *Lifetime effects: The High/Scope Perry Preschool Study through age 40.* Boston, MA: Strategies for Children. Retrieved from www.highscope.org/Research/PerryProject/perry-main.htm

Schweinle, A. & Wilcox, T. (2004). Intermodal perception and physical reasoning in young infants. *Infant Behavior & Development, 27*, 246–265.

Scott, E., & Panksepp, J. (2003). Rough-and-tumble play in human children. *Aggressive Behavior, 29*, 539–551.

Sears, H. (2012). Canada. In J. J. Arnett (Ed.), *Adolescent psychology around the world* (pp. 165–180). New York, NY: Taylor & Francis.

Sears, H. A., Simmering, M. G., & MacNeil, B. A. (2007). Canada. In J. J. Arnett (Ed.), *International encyclopedia of adolescence* (pp. 140–156). New York, NY: Routledge.

Seiffge-Krenke, I. (1997). Imaginary companions in adolescence: Sign of a deficient or positive development? *Journal of Adolescence, 20*(2), 137–154. doi:10.1006/jado.1996.0072

Selah-Shayovits, R. (2006). Adolescent preferences for violence in television shows and music video clips. *International Journal of Adolescence and Youth, 13*(1), 99–112.

Selander, J. (2011). *Cultural beliefs honor placenta.* Retrieved from http://placentabenefits.info/culture.asp

Sellen, D. W. (2001). Comparison of infant feeding patterns reported for nonindustrial populations with current recommendations. *Journal of Nutrition, 131*, 2707–2715.

Sembuya, R. (2010). Mother or nothing: The agony of infertility. *Bulletin of the World Health Organization, 88*, 881–882.

Sen, K., & Samad, A. Y. (Eds.). (2007). *Islam in the European Union: Transnationalism, youth, and the war on terror.* New York, NY: Oxford University Press.

Senghas, A., & Coppola, M. (2001). Children creating language: How Nicaraguan sign language acquired a spatial grammar. *Psychological Science, 12*, 323–329.

Serpell, R. (2011). Social responsibility as a dimension of intelligence, and as an educational goal: Insights from programmatic research in an African society. *Child Development Perspectives, 5*(2), 126–133. doi:10.1111/j.1750-8606.2011.00167.x

Seto, M. C., Babchishin, K. M., Pullman, L. E., & McPhail, I. V. (2015). The puzzle of intrafamilial child sexual abuse: A meta-analysis comparing intrafamilial and extrafamilial offenders with child victims. *Clinical Psychology Review, 39*, 42–57.

Shalatin, S., & Phillip, M. (2003). The role of obesity and leptin in the pubertal process and pubertal growth: A review. *International Journal of Obesity and Related Metabolic Disorders, 27*, 869–874.

Shanahan, L., McHale, S. M., Crouter, A. C., & Osgood, D. W. (2007). Warmth with mothers and fathers from middle childhood to late adolescence: Within- and between-families comparisons. *Developmental Psychology, 43*(3), 551–563.

Shanahan, L., McHale, S. M., Osgood, D. W., & Crouter, A. C. (2007). Conflict frequency with mothers and fathers from middle childhood to late adolescence: Within- and between-families comparisons. *Developmental Psychology, 43*, 539–550.

Shapiro, L. J., & Azuma, H. (2004). Intellectual, attitudinal, and interpersonal aspects of competence in the United States and Japan. In R. J. Sternberg & E. L. Grigorenko (Eds.), *Culture and competence: Contexts of life success* (pp. 187–206). Washington, DC: American Psychological Association.

Shapka, J. D., & Keating, D. P. (2005). Structure and change in self-concept during adolescence. *Canadian Journal of Behavioural Science, 37*, 83–96.

Sharma, T., Guski, L. S., Freund, N., & Gøtzsche, P. C. (2016). Suicidality and aggression during antidepressant treatment: Systematic review and meta-analyses based on clinical study reports. *BMJ, 352*, i65. doi:10.1136/bmj.i65

Shaughnessy, J., Zechmeister, E., & Zechmeister, J. (2011). *Research methods in psychology* (11th ed.). New York, NY: McGraw-Hill.

Shaw, P., Greenstein, D., Lerch, J., Clasen, L., Lenroot, R., Gogtay, N., & Evans, A. (2006). Intellectual ability and cortical development in children and adolescents. *Nature, 440*, 676–679.

Shaywitz, B. A., Shaywitz, S. E., Blachman, B. A., Pugh, K. R., Fulbright, R. K., Skudlarski, P., . . . Gore, J. C. (2004). Development of left occipitotemporal systems for skilled reading in children after a phonologically-based intervention. *Biological Psychiatry, 55*, 926–933.

Shernoff, E. S., & Kratochwill, T. R. (2007). Transporting an evidence-based classroom management program for preschoolers with disruptive behavior problems to a school: An analysis of implementation, outcomes, and contextual variables. *School Psychology Quarterly, 22*(3), 449. doi:http://dx.doi.org/10.1037/1045-3830.22.3.449

Sherrod, L. R., Flanagan, C., & Youniss, J. (2002). Dimensions of citizenship and opportunities for youth development: The what, why, when, where, and who of citizenship development. *Applied Developmental Science, 6*, 264–272.

Sherrod, L. R., Torney-Purta, J., & Flanagan, C. A. (2010). *Handbook of research on civic engagement in youth.* Hoboken, NJ: Wiley.

Shields, S. A. (2008). Gender: An intersectionality perspective. *Sex roles, 59*, 301–311.

Shih, R. A., Miles, J. N., Tucker, J. S., Zhou, A. J., & D'Amico, E. J. (2010). Racial/ethnic differences in adolescent substance use: Mediation by individual, family, and school factors. *Journal of Studies on Alcohol and Drugs, 71*(5), 640.

Shimizu, H. (2001). Japanese adolescent boys' senses of empathy (omoiyari) and Carol Gilligan's perspectives on the morality of care: A phenomenological approach. *Culture & Psychology, 7*, 453–475.

Shiner, R. L., & DeYoung, C. G. (2013). The structure of temperament and personality traits: A developmental perspective. In P. D. Zelazo (Ed.), *The Oxford handbook of developmental psychology: Volume 2: Self and other* (pp. 113–141). New York, NY: Oxford University Press.

Shipman, K. L., Zeman, J., Nesin, A. E., & Fitzgerald, M. (2003). Children's strategies for displaying anger and sadness: What works with whom? *Merrill-Palmer Quarterly, 49*, 100–122.

Shirtcliff, E. A., Dahl, R E., & Pollak, S. D. (2009). Pubertal development: Correspondence between hormonal and physical development. *Child Development, 80*, 327–337.

Shonkoff, J. P., & Phillips, D. A. (Eds.). (2000). *From neurons to neighborhoods: The science of early childhood development.* Washington, DC: National Academy Press.

Shope, J. T. (2007). Graduated driver licensing: Review of evaluation results since 2002. *Journal of Safety Research, 38*(2), 165–175.

Shope, J. T., & Bingham, C. R. (2008). Teen driving: Motor-vehicle crashes and factors that contribute. *American Journal of Preventative Medicine, 35*(3, Suppl. 1), S261–S271.

Shorten, A. (2010). Bridging the gap between mothers and medicine: "New insights" from the NIH Consensus Conference on VBAC. *Birth, 37*(3), 181–183.

Shreeve, J. (2010, July). The evolutionary road. *National Geographic*, 34–50.

Shulman, S., & Connolly, J. (2015). Romantic relationships in emerging adulthood. In J. J. Arnett (Ed.), *Oxford handbook of emerging adulthood* (pp. 230–244). New York, NY: Oxford University Press.

Shulman, S., Laursen, B., Kalman, Z., & Karpovsky, S. (1997). Adolescent intimacy revisited. *Journal of Youth & Adolescence, 26*, 597–617.

Shultz, S., & Vouloumanos, A. (2010). Three-month-olds prefer speech to other naturally occurring signals. *Language Learning and Development, 6*(4), 241–257. doi:10.1080/15475440903507830

Shumaker, D. M., Miller, C., Ortiz, C., & Deutsch, R. (2011). The forgotten bonds: The assessment and contemplation of sibling attachment in divorce and parental separation. *Family Court Review, 49*(1), 46–58.

Shwalb, D. W., & Shwalb, B. J. (2015). Fathering diversity within societies. In L. A. Jensen (Ed.), *Oxford handbook of human development and culture* (pp. 602–617). New York, NY: Oxford University Press.

Shweder, R. A. (Ed.). (2009). *The child: An encyclopedic companion.* Chicago, IL: The University of Chicago Press.

Shweder, R. A., Goodnow, J. J., Hatano, G., LeVine, R. A., Markus, H. R., & Miller, P. J. (2006). The cultural psychology of development: One mind, many mentalities. In W. Damon & R. Lerner (Eds.), & R. M. Lerner (Vol. Ed.), *Handbook of child psychology: Vol. 1. Theoretical models of human development* (6th ed., pp. 716–792). New York, NY: Wiley.

Shweder, R. A., Jensen, L., & Goldstein, W. A. (1995). Who sleeps by whom revisited: A method for extracting the moral goods implicit in practice. In J. J. Goodnow, P. J. Miller, & F. Kessel (Eds.), *Cultural practices as contexts for development* (Vol. 67, pp. 21–39). San Francisco, CA: Jossey-Bass Publishers.

Shweder, R. A., Mahapatra, M., & Miller, J. G. (1990). Culture and moral development. In J. W. Stigler, R. A. Shweder, & G. Herdt (Eds.), *Cultural psychology* (pp. 130–204). New York, NY: Cambridge University Press.

Shweder, R. A., Much, N. C., Mahapatra, M., & Park, L. (1997). The "big three" of morality (autonomy, community, divinity) and the "big three" explanations of suffering. In A. Brandt & D. Rozin (Eds.), *Morality and health* (pp. 119–169). New York, NY: Routledge.

Sidorowicz, L. S., & Lunney, G. S. (1980). Baby X revisited. *Sex Roles, 6*, 67–73.

Siegler, R. S. (1995). How does change occur: A microgenetic study of number conservation. *Cognitive Psychology, 28*, 225–273.

Siegler, R. S. (1996). *Emerging minds: The process of change in children's thinking.* New York, NY: Oxford University Press.

Siegler, R. S., & Ramani, G. B. (2009). Playing linear number board games—but not circular ones—improves low-income preschoolers' numerical understanding. *Journal of Educational Psychology, 101*(3), 545. doi:10.1037/a0014239

Sigelman, C., & Toebben, J. (1992). Tolerant reactions to advocates of disagreeable ideas in childhood and adolescence. *Merrill-Palmer Quarterly, 38*, 542–557.

Sigman, M. (1999). Developmental deficits in children with Down syndrome. In H. Tager-Flusberg (Ed.), *Neurodevelopmental disorders: Developmental cognitive neuroscience* (pp. 179–195). Cambridge, MA: MIT Press.

Signorella, M. L., Bigler, R. S., & Liben, L. S. (1993). Developmental differences in children's gender schemata about others: A meta-analytic review. *Developmental Review, 13*(2), 147–183. doi:10.1006/drev.1993.1007

Silburn, S. R., Blair, E., Griffin, J. A., Zubrick, S. R., Lawrence, D. M., Mitrou, F. G., & De Maio, J. A. (2007). Developmental and environmental factors supporting the health and well-being of Aboriginal adolescents. *International Journal of Adolescent Medicine and Health, 19*(3), 345–354.

Silk, J. B., Beehner, J. C., Bergman, T. J., Crockford, C., Engh, A. L., Moscovice, L. R., … Cheney, D. L. (2010). Female chacma baboons form strong, equitable, and enduring social bonds. *Behavioral Ecology and Sociobiology, 64*(11), 1733–1747. doi:10.1007/s00265-010-0986-0

Silk, J. S., Morris, A. S., Kanaya, T., & Steinberg, L. (2003). Psychological control and autonomy granting: Opposite ends of a continuum or distinct constructs? *Journal of Research on Adolescence, 13*, 113–128.

Silva, C., & Martins, M. (2003). Relations between children's invented spelling and the development of phonological awareness. *Educational Psychology, 23*, 3–16.

Simkin, P. (2013). *The birth partner: A complete guide to childbirth for dads, doulas, and all other labor companions.* Boston, MA: The Harvard Common Press.

Simmons, C. A. (2014). Playing with popular culture–an ethnography of children's sociodramatic play in the classroom. *Ethnography and Education*, 1–14.

Simon, C. A., & Wang, C. (2002). The impact of Americorps on volunteer participants. *Administration & Society, 34*, 522–540.

Simons, L. G., Simons, R. L., & Su, X. (2013). Consequences of corporal punishment among African Americans: The importance of context and outcome. *Journal of Youth and Adolescence, 42*(8), 1273–1285.

Simons, S. H. P., van Dijk, M., Anand, K. S., Roofhooft, D., van Lingen, R., & Tibboel, D. (2003). Do we still hurt newborn babies: A prospective study of procedural pain and analgesia in neonates. *Archives of Pediatrics & Adolescent Medicine, 157*, 1058–1064.

Simons-Morton, B. (2007). Parent involvement in novice teen driving: Rationale, evidence of effects, and potential for enhancing graduated driver licensing effectiveness. *Journal of Safety Research, 38*(2), 192–202.

Simons-Morton, B., & Chen, R. (2009). Peer and parent influences on school engagement among early adolescents. *Youth & Society, 41*(1), 3–25.

Simons-Morton, B. G., Hartos, J. L., & Leaf, W. A. (2002). Promoting parental management of teen driving. *Injury Prevention, 8*(Suppl. 2), ii24–ii31.

Simons-Morton, B. G., Hartos, J. L., Leaf, W. A., & Preusser, D. F. (2006). Increasing parent limits on novice young drivers: Cognitive mediation of the effect of persuasive messages. *Journal of Adolescent Research, 21*, 83–105.

Simons-Morton, B. G., Ouimet, M. C., & Catalano, R. F. (2008). Parenting and the young driver problem. *American Journal of Preventative Medicine, 35*(3, Suppl. 1), S294–S303.

Singer, J. L., & Singer, D. G. (1998). *Barney & Friends* as entertainment and education: Evaluating the quality and effectiveness of a television series for preschool children. In J. K. Asamen & G. L. Berry (Eds.), *Research paradigms, television and social behavior* (pp. 305–367). Thousand Oaks, CA: Sage.

Singerman, J., & Lee, L. (2008). Consistency of the Babinski reflex and its variants. *European Journal of Neurology, 15*, 960–964.

Singh, L., Nestor, S., Parikh, C., & Yull, A. (2009). Influences of infant- directed speech on early word recognition. *Infancy, 14*, 654–666.

Sinha, S. P., & Goel, Y. (2012). Impulsivity and selective attention among adolescents. *Journal of Psychosocial Research, 7*(1), 61.

Sinnott, J. D. (2014). *Adult development: Cognitive aspects of thriving close relationships.* New York, NY: Oxford University Press.

Sippola, L. K., Buchanan, C. M., & Kehoe, S. (2007). Correlates of false self in adolescent romantic relationships. *Journal of Clinical Child and Adolescent Psychology, 36*(4), 515–521.

Sirin, S. R., McCreary, D. R., & Mahalik, J. R. (2004). Differential reactions to men and women's gender role transgressions. *Journal of Men's Studies, 12*, 119–132.

Sirin, S. R., & Rogers-Sirin, L. (2005). Components of school engagement among African American adolescents. *Applied Developmental Science, 9*, 5–13.

Skinner, B. F. (1957). *Verbal behavior.* New York, NY: Appleton-Century-Crofts.

Skoe, E. E., & Gooden, A. (1993). Ethic of care and real-life moral dilemma content in male and female early adolescents. *Journal of Early Adolescence, 13*, 154–167.

Skoog, T., & Stattin, H. (2014). Why and under what contextual conditions do early-maturing girls develop problem behaviors? *Child Development Perspectives, 8*, 158–162.

Slater, A., Riddell, P., Quinn, P. C., Pascalis, O., Lee, K., & Kelly, D. J. (2010). Visual perception. In J. G. Bremner & T. D. Wachs (Eds.), *Wiley-Blackwell handbook of infant development, Volume 1: Basic research* (2nd ed., pp. 40–80). Chichester, UK: Wiley-Blackwell.

Slater, M. D. (2007). Reinforcing spirals: The mutual influence of media selectivity and media effects and their impact on individual behavior and social identity. *Communication Theory, 17*(3), 281–303.

Slobin, D. (1972, July). Children and language: They learn the same way around the world. *Psychology Today*, 71–76.

Slobin, D. I. (2014). The universal, the typological, and the particular in acquisition. In D. I. Slobin (Ed.), *The cross-linguistic study of language acquisition* (Vol. 5, pp. 1–40). New York, NY: Psychology Press.

Slonje, R., & Smith, P. K. (2008). Cyberbullying: Another main type of bullying? *Scandinavian Journal of Psychology, 49*(2), 147–154.

Small, M. (2001). *Kids: How biology and culture shape the way we raise young children.* New York, NY: Anchor.

Small, M. F. (1998). *Our babies, ourselves: How biology and culture shape the way we parent.* New York, NY: Anchor.

Small, M. F. (2005). The natural history of children. In Sharna Olfman (Ed.), *Childhood lost: How American culture is failing our kids* (pp. 3–17). Westport, CT: Praeger.

Smetana, J. G. (1983). Social-cognitive development: Domain distinctions and coordinations. *Developmental Review, 3*, 131–147.

Smetana, J. G. (2005). Adolescent-parent conflict: Resistance and subversion as developmental process. In L. Nucci (Ed.), *Conflict, contradiction, and contrarian elements in moral development and education* (pp. 69–91). Mahwah, NJ: Erlbaum.

Smetana, J. G. (2008). Conflicting views of conflict. *Monographs of the Society for Research in Child Development, 73*(2), 161–168.

Smetana, J. G. (2011). *Adolescents, families and social development: How children construct their worlds.* West Sussex, UK: Wiley.

Smink, F. R. E., van Hoeken, D., & Hoek, H. W. (2012). Epidemiology of eating disorders: Incidence, prevalence, and mortality rates. *Current Psychiatry Report, 14*, 404–414.

Smith, C. (1991). Sex and gender on prime time. *Journal of Homosexuality, 12*, 119–138.

Smith, C., & Denton, M. L. (2005). *Soul searching: The religious and spiritual lives of American teenagers.* New York, NY: Oxford University Press.

Smith, C., & Snell, P. (2010). *Souls in transition: The religious lives of emerging adults in America.* New York, NY: Oxford University Press.

Smith, W. B. (2011). *Youth leaving foster care: A developmental, relationship-based approach to practice.* New York, NY: Oxford University Press.

Smits, J., & Monden, C. (2011). Twinning across the developing world. *PLOS One.* Retrieved from http://journals.plos.org/plosone/article?id=10.1371/journal.pone.0 025239

Snarey, J. R. (1985). Cross-cultural universality of social moral development: A review of Kohlbergian research. *Psychological Bulletin, 97*, 202–232.

Snowden, J. M., Tilden, E. L., Snyder, J., Quigley, B., Caughey, A. B., & Cheng, Y. W. (2015). Planned out-of-hospital birth and birth outcomes. *New England Journal of Medicine, 373*(27), 2642–2653. doi:10.1056/NEJMsa1501738

Snyder, J., Cramer, A., & Afrank, J. (2005). The contributions of ineffective discipline and parental hostile attributions of child misbehavior to the development of conduct problems at home and school. *Developmental Psychology, 41*, 30–41.

Society for Assisted Reproductive Technology (SART). (2014). *Clinic summary report.* Retrieved from https://www.sartcorsonline.com/rptCSR_PublicMultYear.aspx?ClinicPKID=0

Society for Assisted Reproductive Technology (SART). (2017). National summary report. Retrieved from https://www.sartcorsonline.com/rptCSR_PublicMultYear.aspx?ClinicPKID=0

Soderstrom, M. (2007). Beyond babytalk: Reevaluating the nature and content of speech input to preverbal infants. *Developmental Review, 27*, 501–532.

Soken, N. H., & Pick, A. D. (1992). Intermodal perception of happy and angry expressive behaviors by seven-month-old infants. *Child Development, 63*, 787–795.

Sokol, R. J., Delaney-Black, V., & Nordstrom, B. (2003). Fetal alcohol spectrum disorder. *JAMA: Journal of the American Medical Association, 290*, 2996–2999.

Solomon, S. (1981, December 6). The controversy over infant formula. *The New York Times.* Retrieved from http://www.nytimes.com/1981/12/06/magazine/the-controversy-over-infant-formula.html?pagewanted=all

Somerville, L. H., Jones, R. M., & Casey, B. J. (2010). A time of change: Behavioral and neural correlates of adolescent sensitivity to appetitive and aversive environmental cues. *Brain and Cognition, 72*, 124–133.

Son'kin, V. D. (2007). Physical working capacity and energy supply of muscle function during postnatal human ontogeny. *Human Physiology, 33*(3), 326–341.

Sørensen, K., Mouritsen, A., Aksglaede, L., Hagen, C. P., & Morgensen, S. S. (2012). Recent secular trends in pubertal timing: Implications for evaluation and diagnosis of precocious puberty. *Hormone Research in Pediatrics, 77*(3), 137–145.

Sowell, E. R., Thompson, P. M., Holmes, C. J., Jernigan, T. I., & Toga, A. W. (1999). In vivo evidence for post-adolescence brain maturation in frontal and striatal regions. *Nature Neuroscience, 2*, 859–861.

Sowell, E. R., Trauner, D. A., Gamst, A., & Jernigan, T. L. (2002). Development of cortical and subcortical brain structures in childhood and adolescence: A structural MRI study. *Developmental Medicine & Child Neurolog, 44*, 4–16.

Spafford, C. S., & Grosser, G. S. (2005). *Dyslexia and reading difficulties* (2nd ed.). Boston, MA: Allyn & Bacon.

Spelke, E. S. (1979). Perceiving bimodally specified events in infancy. *Developmental Psychology, 5*, 626–636.

Spence, J., & Helmreich, R. (1978). *Masculinity and femininity: Their psychological dimensions, correlates, and antecedents.* Austin, TX: University of Texas Press.

Spence, M. J., & DeCasper, A. J. (1987). Prenatal experience with low-frequency maternal voice sounds influences neonatal perception of maternal voice samples. *Infant Behavior and Development, 10*, 133–142.

Spencer-Rodgers, J., Peng, K., & Wang, L. (2010). Dialecticism and the co-occurrence of positive and negative emotions across cultures. *Journal of Cross-Cultural Psychology, 41*(1), 109–115. doi:10.1177/0022022109349508

Spera, C. (2005). A review of the relationship among parenting practices, parenting styles, and adolescent school achievement. *Educational Psychology Review, 17*, 125–146.

Spitz, R. (1945). Hospitalism: An inquiry into the genesis of psychiatric conditions in early childhood. In A. Freud, H. Hartmann, & E. Kris (Eds.), *The psychoanalytic study of the child* (pp. 53–74). New York, NY: International Universities Press.

Spivak, A. L., & Howes, C. (2011). Social and relational factors in early education and prosocial actions of children of diverse ethnocultural communities. *Merrill-Palmer Quarterly, 57*, 1–24.

Spock, B., & Needlman, R. (2004). *Dr. Spock's baby and child care* (8th ed.). New York, NY: Pocket.

Srinath, B. K., Kumar, P., & Shah, P. S. (2016). Kangaroo care by fathers and mothers: Comparison of physiological and stress responses in preterm babies. *Journal of Perinatology, 36*, 401–404. doi:10.1038/jp.2015.196

Sroufe, L. A. (1996). *Emotional development: The organization of emotional life in the early years.* New York, NY: Cambridge University Press.

Sroufe, L. A., Egeland, B., Carlson, E. A., & Collins, W. A. (2005). *The development of the person: The Minnesota study of risk and adaptation from birth to adulthood.* New York, NY: Guilford.

St. James-Roberts, I., Bargn, J. G., Peter, B., Adams, D., & Hunt, S. (2003). Individual differences in responsivity to a neurobehavioural examination predict crying patterns of 1-week-old infants at home. *Developmental Medicine & Child Neurology, 45*, 400–407.

St. Louis, G. R., & Liem, J. H. (2005). Ego identity, ethnic identity, and psychosocial well-being of ethnic minority and majority college students. *Identity, 5*, 227–246.

St. Petersburg—USA Orphanage Research Team. (2008). The effects of early social-emotional and relationship experience on the development of young children. *Monographs of the Society for Research in Child Development, 73.*

Staff, J., Johnson, M. K., Patrick, M. E., & Schulenberg, J. E. (2014). The Great Recession and recent employment trends among secondary students in the United States. *Longitudinal and Life Course Studies, 5*, 173.

Staff, J., Mont'Alvao, A., & Mortimer, J. T. (2015). Children at work. In R. Lerner (Ed.), *Handbook of child psychology and developmental science* (pp. 345–364.). Hoboken, NJ: Wiley.

Staff, J., Mortimer, J. T., & Uggen, C. (2004). Work and leisure in adolescence. In R. M. Lerner & L. Steinberg (Eds.), *Handbook of adolescent psychology* (2nd ed., pp. 429–450). Hoboken, NJ: John Wiley & Sons.

Stafford, L. (2004). Communication competencies and sociocultural priorities of middle childhood. *Handbook of Family Communication*, 311–332.

Statistic Brain. (2014). Youth sports statistics. Retrieved from http://www.statisticbrain.com/youth-sports-statistics/

Statistics Canada. (2012). 2011 General Social Survey: Overview of Families in Canada – Selected Tables on Families in Canada. Catalogue no. 89-650_X – no. 001.

Steele, J. R. (2002). Teens and movies: Something to do, plenty to learn. In J. D. Brown, J. R. Steele, & K. Walsh-Childers (Eds.), *Sexual teens, sexual media: Investigating media's influence on adolescent sexuality* (pp. 227–252). Mahwah, NJ: Erlbaum.

Steele, J. R. (2006). Media practice model. In J. J. Arnett (Ed.), *Encyclopedia of children, adolescents, and the media* (pp. 533–534). Thousand Oaks, CA: Sage.

Steele, J. R., & Brown, J. D. (1995). Adolescent room culture: Studying media in the context of everyday life. *Journal of Youth & Adolescence, 24*, 551–576.

Steele, R. G., Nesbitt-Daly, J. S., Daniel, R. C., & Forehand, R. (2005). Factor structure of the Parenting Scale in a low-income African American sample. *Journal of Child and Family Studies, 14*, 535–549.

Steinberg, L. (1996). *Beyond the classroom: Why school reform has failed and what parents need to do.* New York, NY: Simon & Schuster.

Steinberg, L. (2000, April). *We know some things: Parent–adolescent relations in retrospect and prospect.* Presidential Address: presented at the biennial meeting of the Society for Research on Adolescence, Chicago, IL.

Steinberg, L., & Levine, A. (1997). *You and your adolescent: A parents' guide for ages 10 to 20* (Rev. ed.). New York, NY: HarperCollins.

Steinhausen, H.-C., Boyadjieva, S., Griogoroiu-Serbanescue, M., & Neumarker, K.-J. (2003). The outcome of adolescent eating disorders: Findings from an international collaborative study. *European Child & Adolescent Psychiatry, 12*, i91–i98.

Stenberg, C. R., Campos, J. J., & Emde, R. N. (1983). The facial expression of anger in seven-month-old infants. *Child Development*, 178–184.

Stenström, A. (2014). *Teenage talk: From general characteristics to the use of pragmatic markers in a contrastive perspective.* London, UK: Palgrave Macmillan. doi:10.1057/9781137430380.0005

Stepick, A., Stepick, C. D., & Labissiere, Y. (2008). South Florida's immigrant youth and civic engagement: Major engagement: Minor differences. In L. A. Jensen & C. A. Flanagan (Eds.), *Immigrant civic engagement: New translation*, Special issue of *Applied Development Science, 12*(2), 57–65. doi:10.1080/10888690801997036

Stern, S. (2002). Sexual selves on the World Wide Web: Adolescent girls' home pages as sites for sexual self-expression. In J. D. Brown, J. R. Steele, & K. Walsh-Childers (Eds.), *Sexual teens, sexual media: Investigating media's influence on adolescent sexuality* (pp. 265–285). Mahwah, NJ: Erlbaum.

Sternberg, R. (1983). Components of human intelligence. *Cognition, 15*, 1–48.

Sternberg, R. (1988). *The triarchic mind: A new theory of human intelligence.* New York, NY: Viking Penguin.

Sternberg, R. J. (2002). Intelligence is not just inside the head: The theory of successful intelligence. In J. Aronson (Ed.), *Improving academic achievement* (pp. 227–244). San Diego, CA: Academic Press.

Sternberg, R. J. (2003). Our research program validating the triarchic theory of successful intelligence: Reply to Gottfredson. *Intelligence, 31*, 399–413.

Sternberg, R. J. (2004). Culture and intelligence. *American Psychologist, 59*, 325–338.

Sternberg, R. J. (2005). The triarchic theory of successful intelligence. In D. P. Flanagan & P. L. Harrison (Eds.), *Contemporary intellectual assessment: Theories, tests and issues* (pp. 103–119). New York, NY: Guilford Press.

Sternberg, R. J. (2007). Intelligence and culture. In S. Kitayama & D. Cohen (Eds.), *Handbook of cultural psychology* (pp. 547–568). New York, NY: Guilford.

Sternberg, R. J. (2010). Assessment of gifted students for identification purposes: New techniques for a new millennium. *Learning and Individual Differences, 20*, 327–336.

Sternberg, R. J., & Grigorenko, E. L. (Eds.). (2004). *Culture and competence.* Washington, DC: American Psychological Association.

Sternberg, R. J., & Nigro, C. (1980). Developmental patterns in the solution of verbal analogies. *Child Development, 51*, 27–38.

Stetler, B. (2013, November 11). Same time, same channel? TV woos kids who can't wait. *The New York Times*, pp. A1, B6.

Steur, F. B., Applefield, J. M., & Smith, R. (1971). Televised aggression and interpersonal aggression of preschool children. *Journal of Experimental Child Psychology, 11*, 442–447.

Stevens, R., Satwicz, T., & McCarthy, L. (2008). In-game, in-room, in-world: Reconnecting video game play to the rest of kids' lives. In K. Salen (Ed.), *The ecology of games: Connecting youth, games, and learning* (pp. 41–66). Cambridge, MA: The MIT Press.

Stevenson, H. C. (2004). Boys in men's clothing: Racial socialization and neighborhood safety as buffers to hypervulnerability in African American adolescent males. In N. Way & J. Y. Chu (Eds.), *Adolescent boys: Exploring diverse cultures of boyhood* (pp. 59–77). New York, NY: New York University Press.

Stevenson, H. W., Lee, S., & Mu, X. (2000). Successful achievement in mathematics: China and the United States. In C. F. M. van Lieshout & P. G. Heymans (Eds.), *Developing talent across the lifespan* (pp. 167–183). Philadelphia, PA: Psychology Press.

Stevenson, H. W., & Zusho, A. (2002). Adolescence in China and Japan: Adapting to a changing environment. In B. B. Brown, R. Larson, & T. S. Saraswathi (Eds.), *The world's youth: Adolescence in eight regions of the globe* (pp. 141–170). New York, NY: Cambridge University Press.

Stevens-Watkins, D., & Rostosky, S. (2010). Binge drinking in African American males from adolescence to young adulthood: The protective influence of religiosity, family connectedness, and close friends' substance use. *Substance Use & Misuse, 45*, 1435–1451.

Stiles, J., & Jernigan, T. L. (2010). The basics of brain development. *Neuropsychology Review, 20*(4), 327–348. doi:10.1007/s11065-010-9148-4

Stoll, B., Hansen, N. I., Adams-Chapman, I., Fanaroff, A. A., Hintz, S. R., Vohr, B.,… Human Development Neonatal Research Network. (2004). Neurodevelopmental and growth impairment among extremely low-birth-weight infants with neonatal infection. *JAMA, 292*, 2357–2365.

Stones, M. J., & Kozma, A. (1996). Activity, exercise, and behavior. In J. E. Birren & K. W. Schaie (Eds.), *Handbook of psychology and aging* (4th ed., pp. 338–352). San Diego, CA: Academic Press.

Stoolmiller, M., Gerrard, M., Sargent, J. D., Worth, K. A., & Gibbons, F. X. (2010). R-rated movie viewing, growth in sensation seeking and alcohol initiation: Reciprocal and moderation effects. *Prevention Science, 11*(1), 1–13.

Strang-Karlsson, S., Räikkönen, K., Pesonen, A.-K., Kajantie, E., Paavonen, J., Lahti, J.,… Andersson, S. (2008). Very low birth weight and behavioral symptoms of Attention Deficit Hyperactivity Disorder in young adulthood: The Helsinki Study of very-low-birth-weight adults. *American Journal of Psychiatry, 165*, 1345–1353.

Strasburger, V. (2006). Super peer. In J. J. Arnett (Ed.), *Encyclopedia of children, adolescents, and the media* (pp. 789–790). Thousand Oaks, CA: Sage.

Straus, M. A., & Donnelly, D. A. (1994). *Beating the devil out of them: Corporal punishment in American families.* New York, NY: Lexington Books.

Striegel-Moore, R. H., & Franko, D. L. (2006). Adolescent eating disorders. In C. A. Essau (Ed.), *Child and adolescent psychopathology: Theoretical and clinical implications* (pp. 160–183). New York, NY: Routledge.

Suárez-Orozco, C. (2004). Formulating identity in a globalized world. In M. Suárez-Orozco & D. B. Qin-Hilliard (Eds.), *Globalization: Culture and education in the new millennium* (pp. 173–202). Berkeley, CA: University of California Press.

Suárez-Orozco, C. (2015). Migration between and within countries: Implications for families and acculturation. In L. A. Jensen (Ed.), *Oxford handbook of human development and culture: An interdisciplinary perspective* (pp. 43–60). New York, NY: Oxford University Press.

Subrahmanyam, K., Greenfield, P. M., & Tynes, B. (2004). Constructing sexuality and identity in an online teen chat room. *Journal of Applied Developmental Psychology, 25*, 651–666.

Subrahmanyam, K., Reich, S. M., Waechter, N., & Espinoza, G. (2008). Online and offline social networks: Use of social networking sites by emerging adults. *Journal of Applied Developmental Psychology, 29*, 420–433.

Suicide Awareness Voices of Education. (2016). Suicide facts. Retrieved from http://www.save.org/about-suicide/suicide-facts/

Sullivan, C., & Cottone, R. R. (2010). Emergent characteristics of effective cross-cultural research: A review of the literature. *Journal of Counseling and Development, 88*, 357–362.

Sullivan, J. L. (2003). Prevention to mother-to-child transmission of HIV—what next? *Journal of Acquired Immune Deficiency Syndrome* (Suppl. 1), *34*, S67–S72.

Sun, J., Dunne, M. P., Hou, X. Y., & Xu, A. Q. (2013). Educational stress among Chinese adolescents: Individual, family, school and peer influences. *Educational Review, 65*(3), 284–302.

Sun, T., Collura, R. V., Ruvolo, M., & Walsh, C. A. (2006). Genomic and evolutionary analyses of asymmetrically expressed genes in human fetal left and right cerebral cortex. *Cerebral Cortex, 16*(suppl.1), i18–i25. doi:10.1093/cercor/bhk026

Super, C., & Harkness, S. (2015). Charting infant development: Milestones along the way. In L. A. Jensen (Ed.), *The Oxford handbook of human development and culture: An interdisciplinary perspective. Oxford library of psychology* (pp. 79–93). New York, NY: Oxford University Press.

Super, C. M., & Harkness, S. (1986). The developmental niche: A conceptualization at the interface of child and culture. *International Journal of Behavioral Development, 9*(4), 545–569. doi:http://dx.doi.org/10.1177/016502548600900409

Super, C. M., & Harkness, S. (1993). The developmental niche: A conceptualization at the interface of child and culture. In R. A. Pierce & M. A. Black (Eds.), *Life-span development: A diversity reader* (pp. 61–77). Dubuque, IA: Kendall/Hunt.

Super, C. M., & Harkness, S. (2009). The developmental niche of the newborn in rural Kenya. In K. J. Nugent, B. J. Petrauskas, & T. B. Brazelton (Eds.), *The newborn as a person: Enabling healthy infant development worldwide* (pp. 85–97). Hoboken, NJ: John Wiley & Sons.

Super, C. M., & Harkness, S. (2010). Culture and infancy. In G. Bremner & T. D. Wachs (Eds.), *Blackwell handbook of infant development, Volume 1* (2nd ed., pp. 623–649). Oxford, UK: Blackwell.

Super, C. M., Harkness, S., van Tijen, N., van der Vlugt, E., Fintelman, M., & Dijkstra, J. (1996). The three R's of Dutch childrearing and the socialization of infant arousal. In S. Harkness & C. M. Super (Eds.), *Parents' cultural belief systems: Their origins, expressions and consequences* (pp. 447–466). New York, NY: Guilford Press.

Susman, E. J., & Rogol, A. (2004). Puberty and psychological development. In R. M. Lerner & L. Steinberg (Eds.), *Handbook of adolescent psychology* (2nd ed., pp. 15–44). Hoboken, NJ: Wiley & Sons.

Sussman, S., Pokhrel, P., Ashmore, R. D., & Brown, B. B. (2007). Adolescent peer group identification and characteristics: A review of the literature. *Addictive Behaviors, 32*(8), 1602–1627.

Svetlova, M., Nichols, S. R., & Brownell, C. A. (2010). Toddlers' prosocial behavior: From instrumental to empathic to altruistic helping. *Child Development, 81*(6), 1814–1827.

Swanson, H., Saez, L., & Gerber, M. (2004). Literacy and cognitive functioning in bilingual and nonbilingual children at or not at risk for reading disabilities. *Journal of Educational Psychology, 96*, 3–18.

Swanson, S. A., Crow, S. J., Le Grange, D., Swendsen, J., & Merikangas, K. R. (2011). Prevalence and correlates of eating disorders in adolescents: Results from the National Comorbidity Survey Replication—Adolescent Supplement. *Archives of General Psychiatry, 68*(7), 714–723. doi:10.1001/archgenpsychiatry.2011.22

Syed, M., & Azmitia, M. (2010). Narrative and ethnic identity exploration: A longitudinal account of emerging adults' ethnicity–related experiences. *Developmental Psychology, 46*, 208–219.

Syed, M., & Mitchell, L. L. (2013). Race, ethnicity, and emerging adulthood: Retrospect and prospects. *Emerging Adulthood, 1*, 83–95.

Syed, M., & Mitchell, L. J. (2015). How race and ethnicity shape emerging adulthood. In J. J. Arnett (Ed.), *Oxford handbook of emerging adulthood* (pp. 87–102). New York, NY: Oxford University Press.

Symons, D. K. (2001). A dyad-oriented approach to distress and mother–child relationship outcomes in the first 24 months. *Parenting: Science and Practice, 1*, 101–122.

Taber-Thomas, B., & Perez-Edgar, K. (2015). Emerging adulthood brain development. In J. J. Arnett (Ed.), *Oxford handbook of emerging adulthood* (pp. 126–141). New York, NY: Oxford University Press.

Taga, K. A., Markey, C. N., & Friedman, H. S. (2006). A longitudinal investigation of associations between boys' pubertal timing and adult behavioral health and well-being. *Journal of Youth and Adolescence, 35*(3), 401–411.

Taillon, G. (2004). *Remote control wars: The media battle for the hearts and minds of our youths.* Frederick, MD: Publish American Baltimore.

Tajfel, H., & Turner, J. (1979). An integrative theory of intergroup conflict. In W. G. Austin & S. Worchel (Eds.), *The social psychology of intergroup relations* (pp. 94–109). Monterey, CA: Brooks-Cole.

Takahashi, K. (1986). Examining the strange-situation procedure with Japanese mothers and 12-month-old infants. *Developmental Psychology, 22*, 265–270.

Takahashi, K., & Takeuchi, K. (2007). Japan. In J. J. Arnett, R. Ahmed, B. Nsamenang, T. S. Saraswathi, & R. Silbereisen (Eds.), *International encyclopedia of adolescence* (pp. 525–539). New York, NY: Routledge.

Takala, M. (2006). The effects of reciprocal teaching on reading comprehension in mainstream and special (SLI) education. *Scandinavian Journal of Educational Research, 50*(5), 559–576. doi:10.1080/00313830600953824

Talbani, A., & Hasanali, P. (2000). Adolescent females between tradition and modernity: Gender role socialization in south Asian immigrant families. *Journal of Adolescence, 23*, 615–627.

Tamaru, S., Kikuchi, A., Takagi, K., Wakamatsu, M., Ono, K., Horikoshi, T., … Nakamura, T. (2011). Neurodevelopmental outcomes of very low birth weight and extremely low birth weight infants at 18 months of corrected age associated with prenatal risk factors. *Early Human Development, 87*, 55–59.

Tamis-LeMonda C. S., Way, N., Hughes, D., Yoshikawa, H., Kalman, R. K., & Niwa, E. Y. (2008). Parents' goals for children: The dynamic coexistence of individualism and collectivism in cultures and individuals. *Social Development, 17*(1), 183–209.

Tan, A. S., Tan, G., & Gibson, T. (2003). Socialization effects of American television on international audiences. In G. M. Elasmar (Ed.), *The impact of international television: A paradigm shift* (pp. 29–38). Mahwah, NJ: Lawrence Erlbaum.

Tanaka, H., & Seals, D. R. (2003). Dynamic exercise performance in master athletes: Insight into the effects of primary human aging on physiological functional capacity. *Journal of Applied Physiology, 95*, 2152–2162.

Tanner, J. M. (1971). Sequence, tempo, and individual variation in the growth and development of boys and girls aged twelve to sixteen. *Daedalus, 100*, 907–930.

Tanon, F. (1994). *A cultural view on planning: The case of weaving in Ivory Coast.* Tilburg, Netherlands: Tilburg University Press.

Tardif, T., Fletcher, P., Liang, W., Zhang, Z., Kaciroti, N., & Marchman, V. A. (2008). Baby's first 10 words. *Developmental Psychology, 44*, 929–938. doi:10.1037/0012-1649.44.4.929

Tarrant, M., North, A. C., & Hargreaves, D. J. (2000). English and American adolescents' reasons for listening to music. *Psychology of Music, 28*, 166–173.

Taylor, A. (2005). It's for the rest of your life: The pragmatics of youth career decision making. *Youth & Society, 36*, 471–503.

Taylor, D. J., Bramoweth, A. D., Grieser, E. A., Tatum, J. I., & Roane, B. M. (2013). Epidemiology of insomnia in college students: Relationship with mental health, quality of life, and substance use difficulties. *Behavior Therapy, 44*, 339–348.

Taylor, J. M., Veloria, C. N., & Verba, M. C. (2007). Latina girls: "We're like sisters—most times!" In B. J. Leadbeater & N. Way (Eds.), *Urban girls revisited: Building strengths* (pp. 157–174). New York, NY: New York University Press.

Taylor, L. (2006). Magazines for adolescent boys. In J. J. Arnett (Ed.), *Encyclopedia of children, adolescents, and the media* (pp. 481–482). Thousand Oaks, CA: Sage.

Taylor, M., Carlson, S. M., Maring, B. L., Gerow, L., & Charley, C. M. (2004). The characteristics and correlates of fantasy in school-age children: Imaginary companions, impersonation, and social understanding. *Developmental Psychology, 40*(6), 1173. doi:http://dx.doi.org/10.1037/0012-1649.40.6.1173

Taylor, M., Hulette, A. C., & Dishion, T. J. (2010). Longitudinal outcomes of young high-risk adolescents with imaginary companions. *Developmental Psychology, 46*(6), 1632–1636. doi:http://dx.doi.org/10.1037/a0019815

Teachman, J. (2007). Military service and educational attainment in the all-volunteer era. *Sociology of Education, 80*(4), 359–374.

Teachman, J. D., & Tedrow, L. (2008). Divorce, race, and military service: More than equal pay and equal opportunity. *Journal of Marriage and Family, 70*(4), 1030–1044.

Telama, R., Yang, X., Viikari, J., Välimäki, I., Wanne, O., & Raitakari, O. (2005). Physical activity from childhood to adulthood: A 21-year tracking study. *American Journal of Preventative Medicine, 28*, 267–273.

Tennant, I. A., Barnett, A. T., Thompson, D. S., Kips, J., Boyne, M. S., Chung, E. E., … Forrester, T. E. (2014). Impaired cardiovascular structure and function in adult survivors of severe acute malnutrition. *Hypertension, 64*, 664–671. doi:10.1161/HYPERTENSIONAHA.114.03230

Terman, L. (1916). *The measurement of intelligence.* Boston, MA: Houghton Mifflin.

Terry, W. S. (2003). *Learning and memory* (2nd ed.). Boston, MA: Allyn & Bacon.

Terry-McElrath, Y. M., Wakefield, M. A., Emery, S., Saffer, H., Szczypka, G., O'Malley, P. M., … Flay, B. R. (2007). State anti-tobacco advertising and smoking outcomes by gender and race/ethnicity. *Ethnicity & Health, 12*(4), 339–362.

Terzian, M. A., Moore, K. A., & Constance, N. (2014). Transitioning to adulthood: The role of supportive relationships and regular religious involvement. *Child Trends, 14*, 1–10.

Teti, D. M., Sakin, K., Kucera, E., Corns, K. M., & Eiden, R. D. (1996). And baby makes four: Predictors of attachment security among preschool-aged first-borns during the transition to sibling-hood. *Child Development, 68*, 579–596.

Thach, B. T. (2009). Does swaddling decrease or increase the risk for Sudden Infant Death Syndrome? *Journal of Pediatrics, 155*, 461–462.

Thacher, P. V. (2008). University students and the "all nighter": Correlates and patterns of students' engagement in a single night of total sleep deprivation. *Behavioral Sleep Medicine, 6*, 16–31.

Thacker, S. B., & Stroup, D. E. (2003). Revisiting the use of the electronic fetal monitor. *Lancet, 361*, 445–446.

Thapar, A., Collishaw, S., Pine, D. S., & Thapar, A. K. (2012). Depression in adolescence. *Lancet, 379*(9820), 1056–1067.

Tharpe, A. M., & Ashmead, D. H. (2001). A longitudinal investigation of infant auditory sensitivity. *AJA: American Journal of Audiology, 10*, 104–112.

Theil, S. (2006). Internet use, HomeNet study. In J. J. Arnett (Ed.), *Encyclopedia of children, adolescents, and the media* (pp. 441–442). Thousand Oaks, CA: Sage.

Thelen, E. (2001). Dynamic mechanisms of change in early perceptual-motor development. In J. L. McClelland & R. S. Siegler (Eds.), *Mechanisms of cognitive development: Behavioral and neural perspectives* (pp. 161–184). Mahwah, NJ: Erlbaum.

Thiessen, E. D., Hill, E. A., & Saffran, J. R. (2005). Infant-directed speech facilitates word segmentation. *Infancy, 7*, 53–71.

Thijs, J., Verkuyten, M., & Helmond, P. (2010). A further examination of the big-fish-little-pond effect: Perceived position in class, class size, and gender comparisons. *Sociology of Education, 83*(4), 333–345.

Thomas, A., & Chess, S. (1977). *Temperament and development.* New York, NY: Brunner/Mazel.

Thomas, A., Chess, S., & Birch, H. G. (1968). *Temperament and behavior disorders in children.* New York, NY: New York University Press.

Thomas, H. J., Connor, J. P., & Scott, J. G. (2015). Integrating traditional bullying and cyberbullying: Challenges of definition and measurement in adolescents—A review. *Educational Psychology Review, 27*(1), 135–152.

Thompson, A. R., & Gregory, A. (2011). Examining the influence of perceived discrimination during African American adolescents' early years of high school. *Education and Urban Society, 43*(1), 3–25.

Thompson, R. A. (2006). The development of the person: Social understanding, relationships, conscience, self. In W. Damon & R. Lerner (Eds.), & N. Eisenberg (Vol. Ed.), *Handbook of child psychology: Vol. 3. Social, emotional and personality development* (6th ed., pp. 24–98). New York, NY: Wiley.

Thompson, R. A. (2012). Whither the preconventional child? Toward a life-span moral development theory. *Child Development Perspectives, 6*(4), 423–429. doi:10.1111/j.1750-8606.2012.00245.x

Thompson, R. A., & Goodvin, R. (2007). Taming the tempest in the teapot: Emotional regulation in toddlers. In C. A. Brownell & C. B. Kopp (Eds.), *Socioemotional development in the toddler years* (pp. 320–341). New York, NY: Guilford.

Thompson, S. K. (1975). Gender labels and early sex role development. *Child Development,* 339–347. doi:10.2307/1128126

Thorne, B. (1993). *Gender play: Girls and boys in school.* New Brunswick, NJ: Rutgers University Press.

Thrane, L. E., Hoyt, D. R., Whitbeck, L. B., & Yoder, K. A. (2006). Impact of family abuse on running away, deviance, and street victimization among homeless rural and urban youth. *Child Abuse & Neglect, 30*(10), 1117–1128.

Tiggemann, M., & Anesbury, T. (2000). Negative stereotyping of obesity in children: The role of controllability beliefs. *Journal of Applied Social Psychology, 30,* 1977–1993.

Tiggemann, M., & Miller, J. (2010). The Internet and adolescent girls' weight satisfaction and drive for thinness. *Sex Roles, 63,* 79–90.

Tiggemann, M., & Slater, A. (2013). NetGirls: The Internet, Facebook, and body image concern in adolescent girls. *International Journal of Eating Disorders, 46,* 630–633.

Tincoff, R., & Jusczyk, P. W. (1999). Some beginnings of word comprehension in 6-month-olds. *Psychological Science, 10*(2), 172–175. doi:10.1111/1467-9280.00127

Titzmann, P. F., Silbereisen, R. K., & Schmitt-Rodermund, E. (2007). Friendship homophily among diaspora migrant adolescents in Germany and Israel. *European Psychology, 12*(3), 181–195.

Tobach, E. (2004). Development of sex and gender: Biochemistry, physiology, and experience. In A. M. Paludi (Ed.), *Praeger guide to the psychology of gender* (pp. 240–270). Westport, CT: Praeger.

Tobin, D. D., Menon, M., Spatta, B. C., Hodges, E. V. E., & Perry, D. G. (2010). The intrapsychics of gender: A model of self-socialization. *Psychological Review, 117,* 601–622.

Tobin, J., Hsueh, Y., & Karasawa, M. (2009). *Preschool in three cultures revisited: China, Japan, and the United States.* Chicago, IL: University of Chicago Press.

Tokunaga, R. S. (2010). Following you home from school: A critical review and synthesis of research on cyberbullying victimization. *Computers in Human Behavior, 26*(3), 277–287. doi:10.1016/j.chb.2009.11.014

Tolman, D. L., Kim, J. L., Schooler, D., & Sorsoli, C. L. (2007). Rethinking the associations between television viewing and adolescent sexuality development: Bringing gender into focus. *Journal of Adolescent Health, 40*(1), e9–e16.

Tomasello, M. (1995). Joint attention as social cognition. In C. J. Moore & P. Dunham (Eds.), *Joint attention: Its origins and role in development* (pp. 103–130). Hillsdale, NJ: Lawrence Erlbaum Publishers.

Tomasello, M. (2003). *Constructing a language: A usage-based theory of language acquisition.* Cambridge, MA: Harvard University Press.

Tomasello, M. (2010). Human culture in evolutionary perspective. In M. J. Gelfand, C. Chiu, & Y. Hong, *Advances in culture and psychology* (Vol. 1, pp. 5–51). New York, NY: Oxford University Press.

Tomasello, M., & Rakoczy, H. (2003). What makes human cognition unique? From individual to shared to collective intentionality. *Mind and Language, 18,* 121–147.

Tomblin, J. B., & Mueller, K. L. (2013). Language and genes. In *eLS.* Chichester, UK: John Wiley & Sons Ltd. Retrieved from http://www.els.net. doi:10.1002/9780470015902.a0006238.pub2

Torney-Purta, J. (1990). From attitudes and knowledge to schemata: Expanding the outcomes of political socialization research. In O. Ichilov (Ed.), *Political socialization, citizenship, education, and democracy* (pp. 98–115). New York: Columbia University Press.

Torney-Purta, J. (1992). Cognitive representations of the political system in adolescents: The continuum from pre-novice to expert. In H. Haste & J. Torney-Purta (Eds.), *New directions for child development: The development of political understanding* (Vol. 56, pp. 11–25). San Francisco, CA: Jossey-Bass.

Torney-Purta, J. (2004). Adolescents' political socialization in changing contexts: An international study in the spirit of Nevitt Sanford. *Political Psychology, 25,* 465–478.

Torney-Purta, J., Amadeo, J.-A., & Richardson, W. (2007). Civic service among youth in Chile, Denmark, England, and the United States. In A. Moore & M. Sherraden (Eds.), *Civic service worldwide: Impacts and inquiry* (pp. 95–132). Armonk, NY: M. E. Sharpe.

Tough, S., Clarke, M., & Cook, J. (2007). Fetal alcohol spectrum disorder prevention approaches among Canadian physicians by proportion of native/Aboriginal patients: Practices during the preconception and prenatal periods. *Maternal and Child Health Journal, 11,* 385–393.

Trahan, L. H., Stuebing, K. K., Fletcher, J. M., & Hiscock, M. (2014). The Flynn effect: A meta-analysis. *Psychological Bulletin, 140,* 1332.

Trainor, L. J., Austin, C. M., & Desjardins, R. N. (2000). Is infant-directed speech prosody a result of the vocal expression of emotion? *Psychological Science, 11,* 188–195.

Treatment for Adolescents with Depression Study (TADS) team, U.S. (2004). Fluoxetine, cognitive-behavioral therapy, and their combination for adolescents with depression: Treatment for Adolescents with Depression Study (TADS) randomized controlled trial. *JAMA: Journal of the American Medical Association, 29,* 807–820.

Treatment for Adolescents with Depression Study Team. (2007). Long-term effectiveness and safety outcomes. *Archives of General Psychiatry, 64,* 1132–1143.

Trehub, S. E. (2001). Musical predispositions in infancy. *Annals of the New York Academy of Sciences, 930,* 1–16.

Trehub, S. E., Thorpe, L. A., & Morrongiello, B. A. (1985). Infants' perception of melodies: Changes in a single tone. *Infant Behavior and Development, 8,* 213–223.

Tremblay, R. E. (2000). The development of aggressive behaviour during childhood: What have we learned in the past century? *International Journal of Behavioral Development, 24,* 129–141.

Tremblay, R. E. (2002). Prevention of injury by early socialization of aggressive behavior. *Injury Prevention, 8*(Suppl. IV), 17–21.

Tremblay, R. E., & Nagin, D. S. (2005). Developmental origins of physical aggression in humans. In R. E. Tremblay, W. W. Hartup, & J. Archer (Eds.), *Developmental origins of aggression* (pp. 83–106). New York, NY: Guilford Press.

Trinh, S. L., Ward, L. M., Day, K., Thomas, K., & Levin, D. (2014). Contributions of divergent peer and parent sexual messages to Asian American college students' sexual behaviors. *The Journal of Sex Research, 51,* 208–220.

Tronick, E. (2007). *The neurobehavioral and social-emotional development of infants and children.* New York, NY: W. W. Norton.

Troseth, G. L. (2003). Getting a clearer picture: Young children's understanding of a televised image. *Developmental Science, 6,* 247–253.

Troseth, G. L., & DeLoache, J. S. (1998). The medium can obscure the message: Young children's understanding of video. *Child Development, 69,* 950–965.

Trost, K. (2012). Norway. In J. J. Arnett (Ed.), *Sweden* (pp. 335–352). New York, NY: Taylor & Francis.

Truglio, R. T. (2007). Sesame workshop. In J. J. Arnett (Ed.), *Encyclopedia of children, adolescents, and the media* (pp. 749–750). Thousand Oaks, CA: Sage.

Trusty, J., Harris, C., & Morag, B. (1999). Lost talent: Predictors of the stability of educational expectation across adolescence. *Journal of Adolescent Research, 14,* 359–382.

Tse, L. (1995). Language brokering among Latino adolescents: Prevalence, attitudes, and school performance. *Hispanic Journal of Behavioral Sciences, 17*(2), 180–193. doi:10.1177/07399863950172003

Tse, L. (1996). Language brokering in linguistic minority communities: The case of Chinese- and Vietnamese-American students. *Bilingual Research Journal, 20*(3–4), 485–498. doi:10.1080/15235882.1996.10668640

Tseng, V. (2004). Family interdependence and academic adjustments in college: Youth from immigrant and U.S.-born families. *Child Development, 75,* 966–983.

Tudge, J. R. H., Doucet, F., Odero, D., Sperb, T. M., Piccinini, C. A., & Lopes, R. S. (2006). A window into different cultural worlds: Young children's everyday activities in the United States, Brazil, and Kenya. *Child Development, 77*, 1446–1469.

Tulving, E. (1983). *Elements of episodic memory*. Oxford, UK: Oxford University Press.

Turiel, E. (1983). *The development of social knowledge: Morality and convention*. Cambridge, UK: Cambridge University Press.

Turiel, E., Killen, M., & Helwig, C. C. (1987). Morality: Its structure, functions, and vagaries. In J. Kagan & S. Lamb (Eds.), *The emergence of morality in young children* (pp. 155–243). Chicago, IL: University of Chicago Press.

Turkheimer, E., Harden, K. P., D'Onofrio, B., & Gottesman, I. I. (2009). The Scarr-Rowe interaction between measured socioeconomic status and the heritability of cognitive ability. In K. McCartney & R. A. Weinberg (Eds.), *Experience and development: A festschrift in honor of Sandra Wood Scarr* (pp. 81–98). New York, NY: Psychology Press.

Turkle, S. (2011). *Alone together: Why we expect more from technology and less from each other*. New York, NY: Basic Books.

Twenge, J. M. (2001). Changes in women's assertiveness in response to status and roles: A cross-temporal meta-analysis, 1931–1993. *Journal of Personality and Social Psychology, 81*(1), 133–145. doi:http://dx.doi.org/10.1037/0022-3514.81.1.133

Twenge, J. M. (2006). *Generation me: Why today's young Americans are more confident, assertive, entitled—and more miserable than ever before*. New York, NY: Free Press.

Twisk, D. A. M., & Stacey, C. (2007). Trends in young driver risk and countermeasures in European countries. *Journal of Safety Research, 38*(2), 245–257.

Tyano, S., Keren, M., Herrman, H., & Cox, J. (2010). *The competent fetus*. New York, NY: Wiley.

Tyler, K. A., Hoyt, D. R., & Whitbeck, L. B. (2000). The effects of early sexual abuse on later sexual victimization among female homeless and runaway adolescents. *Journal of Interpersonal Violence, 15*, 235–250.

Tyler, K. A., & Johnson, K. A. (2006). Pathways in and out of substance use among homeless-emerging adults. *Journal of Adolescent Research, 21*(2), 133–157.

Tyler, K. A., Whitbeck, L. B., Hoyt, D. R., & Cauce, A. M. (2004). Risk factors for sexual victimization among male and female homeless and runaway youth. *Journal of Interpersonal Violence, 19*, 503–520.

Tynes, B., Garcia, E., Giang, M., & Coleman, N. (2010). The racial landscape of social network sites: Forging identity, community, and civic engagement. *I/S: A Journal of Law and Policy for the Information Society, 7*, 1–30.

Tyson, J. E., Parikh, N. A., Langer, J., Green, C., & Higgins, R. D. (2008). Intensive care for extreme prematurity—moving beyond gestational age. *New England Journal of Medicine, 358*(16), 1672–1681. doi:10.1056/NEJMoa073059

Uggen, C., & Blackstone, A. (2004). Sexual harassment as a gendered expression of power. *American Sociological Review, 69*, 64–92.

Umaña-Taylor, A. J. (2005). Ethnic identity and self-esteem: Examining the role of social context. *Journal of Adolescence, 27*, 139–146.

Umrigar, A., Banijee, M., & Tsien, F. (2014). Down syndrome (Trisomy 21). LSUHSC School of Medicine. Retrieved from http://www.medschool.lsuhsc.edu/genetics/down_syndrome.aspx

UNAIDS. (2010). UNAIDS report on the global AIDS epidemic. Retrieved from http://www.unaids.org/globalreport/documents/20101123_GlobalReport_full_en.pdf

UNAIDS. (2017). Leaders from around the world are all in to end the AIDS epidemic among adolescents. Retrieved from http://www.unaids.org/en/resources/presscentre/pressreleaseandstatementarchive/2015/february/20150217_pr_all-in

Underwood, M. K. (2003). *Social-aggression among girls*. New York, NY: Guilford Press.

UNESCO. (2003). *Education in a multilingual world*. Retrieved from: http://unesdoc.unesco.org/images/0012/001297/129728e.pdf

UNESCO (2014). Education: Total net enrollment, lower secondary school. Retrieved from http://data.uis.unesco.org/?ReportId=167.#

UNESCO. (2015). Street children. Retrieved from http://www.unesco.org/new/en/social-and-human-sciences/themes/fight-against-discrimination/education-of-children-in-need/street-children/

UNFPA. (2015). Annual report. Retrieved from http://www.unfpa.org/annual-report

Unger, R. K. (2007). Afterword: From inside and out: Reflecting on a feminist politics of gender in psychology. *Feminism & Psychology, 17*(4), 487–494.

UNICEF. (2011). Breastfeeding initiatives exchange. Retrieved from http://www.unicef.org/programme/breastfeeding/

UNICEF. (2011). *State of the world's children. Adolescence: An age of opportunity*. New York, NY: UNICEF.

UNICEF. (2013). Levels & trends in child mortality: Report 2013. Retrieved from http://www.childinfo.org/files/Child_Mortality_Report_2013.pdf

UNICEF. (2013). Progress toward global immunization goals, 2012: Summary presentation of key indicators. Retrieved from http://www.who.int/immunization/monitoring_surveillance/SlidesGlobalImmunization.pdf?ua=1

UNICEF. (2014). *Committing to child survival: A promise renewed*. New York, NY: Author.

UNICEF. (2014). *The state of the world's children in numbers*. New York, NY: Author.

UNICEF. (2015, October). Neonatal mortality. Retrieved from http://data.unicef.org/child-mortality/neonatal.html

UNICEF. (2016). State of the World's Children. Retrieved from https://www.unicef.org/sowc2016/

UNICEF. (2016). UNICEF Programme Report 2012–2016. Retrieved from https://www.unicef.org/education/files/03_Web_UNICEF1020_PBEA_Final_report_A4_web.pdf

United Nations. (2013). *World population ageing 2013*. New York, NY: Author

United Nations Department of Economic and Social Affairs. (2010). *The world's women 2010: Trends and statistics*. Retrieved from http://unstats.un.org/unsd/demographic/products/Worldswomen/WW_full%20report_color.pdf

United Nations Development Programme (UNDP). (2010). *Human development report*. New York, NY: Author.

United Nations Development Program. (2014). *Human development report*. New York, NY: Author.

United Nations Development Programme (UNDP). (2015). *Human development report*. New York, NY: Author.

United Nations Development Programme (UNDP). (2016). *Human development report*. New York, NY: Author.

Updegraff, K. A., McHale, S. M., Zeiders, K. H., Umaña-Taylor, A. J., Perez-Brena, N. J., Wheeler, L. A., & De Jesús, S. A. R. (2014). Mexican–American adolescents' gender role attitude development: The role of adolescents' gender and nativity and parents' gender role attitudes. *Journal of Youth and Adolescence, 43*, 2041–2053.

U.S. Bureau of the Census. (2010). *Statistical abstract of the United States*. Washington, DC: Author.

U.S. Bureau of the Census. (2011). *Current population survey and annual social and economic supplements*. Washington, DC: Author.

U.S. Census Bureau. (2014). *10 percent of grandparents live with a grandchild, Census Bureau reports* (USCB Publication No. CB14-194). Retrieved from http://www.census.gov/newsroom/press-releases/2014/cb14-194.html

U.S. Department of Defense. (2014). 2014 demographics profile of the military community. Retrieved from http://download.militaryonesource.mil/12038/MOS/Reports/2014-Demographics-Report.pdf

U.S. Department of Health and Human Services. (2016). Trends in teenage pregnancy and childbearing. Retrieved from http://www.hhs.gov/ash/oah/adolescent-health-topics/reproductive-health/teen-pregnancy/trends.html

U.S. Department of Health and Human Services, Children's Bureau, Child Welfare Information Gateway. (2016). Cycle of abuse. Retrieved from https://www.childwelfare.gov/topics/can/impact/long-term-consequences-of-child-abuse-and-neglect/abuse/

U.S. Department of Labor. (2012). Number of jobs held, labor market activity, and earnings growth among the youngest Baby Boomers: Results from a longitudinal survey summary. Economic News Release, Table 1. Retrieved from http://www.bls.gov/news.release/nlsoy.nro.htm

U.S. Department of Transportation. (1995). *The economic costs of motor vehicle crashes, Technical report 1994*. Washington, DC: National Highway Traffic Safety Administration.

U.S. Food and Drug Administration. (2014). *Antidepressant use in children, adolescents, and adults*. Retrieved from http://www.fda.gov/downloads/Drugs/DrugSafety/InformationbyDrugClass/UCM173233.pdf

U.S. National Library of Medicine. (2017). Newborn jaundice. Retrieved from https://medlineplus.gov/ency/article/001559.htm

Utter, J., Neumark-Sztainer, D., Wall, M., & Story, M. (2003). Reading magazine articles about dieting and associated weight control behaviors among adolescents. *Journal of Adolescent Health, 32*, 78–82.

Uusküla, A., Puur, A., Toompere, K., & DeHovitz, J. (2010). Trends in the epidemiology of bacterial sexually transmitted infections in eastern Europe, 1995–2005. *Sexually Transmitted Infections, 86*, 6–14.

Vaillancourt, T., & Hymel, S. (2006). Aggression and social status: The moderating roles of sex and peer-values characteristics. *Aggressive Behavior, 32*, 396–408.

Vaillancourt, T., Brendgen, M., Boivin, M., & Tremblay, R. E. (2003). A longitudinal confirmatory factor analysis of indirect and physical aggression: Evidence of two factors over time? *Child Development, 74*, 1628–1638.

Vainio, A. (2015). Finnish moral landscapes: A comparison of nonreligious, liberal religious, and conservative religious adolescents. In L. A. Jensen (Ed.), *Moral development in a global world: Research from a cultural-developmental perspective* (pp. 46–68). New York, NY: Cambridge University Press.

Vaish, A., Carpenter, M., & Tomasello, M. (2011). Young children's responses to guilt displays. *Developmental Psychology, 47*(5), 1248–1262. doi:10.1037/a0024462

Vaish, A., Missana, M., & Tomasello, M. (2011). Three-year-old children intervene in third-party moral transgressions. *British Journal of Developmental Psychology, 29*(1), 124–130. doi:10.1348/026151010X532888

Vaish, A., & Tomasello, M. (2014). The early ontogeny of human cooperation and morality. In M. Killen & J. G. Smetana (Eds.), *Handbook of moral development* (pp. 279–298). New York, NY: Psychology Press.

Valencia-Martín, J. L., Galán, I., & Rodríguez-Artalejo, F. (2007). Binge drinking in Madrid, Spain. *Alcoholism: Clinical and Experimental Research, 31*(10), 1723–1730.

Valentine, D., Williams, M., & Young, R. K. (2013). *Age-related factors in driving safety*. Austin, TX: Center for Transportation Research.

Valkenburg, P. M., & Peter, J. (2009). Social consequences of the Internet for adolescents. *Current Directions in Psychological Science, 18*, 1–5.

Valkenberg, P. M., & Peter, J. (2011). Online communication among adolescents: An integrated model of its attractions, opportunities, and risks. *Journal of Adolescent Health, 48*(2), 121–127.

Vallejo, M. C., Ramesh, V., Phelps, A. L., & Sah, N. (2007). Epidural labor analgesia: Continuous infusion versus patient-controlled epidural analgesia with background infusion versus without a background infusion. *The Journal of Pain, 8*, 970–975.

van Beinum, F. J. (2008). Frames and babbling in hearing and deaf infants. In B. L. Davis & K. Zajdó (Eds.), *The syllable in speech production* (pp. 225–241). New York, NY: Lawrence Erlbaum.

Vandell, D. L., Burchinal, M. R., Belsky, J., Owen, M. T., Friedman, S. L., Clarke-Stewart, A.,... Weinraub, M. (2005). Early child care and children's development in the primary grades: Follow-up results from the NICHD Study of Early Child Care. Paper presented at the biennial meeting of the Society for Research in Child Development, Atlanta, GA.

Van de Poel, E. V., Hosseinpoor, A. R., Speybroek, N., Van Ourti, T., & Vega, J. (2008). Socioeconomic inequality in malnutrition in developing countries. *Bulletin of the World Health Organization, 86*, 282–291.

Van Doorn, M. D., Branje, S. J., VanderValk, I. E., De Goede, I. H., & Meeus, W. H. (2011). Longitudinal spillover effects of conflict resolution styles between adolescent-parent relationships and adolescent friendships. *Journal of Family Psychology, 25*, 157.

Van Hecke, A. V., Mundy, P. C., Acra, C. F., Block, J. J., Delgado, C. E. F., Parlade, M. V.,... Pomares, Y. B. (2007). Infant joint attention, temperament, and social competence in preschool children. *Child Development, 78*, 53–69.

van Hoof, A. (1999). The identity status approach: In need of fundamental revision and qualitative change. *Developmental Review, 19*(4), 622–647.

Van Horn, K. R., & Cunegatto, M. J. (2000). Interpersonal relationships in Brazilian adolescents. *International Journal of Behavioral Development, 24*, 199–203.

van IJzendoorn, M. H., & Hubbard, F. O. A. (2000). Are infant crying and maternal responsiveness during the first year related to infant–mother attachment at 15 months? *Attachment and Human Development, 2*, 371–391.

van IJzendoorn, M. H., & Kroonenberg, P. M. (1988). Cross-cultural patterns of attachment: A meta-analysis of the Strange Situation. *Child Development, 59*, 147–156.

Van Ijzendoorn, M. H., & Sagi-Schwartz, A. (2008). Cross-culturalpatterns of attachment: Universal and contextual dimensions. In J. Cassidy, Jude & P. Shaver (Eds.), *Handbook of attachment: Theory, research, and clinical applications* (2nd ed.) (pp. 880–905). New York: Guilford Press.

van IJzendoorn, M. H., Schuengel, C., & Bakermans-Kranenburg, M. J. (1999). Disorganized attachment in early childhood: Meta-analysis of precursors, concomitants and sequelae. *Development and Psychopathology, 11*, 225–249.

van IJzendoorn, M. H., Vereijken, C. M. J. L., Bakermans-Kraneburg, M. J., & Riksen-Walraven, J. M. (2004). Assessing attachment security with the Attachment Q Sort: Meta-analytic evidence for the validity of the Observer AQS. *Child Development, 75*, 1188–1213.

Van Noorden, T. H., Haselager, G. J., Cillessen, A. H., & Bukowski, W. M. (2015). Empathy and involvement in bullying in children and adolescents: A systematic review. *Journal of Youth and Adolescence, 44*, 637–657.

van Sleuwen, B. E., Engelberts, A. C., Boere-Boonekamp, M. M., Kuis, W., Schulpen, T. W. J., & L'Hoir, M. P. (2007). Swaddling: A systematic review. *Pediatrics, 120*, e1097–e1106.

Varendi, H., Christensson, K., Porter, R. H., & Wineberg, J. (1998). Soothing effect of amniotic fluid smell in newborn infants. *Early Human Development, 51*, 47–55.

Varendi, H., Porter, R. H., & Winberg, J. (2002). The effect of labor on olfactory exposure learning with the first postnatal hour. *Behavioral Neuroscience, 116*, 206–211.

Vasquez, K., Keltner, D., Ebenbach, D. H., & Banaszynski, T. L. (2001). Cultural variation and similarity in moral rhetorics: Voices from the Philippines and the United States. *Journal of Cross-Cultural Research, 32*, 93–120.

Vasquez, M. J. T., & Fuentes, C. D. L. (1999). American-born Asian, African, Latina, and American Indian adolescent girls: Challenges and strengths. In N. B. Johnson, M. C. Roberts, & J. Worell (Eds.), *Beyond appearance: A new look at adolescent girls* (pp. 151–173). Washington, DC: American Psychological Association.

Vazsonyi, A. T., & Snider, J. B. (2008). Mentoring, competencies, and adjustment in adolescents: American part-time employment and European apprenticeships. *International Journal of Behavioral Development, 32*(1), 46–55.

Vedder, P., & Phinney, J. S. (2014). Identity formation in bicultural youth: A developmental perspective. In V. Benet-Martinez & Y. Hong (Eds.), *Oxford handbook of multicultural identity* (pp. 335–354). New York: Oxford University Press.

Veldhuizen, S., Wade, T. J., Cairney, J., Hay, J. A., & Faught, B. E. (2014). When and for whom are relative age effects important? Evidence from a simple test of cardiorespiratory fitness. *American Journal of Human Biology, 26*, 476–480.

Verkuyten, M. (2002). Multiculturalism among minority and majority adolescents in the Netherlands. *International Journal of Intercultural Relations, 26*, 91–108.

Verma, S., & Larson, R. (1999). Are adolescents more emotional? A study of daily emotions of middle class Indian adolescents. *Psychology and Developing Societies*, 11, 179–194.

Vicary, J. R., Klingaman, L. R., & Harkness, W. L. (1995). Risk factors associated with date rape and sexual assault of adolescent girls. Journal of Adolescence, 18, 289–306.

Vidyasagar, T. R. (2004). Neural underpinnings of dyslexia as a disorder of visuospatial attention. *Clinical and Experimental Optometry, 87*, 4–10.

Vig, S., Chinitz, S., & Shulman, L. (2005). Young children in foster care: Multiple vulnerabilities and complex service needs. *Infants and Young Children, 18*, 147–160.

Vigil, J. M., Geary, D. C., & Byrd-Craven, J. (2005). A life history assessment of early childhood sexual abuse in women. *Developmental Psychology, 41*(3), 553–561.

Vilette, B. (2002). Do young children grasp the inverse relationship between addition and subtraction? Evidence against early arithmetic. *Cognitive Development, 17*, 1365–1383.

Vincent, L. (2008). "Boys will be boys": Traditional Xhosa male circumcision, HIV and sexual socialization in contemporary South Africa. *Culture, Health, and Sexuality, 10*, 431–446.

Visher, E. B., Visher, J. S., & Pasley, K. (2003). Remarriage families and step-parenting. In F. Walsh (Ed.), *Normal family processes* (pp. 153–175). New York, NY: Guilford.

Vlaardingerbroek, J., van Goudoever, J. B., & van den Akker, C. H. P. (2009). Initial nutritional management of the preterm infant. *Early Human Development, 85*, 691–695.

Volk, A., Craif, W., Boyce, W., & King, M. (2006). Adolescent risk correlates of bullying and different types of victimization. *International Journal of Adolescent Medicine and Health, 18*(4), 575–586.

Volling, B. L. (2012). Family transitions following the birth of a sibling: An empirical review of changes in the firstborn's adjustment. *Psychological Bulletin, 138*(3), 497–528. doi:10.1037/a0026921

Vondra, J. L., & Barnett, D. (Eds.). (1999). Atypical attachment in infancy and early childhood among children at developmental risk. *Monographs of the Society for Research in Child Development, 64*(3, Serial No. 258).

von Salisch, M., Oppl, C., & Kristen, A. (2006). What attracts children? In P. Vordere & J. Bryant (Eds.), *Playing video games: Motives, responses, and consequences* (pp. 147–163). Mahwah, NJ: Lawrence Erlbaum.

Votta, E., & Manion, I. (2004). Suicide, high-risk behaviors, and coping style in homeless adolescent males' adjustment. *Journal of Adolescent Health, 34*, 237–243.

Vouloumanos, A., Hauser, M. D., Werker, J. F., & Martin, A. (2010). The tuning of human neonates' preference for speech. *Child Development, 81*(2), 517–527. doi:10.1111/j.1467-8624.2009.01412.x

Vouloumanos, A., & Werker, J. F. (2004). Tuned to the signal: The privileged status of speech for young infants. *Developmental Science, 7*, 270–276.

Voydanoff, P. (2004). The effects of work demands and resources on work-to-family conflict and facilitation. *Journal of Marriage and Family, 66*, 398–412.

Vukman, K. B. (2005). Developmental differences in metacognition and their connections with cognitive development in adulthood. *Journal of Adult Development, 12*(4), 211–221.

Wagner, C. L., & Greer, F. R. (2008). Prevention of rickets and vitamin D deficiency in infants, children, and adolescents. *Pediatrics, 122*(5), 1142–1152.

Wahlstrom, K., Dretzke, B., Gordon, M., Peterson, K., Edwards, K., & Gdula, J. (2014). *Examining the impact of later school start times on the health and academic performance of high school students: A multi-site study*. Center for Applied Research and Educational Improvement. St Paul, MN: University of Minnesota.

Waizenhofer, R. N., Buchanan, C. M., & Jackson-Newsom, J. (2004). Mothers' and fathers' daily activities: Its sources and its links with adolescent adjustment. *Journal of Family Psychology, 18*, 348–360.

Walker, L. J. (1984). Sex differences in the development of moral reasoning. A critical review. *Child Development, 51*, 131–139.

Walker, L. J. (1989). A longitudinal study of moral reasoning. *Child Development, 60*, 157–166.

Walker, L. J. (2013). Exemplars' moral behavior is self-regarding. *New Directions for Child and Adolescent Development, 142*, 27–40.

Walker, L. J., Pitts, R. C., Hennig, K. H., & Matsuba, M. K. (1999). Reasoning about morality and real-life moral problems. In M. Killen & D. Hart (Eds.), *Morality in everyday life* (pp. 371–407). New York, NY: Cambridge University Press.

Wallace, J. M., Yamaguchi, R., Bachman, J. G., O'Malley, P. M., Schulenberg, J. E., & Johnston, L. D. (2007). Religiosity and adolescent substance use: The role of individual and contextual influences. *Social Problems, 54*(2), 308–327.

Wallerstein, J. S., & Johnson-Reitz, K. (2004). Communication in divorced and single-parent families. In A. L. Vangelisti (Ed.), *Handbook of family communication* (pp. 197–214). Mahwah, NJ: Erlbaum.

Walshaw, C.A. (2010). Are we getting the best from breastfeeding? *Acta Paediatria, 99*, 1292–1297.

Wang, Q. (2013). *The autobiographical self in time and culture*. New York, NY: Oxford University Press. doi:10.1093/acprof:oso/9780199737833.001.0001

Wang, S., Baillargeon, R., & Paterson, S. (2005). Detecting continuity violations in infancy: A new account and new evidence from covering and tube events. *Cognition, 95*, 129–173.

Wang, Y., & Fong, V. L. (2009). Little emperors and the 4:2:1 generation: China's singletons. Journal of the American Academy of Child & Adolescent Psychiatry, 48, 1137–1139.

Wang, S., & Tamis-LeMonda C. (2003). Do childrearing values in Taiwan and the United States reflect cultural values of collectivism and individualism? *Journal of Cross-Cultural Psychology, 34*, 629–642.

Wang, W., Vaillancourt, T., Brittain, H. L., McDougall, P., Krygsman, A., Smith, D., … Hymel, S. (2014). School climate, peer victimization, and academic achievement: Results from a multi-informant study. *School Psychology Quarterly, 29*, 360.

Wang, Y., Wang, X., Kong, Y., Zhang, J. H., & Zeng, Q. (2010). The great Chinese famine leads to shorter and overweight females in Chongqing Chinese population after 50 years. *Obesity, 18*, 588–592.

Ward, L. M. (1995). Talking about sex: Common themes about sexuality in the prime-time television programs children and adolescents view most. *Journal of Youth & Adolescence, 24*, 595–616.

Warneken, F., & Tomasello, M. (2006). Altruistic helping in human infants and young chimpanzees. *Science, 311*(5765), 1301–1303. doi:10.1126/science.1121448

Warneken, F., & Tomasello, M. (2007). Helping and cooperation at 14 months of age. *Infancy, 11*(3), 271–294. doi:10.1080/15250000701310389

Warnock, F. F., Castral, T. C., Brant, R., Sekilian, M., Leite, A. M., De La Presa Owens, S., & Schochi, C. G. S. (2010). Brief report: Maternal Kangaroo Care for neonatal pain relief: A systematic narrative review. *Journal of Pediatric Psychology, 35*, 975–984.

Warnock, F., & Sandrin, D. (2004). Comprehensive description of newborn distress behavior in response to acute pain (newborn male circumcision). *Pain, 107*, 242–255.

Warren, S. L., & Simmens, S. J. (2005). Predicting toddler anxiety/depressive symptoms: Effects of caregiver sensitivity of temperamentally vulnerable children. *Infant Mental Health Journal, 26*, 40–55.

Waterman, A. S. (1992). Identity as an aspect of optimal functioning. In G. R. Adams, T. P. Gullotta, & R. Montemayor (Eds.), *Adolescent identity formation* (Vol. 4, pp. 50–72). Newbury Park, CA: Sage.

Waterman, A. S. (1999). Issues of identity formation revisited: United States and the Netherlands. *Developmental Review, 19*, 462–479.

Waterman, A. S. (2007). Doing well: The relationship of identity status to three conceptions of well-being. *Identity, 7*(4), 289–307.

Watkin, P. M. (2011). The value of the neonatal hearing screen. *Paediatrics and Child Health, 21*, 37–41.

Watson, P. (2014). *The age of atheists: How we have sought to live since the death of God*. New York, NY: Simon and Schuster.

Waxman, S. R. (2003). Links between object categorization and naming: Origins and emergence in human infants. In D. H. Rakison & L. M. Oakes (Eds.), *Early category and concept development: Making sense of the blooming, buzzing confusion* (pp. 193–209). New York, NY: Oxford University Press.

Waxman, S. R., & Lidz, J. L. (2006). Early word learning. In W. Damon & R. Lerner (Eds.), & D. Kuhn & R. Siegler (Vol. Eds.), *Handbook of child psychology: Vol. 2. Cognition, perception and language* (6th ed., pp. 299–335). New York, NY: Wiley.

Way, N. (2004). Intimacy, desire, and distrust in the friendships of adolescent boys. In N. Way & J. Y. Chu (Eds.), *Adolescent boys: Exploring diverse cultures of boyhood* (pp. 167–196). New York, NY: New York University Press.

Way, N. (2006). The cultural practice of close friendships among urban adolescents in the United States. In S. Chen, D. C. French, & B. H. Schneider (Eds.), *Peer relationships in cultural context* (pp. 403–425). New York, NY: Cambridge University Press.

Way, N. (2011). *Deep secrets: Boys' friendships and the crisis of connection*. Cambridge, MA: Harvard University Press.

Way, N., Reddy, R., & Rhodes, J. (2007). Students' perceptions of school climate during the middle school years: Associations with trajectories of psychological and behavioral adjustment. *American Journal of Community Psychology, 40*(3–4), 194–213.

Weaver, S. E., & Coleman, M. (2010). Caught in the middle: Mothers in stepfamilies. *Journal of Social and Personal Relationships, 27*, 305–326.

Weber, D. (2006). *Media use by infants and toddlers: A potential for play*. New York, NY: Oxford University Press.

Webster-Stratton, C., Reid, M. J., & Hammond, M. (2001). Preventing conduct problems, promoting social competence: A parent and teacher training partnership in Head Start. *Journal of Clinical Child Psychology, 30*(3), 283–302. doi:10.1207/S15374424JCCP3003_2

Wechsler, D. (2014). *Wechsler intelligence scale for children: Administration and scoring manual* (5th ed.). Bloomington, MN: Pearson.

Wechsler, D. (2014). *Wechsler intelligence scale for children: Administration and scoring manual supplement* (5th ed.). Bloomington, MN: Pearson.

Wechsler, D. (2014). *Wechsler intelligence scale for children: Technical and interpretive manual* (5th ed.). Bloomington, MN: Pearson.

Weekley, A. (2007). Placentophagia: Benefits of eating the placenta. Retrieved from http://www.associatedcontent.com/article/289824/placentophagia_benefits_of_eating_the.html?cat=51

Weichold, K., Silbereisen, R. K., & Schmitt-Rodermund, E. (2003). Short-term and long-term consequences of early vs. late physical maturation in adolescents. In C. Haywood (Ed.), *Puberty and psychopathology* (pp. 241–276). Cambridge, MA: Cambridge University Press.

Weinberg, R. A. (2004). The infant and the family in the twenty-first century. *Journal of the American Academy of Child & Adolescent Psychiatry, 43*, 115–116.

Weinberg, R. A., Scarr, S., & Waldman, I. D. (1992). The Minnesota transracial adoption study: A follow-up of IQ test performance. *Intelligence, 44*, 98–104.

Weiner, I. B. (1992). *Psychological disturbance in adolescence* (2nd ed.). New York, NY: Wiley.

Weinfeld, N. S., Whaley, G. J. L., & Egeland, B. (2004). Continuity, discontinuity, and coherence in attachment from infancy to late adolescence: Sequelae of organization and disorganization. *Attachment and Human Development, 6*, 73–97.

Weir, K. F., & Jose, P. E. (2010). The perception of false self scale for adolescents: Reliability, validity, and longitudinal relationships with depressive and anxious symptoms. *British Journal of Developmental Psychology, 28*(2), 393–411.

Weisgram, E. S., Bigler, R. S., & Liben, L. S. (2010). Gender, values, and occupational interests among children, adolescents, and adults. *Child Development, 81*(3), 778–796.

Weisleder, A., & Fernald, A. (2013). Talking to children matters early language experience strengthens processing and builds vocabulary. *Psychological Science, 24*(11), 2143–2152.

Weisner, T. S. (1996). The 5 to 7 transition as an ecocultural project. In A. J. Sameroff & M. M. Haith, *The five to seven year shift: The age of reason and responsibility* (pp. 295–326). Chicago, IL: University of Chicago Press.

Weisskirch, R. S., Kim, S. Y., Zamboanga, B. L., Schwartz, S. J., Bersamin, M., & Umana-Taylor, A. J. (2011). Cultural influences for college student language brokers. *Cultural Diversity and Ethnic*

*Minority Psychology, 17*(1), 43–51. doi:10.1037/a0021665

Wellman, H. M. (1990). *The child's theory of mind.* Cambridge, MA: MIT Press.

Wendland-Carro, J., Piccinini, C. A., & Millar, W. S. (1999). The role of an early intervention on enhancing the quality of mother–infant interaction. *Child Development, 70*, 713–731.

Wentzel, K. R. (2003). Sociometric status and adjustment in middle school: A longitudinal study. *The Journal of Early Adolescence, 23*, 5–38.

Werner, B., & Bodin, L. (2007). Obesity in Swedish school children is increasing in both prevalence and severity. *Journal of Adolescent Health, 41*, 536–543.

Werner, E., Dawson, G., Osterling, J., & Dinno, N. (2000). Recognition of autism spectrum disorder before one year of age. A retrospective study based on home videotapes. *Journal of Autism & Developmental Disorders, 30*, 157–162.

Werner, E. E., & Smith, R. S. (1982). *Vulnerable but invincible: A study of resilient children.* New York, NY: McGraw-Hill.

Werner, E. E., & Smith, R. S. (1992). *Overcoming the odds: High-risk children from birth to adulthood.* Ithaca, NY: Cornell University Press.

Werner, E. E., & Smith, R. S. (2001). *Journeys from childhood to midlife: Risk, resilience, and recovery.* Ithaca, NY: Cornell University Press.

Werner, L. A., & Marean, G. C. (1996). *Human auditory development.* Boulder, CO: Westview Press.

Westling, E., Andrews, J. A., Hampson, S. E., & Peterson, M. (2008). Pubertal timing and substance use: The effects of gender, parental monitoring and deviant peers. *Journal of Adolescent Health, 42*, 555–563.

Westoff, C. F. (2003). *Trends in marriage and early childbearing in developing countries.* DHS Comparative Reports No. 5. Calverton, MD: ORC Macro.

Whaley, A. L., & Noel, L. (2011). Sociocultural theories, academic achievement, and African American adolescents in a multicultural context: A review of the cultural incompatibility perspective. *Social Psychology of Education, 14*(2), 149–168.

Whaley, D. E. (2007). A life span developmental approach to studying sport and exercise behavior. In G. Tenenbaum & R. C. Eklund (Eds.), *Handbook of sport psychology* (3rd ed., pp. 645–661). Hoboken, NJ: Wiley.

Whitaker, R. C., Wright, J. A., Pepe, M. S., Seidel, K. D., & Dietz, W. H. (1997). Predicting obesity in young adulthood from childhood and parental obesity. *The New England Journal of Medicine, 337*, 869–873.

Whitbeck, L. B. (2009). *Mental health and emerging adulthood among homeless young people.* New York, NY: Psychology Press.

Whitbeck, L. B., Johnson, K. D., Hoyt, D. R., & Cauce, A. M. (2004). Mental disorder and comorbidity among runaway and homeless adolescents. *Journal of Adolescent Health, 35*, 132–140.

The White House. (2011). White House to launch "Digital Promise" initiative. Retrieved from http://www.whitehouse.gov/the-press-office/2011/09/16/white-house-launch-digital-promise-initiative

The White House Initiative on Asian Americans and Pacific Islanders. (2016). Issues and facts: Critical issues facing Asian Americans and Pacific Islanders. Retrieved from https://www.whitehouse.gov/administration/eop/aapi/data/critical-issues

Whiting, B. B., & Edwards, C. P. (1988). *Children of different worlds: The formation of social behavior.* Cambridge, MA: Harvard University Press.

Whitty, M. (2002). Possible selves: An exploration of utility of a narrative approach. *Identity, 2*, 211–228.

Whorf, B. (1939/1956). The relation of habitual thought and behavior to language. In J. B. Carroll (Ed.), *Language, thought & reality: Selected writings by Benjamin Lee Whorf.* Cambridge, MA: MIT Press.

Whyman, M., Lemmon, M., & Treachman, J. (2011). Non-combat military service in the United States and its effects on depressive symptoms among men. *Social Science Research, 40*(2), 695–703.

Wichstrøm, L. (1999). The emergence of gender difference in depressed mood during adolescence: The role of intensified gender socialization. *Developmental Psychology, 35*, 232–245.

Wigfield, A., Eccles, J. S., Yoon, K. S., Harold, R. D., Arbreton, A. J., Freedman-Doan, C., & Blumenfeld, P. C. (1997). Changes in children's competence beliefs and subjective task values across the elementary school years: A three-year study. *Journal of Educational Psychology, 89*, 451–469.

Wigger, J. B., Paxson, K., & Ryan, L. (2013). What do invisible friends know? Imaginary companions, God, and theory of mind. *International Journal for the Psychology of Religion, 23*, 2–14.

Willford, J. A., Richardson, G. A., Leech, S. L., & Day, N. L. (2004). Verbal and visuospatial learning and memory function in children with moderate prenatal alcohol exposure. *Alcoholism: Clinical and Experimental Research, 28*(3), 497–507.

Williams, A. F., & Ferguson, S. A. (2002). Rationale for graduated licensing and the risks it should address. *Injury Prevention, 8*(Suppl. 2), ii9–ii16.

Williams, A. F., Tefft, B. C., & Grabowski, J. G. (2012). Graduated driver licensing research, 2010–present. *Journal of Safety Research, 43*(3), 195–203.

Williams, A. L., Khattak, A. Z., Garza, C. N., & Lasky, R. E. (2009). The behavioral pain response to heelstick in preterm neonates studied longitudinally: Description, development, determinants, and components. *Early Human Development, 85*, 369–374.

Williams, D. R. (2005). The health of U.S. racial and ethnic populations. *Journals of Gerontology, 60B*(Special Issue II), 53–62.

Willinger, M., Ko, C.-W., Hoffman, J. J., Kessler, R. C., & Corwin, M. J. (2003). Trends in infant bed sharing in the United States. *Archives of Pediatrics and Adolescent Medicine, 157*, 43–49.

Wilson, E. O. (2012). *The social conquest of earth.* New York, NY: W.W. Norton.

Wilson, J. Q., & Herrnstein, R. J. (1985). *Crime and human nature.* New York, NY: Simon and Schuster.

Winsler, A., Fernyhough, C., & Montero, I. (Eds.). (2009). *Private speech, executive functioning, and the development of verbal self-regulation.* Cambridge, UK: Cambridge University Press.

Wolak, J., Mitchell, K. J., & Finkelhor, D. (2007). Does online harassment constitute bullying? An exploration of online harassment by known peers and online-only contacts. *Journal of Adolescent Health, 41*(Suppl. 6), S51–S58.

Wolf, J. B. (2007). Is breast really best? Risk and total motherhood in the national breastfeeding awareness campaign. *Journal of Health Politics, Policy and Law, 32*, 595–63.

Wong, S. S., Zhou, B., Goebert, D., & Hishinuma, E. S. (2013). The risk of adolescent suicide across patterns of drug use: A nationally representative study of high school students in the United States from 1999 to 2009. *Social Psychiatry and Psychiatric Epidemiology, 48*, 1611–1620.

Wood, P., & Clay, W. (1996). Perceived structural barriers and academic performance among American Indian high school students. *Youth & Society, 28*, 40–61.

Wood, R. M., & Gustafson, G. E. (2001). Infant crying and adults' anticipated caregiving responses: Acoustic and contextual influences. *Child Development, 72*, 1287–1300.

Wood, W., & Eagly, A. H. (2012). Biosocial construction of sex differences and similarities in behavior. *Advances in Experimental Social Psychology, 46*, 55–123. doi:10.1016/B978-0-12-394281-4.00002-7

Woodhall, S. C., Lehtinen, M., Verho, T., Huhtala, H., Hokkanen, M., & Kosunen, E. (2007). Anticipated acceptance of HPV vaccination at the baseline of implementation: A survey of parental and adolescent knowledge and attitudes in Finland. *Journal of Adolescent Health, 40*(5), 466–469.

Woodward, A. L., & Markman, E. M. (1998). Early word learning. In W. Damon (Ed.), & D. Kuhn & R. S. Siegler (Vol. Eds.), *Handbook of child psychology: Vol. 2. Cognition, perception and language* (5th ed., pp. 371–420). New York, NY: Wiley.

Wooten, M. A. (1992). The effects of heavy metal music on affect shifts of adolescents in an inpatient psychiatric setting. *Music Therapy Perspectives, 10*, 93–98.

World Bank. (2009). Information and communications for development 2009: Extending research and increasing impact. Retrieved from http://www.worldbank.org

World Bank. (2011). India's undernourished children: A call for action. Retrieved from http://web.worldbank.org/WEBSITE/EXTERNAL/COUNTRIES/SOUTHASIAEXT/0,,contentMDK:20916955~pagePK:146736~piPK:146830~theSitePK:223547,00.html

World Health Organization (WHO). (2000). WHO Global Data Bank on Breastfeeding. Retrieved from http://www.who.int/nut/db_bfd.htm

World Health Organization (WHO). (2008). *Worldwide prevalence of anaemia.* Geneva, Switzerland: Author.

World Health Organization (WHO). (2009). *Department of making pregnancy safer: Annual report.* Geneva, Switzerland: Author.

World Health Organization (WHO). (2010). *Towards universal access: Scaling up priority HIV/AIDS interventions in the health sector.* Geneva, Switzerland: Author.

World Health Organization (WHO). (2010). *World Health Statistics 2010.* Geneva, Switzerland: Author.

World Health Organization (WHO). (2011). Cigarette consumption. Retrieved February 21, 2011, from http://www.who.int/tobacco/en/atlas8.pdf

World Health Organization (WHO). (2011) *Global status report on alcohol and health.* Geneva: WHO.

World Health Organization (WHO). (2013). *World malaria report.* Geneva, Switzerland: Author.

World Health Organization (WHO). (2014). *World health statistics.* Geneva, Switzerland: Author.

World Health Organization (WHO). (2015, April 10). Caesarean sections should only be performed when medically necessary. Retrieved from http://www.who.int/mediacentre/news/releases/2015/caesarean-sections/en/

World Health Organization. (2016). Joint child malnutrition estimates —Levels and trends (2016 edition). Retrieved from http://www.who.int/nutgrowthdb/jme_brochure2016.pdf

World Health Organization (WHO). (2017). Genes and human disease. Retrieved from http://www.who.int/genomics/public/geneticdiseases/en/index2.ht ml#SCA

World Health Organization (WHO). (2017). Sex ratio. Retrieved from http://www.searo.who.int/entity/health_situation_trends/data/chi/sex-ratio/en/

World Internet Project. (2012). Center for the digital future at USC Annenberg with 13 partner countries release the first World Internet Project report. Retrieved from http://www.worldinternetproject.net

Wörmann, V., Holodynski, M., Kärtner, J., & Keller, H. (2012). A cross-cultural comparison of the development of the social smile: A longitudinal study of maternal and infant imitation in 6- and 12-week-old infants. *Infant Behavior and Development, 35*(3), 335–347. doi:http://dx.doi.org/10.1016/j.infbeh.2012.03.002

Wrangham, R. (2009). *Catching fire: How cooking made us human.* New York, NY: Basic Books.

Wright, V. C., Schieve, L. A., Reynolds, M. A., Jeng, G., & Kissin, D. (2004). Assisted reproductive technology surveillance—United States 2001. *Morbidity and Mortality Weekly Report, 53,* 1–20.

Wu, L., Schlenger, W., & Galvin, D. (2003). The relationship between employment and substance abuse among students aged 12 to 17. *Journal of Adolescent Health, 32,* 5–15.

Xue, Y., & Meisels, S. J. (2004). Early literacy instruction and learning in kindergarten: Evidence from the early childhood longitudinal study—kindergarten classes of 1998–1999. *American Educational Research Journal, 41,* 191–229.

Yang, B., Ollendick, T. H., Dong, Q., Xia, Y., & Lin, L. (1995). Only children and children with siblings in the People's Republic of China: Levels of fear, anxiety, and depression. *Child Development, 66,* 1301–1311.

Yates, M., & Youniss, J. (1996). A developmental perspective on community service in adolescence. *Social Development, 5,* 85–101.

Yau, J., & Smetana, J. G. (2003). Conceptions of moral, social-conventional, and personal events among Chinese preschoolers in Hong Kong. *Child Development, 74,* 647–658.

Yermachenko, A., & Dvornyk, V. (2014). Nongenetic determinants of age at menarche: A systematic review. *BioMed Research International, 2014.* doi:http://dx.doi.org/10.1155/2014/371583

Yeung, D. Y. L., Tang, C. S. K., & Lee, A. (2005). Psychosocial and cultural factors influencing expectations of menarche: A study on Chinese premenarcheal teenage girls. *Journal of Adolescent Research, 20,* 118–135.

Yip, V., & Matthews, S. (2000). Syntactic transfer in a Cantonese–English bilingual child. *Bilingualism: Language and cognition, 3*(03), 193–208. doi:10.1017/s136672890000033x

Yonker, J. E., Schnabelrauch, C. A., & DeHaan, L. G. (2012). The relationship between spirituality and religiosity on psychological outcomes in adolescents and emerging adults: A meta-analytic review. *Journal of Adolescence, 35*(2), 299–314. doi:10.1016/j.adolescence.2011.08.010

Yoshikawa, H., Weiland, C., Brooks-Gunn, J., Burchinal, M. R., Espinosa, L. M., Gormley, W. T., … Zaslow, M. J. (2013). *Investing in our future: The evidence base on preschool education.* Ann Arbor, MI: Society for Research in Child Development.

Young, A. M., & D'Arcy, H. (2005). Older boyfriends of adolescent girls: The cause or a sign of the problem? *Journal of Adolescent Health, 36,* 410–419.

Young-Hyman, D., Schlundt, D. G., Herman-Wenderoth, L., & Bozylinski, K. (2003). Obesity, appearance, and psychosocial adaptation in young African American children. *Journal of Pediatric Psychology, 28,* 463–472.

Youniss, J. (2006). G. Stanley Hall and his times: Too much so, yet not enough. *History of Psychology, 9*(30), 224–235.

Youniss, J., McClellan, J. A., & Yates, M. (1997). What we know about engendering civic identity. American Behavioral Scientist, 40, 620–631.

Youniss, J., & Smollar, J. (1985). *Adolescent relations with mothers, fathers, and friends.* Chicago, IL: University of Chicago Press.

Youniss, J., & Yates, M. (1997). *Community service and social responsibility in youth: Theory and policy.* Chicago, IL: University of Chicago Press.

Youniss, J., & Yates, M. (2000). Adolescents' public discussion and collective identity. In N. Budwig & I. C. Uzgiris (Eds.), *Communication: An arena of development* (pp. 215–233). New York, NY: Greenwood.

Yu, F., & Patterson, D. (2010). Examining adolescent academic achievement: A cross-cultural review. *The Family Journal, 18*(3), 324–327.

Yuan, S., Fisher, C., & Snedeker, J. (2012). Counting the nouns: Simple structural cues to verb meaning. *Child Development, 83*(4), 1382–1399. doi:10.1111/j.1467-8624.2012.01783.x

Youniss, J., McClellan, J. A., & Yates, M. (1997). What we know about engendering civic identity. *American Behavioral Scientist, 40,* 620–631.

Zach, T., Pramanik, A., & Ford, S. P. (2001). Multiple births. *eMedicine.* Retrieved from www.mypage.direct.ca/csamson/multiples/2twinningrates.html

Zachrisson, H. D., Dearing, E., Lekhal, R., & Toppelberg, C. O. (2013). Little evidence that time in child care causes externalizing problems during early childhood in Norway. *Child Development, 84,* 1152–1170.

Zedd, Z., Brooks, J., & McGarvey, A. M. (2002, August). *Educating America's youth: What makes a difference?* Washington, DC: Child Trends.

Zehle, K., Wen, L. M., Orr, N., & Rissel, C. (2007). "It's not an issue at the moment": A qualitative study of mothers about childhood obesity. *MCN: The American Journal of Maternal/Child Nursing, 32,* 36–41.

Zeidner, M. (1993). Coping with disaster: The case of Israeli adolescents under threat of missile attack. *Journal of Youth & Adolescence, 22,* 89–108.

Zelazo, P. D., Anderson, J. E., Richler, J., Wallner-Allen, K., Beaumont, J. L., Conway, K. P., … Weintraub, S. (2014). NIH Toolbox Cognition Battery (CB): Validation of executive function measures in adults. *Journal of the International Neuropsychological Society, 20*(06), 620–629. doi:10.1017/S1355617714000472

Zell, E., Krizan, Z., & Teeter, S. R. (2015). Evaluating gender similarities and differences using metasynthesis. *American Psychologist, 70,* 10–20. doi:10.1037/a0038208

Zeskind, P. S., Klein, L., & Marshall, T. R. (1992). Adults' perceptions of experimental modifications of durations and expiratory sounds in infant crying. *Developmental Psychology, 28,* 1153–1162.

Zeskind, P. S., & Lester, B. M. (2001). Analysis of infant crying. In L. T. Singer & P. S. Zeskind (Eds.), *Biobehavioral assessment of the infant* (pp. 149–166). New York, NY: Guilford.

Zhang, W., & Fuligni, A. J. (2006). Authority, autonomy, and family relationships among adolescents in urban and rural China. *Journal of Research on Adolescence, 16*(4), 527–537.

Zhao, S., Grasmuck, S., & Martin, J. (2008). Identity construction on Facebook: Digital empowerment in anchored relationships. *Computers in Human Behavior, 24*(5), 1816–1836.

Zheng, F., Li, J., McCall, R., & Groark, C. (2013). Final report of half the sky training and technical assistance evaluation, February 19, 2013. East China Normal University and the University of Pittsburgh Office of Child Development.

Zhong, J., & Arnett, J. J. (2014). Conceptions of adulthood among migrant women workers in China. *International Journal of Behavioral Development, 38,* 255–265.

Zielinski, D. S. (2009). Child maltreatment and adult socioeconomic well-being. *Child Abuse and Neglect, 33,* 666–678.

Zigler, E., & Styfco, S. J. (Eds.). (2004). *The Head Start debates.* Baltimore, MD: Brookes.

Zimmer, C. (2014, December 31). Gene linked to obesity hasn't always been a problem, study finds. *The New York Times.* Retrieved from http://www.nytimes.com/2015/01/01/science/gene-linked-to-obesity-hasnt-always-been-a-problem-study-finds.html

Zimmermann, M. B., Pieter, L. J., & Chandrakant, S. P. (2008). Iodine-deficiency disorders. *The Lancet, 372,* 1251–1262.

Zuckerman, M. (2006). Sensation seeking in entertainment. In J. Bryant & P. Vorderer (Eds.), *Psychology of entertainment* (pp. 367–387). Mahwah, NJ: Lawrence Erlbaum.

Zuckerman, M. (2007). *Sensation seeking and risky behavior.* Washington, DC: American Psychological Association.

Zumwalt, M. (2008). Effects of the menstrual cycle on the acquisition of peak bone mass. In J. J. Robert-McComb, R. Norman, & M. Zumwalt (Eds.), *The active female: Health issues throughout the lifespan* (pp. 141–151). Totowa, NJ: Humana Press.

# Answers

## Chapter 1

**1.** c
**2.** a

## Chapter 2

**1.** d
**2.** c

## Chapter 3

**1.** b
**2.** c

## Chapter 4

**1.** b
**2.** c

## Chapter 5

**1.** c

## Chapter 6

**1.** b

## Chapter 7

**1.** d
**2.** b

## Chapter 8

**1.** d
**2.** d

## Chapter 9

**1.** b
**2.** d

## Chapter 10

**1.** c

## Chapter 11

**1.** b
**2.** a

## Chapter 12

**1.** c
**2.** b

## Chapter 13

**1.** d

# Credits

## Text and Art

**Chapter 1 p. 5 Table 1.1:** Data from Population Reference Bureau. (2013). 2013 World population data sheet. Retrieved from http://www.prb.org/pdf13/2013-population-data-sheet_eng.pdf; **p. 6 Figure 1.1** Data from World Population Ageing 2013. United Nations. http://www.un.org/en/development/desa/population/publications/pdf/ageing/WorldPopulationAgeing2013.pdf; **p. 7 Figure 1.2:** Based on Kaiser Family Foundation (2013); **p. 12 Figure 1.3:** Based on Kaiser Family Foundation (2013); **p. 8** Pearson Education; **p. 12 Figure 1.3:** Pearson Education; **p. 18** Freud, A. (1958) Adolescence. Psychoanalytic Study of the child, 15, 255–278. New York: International Universities Press, Inc.; **p. 19 Figure 1.5:** Pearson Education; **p. 20 Table 1.2:** Pearson Education; Arnett, J. J., Žukauskiene, R., & Sugimura, K. (in press). The new life stage of emerging adulthood, ages 18-29: Implications for mental health. Lancet Psychiatry; UNdata (2014); **Table 1.3:** Arnett, J. J., Žukauskiene, R., & Sugimura, K. (in press). The new life stage of emerging adulthood, ages 18–29: Implications for mental health. Lancet Psychiatry; UNdata (2014); **p. 22 Figure 1.6:** Adapted from: Weisner, T. S. (1984). Ecocultural niches of middle childhood: A cross-cultural perspective. In A. Collins (Ed.), Development during middle childhood: The years from six to twelve. Washington, DC: National Academy Press; **p. 28 Table 1.4:** Pearson Education; **p. 30 Figure 1.7:** Pearson Education; **p. 30 Figure 1.7:** Pearson Education; **p. 31** Keegan, R.T. & Gruber, H.E. (1985) Charles Darwin's unpublished "Diary of an infant," An early phase in his psychological work. In G. Eckhardt, W.G. Bringmann & L. Spring (eds.) Contributions to a history of developmental psychology (pp. 127– 145). New York, NY: Mouton; **p. 32 Table 1.2:** Pearson Education; **p. 34** Based on Fisher, C. B. (2003). A goodness-of-fit ethic for child assent to nonbeneficial research. The American Journal of Bioethics, 3, 27–28.; Rosnow, R. L., & Rosenthal, R. L. (2005). Beginning behavioral research (5th ed.). Upper Saddle River, NJ: Prentice Hall; **p. 33 Table 1.6:** Pearson Education.

**Chapter 2 p. 71** Marsh, M., & Ronner, W. (1996). The empty cradle: Infertility in America from colonial times to the present. Baltimore, MD: Johns Hopkins University Press, **p. 15.**; **p. 41 Figure 2.1, 2.2:** Pearson Education; **p. 43 Figure 2.3:** Pearson Education; **p. 44 Figure 2.4:** Pearson Education; **p. 51 Figure 2.5:** Pearson Education; **p. 52 Figure 2.6:** Pearson Education; **p. 54 Figure 2.7:** Pearson Education; **p. 59 Figure 2.8 and 2.9:** Pearson Education; **p. 59 Figure 2.10:** Data from Markant, J. C., & Thomas, K. M. (2013). Postnatal brain development. In P. D. Zelazo (Ed.), The Oxford handbook of developmental psychology (pp. 129–163). New York: Oxford University Press; **p. 63 Map 2.1:** Pearson Education; **p. 63 Table 2.2:** Data from World Health Organization (WHO) (2009). Monitoring emergency obstetric care: A handbook. Geneva, Switzerland: Author.

**Chapter 3 p. 78 Map 3.1:** Based on WHO (2015); **p. 88 Map 3.3:** Based on UNICEF (2014a, b); **p. 76 Figure 3.1:** Pearson Education; **p. 84 Map 3.2:** Based on UNICEF (2014); WHO (2014); **p. 87 Table 3.1** Source: Based on Montgomery KS. Apgar Scores: Examining the Long-term Significance. The Journal of Perinatal Education. 2000; 9(3):5-9. doi:10.1624/105812400X87716. **p. 93 Table 3.2:** Pearson Education; **p. 99 Table 3.3:** American Academy of Pediatrics [AAP] Section on Breastfeeding, 2016; Godfrey et al., 2009; Feldman & Eidelman, 2003; Ip et al., 2007; Kramer et al., 2008; Schulze & Carlisle, 2010. American Academy of Pediatrics [AAP] Section on Breast-feeding, 2016; Shields et al., 2010; Gibson et al., 2000; Owen et al., 2002; Ip et al., 2007; Schulze & Carlisle, 2010; Ip et al., 2007; Schulze & Carlisle, 2010; **p. 99 Map 3.4:** Pearson Education; **p. 102** Data from Wood, R.M., & Gustafson, G.E. (2001). Infant crying and adults' anticipated caregiving responses; Acoustic and contextual influences. Child Development, 72, 1287–1300; **p. 103 Figure 3.2:** Barr, R.G. (2009) The phenomena of early infant crying and colic, Paper presented at the Centre for Community and Child Health, Melbourne Australia, March 2; **p. 104** Data from Eisenberg et al., 2011; **p. 104** Source: Barr, R.G. (2009). The phenomena of early infant crying and colic, Paper presented at the Centre for Community and Child Health, Melbourne Australia, March 2; **p. 106 Map 3.5:** Data from Parsons, C. E., Young, K. S., Rochat, T. J., Krigelback, M. L., & Stein, A. (2011). Postnatal depression and its effects on child development: A review of evidence from low- and middle-income countries. British Medical Bulletin, 101, 57–79; **p. 108** Nurse-Family Partnership. (n.d.). About: Inclusivity & diversity. Retrieved from http://www.nursefamilypartnership.org/about/Inclusivity-Diversity.

**Chapter 4 p. 113 Figure 4.1:** Centers for Disease Control, 2015; **p. 114 Figure 4.2** Pearson Education; **p. 121 Table 4.1** and **Table 4.2:** Pearson Education; **p. 126 Figure 4.8:** Ervin, R. B., Wang, C. Y., Fryar, C. D., Miller, I. M., & Ogden, C. L. (2013). Measures of muscular strength in US children and adolescents, 2012. NCHS Data Brief, 139, 1–8; **p. 128 Figure 4.9:** Pearson Education; **p. 130 Table 4.3** Sleep guidelines from the National Heart, Lung, and Blood Institute, http://www.cdc.gov/sleep/about_sleep/how_much_sleep.htm; **p. 135 Figure 4.10:** Source: Based on Fryar et al. (2012); **p. 138 Figure 4.12:** Data from GBD 2013 Mortality and Causes of Death Collaborators. (2015). Global, regional, and national age-sex specific all-cause and cause-specific mortality for 240 causes of death, 1990–2013: a systematic analysis for the Global Burden of Disease Study 2013. Lancet, 385(9963), 117–171. http://doi.org/10.1016/S0140-6736(14)61682-2; **p. 139 Map 4.1:** UNICEF (2013). Progress toward global immunization goals, 2012: Summary presentation of key indicators. Retrieved from http://www.who.int/immunization/monitoring_surveillance/SlidesGlobalImmunization.pdf?ua=1.

**Chapter 5 p. 142; p. 181** Bjorklund, D. F. (2007). Why youth is not wasted on the young. Malden, MA: Blackwell Publishing; **p. 148** Source: Flavell, J. H., Miller, P.H., & Miller, S. A. (2002). Cognitive development (4th ed.). Upper Saddle, NY: Prentice Hall; **p. 149 Table 5.1, p. 155 Figure 5.1, p. 157 Figure 5.2:** Pearson Education; **p. 171 Figure 5.4:** Journal of the International Neuropsychological Society. Data from Zelazo et al. (2014); **p. 178,** 179 Gauvain, M. & Nicolaides, C. (2015). Cognition in childhood across cultures. In L. A. Jensen (Ed.), The Oxford Handbook of Human Development and Culture: An Interdisciplinary Perspective (pp. 198–213). New York: Oxford University Press. doi:10.1093/oxfordhb/9780199948550.013.13; **p. 178** Rogoff, B. (1995). Observing sociocultural activities on three planes: Participatory appropriation, guided participation, and apprenticeship. In J. V. Wertsch, P. del Rio, & A. Alvarez (Eds.) Sociocultural studies of the mind (pp. 273–294). New York: NY: Cambridge University Press.

**Chapter 6 p. 184 Map 6.1:** Data from Rubenstein, J. M. (2014). The cultural landscape: An introduction to human geography. New York: Pearson; **p. 186 Figure 6.1:** Data from Internet World Stats 2016, http://www.internetworldstats.com/stats7.htm; **p. 187** Leakey, R. (1994). The origins of human kind. New York, NY: Basic Books; **p. 189 Figure 6.2:** Pearson Education; **p. 191** Gopnik, A., Meltzoff, A. N., & Kuhl, P. K. (1999). The scientist in the crib: Minds, brains, and how children learn. New York, NY: William Morrow; **p. 194 Figure 6.3:** Data from Werker, J. F. (1989, January-February). Becoming a native listener. American Scientist, 77, 54–59. (See also figure in Siegler et al. text, p. 227); **p. 203 Table 6.1:** Bloom, 1998; Clark, 1995; Dale & Goodman, 2004; Fitneva & Matsui, 2015; Menyuk et al., 1995; **p. 208** Charkova, K. D. (2007). A language without borders: English slang and Bulgarian learners of English. Language Learning, 57(3), 369–416. doi: 10.1111/j.1467-9922.2007.00420.x; **p. 208** Orwell, George (1949). 1984. New York: Harvill Secker; **p. 211 Map 6.2:** Pearson Education; **p. 212** Hall, N., & Sham, S. (2007). Language brokering as young people's work: Evidence from Chinese adolescents in England. Language and Education, 21(1), 16–30. doi:10.2167/le645.0; **p. 213** de Abreu, G., & Lambert, H. (2003). The Education of Portuguese Students in England and Channel Island Schools. Final report of research project commissioned by Ministério de Educacão, Portugal.

**Chapter 7** **p. 218 Table 7.1:** Data from Rothbart et al. (2000); Thomas & Chess (1977); **p. 223 Figure 7.1:** Data from Wörmann, V., Holodynski, M., Kärtner, J. & Keller, H. (2012). A cross-cultural comparison of the development of the social smile: A longitudinal study of maternal and infant imitation in 6- and 12-week-old infants. Infant behavior & Development, 35, 335–347. http://www.sciencedirect.com/science/article/pii/S0163638312000410; **p. 227** Murkoff, H. E., Eisenberg, A., Mazel, S., & Hathway, S.E. (2003). What to expect the first year (2nd ed). New York, NY: Workman; **p. 227** Donovan, J., & Zucker, C. (2010, October). Austim's first child. The Atlantic, pp. 78–90. p. 85; **p. 229** Larson, R., & Richards, M. H. (1994, p. 85). Divergent realities: The emotional lives of mothers, fathers, and adolescents. New York, NY: Basic Books; **p. 230** Rousseau, Jean-Jacques. Emilius and Sophia; or, The Solitaries. London: Printed by H. Baldwin, 1783; **p. 230** Aristotle; **p. 230** Larson, R., & Richards, M. H. (1994, p. 85). Divergent realities: The emotional lives of mothers, fathers, and adolescents. New York, NY: Basic Books; **p. 232 Figure 7.3:** Data from OECD Family Database (2012); **p. 233 Table 7.2:** Based on Brent & Melhem (2007); Pfeffer (2006); **p. 239 Figure 7.4:** Data from Robins, R. W., Trzesniewski, K. H., Tracy, J. L., Gosling, S. D., & Potter, J. (2002); **p. 241** Mueller, Claudia M. & Dweck, Carol S. (1998). Praise for Intelligence Can Undermine Children's Motivation and Performance. Journal of Personality and Social Psychology 75, **no. 1**, 33–52; **p. 244** Erikson, E. H. (1958). Young man Luther: A study in psychoanalysis and history. New York: Norton; **p. 245 Table 7.3:** Pearson Education; **p. 244 Figure 7.5:** Pearson Education; **p. 246** Erikson, E. H. (1968). Identity: Youth and crisis. New York, NY: Norton; **p. 248 Table 7.4** Source: Based on Phinney, J. S., & Devich-Navarro, M. (1997). Variation in bicultural identification among African American and Mexican American adolescents. Journal of Research on Adolescence, 7, 3–32.

**Chapter 8** **p. 257** Mensch, B. S., Bruce, J., & Greene, M. E. (1998). The uncharted passage: Girls' adolescence in the developing world. New York: Population Council; **p. 260 Figure 8.1:** Cotter, D. A., Hermsen, J. M., & Vanneman, R. (2014). Brief: Back on track? The stall and rebound in support for women's new roles in work and politics, 1977–2012. Council on Contemporary Families Gender Rebound Symposium, University of Miami, July; **p. 261** Glass, G. V. (1978). Primary, secondary, and meta-analysis of research. Educational Researcher, 5(10), 3–8; **p. 262** Cotter, D. A., Hermsen, J. M., & Vanneman, R. (2014). Brief: Back on track? The stall and rebound in support for women's new roles in work and politics, 1977–2012. Council on Contemporary Families Gender Rebound Symposium, University of Miami, July; **p. 263 Table 8.1:** Gender Differences with Large, Medium, Small, and Negligible Effect Sizes; **p. 267 Figure 8.2:** Muller, M. N., Marlowe, F. W., Bugumba, R, & Ellison, P. T. (2009). Testosterone and paternal care in East African foragers and pastoralists. Proceedings of the Royal Society B, 276, 347–354. Doi: 10.1098/rspb.2008.1028; **p. 269** Mensch, B. S., Bruce, J., & Greene, M. E. (1998). The uncharted passage: Girls' adolescence in the developing world. New York: Population Council; **p. 270** Hilliard, L. J., & Liben, L. S. (2010). Differing levels of gender salience in preschool classrooms: Effects on children's gender attitudes and intergroup bias. Child Development, 81(6), 1787–1798. doi: 10.1111/j.1467-8624.2010.01510.x; **p. 270** Karniol, R., & Gal-Disegni, M. (2009). The impact of gender-fair versus gender-stereotyped basal readers on 1st-grade children's gender stereotypes: A natural experiment. Journal of Research in Childhood Education, 23(4), 411–420. doi: 10.1080/02568540909594670; **p. 270 Figure 8.3:** Hilliard, L. J., & Liben, L. S. (2010). Differing levels of gender salience in preschool classrooms: effects on children's gender attitudes and intergroup bias. Child Development, 81, 1787–1798; **p. 273 Table 8.2** Bem, S. L. (1974). The measurement of psychological androgyny. Journal of Consulting and Clinical Psychology, 42, 155–162; **p. 271** Bem, S. L. (1981). Gender schema theory: A cognitive account of sex-typing. Psychological Review, 88, 354–364. P. 355; **p. 276 Table 8.3:** Bem, S. L. (1974). The measurement of psychological androgyny. Journal of Consulting and Clinical Psychology, 42, 155–162; **p. 277 Figure 8.4:** Data from United Nations. (2010). The World's Women 2010; **p. 277 Table 8.4:** Data from United Nations. (2010). The World's Women 2010; **p. 278 Figure 8.5:** United Nations. (2010). The World's Women 2010; **p. 278** Malcolm X. (1970). By any means necessary: Speeches, interviews, and a letter by Malcolm X. New York: Pathfinder Press.

**Chapter 9** **p. 293 Table 9.1**, **p. 293 Table 9.2:** Pearson Education; **p. 300** Arnett, J. J. (2004). Emerging adulthood: The winding road from the late teens through the twenties. New York: Oxford University Press. P. 54, 53; **p. 289 Figure 9.1** Source: Data from van IJzendoorn, M. H., & Kroonenberg, P. M. (1988). Cross-cultural patterns of attachment: A meta-analysis of the Strange Situation. Child Development, 59, 147–156 **p. 304** Konopka, G. (1985). Young girls: A portrait of adolescence. New York: Harrington Park Press; **p. 305** Ann S. Masten, Ordinary magic. Resilience processes in development, American Psychologist, Vol. 56, No. 3, 227–238, 2001; **p. 299 Figure 9.2** Source: Granic, I., Dishion, T. J., & Hollerstein, T. (2003). The family ecology of adoloscence: A dynamic systems perspective on normative development. In G. R. Adams & M. D. Berzonsky (Eds.), Blackwell handbook of adolescence (pp. 60-91). Malden, MA: Blackwell. **p. 228; p. 313** Gartrell, N., Deck, A., Rodas, C., Peyser, H., & Banks, A. (2005). The national lesbian family study: 4. Interviews with the 10-year-old children. American Journal of Orthopsychiatry, 75(4), 518–524. doi: 10.1037/0002-9432.75.4.518; **p. 300 Figure 9.3** Source: Data from Iacovou, M. (2011). Leaving home: Independence, togetherness, and income in Europe. New York: United Nations Population Division. Re-trieved from http://www.un.org/en/development/desa/population/publications/pdf/expert/2011-10_Iacovou_Expert-paper.pdf; **p. 314 Figure 9.4:** Data from Hernandez, 1997; U.S. Bureau of the Census, 2012.

**Chapter 10** **p. 319 Table 10.1:** Pearson Education; **p. 321 Figure 10.1:** Pearson Education; **p. 322** Wilde, Oscar (1891). The Picture of Dorian Gray. London: Ward, Lock & Co; **p. 324** Chen, X, Wang, L., and DeSouza, A. (2007), "Temperament, socioemotional functioning, and peer relationships in Chinese and North American children" in X. Chen, D.C. French & B.H. Schneider (eds.) Peer Relationships in Cultural Context (pp. 123–146). New York. NY: Cambridge University Press; **p. 326** Ford, C., & Beach, F. (1951). Patterns of sexual behavior. New York: Harper & Row; **p. 339 Figure 10.2** Source: Data from Johnson, S. K., Murphy, S. R., Zewdie, S., & Reichard, R. J. (2008). The strong, sensitive type: Effects of gender stereotypes and leadership prototypes on the evaluation of male and female leaders. Organizational Behavior and Human Decision Processes, 106, 39–60. **p. 337** Larson, R., & Richards, M. H. (1994). Divergent realities: The emotional lives of mothers, fathers, and adolescents. New York: Basic Books. **p. 341 Figure 10.3:** Data from World Health Organization (WHO) (2013). World malaria report. Geneva, Switzerland: Auth; **p. 342 Figure 10.4** Source: Gottfredson .M., & Hirschi, T (1990) A general theory of crime. Standford, CA: Standford University Press p. 125; Osgood, D. W (2009) Illegal behaviour: A presentation to the committee on the science of the adoloscence of the National Academics. Washington, DC. **p. 343 Figure 10.5:** Somerville, L. H., Jones, R. M., & Casey, B. J. (2010). A time of change: Behavioral and neural correlates of adolescent sensitivity to appetitive and aversive environmental cues. Brain and Cognition, 72, 124–133); **p. 346** Arnett, J. J. (2004). Emerging adulthood: The winding road from the late teens through the twenties. New York: Oxford University Press; **p. 348 Figure 10.7:** Based on WHO (2010); **p. 349 Map 10.1:** Based on UNAIDS, GAP Report, 2014; **p. 350 Table 10.2:** Savin-Williams, R. C., & Ream, G. L. (2007). Prevalence and stability of sexual orientation components during adolescence and young adult-hood. Archives of Sexual Behavior, 36(3), 385–394; **p. 344 Figure 10.6** Source: Data from Alexander, B. (2001, June), Radical idea serves youth, saves money. Youth today, pp. 1, 42-44 p. 42.

**Chapter 11** **p. 358** Tobin, J., Hsueh, Y., & Karasawa, M. (2009). Preschool in three cultures revisited: China, Japan, and the United States. Chicago, IL: University of Chicago Press; **p. 361** Shimizu, H. (2001). Japanese adolescent boys' sense of empathy (Omoiyari) and Carol Gilligan's perspectives on the morality of care: A phenomenological approach. Culture & psychology, 7, 453–475. **p. 365 Map 11.1:** Pearson

Education; **p. 368 Map 11.2:** Based on UNESCO (2013); **p. 369** Rohlen, T. P. (1983). Japan's high schools. Berkeley: University of California Press; **p. 372** Thijs, J., Verkuyten, M., & Helmond, P. (2010). A further examination of the big-fish-little-pond effect: Perceived position in class, class size, and gender comparisons. Sociology of Education, 83(4), 333–345. **p. 377 Figure 11.6**: Pearson Education; **p. 378 Figure 11.7** Source: Data from Brant, A.M., Haberstick, B.C., Corley, R.P., Wadsworth, S.J., DeFries, J.C. & Hewitt, J.K. (2009) "The development etiology of high IQ" Behavior Genetics 39, pp 393-405; **p. 379 Figure 11.8** Source: Flynn, J.R. (1999) "The discovery of IQ gains over time" American Psychologist 54 (1999) pp 5-20; **p. 380 Figure 11.9** Eppig, C., Fincher, C.L., and Thornhill, R.(2010). Parasite prevalence and the worldwide distribution of cognitive ability. Proceedings of the Royal Society B, 277, 3801-3808; **p. 361 Table 11.1** Source: Data from Rogoff, B., Correa-Chavez, M. & Cotus, M.N. (2005) "A cultural/historical view of schooling in human development" in Developmental Psychology and Social Change: Research, History and Policy (pp. 225–263) Cambridge University Press; **p. 381 Table 11.2:** Pearson Education; **p. 361 Figure 11.2** Data from UNICEF (2014). State of the world's children. New York: Author.

**Chapter 12** Alwin, D. F. (1988). From obedience to autonomy: Changes in traits desired in children, 1928–1978. Public Opinion Quarterly, 52, 33–52; Rideout, Victoria and Elizabeth Hamel. (2013). The Media Family: Electronic Media in the Lives of Infants, Toddlers, Preschoolers and Their Parents. The Kaiser Family Foundation; Data from Freedom on the Net 2016; https://freedomhouse.org/report/table-country-scores-fotn-2016; Rideout, V. J. (2013). Zero to eight: Children's media use in America, 2013. Washington, DC: Common Sense Media. **Page 11**; Rideout, V. J., Foehr, U. G., & Roberts, D. F. (2010). Generation M2: Media in the lives of 8- to 18-year-olds. Menlo Park, CA: The Henry J. Kaiser Family Foundation. **Page 5**. Rideout, V. J. (2013). Zero to eight: Children's media use in America, 2013. Washington, DC: Common Sense Media. **Page 11**; Rideout, V. J., Foehr, U. G., & Roberts, D. F. (2010). Generation M2: Media in the lives of 8- to 18-year-olds. Menlo Park, CA: The Henry J. Kaiser Family Foundation; Data from Rubenstein, J. M. (2014). The cultural landscape: An introduction to human geography. New York: Pearson; Pew Research Center's Teen Relationship Survey, Sept. 25–Oct. 9, 2014 and Fe**b. 10**–Ma**r. 16**, 2015; Hansen, N., Postmes, T., van der Vinne, N., & van Thiel, W. (2012a). Information and communication technology and cultural change: How ICT changes self-construal and values. Social Psychology, 43, 222–231; Davis, S. S., & Davis, D. A. (1995). "The mosque and the satellite": Media and adolescence in a Moroccan town. Journal of Youth & Adolescence, 24, 577–594; Finkelhor, D., Mitchell, K. J., & Wolak, J. (2000). Online victimization: A report on the nation's youth. Durham, NH: Crimes Against Children Research Center. Retrieved from http://www.unh.edu/ccrc/VictimizationOnlineSurvey.pdf; Greenberg, B. S. (1994). Content trends in media sex. In D. Zillman, J. Bryant, & A. C. Huston (Eds.), Media, children and the family: Social scientific, psychodynamic, and clinical perspectives (pp. 165–182). Hillsdale, NJ: Erlbaum; Huesmann, L. R., Moise-Titus, J., Podolski, C., & Eron, L. D. (2003). Longitudinal relations between children's exposure to TV violence and their aggressiveness in young adulthood, 1977–1992. Developmental Psychology, 39, 201–221; Fisch, S. M., Yeh, H., Zhou, Z., Jin, C., Hamed, M., Khadr, Z.,... Guha, M. L. (2010). Crossing borders: Learning from educational media in four countries. Televizion, 23, 42–45; Olson, C. K. (2010). Children's motivations for video game play in the context of normal development. Review of General Psychology, 14, 180–187; Arnett, J. J. (1996). Metalheads: Heavy metal music and adolescent alienation. Boulder, CO: Westview Press; Currie, D. (1999). Girl talk: Adolescent magazines and their readers. Toronto, Canada: University of Toronto Press; Cragg, A., Taylor, C., & Toombs, B. (2007). Video games: Research to improve understanding of what players enjoy about video games, and to explain their preferences for particular games. London: British Board of Film Classification. Retrieved from http://www.bbfc.co.uk; Liechty, M. (1995). Media, markets, and modernization: Youth identities and the experience of modernity in Kathmandu, Nepal. In V. Amit-Talai & H. Wulff (Eds.), Youth cultures: A cross-cultural perspective (pp. 166–201). New York: Routledge; Pollay, R. W. (1997). Hacks, flacks, and counter-attacks: Cigarette advertising, sponsored research, and controversies. Journal of Social Issues, 53, 53–74.

**Chapter 13 p.451** https://www.unicef.org/education/focus_peace_education.html; **p. 425** Bloom, P. (2013). Just babies: The origins of good and evil. New York: Crown Publishers; **p. 441 Table 13.1** Source: Based on Smith, C. & Denton, M.L. (2005) Soul Searching: The Religious and Spiritual Lives of American Teenagers (Oxford University Press) **p. 425** Schieffelin, B. B. (1990). The give and take of everyday life: Language socialization of Kaluli children. New York, NY: Cambridge University Press; **p. 426** Vaish, A., & Tomasello, M. (2014). The early ontogeny of human cooperation and morality. In M. Killen & J. G. Smetana (Eds.), Handbook of moral development (pp. 279–298). New York: Psychology Press; **p. 427** Hickman, J. R., & DiBianca Fasoli, A. (2015). The Dynamics of Ethical Co-Occurrence: New Directions for Three Ethics Research. In L. A. Jensen (Ed.), Moral development in a global world: Research from a cultural-developmental perspective. New York: Cambridge University Press; **p. 430** Piaget, J. (1932). The moral judgment of the child. New York: Harcourt Brace Jovanovich; **p. 431** Kohlberg, L. (1958). The development of modes of moral thinking and choice in the years 10 to 16. Unpublished doctoral dissertation, University of Chicago; **p. 431** Kohlberg, L. (1981). Essays on moral development, **Vol. 1**: The philosophy of moral development. New York: Harper & Row; **p. 435 Figure 13.1:** Data from Casey, B. J., Getz, S., & Galvan, A. (2008). The adolescent brain. Developmental Review, 28, 62–77; **p. 436 Figure 13.2**: Based on Casey, B. J., Getz, S., & Galvan, A. (2008). The adolescent brain. Developmental Review, 28, 62–77; **p. 441** Smith, C., & Denton, M. L. (2005). Soul searching: The religious and spiritual lives of American teenagers. New York, NY: Oxford University Press; **p. 442** Arnett, J. J. (2004). Emerging adulthood: The winding road from the late teens through the twenties. New York: Oxford University Press; **p. 444 Table 13.2:** Marcelo, K. B. (2007, July). Volunteering among high school students. Retrieved from http://www.civicyouth.org/PopUps/FactSheets/FS07_High_School_Volunteering.pdf; **p. 451 Table 13.3:** Moscardino, U., Scrimin, S., Cadei, F., & Altoè, G. (2012). Mental health among former child soldiers and never-abducted children in northern Uganda. Scientific World Journal, 2012, 1–7; **p. 453 Table 13.4** Based on Alwin, D. F. (1988). From obedience to autonomy: Changes in traits desired in children, 1928–1978. Public Opinion Quarterly, 52, 33–52; **p. 451** Boothby, N., Crawford, J., & Mamade, A. (2009). Mozambican child soldier life outcome study. In B. K. Barber (Ed.), Adolescents and war: How youth deal with political violence, 238–255. New York, NY: Oxford University Press.

## Video Credits

**Chapter 1** **p. 3, 5, 11, 31, 38** Pearson

**Chapter 2** **p. 40, 43, 49, 62, 73** Pearson

**Chapter 3** **p. 75, 77, 92, 94, 98, 101, 104, 109** Pearson

**Chapter 4** **p. 122 , 129, 137, 143, 145** Pearson

**Chapter 5** **p. 147, 149, 151, 154, 155, 156, 167, 175, 177, 181** Pearson

**Chapter 6** **p. 183, 196, 197, 199, 206, 214** Pearson

**Chapter 7** **p. 216, 219, 228, 242, 246, 250** Pearson

**Chapter 8** **p. 252, 253, 255, 261, 275, 280** Pearson

**Chapter 9** **p. 282, 285, 300, 310, 313, 315, 316** Pearson

**Chapter 10** **p. 318, 323, 324, 335, 348, 353** Pearson

**Chapter 11** **p. 355, 364, 376, 382, 387, 389** Pearson; **p. 385** BBC Video

**Chapter 12** **p. 391, 395, 398, 308, 417, 419, 421** Pearson; **p. 408** boclips/Getty

**Chapter 13** **p. 423, 440, 449**, Pearson; **p. 450** BBC Video

# Name Index

## C

## H

## M

# Subject Index

## A

## B

## D

## E

## N



## O



## P

## T